Marc
Damia
Rajya Bhaiya

Microsoft Dynamics CRM 2011

UNLEASHED

SAMS | 800 East 96th Street, Indianapolis, Indiana 46240 USA

Microsoft Dynamics CRM 2011 Unleashed

ISBN-13: 978-0-672-33538-9

ISBN-10: 0-672-33538-7

Library of Congress Cataloging-in-Publication data is on file.

First Printing: September 2011

Trademarks

All terms mentioned in this book that are known to be trademarks or service marks have been appropriately capitalized. Sams Publishing cannot attest to the accuracy of this information. Use of a term in this book should not be regarded as affecting the validity of any trademark or service mark.

Warning and Disclaimer

Every effort has been made to make this book as complete and as accurate as possible, but no warranty or fitness is implied. The information provided is on an "as is" basis. The author and the publisher shall have neither liability nor responsibility to any person or entity with respect to any loss or damages arising from the information contained in this book.

Bulk Sales

Pearson offers excellent discounts on this book when ordered in quantity for bulk purchases or special sales. For more information, please contact:

U.S. Corporate and Government Sales
1-800-382-3419
corpsales@pearsontechgroup.com

For sales outside of the U.S., please contact:

International Sales
+1-317-581-3793
international@pearsontechgroup.com

Associate Publisher
Greg Wiegand

Acquisitions Editor
Loretta Yates

Development Editor
Sondra Scott

Managing Editor
Sandra Schroeder

Project Editor
Seth Kerney

Copy Editor
Mike Henry

Indexer
Tim Wright

Proofreader
Apostrophe Editing Services

Technical Editor
Dylan Haskins

Publishing Coordinator
Cindy Teeters

Book Designer
Gary Adair

Compositor
Mark Shirar

Contents at a Glance

Table of Contents

About the Authors

Marc Wolenik is the CEO of Webfortis—a Microsoft Gold Certified CRM Partner headquartered in San Francisco and with offices in Los Angeles and Seattle.

Rajya Vardhan Bhaiya is the CTO at Webfortis, and he is certified in MCPS, MCSD, MCAD for .NET, MCNPS, and MCTS in SharePoint. His primary focus is .NET development focused specifically in SharePoint and CRM development. Rajya has extensive experience working with technologies such as SharePoint, VoIP systems, Office Communicator, and specifically how they integrate with the Microsoft Dynamics CRM system. Rajya's working experience spans the gamut from simple out-of-the-box environments to complex projects with various integration points and complex customizations.

Damian Sinay, MCP, MCSD, MCAD for .NET, MCTS in SQL Server 2005, SharePoint 2007 and TFS 2010, and MBS CRM 3.0 and 4.0 certified professional, is a partner of Webfortis, a Microsoft Gold CRM Partner consulting company in northern California. Damian is currently a development manager, CRM expert, and a senior .NET developer. He has extensive experience working with all related technologies that make up Dynamics CRM, having worked on projects involving extremely complex customizations, integrations, and implementations for Dynamics CRM customers.

Dedications

As with any project of this type, there are many people that provide help and assistance in all shapes and forms that make up the end result that helps us and the book be successful. Our partnerships and relationships with the folks at Microsoft and other partners inspire us and drive us for continual improvement on a daily basis.

I would like to acknowledge the team at Webfortis for their interest, participation, and overall acceptance that committing to the community of Dynamics CRM users and administrators is the strongest way to differentiate.

—Marc

I want to especially thank Damian and Marc for their support and patience with the book.

—Raj

I want to especially thank Marc for all the patience and help he had while working on the book, as well as to the entire Webfortis team for all their effort on our projects. Finally, I want to dedicate this book to my family; without their support, I would never have had the time to write this book.

—Damian

We Want to Hear from You!

As the reader of this book, *you* are our most important critic and commentator. We value your opinion and want to know what we're doing right, what we could do better, what areas you'd like to see us publish in, and any other words of wisdom you're willing to pass our way.

As an editor-in-chief for Sams Publishing, I welcome your comments. You can email or write me directly to let me know what you did or didn't like about this book—as well as what we can do to make our books better.

Please note that I cannot help you with technical problems related to the topic of this book. We do have a User Services group, however, where I will forward specific technical questions related to the book.

When you write, please be sure to include this book's title and author as well as your name, email address, and phone number. I will carefully review your comments and share them with the author and editors who worked on the book.

Email: feedback@quepublishing.com

Mail: Greg Wiegand
Editor-in-Chief
Sams Publishing
800 East 96th Street
Indianapolis, IN 46240 USA

Reader Services

Visit our website and register this book at informit.com/register for convenient access to any updates, downloads, or errata that might be available for this book.

Introduction

Microsoft took the full three years between the release of its last version (version 4.0) of Customer Relationship Management (CRM) system to release this next version, CRM 2011, and it shows.

CRM 2011 brings to the table more than 500 new features—most, if not all, are outlined within this book. Although every one of those features is an improvement over the previous version, there are a few that really stand out and make this system a game changer with regard to functionality and competition. A few of our personal favorites are

- Native real-time charting and dashboarding in Chapter 21
- Improved user interface in Chapter 7
- Native SharePoint integration in Chapter 17
- Outlook 2010 Integration options in Chapter 13

Additionally, there is one feature that changes not only how this product can be used, but also is indicative of Microsoft's entire position with regard to computing: the dedication to cloud computing.

Microsoft announced at its World Partner Conference (WPC) in July 2010, that it was all in with regard to cloud computing. What this means is that the future is here and applications that previously required extensive infrastructure, IT staff, and multiple supporting applications are no longer necessary. Instead, Microsoft is leading the charge with applications such as CRM, SharePoint, Exchange, and even Office as hosted solutions that can be rented from Microsoft.

With Microsoft Dynamics CRM 2011 Online, the two biggest online limitations in its previous version have been removed: Custom reports can now be deployed in an online instance, and (drumroll) custom code can be deployed and executed on the Microsoft servers. Users benefit from this paradigm shift in that they can now work with solutions that can offer complex aggregate calculations at NO ADDITIONAL COST, (All custom code cycle time is absorbed by the monthly fee paid to Microsoft.) Combine this with the features of the Service Bus offered by Azure, and virtually any limitations that previously existed are nonexistent.

Of course, XRM still plays a major role toward the success of Microsoft Dynamics CRM. Renamed by Microsoft as *Extended CRM*, and carefully worded as not being a platform (so as to not be confused by its successful counterpart, SharePoint), XRM as a deployment model has been successfully deployed countless times. When asked to explain such concepts as XRM and SharePoint versus CRM, we often break them down as follows: XRM has the capability to use the application for anything management: grants, vendors, employees, cows, and so on. When discussing SharePoint versus CRM, we describe them as complementary and refer to SharePoint as an excellent application for unstructured data (such as documents) and CRM as an ideal application for structured data, such as transaction activity (phone calls, invoices, touchpoints, and so forth). Overall, when these concepts are tied together—something now native with CRM 2011—organizations have the ability to manage and control virtually anything.

This book shows you not only how to work with and configure Microsoft Dynamics CRM 2011, but also includes complementary technologies such as

- SharePoint
- Azure
- SQL Server Reporting Services (SSRS)
- SQL Server
- Online versus On Premise options
- Visual Studio and .NET Framework 4.0

Additionally, we'll show you how to get the most from your CRM system. We will delve into how Microsoft Dynamics CRM works, explain why you should set up certain features, and explore advanced configuration and customization options.

To be clear, this book provides an excellent overview of 99% of the application; however, your mileage may vary depending on your requirements. The 1% is often the hardest, most complex, and even the most imaginative. After working exclusively with Microsoft Dynamics CRM for more than seven years, we still frequently see situations and requirements by organizations that we could never have imagined. Additionally, the power of the application continues to increase, delivering options that previously existed only with extensive programming and workarounds.

NOTE

If you believe that that we have omitted anything or would like to share the 1% that your requirements might fall into—write us! Our specific contact information is contained in the chapters preceding these pages, and we have set up an alias that will send any queries to all writers: crmunleashed@webfortis.com. Who knows? Perhaps your story and feedback will be featured in our next book on CRM.

You can use Microsoft Dynamics CRM 2011 to manage virtually anything. This book shows you how.

NOTE

The majority of this book was researched and written using the prereleased version of the Dynamics CRM 2011 software. Every attempt was made to update the contents based on the final version of the software that was released January 2011. However, there may be areas that will not perform as shown because of differences in beta and final software releases.

CHAPTER 1

New Features of Microsoft Dynamics CRM 2011

IN THIS CHAPTER

- Visualizations/Dashboards
- Interface
- Connections
- Custom Activities
- Recurring Events
- Goals and Goal Management
- Processes
- Auditing
- Team Record Ownership
- Field Level Security
- Improved Outlook Integration
- Dynamic Marketing Lists
- Data Management
- Solution Management (drag/drop)
- Mobility
- Web Resources and Azure Integration
- SharePoint Integration
- Dynamics Marketplace

With more than 500 new features (and counting!), this release of Microsoft Dynamics CRM is very exciting. We have taken a handful of some of the best and newest features and attempted to highlight them in this chapter. To be honest, however, one of the best features isn't even listed, and that is the parity that finally exists between the hosted version and the on-premise version of Microsoft Dynamics CRM 2011. In late January, Microsoft launched Microsoft Dynamics CRM 2011—to the cloud first! This was the first enterprise product from Microsoft that had its official launch as a service *before* there was a version you could purchase on premise. This shows that the application as a hosted service was ready for prime time.

Visualizations/Dashboards

Microsoft Dynamics CRM 2011 now offers Dashboards out-of-the-box. Figure 1.1 shows the Microsoft Dynamics CRM Overview Dashboard.

The Dashboards are completely configurable and allow the following capabilities:

- Drill down on the underlying data
- Real-time reporting
- Unlimited usage
- Data visualization outside of just Dashboards and in both Outlook and Internet Explorer referred to as Inline Visualization.

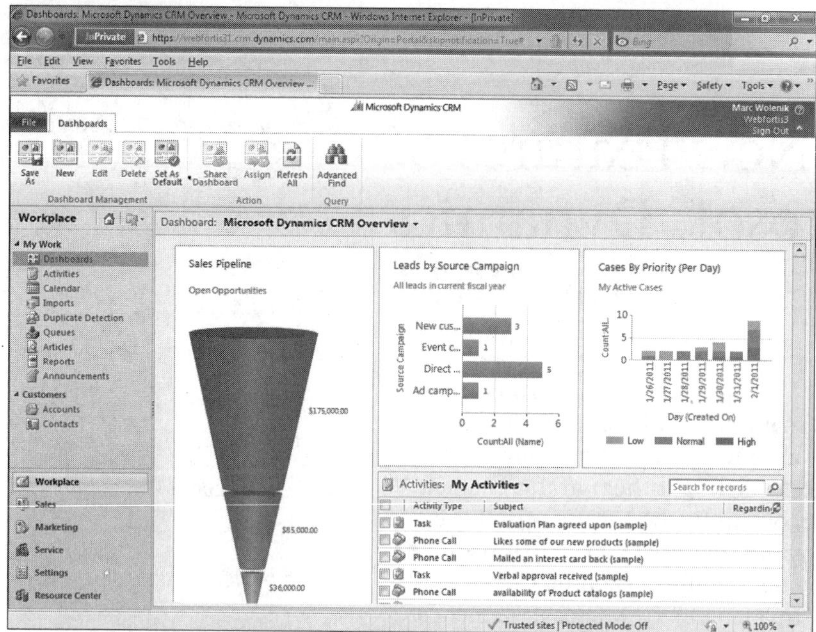

FIGURE 1.1 Microsoft Dynamics CRM Overview Dashboard

The last point is illustrated in Figure 1.2, whereby you see Top Opportunities represented in a chart on the right side of the page—in other words, you don't need to be at the Dashboards section to use the chart features.

Dashboards can be created for the individual users, which can then be shared to the entire organization with just a few clicks.

▶ **SEE** Chapter 21, "Reporting and Dashboards," to learn more about how to create new charts and Dashboards.

Interface

In addition to the listed features that have been added, the interface has been significantly improved. Figure 1.3 shows the new interface from the Account view.

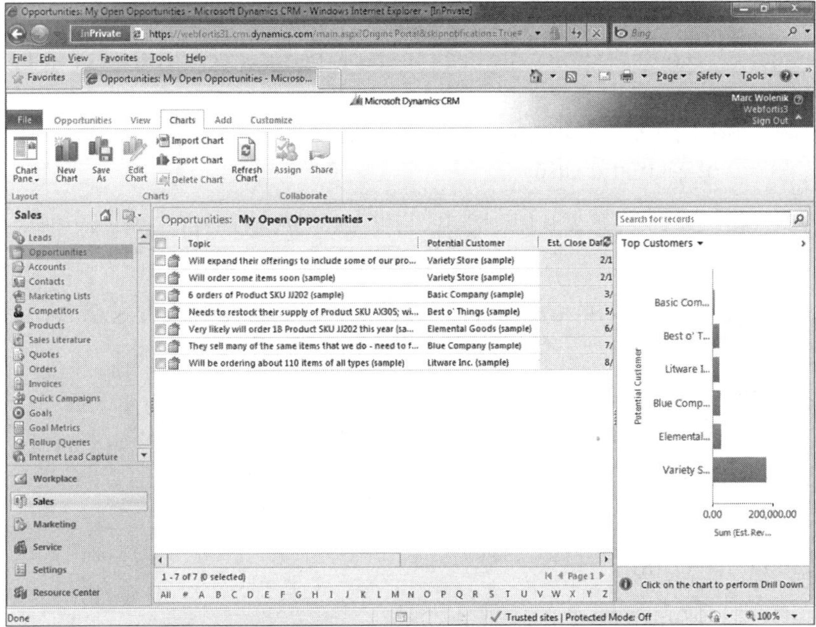

FIGURE 1.2 Top Opportunities represented with a chart.

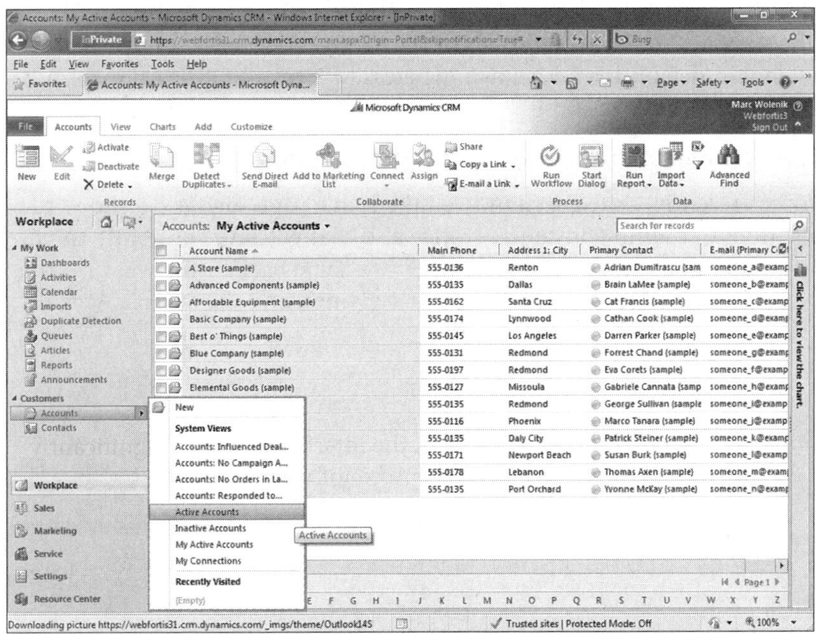

FIGURE 1.3 Redesigned interface for Microsoft Dynamics CRM 2011.

Here are just a few of your favorite features with the new interface:

- The total number of records is shown at the bottom of the interface (instead of just the first 50).
- Users have the ability to select more than one record by using the check box that is added to the record of each grid easily.
- A centralized Home button that you can set to return you to your favorite landing page—or home.

The result of this is simple—the interface is easier to use and requires fewer clicks to get to the information you want/need!

A few of the other changes include

- The tabs on the forms found in previous versions (and limits related to them) have been removed and replaced with sections.
- Contextual ribbon menu.
- Easier breadcrumb navigation.
- Fields have filtered lookups available.
- Filtered form navigation.

Additionally, there is now the ability to have role-based forms based on security roles.

Figure 1.4 shows the standard Account form that has two role-based forms available to it. In Figure 1.4, the standard/default form is shown, whereas in Figure 1.5, the same form is shown, but with minimal data shown on it.

It is the same Account form in both views, but with a different view for each.

There is also a favorites/recently visited section from the home page. Figure 1.6 shows the Recently Viewed list from our sample instance. Notice also that we have the ability to pin our favorites so that they will always be available when we come back to this view (in the example shown, we have pinned Active Accounts, My Activities, and the Sample Account Account record).

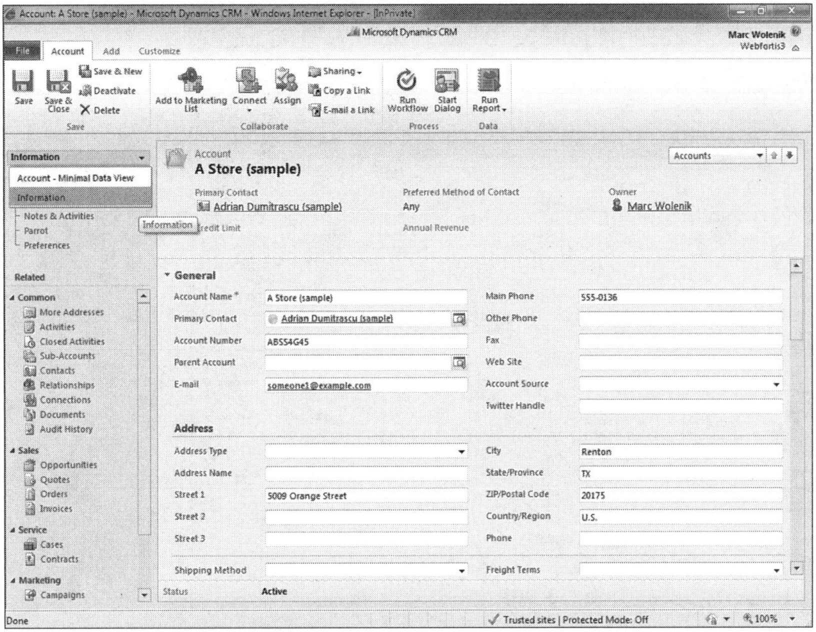

FIGURE 1.4 Two role-based forms.

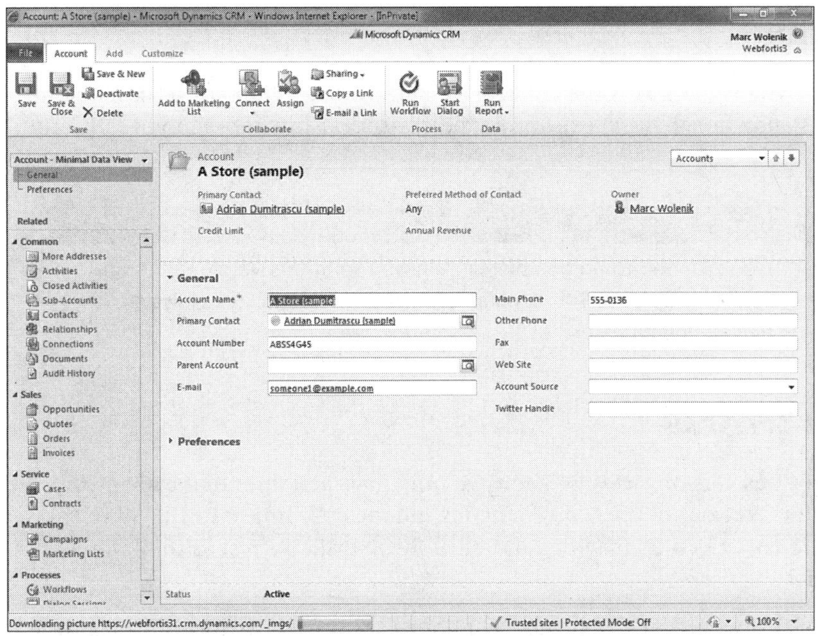

FIGURE 1.5 Two role-based forms—minimal data view.

FIGURE 1.6 Recently Visited from home page.

Connections

New to Microsoft Dynamics CRM is the concept of connections. Different from relationships, connections allow for there to exist any type of relationship between virtually any other entity.

NOTE

Relationships had been planned to be completely removed from this version (and only available if your system was upgraded to support backward compatibility). However, both Relationships and Connections are still available for use.

Custom Activities

A limitation of previous versions was the ability to only have activities that came with Microsoft Dynamics CRM out of the box (email, fax, phone call, and so forth). With this version, organizations can define activities and have them available just as they would with other activities.

A great example of this would be to expand the Phone Call activity as shown in Figure 1.7 in which we have created Inbound and Outbound specific Phone Call activities.

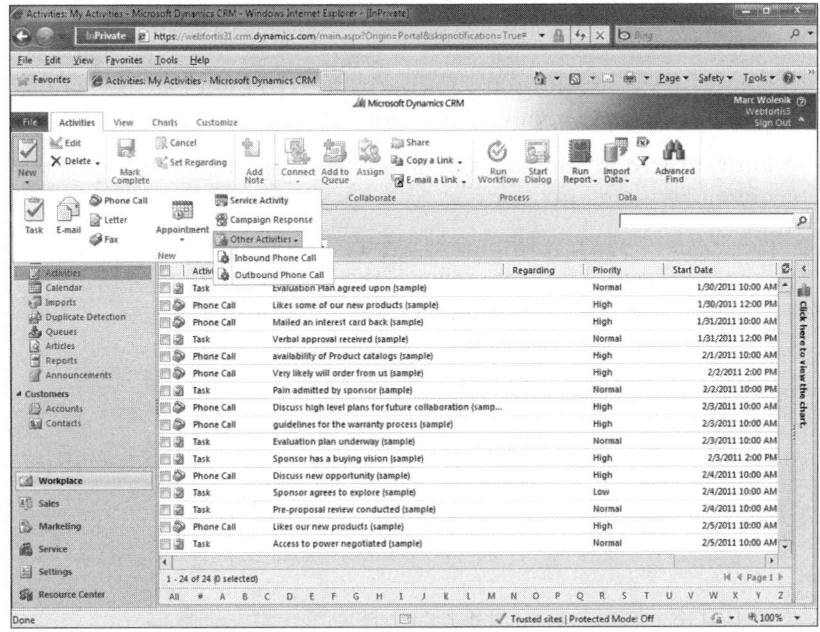

FIGURE 1.7 Custom activities for phone calls.

Recurring Events

The ability to create recurring appointments with the same type of scheduling engine from Outlook is now available.

These appointments are very flexible, can be driven and modified with workflow, know when to cascade, and provide users with the ability to schedule recurrence for important events synchronized directly with their Outlook calendar.

Goals and Goal Management

Previously available only with customization or by using the Sales Forecast Accelerator available from Microsoft/Codeplex, the concept of allowing the organization to track progress has been added to this version.

Goals are extremely flexible and can be defined as not just something to be achieved against cumulative dollar fields/figures, but can also easily be defined to track the total number (that is, the count) of something—for example, the total number of cases closed by a customer service representative.

Processes

Although workflows are still a part of Microsoft Dynamics CRM 2011, they are part of the concept of processes. Processes include both workflow and dialogs.

Workflow is as it previously existed in Microsoft Dynamics CRM—the ability to automate events that do not require user input once started.

Dialogs are interactive events that interact with users to provide a step-by-step interface for the management of a process. Figure 1.8 shows a typical dialog that can be used by individuals in customer service to troubleshoot a computer that won't work.

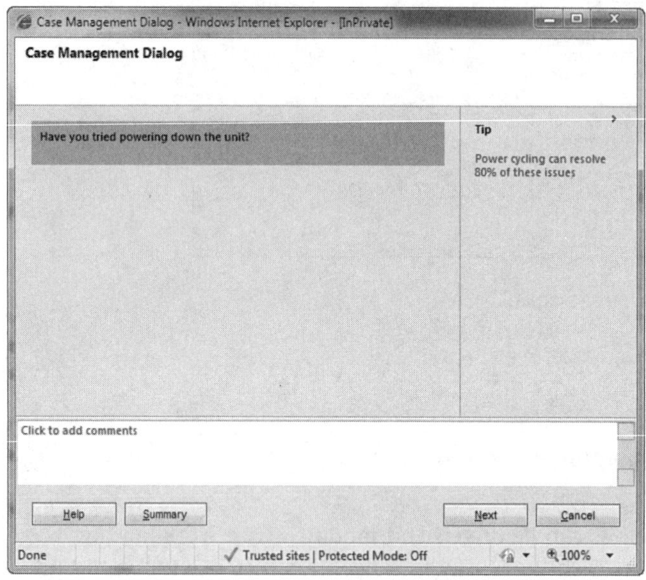

FIGURE 1.8 Dialog for case management.

Processes are supported by Windows Workflow Foundation (WWF) version 4.

▶ For more information about processes, see Chapter 24, "Processes Development."

Auditing

Field-level auditing is now fully supported. Additionally, you can customize where you want auditing to occur. Figure 1.9 shows the new section added to Settings that allows for auditing options to be set.

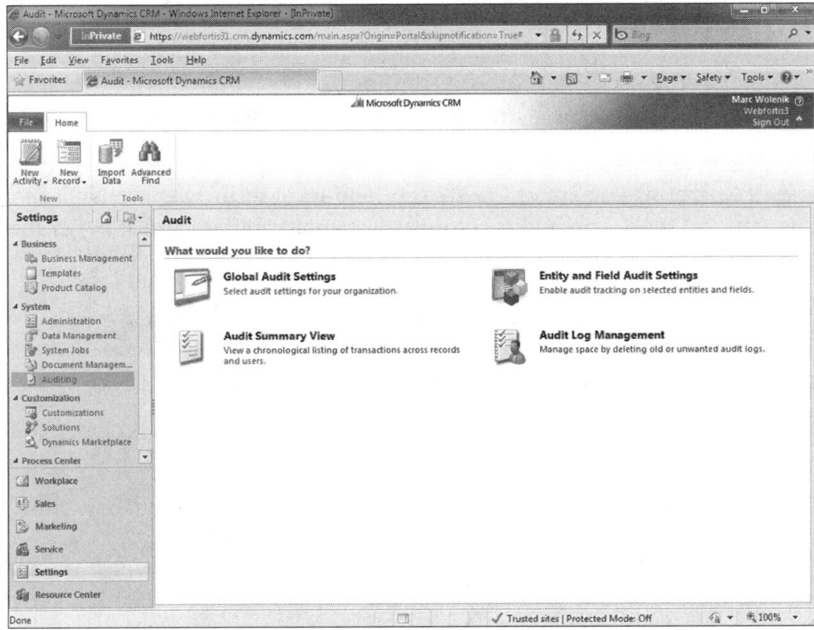

FIGURE 1.9 Auditing features for Microsoft Dynamics CRM 2011.

Auditing captures the following:

- Date and time something was changed
- The old value
- The new value
- The individual who made the change

▶ See Chapter 12, “Settings and Configuration,” for more information on working with auditing.

Team Record Ownership

Groups of people or teams can now own records. This is a hugely valuable feature that extends the concept of record sharing and ownership to allow multiple people to manage records at the same time.

Field-Level Security

Fields can now be hidden at the user level with no additional code required. The field security is defined by user and team; this is unlike record and form security, which is defined by role.

With the first release of Microsoft Dynamics CRM 2011, field-level security is available *only* for custom attributes (that is, those you add to a form). System attributes cannot be set for field-level security.

NOTE

It is anticipated that Microsoft will release an update that will allow this feature to be included for all attributes.

Field-level security is controlled through an added role feature called field security profiles. Figure 1.10 shows the section and a few typical sample field security profiles.

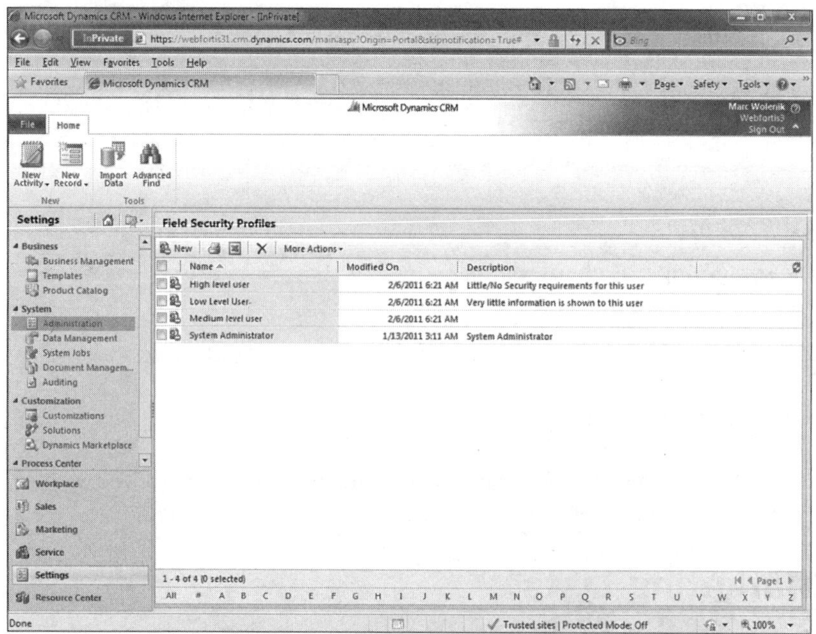

FIGURE 1.10 Field security profiles.

Improved Outlook Integration

Redesigned and using MAPI objects for Outlook integration, Microsoft Dynamics CRM 2011 truly lives within Outlook:

- Information from the entity is available and can be configured to be displayed based on preference directly within Outlook.
- Visualizations or charts are available directly within Outlook.
- Conditional formatting options are available.

Figure 1.11 shows a basic e-mail that is tracked in CRM, but the CRM information is available at the bottom part of the e-mail and is directly navigable by clicking it.

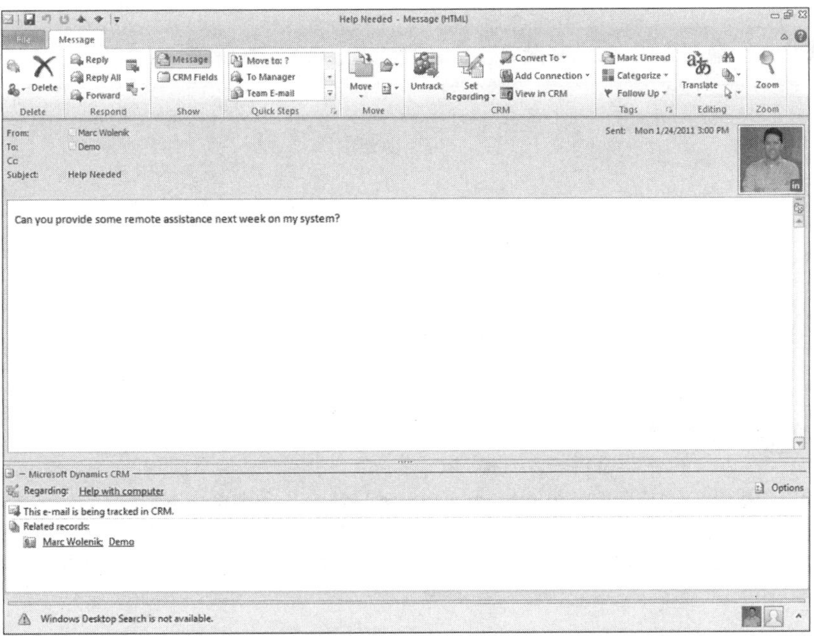

FIGURE 1.11 Tracked e-mail in Outlook.

Figure 1.12 shows Microsoft Outlook with the Accounts selected. Notice the ability to easily navigate using the tabs in Outlook (including pinning favorite views) as well as the information displayed about the record.

Dynamic Marketing Lists

Unlike in previous versions of Microsoft Dynamics CRM, Microsoft Dynamics CRM 2011 allows for marketing lists to be dynamic. What this means is that instead of having to create marketing lists as needed (typically right before they're needed so as to have the most current data and segmentation available), users can define a marketing a list once and have new records that meet the criteria of the marketing list automatically added to the list.

▶ See Chapter 9, "Working with Marketing," for more information on working with marketing lists.

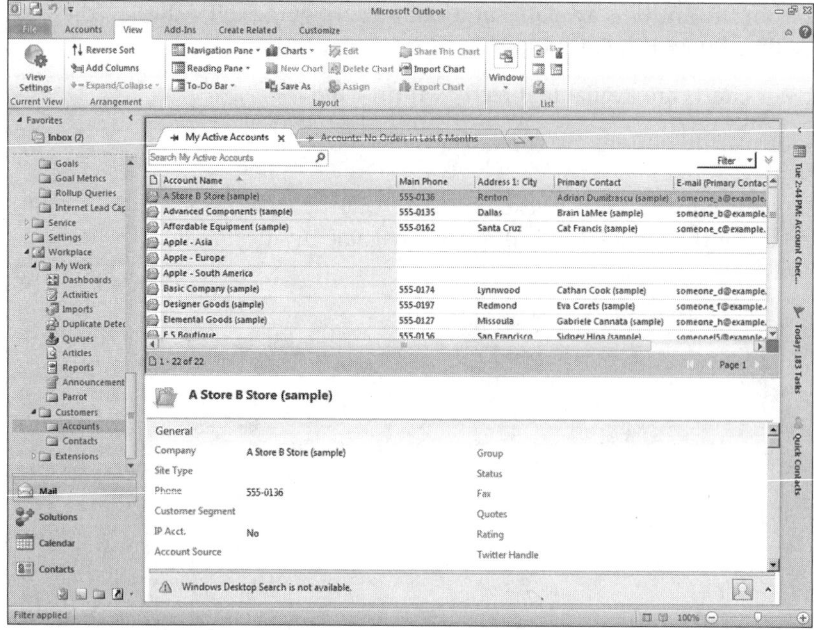

FIGURE 1.12 Accounts as shown in Outlook.

Data Management

The concept of data augmentation is available and supported out of the box. Users now have the ability to export data, work with it directly in Excel, and then reimport the data. Figure 1.13 shows the option that can be selected when exporting data from Microsoft Dynamics CRM 2011.

NOTE

This feature is actually available for users of Microsoft Dynamics CRM 4.0 after applying Rollup 9+ by unhiding the columns exported.

Solution Management

Microsoft Dynamics CRM 2011 now supports the concept of solutions. A solution is the ability to have different layers of customizations in a deployment.

This will result in vast improvements for organizations that want to have a level of control over the customizations applied to a deployment, in that each customization set can be included into a single solution that is deployed and can easily be rolled back.

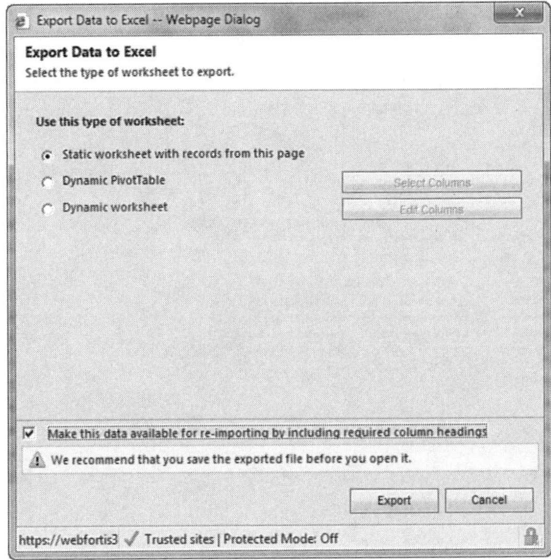

FIGURE 1.13 Data augmentation option.

Additionally, customers can take advantage of the Marketplace and download solutions from ISV publishers and install them directly on their system for testing and usage.

▶ See Chapter 16, "Solution Concepts," for more information on solution management.

Mobility

Supported out-of-the-box is the ability to access the information with any mobile client. Figure 1.14 shows Windows Phone 7 using Microsoft Dynamics CRM.

▶ See Chapter 15, "Mobility," to learn more about mobility options.

Web Resources and Azure Integration

The ability to reference resources such as web pages, JScript, or even Silverlight is now available directly through the application, versus in previous versions that required IFRAMEs.

Leveraging other cloud applications or Azure can now be easily accomplished in Microsoft Dynamics CRM 2011.

▶ See Chapter 18, "Azure Extensions," for more information about web resources and Azure integration.

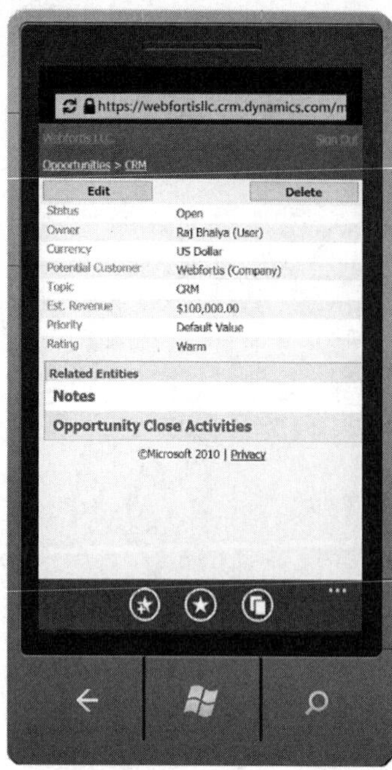

FIGURE 1.14 Sample Windows Phone 7 screenshot.

SharePoint Integration

Document management leveraging Microsoft SharePoint is now fully supported.

Using SharePoint for document management allows organizations to derive the benefits of SharePoint, including

- Document versioning
- Check in and check out
- SharePoint workflow

Additionally, hosted SharePoint – Microsoft Office 365 delivers all the integration options available with SharePoint as well.

Dynamics Marketplace

Similar to the App Store offered by Apple, Microsoft has integrated a centralized location for ISV to publish its applications.

Located directly in Microsoft Dynamics CRM (as shown in Figure 1.15), or by navigating to http://dynamics.pinpoint.microsoft.com/en-US/default.aspx, users can search for features, applications, or customizations that can be downloaded and installed on their system.

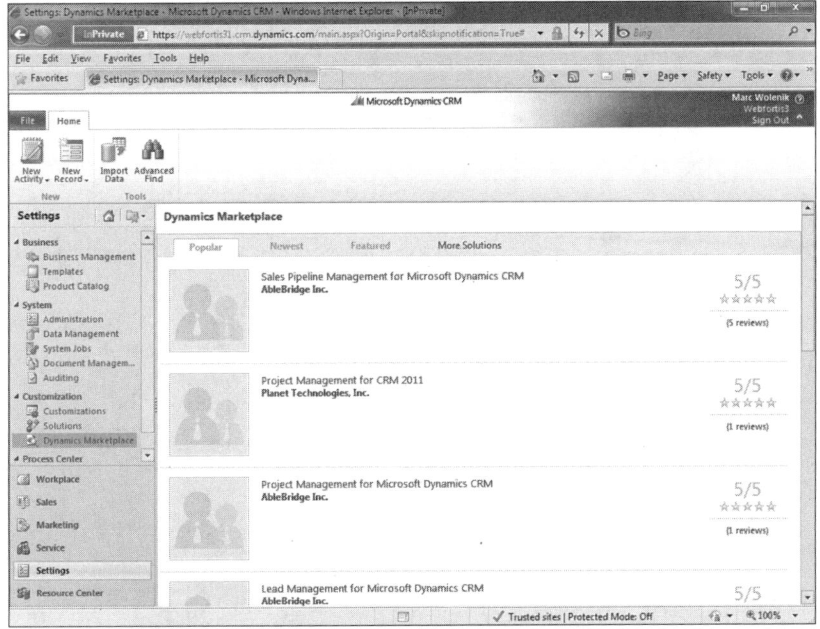

FIGURE 1.15 Dynamics Marketplace in Microsoft Dynamics CRM 2011.

Summary

This chapter listed only some of the most important new changes to Microsoft Dynamics CRM 2011. Although there are too many to list in one chapter, we have attempted to call out or indicate in other chapters where a feature is new or significantly improved from previous versions.

CHAPTER 2

Why Business Needs a CRM System

IN THIS CHAPTER

- Managing Your Business, Customers, and Resources
- People Versus Resource Management
- CRM Versus ERP
- Historical Data and Legal Requirements
- Real-Time and All-the-Time Need for Data
- Lead and Opportunity Management
- Marketing
- Challenges of CRM
- Microsoft Dynamics CRM Is More Than CRM—xRM Explained

As we move beyond a world of data on demand to one where data can provide us with forecasts and complex analysis, our expectations of information that is necessary to do business has changed.

No longer can a customer be told to wait while the accounting department searches for previous invoices or orders. Nor can salespeople be expected to schedule appointments without having access to their delivery and/or route schedules. Now we require the capability not only to access data at any time, but also to have advanced insight into what the data means.

Additionally, marketing efforts are more complex than ever. Internet marketing and e-commerce require a high level of technical sophistication as well as the capability to read and trend various efforts. This places a premium on campaigns that are easy to develop, maintain, and track.

Finally, for customer service, departments within the same organization, as well as different representatives within the same department, need to know about contact history. Who hasn't called a company for a service-related issue, when the call accidentally dropped, only to call back and have a different representative resume where the call left off. Your representative better know the contact history in real time because customers can easily note the difference between companies that solve problems using a CRM system as described and those that don't. Customers might not know whether a company is using a CRM system, but they do know about quality of service received.

Businesses need a CRM system to handle all these things without having to go to different places and involve different departments. The goal of any CRM should be to quickly, easily, and efficiently manage communication with your customers (whether they're current, future, or past customers), employees, and business partners. This includes historical communication, trending data, and associative information.

Managing Your Business, Customers, and Resources

As communication between you and your customers increases, the mechanisms for retrieving the history of communications needs to be more powerful and, at the same time, easier to use. The business model of a dedicated sales representative handling all contact with customers is no longer valid. Regulatory, contractual, and other legal issues are also reasons why communication needs to be tracked. As such, most companies need a centralized form of communication management.

Communication also has many different aspects and usually includes some form of the following:

- Phone calls
- Faxes
- E-mails
- Regular mail (letters)
- Meetings and/or appointments

Without a centralized management system such as a CRM, companies have no way to track and record all these different forms of communication. Instead, the items are completed and recorded in different systems (calendaring for meetings, outbox for e-mail, photocopy/saved document for a letter, and so on) or, worse, hopefully remembered when needed.

Additionally, internal resource management and visibility are more important than ever. With most business, labor division is divided into logic groups (see Figure 2.1), and management needs the ability to control and report on each division.

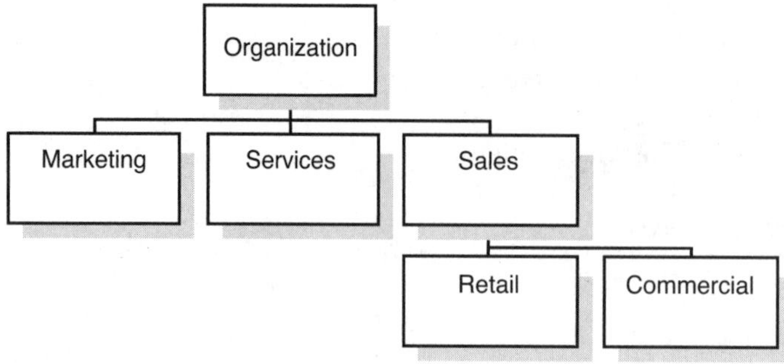

FIGURE 2.1 Business divisions.

Finally, very few, if any, businesses today don't have either a website or e-mail. Certainly, if you're reading this book, it is assumed that you do. Because you send e-mail, you need a mechanism for tracking sent e-mail. Reviewing the sent items in any e-mail program is a great way to do so. By sorting on the To field in the Sent folder, you can see the entire e-mail communication history for each person.

CAUTION

Using just your inbox (as mentioned previously) has several limitations. For example, imagine that we have a business contract with a large company (Company XYZ) and that we want to view all e-mail correspondence related to every contact we've had with that company. We would need to know each person and then search within our sent items for each person. It would be great if we could just create an account named Company XYZ and have all e-mail correspondence for each contact roll up to the company level of Company XYZ automatically. That way, when we needed to check for anything sent to that company, we would see every piece of e-mail sent to every individual who is in some way related to that company. A CRM solution offers this type of ready rollup.

People Versus Resource Management

Managing centralized schedules is one thing, but the capability to also manage the resources necessary for those schedules ties into a business's capability to be ready on all fronts.

A good example of this is an automotive repair shop. The shop needs to have people on hand who not only know how to do the repair, but who also are available to do the repair (and are not working on another repair at the same time). Compound that with the fact that the shop has only three service bays in which to perform the repairs, and this creates a need for a management tool to ensure the following:

- When a customer makes an appointment, you have the resources necessary to complete the job.
- The people with the required skills are available to perform the repairs at the time you want to schedule the job.
- The shop has available room to perform the work.

You can easily see how having all this information in one place and in an easy-to-use manner would facilitate effective management.

NOTE

Not every CRM system has these capabilities, but they should be required of every CRM solution, and Microsoft Dynamics CRM delivers this from its Service Scheduling interface.

CRM Versus ERP

Although an accounting/enterprise resource planning (ERP) system might be able to function as a CRM system, a CRM cannot likely function as an ERP system. Microsoft has a complete ERP option in the form of either AX, NAV, SL or GP (all of which integrate with Microsoft Dynamics CRM quickly and easily).

Some non-Microsoft ERP systems on the market today include

- SAP
- PeopleSoft
- Oracle

The goal of a true ERP system is to unify most or all aspects of a business into a common backbone system. Obviously, at the core of any ERP is a centralized database from which all data is derived. However, several different ways of accessing the data might exist, and users might be using different systems and/or applications that ultimately tie into the main system (and might not even be aware of it).

The reasons for having this unified system are apparent enough, but some downsides to a non-Microsoft CRM/ERP solution do exist:

- **One system and, thus, one way of doing business**—The ERP requires data to be processed and entered (or saved) in the prescribed format. Deviation requires complex customizations and/or business process changes.
- **Cost**—The sheer cost of licensing, integration, and customization associated with an ERP makes it prohibitive except for the largest organizations.
- **Too many options**—In an attempt to be everything to everybody, an ERP might have a huge number of features that make it cumbersome to use.
- **Incapability to quickly adapt to new processes and procedures**—In conjunction with the first point, it is crucial to be able to quickly incorporate new ideas and/or processes that might have positive effects on a company's sales, growth, or revenue.

  Incorporating streamlined processes into a sales process or developing a new interface that enables customers to access their sales history in ways they couldn't do before requires rework that might takes weeks or months and that might not be budgeted for.

CAUTION

When considering a CRM system versus an ERP system, it is important to recognize the preceding points as well as consider the fact that although a CRM can do a lot of things, at its core, it is designed to manage customer relations. It is for this reason that this book addresses everything that Microsoft Dynamics CRM does but will not address things that it may not do. An example of this might be maintaining a general ledger or chart of accounts (functions of an accounting system). Another thing to consider is the CRM functionality that might be promised or built into another system. Our experience has led us to believe that systems that promise CRM-type functionality tend to include only minimal CRM functionality, and much of it appears as an afterthought.

Historical Data and Legal Requirements

Records management involves a complex and varying set of requirements, depending on your business industry, degree of secrecy, and audit requirements. Because business is done by e-mail these days, there are many reasons to maintain complete and full business records.

Although every business undoubtedly has differing requirements, a good example of this is current requirements in place for financial services firms. Rules such as the National Association of Securities Dealers (NASD) Conduct Rule 3010/3110 require that financial security firms establish written procedures for the review of incoming and outgoing written and electronic correspondence (e-mail). Additionally, they must be able to produce evidence of implementation and execution of these procedures or risk sanctions and possibly more severe punitive actions.

Although the implementation of a CRM system might not address every requirement that exists, it can certainly be expected to be a valuable resource to that end.

Real-Time and All-the-Time Need for Data

Businesses need access to data without having to wait. Salespeople need to be able to quickly tell prospective clients about material costs and delivery dates associated with an order. Instead of saying, “I’ll send that to you in an e-mail when I have it all together,” salespeople need to be able to say, “I’ll have that in just a minute.” Otherwise, clients will have already called a competitor, who likely will be able to tell them what they want to know while on the phone.

The ability to empower salespeople with trending and forecasting based on their customers’ previous transactions is no longer an optional or nice-to-have consideration. It is required, and businesses that fail to anticipate the demands of their current and future clients risk falling behind to their competitors who are able to outsell, based on knowing what their customers will want and providing it to them now.

Additional requirements include the ability for clients to self-manage or the ability to provide customers with answers without having to contact your organization. A perfect example of this is a rich and thorough knowledge base that is exposed to the public for searching that they can use to resolve their problems without having to contact you. Additional tools frequently delivered to clients include sales history, trouble-ticket generation, and management, as well as dynamic real-time order processing.

When implementing a CRM solution, it is important to consider how the proposed system will address all these needs and demands.

Lead and Opportunity Management

A typical sales process involves creating leads (potential customers), converting leads to opportunities (sales opportunities), and, finally, making a sale.

As anyone in the business world knows, leads have a delicate nature and a finite life span. We want to encourage their growth and conversion, while not taking them for granted. Thus, we want to be able to tailor marketing material specifically to the leads or prospective customers and, at the same time, be sure they don't receive either information that they aren't entitled to or products that they aren't interested in.

For this reason, we generally don't want to mix leads and opportunities with other customers. We do, however, want to establish them within the CRM system for easy conversion, contact history, and management by other individuals or groups within the organization.

Opportunities are generally related to existing customers. Because it is usually much easier to sell a new service to existing customers than to a new lead, knowing your current customers' needs and sales history will make it easier to improve sales of new services.

It is important, then, for these reasons that leads be segregated and considered as separate when thinking about a CRM system.

Marketing

One of the most requested features of any CRM is marketing capabilities. Marketing is the component that is most closely tied with lead and opportunity generation and conversion, as well as selling new or enhanced services to existing customers. When you think about working with your CRM, marketing should be an area that ties to all other aspects.

It is also important to consider marketing as not just a sales tool. Although the goal of most companies is to sell products and services, not every marketing effort is directly related to that end. Consider company sponsorship at various events, as well as e-mails to customers announcing the addition of a new VP of Development and/or offices at a company. The sponsorship and announcement e-mails are not made to influence direct sales; however, they should be considered marketing because their goal is to make your organization better known, seen as more responsible, or as having better or necessary resources to better service customers.

Of course, when it comes to sales, marketing efforts should also be quantifiable and allow for easy exposure as to the effectiveness of the marketing effort. Consider the idea of creating a spring sale event whose goal is to clear winter inventory from your shelves. With a proper marketing effort, you would be able to specifically target customers who have a strong buying indication for such a sale (because they responded to previous marketing efforts, for example). Alternatively, you might want to tailor your marketing specifically to customers whose previous buying patterns do not indicate that they would participate in such an event, by offering them a strong incentive to do so (something you wouldn't have to offer for the first group of people).

The final piece should be the ability to see what marketing has been done and to which customers. It would be just as irresponsible to send marketing material to customers who have specifically requested not to receive any as it would be to not reach out to regular customers that haven't done business in the last 60 days.

Challenges of CRM

The biggest challenge of any CRM system is user adoption. Without adequate adoption of the system, usage will be minimal and data will not be reliable. As part of that challenge, three other challenges arise:

- Business challenge
- Management challenge
- IT challenge

The business challenge is successful user adoption of the system. This includes users accepting the system as a core business application that all members of the organization can rely on for reliable data. Strong user adoption is usually brought on by ease of use, training, and management support.

TIP

It is not enough just to issue a new business policy from management that requires using CRM as part of a business process. Instead, management needs to fully support its use. To do this, management should ensure that necessary work is done both before and after implementation to support necessary business processes, customizations, and other requirements that make adoption easier. Management also needs to *use* the CRM system to be aware of how users are using the data and making contact with customers.

Some of the issues associated with the IT challenge that should be addressed involve the architecture of the system (including scalability and fault tolerance), the extensibility of the system, and the availability of both tools and people with the skills to support a system.

User adoption in Microsoft Dynamics CRM is easy because users can use it within the Outlook client, an application familiar to most users, so the learning curve is short.

Microsoft Dynamics CRM Is More Than CRM—xRM Explained

Microsoft Dynamics has the ability to be MUCH more than just customer relationship management—it can be an entire framework for the management of anything. What this results in is the concept of replacing the C in CRM with "x," resulting in xRM, which stands for *Anything Relationship Management* (this is also known as *Extended CRM*).

Here are just a few examples that we have seen Microsoft Dynamics CRM used for:

- Vendor Management
- Grant Management
- People/Citizen Management
- Class Management
- Materials Management
- Food Management
- Troop Management
- Supplier Management

The list goes on and the options are limitless with regard to how and what the system can be used for.

NOTE

This book can be used as a guide for xRM. Leveraging the concepts and examples explained you can create a system for your management requirements. For example, after reading Chapters 23, "Customizing Entities," you could easily add a new entity called Vendors, or even modify the existing Account entity to say Vendors and use that going forward.

The benefits of this are obvious:

- A significant amount of work is done to deliver an application that delivers core functionality.
- Native Outlook integration.
- Consistent look and feel.
- Support of Microsoft.

We have seen organizations rollout line of business (LOB) applications using Microsoft Dynamics CRM 2011 in a fraction of the time that they took previously, and the application is solid—very little debugging and/or constant support is required.

Summary

As you can see, a customer relationship management system is more than just a buzzword. It is a powerful tool that, when used correctly, can propel and facilitate relationships among businesses, employees, and customers, as well as increasing efficiency and visibility across an organization.

There is a lot to consider when evaluating CRM systems and functionality; however, it is readily apparent that businesses that fail to provide themselves, their staff, and their customers with the tools that a CRM system provides will have a much more difficult time providing the level of service that customers are growing to expect.

CHAPTER 3

Requirements for CRM 2011

IN THIS CHAPTER

Microsoft Dynamics CRM 2011 is an application that leverages other Microsoft technology. As previously stated, most businesses usually have some of, if not all, the technology required for Microsoft Dynamics CRM 2011, and Microsoft readily admits that if you're not already on the Microsoft platform, the adoption of Microsoft Dynamics CRM for On Premise can be steep because the product requires many core components such as SQL Server, IIS, Active Directory, and so on.

The On Premise version of Microsoft Dynamics CRM is the version that requires the most amount of infrastructure. This is simply because you're dedicating server resources (if not several servers) to host the Microsoft Dynamics CRM application. The other versions (CRM Online and Partner Hosted) require only Outlook, the e-mail router, and/or Internet Explorer.

This chapter deals primarily with the requirements associated with the On Premise requirements. If you are going to be working with the CRM Online version, we recommend you skip to the "Client" section of this chapter because a majority of the material will not apply.

Server

You can deploy Microsoft Dynamics CRM several different ways when considering an On Premise deployment. These include choosing single-server versus distributed-server deployment and determining which version of Microsoft Dynamics CRM to run.

▶ See Chapter 4, "Setting Up CRM 2011," for more information about single-server versus distributed-server deployment.

CAUTION

CRM 2011 Server is supported only on an x64 based architecture computer.

The CRM 2011 Server version has the ability to install individual server roles by using the Microsoft Dynamics CRM Server Setup Wizard. Additionally, you can add a server role, and change or remove installed server roles by navigating to Programs and Features in the Control Panel.

Windows Server Operating system

The operating system requirements for the Microsoft Dynamics CRM 2011 Server are as follows:

- Windows Server 2008 Standard (x64 versions) SP2 or later version
- Windows Server 2008 Enterprise (x64 versions) SP2 or later version
- Windows Server 2008 Datacenter (x64 versions) SP2 or later version
- Windows Web Server 2008 (x64 versions) SP2 or later version
- Windows Small Business Server 2008 Premium x64 or later version
- Windows Small Business Server 2008 Standard x64 or later version

CAUTION

- Windows Server 2008 installed by using the Server Core installation option is not supported for installing and running Microsoft Dynamics CRM 2011 Server.
- Windows Server 2008 for Itanium-Based Systems is not supported for installing and running Microsoft Dynamics CRM 2011 Server.
- The Windows Small Business Server 2008 Standard edition does not include SQL Server. You must have a supported version of SQL Server available to install Microsoft Dynamics CRM on Windows Small Business Server 2008 Standard edition.

Active Directory modes

Active Directory is a Microsoft service that provides authentication and authorization for Windows-based users, computers, and services in a centralized location. It is a necessary component for access into Microsoft CRM 2011. The advantage of leveraging Active Directory is a single system sign-on process; application access can be granted without requiring multiple sign-ons.

The easiest way to think of this is that when users log on to the Windows network, they are essentially logging on to not only the network, but also to all network resources, including printers, file shares, and applications that they have access to. Active Directory works by organizing network objects in a hierarchy.

A forest is the top level of Active Directory. Forests contain domains, and domains contain Organizational Units (OUs) (see Figure 3.1).

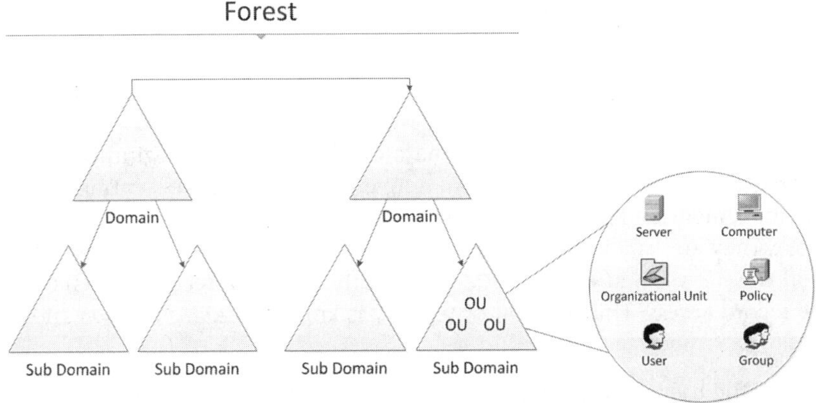

FIGURE 3.1 Graphical display of Active Directory forest, domain, and Organizational Unit.

All Active Directory forest modes (Windows 2003 Native and Windows 2008 forest mode) are supported for Microsoft CRM 2011. However, when installing to a Windows Server 2003 that is a domain member or domain controller in a domain, one of the following Active Directory service modes must be running:

- Windows 2000 Mixed
- Windows 2000 Native
- Windows Server 2003 Interim
- Windows Server 2003 Native
- Windows Server 2008 Interim
- Windows Server 2008 Native

Other Active Directory requirements include these:

- On a server-separated install (in which the CRM SQL Server database is on another computer), the Active Directory domain must contain both the Microsoft CRM 2011 and the SQL Server computer.
- The computer that is running Microsoft CRM 2011 must be on the same domain that has the accounts used to run Microsoft CRM 2011.
- A single OU must house all the Microsoft CRM 2011 security groups (UserGroup, PrivUserGroup, SQLAccessGroup, ReportingGroup, PrivReportingGroup). Note,

however, that the OU does not have to be in the same domain as the computer running Microsoft CRM 2011.

- A one-way trust must exist (in which the user domain trusts the Microsoft CRM 2011 domain) when accessing Microsoft CRM 2011 from another domain.

► For more information about Active Directory, trusts, and domains, go to http://www.microsoft.com/technet/prodtechnol/windows2000serv/technologies/activedirectory/default.mspx.

Active Directory is an integral part of Microsoft Dynamics CRM. From the beginning of Microsoft CRM (starting with the earliest versions), Active Directory was the centralized location for user management and security into the system. When users first attempt to log into the network, they are validating who they are against the information in Active Directory. When on the network, Microsoft CRM uses another internal security mechanism to determine record access. This division of security is known as *Authentication* and *Authorization.*

Authentication (or who the user is) is the process by which a user is verified by providing credentials. In the case of Active Directory, the credentials consist of a username, password, and Windows domain name. In the Windows and Microsoft CRM model, authentication is determined when a user logs on to the network. When a user attempts to access Microsoft CRM, he is not prompted for credentials because he has already been verified (see Figure 3.2).

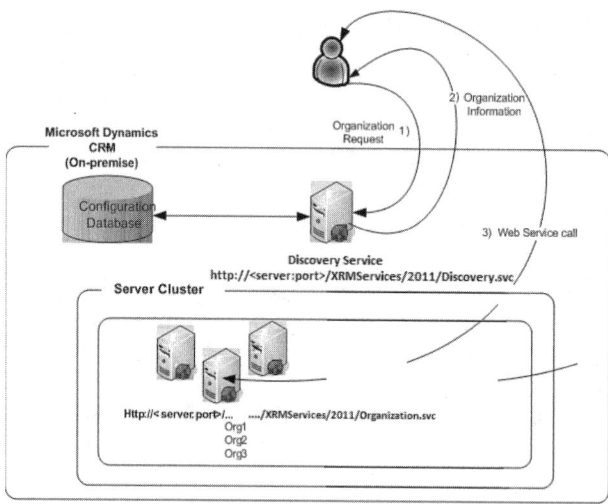

FIGURE 3.2 Active Directory and Microsoft CRM authentication.

Authorization (or what the user can do) is the process by which users are granted the rights to certain resources based on what security levels and permissions they have. For example, a network administrator might have full access rights to the entire system, whereas a secretary might have very limited access rights.

Further, the previous example is specific to the network rights that users have; however, whatever Microsoft Dynamics CRM rights they might have are completely independent of their network rights. As such, the secretary previously mentioned, who has very limited access rights, might be a full Microsoft CRM Administrator and able to do virtually anything in the CRM system, whereas the network administrator might have read-only rights.

If it sounds confusing, it might be easier to think of it like this:

- Users need to be valid network users to be given access to Microsoft Dynamics CRM 2011.
- After being granted access to Microsoft CRM 2011, users need to be given a security role to determine what level of access they have to work within Microsoft CRM 2011.
- There is no inherent correlation between network permissions and Microsoft CRM 2011 permissions.

To explain further, just because users can log on to the network does not necessarily mean they have the rights or the capability to log on to Microsoft CRM 2011. The reason for this is that although Active Directory controls network and network resource access, users must also be set up in Microsoft CRM 2011 as valid users.

For example, if you had 85 people in your organization, but only the CEO has been set up in the Microsoft CRM 2011 as a valid user, only the CEO would be able to access Microsoft CRM 2011; other users would encounter the error shown in Figure 3.3.

The number of valid Microsoft CRM 2011 users that you can have is established by the version of Microsoft CRM 2011 that you purchase, as well as the particular licensing used (see the "Licensing" section of this chapter).

▶ The authorization process is further broken down within Microsoft Dynamics CRM 2011 as outlined in Chapter 12, "Settings and Configuration."

Internet Information Services

Internet Information Services 7.0 (IIS) must be installed and running in Native mode before you install Microsoft Dynamics CRM Server.

TIP

When you install the Microsoft Dynamics CRM Server web application on a computer that is running IIS, Microsoft Dynamics CRM Server Setup will enable HTTP compression by default. If you use a different method to compress HTTP communications, you might want to disable this feature. To do this, start IIS Manager, right-click the Web Sites folder, click Properties, click the Service tab, and then clear the Compress Application Files and Compress Static Files check boxes.

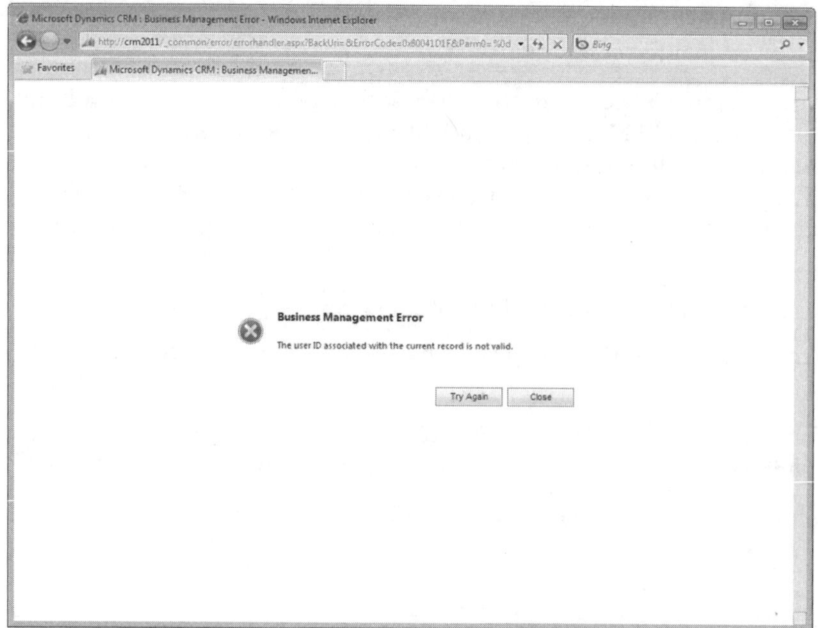

FIGURE 3.3 A valid network user but not added to Microsoft CRM.

Internet-Facing Deployment Requirements

The following items are required for Internet-facing deployments (IFD). This topic assumes you will be using Microsoft Windows 2008 Server as the claims-based authentication solution.

- Access to a Secure Token Services (STS) service, such as the STS called Active Directory Federation Services (ADFS) 2.0.
- The following must be available after you run Microsoft Dynamics CRM Server Setup and before configure IFD:
    - During configuration, you must configure the website to use SSL to configure the Microsoft Dynamics CRM Server Web application. Note that Microsoft Dynamics CRM Server Setup will not configure the website for SSL.
    - For this release of Microsoft Dynamics CRM Server, on the website where the Microsoft Dynamics CRM Server web application will be installed, verify that the Require SSL setting is disabled.
    - Access to the Windows 2008 Server federation metadata XML file from the computer where Microsoft Dynamics CRM Server Setup is run.
    - A valid encryption certificate used for SSL encryption by the Microsoft Dynamics CRM Server website located in the local computer certificate store where Microsoft Dynamics CRM Server will be installed. The certificate can be a wildcard encryption certificate.

ADFS 2.0 requires installation to the default website. Therefore, if you install Microsoft Dynamics CRM Server on a single-computer deployment, the Microsoft Dynamics CRM Server web application must be installed in a website other than the default website.

▶ See Chapter 22, "Forms Authentication" for more information about the IFD configurations.

Database

This section covers the following database components:

- SQL Server Editions
- SQL Server Reporting Services

SQL Server Editions

Any one of the following Microsoft SQL Server editions is required and must be installed, running, and available for Microsoft Dynamics CRM:

- Microsoft SQL Server 2008, Standard Edition, x64 SP1 or later version.
- Microsoft SQL Server 2008, Enterprise Edition, x64 SP1 or later version.
- Microsoft SQL Server 2008 Datacenter x64 SP1 or later version.
- Microsoft SQL Server 2008 Developer x64 SP1 or later version (for non-production environments only).
- Microsoft SQL Server 2008, Workgroup Web, Compact, or Express editions are not supported for running Microsoft Dynamics CRM.
- SQL Server 2000 and SQL Server 2005 editions and are not supported for this version of Microsoft Dynamics CRM.
- Running 64-bit SQL Server versions for Itanium (IA-64) systems in conjunction with Microsoft Dynamics CRM will receive commercially reasonable support. *Commercially reasonable support* is defined as all reasonable support efforts by Microsoft Customer Service and Support that do not require Microsoft Dynamics CRM code fixes.
- Microsoft Dynamics CRM Server supports a named instance of SQL Server when you add or create organization databases.

SQL Server Reporting Services

The following SQL Server Reporting Services editions are required and must be installed, running, and available for Microsoft Dynamics CRM Server:

- Microsoft SQL Server 2008, Standard Edition, x64 SP1 or later version
- Microsoft SQL Server 2008, Enterprise Edition, x64 SP1 or later version
- Microsoft SQL Server 2008 Datacenter x64 SP1 or later version
- Microsoft SQL Server 2008 Developer x64 SP1 or later version (for non-production environments only)

CAUTION

Microsoft SQL Server 2008, Workgroup, Web, Compact, or Express editions are not supported for running Microsoft Dynamics CRM.

32 bits versions of SQL Server are not supported either.

In addition, SQL Server 2000 Reporting Services and SQL Server 2005 Reporting Services editions are not supported with this version of Microsoft Dynamics CRM Server.

When a user who belongs to multiple organizations within a Microsoft Dynamics CRM deployment executes a report, the report executes correctly only if it is executed against that user's default organization.

TIP

To avoid problems that can arise from this, make sure that you use the same deployment of SQL Server Reporting Services for each organization in your Microsoft Dynamics CRM deployment.

Running 64-bit SQL Server versions for Itanium (IA-64) systems in conjunction with Microsoft Dynamics CRM will receive commercially reasonable support. Commercially reasonable support is defined as all reasonable support efforts by Microsoft Customer Service and Support that do not require Dynamics CRM code fixes.

Microsoft Dynamics CRM Reporting Extensions

The Microsoft Dynamics CRM Reporting Extensions is a component that connects the Microsoft Dynamics CRM computer to the SQL Server Reporting Services computer.

Microsoft Dynamics CRM Reporting Extensions Requirements

The Microsoft Dynamics CRM Connector for SQL Server Reporting Services has the following general requirements:

- You must complete Microsoft Dynamics CRM Server Setup before you run Microsoft Dynamics CRM Connector for SQL Server Reporting Services Setup.
- You can install and run only one instance of Microsoft Dynamics CRM Reporting Extensions on a computer that has SQL Server 2008 Reporting Services installed.

- Separate deployments of Microsoft Dynamics CRM cannot share one SQL Server Reporting Services server. However, a single deployment of Microsoft Dynamics CRM that has multiple organizations can use the same SQL Server Reporting Services server.

▶ See Chapter 11, "Reporting," for more information about the Microsoft Dynamics CRM connector for SQL Server Reporting Services.

SharePoint Integration

Microsoft SharePoint is not required to install Microsoft Dynamics CRM 2011, and you can configure the SharePoint server settings after Microsoft Dynamics CRM Server Setup.

To enable Microsoft SharePoint integration, the following Microsoft SharePoint Server editions are required and must be installed, running, and at least one Microsoft SharePoint site collection configured and available for Microsoft Dynamics CRM Server:

- Microsoft SharePoint 2010 (all editions)
- Microsoft Office SharePoint Server (MOSS) 2007

To enable SharePoint functionality, go to the Settings area of the Microsoft Dynamics CRM Web application, and then select Document Management under System group (see Figure 3.4).

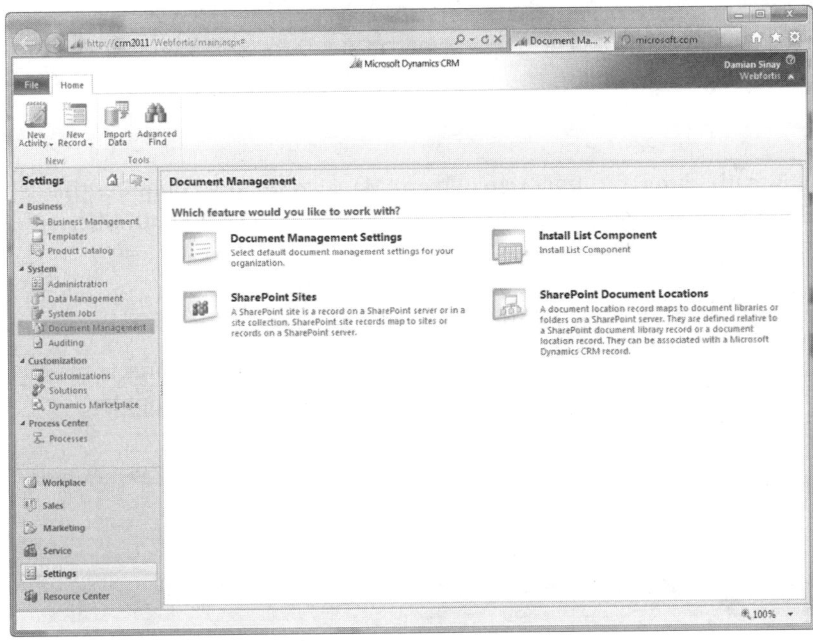

FIGURE 3.4 SharePoint configuration in CRM Web client.

▸ See Chapter 17, "SharePoint Integration" for more information about this configuration.

To have a better SharePoint experience, it is also recommended to install the Microsoft Dynamics CRM 2011 List Component for Microsoft SharePoint Server 2010 that can be downloaded from the Microsoft download website.

E-Mail Router

This section lists the software and application software requirements for Microsoft Dynamics CRM E-mail Router.

There are two separate installers for the Microsoft Dynamics CRM E-mail Router, one for 32 bits and another for 64 bits, notice you cannot install the 32 bits version on a 64-bit Windows operating system.

Microsoft Dynamics CRM E-mail Router Setup consists of two main components: the Microsoft Dynamics CRM E-mail Router Service and the Rule Deployment Wizard. The CRM E-mail Router Service installs the E-mail Router service and E-mail Router Configuration Manager. The E-mail Router Configuration Manager is used to configure the E-mail Router Service. The Rule Deployment Manager component deploys the rules that enables received e-mail messages to be tracked.

NOTE

Unless specified otherwise, E-mail Router supports the latest service pack (SP) for all required software components.

You can install the E-mail Router and Rule Deployment Manager on any computer that is running one of the following operating systems and has network access to both Microsoft Dynamics CRM and the e-mail server:

- Windows 7 (32 or 64 bits)
- Windows Server 2008 (all editions)
- Windows Server 2003 (all editions)
- Windows Vista (32 or 64 bits)
- Windows XP Pro and tablet in (32 or 64 bits)

CAUTION

Windows XP Media Center Edition is not supported for installing and running Microsoft Dynamics CRM E-mail Router or E-mail Router Configuration Manager.

In addition, running Microsoft Dynamics CRM E-mail Router and E-mail Router Configuration Manager (32-bit) is not supported on a Windows Server 64-bit operating system, in Windows-On-Windows (WOW) mode.

Exchange Server

Microsoft Exchange Server is required only if you want to use the E-mail Router to connect to an Exchange Server e-mail messaging system. To do this, the E-mail Router can be installed on any of the previously mentioned Windows or Windows Server operating systems that have a connection to the Exchange Server. The E-mail Router supports the following versions of Exchange Server:

- Exchange 2003 Standard or Enterprise Edition SP2
- Exchange Server 2007 Standard or Enterprise Edition
- Exchange Online
- Exchange Server 2010 Edition or Enterprise Edition

NOTE

Although Microsoft Exchange 2000 Server editions are not supported with these versions of Microsoft Dynamics CRM E-mail Router and Rule Deployment Manager, there is no reason why you couldn't use Exchange 2000 with POP3 access and configure the e-mail router to use native POP3 functionality.

If missing, E-mail Router Setup installs the .NET Framework 4.0 on the computer where you install the E-mail Router.

The Rule Deployment Wizard component must be installed on a computer that is running any of the previously mentioned Windows or Windows Server operating systems and has the Microsoft Exchange Server Messaging API (MAPI) client runtime libraries installed.

- See MAPI client runtime libraries on the Microsoft Download Center at http://go.microsoft.com/fwlink/?linkid=78805.

POP3/SMTP

POP3-compliant e-mail systems are supported for incoming e-mail message routing. SMTP and Exchange Web Services through Exchange Online are the only transport protocol supported for outgoing e-mail message routing.

NOTE

When you use the Forward Mailbox option on the User form, the POP3 e-mail server must provide support where an e-mail message can be sent as an attachment to another e-mail message.

If you install the Microsoft Dynamics CRM E-mail Router to connect to a POP3-compliant or SMTP server, the following standards are required:

- POP3: RFC 1939
- SMTP: RFC 2821 and 2822

Client

You can access Microsoft CRM 2011 in two different ways: by using Microsoft Internet Explorer or by using Microsoft Office Outlook.

Microsoft CRM Client for Internet Explorer

When using the Microsoft CRM Client for Internet Explorer, only Internet Explorer is required. This client is the recommended option when one of the following situations occurs:

- Remote and/or offsite access is necessary.
- Support staff doesn't necessarily need Office.
- A thin client solution is desired.

CAUTION

Note that only Microsoft Internet Explorer can be used as a Microsoft CRM Client, and other browsers, such as Firefox and Opera, are not supported. Although not supported, it is possible to use browsers other than Internet Explorer as a Microsoft CRM client if you enable their IE compatibility functions.

The following versions of Internet Explorer are required:

- Internet Explorer 7
- Internet Explorer 8
- Internet Explorer 9 or later

When using the Microsoft CRM Client for Internet Explorer, the following operating systems are supported:

- Windows 7 (both 64-bit and 32-bit versions)
- Windows Vista (both 64-bit and 32-bit versions)
- Windows XP Professional SP2 or SP3
- Windows XP Tablet PC Edition SP2 or SP3
- Windows XP Professional x64 Edition

To use Microsoft Dynamics CRM Office integration features, such as Export to Excel and Mail Merge, you must have one of the following installed on the computer that is running the Microsoft Dynamics CRM Web client:

- Microsoft Office 2003 with SP3
- Microsoft Office 2007 system
- Microsoft Office 2010

> **CAUTION**
>
> Microsoft Windows 2000 editions are not supported for installing and running the Microsoft Dynamics CRM Web client.

Microsoft CRM Office Client for Outlook

With Outlook, the Microsoft CRM 2011 client is installed directly into Outlook and can be accessed by simply navigating to the Microsoft CRM organization name node (see Figure 3.5).

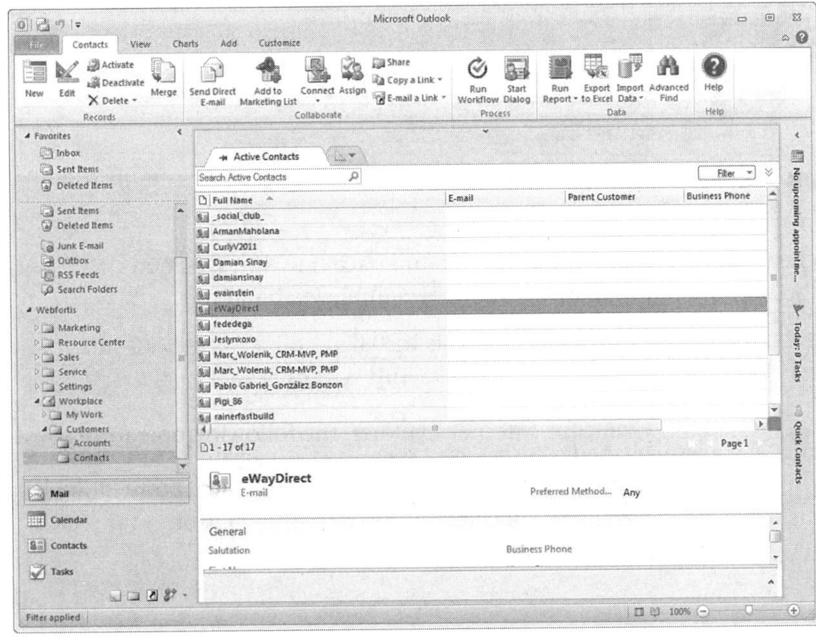

FIGURE 3.5 Microsoft Outlook with Microsoft CRM.

The Microsoft CRM Outlook client comes in two versions, 32 bits and 64 bits. The same client can also run in two modes (online or offline) and can now connects to more than one CRM organization as well as to any Microsoft Dynamics CRM Online organization.

▶ The Outlook client can be either download from http://downloads.microsoft.com or from the CRM Web interface where users will be suggested to download the Outlook client, as seen in Figure 3.6.

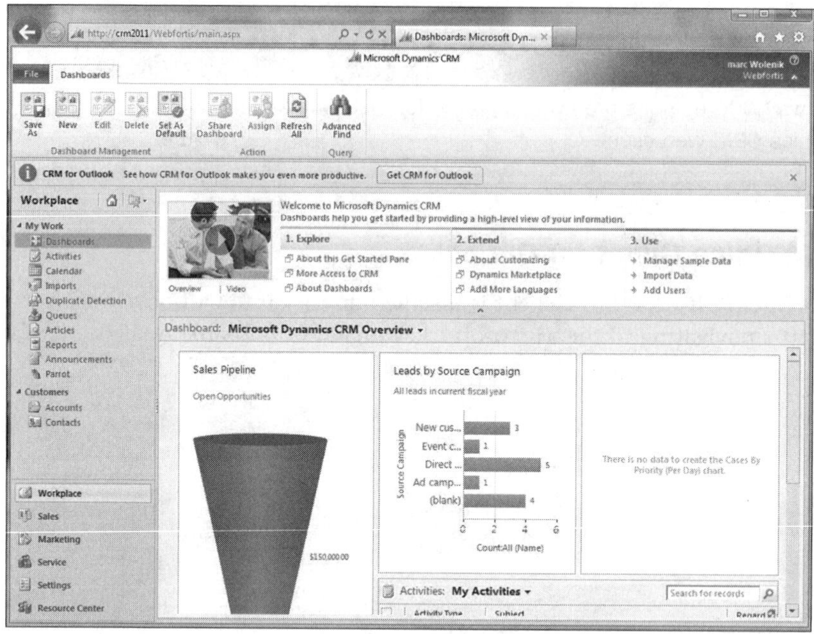

FIGURE 3.6 Microsoft Outlook client download suggestion from Web client.

Notice when the client is downloaded from the web interface only the specific version of the CRM type (online or on-premise) you are running will be downloaded.

On a standard installation online the online access is installed, to install the offline access type, you need to click the Options menu when the Setup Wizard ask for installation type (see Figure 3.7).

Although both features are similar, the Offline Access type has the capability to go offline and enables users to work with CRM data while not connected to the Microsoft CRM server. The offline capabilities are available by clicking the Go Offline button on the CRM tab in the main Outlook ribbon (see Figure 3.8).

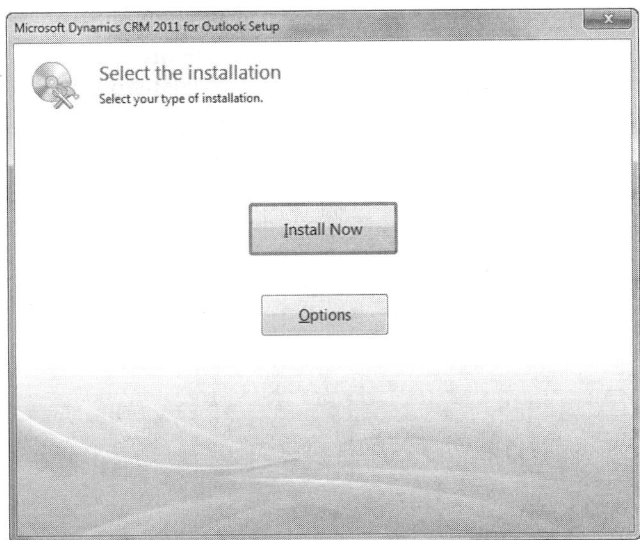

FIGURE 3.7 Microsoft Outlook client installation types.

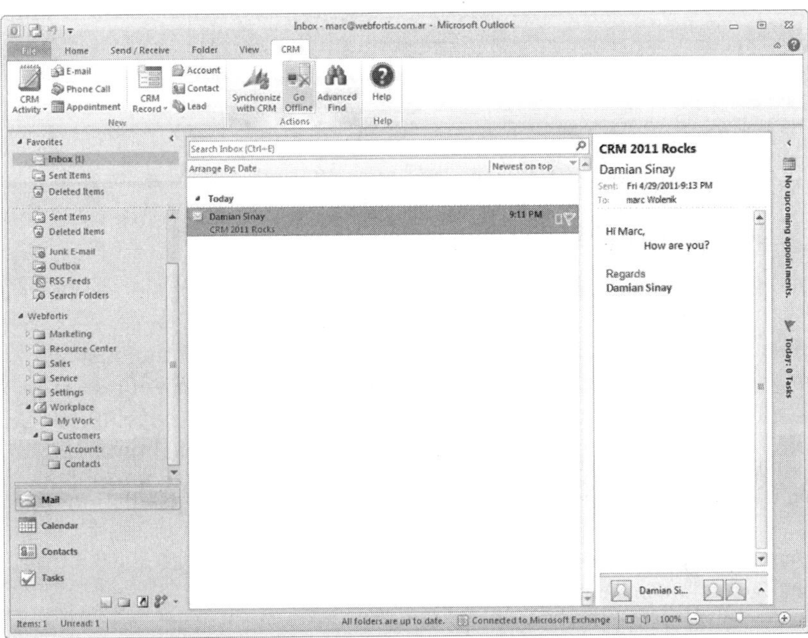

FIGURE 3.8 Microsoft CRM Outlook client while online.

When users have completed their offline tasks and return to the Microsoft CRM 2011 Server, they can click the Go Online button (refer to Figure 3.8), and a synchronization process checks for updated data on both the Microsoft CRM server and the Microsoft CRM Outlook client (see Figure 3.9).

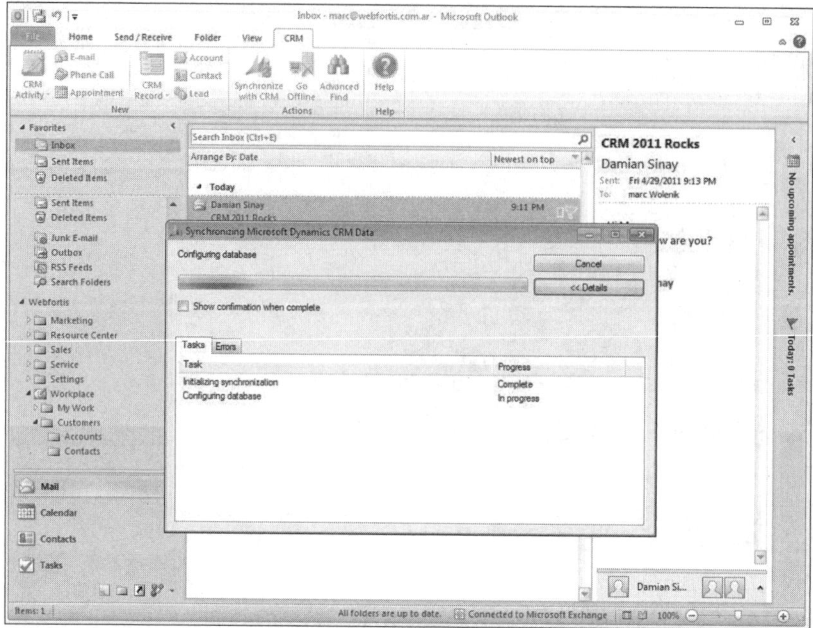

FIGURE 3.9 Microsoft CRM Outlook client synchronizing to go offline.

- Microsoft SQL Server 2008 Express Edition (CRM)
- Microsoft Report Viewer Redistributable 2010

Finally, it should be noted that the Offline Access Client mode does not require installation on a laptop. If you choose to install the Offline Access Client mode on your desktop, it will have the same functionality as the desktop client, but it will install the required components outlined earlier. There are not too many reasons for doing this, however, other than testing and development purposes, because it is unlikely that you'll be taking your desktop offline.

▶ For more information related to the differences in clients, refer to Chapter 16, "Configuration and Customization Tools."

Regardless of which Microsoft CRM client is used, the following operating systems are required for the Microsoft CRM Office client for Outlook:

- Windows 7 (both 64-bit and 32-bit versions)
- Windows Vista (both 64-bit and 32-bit versions)

- Windows XP Professional and Tablet editions with SP3
- Windows Server 2008 and Windows Server 2003 when running with Remote Desktop Services (formerly Terminal Services)

CAUTION

Windows XP Media Center Edition is not supported for installing and running Microsoft Dynamics CRM for Outlook.

In addition, the following components must be installed (and running) before you attempt a Microsoft CRM Office client for Outlook installation:

- Microsoft Office 2003 with SP3 (32-bit version)
- Microsoft Office 2007 (32-bit version)
- Microsoft Office 2010 (32-or 64-bit versions)

The following components are required. However, the installer automatically downloads and installs them as part of the installation process:

- SQL 2008 Express Edition (Offline Access Client mode only)
- .NET Framework 4.0
- Windows Installer (MSI) 4.5.
- MSXML 4.0
- Microsoft Visual C++ Redistributable
- Microsoft Report Viewer Redistributable 2010
- Microsoft Application Error Reporting
- Windows Identity Framework (WIF)

Finally, the Outlook client (either version) cannot be installed on the same server that has Exchange Server on it.

Licensing

With the different versions now available for Microsoft CRM 2011, customers have greater choice for licensing.

The licensing model for Microsoft CRM 2011 has been changed to use only one license key for the version, the server, and Client Access Licenses (CALs). This is a significant improvement over earlier versions that required separate licenses for each.

The Microsoft CRM versions, supported operating systems, and licensing are broken down in Table 3.1.

TABLE 3.1 Summary of Microsoft CRM Versions

Microsoft CRM Version	Supported Operating Systems	Users	Organizations	Computers
Workgroup Edition	• Microsoft Windows Server 2008 • Microsoft Windows Server 2003 (any of the previously listed supported versions) • Microsoft Windows Small Business Server 2008 R2 Enterprise Edition	Five or fewer	Single organization	Single computer
Server Edition	Any of the previously listed supported operating	No user limit	Multiple organizations	Multiple computers

To manage licenses in Microsoft CRM 2011, the Deployment Manager is used on the server. From the Deployment Manager, you can view and upgrade licenses by going to the License tab in the deployment properties dialog (see Figure 3.10).

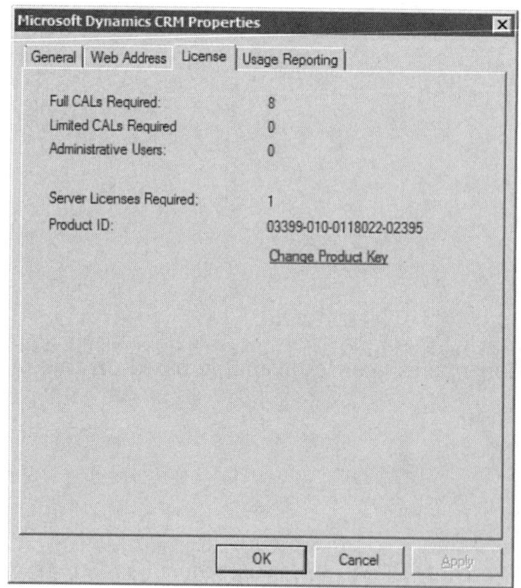

FIGURE 3.10 Microsoft Dynamics CRM Deployment Manager.

Microsoft CRM 2011 uses named licenses (or user CALs) as well as machine licenses (or device CALs) as its licensing model. Named licenses require that every user who accesses the Microsoft CRM 2011 must have a license. If that user leaves the company or no longer needs to use the CRM, the license can be transferred to another individual; however, the previous individual then no longer has access to Microsoft CRM 2011. Machine licenses allow a single computer to be licensed to Microsoft CRM 2011, and multiple users can use the same machine provided they aren't accessing it simultaneously. This is a significant improvement with regard to licensing when you consider call centers or similar organizations that operate around the clock. Named and Machine CALs can be mixed in a deployment.

Two different kinds of Microsoft CALs are available with Microsoft CRM 2011:

- **Full**—Full system functionality is granted to a user with this type of license. These users have full system access and full permission to modify records, limited only by whatever security role and privileges might be set for them.
- **Limited-use**—This CAL is a read-only CAL and comes in two options: Administrative or Read-only. With this license, users have the ability to view all areas and records in Microsoft CRM 2011. However, they cannot make any changes. The Administrative version gives users the ability to modify records only in the Settings area.

NOTE

The licensing differences apply only when Microsoft CRM 2011 is accessed via the web client. To use the Outlook client, you must have the Full CAL.

Microsoft makes CRM licensing available in the following different ways:

- Retail
- Volume

You can purchase retail licensing from any vendor that sells software.

Volume licensing is a method by which Microsoft makes licenses available based on the following criteria:

- Size of the purchasing organization
- Type of licensing desired
- Licensing term desired
- Payment options

When purchasing licenses through volume licensing, customers also can add Software Assurance (SA). SA enables customers to upgrade their software if Microsoft releases a newer version within a certain timeframe. Customers then can purchase software and not worry about it being obsolete and/or having to repurchase again when a new version comes out.

Volume licensing is broken down into the following four methods:

- **Open License**—Organizations that Microsoft considers small or midsized (usually with fewer than 250 computers) have the option to purchase licensing and receive benefits such as discounts, Software Assurance (mentioned previously), and easy deployment and management. The only restrictions on open licensing are that a minimum of five licenses must be purchased at a time, and payment is expected at the time of the transaction. These specific licensing options are available with Open License:
  - Open Value
  - Open Business
  - Open Volume

Each option has different advantages, depending largely on your business needs.

> To learn more about these options, go to www.microsoft.com/licensing/programs/open/overview.mspx.

- **Select License**—Organizations have the option to create a payment plan and are given discounts based on the amount of software ordered. Generally, the Select License option is reserved for organizations that have more than 250 computers.
- **Enterprise Agreement**—Enterprise Agreement licensing is similar to the Select License option, but there are more significant discounts (usually reserved for larger orders).
- **Enterprise Subscription Agreement**—This is a subscription-based model similar to the Enterprise Agreement option. However, because the software is not purchased, it offers discounts at a greater rate. Again, this option is usually reserved for organizations with more than 250 computers.

Although you can purchase the Microsoft CRM 2011 licenses via retail methods, we recommend purchasing licensing through volume licensing rather than retail if possible.

If you are a developer or an ISV, or if you are interested in enhancing or working with some of the features of Microsoft CRM 2011, you might want to consider acquiring an MSDN license, which includes a copy of CRM for development purposes.

> You can find more information about the MSDN program at www.microsoft.com/msdn.

Upgrading

Existing Microsoft Dynamics CRM 4.0 customers who would like to upgrade to 2011 can select whether they want to convert their named/user CALs to either a user or device CAL. Additionally, customers that have Microsoft Dynamics 2011 Professional Edition can upgrade their server and external connector licenses to Microsoft Dynamics CRM 2011 Professional version.

The upgrade path for Microsoft Dynamics CRM 4.0 Workgroup is unavailable at time of press, so be sure to check the Microsoft website for more information at www.microsoft.com/dynamics.

External Connector Licensing

A special license known as the *External Connector License* is required when you want to work directly with the data contained in your Microsoft Dynamics CRM database for any purpose. This is common when organizations want to extend functionality of case creation to their external customer facing websites, for example. In this scenario, a user could go to the organizations website, log in, and create a case directly in the website. The information would then be processed within Microsoft Dynamics CRM as a new case and assigned to either a support queue or user. Because this type of functionality requires us to touch Microsoft Dynamics CRM data, we need one an external connector license. This type of license has changed on this version of CRM 2011 and has the following limitations:

- Read only access to entities, activities, and custom entities and activities.
- Data privileges to create entity and custom entity records.
- Data privileges to append to, and update entity and custom entity records.
- No delete, share, and assign privileges are supported.

Basically the connector allows you to do most of the operations you want with the database, including reading, writing, but not deleting. The read-only connector enables you to display only information from the database and not update it in any fashion. The latter would be helpful if you wanted to share information with your organization or external partners relating to Microsoft Dynamics CRM data, such as upcoming sales and/or caseloads.

Either of these licenses is available with the CRM 2011 Server on-premise; however, neither is available with the Workgroup Server 2011 edition. If you are working with the Workgroup edition and want to use a connector for whatever reason, you must upgrade to the CRM 2011 Server version.

Windows Users

Note that Microsoft Windows has separate CAL requirements and, hence, can place restrictions on Microsoft CRM users. A good example of this is the 75-user limit on Windows Small Business Servers. The Professional Edition of Microsoft CRM 2011 supports an unlimited number of users, but each user must be listed in Active Directory. Active Directory in SBS supports only 75 users, so you can have only 75 users in Microsoft CRM 2011.

Carefully consider this when planning the infrastructure.

Summary

There are several different configuration options for both the Microsoft Dynamics CRM server and its clients.

When working with an On Premise version of Microsoft Dynamics CRM, be sure that all the components listed previously are installed and correctly configured.

Finally, the related licensing options have been greatly improved, as well as the ability for customers to upgrade.

CHAPTER 4

Setting Up CRM 2011

IN THIS CHAPTER

This chapter is effectively split into two parts: setting up CRM 2011 Online and setting up CRM 2011 On Premise.

We have included the setup of CRM Online as a step-by-step process, and although current at the time of publication, it is highly subject to change as Microsoft continues to improve the sign-up process, steps, and overall requirements.

NOTE

This chapter does not apply to anything related to partner hosted (except for partners wanting to set up their servers for customers) because the process for customers is unique to the partner requirements.

CRM Online

Setting up CRM 2011 Online server is really nothing more than provisioning the service from Microsoft and can now be done with just a few steps. The Outlook client still requires installation. However, the steps are the same as the On Premise setup, which is explained later in this chapter.

▶ Refer to Chapter 13, "Client Configuration Options," for more information about the Outlook setup.

NOTE

At the time this book was published, Microsoft had a free trial of the software for 30 days, and we don't anticipate this offer disappearing anytime soon. This is a great way to get a free month of use because the trial can easily be converted to a full production system.

TIP

Although you can provision, and perform all the steps listed in this book without the benefit of a partner, we *strongly* recommend engaging the assistance of a partner for advice, recommendation of best practices, and troubleshooting. Our company, Webfortis, currently has several Quickstart packages to help you get up and running. (These packages start at zero cost [initial provisioning, setup, and training] and go up to several thousand dollars depending on requirements.)

For more information about our offerings, please refer to http://crmonline.webfortis.com.

To start service with CRM 2011 Online, follow these steps:

1. Using Internet Explorer, navigate to http://crm.dynamics.com.
2. Select the Get Started! button, as shown in Figure 4.1.

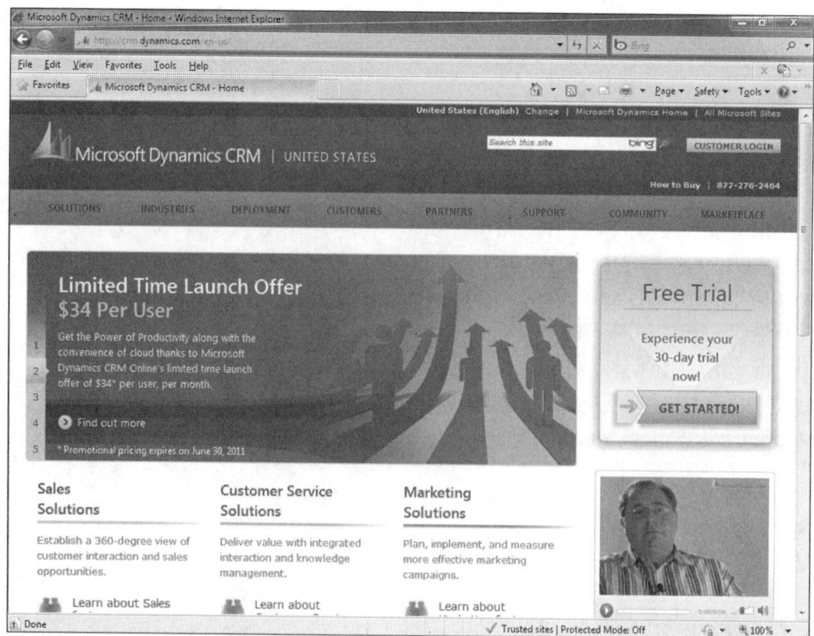

FIGURE 4.1 Microsoft CRM Online home page.

3. Select the Sign Up Now! button on the next screen, which takes you to the Provisioning Wizard, as shown in Figure 4.2.

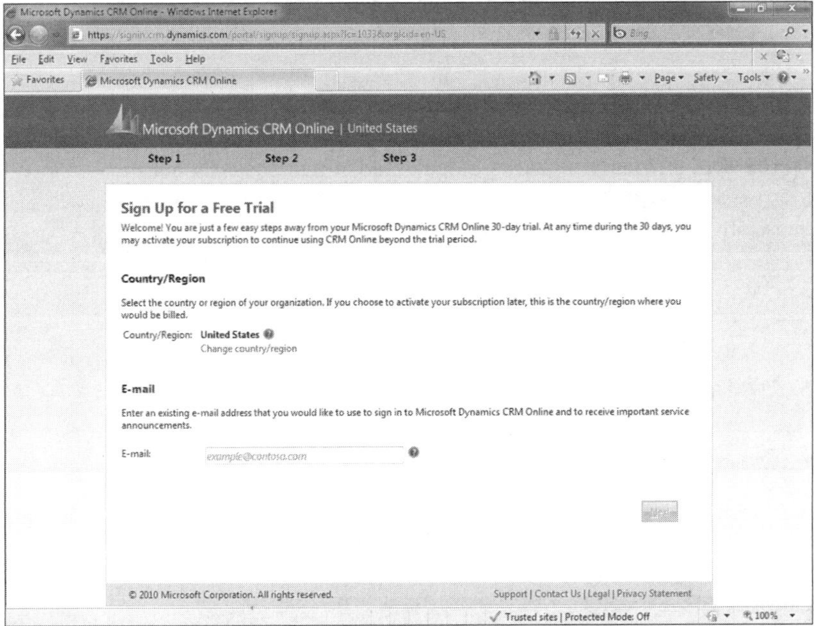

FIGURE 4.2 Microsoft CRM Online Provisioning Wizard—step 1 of 3.

4. Select your country/region as the first option, and then select the e-mail that will be the primary contact e-mail associated with the account. Click Next to continue.

   The system will validate the e-mail entered against the Windows Live ID database, and if there is a Windows Live ID (WLID) account associated with the e-mail, you'll be prompted through to the next screen in the wizard. Otherwise you will be prompted through the WLID setup/sign-in process, returning you back to step 2 when completed.

5. Enter the captcha value and accept the terms of service as shown in Figure 4.3.

NOTE

The captcha shown on your signup will be different from the one shown in Figure 4.3.

6. Complete the sign-up information as shown in Figure 4.4, and then click Finish to continue.

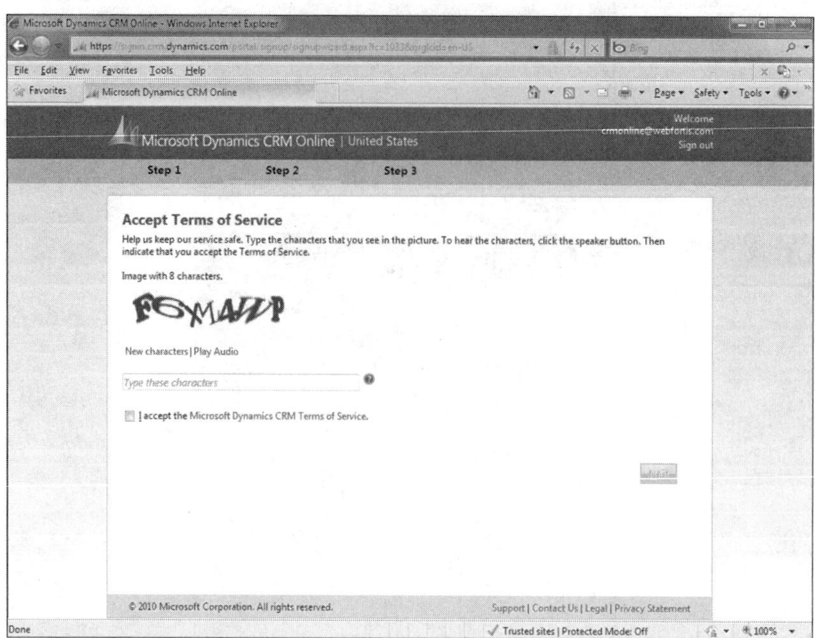

FIGURE 4.3 Microsoft CRM Online Provisioning Wizard—step 2 of 3.

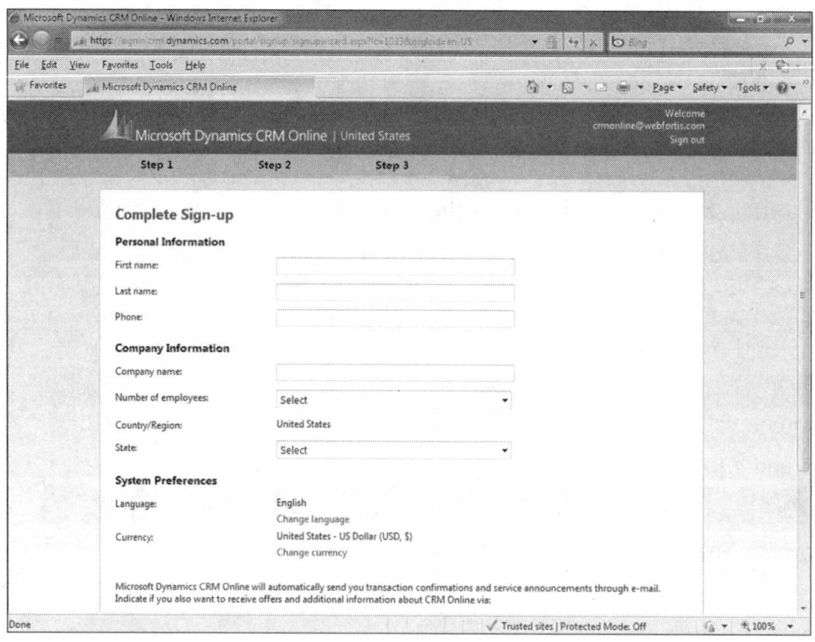

FIGURE 4.4 Microsoft CRM Online Provisioning Wizard—step 3 of 3.

CAUTION

It is at step 6 where you set both the base language and the base currency. Neither of these can be changed after provisioning, so if either is different than shown, make the changes *before* clicking Finish.

7. The system will start the process of provisioning on the Microsoft servers (see Figure 4.5).

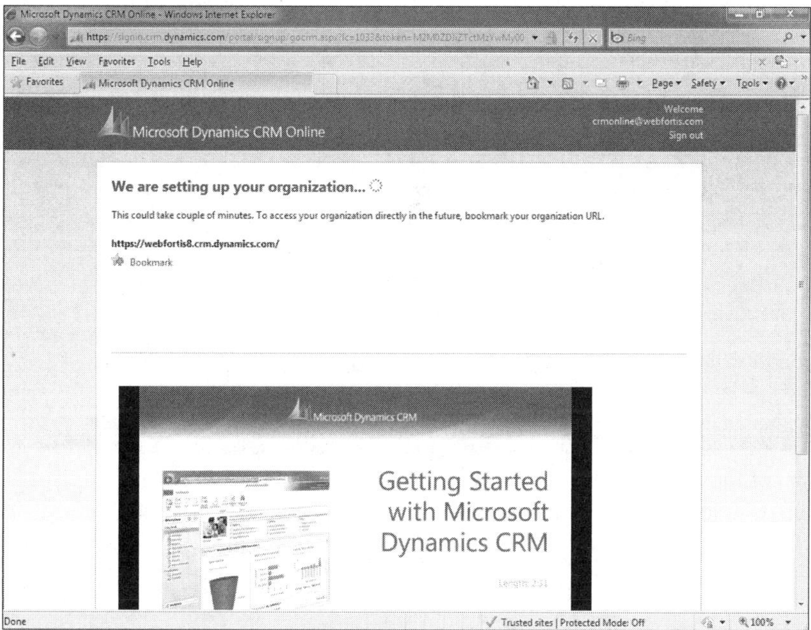

FIGURE 4.5 Microsoft CRM Online organization provisioning.

When complete, the application is ready for usage, as shown in Figure 4.6.

NOTE

The final URL of your organization might or might not include your organization name (see Figures 4.5 and 4.6). The option for vanity or custom URLs is a feature that is not guaranteed by Microsoft now. Therefore, don't be surprised if your final URL is the organization unique name—for example, https://crmnaorg9c121.crm.dynamics.com/ or similar.

Now you are done with the setup of your instance of CRM Online and have only to add users, configure the application, and install the Outlook clients (if desired).

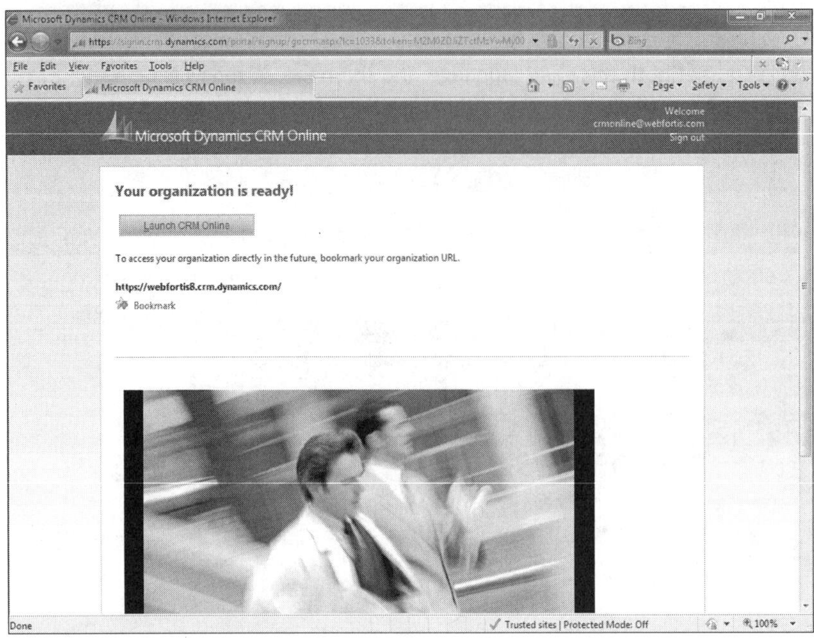

FIGURE 4.6 Microsoft CRM Online Organization is ready for use.

NOTE

With the exception of the "Microsoft Dynamics CRM Clients" and "Microsoft Dynamics CRM Online Setup" sections, virtually everything else in this chapter applies to the On Premise setup.

▶ Be sure to review Chapter 3, "Requirements for CRM 2011," for hardware and software requirements related to CRM 2011.

Single- Versus Multiple-Server Deployment

You can deploy Microsoft Dynamics CRM across multiple servers or on a single server. Although the method of deployment depends on your system requirements and server availability, some restrictions govern which version you can deploy and how you can do so.

Single-Server Deployment

In a single-server deployment, a single server can perform all these functions:

- Domain controller
- Microsoft Dynamics CRM Server

- SQL Server
- SQL Server Reporting Server (SRS)

It is important to consider these when planning the deployment because the resource requirements for any one of these functions can be extensive. Thus, we recommend considering a multiple-server deployment whenever you might be using the server for more than just Microsoft Dynamics CRM.

Microsoft Dynamics CRM 2011 Workgroup edition is limited to a single computer running Microsoft Dynamics CRM Server, so it is the most common usage of a single server deployment.

▶ Refer to Chapter 3 when considering a single-server deployment.

4

Multiple-Server Deployments

Microsoft CRM Server can be spread across multiple servers during deployment (and later, if necessary). Multiple servers offer these benefits:

- Scalability
- Performance
- Server resource allocation and control
- Shortened disaster recovery time
- Server roles

Server roles provide the capability to deploy specific services and components to different computers for scaling and performance benefits.

You can select two predefined server role groupings when installing Microsoft Dynamics CRM under the Custom Setup process, as shown in Figure 4.7. By default, both server role groupings are installed with a typical install.

- The Front End Server role provides the Microsoft Dynamics CRM web user interface and services.
- The Back End Server role provides the asynchronous services, such as the Workflow and Bulk E-mail services and the Sandbox Processing Service to run code with partial trusts security restrictions.
- The Deployment Administration Server role provides the tools and services necessary to manage CRM deployments and organizations.

The Front End Server role is divided in the following components:

- **Web Application Server**—Provides the necessary components and web services needed to run the web application server and to connect the CRM Outlook client that is used to connect users to Microsoft Dynamics CRM data

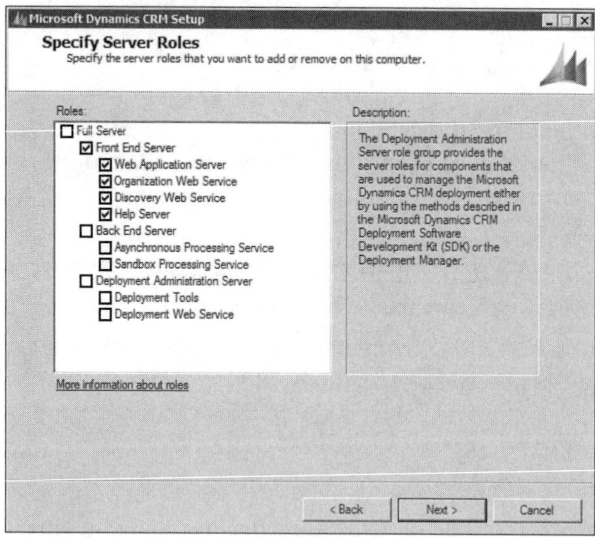

FIGURE 4.7 Role grouping options during custom setup.

- **Organization Web Service**—Installs the components needed to run the Microsoft Dynamics CRM external applications that uses the methods described in the Microsoft CRM SDK
- **Discovery Web Service**—Installs the components required for users to find the organization that they are a member of in a multitenant deployment
- **Help Server**—Provides the components needed to make Microsoft Dynamics CRM Help available to users

The Back End Server role is divided in the following components:

- **Asynchronous Processing Service**—Processes queued asynchronous events, including the following:
  - Workflow
  - Data import
  - Bulk e-mail
- **Sandbox Processing Service**—Provides an isolated partial trust environment to run custom plug-in codes or workflows in a more secure environment

The Deployment Administration Server role is divided in the following components:

- **Deployment Tools**—Installs the components required to manage the deployment by using the methods described in the Software Development Kit (SDK), such as creating an organization or removing a Deployment Administrator role from a user

- **Deployment Web Service**—Provides the service needed to deploy applications by custom application that follows the Microsoft SDK to automate deployments

TIP

Keep in mind that no role exists specifically for workflow services. Instead, you must deploy the Asynchronous Processing Service because this service handles workflow.

Another consideration related to multiple-server deployments is the Microsoft CRM LAN topology. The topology should include the Microsoft Dynamics CRM Server as well as both Active Directory and SQL Server on the same LAN, primarily because of the large amount of network traffic that they create and use. Failure to have a permanent high-speed network connection between any of these computers can seriously affect performance and possibly cause data corruption.

Microsoft recommends using a topology similar to this:

- Team topology (two servers)
    - Computer 1: Running Windows Server 2008, Windows Server 2003, or Windows 2000 Server as a functioning domain controller. If the computer is running Windows Server 2003, it may also run Microsoft Exchange 2003.
    - Computer 2: Running Windows Server 2008, SQL Server 2008, SQL Server 2008 Reporting Services, and Microsoft Dynamics CRM Server.
- Division topology (five servers)
    - Computer 1: Running Windows Server 2008, Windows Server 2003 as a functioning domain controller
    - Computer 2: Running Windows Server 2008, Windows Server 2003 as a secondary domain controller
    - Computer 3: Running Windows Server 2008 and Microsoft Dynamics CRM Server
    - Computer 4: Running Windows Server 2008 or Windows Server 2003, Microsoft SQL Server 2008, and SQL Server 2008 Reporting Services
    - Computer 5: Running Windows Server 2008 or Windows Server 2003, Microsoft Exchange Server, and the e-mail router
- Multiforest and multidomain Active Directory topology

For very large user bases that span multiple domains and, in some cases, forests, the following configuration is supported:

- Forest A: Parent Domain
    - Computer 1: Running Windows Server 2008, Windows Server 2003 as a functioning domain controller
    - Computer 2: Running Windows Server 2008, Windows Server 2003 as a secondary domain controller
    - Computer 3: Running Windows Server 2008 and Microsoft Dynamics CRM Server
    - Computer 4: Running Windows Server 2008 and Microsoft SQL Server 2008
    - Computer 5: Running Windows Server 2008 or Windows Server 2003 and SQL Server 2008 Reporting Services
    - Computer 6: Running Windows Server 2008 or Windows Server 2003, Microsoft Exchange Server, and the Microsoft Dynamics CRM e-mail router
- Forest A: Child Domain
    - Computer 7: Running Windows Server 2008, Windows Server 2003 as a functioning domain controller
    - Computer 8: Running Windows Server 2008, Windows Server 2003 as a secondary domain controller
    - Computer 9: Running Windows Server 2008 or Windows Server 2003 and Microsoft Exchange Server
    - Forest B: Parent Domain
    - Computer 10: Running Windows Server 2008, Windows Server 2003 as a functioning domain controller
    - Computer 11: Running Windows Server 2008, Windows Server 2003 as a secondary domain controller
    - Computer 12: Running Windows Server 2008 or Windows Server 2003 and Microsoft Exchange Server

Setup Process

When installing Microsoft Dynamics CRM for the first time, it is a good idea to confirm that all the requirements for Microsoft Dynamics CRM listed in Chapter 3 are configured properly, are running, and have the most updated service packs.

Additionally, you must have the following as part of the Microsoft CRM Dynamics Server setup process:

- Microsoft CRM license code
- Desired Microsoft Dynamics CRM server type (application, platform, or both)
- Organization name

- Organization friendly name
- Desired base currency
- Location/port of the Microsoft Dynamics CRM web site
- Location of Microsoft SQL Server
- Location of SQL Server Reporting Services Report Server
- E-mail router server name (optional)

It is not necessary to have the Microsoft Dynamics CRM server set up to install the Microsoft CRM Dynamics Outlook clients; however, you cannot configure the clients with the Microsoft Dynamics CRM server until the server is set up.

Microsoft Dynamics CRM Server Setup

When setting up Microsoft Dynamics CRM, it is recommended to set up the server first and then the e-mail router. Although you can install the e-mail router before you install Microsoft Dynamics CRM, it is recommended that you first install Microsoft Dynamics CRM because the service accounts that are necessary to run the e-mail router service are automatically added when you specify the incoming e-mail server during the setup process.

Follow these steps to complete the Microsoft Dynamics CRM installation:

1. Start the setup process by launching the CRM2011-Server-ENU-amd64.exe file from the root directory. The setup screen appears (see Figure 4.8), and you are given the option to download updated installation files.

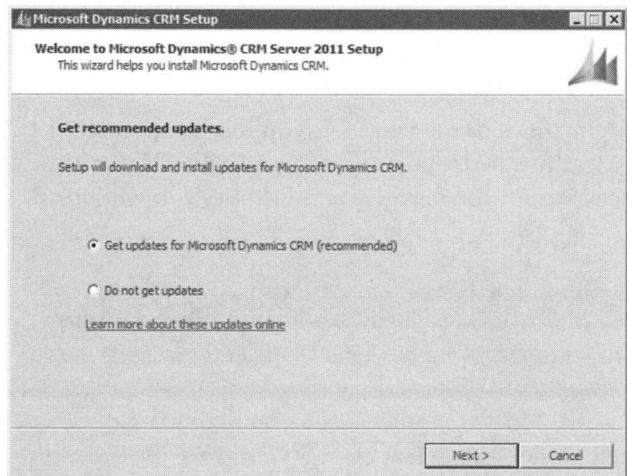

FIGURE 4.8 Microsoft Dynamics CRM setup screen.

TIP

Although you can update Microsoft Dynamics CRM after you've installed it, it is recommended that you get the updates from Microsoft at this point in the setup. They are then automatically downloaded to ensure that your installation goes smoothly.

2. Click Next to continue.
3. Enter your license code (see Figure 4.9). When you have finished entering your license code, a message appears with your license status summary; it should match your license agreement from Microsoft. Click Next to continue.

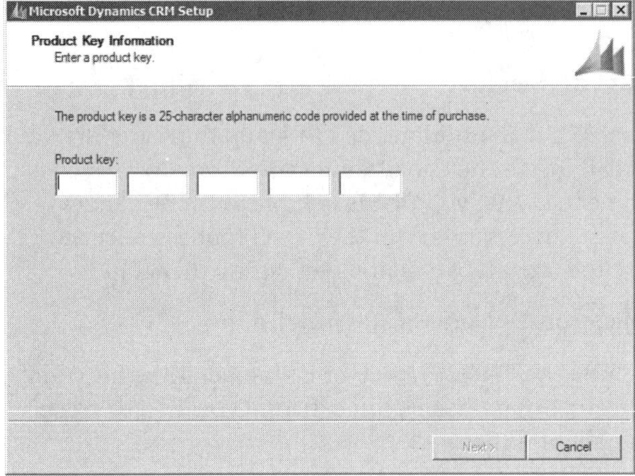

FIGURE 4.9 Microsoft Dynamics CRM license code prompt.

4. Accept the license agreement and click I Accept to continue.
5. The installer then performs a system check to see whether required components necessary for the installation to continue are installed (see Figure 4.10). If you are not missing any components necessary for the installer to continue, you will not see this screen.

NOTE

This check is for the installer only. If you are missing or have misconfigured required Microsoft Dynamics CRM components such as SQL Server Reporting Services, you might be able to continue from this screen; however, you will receive an error when the installer performs a system requirements check as the last step.

Missing installer components will be installed for you when you click Install. After setup confirms that all required components are installed, click Next to continue.

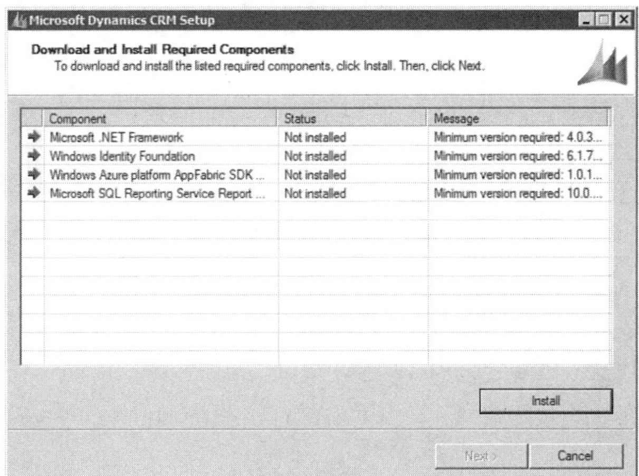

FIGURE 4.10 Microsoft Dynamics CRM installer check for missing components.

6. You must specify the setup installation location on the next screen (see Figure 4.11). Click Next to continue.

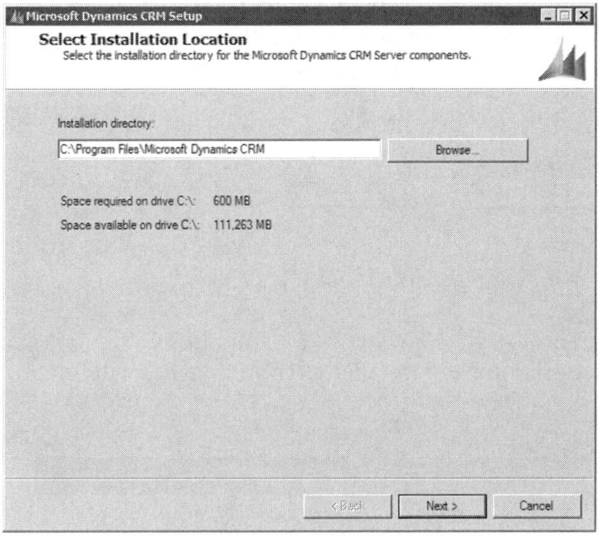

FIGURE 4.11 Microsoft Dynamics CRM installation location.

7. You have the option to install different server roles (mentioned previously in this chapter). You can choose which (or all) server roles you would like to set up (see Figure 4.12). For this installation, select a Full Server installation. Click Next to continue.

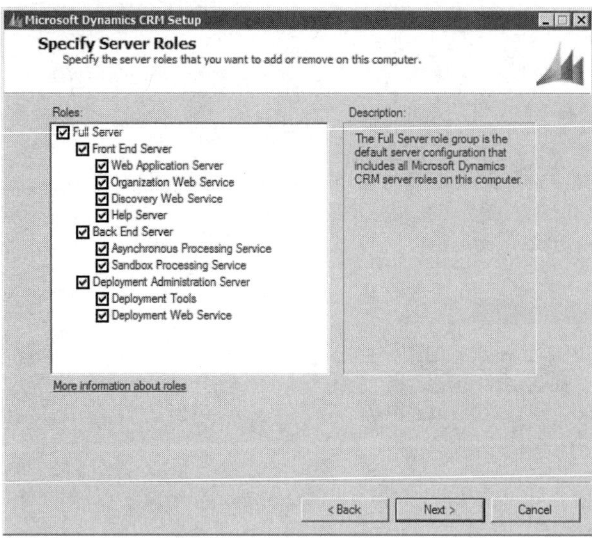

FIGURE 4.12 Microsoft Dynamics CRM installer with the predefined server roles options displayed.

8. Select the SQL Server that will be used for Microsoft Dynamics CRM (see Figure 4.13). By default, no SQL Servers are listed. However, clicking the Refresh option next to the drop-down shows SQL Servers identified on the network.

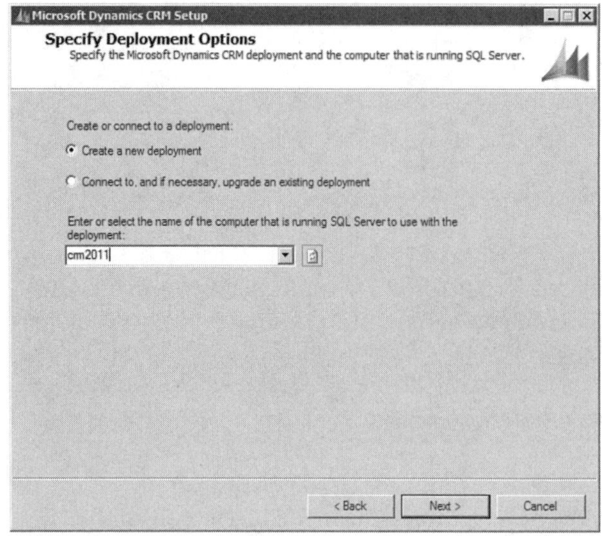

FIGURE 4.13 Microsoft Dynamics CRM Select SQL Server setup.

Additionally, by default, the database option is Create New Deployment. If you already have an existing Microsoft Dynamics CRM deployment, you can select Connect to Existing Deployment, and Setup will use that deployment during setup. If you selected a deployment from a previous version of CRM, this option will also upgrade the deployment. Click Next to continue.

9. Select the organization unit to be used for Microsoft Dynamics CRM (see Figure 4.14). Clicking Browse connects to the active directory, which allows you to select the organization unit. Click Next to continue.

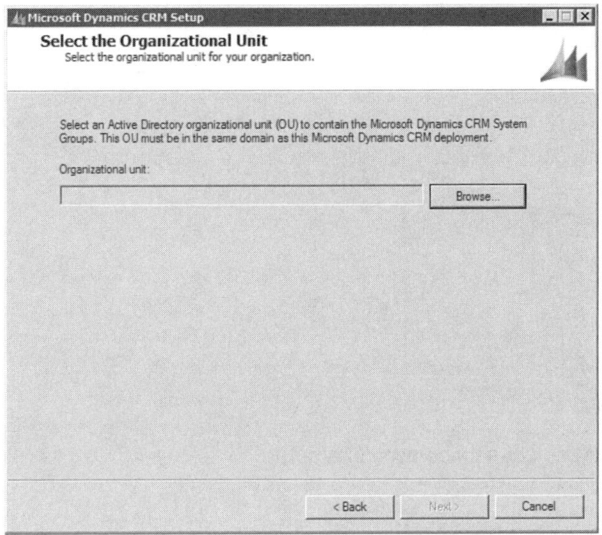

FIGURE 4.14 Microsoft Dynamics CRM select organization unit setup.

NOTE

It is important to have domain administrator rights to perform this deployment mentioned in step 9.

10. Select the service accounts to be used for Microsoft Dynamics CRM (see Figure 4.15). Although it is recommended to use different accounts with minimum privileges for each service, we can use the default NETWORK SERVICE account for this quick installation. If you use domain accounts, you will need to configure the SPNs (Service Principal Names) for each domain account. Click Next to continue.

11. Select the web site where you want Microsoft Dynamics CRM to be installed (see Figure 4.16).

    By default, the application is loaded onto the Default Web Site using server bindings (port) 80. However, if Create New Web Site is selected (see Figure 4.17), the website is created using server bindings on the port you enter in the text box (by default, it is 5555). The difference is whether you want to dedicate your port 80 for Microsoft Dynamics CRM's exclusive use; other web applications will then not be able to use that port.

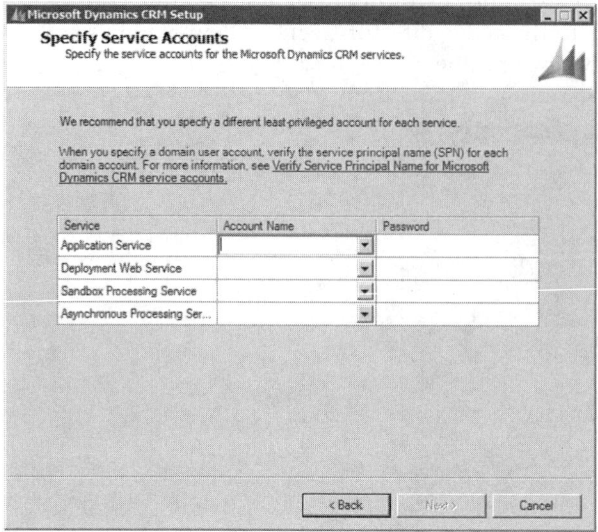

FIGURE 4.15 Microsoft Dynamics CRM select service accounts setup.

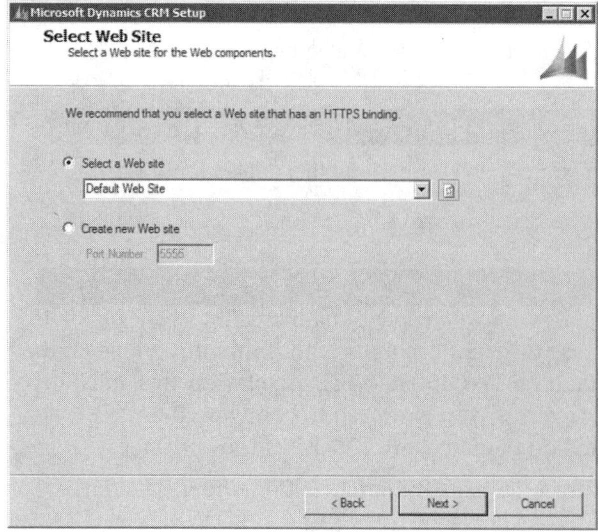

FIGURE 4.16 Microsoft Dynamics CRM Web Site selection for installation.

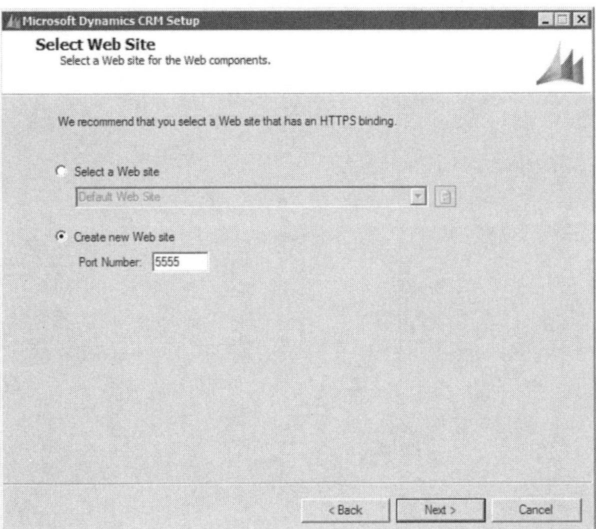

FIGURE 4.17 Microsoft Dynamics CRM new web site selected. Notice that server binding is selected instead of 80.

CAUTION

Because port 80 is the default port for web traffic, carefully consider your options when selecting this setting. If you're unsure or you have other web-based applications that you are running (or would like to run from this server), we recommend you select the Create New Web site option.

12. Click Next to continue.
13. Enter the E-mail router server name (see Figure 4.18). The e-mail router can be installed on a server with Microsoft Exchange 2010 or on a computer that has a connection to an Exchange server. Additionally, because Exchange is not required, you can install the e-mail router on any POP3-compliant e-mail server.

TIP

If you are installing the e-mail router on a computer that previously had the Microsoft CRM 4.0 Router installed on it, you must manually remove the Microsoft CRM 4.0 Router before installing the Microsoft Dynamics CRM e-mail router.

If you elect to install the e-mail router later, leave the field blank and click Next.

▶ For more information on how the e-mail router works, see Chapter 14, "E-mail Configuration."

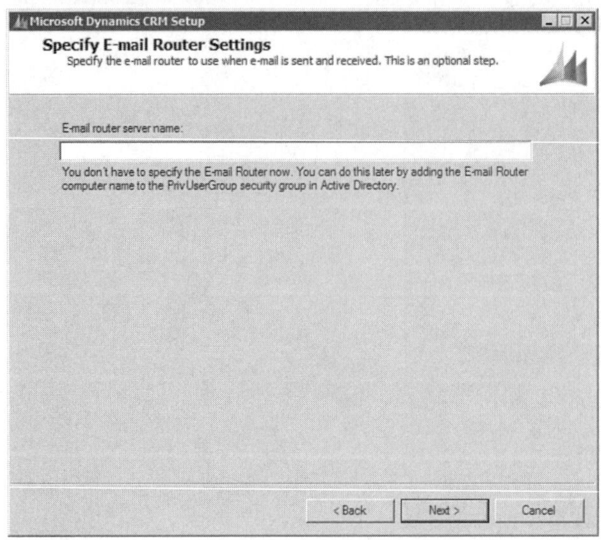

FIGURE 4.18 Microsoft Dynamics CRM e-mail router settings setup.

14. The Display Name field is the long name or descriptive name of your organization, and it has a 250-character limit. The Name field is the name of your organization, and it has a 30-character limit. (See Figure 4.19.)

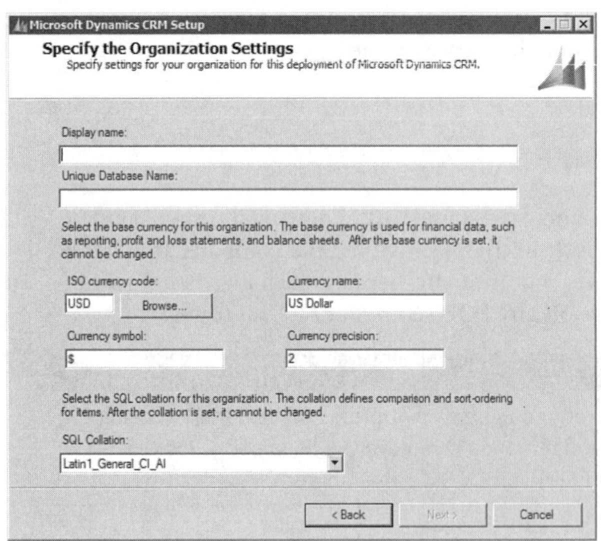

FIGURE 4.19 Microsoft Dynamics CRM organization settings.

15. Select the ISO currency code from the pop-up after selecting Browse (see Figure 4.20). This information is necessary for Microsoft Dynamics CRM to create an organizational database. Click Next to continue.

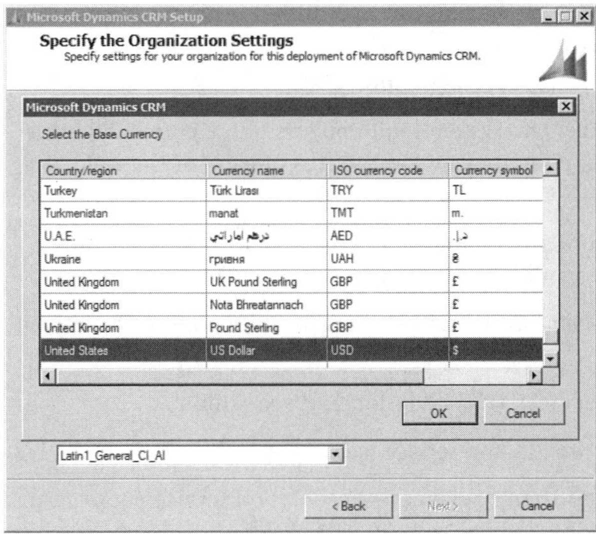

FIGURE 4.20 Microsoft Dynamics CRM ISO currency code selection screen.

16. Enter the Reporting Services Server (see Figure 4.21). As indicated, make sure that you specify the Report Server URL and not the Report Manager URL. If you're unsure of the difference, you can open a browser window and enter the URL to verify that it is not the Report Manager URL. Click Next to continue.

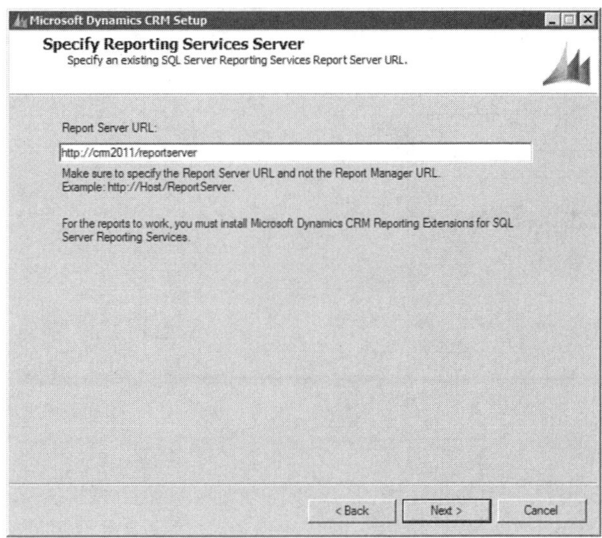

FIGURE 4.21 Microsoft Dynamics CRM Reporting Services Server setup.

17. Select whether you want to participate in the Customer Experience Improvement Program (CEIP), and click Next to continue.
18. Select the installation location. Click Next to continue.
19. The last step of the setup involves the system requirements (see Figure 4.22). This is where the proper installation, configuration, and status of each of the following are confirmed:
    - **Microsoft Windows Operating System**—Version and service pack status. Additional checks include pending restart status.
    - **Microsoft CRM Server User Input**—License, organization, and ISO specification.
    - **Internet Information Services (IIS)**—Version and accessibility.
    - **Microsoft SQL Server**—Version and service pack status.
    - **Microsoft SQL Server Reporting Services**—Version and service pack status. Also checks the specified URL entered because part of the setup can be resolved to the Report Server.
    - **Active Directory**—Whether Active Directory is accessible and whether the specified security account has the necessary permissions.

If any errors arise with these components, you must correct them before continuing with the installation. When everything is resolved, click Next to continue.

When you have completed the Microsoft Dynamics CRM setup, you will be able to access the application by opening your browser and navigating to the URL you selected previously. Usually, this is http://localhost or http://localhost:5555, depending on the bindings selected.

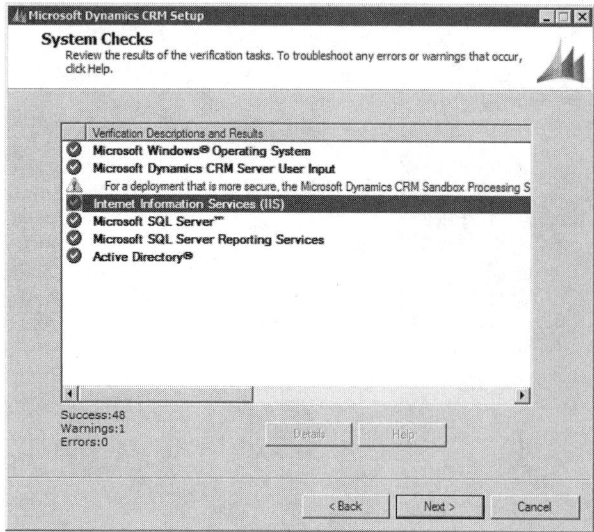

FIGURE 4.22 Microsoft Dynamics CRM system requirements verification.

Additional Steps

After the server is set up, there are a few other tasks that either need to be completed for full functionality or are recommended, depending on the type of server install you've selected.

Reporting Extensions for SSRS Setup

The Reporting Extensions for SSRS Setup is required for Microsoft Dynamics CRM reporting and by default; the Reporting Extensions for SSRS is installed as part of the Microsoft Dynamics CRM installation process when performing the installation. However, unlike the e-mail router, Microsoft Dynamics CRM Server setup must be completed before you install the Reporting Extensions for SSRS Setup as part of the installation. Additionally, installation must be done on the computer that has the Microsoft SQL Server Reporting Services (SRS) that you will use for your installation of Microsoft Dynamics CRM.

When completing the CRM 2011 setup after successful installation, you will be prompted to install the Reporting Extensions for SSRS Setup (see Figure 4.23).

The Reporting Extensions for SSRS Setup can be installed later and you can find the setup files in the Microsoft CRM Server CD/DVD under the SrsDataConnector folder.

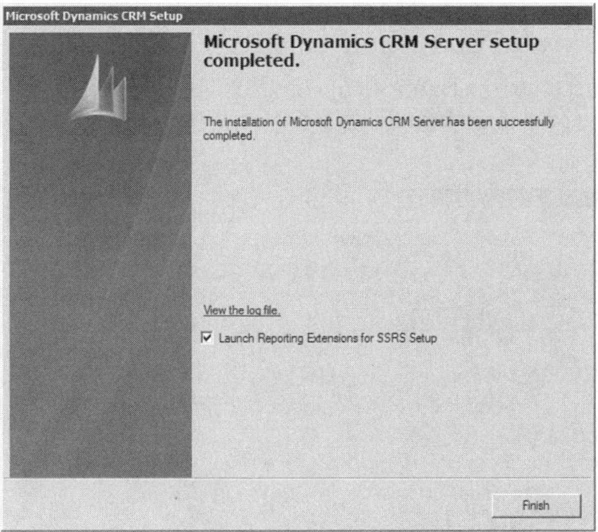

FIGURE 4.23 Microsoft Dynamics CRM setup completed.

To install the Reporting Extensions for SSRS Setup, follow these steps:

1. The Reporting Extensions for SSRS Setup Wizard prompts you to download installation files (see Figure 4.24). Click the Get updates for Microsoft Dynamics CRM (recommended) option, and click on Next.
2. Accept the Microsoft Dynamics CRM Reporting Extensions license agreement and click I Accept to continue.

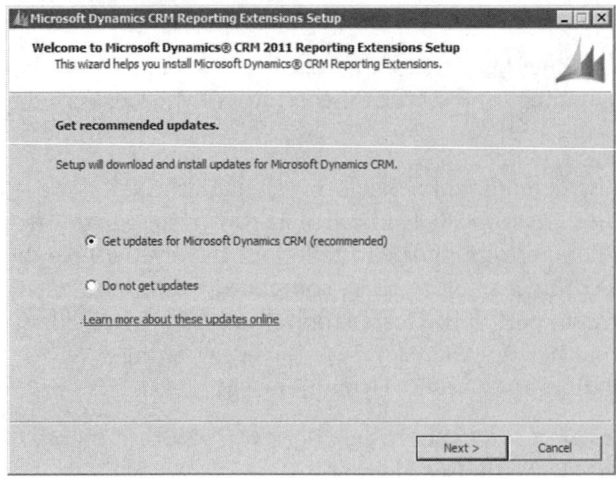

FIGURE 4.24 Reporting Extensions for SSRS Setup Wizard get recommended updates.

3. Specify the name of the computer that has the Microsoft Dynamics CRM SQL Server configuration database (see Figure 4.25). The configuration database for Microsoft Dynamics CRM is named `MSCRM_CONFIG`. Click Next to continue.
4. Specify the name of the SSRS instance (see Figure 4.26). The SSRS instance name is where you have the Report Server database installed. Click Next to continue.

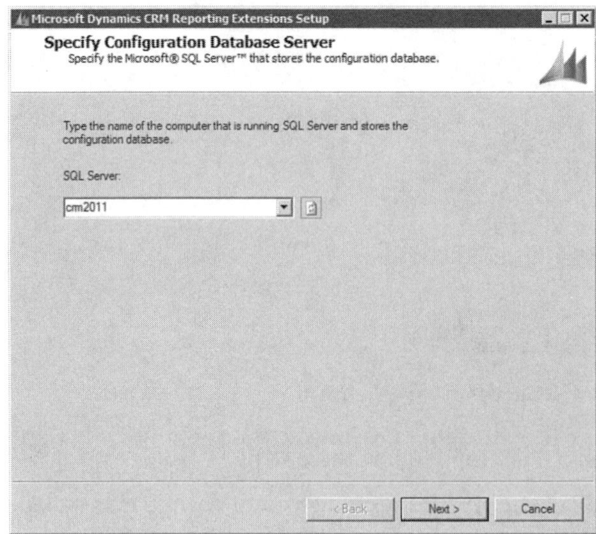

FIGURE 4.25 Reporting Extensions for SSRS Setup database configuration screen.

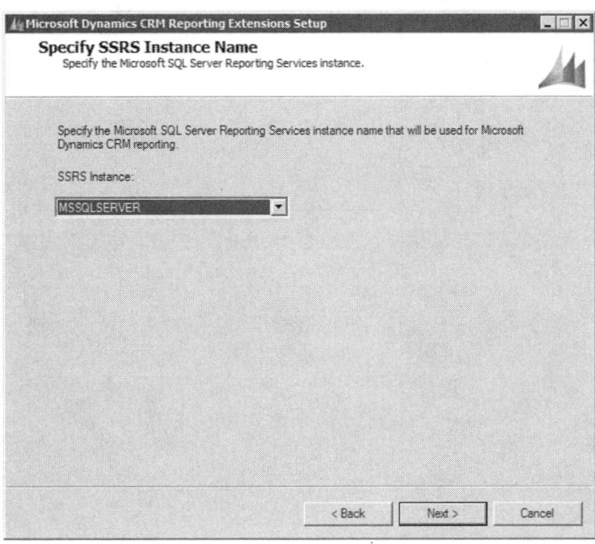

FIGURE 4.26 Reporting Extensions for SSRS Setup SSRS instance configuration screen.

5. You must specify the setup installation location on the next screen (see Figure 4.27). Click Next to continue.

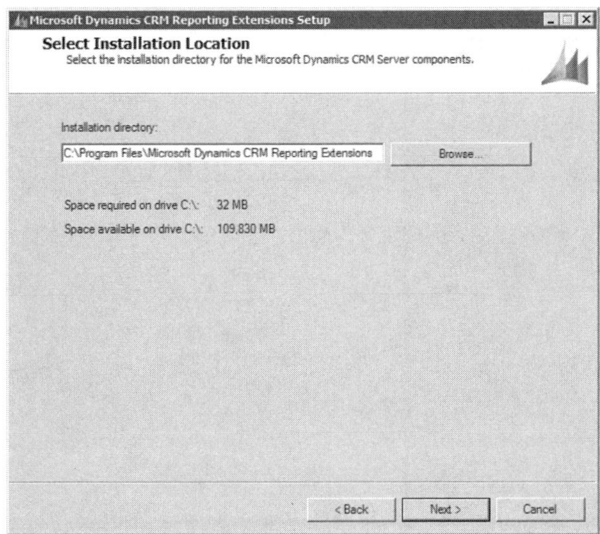

FIGURE 4.27 Reporting Extensions for SSRS Setup Installation location.

6. System requirements are verified and, if necessary, must be corrected before you continue the setup process (see Figure 4.28). When all requirements are met, click Next to continue.

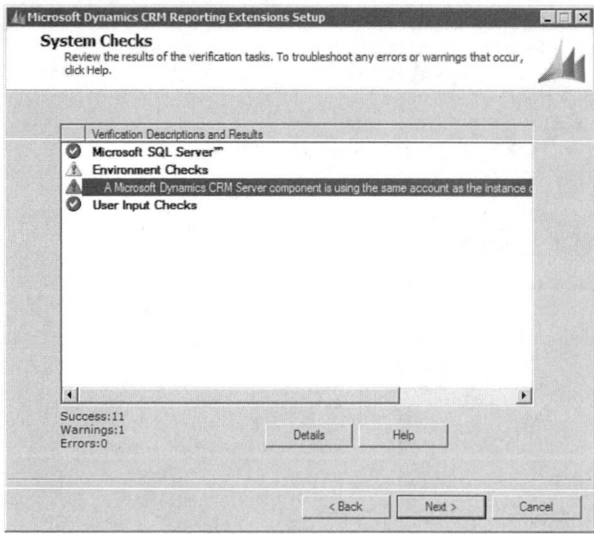

FIGURE 4.28 Reporting Extensions for SSRS Setup missing components check.

7. A Service Disruption warning message will alert you that the SQL Server instance will be restarted during the setup (see Figure 4.29). When all requirements are met, click Next to continue.

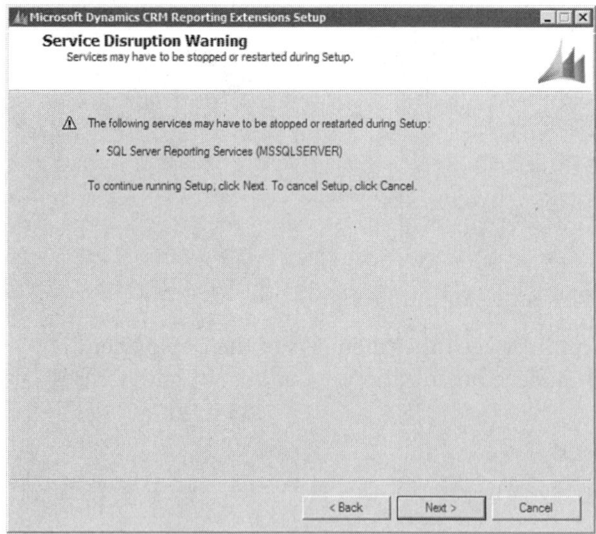

FIGURE 4.29 Reporting Extensions for SSRS Setup Service Disruption warning.

8. The setup summary screen appears. You can make any corrections at this time by clicking Back. Click Install to continue.

9. The installer then installs the Microsoft Dynamics CRM Data Connector and, when completed, displays a completion screen (see Figure 4.30). Click Finish to complete the installation.

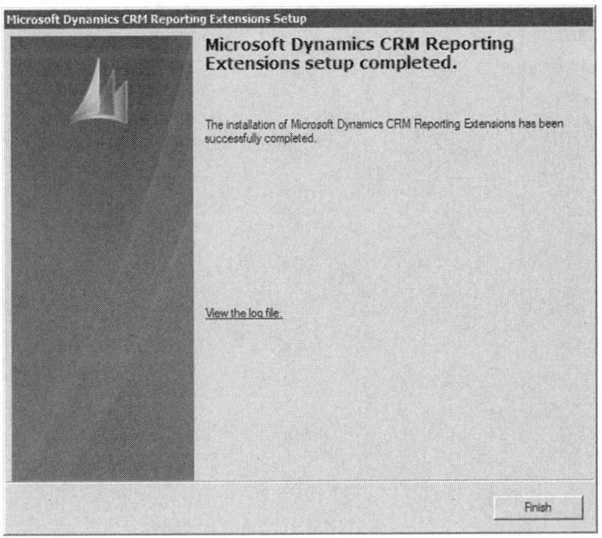

FIGURE 4.30 Reporting Extensions for SSRS Setup completion.

Deployment Manager

To create new organizations and manage your licenses and database, you will need to use the Deployment Manager. The Deployment Manager is found on the CRM server by going to Start, Programs, Microsoft Dynamics CRM 2011, and selecting Deployment Manager (see Figure 4.31).

You must be a member of the Deployment Administrators group; otherwise, you will receive an error when you try to launch it. By default, the user who performs the installation of Microsoft Dynamics CRM will be added to this group.

With the Deployment Manager, you can manage other members of the Deployment Administrators group, and set up and manage organizations, your servers, and licenses (see Figure 4.32).

To add users to the Deployment Administrators group, they must be added through the Deployment Manager. Users can be added by right-clicking the Deployment Administrators node and selecting New Deployment Administrator.

To provision a new organization, follow these steps. (You must have a Microsoft Dynamics CRM version that supports multiple organizations to add new organizations to your system.)

1. Right-click Organizations, and select New Organization.

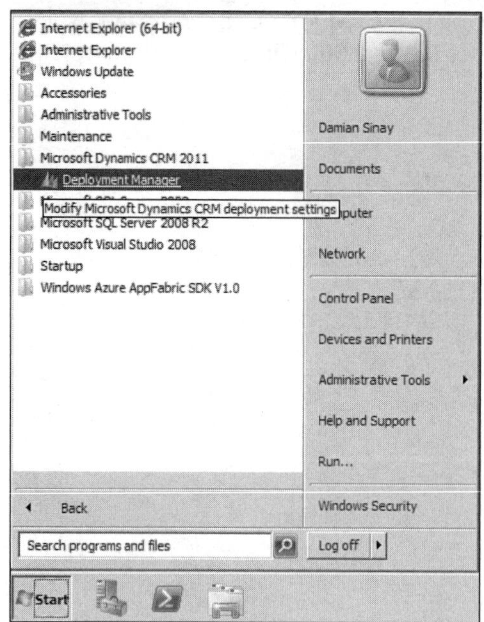

FIGURE 4.31 Location of Deployment Manager.

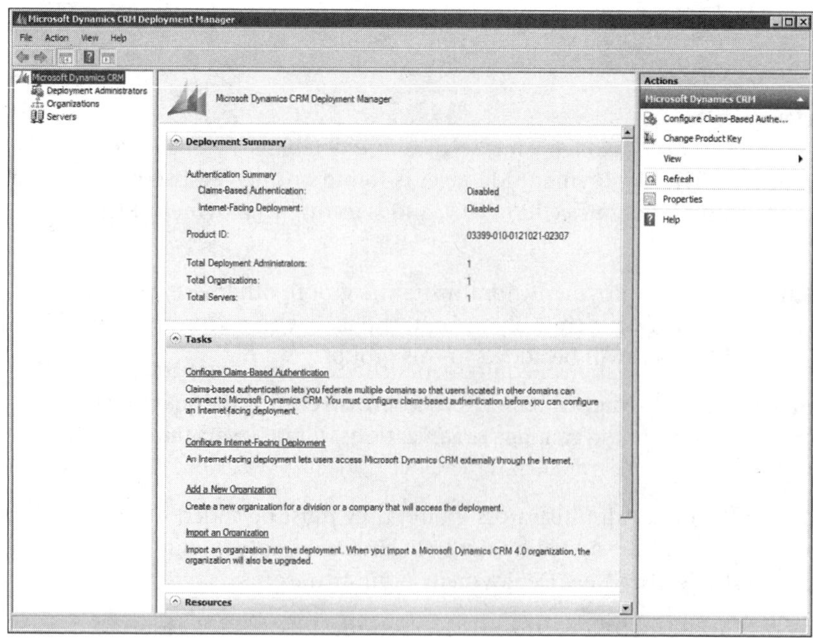

FIGURE 4.32 Deployment Manager.

2. Complete the required fields in the New Organization Wizard by entering the display name, unique database name, and selecting a base currency by selecting the Browse button and then selecting a currency from the displayed currency options. When you're ready to continue, your form should look similar to Figure 4.33. Select Next to continue.

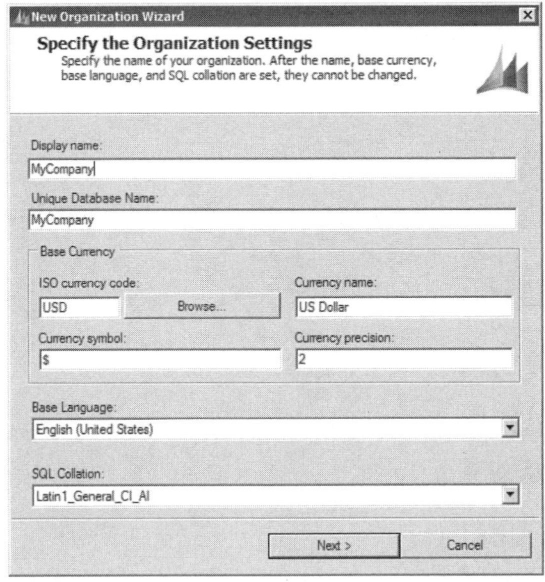

FIGURE 4.33 New Organization Wizard.

3. Select whether you'd like to participate in the Customer Experience Improvement Program, and select Next to continue.
4. Enter the location of your SQL Server (see Figure 4.34). Select Next to continue.
5. Enter the URL for your Reporting Services Server (see Figure 4.35). Select Next to continue.
6. The system will perform a Systems Requirements check on the organization information, SQL Server, and reporting services information entered. If there are any problems (such as an incorrect reporting server URL), they will be indicated and must be corrected prior to continuing by selecting Back or Cancel. Select Next to continue.
7. The entered information will be presented for a final review. If any corrections need to be made, you can select Back and make them. Select Create to create the organization.
8. The system will provision the new organization, and when complete, return a confirmation that the new organization has been created. It can then be managed in the Deployment Manager (see Figure 4.36).

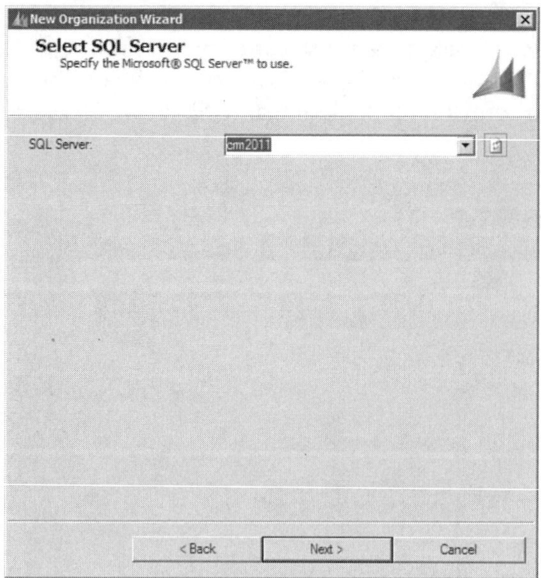

FIGURE 4.34 New Organization Wizard—select SQL Server.

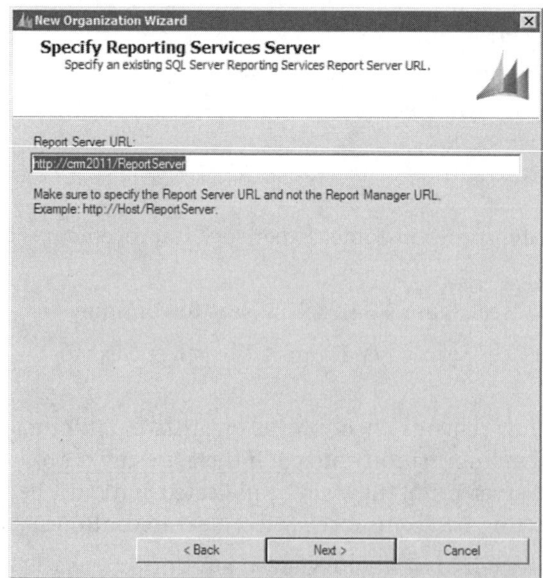

FIGURE 4.35 New Organization Wizard—enter Reporting Services Server URL.

Additional options that can be performed within the organization node are the ability to delete, edit, or disable and enable an existing organization. It is important to note that an organization must first be disabled prior to being deleted. Additionally, a deleted organization has its organization information deleted only from the configuration database—the organization database remains and must be removed manually by using SQL tools.

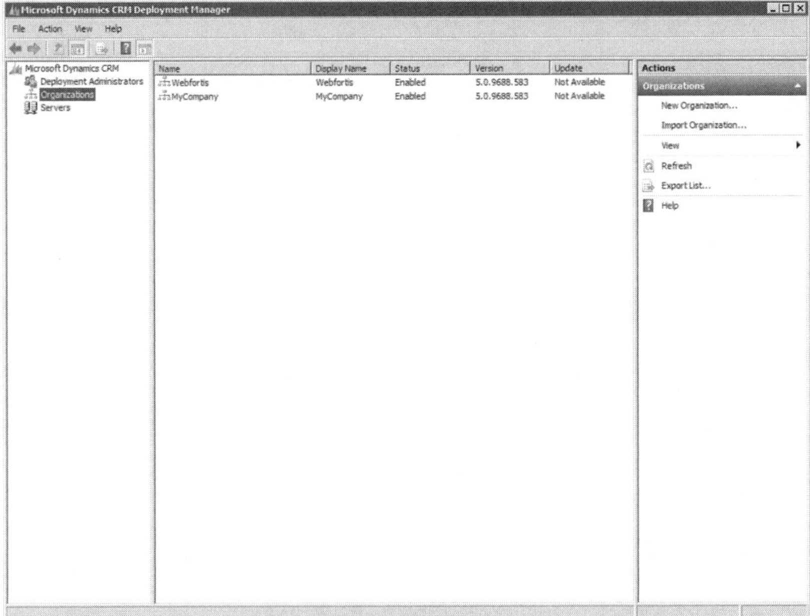

FIGURE 4.36 Deployment Manager with new organization.

The edit options enable you to easily change an organization name, the SQL Server, and the SRS Server. This is usually done when a database is moved to a new server.

The Server option displays information about the server, Microsoft Dynamics CRM version, and the role, whereas the License option displays information relevant to the Microsoft Dynamics version and users.

If you select the root node that says Microsoft Dynamics CRM and click on properties, you will get a summary of the licenses used in the license tab (see Figure 4.37).

The Deployment Manager is also used to configure the claims-based authentication and the Internet-facing deployments.

▶ For more information about how to perform these configurations refer to Chapter 22, "Forms Authentication."

Microsoft Dynamics CRM Clients

With a fully functional Internet Explorer–based interface as well as the Microsoft Dynamics CRM Outlook client, users can choose how they want to work with Microsoft Dynamics CRM.

Regardless of which client you choose to work with, the CRM website should be added as a trusted site on the client computers to avoid any security messages or a prompt for authentication. To do this, complete the following steps:

1. Navigate to the Control Panel by going to Start, Control Panel.

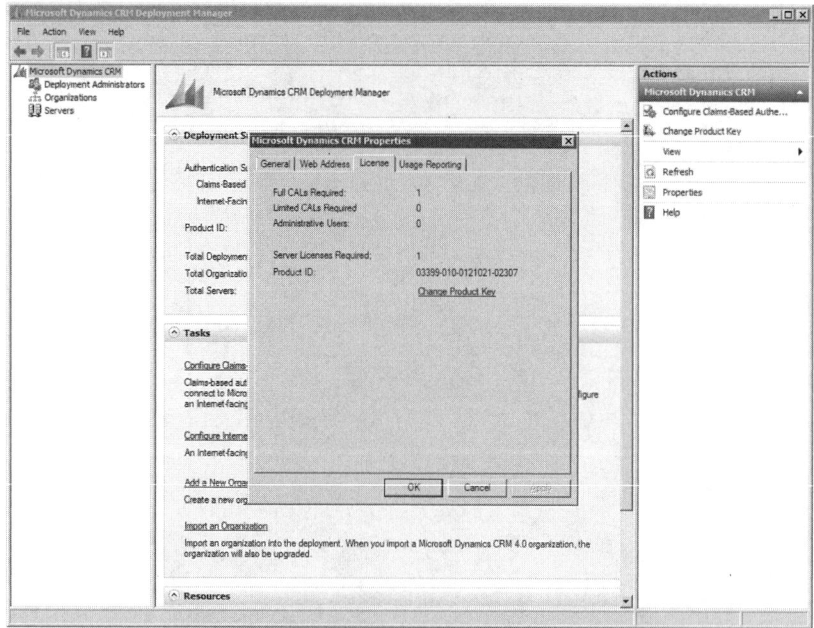

FIGURE 4.37 Deployment Manager displaying licensing information.

2. Launch Internet Options.
3. Select the Security tab.
4. Click Trusted Sites; then click the Sites button.
5. On the Trusted Sites dialog page, enter the URL to your CRM website. Be sure to include the http:// or https:// if your server uses a secure (SSL [secure sockets layer]) connection. Uncheck Require Server Verification (https:) for all sites in this zone if you are not running your CRM over a secure connection.
6. Click Close and OK to close the Internet Options dialog page.

You are now set to install or configure one of the Microsoft CRM clients.

Internet Explorer

When accessing Microsoft Dynamics CRM from Internet Explorer, users merely have to enter the URL for their Microsoft CRM installation. A default installation URL consists of http://*<servername>*:5555 or http://*<servername>*, where *<servername>* is the name of the CRM server. When users are authenticated on the same network, Microsoft Dynamics CRM loads in the browser automatically. If users are connecting to the Microsoft CRM Server via the Internet, they receive a Microsoft Windows authentication request consisting of username and password after they request use of the application by default; however, you can also set this to use forms (IFD) or passport authentication.

▶ Refer to Chapter 22 for more information about how to access the CRM server when IFD is enabled.

With this version of Microsoft Dynamics CRM, the application is set by default to not run in application mode, and it loads as a tabbed page in Internet Explorer 8 (see Figure 4.38).

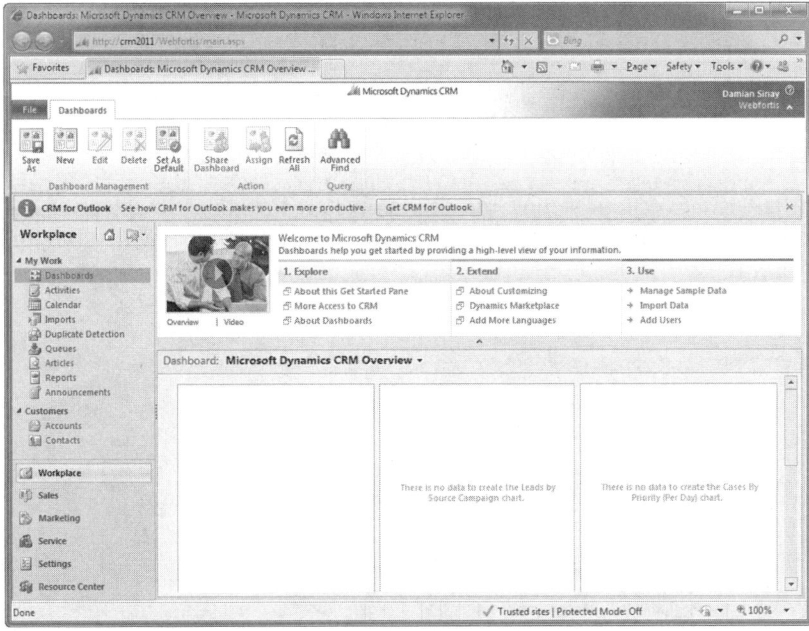

FIGURE 4.38 Microsoft Dynamics CRM tabbed browsing interface.

Application mode hides the URL address information in the Internet Explorer window, and, when used, it acts more like a Windows application. If you want to use application mode, be sure users don't have a pop-up blocker installed, or they will have trouble opening the CRM web application.

As you can see on Figure 4.38, the first time users enter the CRM Web application interface they will be presented with a yellow bar with a direct link to download the Outlook client. After installing the Outlook client or clicking the X button on the right, this message will no longer be displayed to the user.

Outlook Client

The Outlook client is available in two different modes:

- CRM for Outlook
- CRM for Outlook with Offline Access

As explained in Chapter 3, the versions are essentially the same (the Laptop version has offline support), and only one installation package exists for both.

An important addition to Microsoft Dynamics CRM with regard to the Outlook client is that it is now broken down into two steps:

- Installation
- Configuration

Installation To install either version of the Outlook client, start the client setup application found on the Microsoft Dynamics CRM web application interface as shown on Figure 4.39 and follow these steps:

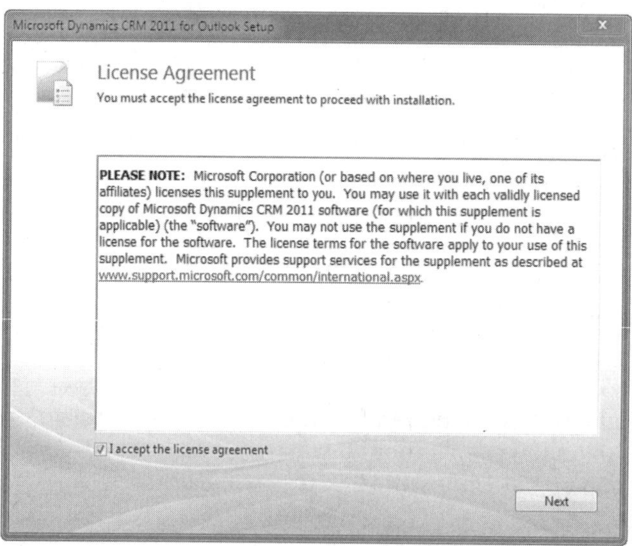

FIGURE 4.39 Microsoft Dynamics CRM 2011 for Outlook setup license agreement.

1. Start the client installation by launching the setup application CRM2011-ClientOnPremiseInstaller-ENU.exe.
2. The license terms from Microsoft are displayed. You must accept the license agreement to continue. After you do so, click Next to continue.
3. Click Options if you want to install the Offline Access; otherwise, clicking Install Now will only install the online access (see Figure 4.40).
4. If you clicked Options, you will be able to check the offline capability as well as to change the installation location (see Figure 4.41). Click Install Now to continue.

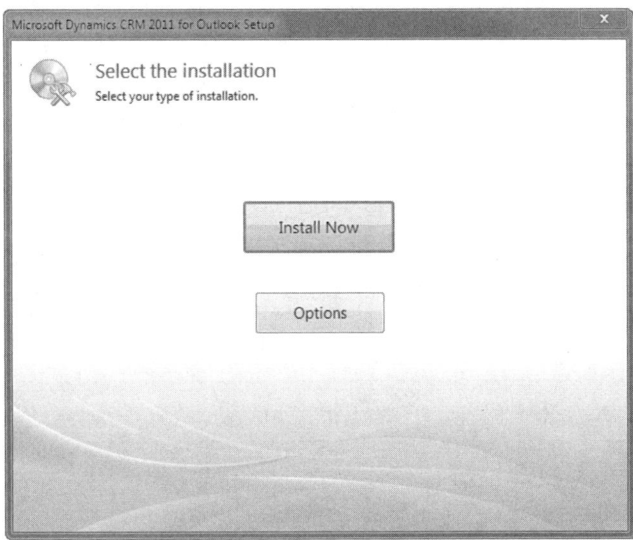

FIGURE 4.40 Microsoft Dynamics CRM 2011 for Outlook setup.

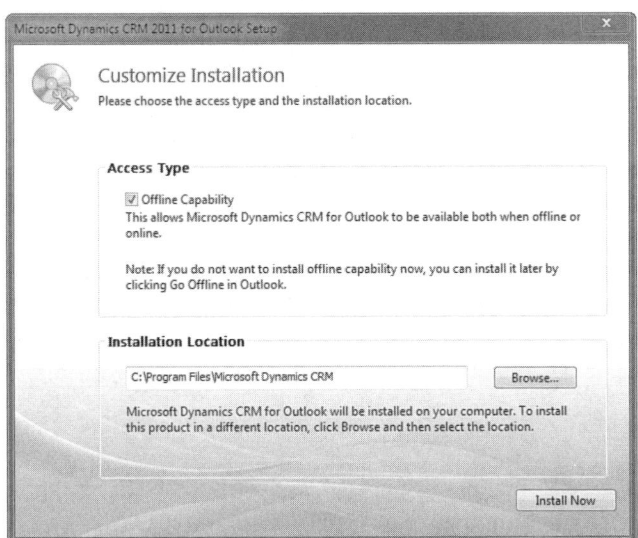

FIGURE 4.41 Microsoft Dynamics CRM 2011 for Outlook setup customize installation.

5. The installer will download prerequisites and will install them automatically. The program will install and when setup is completed, you will see a completed confirmation (see Figure 4.42).

4

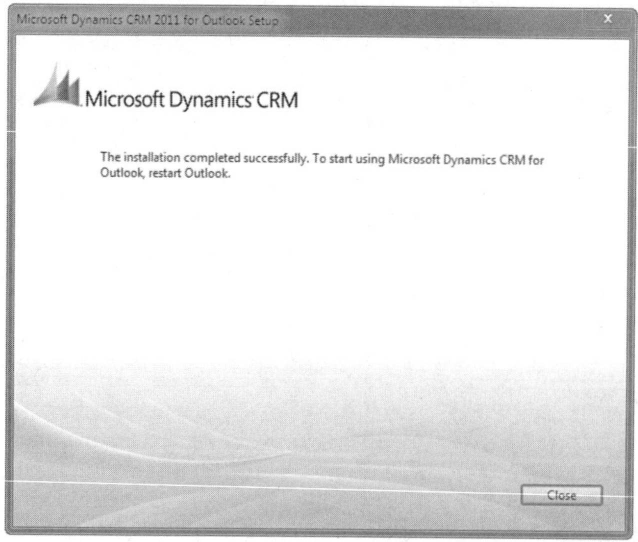

FIGURE 4.42 Microsoft Dynamics CRM 2011 for Outlook setup confirmation.

Configuration After the Outlook client has been installed on to your system, it must be configured. To configure the Outlook client, follow these steps (note that Outlook must be closed before running the configuration or you will get an alert to close it):

1. Navigate to Start, All Programs, Microsoft Dynamics CRM 2011, and select Configuration Wizard. The Configuration Wizard will start (see Figure 4.43).
2. Enter the server information. For On Premise installations, this is usually http://*<servername>* or http://*<servername>*:5555. For either Microsoft CRM Online or hosted servers, enter the URL information that you received from them (see Figure 4.43). For Microsoft CRM Online, select "CRM Online"; you will be prompted for authentication to Windows Live ID, which authenticates and shows your available organizations.

CAUTION

Keep in mind that the machine must be joined to the domain where the CRM server is installed, and you must be a valid CRM user or the setup won't let you continue.

3. If the CRM server address you entered has more than one organization, you will be asked to choose one organization in this step (see Figure 4.44). If your server contains only one organization, this step will be skipped. Select OK to continue.
4. The setup will configure the Outlook client for the selected organization. When the setup finishes, it will show the configuration complete dialog box (see Figure 4.45).

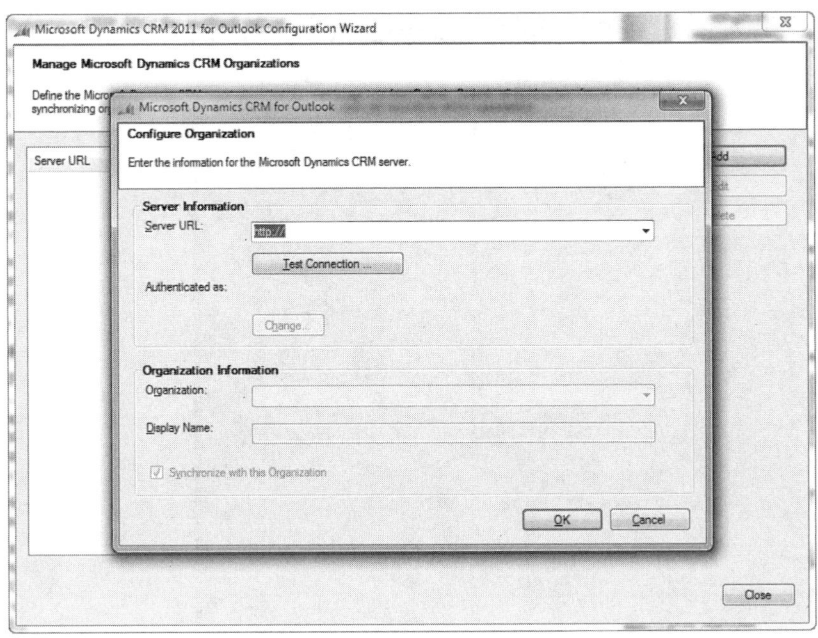

FIGURE 4.43 Microsoft Dynamics CRM 2011 for Outlook Configuration Wizard.

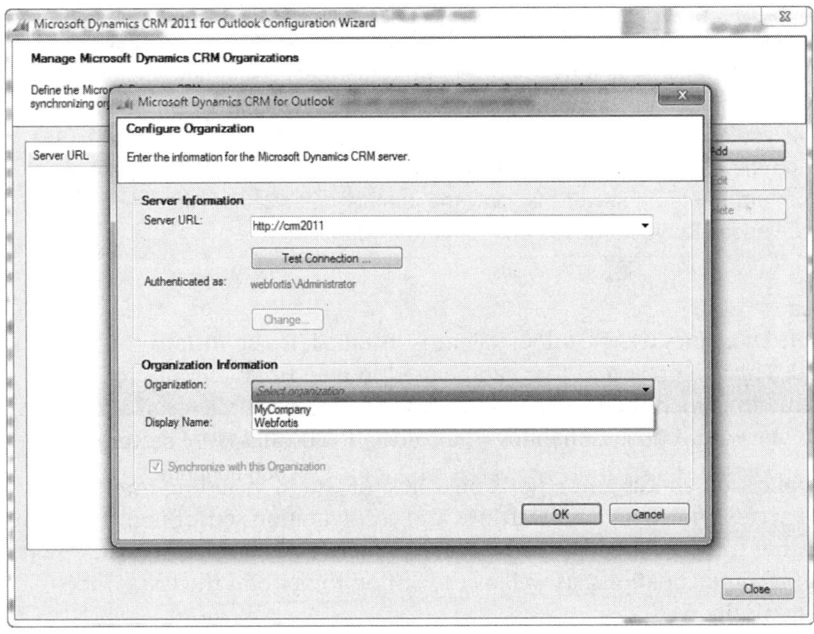

FIGURE 4.44 Selecting organization.

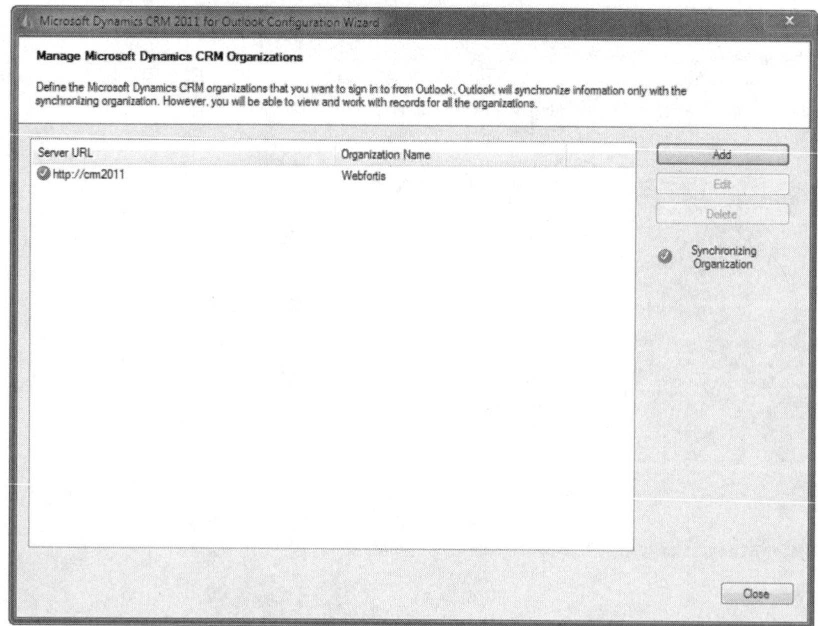

FIGURE 4.45 Configuration complete.

NOTE

This new version of CRM 2011 has a new and very welcome feature that now enables you to configure the Microsoft outlook client to work with more than one organization at the same time, as you can see on Figure 4.45. You can configure additional organizations by clicking on the Add button, which is useful when you work for different organizations. It is important to note however that only the primary organization can synchronize the Calendar, Contacts, Tasks and Email with Outlook.

Outlook Diagnostics

When the Microsoft Dynamics CRM Outlook client is installed, it also installs the Outlook Diagnostics Wizard. This is a great tool that can be used to help troubleshoot problems with the CRM client. To launch the wizard, go to Start, All Programs, Microsoft CRM, and select Diagnostics. The wizard opens, enabling you to run diagnostics (see Figure 4.46).

The diagnostics application checks and reports on a host of issues, including Internet connectivity, CRM access and credentials, settings and configuration settings on the client machine, and whether there are any required updates. When it has finished, it will report on the results with recommendations, as well as the option to perform the fixes if it is able to do so automatically.

If you select Support Mode, you can select which of the checks it should run, whether certain synchronization should be turned on or off for the diagnostics, as well as whether it should generate support files for advanced troubleshooting.

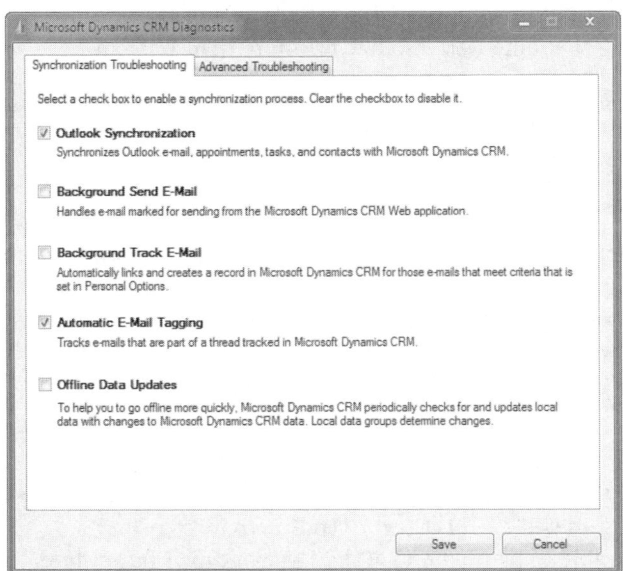

FIGURE 4.46 Microsoft Dynamics CRM diagnostics.

Upgrading from Previous Versions

The only supported upgrade to Microsoft CRM 2011 is an upgrade from Microsoft 4.0. If you're running a version of Microsoft CRM prior to 4.0 (that is, 1.0, 1.2, or 3.0), you must first upgrade to 4.0 and then to 2011. Additionally, there is no support for Microsoft Dynamics 4.0 Mobile Express, and it should be uninstalled prior to attempting an upgrade. (Microsoft Dynamics CRM 2011 comes with Mobile Express by default.)

NOTE

Upgrading Microsoft CRM 1.0, 1.2, or 3.0 to Microsoft 4.0 is not discussed because that topic is beyond the scope of this book.

Considerations when upgrading:

- **Customizations**—The upgrade process attempts to upgrade all published customizations automatically, but all unpublished customizations will be lost. Make sure that all customized forms are fully published before you upgrade. Furthermore, an entity might not be upgraded if it is missing required fields. If you encounter this problem, be sure to check the setup log file. Also because the JavaScript object model has been changed on this version, you might need to disable some JavaScript code you have on CRM 4.0 before starting the migration, or you will get lot of errors on the customized entities for the onload and onsave events that you will have to manually fix after the migration is completed. One web resource of type Script will be created for every entity and event that had code previous. It might be a good thing to review the codes because there might be duplicated functions you could now avoid on this new version by reusing the same web resource for more than one entity.

- **Reports**—Because CRM 4.0 can also use SSRS 2008 and almost most of the implementation uses it, report migration typically isn't a problem.
- **Ownership issues**—Reports are given organization ownership and are available to all users.
- **Plug-ins**—Even though this new version of CRM 2011 uses .NET Framework 4.0, CRM 4.0 plug-ins will run without any problems on CRM 2011. However, if you want to make any change or update on the plug-in code, you will have to migrate the code and reference the new CRM 2011 SDK assemblies, which will also involve reworking the code to follow the new classes for plug-ins that have drastically changed.
- **Workflow**—Even though this new version of CRM 2011 uses .NET Framework 4.0, workflows made for CRM 4.0 that runs on .NET Framework 3.5 are supported and can run without any problems on CRM 2011. Custom code activities created on previous versions will only be able to be used on CRM 2011 workflows but not on CRM 2011 dialogs.

Although Microsoft Dynamics CRM 2011 supports an in-place upgrade, the following steps are recommended as part of the upgrade process:

1. Back up the existing Microsoft CRM 4.0 databases. This includes the SQL Server configuration CRM database and all the organizations databases for CRM. The database names are formatted as <*organizationname*>_MSCRM and MSCRM_CONFIG.
2. Back up all reports, including any custom and modified reports from the existing Microsoft Dynamics CRM application. This can be done by performing a backup of the ReportServer database.
3. Export and back up all customizations from the Microsoft CRM 4.0 application. This needs to be done from the CRM web interface by going to Settings, Customizations, Export Customizations.

When you have completed and verified these steps, follow the steps previously outlined in the "Microsoft Dynamics CRM Server Setup" section of this chapter to upgrade the Microsoft CRM 4.0 server to a Microsoft Dynamics CRM 2011 server. After the installer completes its system check (step 5) and installs any missing components, it automatically recognizes that Microsoft CRM 4.0 is installed (see Figure 4.47). Click Next to continue.

By default, Microsoft CRM 4.0 is upgraded with both application and platform server roles as part of the upgrade.

Complete the remaining steps outlined. When the installation finishes, you are prompted to restart your computer.

On a multitenant environment, when upgrading a Microsoft CRM 4.0 Enterprise version from the setup with multiple organizations, only the default organization will be migrated and other organizations will be disabled, so you will have to go to the Deployment Manager and upgrade one by one.

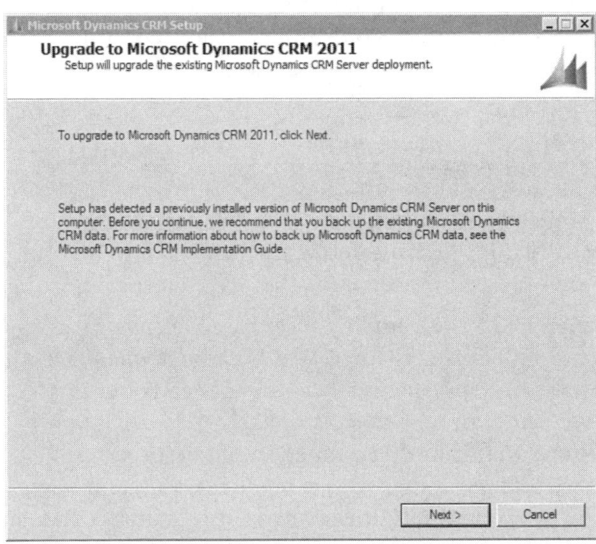

FIGURE 4.47 Microsoft Dynamics CRM/Microsoft CRM 4.0 upgrade notification.

If you encounter any issues not mentioned here, check the setup log that is created when the server installation completes.

Setting Up Your Business in Microsoft Dynamics CRM 2011

Regardless of which version and platform of Microsoft Dynamics CRM you're working with, after you complete setting up your system, you need to configure your business. Microsoft Dynamics CRM is extremely flexible and can be made to work with virtually any business. When working with Microsoft Dynamics CRM Online, the wizard walks you through many of the setup steps; however, there are still many things that can be configured, and it is helpful to know about the options if you want to change the configurations. If you're not using Microsoft Dynamics CRM Online, you need to perform these settings.

The following list represents some of the things that need to be configured.

▶ For a complete list of all settings and configuration options, as well as more information related to everything below, refer to Chapter 12, "Settings and Configuration."

- **Organizations**—When considering working with your organization, you'll want to consider the hierarchy of your organization as well as how it is structured. Within Microsoft Dynamics CRM, there are options to break out your organization by business unit, territories, and sites. When thinking about how to configure your organization, it is helpful to spend some time preparing how it should be structured within the Microsoft Dynamics CRM 2011 framework, both how it is now, as well as how you believe it will be in six months to two years from now.

- **Business Units**—Business units are important and can be used by even the smallest organizations to easily control access and divide records. A new change on this version of CRM 2011 allows business units to be changed or deleted after created.

CAUTION

Keep in mind that business units must be disabled before they can be deleted. It is a good idea to think about how they will work within your organization.

- **Users**—Because Microsoft Dynamics CRM 2011 employs user-based licensing, determining who will need access to the system is very important because it will affect not only the cost, but also how users in the system will work together. For example, if only customer service people are using the system, it is unlikely that you'll be using the Leads functionality because that is mostly a function of salespeople. Another example is when you have both customer service representatives and salespeople in the system but not your marketing staff; then Microsoft Dynamics CRM marketing functionality will likely be underutilized.

TIP

It is a good idea to outline who needs to use the system immediately, as well as anticipated users, so that you can plan for both growth and other licensing requirements. We have found that initial estimates of users are usually light because the system is so powerful and easy to use that when users see it, they want to work with it. With the new licensing options for Microsoft Dynamics CRM 2011, this isn't as prohibitive as it was in earlier versions.

Although users are established in the system, they can be deactivated, and other users can use the license.

CAUTION

Note that the practice of letting someone use the license of a deactivated user is not recommended for routine use. This practice should only be used when users leave the company or no longer need access to the Microsoft Dynamics CRM system.

Managing users is easy, and unlike previous versions, the ability to quickly and easily add one or multiple users to the system is now available directly from the application interface by navigating to Settings, Administration, and selecting New from the Users option.

If you are working with Microsoft Dynamics CRM Online, you have the option to create users when you first perform your system setup via the Setup Wizard. Additionally, and only available with Microsoft Dynamics CRM Online, you have the option to send invitations to the newly added users via their entered e-mail addresses. If you select this option, the users are sent an e-mail that explains how to access Microsoft Dynamics CRM Online.

- **Customers**—Microsoft Dynamics CRM defines customers in two ways: Accounts and Contacts. These entities can be easily renamed if your organization requires it (for example, Companies and Customers instead of Accounts and Contacts). Working with customers is explained fully in Chapter 6, "Working with Customers." However, at this point, it is important to consider the account and contacts structure when migrating from other CRM applications because other systems might use a different hierarchy, and data will need to be migrated using this structure. If this is your case, consider referential accounts and contacts where accounts have a parent–child relationship (for example, there might be an account called Joe's Auto that has two subaccounts called Joe's Auto—Retail and Joe's Auto—Commercial, and contacts that report directly to either of these, but none to the master parent account of Joe's Auto), or work with business units instead.

  Additionally, although both accounts and contacts are considered customers, you will likely have a mix of records contained within these records. For example, your account records might have supplier and/or vendor records, as well as their contact information.

- **Roles**—Microsoft Dynamics CRM 2011 is role-based, and every user must have a valid role to work within the system. This is outlined in Chapters 3 and 12; however, it is important to recognize the difference in roles that might exist between a user on the network and Microsoft Dynamics CRM 2011.

  The roles that come by default with Microsoft Dynamics CRM 2011 are well defined; however, be sure to review the permissions carefully when utilizing them. The most common cause of users having problems working within their system is related to their permissions. Additionally, be sure whichever role you set for your users has the level of control that you expect.

- **Queues and Teams**—Queues and teams are a powerful way of setting up your system to ensure that both record load is leveled and records can be shared when required.

- **E-mail**—When setting up e-mail with Microsoft Dynamics CRM 2011, there is a host of new options that easily extend functionality, regardless of what you're using for your e-mail server.

TIP

Be sure to carefully check your settings for e-mail tracking. Occasionally, users will set the tracking of e-mails to All for their mailbox, and later find that their personal messages are appearing in Microsoft Dynamics CRM 2011. We generally recommend setting the All option for dedicated mailboxes, such as support@yourdomain.com or sales@yourdomain.com.

Summary

Within this chapter, we reviewed how to set up Microsoft Dynamics CRM 2011, with consideration given to both the architecture as well as the business for both On Premise and Microsoft Dynamics CRM Online. It is important to realize that these can be related or unique processes, and an understanding of what options are available can dictate a successful or failed implementation.

CHAPTER 5

Working with the Ribbon Menu

IN THIS CHAPTER

- Get Started Pane
- Contextual Features—List Tools
- Common Usage and Functions
- Ribbons in Outlook
- Customizing

Introduced in this version of Microsoft Dynamics CRM, the Ribbon menu is a graphical display of functions available to users as they navigate throughout the application.

Although a majority of this chapter is applicable to both Outlook and Internet Explorer, the section "Ribbons in Outlook" looks specifically at the Outlook ribbon menu options.

The Ribbon menu is what is commonly referred to as a "smart" ribbon. That means that it does several things based on your actions. Examples of this include

- If you resize the application, the Ribbon icons resize as well.
- It is contextually aware of what you are working on—both with the list tools that open, as well as actual menu options. For example, if you select two records, you have the merge option; however, if you select more than two records, the merge option is not available because you cannot merge more than two records at a time.
- The Ribbon menu options are varied. There are options that have large icons, small icons, and options that drop-down and give a variety of choices.

Figure 5.1 shows the Ribbon menu along the top, as well as the Get Started pane right below it.

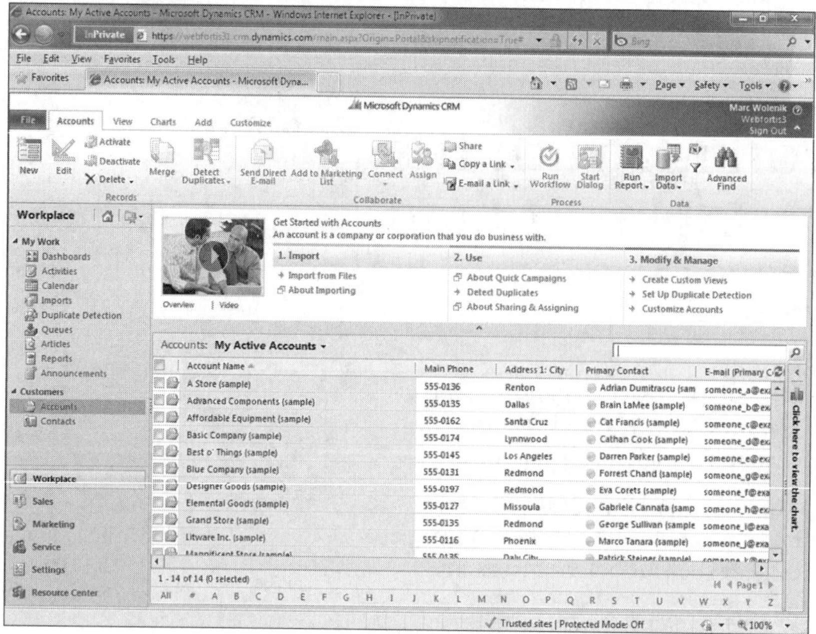

FIGURE 5.1 Ribbon menu and Get Started pane.

Get Started Pane

The Get Started pane is a prebuilt section that gives users quick tips and training options, as well as quick launch settings to various functions.

NOTE

For the examples in this chapter, we're not going to use the Get Started pane and have collapsed it by selecting the chevron at the bottom of it. Figure 5.2 shows the same page with the Get Started pane collapsed. If you would like to permanently hide the Get Started pane, navigate to File, Options, and then unselect Show Get Started Panes on All Lists, as shown in Figure 5.3, or by navigating to System settings and disabling it for the organization.

Additionally, notice that it will also remember the state that you leave the Get Started pane in. So, for example, if you close it for Accounts, it will remain closed until you open it again, but other entities will open by default until you close or hide it for them.

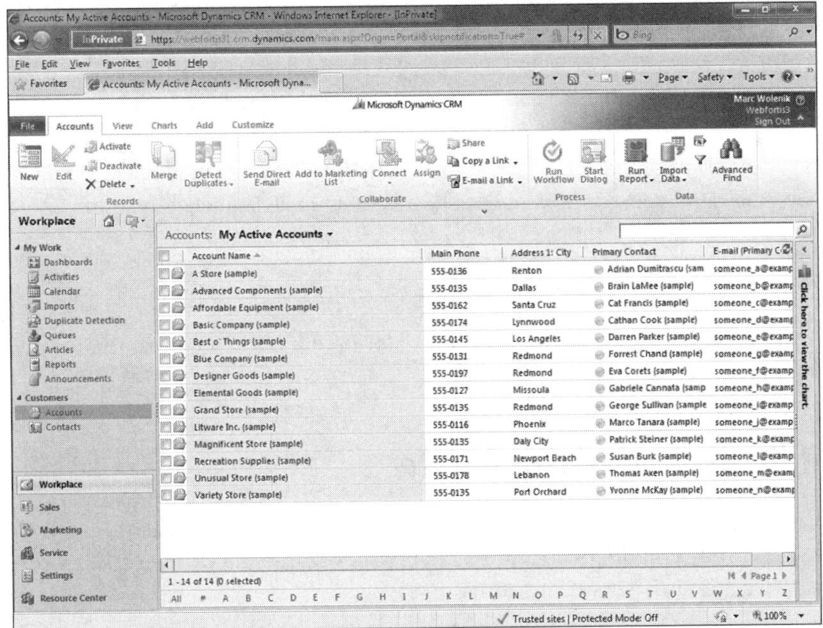

FIGURE 5.2 Ribbon menu and Get Started pane collapsed.

Set Personal Options -- Webpage Dialog

Set Personal Options

Change the default display settings to personalize Microsoft Dynamics CRM, and manage your e-mail templates.

General | Workplace | Activities | Formats | E-mail Templates | E-mail | Privacy | Languages

Select your home page and settings for Get Started panes

Default Pane: Workplace — Default Tab: Dashboards

☐ Show Get Started panes on all lists

Set the number of records shown per page in any list of records.

Records Per Page: 50

Select the default mode in Advanced Find

Advanced Find Mode: ◉ Simple ○ Detailed

Set the time zone you are in

Time Zone: (GMT-08:00) Pacific Time (US & Canada)

Select a default currency

Currency

Support high contrast settings

Select this option if you are using the High Contrast settings in your browser or operating system.

☐ Enable high contrast

View your user information.

Help — OK — Cancel

https://webfortis31.crm.dynamics.com/tools/personalsettings/dialogs/personalsettings.aspx — Trusted sites | Protected Mode: Off

FIGURE 5.3 Show Get Started panes on all lists.

NOTE

Although the Get Started pane does provide some benefit to the new user, we find that the real estate it uses mandates turning it off. Throughout this book you will rarely see it.

Additionally, if you would like to modify the Get Started pane, the SDK explains how to customize it by creating HTML files. This is especially helpful in providing inline help to users for new, custom entities.

▶ See Chapter 23, "Customizing Entities," for more information and examples related to customizing HTML files.

Contextual Features—List Tools

The Ribbon menu changes based on both what you are working with as well as the selected area of the form that you are on. Figure 5.4 shows a completely different Ribbon menu when selecting Dashboards versus Accounts.

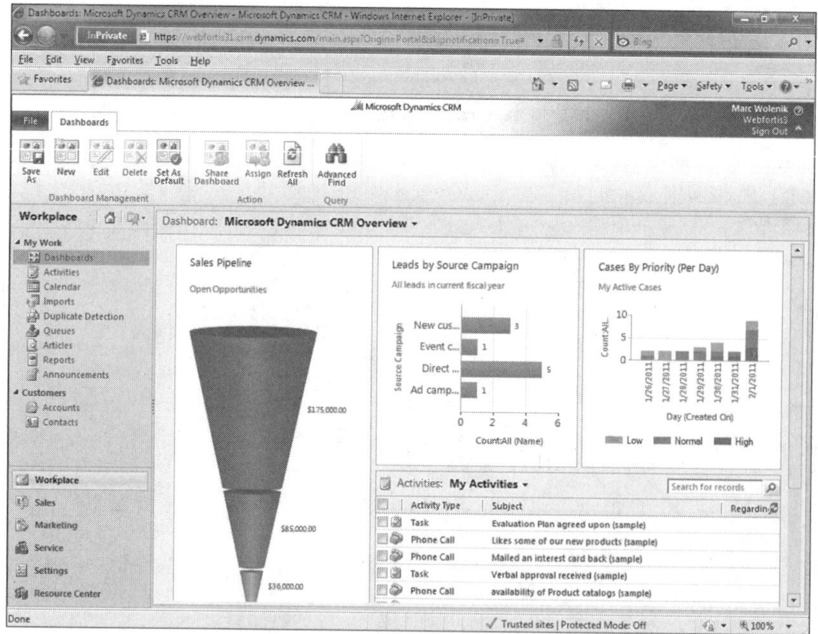

FIGURE 5.4 Ribbon menu for Dashboards.

Additionally, the options are available (or light up) when you have selected records (as shown in Figure 5.5), or when you have saved a record for a specific entity (see Figure 5.6 and Figure 5.7).

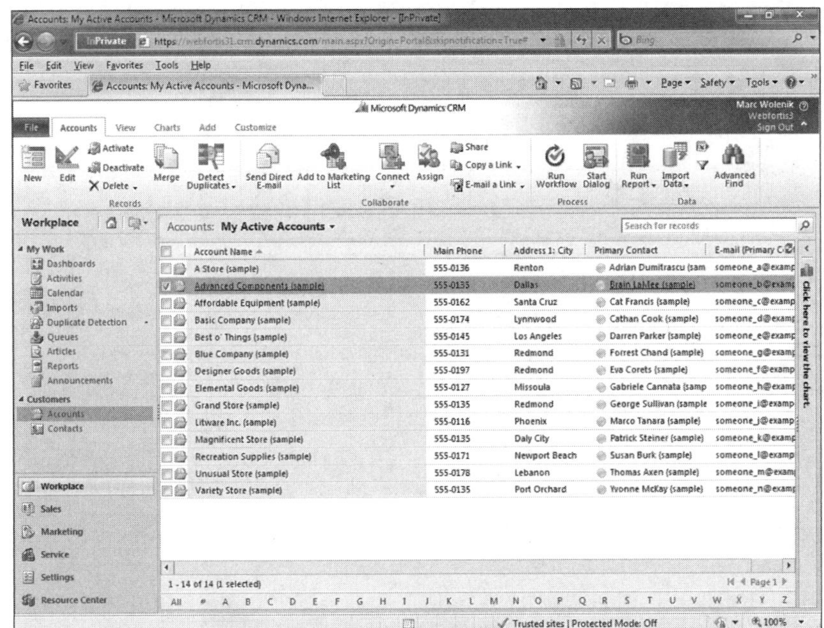

FIGURE 5.5 Ribbon menu for Accounts with an Account selected.

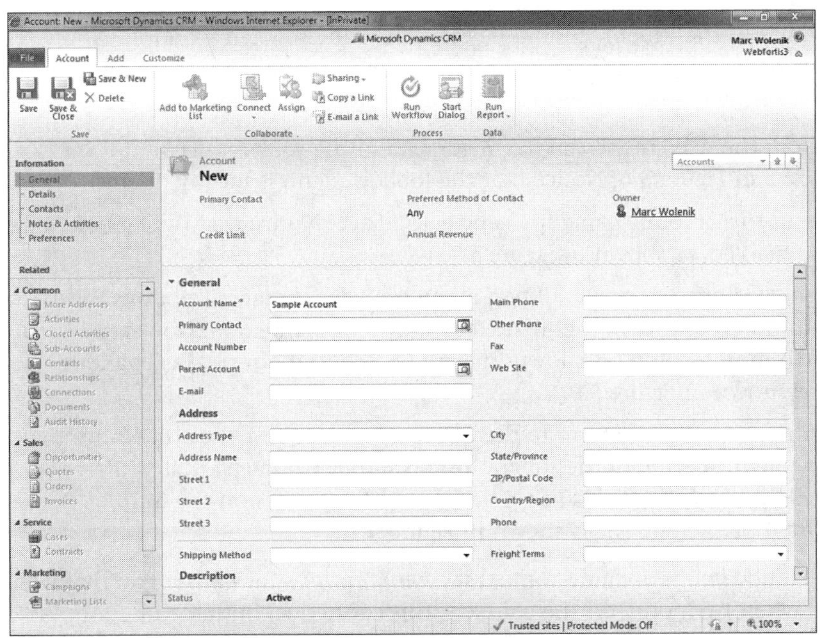

FIGURE 5.6 New Account—not saved yet.

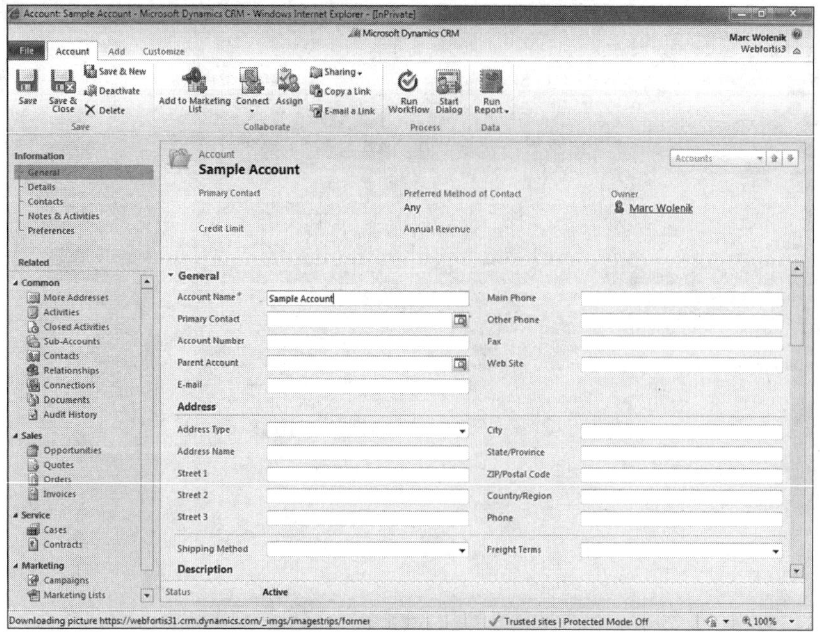

FIGURE 5.7 New Account saved with Ribbon menu options.

The contextual nature of the Ribbon should be especially noted when working with subitems on a form, as we're going to show in the following example of working with an Account.

1. Select New from the Account screen (see Figure 5.5). A new, blank Account form opens, as shown in Figure 5.6. Notice that the Ribbon menu is mostly disabled.
2. Enter a value in the Account name field and select Save. Notice that the Ribbon menu is now enabled, as shown in Figure 5.7.
3. Notice that the options across the Ribbon menu include the default options for the Account (with the Account tab highlighted as shown in Figure 5.7). However, we also have the option for Add (as shown in Figure 5.8) and if our privileges allow, Customize, as shown in Figure 5.9.
4. Navigate further down on the form to the Contacts section and select it. Notice that there is a *new* menu specific to the subgrid (for example, Contacts) that you've selected called List Tools/Contacts (if we had selected Activities on the form, it would say List Tools/Activities), as shown in Figure 5.10.

The ribbon has been updated to include contextual menu options for the subgrid that we have selected, and when we mouse off the contacts, this contextual option will disappear.

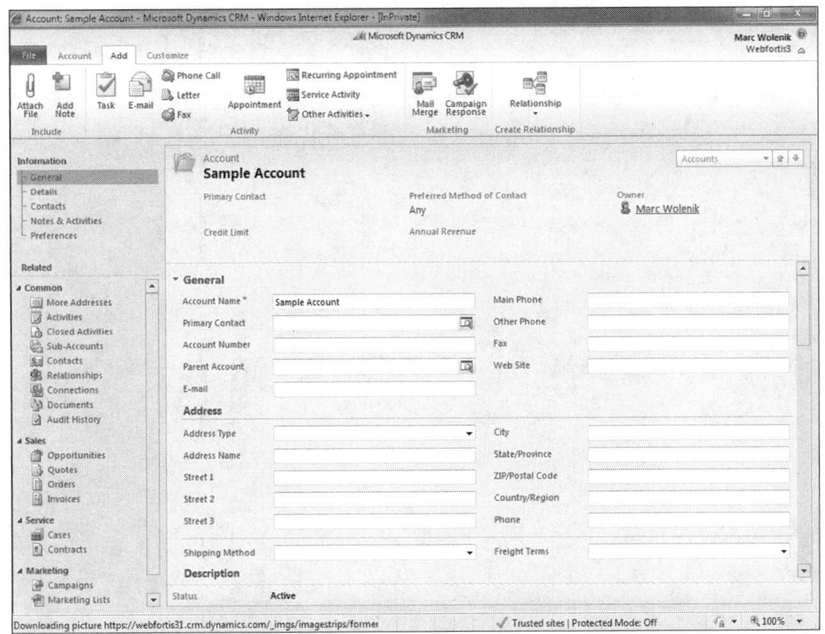

FIGURE 5.8 New Account with Add tab from Ribbon selected.

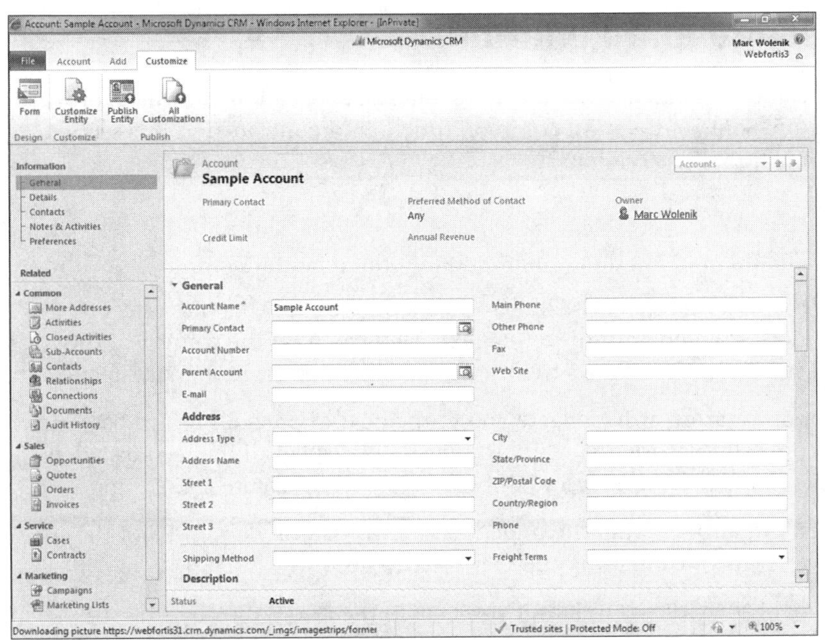

FIGURE 5.9 New Account with Customize tab from Ribbon selected.

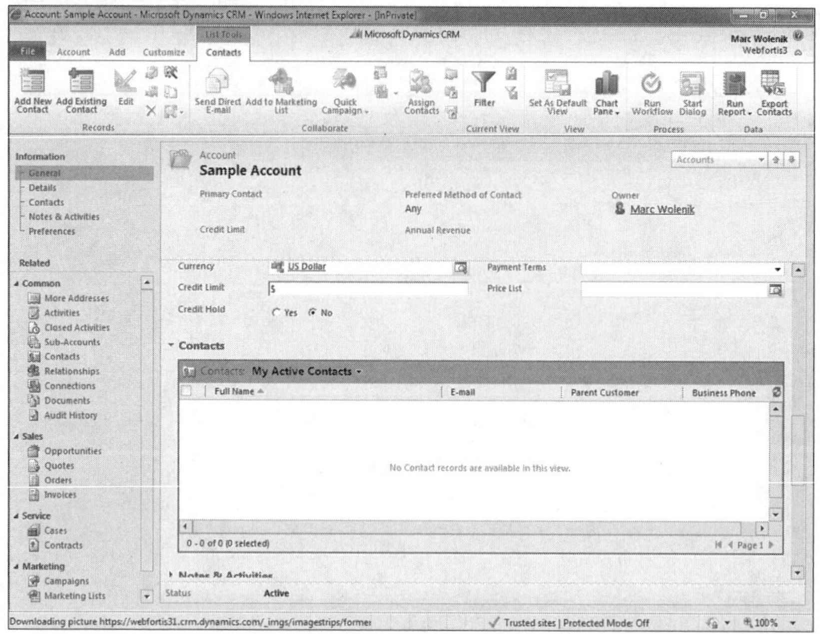

FIGURE 5.10 Contacts List Tools Ribbon option.

Common Usage and Functions

There are several features that are common throughout the application, regardless of what record type you're on. Some of the most common functions are included in this section and will apply to a majority of situations.

Record Navigation

Although not necessarily a feature of the Ribbon menu, Microsoft Dynamics offers the ability to quickly move from one record to the next, even based on the context of the underlying record set. Figure 5.11 shows the list navigation when an Account is opened.

Selecting the up or down arrow will navigate you to the next or previous record based in the underlying record set. Selecting the word Accounts will display all the records, allowing you to navigate to the individual record directly, as shown in Figure 5.12.

From this view, you can also see what the underlying record set, or view, is. From the example that we've shown, we are using the View: Active Records.

This works with any of the views as well as if you launch the record directly from the Advanced Find. (It will display View: Account Advanced Find View.)

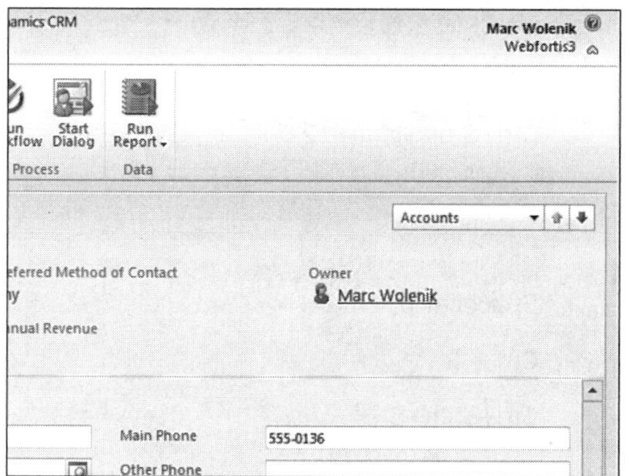

FIGURE 5.11 Account record navigation.

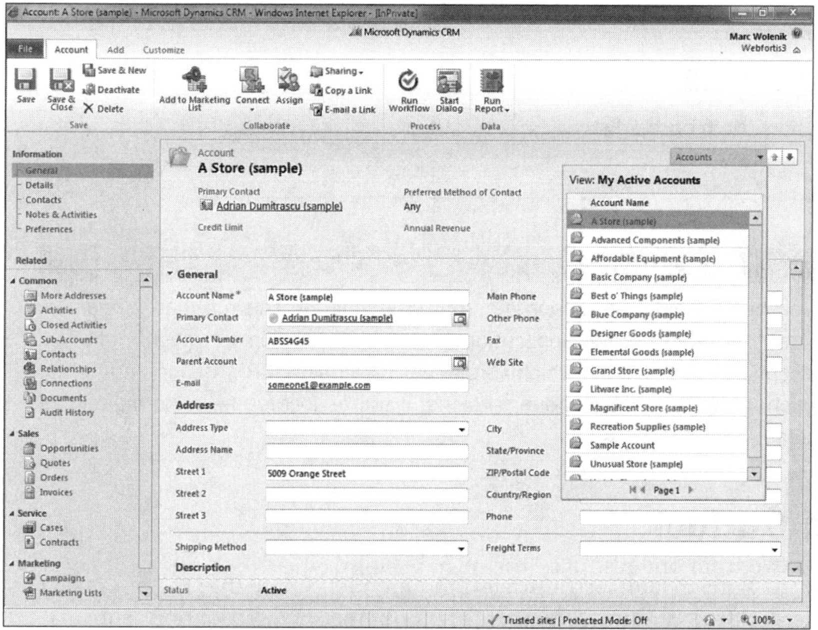

FIGURE 5.12 Account record navigation—specific record selection.

Keyboard Shortcuts

Although the Ribbon menu is extremely helpful, it does not provide complete parity between keyboard strokes and usage. However, there are some keyboard shortcuts that you can use while working with Microsoft Dynamics CRM 2011, as shown in Table 5.1.

TABLE 5.1 Keyboard Shortcuts for Microsoft Dynamics CRM 2011

Action	Keyboard Shortcut
Save	Ctrl+S or Shift+F12
Save and close	Alt+S
Close and lose edits	Esc
Open search	Spacebar or Enter
Delete	Ctrl + D
Save and New	Ctrl+Shift+S
Next field on a form	Tab
Previous field on a form	Shift+Tab
Open the lookup menu	Alt+Down Arrow
Open the list menu	Ctrl+Shift+2
Navigate to next item on the list	Ctrl+>
Navigate to the previous item on the list	Ctrl+<
Autocomplete lookups	Ctrl+K

TIP

You can completely hide/unhide the Ribbon menu by selecting the chevron that is near the Sign Out text at the top left of the application. Notice that you might or might not see the Sign Out option depending on which version you are using. CRM Online and IFD have this option; however, without these versions, it will be located near the organization name instead.

Ribbons in Outlook

Figure 5.13 shows the same default Account view in Outlook. Notice that the options are the same as in Internet Explorer; however, there are a number of other options shown.

TIP

While working in Outlook, your first tab might or might not be the same as the examples shown, depending on what options you selected to have available.

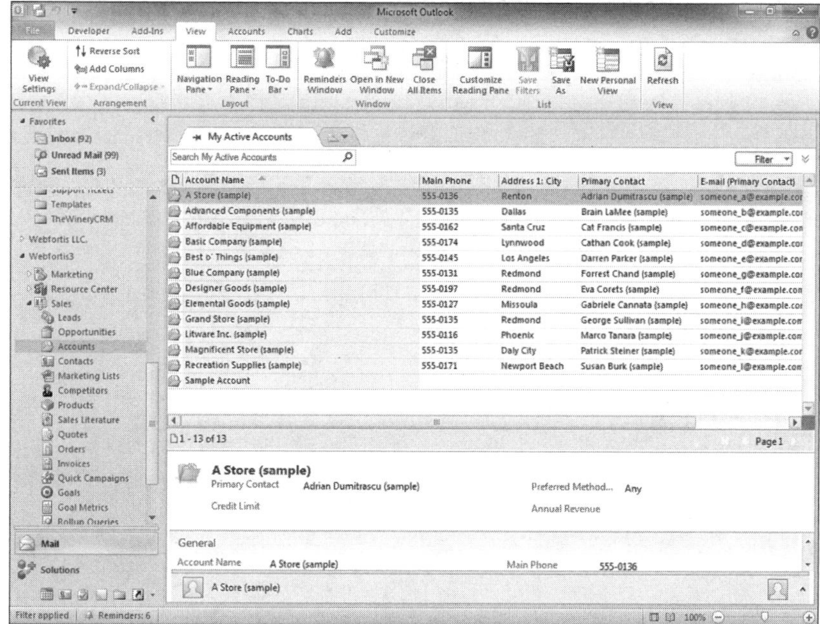

FIGURE 5.13 Account ribbon menu in Outlook.

The other CRM options include

- ▶ Charts
- ▶ Add
- ▶ Customize

The remaining options (as shown) are Outlook options, and include

- ▶ Developer
- ▶ Add-Ins
- ▶ View

Users can customize the tabs by right-clicking the Ribbon and selecting Customize the Ribbon, as shown in Figure 5.14.

Figure 5.15 shows the tabs that are available with the Microsoft Dynamics CRM for Outlook. Unselecting tab options will hide them.

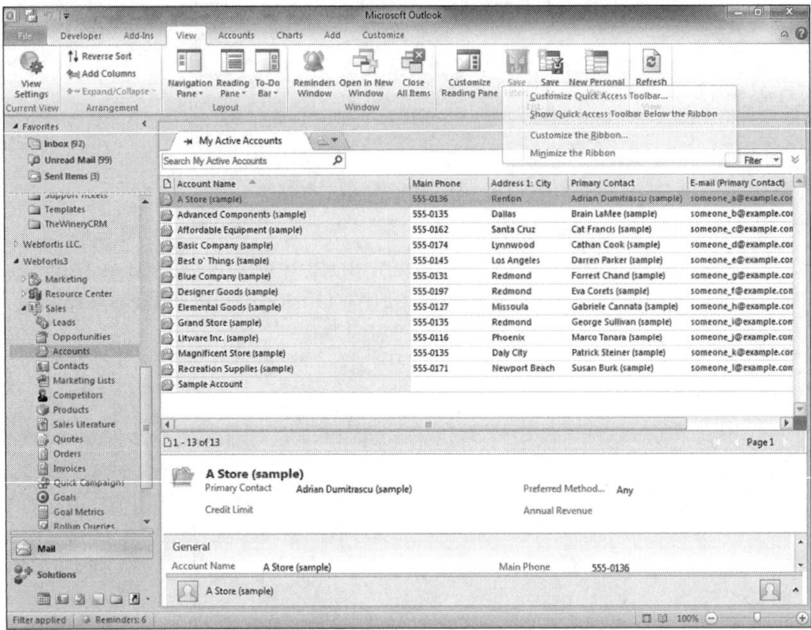

FIGURE 5.14 Customize the ribbon in Outlook.

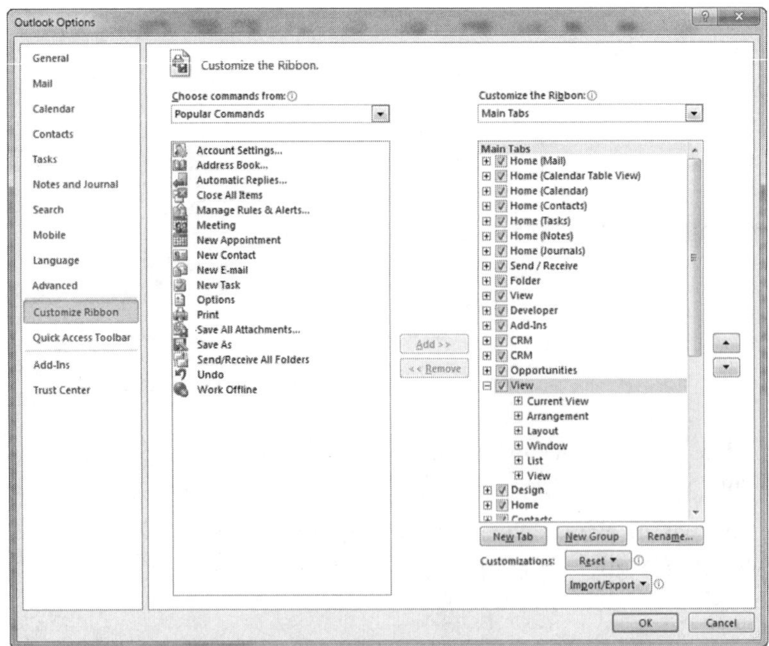

FIGURE 5.15 Tab options for the Ribbon.

CAUTION

Be careful removing tabs for Outlook. Doing so might remove functionality required for CRM and could result in your having to restore the missing options (or reinstall the client).

Conditional Formatting

Using the Outlook View tab, we can apply conditional formatting to the records as they are shown in Outlook. This feature will work for both native Outlook data (that is, emails) as well as CRM data.

TIP

Conditional formatting is a very powerful feature and allows for calling out underlying data directly in Outlook.

To apply conditional formatting, follow these steps:

1. Select the View tab, and select View Settings (as shown in Figure 5.16).

FIGURE 5.16 Advanced View Settings—Launched from the View Settings option of the View Ribbon menu.

2. The Advanced View Settings will open (as shown in Figure 5.16). Select Conditional Formatting.
3. The Conditional Formatting Wizard will open. Select Add and enter a name for the condition, as shown in Figure 5.17. In our example, we're going to highlight Accounts that have high dollar values.
4. Next select the font that you would like to apply to those accounts that meet the criteria by selecting the Font button. In our example, we're going to set the size equal to 12 and the color to red, as shown in Figure 5.18. Select OK to return to the Conditional Formatting Wizard.

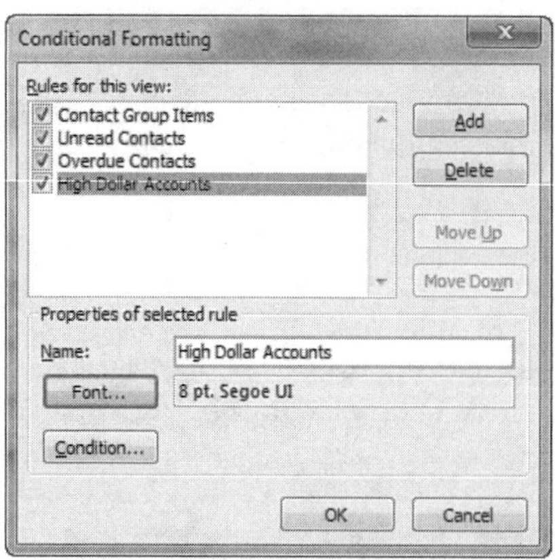

FIGURE 5.17 Conditional Formatting Wizard.

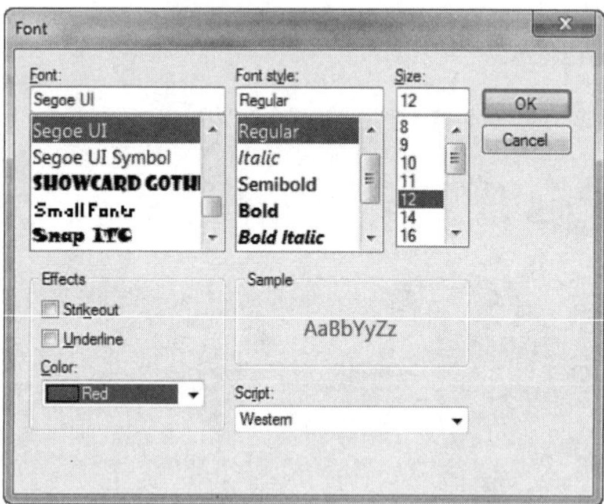

FIGURE 5.18 Setting the font.

5. Now select the condition to be applied by clicking the Condition button.
6. The filter opens (as shown in Figure 5.19). Select the Advanced tab, and select the Field button.
7. Select user-defined fields in the folder (the last option), and then the field you would like to apply the filter to. In our example, we're going to select the attribute Credit Limit from the Account, as shown in Figure 5.20.

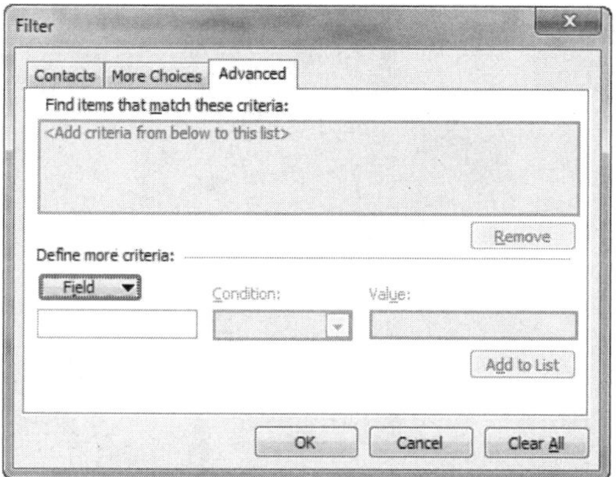

FIGURE 5.19 Setting the filter.

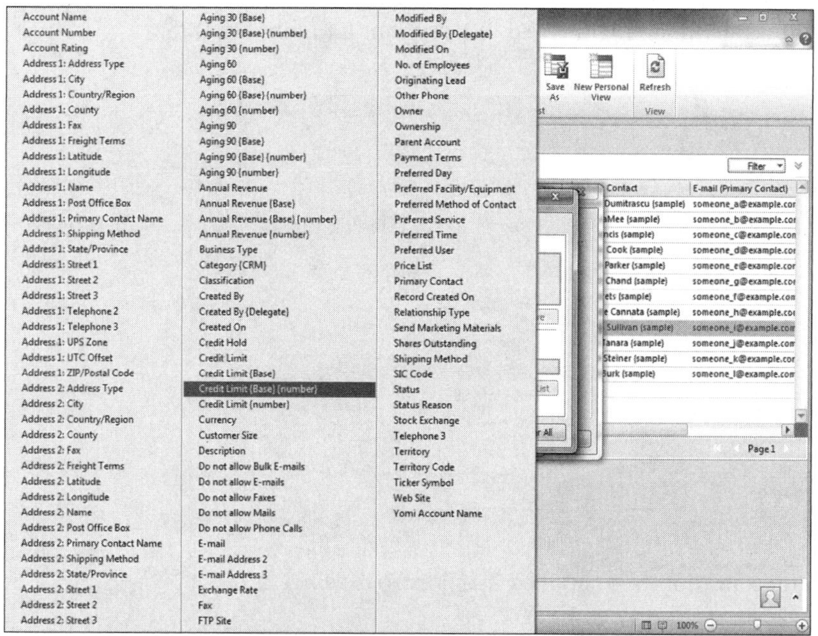

FIGURE 5.20 Selecting the attribute.

8. Complete the filter selection. In our example, we're going to select all Accounts that have a credit limit of at least $10,000, as shown in Figure 5.21.
9. Click Add to List to add the criteria to the list, and then click OK three times.

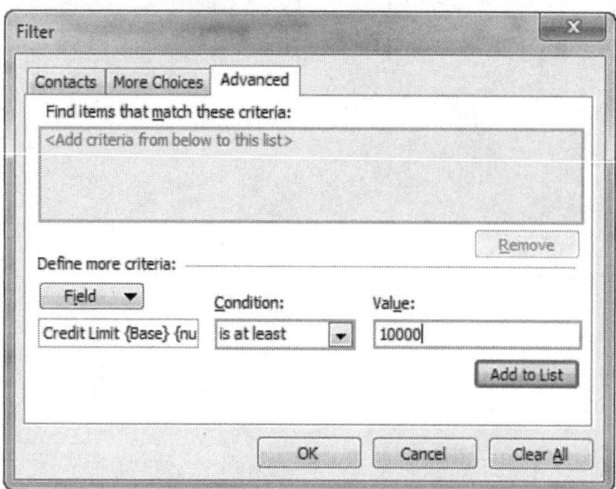

FIGURE 5.21 Setting the filter values.

10. The result will be shown as in Figure 5.22. All the records that have at least a $10,000 credit limit will be highlighted in a red font and font size 12.

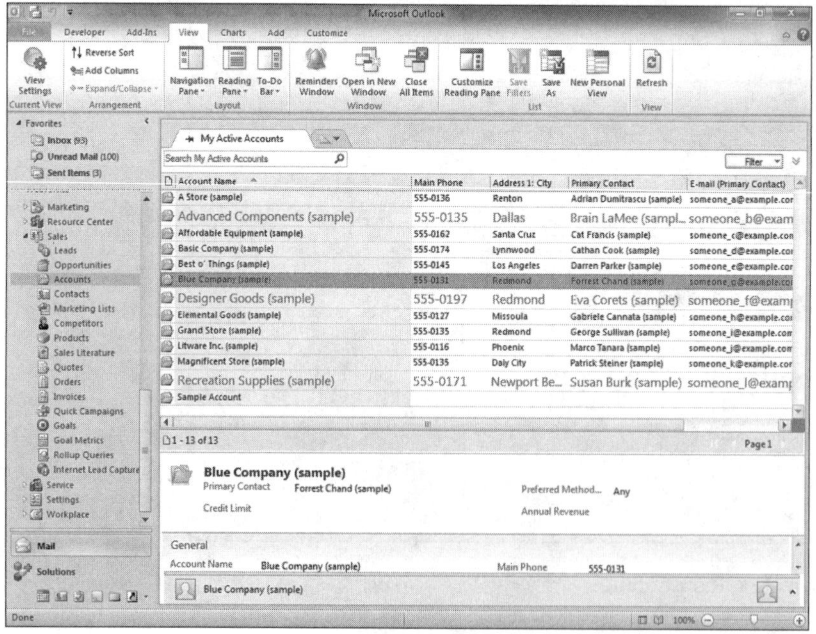

FIGURE 5.22 Conditional formatting applied.

As users update the records, they will be dynamically updated in this view, and provided you have saved your criteria, this is the view that will be presented to users when they return to Accounts.

Customizing

You can customize the Ribbon menu by modifying the underlying Ribbon XML. The Microsoft Dynamics CRM SDK has information and a complete example on how to do this.

The Microsoft Dynamic CRM SDK can be downloaded from the Microsoft download website by searching for "CRM 2011 SDK."

▶ See Chapter 23, "Customizing Entities," for more information on customizing the Dynamics CRM SDK.

Summary

The Ribbon menu provides both a contextual and a graphical way of using the application.

The overview in this chapter should make a number of the new options that are available with Microsoft Dynamics CRM 2011 easier to work with and understand.

CHAPTER 6

Working with Customers

IN THIS CHAPTER

- Accounts
- Contacts

Customers are defined in several different ways. When working in a conventional environment, customers are individuals or organizations that you have conducted business with. When considering an xRM deployment of Microsoft Dynamics CRM, your customers will typically become whatever the "x" designation is.

Examples of this might include

- Vendors
- Employees
- Recruits
- Grants
- Patients
- Suppliers

NOTE

Considering an xRM deployment requires a thorough understanding of the base entities in Microsoft Dynamics CRM prior to deploying. Our recommendation is to thoroughly read through this book in its entirety to gain the required level of understanding prior to attempting a build-out of an xRM deployment. The reason for this is that knowing when, where, and why to use native base entities versus custom ones, can result in significantly easier support and maintenance in the long term.

When working with Customers, you'll become familiar with two entities: Accounts and Contacts. Both can contain records that organizations can consider Customers. In fact, when associating parent/child records to Customers (as on the Contact form where it says Parent Customer), you select either an Account or a Contact value. As such, consider Customers in Microsoft Dynamics CRM to be equal to either of these entities.

TIP

It is sometimes helpful to rename Accounts to Companies, and Contacts to Customers—something that can easily be done by editing its display name under Settings and Customization.

▶ For more information about settings and customization, see Chapter 23, "Customizing Entities."

Often times we hear customers asking about Leads in Microsoft Dynamics CRM as customers and it is important to remember that, when using Microsoft Dynamics CRM, Leads are *potential* customers, not actual customers. Although we have seen in rare cases Leads being used as customers, it is not common with a base build because there is no out-of-the-box many-to-one relationship for common necessary entities such as Contacts and Invoices.

When considering a sales process and Microsoft Dynamics CRM, it is important to realize that unlike Leads, Opportunities do require a reference to an existing Customer (that is, an Account or Contact), and as such use of the Opportunity entity requires some thought prior to usage.

▶ See Chapter 8, "Working with Sales," for greater depth on working with Opportunities and Leads.

Accounts

In very general terms, users should consider Accounts as businesses or organizations. Some Accounts have many contacts associated with them (such as a normal customer that has two dozen employees with whom you have contact on some level); other Accounts have no contacts associated with them. (The Internal Revenue Service might be a good example of this.)

The Account entity can be used not only for businesses you sell to, but also for vendors you purchase from, again tracking contacts that work for the vendor.

Finally, although not generally common, another use for Accounts is to track competitors. This situation arises if you have a lot of information about competitors (such as individual employee data) or if the existing Competitor entity (found in the Sales area) in Microsoft Dynamics CRM is not sufficient enough for your needs.

The most common usage types for Accounts can actually be found in the Relationship Type drop-down list (see Figure 6.1):

- Competitor
- Consultant
- Customer
- Investor
- Partner
- Influencer
- Press
- Prospect
- Reseller
- Supplier
- Vendor
- Other

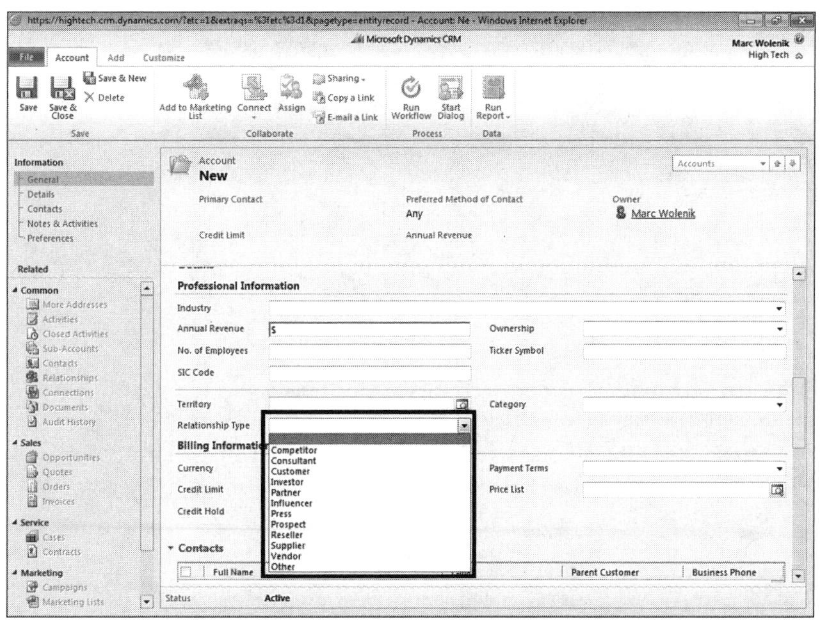

FIGURE 6.1 Default relationship type shown on the Account form.

NOTE

Typically, we don't recommend using Accounts to track competitors. We recommend augmenting the out-of-the-box Competitor entity found in the Sales area with customizations, as necessary, and using it instead. The reason for this is that, when you close Opportunities in Microsoft Dynamics CRM, you have the option to tie lost opportunities to only the Competitor entity (and not other Accounts or Contacts). Therefore, you effectively lose visibility into competitors' win/loss metrics relating to your opportunities when you don't use the Competitor entity.

Because of the amount of time spent by most users working with Customers, we have taken extra effort in this chapter to explain most, if not all, the fields on the Account and Contact forms.

General Area

When working with Accounts, only two fields are required by default: Account Name and Owner. (However, you can easily customize the form to make other fields required if your business needs require it.) Because the Account Name is the first field shown on the default quick find view (see Figure 6.2), it is important to be descriptive here.

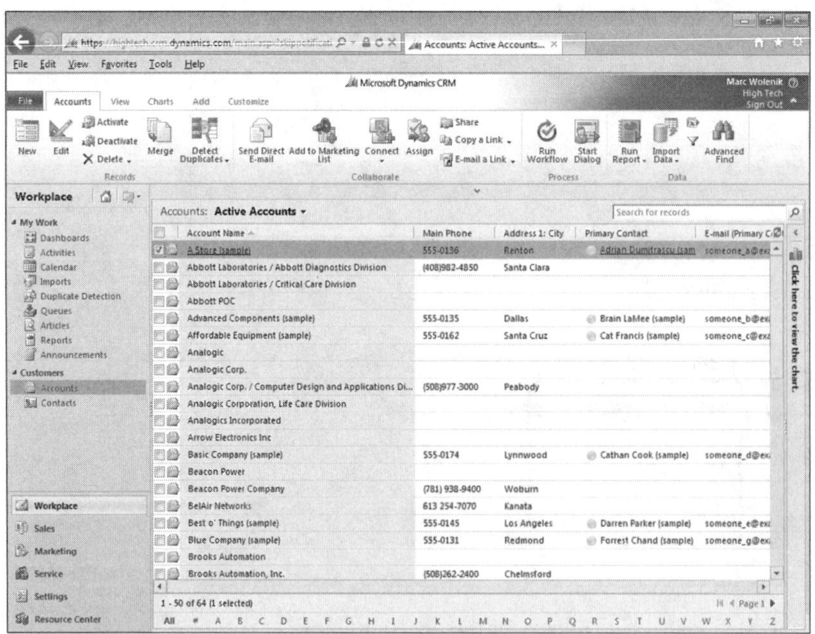

FIGURE 6.2 Active Accounts with Account Name shown.

CAUTION

Because the Account Name field has no built-in functionality to avoid duplicates, be sure to add a Duplicate Detection Rule on Account Name if you have concerns about duplicates here. See Figure 6.3 for an example of a duplicate detection warning when entering a duplicated account name and duplicate detection is on for Account Name.

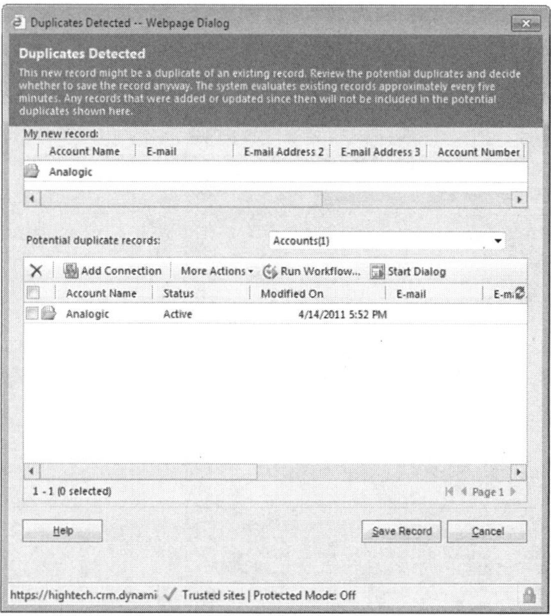

FIGURE 6.3 Duplicate detection example when entering a duplicate Account name.

▶ See Chapter 24, "Workflow Development," for more information about duplicate detection rules.

By default, the Owner (located on theAdministration section) is set to the user who created the record; however, you can change this to select another user in the system.

NOTE

A new feature in this version is the ability to assign record ownership to not just users, but also teams. This has a significant impact in that multiple users' rights to records can now be set/shared by using the Owner field.

TIP

Be sure that the user has permissions to view the record. If not, you will receive a security warning prompt indicating that the user doesn't have the necessary security permissions to access the record, and you cannot assign it to him.

To add a new Account, select New from the Ribbon interface (see Figure 6.4) and the new Account form opens.

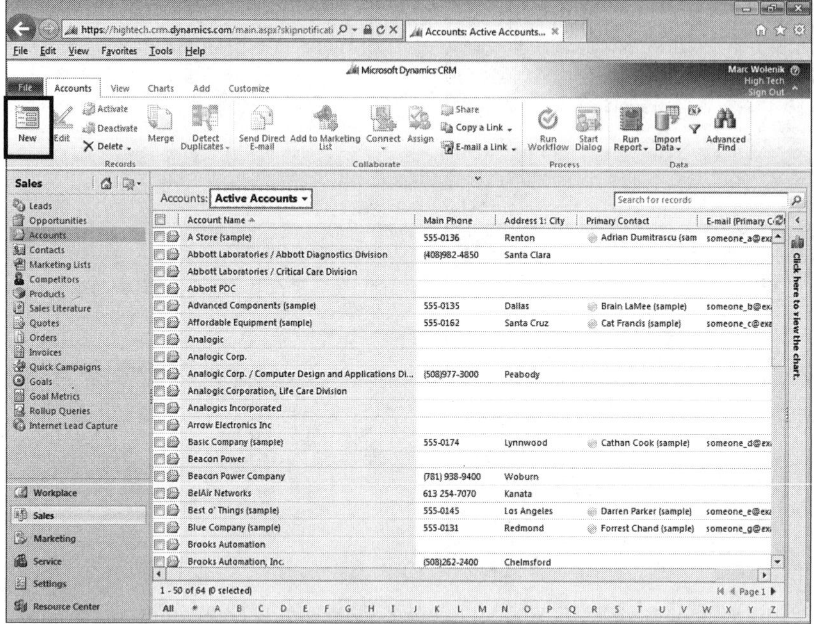

FIGURE 6.4 Adding a new Account from the Ribbon.

Besides the two required fields previously indicated, the following comprise the list of fields that can be used:

- **Account Number**—This free-form entry field can be used to enter any number or alphanumeric combination. This field can be tied to existing ERP, Accounting, or other systems for quick-and-easy reference. In that case, we recommend setting the value to read-only or similarly controlling it so that it can be modified only through an approved business process. Again, as noted earlier with the Account Name, duplicate entries are not checked on this field by default; therefore, it is possible to enter the same Account Number unless you have a duplicate detection rule running here as well.
- **Parent Account**—The Parent Account field is used when the Account rolls up to another Account. An example of this is a customer that has several different business units that report to a corporate entity.

- **Primary Contact**—The Primary Contact field ties to the Contact record. This is not a required association, but the Primary Contact is shown on the Account Quickview by default and can make similar Accounts easier to identify and work with.
- **Currency**—The Currency field enables users to select the primary currency that this entity deals with. You must select a currency option here to work with other attributes of the form (such as the Annual Revenue field on the Details tab). The currency options shown are only those that the system administrator has set within the system. It should be noted that this field automatically populates to the default currency specified when CRM was first installed. However, it can be changed as required on an account-by-account basis.

▶ For more information about currency, see Chapter 12, "Settings and Configuration."

TIP

It is important that the Currency field is populated when working with imported records because it will not populate by default when importing records, and you will receive an error when trying to add values to any Currency value field.

- **Main Phone, Other Phone, and Fax**—These free-form entry fields accept any alphanumeric value. Because any value is accepted here, you might want to enforce entry standards by using scripting. For more information about working with scripts, see Chapter 23.
- **Website**—The Website field accepts any value and automatically formats it as a URL by prepending the entered value with http://. (If the entered value already has http://, it uses the entered value.) Users can double-click the entered value to go directly to the website, which opens in a new window.
- **Email**—The Email field accepts an address for any domain. However, a check is done to be sure that it is properly formatted as an email address. This is an important field because the system prompts you with errors if you try to send an e-mail to the Account and this value is missing (see Figure 6.5). Additionally, when a user double-clicks on the entered value in this field, a new window opens prepopulated with the email address selected.

  Additional considerations around the E-mail field are duplicate detection jobs. By default, Microsoft Dynamics CRM comes with at least three email duplicate detection rules, one of which is used for detecting duplicate Account names (found in Settings, Data Management, Duplicate Detection Rules). By default, the email rules look at the e-mail addresses of Accounts, Contacts, and Leads, so if you enter a duplicate e-mail, you will be warned, as shown in Figure 6.3.

▶ For more information about duplicate detection rules, see Chapter 24.

The remaining fields on the General tab consist of address information. These fields are also available in the More Addresses option on the left navigation if an Account has multiple addresses.

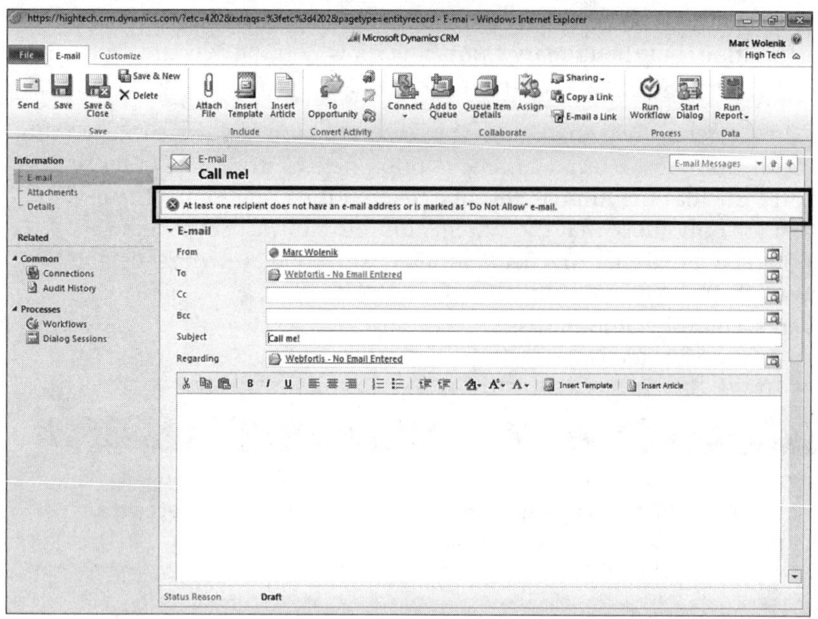

FIGURE 6.5 Error message when creating an E-mail Activity task for an Account that does not have an e-mail address.

Details Area

Options on the Details panel (see Figure 6.6) follow:

- **Territory**—If you have set up your CRM to use Territories, you can select one of them here. For more information on setting up Territories, refer to Chapter 12.
- **Annual Revenue**—The Annual Revenue field is a free-form field that requires you to enter the base currency for the Account on the General tab. If you have selected a currency and entered a value here, and then try to change the currency, you receive an error message that you must remove the entered value before setting the currency again.
- **Credit Limit**—Similar to the Annual Revenue field, you must select a currency value to enter a value here.
- **Price List**—When using different Price Lists for your organization, you can select the preferred Price List here.
- **Billing Information - Credit Hold and Payment Terms**—You can select these fields when setting up the Account, and you can change them during the Account's life. (If you are thinking about integrating CRM into an existing ERP or other accounting system, the fields in the Billing Information section get special attention.)

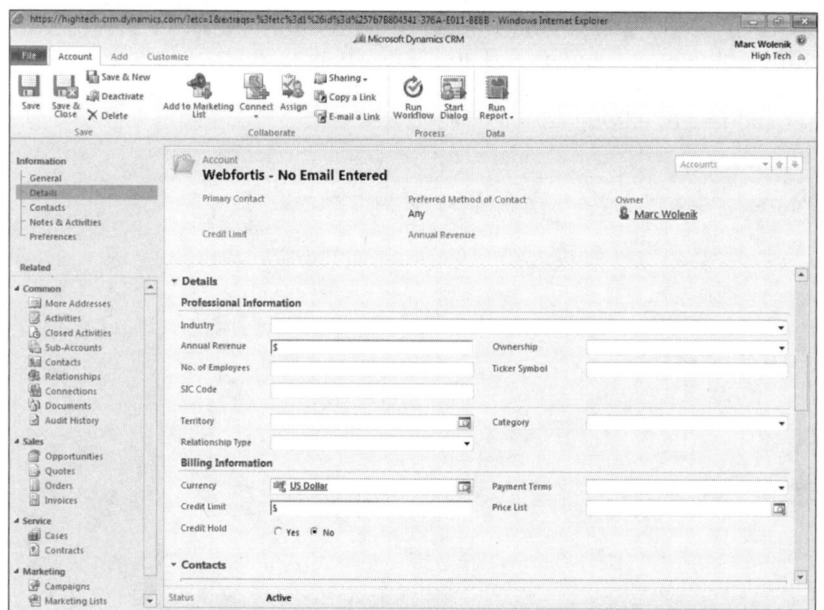

FIGURE 6.6 Account creation Details section.

NOTE

When working with integration between Microsoft Dynamics CRM and an accounting system, the Billing Information section is a common area that is referenced with the integration because this type of information is much more commonly held with the accounting system.

Other options on the Details tab include Category, Industry, Ownership, No. of Employees, Ticker Symbol, and Description; these are fairly self-explanatory. The SIC Code is the Standard Industrial Classification code used to specify what industry this Account belongs to.

▶ You can find more information about SIC codes and the code values at www.sec.gov/info/edgar/siccodes.htm.

Contacts

The Contacts area shows the contacts that are associated to the selected Account.

By default there are no contacts associated to a new Account, and you have to either add a new contact or add an existing contact.

To do so, select anywhere on the grid (notice the outline will turn blue) and a new menu bar will appear on the ribbon (see Figure 6.7). This is known as a contextual ribbon and is specific to the selected area (in this case the contacts). From here you can perform the functions required to adding or editing contacts associated to the Account.

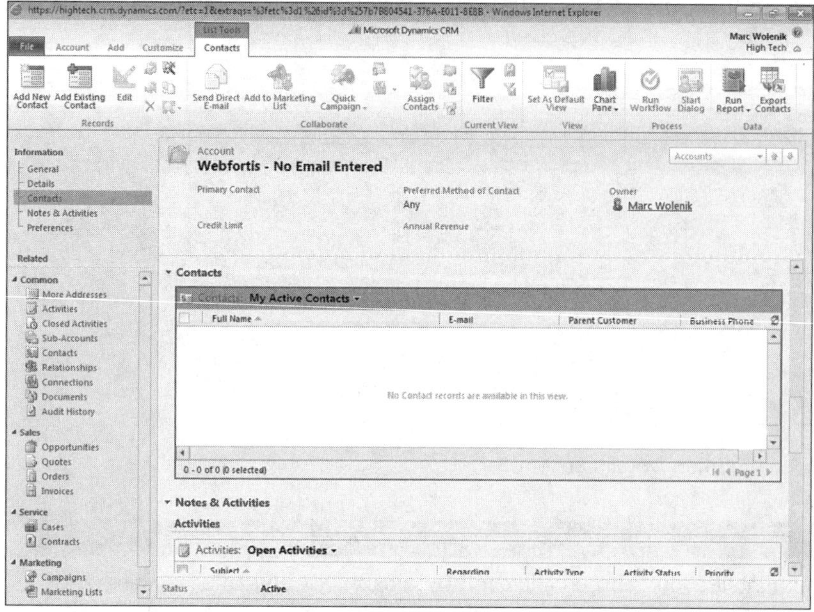

FIGURE 6.7 Account Contacts section.

Notes & Activities

The Notes & Activities section displays (similarly to the Contacts) inline information about any activities that are pending for the selected Account (shown in Figure 6.8).

Preferences

Options on the Administration panel (see Figure 6.9) follow:

- **Owner**—As stated earlier, the Owner field is automatically populated when the record is created. However, you can change this if the new owner user or team has the necessary permissions.
- **Originating Lead**—This field is populated only when an Account is converted from an originating Lead and cannot be changed. If the Account is not converted from a Lead, this field is blank.

▶ For more information about Price Lists, see Chapter 12, "Settings and Configuration."

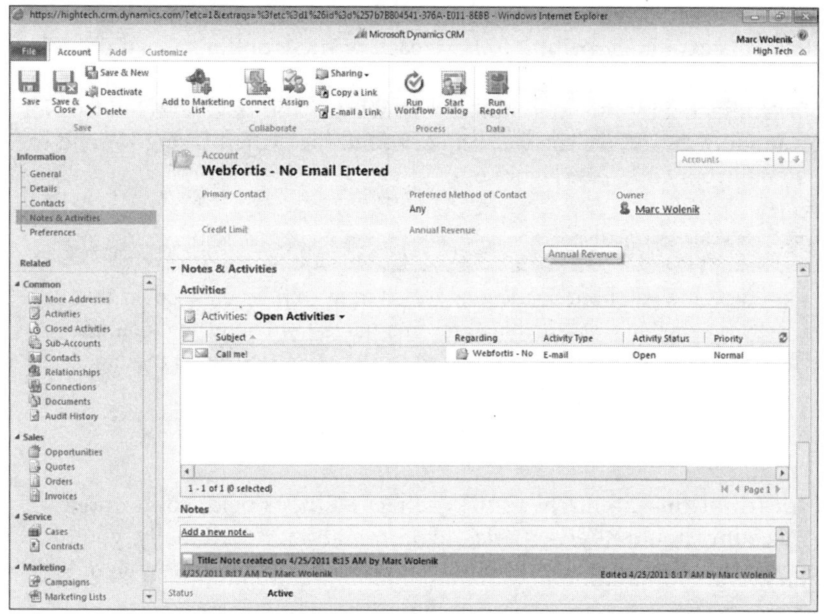

FIGURE 6.8 Account creation Notes section.

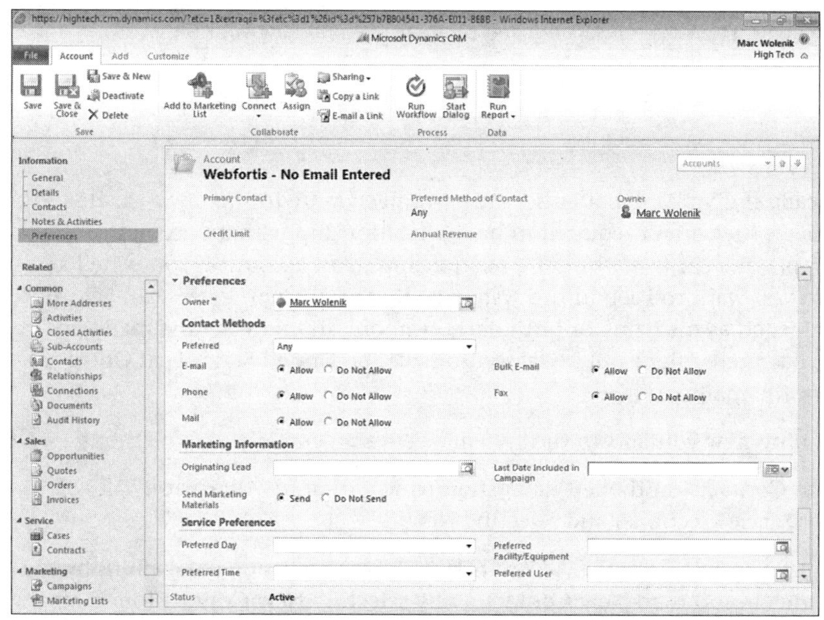

FIGURE 6.9 Account creation Preferences section.

- **Contact Methods**—When selecting the Contact Methods, the system defaults all values to Allow. It is extremely helpful to have each of these options when doing bulk activities such as e-mail campaigns because you can exclude Accounts that do not want to be contacted by this method. Additionally, if you have selected Do Not Allow for the e-mail, you receive the warning error message when trying to send the Account an e-mail from CRM (see Figure 6.5).

NOTE

Although the system prevents you from sending an e-mail from CRM to an Account that has Do Not Allow set for e-mail in CRM, nothing prevents users from sending e-mail to an Account directly from Outlook that is set in CRM to Do Not Allow (provided the email is not tracked).

- **Marketing Information**—Similarly, to the Contact Methods field, you can set whether the Account should receive marketing information. Additionally, you have the option to view the date that the Account was last included in a campaign.
- **Service Preferences**—If the Account has any kind of service preferences, you can record that here. This is especially helpful in recording preferences for quick look up by Account.

▶ To learn more about service preferences, see Chapter 10, "Working with Service."

Contacts

Contacts are typically individuals that either are customers or are in some way related to an account. Although they aren't required to have a relationship with an account, they often do. An example of a contact without a relationship to an account is someone like the mailman, who you want to keep in the system so that all the employees can get information about him (such as his name or birth date; everyone should wish the mailman happy birthday!), but there might not be reason to have the United States Post Office as an account just for the mailman.

When creating/adding new contacts to the system, there are generally easy methods:

- Navigating to Contacts on the left navigation pane (either in Workplace, Sales, Marketing or Service sections) and selecting New.
- Creating a new Contact from the Accounts form (on the left side navigation) by selecting Contacts and then New Contact, or by selecting New Contact found on the Ribbon bar under list Tools/Contacts.
- Creating a new Contact by navigating to the File tab and then selecting New Record, Contact. (Doing it this way does not prepopulate the parent customer however.)

The first method enables you to select the Parent Customer (if applicable), whereas the second method prepopulates that information for you. (In addition to the Parent Customer, the address information and currency information are populated from the Account that spawned the new Contact form, and is therefore the recommended method.)

It is important to understand when working with Contacts that they inherit Account information only if they are propagated from the Account. This is important because different Accounts may have different currencies associated with them.

General Section

By default, Contacts have two required fields. One, on the General section, is Last Name; the other, on the Administration section, is Owner. The First Name field is a Business Recommended field, so we always recommend using it whenever possible (see Figure 6.10).

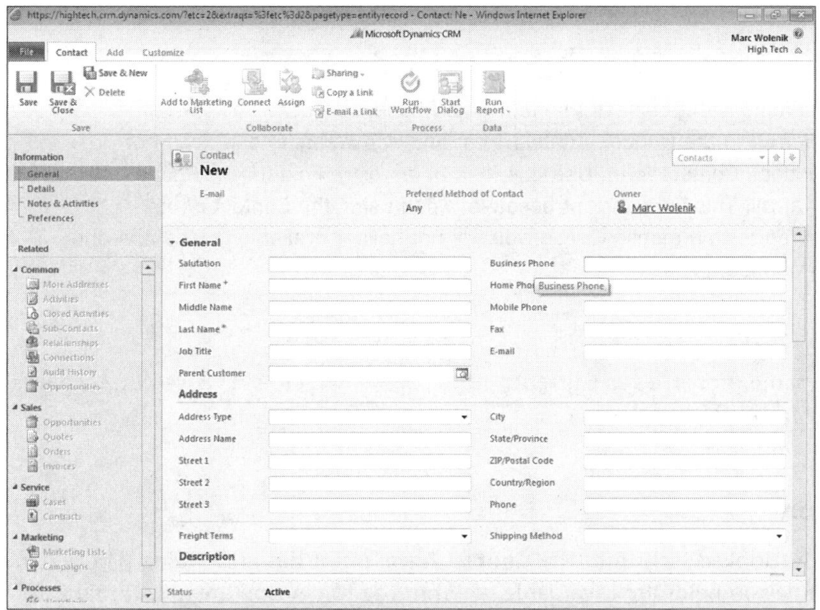

FIGURE 6.10 Creating a new Contact interface.

Parent Customer is a very important field: By populating it, you create a relationship between the Contact and the Customer. As discussed in the earlier section, "Accounts," if you enter a value in this field (either an Account or a Contact), the Contact you're working with shows up as either a Subcontact (if you enter a Contact Customer) or a Contact (if you enter an Account Customer) related to that entry. Additionally, this relationship facilitates the rollup of all information (Activities, Opportunities, Quotes, Orders, etc.) from the contact to the Account allowing you to get a consolidated view of all activities relating to the Account and associated Contacts.

NOTE

As indicated, the Parent Customer can be either an Account or a Contact. This has an interesting effect on the Outlook client that displays this field as the Company. If you select a Contact, Outlook displays that person as the Company.

As mentioned, in addition to Parent Customer, you should populate the other fields on this form (Salutation, Middle Name, Job Title, Street 1, Street 2, Street 3, City, State/Province, Business Phone, Home Phone, Mobile Phone, Fax, Email, Zip/Postal Code, and Country/Region) as necessary because they will all correlate to a Contact in Microsoft Outlook.

TIP

Do not confuse Phone with Business Phone, Home Phone, or Mobile Phone—all of which are transferred to the Outlook Contact form and vice versa. Phone does not appear in the Outlook Contact form. Use this field as an extra field for the Phone entry or do not use it at all. This is important because, when using the Contacts from Outlook to synchronize to a mobile device, you will not have it available unless it is one of the previous mapped fields.

Currency has the same properties as Currency in Accounts, which is reviewed in Accounts, Details previously in this chapter.

Details Section

This is the most overlooked section in the Contact form, but it has great value. The Professional Information fields are invaluable when trying to develop organizational information, and the Personal Information fields are of great benefit when you need to know salient details about the Contact. The Description field is used for general information relevant to the contact that isn't likely to change (see Figure 6.12).

NOTE

The Birthday field is a great excuse for customer contact. Who wouldn't like to receive a call, e-mail, or small gift from a vendor on their birthday?

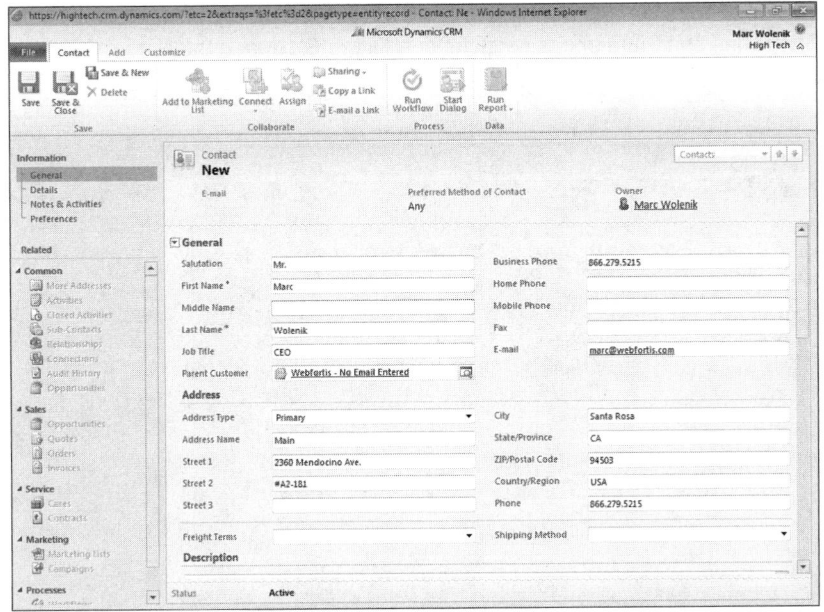

FIGURE 6.11 Sample Contact in CRM.

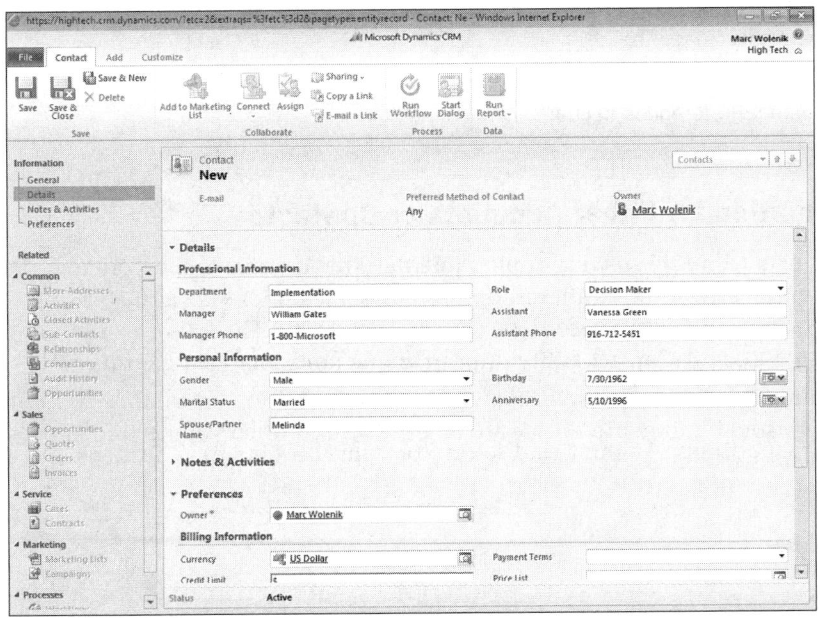

FIGURE 6.12 Contact Details section.

▶ Refer to the "Accounts" section covered earlier in this chapter for more information on the Notes & Activities and Preferences sections see Figure 6.13) and the Notes panel (see Figure 6.14).

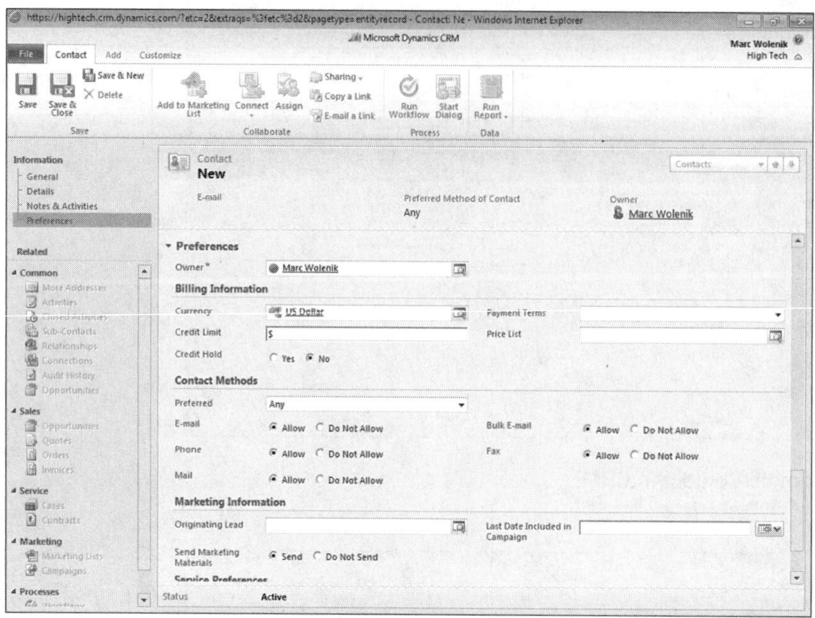

FIGURE 6.13 Contact Preferences section.

General Information for Either Accounts or Contacts

The information included in this section applies to either the Account or the Contact entity forms. As with many of the entities in the system, some options are available only after the record is saved. (It doesn't need to be closed—just saved.) The following options are available for the Account/Contact entity prior to saving (and completing Business Required fields):

- New (Lead, Opportunity, Account, and so on from the File Ribbon)
- Save
- Save and Close
- Save and New
- Close

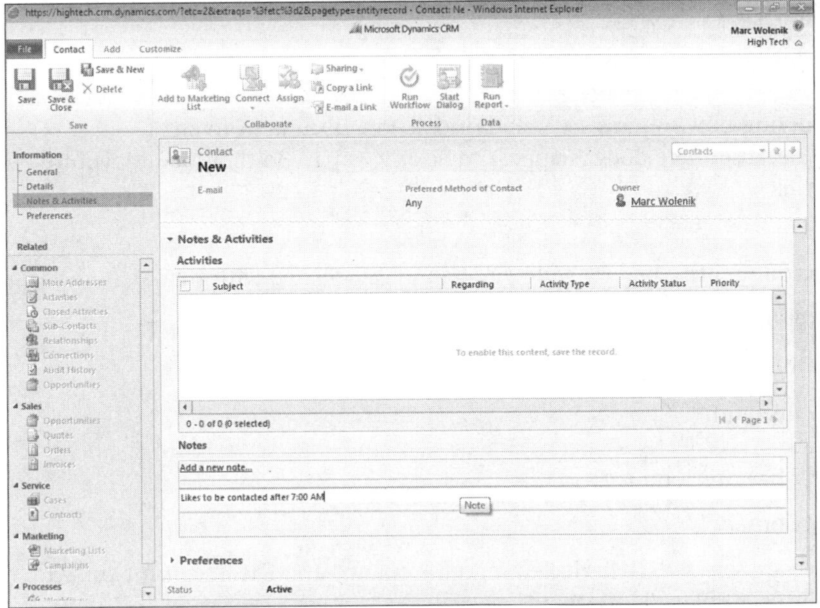

FIGURE 6.14 Contact Notes & Activities Section.

If you attempt to close the record after you have already started to enter data, you receive a warning prompt if Business Required fields are blank (in the case of Accounts, Account Name and Owner; in the case of Contacts, Last Name and Owner).

The following options are available after saving:

- All options listed previously
- Delete
- Deactivate
- Assign
- Sharing
- Add to Marketing List
- Add Connection
- Run Report
- Print Preview
- Run Process
- Start Dialog

- Copy and Email a Link
- All the options on the 'Create Related' ribbon

So, if you're wondering how to send an e-mail or upload a document to an Account/Contact because there doesn't appear to be any way to do that, be sure you've saved the record first.

Reports

By default, the Account entity has the following reports associated with it:

- Account Overview
- Account Summary
- Products by Account

The Contact entity has this report:

- Products by Contact

When any of these are selected, the selected report is opened and the Account/Contact you're working with is displayed by default.

▶ Refer to Chapter 11, "Reporting," for more information about reports.

Common, More Addresses

More Addresses (shown in Figure 6.15) is generally used when an Account/Contact has multiple locations. This can include different departments within an organization at a different organization, different shipping addresses, or different primary addresses. The Address Name field (not the Address Type field) should differentiate them because it is displayed on the Quickview form.

Common, Activities

Activities are where all future events are shown. Figure 6.16 shows the activities for our selected account with the default view shown of Open Activity Associated View.

When a new activity is created (either in CRM or in Outlook (provided it is tracked to CRM)), then it will be shown here until it is marked as closed.

NOTE

Even if you set the date for something as previous to today's date, the activity will remain open until it is marked as closed. One way to address this is to create a workflow that automatically closes all activities with a prior date; however you risk closing items that should remain pending.

Common, Closed Activities

After activities are marked as completed, they will be shown in the Closed Activities (as shown in Figure 6.17).

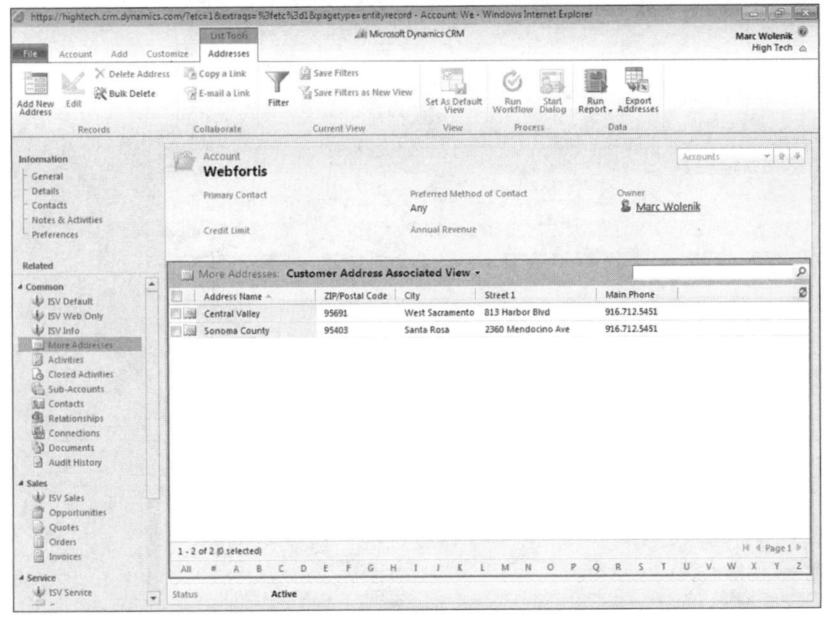

FIGURE 6.15 Account More Addresses.

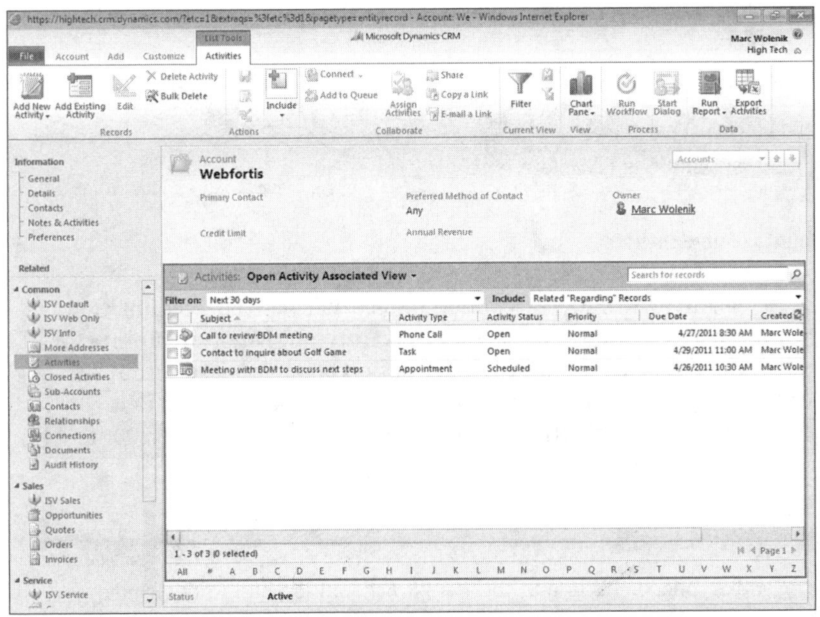

FIGURE 6.16 Account Activities.

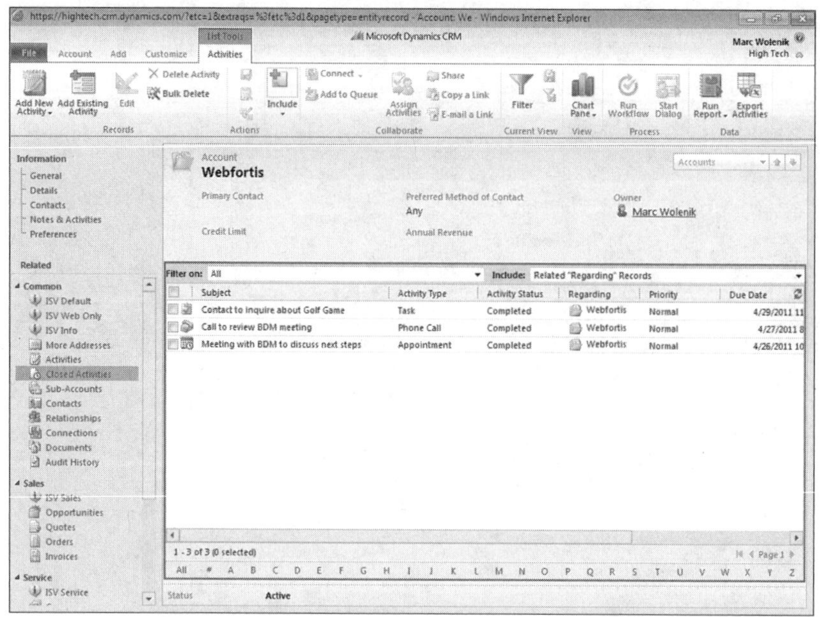

FIGURE 6.17 Account Closed Activities.

Closed activities have limited properties and editability as they become read-only after being marked as completed.

NOTE

The only way to mark an email as complete is to send it.

Common, Sub-accounts/Sub-contacts

The Sub-accounts/Sub-contacts section is an easy way to view associated Accounts/Contacts (see Figure 6.18). Any Account/Contact that has the Account/Contact you're working with listed as its Parent Account for Accounts and Parent Customer for Contacts appears here. Additionally, if you select the option New Account within the subaccount, or New Contact within the subcontact, you can quickly create a new Account/Contact that inherits several attributes of the Account/Contact you're working with, such as Currency and Parent Account or Parent Customer.

TIP

The key to working with subaccounts is that the Parent Account is used to determine the subaccount relationship (The same is true for subcontacts and the Parent Customer). If you're working with Accounts and select an existing Account as a Parent Account, the Account you're working with then shows as a subaccount of the Account you selected.

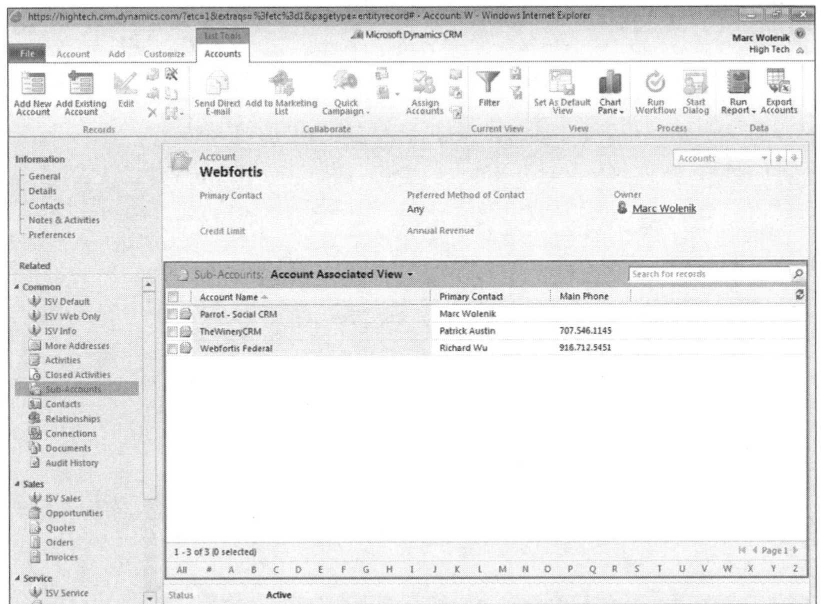

FIGURE 6.18 Account Sub-Accounts

NOTE

The nesting level is only one deep. So, if you have Account 1 and make Account 2 a subaccount (by selecting Account 1 as the Parent Account), you will see Account 2 as the subaccount for Account 1. However, if you add a new subaccount to Account 2, called Account 3, you will not see Account 1 when you look at subaccounts for Account 1. This is because you see only the Accounts that have the Account you're working with listed as Parent Accounts as subaccounts.

The Contacts section shows all Contacts that are associated with this Account/Contact.

▶ For more information on Contacts, refer to the "Contacts" section in this chapter.

Common, Relationships

It is quite common for Accounts to have relationships with other Accounts or Contacts that don't fit within the role of a subaccount or work directly for the Account. A good example of this might be an Account that manufactures ice cream and an Account that produces milk. Although they have no hierarchal relationship, without the milk Account, the ice cream Account can't manufacture ice cream. As such, you would add a relationship between the two Accounts here to record this type of relationship.

You can create relationships between either an Account or Contacts using this form (see Figure 6.19).

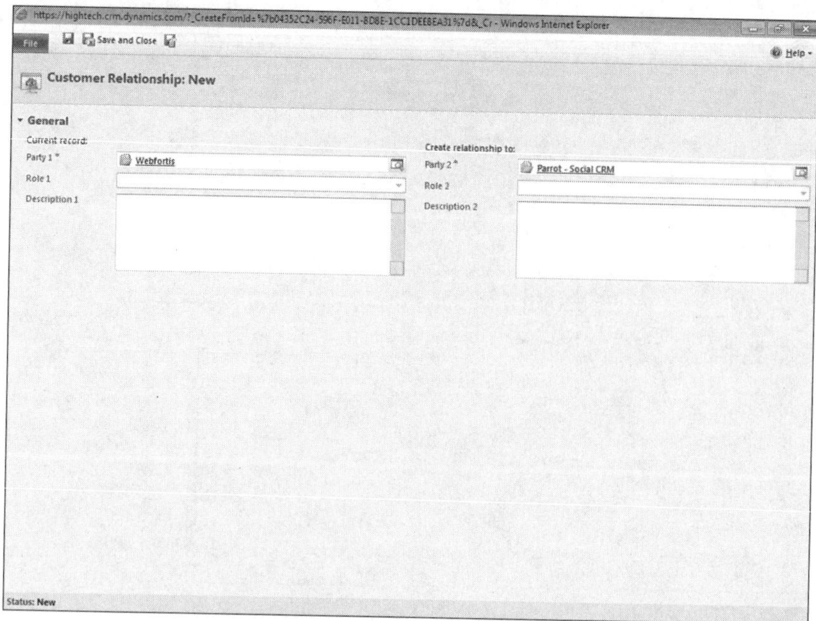

FIGURE 6.19 Relationships.

When adding the relationship, you must select the Account or Contact you want to relate. If you have created relationship roles, you can select them here as well as enter a further description related to the relationship.

▶ For more information about setting up relationship roles, see Chapter 12, "Settings and Configuration."

NOTE

You can select from Customers (Accounts or Contacts) only when creating relationships. However, when working with the Opportunities form, you can create a relationship between the Opportunity and an Account or Contact. (The option to easily associate a relationship between the Account you're working with and an Opportunity is available via the top Actions menu, but that relationship is visible only on the Opportunity Entity.)

Relationships are a great way to record relations of a nonbusiness nature, such as friendships, family and relatives, and other nonbusiness organizations. They provide a quick-and-easy way to view relationships with an Account that are nonhierarchal in nature.

TIP

When working with Advanced Find, be sure not to use the attribute Relationship Type when attempting to query on existing relationships. The Relationship Type attribute relates to the drop-down option found on the General panel of the Account form. Instead, be sure to select Related Customer Relationships (either Party 1 or Party 2) and select either Role 1 or Role 2.

▶ See Chapter 19, "Advanced Views and Connections," for more information about relationships.

Common, Connections

Connections can be established directly to the Account or Contact record from here. See Figure 6.20 for an example of creating a connection.

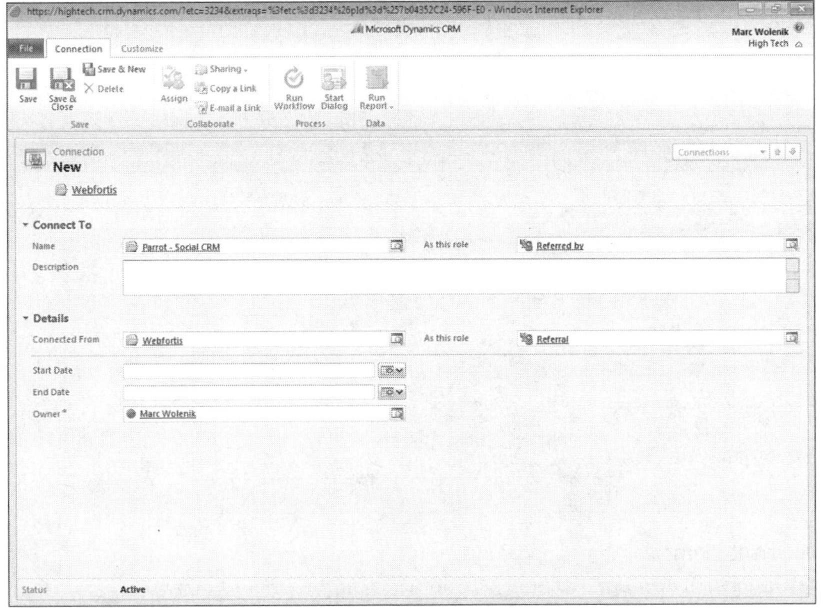

FIGURE 6.20 Connection creation.

▶ For more information about working with connections and how they differ from relationships, please refer to Chapter 5 and Chapter 19.

Common, Documents

With the inclusion of SharePoint services in Microsoft Dynamics CRM 2011, SharePoint document libraries are now easily referenced and directly accessible from the Account or Contact entities. Figure 6.21 show how to add a document location and Figure 6.22 shows the created document library accessible via the Account, Documents link.

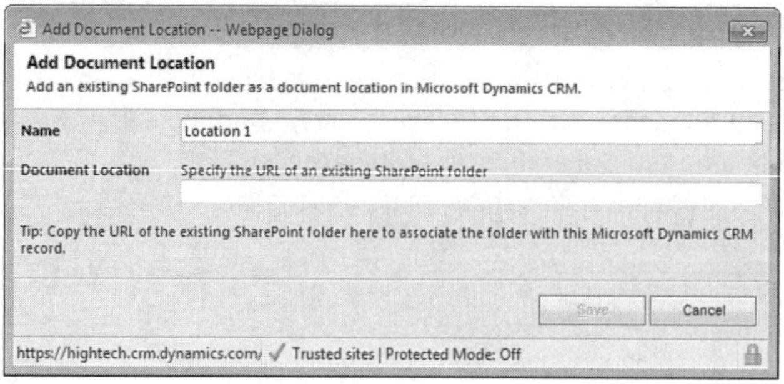

Add Document Location -- Webpage Dialog

Add Document Location

Add an existing SharePoint folder as a document location in Microsoft Dynamics CRM.

Name: Location 1

Document Location: Specify the URL of an existing SharePoint folder

Tip: Copy the URL of the existing SharePoint folder here to associate the folder with this Microsoft Dynamics CRM record.

Save | Cancel

https://hightech.crm.dynamics.com/ ✓ Trusted sites | Protected Mode: Off

FIGURE 6.21 Creating a document location or association.

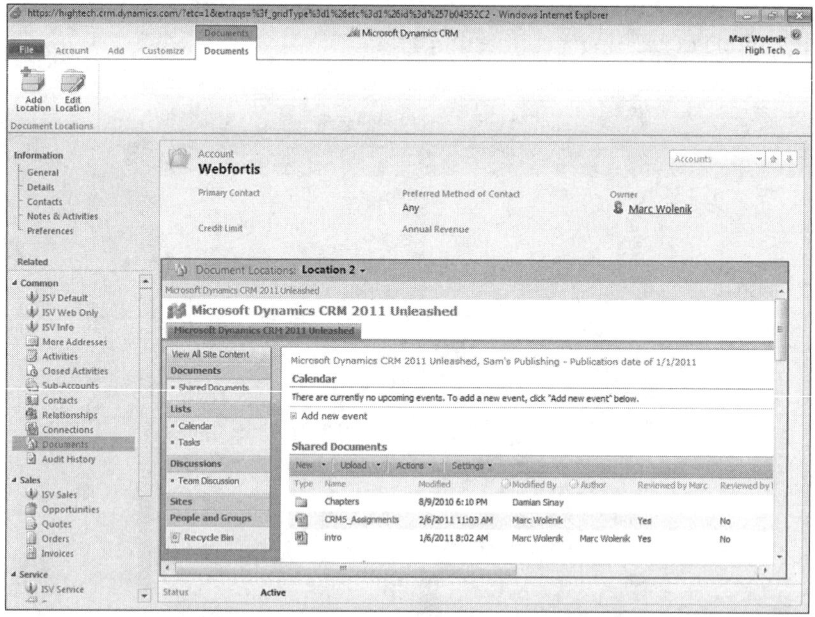

FIGURE 6.22 Document Library.

Although Document libraries can be created from any entity in CRM, they are created by default on Account, Article, Lead, Opportunity, Product, Quote and Sales Literature.

▶ See Chapter 17, "CRM 2011 SharePoint Integration," for instructions on how to set up SharePoint servers for document library usage.

Common, Audit History

Assuming auditing is enabled and applied to the entity (see Chapter 29, "Data Management," for information on how to manage audit settings), the audit history for the attributes of this entity will be visible here.

Figure 6.23 shows an example of the audit history displayed when the Account name was changed. Figure 6.24 shows the detail of the selected audit row.

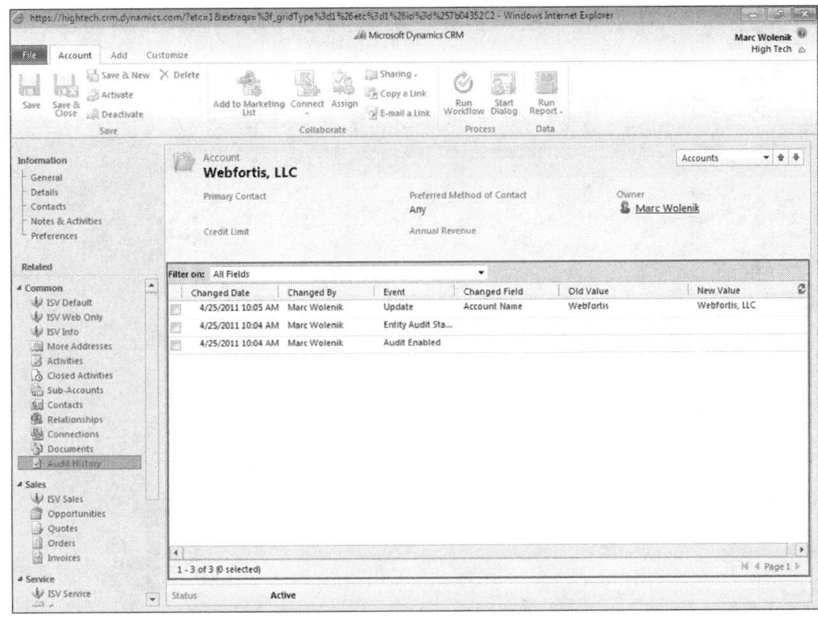

FIGURE 6.23 Audit history displayed.

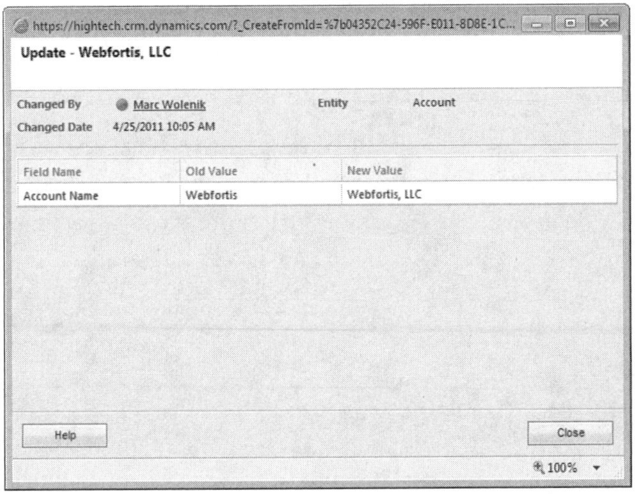

FIGURE 6.24 Audit values displayed.

Processes, Workflows and Dialog Sessions

Any processes (previously referred to as *workflow*) that have been run or are currently running that affect the Account you're working with are displayed here (see Figure 6.25 and Figure 6.26). You can bulk delete, enable/disable filters, cancel, resume, postpone or pause any process from More Actions located at the top of the Quickview.

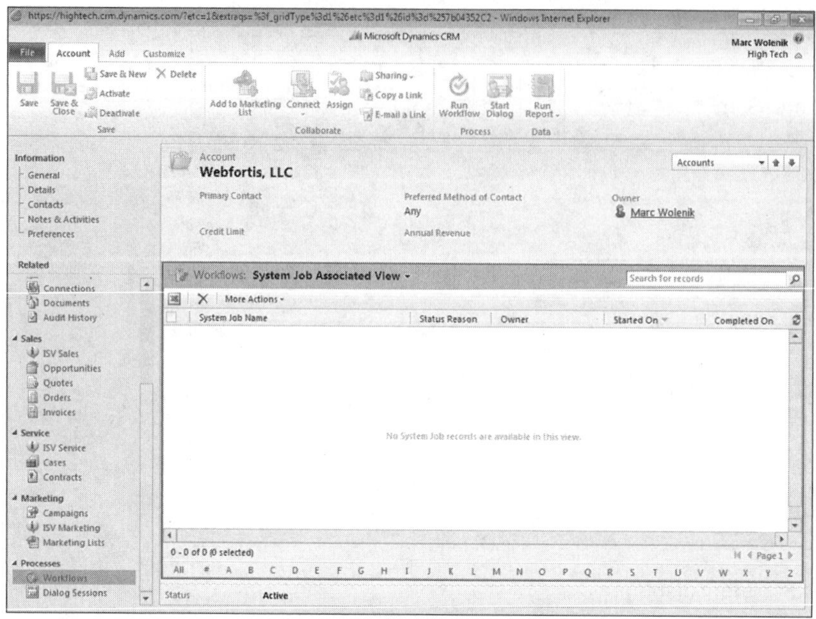

FIGURE 6.25 Account processes interface.

Additionally, you can open any process listed here to see further information about it, such as what the process was responsible for, when it started, and when it completed.

▶ See Chapter 24 for more information about how processes work.

Processes and Dialog Sessions are broken down separately to allow management of them by processes.

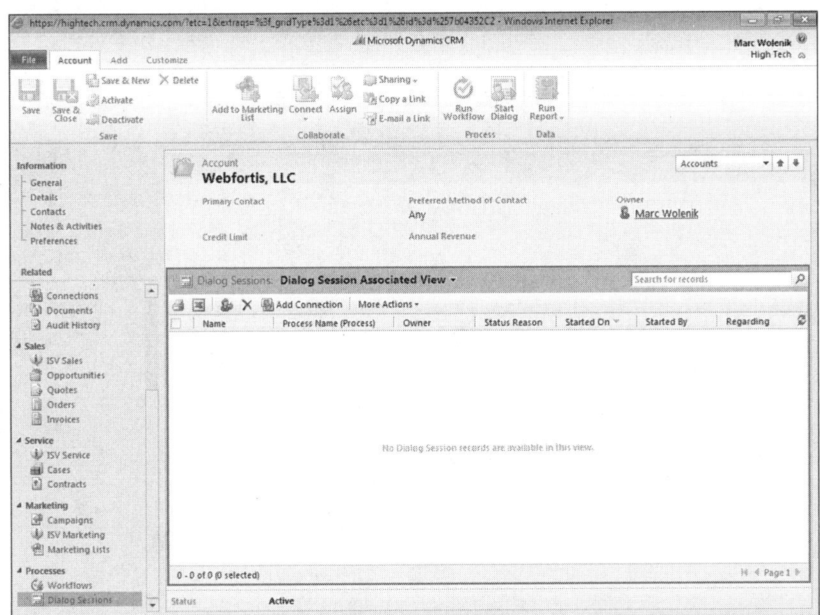

FIGURE 6.26 Account Dialog Sessions interface.

Summary

In this chapter, we discussed when a Customer is an Account or a Contact when working with Microsoft Dynamics CRM, as well as how to use the Accounts and Contact entities in depth.

When working with Accounts and Contacts, understanding how they work and relate is an important concept when working with your Customers, and typically these two entities are the cornerstone of Microsoft Dynamics CRM 2011.

CHAPTER 7

Working with the Workplace

IN THIS CHAPTER

- Dashboards
- Activities
- Calendar
- Imports
- Duplicate Detection
- Queues
- Articles
- Exporting Data
- Personalize Workplace with Personal Options

The Workplace, as it's referred to in Microsoft Dynamics CRM, is where most end users will spend a lot of their time. It is important to understand the various features that make up the Workplace, as well as how to customize it for your needs.

You can customize the Workplace to include Sales, Marketing, Service, and Scheduling (see Figure 7.1). However, this chapter covers only the core components; other chapters discuss those other modules specifically.

▶ Although Customers, Accounts, and Contacts are included in the Workplace, refer to Chapter 6, "Working with Customers," for information on working with them.

TIP

By default, the only items in the My Workplace area are My Work and Customers. To add or remove the other modules mentioned earlier (Sales, Marketing, and so on), review the last section in this chapter, "Personalize Workplace with Personal Options."

Dashboards

Dashboards are now included by default with Microsoft Dynamics CRM and are available in both Internet Explorer and Outlook.

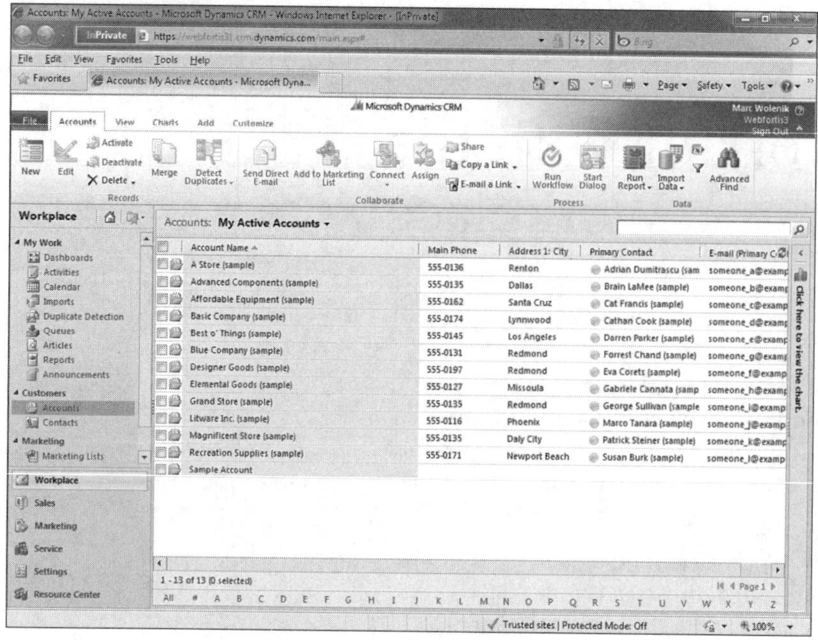

FIGURE 7.1 My Workplace (with Marketing added to it).

Figure 7.2 shows the main Dashboard page, with the option to select between Dashboards.

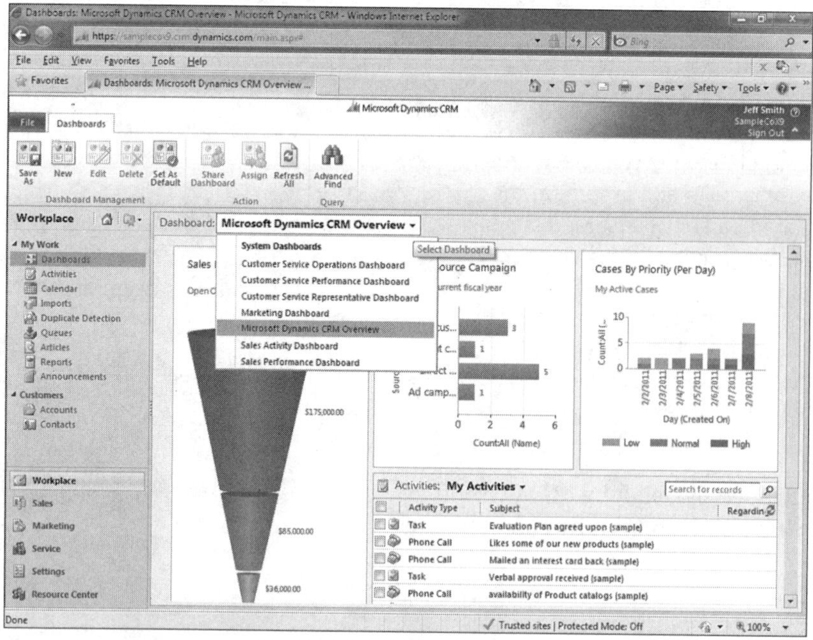

FIGURE 7.2 Dashboards from the workplace.

▶ For more information about Dashboards, refer to Chapter 21, "Reporting and Dashboards."

Activities

Work gets assigned, completed, and reported on through activities. Combined with queues, explained further in this chapter under "Queues," activity management offers a good reflection of the status of work in an organization.

An activity can consist of the following:

- Task
- Fax
- Phone Call
- E-mail
- Letter
- Appointment
- Service Activity
- Campaign Response
- Recurring Appointment
- Custom Activity

When you select the New button to create a new activity, you will be prompted to select the type of the activity (see Figure 7.3).

After an activity is created, it can be assigned to another user or queue, as long as it has the necessary permissions.

Additionally, and new to this version of Microsoft Dynamics CRM, you can assign activities to teams, as shown in Figure 7.4.

Figure 7.5 shows the Activities view with the record ownership. Notice the records that have specific owners, versus those that are owned by teams.

▶ Teams are explained in further detail in Chapter 12, "Settings and Configuration."

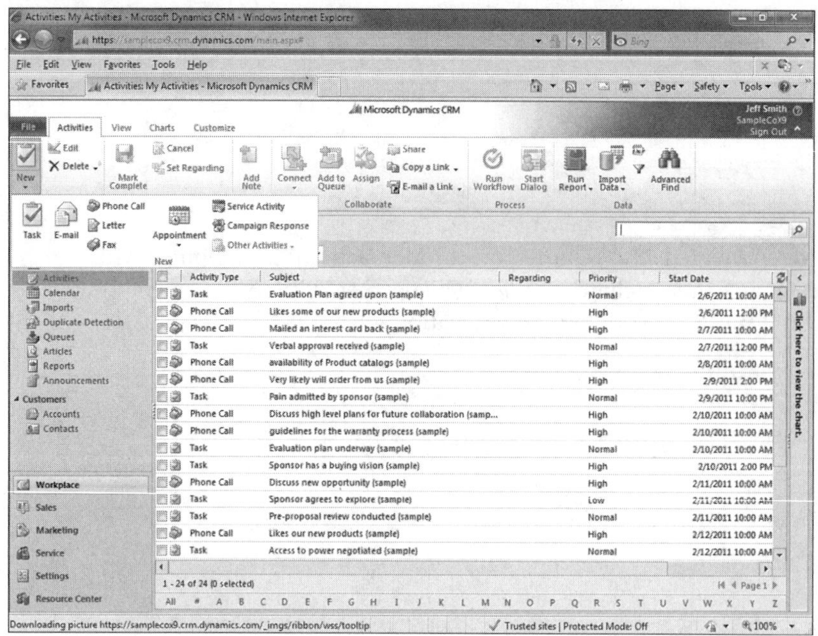

FIGURE 7.3 Activities list.

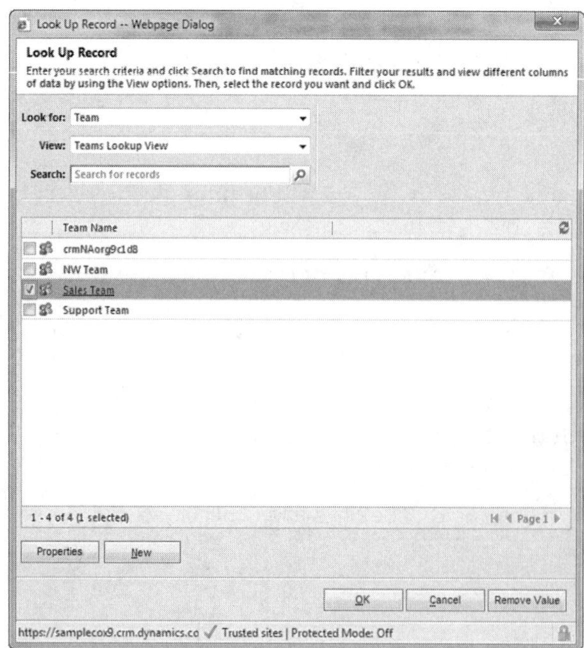

FIGURE 7.4 Assigning an activity to a team.

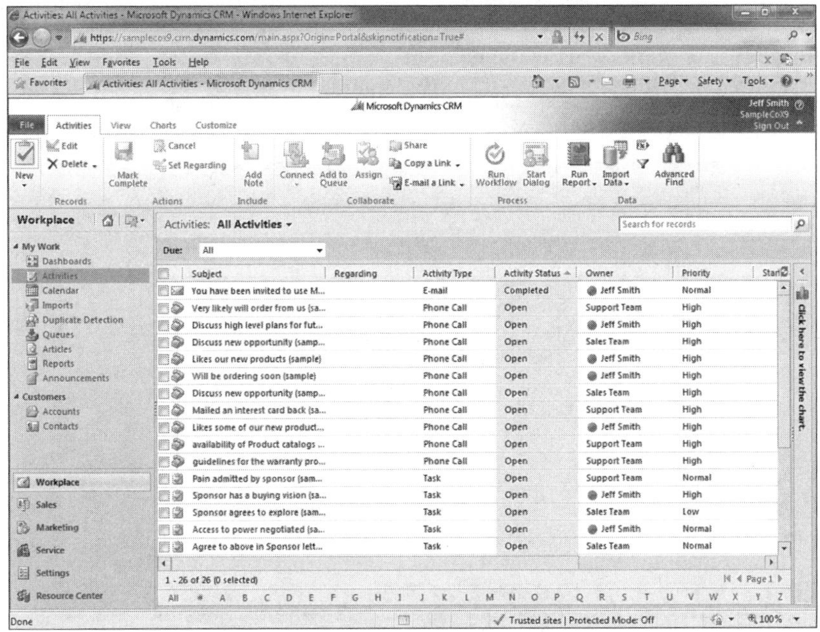

FIGURE 7.5 Viewing records owned by teams.

Bulk Editing

With Microsoft Dynamics CRM 2011 and the addition of the ability to multiselect records in grid view, you can now edit Activities in bulk.

NOTE

The options for bulk editing are dependent on the types of activities you've selected—for example, you cannot Mark Complete activity types that are not the same.

Table 7.1 lists the following actions available on activities when selected in bulk.

TABLE 7.1 Bulk Edit Options

	Edit	Add Notes	Mark Complete	Cancel	Set Regarding	Delete	Assign	Add to Queue
Tasks	X	X	X	X	X	X	X	X
Fax	X	X	X	X	X	X	X	X
Letter	X	X	X	X	X	X	X	X
Phone Call	X	X	X	X	X	X	X	X
E-Mail	X		X	X	X	X	X	X

TABLE 7.1 Bulk Edit Options

	Edit	Add Notes	Mark Complete	Cancel	Set Regarding	Delete	Assign	Add to Queue
Appointment	X	X	X	X	X	X	X	X
Service Activity	X	X	X	X	X	X	X	X
Campaign Response	X	X	X	X	X	X	X	X
Recurring Appointment		X						
Custom Activity Types	X	X	X	X	X	X	X	X
Campaign Activity	X	X	X	X		X	X	X

CAUTION

There are some limitations when editing activities in bulk because there are some attributes that cannot be edited while in bulk edit. An example of this is the start and end times of appointments and service activities.

You should consider some other important properties when working with activities:

- Regardless of whether you set the duration and due dates (the fields you use to set the date when the activity is or should be performed), appointment and service activities are the only activities that show up on the Microsoft CRM Calendar. For more information about the Microsoft CRM Calendar, see the "Calendar" section later in this chapter.
- After you close an activity, you cannot edit or reopen it (with the exception of Campaign Responses). Table 7.2 outlines what you can do to an activity (besides deleting it, adding a connection, or adding to queue) that has been marked as closed.

TABLE 7.2 Actions Available on Closed Activities

Activity	Actions Available After It Has Been Closed
E-mail	Forward, Reply To, Convert to Opportunity, Case, or Lead
Task	No further action
Phone Call	No further action
Fax	No further action
Letter	No further action

TABLE 7.2 Actions Available on Closed Activities

Activity	Actions Available After It Has Been Closed
Appointment	No further action
Campaign Response	Copied or Reactivated

- Some, but not all, Activities have the option to be converted to another activity type. An example of this is a received email that can be converted to an Opportunity, Case, or Lead.
- Reminders (similar to Outlook pop-up reminders) are not available using either version of the CRM clients. However, you can set reminders in Outlook by setting a reminder for an appointment and then saving the appointment as a Microsoft CRM activity by selecting Track in CRM for the entered appointment. In doing so, you promote the activity to Microsoft Dynamics CRM, and a reminder is set in Outlook.

CAUTION

Activities created in CRM are synchronized with the Outlook client, but reminders are not set for them; be sure to set all appointments directly in Outlook and promote to CRM if your business requires reminders.

- You can create an activity for more than one record at a time. For example, if you wanted to be sure to send holiday cards to every active account, you would not want to have to create the activity for every account. You can create a Quick Campaign and set this task as the Campaign Activity.

  To create a Quick Campaign, open the Advanced Find and select the records you want to set the activities on. Then select Create Quick Campaign to open the wizard.

▶ For more information on creating Quick Campaigns, refer to Chapter 9, "Working with Marketing."

Before closing but after saving Fax, Appointment, Phone Call, Task, E-mail, and Letter activities, you can convert these to an Opportunity or a Case from the Ribbon menu where it says Convert Activity (see Figure 7.6).

- You can convert Campaign Response activities into a new Lead, an existing Lead, or a new Quote, Order, or Opportunity record for an existing customer (see Figure 7.7).
- Duration time entered for activities is converted to hours when the duration exceeds one hour. The displayed value shows the rounded hour total, but the actual value (in minutes) is stored in the database and is used for total billing time when working on cases.

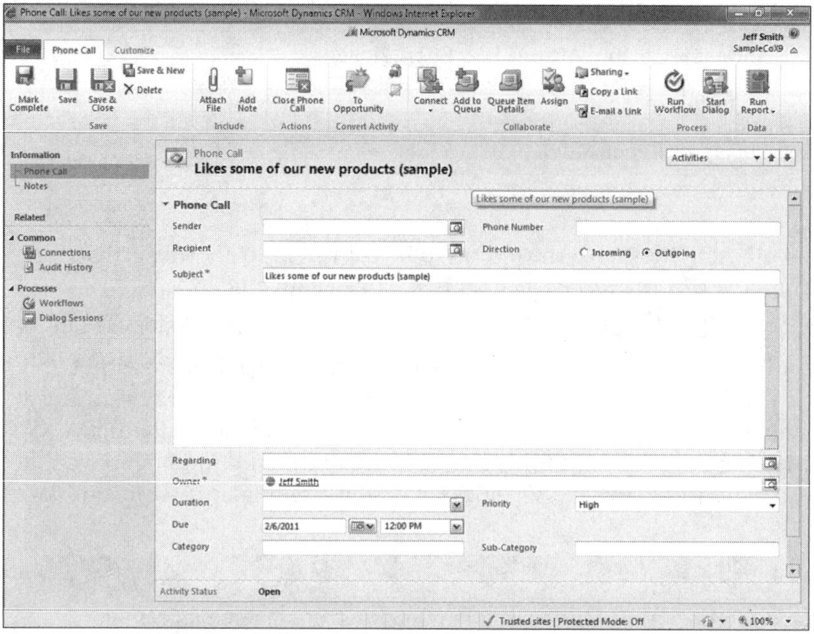

FIGURE 7.6 Convert activity.

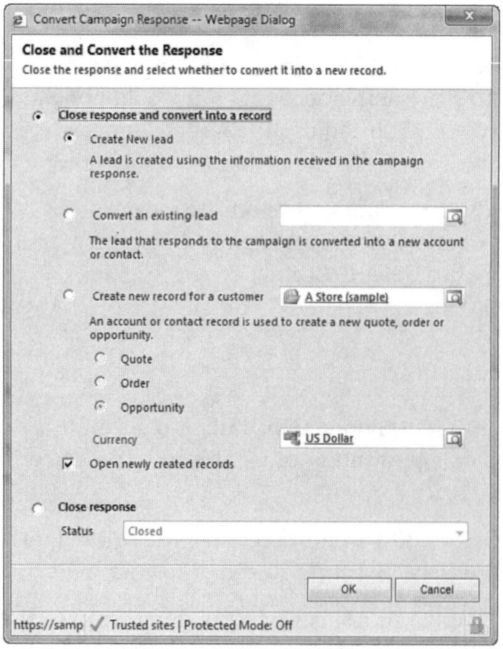

FIGURE 7.7 Converting a Campaign Response option.

TIP

Although it seems contrary, the Category and Subcategory fields have no correlation with either categories in Outlook or subjects in CRM. They are free-form entry fields that are often used by users that can incorporate business logic (such as setting the Category equal to Billable, for example).

Task

Task activities (see Figure 7.8) are those that have some kind of action that doesn't fall within the other categories. The Task activity will be the one most commonly used when the work doesn't fit neatly within the existing activity types (Appointment, Phone, and so on). As such, the Task activity is considered the catchall activity.

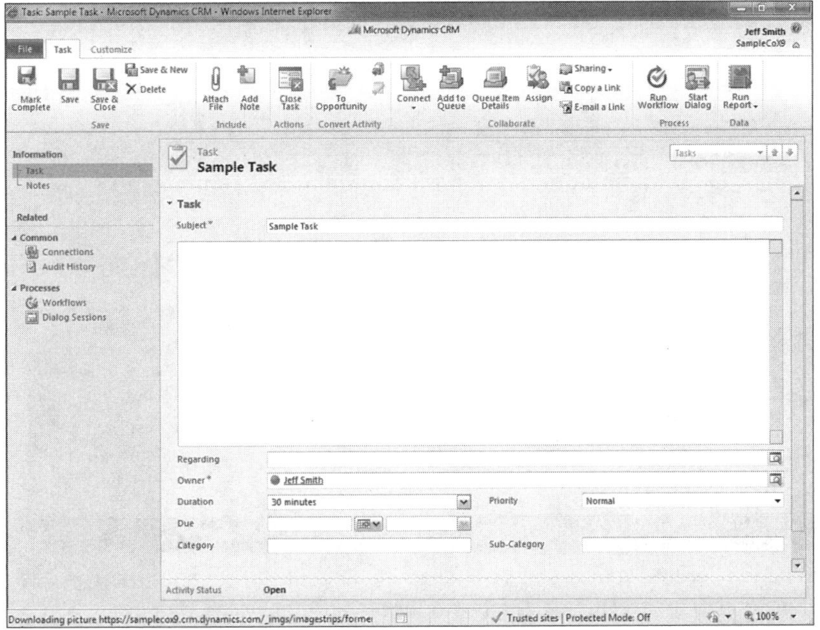

FIGURE 7.8 Task activity.

An example of a Task activity might be the preparation of a document or a reminder to yourself to put your golf clubs in your car before you leave in the morning.

When working with the new Task activity form, Subject and Owner are the only required fields in creating a Task. The area directly below the Subject field is generally reserved for details related to the Subject, but you can include those details on the Notes section if you prefer.

CAUTION

The Regarding field is not required by default. However, if you do not complete this field, the Task will not be part of a record's history. This is acceptable if you are creating Tasks for yourself such as when preparing a document. However, if the preparation of a document Task is for an existing customer, Lead, or other entity, you should enter that information so that the document preparation record becomes part of the related record.

The Regarding field can be related to any of the following entities:

- Account
- Campaign (or Campaign Activity)
- Invoice
- Lead
- Opportunity
- Case
- Contact
- Contract
- Order
- Quote
- Any custom entity that has the activities relationship check box set

NOTE

It is important to remember that you can easily change the Regarding field after setting it. Usually, it is a good idea to get into the practice of associating activities with existing entities so that the Task history is available when working with the entity.

Tasks are synchronized with Outlook, allowing Task activities to be created and managed within either application. Additionally, you can create Task activities directly within Outlook, which can be promoted to Microsoft Dynamics CRM. Because you can synchronize your mobile device with Tasks in Outlook, you close a Task activity directly within Microsoft Dynamics CRM, Microsoft Outlook, or your mobile device.

Fax

Fax activities (see Figure 7.9) are those related to either incoming or outgoing faxes. Fax activities are designed to have the actual fax attached to the Notes section of the activity; they are not used to actually send faxes by default.

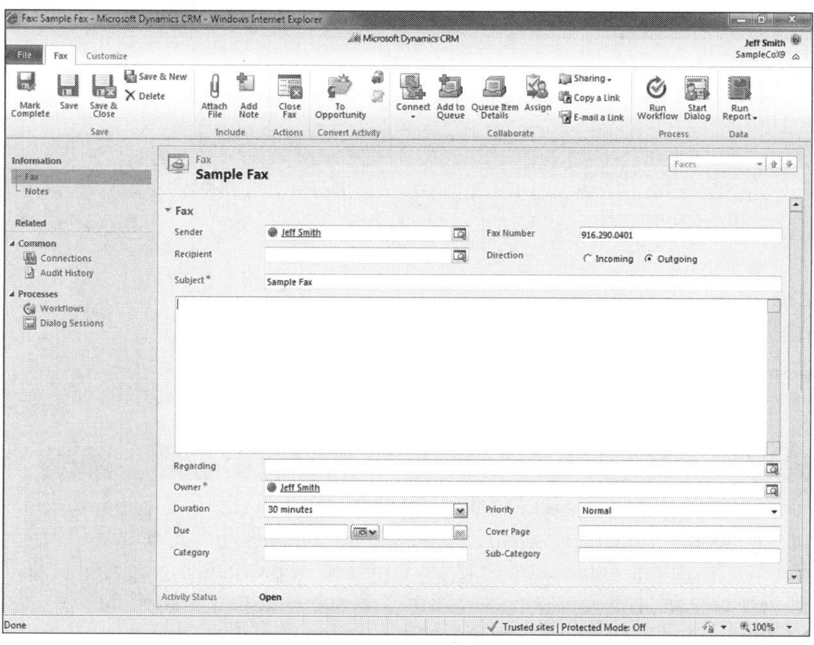

FIGURE 7.9 Fax activity.

TIP

Although no included functionality covers sending or receiving faxes directly from Microsoft CRM, previous versions offered several options. These included the Business Data Lookup snap-in to look up and view Microsoft CRM Data directly in Word, Excel, or Outlook. With this functionality, data from CRM could be added directly to the Word document and saved directly within CRM as an activity.

Phone Call

Similarly to faxes, Phone Call activities are phone calls either sent or received (see Figure 7.10). It is good practice to be sure to have all staff enter this information routinely so that it is available to all CRM users when viewing the Customer record.

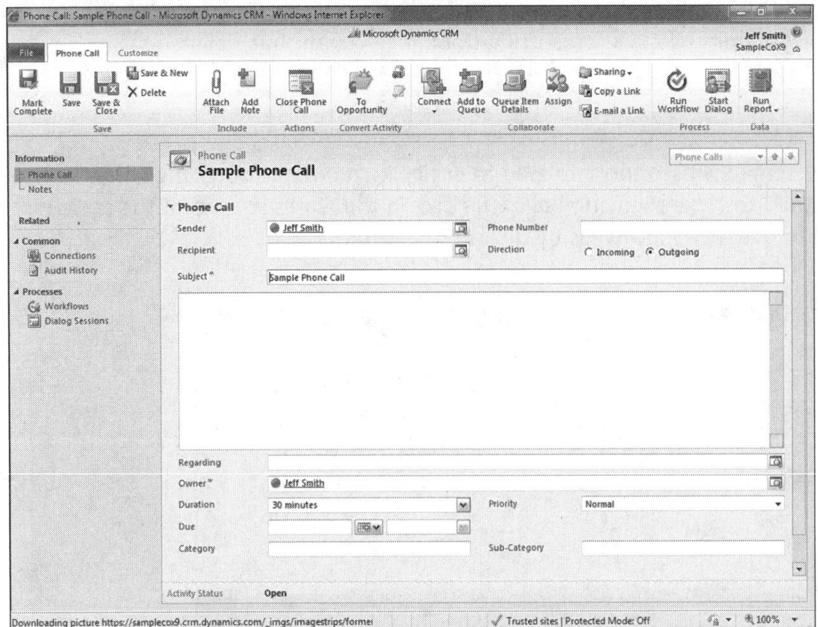

FIGURE 7.10 Phone Call activity.

TIP

Microsoft Dynamics CRM can be extended to TAPI-compliant phone systems to perform a wide number of functions, including automatically dialing the number reflected on a record. TAPI stands for Telephony Application Program Interface. It provides a programming interface for applications with your phone system. The scope of this custom functionality and integration exceeds this book; several third-party components offer this type of functionality, and it can be integrated with some programming.

E-Mail

E-mail activities are activity records that indicate either an incoming or an outgoing e-mail. Similar to faxes, they don't necessarily indicate an actual e-mail; rather, they indicate an E-mail activity that has occurred (e-mail has been sent) or will occur. (E-mail activity should be sent on the due date.)

E-mail activities create a record whereby the E-mail is sent to the Account, Contact, Lead, Queue, or User listed in the To, Cc, or Bcc fields. The Subject of the E-mail activity is the subject of the e-mail, and the Text is the body of the email. Any attachments to the E-mail activity are included.

After an E-mail activity has been sent (via the Send button at the top of the E-mail activity), it is automatically closed and available on the History tab. Figure 7.11 shows an unsent E-mail.

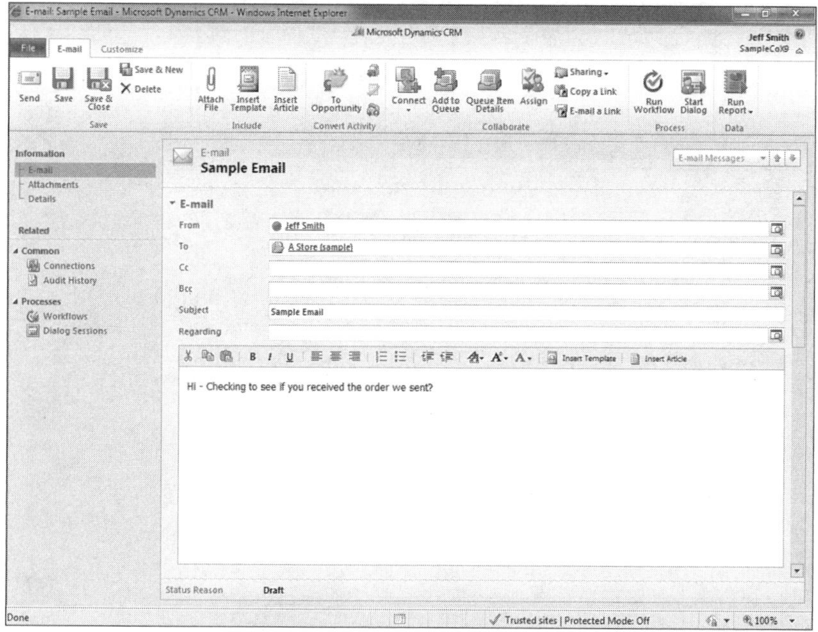

FIGURE 7.11 E-mail activity.

Figure 7.12 shows the received E-mail. Notice the Microsoft Dynamics CRM token of CRM:0001002 in the subject line of the received E-mail in Figure 7.12. The optional CRM token is used for tracking purposes and is automatically added to CRM E-mails.

▶ For configuration options, as well as tracking options other than with the tracking token, see Chapter 12.

You should consider several things when sending e-mails from Microsoft Dynamics CRM:

- The recipients must have a valid e-mail address as part of their record.
- The recipients must have Allow E-mail set to Allowed on their Contact methods.
- Microsoft Dynamics CRM must be set up and configured to send e-mails from the application.

▶ Refer to Chapter 14, "E-Mail Configuration," for more information on how to set up Microsoft Dynamics CRM to work with e-mails.

CAUTION

If any of these settings are not correct, you might receive a yellow alert on the activity, warning that the e-mail could not be sent and requiring investigation and correction.

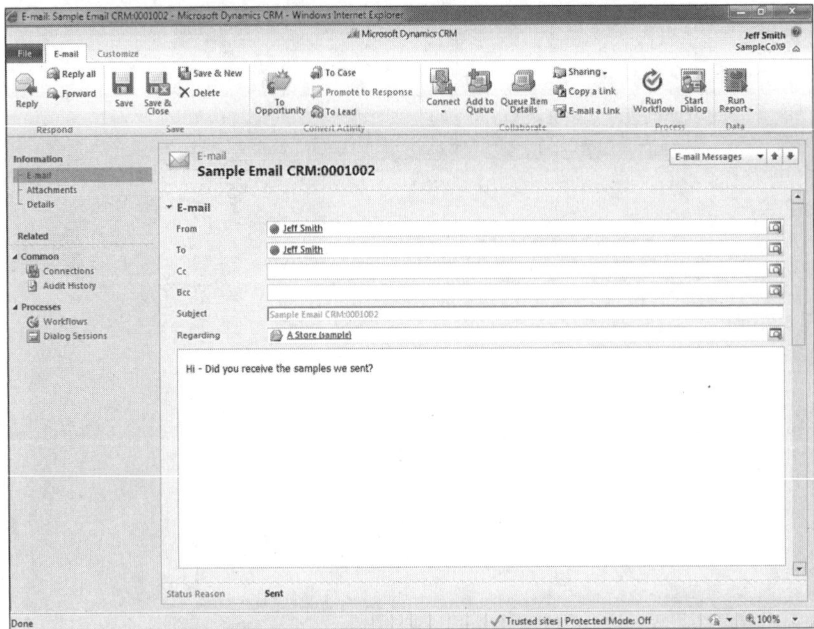

FIGURE 7.12 Received E-mail.

Letter

Letter activities indicate when a letter has been sent or received (see Figure 7.13). As with faxes, the Letter activity is designed to have the actual letter associated with it.

If you want to create a letter using mail merge, you can create the letter and then automatically set activities associated with the merge.

Appointment

You can use an Appointment activity to schedule users for appointment-type activities (see Figure 7.14).

Both the Required and Optional fields allow multiple records consisting of Accounts, Business Units, Contacts, Facility/Equipment, Lead, Team, or Users.

TIP

To rapidly enter information in the Required or Optional fields, enter the names separated with a semicolon. The system attempts to resolve the entered information automatically; where it is unable to do so, it displays a warning enabling you to either select from the quick-find (with multiple matches) or create a new entry (see Figure 7.15).

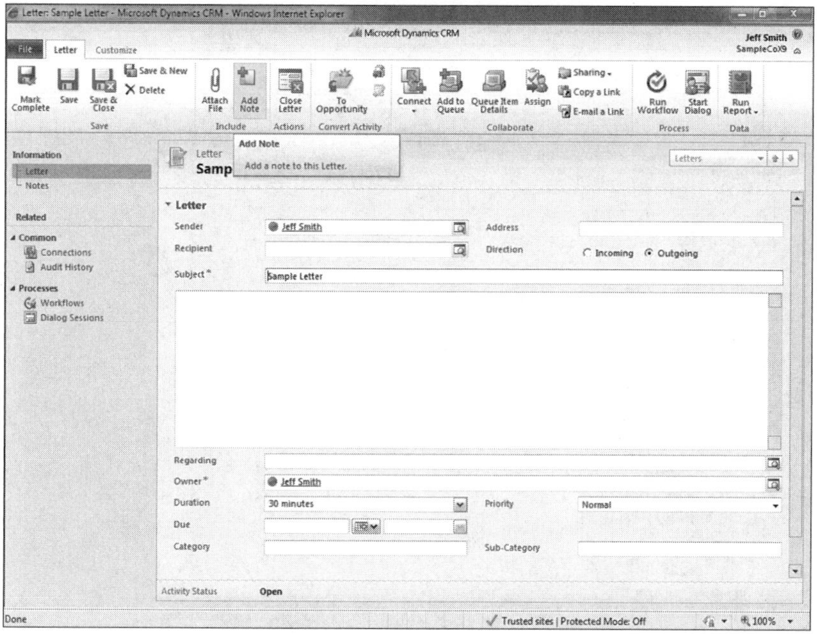

FIGURE 7.13 Letter activity.

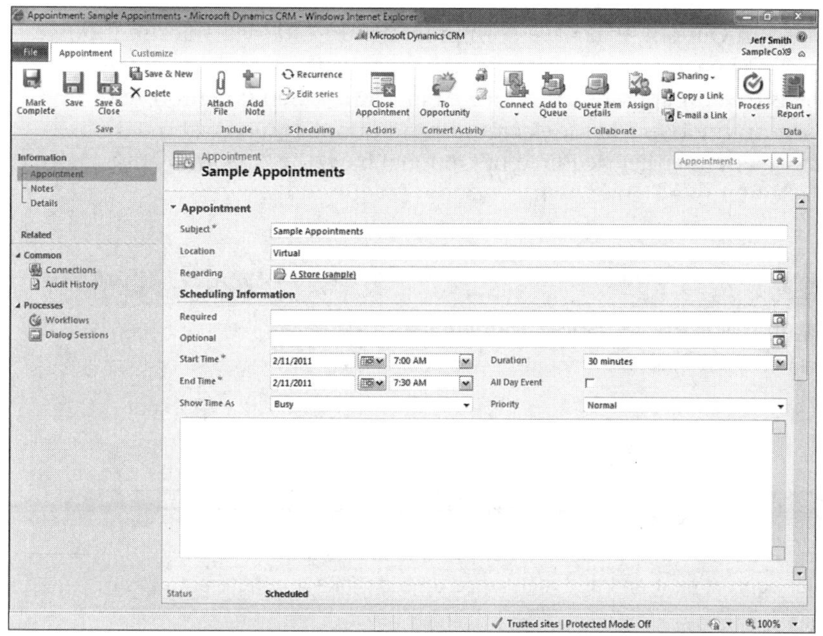

FIGURE 7.14 Appointment activity.

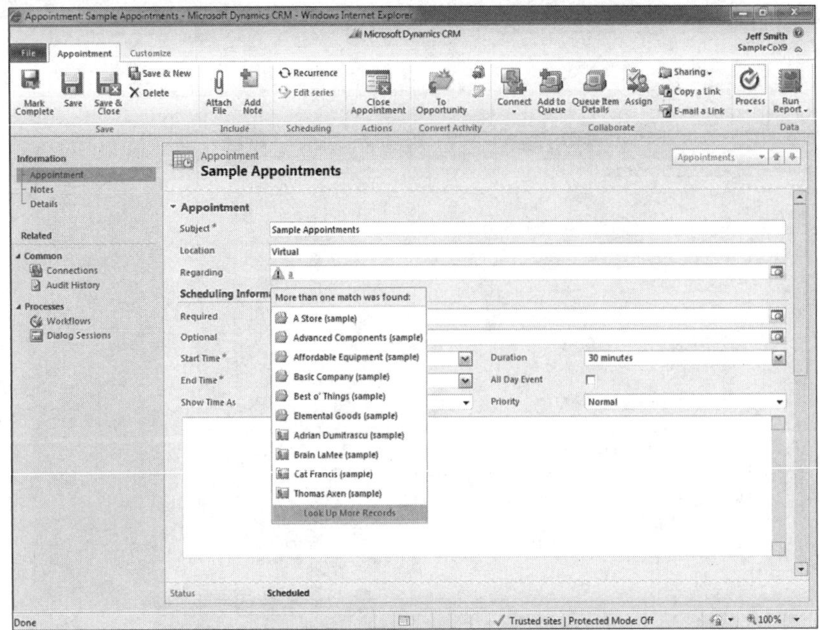

FIGURE 7.15 Appointment activity warning.

Appointments created in Outlook that have been promoted to CRM via Track in CRM are visible in the Activities pane as an Appointment activity and also appear on the Service Calendar. The same is true for appointments created in CRM: When synchronized with Outlook, they appear on the User's Outlook calendar. Additionally, users who have been added to the appointment as either Required or Optional have the Appointment activity show up on their calendar (see Figure 7.16).

TIP

Appointment activities whose start date and/or due date have passed do not become completed by default. They must be manually set as completed either before or after the date has passed.

NOTE

Notice the Recurrence option at the top of the appointment as shown in Figure 7.14. You can start a regular appointment and add recurrence to it to make it a recurrent activity.

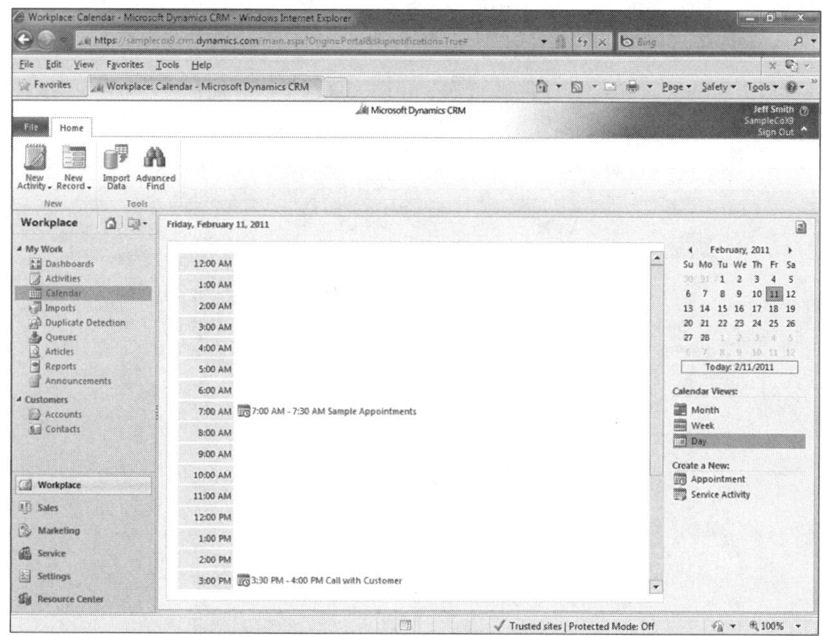

FIGURE 7.16 Appointment activity on the calendar.

Recurring Appointments

Recurring appointments are similar to appointments; however, they have the added benefit of being able to be recurrent. Figure 7.17 shows a recurring activity.

NOTE

The system will support only recurrent appointments, not recurrence in other activities (such as tasks).

To schedule the recurrence, select the Recurrence Ribbon option. The Appointment Recurrence Wizard will open (as shown in Figure 7.18), enabling you to set the rules associated with recurrence—just as you would within Outlook.

After the recurrence is set, you will see the schedule in a yellow bar across the top (as shown in Figure 7.17).

Upon saving, the system will do a check and validate availability of the resources. If there is no conflict, the records for the recurrent activity will be saved. If there is a conflict, the schedule engine will notify you prior to saving as shown in Figure 7.19.

You have the option to cancel and change the appointment, or just choose Ignore and Save. If you choose Ignore and Save, the appointment will be scheduled and the resource will be double-booked for the times. Figure 7.20 shows the recurring appointment double-booking on the user's calendar.

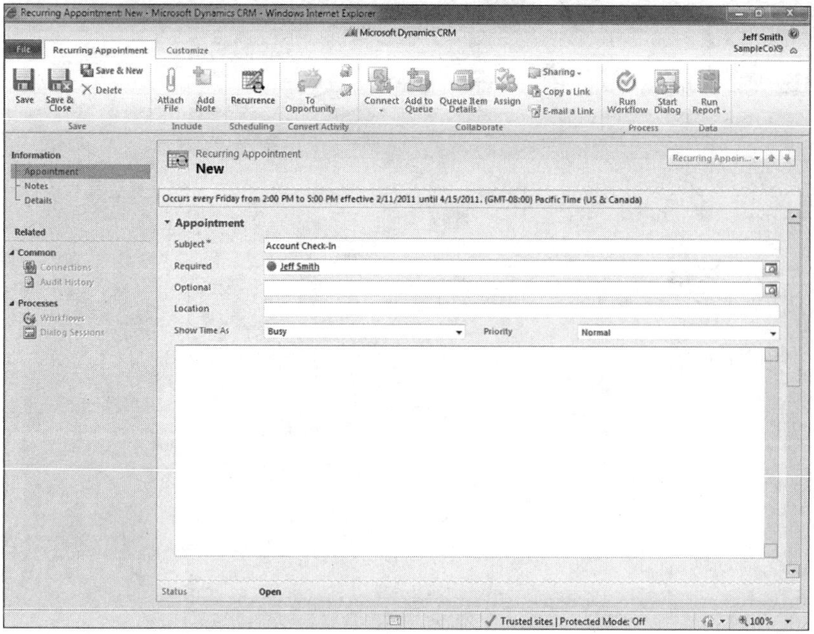

FIGURE 7.17 Recurring activity.

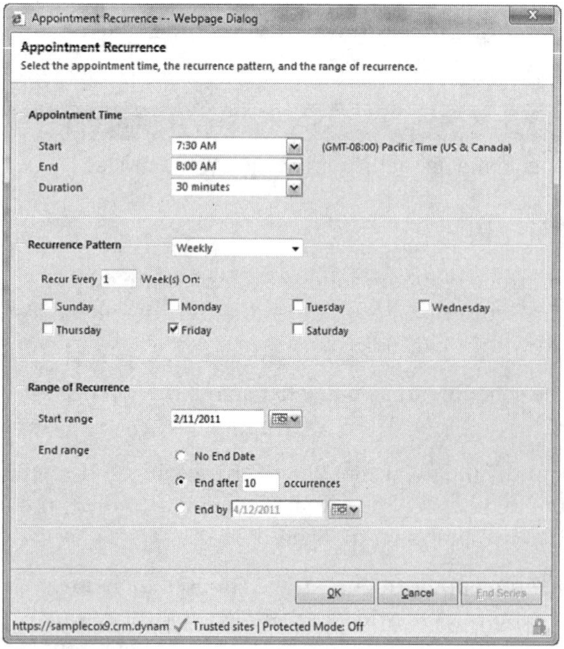

FIGURE 7.18 Recurring Activity Wizard.

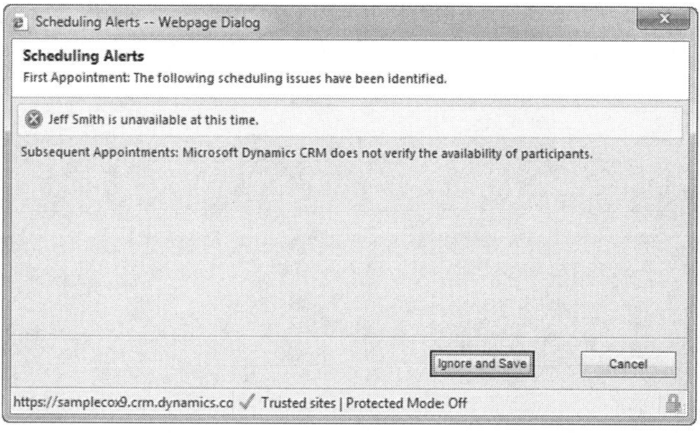

FIGURE 7.19 Recurring activity scheduling alert.

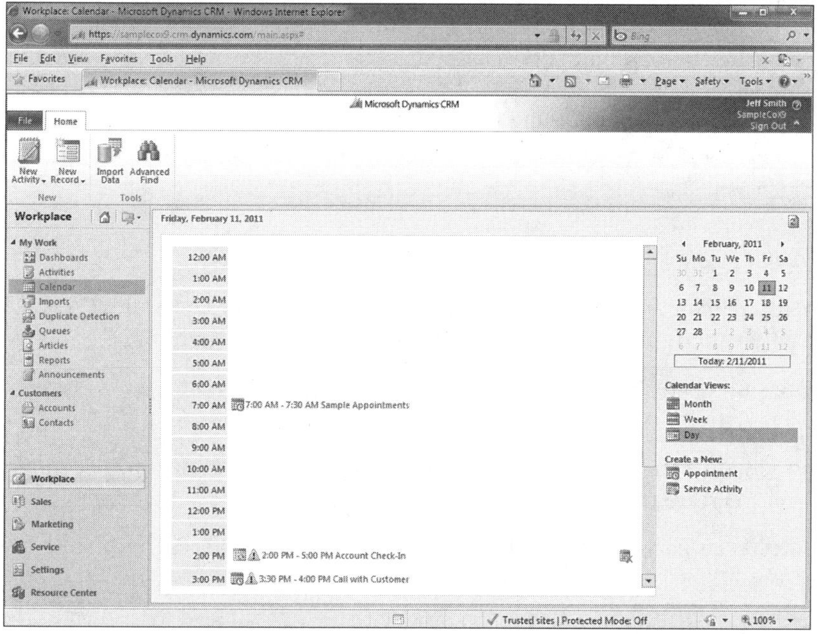

FIGURE 7.20 Recurring activity double-booking.

NOTE

Notice that in Figure 7.20 there is the option to delete the appointment directly from the calendar. This is a feature available only for recurrent appointments.

When you go to delete a recurring appointment, you are given the option to modify the appointment or the series, as shown in Figure 7.21.

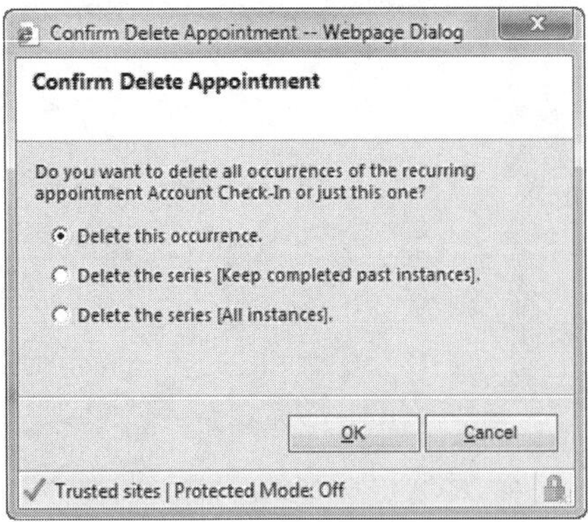

FIGURE 7.21 Confirm Appointment Deletion dialog

TIP

If you move recurrent appointments in Outlook, you will move only the single appointment (not the series) and recurrent appointment will be converted to a regular appointment.

Service Activity

As with appointments, service activities are scheduled on the Microsoft Dynamics CRM Calendar. Service Activity activities require a subject and a service (see Figure 7.22).

Failure to add any resources creates a scheduling alert notifying you, No Resources Have Been Selected for This Activity (see Figure 7.23).

You can ignore and schedule the activity by selecting Ignore and Save. However, selecting Schedule enables you to create the Service Schedule activity (see Figure 7.24).

▶ For more information on working with service scheduling, refer to Chapter 10, "Working with Service."

TIP

Reminders are not sent automatically to either customers or resources for service activities, but you can have reminders sent automatically by creating workflow to do just that.

▶ Refer to Chapter 24, "Processes Development," for more information on working with workflows.

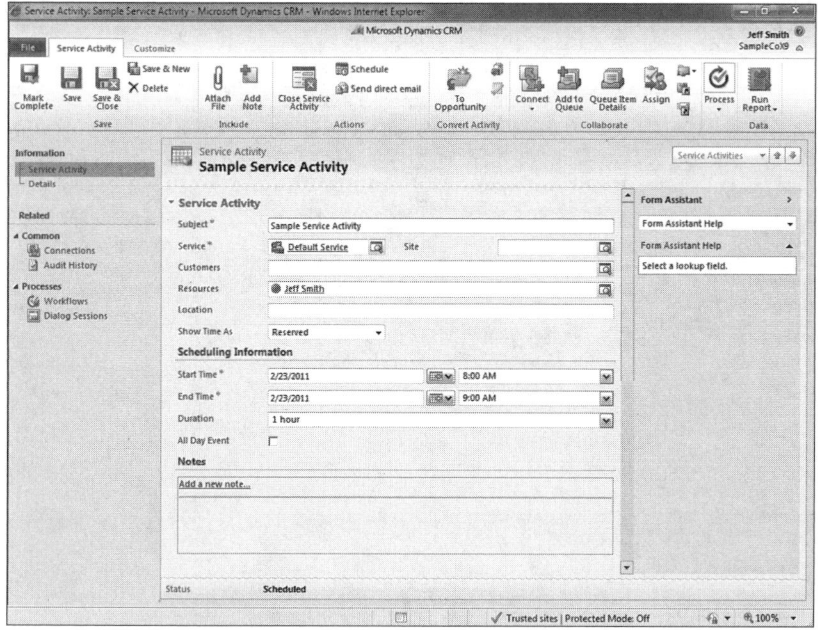

FIGURE 7.22 Service activity.

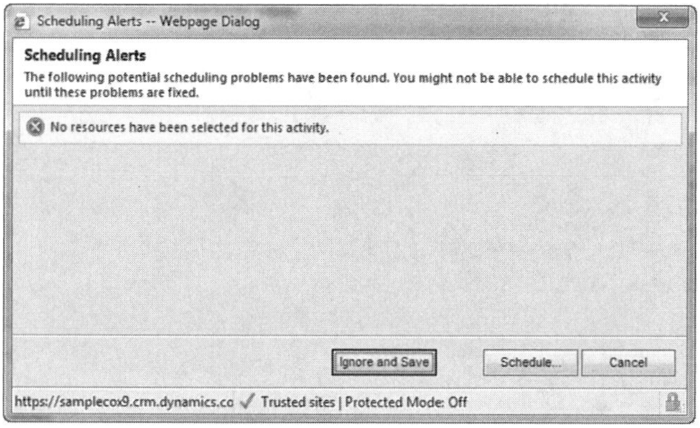

FIGURE 7.23 Scheduling alert.

Campaign Response

The Campaign Response activity is a record indicating a response received in response to a campaign. The Campaign Response activity found in My Workplace is the same type found on the Marketing tab, under Campaigns, Campaign Responses. Both require the Parent Campaign and Subject fields and include other information fields specific to campaigns (see Figure 7.25).

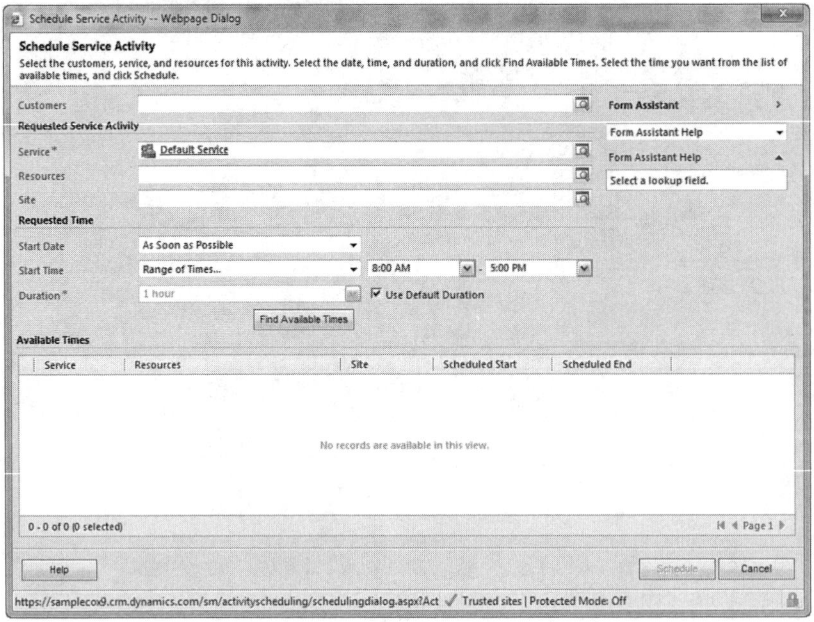

FIGURE 7.24 Schedule Service Activity

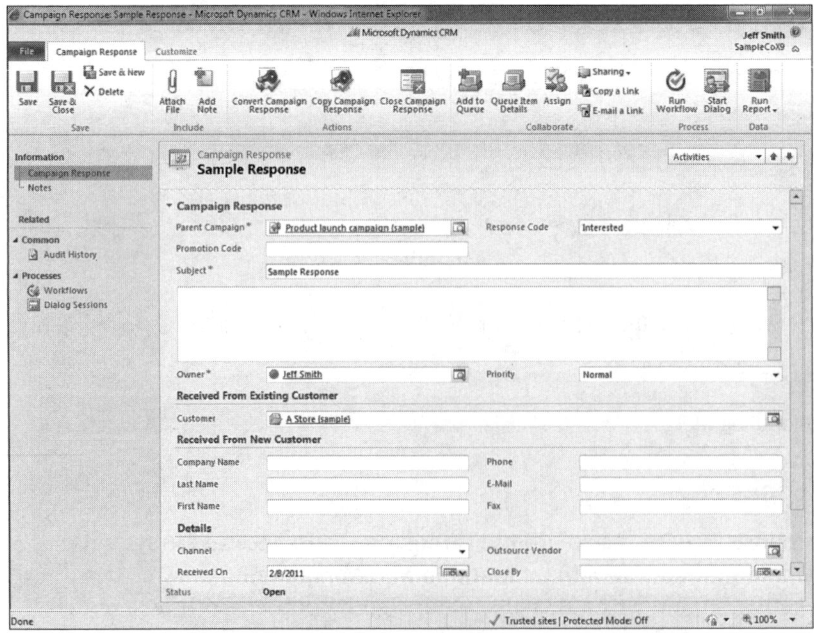

FIGURE 7.25 Campaign Response activity.

It is helpful to know that Campaign Response activities are sort of an activity hybrid specific to campaigns. For example, they can consist of an e-mail, phone call, fax, letter, or appointment—they even have an Others designation for word of mouth.

▶ See Chapter 9, "Working with Marketing," to learn about working with campaigns and related marketing efforts.

Custom Activities

Custom activities are those activities that have been created as new entities, with the selection set defining the entity as an activity entity (as shown in Figure 7.26).

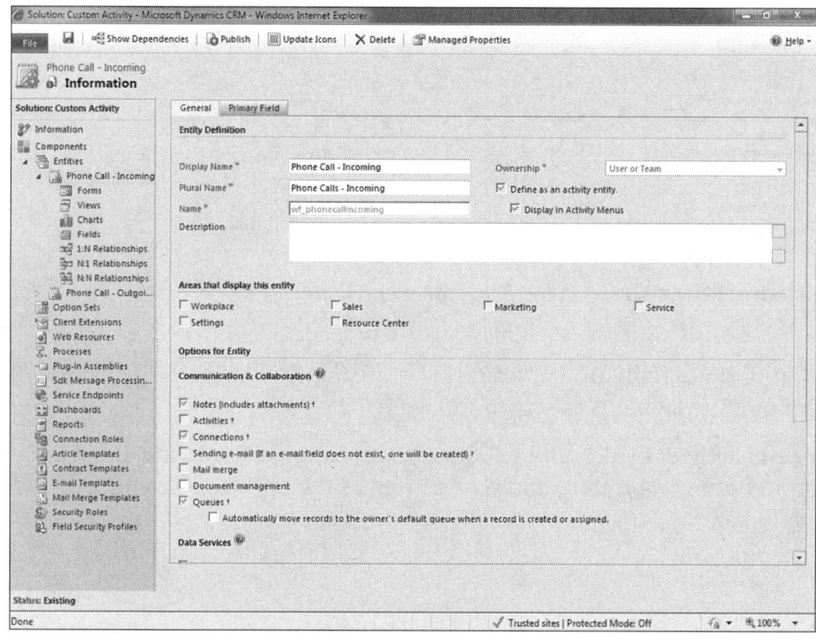

FIGURE 7.26 Custom activity entity.

TIP

An entity can only be set as an activity entity during initial creation.

Custom activities can be almost anything you would like them to be, and they have the benefit in showing in the activities area in CRM and Outlook, provided you have selected the Display in Activity Menus option shown in Figure 7.26. Figure 7.27 shows the activities we have created with the option selected.

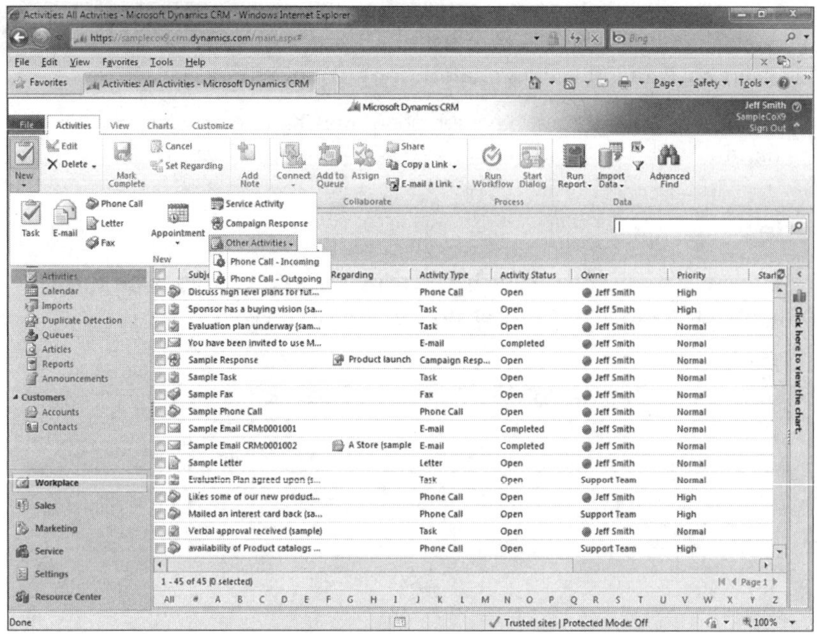

FIGURE 7.27 Custom activities shown in the Activities menu.

Upon initial creation of the activity (in our example we created a vanilla activity called Phone Call – Incoming), the layout is as shown in Figure 7.28.

Notice that our custom activity by default includes a relationship to Regarding, as well as the Convert option to both Opportunity and Case as well as the option to Promote to Response in the menu bar.

Calendar

The Calendar is used to display information related to any appointments or service activities that have been scheduled for you (see Figure 7.29).

TIP

The Calendar displays the current day by default. However, this setting can be changed by adjusting the default Calendar view in personal options, which is explained later in this chapter.

By selecting the options from the far navigation, you can change the view to months or weeks. Additional options enable you to create a new appointment or service activity with the selected day entered as the default start time for the activity. Finally, the far navigation also displays a mini Calendar that you can use to quickly navigate to a specific month, week, or date.

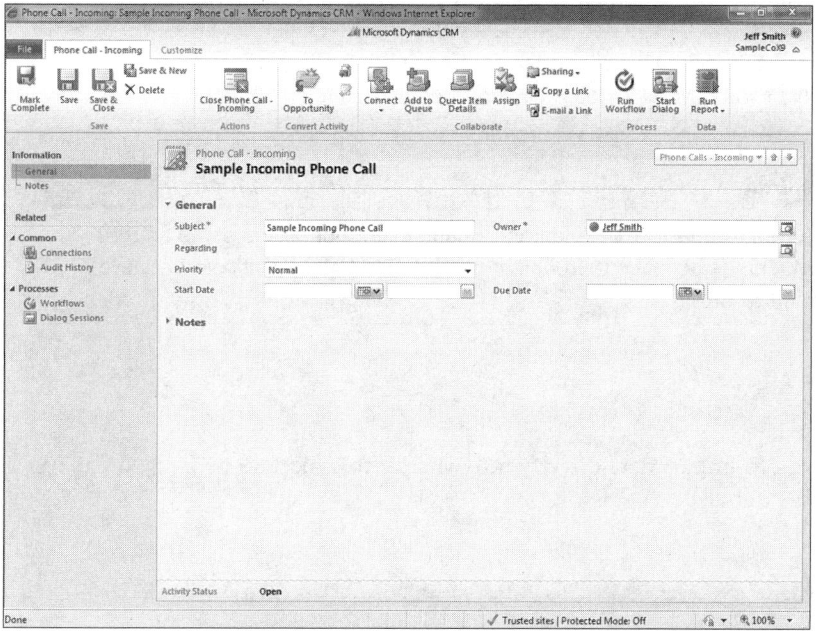

FIGURE 7.28 Custom activity entity.

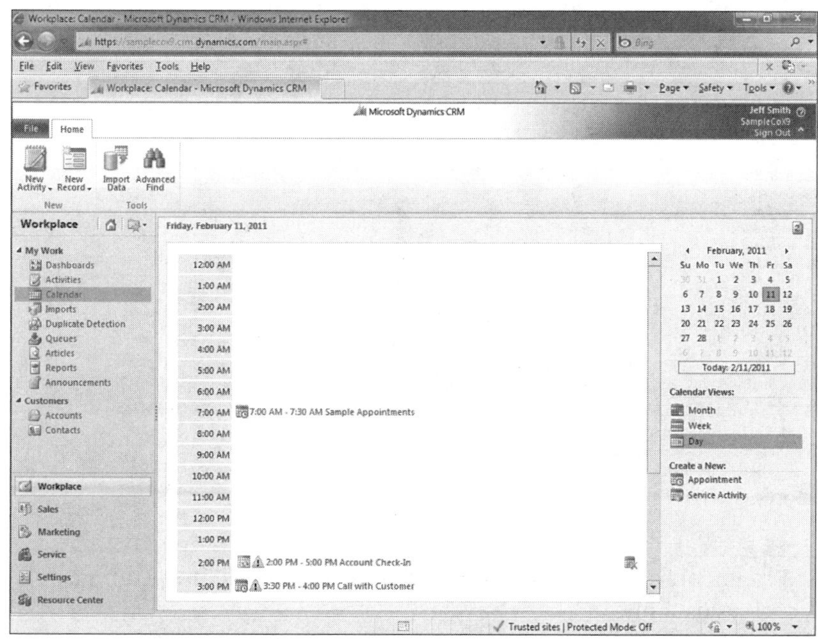

FIGURE 7.29 Calendar.

7

TIP

Navigating to a specific month, week, or day on the mini Calendar does not move the main Calendar until you have selected a day on the mini Calendar.

NOTE

It is important to realize that the Calendar in Outlook might *not* be the same as the Calendar in CRM. This is because there might be appointments in Outlook that have not been promoted to CRM.

Imports

Imports enables you to import data directly into Microsoft Dynamics CRM. Figure 7.30 shows the Imports interface.

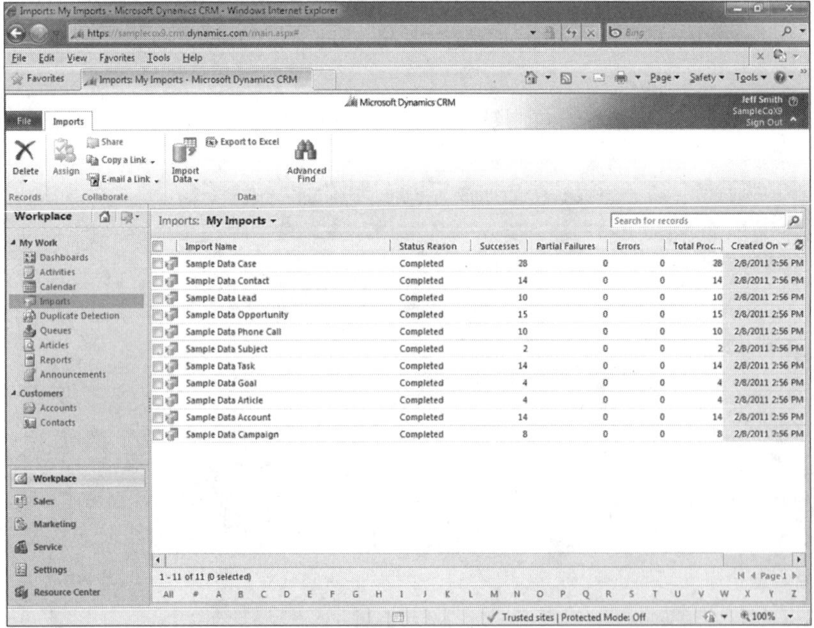

FIGURE 7.30 Imports.

Imports can be used to import data directly into the system. This would happen for a variety of reasons, such as data migration.

▶ See Chapter 29, "Data Management," for more examples and a more exhaustive look at Data Migration when considering data migration from other CRM systems.

There are other more common uses for performing a data import; for example, if you returned from a convention and wanted to upload all the new contact data you collected while there. To do this, navigate to Imports, select New, and follow the wizard steps for importing a CSV file.

TIP

The Import Wizard that is found in Tools, Import Data is the same Import Wizard that is launched by going to Imports and selecting Import Data New.

In our example, we assume we have two contact records in Excel format with header values of First Name, Last Name, and Full Name. Because we have the minimally required fields for a contact of First Name and Last Name, the import will accept the job. You can, however, add additional fields if you like. We need to save the Excel document in CSV format and then you're ready to import the data by going to Imports or by navigating to File, Tools, Import data (see Figure 7.31).

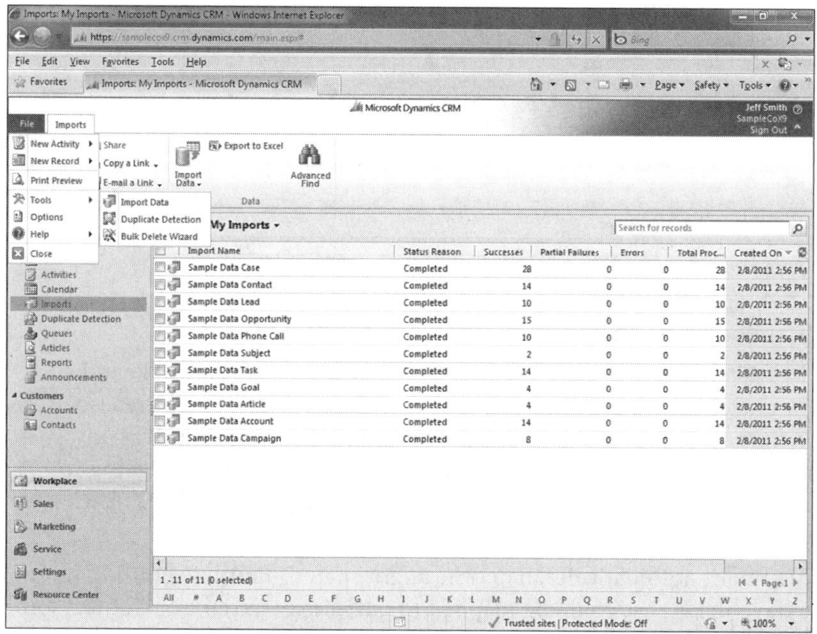

FIGURE 7.31 Imports.

TIP

Not every field will accept changes. In our example, any changes made to Full Name will not be accepted, and you'll receive a warning during the reimport process about this field.

1. Select Import Data to display the Import Data Wizard from the Imports area (refer to Figure 7.31). Enter the file by selecting Browse and navigating to the file (see Figure 7.32). Select Next to continue.

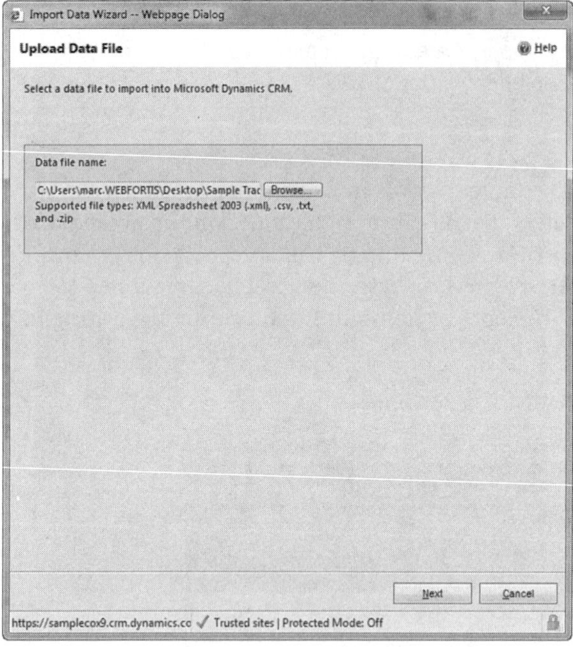

FIGURE 7.32 Selecting file to import.

2. When uploaded, you have the option to review the uploaded file summary and make modifications to the delimiter settings if necessary (see Figure 7.33).
3. The option to select a data map is presented (see Figure 7.34). If the data can be mapped automatically, you can select the first or second option. There are also more sophisticated data maps for BCM and Salesforce.com migrations, as well as any custom data maps that might have been created. In our example, we're going to choose the second option for generic mapping to Accounts and Contacts. Click Next to continue.
4. The source file might automatically map or it might map to multiple entities. In our example, we have fields that could be mapped to either the Account or Contact entities, so we're presented with a mapping option as shown in Figure 7.35. Click Next to continue.

Import Data Wizard -- Webpage Dialog

Review File Upload Summary

Help

The following data will be imported into Microsoft Dynamics CRM.

1 file uploaded.

File Name	Size
Sample Trade Show Contacts.csv	1 KB

Delimiter Settings

Select the field and data delimiters. If there is more than one file, these delimiters will be applied to all files that you want to import.

Field delimiter: Comma (,)

Data delimiter: Quotation mark (")

First row contains column headings

Back Next Cancel

https://samplecox9.crm.dynamics.co Trusted sites | Protected Mode: Off

FIGURE 7.33 Review file upload summary.

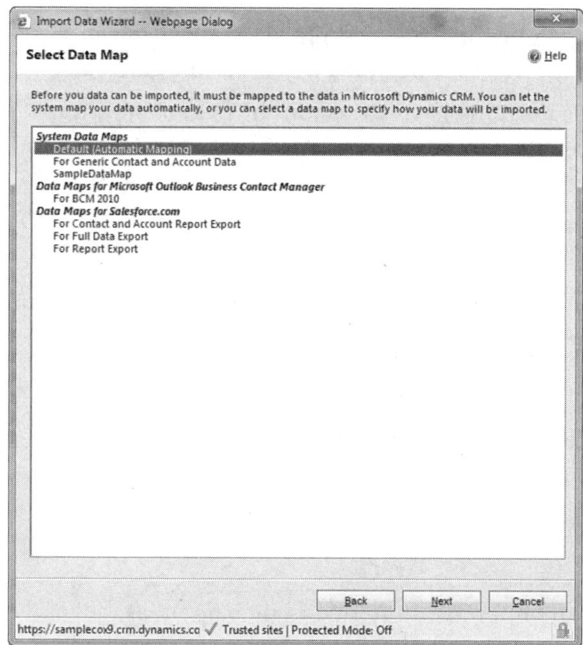

FIGURE 7.34 Select data map.

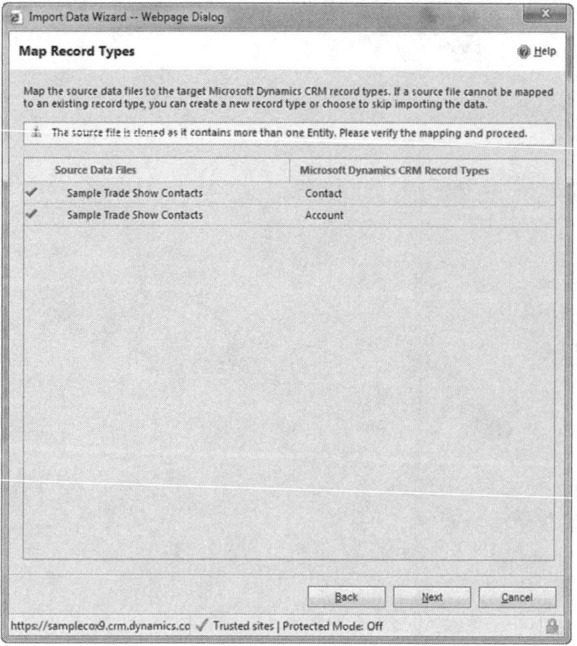

FIGURE 7.35 Map record types.

5. Because we had a cloned mapping in the previous screen and unmapped fields, we need to select the entity and our attributes for mapping as shown in Figure 7.36.
6. Select Contact on the left, and the mapping is presented on the right as shown in Figure 7.37. We can manually map the fields from our spreadsheet to the entity. You can easily see the required versus the optional fields for mapping. If you chose not to map all the fields, select Next, and you'll be presented with a warning message as shown in Figure 7.38. Click OK to continue.
7. We have the option to review the mapping summary as shown in Figure 7.39. Click Next to continue.
8. Select to whom the records should be assigned and whether to import duplicate records (see Figure 7.40). Select Next to continue.
9. The import is submitted and we are shown a final confirmation screen (see Figure 7.41).
10. The Imports screen shows the status of the import under Status Reason. Selecting the refresh icon updates the status of the import. When completed, Completed displays as the Status Reason (see Figure 7.42).
11. Opening the Imports record displays information related to the import, as well as the actual contacts updated and any failures in detail (see Figure 7.43). Any upload failures can be exported exclusively and then reimported without having to reimport the entire job again.

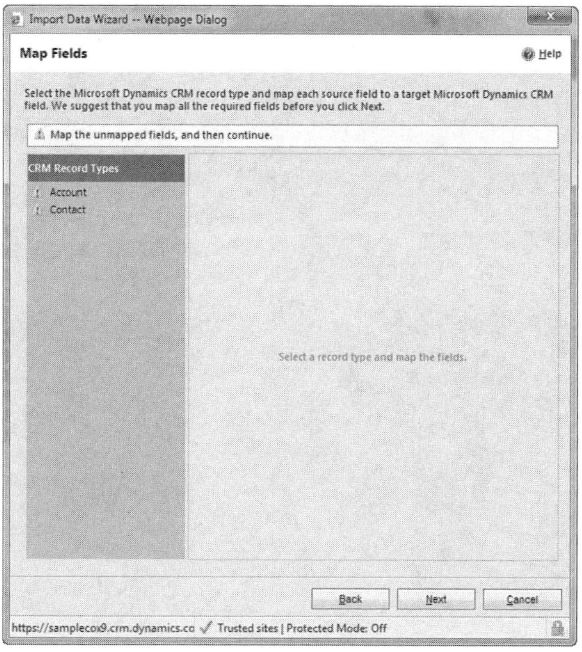

FIGURE 7.36 Map fields.

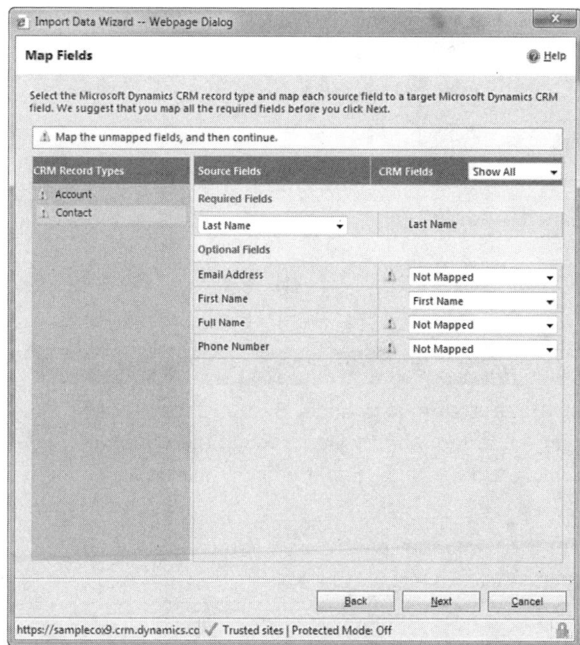

FIGURE 7.37 Unmapped fields alert.

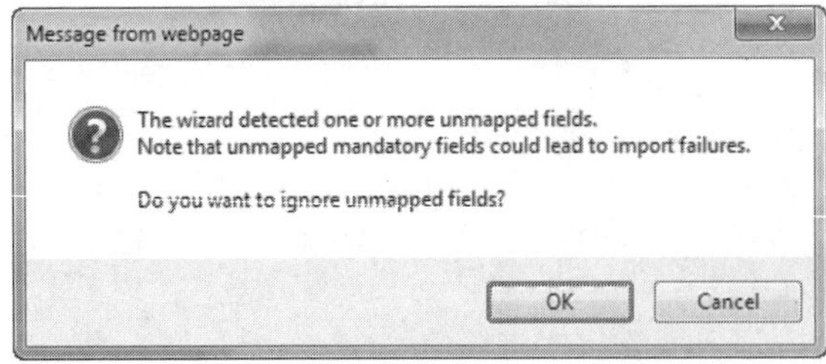

FIGURE 7.38 Unmapped field warning.

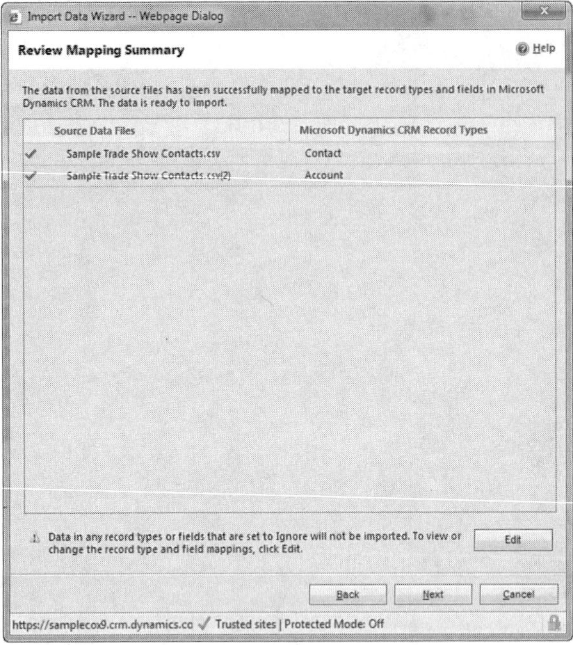

FIGURE 7.39 Review mapping summary

TIP

For the previous example, you will notice three system jobs under System Jobs. These system jobs are created when records are imported, and they go through the status of Submitted to Parsing (parsing), Transforming to Importing (transforming), and finally Importing to Completed (importing).

Imports are technically system jobs, with the Owner set as the user. You can find them in the System Jobs section of the Settings area.

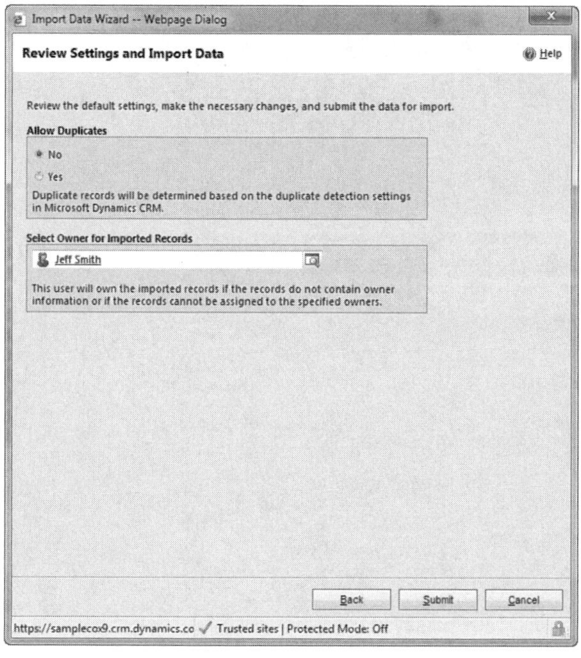

FIGURE 7.40 Import Data Wizard—assign records and select duplicate option.

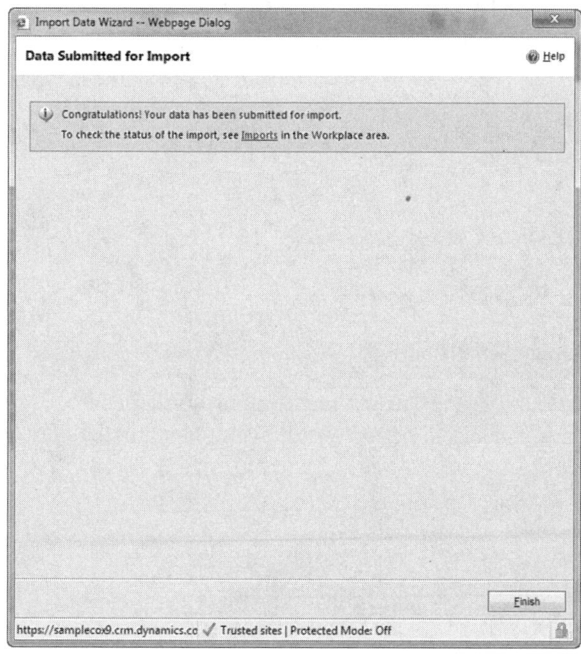

FIGURE 7.41 Import Data Wizard—data submitted for import.

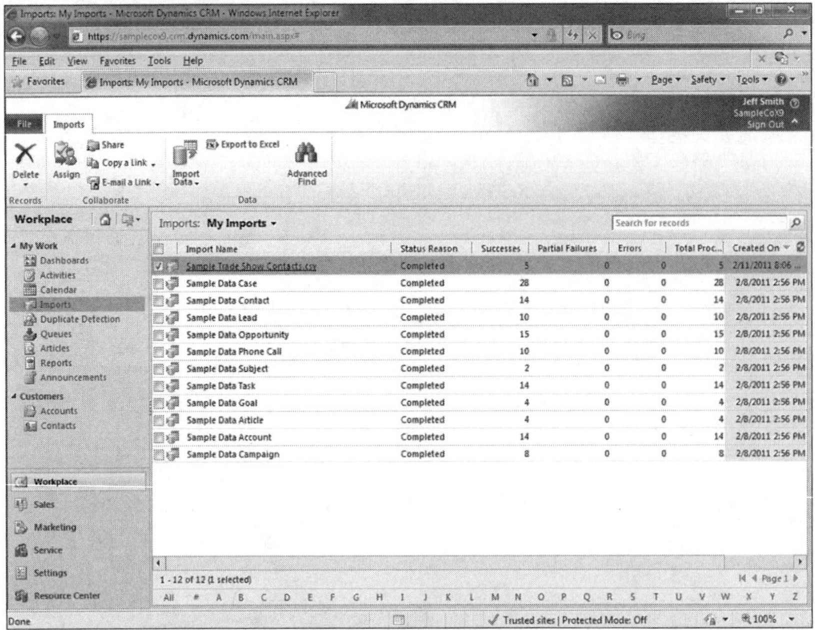

FIGURE 7.42 Completed import in My Imports.

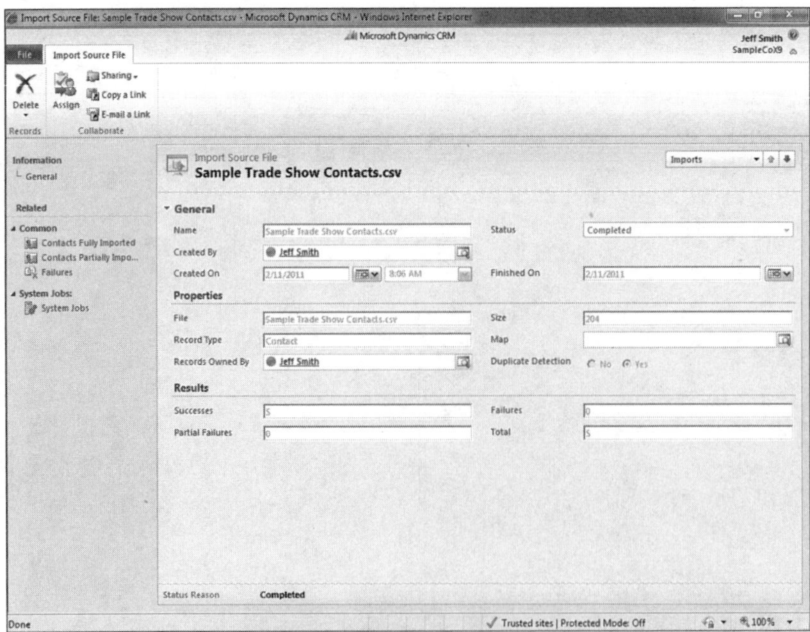

FIGURE 7.43 Import details.

If you select Delete as shown in Figure 7.44, you have the following options:

- Delete Import Source File
- All Records Imported to This Entity During This Import
- All Imported Records from the .zip File

This allows you to easily roll back the import and related records.

▶ For additional information about working with importing data, see Chapter 29.

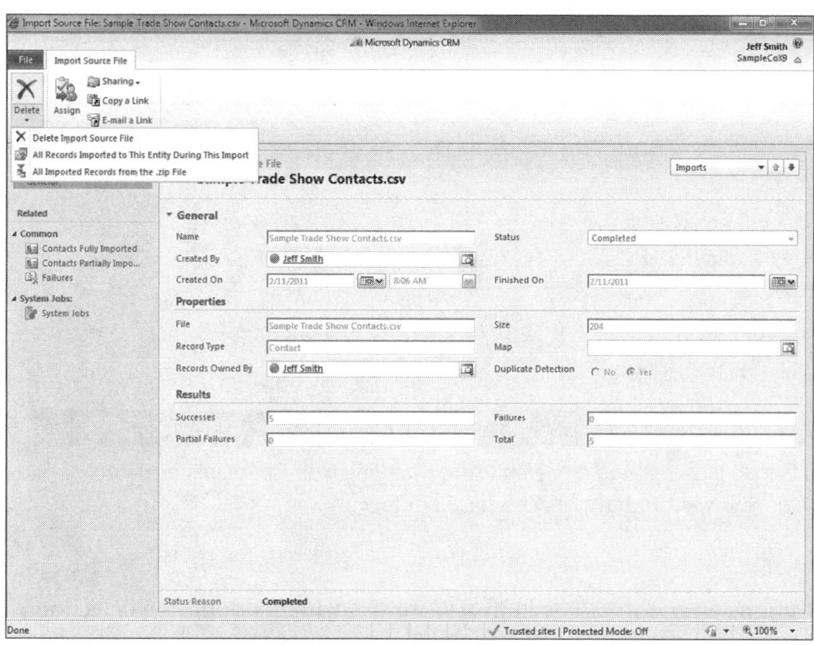

FIGURE 7.44 Delete options.

Duplicate Detection

Duplicate detection provides the system with the ability to control duplicates, and users can choose whether to accept the data.

To create a duplicate detection job, you must enable Duplicate Detection in Settings, Data Management, Duplicate Detection Rules, and at least one rule for duplicate detection must exist for the selected record type. By default, several rules exist: two for Accounts, one for Contacts, and one for Leads with the same e-mail address (see Figure 7.45). These rules are applied when working with duplicate detection in the My Workplace area. New rules added here also apply to any new duplicate detection jobs that will be run on a per-entity basis.

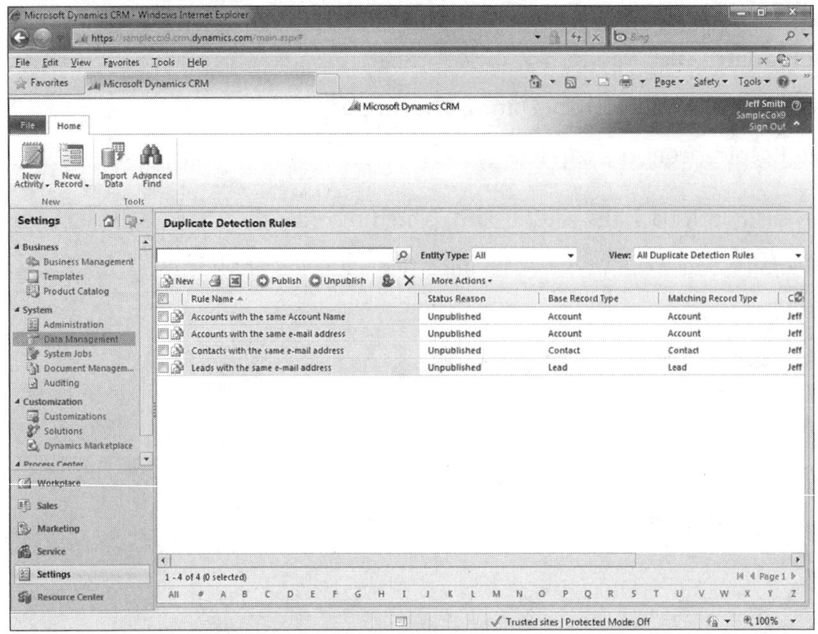

FIGURE 7.45 Duplicate detection rules from Settings, Data Management.

NOTE

The rules are in Unpublished status by default when working with CRM Online. Be sure to publish the rules you want to have applied for them to work.

The duplicate detection settings in this section also control whether duplicate detection is enabled when records are created or updated, when Outlook goes offline to online, and during data import.

▶ To learn about creating more rules and to work with the other Data Management options, see Chapter 12, "Settings and Configuration."

Although the rules check for duplicates, it might still be possible to create duplicates within the system. This is because, when adding records to Microsoft Dynamics CRM, the codes used for the detection of duplicates, or match codes, are updated only every five minutes. Therefore, it is possible to enter a duplicate record right after creating a rule, and the rules will appear not to work. However, if you wait five minutes and then attempt to add a record, you should see an alert similar to the one shown in Figure 7.46.

For this reason, you might want to run duplicate detection manually from My Workplace.

To create a new duplicate detection job, follow these steps:

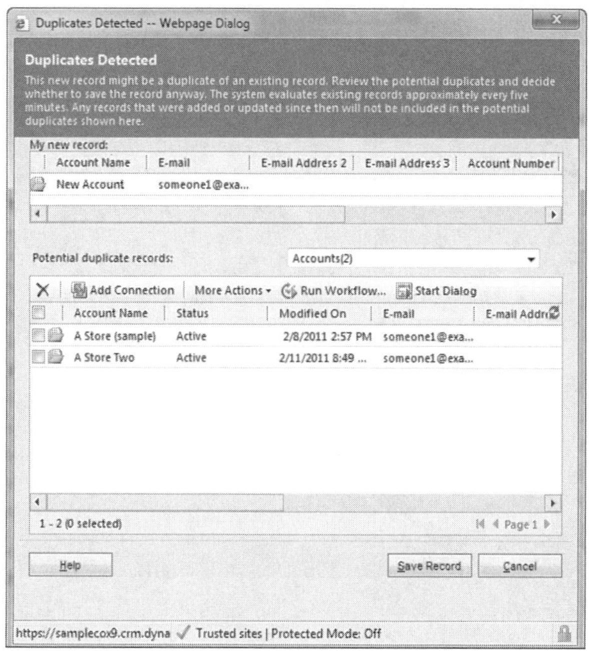

FIGURE 7.46 Duplicates Detected dialog box.

1. Navigate to Duplicate Detection in My Work found in the Workplace area, and select New. The Duplicate Detection Wizard starts.
2. After the welcome screen appears, select Next to continue. A screen similar to the Advanced Find appears, but unless you've created duplicate detection rules to work on other entities, it is limited to Accounts, Contacts, or Leads by default because those entities have rules associated with them by default (see Figure 7.47). You can apply any kind of advanced criteria to the selected entity or you can leave it blank (with no criteria) to check all records. Our example checks all account records created within the last two hours only.

   If desired, you can preview the records to ensure that the selected criteria will actually examine the records you want to check by selecting Preview Records. Click Next to continue.

TIP

You can launch duplicate detection directly from an Advanced Find by selecting Detect Duplicates from the More Actions drop-down menu.

By default, all records of the selected entity are chosen, including deactivated records. You can easily set this within the Duplicate Detection Find to check for only records in which Status is equal to Active.

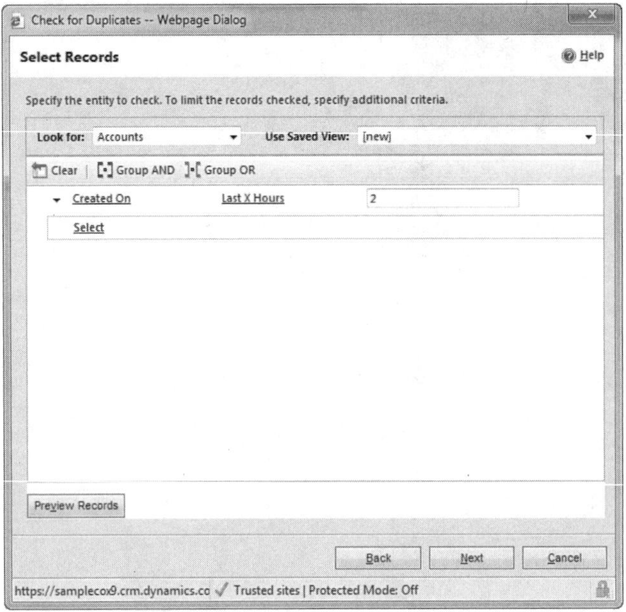

FIGURE 7.47 Duplicate detection find.

3. The Select Options are displayed with naming options, as well as the start time and whether the job should be scheduled for recurrence (see Figure 7.48). The e-mail options enable you to have an e-mail sent to you as well as other selected users when the job is completed. Click Next to continue and then Finish to complete the duplicate detection job.

4. The job is now scheduled and, if selected for immediate running, starts running. The Status Reason displays the status of the job; you can refresh this by clicking the refresh icon. (Depending on the quantity of records in the system, this process might take a long time to complete.) When completed, the Status Reason will display Succeeded or Failed (see Figure 7.49). You can double-click the record to check the status.

5. Opening the duplicate detection job displays general information about the job. The View Duplicates option from the near navigation displays any duplicates that were found as part of the job (see Figure 7.50).

6. To correct any duplicates, select the options from the menu bar above the bottom list. You have these options for dealing with a duplicate record:

   a. Deleting the record.

   b. Editing, deactivating, or activating the record from the More Actions drop-down menu. Because you can edit only an active record, you might need to activate the record.

   c. Merge the records either Automatically or by selecting the Master record from the Merge drop-down menu.

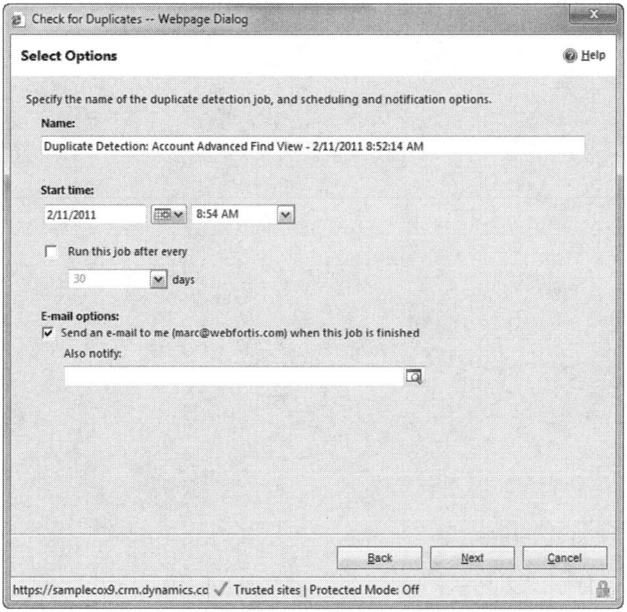

Check for Duplicates -- Webpage Dialog

Select Options

Help

Specify the name of the duplicate detection job, and scheduling and notification options.

Name:

Duplicate Detection: Account Advanced Find View - 2/11/2011 8:52:14 AM

Start time:

2/11/2011 8:54 AM

Run this job after every

30 days

E-mail options:

Send an e-mail to me (marc@webfortis.com) when this job is finished

Also notify:

Back Next Cancel

https://samplecox9.crm.dynamics.co Trusted sites | Protected Mode: Off

FIGURE 7.48 Duplicate options.

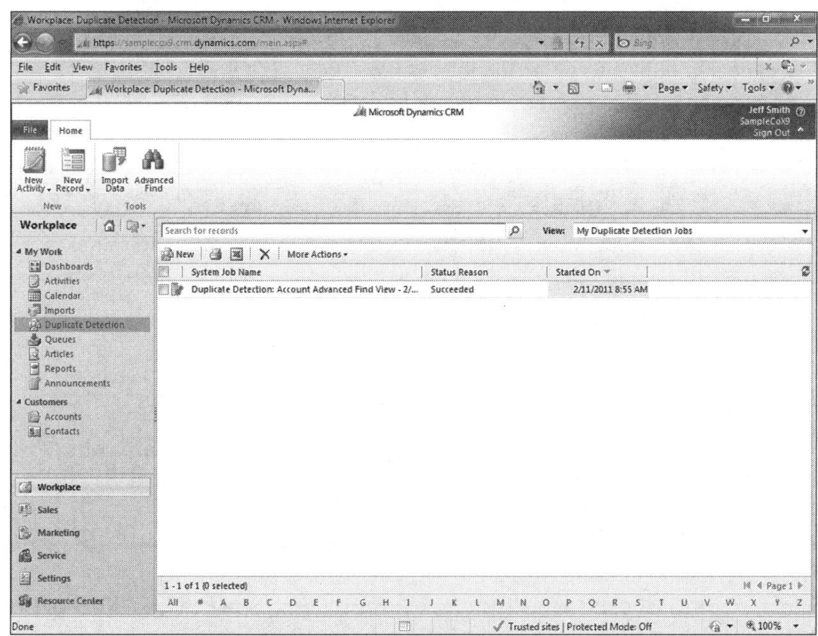

FIGURE 7.49 Duplicate detection jobs.

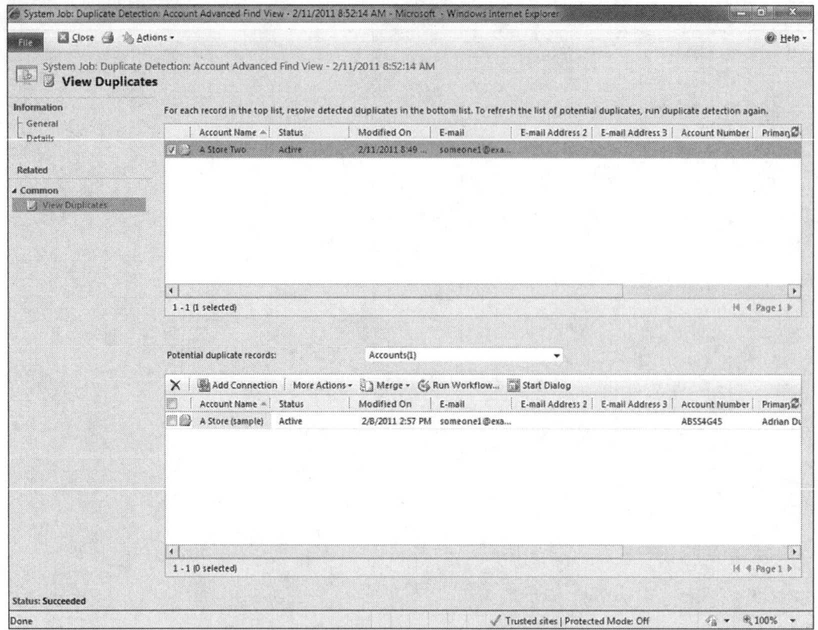

FIGURE 7.50 Duplicates found on the duplicate detection job.

TIP

Only completed or canceled duplicate detection jobs can be deleted. If you want to delete a job that is pending, cancel it and then delete it.

TIP

Similarly to duplicate detection jobs, imports are technically system jobs, with the owner set as the user. Imports are found in the System Jobs section of the Settings area.

Queues

You can think of queues as holding areas (or containers) that contain almost anything (unlike in previous versions that only held activities).

Figure 7.51 shows queues that we have both system assigned, as well as a few that we have created.

Unlike in the previous version of CRM where there was only two queues by default, there is a now a default queue setup for every user and team with the user and team name in Microsoft Dynamics CRM 2011, and these queues are available for everyone to use. Figure 7.52 shows the default Case entity customization with the Queue selection. This option is available for all entities, including new custom ones.

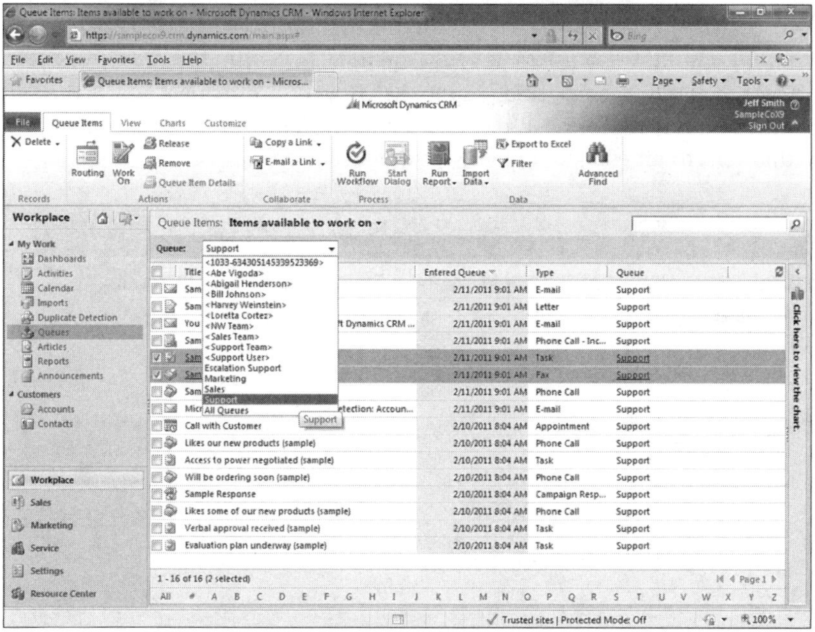

FIGURE 7.51 Queues.

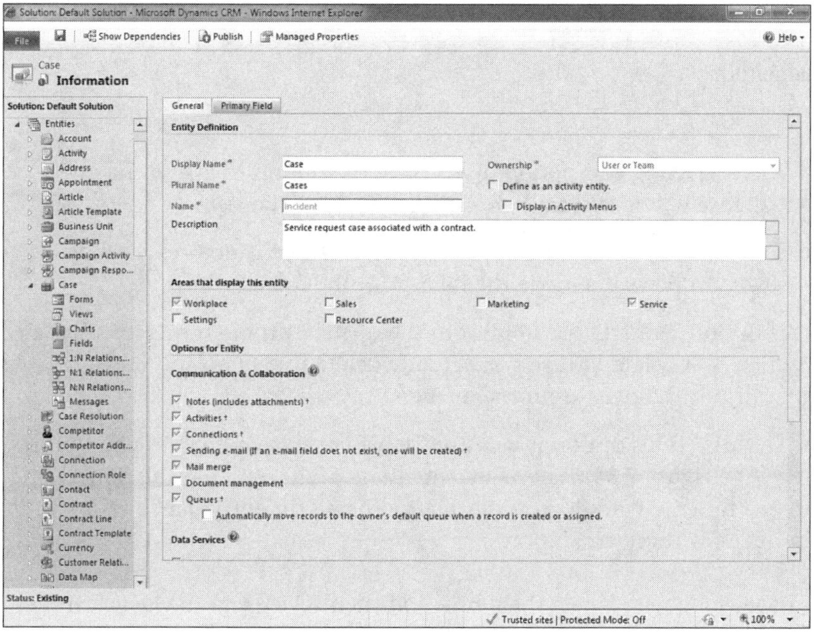

FIGURE 7.52 Queue options for entities.

When working with queues, you have the following options:

- **Routing**—Enables you to move (or route) a queue item for a number of purposes; however, the best example is escalation. Suppose that a service request enters the queue at 9:00 A.M., but it hasn't been resolved by 10:30 A.M.—routing can take over and escalate the item to an escalated queue for quicker support.

TIP

Unlike in previous versions where routing could not be controlled, we can set routing to occur automatically (see Figure 7.53).

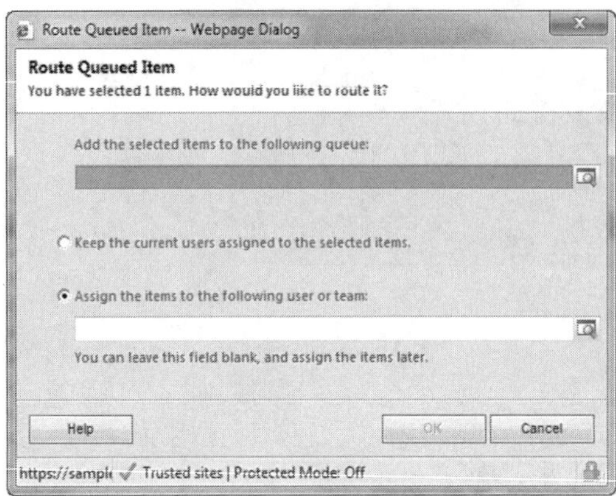

FIGURE 7.53 Queue routing.

- **Work On**—When selecting this option, users have the option to assign the queue item to either themselves or select other teams to work on the item.
- **Release**—Selecting this option on a queue item means there is no one working on the item. However, it does *not* remove the item from the queue.
- **Remove**—This option removes the item from the queue. Although this icon has a red X on it similar to a delete, it does not actually delete the item—it is still available in the system, but it is removed from the queue.
- **Queue Item Details**—This option is a customizable entity that enables you to track the queue item (see Figure 7.54). This is extremely helpful from an escalation standpoint if you need to write workflows for escalation based on entry date or amount of time spent in queue without resolution.

To move items to a specific queue, select the items, and then select Add to Queue on the Ribbon menu. You will have the option to select which queue to move them into (as shown in Figure 7.55).

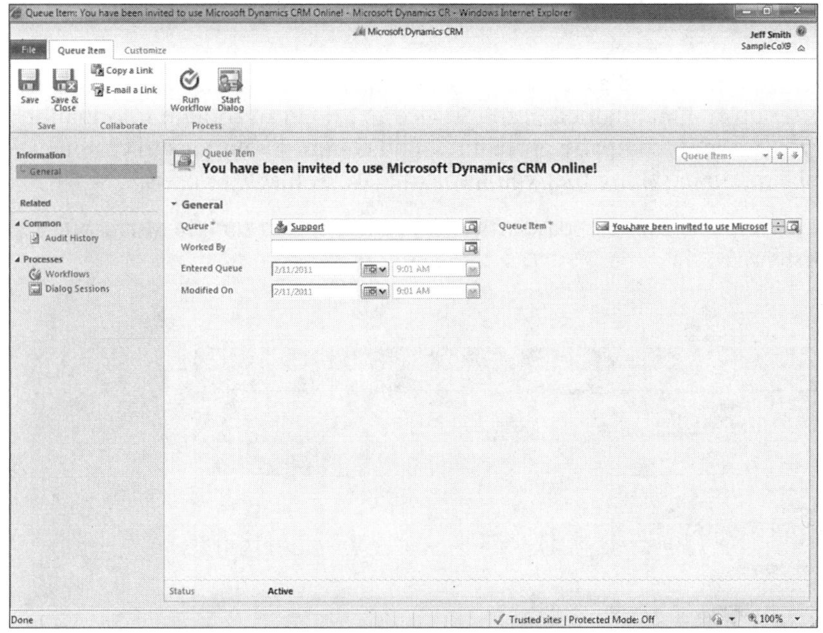

FIGURE 7.54 Queue item details.

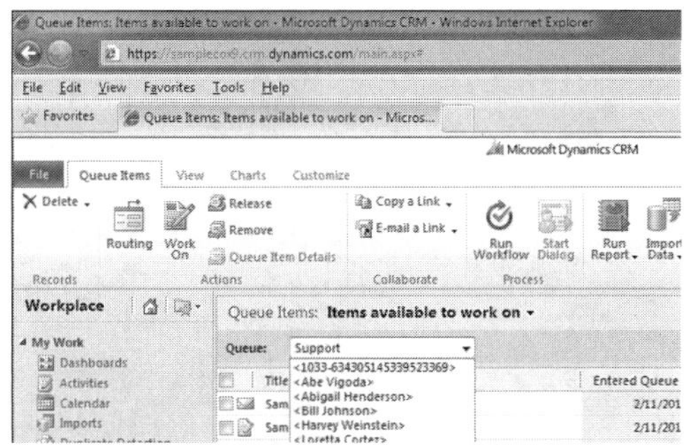

FIGURE 7.55 Queue selection.

The queue item details are used similarly to how Assign was used in the previous version of CRM.

▶ For more information about additional queue setup, see Chapter 12.

Articles

Articles enable users to quickly and easily search the company's knowledge base. The knowledge base is set up and maintained in the Service area and can contain information such as product specifications, company procedures, and common solutions to customer and employee problems, or anything that you want to make available to users.

Figure 7.56 shows a sample knowledge base article that exists in our sample Microsoft Dynamics CRM system.

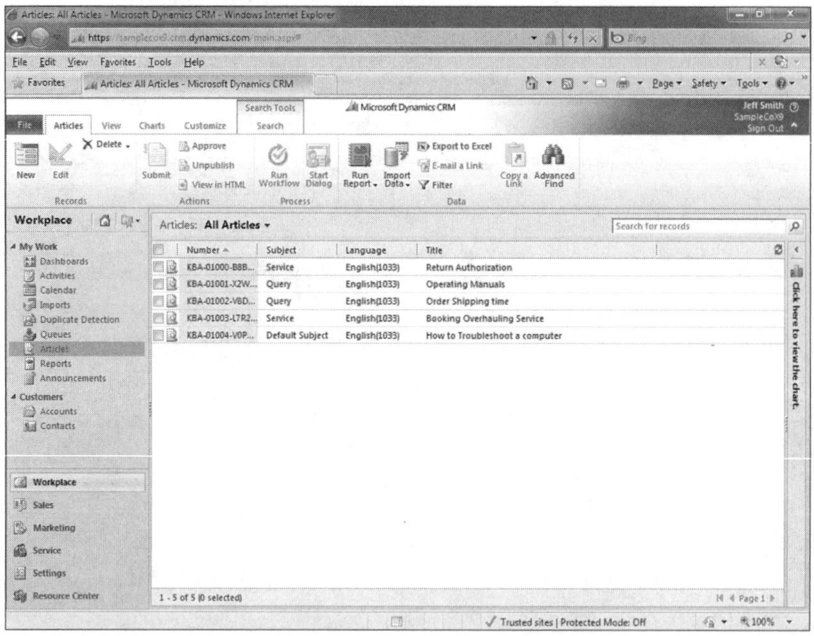

FIGURE 7.56 Knowledge base article.

Using this knowledge base article as our example, we can use the Articles tab to search for it among the many knowledge base articles that might exist.

Using the search features from the Search Tools menu on the Ribbon menu, we can select the criteria and where to search for articles (see Figure 7.57). Options include searching using the exact text entered or similar text via Use Like Words. The latter option includes a pseudoheuristic search that matches words with their corresponding tenses. For example, a search for submit would match *submitting*, *submits*, and *submitted*. After you find an article, you can view, print, or e-mail it.

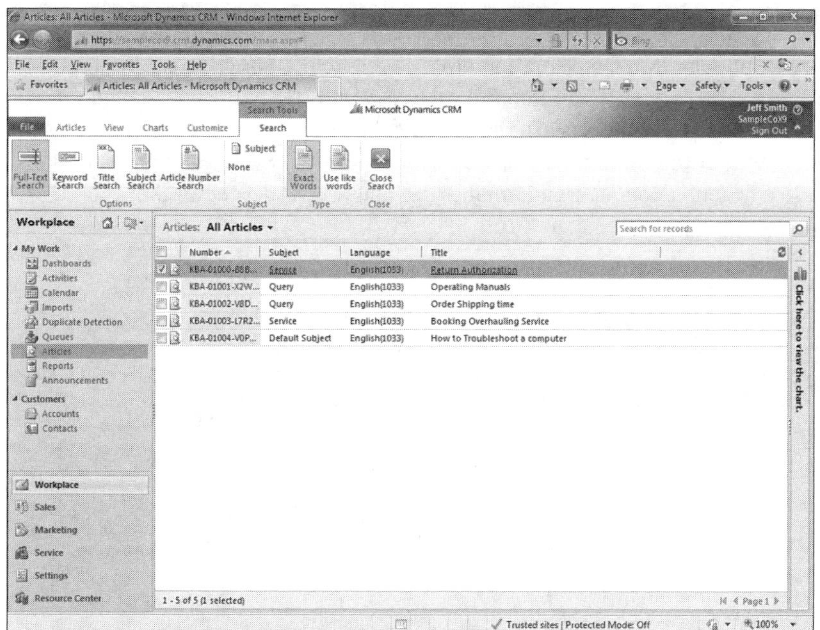

FIGURE 7.57 Knowledge Base Articles searching.

TIP

If an article doesn't appear in the Articles area, the system might not have indexed it yet. Normally, it takes up to 15 minutes for articles to be approved and made available in the Articles area.

TIP

You might have the ability to view unapproved/unpublished articles, provided your role is sufficient. Typically only published and approved articles are available to users.

▶ For more information about creating and working with the Knowledge Base, see Chapter 10, "Working with Service," as well as Chapter 12.

NOTE

Two other areas available in the Workplace that are discussed in other chapters are the Reports and Announcements areas. The Reports area is where you run, manage, and create Microsoft Dynamics CRM reports. The Announcements area displays any unexpired announcements that the system administrator has set in the Settings area. These can include any general company information or industry-specific news that you want to share with your users (see Figure 7.58).

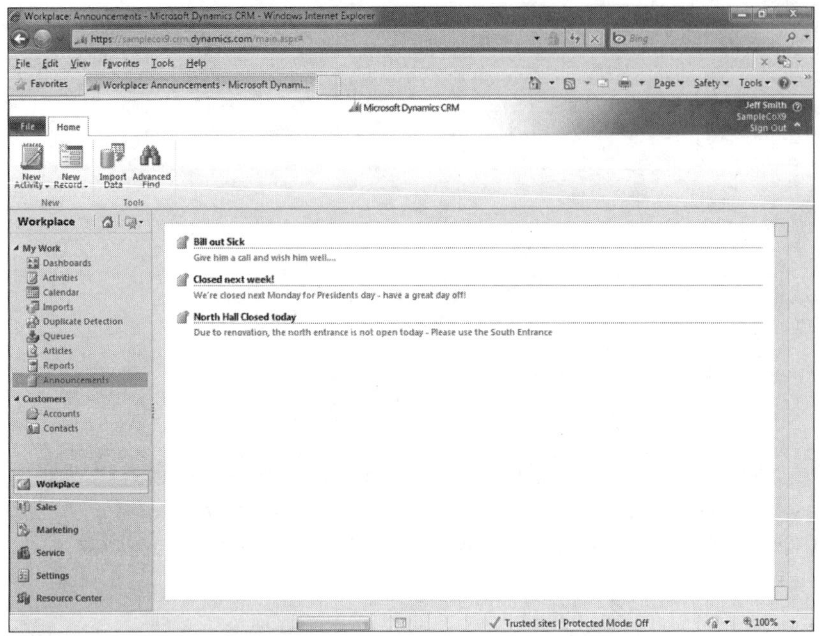

FIGURE 7.58 Announcements.

▶ For more information on working with reports, see Chapter 21, "Reporting and Dashboards." For more information about working with announcements, see Chapter 12.

Exporting Data

Virtually every area of Microsoft Dynamics CRM has the ability to export to Excel. In addition to being able to export using the Advanced Find, you can select the Excel icon within Microsoft Dynamics CRM (see Figure 7.59).

Exporting data enables you to perform advanced manipulation and reporting within the familiar interface of Excel.

Additionally, you can select the option to make the data available for reimporting after export, which allows for easy manipulation of the data in Excel.

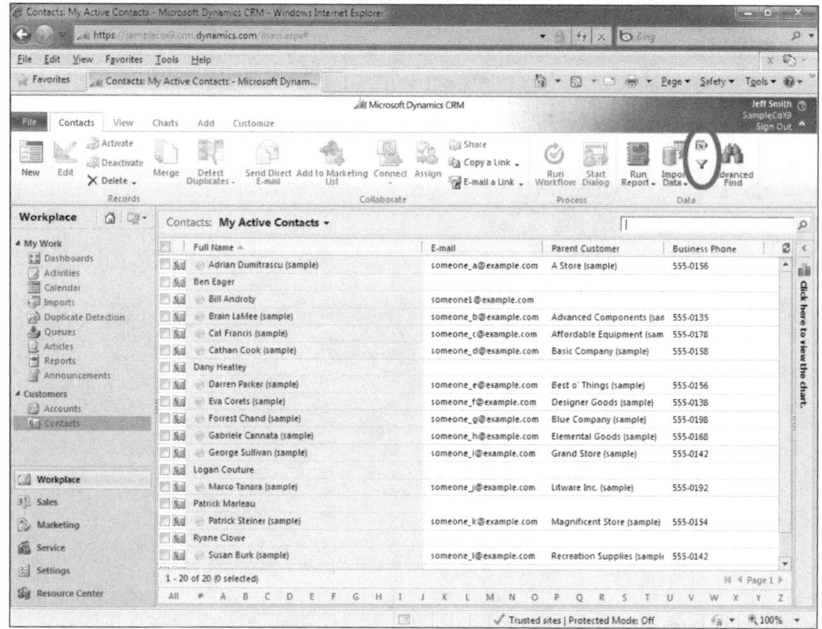

FIGURE 7.59 Excel icon in Contacts.

To export data from an entity, follow these steps:

1. Navigate to the entity that contains the records you want to export. In this example, you'll export all inactive contacts. To do this, navigate to Contacts and then select Inactive Contacts from the drop-down view. Select the Excel icon to display the Export Data to Excel dialog box (see Figure 7.60).
2. The Export to Data to Excel dialog box has three options:
   a. **Static Worksheet with Records from This Page**—This option exports the records on the page, with only the columns that are visible on the view from the page. By default, the inactive contacts have only Full Name, Parent Customer, and Business Phone, so those will be the only fields exported. You can modify your view and additional columns by going to Settings, Customize and adding columns to the view, if necessary.
   b. **Dynamic Pivot Table**—When selected, the Select Columns button becomes enabled, enabling you to optionally add additional columns to the export (see Figure 7.61). After you're finished adding columns, you can export the data by selecting Export, and Excel will open in Pivot Table Design mode, enabling you to drag and drop to create pivot tables. This option is generally used to manipulate and report on data from Microsoft Dynamics CRM.
   c. **Dynamic Worksheet**—Selecting this option will enable you to add new columns (as described in the first option, Static Worksheet with Records from

This Page); however, the columns are only added for the purpose of export and do not change the underlying view (see Figure 7.62).

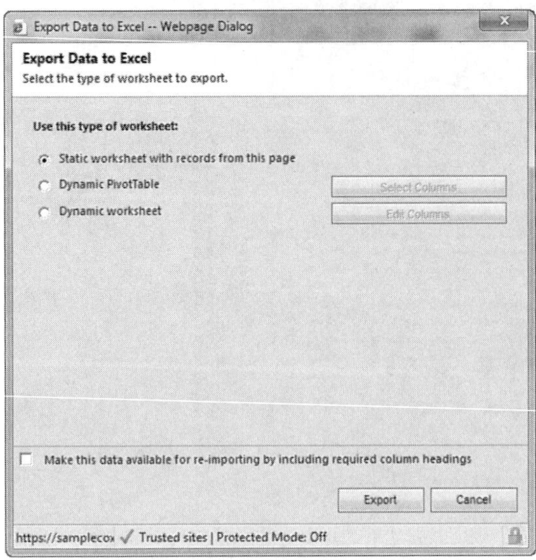

FIGURE 7.60 Export Data to Excel dialog box.

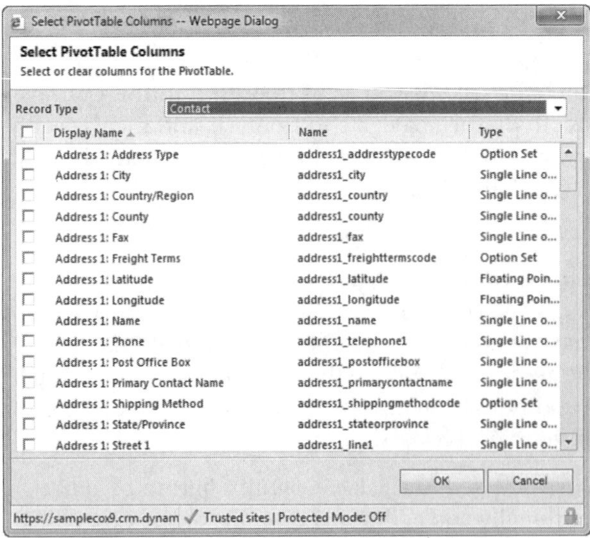

FIGURE 7.61 Select columns to export.

NOTE

The option to make the data available for reimporting is only available with the static worksheet option.

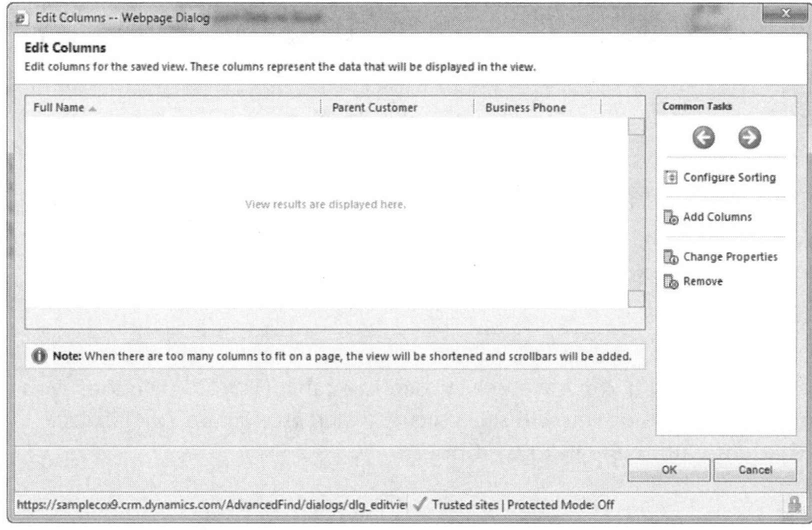

FIGURE 7.62 Select columns to add for export.

3. For our example, we'll select the Dynamic Worksheet option, and add three columns consisting of First Name, Last Name, and Credit Limit (see Figure 7.63). Select OK twice, and then choose Export to export the data to Excel.

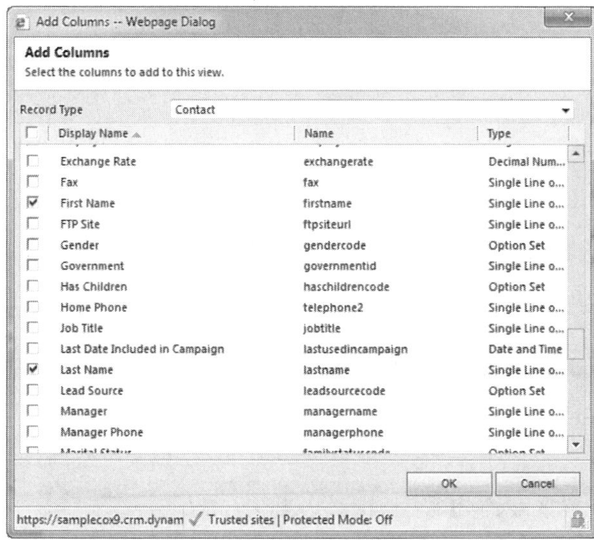

FIGURE 7.63 Select columns to edit for export.

TIP

To export data, you must have the appropriate permissions in security roles that allows exporting.

TIP

Both the dynamic pivot table and the dynamic worksheet require Microsoft Dynamics CRM for Outlook installed to view exported data.

4. Open Microsoft Excel, and if you have not chosen to enable Data Connections, you might have to enable them or you will see a security alert (see Figure 7.64). Select Enable This Content, and then OK to continue.

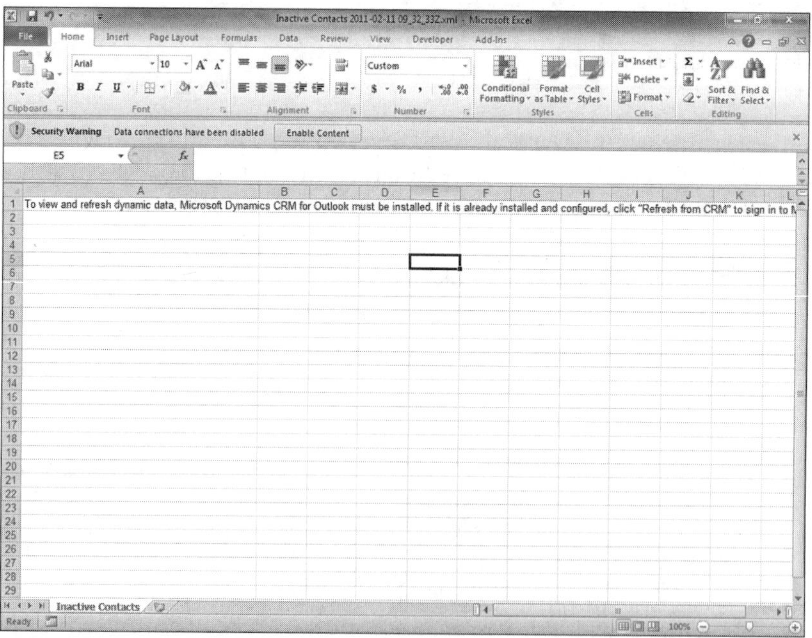

FIGURE 7.64 Microsoft Office Excel data connection security warning alert.

TIP

In Step 4, you might have to choose Refresh from CRM as shown in Figure 7.65 to bring the data into Excel.

5. When the content downloads, it is displayed in Excel, as shown in Figure 7.66.

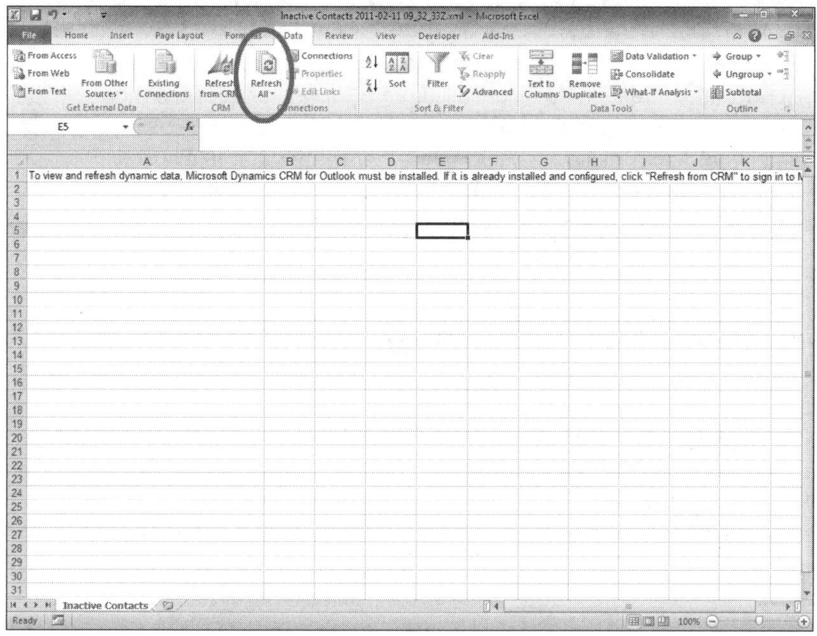

FIGURE 7.65 Microsoft Office Excel Refresh from CRM option in Excel.

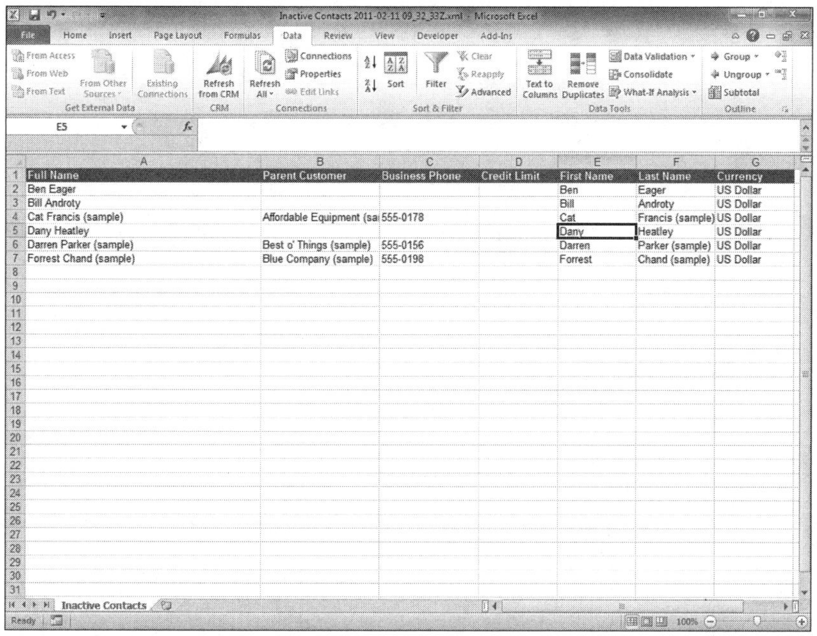

FIGURE 7.66 Microsoft Office Excel with CRM data.

TIP

Notice in Figure 7.66 that the Data tab is selected and there is an option to Refresh from CRM. Microsoft Excel will refresh automatically from CRM when it reopens; however, if you want to reflect changes made to your data without closing and reopening, you can select this option. Additionally, it is important to remember that this is only one-way. Changes made to your data in Excel will not be pushed up to CRM. Rather, they must be reimported following the steps outlined here.

Personalize Workplace with Personal Options

One of the most powerful aspects of the Workplace is that you can personalize or customize it. To customize it, select Options from the File drop-down menu (using either client). Notice that you need to select the Tools menu option in the CRM toolbar, not the similarly named menu item on Internet Explorer when working with the web client. When working with the CRM client for Outlook, this option is available by selecting File from the top menu bar and then CRM, followed by the Options button (as shown in Figure 7.67).

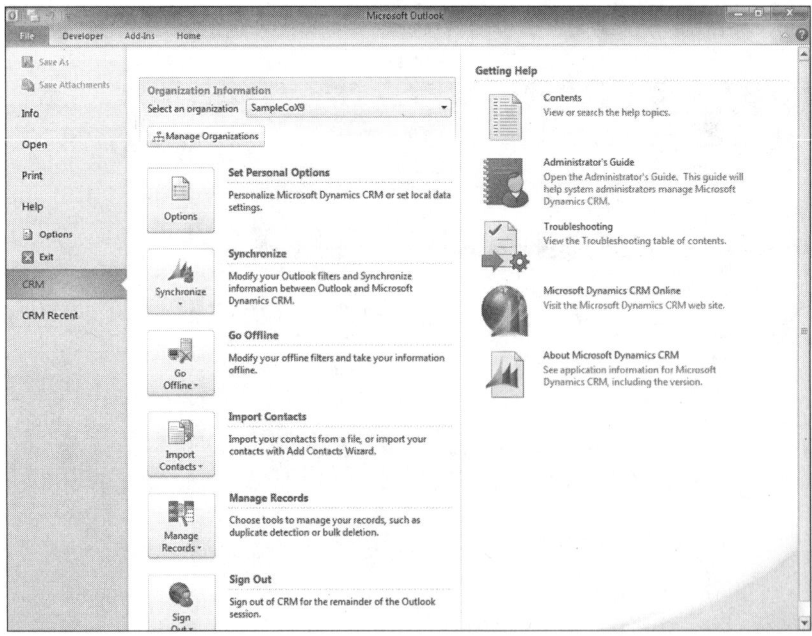

FIGURE 7.67 Microsoft CRM Options in Outlook.

You will encounter a few differences with setting the Personal Options when working with the Outlook client versus the web client options window. We have indicated the differences accordingly. The options to personalize include the following:

- **General**—Available on both Web and Outlook clients, however there is neither a default pane nor a time zone selection option in the Outlook client.
- **Synchronization**—Outlook client only.
- **Workplace**—Available in both web and Outlook clients.
- **Activities**—Web client only.
- **Formats**—Available in both web and Outlook clients.
- **E-mail Templates**—Available in both web and Outlook clients.
- **E-mail**—Available in both web and Outlook clients; however, there is no Outlook integration options available in the web version.
- **Address Book**—Available in the Outlook client only.
- **Local Data**—Available in the Outlook client only.
- **Privacy**—Available in both web and Outlook clients.
- **Languages**—Available in both web and Outlook clients.

It is important to remember that the settings made here are personal to only the user profile making the changes. When set, they are applied to whichever client the user uses and will have no effect on other users.

General Options for Both Web and Outlook Clients

The General options include the capability to set the general layout, view, and options (see Figure 7.68).

Default pane (available only in the web client) refers to which area receives the focus and is expanded by default when the system is started. By default, this is set to Workplace, but you can set it to any pane. This is very helpful if you work in the marketing department, for example—you can have that area selected when you open Microsoft Dynamics CRM. We personally set the default pane to Settings because we do so much work on the configuration of Microsoft Dynamics CRM. Similarly, you can set the default tab or the node where the start page opens (web client only).

The option to show the Get Started panes exists here and as we have mentioned previously, we have turned it off for real estate purposes.

Select Which Forms to Use enables you to set whether to use Microsoft Dynamics CRM forms for the indicated items or use the native Outlook forms. Because Microsoft Dynamics CRM is so closely integrated with Outlook, either form works provided that the Outlook forms are promoted to CRM (Outlook client only).

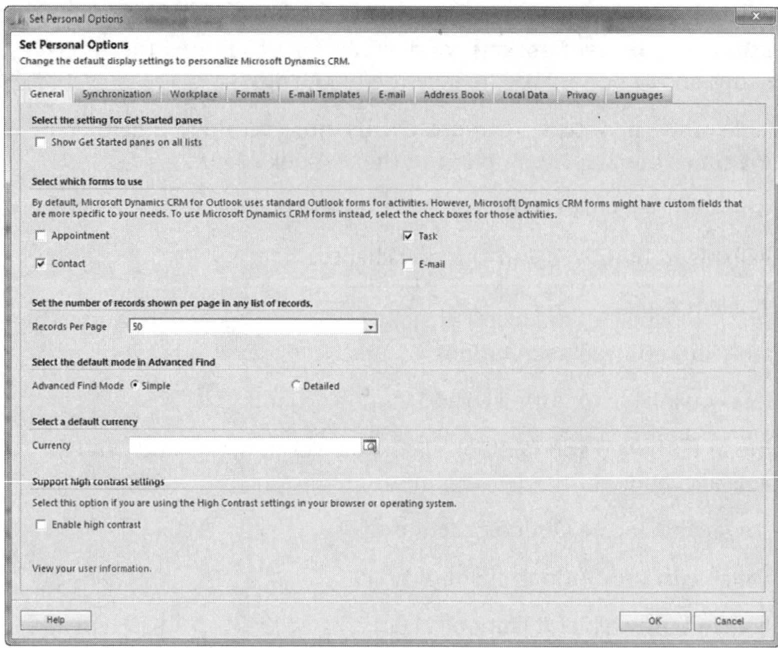

FIGURE 7.68 Personal Options, General (Outlook Client).

TIP

Customizations to Microsoft Dynamics CRM forms are not available if you select to work with the Outlook forms. An example of this might be adding a new field to the Contact record that tracks the industry of the contact. This field will not be on the Outlook form.

Number of Records Displayed Per Page is a global setting (for your user only) that sets the maximum number or rows, or records, to display on any list of records. The maximum is 250. If you frequently work with large record sets, you might want to set it to the maximum for less paging requirements (both web and Outlook clients).

TIP

We've noticed in our testing that the larger the number you select for rows, the longer it takes for the page to load. This is because more records need to load on a given page, thereby slowing the load time. Additionally, there is no easy way to change this number to greater than 250.

Default Mode for Advanced Find is the option to select between Simple and Detailed. Simple mode doesn't display the query/filter options; Detailed mode shows and lets you modify the query/filter options. Note that, regardless of the setting here, you can select either mode when working with the Advanced Find by selecting Hide Details or Show Details on the form manually (both web and Outlook client).

The Time Zone option enables you to select and set the time zone for your area/region. Note that this might be different from where the server is located, and it can affect how you use Microsoft Dynamics CRM (web client only).

Default Currency enables users to select which currency should be set as the default currency when new records are created (both web and Outlook clients).

High Contrast improves the display of Microsoft Dynamics CRM and is generally used by vision-impaired users while Windows is running in High Contrast mode.

At the bottom of the web client is the View Your User Information link. When clicked, it takes users to view their profile.

Synchronization for Outlook Client Only

To modify how Outlook synchronizes with Microsoft Dynamics CRM, you make changes here (see Figure 7.69).

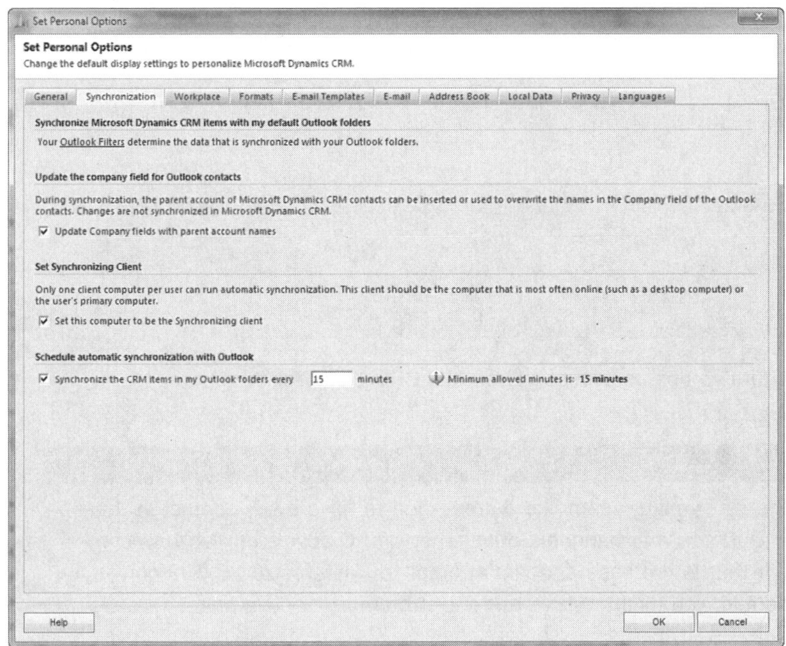

FIGURE 7.69 Personal Options, Synchronization (Outlook client).

Outlook can synchronize any task, phone call, letter, or fax that you are the owner of, as well as appointments for which you're listed as an attendee. Contacts are a little trickier.

Only the contacts that you've specified in the Local Data settings are synchronized. You can navigate to the Local Data settings by clicking Local Data or by navigating to CRM, Modify Local Data Groups from the Outlook client.

By default, Local Data synchronizes only contacts for which you are listed as the owner. This prevents problems when organizations have a huge number of contacts from all of them synchronizing with Outlook. However, if you want to have every contact in the organization, or if you want to have all of your contacts as well as all the contacts your employees own, you can dynamically set that value here. Figure 7.70 shows the option available from Outlook that can be accessed by going to CRM from the top menu and selecting Modify Local Data Groups.

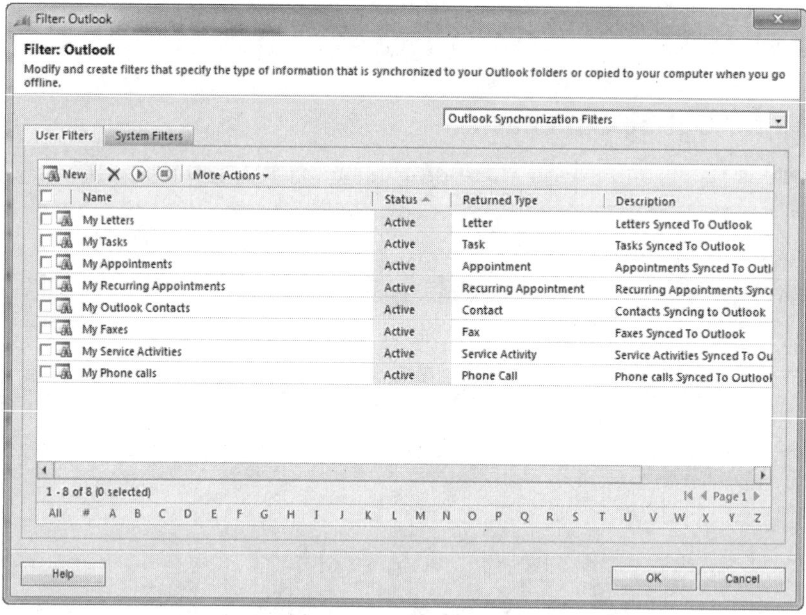

FIGURE 7.70 Local data groups as accessed from the CRM client for Outlook.

TIP

Remember that although it might seem like a great idea to have every contact in the organization in your Outlook, your handheld phone/pocket PC device probably synchronizes with Outlook. If that is the case and you attempt to synchronize 25,000 contacts with your handheld, you might quickly run out of memory or have an unmanageable device.

Updating the Company field is an option because previous versions required a workaround to display it. It is highly recommended that you have this checked because it displays the parent account name in the Company field.

NOTE

Unlike other fields, the Company field synchronization is one-way. Changes to this field are pushed down from CRM to Outlook, but they are not pushed from Outlook to CRM (and in fact changes to the Company field in Outlook will be overwritten by CRM during the next Synchronization).

When setting the synchronizing client, it is necessary to consider changing this option only if you have more than one computer. If so, consider which computer you will use most often and set that computer as the primary client. If you use more than one computer with the Outlook client, Microsoft Dynamics might prompt you to set this.

Synchronization with CRM occurs every 15 minutes or as often as the automatic synchronization is set. This is optional: You can set synchronization manually by going to CRM, Synchronize with CRM.

- **Workplace**—Within the Workplace, you can set which areas you want to have quick-and-easy access to, such as Sales, Marketing, Service, or Scheduling.
- **Activities (web client only)**—You can set the default view for the Calendar to day, week, or month, and you also can set the default work hours.
- **Formats (web client only)**—Here you select the format for how you want information such as numbers, currencies, time, and dates: You can select from the defaults or customize these specifically to your region.
- **E-mail Templates**—Enable you to create and modify your personal e-mail templates, as well as promote them to the organizational level.

▶ For more information about working with e-mail templates, see Chapter 12.

- **E-mail (both web and Outlook clients)**—Setting the configuration Allow the E-mail Router to Send and Receive E-mail on Your Behalf enables Microsoft Dynamics CRM to send e-mails directly from CRM with your credentials (web client only). You also can determine how e-mail messages are tracked in Microsoft Dynamics CRM here (both web and Outlook client).

▶ For more information about both of these options, see Chapter 14, "E-Mail Configuration."

- **Address Book**—This option allows you to select Synchronizing record types and sets the reconciliation for CRM records.
- **Local Data**—The local data options enable you to set the frequency as well as how duplicate records are handled during synchronization.
- **Privacy (both web and Outlook clients)**—Checks to see how to send error information to Microsoft related to problems with Microsoft Dynamics CRM.

- **Languages (both web and Outlook clients)**—With this setting you can set the user interface and help language. The only options available are those that the system administrator has installed and made active. However, users can customize their Microsoft Dynamics CRM experience based on their preferred language.

NOTE

The base language is set when Microsoft Dynamics CRM is first loaded and cannot be changed. Additionally, setting the language here changes only the way the Microsoft Dynamics interface is displayed. Data contained within the system will not change.

▶ For more information on working with languages, see Chapter 12.

Summary

The Workplace is where users will spend most of their time managing activities and customers. It is very customizable, and there are several options that enable you to extend the functionality related to customers, the Calendar, and tasks directly to mobile devices through Outlook.

Activities are how work gets assigned, managed, and completed. This chapter explained how to work not just with activities, but also how to assign them to users and queues. Activities are used to drive tasks, as well as many reports that rely on activities (the Neglected Accounts report, for example) and should be used to record every customer contact.

Duplicate detection, as well as how to work with data that can be exported and imported, showed how easy it is to work with data both in and out of the CRM application. It is important to remember that when working with dynamic data in Excel, it will be refreshed from the underlying data source, and you might open a spreadsheet that doesn't contain data (or has new data) other than you originally were working with.

CHAPTER 8

Working with Sales

IN THIS CHAPTER

- Leads
- Opportunities
- Competitors
- Products
- Quotes, Orders, and Invoices
- Goals, Goal Metrics, and Rollup Queries

The Sales area in Microsoft Dynamics CRM is where you work with current and prospective customers. Here you manage Leads and Opportunities, and where the only workflow other than the Knowledge Base approval process is included with Microsoft Dynamics CRM by default. The workflow is presented via the Lead conversion process when a user selects Convert Lead from the top menu. The Lead is either qualified and converted to a customer, or disqualified and deactivated.

▶ Other sections in the Sales area such as Accounts, Contacts, are explained in Chapter 6, "Working with Customers." Marketing Lists, Sales Literature, and Quick Campaigns are included in Chapter 9, "Working with Marketing." Therefore, these topics are not covered in this chapter.

Leads

Leads are not customers but rather potential customers. This is an important distinction because it provides a needed level of separation when working with your customer base. As explained later in this chapter, Leads are converted to customers when they become qualified. If they are disqualified, they remain as an inactive Lead.

Using Leads properly can provide rich insight into your organization on several levels. Because Leads are not yet qualified (they are potential customers who haven't yet met internal criteria to be converted to customers), they should be considered the customer entry point into the CRM system. Although it is certainly possible that you will be adding Accounts and Contacts directly into Microsoft Dynamics CRM, entering Leads enables you to manage what new customers might be interested in your products, how your salespeople are cultivating their new customer base, and what kind of criteria is being used to convert Leads to customers.

As mentioned earlier, Leads are also used for specific marketing efforts. Any growing business usually aims to add new customers, and the capability to create marketing efforts tailored to interested customers is much more efficient than preparing marketing for everyone.

When creating a Lead, you must specify the Topic (or what the Lead pertains to—this can be the specific product or service specific to the Lead), the Last Name, and the Company Name by default (see Figure 8.1). These fields are used when the Lead is qualified and converted to Account, Contact, or Opportunity.

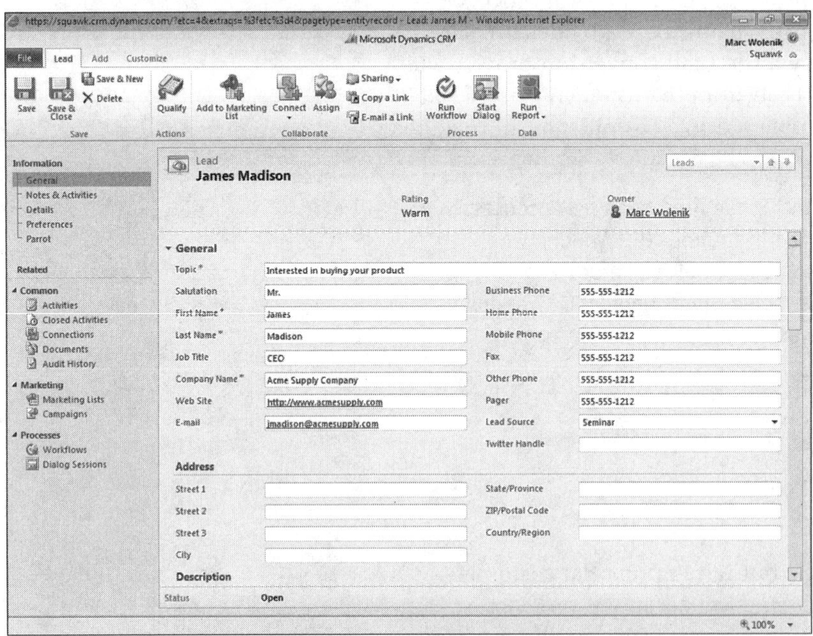

FIGURE 8.1 New Lead, General tab.

To create a new Lead, navigate to Sales, Leads and select New.

Figure 8.1 shows a new Lead entered and saved.

NOTE

There is no lookup for or association with any existing data in the CRM system other than Currency found lower on the form in the Details section. This is because the Lead is a new record and is not related to any existing record. If you're creating a Lead and want to associate it with an existing customer, you probably want to work with Opportunities, which is explained in the next section.

CAUTION

When working with Leads, you cannot include potential sales information anywhere other than the Notes and Description fields. This is because Leads are considered potential customers, not potential sales. This is an important distinction: Potential sales information should be captured with an Opportunity, not a Lead.

Although the remaining fields on the form and tabs are not required, it is helpful to populate them; the information entered and saved automatically carries over to the converted Account, Contact, and Opportunity records when they have been qualified.

Most of the information on the various sections is self-explanatory, with the exception of Rating found in the details section. This is a self-assessment of the Lead itself and can be Cold, Warm, or Hot. When used properly, it can drive workflow events, such as a callback by the sales manager within one day if the Lead is hot, or within five days if the Lead is Cold, for example.

The Lead Source drop-down list shown in Figure 8.2 offers a great way of running reverse metrics on a trade show or seminar. You can easily add to this drop-down list by customizing the leadsourcecode attribute and adding specific events that your company might sponsor or attend. Figure 8.3 shows the customization options for this field and the addition of a new event called Microsoft Convergence, which is shown in the drop-down list in Figure 8.2. To make this customization, navigate to Customization at the top of the form, select Customize Entity, and then select the Source of Lead field to modify.

Using this information, you can easily determine who was contacted and at which event by querying on this field.

▶ Refer to Chapter 16, "Solution Concepts," for more information on how to fully customize Microsoft Dynamics CRM entities.

The Preference section of the Lead form enables you to set the Owner, which, by default, is populated with the user who created the record, the Status Reason, and the Source Campaign. When working with unqualified or new Leads, the Status Reason enables you to select whether the Lead is new or contacted. When a Lead is converted, the Status Reason changes to Qualified if the Lead was converted to a customer, or it changes to the reason it was disqualified (as selected during the conversion process). The Source Campaign enables you to tie the Lead to any campaign generated from Microsoft Dynamics CRM.

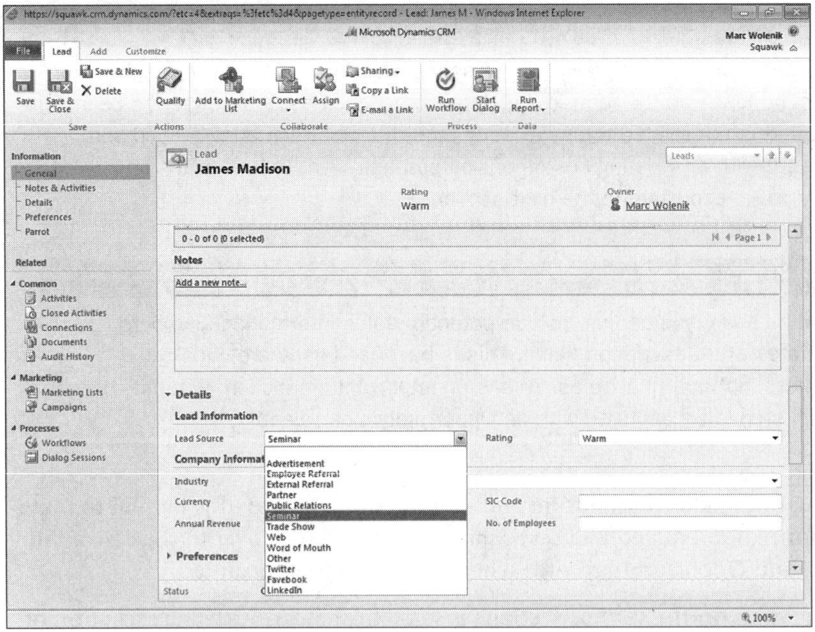

FIGURE 8.2 Lead source options.

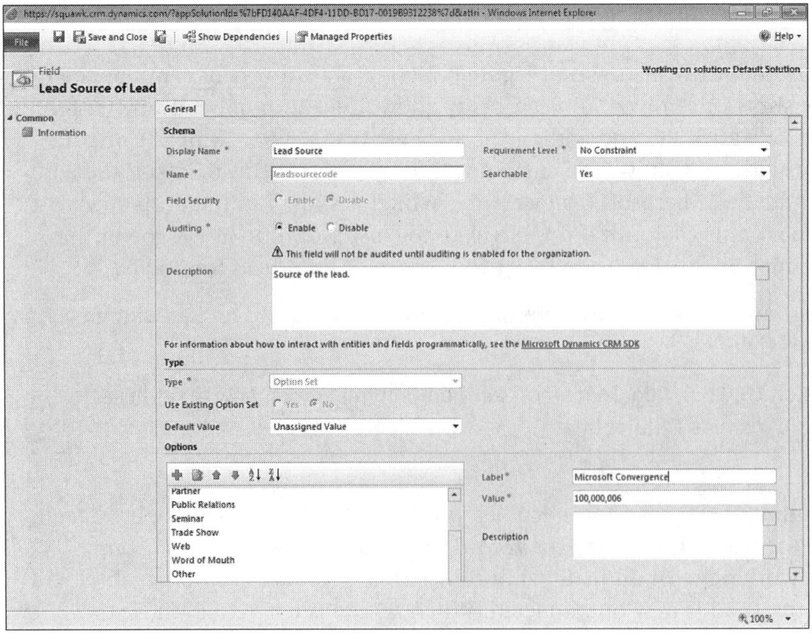

FIGURE 8.3 Add a new value to the lead source.

The Contact Methods and Marketing Information are the same as found on the Account and Contact forms (see Figure 8.4).

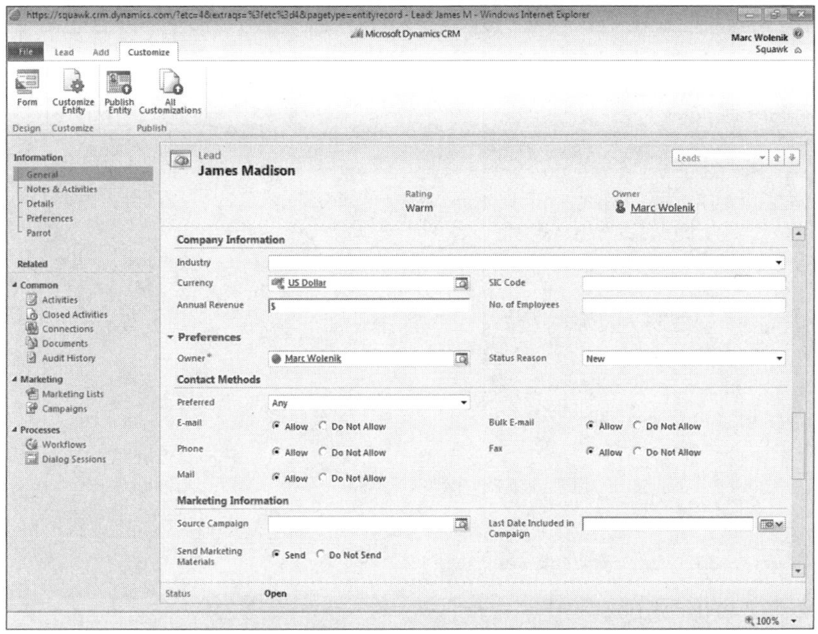

FIGURE 8.4 New Lead, Preferences section.

The options in the Ribbon menu (after it is saved) include the capabilities to Assign, make a connection, or convert the Lead (via the Qualify button), which we explain in the next section.

Converting Leads

As mentioned at the beginning of this chapter, the only sales force automation (SFA) included by default in Microsoft Dynamics CRM is in Lead conversion. All other SFA is customizable by creating specific Microsoft Dynamics CRM workflow.

Leads are converted to customers when they have met internal qualifications and become customers. Internal qualifications can be anything from a Lead indicating that he is ready to buy, to a background/credit check and line of credit approval prepared by your accounting department. Additionally, Leads are converted to disqualified customers (and removed as active Leads) through the conversion processes for a variety of reasons, such as Lead disinterest or an inability to contact.

To convert a Lead, select the Qualify option from the Ribbon menu. The Convert Lead form opens, as shown in Figure 8.5.

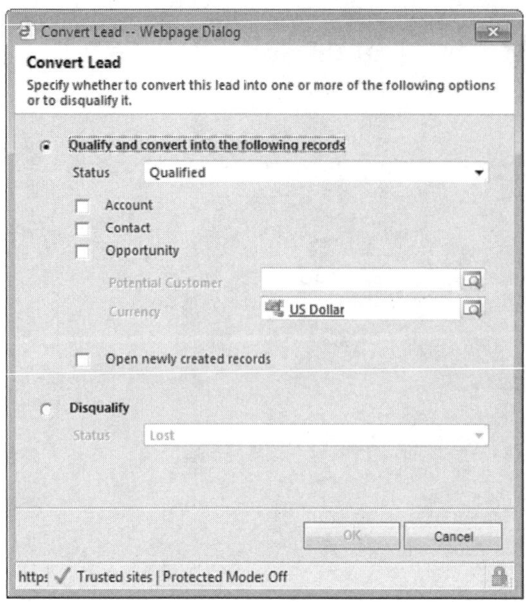

FIGURE 8.5 Convert Lead dialog box.

Lead conversion in Microsoft Dynamics CRM enables you to quickly create the necessary customer records in Microsoft Dynamics CRM by automatically creating an Account, a Contact, or an Opportunity automatically from the existing information on the Lead. When a Lead is converted (either qualified or disqualified), the original Lead record status is changed to indicate the new status of the Lead, and the Lead is closed. When a Lead is closed, no further edits can be made to it unless it is reactivated. You can reactivate any closed Lead by opening the closed Lead and selecting Reactivate Lead from the Actions drop-down list (see Figure 8.6). Any activities will remain with the Lead regardless of whether it is active or deactivated.

CAUTION

It is important to know that when a Lead is reactivated for whatever reason, any qualified records that might have been generated (such as Accounts, Contacts, or Opportunities) continue to exist. You can end up creating duplicate records if you frequently reactivate closed Leads.

If the Lead fails to qualify, select Disqualify (see Figure 8.5). Select from the drop-down options listed in the Status and click OK. This closes the Lead and sets its status to whatever value was selected.

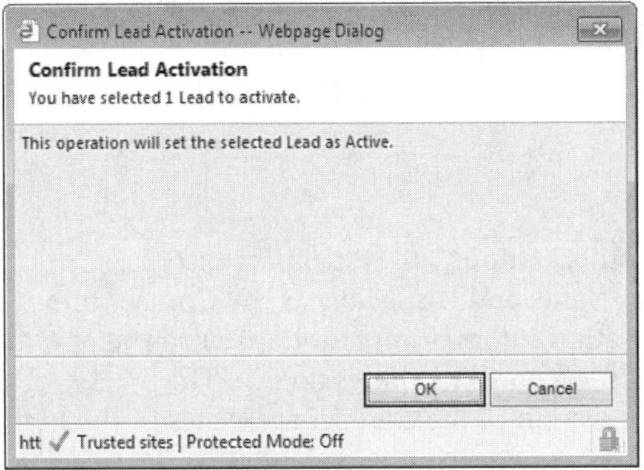

FIGURE 8.6 Lead activation.

If the Lead has qualified, select Qualify and select whether to convert the Lead record into a new Account, Contact, or Opportunity record. It is possible to convert the Lead directly to one or all of the options. The effects of either of the options are as follows:

- If Account is selected, regardless of the other options, a new Account record is created, with the value entered for Company Name in the Lead record as the Account Name. The Lead address, details, and administration information also transfer to the new Account record, but the notes do not because it is assumed that the notes are Lead notes, not Account notes. The Originating Lead field on the Preference section of the Account associates to the Lead (see Figure 8.7).

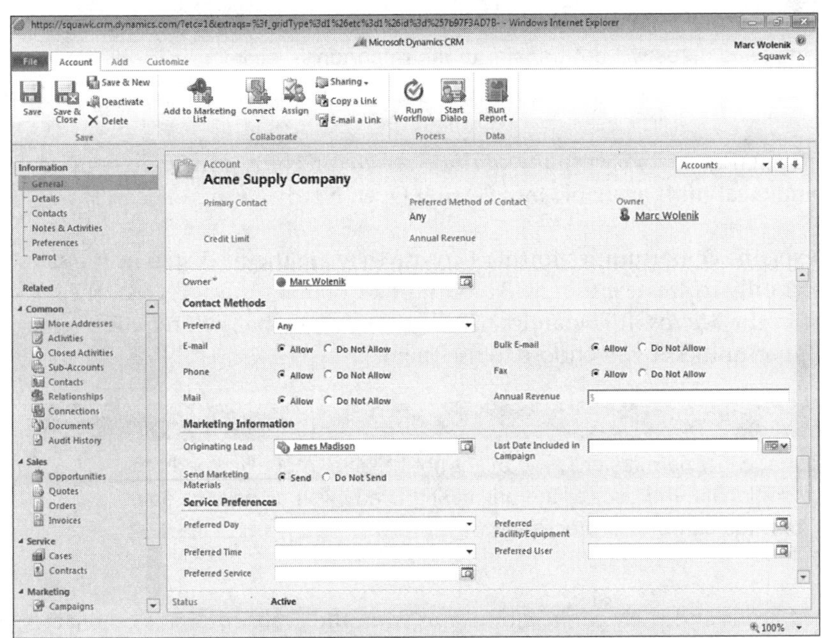

FIGURE 8.7 Originating Lead field on the Account Administration tab.

TIP

Keep in mind that you can still check the original Lead notes by opening it and checking the notes there.

- If Contact is selected, regardless of the other options, a new Contact record is created, with the values entered for First Name and Last Name as the Contact information. The Lead address and administration information also transfer to the new Contact record, but similar to creating an Account, the notes do not. The Originating Lead field on the Preference section of the Contact associates to the Lead (similar to Figure 8.7).
- If both Account and Contact are selected, the Account record will have the Contact record as the Primary Contact field, and the Contact record will have the Account record in the Parent Customer field.
- If Opportunity is selected and either Account or Contact is selected, a new Opportunity is created (along with the selected Account and Contact records). However, if Opportunity is selected and neither Account nor Contact is selected, you must associate the Lead with an existing customer. If the Lead is associated with an existing customer, the Lead information stays with the Lead record. The Originating Lead and the Source Campaign fields on the Administration tab of the Opportunity will associate with the Lead.

TIP

Remember that the Lead notes will not transfer to the Opportunity record.

- The option to open and work with any of these selected records immediately upon conversion and creation is available by selecting Open Newly Created Records.

The next section explains Opportunities further because they are the next step in the sales process. If you select only to create either an Account or a Contact from the Lead, the customer will exist in the Microsoft Dynamics CRM customer base but will require you to manually create Opportunities if you choose to use them.

CAUTION

Depending on your security permissions, you might not be able to qualify Leads that you do not own. Additionally, the user of the originating Lead owns all newly created records created from the conversion process.

You can view closed Leads and their conversion status from the Leads interface by selecting Closed Leads from the view (see Figure 8.8). You can reactivate any Lead by opening it and selecting Reactivate Lead from the Actions drop-down list, as explained earlier.

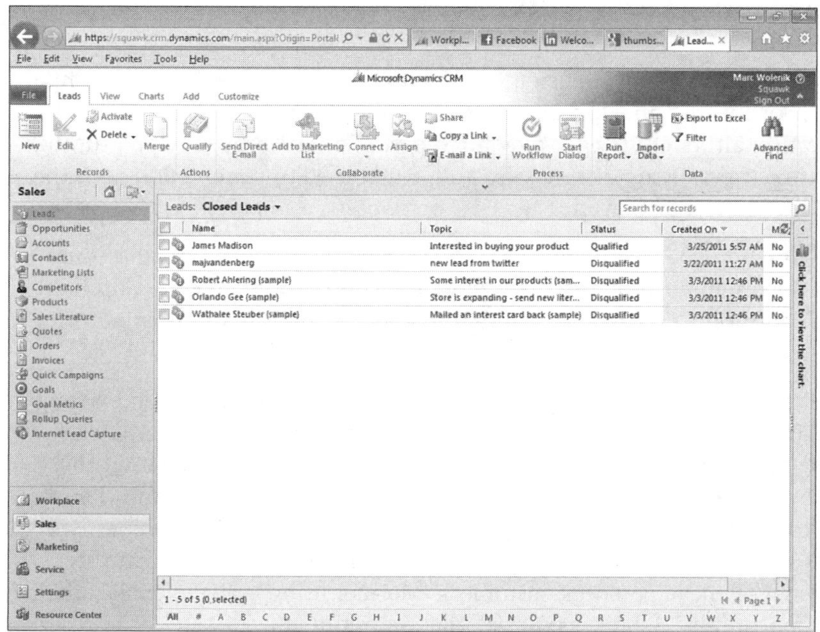

FIGURE 8.8 View closed Leads.

Closed Leads should be an important auditing tool of your organization because these Leads can be analyzed for the effectiveness of your sales team and to determine which campaigns created how many Leads.

Microsoft Dynamics CRM includes these tools that enable you to query on their status:

- Two reports, the Lead Source Effectiveness report and the Neglected Leads report, found in the Report section of My Work
- Capability to view closed Leads from Lead view
- More complex queries using Advanced Find to determine conversion dates, as well as Opportunities and customer records, or associations with existing customer records

Finally, you can also convert Leads in groups, if required, instead of having to do it one by one. To convert multiple Leads, you can either add them to a marketing list as marketing list members and then select Convert Lead from the Ribbon menu, or simply select multiple records from the Lead view and then select the Qualify button from the Ribbon menu.

▶ For information about working with marketing lists, refer to Chapter 9, "Working with Marketing."

Opportunities

Just as a Lead can ultimately lead to a customer, an Opportunity is considered a potential sale to a customer. For this reason, Opportunity records must associate with existing customer records. Also, although it is not a required part of a sales process, Opportunities provide insight into potentially upcoming sales and, when used in conjunction with the Sales Pipeline report, can forecast revenue by date, probability, and potential revenue.

Opportunities tie closely to Quotes, Orders, and Invoices because they use the base information found on the originating Opportunity when they are being created. Additionally, Opportunities are commonly created from Leads and contain the base information from the originating Lead.

Opportunities are created when "an opportunity" to make a sale is found for an existing customer. Although Opportunities require the existence of a customer record, you can easily create a new Account or Contact record to associate the Opportunity with if the customer is new. By doing this, however, you skip the step of creating Leads and then converting Leads to customers and Opportunities. This might be how your business works. Perhaps your sales cycle is very quick, and Leads are not something that you cultivate. However, if you generally have potential customers, consider using Leads to qualify them and then using Opportunities to build potential sales around them.

For this example, you'll create a new Opportunity; however, you could easily work with an Opportunity that was created as part of the conversion process from a Lead.

Creating a New Opportunity

To create a new Opportunity, navigate to Opportunities in the Sales area and select New. The required fields for an Opportunity are Topic, Potential Customer, and Currency (see Figure 8.9). The Potential Customer field can be any existing active Account or Contact.

Although the Price List is not required, you cannot add any products to the Opportunity until you have selected one. Probability is a field designed to contain a number between 1 and 100 to represent the probability of a close. This example uses a probability of 50—that is, a 50% chance that we'll be able to convert this Opportunity into a sale—and a forecasted value of 50% of the estimated revenue. The probability is a free-form field that is used for forecasting purposes and frequently adjusted by workflow automatically. The Estimated Close Date indicates the date that the Opportunity might be converted to a sale, which is necessary for forecasting when considering sales. Failure to enter the Estimated Close Date prevents the Opportunity from appearing on the Sales Pipeline report. The Rating indicates the overall rating of the Opportunity; you can change this in the customization screen to include ratings that might fit your organization better.

The Estimated Revenue section defaults to System Calculated and, when first created, has a total value of $0. When products are added to the Opportunity, the estimate revenue adjusts accordingly. Alternatively, you can select User Provided and enter any value into the Estimated Revenue text box. If User Provided is selected, however, adding products and clicking Recalculate will have no effect on the Estimated Revenue.

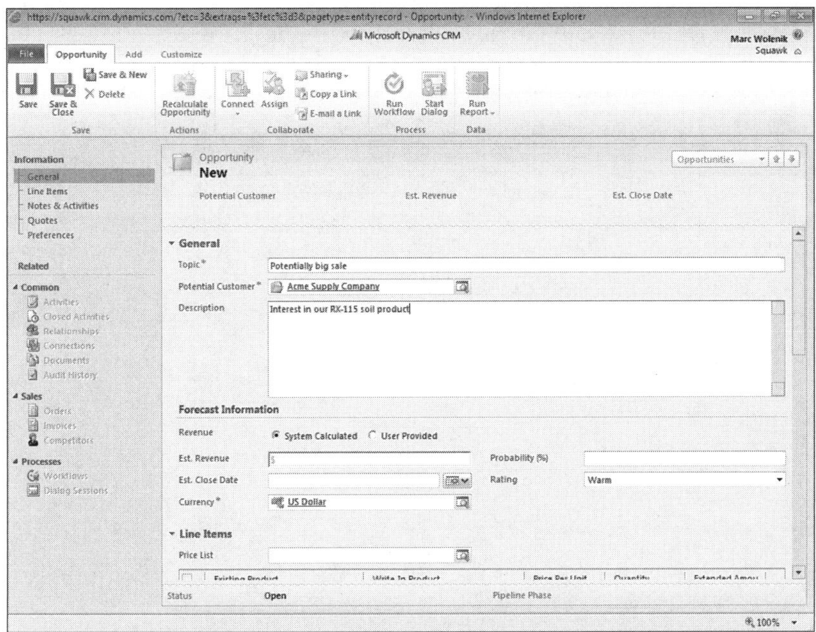

FIGURE 8.9 New Opportunity form.

The Preferences section contains record ownership information, originating Lead, Status, and Source Campaign (see Figure 8.10). The Source Campaign information is populated only when a Lead has this information and is converted to an Opportunity; when you change the Opportunity record, you cannot edit the Originating Lead and the Source Campaign information.

The options in the Ribbon menu of an Opportunity (after it is saved) include the capability to Close the Opportunity as either Won or Lost and Recalculate the Opportunity.

Add Products to an Opportunity

To create a complete Opportunity, including adding products, follow these steps:

1. Select New from the Sales, Opportunity area.
2. Complete the Topic, Potential Customer, and Currency selection.
3. Select whether the Opportunity Estimated Revenue should be calculated by the system or user. Because you'll have the system calculate the estimated revenue for this example, leave the Revenue as System Calculated.
4. Enter the Probability, Estimated Close Date, and Rating. Before you can add products, you must also select the Price List (see Figure 8.11).

▶ For information on constructing your Price Lists, refer to the "Product Catalog" section in Chapter 12, "Settings and Configuration."

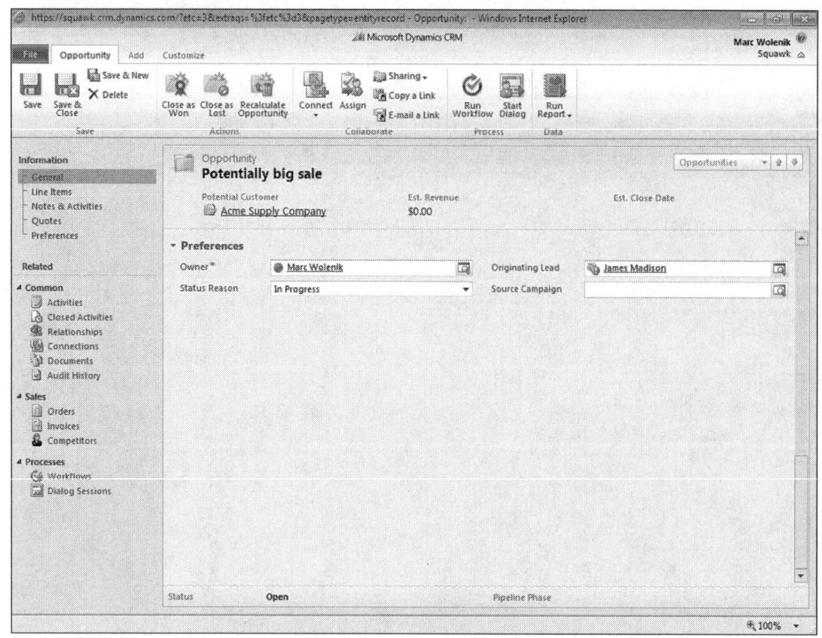

FIGURE 8.10 New Opportunity, Preferences section.

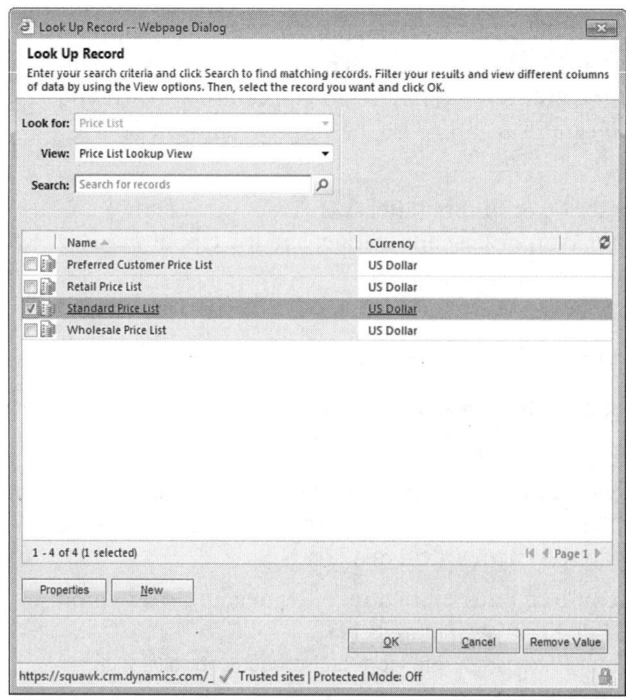

FIGURE 8.11 Price List selection.

5. After you select the Price List, click Save. Then select the products section box immediately below the Price List. It will highlight and the Ribbon menu will display List Tools specific for the section, allowing you to add, edit, or delete new opportunity products (see Figure 8.12).

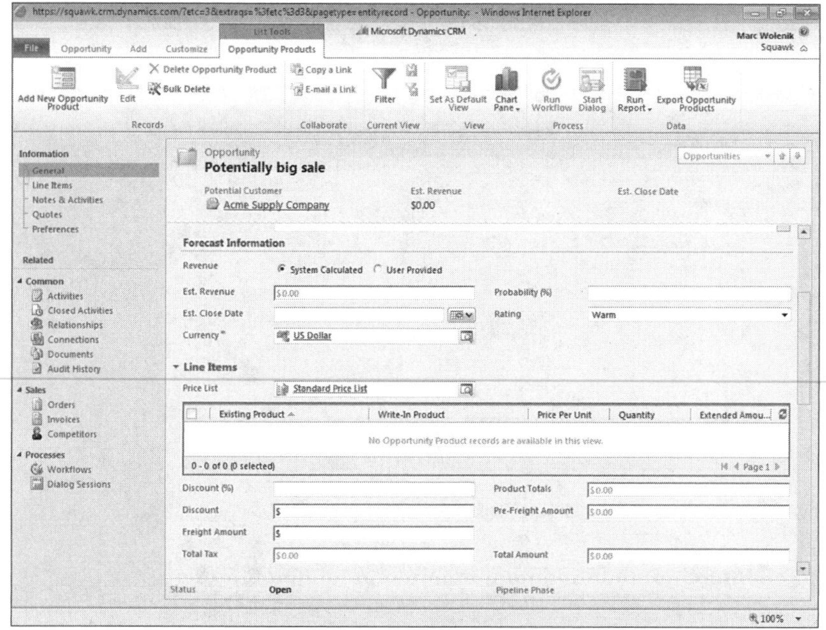

FIGURE 8.12 List Tools displayed for product addition.

6. Select Add New Opportunity Product for our example (see Figure 8.13).

7. Either look up or enter the product, select the applicable unit, and enter the quantity as well as any discount you want to give (if any). You can click Save to view the information before closing the form (see Figure 8.13). In the example, we've added a quantity of 11 products and set a price of $450 per unit; because we didn't include any discount, the extended amount is $4,950 (see Figure 8.14).

TIP

If you want to edit the quantity or discounts, you must double-click the product line, not the underlined name of the product. If you select the product name, the product details screen opens.

8. Navigating back to the main or Information screen, you should now see the Estimated Revenue at $4,950 at the top navigation of the Opportunity (see Figure 8.14).

You can add products that are in your product catalog or write in products. Write-in products are covered in the "Quotes" section later in this chapter.

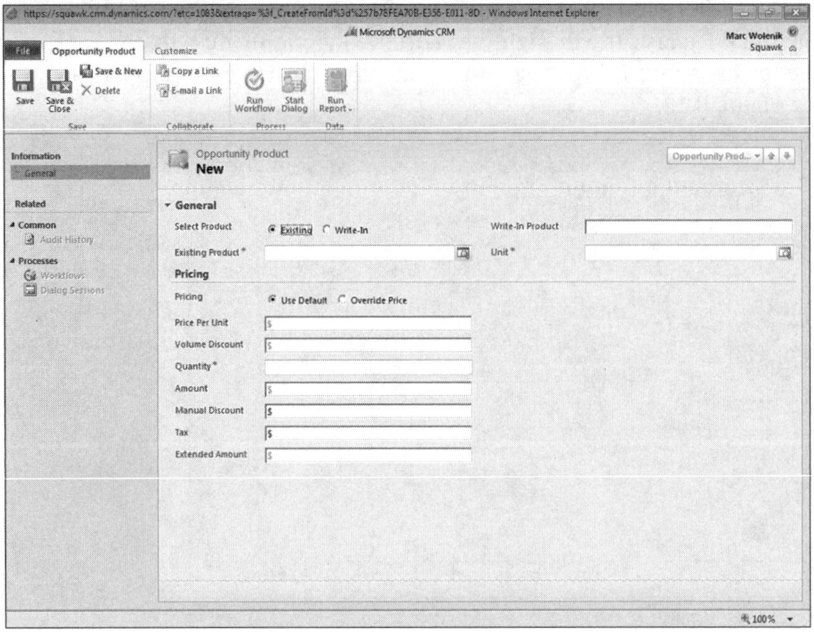

FIGURE 8.13 New Opportunity Product dialog box—Add new product.

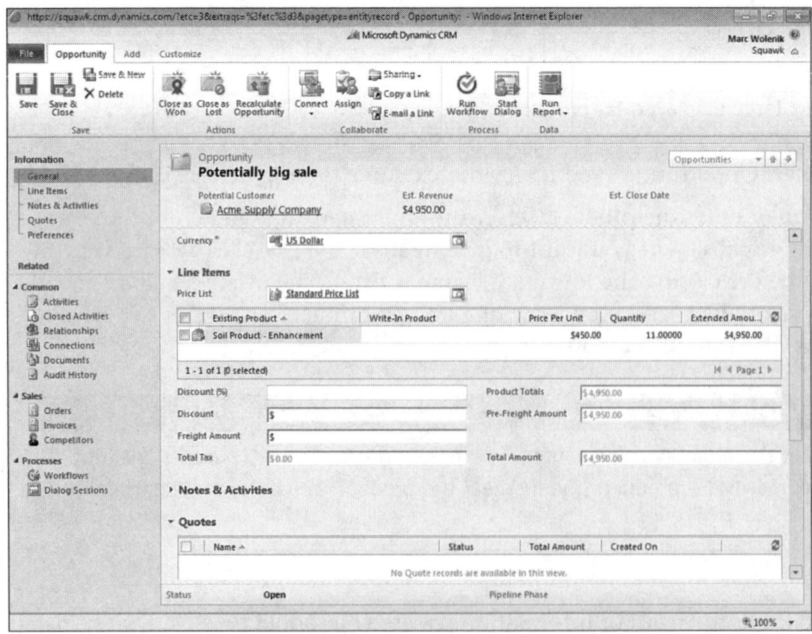

FIGURE 8.14 Products added as Line Items on the Opportunity Form.

Additional Options and Tools

The handy Recalculate option enables you to easily recalculate the estimated revenue, save and close, and then reopen the form when adjusting pricing for products. A common use of this is when you are building an Opportunity and want to change the underlying Price List for it, or you are adding Products and need to be sure you have the underlying calculations correct.

Another important tool when working with Opportunities is the Pipeline Phase. This is found in the lower-right corner of the Opportunity (see Figure 8.15). The Pipeline Phase was previously referred to as the Step Name in previous versions of CRM and uses the attribute stepname to show the current phase in the sales pipeline for the opportunity.

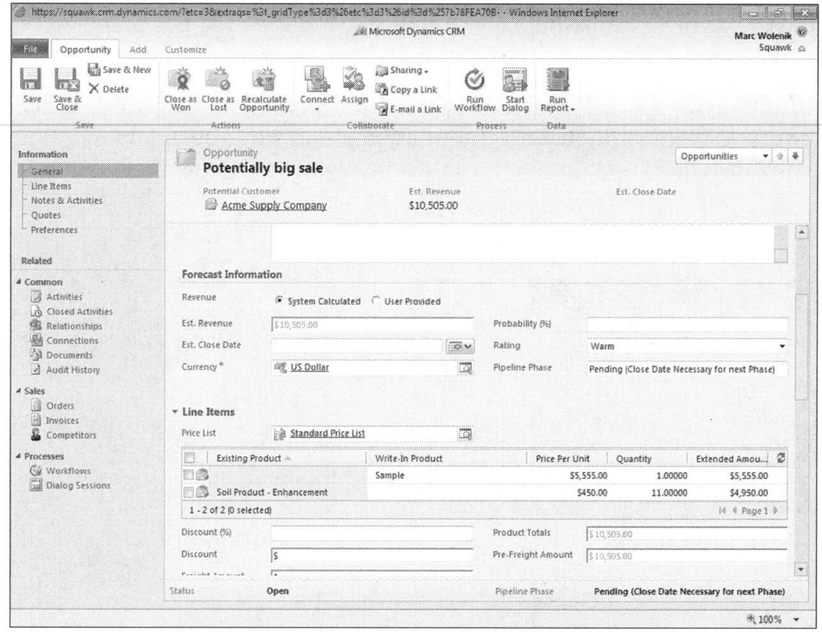

FIGURE 8.15 New Opportunity Pipeline Phase.

Additionally, we've modified the form to add the stepname field to the form so that it can be updated manually, as shown in Figure 8.15. However, this is typically updated via workflow.

NOTE

Because previous versions of CRM had stages only for Opportunity sales processes, it is important to understand the distinction between the stages and workflow steps.

Stages are collections of steps that must be labeled with a descriptive label (shown as the current status when viewing the workflow). *Steps* are the workflow items that operate within predefined stages. Both can be used extensively when working with the Opportunity entity to manage sales processes.

▶ Refer to Chapter 24, "Processes Development," for more information about working with workflows.

Closing Opportunities

Before you close an Opportunity, you can associate Quotes, Orders, and Invoices with it. When the Opportunity has been realized (by either winning or losing the business), you must close it. Closing Opportunities helps you effectively manage forecasted sales.

To close an Opportunity, select Close Opportunity from the Actions drop-down list. When closing an Opportunity, you are prompted for information about why you are doing so, which is pre-populated by your selection of either Close as Won or Close as Lost (see Figure 8.16).

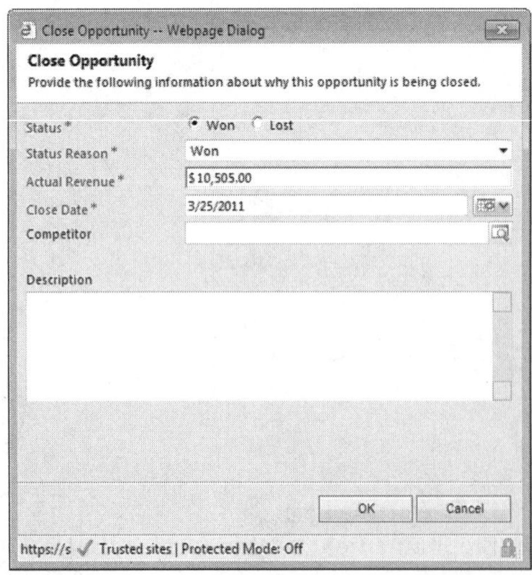

FIGURE 8.16 Close Opportunity dialog box.

When an Opportunity is closed, it is either Won or Lost. Selecting the status as Won when closing an Opportunity indicates that the revenue associated with the Opportunity has been realized and that the business has been closed (or will be on the date indicated). When you select Lost, you indicate that the Opportunity is no longer viable; either it has been lost to a competitor or the customer is no longer interested.

TIP

You cannot close an Opportunity (as either Won or Lost) if active or draft Quotes are associated with it. To close the Opportunity, you must first close the active or draft Quotes.

After you close the Opportunity, it can no longer have new Quotes, Orders, and Invoices associated with it unless it is reopened. You can easily reopen an Opportunity by selecting Reopen Opportunity from the Ribbon menu (see Figure 8.17).

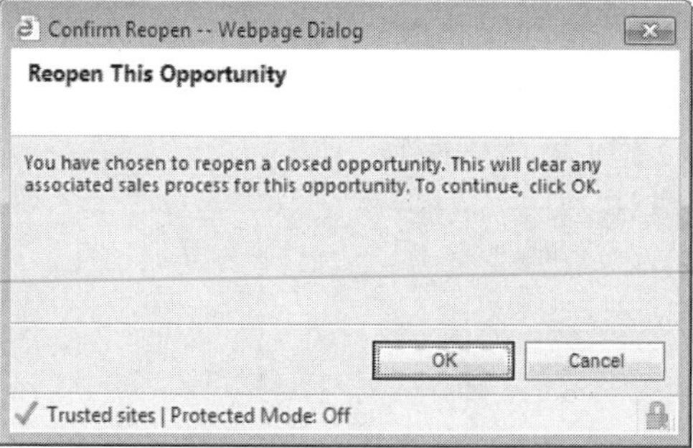

FIGURE 8.17 Reopen Opportunity option.

TIP

Closing an Opportunity does not affect the Probability Rating of the Opportunity. Depending on your situation, this might be fine, but you might end up closing Opportunities with a 0 Probability Rating as Won. Based on your business needs, you might want to consider adding a custom workflow that updates the Probability Rating to 0 if you close the Opportunity as Lost, and 100 if you close the Opportunity as a Win.

If you reopen a closed Opportunity, all related sales processes for the Opportunity are cleared.

Competitors

Managing your competitors is just as important as managing your customers. The more you know about your competition, the better you'll be able to compete.

Microsoft Dynamics CRM can track competitors associated with your Opportunities and Sales Literature, which provides rich information to your sales force when working with either of these records. Additionally, as previously explained in the "Opportunities" section in this chapter, closed Opportunities that are lost can be associated with competitors. Doing so provides the underlying data for the default Competitor Win Loss report.

TIP

Although the functionality for working with competitors exists within the Sales module of Microsoft Dynamics CRM, competitors apply only to Opportunities and Sales Literature, not Leads. If you are interested in tracking competitors against your Leads, you must extend the functionality of Microsoft Dynamics CRM by adding a relationship for Leads and competitors.

The Competitor record is considered a high-level overview of the competitor's company, related analysis, and associated products (see Figure 8.18).

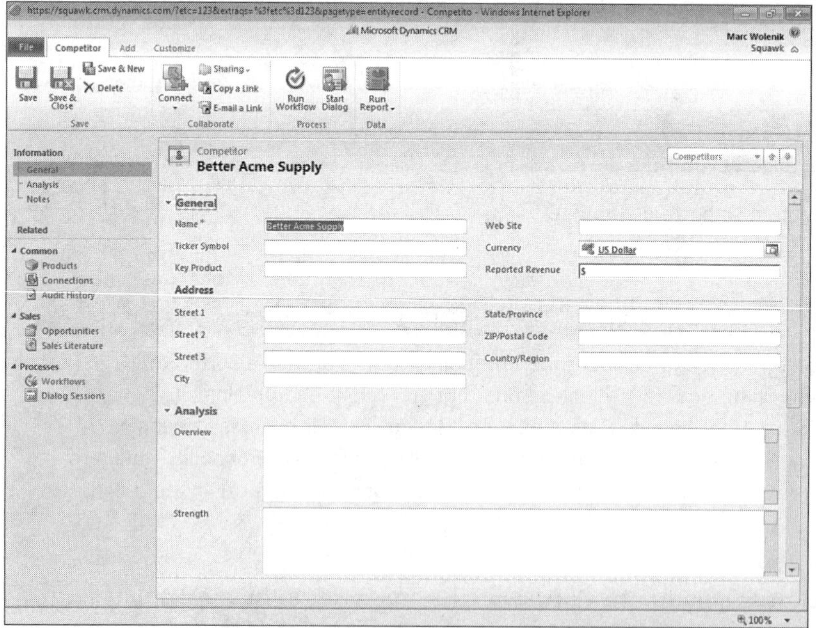

FIGURE 8.18 Competitor form.

When working with Competitor records, you can easily add key information about the competitor on the General section (see Figure 8.17) and include overview information as well as strengths, weaknesses, opportunities, and threats (SWOT) on the Analysis section.

In addition to capturing analysis information, you can show what products your competitor is selling that directly match yours. Because of the way Microsoft Dynamics CRM works, Competitor Products are limited to the products contained within your product catalog (see Figure 8.19).

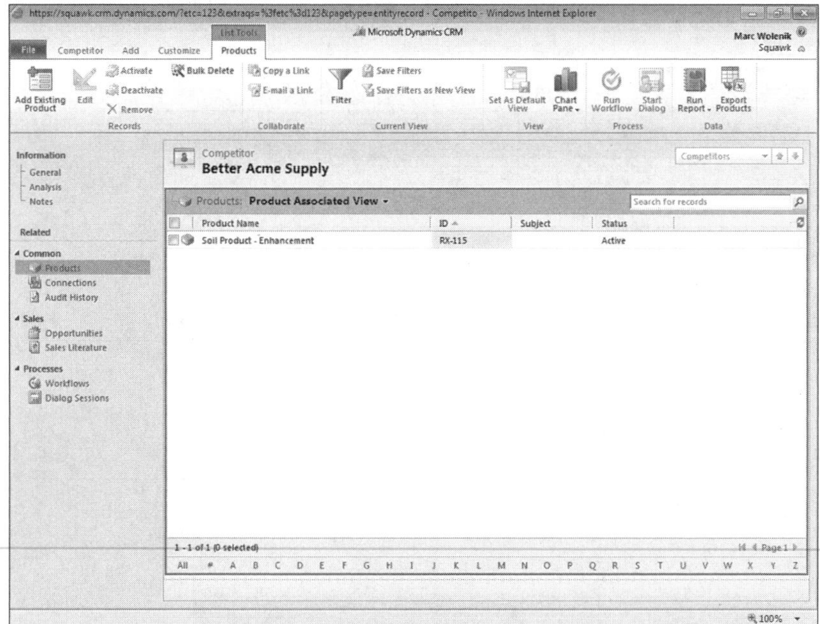

FIGURE 8.19 Competitor products.

TIP

If you want to show information related to other product lines or similar ones, consider including that information in the Notes section or creating a new entity to track this information.

Products

Products in the Sales area show the products available to sell. Unlike in previous versions, new Products can be created directly from this interface, provided the necessary security permissions exist to do so (see Figure 8.20). You can also add Products in the Settings, Product Catalog area.

▶ See Chapter 12 for more information about working with Products.

Quotes, Orders, and Invoices

Microsoft Dynamics CRM includes functionality for working with Quotes, Orders, and Invoices. They are defined as follows:

- **Quote**—A proposed offer for products or services for an existing customer. The Quote can include specific payment terms, a discount, and delivery terms.
- **Order**—An accepted Quote.

- **Invoice**—A billed Order.

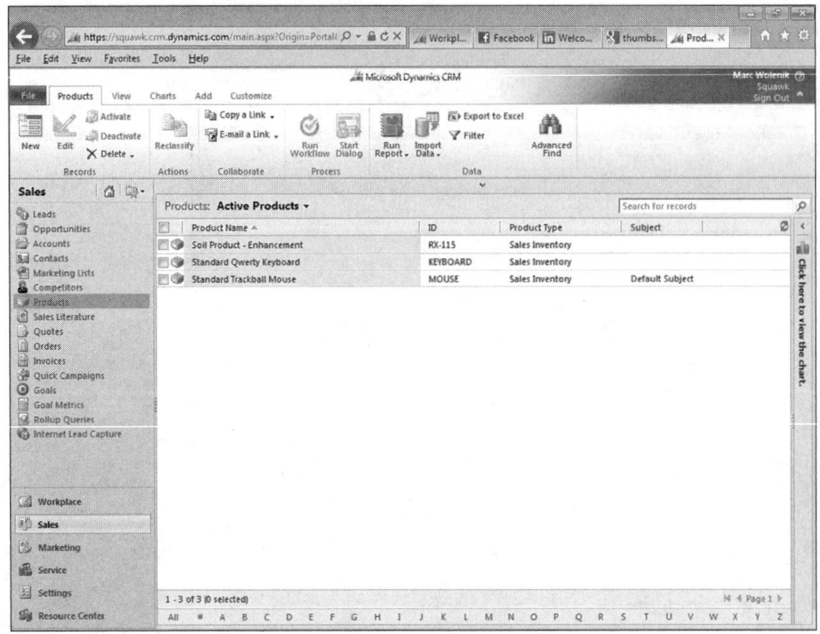

FIGURE 8.20 Product List from the Sales area.

Additional features apply to these entities:

- Multiple pricing lists/models
- Line-item discounting based on volume, customer type, or manual overrides
- Quote-level discounting

NOTE

It is important to understand how Quotes, Orders, and Invoices work with Microsoft Dynamics products, particularly product inventory. Although Microsoft Dynamics CRM has the functionality to create Orders, Quotes, and Invoices, it is not designed to be a stock-control application. If you want to affect inventory levels (quantity on hand, for instance), you must do this either with custom workflows or by integrating an accounting/ERP system. That system should also be used to handle additional calculations such as sales tax and value added tax (VAT).

Quotes

As the name implies, a Quote in Microsoft Dynamics CRM is an offer to sell your products or services for a certain price. When working with a Quote from an associated Opportunity, you can generate the Quote using some, all, or none of the product items on the Opportunity. This provides the flexibility to create Quotes based on a number of criteria, such as mixed product-delivery dates, other optional products (referred to as *write-in products*), and discounts.

Several common scenarios and status arise when working with Quotes and existing Opportunities. A common example is an Opportunity that might be realized within the next three months for $25,000. During this time period, you might prepare a Quote and submit it to the customer for review. The customer might decide to move forward with the Quote and agree to the sale. You would complete the sales process and close the Opportunity as Won. Another scenario might be a 12-month Opportunity with multiple sales activities associated with it—in this example, it could be product sales every 30 days. Instead of creating 12 Opportunities, you could create one Opportunity for the total amount and then create 12 associated Quotes (and Orders and Invoices). This is a little tricky from a forecasting perspective, however, because your realized/earned dollars will be represented on the Invoices, and your estimated revenue will be consistent with a single close date.

Quotes do not need to have an associated Opportunity to them; however, there are some advantages to working with them when there is an Opportunity.

- Quotes can easily get product information from the Opportunity.
- When a Quote is spawned from an Opportunity directly (by selecting Quote from the Opportunity record rather than selecting Quote from the Sales area), the Quote information is autopopulated with the underlying customer information.
- Although it might not apply to your organization, business rules can be enforced if you require Quotes to have an active/open Opportunity.

NOTE

New to this version of Microsoft Dynamics CRM 2011 is the ability to reflect both negative quantity and sales amounts. Previous versions of Microsoft Dynamics CRM did not allow this functionality.

As with Orders and Invoices, you can create a Quote by selecting Quotes from the Sales area and selecting New (see Figure 8.21).

When working with Quotes, it is important to understand their status options:

- Draft
- Active
- Won
- Closed

Figure 8.22 illustrates how a Quote correlates to an existing customer, Products/Price Lists (required), and Opportunities (optional), and also shows the status options.

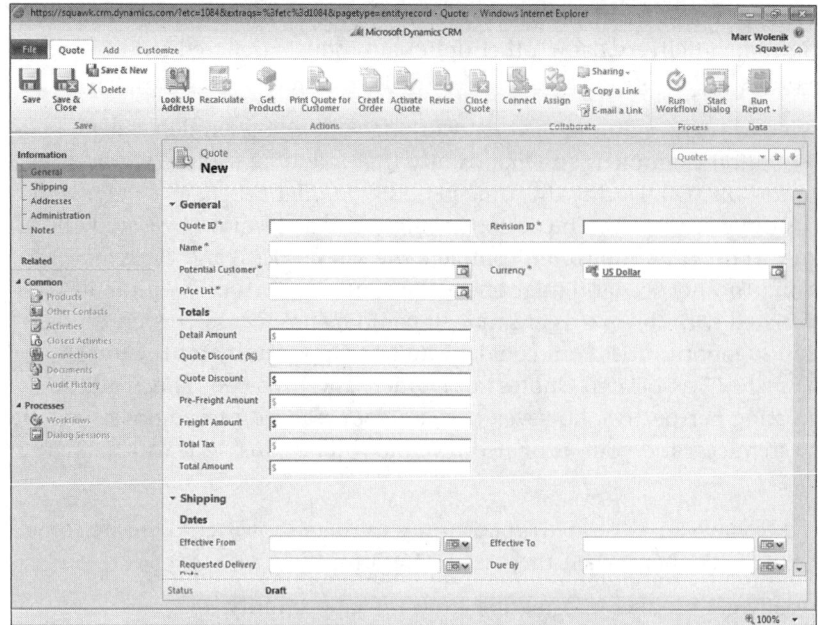

FIGURE 8.21 New Quote option.

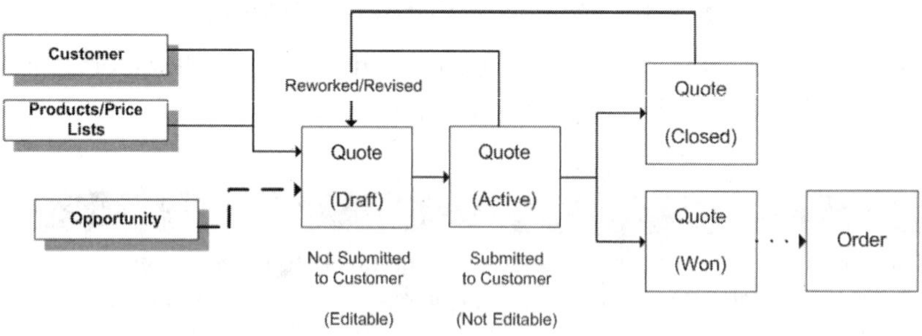

FIGURE 8.22 Quote lifecycle.

A Quote likely will be revised many times, and Microsoft Dynamics CRM has built-in functionality via the Draft and Active status for this.

Draft Status

When a Quote is in Draft status, it has been created but generally not ready to be submitted to customers. This is the only time Quotes can be completely modified with products added or removed, and discounts applied as well as deleted (see Figure 8.23).

General Section After the Quote is created, it automatically sets the Quote ID using the auto-numbering set up by the system administrator. You can change this by configuring Auto-Numbering in the Settings area. The Revision ID is automatically established and set as 0 when first created. If the Quote is revised, it will go from Active to Draft status and the Revision ID will automatically increase. You can modify the name of the Quote, but it is the same as the Opportunity that spawned it and blank if it is not associated with an Opportunity. The potential customer, Currency, and Price List must be selected and are also the same as the Opportunity that spawned it; with the exception of Currency (which defaults to the base Currency), these are blank if there is no associated Opportunity.

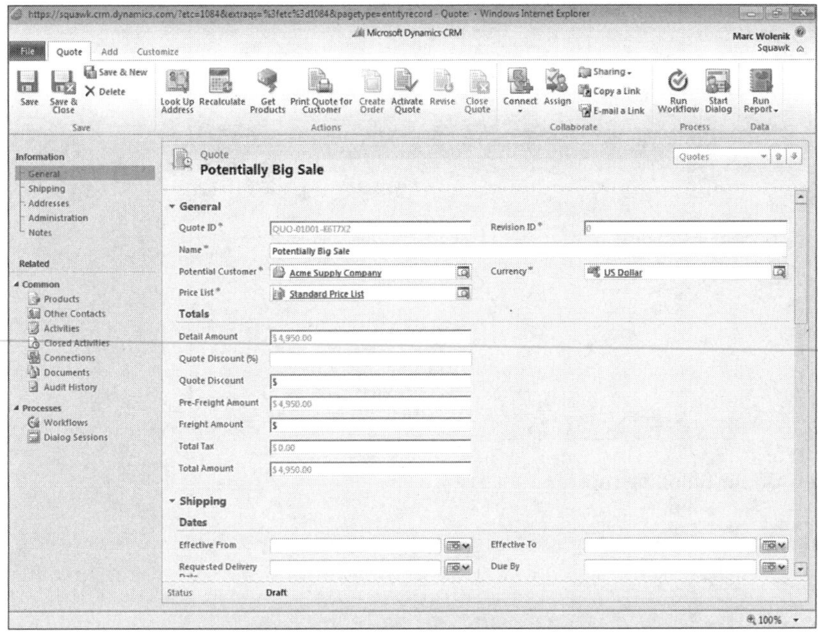

FIGURE 8.23 New Quote in Draft status.

▶ Refer to Chapter 12 for more information about working with the Auto-Numbering option.

Shipping Section The Shipping section has effective dates that you can select to set for how long the Quote is valid for and to set delivery and due dates. Additionally, you can select the shipping method, payment, and freight terms (see Figure 8.24).

Addresses Section The Address tab enables you to easily set where the Quote should be billed and shipped to. By default, this information is blank, regardless of whether the customer has this information on file. You can either manually enter it here or select Look Up Address on the Ribbon menu. If you select Look Up Address, the dialog box shown in Figure 8.25 appears.

From this dialog box, you can select to autopopulate either the Bill To Address or the Ship To Address information with address information from customer records. When you select the lookup option, you can see the addresses that you have on file, listed by Address Name (see Figure 8.26).

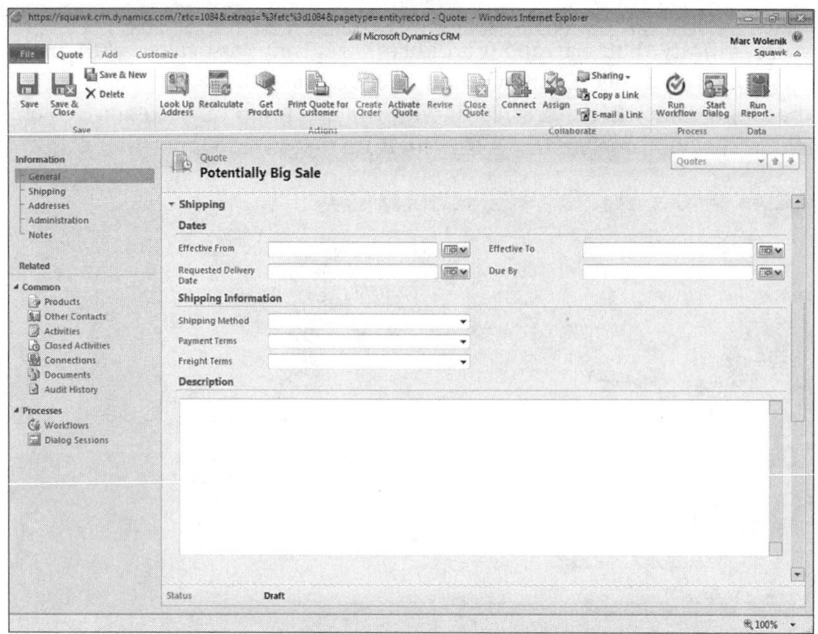

FIGURE 8.24 New Quote Shipping tab.

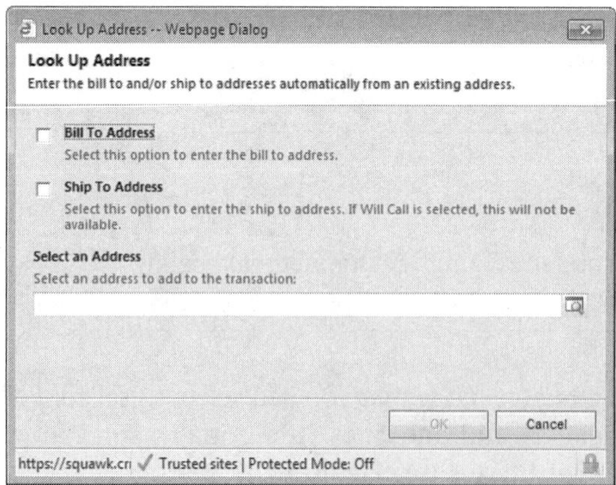

FIGURE 8.25 Look Up Address dialog box.

TIP

This pulls only from the More Addresses section of the selected customer. If you don't have separate address information for the selected customer, you won't have this option.

This example has only one address on file for the customer, but we select it as the address for both the Bill To and Ship To addresses (see Figure 8.27).

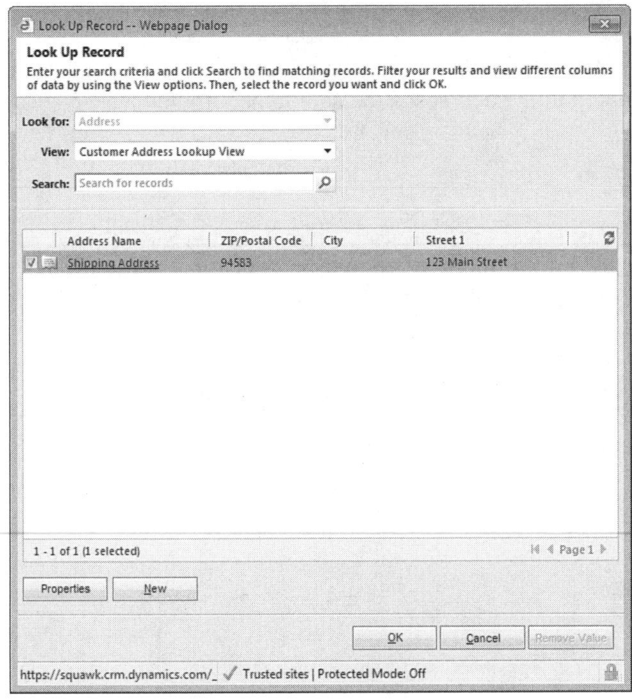

FIGURE 8.26 Look Up Record dialog box, select addresses.

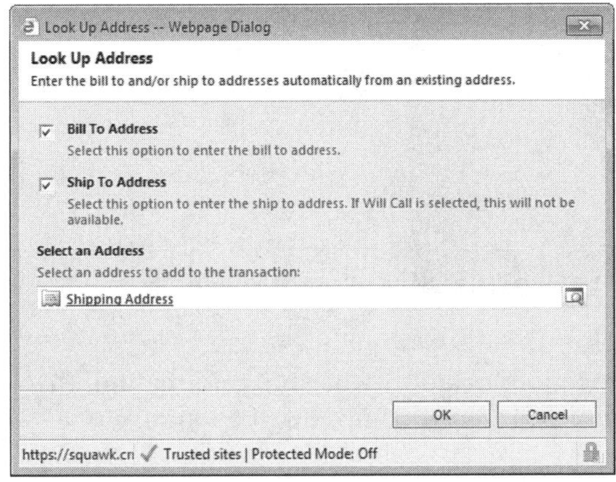

FIGURE 8.27 Look Up Address dialog box selected.

After you select this, click OK. The address information is then populated on the Addresses tab.

TIP

The Look Up Address option overwrites any existing address information entered. If you want to edit or add information related to the addresses, be sure to perform the lookup first and then edit it.

If the Quote will be picked up, you can select Will Call to lock and disable the Ship to Address information (see Figure 8.28). Additionally, if you select Will Call and then select Look Up Address, you cannot select a Ship to Address.

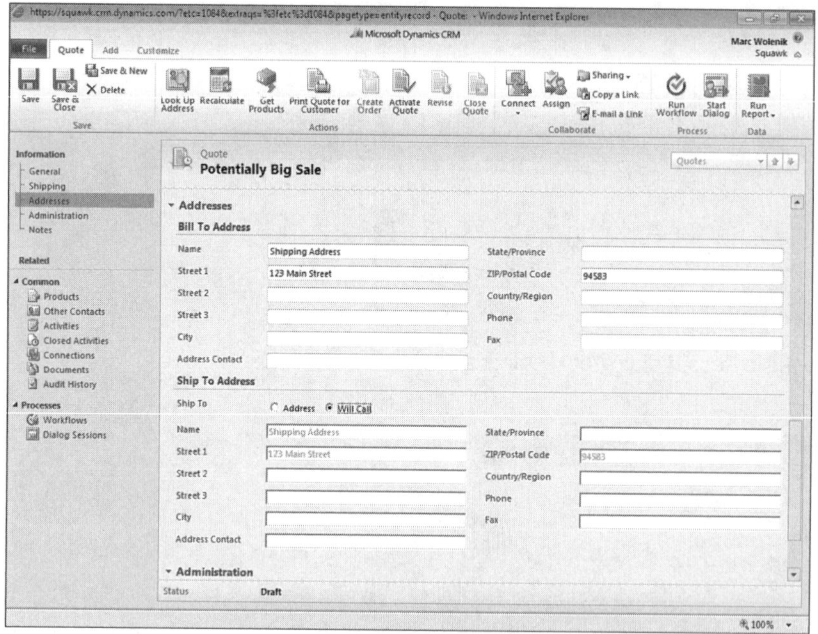

FIGURE 8.28 Completed address information with Ship To selected as Will Call.

Administration Section The Administration section includes ownership information, the status reason, and the underlying Opportunity and Source Campaign, if applicable (see Figure 8.29).

Options in the Draft Status When in Draft status, the Quote has a large amount of flexibility. Options exist to add products (both existing and write-in) and perform a number of actions from the Actions drop-down list. These options include the following:

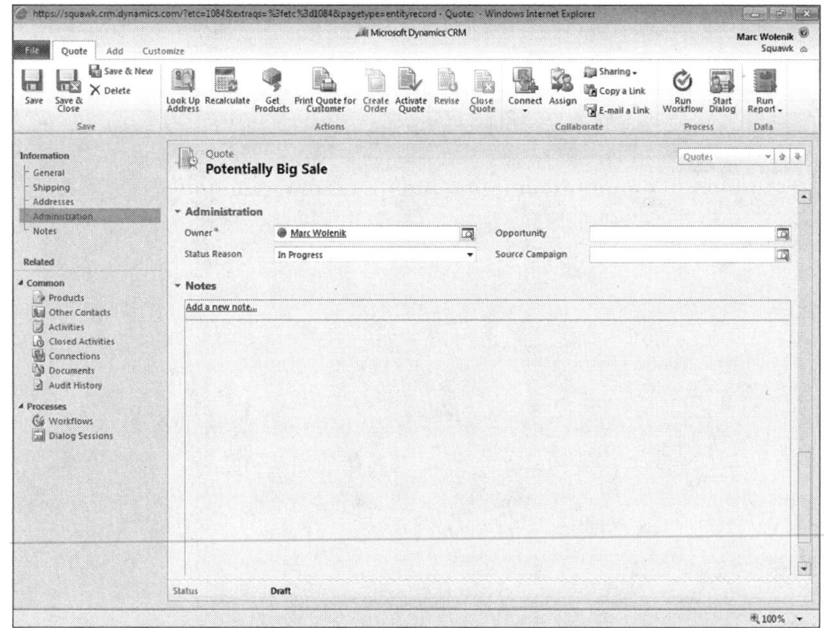

FIGURE 8.29 Administration section.

- Add Existing Products
- Add Write-In Products
- Delete the Quote
- Recalculate
- Look Up Address
- Get Products
- Activate Quote
- Print Quote for Customer
- Run the Quote Report

Add Existing Products You can add products to the Quote in several ways:

- If the Quote is spawned from an Opportunity, the products are automatically listed on the Existing Products tab (see Figure 8.30).

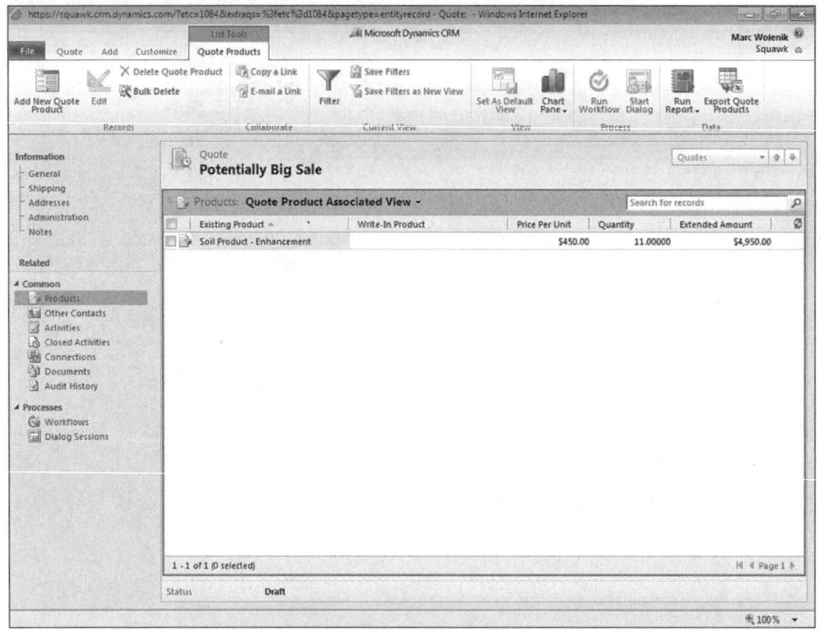

FIGURE 8.30 Products added automatically to a Quote.

- You can add an existing product to the Quote, regardless of whether the product is on the underlying Opportunity, by selecting New Quote Product from the Existing Products tab (see Figure 8.31).
- Select Get Products from the Ribbon menu. This option automatically adds the product list from any existing Opportunity (see Figure 8.32).

Add Write-In Products If your product catalog doesn't have the product, you can manually create it on-the-fly by selecting Write-In Products and then New Quote Product. The Quote Product screen opens and allows you the option to select Write In (refer to Figure 8.31).

From this screen, you can add virtually anything, completing the necessary fields. The Quote reflects the new total, including this information. (You might need to select Recalculate on the Ribbon menu to adjust the totals after you modify the products.)

Delete the Quote The Quote can be deleted only when in Draft status. To delete a Quote, select Delete from the Actions drop-down list or from the top menu bar.

Recalculate As explained previously, the Recalculate option enables you to update the totals and other amounts on the Quote when you modify the Quote. This is helpful because without this functionality you would have to save, close, and reopen the Quote to have it recalculate.

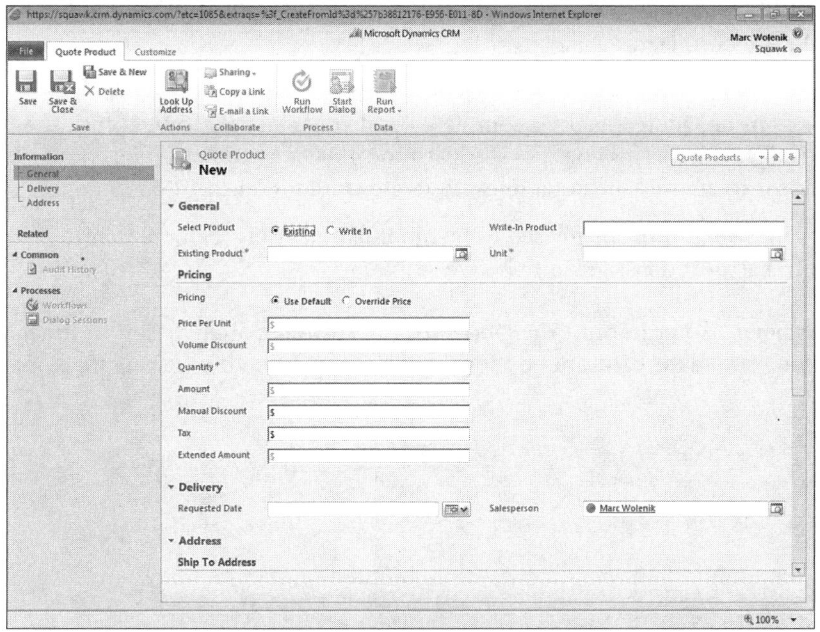

FIGURE 8.31 Products added by selecting New Quote Product.

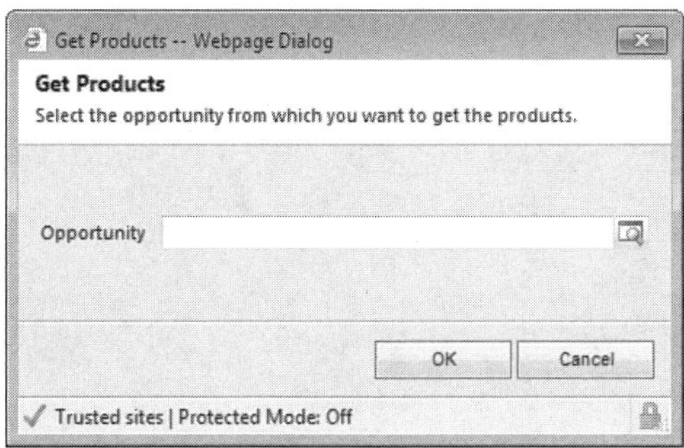

FIGURE 8.32 Products added by selecting Get Products.

Look Up Address The Look Up Address functionality was explained previously when working with the Addresses tab of the Quote.

Get Products Get Products enables you to add products from existing Opportunities. Note that the Get Products option enables you to get the products on any existing Opportunity, as well as the existing Opportunity that might have spawned the Quote.

Therefore, it is possible to duplicate the Product List on the Existing Products if you have already populated it (refer to Figure 8.32).

Activate Quote When the Quote has been completed and you are ready to send it to the customer, you must activate it. This changes the status of the Quote to Active and prevents further modifications. To activate a Quote, select Activate Quote from the Ribbon menu.

When the Quote is Active, it must be revised to be modified. Revising a Quote is explained further in the upcoming section "Active Status."

Print Quote for Customer You can print the Quote for the customer at any point in time by selecting the Print Quote for Customer option from the top menu bar (see Figure 8.33).

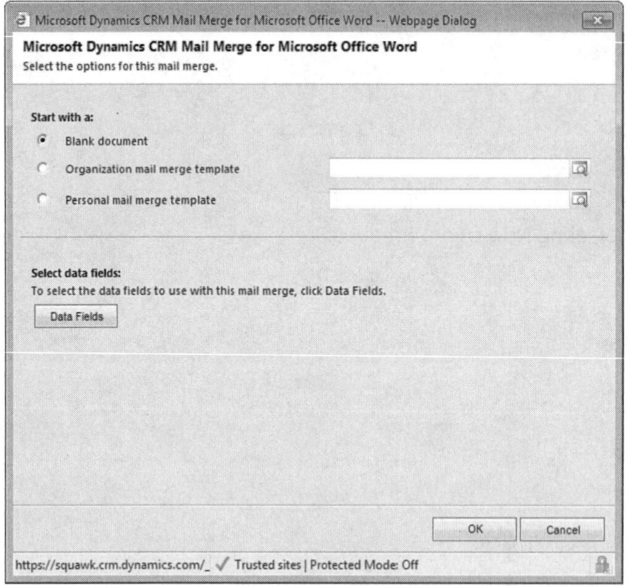

FIGURE 8.33 Print Quote for Customer.

When the Print Quote option is selected, a mail merge is started that enables you to merge data fields from the Quote into a Microsoft Word document.

The mail merge enables you to select a template language and merge to either a blank document or an organizational or personal template, as well as select the data fields. By default, Microsoft Dynamics CRM comes with an organizational template for Quotes called Quote for Customer.

TIP

If you select the Print Quote option, be sure you have customized it for your organizational layout requirements by modifying the Quote template report.

Active Status When a Quote moves to Active status, it has been or will be shortly submitted to the customer and therefore can't be edited (see Figure 8.34).

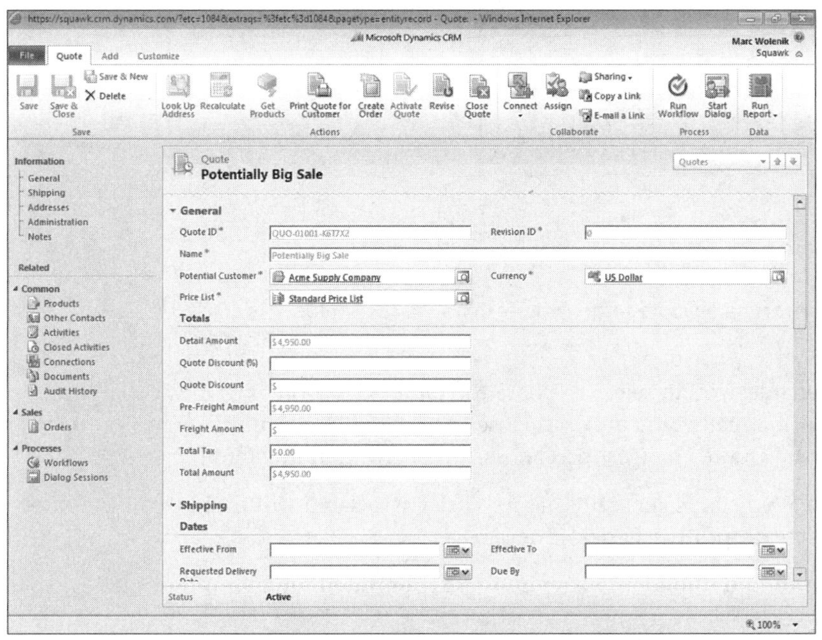

FIGURE 8.34 An Active Quote—notice that it is disabled and cannot be edited.

If modifications are necessary, you can revise the Quote by selecting Revise from the Ribbon menu. Revising a Quote closes the existing Quote, opens a new Quote with a status of Draft, and assigns a new Revision ID. The Quote ID remains the same, however.

Revise, Close, or Convert the Quote to an Order At this point, the Quote can be revised, closed, or Won—converted to an Order. To convert a Quote to an Order, either select Create Order from the top menu or select Create Order from the Ribbon menu.

Selecting Create Order opens the Create Order dialog form (see Figure 8.35).

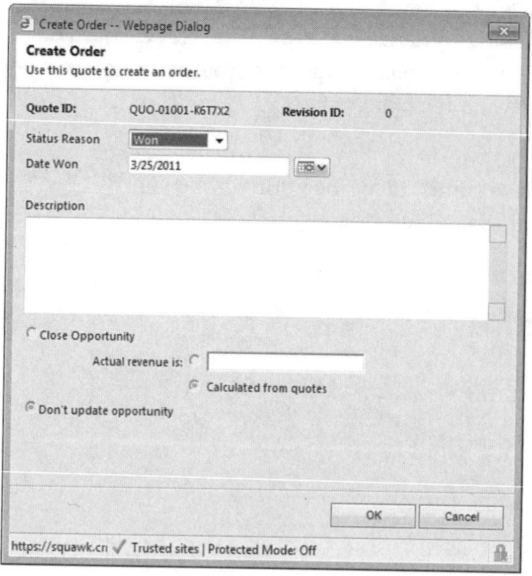

FIGURE 8.35 Converting a Quote to an Order—updating the status.

The dialog form enables you to select the date the Order was Won and to calculate the revenue or enter it manually; you also can close the related Opportunity. After you select OK, the status of the Quote changes to Won and the corresponding Order opens.

A Quote that is in Won status generally has an Order associated with it, but you can select Create Order and create another Order, if necessary.

Quotes that are in Closed status can be revised and reactivated for approval or made active.

Orders

An Order is created when a customer is ready to make a purchase. The customer either has accepted the Quote or is ready to make a purchase regardless of a Quote.

TIP

Keep in mind that a Quote is not required to create an Order. While an Order can be spawned from a Quote, Orders are separate entities and many have no Quote correlation. (However this is something that you could theoretically manage with a plug-in.)

Figure 8.36 illustrates how an Order correlates to an existing customer (required), Products/Price Lists (required), Opportunities (optional), and Quotes (optional).

When working with Orders, it is important to understand their different status options:

- Active
- Fulfilled
- Cancelled

An Active Order can be deleted, canceled, and edited (see Figure 8.37). Editing an Active Order includes updating products associated with the Order, as well as discount, shipping, and address information. The section options for Shipping, Addresses, Administration, and notes are similar to those defined in Quotes.

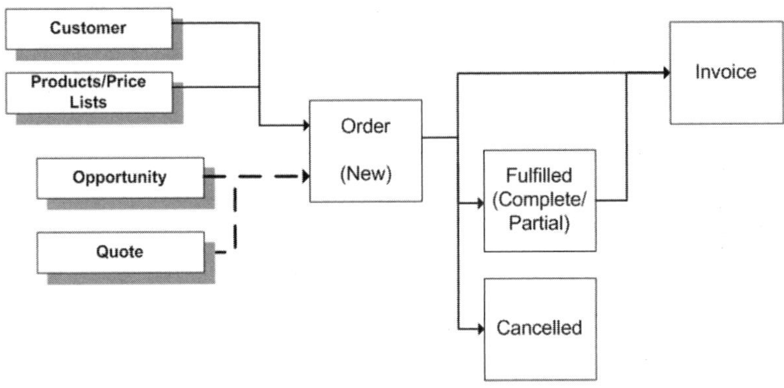

FIGURE 8.36 Order lifecycle.

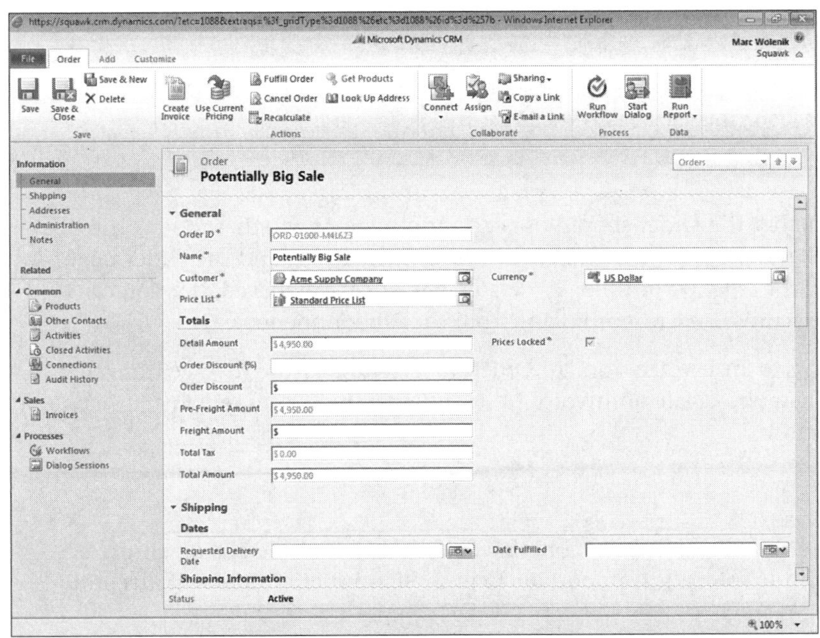

FIGURE 8.37 Active Order.

An Order that has been Fulfilled has had its products shipped or delivered. To fulfill an Order, select Fulfill Order from the Ribbon menu. The Fulfill Order dialog box then opens (see Figure 8.38).

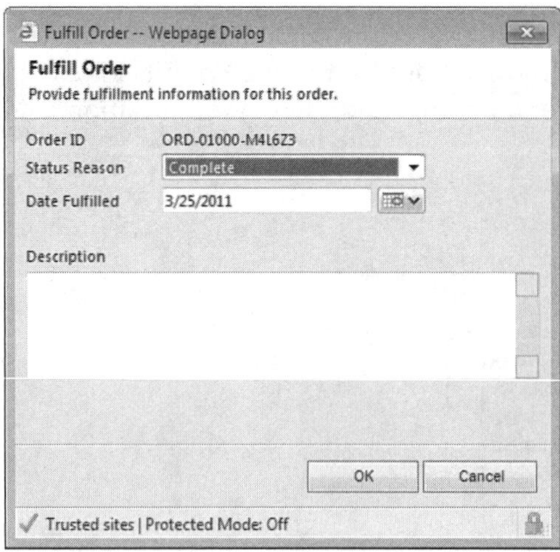

FIGURE 8.38 Fulfill Order dialog box.

This dialog box enables you to indicate that the order has been shipped.

CAUTION

When selecting how to fulfill the Order, remember that you cannot edit the Order after you select any option. This includes selecting Partial Fulfillment.

You can select whether the Order should use current pricing or whether to lock the pricing. This is a helpful option when there are price fluctuations and the Order might remain unfulfilled for a period of time. By default, the prices are locked, but you can change that by selecting Use Current Pricing from the Ribbon menu.

Finally, you can create an Invoice from an Order by selecting Create Invoice from the Ribbon menu. When you create an Invoice from an Order, the Order remains in Active status until it is fulfilled.

Invoices

When the terms of the sale have been completed, the sale is recorded using an Invoice. When working with Invoices, it is important to understand their different status options:

- Active
- Closed

Figure 8.39 illustrates how an Invoice correlates to an existing customer (required), Products/Price Lists (required), Opportunities (optional), and Quotes (optional).

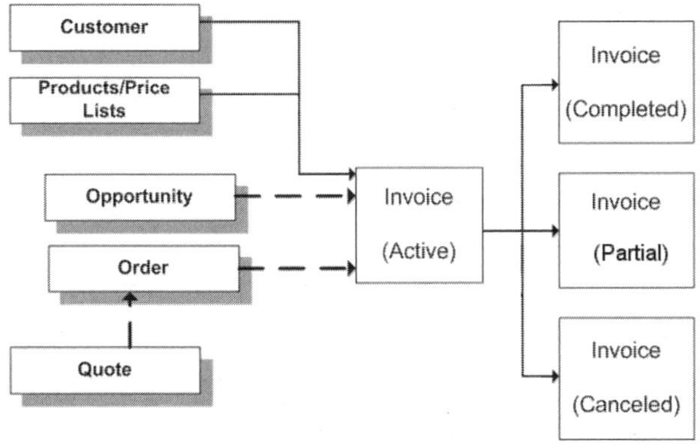

FIGURE 8.39 Invoice lifecycle.

An Invoice is very similar to an Order, in that you can perform the following actions:

- You can add new products from your product catalog.
- You cannot add new write-in products.
- You can perform various functions on the Invoice, including selecting whether to use current or locked pricing and recalculate accordingly.

Figure 8.40 illustrates an active Invoice. The tab options for Shipping, Addresses, Administration, and Notes are similar to those defined in Quotes.

As with Orders fulfillment, if you mark an Invoice as Paid, you have the option to select Partial or Complete (see Figure 8.41).

TIP

Regardless of your selection, after you mark an invoice as Paid or Partial, you cannot edit it.

NOTE

When working with a back-end accounting or ERP system, you might often create and manage Orders in Microsoft Dynamics CRM and have them posted (when approved) in the back-end/ERP system. Doing so can enforce more complex business rules (such as VAT calculations), and the back-end/ERP posting process should be responsible for creating an Invoice record in Microsoft Dynamics CRM so that sales staff can see the process status without having to navigate to its ERP system.

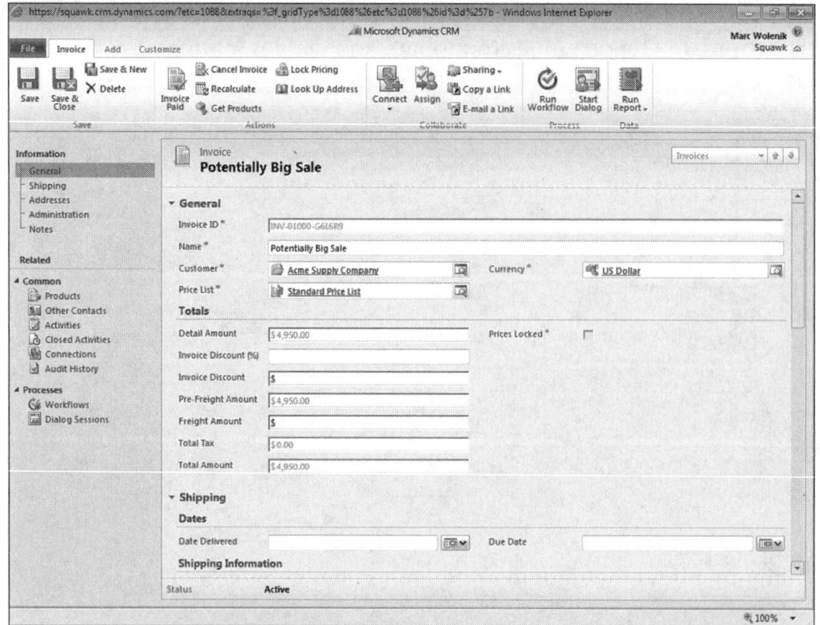

FIGURE 8.40 Active Invoice.

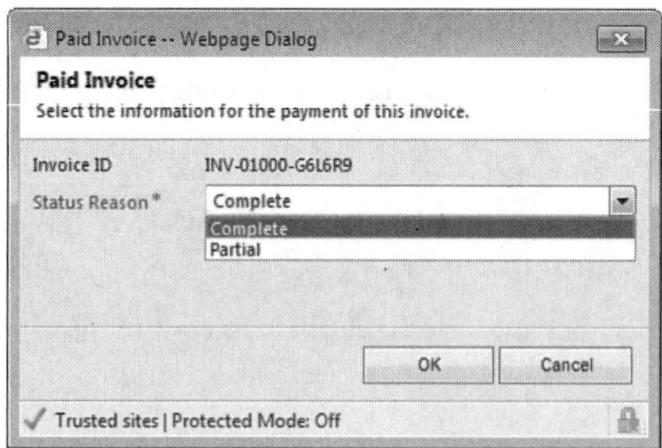

FIGURE 8.41 Marking an Invoice as Paid.

▶ Extending functionally of the Sales Quotes, Orders, and Invoices to specific back-end/ERP systems exceeds the scope of this book. You can learn more about extending functionality in our previous book by Sam's Publishing, *Microsoft Dynamics CRM 4.0 Integration Unleashed*.

Goals, Goal Metrics, and Rollup Queries

Goals allow for the organization to capture and track their achievements. The nicest aspect to goals is that they are not singularly revenue based (that is, the total sum of something sold for a given period), but rather can be aggregate based (such as the total number of cases closed). As such, they provide a robust format for capture performance metrics.

To create Goals, you first need to create Goal Metrics and Rollup Queries. Goal Metrics are used to determine which metric you want to use to measure your goal (count or amount), and rollup queries are the specific field you want to pull the data from.

By default, you will find at least three Goal Metrics included with the system. These are shown in Figure 8.42 and consist of the following:

- Number of cases
- Number of product units
- Revenue

Define Goal Metrics

To create a new Goal, select New and then follow the steps on the Goal Metric interface (see Figure 8.43).

1. Define the metric by entering the name and the metric type. The metric type can be either count or amount. For our example we're going to track the amount of new leads created.

   If you select Track Stretch Target, you have the option to use this metric to have a stretch target field.

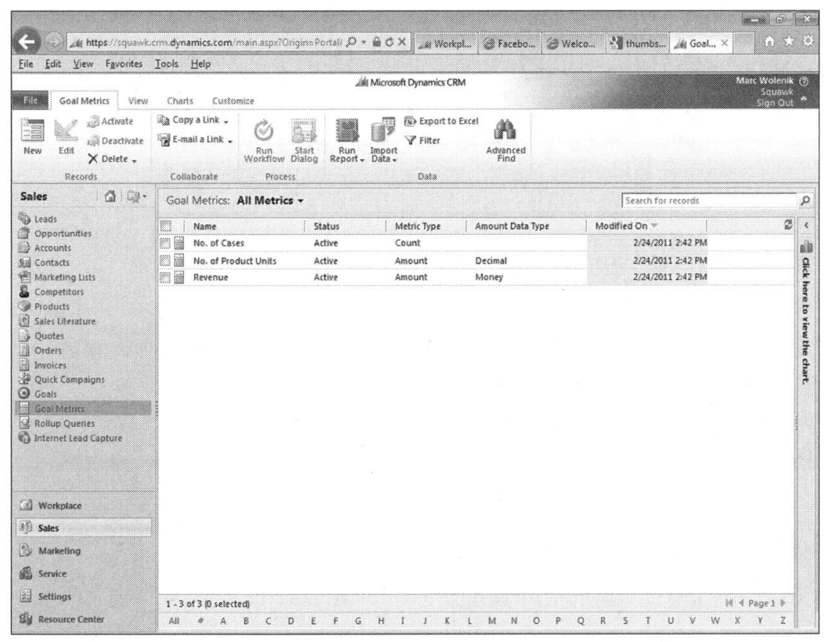

FIGURE 8.42 Default Goal Metrics.

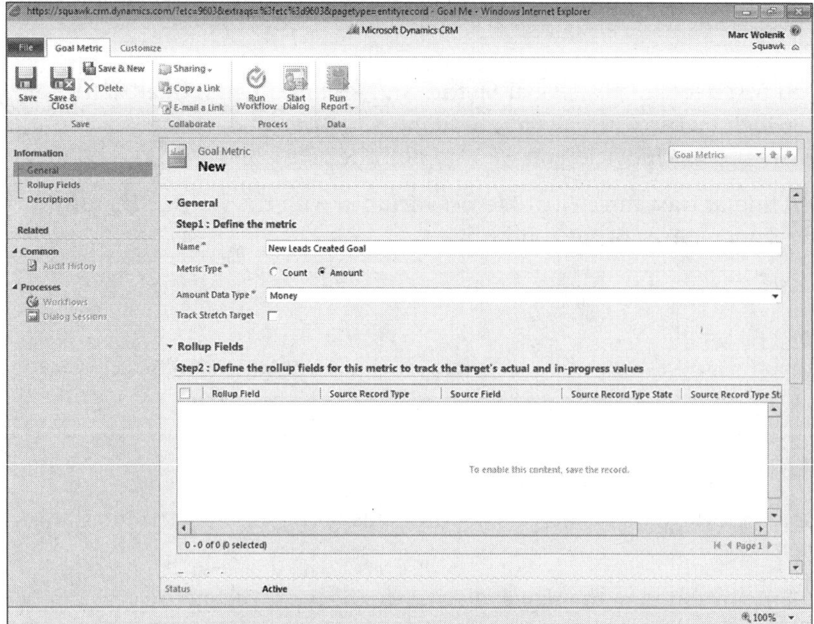

FIGURE 8.43 New Goal Metric.

2. Next, you need to create a new Rollup field that tracks the metric data by selecting Add New Rollup Field from the Ribbon menu.

TIP

You will not be able to create a new rollup metric or add a new one until the form is saved and you are presented with the List Tools Ribbon menu, as shown in Figure 8.44.

3. Select the field to rollup as Actual (money).
4. Complete the source data fields
5. Complete the date field that comprises the rollup. Figure 8.45 illustrates our example for the rollup field created.
6. Click Save to complete the action related to creating the Goal Metric and the Rollup Query associated to it.

Create New Goal

We are now ready to create a Goal by completing the following steps:

1. Navigate to Goals and select New from the ribbon menu. Figure 8.46 shows the new Goal interface.

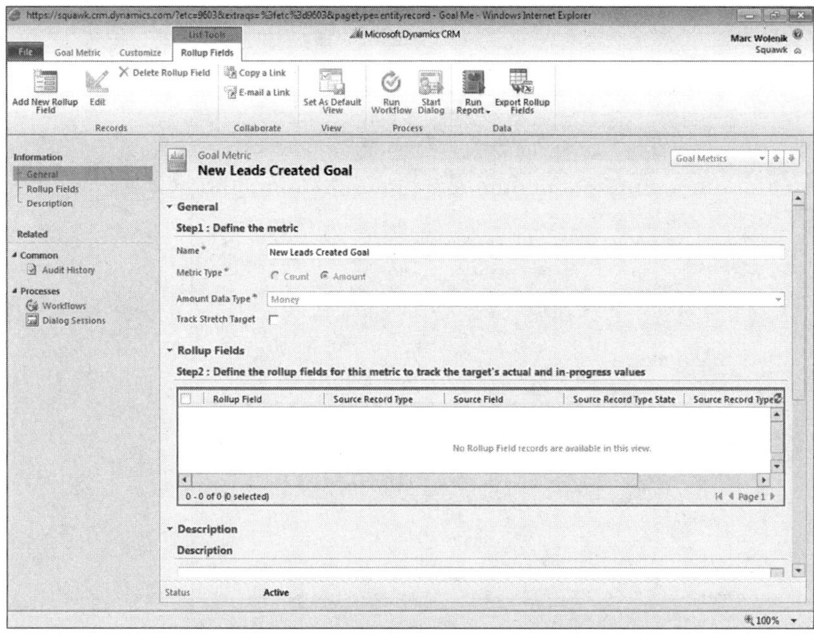

FIGURE 8.44 List Tools option for Rollup Field on a Goal Metric.

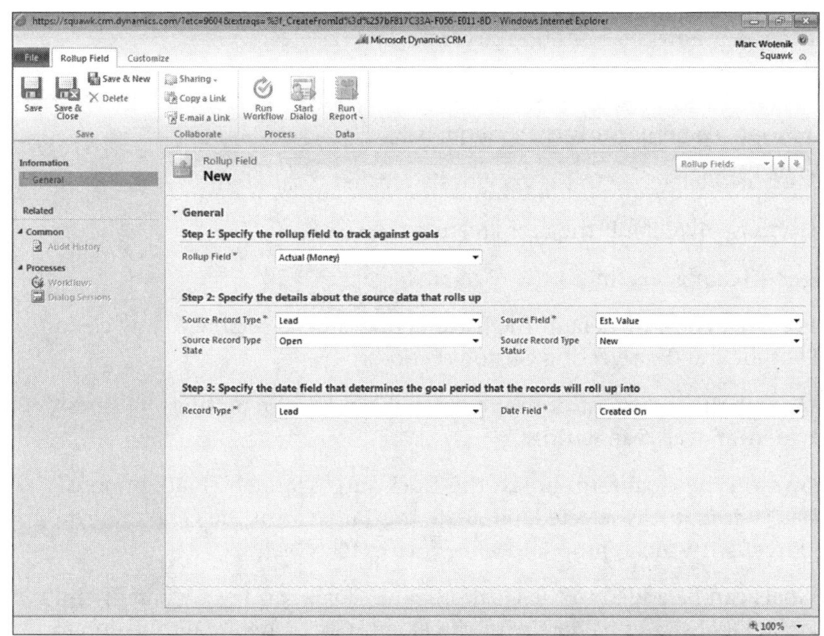

FIGURE 8.45 Rollup field.

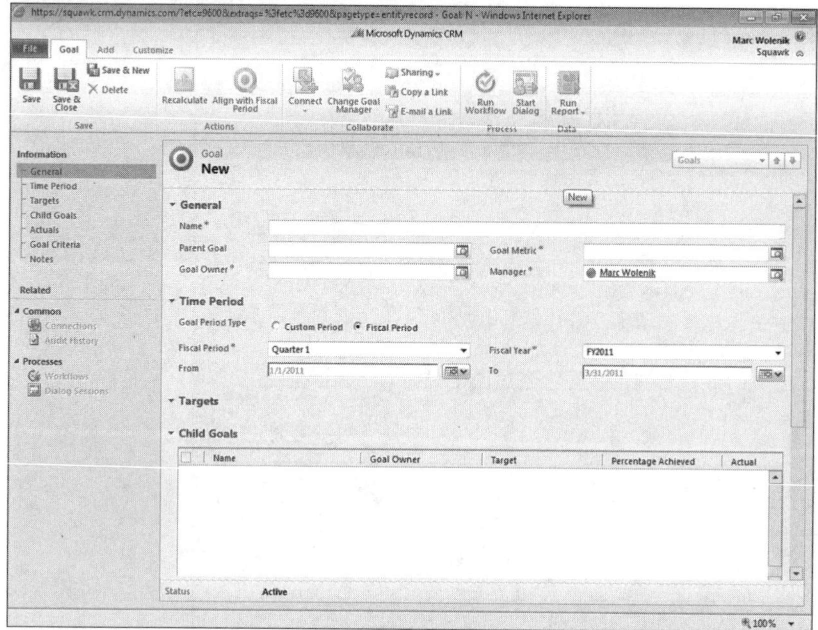

FIGURE 8.46 Goal.

2. Next, complete the following fields on the form:

   - **Name**—The name of the Goal.
   - **Parent Goal**—Whether this is a Child Goal.
   - **Goal Metric**—Reference to the previously created Goal Metric.
   - **Goal Owner**—By default the user creating the Goal.
   - **Manager**—Team goals roll to the users manager.
   - **Goal Period Type**—By default the fiscal period, but selectable to any custom period you define (by selecting Custom Period).
   - **Fiscal Year**—Either current or future years. (This is set in Settings, Business Management, Fiscal Year Settings.)

Targets are not shown on the Goal form unless the Track Target Stretch Goal option is selected on the Goal Metric. If it is selected, populate the Target with the Goal's target value and Stretch Target with the appropriate value for Stretch Goal.

Additional Child Goals can be added to the Goal. Because Goals can have a parent-child relationship, the Child Goal shares its data with the Parent Goal when it is rolled up to the parent level.

CAUTION

The Parent and Child Goals must have the same goal metric and time period.

Results of the Goals are shown in the Actuals section on the form.

TIP

Actuals data is run once every 24 hours (as found in system settings, Goals tab); however. you can select the Recalculate button at the top of the form to refresh the data.

Set Goal Criteria

Finally, the Goal Criteria lets you set criteria that is used for rolling up actuals data against the goal.

- **Roll up only from child goals**—Sets the goal as a summary of only child goals, or as a summation of both child and parent goals.
- **Record set for rollup**—This limits the rollup to include only the owner or all records and has an effect on the underlying data depending on desired results.
- **Rollup Query**—This is Actual, In-Progress, or a Custom Rollup Field used to select the query used for rollup.

When working with Parent and/or Child goals, the typical scenario is a manager that has multiple sales people that comprise their total/overall goal and typically the sales people goals are child goals that are summarized into the manager's goal.

Summary

This chapter illustrated how to work with the Sales area of Microsoft Dynamics CRM. The most important aspects to remember in this chapter are that Leads are separated from your regular customer base and that you can convert them to Accounts, Contacts, or Opportunities using the included sales force automation (SFA).

Additionally, this chapter explained how to manage and use Opportunities, and we thoroughly examined Quotes, Orders, and Invoice functionality, as well as reviewing their integration options with regard to back-end accounting systems. Because Microsoft Dynamics CRM is not designed to be a stock control, accounting, or invoicing system, we recommend considering integrating with other applications (ERP/accounting systems) for that requirement.

Finally we reviewed the features provided with Goals and Goal management. It is important to remember that a number of sales charts available by default on the dashboards use the goal data for performance indicators.

CHAPTER 9

Working with Marketing

IN THIS CHAPTER

- Marketing Lists
- Campaigns
- Sales Literature
- Quick Campaigns

A powerful feature that sets Microsoft Dynamics CRM ahead of its competitors is its capability to build, manage, track, and report on the effectiveness of marketing efforts. When thinking about marketing, consider how you currently market. Do you want to send the same sales literature to potential customers as you would to existing customers? Probably not. Therefore, when you're considering creating a marketing campaign, consider your audience.

NOTE

Microsoft Dynamics CRM refers to any kind of targeted marketing effort as a Campaign, with differences between a Quick Campaign and Campaign, which we explain later in this chapter.

Typically, marketing efforts designed to appeal to existing customers include incentives to buy more, reestablish buying after a lapse, or appeal to customers to purchase from you in other ways. Marketing efforts designed around potential customers are usually very different in that generally you want to appeal to them to start purchasing from you.

Thousands of books and companies specialize in how to market to potential and existing customers. We're by no means attempting to explain how best to market for your organization. Instead, we're explaining in depth the marketing features Microsoft Dynamics CRM provides so that when you want to market your organization, products, or personnel, you will have a solid understanding of how Microsoft Dynamics CRM can do so.

This chapter reviews the items specific to marketing found on the Marketing tab, such as Marketing Lists, Campaigns, sales literature, and Quick Campaigns, as well as other areas within the application that touch on marketing.

▶ For information about the other aspects of the Marketing tabs, such as Leads or Products, refer to Chapter 8, "Working with Sales." For information about Accounts and Contacts, refer to Chapter 6, "Working with Customers."

Marketing Lists

Marketing Lists are great tools for managing marketing efforts. You can use Marketing Lists to create a list of members that will receive the marketing material. The members can be made up of either existing customers (Accounts or Contacts) or potential customers (Leads). There is no way to prepare a single Marketing List for both existing and potential customers, so if you need to do so, consider creating two or more Marketing Lists.

After they're created, you can directly market to Marketing Lists via a Mail Merge, a Quick Campaign, or a Campaign.

TIP

After you have created a Marketing List, you cannot change its base entity assignment (for example, from an Account Marketing List to a Leads Marketing List). You must create a new Marketing List if you need to use a different base entity.

To create a new Marketing List, navigate to the Marketing area, and then select Marketing Lists, New.

As shown in Figure 9.1, we've created a new Marketing List by completing the Name and Member Type fields of the Marketing List and saving the list. Note that the only member types allowed are Account, Contact, and Lead.

Other attributes on the Marketing List include the Source, which can be any free form value, the Currency and Cost, and whether new members can be added to the list by selecting whether the list is Locked. Additionally, notice in the lower-left corner the Status of the Marketing List. By default, new Marketing Lists are active, but you can easily deactivate them when necessary by selecting Deactivate from the More Actions drop-down menu.

TIP

Be sure not to lock the Marketing List by selecting the Locked radio option (as shown in Figure 9.1) before you've added the members to it. You will be unable to perform any additions or subtractions to the membership if it is locked. (Of course, you can always unlock a Marketing List if you need to by opening the Marketing List and changing the Locked option.)

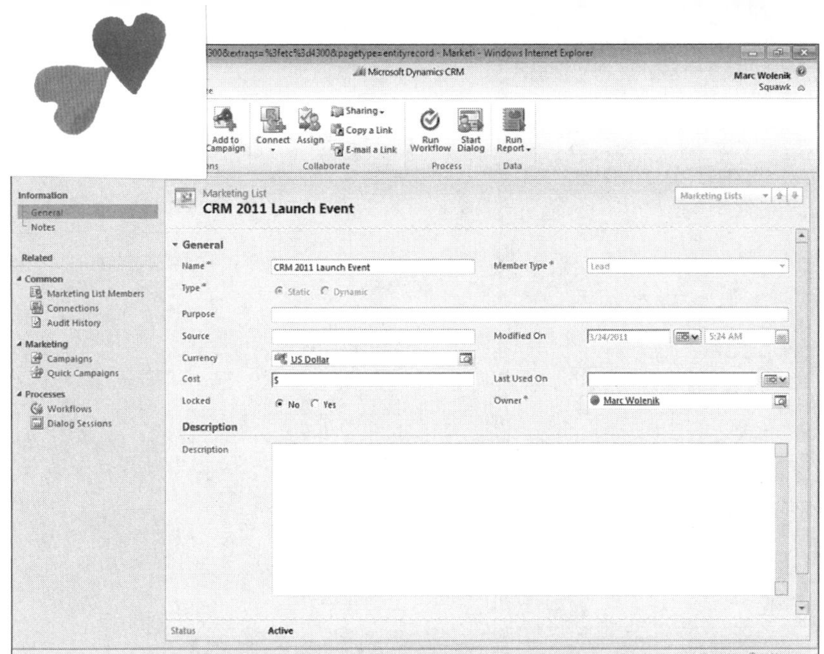

FIGURE 9.1 New Marketing List for Leads.

A new feature to Microsoft Dynamics CRM 2011 is the ability to have dynamic Marketing Lists. This option is available by selecting the type—either static or dynamic. By default the option is set to Static, which means that after the list is created, the members are not updated. If Dynamic is selected, the Marketing List members will be updated whenever the list is used.

NOTE

Dynamic lists can't be converted to static lists, but they can be *copied* to static lists. This option is on the Ribbon menu of any dynamic list.

To add members to the Marketing List, select Marketing List Members from the near navigation, and select Manage Members from the top quick-view menu (see Figure 9.2). As with many of the forms in Microsoft Dynamics CRM, the Marketing List must first be saved before members can be added.

When adding members, you have four different options:

- Use Lookup to Add Members
- Use Advanced Find to Add Members
- Use Advanced Find to Remove Members
- Use Advanced Find to Evaluate Members

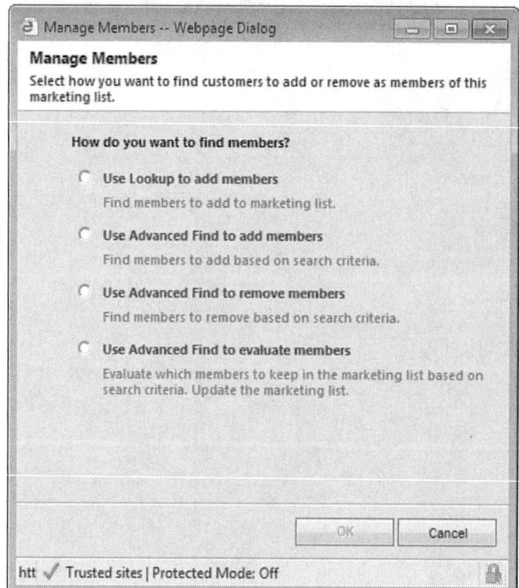

FIGURE 9.2 Manage Members display.

These options are interchangeable, and you can use them at any time if the list has not been locked. This is helpful if you have specific criteria to query on because you can add, remove, or evaluate members before or after they've been added to the Marketing List to ensure that you are marketing to the correct members.

NOTE

Members of Marketing Lists cannot be added more than once. This is a nice feature because sometimes you need to use the previous options more than once. For example, you might use Advanced Find to find all members located in a certain geographic area, and then use Lookup to add more members that might or might not be in the geographic area you previously selected. If the new members are already on the Marketing List, they will appear only once, ensuring that they don't receive duplicate marketing material.

Use Lookup to Add Members

Using Lookup to add members displays the Look Up Records dialog box for the base entity of the Marketing List (in this case, Leads) and enables you to search and add quickly and easily by selecting active records and adding them to the right-pane navigation (see Figure 9.3).

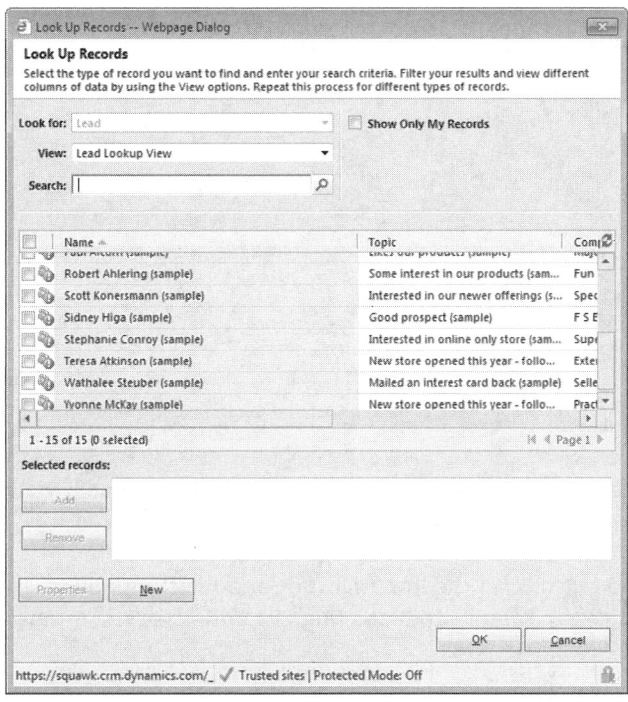

FIGURE 9.3 Look Up Records dialog box.

Use Advanced Find to Add Members

Using Advanced Find enables you to add complex (or previously saved) criteria to ensure that you find only the specific members to whom you want to market.

In the following example, we've created a query using Advanced Find to add only qualified Leads that have been created in the last two months (see Figure 9.4). It is important to note that Advanced Find will be blank until you create your query.

You can easily adjust this query to include Contacts that have not placed an order with you in x number of months, have x number of sales with you over the last x number of months, or any similar criteria using the Advanced Find features.

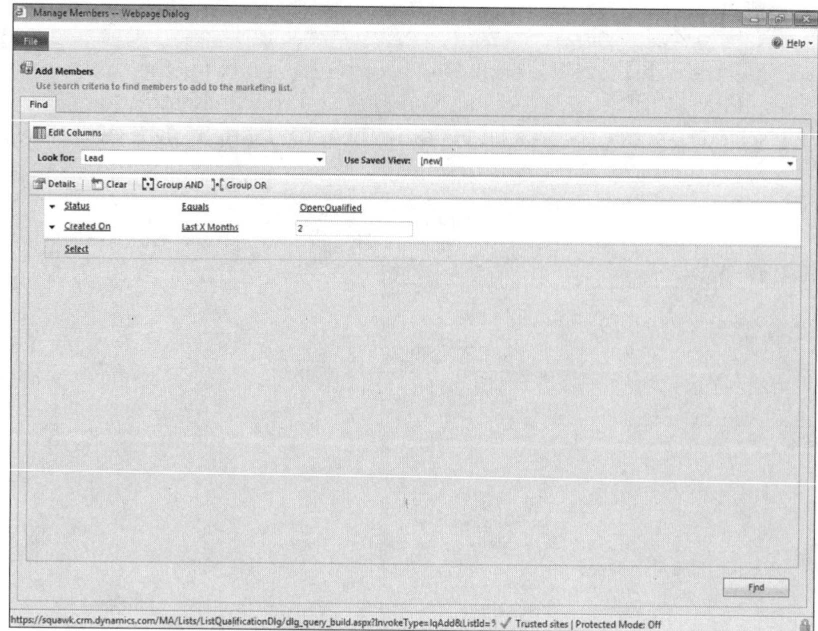

FIGURE 9.4 Advanced Find dialog box.

After you've prepared your query, select the Find button to view members that match your query logic. You have the option to select individual members from the results, or to simply add all members returned by the search to the Marketing List by making the appropriate selection from the radio buttons on the lower-left side and selecting Add to Marketing List (see Figure 9.5—Notice the Remove to Marketing List options at the lower-left side of the form).

Use Advanced Find to Remove Members

Similar to using Advanced Find to add members, you can use the Advanced Find to remove members. This method enables you to add complex query logic via Advanced Find and remove any members that match your entered criteria.

Use Advanced Find to Evaluate Members

Also similar to using Advanced Find to add members (as explained previously), using Advanced Find to evaluate members enables you to use the existing membership list to evaluate with any additional logic whether to keep existing members after you've applied the new logic.

When the Marketing List has the desired members in it, you can lock it to prevent any further modifications to the membership.

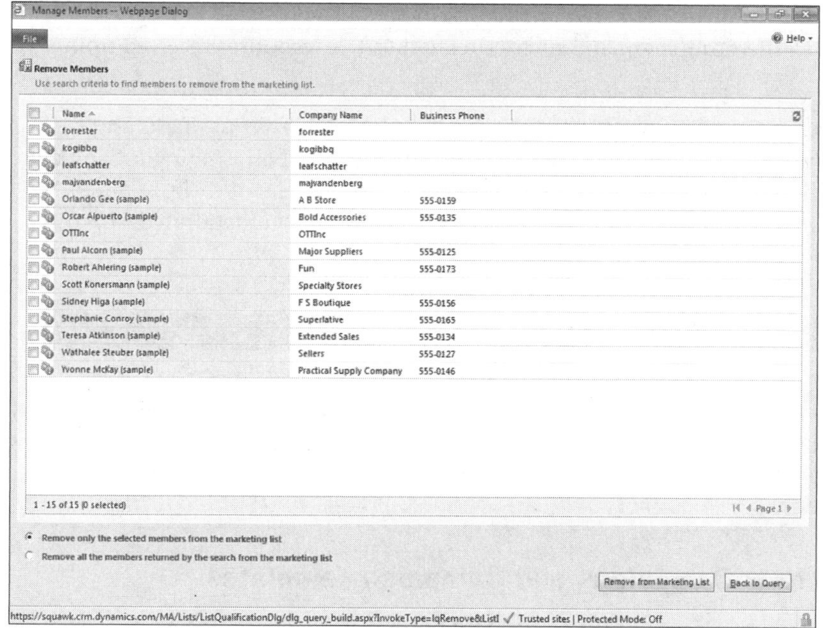

FIGURE 9.5 Advanced Find dialog box..

Other Marketing List Features

After you have created Marketing Lists, you can perform several functions with them. You can use them interchangeably on multiple Campaigns or Quick Campaigns. You can merge them (provided the base entity of each is the same—for example, both lists are Accounts, Contacts, or Leads) by going to the More Actions drop-down menu and selecting Copy To. You can easily see where and which Campaigns or Quick Campaigns have been used by opening any Marketing List and selecting Campaign or Quick Campaign from the near navigation.

Campaigns

Campaigns are structured events that enable you to create and manage targeted marketing efforts. Campaigns differ from Quick Campaigns in that Campaigns can work with multiple marketing lists (Quick Campaigns can only work with single marketing lists), can have complex activity distribution (Quick Campaigns can only have a single activity type), and can have complex planning and management information. However, both Campaigns and Quick Campaigns can receive campaign responses. The actual marketing effort can be virtually anything—a new product announcement, company exposure at a popular event, or even an effort to convince previous customers to buy products again.

Campaigns allow for the structured creation of Tasks related to planning the Campaign, Activities specific to the Campaign, and metrics related to the responses received from a Campaign.

In this section, we create a Campaign example that involves some simple Tasks and Activities to illustrate how a Campaign might work. Obviously, when creating a Campaign for your organization, you want to consider your specific needs related to Tasks and Activities, but using the examples provided can give you a solid foundation for working with Campaigns.

TIP

Campaigns in Microsoft Dynamics CRM are designed to define, create, task, and track marketing efforts from beginning to end. They can have multiple Tasks and Activities associated with them, and they allow for a large amount of structure. Consider using a Quick Campaign (explained later) if your organization won't benefit from the structure Campaigns provide.

Working with New Campaigns and Campaign Templates

When working with new Campaigns, you have two options: a new Campaign or a new Campaign template. A Campaign template is used when you anticipate needing to use the Campaign and its related Tasks and Activities again.

When working with Campaigns and Campaign templates, you can easily manage which one to work with by viewing the Template Status on the quickview (see Figure 9.6).

Campaign templates differ from Campaigns in that they must be converted to Campaigns (from the Ribbon menu) to be used to record Campaign responses against.

You can copy the Campaign templates as a Campaign or as a template from the Ribbon menu when opened. The Campaign template generally won't include any scheduling data because it a reusable template, and that information is generally populated only when an actual Campaign is planned.

To create a new Campaign, follow these steps:

1. Navigate to Campaigns in the Marketing area and select New. For this example, you create a Campaign without using a template and start on the General section. As with most entities in CRM, the top menu and the near navigation are disabled until you save the Campaign, at which time you can work with these objects, as shown in Figure 9.7.
2. Enter a descriptive name of the Campaign, and select the status reason for the Campaign. Because you're creating a new Campaign, leave it at the default of Proposed. You can enter a campaign code or have the system assign an automatic campaign code to your Campaign by leaving it blank; however, after the Campaign has been saved, you cannot edit this field. Selecting a campaign type tells others the type of Campaign that it is. By default, Currency is the system base currency, and the Expected Response defaults to 100 responses.

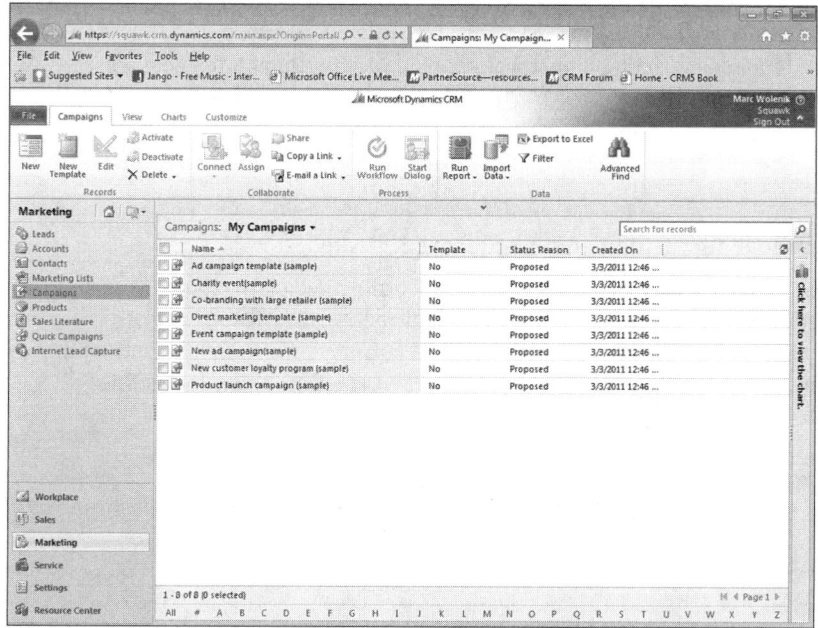

FIGURE 9.6 Campaigns quickview.

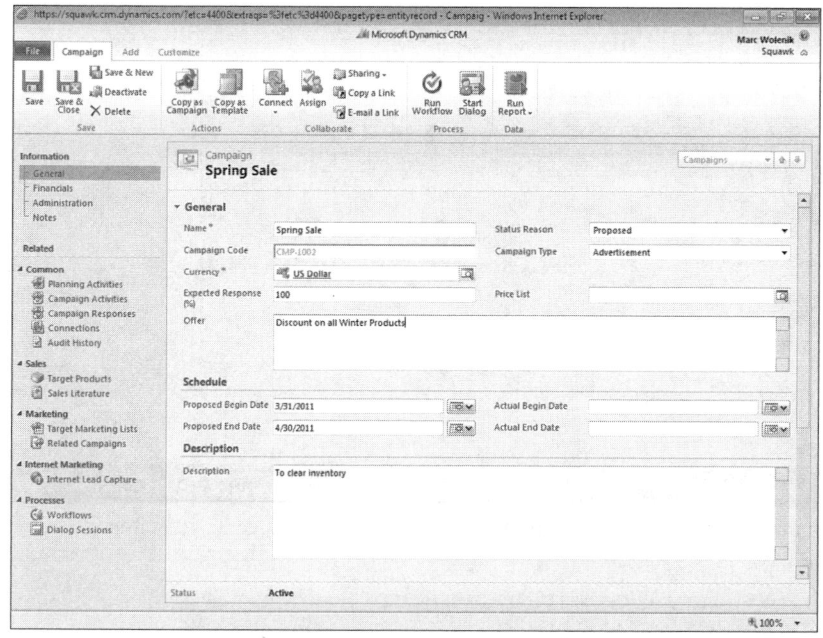

FIGURE 9.7 New Campaign.

TIP

Although it is not required, selecting a price list enables you to compare the cost versus revenue generated from the Campaign. The Offer field is used to explain the detail of the Campaign.

3. Enter the schedule information and description, if desired.
4. Select the Financials section and enter the budget allocated, miscellaneous costs, and the estimated revenue for the Campaign (see Figure 9.8). The Total Cost of Campaign calculates automatically and, because you have no Activities yet, equals the miscellaneous costs only. When we add costs to the Campaign by adding Campaign Activities, costs will automatically be shown here.

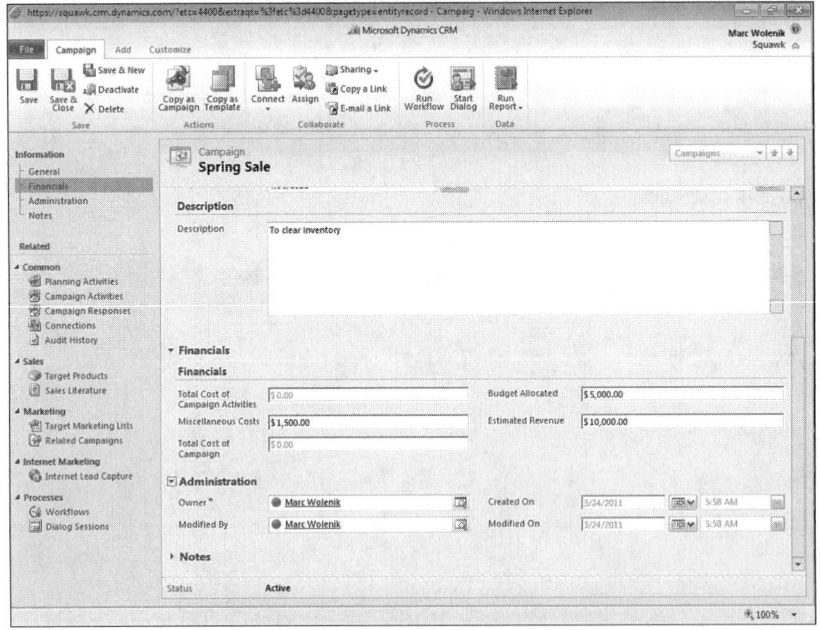

FIGURE 9.8 New Campaign, Financials.

TIP

You may have to save, close, and reopen the form prior to seeing the costs reflected.

5. You can add/edit information on the Administration and Notes tabs, if desired.

   Now that you've created the basic framework for the Campaign, you need to add any Planning Tasks associated with the Campaign.

TIP

Be sure to save the Campaign prior to adding any Planning Tasks to it.

6. Planning Activities are simply Activities, with the Regarding field set to the Campaign. Navigate to the Planning Activities and select New Activity to create a Planning Activity (see Figure 9.9).

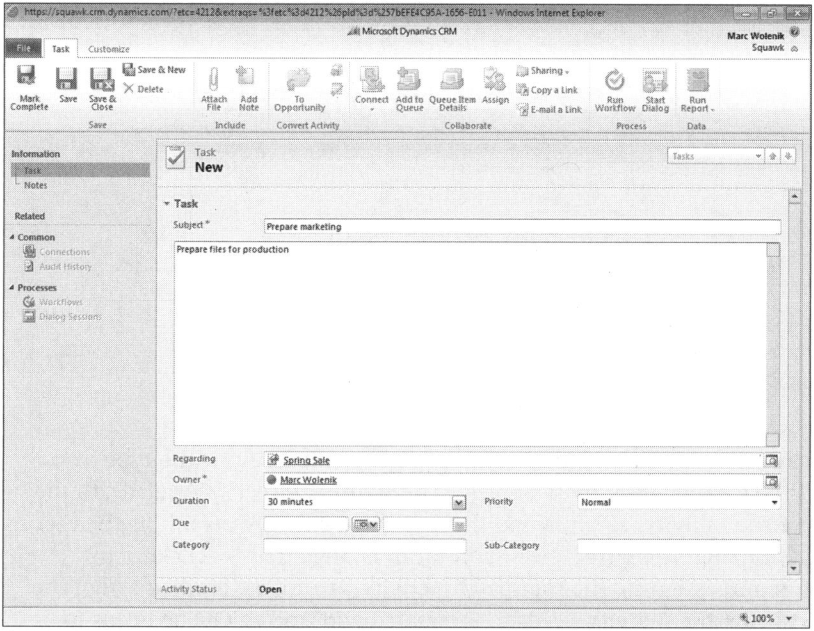

FIGURE 9.9 New Campaign, Planning Tasks.

7. As with any Activity, after you have created it, you can assign it to another user or queue. It will appear as an Activity in the assigned User's My Work and will have associated follow-up Tasks or Activities assigned to the user if added.

8. For this Campaign, you'll have only one Activity. Normally, however, a Campaign has several Planning Activities. If the Campaign will be reused, the Planning Activities likely will be common to the Campaign; it might make sense to convert the Campaign to a Campaign template from the More Actions drop-down menu when you finish adding the necessary Planning Tasks to the Campaign.

Adding Campaign Activities

You have only one Activity, so you add a Campaign Activity next.

1. Campaign Activities are different from common Activities and are specific to the Campaign. To add Campaign Activities, navigate to Campaign Activity, and select Add New Campaign Activity from the Ribbon menu (see Figure 9.10).

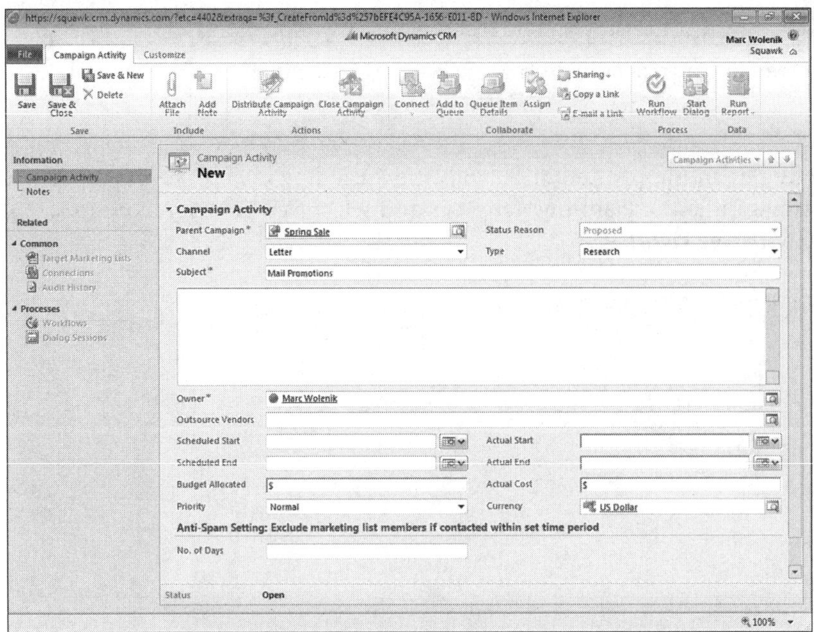

FIGURE 9.10 New Campaign, Campaign Activity.

2. Select the channel or method of marketing specific to this Activity, the type of Activity, and the Campaign Activity Subject. The channel directly correlates to the distribution of the Activity, as explained shortly. The owner, by default, is the user creating the Campaign Activity. However, you can change that by clicking the Lookup button and assigning the Campaign Activity to another user. To assign the Activity to a queue, the Activity needs to be created and Add to Queue needs to be selected from the Ribbon menu. Select any outsource vendors that might be used with this particular Task, and enter the scheduled start and end dates and any budget allocated. The Anti-Spam setting excludes members from receiving any marketing material by preventing the Activity from being distributed to the member for the number of days entered.
3. Campaign Activities must be assigned to Marketing List members by being distributed to the members of the associated Marketing Lists. Distribution simply means assigning the specified Activity to the owner of the member in the Marketing List. Before distribution of Campaign Activities, you must set which Marketing Lists to use as part of this Campaign.
4. To add Marketing Lists, navigate to the near navigation on the Campaign form and select Target Marketing Lists; then click Add (see Figure 9.11).
5. From here, you can easily add any existing Marketing Lists or create a new one. After you select one, you are prompted whether to include the Marketing List in any undistributed Campaign Activities (see Figure 9.12).

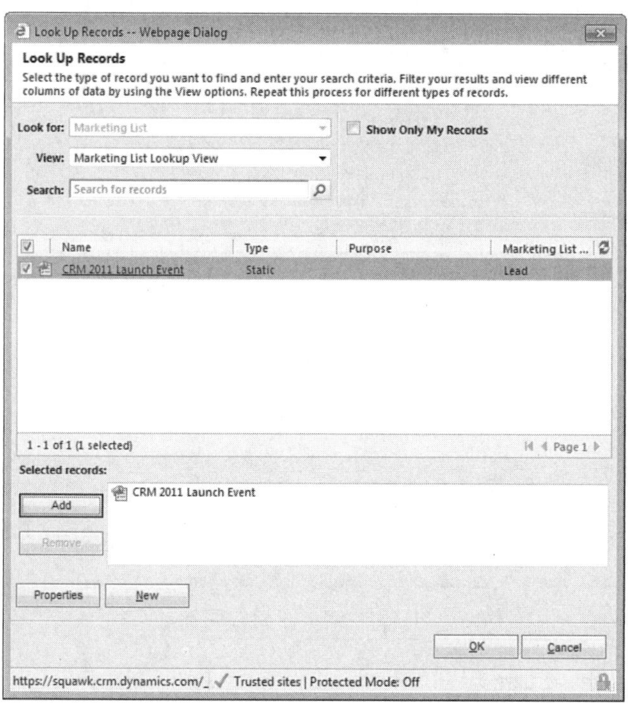

FIGURE 9.11 New Campaign, Add Marketing List.

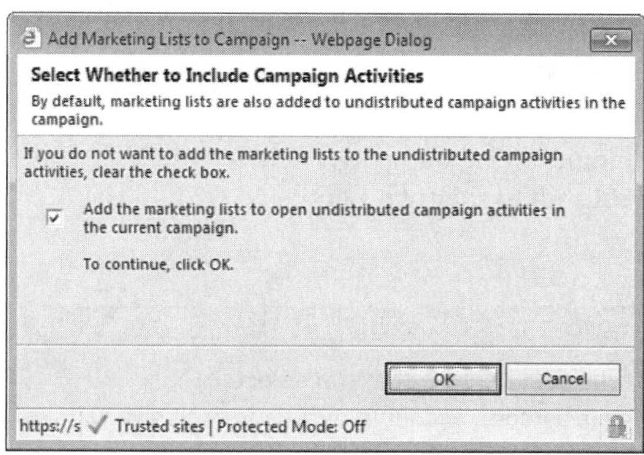

FIGURE 9.12 Add Marketing Lists to Campaign dialog.

6. Because you have already started a Campaign Activity in this example, leave the option checked. The selected Marketing List automatically associates with your Campaign Activity (see Figure 9.13).

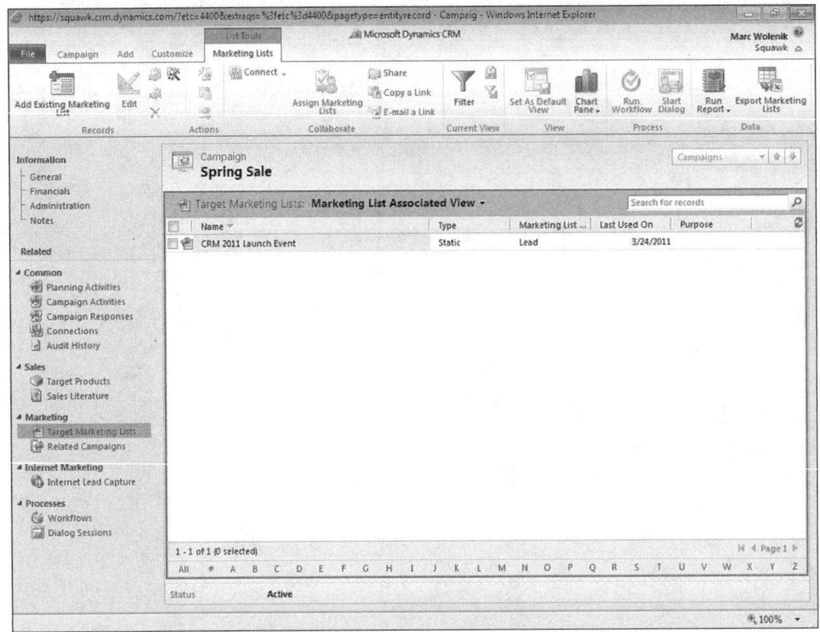

FIGURE 9.13 Campaign Activity Marketing List.

7. Now that you've created the Campaign Activity and associated a Marketing List, you can assign the Campaign Activities from the Ribbon menu. To do this, navigate to Campaign Activities (on the near navigation), and select the Campaign Activities.
8. The Activities are assigned to the designated owners and appear as open Activities for each member in the Marketing List.
9. Be sure to complete the actual cost amount of the Campaign Activity when completed because that information rolls up to the total Campaign cost on the Campaign Financials tab.

NOTE

When working with Mail Merge Campaign Activities, be sure that the selected Marketing Lists are all the same base entity (Contacts, Accounts, or Leads exclusively); otherwise, the merge will fail. If you need to create a Mail Merge Campaign Activity for mixed entities, create separate Campaign Activities for each entity.

10. The last part of Campaigns is the Campaign Responses. As the name indicates, Campaign Responses are responses that your organization receives in response to a Campaign. They are very useful in determining the effectiveness of Campaigns and can indicate many things, such as geographic trending, responsiveness to Campaign

particulars such as discounts and other incentives, and how well your target audience is receiving the Campaigns. It is important to note that Campaign Responses are responses received from potential customers in response to your Campaign, not automated responses sent to your customers as part of your Campaign. You can automatically convert Campaign Activities to Campaign Responses or you can manually create them.

11. In addition to manually creating a Campaign Response by selecting New on the Campaign Response tab located on the near navigation of the Campaign, you can create Campaign Responses by selecting a new Activity type of Campaign Response or by importing records into the system as Campaign Responses by using the Import Data Wizard. This last method is useful when you're working with a large number of records offline because you can easily manipulate them and then tie them to the Campaign as responses when uploaded. Figure 9.14 shows a newly added and saved Campaign Response.

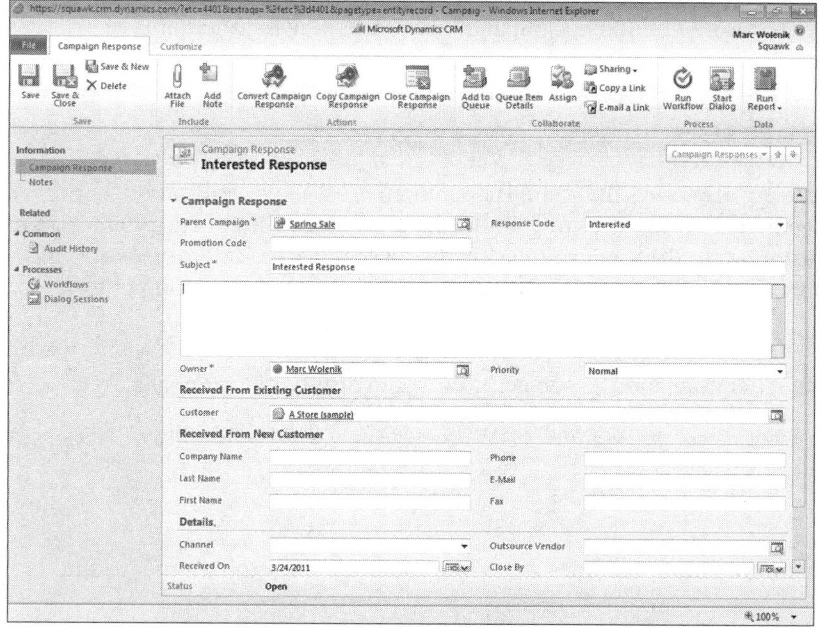

FIGURE 9.14 Campaign Response.

12. The last method for creating a Campaign Response is via e-mail responses if e-mail tracking has been enabled in settings. When an e-mail is sent in response to a Campaign, the incoming e-mail can be automatically created as a Campaign Response.

Convert Campaign Responses

When a Campaign Response has been entered and saved, you can select Convert Campaign Response, which is located in the Ribbon menu bar of Figure 9.14. When selected, this will allow you to close the response and convert the record as follows:

- ▶ Convert into a new Lead
- ▶ Convert an existing Lead into a new Account or Contact
- ▶ Create a new Quote, Order, or Opportunity for an existing customer
- ▶ Simply close the response and mark it as completed or canceled

As a final note, it is important to realize that although the Campaign Response functionality previously described is applicable to Campaigns and Quick Campaigns, the three Campaign reports available in the Reports area (Campaign Activity Status, Campaign Comparison, and Campaign Performance) are applicable only to Campaigns by default. These reports are powerful and display Campaign information in a manner that is easy to understand and useful for determining metrics on Campaigns. We recommend frequently reviewing both of them when building Campaigns as well as viewing the status of executed Campaigns.

Sales Literature

Found in the Marketing area, sales literature is documentation about your products designed to be used by your sales force to gain deeper knowledge about your products and can be given to customers to drive sales. Additionally, sales literature can provide specific instructions on how to use a given product or services, as well as identify competitors.

To create a new piece of sales literature, first select New (see Figure 9.15).

Enter the title of the literature and the subject from your corresponding Subject Tree.

▶ For more information about working with subjects, refer to Chapter 12, "Settings and Configuration."

Additional optional information includes employee contact, type, expiration date, and description.

NOTE

Although the Expiration Date field has no functionality other than to tell the salesperson when it expires, it would be easy to add another custom view to the Sales Literature interface that shows only current or nonexpired sales literature.

Sales attachments can have as many pieces of documentation as desired. To create a new sales attachment document, select Sales Attachment, New (see Figure 9.16).

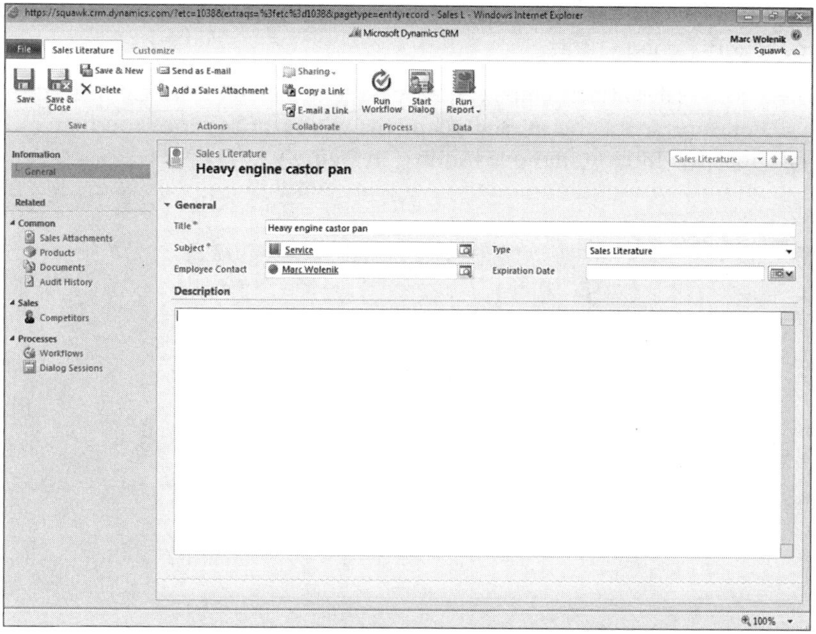

FIGURE 9.15 Sales literature.

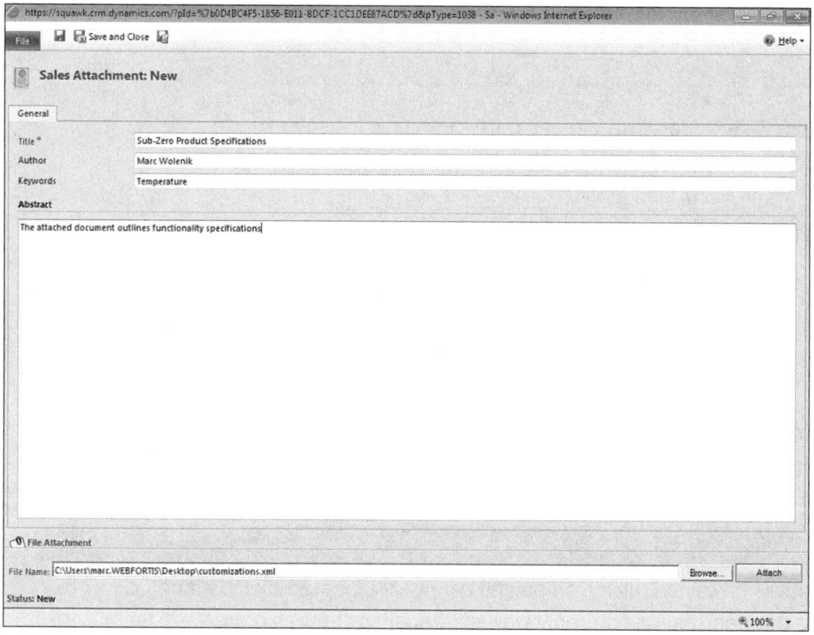

FIGURE 9.16 Sales attachments.

Additional functionality available when working with sales attachments is the capability to add products and identify competitors.

Unlike in previous versions, sales attachments can now be sent directly from CRM. To do so navigate to Sales Literature, select the sales attachments you want to send, and then select Send as E-Mail from the Ribbon menu (as shown in Figure 9.17).

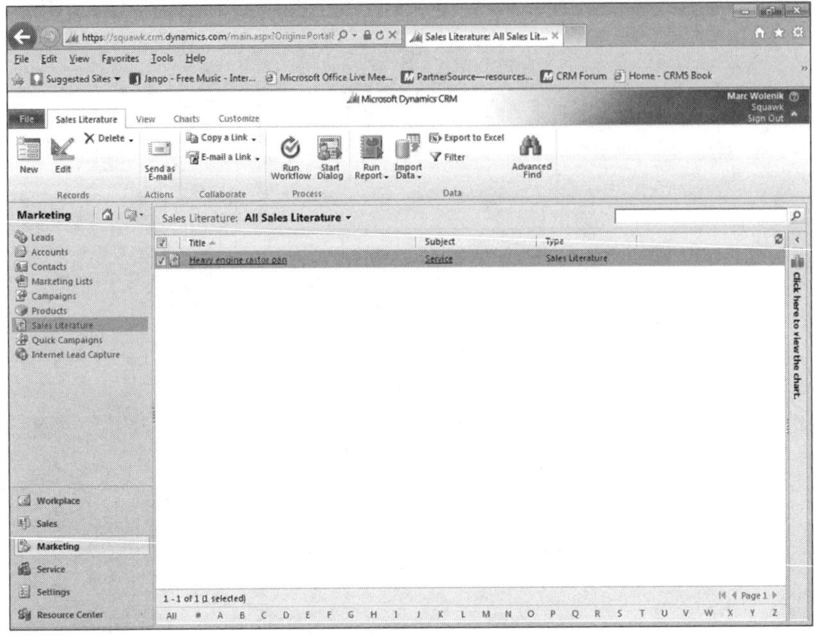

FIGURE 9.17 Send Sales Literature directly from CRM.

Quick Campaigns

A Quick Campaign is a simplified version of a Campaign: Unlike Campaigns, which can contain many Activities, Quick Campaigns have one Activity. The capability to create a Quick Campaign is easy, using a wizard that you can launch from Advanced Find or directly from the Account, Contact, or Lead forms.

When discussing Quick Campaigns, we must consider two aspects: their creation and status. We review both in this section.

NOTE

It is counterintuitive: however Quick Campaigns *cannot* be created by selecting Quick Campaigns from the near navigation (only viewed/managed there). To create a quick campaign, follow the steps in the following sections.

Creating Quick Campaigns

As indicated, creating Quick Campaigns is easy. To launch a Quick Campaign, click the button Create Quick Campaign from either the Contact, Account, or Lead forms. For this example, you launch a Quick Campaign from Advanced Find using the Contacts entity.

1. Open Advanced Find and select Contacts as the base entity. You'll do a targeted Quick Campaign for all your Contacts in the state of California (see Figure 9.18). Select Find to continue.

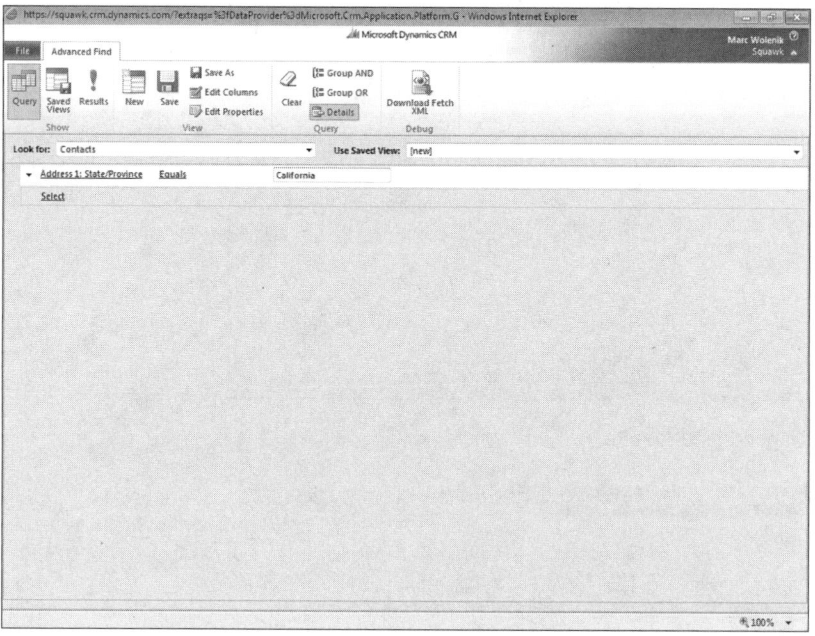

FIGURE 9.18 Advanced Find for Contacts in California.

2. From the results screen, select Create Quick Campaign, and select the option indicated (see Figure 9.19). In this example, select All Records on All Pages. The Quick Campaign Wizard starts and welcomes you (as shown in Figure 9.20). Click Next to continue.

3. Enter the name of the Campaign, and click Next to continue. Select the Activity Type of the Quick Campaign, as well as who will own the Activities (see Figure 9.21). If the Activity type selected is an e-mail (as in our example), the system can automatically send the e-mails and close the Activities, if selected. Otherwise, the Activities will belong to the selected owners as pending and will require action by them to close them out.

4. Because you've selected e-mail, we're prompted to enter the e-mail information shown in Figure 9.22. If you had selected another Activity, you would be prompted to complete the appropriate fields for that Activity. Our example is a simple e-mail, which has the downside of limited customization. If we were to use the Channel

option of Letter via Mail Merge, we could personalize the letter fully as well as include additional data fields. Click Next to continue, and then Create to create the Quick Campaign.

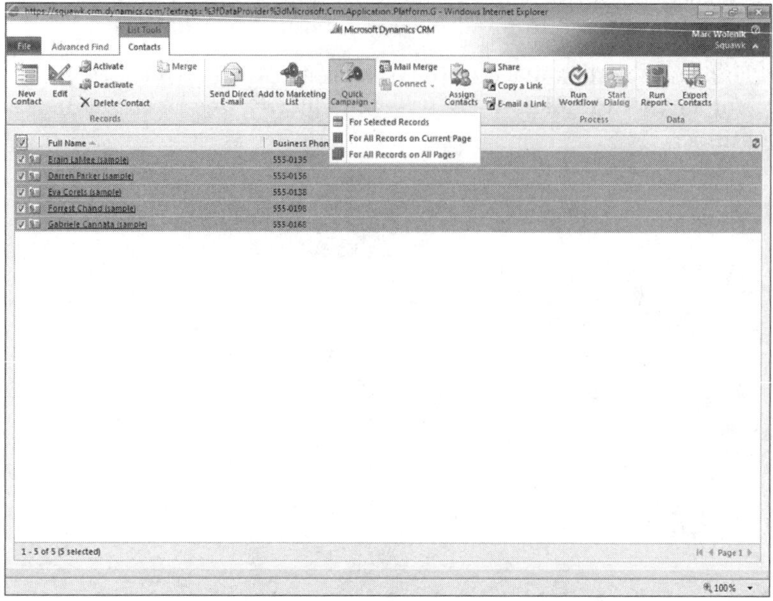

FIGURE 9.19 Advanced Find results.

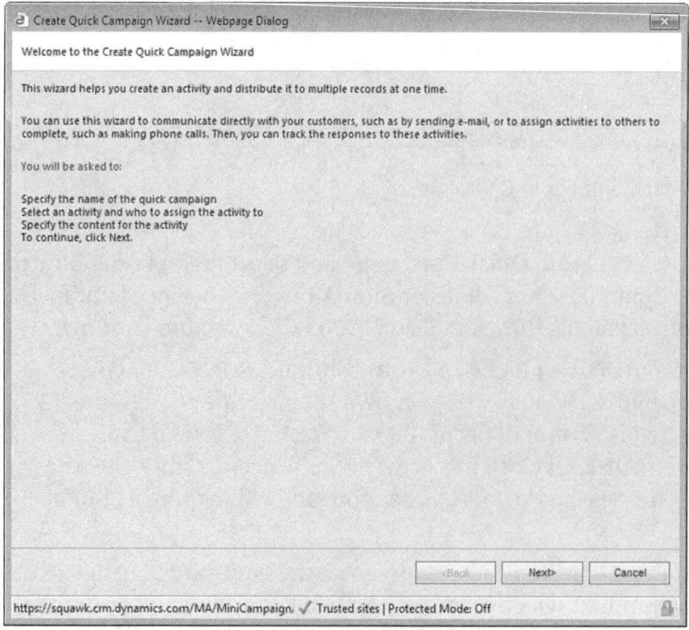

FIGURE 9.20 Quick Campaign Wizard.

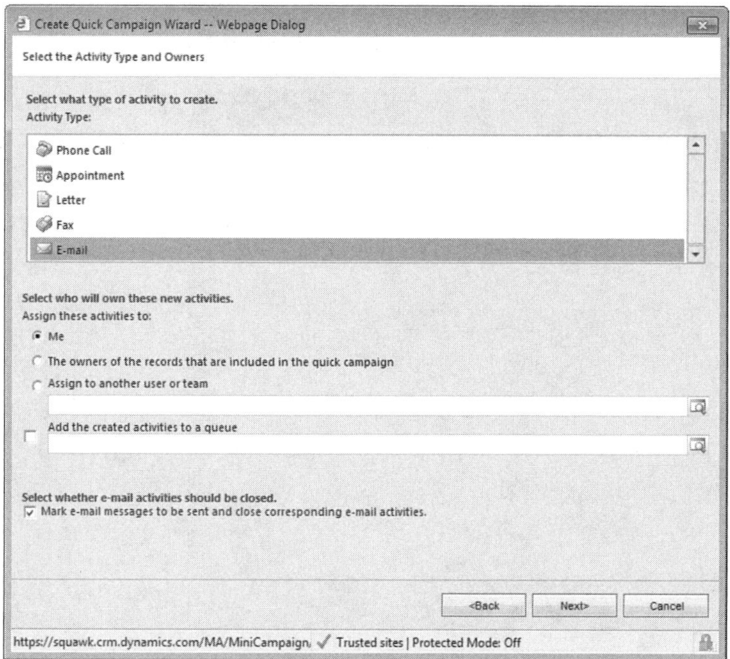

FIGURE 9.21 Activity type.

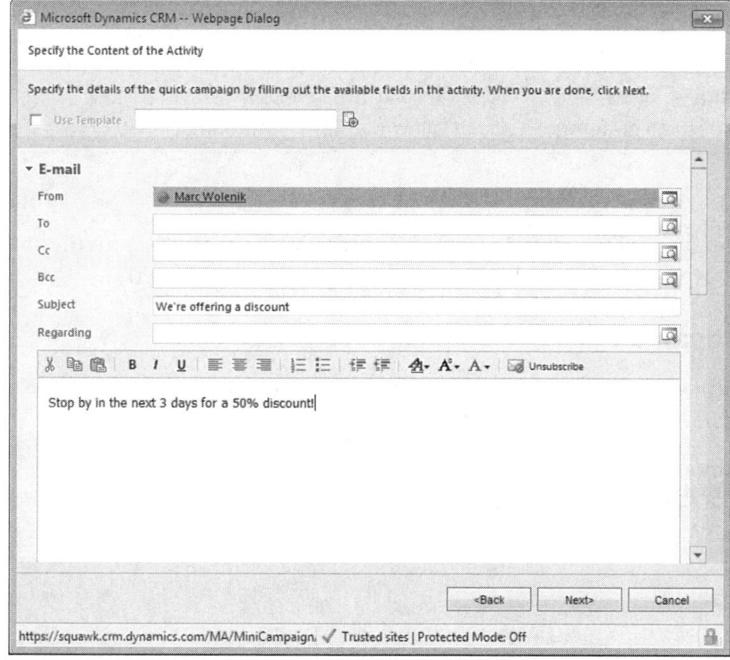

FIGURE 9.22 E-mail Activity type.

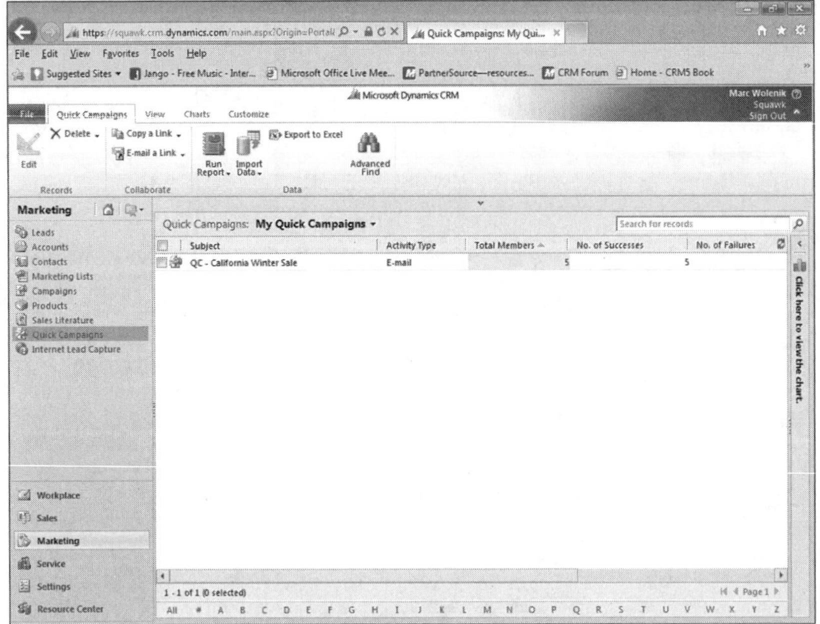

FIGURE 9.23 Marketing, Quick Campaigns.

NOTE

To use the Unsubscribe option, select some text in the body of the e-mail by highlighting, and click the Unsubscribe button (for example, add and select the following text: **To stop receiving our e-mails, click here**). This will format the selected text as a link that users can click to set their preferences to not allow marketing materials.

5. The wizard completes and the Activity is created. It waits in the person's Activities to complete unless it was an e-mail (in which case the e-mail goes out directly).

Status of Quick Campaigns

Although you can't launch Quick Campaigns directly from the Quick Campaign node of the Marketing area, you can monitor their status from there (see Figure 9.23).

Open a Quick Campaign by double-clicking it to bring up information about the success and failure of the Quick Campaign (see Figure 9.24).

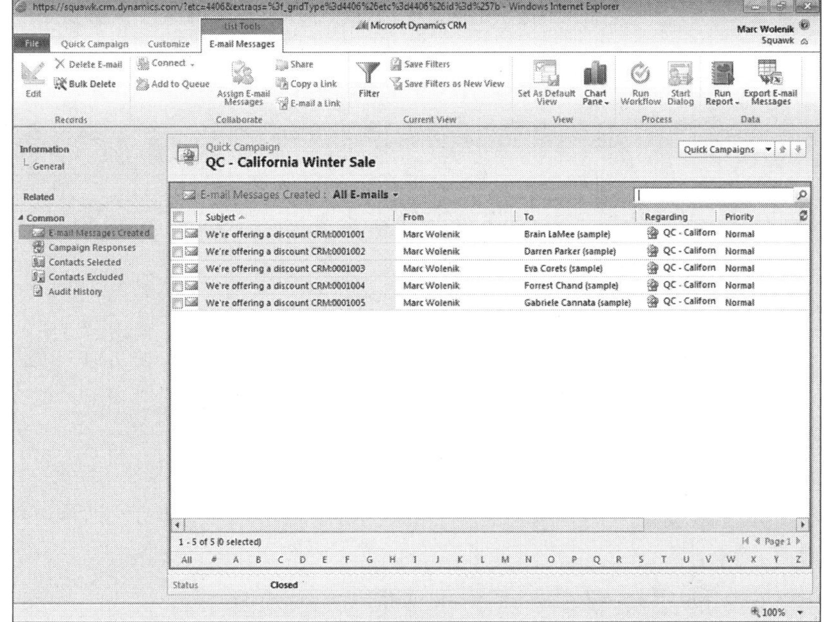

FIGURE 9.24 Quick Campaigns status.

In reviewing the form, you can easily see what the Quick Campaign was for and who received e-mail messages by selecting E-mail Messages Created from the near navigation. Additionally, you can track any responses to the Quick Campaign, just as you would for a regular Campaign. Finally, you can easily see which Contacts received the e-mail and which were excluded and why by examining the details found in each node (for example, a Contact selected didn't have a valid e-mail).

Summary

In reviewing the Marketing options for Microsoft Dynamics CRM, it is easy to see that Microsoft Dynamics CRM offers a full set of marketing options and capabilities. From its powerful Campaign-management features to its quick-and-easy Quick Campaigns, you can easily market to existing and potential clients, report on results, and determine which marketing efforts worked.

CHAPTER 10

Working with Service

IN THIS CHAPTER

- Service and Services Activities Explained
- Services
- Service Calendar
- Cases
- Articles
- Contracts
- Goals, Goal Metrics, and Rollup Queries

Service and Services Activities Explained

Services are the best way to manage resources such as time and materials within the organization. *Resources* can consist of users, resource groups, or teams, and *materials* are defined as a facilities or equipment.

A *service* is basically anything that involves resource time and materials. It is different from a product, for which you have to manage stock and quantities. With a service, the critical considerations are the time allocated to the necessary resources and the stock of materials. For example, imagine that an IT company has two technicians who can repair computers. When one goes to a client to repair a computer, that technician might take one hour or more to perform the work and, depending on the service required, might need to use materials such a new CD-ROM or computer part. You can schedule all these tasks in Microsoft Dynamics CRM via service activities. Although you can also schedule this service as an appointment, the difference between them is that a service activity has an associated service. You use appointments for meetings with clients that do not involve performing any service.

When service activities are scheduled, they appear on the user's CRM calendar (found in My Service); when working with the Outlook client, they appear as appointments on the Outlook calendar.

TIP

When working with the Outlook client, there is full-featured functionality for services unless you are offline. When offline, the Service Calendar is unavailable; however, appointments can still be viewed on the Outlook calendar.

The Service area of Microsoft CRM has the following options, by default:

- Service Calendar
- Cases
- Accounts
- Contacts
- Articles
- Contracts
- Products
- Services
- Goals
- Goal Metrics
- Rollup Queries

▶ These options can be customized from the Site Map entity, as explained in Chapter 23, "Customizing Entities."

▶ The Accounts, Contacts, and Products options are specifically covered in Chapter 6, "Working with Customers," and Chapter 8, "Working with Sales," and therefore are not covered here.

Services

The service activities use services to define and configure how time and resources will be managed when a user schedules a service activity.

For example, consider an IT company that has a service called Network Installation, which might take three hours to complete and that requires one of the three technicians to go to the customer's office.

To set up this service example, follow these steps:

1. Go to the Service area and click Services. Then click the New button on the Ribbon. The New Service form appears (see Figure 10.1).

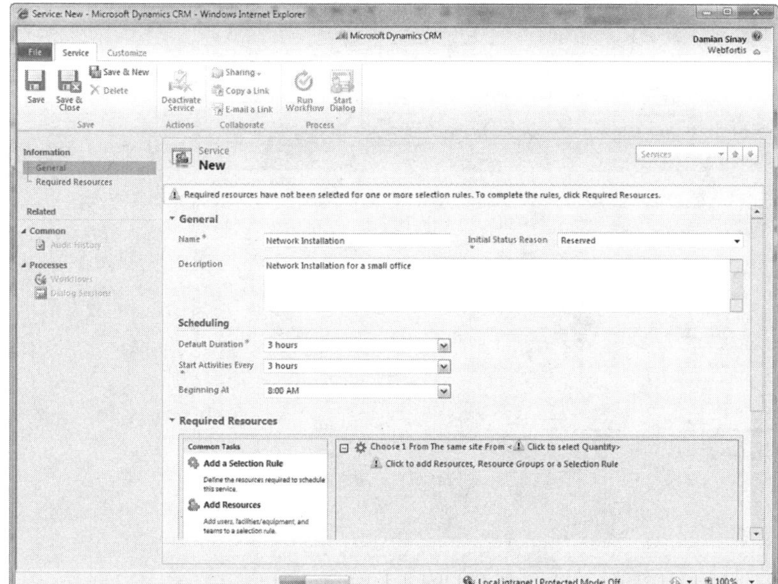

FIGURE 10.1 New Service window interface.

By default, each service has the following required fields:

- Name
- Initial Status Reason
- Default Duration
- Start Activities Every

To configure the resources needed to accomplish the service, navigate to the Required Resources tab (see Figure 10.2).

Select the first option from the tree displayed on the right that says Choose 1 from the Same Site from <Click to Select Quantity>, and double-click it to display the window shown in Figure 10.3.

If you don't see the Scheduling Details fields, click on the arrow at the right of that title to expand the section.

This example requires only one technician to perform the service, so you can close this window (if you were going to need more than one technician, you would change the values here to reflect the number needed). Select the child option that says Click to Add Resources, Resource Groups, or a Selection Rule. The window shown in Figure 10.4 displays the available resources that you want to assign.

TIP

Click the Search for Records button (the one with a magnifying glass icon) to display all available records on the left.

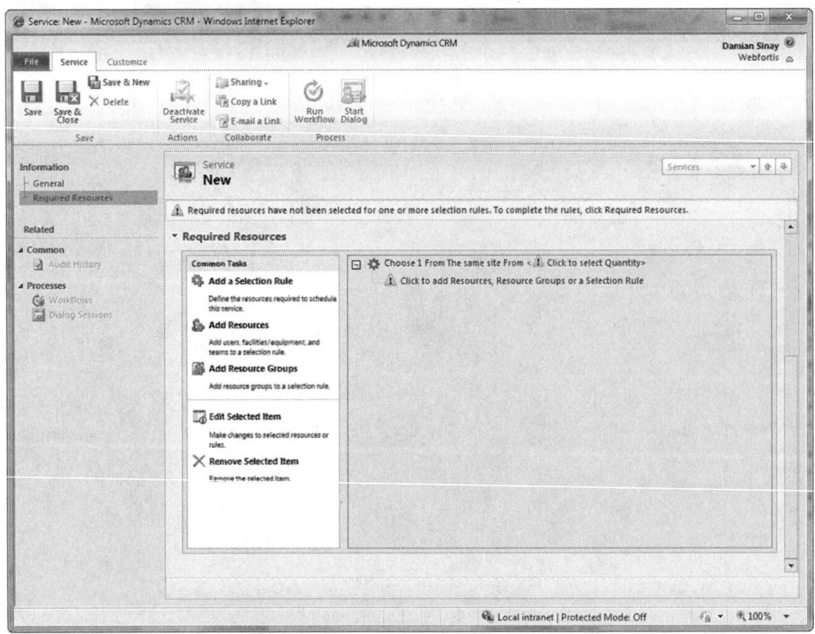

FIGURE 10.2 Configuring required resources.

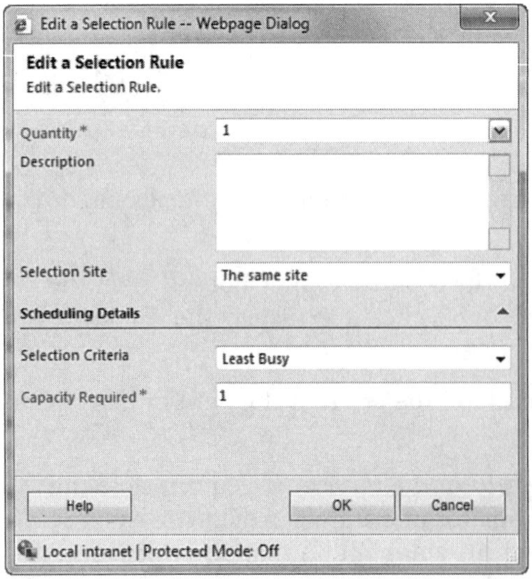

FIGURE 10.3 Editing a selection rule.

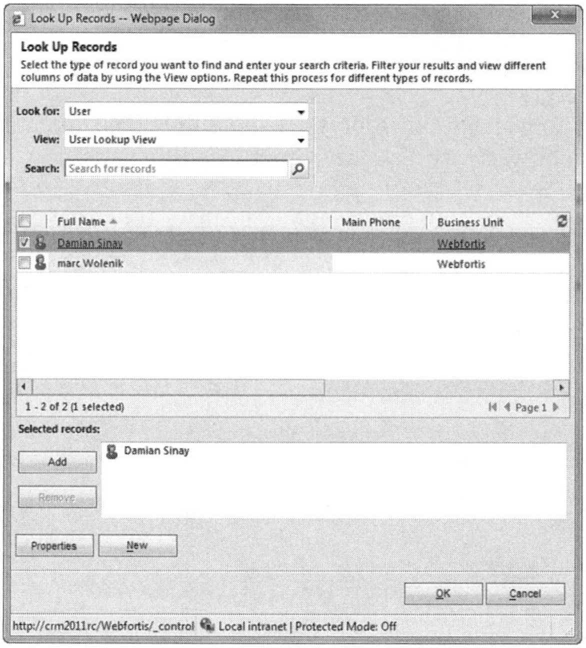

FIGURE 10.4 Adding resources to a selection rule.

Select the users you want to include from the left list box and click the Add button to move them to the Selected Records list and click OK to close this dialog.

If you add more than one user, you will be asked whether you want to create a new resource group, which is useful for reusing the same group of users on other services instead of selecting the users one by one (see Figure 10.5).

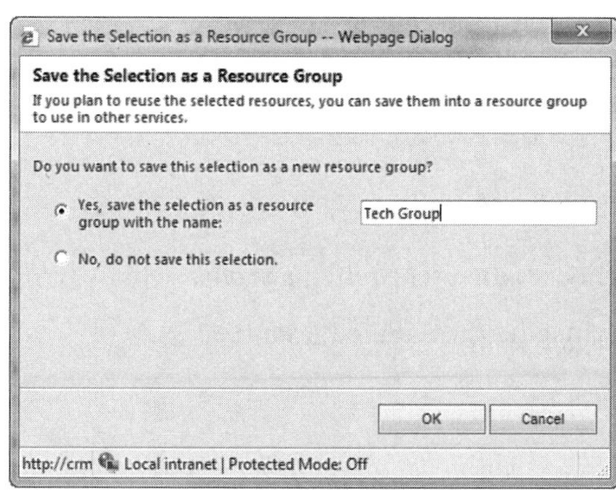

FIGURE 10.5 Saving the selection as a resource group.

To further work with services, you might need to create Facility/Equipment and Resource Groups, if you haven't done so yet. You can do this by going to Settings, Business Management.

Facility/Equipment refers to the ability to manage either locations or, as the name implies, equipment as part of the service-scheduling activity. Resource Groups is just a basic grouping that can be reused.

▶ See Chapter 12, "Settings and Configuration," for detailed information about how to add and manage these kinds of entities.

After you select the required resources, you will see them, as shown in Figure 10.6.

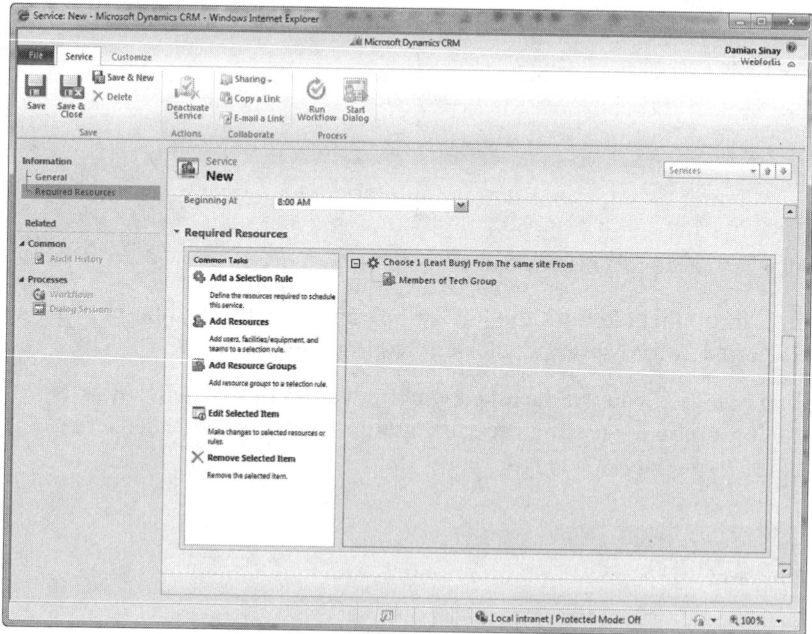

FIGURE 10.6 Required resources.

These resources are the ones the user must choose when scheduling a service activity.

You also can perform some common tasks managing the required resources:

- Add a Selection Rule
- Add Resources
- Add Resource Groups
- Edit Selected Item
- Remove Selected Item

TIP

Unfortunately, the Service entity doesn't support customizations. If you want to customize it, consider adding a new custom attribute for your business services.

Click Save and Close button to finish with the new service creation.

Service Calendar

The Service Calendar checks resource availability and schedules appointments for the resources. Figure 10.7 shows the Service Calendar interface. When a customer calls to request a service, you can easily manage a general agenda and reserve or request a time for a resource or equipment based on the requested service. Additionally, you can manage the existing schedules and make changes, if necessary.

By default, the Service Calendar is displayed showing the time and usage allocation for facility/equipment, as well as the tasks scheduled for the users.

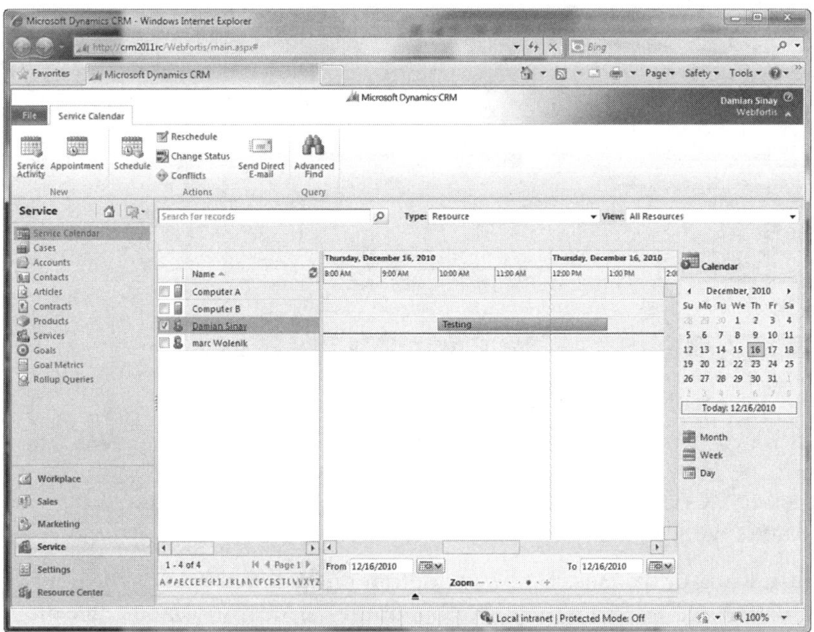

FIGURE 10.7 Main Service area interface.

NOTE

The Service Calendar is available only to users with System Administrator or one of the Scheduler roles. If users do not have these roles, they see the time allocated on their personal calendars as appointments, which are accessed by going to Workplace, My Work, Calendar.

As you can see in Figure 10.8, each activity state has a different color so that you can easily recognize its status.

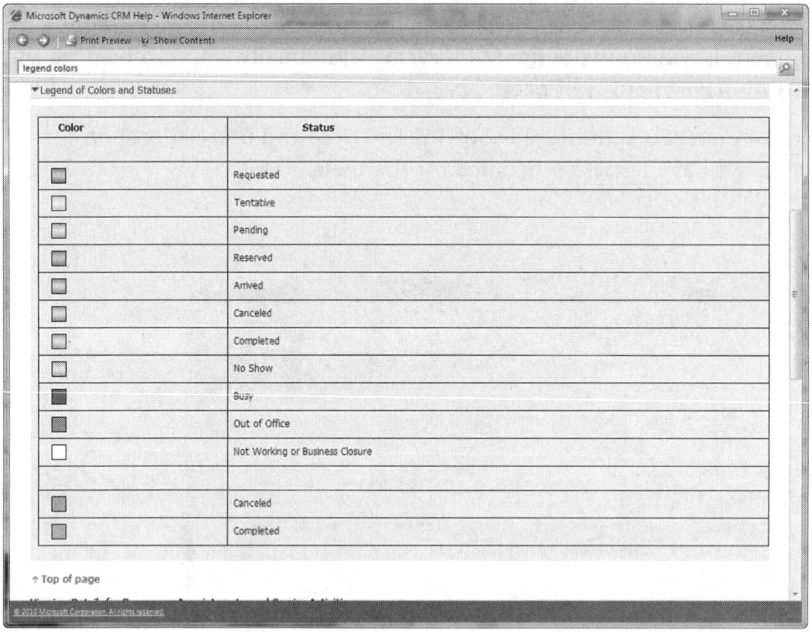

Microsoft Dynamics CRM Help - Windows Internet Explorer

Print Preview Show Contents Help

legend colors

Legend of Colors and Statuses

Color	Status
■	Requested
□	Tentative
■	Pending
■	Reserved
■	Arrived
■	Canceled
■	Completed
■	No Show
■	Busy
■	Out of Office
□	Not Working or Business Closure
■	Canceled
■	Completed

Top of page

FIGURE 10.8 Color table for a service activity's status.

You can display the Service Calendar by month, week, or day, and you can also display it within a custom date range specified.

To view it by month, week, or day, select the View option in the lower right of the interface. For a custom date range, navigate to the bottom of the calendar view and enter the date range.

TIP

You can use the calendars next to the date input fields to more easily select a date.

If you have many resources and equipment, you can easily locate a resource by using the search text box at the top by typing the first few letters of the resource name.

The Service Calendar shows the two types of activities you can create from this interface: the service activity and the appointment activities.

Service Activity

A service activity helps you schedule appointments for resources associated with a service. Before creating service activities, you must define and create your business services as discussed in detail earlier in the "Services" section of this chapter.

To create a new service activity from the Service Calendar interface, click the Service Activity button on the Ribbon (see Figure 10.9).

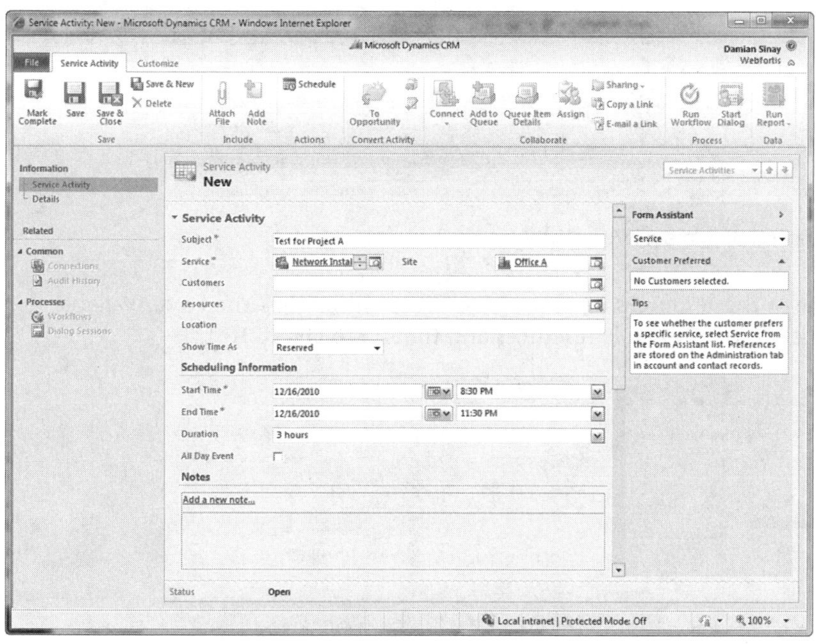

FIGURE 10.9 New service activity.

When creating a new service activity, you are required to enter a subject, a service, and the time (start and end dates) for the activity. Depending on the service selected, you might also be required to select one or more resources or equipment. If so, after selecting the service, click the Schedule button from the top Ribbon.

A new window opens for scheduling a service. In this example (see Figure 10.10), the Form Assistant displays the resources that are available for completion in the Resources field. When the Resources field has the focus, you will see Service Rule options in the Form Assistant that must be selected. In this example, one of the displayed resources must be selected (see Figure 10.10).

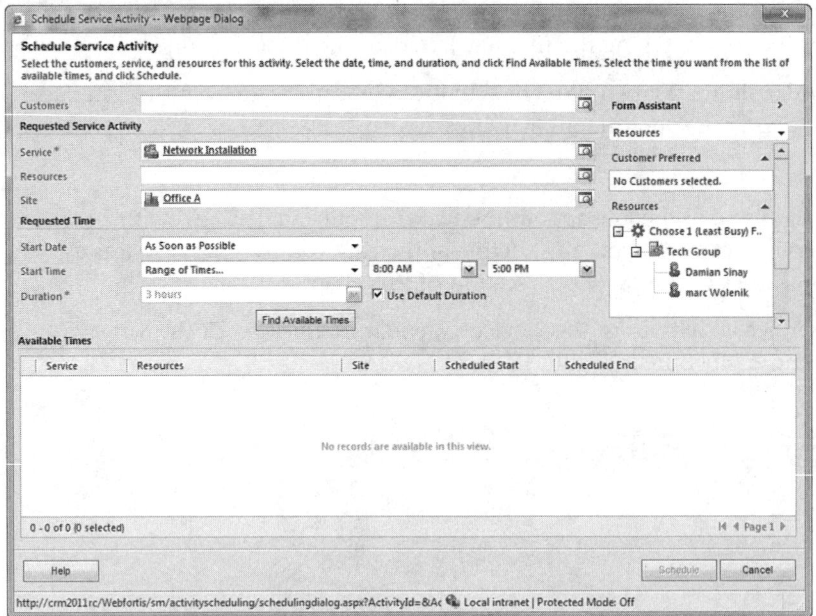

FIGURE 10.10 Scheduling a service activity.

You can select one of the resources from the Form Assistant or click the Find Available Times button to list all the available resources and times (see Figure 10.11).

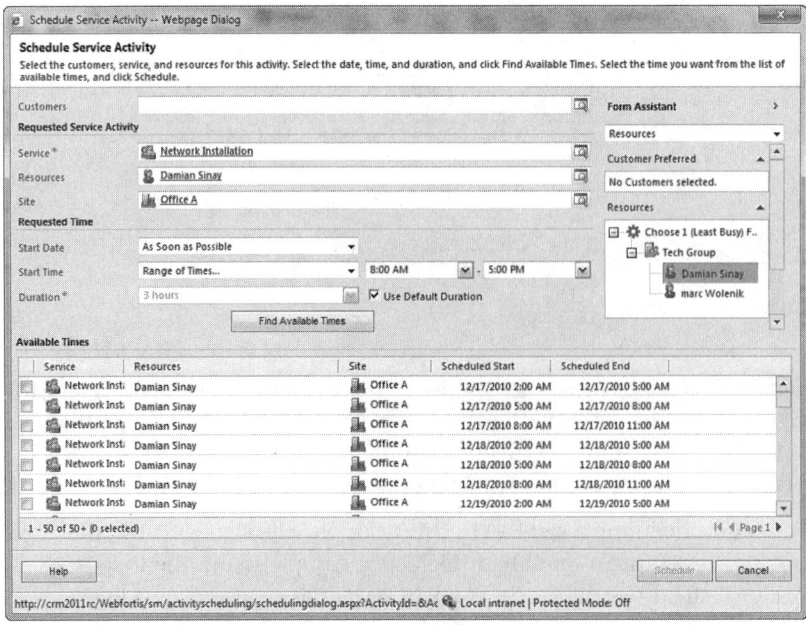

FIGURE 10.11 Selecting resources.

NOTE

If you see errors when clicking on the Find Available Times button, it might be because the resources didn't have a site specified. Be sure the facilities and users have one site set.

Select the resource that matches your desired time availability and click the Schedule button. Notice that you might have to select more than one resource, depending on how the service was initially defined.

Finally, click Save and Close to finish the service activity. This closes the window, and you will see the scheduled activity on the Service Calendar. Each affected user sees the service activity on his or her calendar that is in the Workplace area (see Figure 10.12).

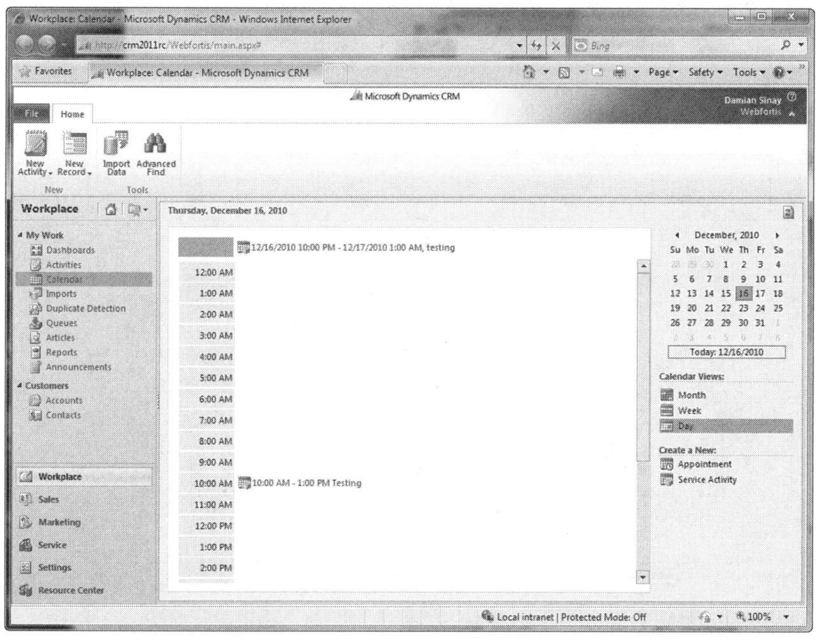

FIGURE 10.12 User workplace calendar.

TIP

By default, users are not notified via e-mail when you schedule a service activity for them. However, you can easily customize that by creating a custom workflow for the Service Activity entity.

▶ Refer to Chapter 24, "Processes Development," for more details about how to create custom workflows and processes.

You can easily reschedule service activities, if necessary. For example, suppose that a customer has to reschedule an appointment. The Customer Service Representative could easily do that by clicking the Reschedule button and then checking the next available time to verify availability of the resources to the service to be rescheduled.

TIP

Another hidden pane, at the bottom of the window, shows resources and facility details. If you click the black arrow located in the middle bottom of the main Service Calendar window, another panel displaying the selected resource details appears (see Figure 10.13).

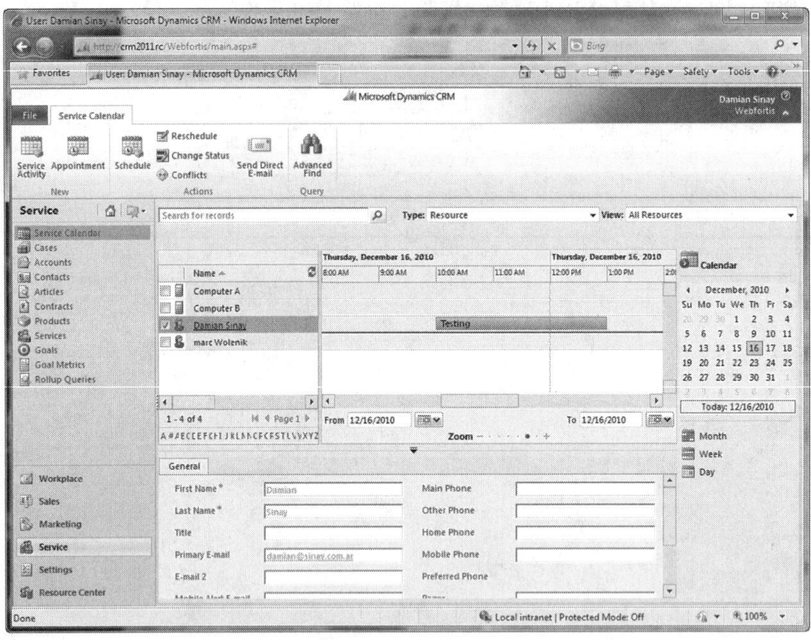

FIGURE 10.13 Resource details panel expanded.

Managing Users' Working Time You can change the working hours for a user from the Service Calendar. You open a user's details by selecting and then double-clicking the user. Navigating then to the Work Hours tab from the Details section, you can see and configure the user's working times.

Suppose the user Damian is going on vacation from 1/15 to 1/30. You can easily set up these days as time off to prevent other users from scheduling appointments or service activities with him. From the Set Up menu that is inside the Monthly View tab, click Time Off to configure the holidays, as shown in Figure 10.15.

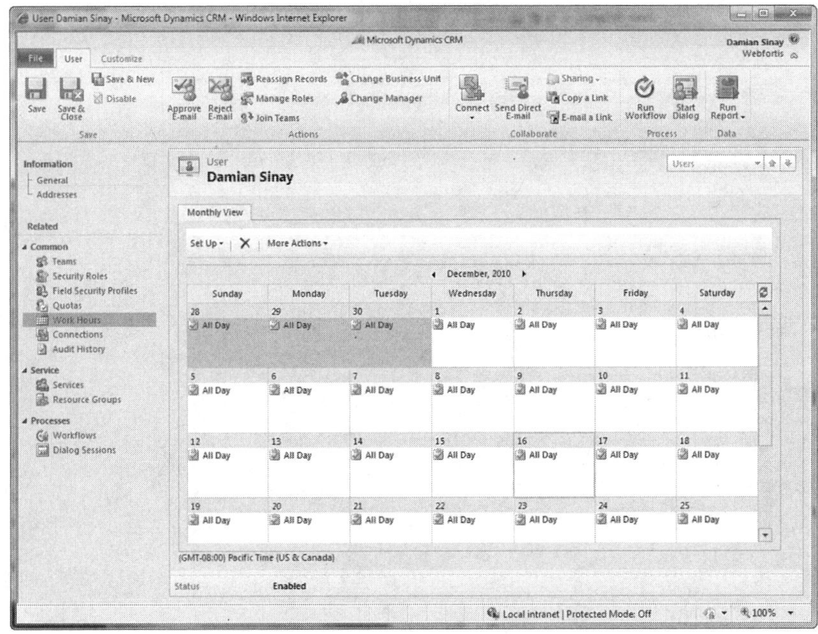

FIGURE 10.14 Work Hours tab for a user.

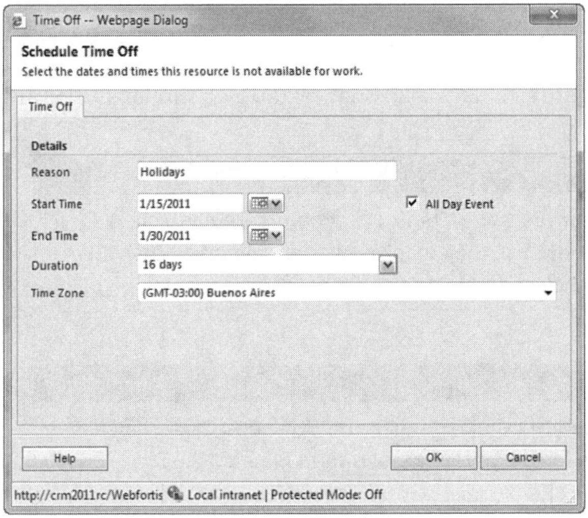

Time Off -- Webpage Dialog

Schedule Time Off

Select the dates and times this resource is not available for work.

Time Off

Details

Reason: Holidays

Start Time: 1/15/2011 — All Day Event

End Time: 1/30/2011

Duration: 16 days

Time Zone: (GMT-03:00) Buenos Aires

Help — OK — Cancel

http://crm2011rc/Webfortis Local intranet | Protected Mode: Off

FIGURE 10.15 Configuring time off.

Figure 10.16 shows how the work hours are displayed after configuring time off.

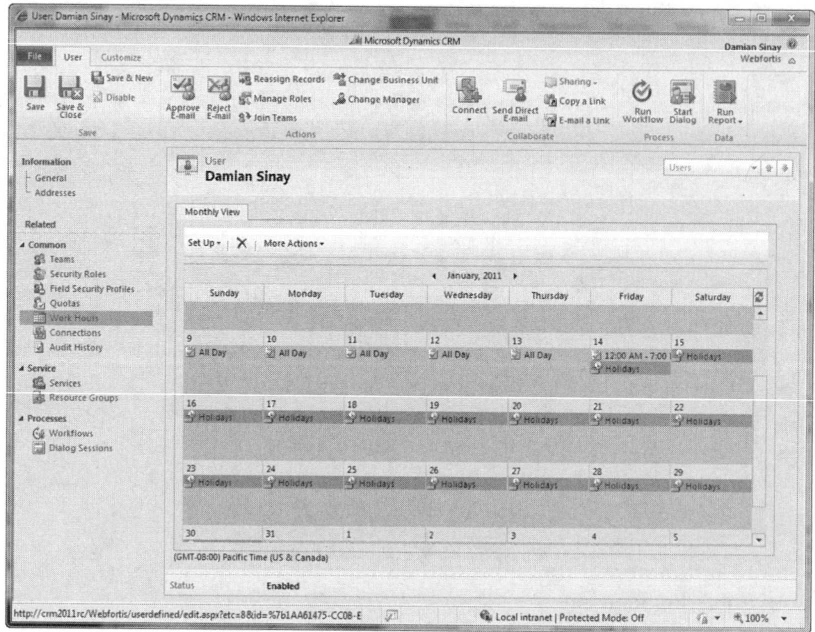

FIGURE 10.16 Work hours with holidays.

You can use this same process to configure sick days, personal errands, or similar situations.

NOTE

Even though the work hours for the user are set as time off, other users can schedule activities for this user on those days. However, they receive an alert message that the user is scheduled for time off so that they can change the dates, if necessary.

TIP

For general holidays when the business will be closed, use the Business Closures calendar in the Settings, Business Management option, as shown in Figure 10.17.

Appointment

Appointments differ from service activities because they don't need to have a service associated with them. To create a new appointment, go to the Service area, select Service Calendar, and then click Appointment. Figure 10.18 illustrates the Appointment window.

The required fields are the Subject field and the start and end times for the appointment. If you want, you can specify the required resources or materials necessary for the appointment and the optional resources.

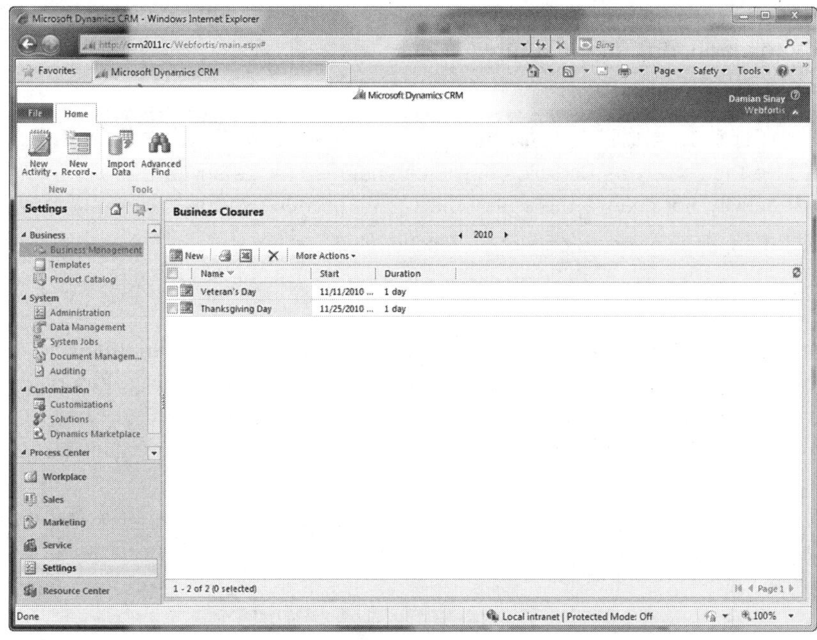

FIGURE 10.17 Business Closures interface.

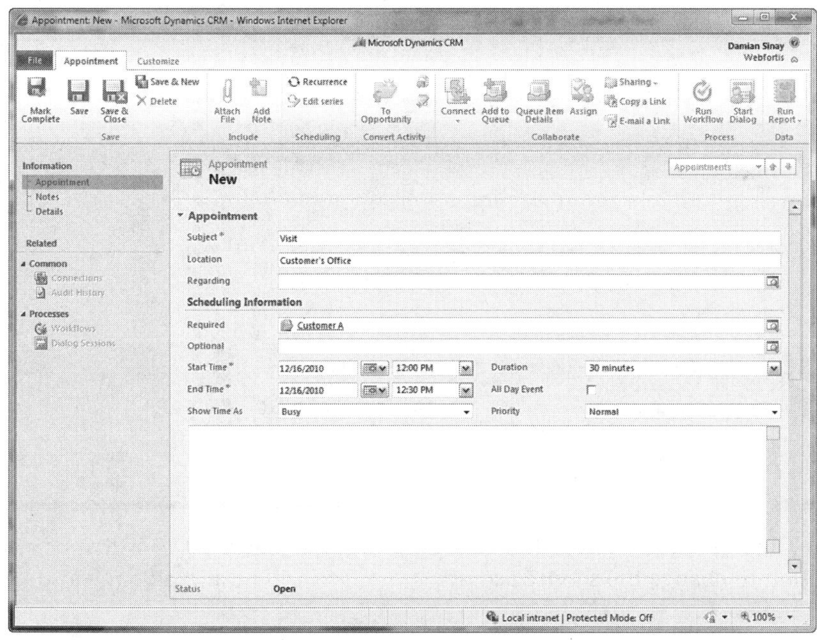

FIGURE 10.18 Creating a new appointment.

After the appointment is created, you can save the activity as Completed, or you can convert the activity to an opportunity or a case.

CAUTION

If you choose to save the activity as Completed, you can neither change any of the properties for that activity, nor change the status back to its previous status.

Unlike service activities, appointments cannot be rescheduled.

When you create a service activity, you can set its initial status to Open or Scheduled where Open can be Requested or Tentative and Scheduled can be set as Pending, Reserved, In Progress, or Arrived. To change the status of a service activity, select the activity first and then click on the Change Status button (see Figure 10.19).

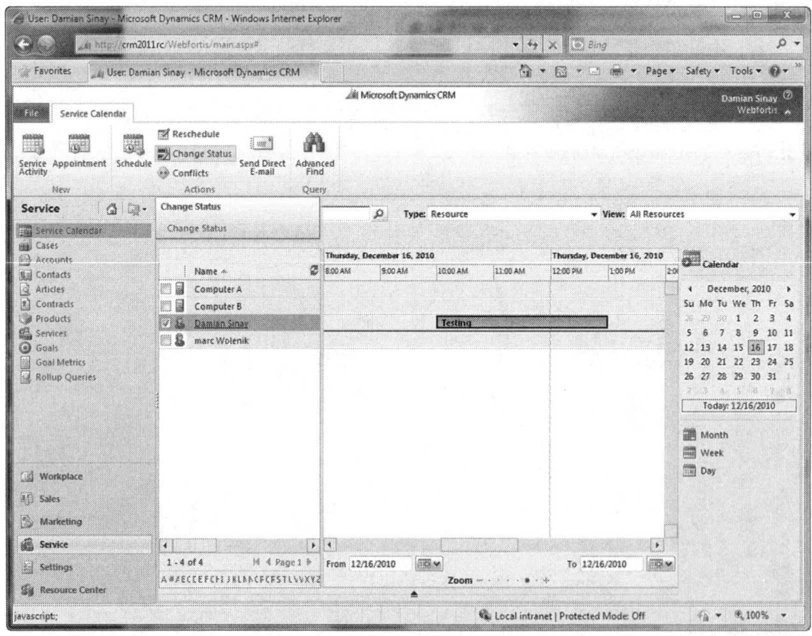

FIGURE 10.19 Changing a service activity's status.

After you click the Change Status button, the dialog displayed in Figure 10.20 will appear, giving you the option to change the service activity status. You will be also able to close the activity and complete it.

A new and welcome feature related to appointments in CRM 2011 is that you can now create a recurring appointment. For example, if you have to meet a client once a week for two months, you can now configure this by clicking the Recurrence button on the

Ribbon. In Figure 10.21, you can see the options you can use to set the recurrence; they are the same you are used to use in Microsoft Outlook.

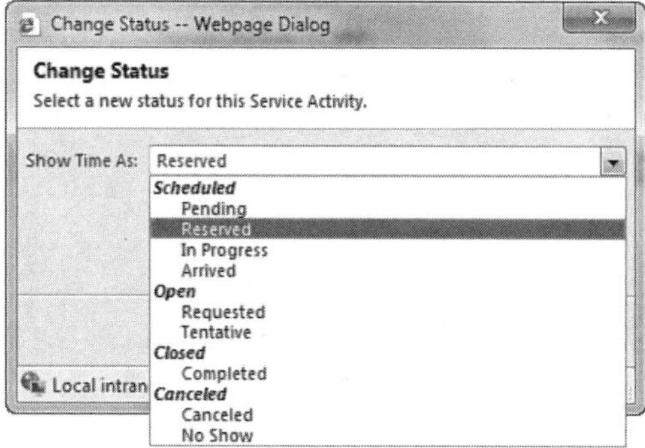

FIGURE 10.20 Changing a service activity's status to Completed.

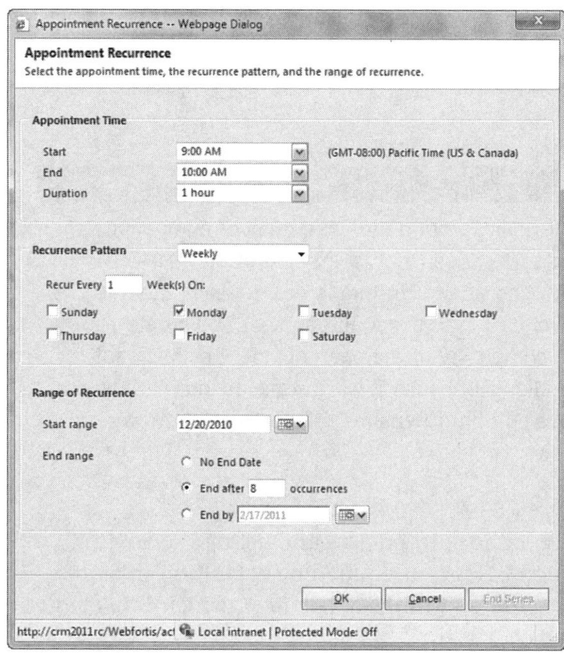

FIGURE 10.21 Appointment recurrence.

Cases

Cases are normally used to track customer problems, questions, and issues. Each case is assigned a unique identifier with a prefix of CAS by default, which you can customize from Settings, Administration, Autonumbering.

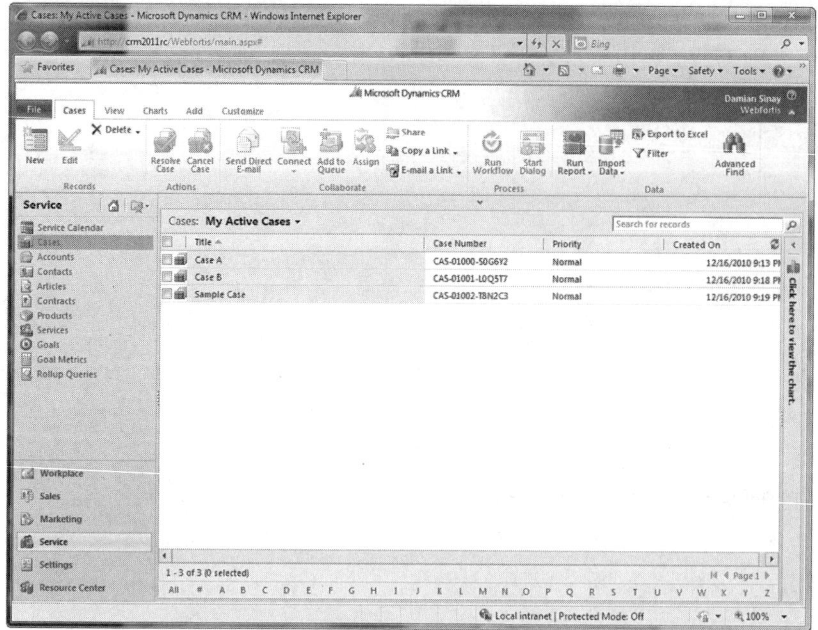

FIGURE 10.22 Cases interface.

NOTE

We are frequently asked if there is any flexibility around the case number numbering scheme because it can be unfriendly in some cases (that is, instead of CAS-01002-T8N2C3, something more like CAS-5401). The answer to this is no. However, there is no reason why you cannot create your own plug-in that will autonumber and create a case number for you. The reason for the complexity of the case numbers by Microsoft Dynamics CRM is because of the offline client. Because it will not necessarily be connected to the server, it needs a complex algorithm to ensure uniqueness—even when offline—hence the case numbers as shown.

Before starting to work with cases, it is a good idea to prepare and define the Subject, explained later in this chapter. Even though his is not required by default on this new version of Dynamics CRM 2011, it can be entered in the Subject field, which is related to the Knowledge Base. To create a new case, click New.

After selecting the subject, you can move to the Notes and Article tab and look up the Knowledge Base (KB) articles associated with the selected subject (see Figure 10.24). You can do this by using the Form Assistant on the right side of the window or by opening the Article pop-up.

After entering the required values, click Save and Close to create the new case.

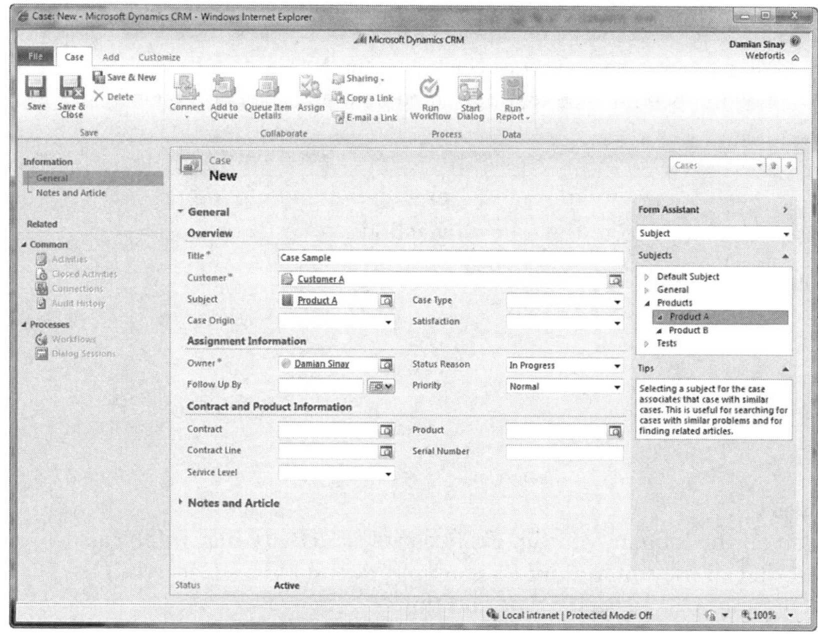

FIGURE 10.23 Creating a new case.

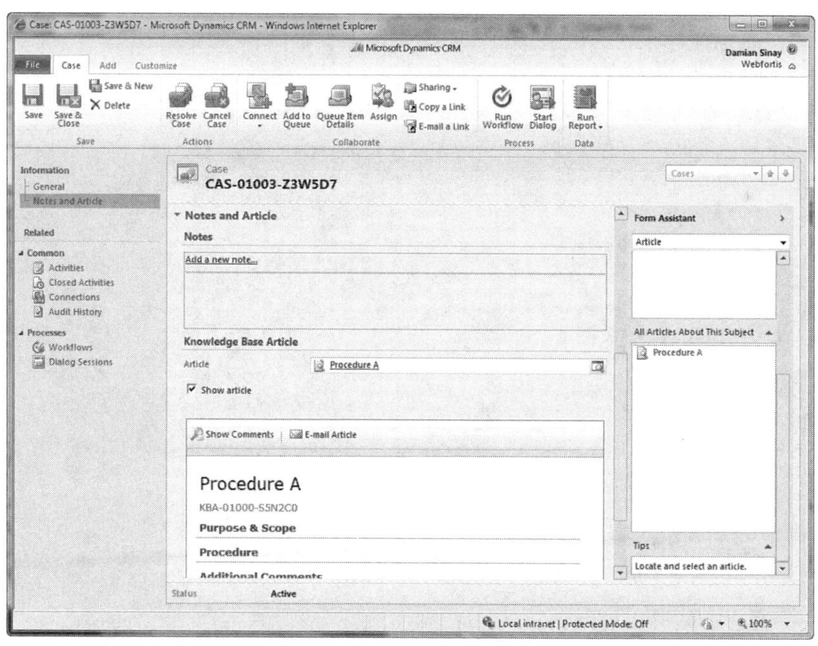

FIGURE 10.24 Associating a Knowledge Base article to a case.

> **TIP**
>
> You can also create a case from an activity by converting the activity to a case. This is useful when you need to open a case that originated from an e-mail or a phone conversation.

After creating a case, you can perform the following actions:

- Add related activities
- Delete Case
- Resolve Case
- Cancel Case

Add Related Activities

Clicking the Add tab on the Ribbon, you can easily create an activity that will be associated with the case. You can use this option, for example, to add a reminder to call the customer with the resolution at a specific date and time.

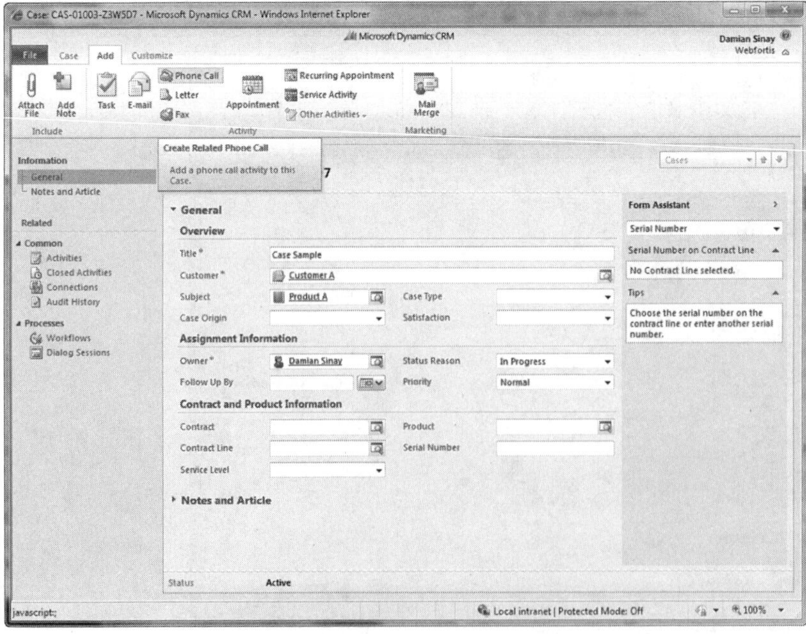

FIGURE 10.25 Adding a related activity.

Delete Case

This option deletes the case and its associated records and activities. This operation requires a confirmation, and there is no way to roll it back.

Resolve Case

Resolve the case by opening the case and clicking Resolve Case on the Ribbon. This opens the Resolve Case dialog shown in Figure 10.26, where you can enter the resolution description and billable time.

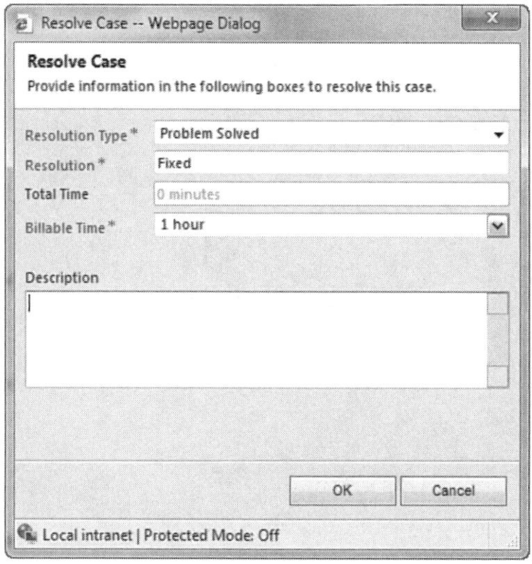

FIGURE 10.26 Resolve Case dialog.

> **CAUTION**
>
> After a case is resolved, you cannot edit its properties. If you want to make a change to a resolved case, you must reactivate it by selecting Reactivate from the Actions menu, making your changes, and then resolving it again.

Cancel Case

This option changes the case status to Cancelled. You can reactivate the case later, if necessary. After you select this option, a confirmation dialog appears.

> **CAUTION**
>
> To cancel a case, you cannot have an open activity associated with the case.

Reports

There are some predefined reports built for cases that you can run for the selected record or based on all records. To see these reports from the Cases interface, click the Report icon as shown in Figure 10.27.

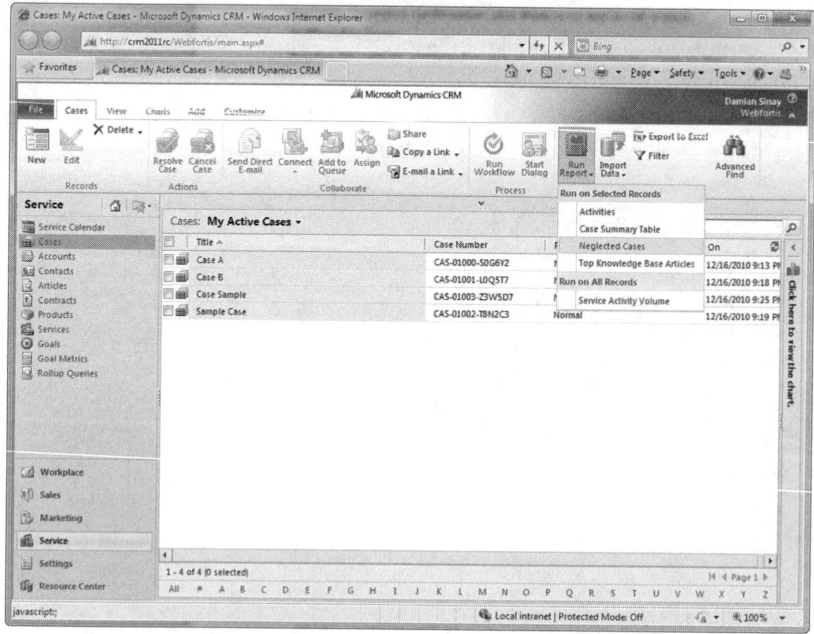

FIGURE 10.27 Case-related reports.

The available reports are

- Activities
- Case Summary Table
- Neglected Cases
- Top Knowledge Base Articles
- Service Activity Volume

Figure 10.28 shows the Case Summary Table report.

TIP

If the predefined reports don't meet your needs, you can easily create custom reports using the New Report Wizard.

▶ For more information about working with reports, see Chapter 11, "Reporting." To learn more about accounts and contacts, refer to Chapter 6.

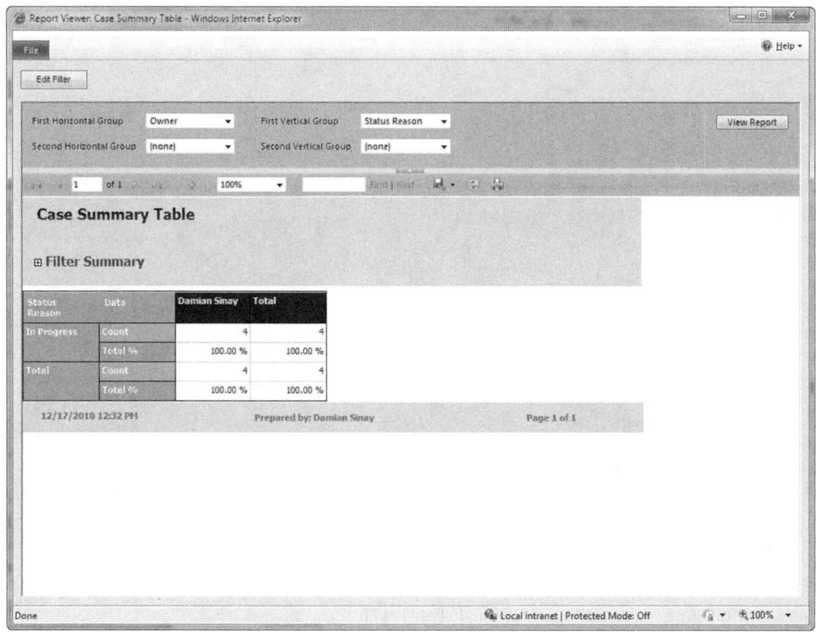

FIGURE 10.28 Case Summary Table report.

Articles

Articles used to be called Knowledge Base, or KB, in previous versions of CRM. It is a common repository where users can share their experience and solutions for common issues and customers' questions.

Articles has a small predefined workflow:

1. Anyone with the right permissions can create articles.
2. Articles are submitted for review.
3. A higher-level permissions user reviews articles and approves or disapproves them.
4. When approved, articles are published.

Figure 10.29 shows the steps involved in this workflow.

Before you start writing articles, it is important to consider the following things:

- Be sure to prepare the right article templates so that you have a consistent Knowledge Base of articles. You can manage templates by going to Settings, Templates, Articles Templates (see Figure 10.30).
- Be sure to set up the topics where you want people to submit their articles so that users can search for them more easily after they are published. You can do this by going to Settings, Business Management, Subjects (see Figure 10.31).

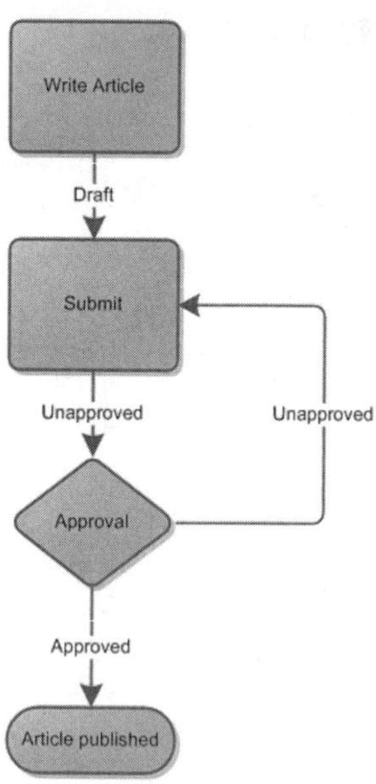

FIGURE 10.29 Knowledge Base workflow.

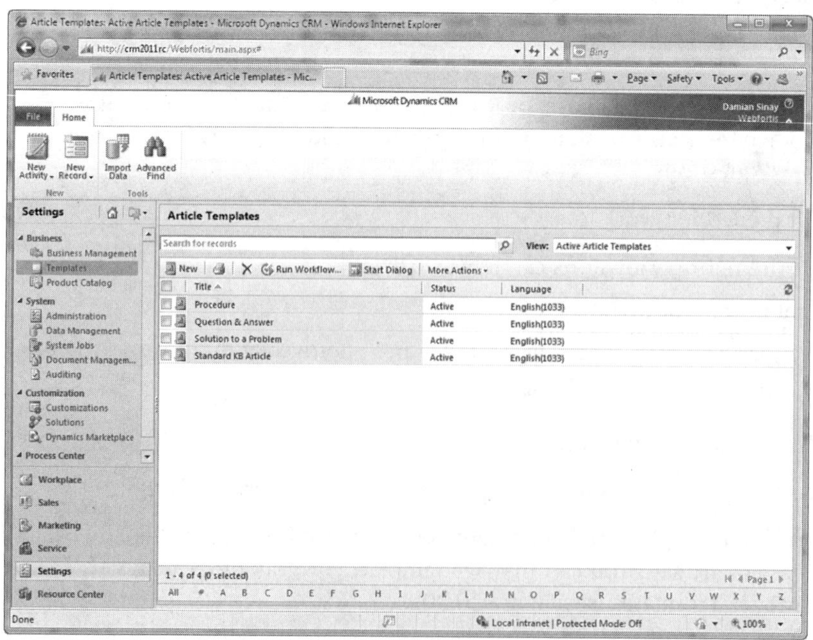

FIGURE 10.30 Managing article templates.

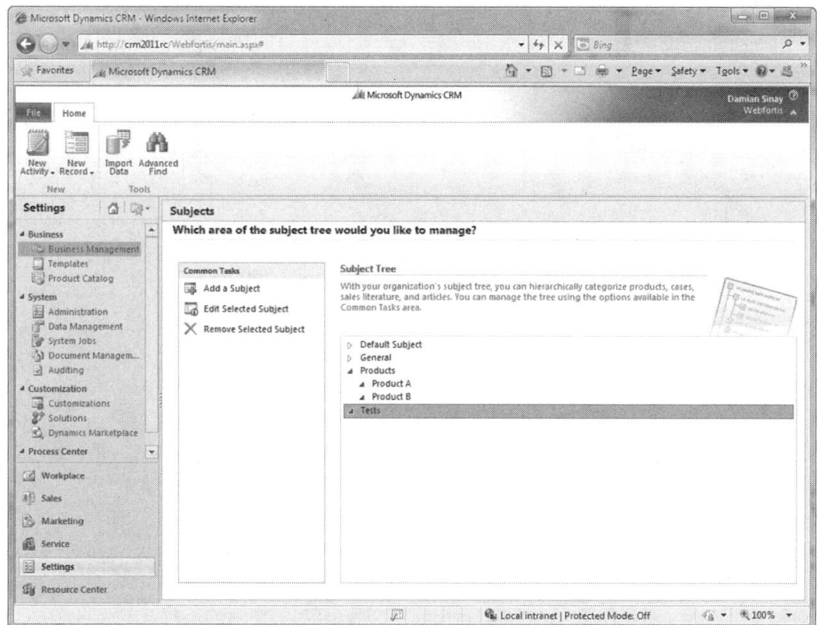

FIGURE 10.31 Configuring the subject tree.

- Be sure to set up the right permissions for the users who can write and submit articles, the users who can approve or reject the articles, and the users who can publish the articles.

By default, users with a CSR (Customer Service Representative) role can only write and submit articles; CSR Managers can approve, reject, and publish articles.

Figure 10.32 shows the default interface when you access the Articles interface as Administrator.

This interface is divided into the following views:

- All Articles
- Draft Articles
- Published Articles
- Unapproved Articles
- Unpublished Articles

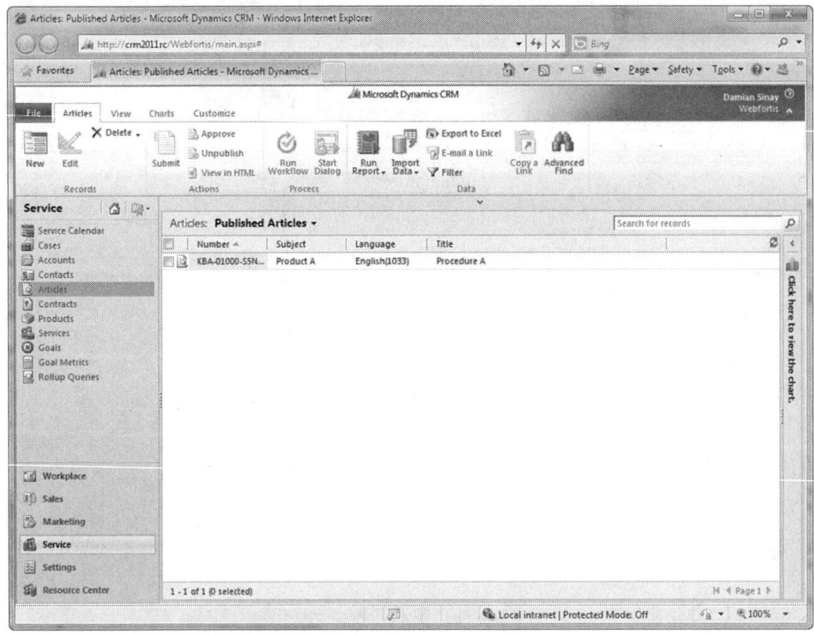

FIGURE 10.32 Articles interface.

No matter which view you are using, you can always create a new article. To create a new article, follow these steps:

1. Click the New button on the Ribbon. You will see the window shown on Figure 10.33.

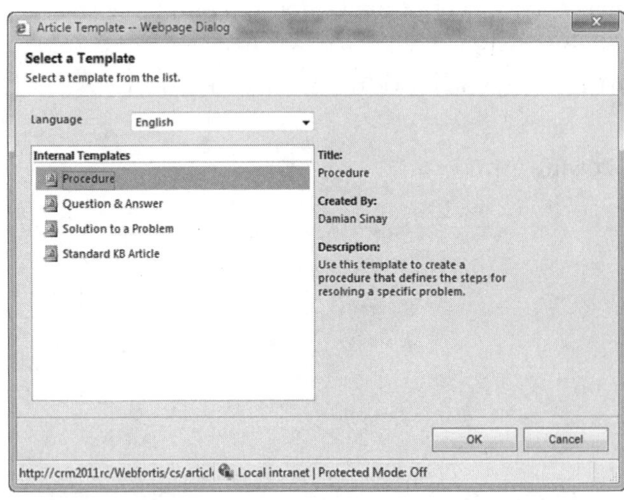

FIGURE 10.33 Selecting a template.

Microsoft Dynamics CRM 2011 also enables you to create articles for different languages, depending on the language packs you have installed. You can also create an article for any specific language, or you can create an article for All Languages if you want to have the article available for everybody.

▶ For more information on language packs, see Chapter 12.

2. Select the language and select a template from the list. Notice that the internal templates vary depending on the language selected. Click the OK button to continue.

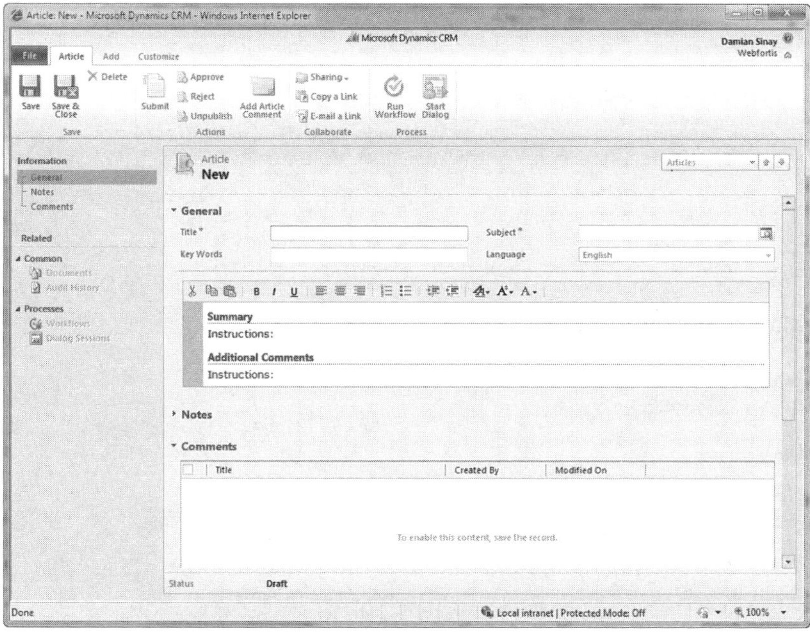

FIGURE 10.34 Writing a Knowledge Base article based on the Standard KB Article template.

3. Enter the title and subject, which are required for any article. The body format of the article depends on the selected template. It is recommended that you enter keywords for a faster search and lookup of the articles.
4. Click Save and Close to continue.

Subjects

To create new subjects, you must be logged in as System Administrator. Click Settings, Business Management, Subjects, click on any existing subject in the Subject Tree, and click the Add a Subject link from the Common Tasks list box as shown in Figure 10.36.

All articles go directly to the Draft folder when created, which means that they aren't available to users until the article is published.

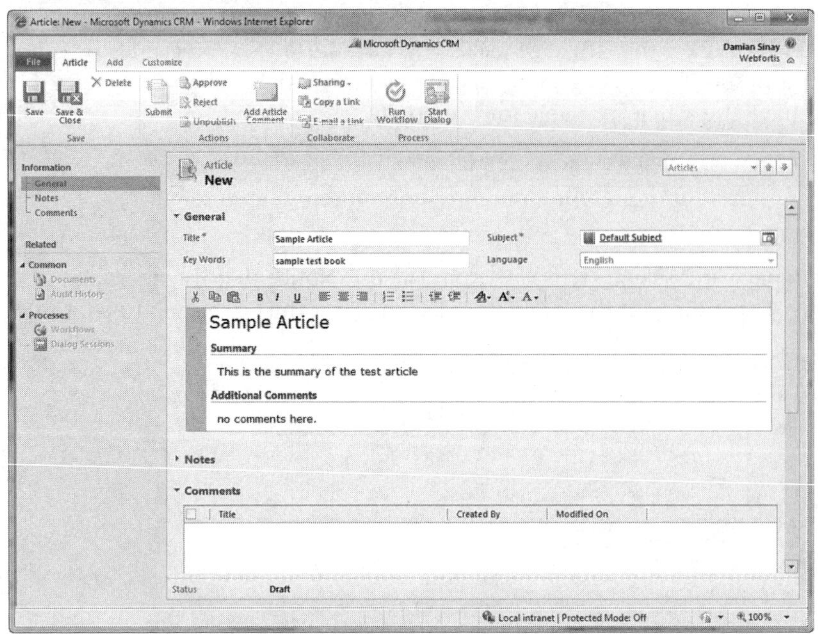

FIGURE 10.35 Writing a KB article.

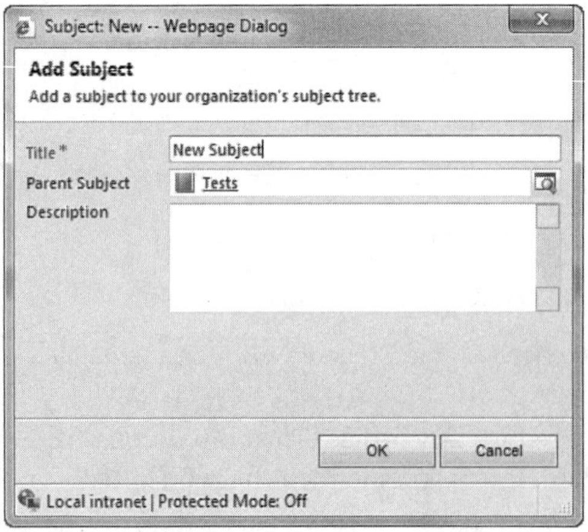

FIGURE 10.36 Subject Tree options.

Submitting an Article

An article must be submitted before it can be approved or disapproved. To submit an article, you must move to the Draft Articles view, select the article you want to submit, and click the Submit button that is on the Ribbon. You receive a dialog alert to confirm the operation, as shown in Figure 10.37.

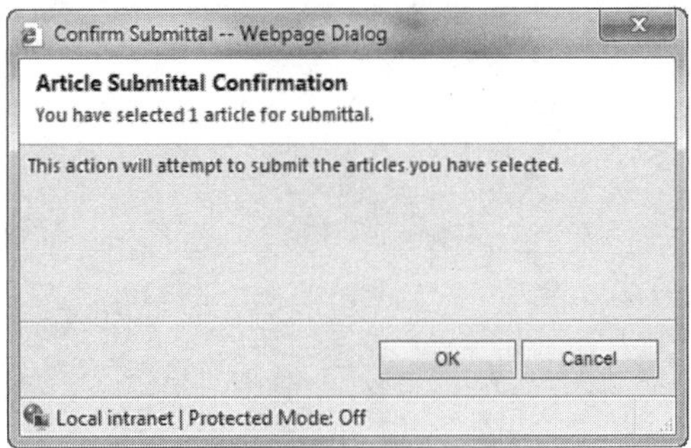

FIGURE 10.37 Article submission.

Click OK to submit the article. The article will be moved to the Unapproved Articles view.

Approving an Article

To approve an article, move to the Unapproved Articles view and select the article you want to approve; then click the Approve button on the Ribbon (see Figure 10.38).

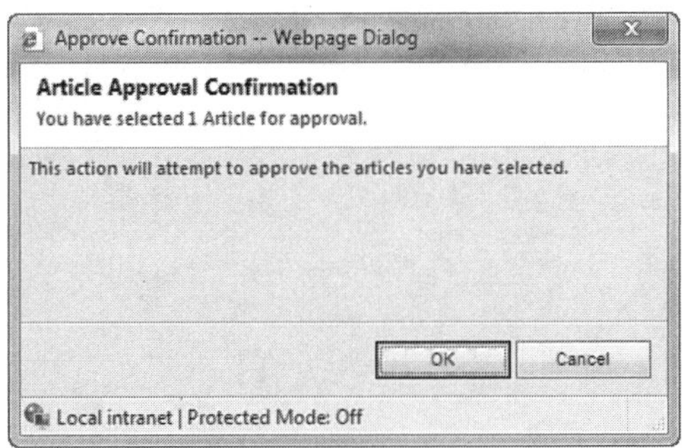

FIGURE 10.38 Article approval.

Approved articles move to the Published Articles view, where they are ready and available for other users.

Rejecting an Article

To reject an article, open the article located in the Unapproved Articles view and click the Reject button (see Figure 10.39).

This enables you to enter the rejection reason (see Figure 10.40).

After you click OK, the article moves back to the Draft Articles view. If the user who wrote the article wants to see the comments and reason about the rejection, he will have to move to the Draft queue, select the article, double-click it to open it, and move to the Comments tab to see the rejection reasons (see Figure 10.41)

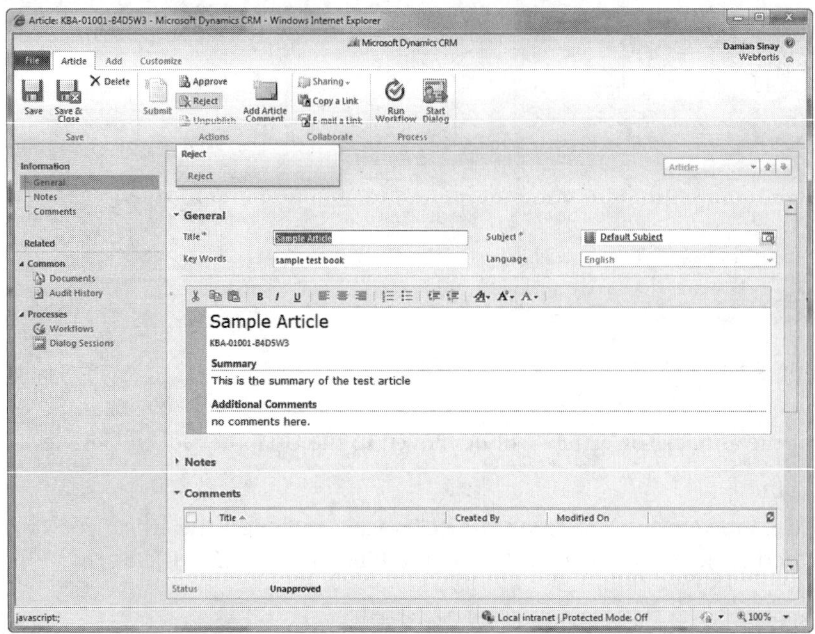

FIGURE 10.39 Article review for rejection.

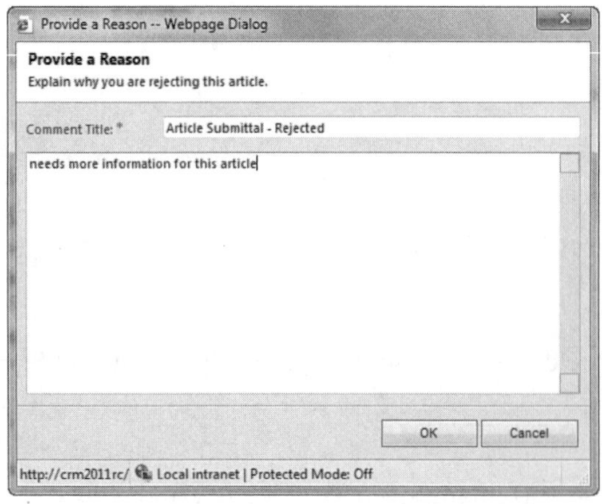

FIGURE 10.40 Article rejection.

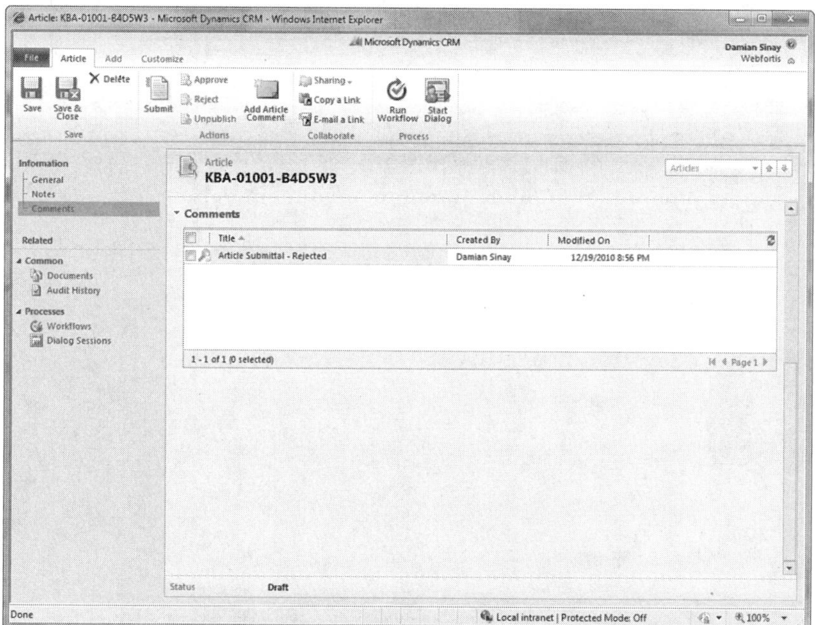

FIGURE 10.41 Article rejection reasons.

TIP

The article default workflow doesn't send alerts when a user submits, approves, or rejects an article, so a good practice would be creating a custom workflow for Article and/or Article Comment entities so that the users can be notified via e-mail when an article is submitted, approved, or rejected.

▶ See Chapter 24 for more information about how to create custom workflows.

Reports

A predefined report built for the Knowledge Base shows the top articles that are associated and used on cases.

CAUTION

The Top Knowledge Base articles report will be empty if you do not have at least one case record associated with the Knowledge Base articles.

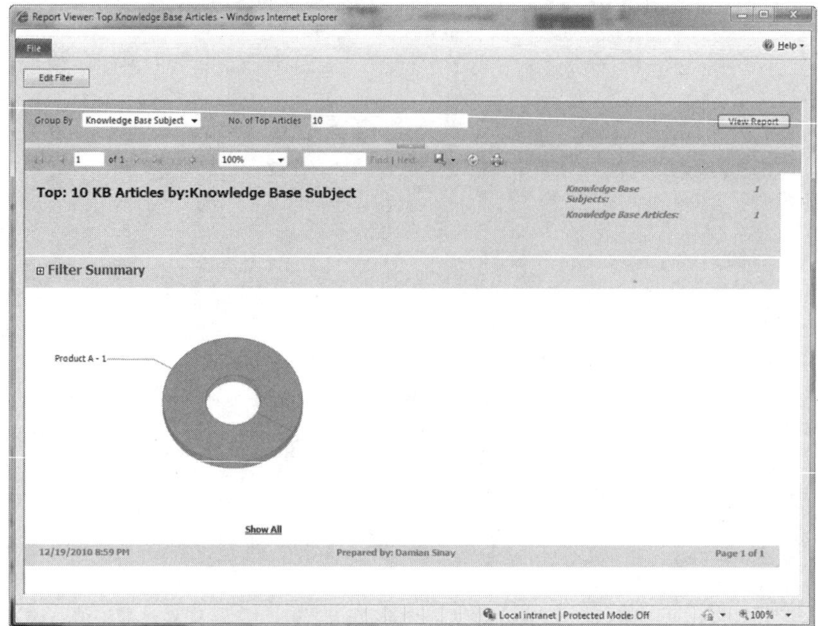

FIGURE 10.42 Top Knowledge Base articles report.

Articles Security

The Knowledge Base is not available to all the roles, by default. For example, the Salesperson role doesn't have access to create new articles, whereas a Customer Representative does. Of course, you can customize and change this configuration as necessary.

Contracts

Contracts are created from a template that is defined by a language. A *contract* is group of services and products that you sell to a client during a period of time. On a contract, you define when you start providing services to a customer and when you finish; both dates are required when you create a contract. Each contract also has billing information associated with it, such as which client you will bill, to what address you will send invoices, and billing frequency (monthly, quarterly, annually, and so on). The products you sell are defined in contract lines, where you can enter product details such as the quantity, the time you will include for support cases, and the total price and discounts.

To create new contracts, follow these steps:

1. Navigate to the Contracts section within the Service tab, and click New.
2. Select the language and then select a template (see Figure 10.43). Notice that the template depends on the language selected. To create a new template, go to Settings, Templates, and select the Contract Templates option.

▶ See Chapter 12 for more information on how to manage and create new templates.

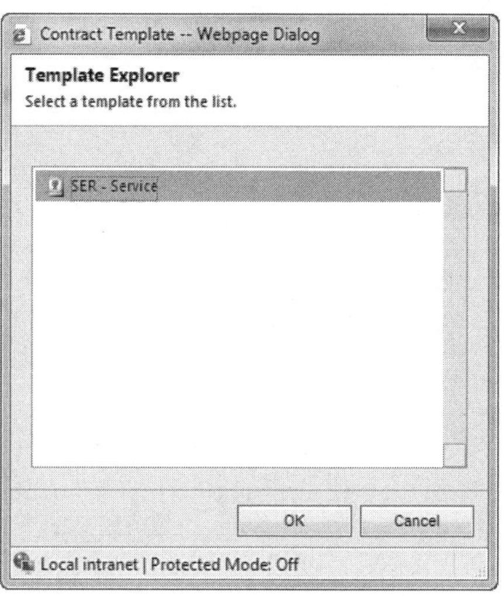

FIGURE 10.43 Selecting a contract template for a new contract.

3. Enter the required fields: Contract Name, Customer, Contract Start Date, Contract End Date, Billing To Customer, and Currency (see Figure 10.44). Click Save to continue.

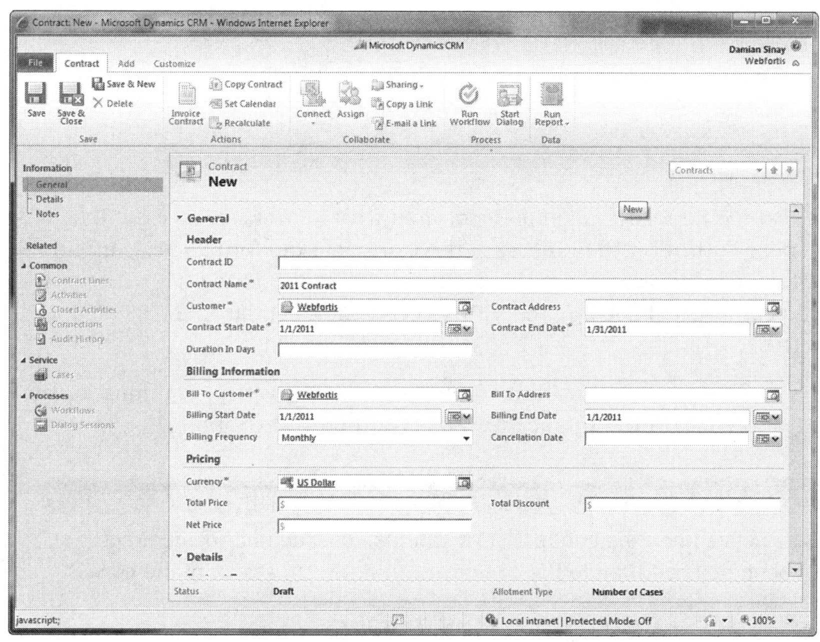

FIGURE 10.44 Creating a new contract.

4. Go to the Contract Lines tab inside the Common section, and click the Add New Contract Line button on the Ribbon.
5. Enter the required fields (see Figure 10.45).

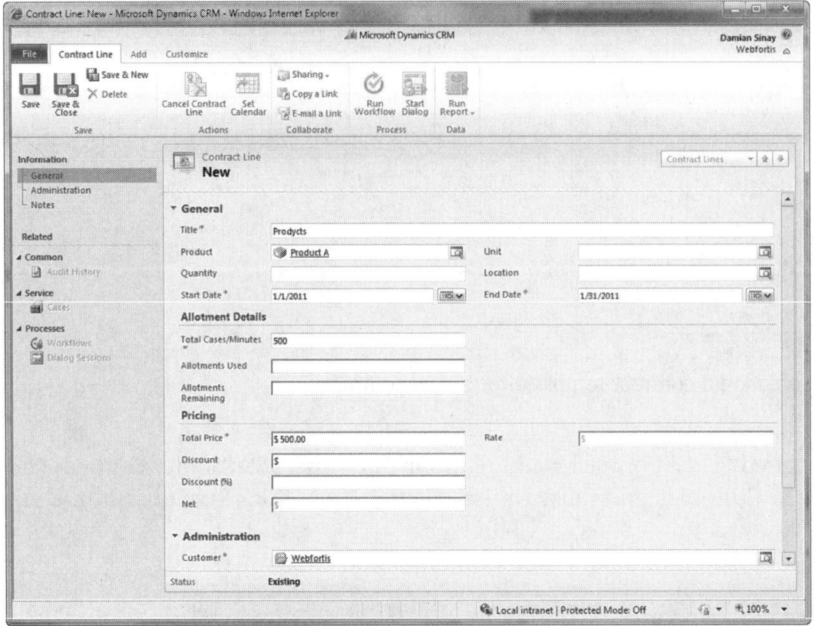

FIGURE 10.45 Adding a new contract line.

6. Click Save and Close.

Each contract line also has a specific calendar associated with it. You can access it by clicking on the Set Calendar button on the Ribbon of the Contract Line form. This is useful for customer representatives to know whether the client should be supported 24 × 7 or only at regular times. You can use a check box to easily convert the calendar to 24 × 7 support, as shown in Figure 10.46.

After the contract is created, its status is Draft. To make a contract active, you must open the contract record, and click on the Invoice Contract button on the Ribbon.

NOTE

The contract will be active when the contract start date has passed and the contract end date has not been reached. Before the contract start date, the status of the contract will say Invoiced.

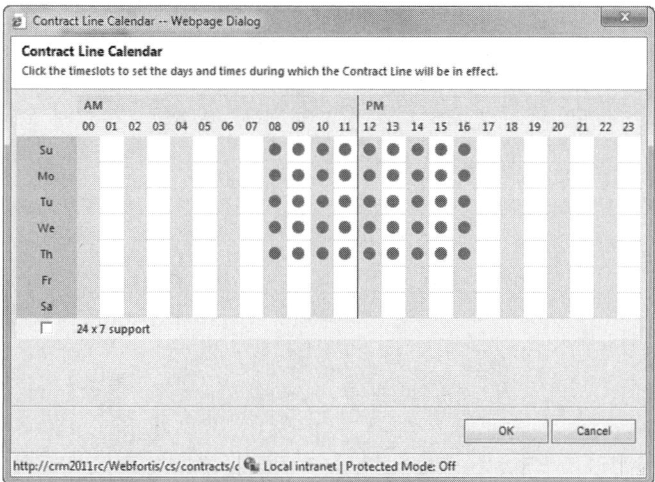

FIGURE 10.46 Contract line calendar.

Goals, Goal Metrics, and Rollup Queries

▶ Refer to Chapter 8, "Working with Sales" for information related to Goals, Goal Metrics, and Rollup Queries.

Summary

The Service area is a valuable and important part of Microsoft Dynamics CRM. When used correctly, you have a centralized view of calendars and schedules, and can easily perform scheduling tasks.

When working with cases, it is important to remember a key feature: The summary of the activities that make up the case (and therefore the case resolution) are the resultant work effort—something neither expressed nor available on the main Case entity by default. We commonly see organizations request the ability to see case resolution times and the ability to quickly/easily track times directly against the Case entity. (An example of this might be a spinning/countdown clock when the form is opened/being worked on.) Microsoft Dynamics CRM does NOT support this requirement without custom development; however, the actual work to put this in place is actually quite minimal. The majority of effort in putting something like this together is in defining the actual business process and how best to implement. (For example, does the clock start automatically on open or does the user click a button to start? What happens on form load—does the clock stop or does it stay open until proactively stopped?)

You have learned how to work with services in Microsoft Dynamics CRM 2011 by using the Service Calendar, working with cases to track customer's issues, working with contracts, and managing the articles as a common place to share typical business procedures.

CHAPTER 11
Reporting

IN THIS CHAPTER

This version of Microsoft Dynamics CRM features improved reporting capabilities. Reports are more dynamic and flexible, and a reporting wizard is included that enables users to create basic reports on the fly and share them with the organization.

Additionally, reporting options are greatly increased with CRM Online. Before Microsoft Dynamics CRM 2011, your reporting options with CRM Online were limited to existing reports, advanced find views, or a custom reporting solution that typically required an on-premise reporting server. Now, however, reports can be created and uploaded directly to CRM Online and the limitations that previously existed are lessened.

NOTE

There are still some limitations with CRM Online. See the "Report Wizard" section in this chapter to learn about SQL versus Fetch limitations and how to address and overcome them.

Reporting Defined

Microsoft Dynamics CRM uses Microsoft SQL Server Reporting Services (SSRS) as the engine for creating and rendering reports. SSRS is a separate application that you can install on a different server than SQL Server or even the Microsoft Dynamics CRM Server if desired. Microsoft

Dynamics CRM then connects to SSRS by using the reporting services URL, as specified during installation.

The CRM Reporting Extensions are not required during a normal, non-IFD installation. For IFD installations, or when you make modifications to the default setup, you must install the CRM Reporting Extensions for SSRS to avoid the error shown in Figure 11.1.

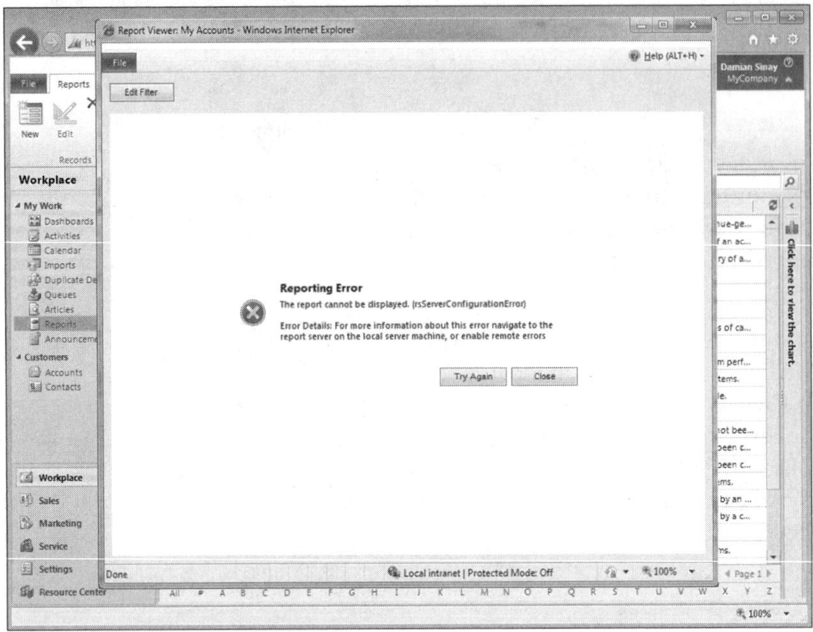

FIGURE 11.1 Reporting error.

▶ To install the CRM Reporting Extensions for SSRS, follow the steps outlined in Chapter 4, "Setting Up CRM 2011."

After the Reporting Extensions are installed, you can access reports in Microsoft Dynamics CRM from the main reporting interface, which is found in the Workplace area (see Figure 11.2), or directly from various entities in the system (Accounts, Contacts, and so on).

CAUTION

When viewing reports in the system, you can see all available reports; however, you might or might not be able to display the underlying data, depending on your permissions.

When working with an entity record, such as Contacts shown in Figure 11.3, you can run specific entity reports without needing to access the main Reports area.

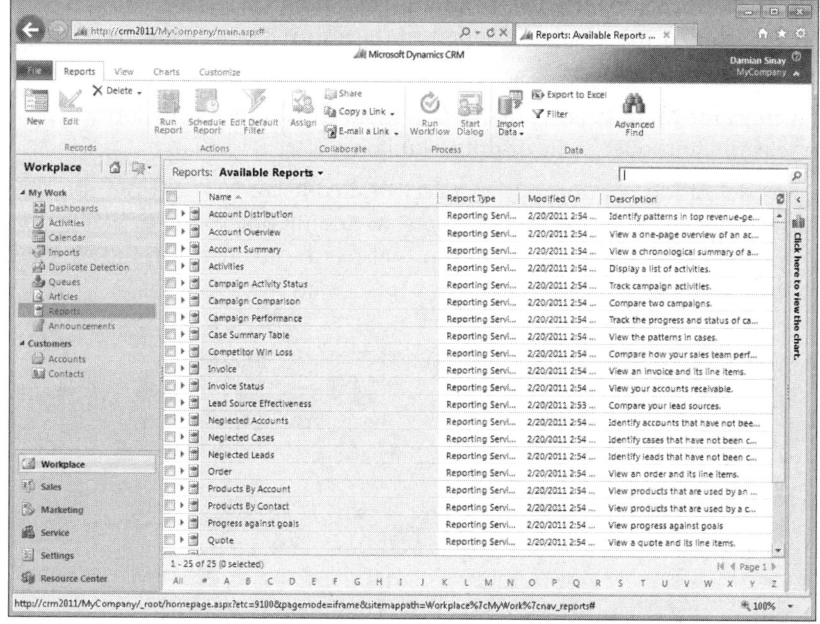

FIGURE 11.2 Reports in the Workplace area.

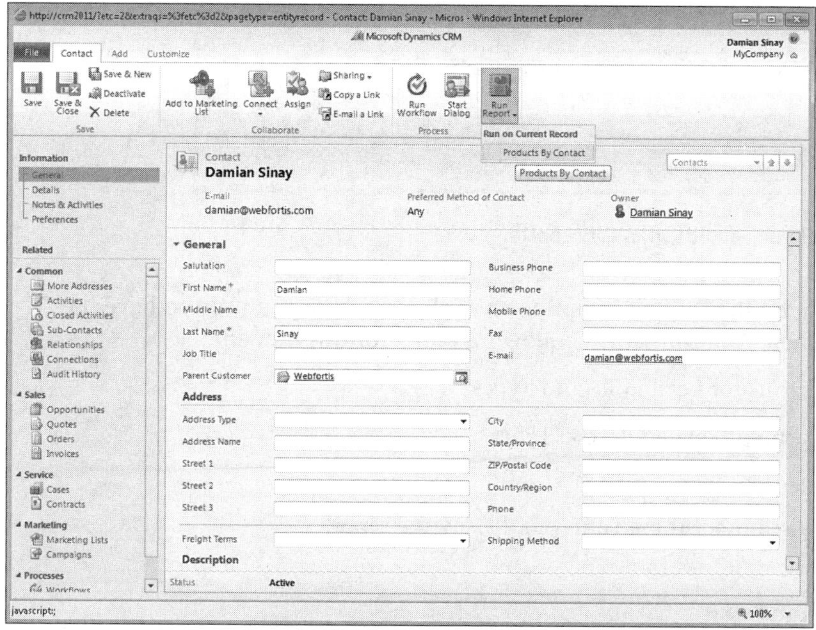

FIGURE 11.3 Reports from the Contacts entity.

Although some reports are already configured to run directly from the entity, you can easily configure a report so that it is available as part of the entity if you desire, as is shown in Figure 11.3. To do so, follow these steps:

1. Select a report from the Main Reports interface located in Workplace, Reports, by clicking it to select it, and select Edit from the Ribbon.
2. When the report definition window opens, select Related Record Types from the Categorization section and then click the . . . button. Adding one of the available values to the selected values enables you to run that report directly from the selected entity (see Figure 11.4).

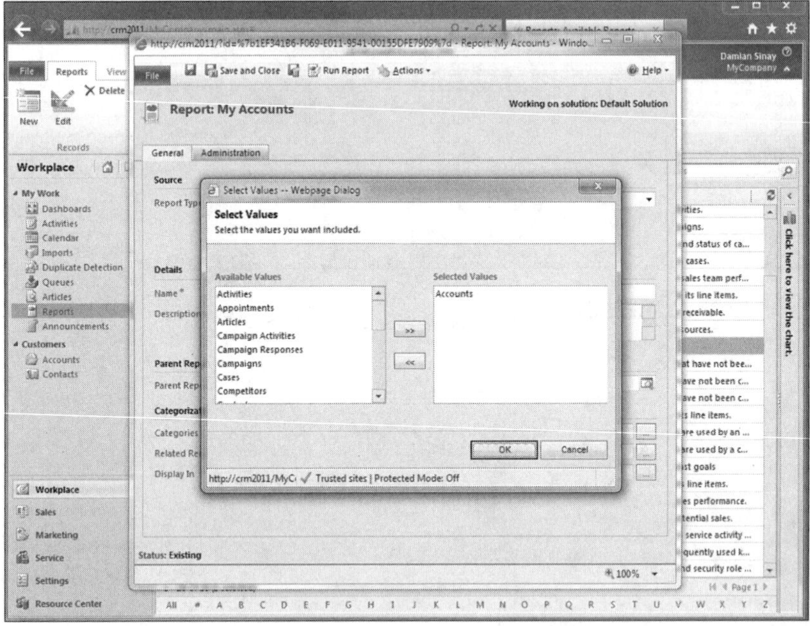

FIGURE 11.4 Related record types for reports.

3. You can also use the Display In option to configure where you want to have the reports available. You can set the following values for this property:
   - Forms for Related Record Types
   - Lists for Related Record Types
   - Reports Area

   You can choose any of these values to display the report.

Reports Filters

All reports in CRM have a special feature that enables you to prefilter the underlying data when you run a report. You can configure this feature on the first screen when you double-click on a report (see Figure 11.5).

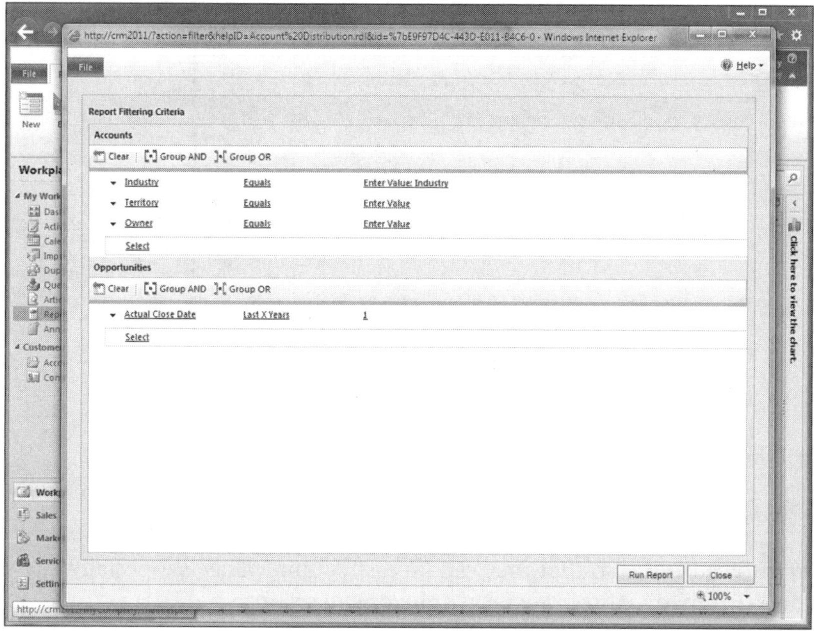

FIGURE 11.5 Report filtering criteria.

Here you will see the report criteria that were defined as part of the report definition during initial report creation. Although you can manually change these values and properties every time you run a report, you can also change the default filtering criteria by editing the report definition. To do so, go to the main Reports option located in Workplace, Reports, click on the report you want to modify, and then select Edit Default Filter from the Ribbon (see Figure 11.6).

Make any necessary changes, and then click the Save Default Filter button to save your changes.

CAUTION

Keep in mind that changes to the Edit Default Filter will affect all users running the report.

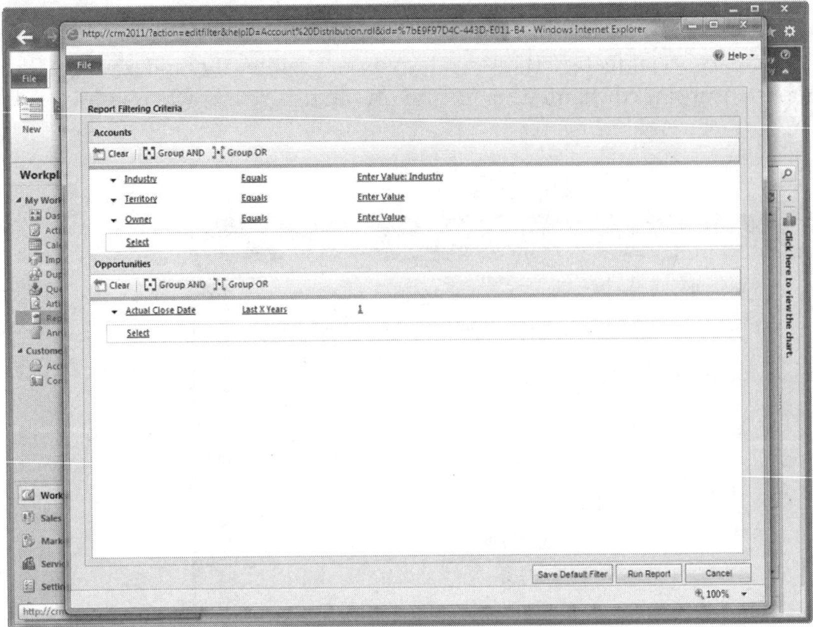

FIGURE 11.6 Modifying the default report filtering criteria.

Categories

Reports are divided into categories so that they can be easily found. This is especially useful when working with many custom reports in the organization.

By default, only the following four categories are created in the system, but you can easily create more as necessary:

- ▶ Administrative Reports
- ▶ Marketing Reports
- ▶ Sales Reports
- ▶ Service Reports

Each category has a predefined view to filter and is easily accessible, as shown in Figure 11.7.

A new feature of CRM 2011 allows the user to access the reports categories or views with fewer clicks than the previous version. So, if you are not in the reports page and you are in another page such as accounts, you can use the shortcut menu that becomes available when you pass the mouse over the Reports menu option in the sidebar, as shown in Figure 11.8.

To set a category on a report, select the report from the Reports interface and then click the Edit button from the Ribbon. Click the . . . button under the last section labeled Categorization next to the field Categories, and then select the required categories for the report (see Figure 11.9).

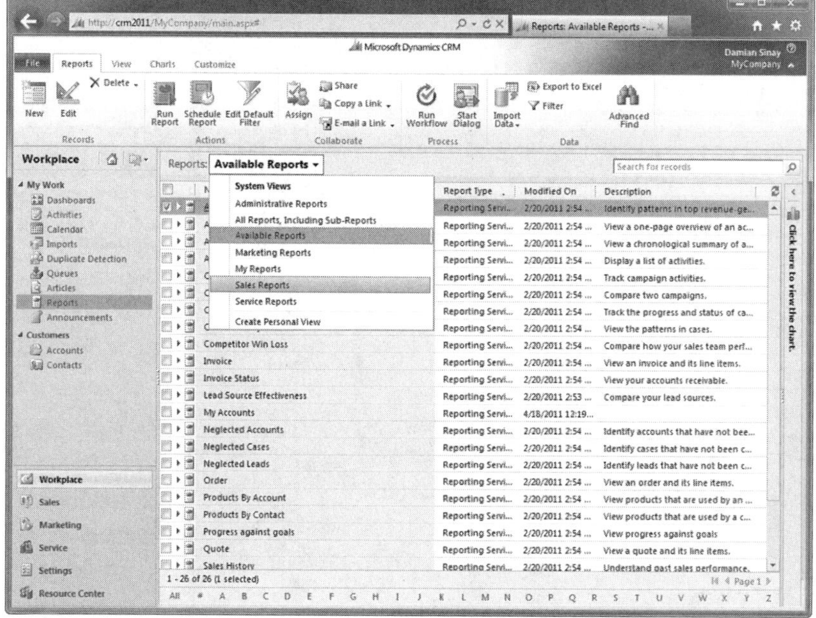

FIGURE 11.7 Report Categories.

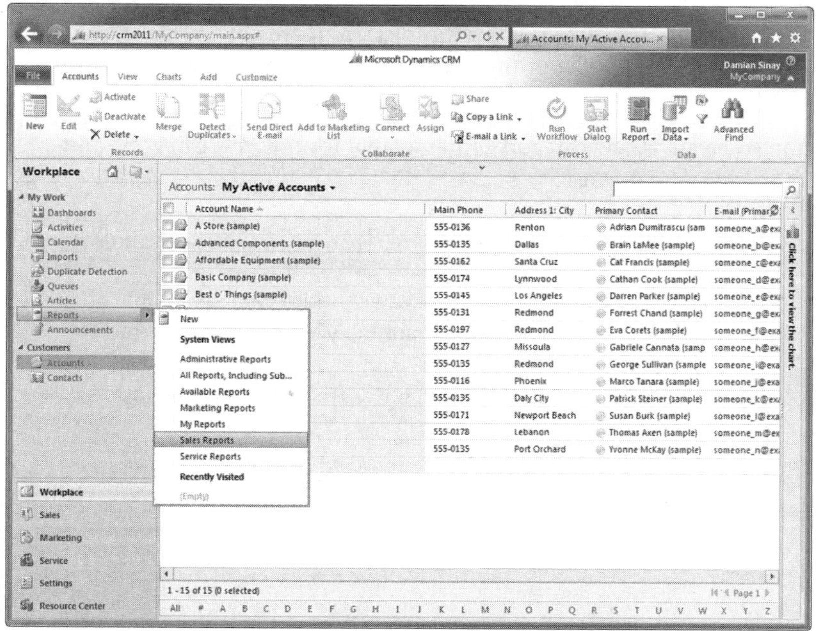

FIGURE 11.8 Report categories view.

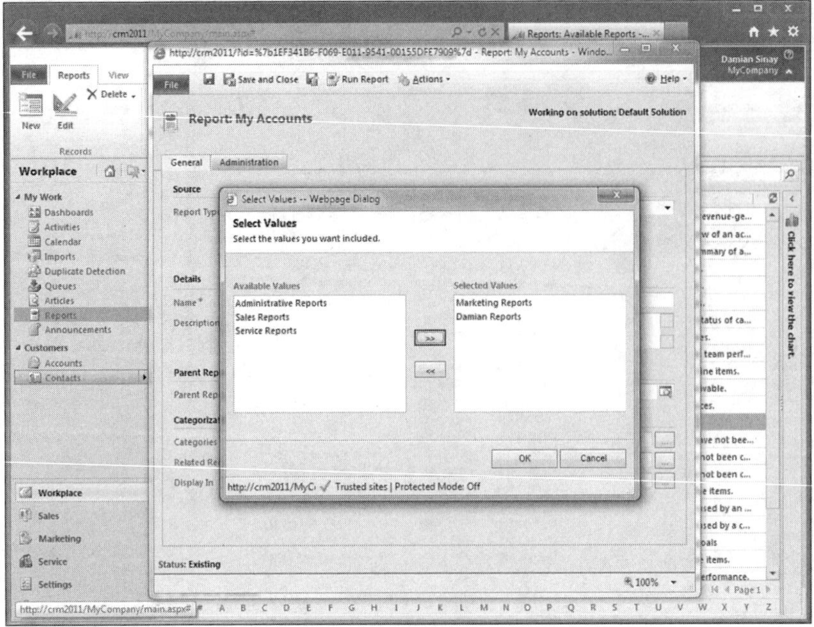

FIGURE 11.9 Associating report categories.

To create new report categories, navigate to the Administration area in the System group in Settings and click System Settings. Select the Reporting tab to edit the categories, as shown in Figure 11.10.

Click the Add button to create a new category, enter a label for the new category, and then click OK twice to close the dialogs.

TIP

If you would like to use the new category in the shortcut list, which was shown in Figure 11.8 as part of the report, you will need to create the view with the new category manually.

▶ For details about how to create custom views refer to Chapter 23, "Customizing Entitles."

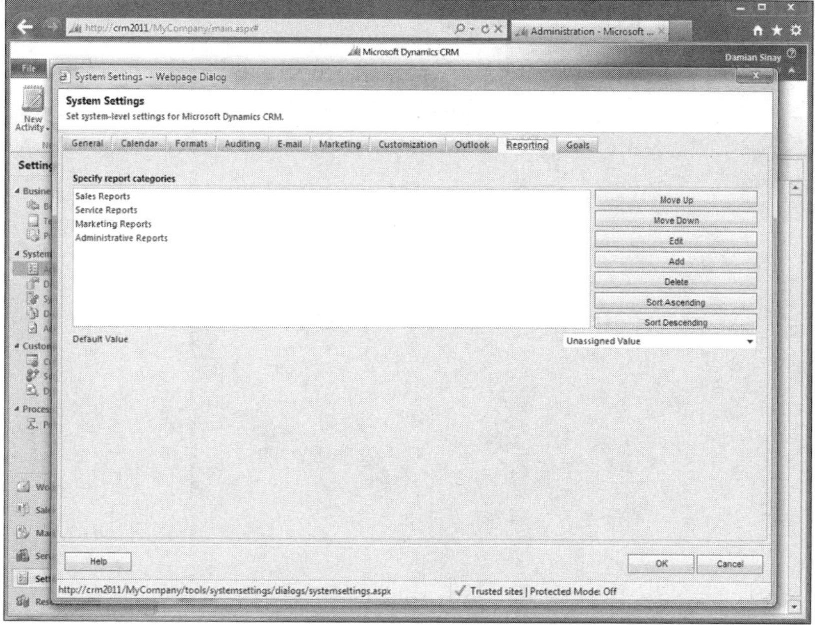

FIGURE 11.10 Managing reporting categories.

Administration

When editing a report (by selecting a report and then selecting Edit from the Reports Ribbon), there are two tabs: General and Administration. The Administration option is used to configure the administrative options for the report. By using the options on the tab, you can set the owner of the report and whether the report should be viewed by the user or by the entire organization (see Figure 11.11).

TIP

You can also change the report owner by selecting Assign from the Actions drop-down.

Report Wizard

The Report Wizard enables users to build basic reports without development knowledge by providing an easy-to-use interface for doing so. With Microsoft Dynamics CRM 2011, reports are generated using native Fetch-based queries through a new data source that is now available to support Fetch queries that can be found in the Report Manager with the name of MSCRM_FetchDataSource. Additionally, the final reports are actually Microsoft SQL Server Reporting Services reports, or `.rdl` files, which you can further manipulate using a more advanced editing tool such as Visual Studio.

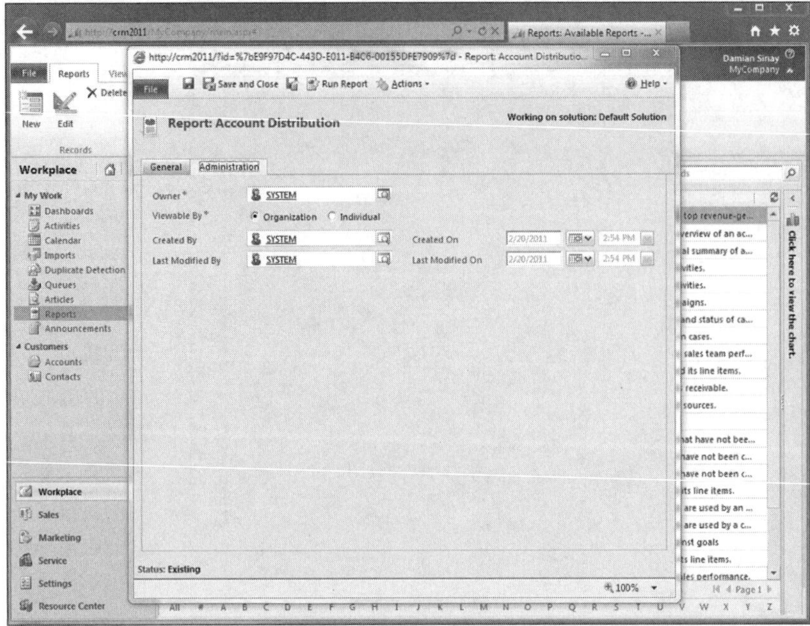

FIGURE 11.11 Report administration.

NOTE

As with previous versions, reports built with the Report Wizard can be edited using Visual Studio. This is typically done to increase performance, layout, and report complexity. To do so, you need to download and install a Visual Studio plug-in called Microsoft Dynamics CRM 2011 Report Authoring Extension(CRM2011-Bids-ENU-i386.exe),which needs to be installed to use the required Fetch data source type to parse the Fetch queries that exist in the reports data source generated by the Report Wizard.

CAUTION

When working with reports, be sure to consider the fact that although you can continue to use data source type as SQL (typically used to query older reporting versions), be aware that CRM Online will not support SQL queries for security reasons, and the Fetch Extension needs to be used instead.

For users that are not familiar with the Fetch XML query schema, this new version enables users to create any query with the Advanced Find tool and easily download or view the Fetch XML generated by this tool for reuse on custom reports.

An example of a fetch XML query is as follows

```
<fetch>
  <entity name="account" enableprefiltering="1" >
  <attribute name="name" />
</entity>
</fetch>
```

This code would be equivalent to the following SQL query:

```
select name from FilteredAccount
```

Noticed the enableprefiltering attribute in the entity node allows the query to user prefilters.

To use the Report Wizard, follow these steps:

1. Navigate to Workplace and then Reports. Select New, which opens the dialog shown in Figure 11.12.

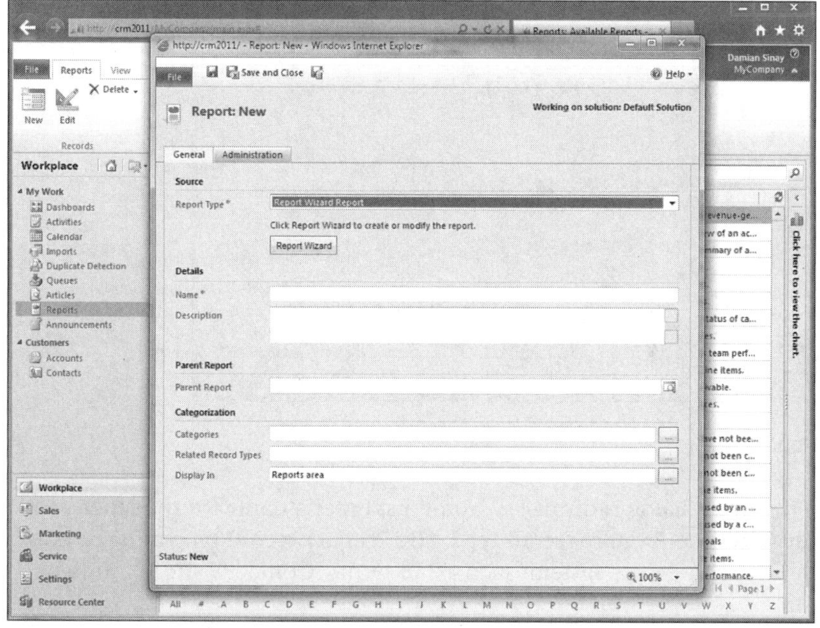

FIGURE 11.12 New report.

2. The Report Type option defaults to Report Wizard Report, which is the one used in this example. If you had created an external report, such as one using Visual Studio, you would select Existing File and upload the file directly. Link to a Web Page enables you to link to a web page that contains a report on a custom web page, such as what we could do for a Silverlight report.
3. Click the Report Wizard button to start the wizard. After it starts, you have two options for creating a new report:

- Start a New Report
- Start from an Existing Report

The second option only enables you to create a new report from a report that was previously generated through this wizard and to make edits to an existing report through the wizard. In this example, you'll create a new report by selecting the first option and clicking Next to continue.

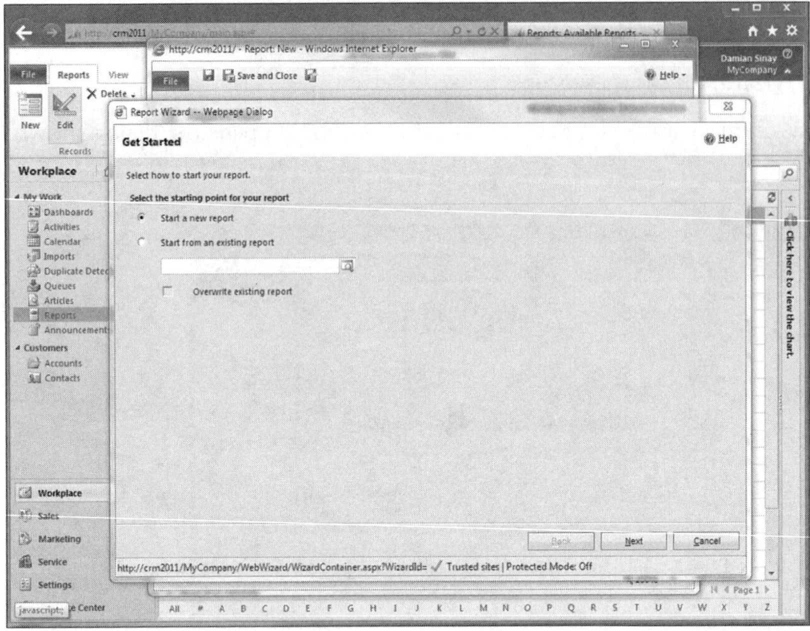

FIGURE 11.13 Report Wizard.

4. The Report Properties dialog is displayed. You must enter a name for the report, and you also must select the Primary record type. The Primary record type must be one of the entities available in the system, such as Accounts, Contacts, and so on (see Figure 11.14).

   Click Next to continue.

NOTE

The Related record type option values depend on the entity you select on the Primary record type. It shows all the entities related to the primary entity selected. For example, we will select Contacts as the Related record type so that we can create a report of the Contacts by Account.

5. Select the default report filters for the primary or related record types selected in the previous step (see Figure 11.15).

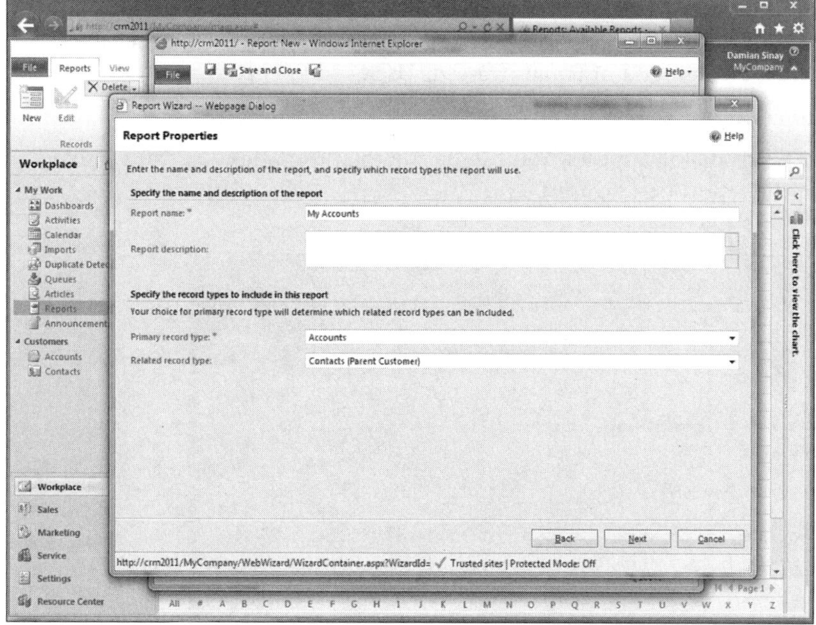

FIGURE 11.14 Report properties.

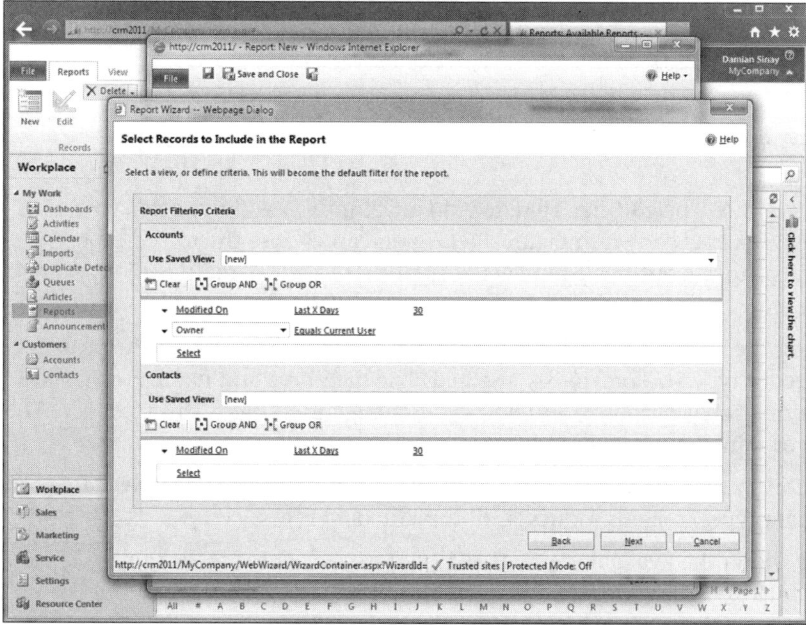

FIGURE 11.15 Report Wizard report filtering criteria.

You can use a previously used view or create a new one. To add a new filter, click the Select link and select the property you want to use. In this example, we selected the property Owner with criteria of Equals Current User.

Click Next to continue.

6. The Lay Out Fields dialog appears. You can define the properties you want to have displayed on the report (see Figure 11.16).

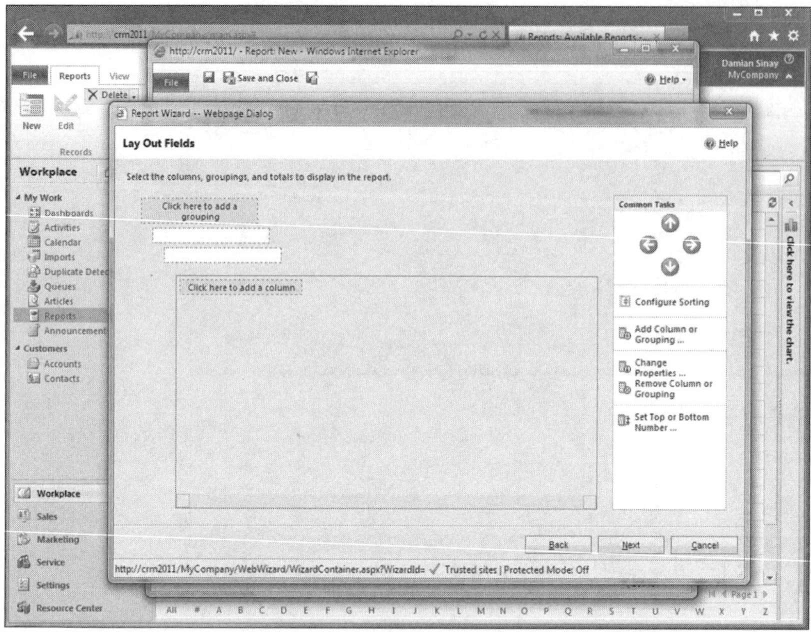

FIGURE 11.16 Lay out fields.

7. Select the main box labeled Click Here to Add a Column to add the fields you want to see in the report. As shown in Figure 11.17, you can choose the record type, which is limited to the entities you selected as primary and related record types in the previous steps.

8. After selecting the record type, select the column, which will be any of the properties of the record type you previously selected. The data type and name are displayed only for informational purposes, and you can't change them from this interface. The only thing you can change is the column width in pixels.

   The last option in the Add Column dialog is called Summary Type. It is available for only some data types, such as money and numeric data types.

   Figure 11.18 shows the available options that you can select for the summary type. (They are similar to SQL aggregate functions.)

9. If any of the summary types were used, it would be a good idea to configure the grouping by selecting the box labeled Click Here to Add a Grouping.

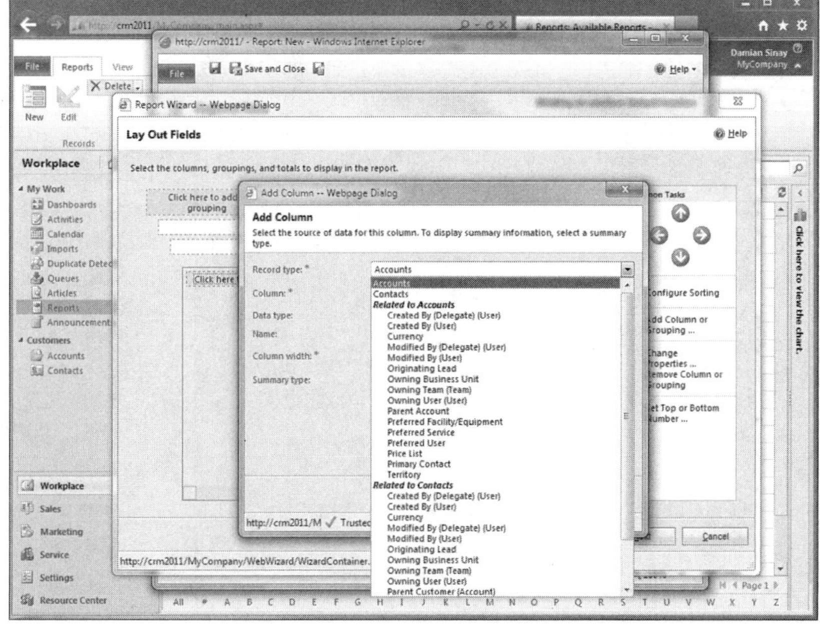

FIGURE 11.17 Adding columns to the report.

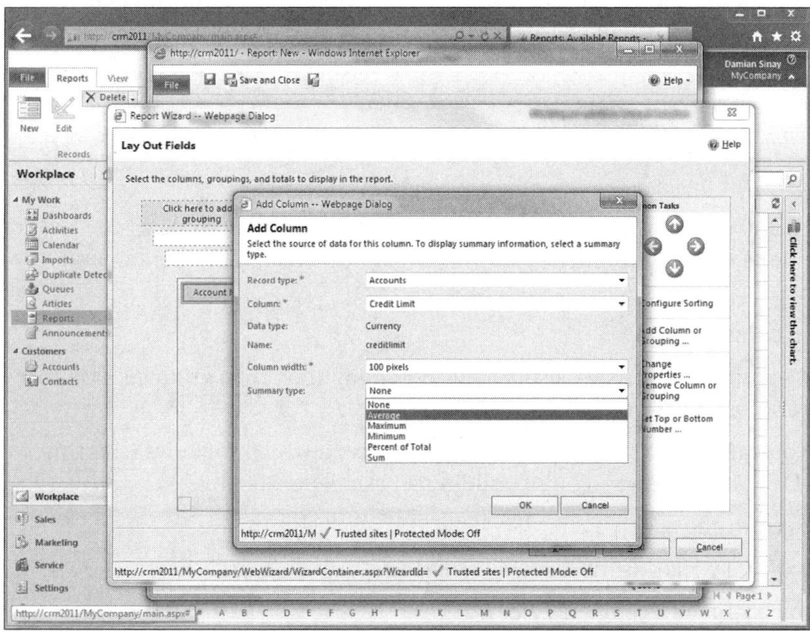

FIGURE 11.18 Summary types.

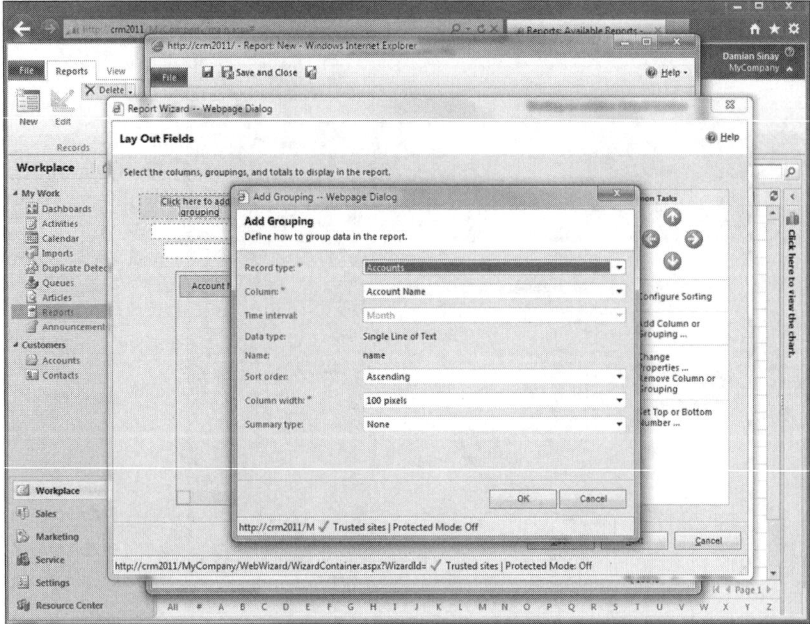

FIGURE 11.19 Add grouping.

The columns that you can select in the grouping are based on any of the entities previously selected.

NOTE

You can create up to three different groupings that will be nested among themselves.

The Time Interval option is available only for fields that have datetime as their data type. The options enable grouping by day, week, month, year, fiscal period, and fiscal year.

Click Next to continue.

10. After defining which columns to display and how they should be grouped, you can specify their format (see Figure 11.20).

    From here, you can select the basic format of the report, which includes Charting. Select Table Only here because you're building a basic report for this example.

    Click Next to continue.

11. The last step of the wizard is the Report Wizard Summary.

    Click Next to continue (see Figure 11.21).

12. The report is generated and the results are displayed (see Figure 11.22). Note that there might be a delay while the report is being generated.

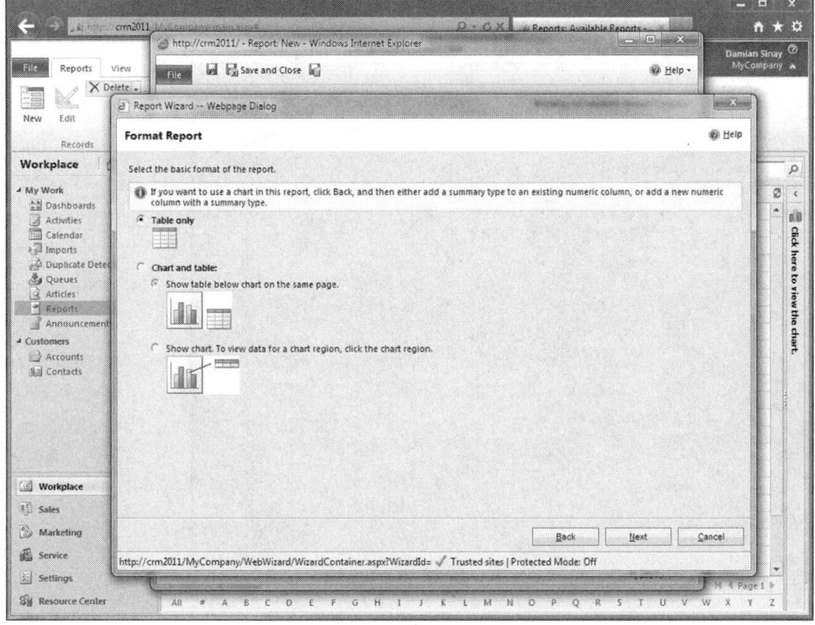

FIGURE 11.20 Format report.

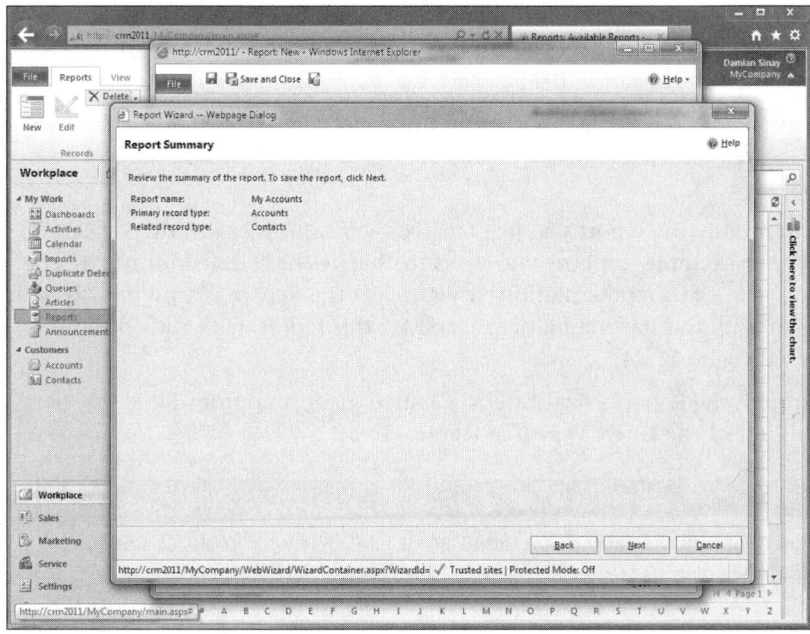

FIGURE 11.21 Report summary.

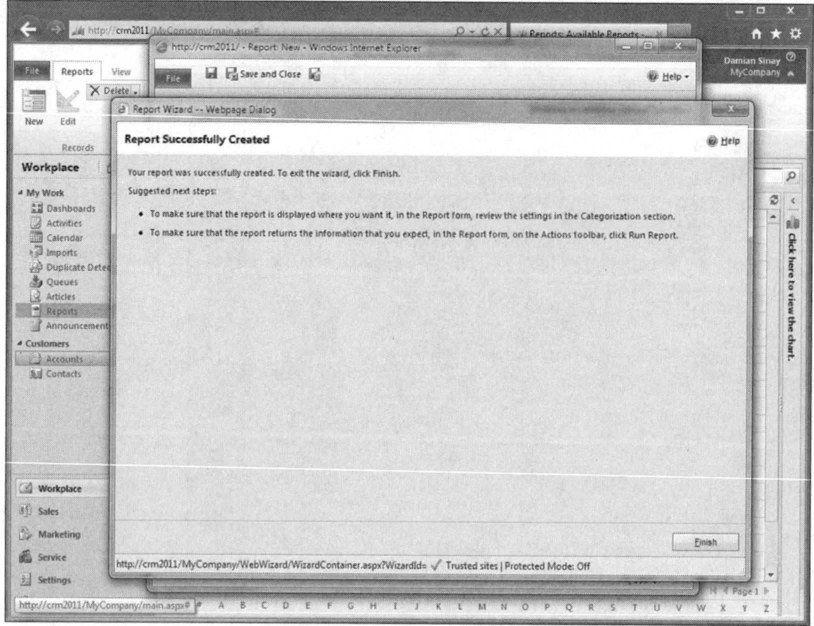

FIGURE 11.22 Report successfully created.

13. Click Finish to close the wizard. If necessary, you can now select, and edit the properties of the report. Notice that the wizard has automatically populated the name of the report and the categorization fields.
14. To test the new report, select the report from the Reports interface, and either select Run Report, located on the top menu of this dialog, or double-click the report name (see Figure 11.23).
15. If you want to modify the report you just created, you can easily run the Report Wizard again. For example, suppose you want to change the selected format from a table to a graphical chart representation. If you select the Report Wizard button, the report will start with the starting point selected for this report, with the option to overwrite it (see Figure 11.24).
16. Continue through the Report Wizard steps. Change the format from Table to Chart and Table, and select the Chart Type (see Figure 11.25).

NOTE

The Pie Chart type might be disabled if you didn't select the Sum or Percent of Total option in the Summary columns.

17. Click Next to customize the chart format. You can select the labels of the x-axis and y-axis, as well as the fields for them, as shown in Figure 11.26.

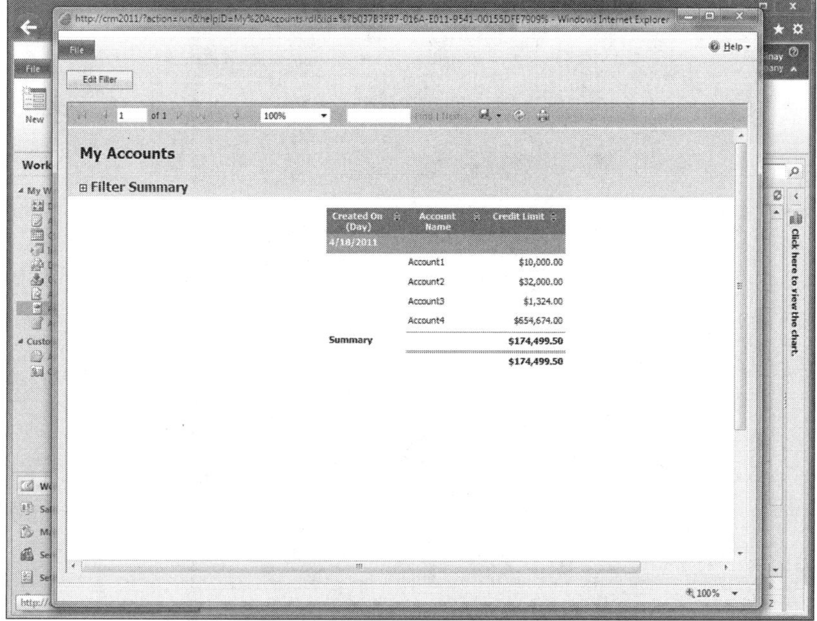

FIGURE 11.23 Running the report.

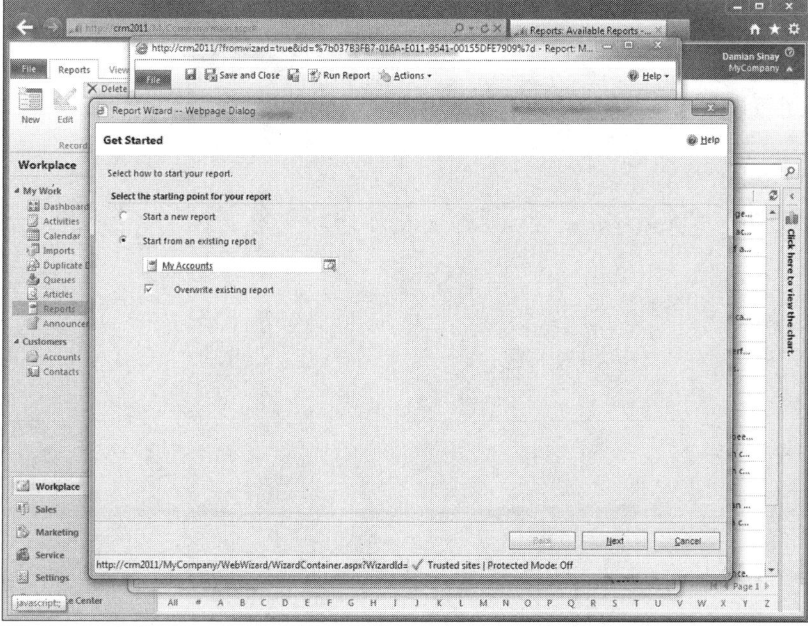

FIGURE 11.24 Modifying the report.

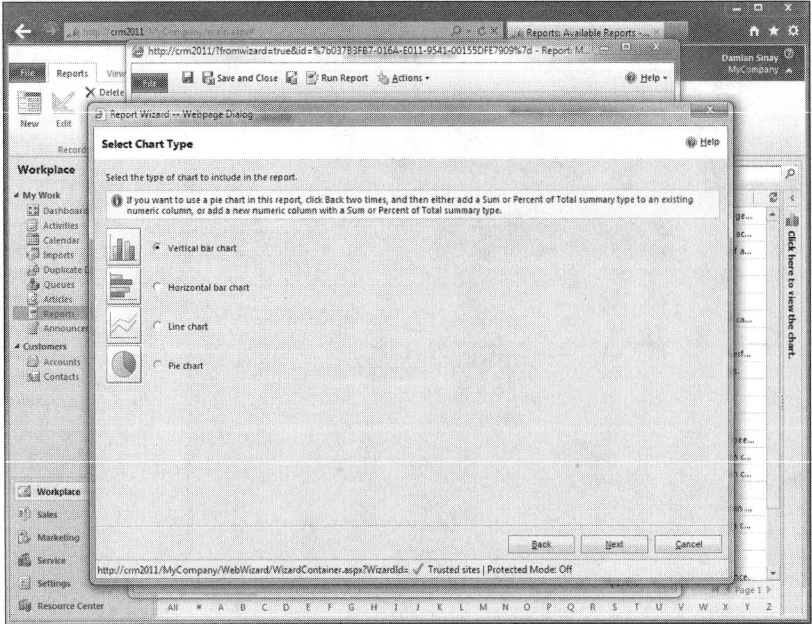

FIGURE 11.25 Select chart type.

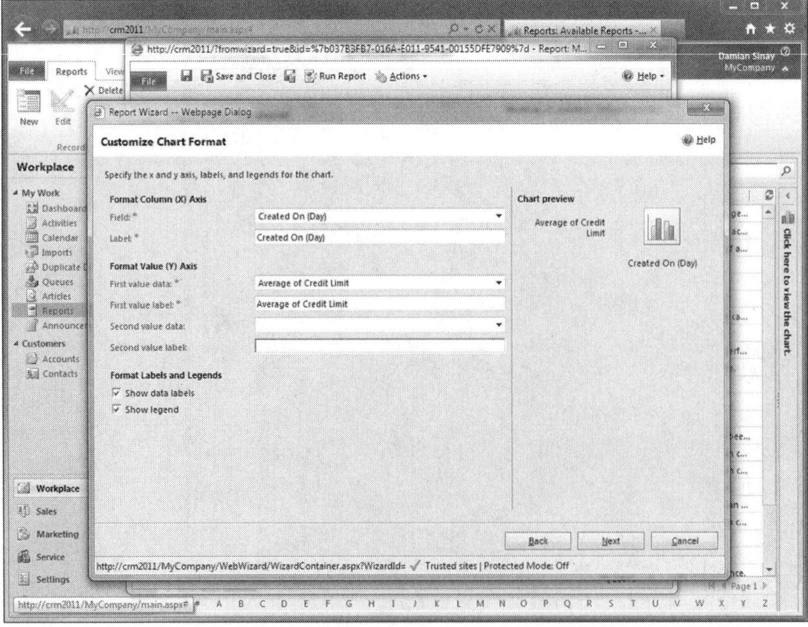

FIGURE 11.26 Customize chart format.

18. Click Next to go to the summary screen for review, and then click Next to modify the report. Now if you run the report, it will appear as shown in Figure 11.27.

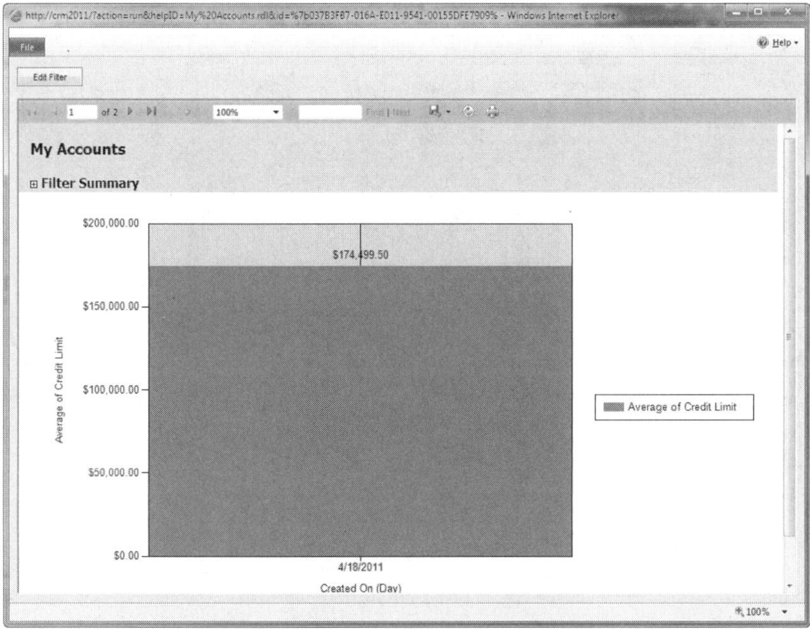

FIGURE 11.27 Running the report with the Chart format.

Scheduled Reports

SRS has many advanced features that are closely integrated in this version of Microsoft Dynamics CRM. For example, you can schedule report execution.

This is a great feature that many organizations use to proactively receive data. For example, the CFO typically would like to see all orders entered into the system for the week—SSRS can generate this report automatically every Friday morning and then e-mail the report to the CFO, with no user intervention, so that when he arrives in the office in the morning there is an e-mail from CRM with the report attached.

To access this feature from the Reports interface, select a report, and then select Schedule Report from the Reports Ribbon (see Figure 11.28).

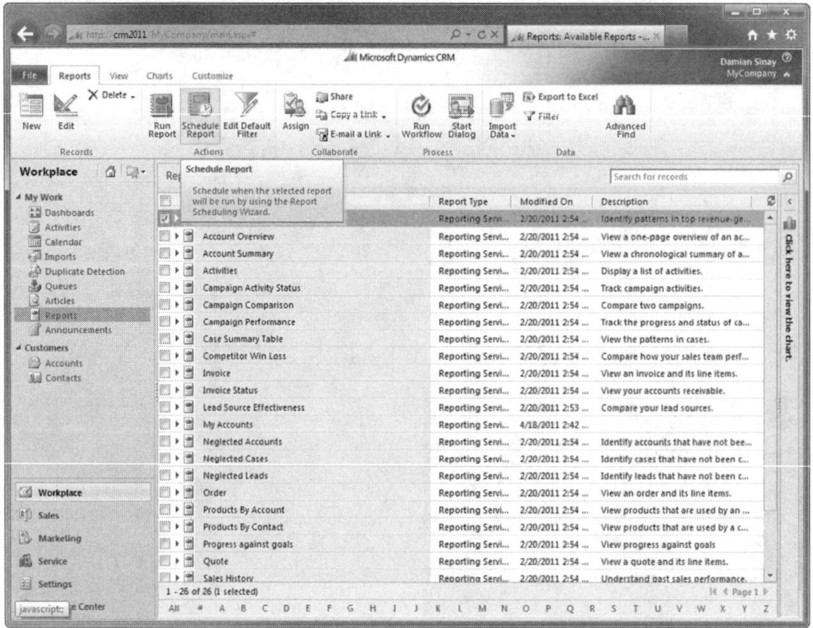

FIGURE 11.28 Schedule report.

NOTE

By default, only administrators have access to this feature. To give this feature to a lower-privileged role, an administrator must grant permission in the Add Reporting Services Reports security option under Miscellaneous Privileges in the Core Records tab of the security role configuration interface that can be accessed from the Settings area, Administration section; click on Security Roles, and then double-click the role you want to customize. Figure 11.29 shows this permission added to the Customer Service Representative role.

The Report Scheduling Wizard starts and presents two options (see Figure 11.30):

- On Demand
- On a Schedule

On Demand

On-demand reports generate a snapshot as soon as you finish the wizard.

Depending on the report selected, you must specify values for the report parameters, as shown in Figure 11.31.

Miscellaneous Privileges			
Add Reporting Services Reports	●	Bulk Delete	○
Delete Audit Partitions	○	Manage User Synchronization Filters	○
Publish Duplicate Detection Rules	○	Publish E-mail Templates	○
Publish Mail Merge Templates to Organization	○	Publish Reports	○
View Audit History	○	View Audit Partitions	○
View Audit Summary	○		

FIGURE 11.29 Setting permissions for scheduling reports.

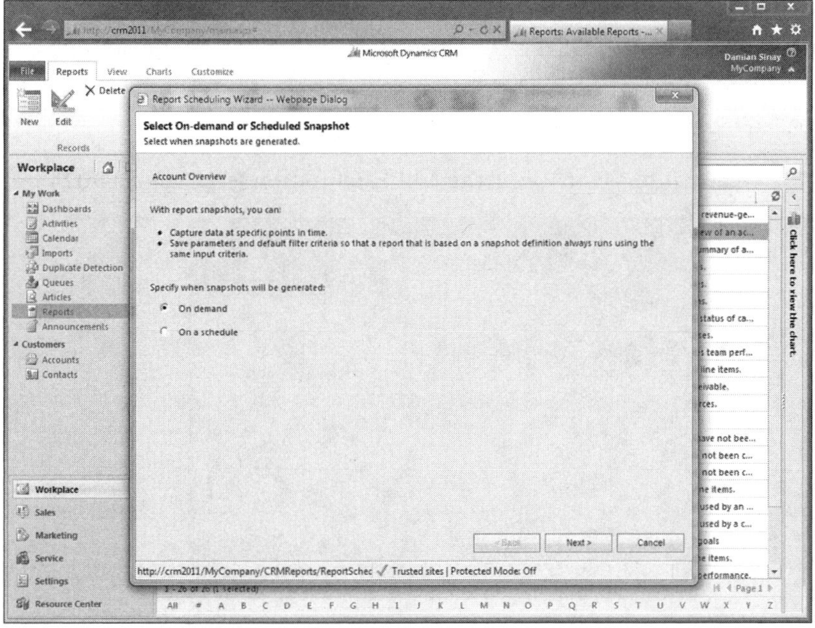

FIGURE 11.30 Report Scheduling Wizard.

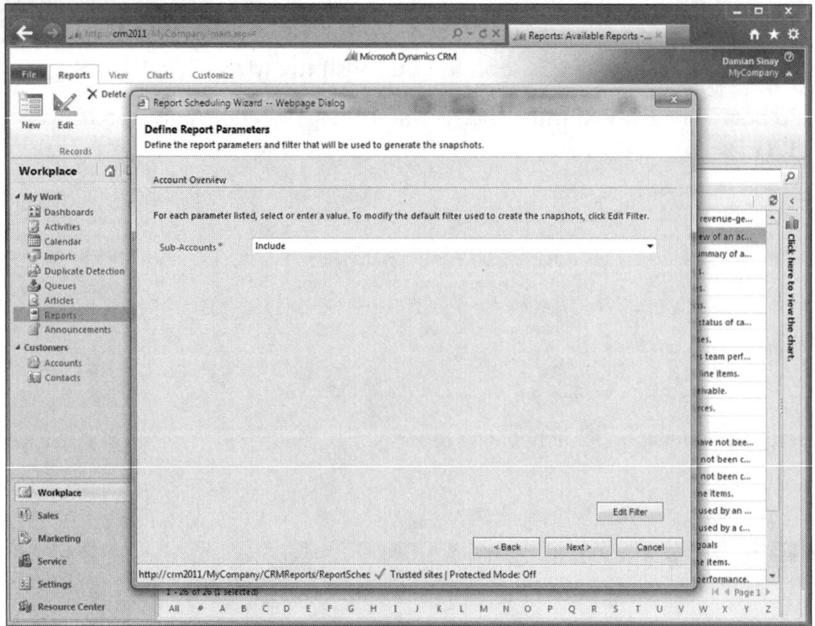

FIGURE 11.31 Define report parameters.

You can also edit the default filters by clicking the Edit Filter button (see Figure 11.32).

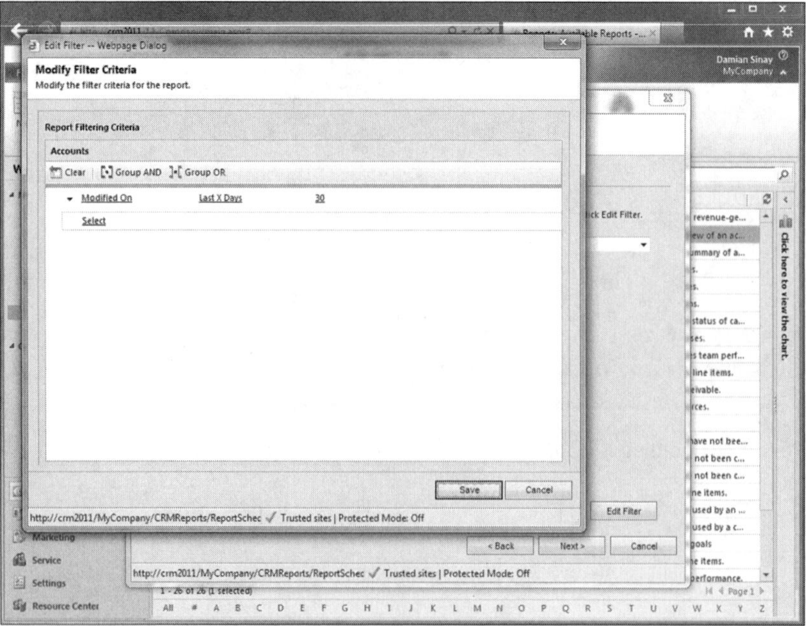

FIGURE 11.32 Modify filter criteria.

After you click Next, you can choose whether to generate the report snapshot now or just save the report snapshot definition for later use (see Figure 11.33).

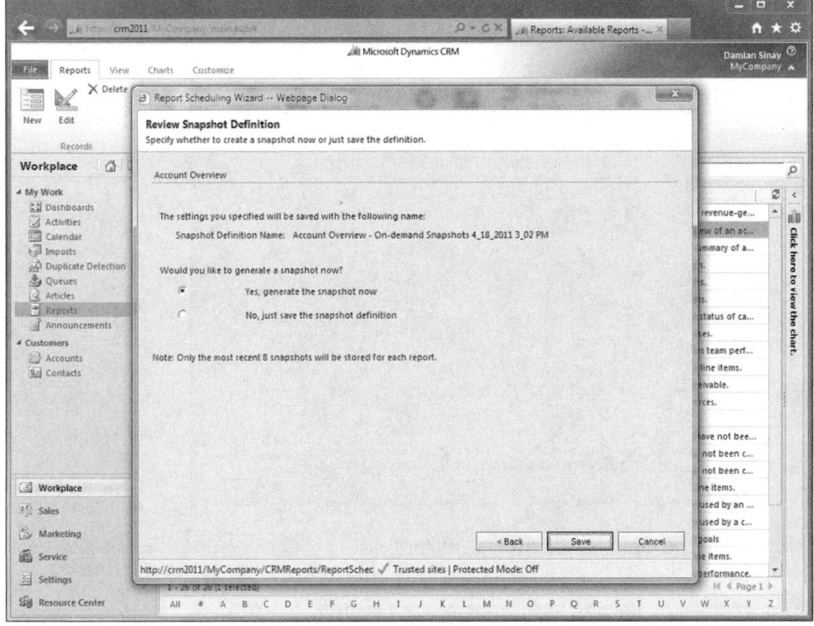

FIGURE 11.33 Review snapshot definition.

If you choose the first option and then select Save, the new snapshot is generated and the overview is detailed, as shown in Figure 11.34.

This screen contains all the necessary instructions to access and view the snapshot report that was just created.

Click Finish to close the wizard. You will then see the snapshot shown in Figure 11.35.

On a Schedule

Selecting On a Schedule enables you to select the frequency of the report execution, as well as the time when you want the report to execute (see Figure 11.36). The available options for the frequency are as follows:

- Once
- Hourly
- Daily
- Weekly
- Monthly

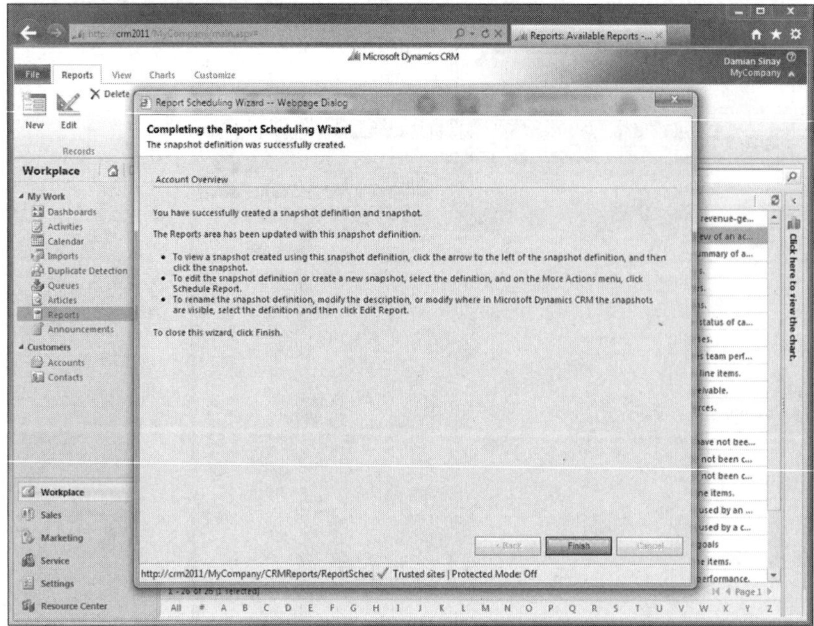

FIGURE 11.34 Completing the Report Scheduling Wizard.

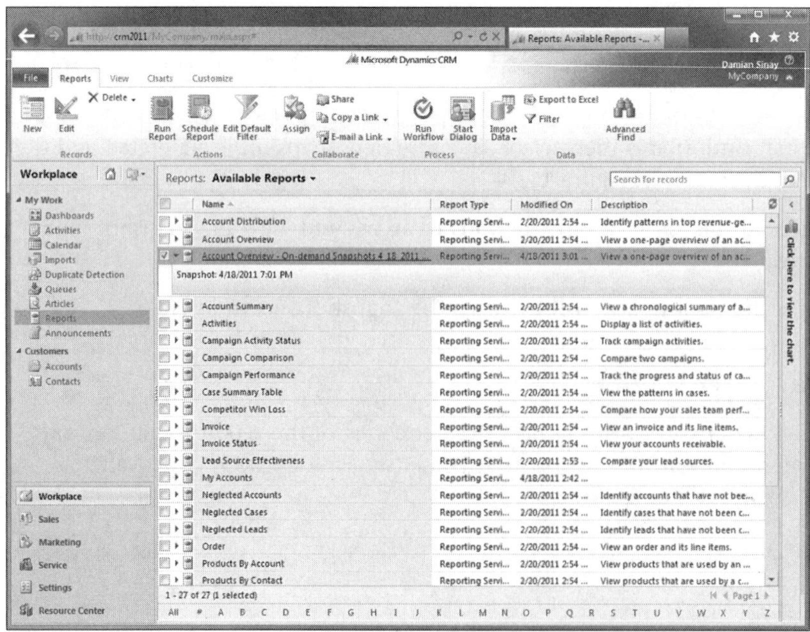

FIGURE 11.35 Snapshot report.

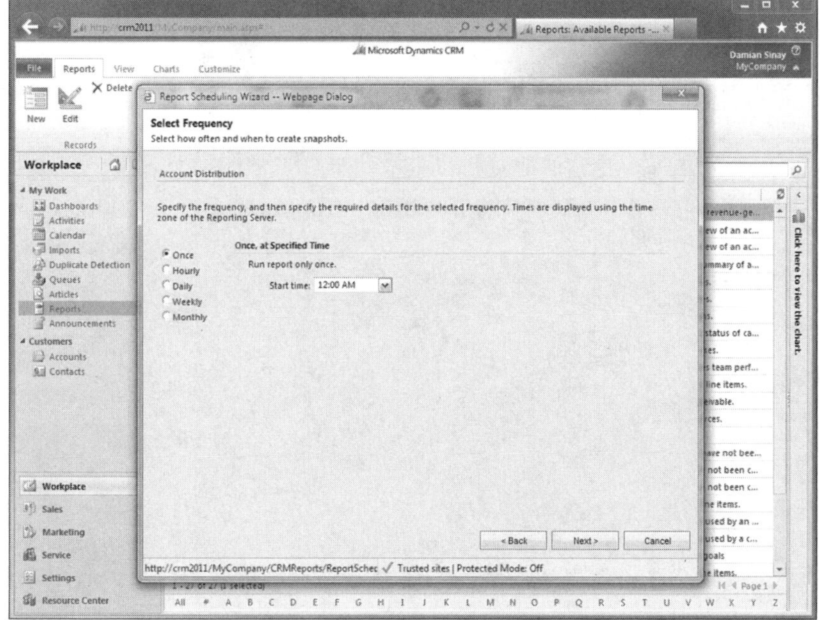

FIGURE 11.36 Select Frequency for Once option.

Depending on the desired frequency, different options display. For example, if you select Once, you can select only the Start Time. But if you select Hourly, you can select the number of hours and minutes you want the report to be run (see Figure 11.37).

Similarly, the options change for Daily, Weekly, and Monthly.

Select the Start Date and the End Date for the report (see Figure 11.38).

TIP

Leave the End Date blank if you want the report to be generated forever.

After you set the starting and ending dates, you can define the report parameters and edit the default filters for the report. These interfaces are similar to the ones in the On Demand option, explained previously. When you have defined the parameters, click Next. The Overview is presented so that you can review the scheduling report settings (see Figure 11.39).

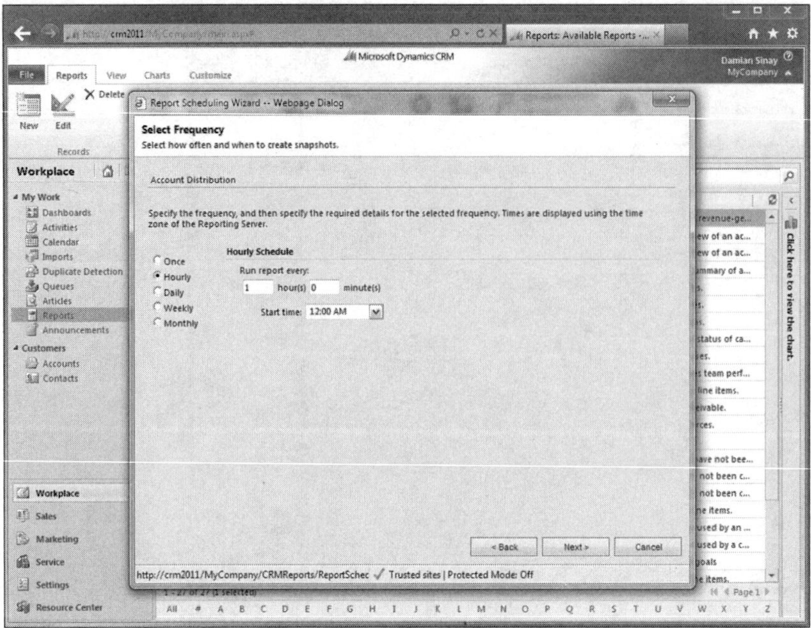

FIGURE 11.37 Select Frequency for Hourly option.

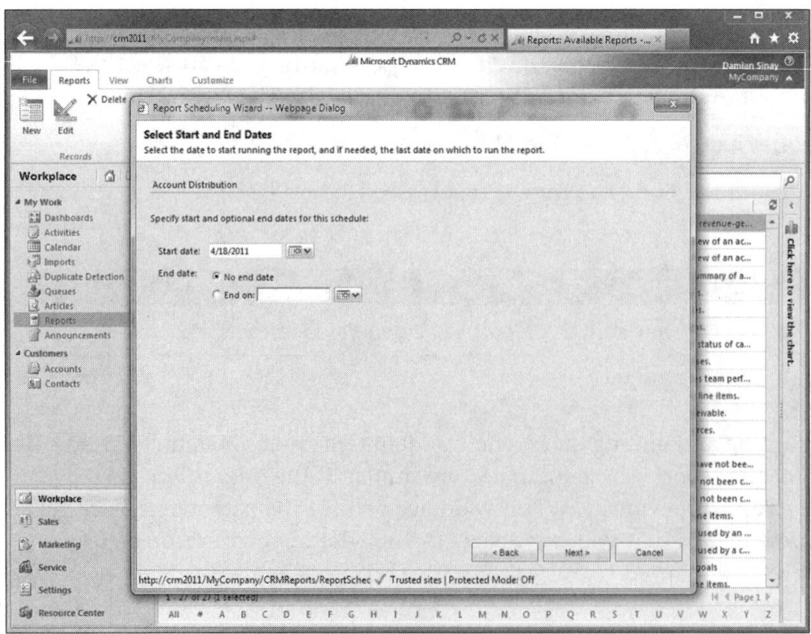

FIGURE 11.38 Select start and end dates.

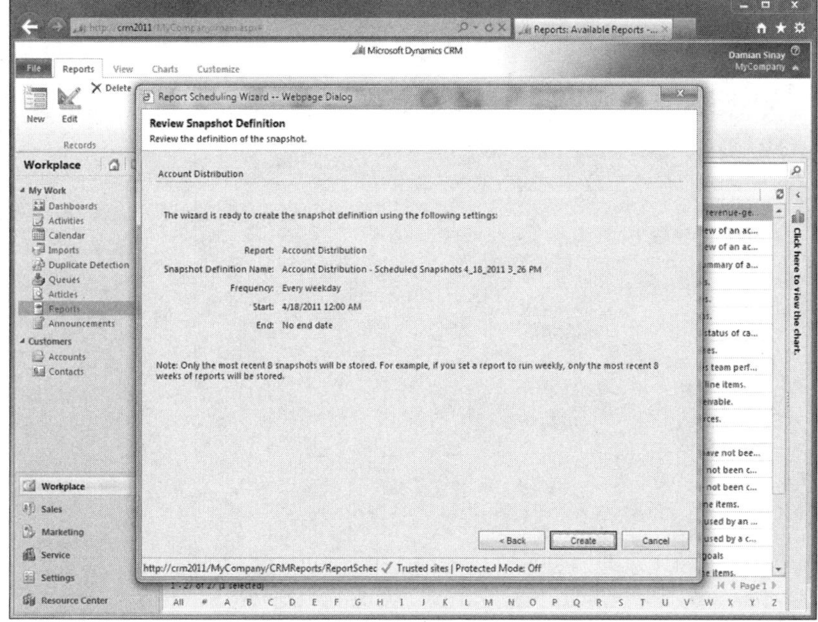

FIGURE 11.39 Review snapshot definition.

CAUTION

If errors occur when you're trying to schedule a report, the SRS server most likely is not configured properly with a valid execution account. To check or change this, start the Reporting Services Configuration Manager application that is inside the Microsoft SQL Server 2008 R2 programs group and inside the Configuration Tools (see Figure 11.40).

Exporting

You can export all Microsoft Dynamics CRM reports and report data in the following formats:

- XML file with report data
- CSV (comma delimited)
- Acrobat (PDF) file
- MHTML (web archive)
- Excel
- TIFF file
- Word

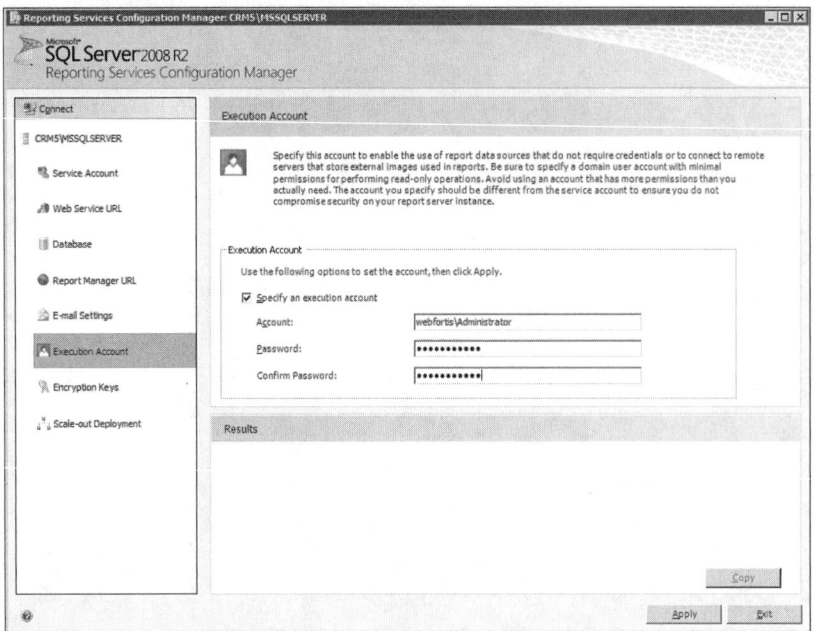

FIGURE 11.40 Execution account configuration.

This option is available in the top navigation bar of any report as a drop-down near Export. It allows reports within Microsoft Dynamics CRM to be completely portable and enables you to easily manipulate the data.

To export the actual report definition (not just the report format or data), select the report you want to export from the Reports interface and select Edit Report from the Reports Ribbon. When the report properties window appears, go to the Actions menu and select Download Report, as shown in Figure 11.41.

This option enables you to download the report in its Report Definition Language (RDL) format. This is the standard SRS extension based on XML that you can edit using an editor such as Visual Studio 2008, previously mentioned in this chapter.

▶ Refer to the Chapter 21, “Reporting and Dashboards,” for advanced report customization.

When working with a multitenant environment (more than one organization), it is important to remember that each organization has its own set of reports. As such, you might want to make some custom reports available across all organizations. The only way to do that is to export the report definitions to your local machine or server and then move them to another organization or implementation.

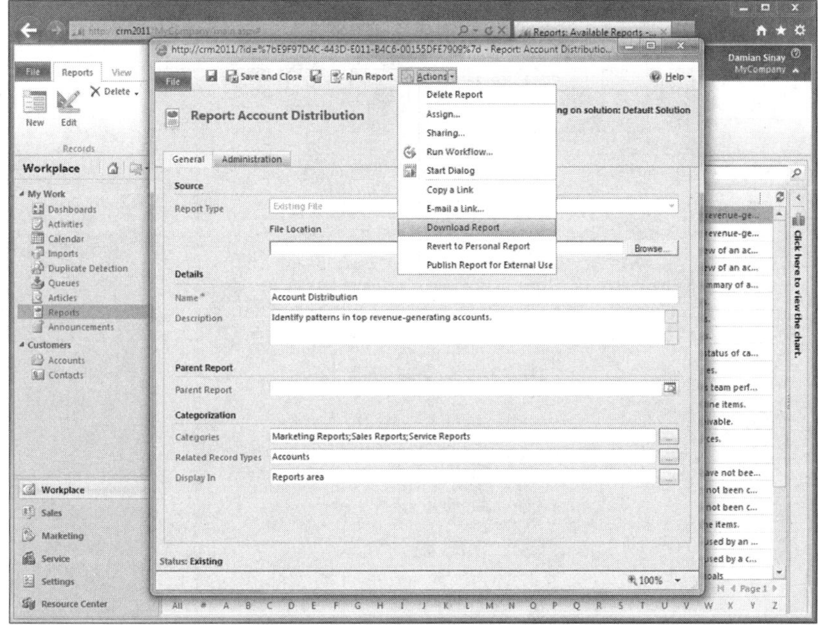

FIGURE 11.41 Download report.

TIP

Reports also belong to one solution that can be easily moved to one deployment to another. Solution is a new concept added on CRM 2011 that changes the way the CRM customizations are managed; to learn more about Solutions, refer to Chapter 16.

Advanced Features

Apart from running, creating, editing, and/or downloading reports, there are other actions you can perform when working with reports as detailed next.

Sharing Reports

Any reports that you create are available to you. If you want to share your custom report with a user who has lower privilege role levels, select the report from the main Reports interface, and select Share from the Reports Ribbon (see Figure 11.42).

From this interface, you can give the following permissions to users:

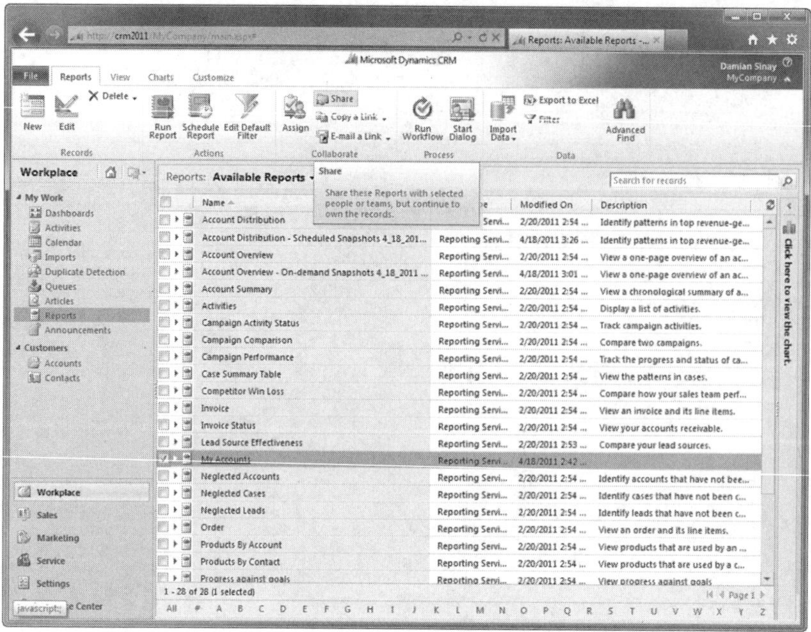

FIGURE 11.42 Sharing reports.

- **Read**—Enables the user to run the report.
- **Write**—Enables the user to modify the report definition and to change the properties and default filters.
- **Delete**—Enables the user to delete the report
- **Append**—Not applicable.
- **Assign**—Enables the user to change the owner of the report. This setting also gives write permission to the user for the report.
- **Share**—Enables the user to share the report with other users.

NOTE

If you add only read permissions to a user, that user will be able to share the report with other users even though you didn't select the Share option. This is because the default permissions are set to allow sharing between users. Of course, the user can give only read permissions to the other users, but carefully consider the implications of each permission before you set them. Figure 11.43 illustrates the sharing options available with reports.

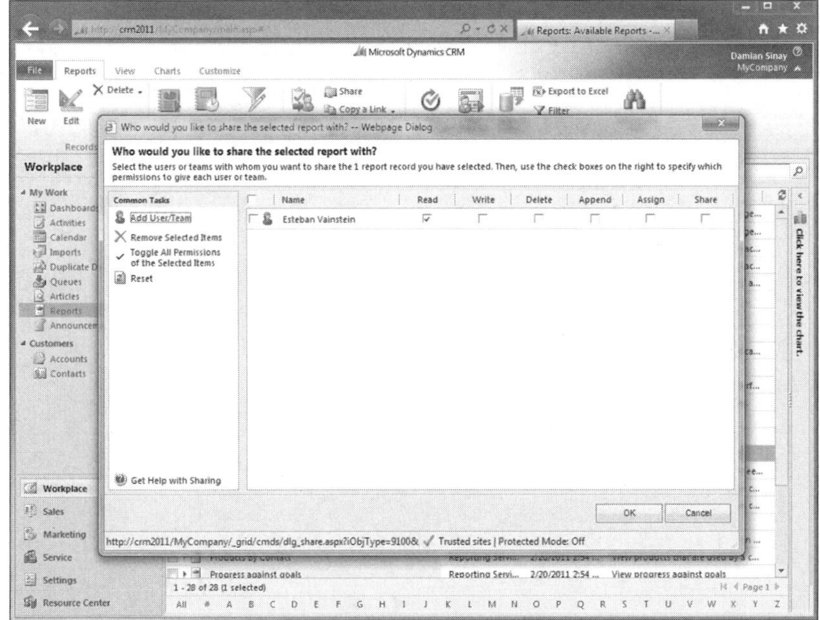

FIGURE 11.43 Reports-sharing permissions.

Exposing Reports to SRS

As with previous versions of Microsoft CRM, this version of Dynamics CRM doesn't expose every report in the SRS Manager application. If you want to use a report from another application, the reports must be published. For example, if you go to the Report Manager application of SRS, you will see a folder created for the organization; however, it is empty (see Figure 11.44).

So, where are the reports now? All the predefined reports are now on a different common folder for all the organizations in the system; this folder is called SharedReports. In this folder you will see all the out-of-the-box reports created (see Figure 11.45). Every custom report you will create using the Report Wizard or every report snapshot will be placed in the organization name folder as it was on the previous version.

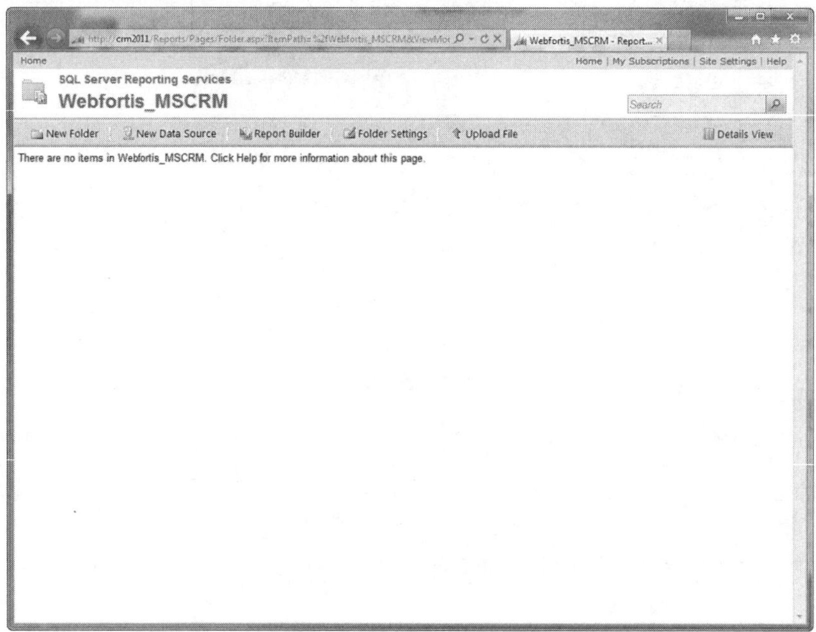

FIGURE 11.44 Report Manager.

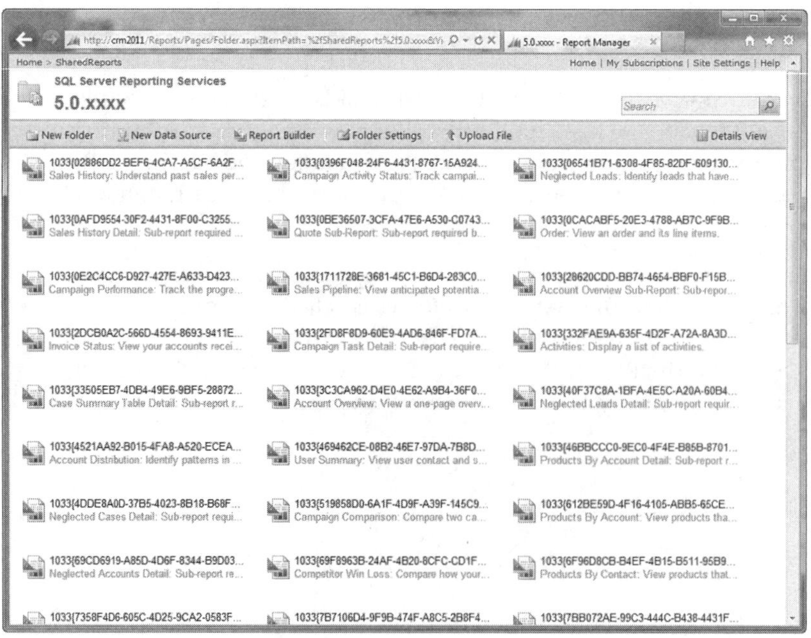

FIGURE 11.45 CRM 2011 reports in Report Manager.

If you need to use any of these reports or expose them to another application, you need to go to the CRM interface, select the report you want to expose, select Edit Report, and then select Publish Report for External Use from the Actions drop-down (see Figure 11.46).

After you select this option, no confirmation or message states that the operation was completed. In fact, the only way to verify that it was published is to go to the Report Manager web application and navigate to your CRM organization folder. You will see that the report is now available (see Figure 11.47).

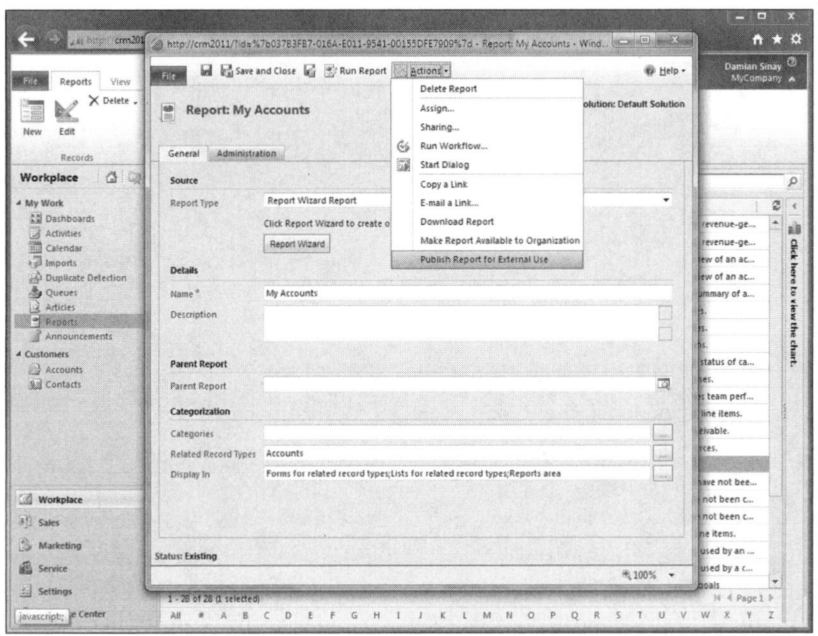

FIGURE 11.46 Publish report for external use.

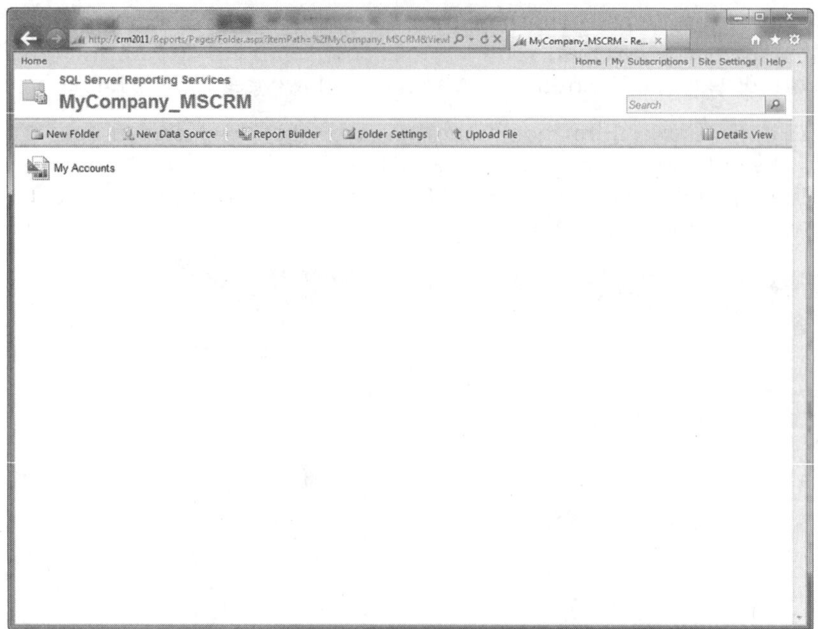

FIGURE 11.47 CRM report exposed in the Report Manager for external use.

Summary

This chapter described how Microsoft Dynamics CRM manages reports and how you can create new reports easily with the Report Wizard. We also reviewed the report scheduling feature and how to export reports for backups or redeployment purposes. Finally, we reviewed the advanced features of the reports.

CHAPTER 12

Settings and Configuration

- Business
- System
- Customization

Proper setup and configuration of Microsoft Dynamics CRM is critical to a successful implementation.

As you have seen in the previous chapters, and as we make clear in this chapter, the Settings area drives most of the core functionality for Microsoft Dynamics CRM. From user setup, to template management, to language options and workflows, the Settings area quickly becomes the place to go for proper configuration and tuning of your business.

NOTE

The Settings area should be a carefully controlled access point. If you want to remove access (aside from role membership, as you'll see later in this chapter), you can modify the site map so that it will not appear.

▶ Refer to Chapter 23, "Customizing Entities," for more information about working with the site map.

Any good implementation should consist of at least two main components when considering Microsoft Dynamics CRM. The first component is the physical setup. For on premise solutions, this includes everything from loading the application on the server to ensuring that a proper backup strategy is in place. For hosted solutions, this should include proper setup and configuration of client access. The second component is the configuration and customization of the application. Configuration and customization in this sense refers to how the application works in response to how you need it to work. As an example of this, Microsoft

Dynamics CRM has no default processes when it is first loaded. Your business might never need a workflow built, but most business that use Microsoft Dynamics CRM can really benefit from them.

▶ We strongly recommend reading the workflow information in Chapter 24, "Processes Development" when considering building any workflow.

NOTE

Although there are no processes included, Microsoft has included a basic form of sales force automation (SFA) in the form of Lead conversion.

▶ Refer to Chapter 8, "Working with Sales," for more information on working with SFA.

Additional considerations related to configuration include the previous components already mentioned: setting up users, choosing which languages to deploy, selecting the currency types, and so on.

Business

The Business section is an area that deals with business functions and components (as opposed to the System section that deals with system functions). The following subsections are available in Business:

- Business Management
- Templates
- Product Catalog

Business Management

Located in the Settings area, the Business Management page has the following options:

- Fiscal Year Settings
- Goal Metrics
- Business Closures

- Facilities/Equipment
- Queues
- Resource Groups
- Salespeople with Quotas
- Sales Territories
- Services
- Sites
- Subjects
- Currencies
- Connection Roles
- Relationship Roles
- Internet Marketing

Figure 12.1 shows the Business Management interface.

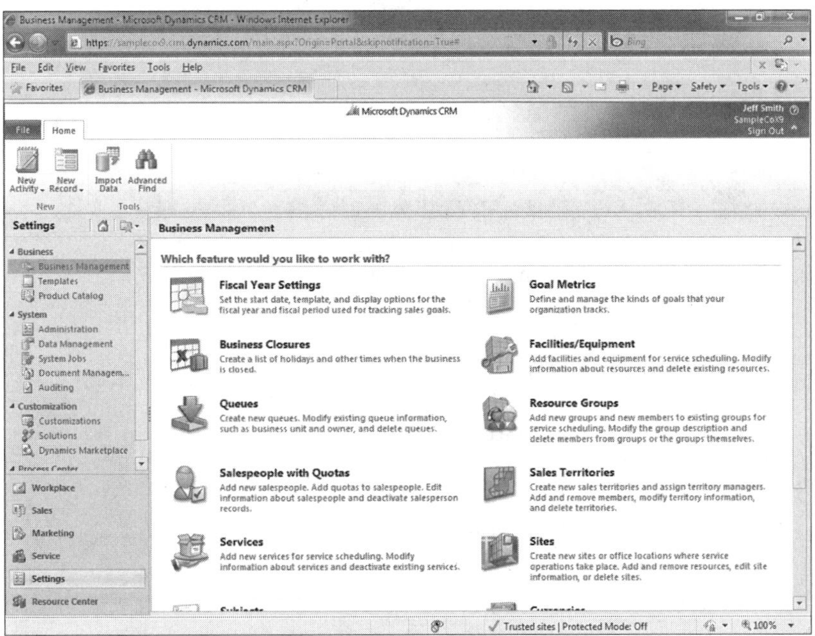

FIGURE 12.1 Settings, Business Management.

Fiscal Year Settings

To work with sales Quotas, you must set the Fiscal Year Settings. Be careful when setting the fiscal period; it should not be changed, as it will affect reporting (see Figure 12.2).

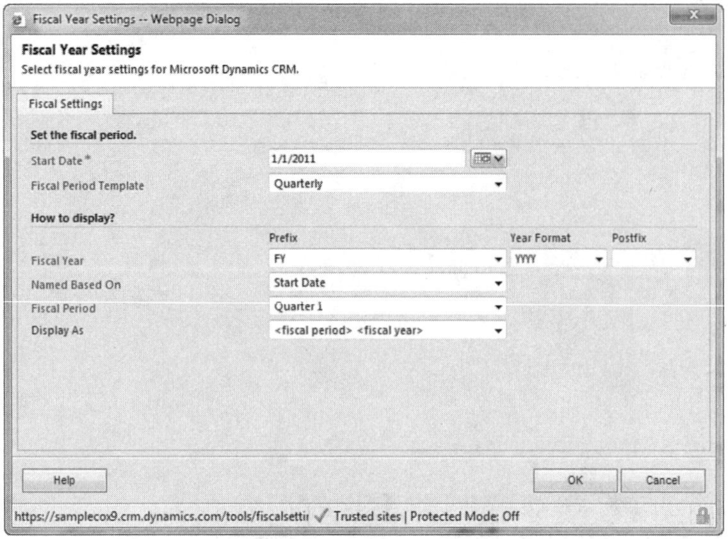

FIGURE 12.2 Fiscal Year Settings.

TIP

Sales Quotas are being deprecated and Goals should be used instead. Refer to Chapter 8, "Working with Sales" for more information about Goals.

The following fields are available when setting the Fiscal Year Settings:

- **Start Date**—The year the fiscal year starts
- **Fiscal Period Template**—The description of how the fiscal year is divided
- **Fiscal Year**—The fiscal year display options
- **Named Based On**—Whether the displayed name is based on the start or end of the fiscal year
- **Fiscal Period**—The fiscal period abbreviation
- **Display As**—How the fiscal year is displayed

TIP

As previously indicated, setting the Fiscal Year enables you to set Quotas on users.

Goal Metrics

Although the concept of quotas still exist within the system, goals have been added and brings goal management as an easy-to-use and manage option.

Selecting Goal Metrics from the Business Management interface brings you to the Goals Metrics page on the Sales section (see Figure 12.3).

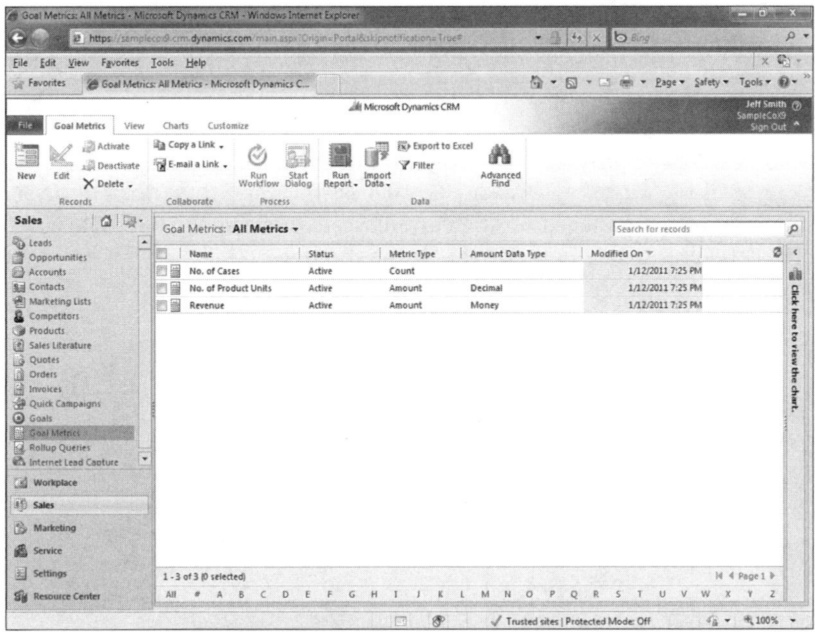

FIGURE 12.3 Goal Metrics interface.

▶ For more information about goals, refer to Chapter 8.

Business Closures

Business Closures are useful for managing service Activities. A user cannot schedule Activities during a time when a Business Closure is designated unless the Do Not Observe option is selected (The Do Not Observe option is selected when working with Resources and setting up Work Hour schedules).

When creating the Business Closure, you have the option to create it as a full-day, multiple-day, or part-of-the-day event (see Figure 12.4).

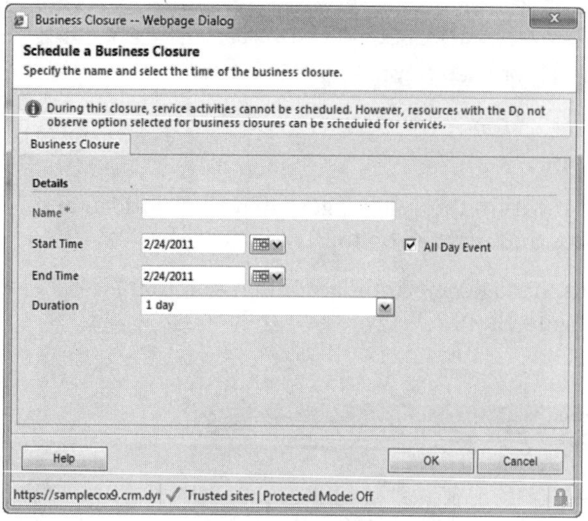

Business Closure -- Webpage Dialog

Schedule a Business Closure

Specify the name and select the time of the business closure.

During this closure, service activities cannot be scheduled. However, resources with the Do not observe option selected for business closures can be scheduled for services.

Business Closure

Details

Name *

Start Time 2/24/2011 All Day Event

End Time 2/24/2011

Duration 1 day

Help OK Cancel

https://samplecox9.crm.dy Trusted sites | Protected Mode: Off

FIGURE 12.4 Adding designated Business Closures.

By default, Business Closures are managed on the current year. To create Business Closures for another year, select the year toggle near the top of the interface.

Facilities/Equipment

Services use Facilities/Equipment when scheduling resources (see Figure 12.5).

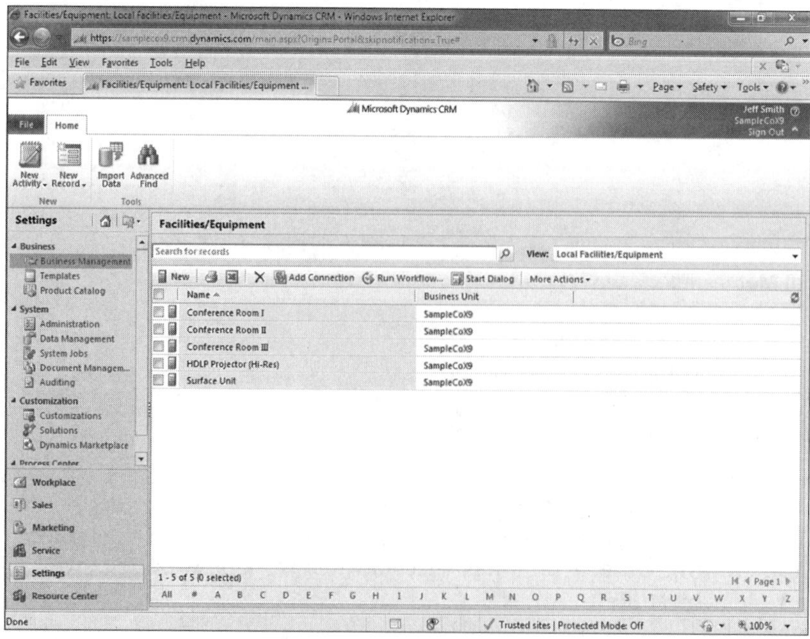

FIGURE 12.5 Facilities/Equipment.

Facilities/Equipment is necessary when performing scheduling because it makes up the Resources component. It differs from a business location because it makes up the necessary services component to complete a service task. If a business location is needed, add a Site, as explained later in this chapter.

▶ For more information on service scheduling, refer to Chapter 10, "Working with Service."

Queues

Queues serve as general access areas that are used to store items (unlike in previous versions, all custom entities can be stored in Queues now). You can set up custom Queues to automatically process incoming e-mail and convert them to Activities (waiting assignment in a Queue).

Unlike in the previous version of CRM where there was only two Queues by default, there is a now a Default Queue setup for every user and team with the user and team name in Microsoft Dynamics CRM 2011, and these queues are available for everyone to use. Figure 12.6 shows all Queues (by selecting the view option).

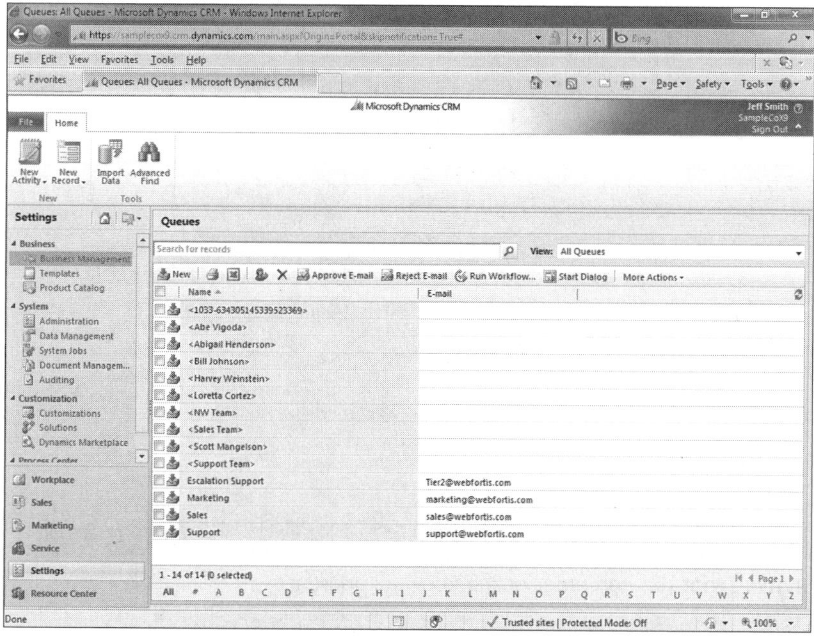

FIGURE 12.6 All Queues.

NOTE

Notice that the users' Queues (shown in Figure 12.6) are pre- and post-pended with < and >, respectively. This is established on the user setup page where it asks for the Default Queue assignment. If a Queue is not established, it defaults to this format.

Default Queues are provided so that items can be routed automatically when an item is created (or is assigned via a change of ownership).

To create a Queue, follow these steps:

1. Navigate to Settings, Business, Business Management, Queues. Select New to create a new Queue.
2. Enter the Queue name, and the owner.
3. Enter the e-mail address that the Queue will use to gather incoming e-mails and automatically convert them to Activities if desired (see Figure 12.7).

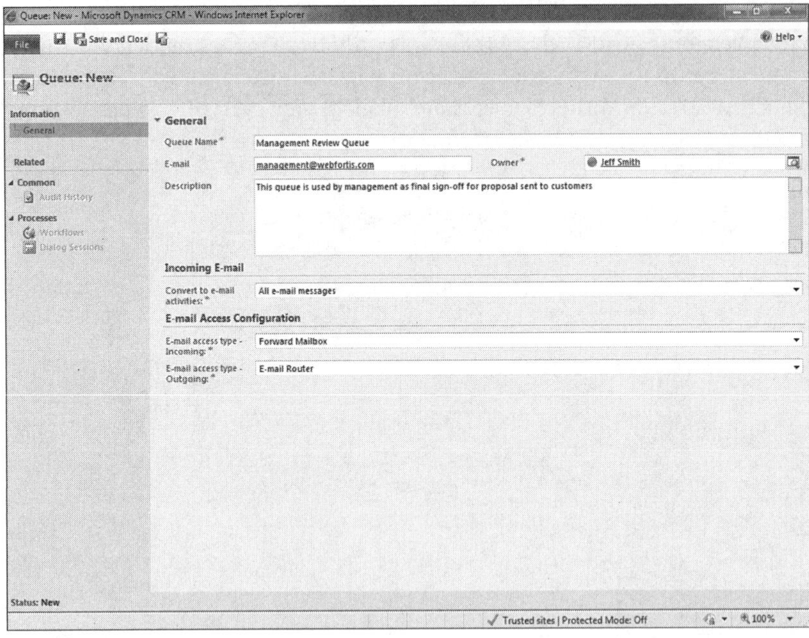

FIGURE 12.7 Queue setup.

TIP

In step 3, keep in mind that you can enter only one e-mail address.

4. Select how Microsoft CRM should work with e-mails received by the e-mail address entered for the Queue. By default, the system processes all incoming e-mail messages and converts them to Activities. However, you can set from the drop-down menu to process only incoming e-mails that are in response to other e-mails previously sent from CRM or only e-mails received that resolve to existing CRM Leads, Contacts, or Accounts.

5. Configure how e-mail access should work for both incoming and outgoing.

▶ or more information about configuring e-mail access, refer to Chapter 14, "E-Mail Configuration."

Queues can be activated, deactivated, or deleted. If a Queue is deactivated, all items are removed, and if it is reactivated, it will remain empty until used again. Queue deletion requires all queue items to be moved to another queue.

NOTE

To move items from Queue to another, navigate to Workplace and select the Queue to be deleted. Select All Items from the Queue Items Ribbon option and then click Routing from the Ribbon menu and after you select a queue, all items will be moved.

Unlike in previous versions, Queues now offer the ability to set security on them using roles (as explained further in this chapter). Additionally, the Queue entity can be customized to extend its functionality beyond a vanilla implementation. Finally, one of the most significant improvements is the concept of *Working On*, which allows the owner of a record to maintain ownership, but another person can be the Working On user (which is found on the Queue Item record, via the Queue view Ribbon button).

Resource Groups

Resource Groups consist of a grouping of users, teams, facility/equipment, or other resource groups for the purposes of service scheduling.

To create a Resource Group, select New and enter the name of the Resource Group (see Figure 12.8).

After you save the Resource Group, you can add resources (see Figure 12.9).

▶ For more information on service scheduling, refer to Chapter 10.

Salespeople with Quotas

Available only after the fiscal year has been set and Quotas have been assigned to users, the Salespeople with Quotas option is available from Settings, Business, Business Management. It shows users who have Quotas assigned to them from this interface.

NOTE

This feature is added for backwards compatibility. It is now recommended that organizations use the Goals and Goals Metrics for Quota Management.

Sales Territories

Sales territories are the grouping of users into one territory, with a common manager specific to the territory.

Figure 12.10 shows a number of sample territories with Manager assignment to each one.

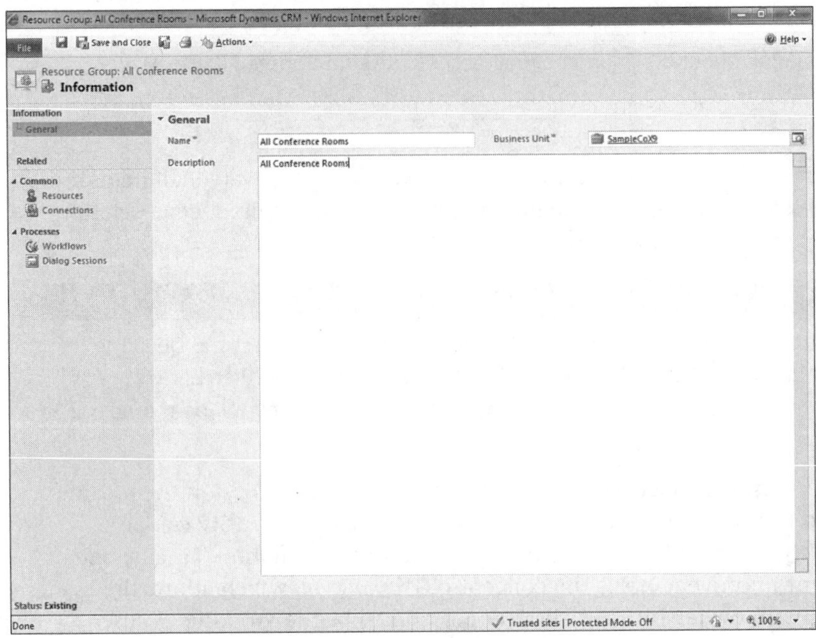

FIGURE 12.8 Creating a new Resource Group.

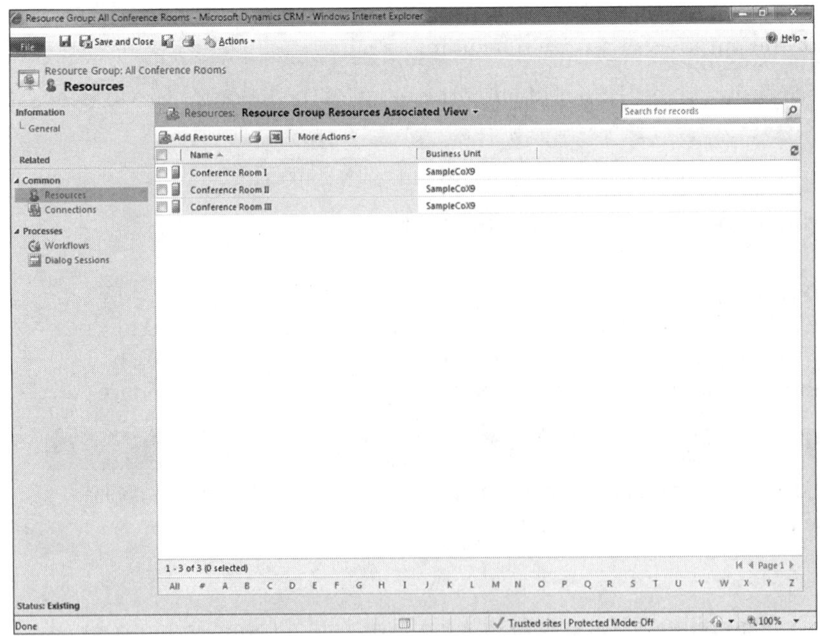

FIGURE 12.9 Resources added to the Resource Group.

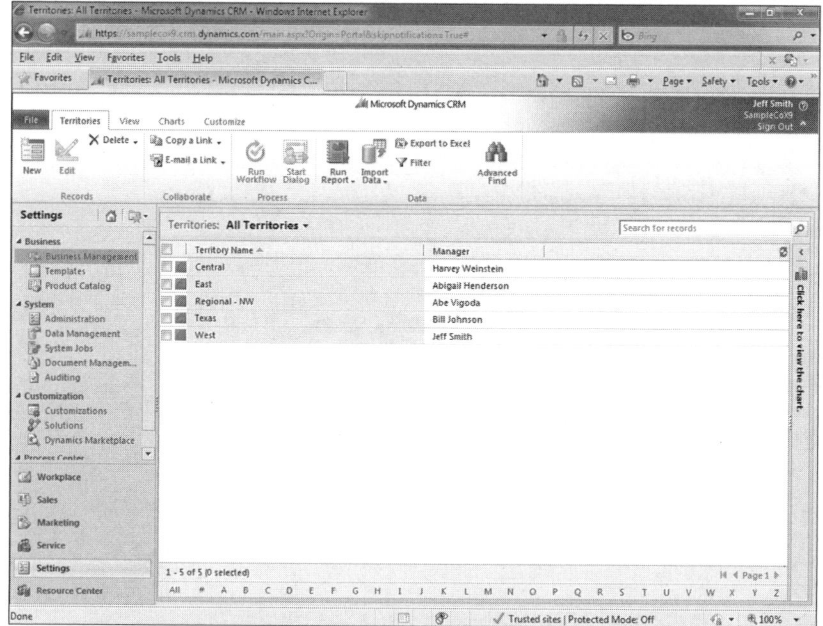

FIGURE 12.10

NOTE

The territory manager is not necessarily the user's manager.

TIP

Because users can be assigned to only one territory, if you want to assign a user to more than one of your existing territories, you must create a new territory that covers the existing ones and assign the user to that new territory.

To create a new territory, select New, and enter the territory name and, if applicable, the territory manager (see Figure 12.11). Users in territories are either users or a manager.

Select users to add to the territory. Because users can be assigned to only single territory, they are removed from any previously assigned territories when assigned to the new one (see Figure 12.12).

Territories are very useful for summarizing data in sales reports, as well as obtaining various metrics data on Activities by territory.

The territory manager is used for reporting and/or workflow purposes.

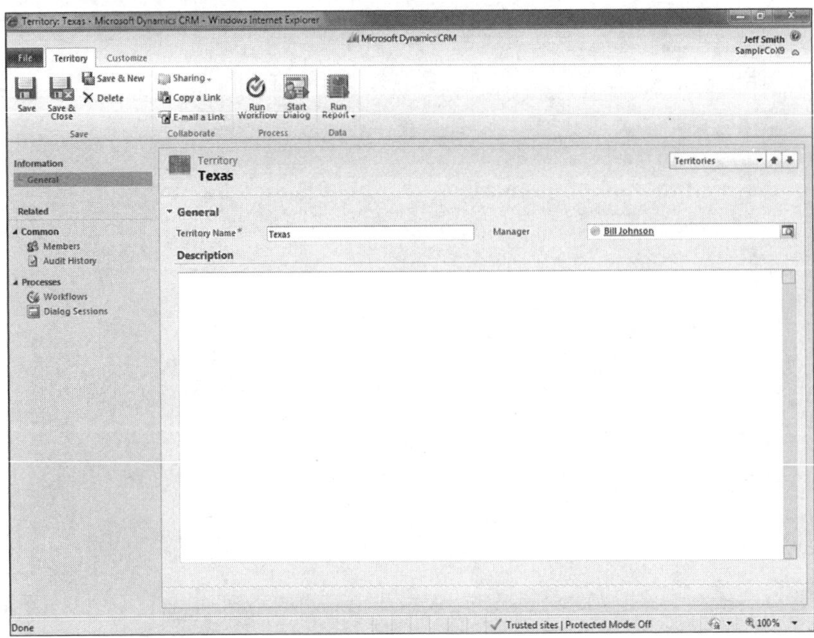

FIGURE 12.11 Creating a new territory.

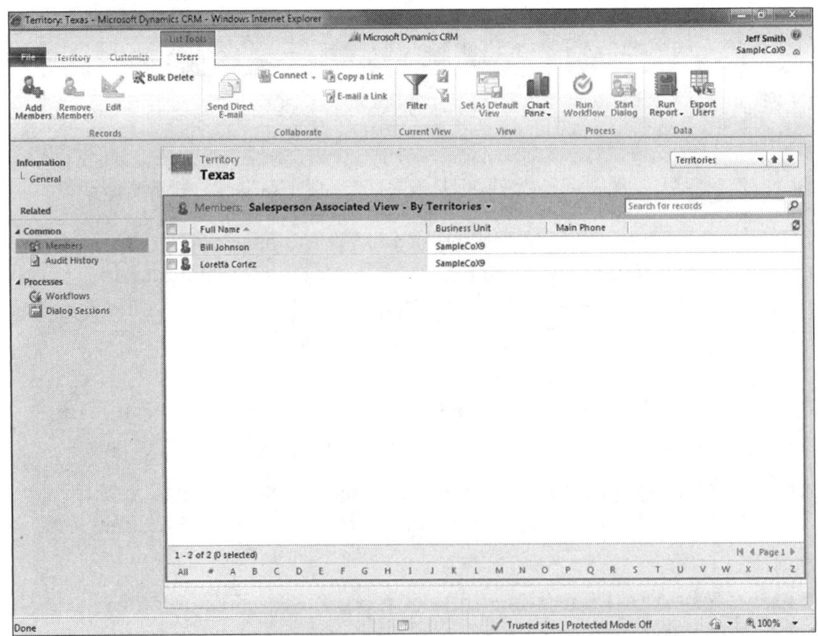

FIGURE 12.12 Assigning users to a territory.

Services

Services are activities performed by one or multiple resources that are scheduled using the Service Scheduling module.

▶ For more information about working with services, refer to Chapter 10.

Sites

Sites are the physical locations where work is done and resources are to be assigned in the service scheduling. When creating a site, the only required information is the location name (see Figure 12.13).

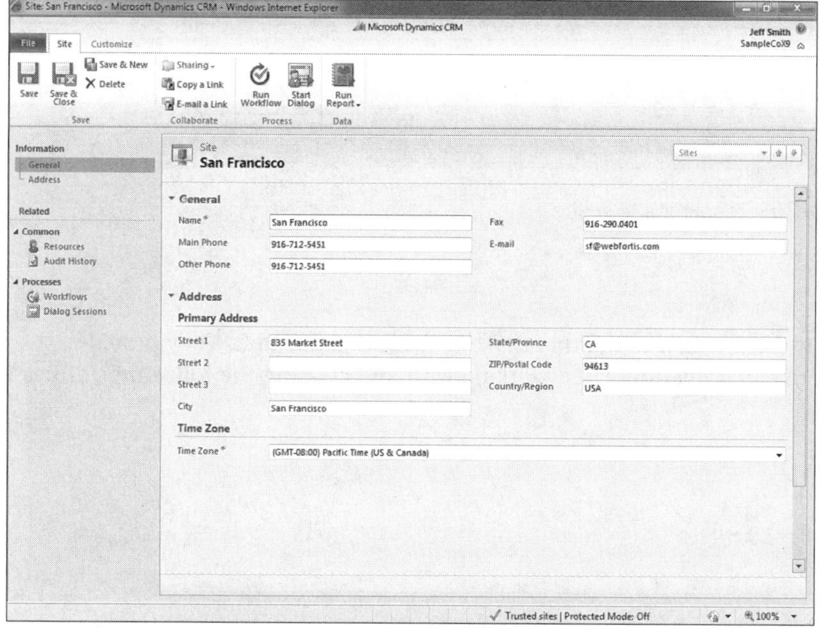

FIGURE 12.13 Creating a site.

After the site has been created, you can assign resources consisting of either users or facility/equipment to it (see Figure 12.14).

▶ For more information on service scheduling, refer to Chapter 10.

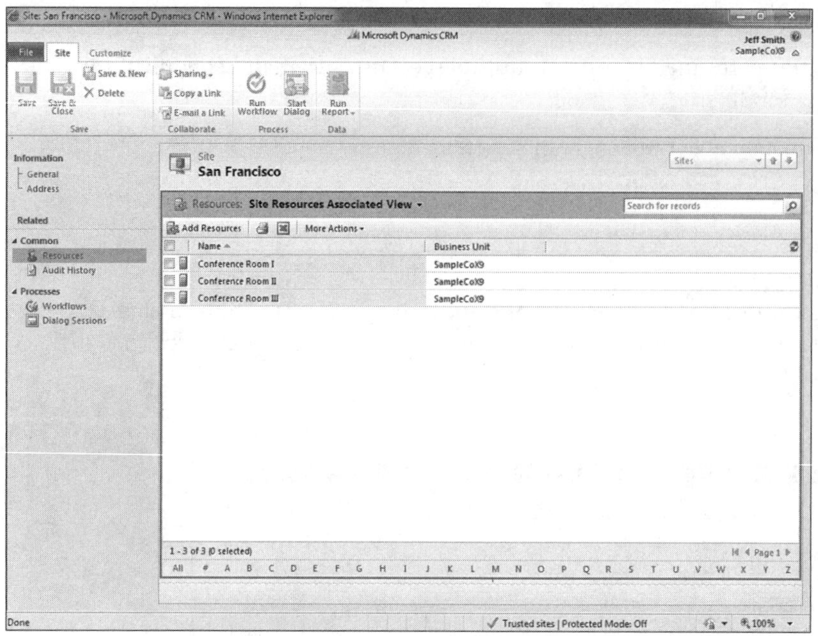

FIGURE 12.14 Adding resources to a site.

Subjects

Subjects relate to the individual topics that make up your organization. They provide context and are a required relation when working with and creating the following entities:

- Cases
- Sales Literature
- Knowledge Base Articles
- Products

Generally, Subjects include information related to these entities and are hierarchal in nature (see Figure 12.15).

To create new Subjects, select the node that is the parent of the new Subject on the Subject Tree, and then select Add a Subject. By default, the Parent Subject populates with the Subject previously selected. Enter a value in the Title and any corresponding description (see Figure 12.16). Selecting OK adds the entered Subject to the Subject Tree, making it available for selection when working with the previous entities.

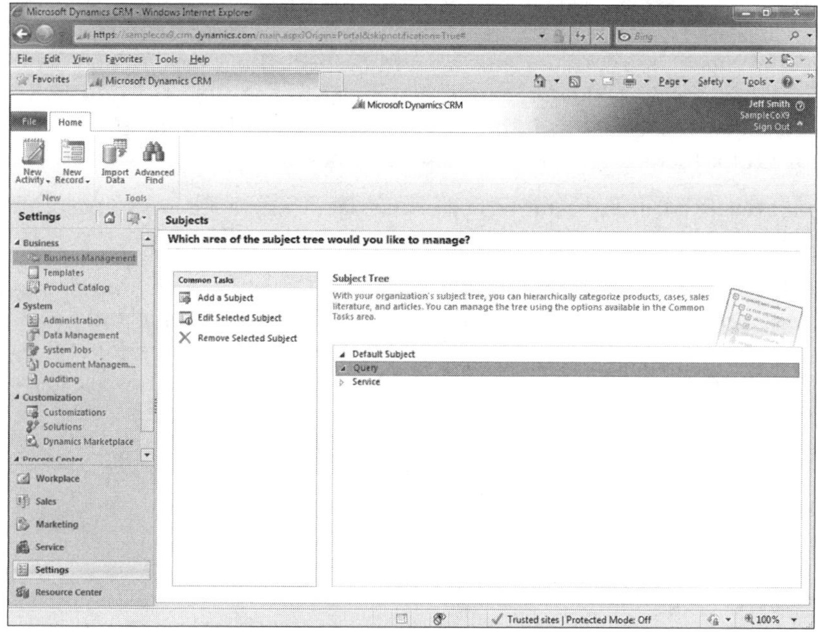

FIGURE 12.15 Sample company Subject hierarchy.

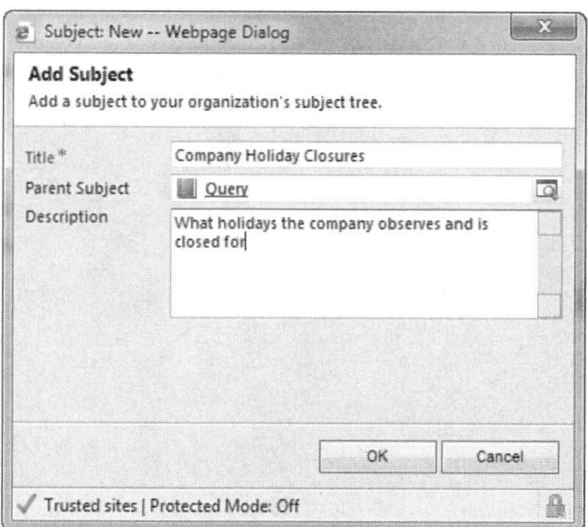

FIGURE 12.16 Adding a new subject.

TIP

Carefully consider setting up the Subject Tree for your products. Although an association is not required, Subjects let you effectively categorize products for searching and reporting. When setting up the Subject Tree for Products, the Subjects will usually be at a more general level than the actual product. For example, a Subject might be Computers, and actual products associated might be Laptop, Desktop, and Handheld.

Currencies

As with languages, Currencies are added and managed from the Settings page. When they are added and active, they are available to the user. When a Currency other than the base Currency is used, the values associated with the record are converted (based on the conversion rate entered for that Currency) to the base Currency.

Although you cannot delete a Currency if it has been associated with a record, you can disable it, preventing it from being used on any new records.

To add a new Currency option, select New and then select the Currency Code from the lookup (or select Custom to enter a new custom currency). The Currency name and Currency symbol populate automatically, but you can change this information, if necessary. Finally, enter the currency conversion rate. This is the amount at which the selected Currency converts to the base Currency rate (see Figure 12.17).

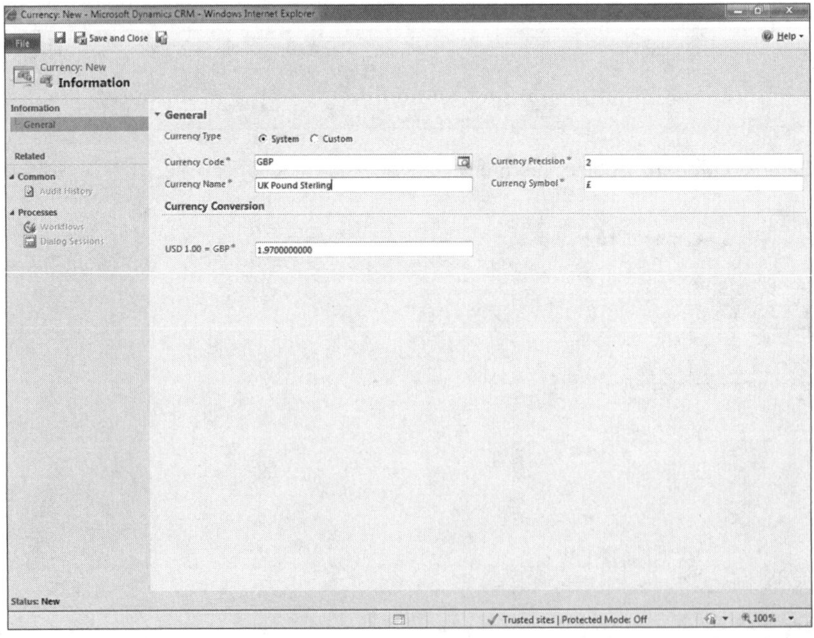

FIGURE 12.17 Creating a new Currency.

NOTE

The conversion rate entered for a Currency remains at that rate until a system administrator updates it. Potentially, inaccurate data can be reported if the conversion rate is not updated relatively frequently, based on the selected Currency conversion fluctuations. One consideration might be to extend the functionality of Microsoft Dynamics CRM by calling a web service to automatically calculate conversion on a monthly, weekly, daily, or even hourly rate.

▶ For more information on extending Microsoft Dynamics CRM, refer to Chapter 26, "Web Services."

After new currencies are created, different currencies can be assigned to transactions such as Quotas, Orders, Invoices, and Price Lists. When this happens, Microsoft Dynamics CRM converts the money fields to the base currency using the exchange rate entered for the selected currency.

It is important to understand when this conversion might happen because transactions can happen over a period of time, during which exchange rates might have been changed. An example of this is a Quote that was created, but that waited for approval for three months. During that time, the exchange rate could have been adjusted several times.

Exchange rates are updated when Quotes, Orders, Invoices, or Price Lists are created or when any field is updated that relates to currency. Additionally, if the state of the entity changes, exchange rates are recalculated.

NOTE

It is important to note that changing a currency rate will have no effect on any entity that is using that currency, unless one of the conditions previously mentioned (updated or has its state change) is met. Because of this, you could view a transaction that has an old exchange rate unless you explicitly update it by changing the values or changing the entity state.

Connection Roles

Replacing Relationship Roles, Connection Roles are a more flexible variant of establishing a relationship (or connection) to other records. Figure 12.18 shows the default connection roles that are available.

To create a new Connection Role, select New and follow the steps as shown in Figure 12.19.

After they are established, the Connection Roles will be available on the entity level (where selected in step 2) for reporting/management.

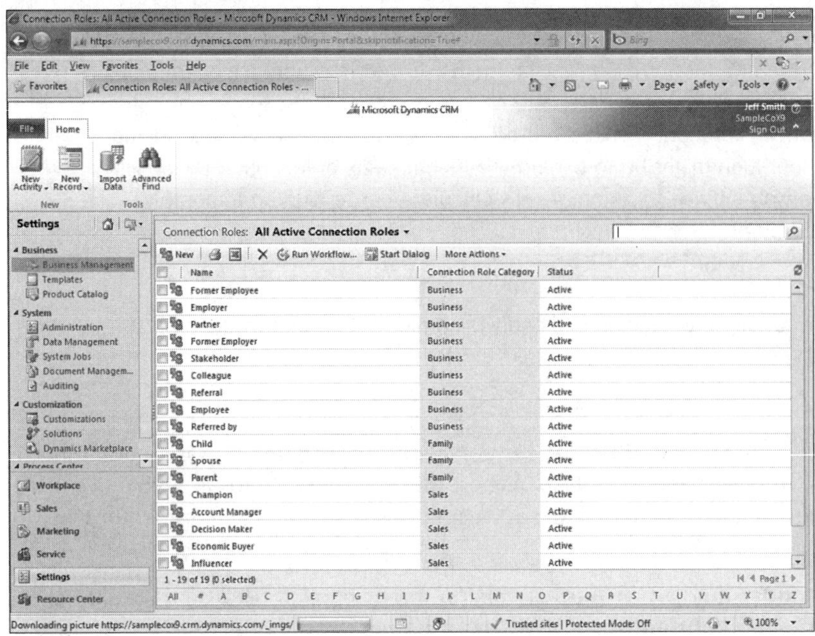

FIGURE 12.18 Default Connection Roles.

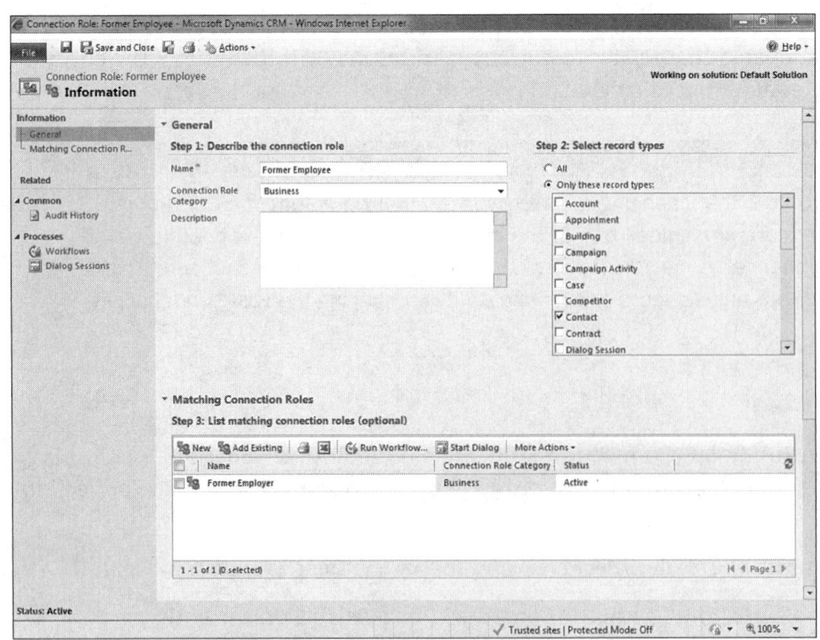

FIGURE 12.19 Creating a new Connection Role.

Relationship Roles

Relationship Roles are available only for Accounts, Contacts, and Opportunities. They are designed to enable users to configure relationship types that might exist between records of these entities in the system. Relationship Roles can be used for any kind of relationship, including business, familiar, and social ones.

NOTE

As previously noted in Connection Roles, Relationship Roles were to have been removed from Microsoft Dynamics CRM 2011 completely (available only for upgraded instances for backward compatibility), however they appear to have shipped with the final product. As such, you have the option to use either Connection Roles or Relationship Roles. It is both our and Microsoft's recommendation to use Connection Roles to manage your relationships going forward because they are much more flexible and easier to use (and Relationship Roles will probably be completely deprecated in the near future).

To create a new Relationship Role, select New and enter the required field information for Role Name (see Figure 12.20). Although it is not required, if you do not make a selection for Account, Contact, or Opportunity, the Relationship Role will be active but not available to use on any entity.

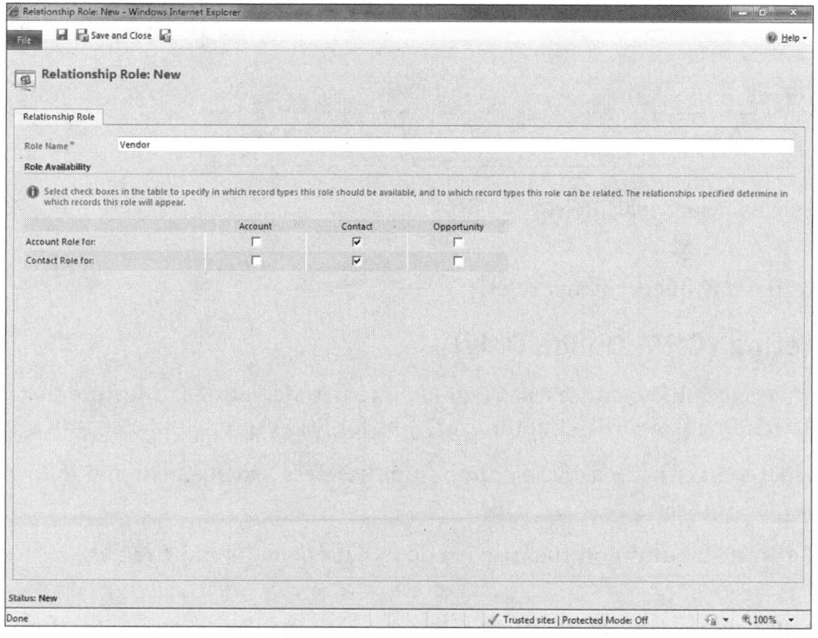

FIGURE 12.20 Creating a Relationship Role.

When creating the relationship, you can set the type of relationship based on the Relationship Roles that have been created. Because we've created only one Relationship Role in this example, called Vendor, we'll select it only for the sample Contact, not the sample Account shown (refer to Figure 12.20).

Navigating to the Relationships for the sample Contact, you can easily see the role (see Figure 12.21).

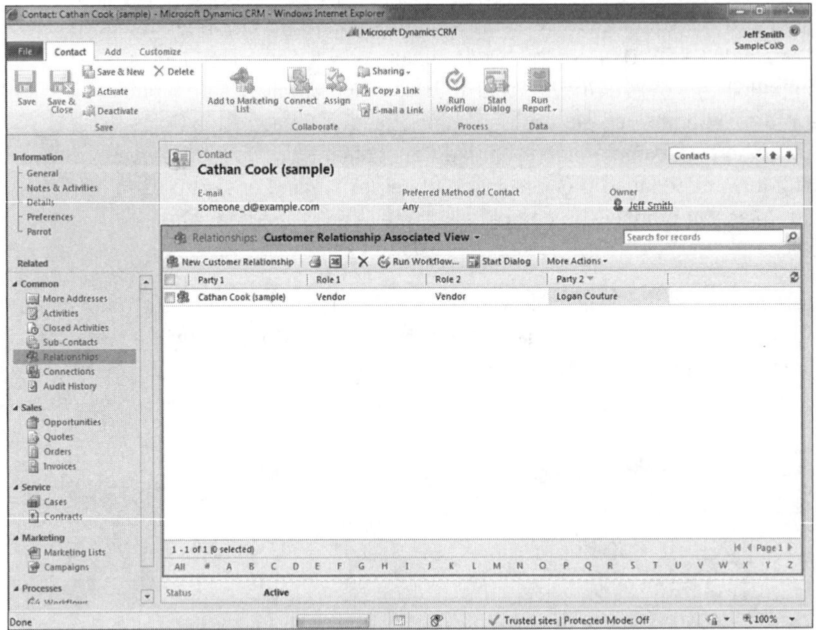

FIGURE 12.21 Sample Relationship Role.

After setup, users can easily query on any roles.

Internet Marketing (CRM Online Only)

Available only with Microsoft Dynamics CRM Online, Internet Marketing is a feature that provisions up to 10 landing pages with built in workflow for lead capture and assignment.

To work with Internet Marketing, select the option from Business Management and follow the steps below.

1. Select the Get Started! button on the new window that opens (as shown in Figure 12.22).
2. The service will be activated, which might take a few minutes. You can monitor the process by selecting the Refresh text at the top of the page (as shown in Figure 12.23).
3. After activation, you need to create a new landing page as shown in Figure 12.24. Select Create a New Landing Page to continue.

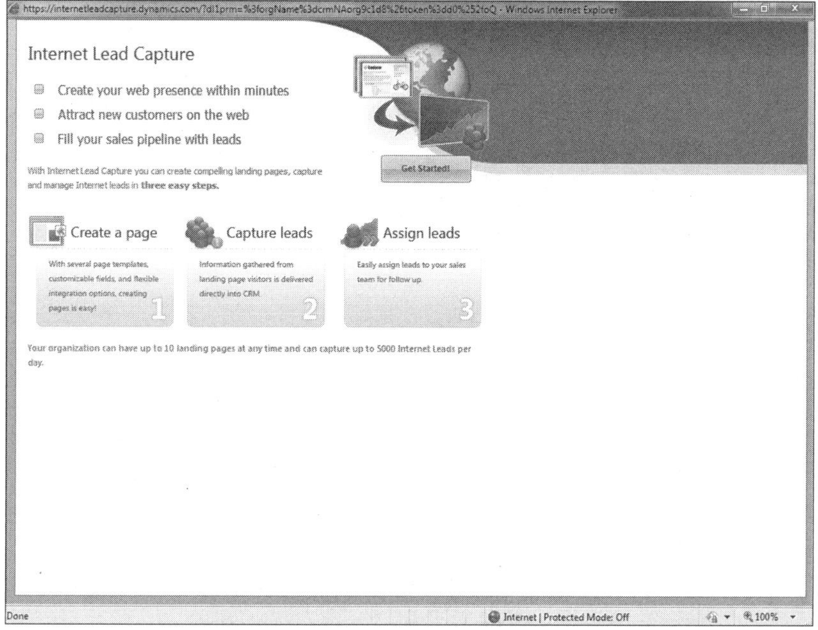

FIGURE 12.22 Internet Lead capture.

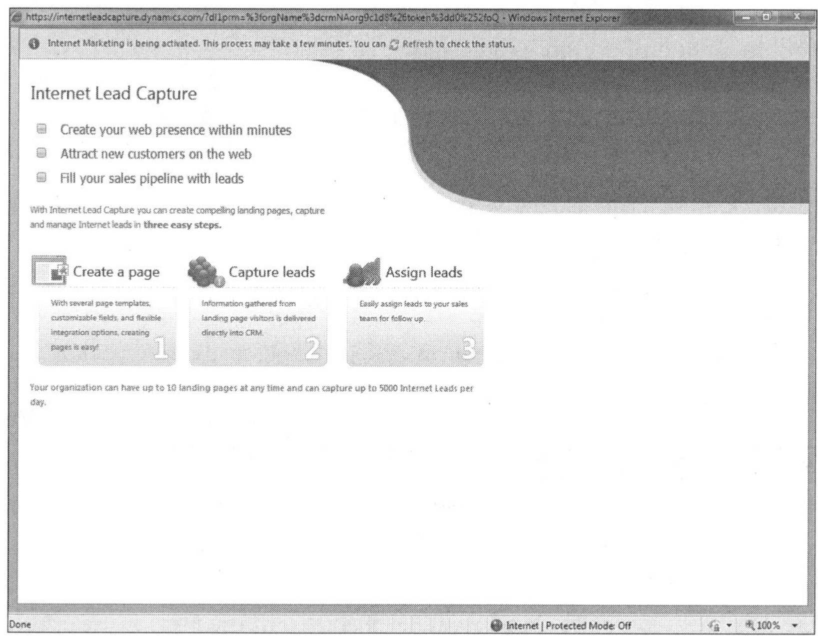

FIGURE 12.23 Internet Lead capture—service activation.

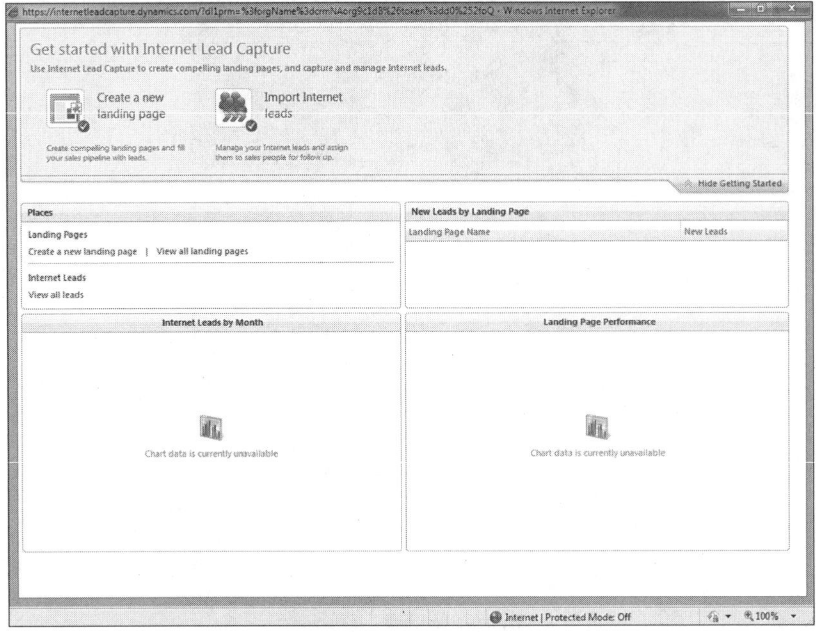

FIGURE 12.24 Internet Lead Capture Wizard.

4. Create the landing page from the wizard as shown in Figure 12.25 by selecting Create Page on the Action option for Lead Capture Page.

TIP

In addition, you can optionally create a custom form for lead capture and fields. If you don't create a custom form, you can use the default one available.

5. Using the Landing Page Wizard, follow the steps for setting up the page appearance by selecting the page URL, layout, and theme (as shown in Figure 12.26). Click Next to continue.

NOTE

The organization name and page name cannot contain any spaces or apostrophes.

6. Customize the page elements—the elements are available from the previous selection (for example, if you included a form as the layout, you would customize the form here), as shown in Figure 12.27. Click Next to continue.

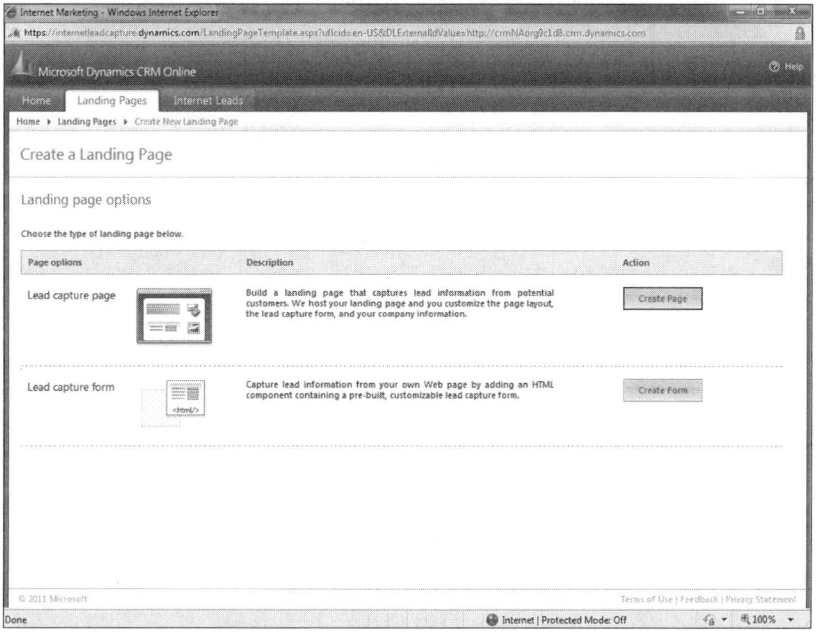

FIGURE 12.25 Internet Lead capture—create new landing page.

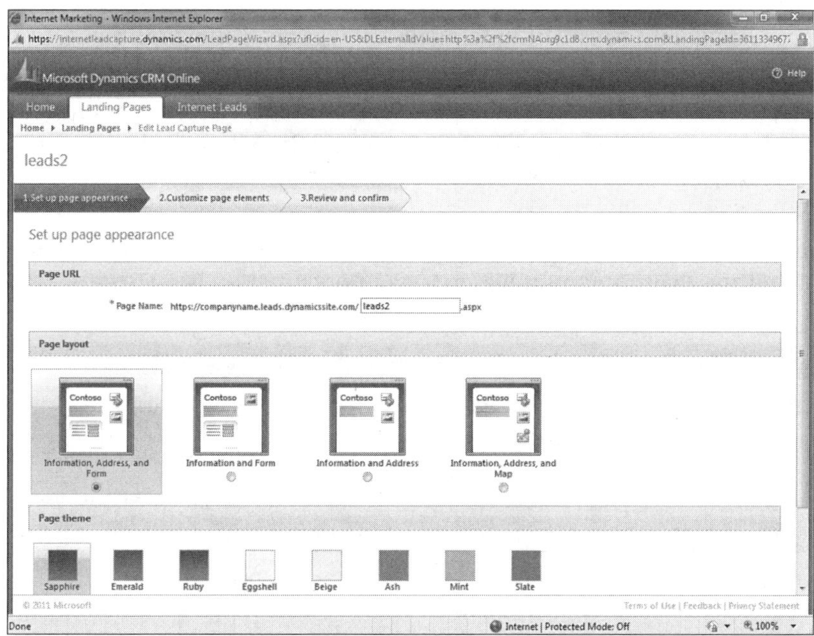

FIGURE 12.26 Internet Lead capture—set up page appearance.

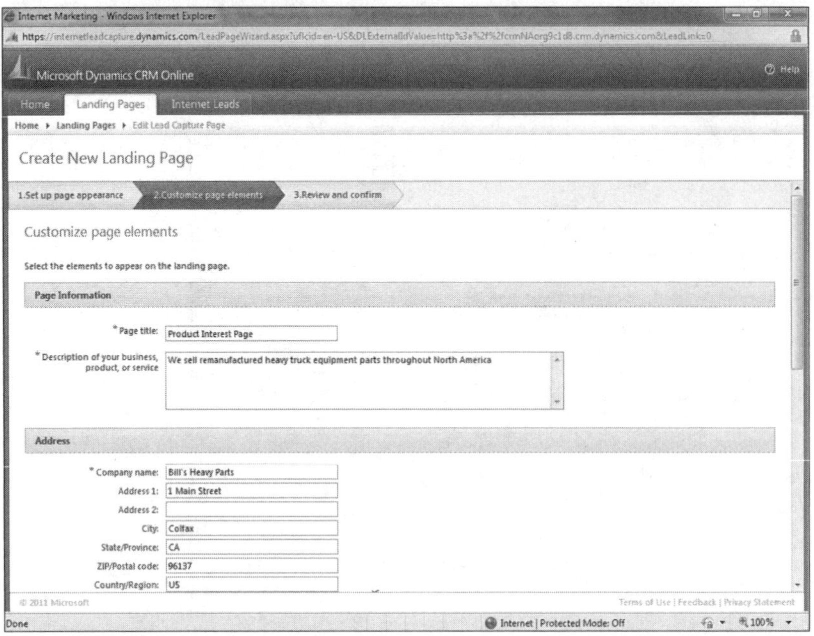

FIGURE 12.27 Internet Lead capture—customize page elements.

7. Review the page layout and select Finish to publish the page (as shown in Figure 12.28).
8. The landing page is set up and you have the option to turn the page off or on, preview the page, or edit the page as shown in Figure 12.29. Selecting the URL or the link that says Open in Browser will open your page in a new browser (see Figure 12.30).
9. Provided you added a form to your landing page, you will start to see metrics upon customers submitting their form information to your organization (see Figure 12.31).

TIP

Any leads will show as New Leads by Landing Page, and selecting the New Leads number will bring you to the Internet Leads page, as shown in Figure 12.32.

NOTE

The leads shown are *not* available in CRM yet. They have to be assigned to a user prior to being available in CRM. Step 10 illustrates how to do this.

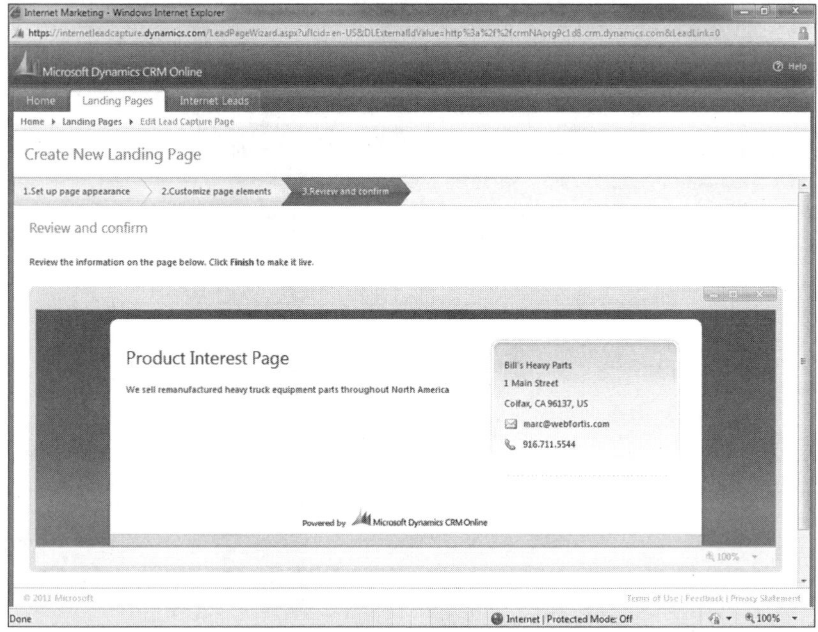

FIGURE 12.28 Internet Lead capture—customize page elements.

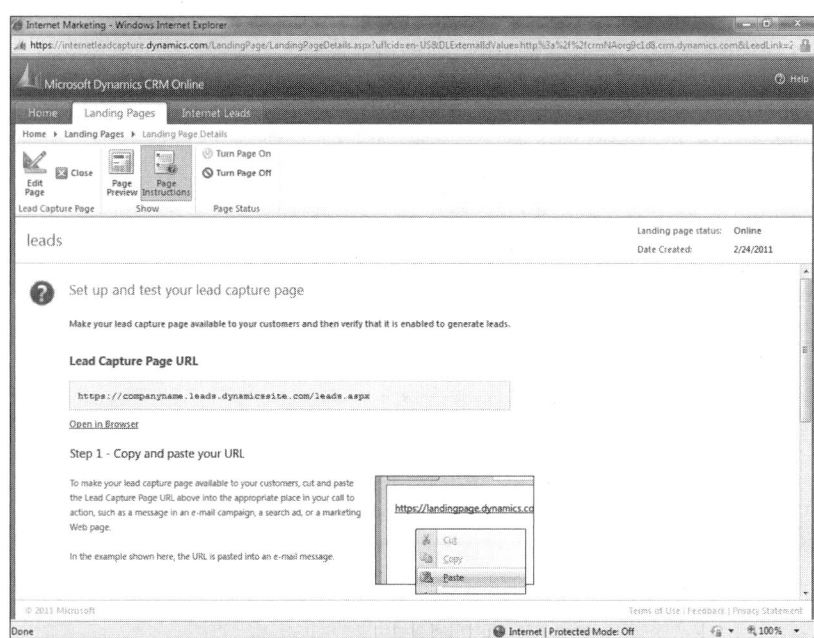

FIGURE 12.29 Internet Lead capture—setup and test the page.

12

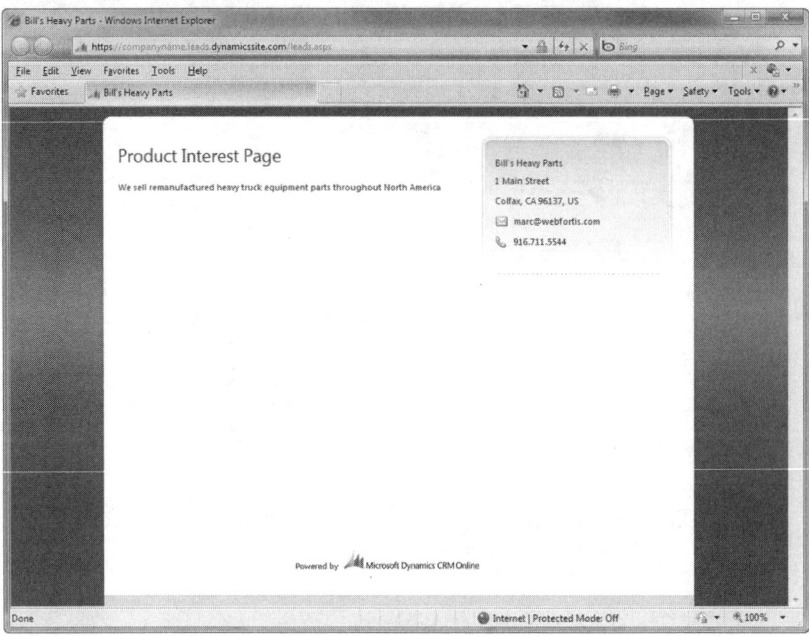

FIGURE 12.30 Internet Lead capture—custom lead page.

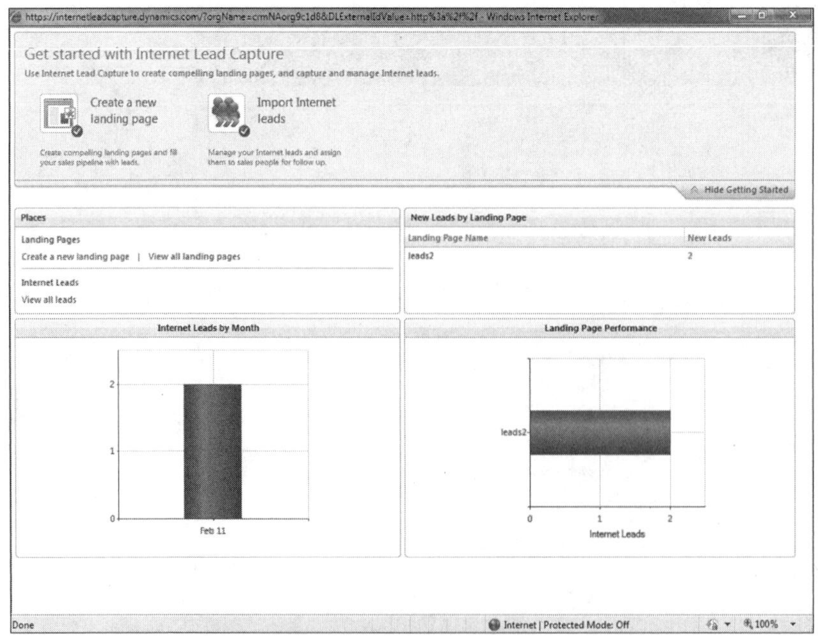

FIGURE 12.31 Internet Lead capture—lead Dashboard.

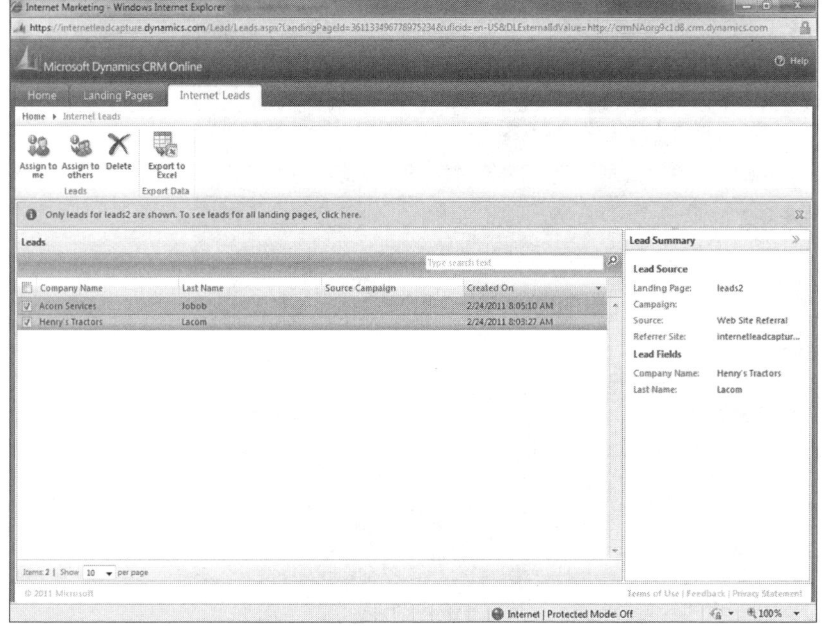

FIGURE 12.32 Internet Lead capture—leads.

10. Select the leads that you would like to import from Figure 12.32 and select from the Ribbon menu either Assign to Me or Assign to Others. Then click Assign as shown in Figure 12.33. The leads are now available and waiting for the next action.

Templates

Templates facilitate the management of predefined Articles, Contracts, e-mails, and Word mail merges. E-mail Templates can be built to dynamically include context-sensitive information such as senders or receivers.

Four different template categories exist:

- Article Templates
- Contract Templates
- E-mail Templates
- Mail Merge Templates

Templates can be active or inactive, and can be in any language that the system administrator makes available.

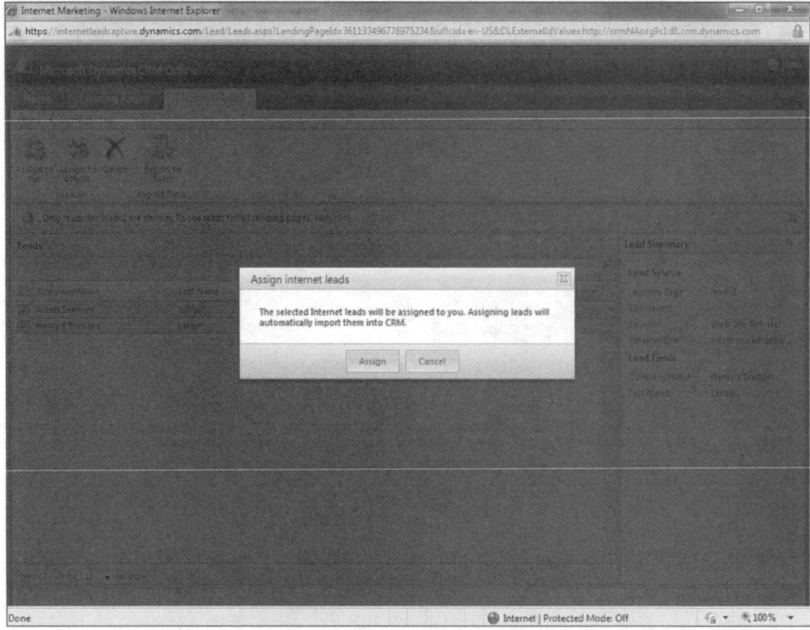

FIGURE 12.33 Internet Lead capture—lead assignment

NOTE

Data Management Templates exist under System, Data Management, not here.

Article Templates

Article Templates are used when working with the Knowledge Base (found in the Service section of Microsoft Dynamics CRM).

They can include formatted titles, sections, and section titles.

Contract Templates

Contract Templates are used to manage Contracts and include information such as the billing frequency and the service allotment.

E-mail Templates

E-mail Templates are the richest templates because they allow for specific customizations specific to the sender and receiver. E-mail Templates have several core properties that make up how they work:

- Template Type
- Viewable By
- Language

Template Type The template type is selected when the template is first created (see Figure 12.34).

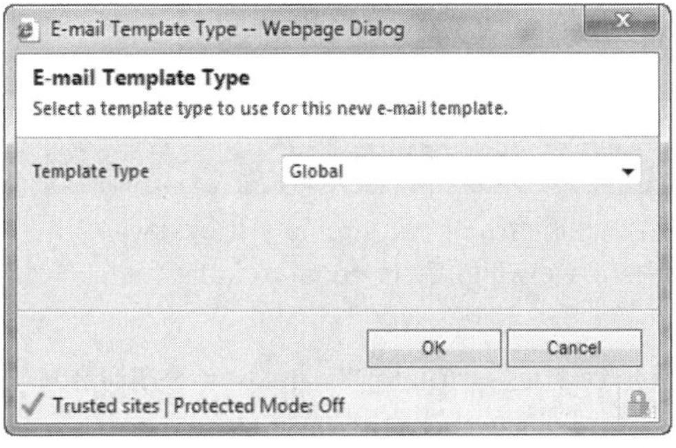

FIGURE 12.34 Template type.

Selecting the template type determines what data fields are available to work with on the template. Table 12.1 describes which data fields are available with the template type.

TABLE 12.1 Template Type/Entity Data Fields Available

Template Type	Entity Data Fields Available
Global	User
Lead	User, Lead
Opportunity	User, Account, Contact, Opportunity
Account	User, Account, Contact
Contact	User, Account, Contact
Quota	User, Account, Contact, Quota
Order	User, Account, Contact, Order
Invoice	User, Account, Contact, Invoice
Case	User, Account, Contact, Case
Contract	User, Account, Contact, Contract
Service Activity	User, Account, Contact, Service Activity, Site, Service
System Job	User, System Job

Viewable By Viewable By is a property that identifies where the E-mail Template is available. The entire organization can view and use Templates created in the Settings area (assuming that everyone has have adequate permission from the Security Role).

Users can create their own E-mail Templates from their personal options, and, by default, the permissions on their personal templates are set at Individual. You can promote these templates to an organizational level and use them across the organization by selecting Make Template Available to Organization from the Actions drop-down menu. For more information about working with individual templates, see Chapter 7, "Working with the Workplace."

TIP

The user who owns the personal template or the administrator can promote it by navigating to All E-mail Templates and selecting it where Viewable By is equal to Individual.

Language The Language property is the language of the template. By default, templates are displayed in the view as All E-mail Templates and show only the base language templates. If a new template is created and another language is selected, it will not show in All E-mail Templates—you must select All Language E-mail Templates to see the templates that exist outside of the base template.

As with the rest of the system, the only language options are those that the system administrator has loaded and made available in the Languages section of Settings.

When creating a template, follow these steps:

1. Select New and select the template type (refer to Figure 12.34).
2. Select the language, the title, and, optionally, the description. These are specific to the template properties, and the recipient will not see them.
3. The recipient will see the Subject and the body, and these are available for dynamic content. To enter dynamic content, place the cursor in either the Subject or the body, and click the Insert/Update button at the top of the form. (If the cursor is in the title or the description, the dynamic fields will be placed in the body by default.) The Data Field Values interface then opens, enabling you to add data fields. Click Add to add a data field (see Figure 12.35).

TIP

The Default Text option enables you to enter alternative text in cases when the selected data field is blank.

---

4. Select the record type to work with. By default, the user record information will always be available, along with content-specific information related to the template type (refer to previous discussion on template type).
5. Select the attribute from Record Type and add it to Data Field Values. Selecting more than one value causes Microsoft Dynamics CRM to add only one value from the list—whichever one it finds first. Additionally, each data field must be added uniquely. An example might be the name of the Contact. If you select First Name and then Last Name as part of the same data field, Microsoft Dynamics CRM uses

the First Name (if available), not the Last Name. If the First Name is not available, it uses the Last Name. If neither is available, it uses the default text entered. If there was no default text, this will be blank. Format the text and/or dynamic areas as desired (see Figure 12.36).

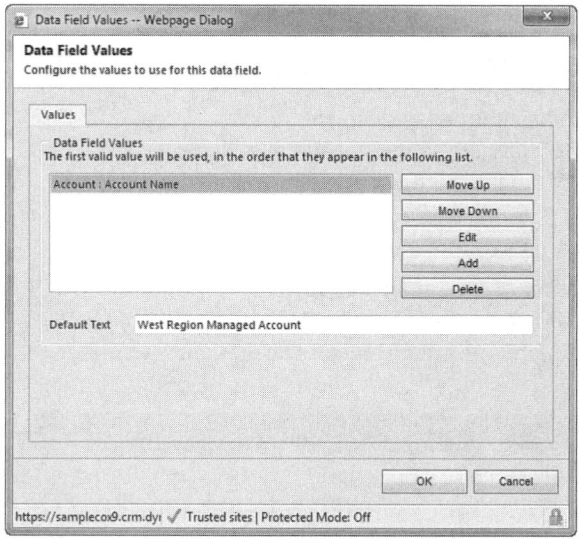

FIGURE 12.35 Insert/Update for a template.

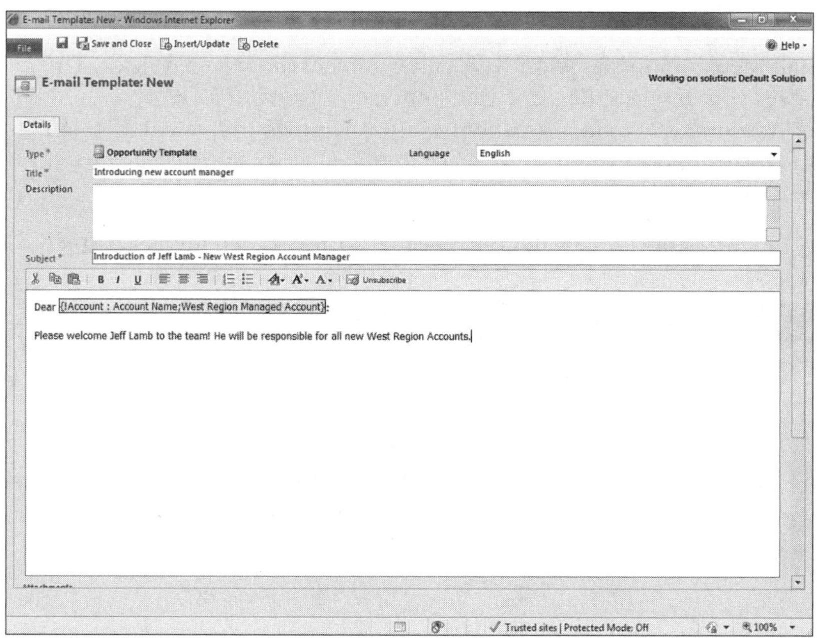

FIGURE 12.36 Formatted template.

NOTE

Unlike in previous versions, templates can now have attachments. To add an attachment to a template, scroll down to the bottom of the template and add an attachment.

TIP

You can include an image in a template as either an attachment, or you can copy and paste the image from any public website. Navigate to the website and then copy and paste the image directly into the body of the template.

Another use for templates is in the creation of an e-mail signature. To do this, create a template with Template Type equal to Global and add the desired signature values. When creating an e-mail, select the Insert Template option and insert the Signature template.

TIP

You can add multiple templates to a single e-mail.

Mail Merge Templates

Mail Merge Templates are powerful because they allow for the creation of formatted Word documents with data from Microsoft Dynamics CRM.

To create a new Mail Merge Template, select New and complete the required fields. The categorization enables you to select the associated entity, consisting of a Quote, Opportunity, Lead, Account, or Contact. The ownership defaults to Individual, but you can change that to Organizational when completed. Template language is limited to the language options installed and made active by the system administrator.

File Attachment is the merge document that is associated with the Mail Merge Template.

NOTE

The only acceptable files for Mail Merge templates are Microsoft Office Word documents saved in Office XML format.

Figure 12.37 shows a Mail Merge Template associated to the Contact entity.

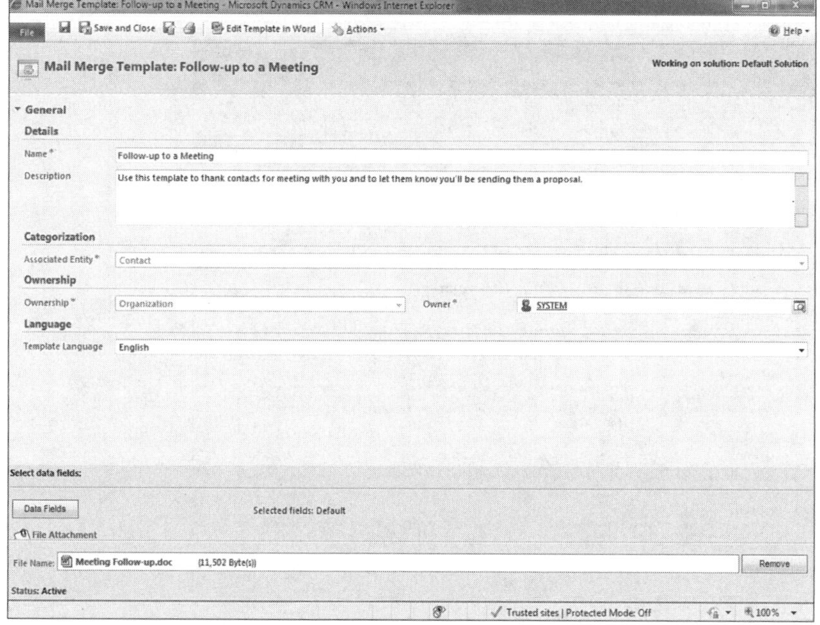

FIGURE 12.37 Mail Merge Template.

▶ Refer to Chapter 7 for details about creating Mail Merge Templates.

Product Catalog

Information about the products being sold is managed in the Product Catalog. You must set up four areas:

- Discount Lists
- Unit Groups
- Price Lists
- Products

To set up products, it is recommended that you set up the areas in the order listed, but you can edit them in any order.

TIP

Although they're not listed in the previous list, products associated with both Currencies are classified by Subject. If you're setting up a large Product List, it might make sense to build the Subject categories and add whatever Currencies you want to work with before you start working with products because editing each product later might be time-consuming.

Figure 12.38 shows the Product Catalog and the four areas that must be set up.

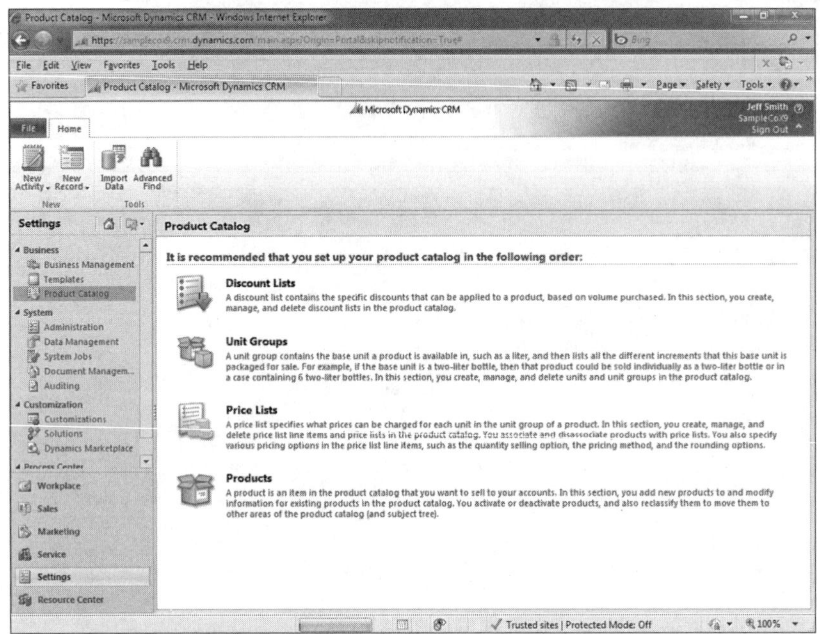

FIGURE 12.38 Product Catalog.

NOTE

Many Microsoft Dynamics CRM users will undoubtedly be interested in having their Product Catalog managed by another application—typically, their accounting or ERP system. This is a best practice and highly recommended. It is typically handled programmatically and can be configured for almost any type of ERP/accounting system.

Discount Lists

Commonly referred to as *discount schedules,* Discount Lists allow discounts to be given based on quantity. Discounts can be based on either percentage or amount of the quantity ordered within an entered range (see Figure 12.39).

When thinking about setting up Discount Lists, consider how you want the discount to be applied. Table 12.2 shows an example of how a Discount List might work using percentages.

TABLE 12.2 Discount List Using Percentages and Amounts

Beginning Quantity	Ending Quantity	Percentage Discount
1,000	5,000	3.50
5,001	25,000	5.00
25,001	100,000+	7.50

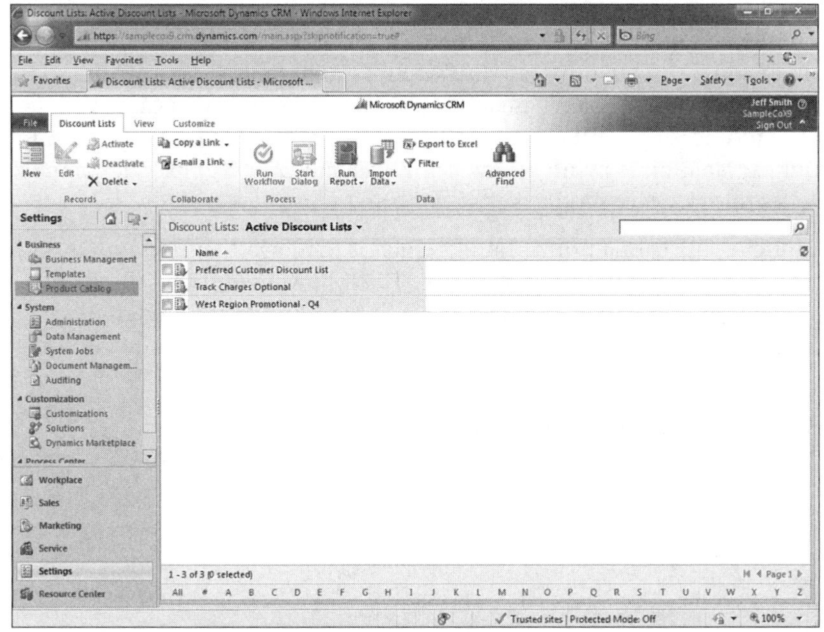

FIGURE 12.39 Discount List configured for varied quantities.

To set up a Discount List with amounts, this could work as follows:

Beginning Quantity	Ending Quantity	Amount Discount
1,000	5,000	$ 50.00
5,001	25,000	$ 150.00
25,001	100,000+	$ 500.00

In both cases, no discount will be applied if the quantity ordered is less than 1,000.

You can create as many Discount Lists as necessary and, although not required, associate them with different Price Lists and Price List Items (see the "Price Lists" section later in this chapter).

Unit Groups

Unit Groups determine groupings of how products are to be sold. The typical example of unit groups is a can of soda. The quantity (or Unit Group) is determined on how the soda is purchased because it is possible to purchase a single can, a six-pack, and a case consisting of 12 or 24 cans. Additionally, Unit Groups can consist of minutes, hours, and days for services offered. Our explanation is by no means definitive, and Unit Groups can comprise any level of quantities for whatever products your company sells.

Each of these quantities consists of a primary unit, which is the lowest level of unit available and, in the case of services, could be at any level. The following example shown in Figure 12.40 illustrates a services company that sells its services by the second (granted, this is a somewhat far-fetched scenario, but it clearly illustrates how to set up quantities).

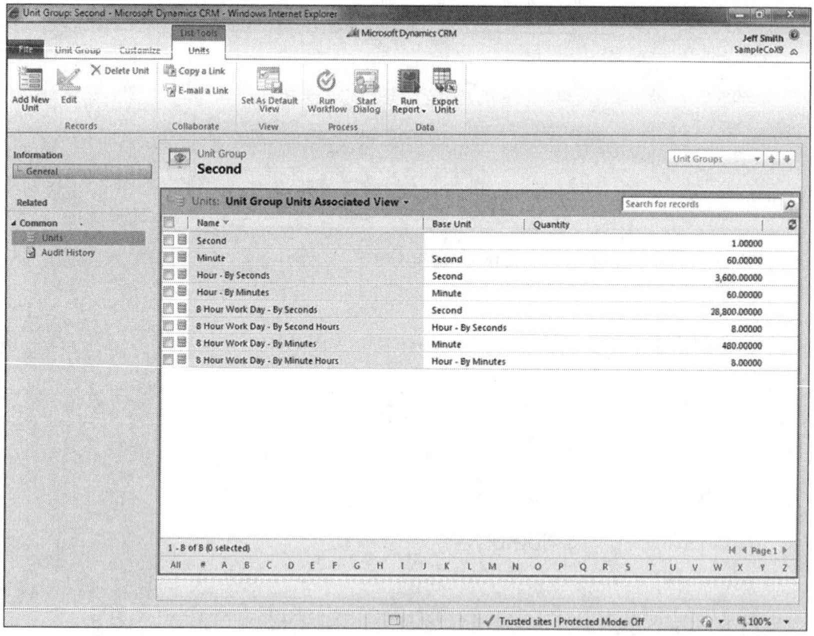

FIGURE 12.40 Unit Group for services by the second.

Note that, in this example, the last four lines for "8 Hour Work Day" are all the same—they all charge 8 hours for the day, but they comprise different quantities of the base unit.

Unit Groups are associated with products, as well as the default unit for the product.

Price Lists

Price Lists make up groupings of products with associated pricing. If you don't have varied pricing for any reason, you could easily set up a single Price List (called Standard Price List, Default Price List, or similar) with all your products and their pricing on it. Additionally, it might be common to have only a small number of prices lists, such as

Retail and Wholesale. However, no limit governs the number of available Price Lists—you can create multiple prices lists by customer, region, time of year, or other consideration.

TIP

Too many Price Lists can create confusion when your salespeople are attempting to build Quotes, Orders, or Invoices. If you use many Price Lists, be sure to use a comprehensive naming strategy to ensure that the right list is used.

Although you need to create Price Lists next in the hierarchy, they aren't completed until you add products to each list. Fortunately, you can do this in the final step when the products are built, and, if necessary, you can return to the Price List Items for each Price List to edit the items associated with them.

Price Lists consist of the currency, name, and start/end date that the Price List is applicable for, as well as Price List Items (see Figure 12.41).

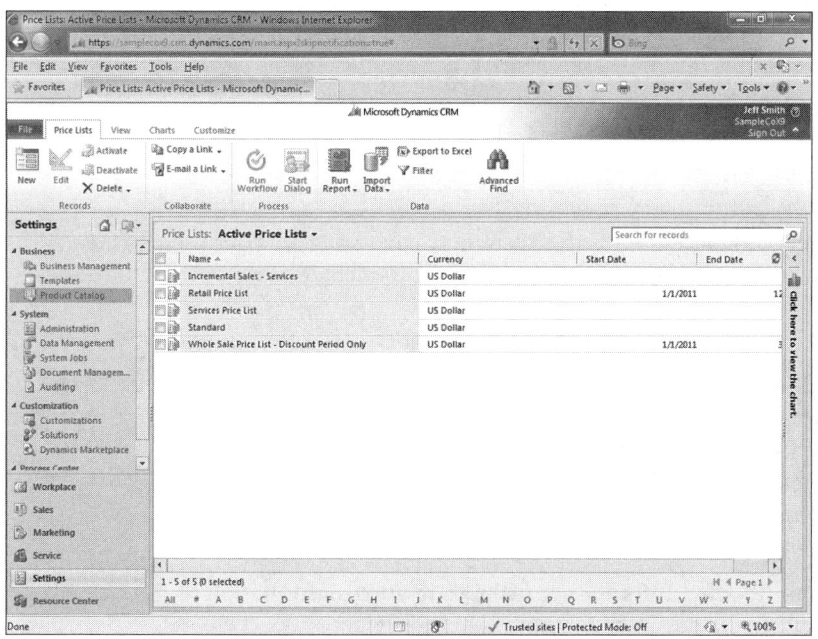

FIGURE 12.41 Price Lists.

NOTE

Although you can configure the Start and End dates for the Price List, they are not enforced, and users can continue to use them after the date has passed. You must manually deactivate or delete them after the date has passed to prevent them from being used.

TIP

You can easily set up Price Lists in conjunction with Discount Lists for promotional and seasonal pricing for specific products. To do this, create a new Discount List with the discount and quantity of discount. (For this scenario, in which the promotional pricing would apply to every item, regardless of quantity, the beginning quantity would be 1, and the ending quantity would be whatever maximum level you wanted to set.) Create a new Price List and add existing products and units, as well as the Discount List you previously set up. Be sure to name both the Price List and the Discount List accordingly so that you'll know what they are for.

Price lists must be activated prior to being available for use. To do so, navigate to the Active Price list display, select the price lists and then select Activate from the Ribbon menu.

Products

Products is where you set up and maintain the products you sell. Several aspects make up a product:

- Product Information
- Substitutes
- Price List Items
- Kit Products

Although we review product setup in this section, it is possible for your users to create products as Write In products. Write In products are products that are not set up in the Product Catalog.

TIP

Be sure to monitor the use of Write In products by your salespersons. Frequently, salespeople will use Write In products to manipulate the system to sell products that are in the Product Catalog to create product discounts or solve other limitations that aren't normally available.

Product Information Product Information includes required information of ID, Name, Unit Group, Default Unit, and Decimals Supported (see Figure 12.42).

Additionally, it is important to set the Product Type. In the previous example, we selected Services, but you can set this to Sales Inventory, Miscellaneous Charges, or Flat Fees as well.

The Description tab enables you to enter vendor information as well as weight and volume information. This is helpful for automation and shipping routines that might be incorporated into the system related to e-commerce situations.

Substitutes Substitutions are products from the Product Catalog that can be substituted for the product being created or edited. Substitutions are not the same as Write In prod-

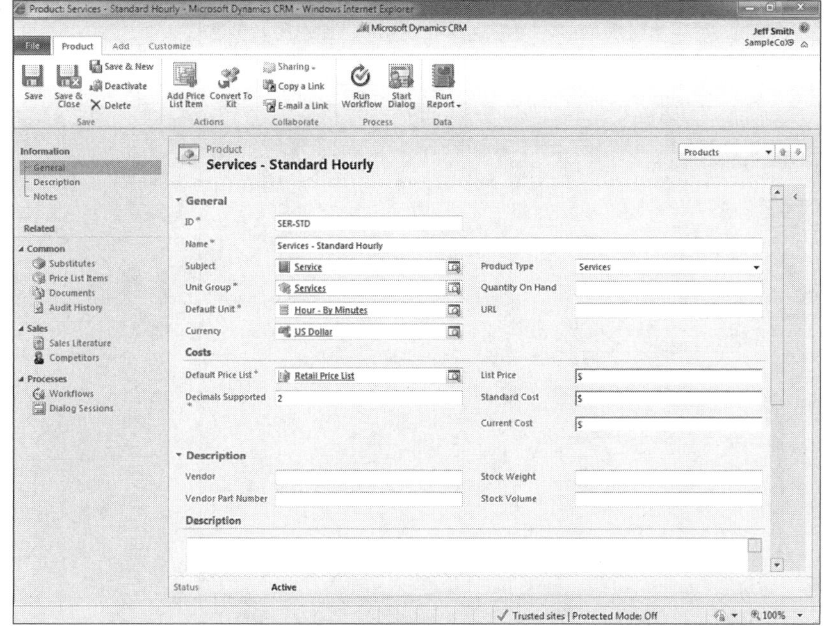

FIGURE 12.42 Product Information.

ucts that can consist of any item; these are predefined substitutions for the product being edited.

Price List Items The Price List Items are the product groupings applicable to the product, as well as their association to the actual product and units (see Figure 12.43).

Additional important options include Quantity Selling Option, which, in the example shown, enables you to sell in any fashion. This is good because we've selected hours as our product, and we want to invoice in only 15-minute increments, or 1/4 quantity.

Kit Products Kit Products are a number of products bundled as a kit for purposes of selling as a group. A Kit Product has a single price that makes up each item in the kit. To create a Kit Product, select the product and, from the More Actions menu, select Convert to Kit. (Similarly, if you want to demote a Kit Product to a regular product, select Convert to Product.) An example of a Kit Product might be a 1-hour service call on a computer that includes a new mouse and a new computer (see Figure 12.44).

System

The System features of the system are those that should be carefully controlled and be given limited access, as the changes can have severe affects including revoking permissions to intended users. It is typical for an organization to limit access to the System features to only one or two System Administrators.

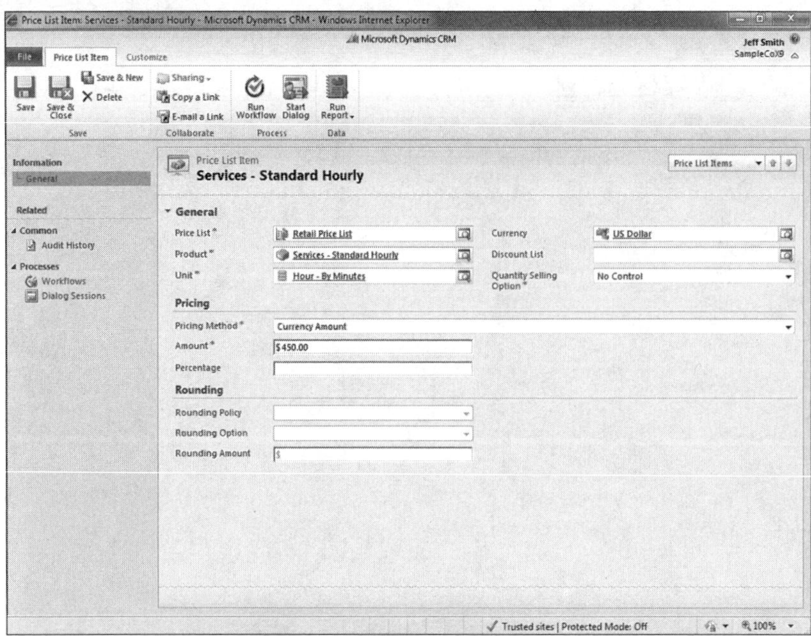

FIGURE 12.43 Product Price List information.

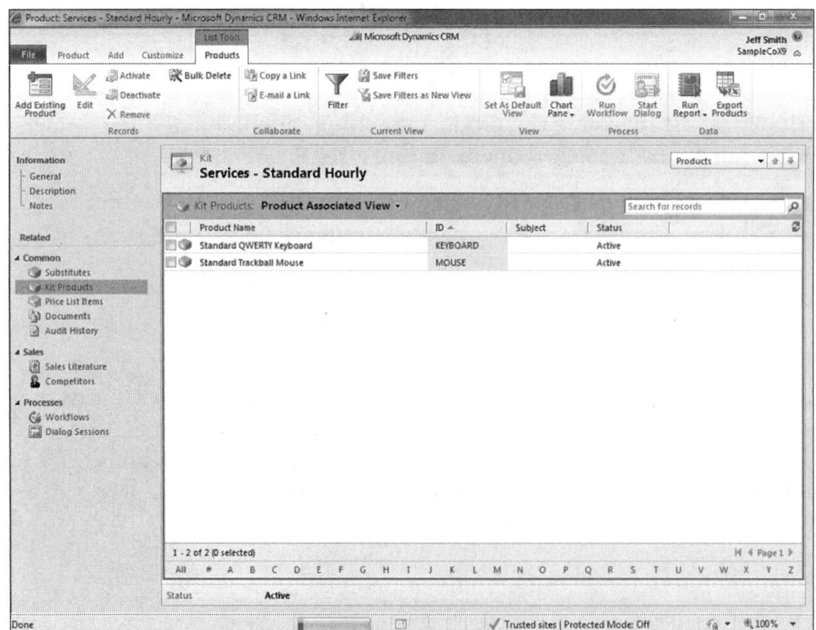

FIGURE 12.44 Kit Product example.

Administration

Administration is where a majority of the System setup, configuration and maintenance is performed.

The Administration page has the following options:

- Announcements
- Auto-Numbering
- Business Units
- System Settings
- Security Roles
- Field Security Profiles
- Teams
- Users
- Languages
- Privacy Preferences
- Billing (CRM Online only)
- System Notifications (CRM Online only)
- Product Updates (Partner hosted or on premise only)
- Subscription Management (CRM Online only)

Figure 12.45 shows the Administration screen from the Settings area with the On Line options visible.

Announcements

Announcements enable you to easily communicate with your CRM users by creating messages that display by default in the My Workspace, Announcements section of Microsoft Dynamics CRM (see Figure 12.46).

Announcements are listed by creation date, with the most recent at the top. When creating Announcements, select New and complete the required information (see Figure 12.47).

Announcements have four properties:

- Title
- Body
- URL
- Expiration Date

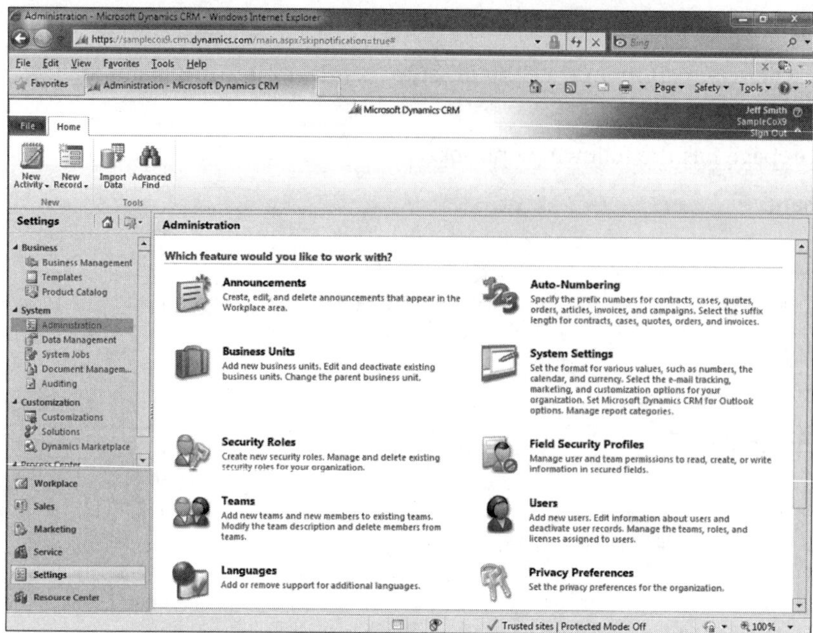

FIGURE 12.45 Settings, Administration screen.

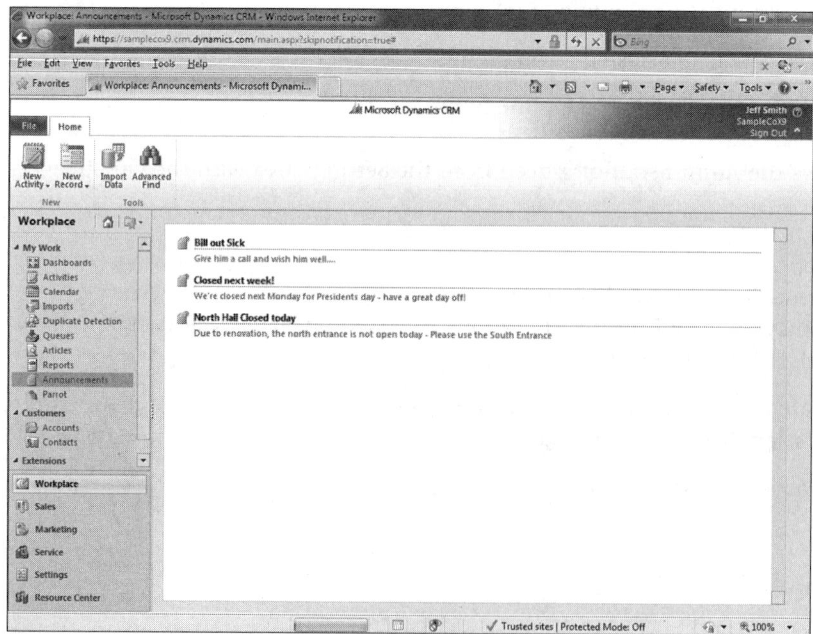

FIGURE 12.46 Announcements in My Workplace.

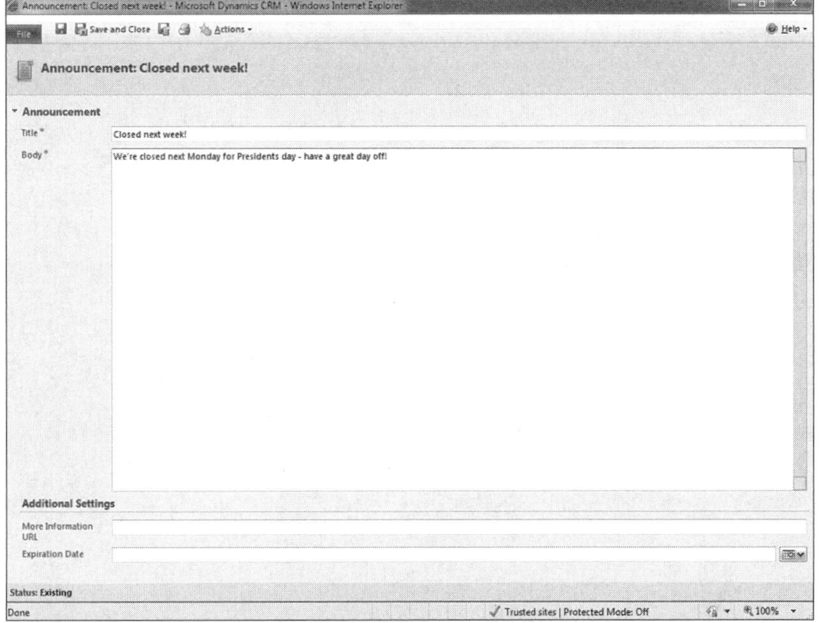

FIGURE 12.47 Creating new Announcements.

The two required fields are Title and Body. URL is optional; however, when entered, it displays on the main Announcements page, allowing Users to navigate directly to the entered URL. Finally, Expiration Date is an optional value that automatically hides the Announcement after the date has expired. After the Announcement has expired, there is no way to reactivate it—you must create a new one.

NOTE

Announcements do not support either rich formatting or documents attached to them. If you need to refer to external documents, consider placing them on a common web directory and inserting the URL into the documents.

Auto-Numbering

By default, Microsoft Dynamics CRM auto-numbers the following entities incrementally:

- Contracts
- Cases
- Articles
- Quotas

- Orders
- Invoices
- Campaigns

With the exception of Articles, you can adjust the suffix length (see Figure 12.48).

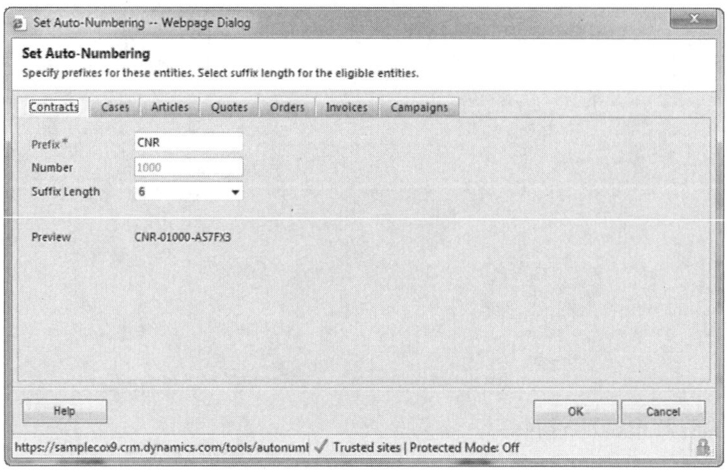

FIGURE 12.48 Auto-numbering options.

NOTE

Changing a prefix number to a new value applies to newly created records; it does not change existing records.

Business Units

You control access to information across the organization with Business Units, Teams, and territories. With Microsoft Dynamics CRM, you can create multiple Child Business Units and assign users that have access to only the information within their Business Unit, not their Parent Business Unit.

When Microsoft Dynamics CRM is first installed, you specify the Parent Business Unit as the organization name during the installation. This is the default Business Unit that will derive any Child Business Units. If your organization is relatively small or has no separated Business Units (other than the organization itself), there is little reason to make any changes to the Business Units. As such, you end up with one Business Unit with the same name as your organization. However, if you have multiple Business Units, you will want to configure them here.

NOTE

You may have multiple Child Business Units (see Figure 12.49), but you cannot disable the Parent Business Unit (which is created during setup). New to this version of CRM, you can now change the Parent Business Unit (to correct a spelling error, or because the wrong Business Unit was assigned as the Parent, and so on). Previous versions required that you must uninstall and completely reinstall Microsoft Dynamics CRM with the correct Business Unit specified.

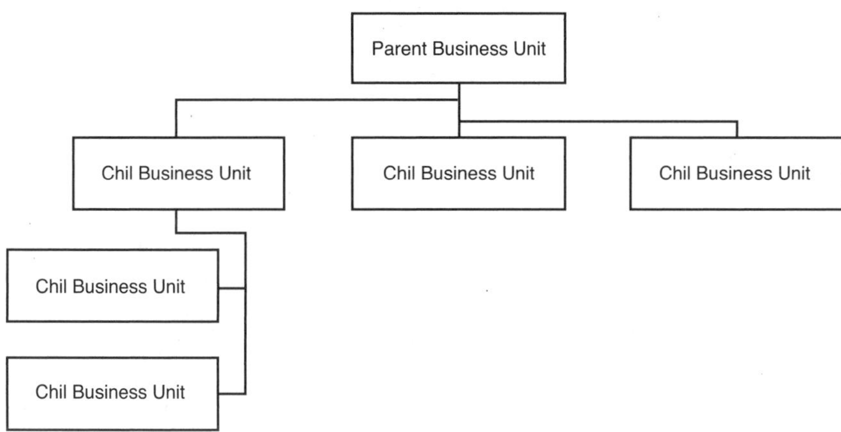

FIGURE 12.49 Parent and Child Business Units.

Because of the way the Security Roles work, it is important to consider setting up both Business Units and the Security Roles. (For more information about Security Roles, see the "Security Roles" section later in this chapter.) Additionally, because Users are assigned Business Units as a required field for their setup, when you disable a Business Unit, all users assigned to that Business Unit (and any Child Business Units) are deactivated and cannot log in to the system until they are reassigned to an active Business Unit.

NOTE

Users are not deactivated or deleted if the Business Unit is deactivated. They remain valid/active users in the system, but they cannot log in because their Business Unit is disabled. This is an important distinction because they continue to consume a Client Access License (CAL), even though they have no access to the system. A user can be moved to a different Business Unit after the original Business Unit is deactivated if necessary.

▶ For more information about working with Users, see the "Users" section later in this chapter.

By default, when viewing the Business Units from the Administration screen, the Active Business Units appear with their Parent Business Unit (see Figure 12.50).

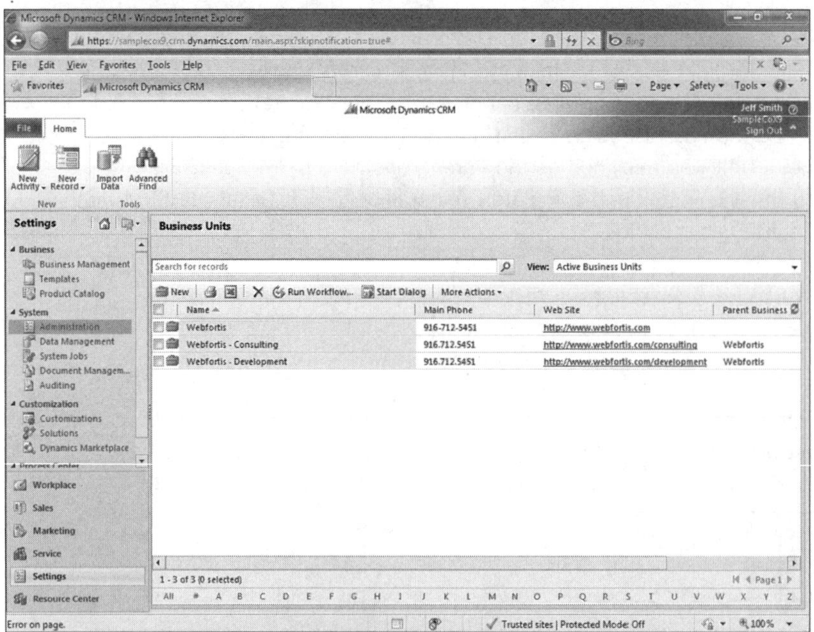

FIGURE 12.50 Business Unit view.

By selecting More Actions on this screen, you can enable a deactivated Business Unit, disable an active Business Unit, and change the Parent Business of a Child Business Unit. To create a new Business Unit, select New on the main Business Unit Administration screen (see Figure 12.51).

The new Business Unit screen has two required fields that must be populated (refer to Figure 12.51). The first is the name of the Business Unit, and the second is the Parent Business Unit.

By default, the Parent Business Unit is populated with the Organization Business Unit (or Master Business Unit), but you can change this to a Child Business Unit if you want. As mentioned previously, you must have a Parent Business Unit for any new Business Units that are created.

NOTE

You can disable Business Units after creating them, but you cannot delete them until they are disabled.

After you enter the desired name and select the Parent Business Unit, click Save to enter specific address information related to the Business Unit, as well as to begin to build out organizational information specific to the Business Unit (see Figure 12.52).

FIGURE 12.51 New Business Unit.

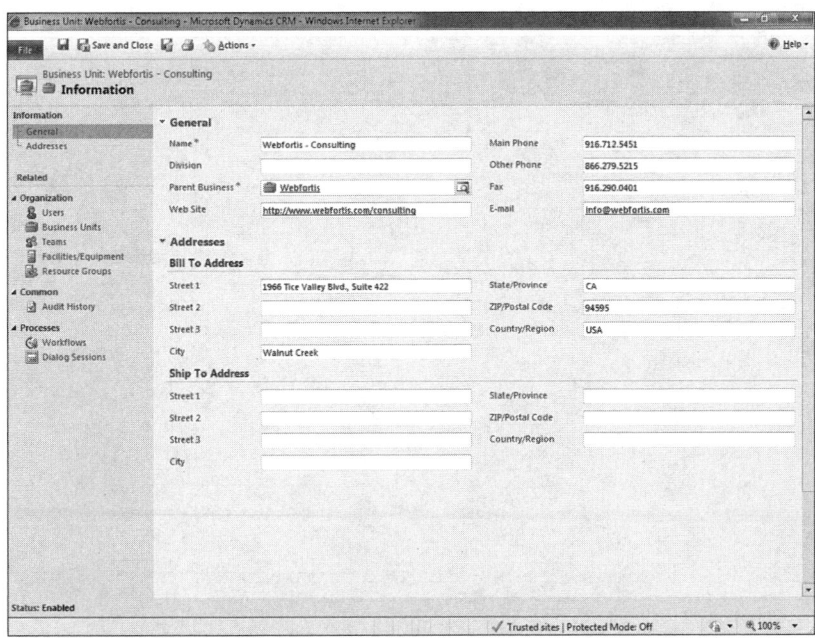

FIGURE 12.52 Saved new Business Unit.

TIP

Although the Parent Business Unit appears to be locked, you can easily change it by selecting Actions, Change Parent Business.

Security Roles are specific to Business Units, with certain limitations. The Organizational information options are on the near navigation of the Business Unit:

- ▶ Users
- ▶ Business Units
- ▶ Teams
- ▶ Facilities/Equipment
- ▶ Resource Groups

For more information on Security Roles, see the "Security Roles" section later in this chapter.

Users Selecting Users shows you who is assigned to that Business Unit (see Figure 12.53).

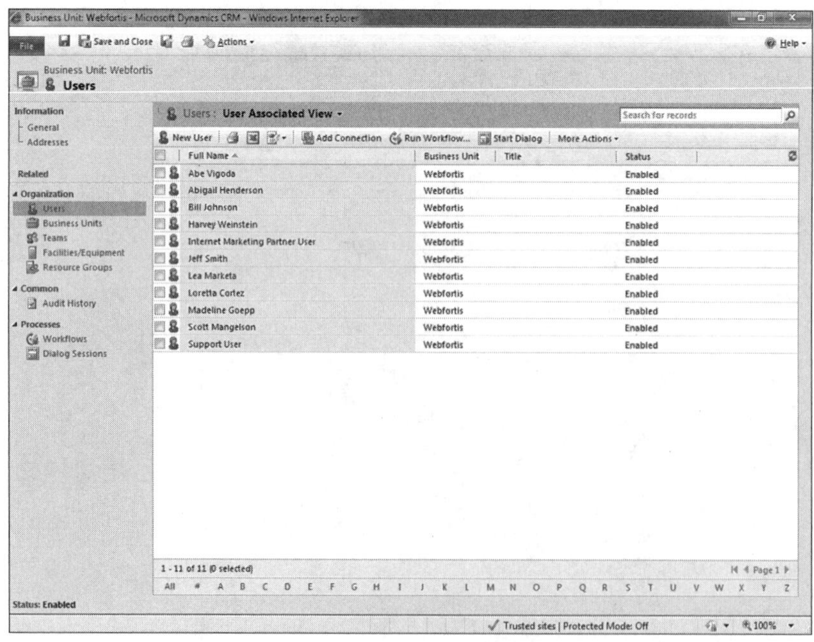

FIGURE 12.53 Business Unit Users.

User assignment to Business Units is explained in greater detail later in this chapter in the "Administration—Users" section. However, when adding users, be aware of the following:

- Only users who have *not* been added to the CRM can be added to newly created Business Units from the New Business Unit screen. If you want to assign Users to a newly created Business Unit who are already in the system, you must first navigate to the user (Settings, Users) and select Change Business Unit from the Actions or More Actions drop-down options.
- You cannot move the current user (that is, the user who is logged in) to a Business Unit. Instead, you must delegate access to another user and either request that the other user make the changes or log in as the other user and make the changes. (Be sure to grant the necessary Security Role of either System Administrator or System Customizer to the other user before you attempt to make this change.)
- Only users who are assigned to the Business Unit you're working with appear on the Users screen. To see users of Child Business Units, you must select the Child Business Units separately.
- When users are moved from an existing Business Unit to a new Business Unit, all role information is removed, and it must be manually reassigned.

Business Units Business Units displays the Child Business Units of the selected Business Unit (see Figure 12.54).

NOTE

Note that in the same way Subcontacts work on the Contacts form, only the direct Child Business Units display on the screen. To view Child Business Units that might exist, you must select the Child Business Unit and navigate to the Business Units section of the Child Business Unit.

From here you can easily create a new Child Business Unit by selecting New Business Unit. You can also enable and disable any existing Business Units displayed.

Teams Because Teams are specific to Business Units, selecting Teams shows you which Teams are assigned to that Business Unit (see Figure 12.10). Teams are explained in greater detail later in this chapter in the "Administration—Teams" section.

Facilities/Equipment As with Teams, Facilities/Equipment is specific to Business Units. Selecting Facilities/Equipment shows you what Facilities/Equipment is assigned to that Business Unit (see Figure 12.56). Facilities/Equipment is explained in greater detail later in this chapter in the section "Business Management—Facilities/Equipment."

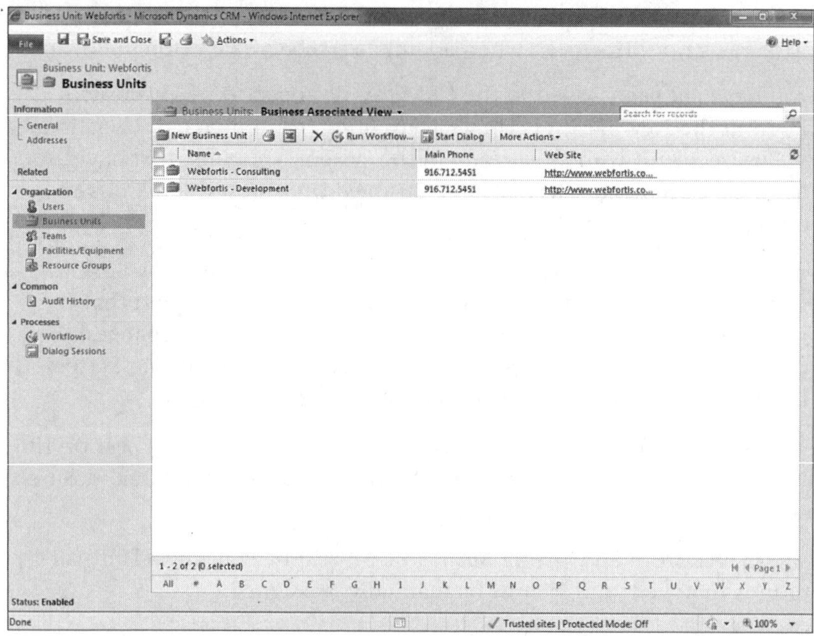

FIGURE 12.54 Business Units.

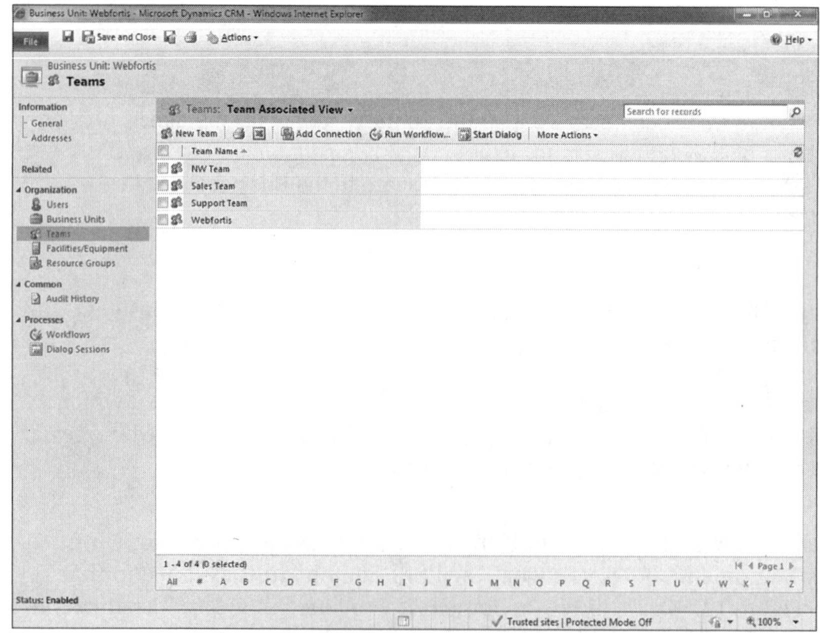

FIGURE 12.55 Business Unit Teams.

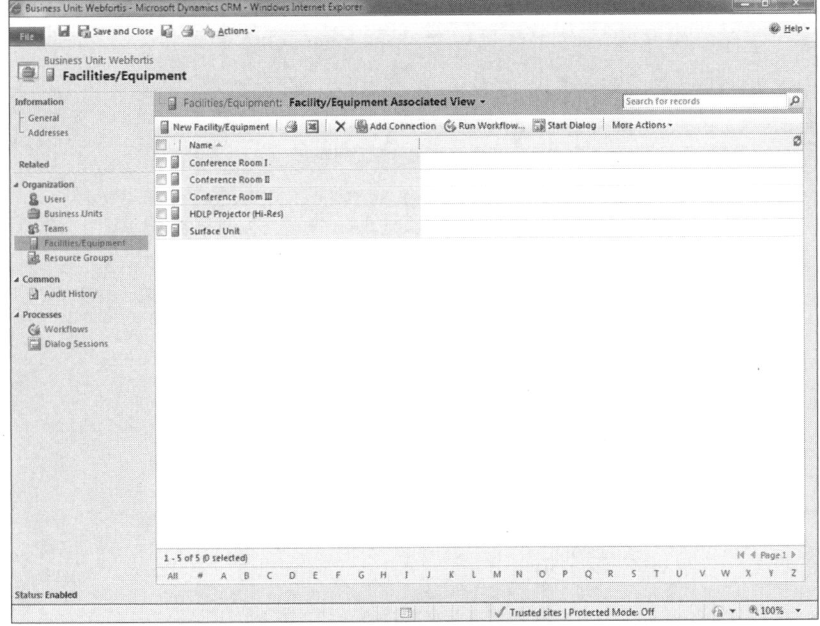

FIGURE 12.56 Business Unit Facilities/Equipment.

Resource Groups As with both Teams and Facilities/Equipment, Resource Groups are specific to Business Units. Selecting Resource Groups shows you what Resource Groups are assigned to that Business Unit (see Figure 12.57).

Resource Groups are explained in greater detail later in this chapter in the section "Business Management—Resource Groups."

NOTE

Every time a business unit is created, a new team is created with the new business unit name.

System Settings

Located on the main Administration page after selecting Settings, the System Settings interface is similar to (and often confused with) the User Options interface. Here you make systemwide settings that affect all users (unlike the User Options).

The System Settings interface is divided into seven tabbed sections (see Figure 12.58).

The sections are as follows:

- General
- Calendar

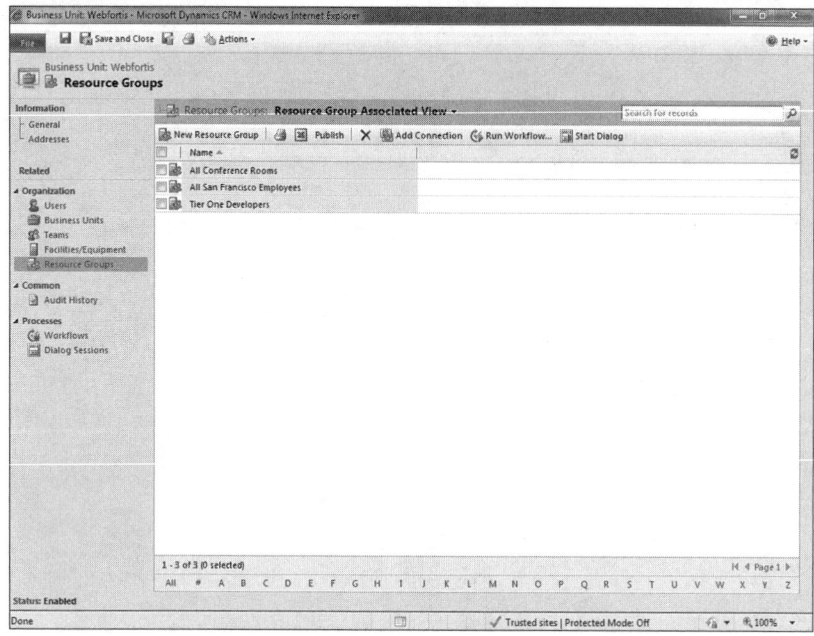

FIGURE 12.57 Business Unit Resource Groups.

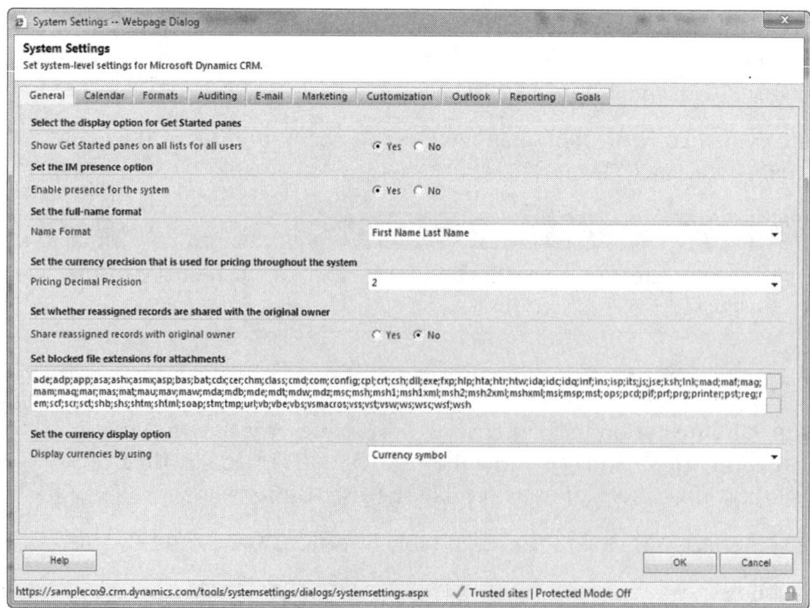

FIGURE 12.58 System Settings.

- Formats
- Auditing
- E-mail
- Marketing
- Customization
- Outlook
- Reporting
- Goals

General

In the General section, you can set and change the following options:

- **Show Get Started Panes**—Set this to either off or on for global settings of the Get Started Panes.

NOTE

This setting will affect all entities. To set individual entities, navigate to that entity, and then minimize the pane—the system will remember that setting and not display it the next time you navigate to it (however, this is an individual user setting).

- **Set the IM presence option**—Set whether instant messaging will display the current presence status for users, Contacts, Opportunities, or Leads.
- **Full-name format**—This is the default way the user and customer names are displayed when using Microsoft Dynamics CRM.

NOTE

If you select to change the full-name format, you will only be able to change the format on new records added to the system. All existing records will continue to display in the original format. Although it can take some effort, one way of correcting this for existing records is to export all of them, delete or deactivate them, and then re-import them. They will take on the new format during re-import. Be sure to carefully consider this prior to attempting because it might be more trouble than it's worth.

- **Currency precision**—When working with Currency fields throughout Microsoft Dynamics CRM, you can set the level of precision (from 0 to 4) for the decimal.

- **Reassigned record sharing**—This option enables you to specify whether an entity is shared with the original owner by default when it is reassigned, or whether the new owner assumes complete ownership of the entity. By default, this is set to No.
- **Blocked file extensions**—By default, the listed file extensions are blocked and prevented from being uploaded. Attempting to upload a document with one of the blocked file extensions listed will result in an error when trying to upload (see Figure 12.59).

FIGURE 12.59 File upload error.

These are the recommended and default extensions designed to keep your system safe and prevent malicious files from being uploaded. However, you can edit this list as you see fit.

- **Currency display option**—You can choose to display either the Currency symbol (in the case of U.S. dollars and euros, this would be $ and e, respectively) or the Currency code (again, in the case of U.S. dollars and euros, this would be USD and EUR, respectively).

Calendar

From here you can set the scheduling options with regard to the maximum durations of an appointment in days.

Figure 12.61 shows the error that you'll receive when you try and schedule an appointment and it exceeds the amount set here.

Users are alerted to this error, but have the option to ignore and save and continue.

Formats

The Formats section enables you to customize how Microsoft Dynamics CRM formats data such as dates, times, and numbers (see Figure 12.62).

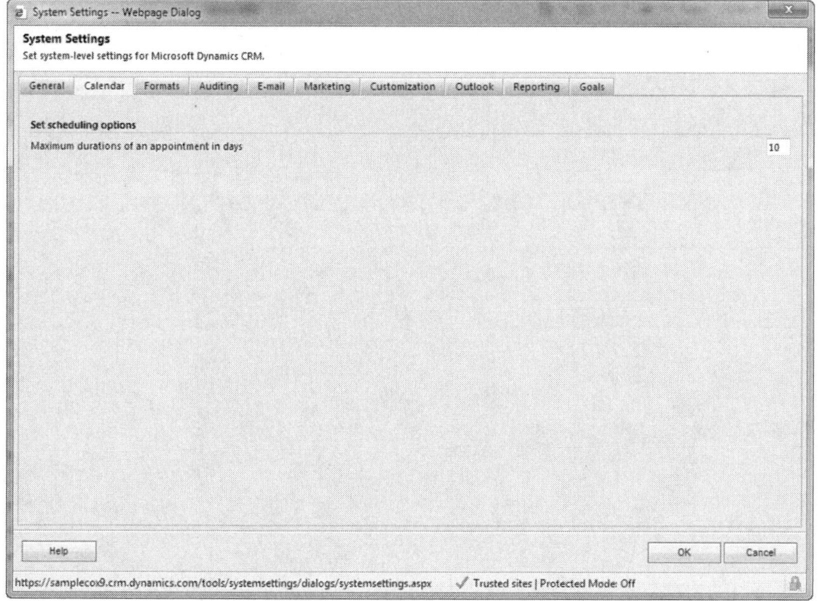

FIGURE 12.60 Calendar options.

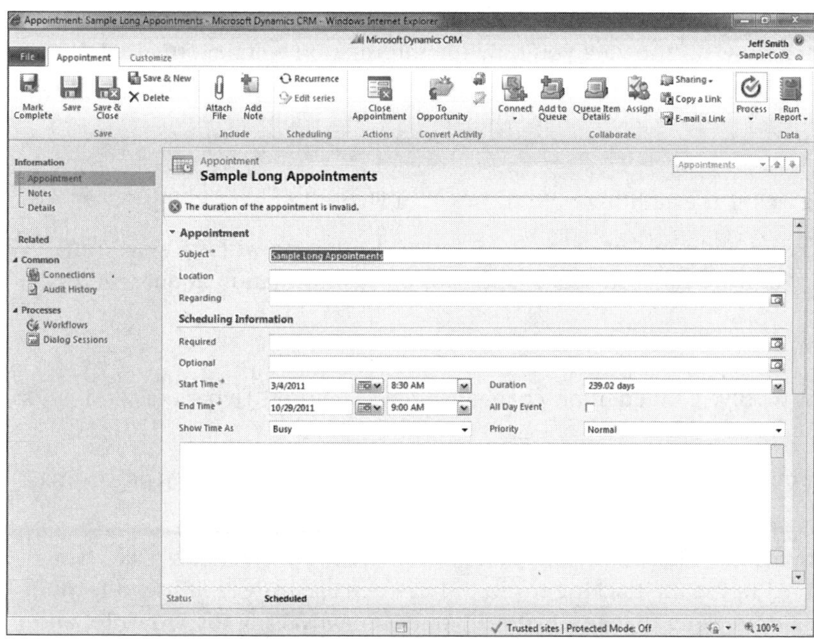

FIGURE 12.61 Appointment duration is exceeded.

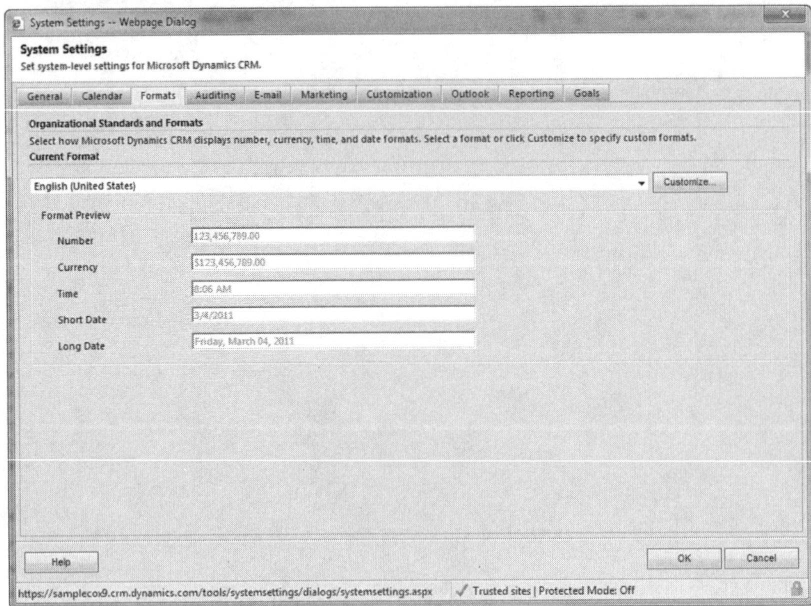

FIGURE 12.62 Format options.

Selecting a value from the drop-down menu populates the default values for the selected region in the Format Preview, showing you how the information will be formatted. If you need to further edit them for regional, custom formats or other settings, select Customize (refer to Figure 12.62) and make advanced configurations (see Figure 12.63).

Auditing

To enable auditing, select the auditing option shown in Figure 12.64.

Regardless of your individual entity or attribute settings, auditing will not start until this enabled. See "Auditing" later in this chapter for more information about working with this feature.

E-mail

The E-mail options involve configuration changes to how Microsoft Dynamics CRM works with e-mail (see Figure 12.65).

- **Configure e-mail processing**—This option helps the E-Mail router by processing only e-mails that have met the selected criteria.
- **E-mail correlation**—As with previous versions of Microsoft Dynamics CRM, you are not required to use the tracking token to track e-mails. Instead, it uses a feature known as Smart Tracking that automatically tracks e-mails using the From, To, and Subject to match the e-mail. For a variety of reasons, this correlation might not be 100% accurate. (Common reasons why you might lose correlation are if somebody changes the Subject or if the e-mail is forwarded to another individual.) If you

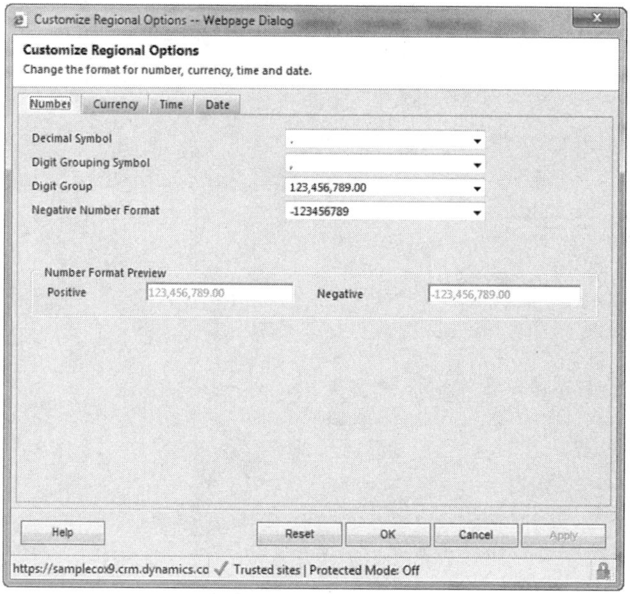

Customize Regional Options -- Webpage Dialog
Customize Regional Options
Change the format for number, currency, time and date.
Number Currency Time Date
Decimal Symbol .
Digit Grouping Symbol ,
Digit Group 123,456,789.00
Negative Number Format -123456789
Number Format Preview
Positive 123,456,789.00 Negative -123,456,789.00
Help Reset OK Cancel Apply
https://samplecox9.crm.dynamics.co Trusted sites | Protected Mode: Off

FIGURE 12.63 Customize regional options.

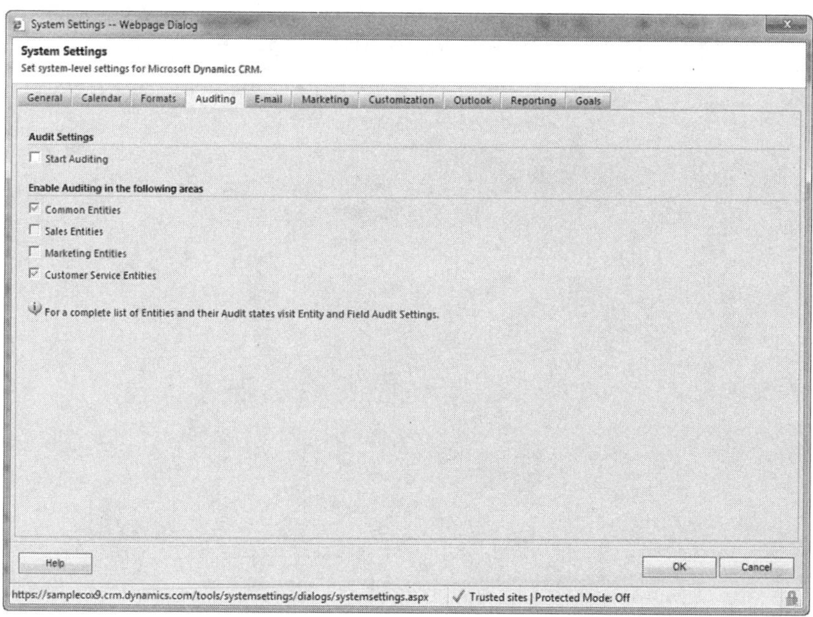

FIGURE 12.64 Auditing settings.

require 100% correlation, you should use the tracking token. The tracking token automatically appends itself to the Subject of all outbound e-mails in whatever form you select on this tab (see Figure 12.66).

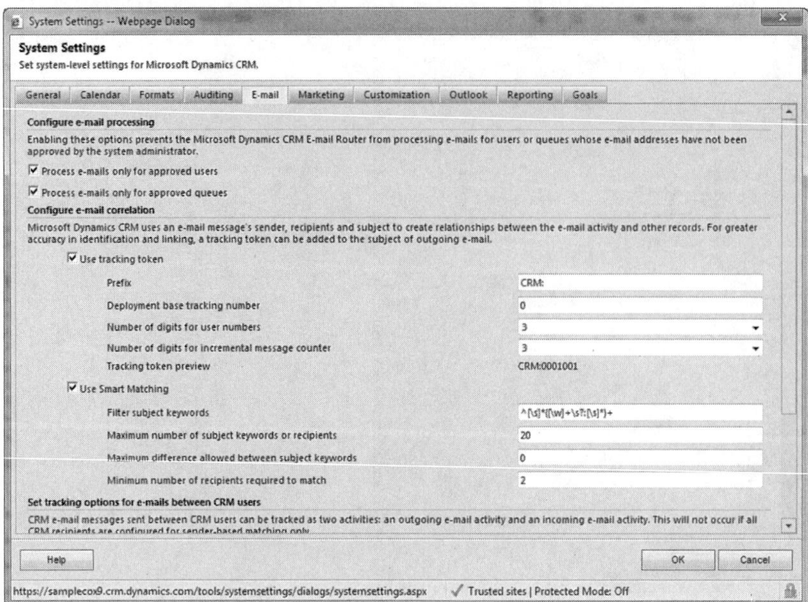

FIGURE 12.65 E-mail setting options.

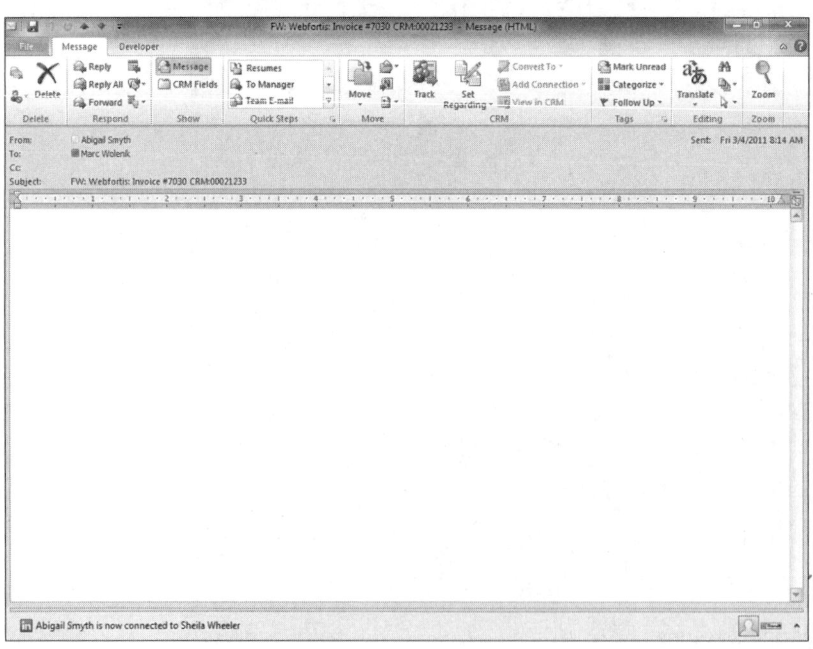

FIGURE 12.66 E-mail with tracking token in the Subject line.

NOTE

The prefix of the tracking token cannot be blank, can contain spaces, and has a maximum value of 20 characters.

Figure 12.65 shows how the tracking token is structured, as well as options available to tune the Smart Matching feature.

Notice the Track and CRM button in Figure 12.66. This is used to promote an email received in Outlook into CRM and can be used to untrack an item.

- **CRM User tracking options**—By default, when a user sends a CRM e-mail to another CRM User, both e-mails are recorded as an Activity for the selected record (one Activity of type = 'e-mail' outgoing and one Activity of type = 'e-mail' incoming).
- **E-mail form options**—Select whether to restrict e-mail message content via secure frames and whether to allow messages with unresolved e-mail recipients. Secure frames are used to prevent malicious code execution that might exist when opening e-mails in CRM. Unresolved e-mail recipients are recipients that are not found in the Account, Contact, Lead, or User e-mail address fields.
- **File size limitations**—Enter the file size allowed for uploading attachments to e-mails. The default is 5,120Kb (5MB) and the maximum value is 8,192Kb (8MB).

Marketing

The Marketing options allow for powerful and easy management related to marketing when using Microsoft Dynamics CRM (see Figure 12.67).

- **Enable Direct E-mail via Mail Merge**—By default, users can send e-mail as Campaign Activities using the Mail Merge feature. If you want to prevent this functionality, change the value here.
- **Create Campaign Responses for Incoming E-mail**—If e-mail tracking is enabled, you can configure Microsoft Dynamics CRM to automatically create a Campaign Response for incoming e-mail. This is enabled by default.
- **Auto-unsubscribe**—Again, if e-mail tracking is enabled, you can configure Microsoft Dynamics CRM to change the value on the customer record of Do Not Send Marketing Material to True if an unsubscribe e-mail is received. Furthermore, you can configure whether the customer will receive an acknowledgment of the unsubscribe request and select a template for this acknowledgment.

The Unsubscribe option is available when preparing marketing by inserting an option allowing users to click a link that allows them to unsubscribe from future marketing campaigns.

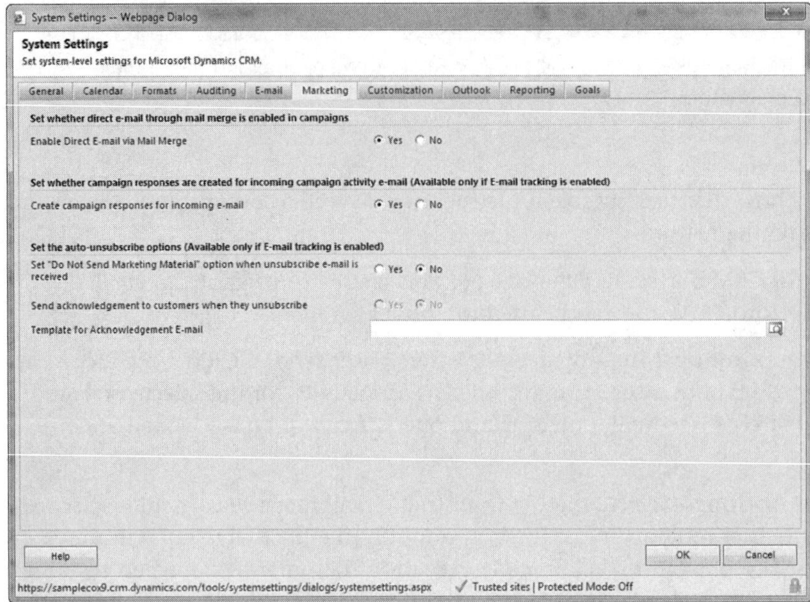

FIGURE 12.67 Marketing settings.

▶ See Chapter 9, "Working with Marketing," for more information about working with this feature.

Customization

Set whether Microsoft Dynamics CRM opens in Application mode (full browser screen for CRM usage only) as shown in Figure 12.68.

TIP

When working in Application mode, you can press Ctrl+N to open a new window. The application will open with Application mode off for as long as that new browser is opened.

Outlook

Distinctly separate from the e-mail options, the Outlook options provide options specifically designed for Outlook (see Figure 12.69).

- **E-mail promotion options**—Incoming e-mail to Outlook is automatically promoted to CRM based on the user settings configured. The options here set whether the e-mail is eligible for promotion as it arrives, performs the actual promotion at specified intervals, and sends pending CRM specific e-mail at the specified interval.

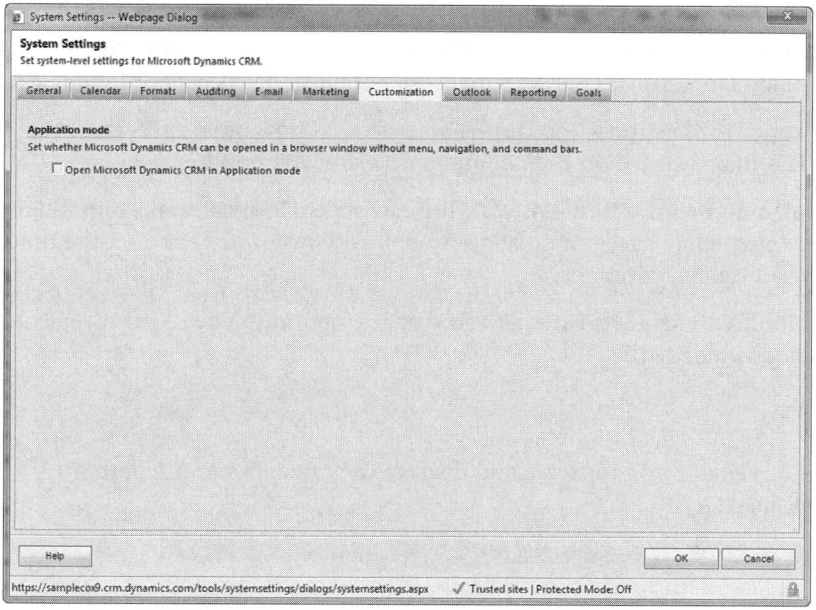

System Settings -- Webpage Dialog
System Settings
Set system-level settings for Microsoft Dynamics CRM.
General
Calendar
Formats
Auditing
E-mail
Marketing
Customization
Outlook
Reporting
Goals
Application mode
Set whether Microsoft Dynamics CRM can be opened in a browser window without menu, navigation, and command bars.
Open Microsoft Dynamics CRM in Application mode
Help
OK
Cancel
https://samplecox9.crm.dynamics.com/tools/systemsettings/dialogs/systemsettings.aspx
Trusted sites | Protected Mode: Off

FIGURE 12.68 Customization options.

System Settings -- Webpage Dialog
System Settings
Set system-level settings for Microsoft Dynamics CRM.
General
Calendar
Formats
Auditing
E-mail
Marketing
Customization
Outlook
Reporting
Goals
Set e-mail promotion options for Microsoft Dynamics CRM for Outlook
Perform checks as new e-mail is received
Yes
No
Promote incoming e-mail every
10
minutes
Send pending CRM e-mail every
10
minutes
Set whether users can schedule synchronization in Microsoft Dynamics CRM for Outlook
Users can schedule synchronization
Yes
No
Minimum Time between synchronizations
15
minutes
Set whether users can update their local data in the background in Microsoft Dynamics CRM for Outlook
Users can schedule background local data synchronization
Yes
No
Minimum time between background local data synchronizations
15
minutes
Set schedule for address book synchronization in Microsoft Dynamics CRM for Outlook
Users can schedule background address book synchronization
Yes
No
Minimum time between address book synchronizations
1
hours
Set whether users see "Get the Outlook client" in the Message Bar
Outlook client is advertised to users in the Message Bar
Yes
No
Help
OK
Cancel
https://samplecox9.crm.dynamics.com/tools/systemsettings/dialogs/systemsettings.aspx
Trusted sites | Protected Mode: Off

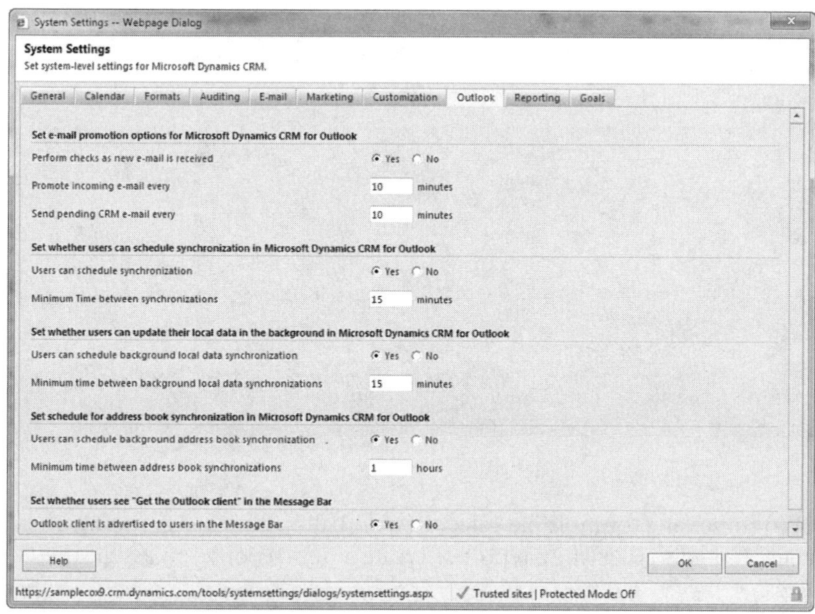

FIGURE 12.69 Outlook options.

- **User schedule synchronization**—You can set whether users can manually schedule synchronization from Outlook and at what interval synchronizations this should occur. For optimal performance, set this to no less than the recommended default of 15 minutes.
- **Local data synchronization**—You can set whether and how often users can update the data that is stored on their computers to use when offline.
- **Address book synchronization**—As with the user schedule synchronization, this enables users to schedule background address book synchronization and set the time interval between synchronizations.
- **Get the Outlook Client**—Sets whether users see the option to download the client (if not already downloaded).

Reporting

The Reporting options enable you to create and manage the categories that reports are grouped into (see Figure 12.70).

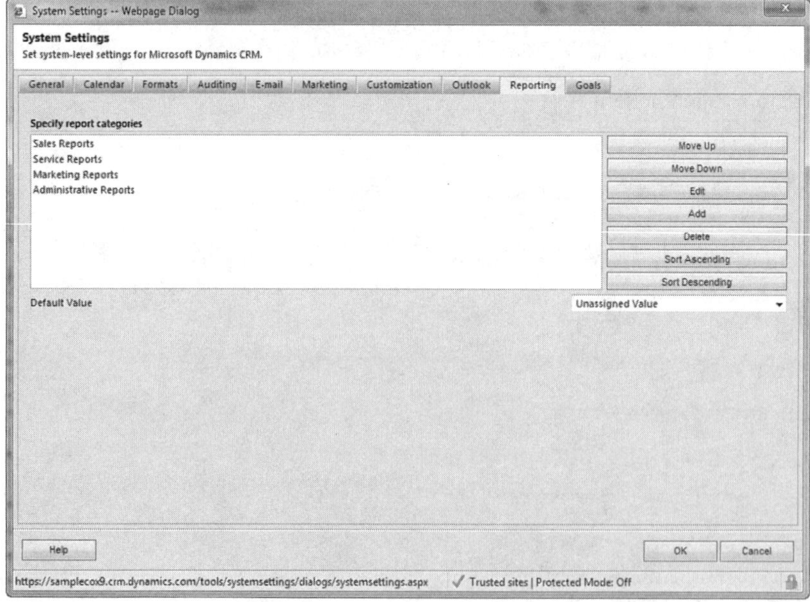

FIGURE 12.70 Reporting options.

Reports can belong to none, one, or multiple categories, and allow for easy grouping of different kinds. When you edit an existing report or create a new report, you assign the categories listed here.

NOTE

If you add a new category here, you can assign it to new or existing reports; however, it is not an available option in the Report views until you create a View for the new category.

Goals

Goals options enable you to set the expiration time and roll-up frequency (see Figure 12.71).

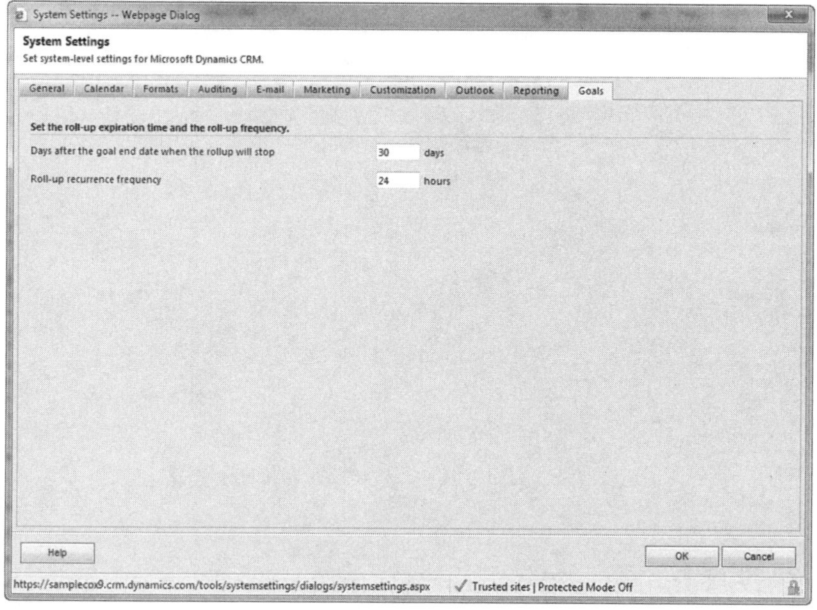

FIGURE 12.71 Goals options.

Security Roles

Microsoft Dynamics CRM controls user permissions with Security Roles (see Figure 12.72).

NOTE

Although Microsoft Dynamics CRM integrates tightly with Active Directory to determine its user base, permissions established in Active Directory have no correlation with users in Microsoft Dynamics CRM. As such, it is quite possible to have an Active Directory membership of Enterprise Administrator, but be in Read-Only User Mode or have a minimal role setting in Microsoft Dynamics CRM and vice versa.

By default, the following Security Roles are included with Microsoft Dynamics CRM 2011:

- CEO-Business Manager
- CSR Manager
- Customer Service Representative
- Delegate
- Internet Marketing Partner User Role
- Marketing Manager

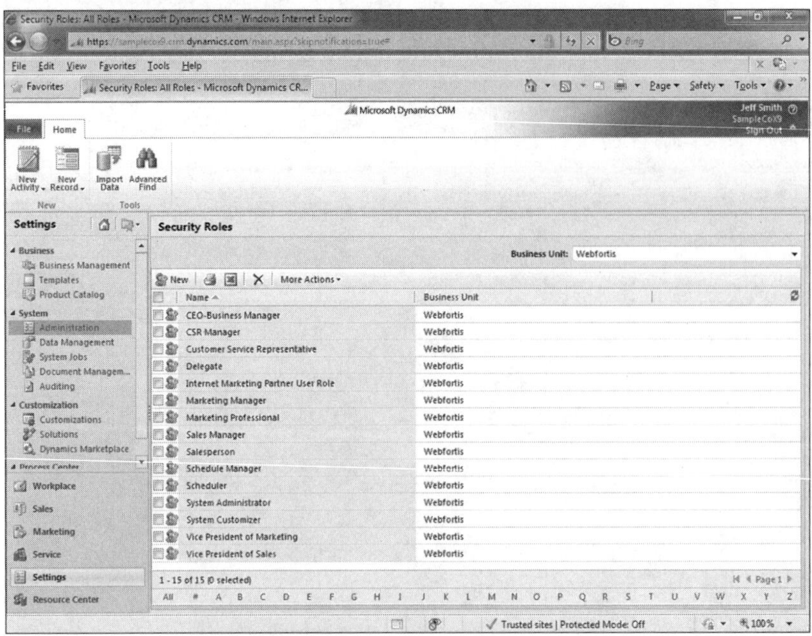

FIGURE 12.72 Security Roles.

- Marketing Professional
- Sales Manager
- Salesperson
- Schedule Manager
- Scheduler
- System Administrator
- System Customizer
- Vice President of Marketing
- Vice President of Sales

With Microsoft Dynamics CRM, Security Roles are flexible and easily created, and extend security to custom entities. By default, new Security Roles are created on the Organizational level and inherited by Child Business Units, regardless of which Business Unit is selected from the Security Roles Administration screen. Additionally, with regard to how Security Roles are inherited:

- New Security Roles are automatically created on the Master Business Unit and inherited to all Child Business Units.

- Copied Security Roles are created on the selected Business Unit, are available only on the selected Business Unit, and are inherited by all Child Business Units of the selected Business Unit (not any Parent Business Units).
- Inherited Security Roles cannot be modified or deleted. To make changes to inherited Security Roles, you must select the Business Unit that the Security Role is assigned to and then make changes there. All changes are inherited to Child Business Units.

Based on this, if a specific Security Role is required on a Child Business Unit, you must create a new Security Role, navigate to the Child Business Unit, and select Copy Role from the More Actions drop-down menu. After you copy the Security Role, you cannot modify it. The Security Role also will apply only to the Business Unit and any children where it was copied.

To view the specific access granted by any role, double-click the desired role to bring up the Role Settings screen (see Figure 12.73).

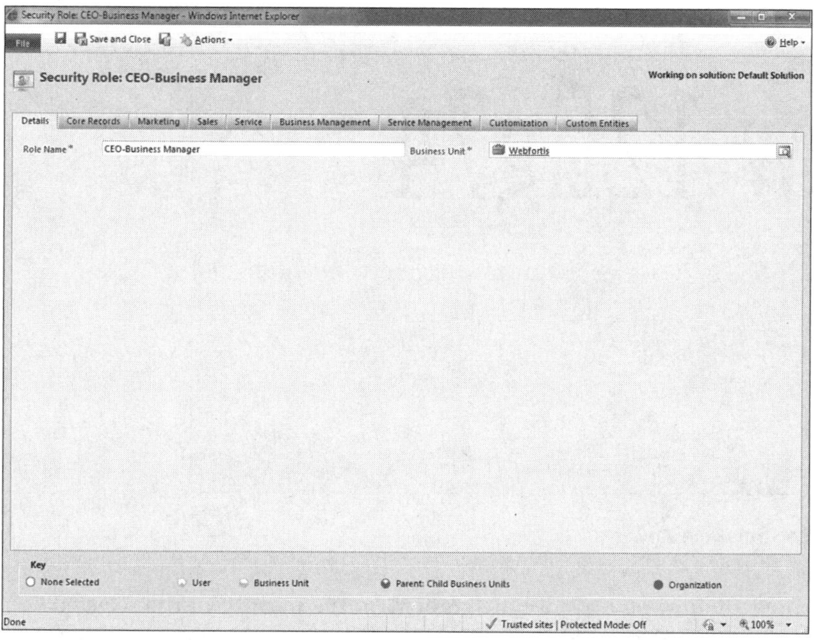

FIGURE 12.73 Role settings for CEO-Business Manager.

The tabs across break out the major access points within Microsoft Dynamics CRM 2011:

- Details
- Core Records
- Marketing

- Sales
- Service
- Business Management
- Service Management
- Customization
- Custom Entities

Before we explain each of the sections, it is important to review the Key at the bottom of each form; it applies to all tabs except the Details tab (see Figure 12.74).

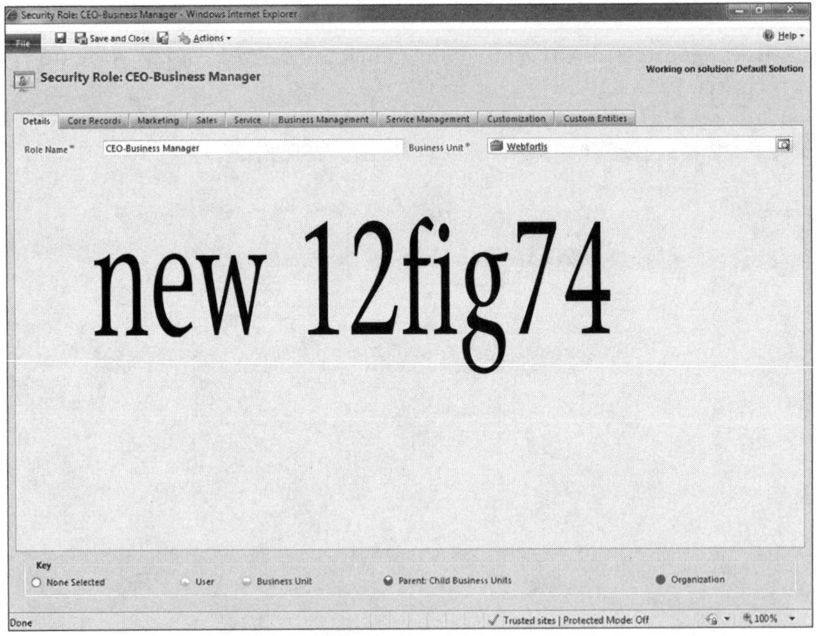

FIGURE 12.74 Security Role Key.

The symbols indicated are how permissions are granted on the records for the selected Security Role. Records within Microsoft Dynamics CRM 2011 have either organizational permissions or user permissions. When applying permissions, you select the entity (for example, Account, Contact, or Lead) and then associate the action with the record (Create, Read, Write, and so on) and, finally, the level of access (as indicated on the Key).

The level of access is explained as follows:

- **None Selected**—The user cannot perform the selected action.
- **User**—The user can perform the selected action only on the records that he or she owns.

- **Business Unit**—The user can perform the selected action on records owned by anyone in the Business Unit that this User belongs to, but not Child or Parent Business Units.
- **Parent: Child Business Units**—The user can perform the selected action on records within his or her Business Unit (same as Business Unit access), and perform the selected action on any Child Business Units of his or her Business Unit (but not the Parent Business Unit).
- **Organization**—The user can perform the selected action on any record within the organization.

NOTE

Some entities either can't have permission levels set on them or have only limited options. In the first case, where there is no ability to set a permission level, this is usually because that functionality doesn't exist, so there is no reason to set permissions on it. An example of this is on the Business Management tab, for the entity User and the action Delete. Because Users can't be deleted (only deactivated), there is no capability to set a permission level on it.

Carefully consider how you want to set permissions by selecting the level of access for the selected role; Users might have trouble accessing records without the correct permissions.

TIP

If you want to share only some records between users, consider using Teams. Team membership is often used to allow access to records that users normally don't have access to. For more information about Teams, see the "Teams" section later in this chapter.

You can set security levels across all entities by clicking the action label at the top of the screen.

NOTE

When setting permissions for Security Roles, no option enables you to secure individual fields or individual records through this interface. Instead, the permissions selected apply to all records of the selected type. (For example, if Read permission for Account is granted to a role, the user will have the capability to read all Account records.)

Review the section on Field Level Security later in this chapter for more information about how to secure individual fields.

TIP

You cannot update or modify the System Administrator role. This ensures that permissions aren't accidentally denied within that role, preventing access to make corrections.

Details

The Details tab displays the Security Role name and the Business Unit that the role applies to (refer to Figure 12.74). If the Security Role is an inherited role (as previously described), you cannot change the role name.

Core Records

As its name implies, permissions for general or core access to the system are set in Core Records. Access from everything to Accounts, Contacts, Leads, and so on is controlled on this screen (see Figure 12.75).

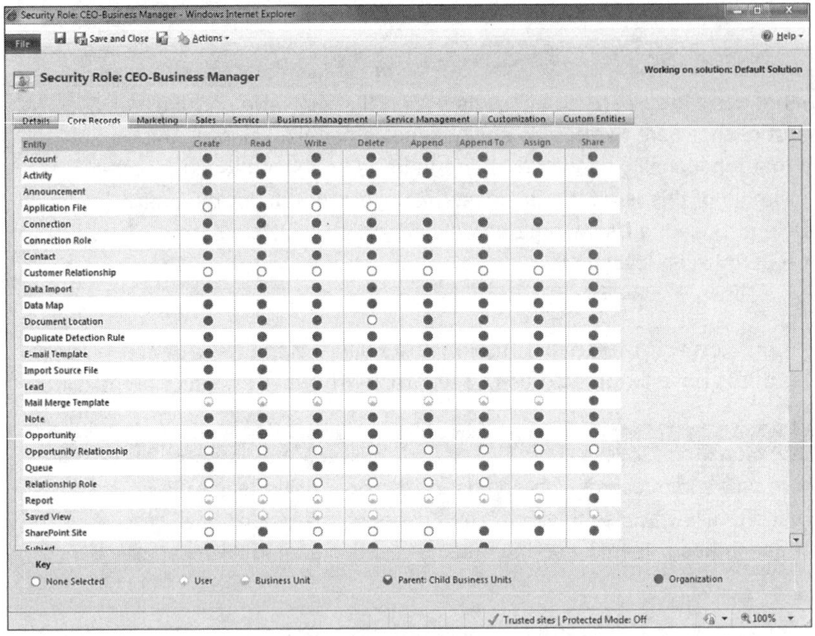

FIGURE 12.75 Security Role—core records.

NOTE

Entities that you can't set on the core records are available on the other tabs. For example, the capability to set permissions on the Case entity is not available in the core records interface because Case is a service entity and, therefore, is found on the Service tab. If you don't find the entity you want to set, be sure to check all the tabs across the top.

The permission options are divided across the top, whereas the entities affected are listed in rows (see Figure 12.75). The permissions (or privileges) are as follows:

- **Create**—The ability to create a new record

- **Read**—The ability to open and read an existing record
- **Write**—The ability to make and save changes to an existing record, including deleting data from the record (however, not to delete the entire record)
- **Delete**—The ability to delete an existing record
- **Append**—The ability to append the current record to another record
- **Append To**—The ability to append a different record to the current record
- **Assign**—The ability to assign the record to another user
- **Share**—The ability to share the record with another user

NOTE

The difference between Append and Append To is that Append enables you to append the current record to another record, whereas Append To gives you the ability to append another record to this record.

Additional options include Miscellaneous Privileges, located at the bottom of the form, and include options such as the capability to publish various objects and add reports.

Marketing

Marketing has the same permission options listed in Core Records (see Figure 12.76).

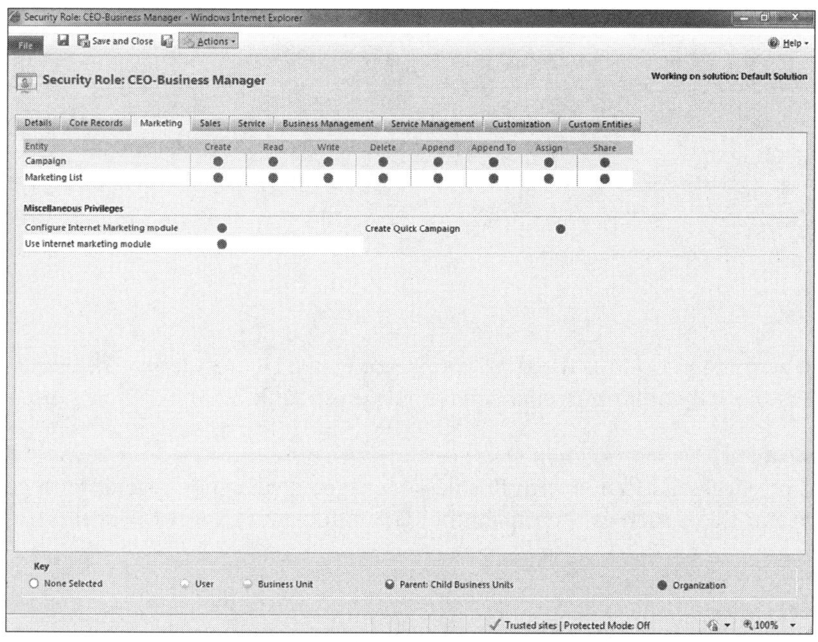

FIGURE 12.76 Security Role—marketing records.

The only marketing miscellaneous privilege is Create Quick Campaign. Note that Quick Campaigns are different from Campaigns, and the only permission for a Quick Campaign is the ability to create one.

▶ Refer to Chapter 9 to review the differences between Campaigns and Quick Campaigns.

Sales

Sales has the same permission options listed in Core Records (see Figure 12.77). The three miscellaneous privileges give a user with this role the ability to override pricing on the Quota, the Invoice, or the Order.

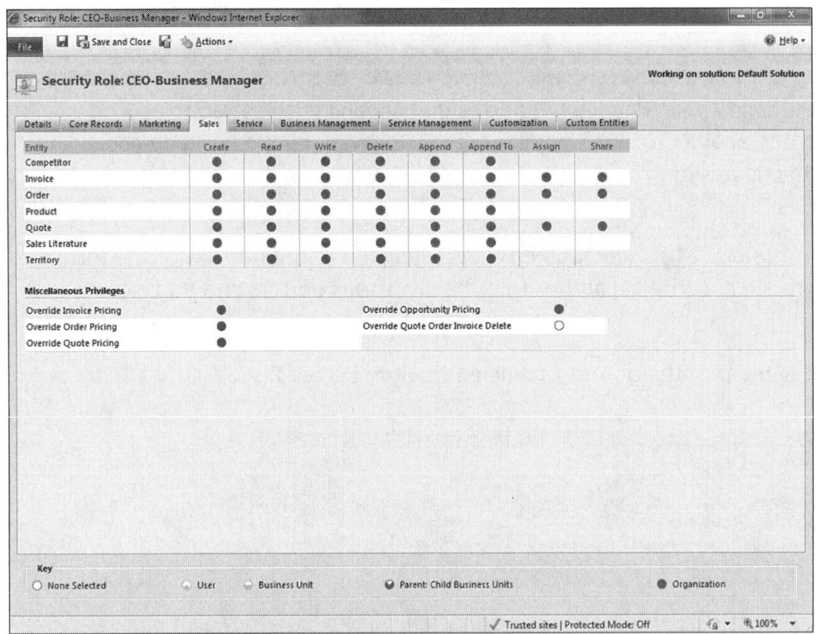

FIGURE 12.77 Security Role—sales records.

Service

Sales has the same permission options listed in Core Records (see Figure 12.78). The ability to publish Articles is the only other miscellaneous privilege available on the Service tab.

Business Management

The miscellaneous privileges associated with Business Management include several settings that can affect usage of CRM, such as the capabilities Go Offline and Export to Excel (see Figure 12.79).

Service Management

Service Management has the same permission options listed in Core Records, with the exception of the capability Assign and Share (see Figure 12.80).

Security Role: CEO-Business Manager - Windows Internet Explorer

File | Save and Close | Actions | Help

Security Role: CEO-Business Manager

Working on solution: Default Solution

Details | Core Records | Marketing | Sales | Service | Business Management | Service Management | Customization | Custom Entities

Entity	Create	Read	Write	Delete	Append	Append To	Assign	Share
Article	●	●	●	●	●	●		
Article Template	●	●	●	●		●		
Case	●	●	●	●	●	●	●	●
Contract	●	●	●	●	●	●	●	●
Contract Template	●	●	●	●		●		

Miscellaneous Privileges

Publish Articles ●

Key: None Selected | User | Business Unit | Parent: Child Business Units | Organization

Trusted sites | Protected Mode: Off | 100%

FIGURE 12.78 Security Role—service records.

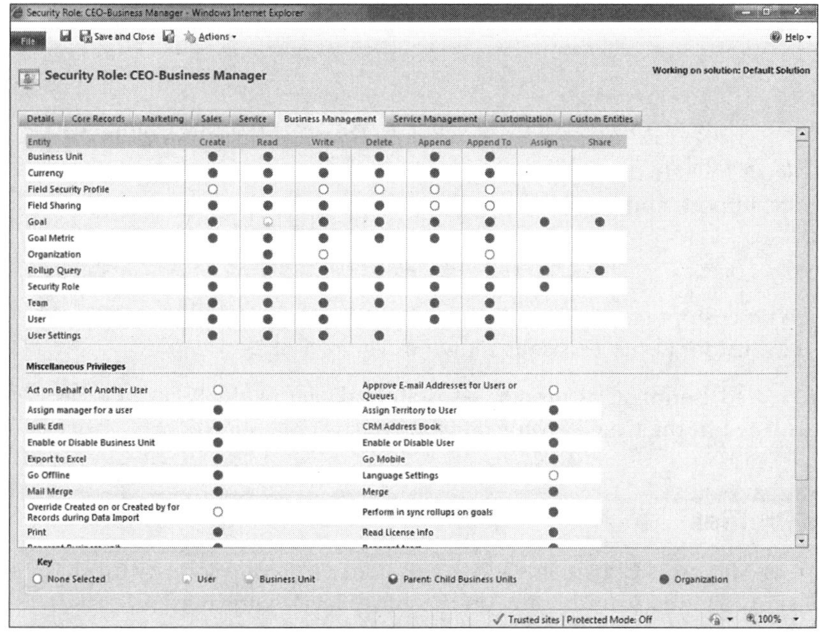

FIGURE 12.79 Security Role—business management records.

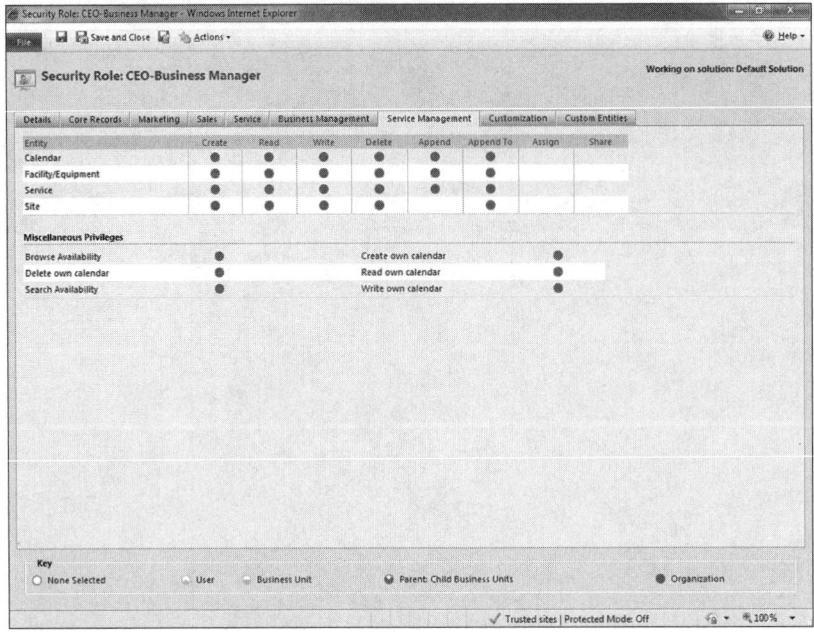

FIGURE 12.80 Security Role—service management records.

The miscellaneous privileges enable the user to search and browse.

Customization

Customization has the same permission options listed in Core Records (see Figure 12.81).

Miscellaneous privileges include the capability to work with ISV extensions, execute workflow jobs, and export, import, and publish customizations.

Custom Entities

By default, there are no custom entities. The Custom Entities tab gives the options to set permissions only if a Custom Entity exists (as shown in Figure 12.82).

When an entity is created, permissions need to be established across the Security Roles and are the same as listed in the Core Records previously.

Field Security Profiles

New to this version of Microsoft Dynamics CRM is the ability to set up security on specific fields (previous versions allowed security only on the entity level) known as Field Level Security (also known as FLS).

When working with Field Level Security, Field Security Profiles need to be created, and then applied to either Teams or users.

Security Role: CEO-Business Manager - Windows Internet Explorer

File | Save and Close | Actions | Help

Security Role: CEO-Business Manager

Working on solution: Default Solution

Details | Core Records | Marketing | Sales | Service | Business Management | Service Management | Customization | Custom Entities

Entity	Create	Read	Write	Delete	Append	Append To	Assign	Share
Attribute Map	○	●	○	○	○	○		
Customizations	○	●	○	○				
Dialog Session	●	●	●	●	●	●	●	●
Entity	○	●	○	○				
Entity Map	○	●	○	○		○		
Field	○	●	○	○				
Import Job		○	○	○				
Option Set	○	●	○	○				
Plug-in Assembly	○	●	○	○				
Plug-in Type	○	●	○	○				
Process	●	●	●	●	●	●	●	●
Publisher	○	○	○	○	○	○		
Relationship	○	●	○	○				
Sdk Message	○	●	○	○				
Sdk Message Processing Step	○	●	○	○				
Sdk Message Processing Step Image	○	●	○	○				
Sdk Message Processing Step Secure Configuration	○	○	○	○				
Service Endpoint	○	○	○	○				
Solution	○	○	○	○	○	○		
System Chart	●	●	●	●				
System Form	○	●	○	○				
System Job	○	●	●	○	○	●	●	○
View	●	●	●	●				
Web Resource	○	●	○	○				

Key

None Selected | User | Business Unit | Parent: Child Business Units | Organization

Trusted sites | Protected Mode: Off | 100%

FIGURE 12.81 Security Role—customization records.

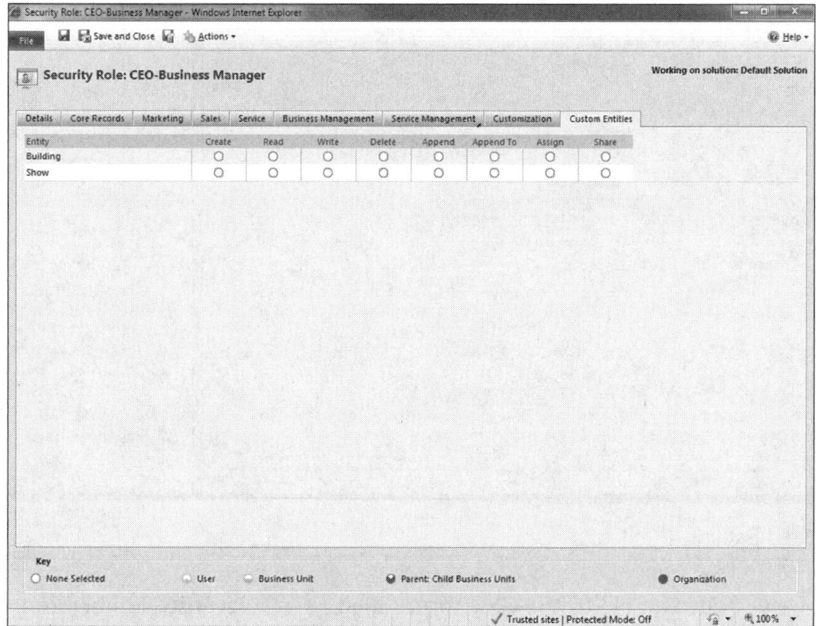

FIGURE 12.82 Security Role—custom entities.

NOTE

The profiles created are completely separate from the security roles created.

NOTE

Field Level Security is only available to custom attributes. It is anticipated that the option for system attributes will be part of a future update rollup from Microsoft.

NOTE

If you create Field Security Profiles and then select Field Permissions, but don't see any records, it is because you haven't created any custom fields with field security enabled yet.

Figure 12.83 shows what the various profiles look like from the Administration page.

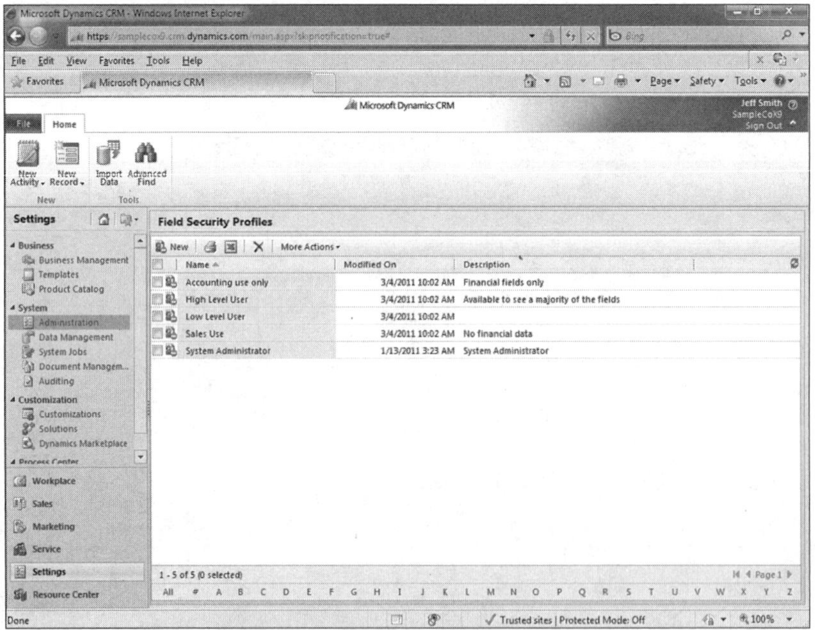

FIGURE 12.83 Field Security Profiles.

For our example, we've added a field to the Case form called Drivers License Number and selected Field Security to Enabled as shown in Figure 12.84.

Once the field is added to the form (as shown in Figure 12.85), it is reflected with a key icon to show that it has some level of security applied to it.

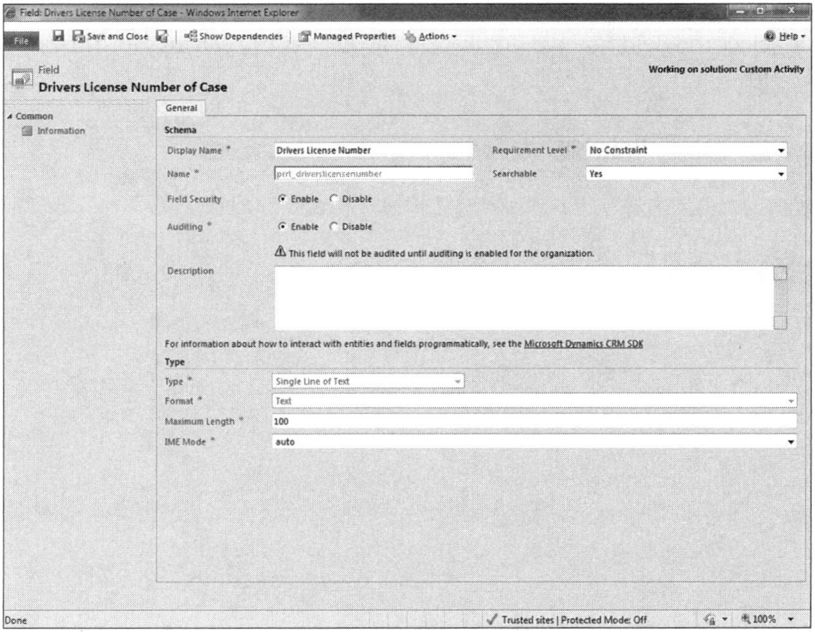

FIGURE 12.84 New field called Drivers License Number with Field Security settings shown.

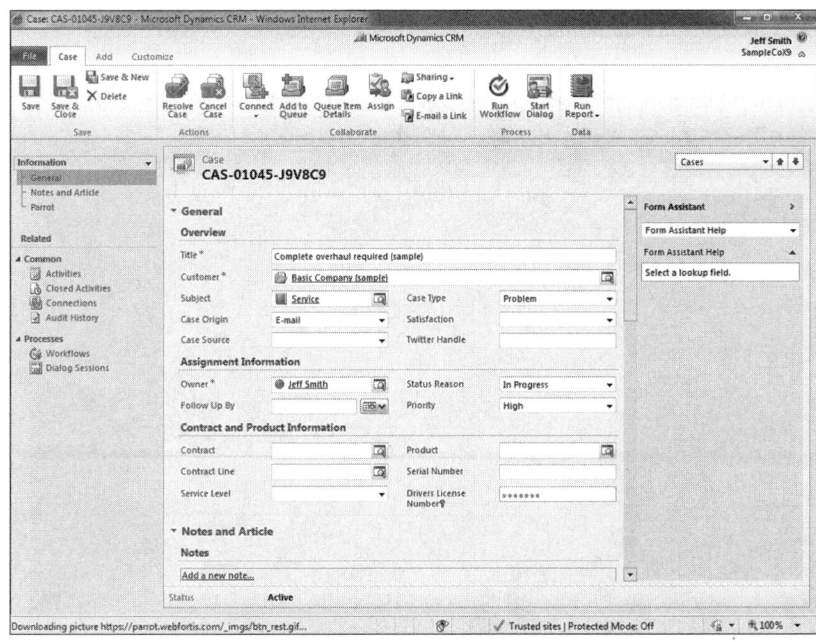

FIGURE 12.85 Case form with secured field on it.

To enforce the security, select one of the profiles, and select Field Permissions on the near navigation and the select the field you would like to edit the security settings for (as shown in figure 12.86).

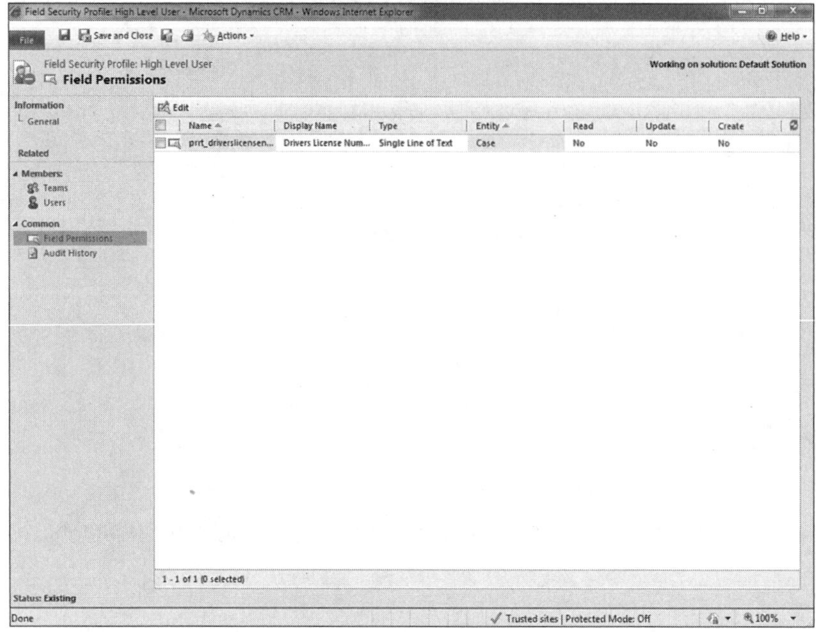

FIGURE 12.86 Field Security Profile settings.

Clicking Edit opens the Field Security settings specific for that field and gives you the ability to set the permission in a variety of ways (see Figure 12.87).

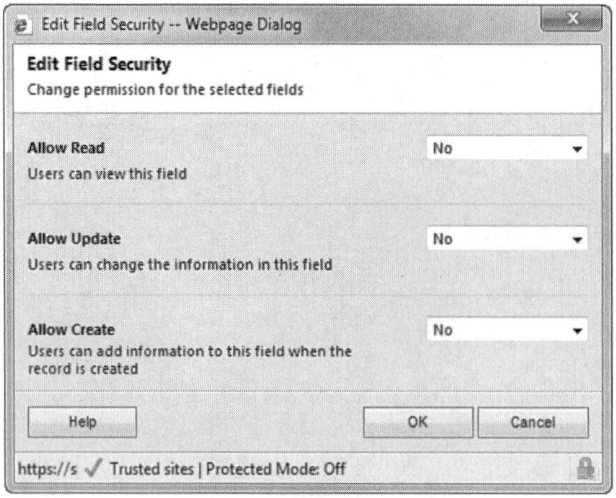

FIGURE 12.87 Field Security settings.

Because we have multiple profiles, the same field can be reflected differently depending on which profile is assigned. This results in a very dynamic and flexible approach to security.

> **NOTE**
>
> As with Security Roles, users can receive multiple Field Level Security Profiles and the least restrictive one will win.

Teams

The concept of Teams in Microsoft Dynamics CRM is designed around the idea that members of a Team can share records that members wouldn't ordinarily have access to. An example of this is users in different Business Units who belong to the same Team. These users could view records across the business units by sharing them. Figure 12.88 shows the Team interface found in Settings, Administration.

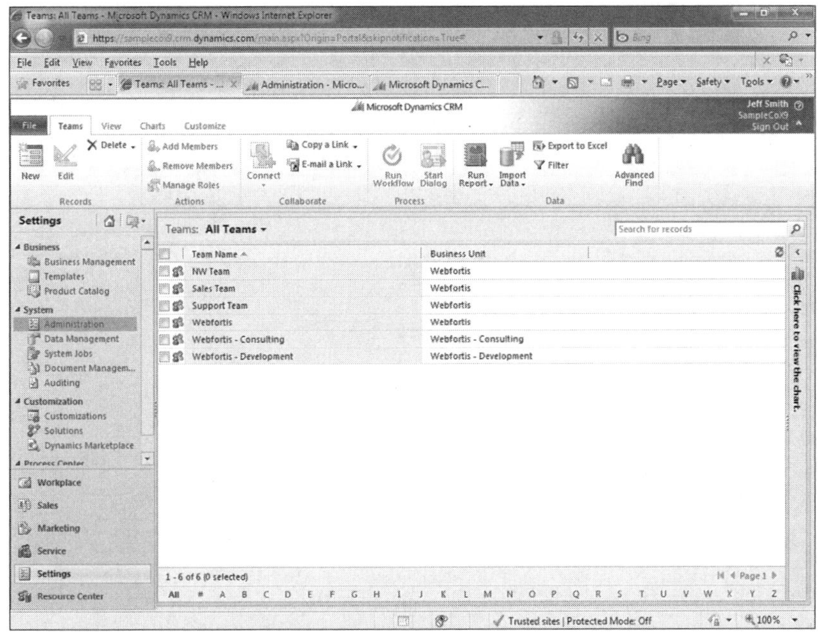

FIGURE 12.88 Teams in Microsoft Dynamics CRM.

There is a default Team established when an organization is deployed. The default Team is the same as the root Business Unit, and there is a new Team created for every Business Unit created. The only way to delete the created team is to first delete the correlating Business Unit.

NOTE

If your organization was upgraded, there will be a new Team created for each Business Unit in the organization.

The process of creating and managing Teams in Microsoft Dynamics CRM is very straightforward. To create a new Team, follow these steps:

1. Navigate to Settings, Administration, Teams (see Figure 12.88). Select New.
2. Enter the Team name and select the Business Unit and the administrator. (The administrator is the owner of the team.) By default, the root Business Unit is selected (see Figure 12.89).

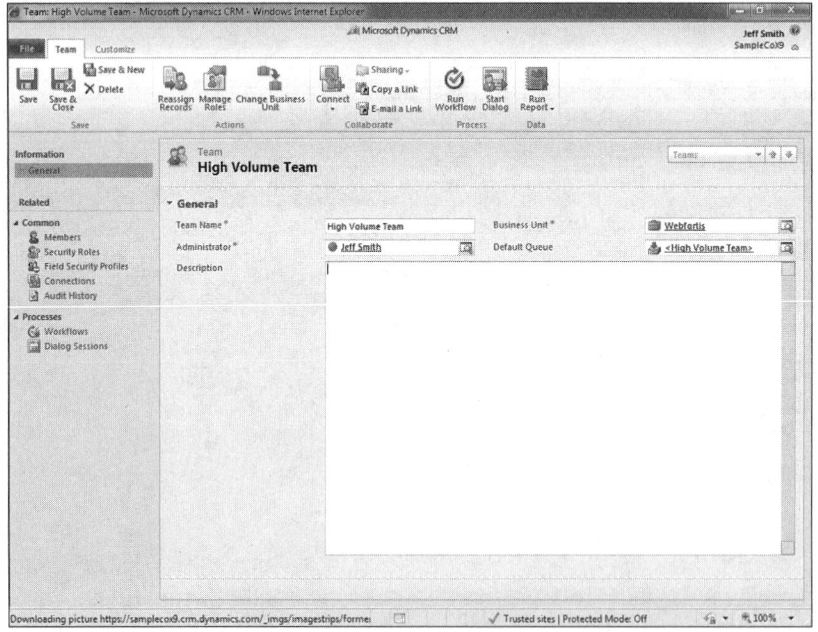

FIGURE 12.89 Creating a new Team in Microsoft Dynamics CRM.

Optionally, enter the Default Queue. If you don't enter a value, a new queue with the team name pre- and post-pended with < and >, respectively, will be created automatically and the team will own the queue (as shown in Figure 12.89).

1. Click Save to enable the near navigation options.
2. Select the users from the system who will be part of the Team by clicking Add Members (see Figure 12.90). Click Add then OK to continue.

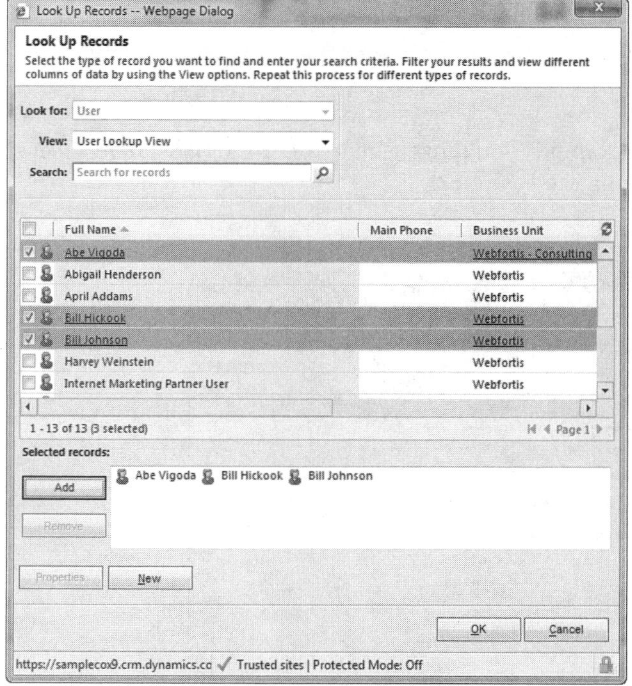

FIGURE 12.90 Adding members to a new Team in Microsoft Dynamics CRM.

3. Because Teams can have record ownership in this version of Microsoft Dynamics CRM, they need to have a security role set for them. Just like with new members, they are created without one and need to be set. Additionally, you can set up the Field Security Profiles for the Team at this point.

Because Microsoft Dynamics CRM 2011 offers users the ability to assign records to Teams (instead of earlier versions that only allowed sharing), it is important to outline the differences between sharing and assignment.

Sharing a record has the following effects:

- You retain ownership of the record.
- You give permission for the record to be read, edited, or deleted.

Assigning a record has the following effects:

- You lose ownership of the record (and the new owner has permission to do whatever his security context allows).

As such, be sure to assign or share appropriately.

Now that you have created your Team, sharing records with the Team is very simple. Follow these steps:

1. Navigate to a record. In this example, you'll navigate to a Lead in the system. Select Sharing from the Ribbon menu (see Figure 12.91).

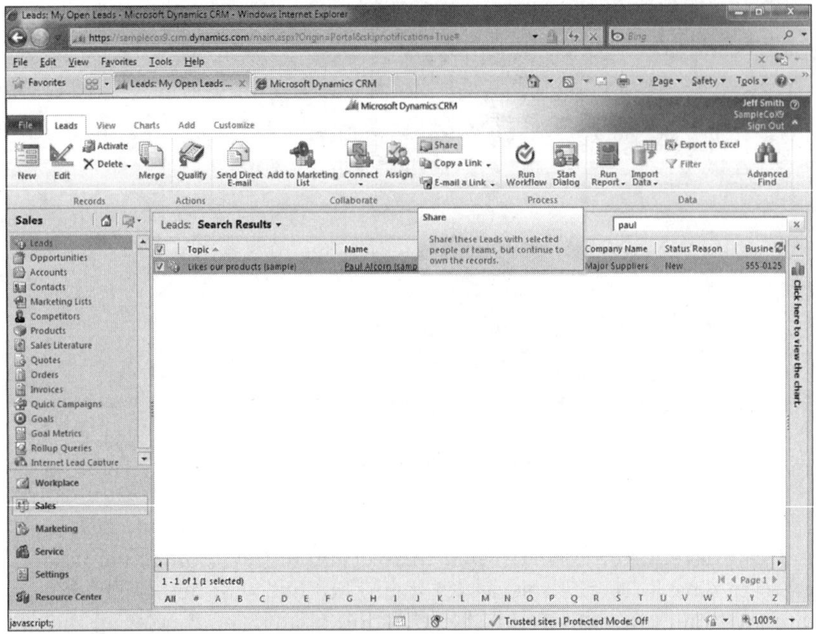

FIGURE 12.91 Sharing a Lead in Microsoft Dynamics CRM.

2. The sharing interface appears (see Figure 12.92). Select Add User/Team to continue.
3. Select to share the record with either a User or a Team (see Figure 12.93).
4. Select from the available Teams, and add them. Click OK to continue.
5. The selected Team is now available on the sharing interface, and you can give it access for either read, write, delete, append, assign, or share (see Figure 12.94).

To assign a record to a team, select Assign from the Ribbon menu (as shown in figure 12.95).

Navigate and select the team to assign it to and select OK. The record will assign to that Team.

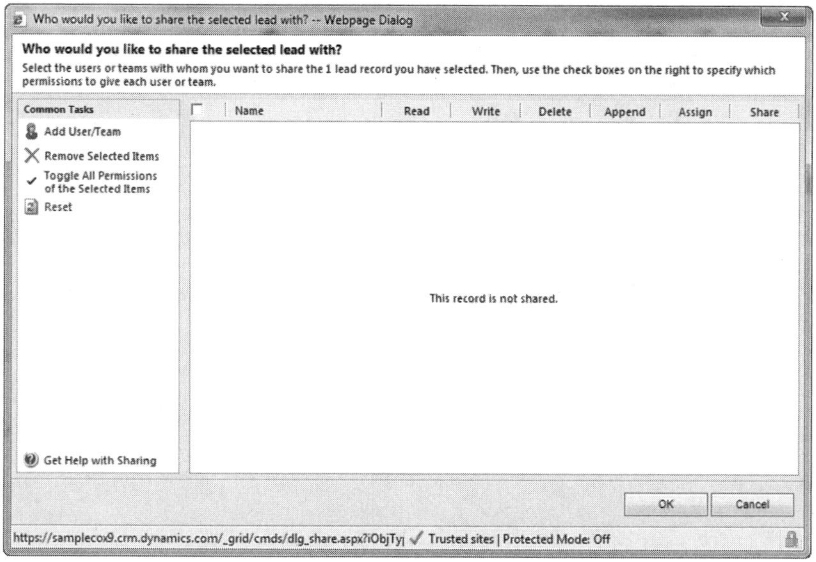

FIGURE 12.92 Sharing interface.

NOTE

If you have not yet assigned a security role to your team, you will see a Team Roles Error (as shown in Figure 12.96). To correct this, navigate to the team and assign the appropriate security role.

Users

Found on the Administration option from the Settings area, Microsoft Dynamics users are created and managed in the Users section (see Figure 12.97).

When working with the Users interface, you can perform several different operations:

- Add a new user
- Enable or disable users
- Manage user roles
- Change Business Units
- Change managers
- Approve/reject e-mails
- Send invitation (CRM Online only)
- View users

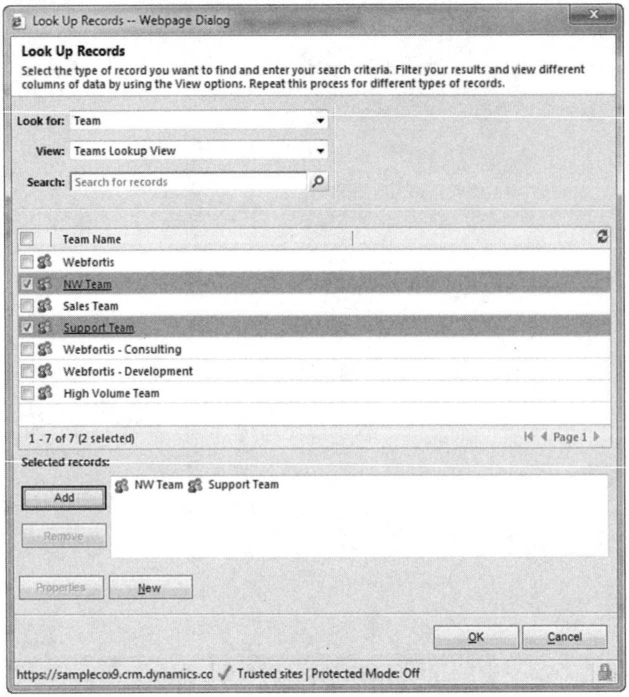

FIGURE 12.93 Look Up Records page.

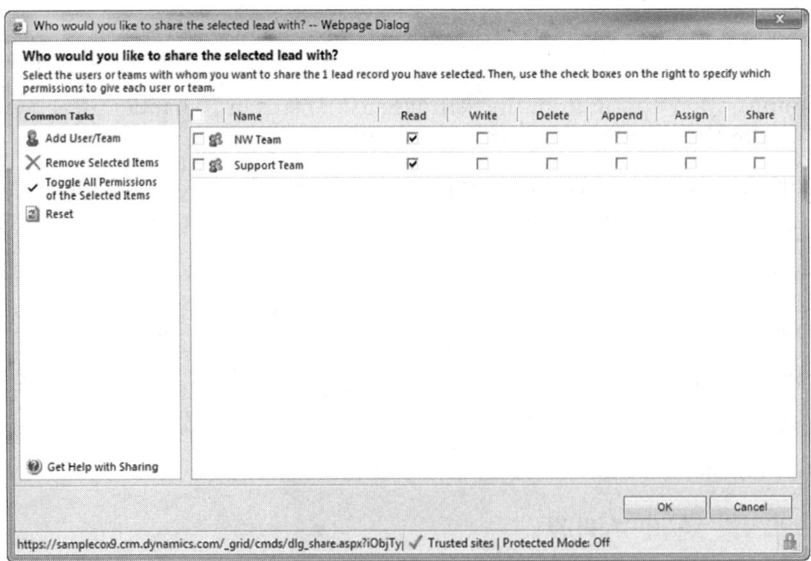

FIGURE 12.94 Sharing a record.

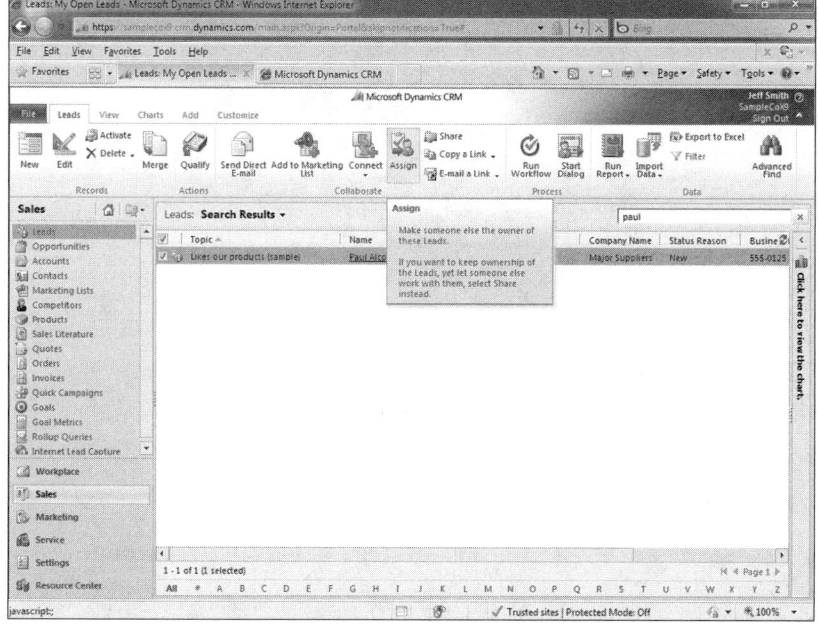

FIGURE 12.95 Assign a record.

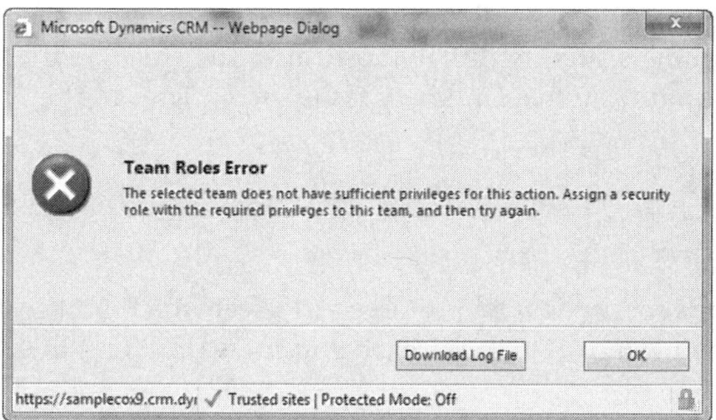

FIGURE 12.96 Record assignment error.

These options and their locations are explained further in the following sections.

Add a New User To add a new user, select the New option and then User, located in the upper-left corner and follow the steps outlined next to complete the user addition.

NOTE

If you do not have a New option here, you might not have sufficient rights or privileges to create new users.

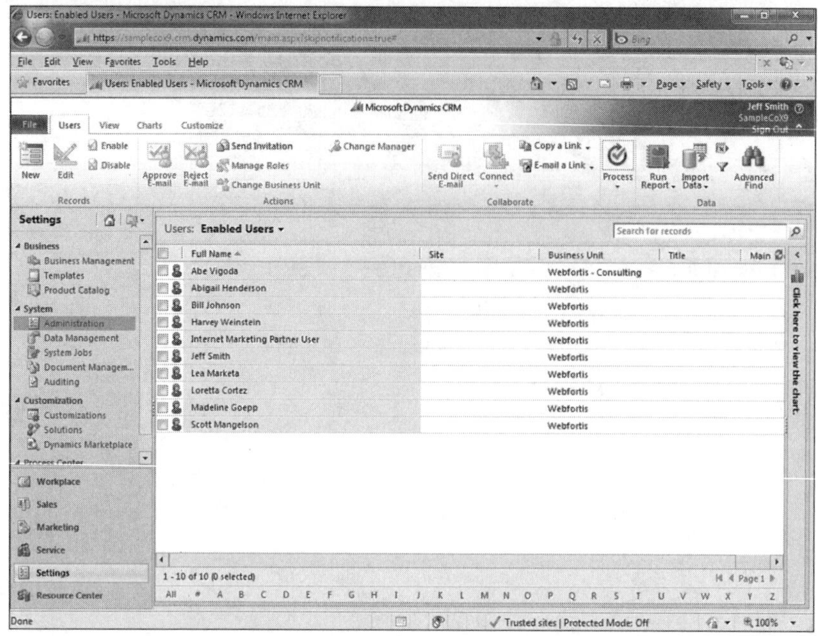

FIGURE 12.97 Users.

CRM Online Adding users for CRM Online is slightly different as it uses the email address as the primary key, rather than a lookup into Active Directory (as is shown later in the chapter).

To add new users, follow these steps:

1. Select New.
2. If you have multiple Business Units set up, you will be asked to select which unit to assign the new user to (as shown in Figure 12.98). Select the Business Unit, and then Next to continue.
3. Select the security role to assign the user. You must select at least one, and if you are going to add more than one user, all users that you add will receive the security role designated here (as shown in Figure 12.99).
4. Add the users by adding the First and Last Name as well as their e-mail and then clicking Add >> (as shown in Figure 12.100). You can add one or multiple users here (depending on how many users you have available with your subscription). Click Next to continue.

NOTE

It is important to realize that the e-mail that is used must be associated with a Windows Live ID (WLID). WLIDs are free and can be associated with any e-mail address.

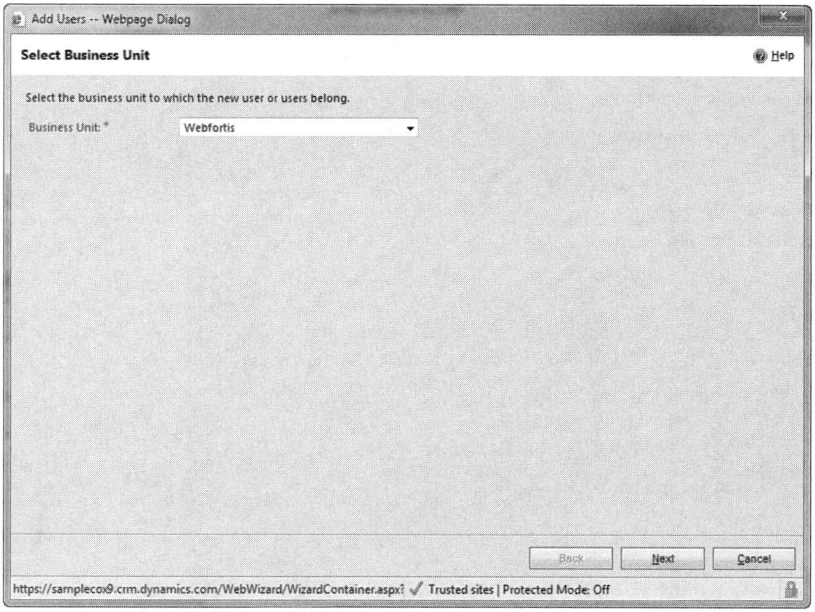

FIGURE 12.98 Select Business Unit.

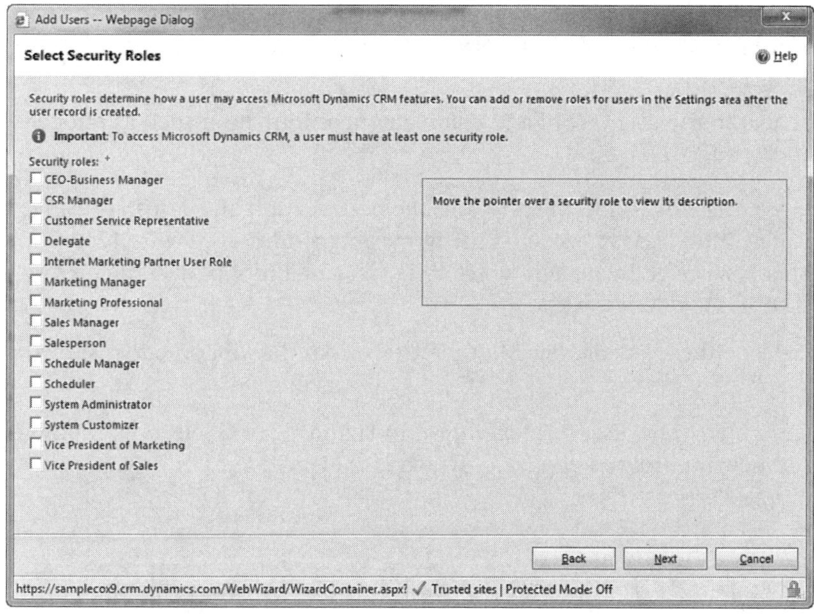

FIGURE 12.99 Select security role.

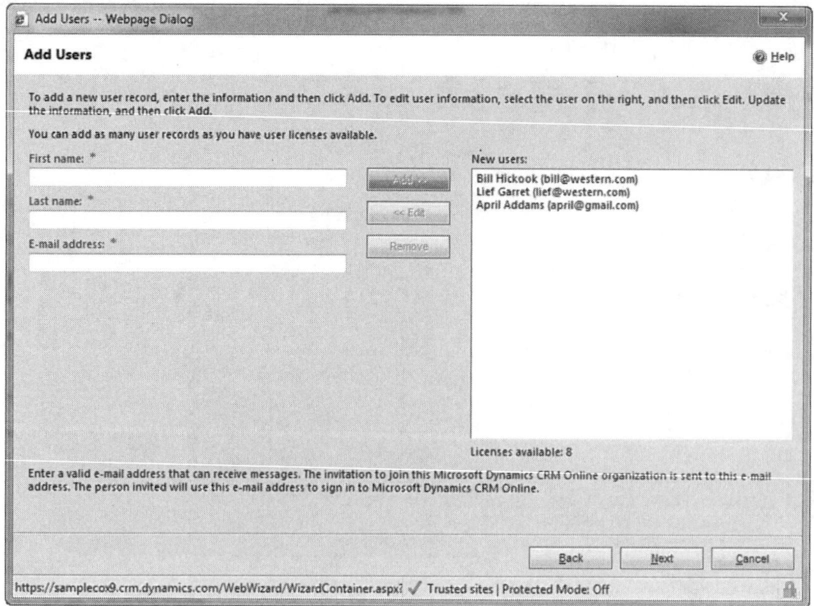

FIGURE 12.100 Add users.

5. Select whether the users should be added and sent invitations immediately, or have invitations sent later. Click Create New Users to complete the new user setup (as shown in Figure 12.101).
6. Optionally, return to the user record and complete the information such as phone number, territory, and so on.

The users will receive an e-mail asking them to join the organization and can start using the system immediately after they've accepted the terms and conditions. Figure 12.102 shows the e-mail that is received by default when users are added (notice also the provision to create a WLID if one doesn't exist).

CRM On Premise Select either New or New Multiple Users from the Ribbon bar as shown in Figure 12.103.

Selecting New opens a blank new user form as shown in Figure 12.104. Selecting 'Multiple Users' opens the add new multiple users wizard, which is explained later in this chapter under 'Adding Multiple Users'.

NOTE

After you add users to the CRM system, you can only deactivate them; you cannot delete them. For that reason, you can "add" a user only once. If you have already added a user and you don't see him or her, be sure to check the Disabled Users view to see whether that user has already been added.

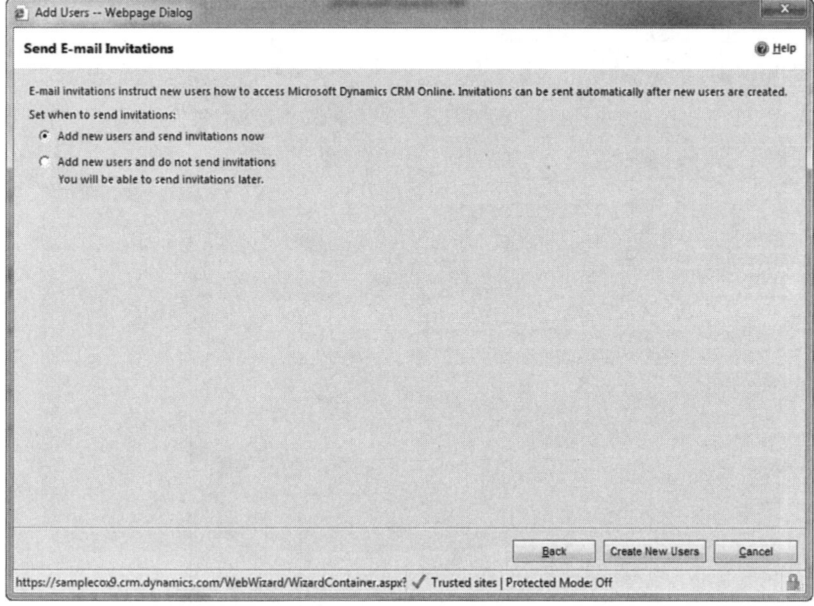

FIGURE 12.101 Send e-mail invitations to new users.

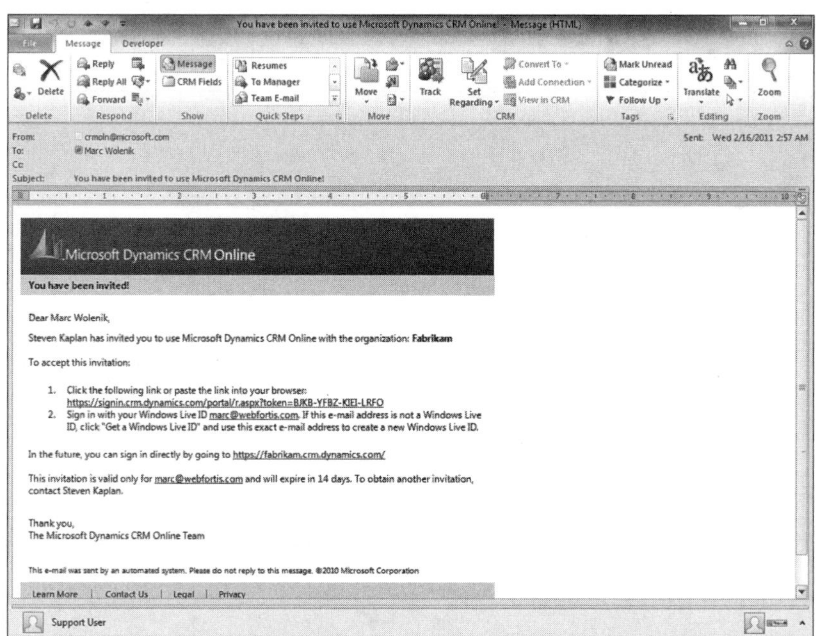

FIGURE 12.102 Invitation e-mail.

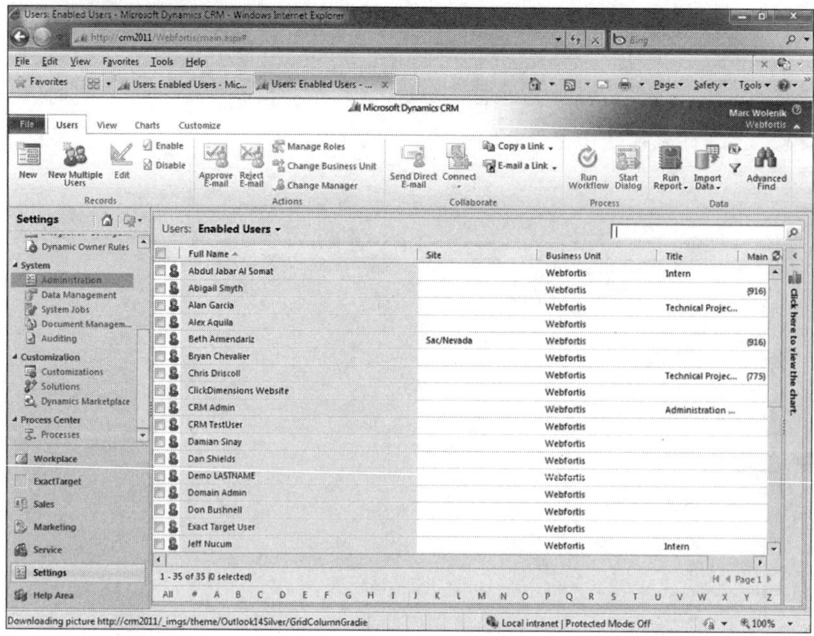

FIGURE 12.103 New User option—CRM On Premise.

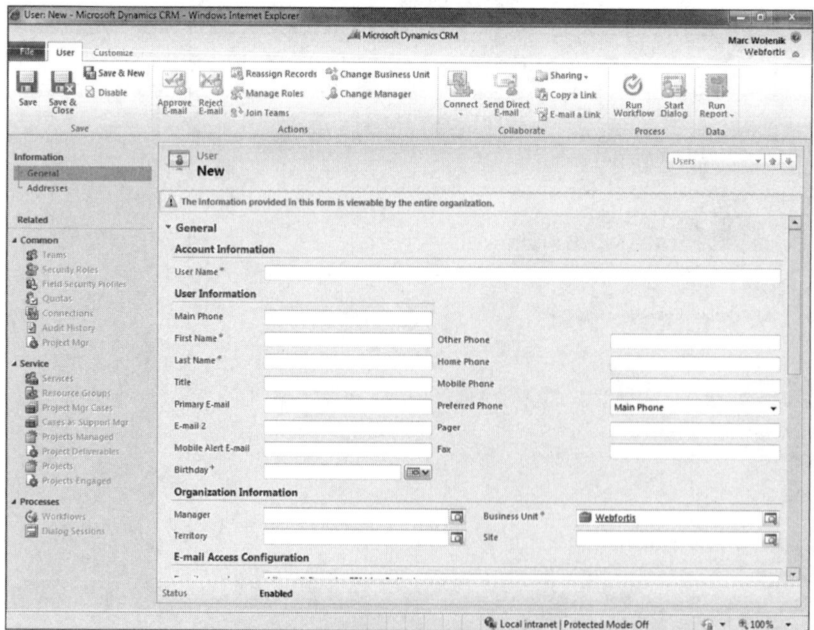

FIGURE 12.104 New User Form—CRM On Premise.

Complete the user name first—when you enter this information and move to the next field, automatic resolution is attempted on the entered value, and other fields are populated. If auto-population does not occur, be sure to enter the exact first and last name as well as the e-mail address for the user that exists in the AD. An example of this is <domain>\<user name>, where <domain> is the domain for your organization, and user is the domain username.

The remaining fields in the User Information section are optional and allow for richer reporting on users across the organization. We usually recommend completing at least the primary e-mail so that the user can receive e-mails. If no e-mail is entered, events (such as workflows and system alerts) that need to send e-mails to users will fail.

TIP

If your organization is not using another tool for user management, such as human resource management, you might want to consider this for management. You can customize it to include other fields, and you can easily report on it using Advanced Finds.

Organizational information: The default Master Parent Unit automatically populates Business Units, but you can change this to any available Business Unit before you click Save. After you save the record, you must select Change Business Unit from the Ribbon menu to change the Business Unit.

Similar to Business Units, you must set the Manager before you click Save: After you save the record, you must select Change Manager from the Ribbon menu to change or set the Manager.

Territory and Site are optional lookup fields. If you have not created any territories or sites in the system, you can leave these blank.

▶ Although not required, Service Activities can use sites. Refer to Chapter 10, “Working with Service,” for more information about configuring Service Activities.

E-mail access configuration: Here you set the two options for e-mail access type configuration (Incoming and Outgoing), with the default of Microsoft Dynamics CRM Client for Outlook.

▶ For more information about these values, refer to Chapter 14, “E-mail Configuration.”

Client access license—You can set the access mode for users to the following:

- Read-Write
- Administrative
- Read

Read-Write allows full access to the system, provided they have the security permissions to access. This Access type consumes a CAL.

Administrative does not consume a CAL, but only grants permission to the limited administrative areas of the system.

Read consumes a CAL (but one that is significantly less expensive than a full Read-Write CAL) and allows full access in a read-only capacity to the system.

License type can be set for the following:

- ▶ Full
- ▶ Limited
- ▶ Device Full
- ▶ Device Limited

▶ See Chapter 3, "Requirements for CRM 2011," for more information about the licensing models.

Addresses You can add Mailing and Other Address information to the user record as well (see Figure 12.105).

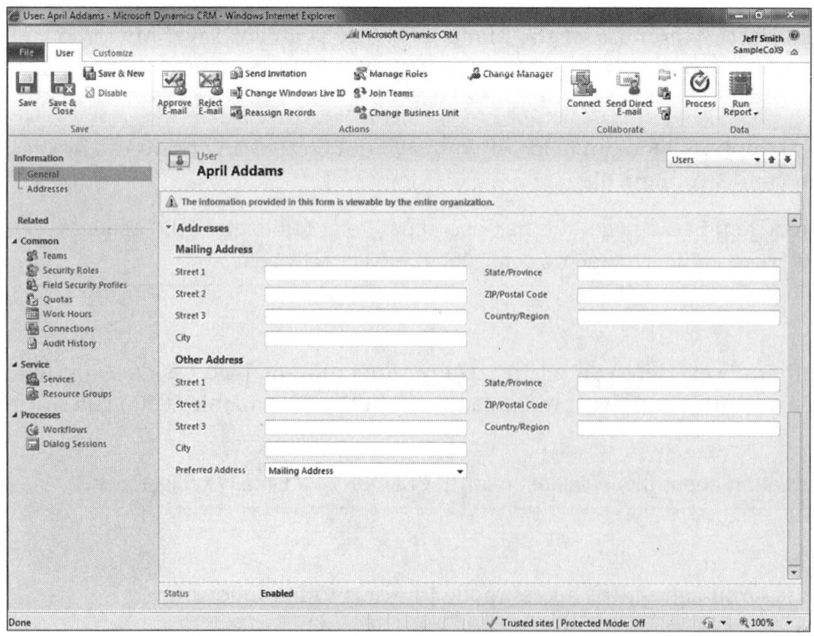

FIGURE 12.105 New User addresses.

Teams After you have successfully created and saved a user, that user can join existing Teams by selecting Teams from the near navigation (see Figure 12.106).

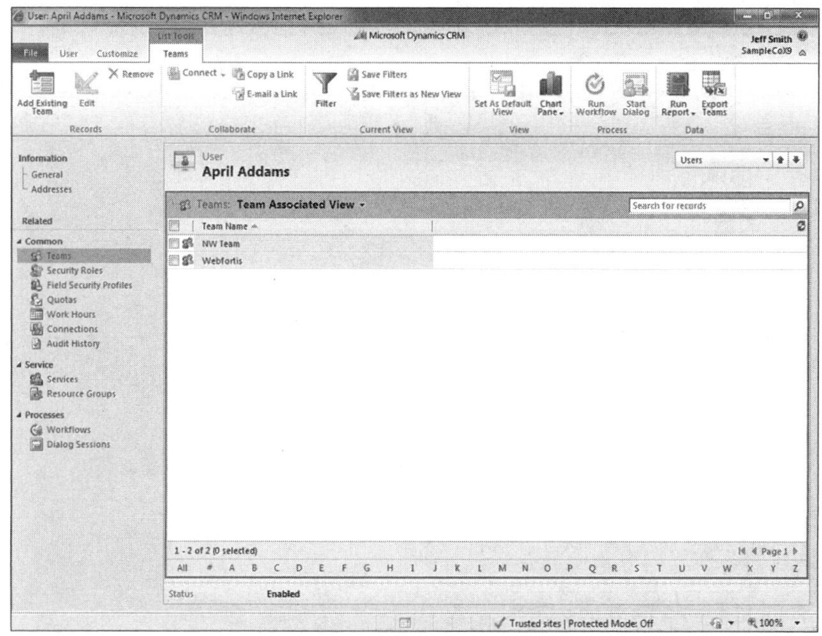

FIGURE 12.106 Team membership for a new user.

By default, users have no Team membership.

To join a Team, select Add Existing Team. Select the lookup icon to view all available Teams (see Figure 12.107).

Users can belong to none, one, or many Teams. If they do belong to a Team, they benefit from Team record sharing.

For more information about Teams, see the "Teams" section earlier in this chapter.

Security Roles For users to be able to do anything in Microsoft Dynamics CRM, they must be assigned a Security Role. Security Roles are explained later in this chapter; however, after a user has been created, or if the user has had its Business Unit changed, that user has no Security Roles and must be assigned one before he can use the system (see Figure 12.108).

To grant them access to a role, select Manage Roles and select which roles you want the user to belong to (see Figure 12.109).

Look Up Records -- Webpage Dialog

Look Up Records

Select the type of record you want to find and enter your search criteria. Filter your results and view different columns of data by using the View options. Repeat this process for different types of records.

Look for: Team

View: Teams Lookup View

Search:

Team Name
Webfortis
NW Team
Sales Team
Support Team
Webfortis - Consulting
Webfortis - Development

1 - 6 of 6 (0 selected) Page 1

Selected records:

Add

Remove

Properties New

OK Cancel

https://samplecox9.crm.dynamics.co Trusted sites | Protected Mode: Off

FIGURE 12.107 Joining Teams for a new user.

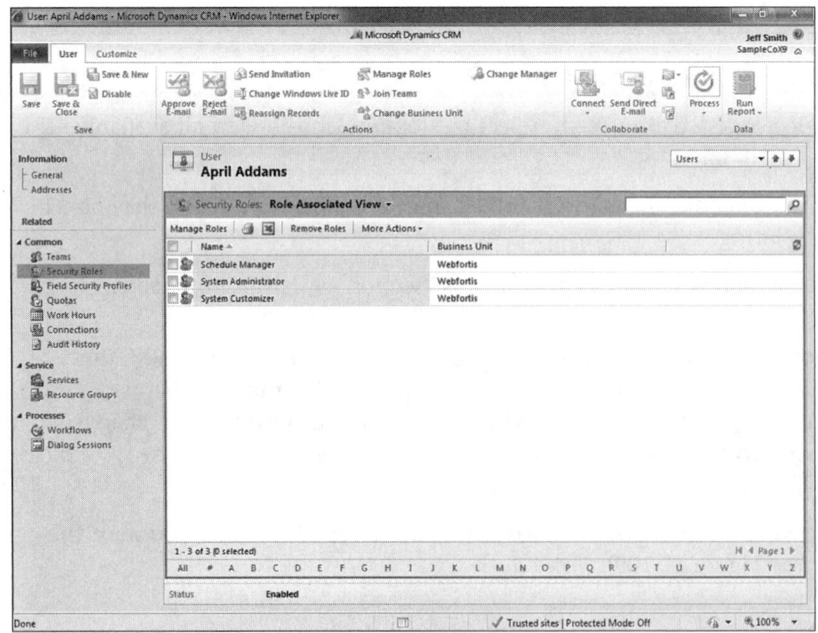

FIGURE 12.108 Role membership for a user.

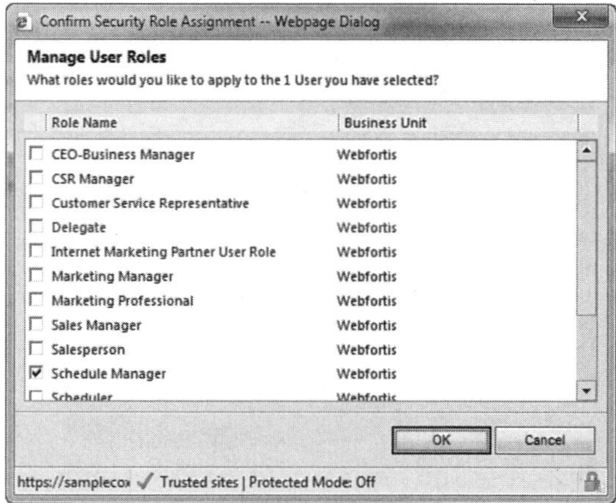

FIGURE 12.109 Security Role selection.

NOTE

Users must belong to at least one role, and their permissions are based on the highest role selected. If the user has both the restrictive role of Customer Service Representative as well as the System Administrator role, they will have System Administrator rights throughout the system. See the "Roles" section earlier in this chapter on creating new roles if you need to mix permissions between roles.

Field Security Profiles As explained earlier in this chapter, Field Security Profiles are established per user by selecting this option from the near navigation (as shown as the option below Security Roles in Figure 12.108).

Quotas Quotas (as shown in Figure 12.110) are deprecated in this version and included for backward compatibility only.

For Quota functionality, work with Goals and Goal Management as explained in Chapter 9, "Working with Marketing."

Work Hours Work Hours is the mechanism whereby you can control users' schedules and schedule activities (see Figure 12.111).

▶ Chapter 10, "Working with Service," discusses how the service calendar and scheduling engine works with Work Hours.

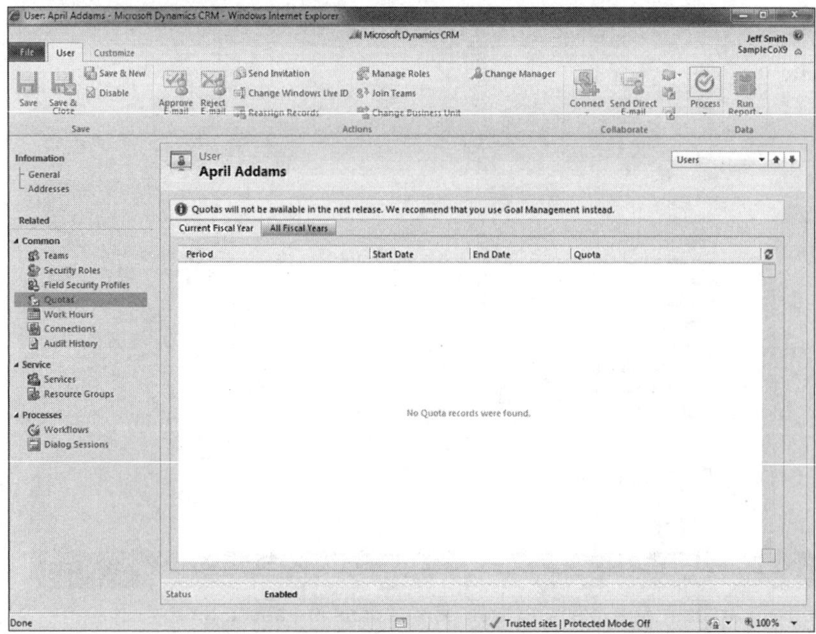

FIGURE 12.110 User Quotas.

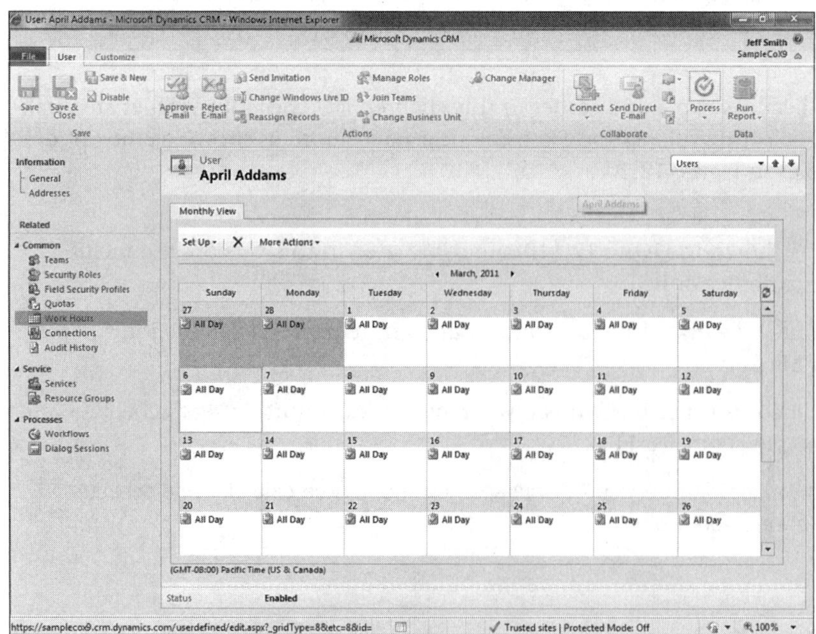

FIGURE 12.111 Work Hours.

Services When viewing an existing user record, any service records associated with the user are available by selecting Services from the Service option on the near navigation (see Figure 12.112). A service is any work performed for a customer by a user and resources. By default, a new user will have no services associated with it.

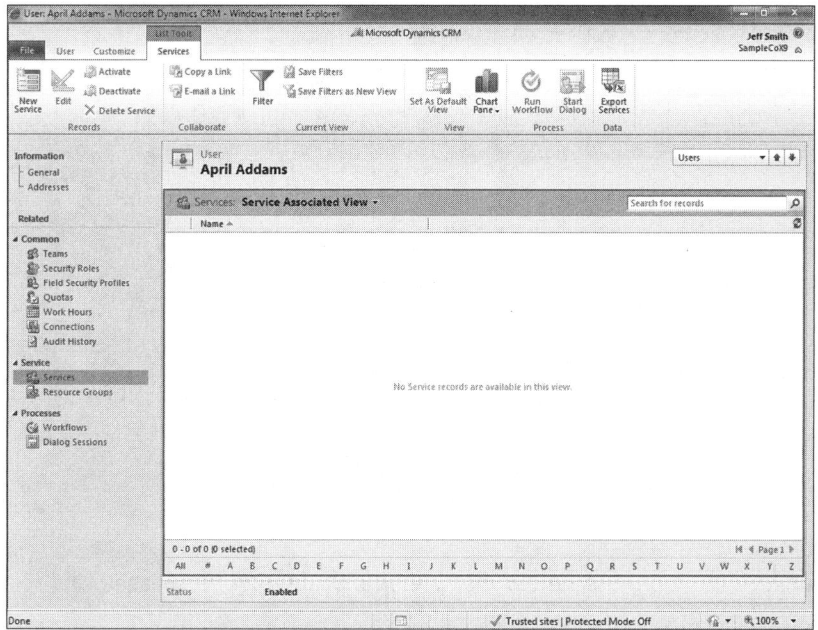

FIGURE 12.112 Services for the selected user.

▶ For more information about creating and working with services, refer to Chapter 10.

Resource Groups You can add users to existing Resource Groups by selecting Resource Groups from the near navigation (see Figure 12.113). A Resource Group is a collection of users, facilities, or equipment. The advantage to having them is that they can be scheduled interchangeably. For example, a Resource Group of everyone who works for you that is qualified to service a particular line of cars can be grouped. Then, when you need to schedule that service, you'll pick from that group instead of among individual employees.

For more information about Resource Groups, refer to the "Resource Groups" section later in this chapter.

Processes Here you can see any completed workflows or dialog sessions that were run on the User entity. Because this is for a new user, you won't see any available here unless you have a workflow built for the Create event of the User entity when initially setting up your system.

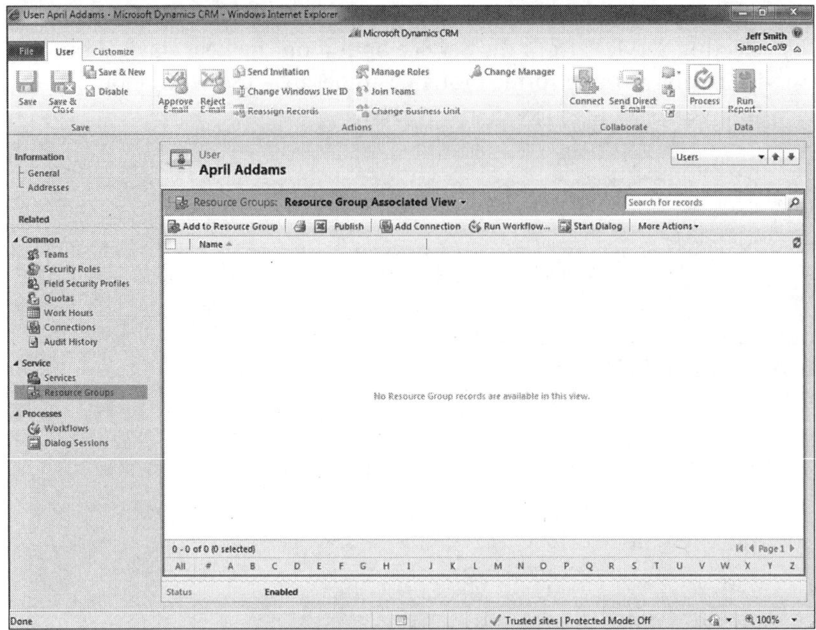

FIGURE 12.113 Resource Groups.

▶ For more information about process development, refer to Chapter 24, "Processes Development."

Adding Multiple Users (CRM On Premise Only) You can easily add multiple users at one time. To do so, select the New option on the Users page and then select Multiple Users.

The Add Users Wizard opens.

To complete the wizard, follow these steps:

1. Select the Business Unit and click Next to continue (see Figure 12.114).
2. Select which Security Roles the Users will belong to (see Figure 12.115). As with individual Users, all Users must have at least one Security Role to be able to use the system. When setting the roles for multiple Users, all Users who will be added will receive the same Security Roles selected. Click Next to continue.

NOTE

If you don't select Security Roles, the users will still be created, but you will receive an alert after they have been added that you must assign at least one Security Role to the new users. When you are adding many users, this can be time-consuming, so consider adding the role here.

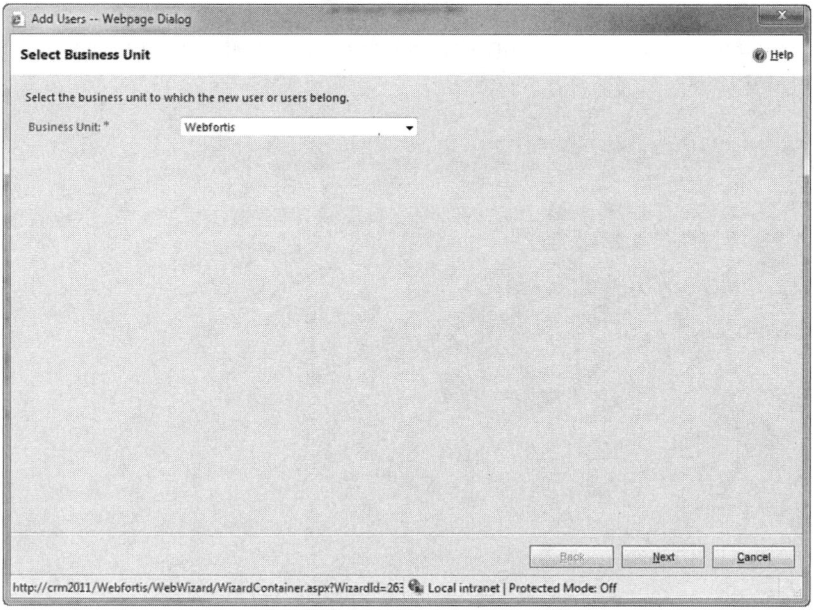

Add Users -- Webpage Dialog

Select Business Unit

Help

Select the business unit to which the new user or users belong.

Business Unit: * Webfortis

Back Next Cancel

http://crm2011/Webfortis/WebWizard/WizardContainer.aspx?WizardId=263 Local intranet | Protected Mode: Off

FIGURE 12.114 Add Users Wizard.

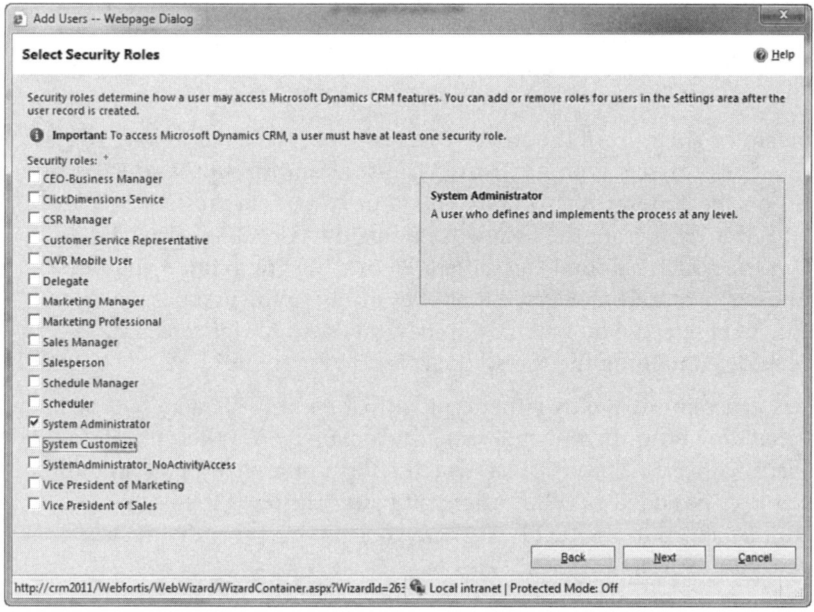

FIGURE 12.115 Selecting Security Roles with the Add Users Wizard.

3. Select the licensing for the users (see Figure 12.116). The Access Type, the license type, and the e-mail access configuration selected will apply to all users to be added. Click Next to continue.

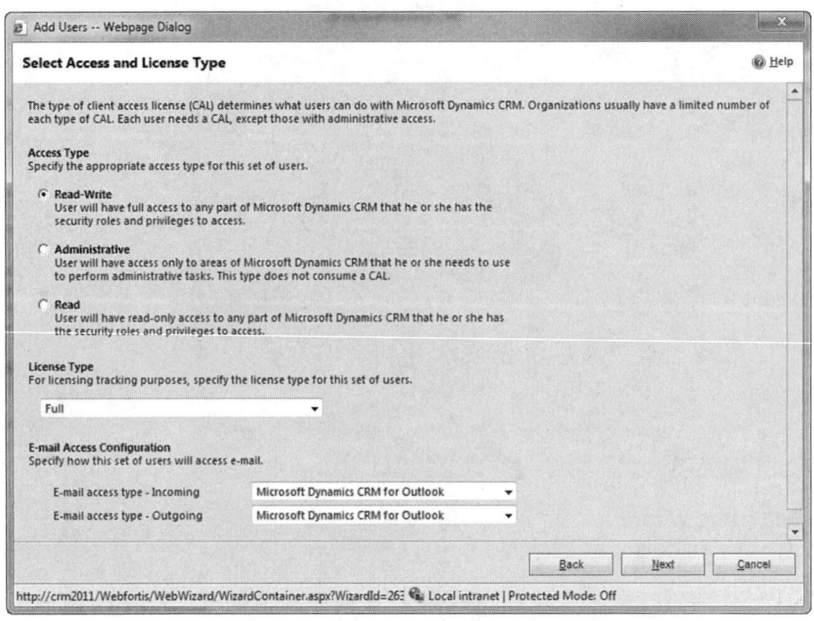

FIGURE 12.116 Selecting the license type with the Add Users Wizard.

4. Select the domain or group from the Active Directory that the Users belong to (see Figure 12.117). If Select Users from All Trusted Domains and Groups is selected, all available Users on the current trusted domain and/or groups are presented on the next screen. If Select Users from the Following Domain or Group is selected, the option to select the specific group is presented. Be sure the group node you select contains your users; if a node is selected that does not have the users, it will not show up on the next screen; you will have to navigate back to this screen to select an alternative node containing the users. Click Next to continue.

5. Select the users you want to add by either typing their names separated by a semi-colon, or by searching from them by selecting the lookup icon. When the lookup dialog box opens, either enter your Users' search criteria or leave it blank to return all users available to be added to CRM. After you have confirmed the users to be added, they will be added to the text box where you can remove individuals if necessary (see Figure 12.118).

TIP

Only users who have not been already added to Microsoft Dynamics CRM are available to be added.

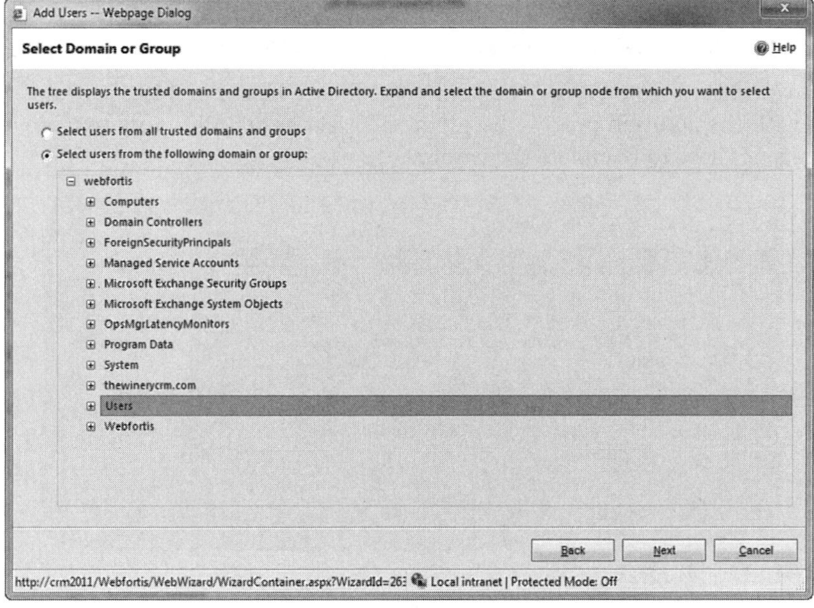

FIGURE 12.117 Selecting a domain or group with the Add Users Wizard.

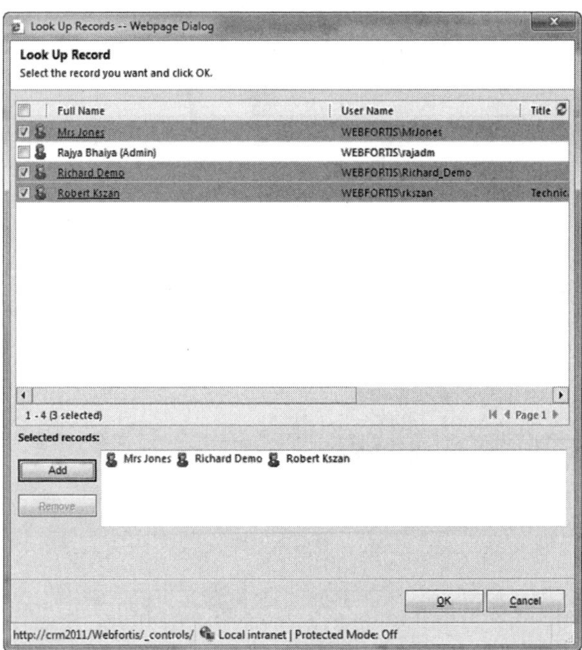

FIGURE 12.118 Selecting users with the Add Users Wizard.

6. Click OK, and then Create New Users to continue.
7. The users are added to Microsoft Dynamics CRM. This step might take several minutes.
8. When this is completed, you will see the Finish screen (see Figure 12.119). Any alerts or problems with the addition process display here. Select either Add More Users to add more users or Close to complete the wizard.

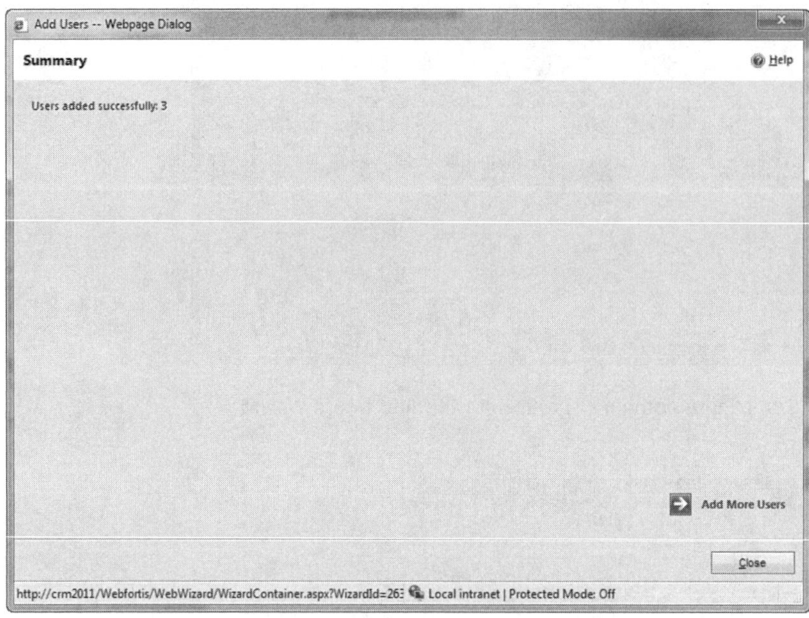

FIGURE 12.119 Finishing the Add Users Wizard.

Enable or Disable Users From the Ribbon menu, you can either enable or disable selected users. By disabling a user, you remove her license, and you can add a new user to use that license if you want.

NOTE

Disabling users might cause any existing workflows or system jobs that the user has created or owns to fail.

Manage User Roles From the Ribbon menu, you can manage selected users' roles. Microsoft Dynamics CRM is role-based, which provides a powerful mechanism to manage users. Because users must belong to at least one role, but can belong to more, it is important to remember that the user will have the permissions from a higher role.

NOTE

You can select multiple users at the same time, by selecting one or more on the left checkbox option. Thus, if you select a single user, only the existing roles display. If you select multiple users, no roles are selected, by default.

Change Business Units Available as an option from the Ribbon menu, you can change selected users' Business Units (see Figure 12.120).

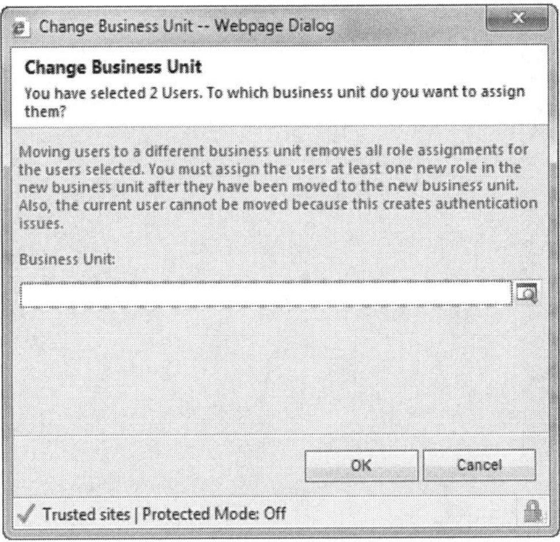

FIGURE 12.120 Changing a Business Unit.

For more information about Business Units and the effects of changing users' assigned Business Units, refer to the previous section named "Business Units."

Change Managers Available as an option from the More Actions drop-down menu, you can change the selected User Manager (see Figure 12.121).

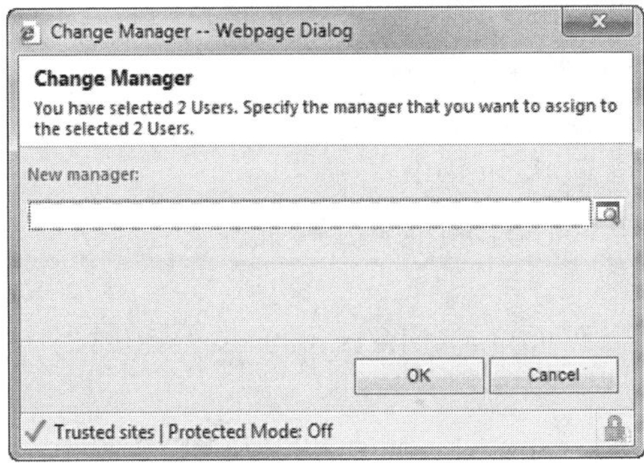

FIGURE 12.121 Changing the Manager.

You can set another user as the Manager (provided that the selected user is not one previously selected as the Change Manager) as the Manager of the selected users.

Send Invitation (CRM Online Only) When adding new users for CRM Online, the users must accept the invitation and associate their login with a Passport/WLID account. During the setup process of users for CRM Online, you have the option to send them an invitation. If they don't receive it or you need to resend it for any reason, you can select Send Invitation from the Ribbon menu (see Figure 12.122).

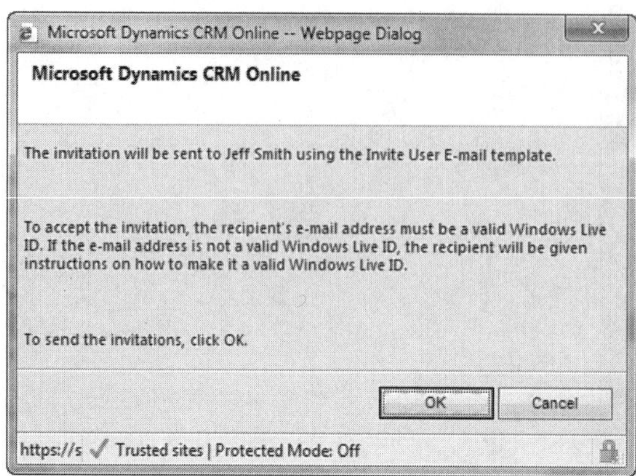

FIGURE 12.122 Send a CRM Online invitation to a user.

View Users When working with the main users interface, these are the default system views for a user:

- **Administrative Access Users**—Shows all enabled users with administrative access permissions
- **Disabled Users**—Shows all users who are disabled
- **Enabled Users**—Shows all users who are active
- **Full Access Users**—Shows all enabled users who have a Full Access CAL
- **Local Business Users**—Shows all enabled users who report to the selected Business Unit Organization that the logged-in user is working with
- **My Connections**—Shows all enabled users who have the current user as their connection
- **My Direct Reports**—Shows all enabled users who have the current user as their manager
- **Read-Only Access Users**—Shows all enabled users who have a Read-Only Access CAL
- **Subsidiary Users**—Shows all enabled users who report to Child Business Units

- **Users Invitation Status**—Shows all enabled users and their invitation status (CRM Online only)

Languages

Microsoft Dynamics CRM is incredibly multilingual. It can serve as many languages are available, enabling users to select what language they want to work with.

Language selection works by translating most of the labels within Microsoft Dynamics CRM to the selected language. In rare cases when the language is unavailable to translate, the translation falls back to the installed base language. Note that setting a different language does not translate the data information contained within Microsoft Dynamics CRM.

TIP

When using right-to-left languages, such as Hebrew and Arabic, the language and the navigation pane displays from right to left as well. That is why the navigation pane in Microsoft Dynamics CRM is continually referred to as the "near navigation" instead of the "left navigation."

NOTE

Although customizations must be done in the base language, they can be translated so that they are viewed in a different language.

To allow a different language, select Languages, and select the language you would like to have deployed on the system. Click Apply, and then click OK.

The system will provision the language and will be available to users.

By default, installed languages are disabled and must be enabled.

Users can now select which language they want to work with by navigating to Tools, Options, and selecting the Languages tab (see Figure 12.123).

Only the languages that have been enabled are available for users to select.

NOTE

There is a special setting in the Business Management Role under Miscellaneous Privileges called Language Settings. It allows the enabling and disabling of languages. If you're unable to perform language configuration changes, be sure to check your role settings for this permission.

TIP

Check the Mail Merge Templates after the language packs have been installed. Several different ones are loaded with each language installed.

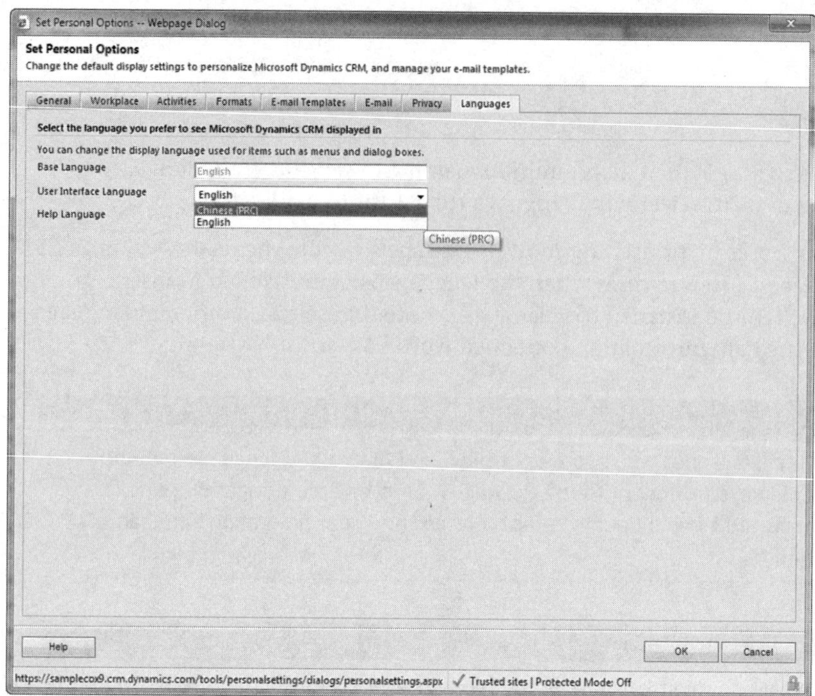

FIGURE 12.123 Installed languages available to users.

Privacy Preferences

Privacy Preferences enables you to specify both whether you will see an error message and whether that error message will be sent to Microsoft (see Figure 12.124).

The default for this is established when Microsoft Dynamics CRM is installed, and we recommend participation because it will improve future products and releases.

Billing (CRM Online Only)

Found only with CRM Online, the Settings/Administration area has a Billing option that allows CRM Online administrators to set payment and billing options.

When you select the Billing option, a new window opens that verifies your Windows Live ID and then takes you to the billing and account management interface for your CRM Online account (see Figure 12.125).

From this interface, you can add account delegates, view your payment details, and see what services you are using.

System Notifications (CRM Online Only)

As with the Billing option explained previously, the System Notifications options are found only with CRM Online in Settings, Administration.

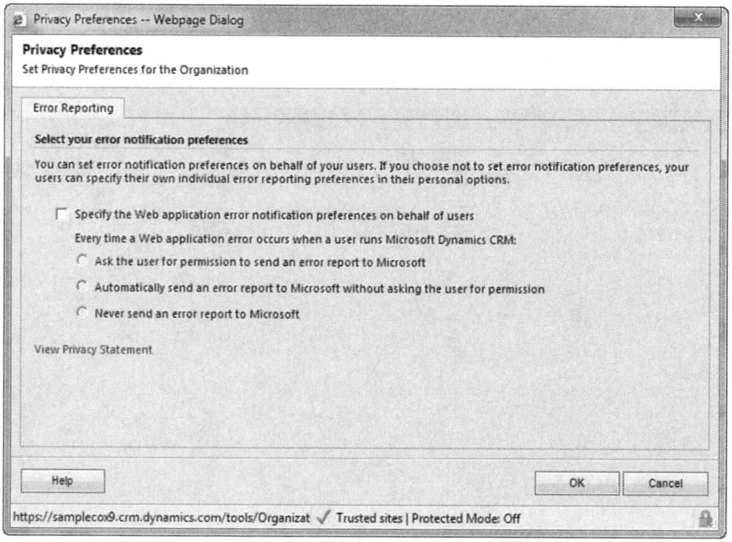

Privacy Preferences -- Webpage Dialog

Privacy Preferences

Set Privacy Preferences for the Organization

Error Reporting

Select your error notification preferences

You can set error notification preferences on behalf of your users. If you choose not to set error notification preferences, your users can specify their own individual error reporting preferences in their personal options.

- [ ] Specify the Web application error notification preferences on behalf of users

Every time a Web application error occurs when a user runs Microsoft Dynamics CRM:

- ( ) Ask the user for permission to send an error report to Microsoft
- ( ) Automatically send an error report to Microsoft without asking the user for permission
- ( ) Never send an error report to Microsoft

View Privacy Statement

Help | OK | Cancel

https://samplecox9.crm.dynamics.com/tools/Organizat ✓ Trusted sites | Protected Mode: Off

FIGURE 12.124 Privacy Preferences.

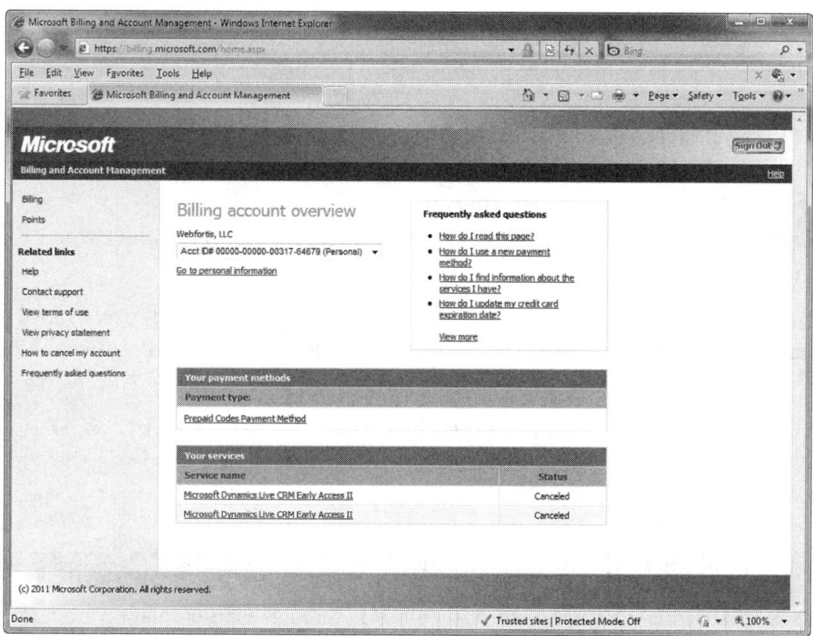

FIGURE 12.125 Billing and Account Management interface.

The System Notifications Status screen is used to show information related to your CRM Online account (see Figure 12.126).

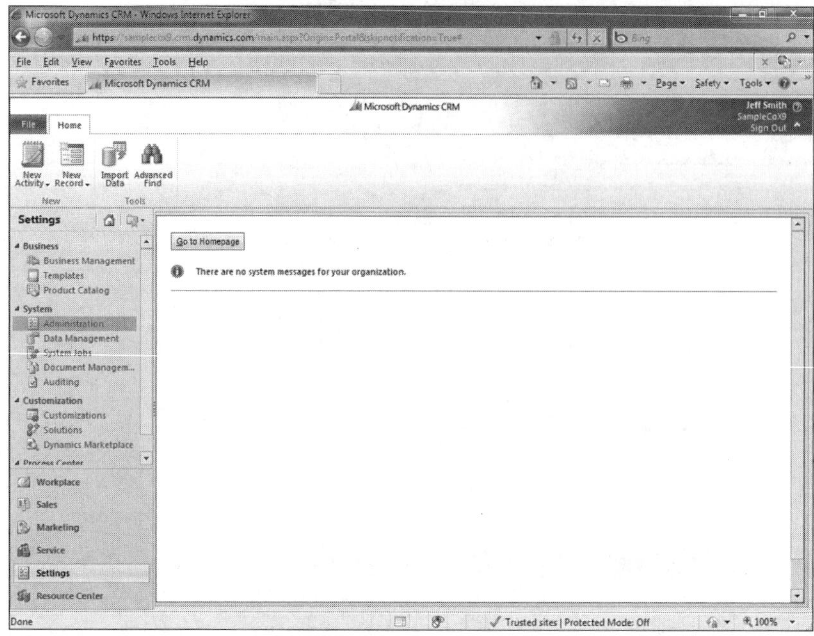

FIGURE 12.126 CRM System Notifications.

Product Updates (Partner Hosted or On Premise Only)

Product Updates enables you to sign up for the Microsoft Dynamics CRM Product Update newsletter (see Figure 12.127).

A Windows Live ID is required to complete the registration. When subscribed, users can receive communications from Microsoft related to Microsoft Dynamics CRM Product Updates.

A Windows Live ID is an account that is set up, verified, and administrated by Microsoft. With Windows Live, you can verify your identity by any system using the Live/Passport network.

NOTE

Microsoft Dynamics CRM product updates are now delivered through the automatic update service automatically. This signup is simply a newsletter informing you of information related to the updates (not the actual updates themselves).

Subscription Management (CRM Online Only)

Subscription Management is used to show information related to your CRM Online account such as the number of licenses you have available and your total storage available

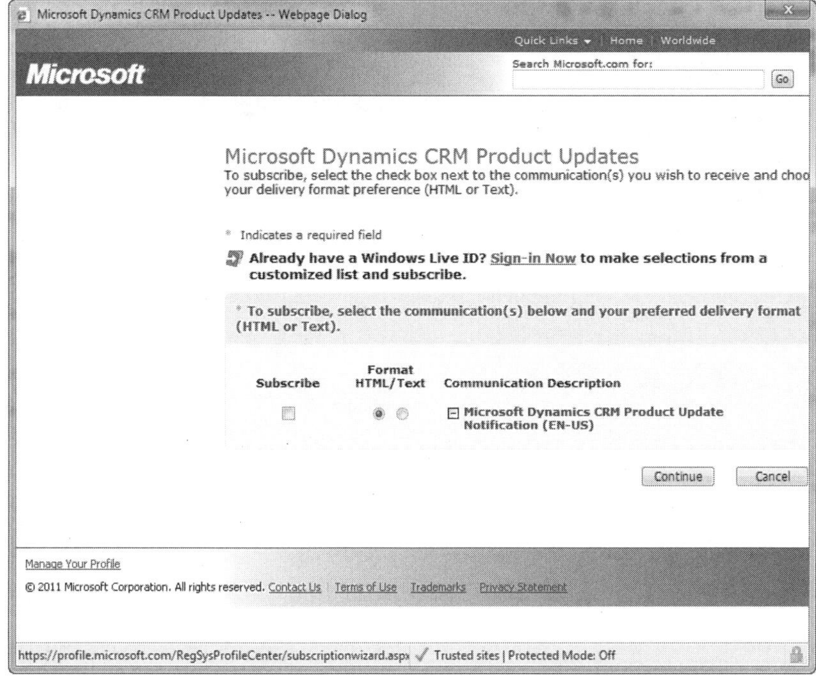

FIGURE 12.127 Product Updates.

12

and used (as shown in Figure 12.128). This information will be particular to your organization and the plan that you've purchased.

Data Management

Data Management is designed to easily manage the following:

- Duplication Detection Settings
- Duplicate Detection Rules
- Duplicate Detection Jobs
- Bulk Record Deletion
- Data Maps
- Imports
- Templates for Data Import
- Sample Data

▶ Data Management is covered in Chapter 29, "Data Management."

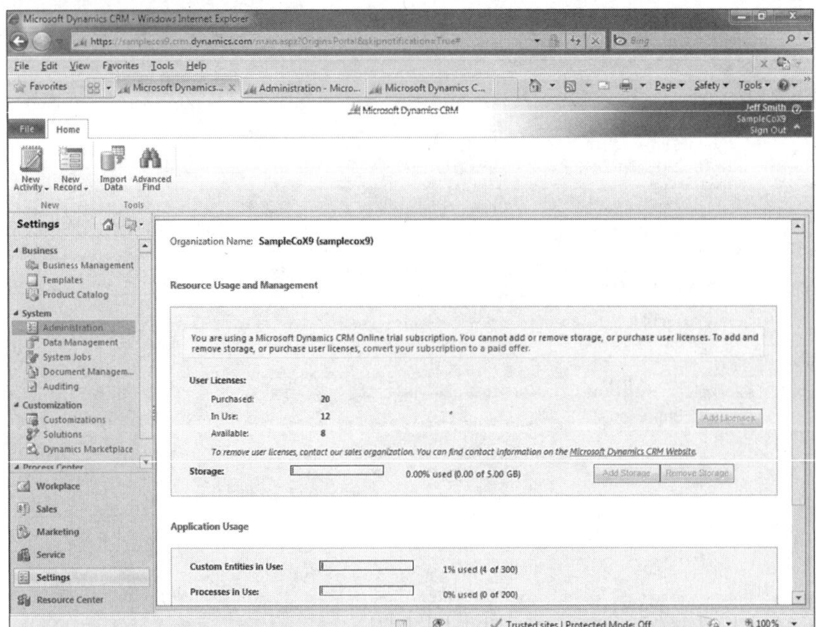

FIGURE 12.128 Subscription Management.

System Jobs

Just as every entity in Microsoft Dynamics CRM has a workflow entity association to it that displays any workflow used by that entity, the system itself has workflow. This workflow is referred to as a *System Job*, and it generally runs in the background. The System Jobs interface provides the capability to view the status of System Jobs and cancel, postpone, pause, or resume them by selecting these options from the More Actions drop-down menu.

By default, the interface displays the System Jobs and their status (see Figure 12.129).

You can open any of the displayed jobs by double-clicking them, and any errors are displayed here.

TIP

What's in a name? Generally, a lot of System Jobs are labeled as Matchcode Update Jobs. The term *Matchcode* refers to the match conditions of the base record to the matching record in duplicate detection rules. The Matchcode conditions are limited to 450 characters.

Document Management

Document Management is where you can manage your SharePoint settings. There are four options here:

- Document Management Settings

- Install List Component
- SharePoint Sites
- SharePoint Document Locations

▶ Document Management is covered in Chapter 17, "CRM 2011 SharePoint Integration."

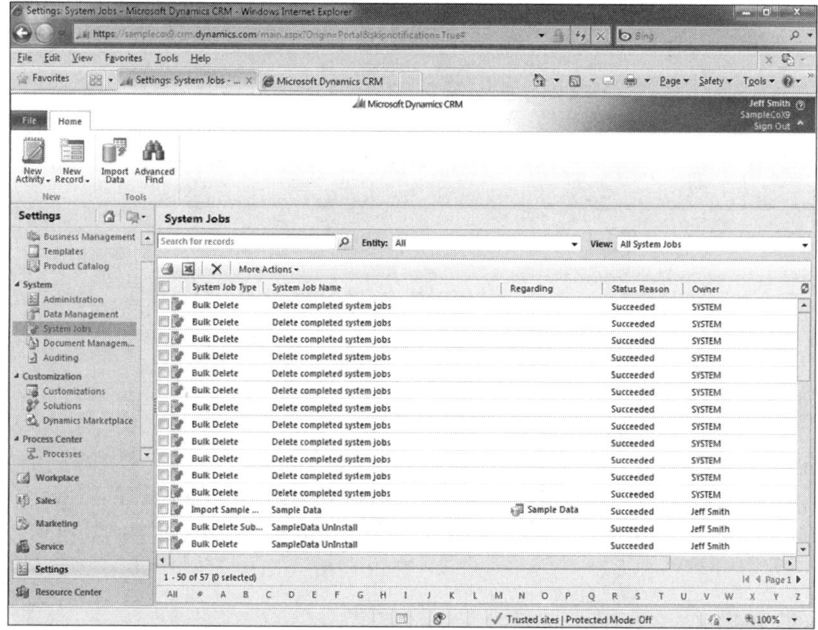

FIGURE 12.129 System Jobs.

Auditing

Auditing gives us the ability to record changes made by any record update, creation or deletion—on either the attribute or entity level.

The four options are as follows:

- Global Auditing Settings
- Entity and Field Audit Settings
- Audit Summary View
- Audit Log Management

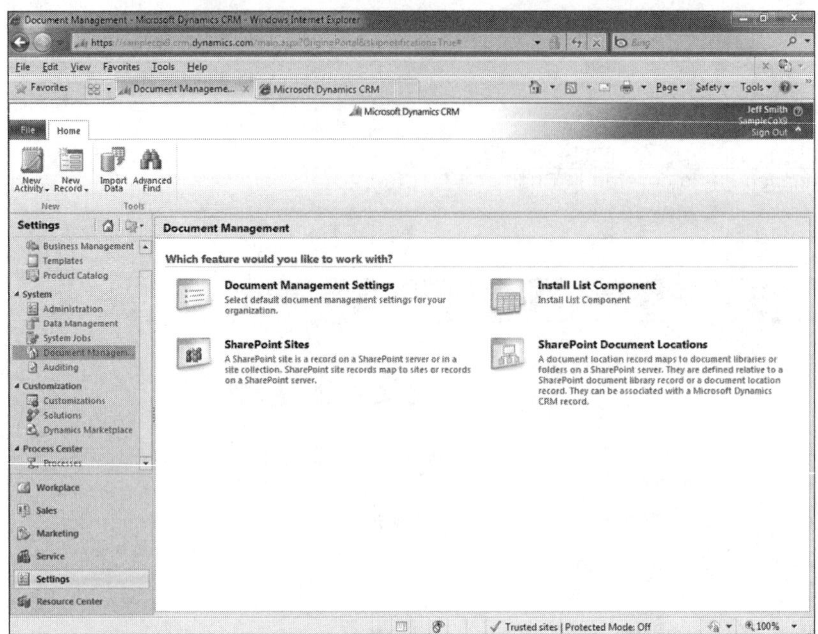

FIGURE 12.130 Document Management.

Global Auditing Settings

This opens the system settings interface (as explained earlier in this chapter) and allows the global setting to be turned on or off (see Figure 12.131). It must be on for auditing of any type to be active.

Entity and Field Audit Settings

When selected, this opens the default solution for Edit view and allows auditing to be set.

As shown in Figure 12.132, the entity audit status is shown in the column.

This is critical because even though you can enable auditing on the attribute level, if you have not enabled auditing on the entity level, auditing will not occur.

To enable auditing on the attribute level, expand the entity you want to work with, and select fields (as shown in Figure 12.133).

Select a field that you want to enable (or disable) auditing on, and double-click to open the details.

Change the value on the attribute for Auditing and select Save and Close (as shown in Figure 12.134).

Auditing will now occur on that field going forward.

Audit Summary View

This is a summary view of both the audits that occurred in the system, as well as any audit changes (that is, enabling or disabling auditing).

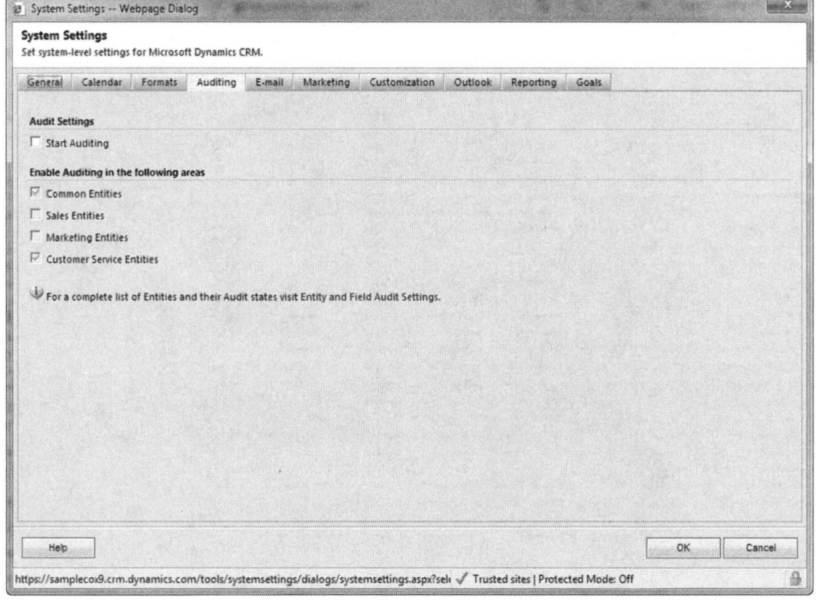

FIGURE 12.131 Auditing System Setting.

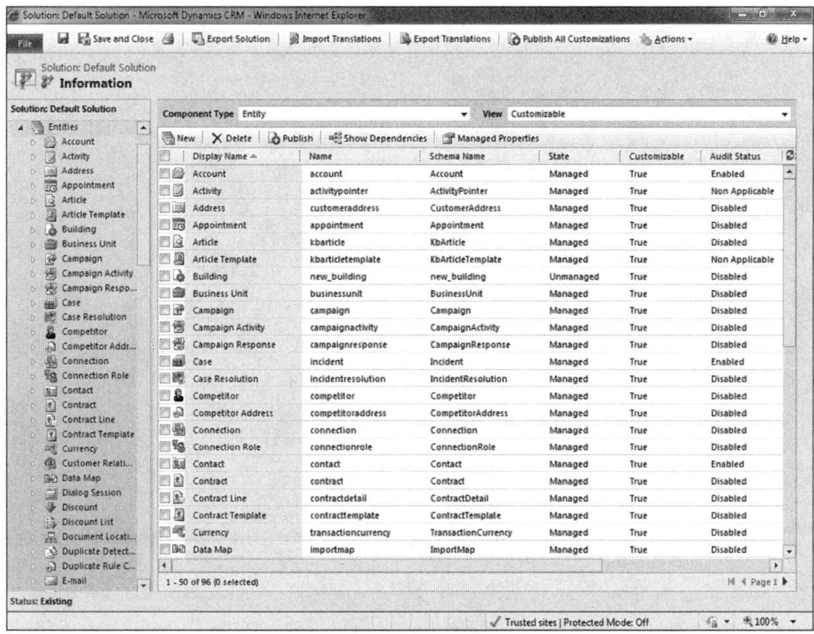

FIGURE 12.132 Entity Auditing options.

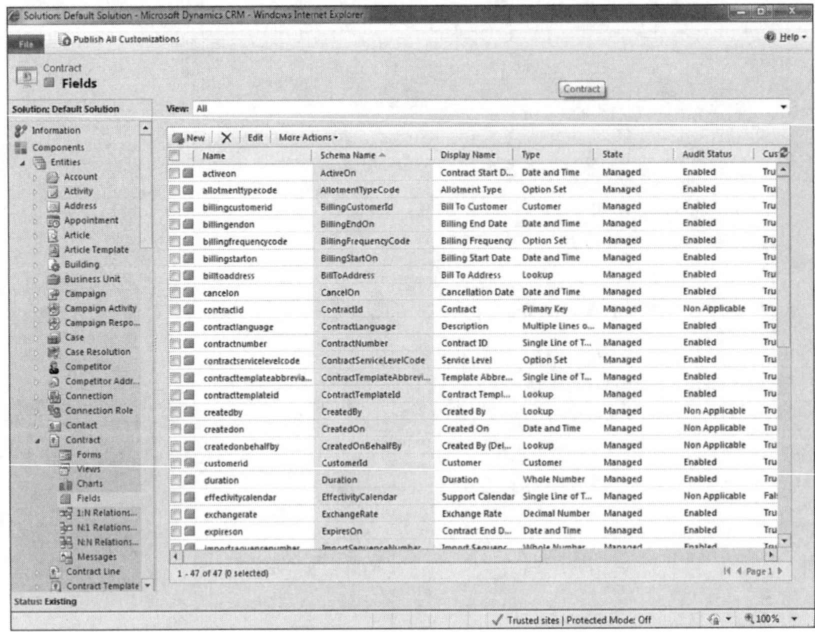

FIGURE 12.133 Attribute Auditing options.

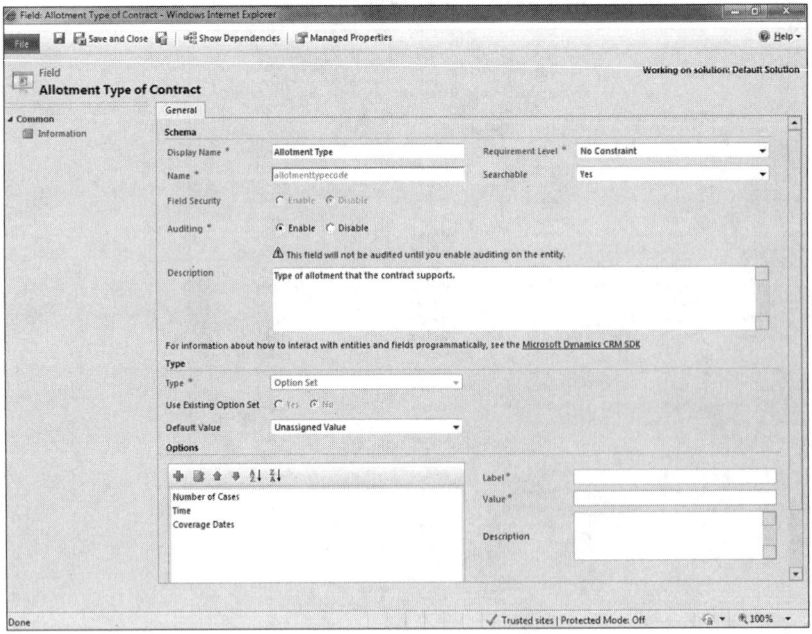

FIGURE 12.134 Enable attribute auditing options.

Figure 12.135 shows the summary view that is shown in a system with auditing enabled.

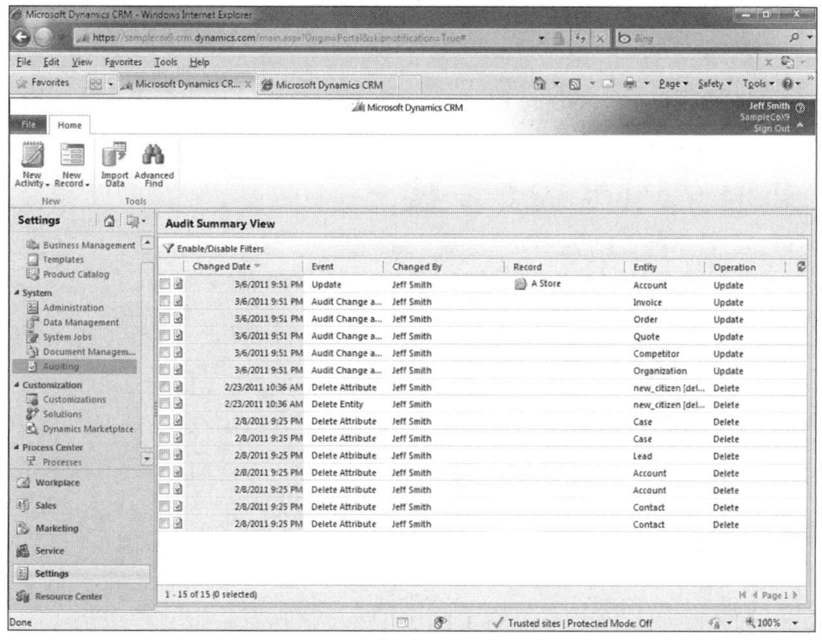

FIGURE 12.135 Audit summary view.

The first line in the view is where we disabled auditing on Account:Address 1:Street, and if you double-click the row, you can see the details (as shown in Figure 12.136). This is different from the second row, which has the actual audit values on the record level shown when selected (see Figure 12.137).

Audit Management Log

This allows users to delete audit logs. When you delete a log however, you will lose the audit history.

Customization

The Customization area is where Microsoft Dynamics CRM can be modified extensively.

> ▶ Refer to Chapters 16, "Solution Concepts," 20, "Advanced Configuration and Customization," and 23, "Customizing Entities," for information about working with customizations.

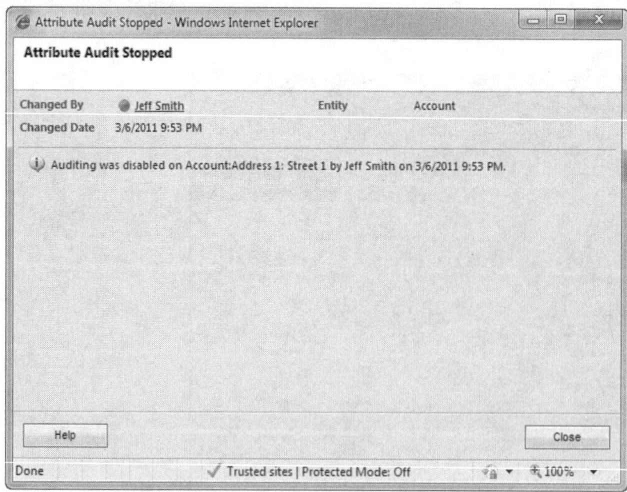

FIGURE 12.136 Attribute auditing changes.

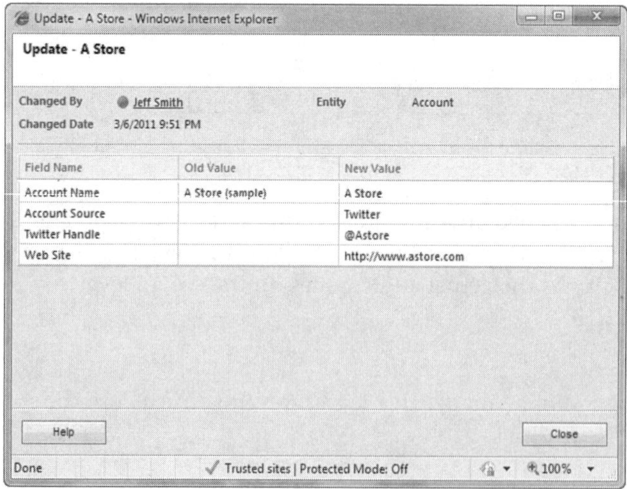

FIGURE 12.137 Actual attribute value changes.

▶ You can create and manage processes from the Process Center. For more information on working with processes, refer to Chapter 24, "Processes Development."

Dynamics Marketplace

The Dynamics Marketplace is a link that takes users to the Microsoft Dynamics Marketplace within Microsoft Dynamics CRM (as shown in Figure 12.138).

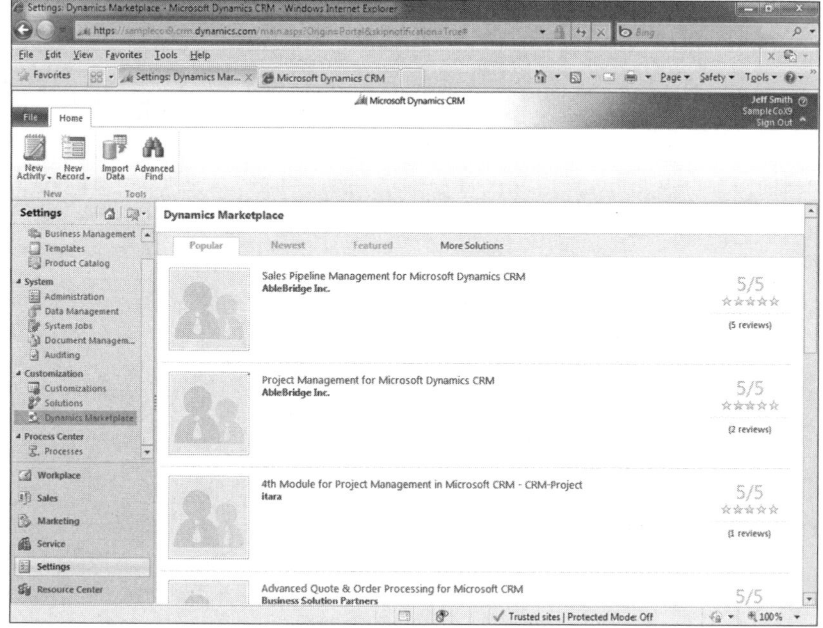

FIGURE 12.138 Actual Attribute value changes.

Summary

This chapter reviewed the areas that make up the Settings area for CRM and discussed how they are important and relevant to setting up, maintaining, and managing your business. Additionally, this chapter detailed how to configure the security of CRM through the use of Roles and Business Units.

You will visit many aspects of the Settings area only occasionally, but others are dynamic (such as adding and removing users and permissions, activating and deactivating Product Lists, and creating customizations for the system) and will be used often.

Hopefully, this chapter has illustrated the importance of becoming familiar with the different Settings areas because it will be a frequently accessed resource area for system administrators.

CHAPTER 13

Client Configuration Options

IN THIS CHAPTER

- Internet Explorer Client (Web Client)
- Microsoft Dynamics CRM 2011 for Outlook
- Advanced Configuration
- Previous Version Compatibility

Microsoft Dynamics CRM has always offered to users the ability to work within Outlook seamlessly. The Outlook integration provided by Microsoft Dynamics CRM tightly delivers CRM data in and through Outlook so that users can truly work in one place without having to navigate to separate applications.

Some of the new features provided with this version of Microsoft Dynamics CRM Outlook connector include

- Full MAPI integration
- Customizable views of CRM data in Outlook
- Ribbon enhancements
- Data filters
- E-mail enhancements

When accessing the full Microsoft Dynamics CRM client, users have two options for accessing the application:

- Internet Explorer (IE) client (web client)
- Outlook (Microsoft Dynamics CRM for Outlook)

Additionally, users can access the application directly using mobile or custom solutions; however, the full client experience is limited to these options.

CAUTION

At the time this book was published, Microsoft Dynamics CRM will not run on any web browser other than Internet Explorer version 7 or greater. There is some talk that application functionality will be ported across other browsers. However, this is not anticipated prior to early 2012 at the earliest.

Although this chapter covers both client options for Microsoft Dynamics CRM 2011, with the exception of the next section, the focus of this chapter is the Outlook client.

Internet Explorer Client (Web Client)

As shown in Figure 13.1, Microsoft Dynamics CRM has full-featured functionality using only Internet Explorer.

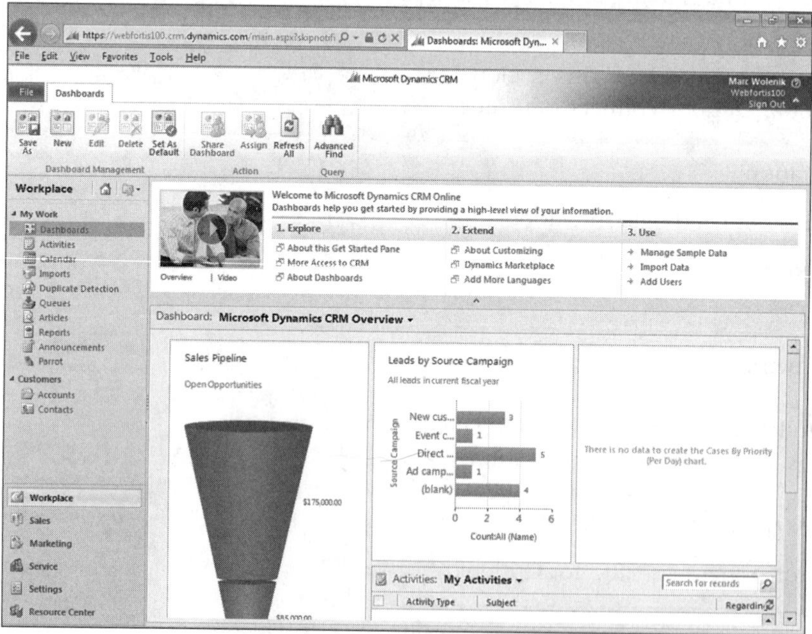

FIGURE 13.1 Internet Explorer client (web client)—as shown in IE 9.

The following operating systems are supported for the Microsoft Dynamics CRM web client:

- Windows 7 (all versions)
- Windows Vista (all versions)
- Microsoft Windows XP Professional SP3
- Microsoft Windows XP Home SP3

- Windows XP Media Center Edition SP3
- Microsoft Windows XP Tablet SP3

The following versions of Internet Explorer are required:

- Internet Explorer 9 or a later version
- Internet Explorer 8 or a later version
- Internet Explorer 7 or a later version

To use several of the Office features available within the web client, such as exporting to Excel, the following minimum components must also be installed on the client computer:

- Microsoft Office 2003 SP3 or later version
- 2007 Microsoft Office system SP2 or later version
- Office 2010

When considering using the Internet Explorer client for Microsoft Dynamics CRM, the following pros and cons should be considered:

Pros:

- Lightweight, almost always available (guest computers and so forth)
- Little or no configuration required to use

Cons:

- Ability to correlate (or track) e-mails to CRM does not exist using Outlook
- Requires use of another application (instead of just using Outlook)
- No offline availability/access (requires Internet connection)

CAUTION

At the time this book was published, Microsoft Dynamics CRM web client and Outlook Web Access (OWA) have no integration options. As such, if you are used to accessing your e-mail from your corporate network using Internet Explorer, you will be unable to access any level of integration, and the two applications will interact independently.

Microsoft Dynamics CRM 2011 for Outook

The integration with Microsoft Dynamics CRM and Outlook is known officially as "Microsoft Dynamics CRM 2011 for Outlook." However it is commonly referred to as "the Outlook connector," and it brings Microsoft Dynamics CRM 2011 into Outlook for a single and unified user experience.

Unlike other applications (or competitors), users can use Microsoft Dynamics CRM within Microsoft Outlook. Additional benefits include

- Integrated e-mail tracking options
- Ability to quickly convert e-mails to Cases, Leads, or Opportunities
- Add Connections
- Visualize data quickly and easily

Figure 13.2 shows Microsoft Outlook with the Microsoft Dynamics CRM client installed.

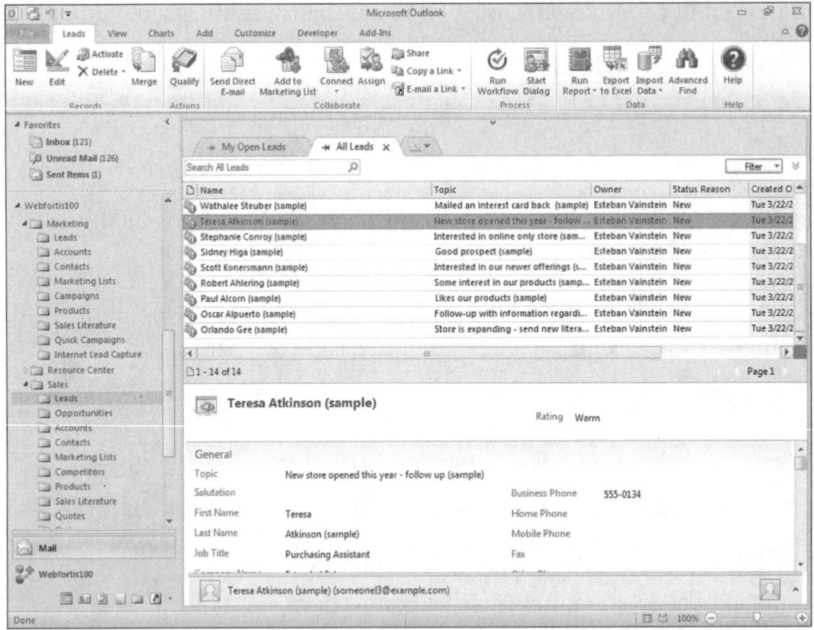

FIGURE 13.2 Microsoft Dynamics 2011 for Outlook.

Requirements

Although the Microsoft Dynamics CRM client works on both x64 and x86 machines, these are the following minimum hardware requirements:

- **Processor**
    - 32-bit—750MHz or comparable
    - 64-bit—1.5GHz processor
- **Memory**—2GB RAM
- **Hard disk**—1.5GB of available hard disk space
- **Display**—Super VGA with a minimum resolution of 1024×768

In addition to the hardware requirements, the following software requirements exist as well:

- Windows 7 (both 64-bit and 32-bit versions)
- Windows Vista (both 64-bit and 32-bit versions)
- Microsoft Windows XP Professional SP3
- Microsoft Windows XP Tablet SP3
- Windows XP Professional x64 Edition

As noted previously in this chapter, Microsoft Dynamics CRM requires Internet Explorer for use of the web client. However, Internet Explorer version 7 (or later version) must be installed on the client computer, as well as the following Microsoft versions of Microsoft Office:

- Microsoft Office 2003 with SP3 or later version
- 2007 Microsoft Office system
- Office 2010
- Indexing service (must be installed and running)

CAUTION

Browsers other than Microsoft Internet Explorer and versions of Internet Explorer prior to version 7 are not supported.

Because Microsoft Dynamics CRM for Outlook is supported in both 64- and 32-bit versions, you can install either one on your computer, provided you are running Windows 64-bit. However, you must have a 64-bit version of Microsoft Office 2010 to install the 64-bit version of the client. (Otherwise you will see a compatibility error.)

Client Setup

Similar to previous versions of Microsoft Dynamics CRM, the Outlook client configuration is broken down into two separate processes:

- Client installation
- Client configuration

After the client is installed, it must be configured for usage before it can be used.

Client Installation

To install Microsoft Dynamics CRM for Outlook, follow these steps:

1. Ensure that Outlook has been run at least once on the client computer. Running Outlook once creates an Outlook profile for the user, and Microsoft Dynamics CRM for Outlook uses that profile for installation.
2. Download to the client install file, and double-click it to start the installation. They can be found by searching Microsoft for CRM Outlook Client, or by clicking on the yellow notification on the web client to download the Outlook client Get the Outlook Client and will be the following format:
   - CRM2011-Client-ENU-i386.exe (for 32-bit installations)
   - CRM2011-Client-ENU-amd64.exe (for 64-bit installations)

NOTE

The Get the Outlook Client message can be turned off by selecting the X on the far right. Additionally, you can set the system to not display this message in System Settings, Outlook, as shown in Figure 13.3. This is helpful for organizations such as help desk operations, which have no need for the Outlook client.

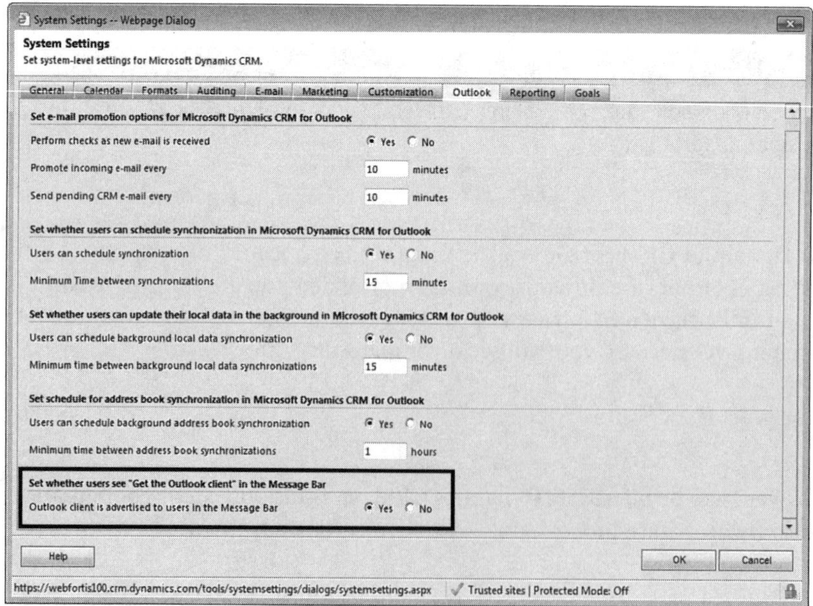

FIGURE 13.3 System settings for displaying the message for the Outlook client.

During installation, the following components will be installed if they are missing:

- Microsoft .NET Framework 4.0
- Microsoft Windows Installer (MSI) 4.5
- MSXML 4.0
- Microsoft Visual C++ Redistributable
- Microsoft Report Viewer 2010
- Microsoft Application Error Reporting
- Windows Identity Framework (WIF)

If Offline Access is selected, Microsoft SQL Server 2008 Express Edition will be installed as well.

TIP

You can install the Offline Access at a future date.

1. Accept the licensing agreement to continue, as shown in Figure 13.4.

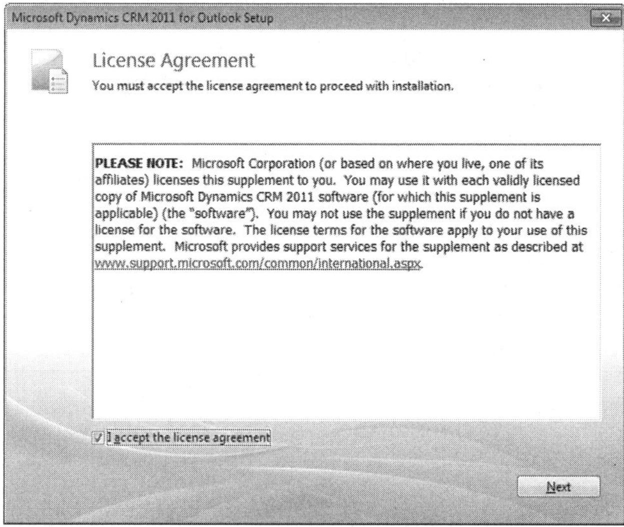

FIGURE 13.4 Licensing agreement.

2. Select Install Now to install the client, or select Options to change whether to install the Offline capabilities and the installation location.
3. The client will install and when completed, you will be asked to restart Outlook, as shown in Figure 13.5.

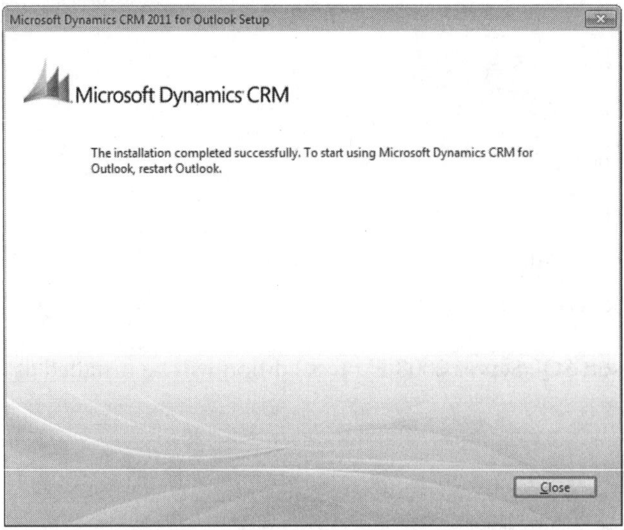

FIGURE 13.5 Successful installation of the client component.

TIP

If your Internet connection is less than 300Kbps, installation of the Outlook client might fail. Ensure that your network connection is reliable and available at speeds above 300Kbps to avoid installation problems.

Microsoft Dynamics CRM is now successfully installed on the client computer and is pending only configuration.

Client Configuration

With the client successfully installed, we need to configure it to work with the CRM organization.

To configure the client, either open Outlook after installation, or select Start, All Programs, Microsoft Dynamics CRM 2011, Configuration Wizard, and follow these steps:

1. Configure the organization by entering the server URL in the first drop-down box (see Figure 13.6) and then selecting Test Connection.

   If you have an on-premise deployment, this URL format should be in the following format:

   ```
   <<servername>>:<<Port>>
   ```

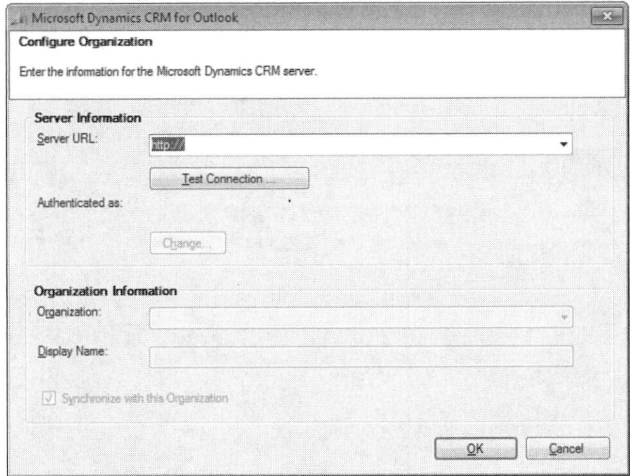

FIGURE 13.6 Client configuration.

Figure 13.7 shows a properly configured on-premise configuration.

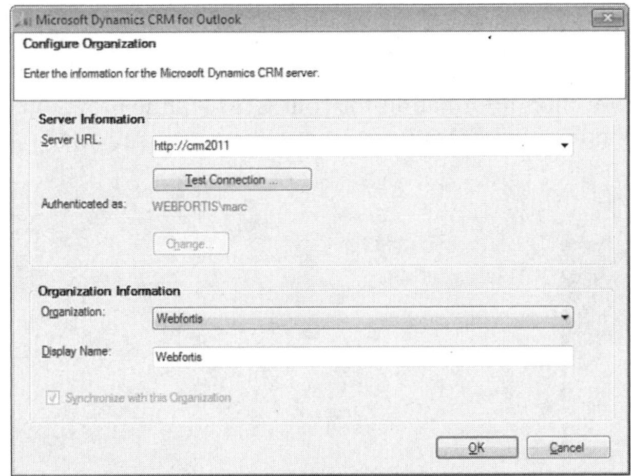

FIGURE 13.7 On-premise client configuration.

TIP

Notice that because our CRM server is installed on the default port 80, it is not necessary to enter the port information. When you select Test Connection, the Configuration Wizard uses your current AD information for verification/authorization.

2. If you have an online deployment (that is, you are connecting to Microsoft Dynamics Online), you will select CRM Online from the Server URL drop-down (see Figure 13.8), and then select Test Connection.

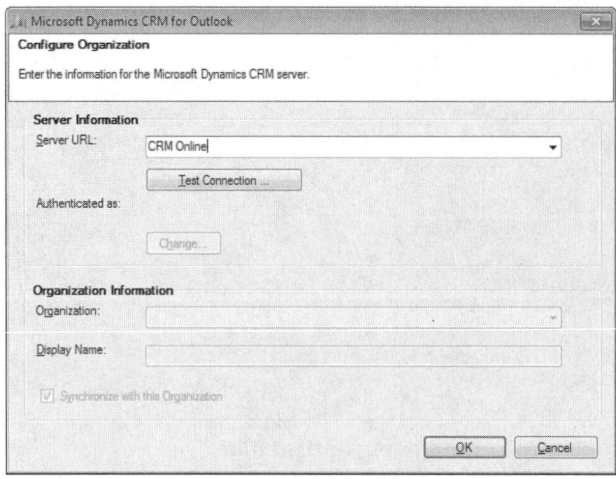

FIGURE 13.8 CRM Online client configuration.

3. When you select Test Connection, you are presented with an authorization option that stores and caches your connection information for your CRM Online provision (see Figure 13.9). Enter your Windows Live ID (WLID) information here and select OK to continue.

FIGURE 13.9 Windows Live ID Information.

Figure 13.10 shows the proper configuration for a CRM Online instance.

4. The next step is to select the organization from the Organization Information drop-down. If you only have one organization, this option will automatically be selected, as you saw in Figure 13.7. In cases where you have multiple organizations (or in the

case of CRM Online where you have multiple associations to the same Windows Live ID), you need to select the organization with which you want to integrate, as shown in Figure 13.11.

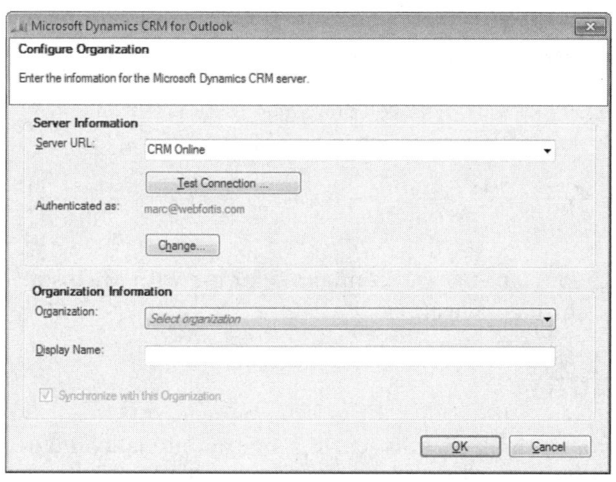

FIGURE 13.10 CRM Online client configuration.

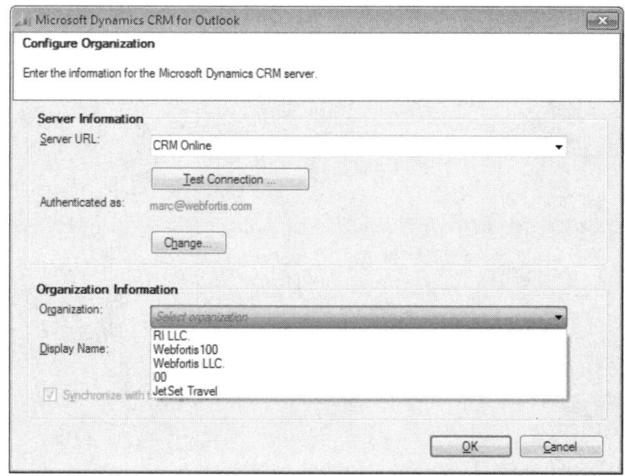

FIGURE 13.11 CRM Online client configuration with multiple organizations.

5. After you select the organization, you have the option to change the display name and set whether you should synchronize with the organization. Setting the Synchronization option is done when you have multiple organizations attached to a single Outlook instance—something that is a new feature with this version of Microsoft Dynamics CRM.

Although you can have multiple organizations attached to Outlook, you can only have one synchronizing organization. This is especially important when considering the fact that when you go to track an item in CRM from Outlook, it will track to the synchronizing organization, regardless of how many different CRM organizations you have in Outlook.

NOTE

Having multiple organizations in one Outlook would happen only when there is a business need for multiple or completely different organizations to be accessed through a single Outlook interface.

Now the Microsoft Dynamics CRM client is loaded and configured for use with Microsoft Outlook and can be accessed via the left-side navigation.

Advanced Configuration

With the Microsoft Dynamics CRM for Outlook client installed, some additional configuration options can be made. To find these options in Microsoft Outlook 2010, navigate in the near navigation to File, and then select CRM (as shown in Figure 13.12).

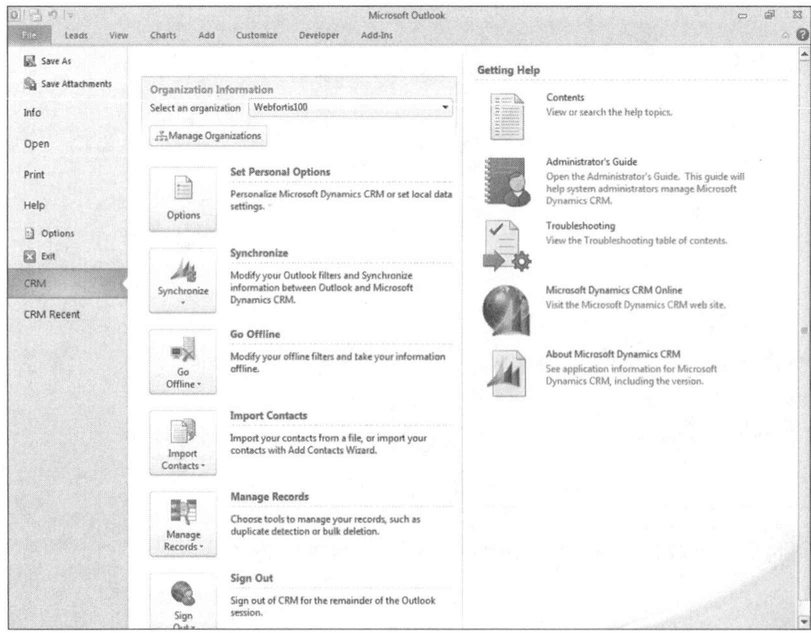

FIGURE 13.12 Microsoft Outlook 2010 CRM option.

- **Options**—The configuration options shown enable you to set personal and local data options.

- **Synchronize**—Perform a manual synchronization (instead of waiting the default 15 minutes) for data between CRM and Outlook. Additionally, it is here where you set the data filters, as shown in Figure 13.13.

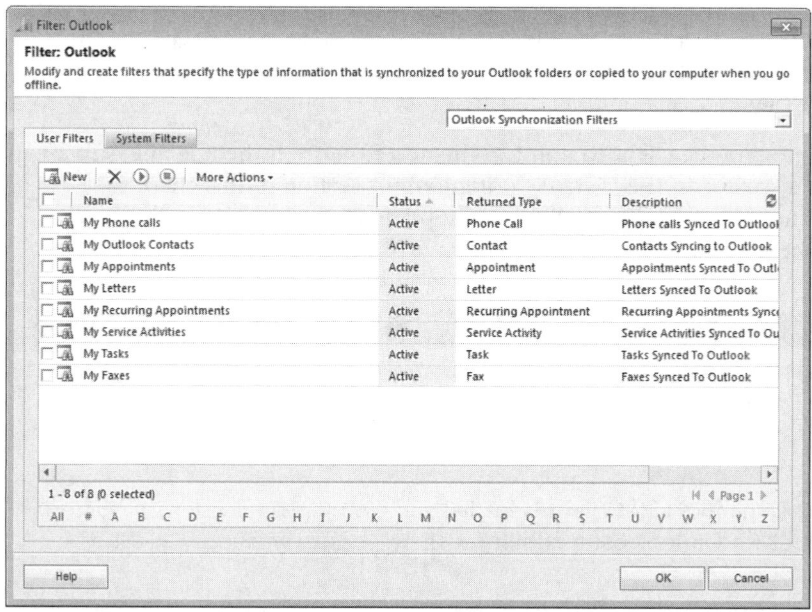

FIGURE 13.13 User data filters.

CAUTION

Be sure to notice the option to select the either Outlook Synchronization Filters or Offline Synchronization Filters in the drop-down. Selecting either of these options presents different values in the user versus system filters.

- **Go Offline**—Take the data offline and set the filters for doing so.
- **Import Contacts**—Allows you import data as contacts.
- **Manage Records**—Perform duplicate detection or perform bulk updates.
- **Sign Out**—This will sign you out of your CRM session.

TIP

Although you can upgrade the Outlook client, it must match the base architecture. Therefore, if you want to upgrade the 32-bit client for CRM 4.0 to the 64-bit client for CRM 2011, you must uninstall and reinstall because it is not supported.

Previous Version Compatibility

This section briefly discusses how Microsoft Dynamics CRM 4.0 for Outlook is compatible with Microsoft Dynamics CRM 2011.

As more and more enterprise organizations use Microsoft Dynamics CRM, Microsoft anticipates increasingly complex upgrade scenarios. As such, provided that Update Rollup 7 (or greater) is installed with Microsoft Dynamics CRM 4.0 for Outlook, the client is compatible with Microsoft Dynamics CRM 2011.

Users must still configure the client to point to the new instance if the upgrade is to a new server, which was discussed in the "Client Configuration" section of this chapter. However, system administrators can make an appropriate DNS entry that redirects users automatically to the new server.

TIP

Although the CRM 4.0 Outlook client can be used with Microsoft Dynamics CRM 2011, offline access works only if the client and server versions match.

Now the Microsoft Dynamics CRM client is loaded and configured for use with Microsoft Dynamics CRM 2011 for Outlook compatibility with Microsoft Dynamics CRM 4.0.

CAUTION

There is no backward compatibility with the clients, which means that you cannot use your Microsoft Dynamics CRM 2011 for Outlook to access a CRM 4.0 environment. In addition, it is not possible to have both clients installed on the same machine.

For a complete guide to upgrading, as well as system compatibility options, download the installation guide from Microsoft at msdn.microsoft.com.

Summary

Providing a best-in-class experience for users (by delivering CRM functionality from within Outlook), the Outlook Client is both easy to install, set up, and maintain.

It should be noted that although the application can be accessed via either Outlook or Internet Explorer, Internet Explorer is still required in both cases.

CHAPTER 14

E-Mail Configuration

IN THIS CHAPTER

The new E-mail Router allows organizations to cluster the service for higher uptime and scalability. Because configuring the e-mail services for either incoming or outgoing e-mails is not a simple task, we have taken extra effort in this chapter to explain how to make the necessary configurations. Depending on your users and implementation needs, you can decide which configuration is best for your organization.

NOTE

The e-mail settings are not set up during server installation to permit users to configure their preferred configuration.

Overview

Microsoft Dynamics CRM provides the following e-mail processing options:

- Microsoft Dynamics CRM for Microsoft Office Outlook and Microsoft Dynamics CRM for Outlook with Offline Access.
- The E-mail Router manages both incoming and outgoing messages.
- The E-mail Router also supports POP3 e-mail systems for incoming messages and SMTP e-mail systems for outgoing messages.
- Microsoft Dynamics CRM e-mail messages are sent asynchronously by using E-mail Router.

Microsoft Dynamics CRM for Outlook

Microsoft Dynamics CRM for Outlook can also be used to perform the following tasks:

- Deliver received e-mail messages to Microsoft Dynamics CRM
- Send e-mail messages generated from Microsoft Dynamics CRM

CAUTION

Similar to the previous version of Microsoft Dynamics CRM, Microsoft Dynamics CRM for Outlook does not require the E-mail Router to process Microsoft Dynamics CRM e-mail messages. However when it is not used, the only time CRM will be able to process e-mails into the CRM system is when Outlook and the Dynamics CRM client are running—hence situations can arise where important e-mails might be sent and received by the organization but are not acted upon by CRM because the individuals' Outlook is not running and has not processed the e-mail yet.

E-mail Router

The CRM E-mail Router is a piece of software that receives messages from a service and forwards the messages to another service. For example, the messages are received from the CRM Server, and they are forwarded to Microsoft Exchange or to the configured e-mail server, or vice versa.

The E-mail Router performs the following tasks:

- Routes incoming email message to Microsoft Dynamics CRM
- Sends e-mail messages generated from Microsoft Dynamics CRM

The CRM E-mail Router comes as a separate installation and must be installed after the CRM Server installation. You can install the CRM E-mail Router on a separate server; this doesn't need to be the same server where you have Microsoft Exchange Server installed or the same machine where you have the CRM Server installed. You can even install it on a separate server or computer running Windows 7, Windows Vista Business, or Enterprise because those are the versions that can be joined to a domain. The computer that you install E-mail Router on must have a connection to the Exchange Server or POP3 e-mail server. Also, the server is not required to be a member of the same domain as the CRM Servers.

NOTE

You might also be required to install the Microsoft Exchange Server MAPI Client and Collaboration Data Object component before installing the CRM E-mail Router.

The E-mail Router contains the following components:

- E-mail Router service and program files.
- E-mail Router Configuration Manager.
- Rule Deployment Wizard. This wizard lets you deploy rules that are used to route e-mail messages to a forward mailbox.

CAUTION

The Rule Deployment Wizard does not work with POP3/SMTP e-mail servers.

Configuring the E-Mail Services

By default, users must use the Microsoft Outlook client to be able to send and track incoming e-mails in Microsoft Dynamics CRM Send E-Mail button, as shown in Figure 14.1.

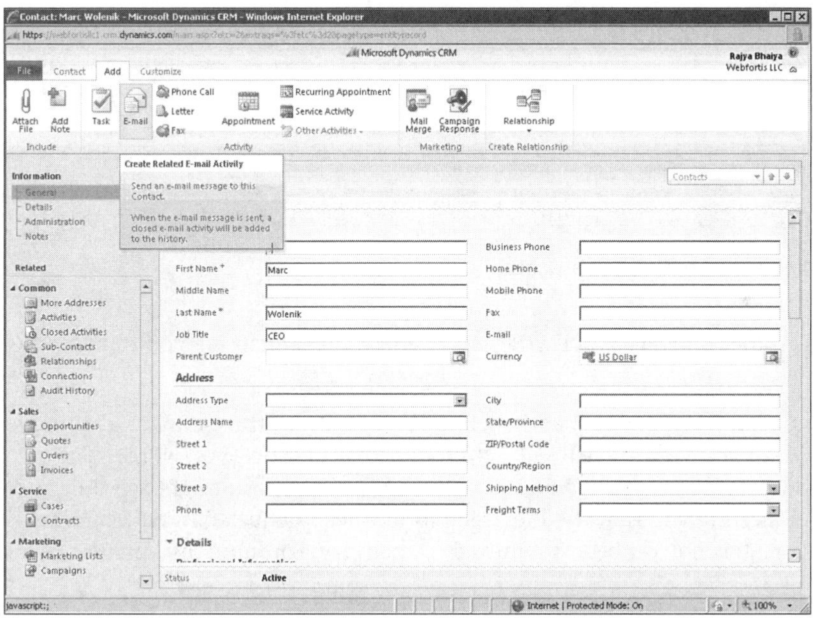

FIGURE 14.1 Sending direct e-mail to a Contact from Microsoft Dynamics CRM.

CAUTION

If you do not install the Outlook client and you send a direct e-mail to a Contact using the CRM web interface, the e-mail will not be sent without a CRM router.

Notice the tooltip in Figure 14.1 says Create Related E-mail Activity. That is because the Contact is not only used in the To field but also in the Regarding field, which is another field that is used by Microsoft Dynamics CRM to make the e-mail activity relate to the Contacts (see Figure 14.2). For example, you might change the To address and send the e-mail to another person, which would be also related to the first Contact, and you will see the e-mail in the history of both Contacts.

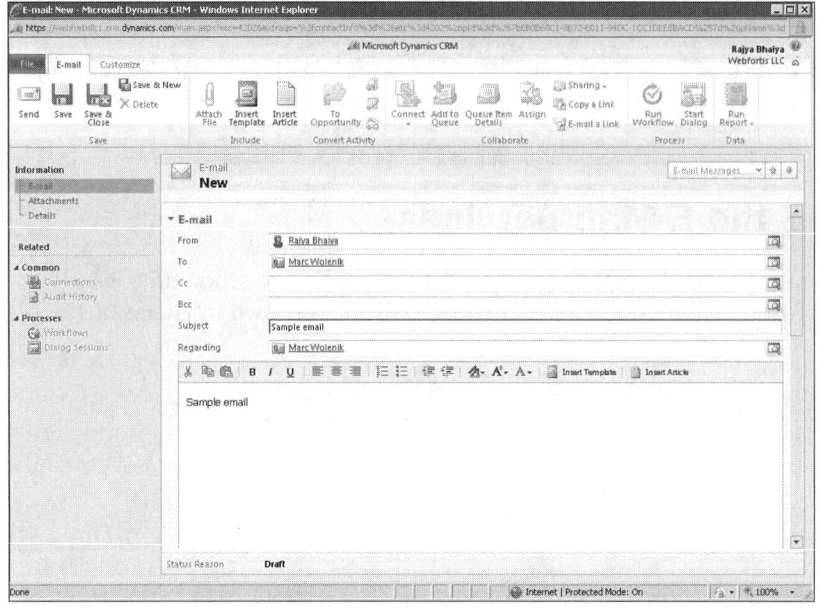

FIGURE 14.2 Composing an e-mail to a Contact.

Figure 14.2 displays what happens when you select Send E-mail, enabling you to compose a new e-mail.

However, after you compose the e-mail and click the Send button, the e-mail might not go out as expected. When you view the Closed Activity for that Contact, you will see the e-mail is there. However, when you open the e-mail you just sent, you might see the yellow warning bar alerting you that the message has not been delivered, with a message such as "This message has not yet been submitted for delivery. For more information, see help" (see Figure 14.3).

When the user setting for outgoing is selected to Microsoft Dynamics CRM for Outlook, the user must have the Microsoft Dynamics CRM for Outlook installed and running. The alternative option is to use e-mail router; this option does not require Outlook to be running (see Figure 14.4).

You need to consider a few factors when using the Outlook client to send e-mails. First, the e-mails are actually going out through Outlook. This happens when the user starts Outlook, and Outlook synchronizes with the CRM Server. If the user prepared several e-mails through the web application and didn't open the Outlook application for a long time (for example, a month), the e-mails won't be sent until the User opens Outlook. This can be a real problem, for obvious reasons.

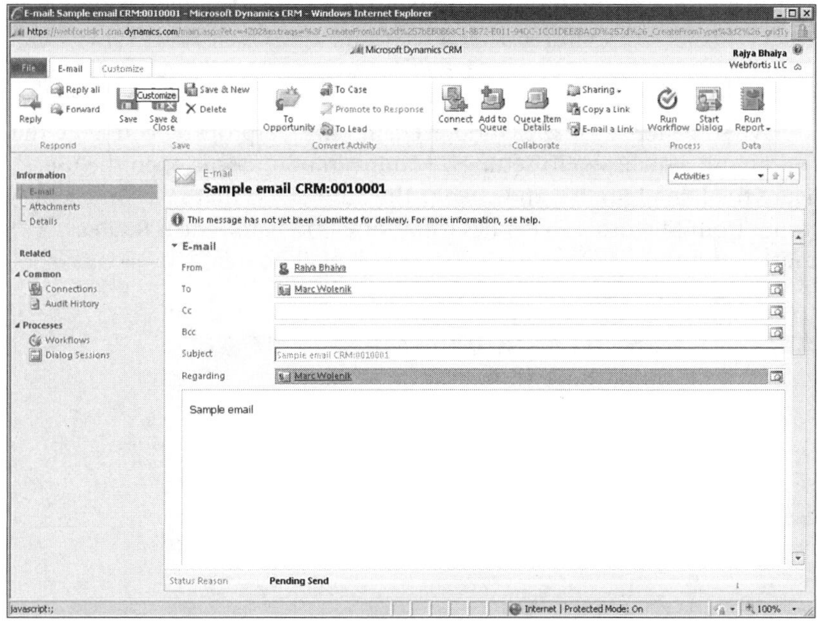

FIGURE 14.3 Warning message alert for undelivered e-mail.

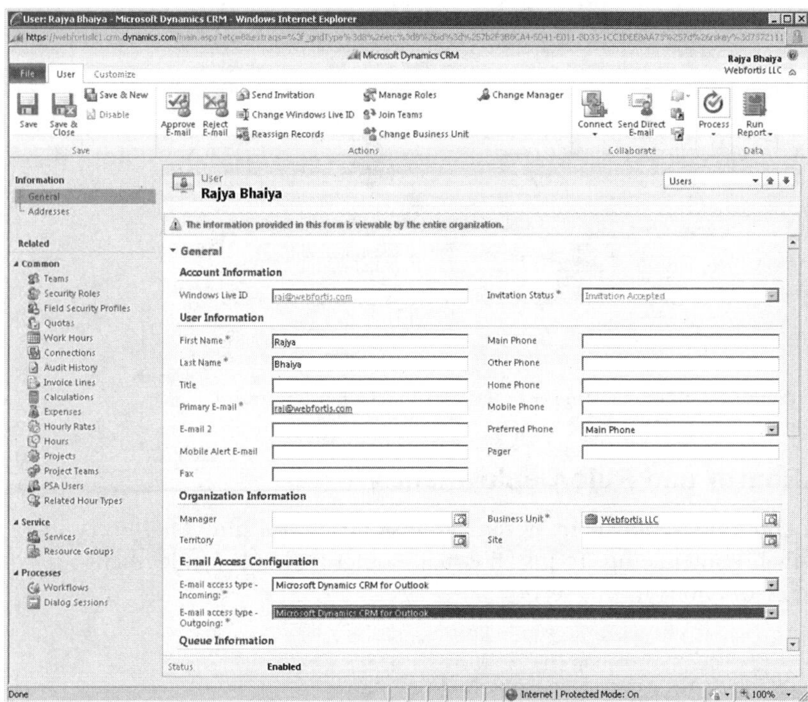

FIGURE 14.4 Outlook client e-mail options.

Using Outlook as the e-mail gateway is the default configuration, and you must consider whether this configuration will work well with your business. If you want to have the e-mails composed through the web application sent out directly (not through Outlook), you must install and configure the CRM E-mail Router as described later in this chapter. Also, you will need to configure each user's preferences to use the E-mail Router, as shown in Figure 14.5. This is something that will have to be configured for every user because you might want to have some users use the Outlook client only. To properly configure the E-mail Router for outbound e-mails, go to Settings, Administration, Users, open the user you want to configure the E-mail Router, and change the drop-down that says E-mail Access type—Outgoing from Microsoft Dynamics CRM for Outlook to E-mail Router. (Remember, you must first install and configure the CRM E-mail Router.)

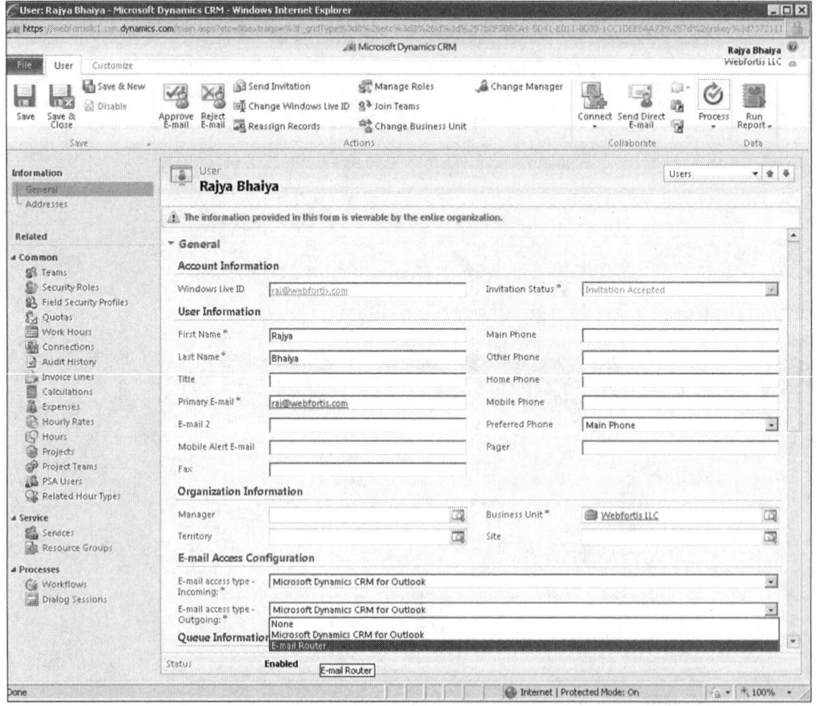

FIGURE 14.5 Configuring outgoing e-mail access type to use E-mail Router.

Install E-mail Router and Rule Deployment Wizard

The E-mail Router and Rule Deployment Wizard are installed by running Microsoft Dynamics CRM E-mail Router Setup. To install E-mail Router and Rule Deployment Wizard, follow the instructions in this section.

To install and configure E-mail Router on a server named WebfortisEX01, follow these steps:

1. Log on to WebfortisEX01 as a Domain User with Local Administrator permissions.
2. Locate the installation files. Navigate to the emailrouter folder, and double-click Setupemailrouter.exe.
3. On the Welcome page, select whether you want to update Microsoft Dynamics CRM Server Setup. It is recommend to download the latest version from the Web. To do this, click Update Installation Files, wait until the update process is complete, and then click Next.

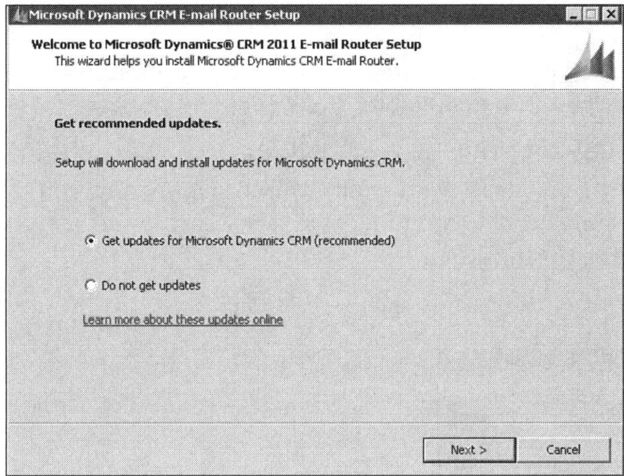

FIGURE 14.6 Get recommended updates.

4. On the License Agreement page, click I Accept.

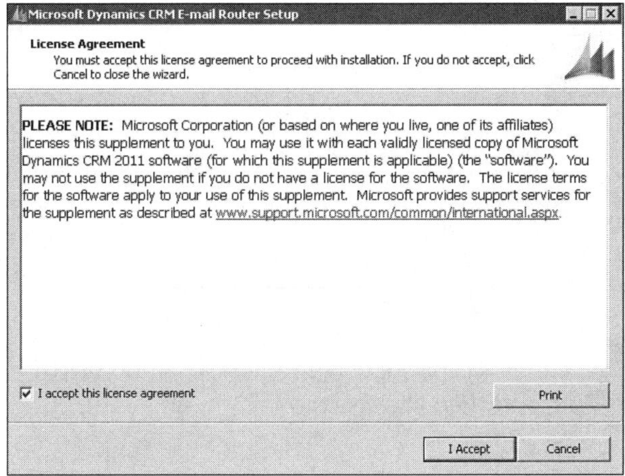

FIGURE 14.7 License Agreement.

5. The Install Required Components page appears.

CAUTION

If you have already installed the required components, this page will not appear.

6. If you have not installed the required components that are listed, you can install them now. Click Install. When the components are installed, the status column will change from Missing to Installed, and you can click Next to continue.
   a. On the Select Router Components page, select either or both options:
      i. **Microsoft Dynamics CRM E-mail Router Service.** This option installs the E-mail Router service and E-mail Router Configuration Manager.
      ii. **Rule Deployment Wizard.** This option installs the Rule Deployment Wizard used to deploy rules for forward mailbox users. Optionally, you can install this wizard on another computer that has access to the Exchange Servers in the organization.

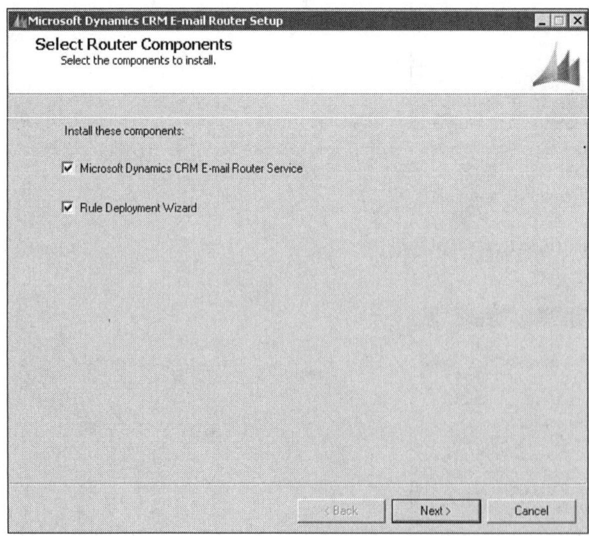

FIGURE 14.8 Select Components.

7. On the Select Install Location page, either accept the default file installation directory or browse for a different location, and then click Next.

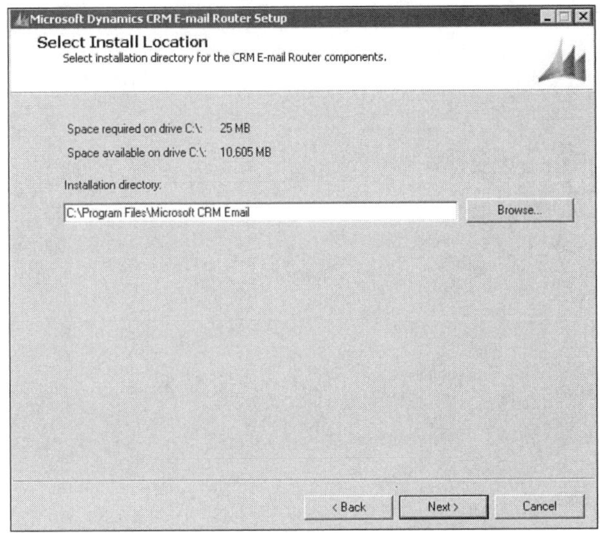

FIGURE 14.9 Select Install Location.

8. The System Requirements page appears. This page is a summary of all system requirements for a successful E-mail Router installation. Failed tests must be corrected before installation can continue. If there is a problem that will take time to correct, cancel Setup at this point, fix the problem, and restart Setup. When all tests are successful, click Next.

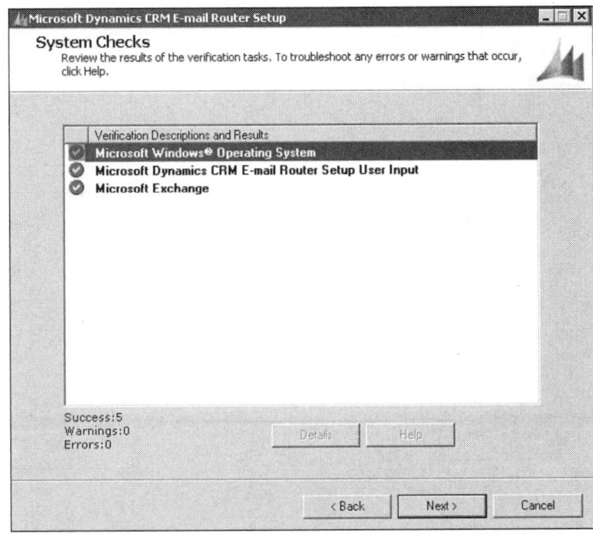

FIGURE 14.10 System Checks.

9. The Ready to Install the Application page appears. Click Install.

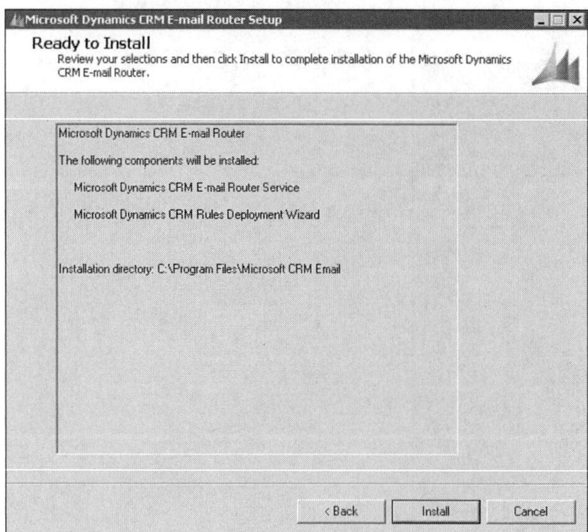

FIGURE 14.11 Ready to Install.

10. After E-mail Router Setup is finished installing files, click OK.

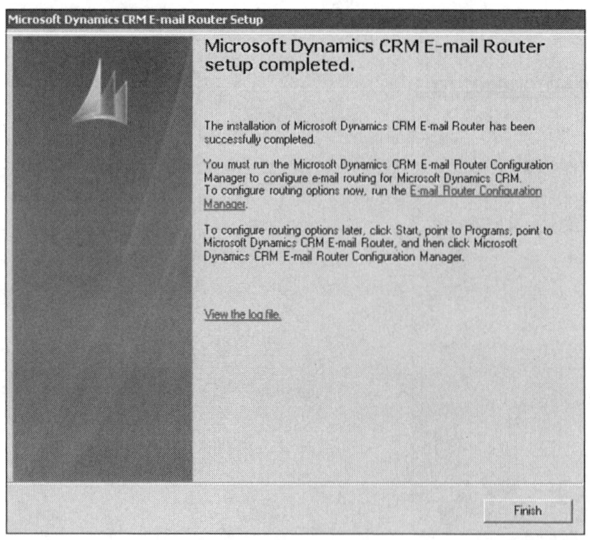

FIGURE 14.12 Installation Result.

NOTE

By default, Microsoft Dynamics CRM users are set with both the incoming e-mail server type and the outgoing e-mail server type of Microsoft Dynamics CRM for Outlook. For web application users, you must change the incoming type to E-mail Router or Forward Mailbox, and the outgoing type to E-mail Router for each user.

Install E-mail Router on Multiple Computers

You can now deploy and run the Microsoft Dynamics CRM E-mail Router on multiple computers in a Microsoft cluster to provide high availability and failover functionality. In Windows Server 2008 it is known as *failover clustering*. Both of these server clustering technologies are supported with the E-mail Router. Establish the cluster using standard windows standard practices.

CAUTION

The E-mail Router will only support an active/passive cluster deployment, and it does not support an active/active cluster deployment.

Install the E-mail Router to the Active Primary Node in the Cluster

1. Run E-mail Router Setup on the active primary node in the cluster.

TIP

You do not have to install the E-mail Router on a computer that is running Microsoft Exchange Server. Therefore, it is recommended installing the E-mail Router as the only application on a cluster.

2. First, open the E-mail Router Configuration Manager on the first node, and configure the E-mail Router. Verify that the E-mail Router is routing messages correctly to and from the Microsoft Dynamics CRM and e-mail systems.
3. Copy all E-mail Router application files to the common storage or shared hard disk. By default, the files are located at *Drive*:\Program Files\Microsoft CRM Email.
4. The following files must be located on the common storage or shared disk so that they can be moved to the secondary node in the event of a failover.
   a. Microsoft.Crm.Tools.EmailAgent.Configuration.bin
   b. Microsoft.Crm.Tools.EmailAgent.SystemState.xml
   c. Microsoft.Crm.Tools.EmailAgent.xml
   d. Microsoft.Crm.Tools.Email.Management.config
   e. EncryptionKey.xml (if encryption is enabled)

5. Update the following Windows Registry settings to allow the E-mail Router to use the shared disks.
6. HKEY_LOCAL_MACHINE\SYSTEM\CurrentControlSet\Services\MSCRMEmail
7. Change the ImagePath value to point to the shared disk drive where the E-mail Router files.

TIP

You will need to restart the Microsoft CRM Email Router service for these changes to take effect.

CAUTION

The E-mail Router files should be manually secured on the common storage or shared disk. We recommend that you grant full control only to the service account running the E-mail Router service ("Microsoft CRM E-mail Router") and to those administrators who might have to update configuration files manually.

Install the E-mail Router to the Passive Node in the Cluster

1. Run E-mail Router Setup on the second node in the cluster.
2. Update the following Windows registry settings to allow the E-mail Router to use the shared disks.
3. HKEY_LOCAL_MACHINE\SYSTEM\CurrentControlSet\Services\MSCRMEmail

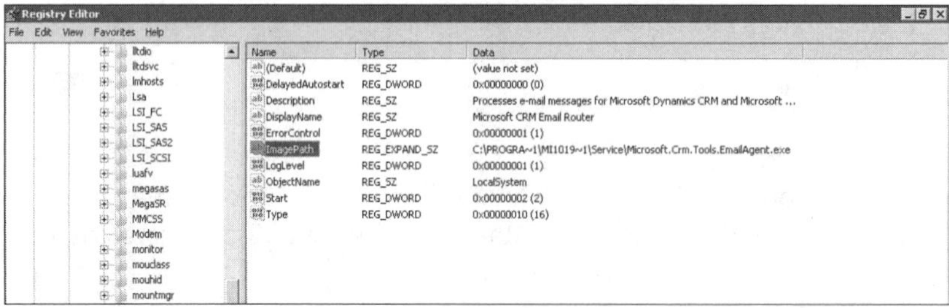

FIGURE 14.13 ImagePath in Registry.

4. Change the ImagePath value to point to the shared disk drive where the E-mail Router files.

TIP

You will need to restart the Microsoft CRM E-mail Router service for these changes to take effect.

Do not run E-mail Router Configuration Manager, and do not copy the files to the shared hard disks. Because the configuration files are placed on the shared disks, they are automatically available on the passive server.

Create the Generic Resource Service to Manage the MSCRM E-mail Router Service on the Cluster

1. On each node in the cluster, set the Microsoft CRM Email Router Service to manually start on Windows start.
2. Ensure that each of the nodes is a member of the PrivUserGroup {GUID} in Active Directory.
3. In the Failover Cluster Management, create a generic resource service with the following parameters:
    - **Name**—Create a descriptive name for the generic resource service, such as MSCRM E-mail Router.
    - **Resource type**—Generic Service.
    - **Group**—Cluster Group.
    - **Possible owners**—Add all nodes in the cluster.
    - **Dependencies**—If you are using Exchange Server and you have installed the E-mail Router on the Exchange Server (not recommended), add Microsoft Exchange Information Store. Otherwise leave just enter the network name registration in DNS.
    - **Service Name**—Microsoft CRM Email Router.
    - **Start Parameters**—Leave blank.
    - **Use Network Name for computer Name**—Leave unchecked.
    - Do not checkpoint any Registry keys.
4. Bring the resource online. If it is necessary, configure the resource properties such as the failover policies.

Verify and Monitor the Cluster

Open Cluster Management and force a failover. Please ensure that you see the services stop on node 1 and failover to note 2.

E-mail Router Configuration Manager and Configuration Profiles

The E-mail Router Configuration Manager is a tool that enables you to configure the E-mail Router. This is typically installed on the server running E-mail Router. All configurations are saved in the Microsoft.Crm.tools.EmailAgent.xml file.

You must configure at least one incoming e-mail profile and one outgoing e-mail profile to enable the E-mail Router to route e-mail to and from of your Microsoft Dynamics CRM organization. Depending on the complexity of your organization's e-mail system, you might have to create multiple incoming and outgoing configuration profiles. For example, if your organization requires incoming E-mail Router services for multiple e-mail servers, you will have to create one incoming configuration profile for each e-mail server.

CAUTION

A single instance of E-mail Router that has a variety of e-mail profiles is not a certified configuration. For example, do not configure the same instance of E-mail Router to retrieve e-mail from an on-premise Exchange Server and Exchange Online.

Authentication Types

Authentication for the E-mail Router is required for the connections to the e-mail system and the users' mailbox for each incoming and outgoing e-mail profile.

Exchange Server supports only Windows Authentication for the incoming profiles. Exchange online supports Clear Text Authentication.

For POP3-compliant servers, incoming profiles can use NTLM or Clear Text authentication.

NOTE

Clear Text authentication transmits unencrypted user names and passwords. If you use Clear Text authentication, we recommend that you do this only with Secure Sockets Layer (SSL). The Use SSL option should be selected and the Network Port field (on the Advanced tab) must be set to a value appropriate for your environment. Verify your POP3 server requirements with your e-mail administrator.

Outgoing (SMTP) profiles support Windows Authentication, Exchange online, Clear Text, and Anonymous authentication types.

TIP

Anonymous SMTP is only valid for internal, non-Internet-facing SMTP servers. Many SMTP servers do not support anonymous authentication. To ensure uninterrupted e-mail flow from the E-mail Router, verify your SMTP server requirements with your e-mail administrator.

Access Credentials

Depending on how you set the other configuration profile options, the following options are available for specifying the username and password that the E-mail Router will use to access each mailbox the profile serves.

CAUTION

If you use access credentials that are valid for the e-mail server but not for a particular mailbox, a 401 Access Denied error will be generated when you test access.

Incoming profiles support the following access credentials:

- **Local system account**—This option requires a machine trust between the computer where the E-mail Router is running and the computer where the Exchange Server is running. The E-mail Router must be included in the PrivUserGroup security group. For incoming profiles, this option is available only for Exchange Server (not for other POP3-compliant e-mail servers).
- **User specified**—This option requires that each user enter their username and password in the Set Personal Options dialog box (available in the Options under the File menu of the Microsoft Dynamics CRM Web client). This enables the E-mail Router to monitor mailboxes by using each user's access credentials. When users change their domain password (for example, when it expires), they must update their password in Microsoft Dynamics CRM so that the E-mail Router can continue to monitor their mailbox. This option is available only in the On-Premise version of the product.
- **Other specified**—This option enables the administrator to configure the E-mail Router to connect to user mailboxes as a specified user. The specified user must have full access to all the mailboxes that the incoming profile will serve.

Outgoing profiles support the following access credentials:

- **Local system account**—This option requires a machine trust between the computer where the E-mail Router is running and the computer where Exchange Server is running. The E-mail Router must be included in the PrivUserGroup. For more information, see the Microsoft Dynamics CRM Installing Guide. For outgoing profiles, this is the only option available if you select the Anonymous authentication type.
- **Other specified**—This option enables the administrator to configure the E-mail Router to send e-mail messages on each user's behalf by using the access credentials of a specified user account that has full access to all the mailboxes that the outgoing profile will serve.

Configuring E-mail Routing for Multiple Configurations and Deployments

You can add or edit an E-mail Router configuration, which contains a single incoming and outgoing method that routes e-mail to the e-mail server. In the configuration, you must specify the following components:

- A name for display and reference
- Whether the configuration is incoming or outgoing
- The e-mail transport type, such as Exchange or Exchange online or POP3 for incoming, and SMTP for outgoing

In addition, you can add or edit E-mail Router deployments. An E-mail Router deployment contains a URL to a Microsoft Dynamics CRM Server computer, one incoming configuration, and one outgoing configuration. In an E-mail Router deployment object, you specify the following components:

- A name for display and reference (required)
- A URL to the Microsoft Dynamics CRM Server computer (required)
- A default incoming configuration (optional)
- A default outgoing configuration (optional)

Configuring the CRM E-mail Router

If you are using your local SMTP server, configure the relay restrictions property and have the reverse DNS records set for the server IP address. Also be sure that the domain is configured properly to avoid being blacklisted for spam.

You can also use Exchange online to send emails.

Creating the Incoming Profile

To create another profile for the incoming e-mail, select New, located on the right of the application. Figure 14.14 shows a new profile using Microsoft Exchange Server.

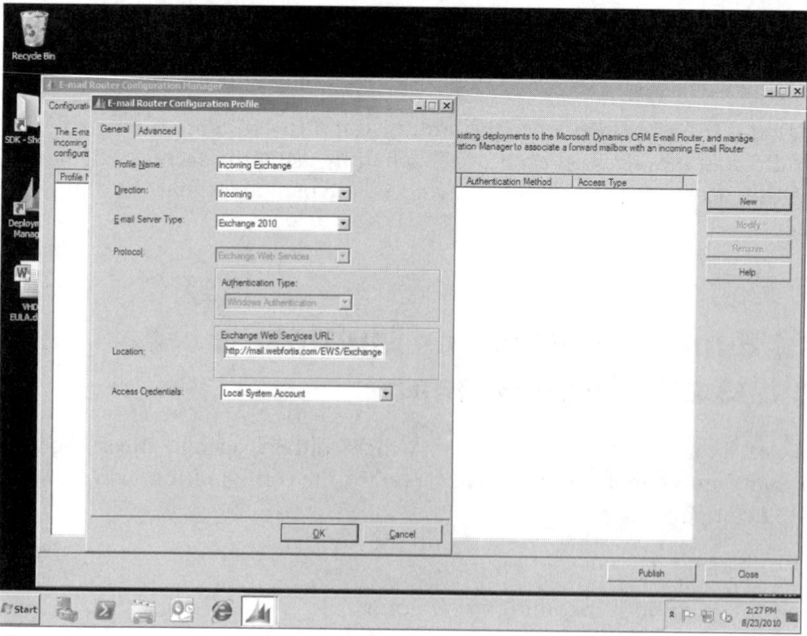

FIGURE 14.14 Configuring incoming profile for Exchange.

You also have the option to use the POP3 protocol for incoming e-mails if you don't use Microsoft Exchange Server (see Figure 14.15).

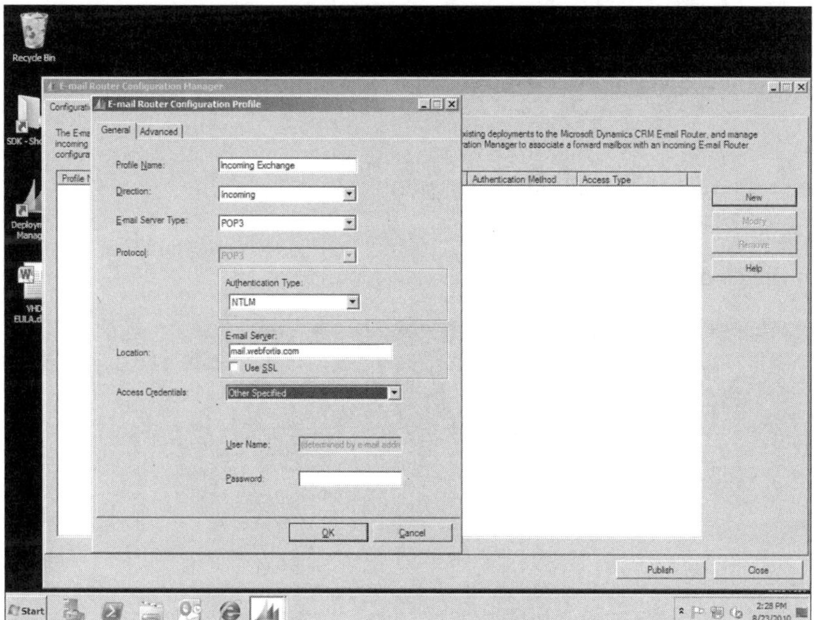

FIGURE 14.15 Configuring incoming profile for POP3 protocol.

NOTE

If you want to use the POP3 protocol with Microsoft Exchange 2007/2010, be aware that this service is disabled by default on Microsoft Exchange 2007/2010. To enable it, go to Services (inside the Administrative tools in the Control Panel) and double-click the service with the name Microsoft Exchange POP3 to open the settings. Change the startup type to Automatic, click the Apply button, and then click the Start button.

CAUTION

Because Exchange 2007 and 2010 will not allow you to use POP3 for the administrator account, you need to create a separate account for using the POP3 accounts.

The Server field under the Location area must be a valid URL with http:// or https:// for the Microsoft Exchange option or a valid address without the protocol for the POP3 option.

The authentication type supported for Exchange can only be Windows Authentication.

The authentication types supported for POP3 are NTLM and Clear Text. If you are going to use the latter, it is recommended you use SSL to secure the user's credentials over the network. For the credentials, you have the option to have the user specify one (discussed in the next section "Deployments") or enter a fixed username and password when creating the incoming profile.

To test the POP3 or exchange info, you need to create an incoming profile. You can use the Microsoft Outlook application and create an account manually to be sure you have the right connection and credential information.

Deployments

First configure the profiles for the email transport options:

1. Open Email Router Configuration Manager.
2. Click New in the Configuration Profiles tab.

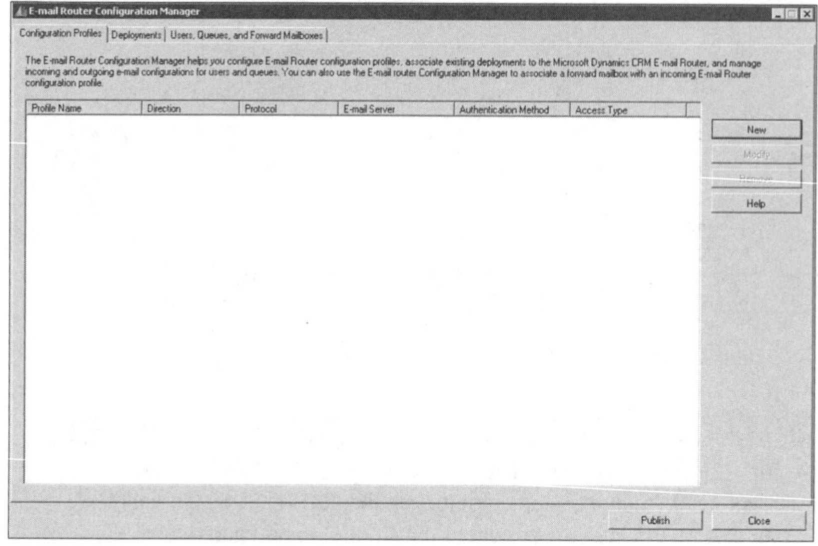

FIGURE 14.16 E-mail Router Configuration Manager

3. Create a profile for Incoming with the following values:
   a. Profile name: Incoming
   b. E-mail Server Type: Exchange 2010
   c. Location: Use Autodiscovr
   d. Access Credentials: Local System Account
4. Click OK.
5. Create a profile for Outgoing with the following values:
   a. Profile name: Outgoing
   b. E-mail Server Type: SMTP
   c. Authentication: Windows Authentication
   d. Location: mail.webfortis.com
   e. Access Credentials: Local System Account
6. Click Publish

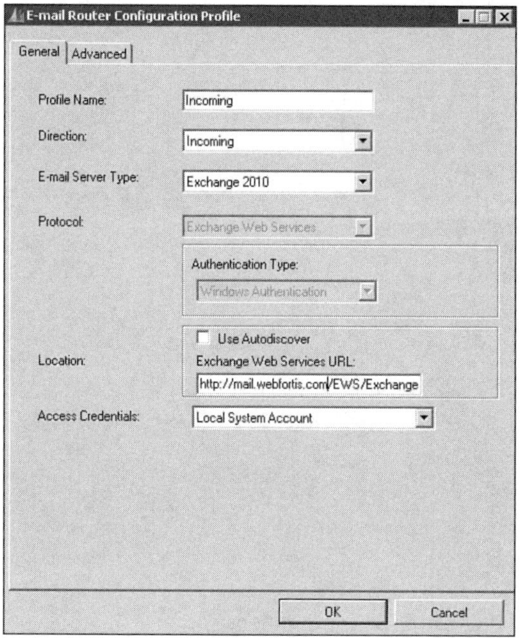

FIGURE 14.17 Incoming Profile.

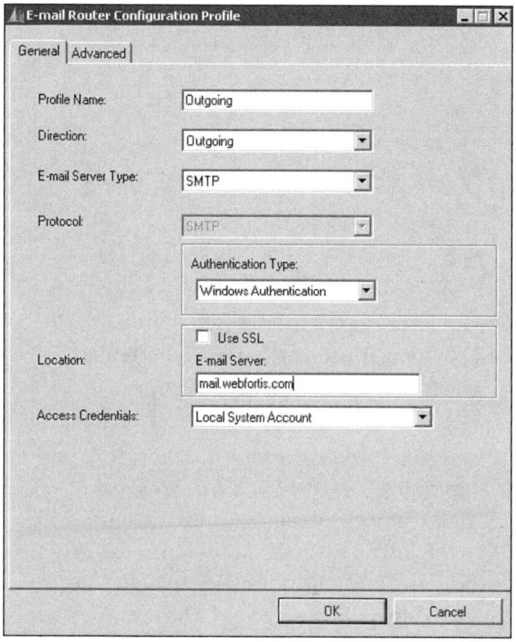

FIGURE 14.18 Outgoing Profile.

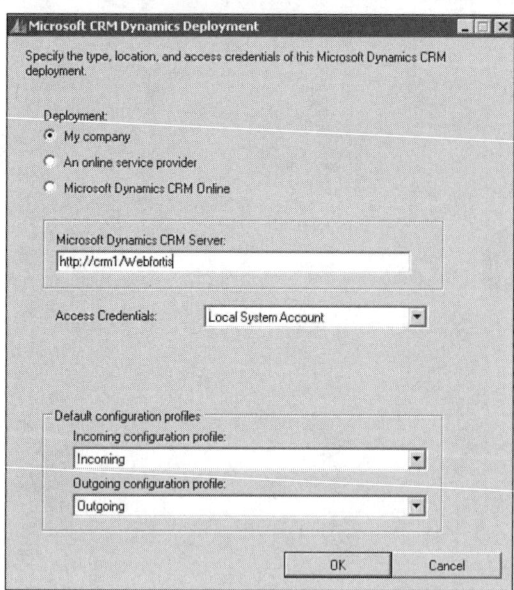

FIGURE 14.19 Configuring deployment for On-Premise CRM organizations.

After configuring the profiles, you need to create and set up a deployment where you want to use and apply the profiles. Notice you will be able to set the profiles for each user after configuring the deployment in the next section, "Users, Queues, and Forward Mailboxes."

You can configure two types of deployments:

- My Company
- An online service provider
- Microsoft Dynamics CRM Online

The first option, My Company, is used with On-Premise deployments (see Figure 14.19). The second option, which is an Online Service Provider, is used when IFD is enabled.

▶ For more information about IFD, see Chapter 22, "Forms Authentication."

Enter the appropriate values for the Microsoft Dynamics CRM Server (http://<server-name>/<organization>). Enter the access credentials and select the default configuration profiles. In this case, we selected our newly created profiles of INCOMING and OUTGOING, created in the previous section. The incoming and outgoing profiles selected here will be the default options for the users and queues, but you can change these values for each user in the following section, if desired.

User, Queues, and Forward Mailboxes

Select the deployment from the top drop-down list, and click Load Data to see the Users and Queues tab, as shown in Figure 14.20.

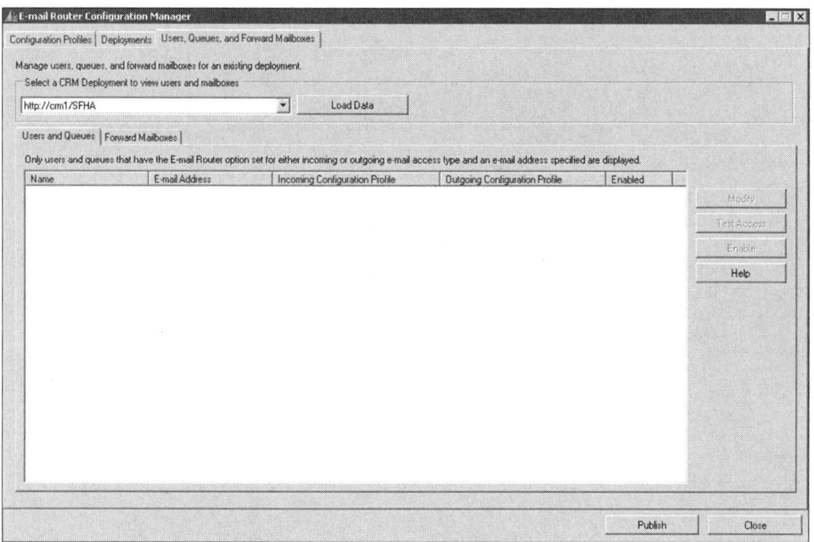

FIGURE 14.20 Users and queues.

NOTE

Only the users and queues configured to use the E-mail Router are shown here.

Forward Mailboxes

Forward mailboxes are used to process incoming e-mails, and they require a dedicated mailbox to receive and forward them. There are a couple of reasons why you might want to use them. Primarily, you can use a single set of credentials for a single mailbox; however, there is a benefit in polling (only one mailbox is polled) as well as using taking advantage of Exchange forwarding rules.

Forward mailboxes functionality to process incoming e-mails without using Microsoft Outlook. This option works only with Microsoft Exchange Server, and it requires having a dedicated mailbox to process the incoming e-mails. The users or queues that want to use this option must have some rules deployed that you can create using the Rule Deployment Wizard, described later in this chapter.

The E-mail Router Configuration Manager Forward Mailboxes configuration is shown in Figure 14.21.

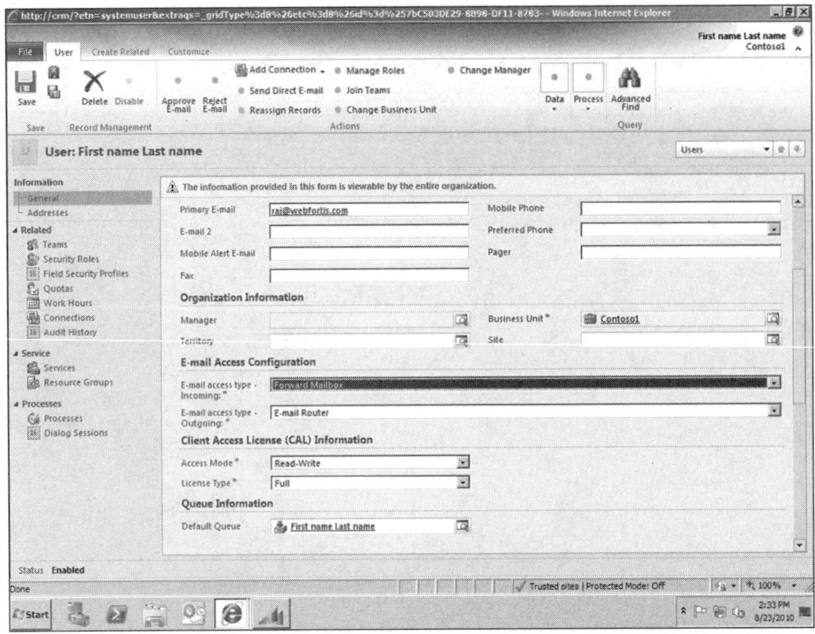

FIGURE 14.21 Forward mailboxes.

The e-mail is first received by the User's mailbox and then is forwarded to the Router mailbox.

NOTE

Many users can forward their e-mails to the same router mailbox.

The CRM E-mail Router Service polls the Router mailbox looking for incoming messages. When it finds an e-mail, it inserts that e-mail into CRM as a new E-mail activity for the user or queue that forwarded the e-mail. The e-mail is then deleted from the Router mailbox, depending on the configurations.

Microsoft recommends this technique if you are using Microsoft Exchange Server as your primary e-mail server. However, you don't actually need to set up a forward mailbox to receive e-mails. The incoming profile configured to use Exchange will be sufficient in most cases.

The outgoing e-mails are processed asynchronously, and the default polling is scheduled for every 1,000 seconds (about 15 minutes), so you must wait that time before the e-mails are actually sent.

TIP

To increase the speed at which outgoing e-mails are sent, you can edit the configuration file Microsoft.Crm.Tools.EmailAgent.xml (which is usually located at C:\Program Files\Microsoft CRM Email\Service) and find the SchedulingPeriod element. We recommend changing its default value to 10 seconds.

Tracking Incoming E-mails

You can track incoming e-mails in two ways:

- By using the CRM tracking token
- Through message filtering and correlation

The tokens work by appending a code in the subject of the e-mail with a form similar to CRM:0001006.

▶ To learn more about how to configure this in the system options, see Chapter 12, “Settings and Configuration.”

The filtering and correlation to track incoming e-mails involves a method that doesn’t require appending data on the e-mail’s subject line. Instead, it uses an intelligent way to figure the thread of the e-mail using the e-mail’s sender, the e-mail’s recipient, the e-mail subject, and any CC. This method is not 100% effective, but you can use it if you don’t want the CRM tracking tokens to alter the e-mails.

TIP

By default, only incoming e-mails that are received as a response to an e-mail sent from Dynamics CRM are tracked. If you want CRM to track all incoming e-mails, you must change your personal settings from the web application by going to File, Options, and then going to the E-mail tab.

You can select to track all e-mails, the e-mails that are responses to CRM e-mails, or the e-mail messages from CRM Leads, Contacts, and Accounts.

NOTE

The option that says Allow E-mail Router to Use My Credentials to Send and Receive E-mail on My Behalf is available only if your user is configured to receive or send e-mails through the CRM E-mail Router.

You can see all the incoming e-mails CRM tracks by going to Workplace, Activities, and then changing the type drop-down from All to E-mail.

One of the most common issues related to received e-mails is that the From e-mail address sometimes can't be mapped properly. This is shown with an alert red icon with a question mark on it (see Figure 14.22).

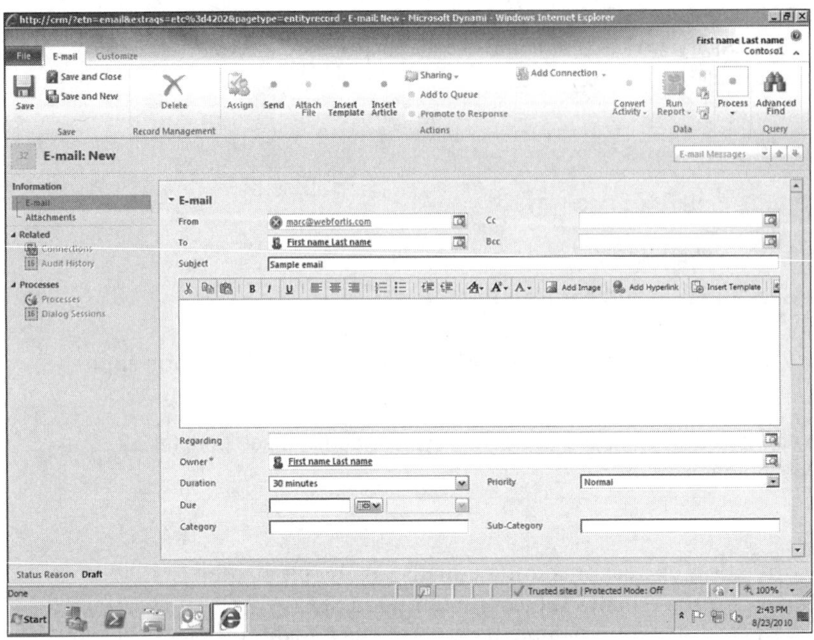

FIGURE 14.22 E-mail with an unmapped From address.

This can happen for two reasons: Either the e-mail address doesn't match any existing e-mail address on any Lead, Contact, User, or Account record in the system organization, or more than one system record exists with the same e-mail address and CRM doesn't know which one it should be mapped to. In either case, the user must map the e-mail address manually by opening the e-mail and clicking the red e-mail address. The dialog box shown in Figure 14.23 illustrates how to allow the user to resolve the issue by selecting an existing record or by creating a new one.

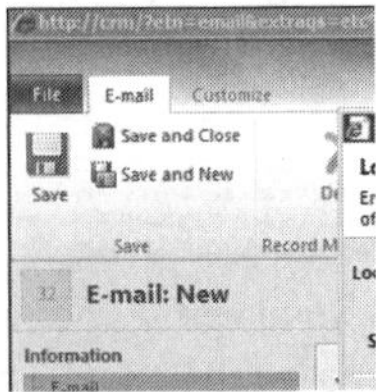

FIGURE 14.23 Resolving unmapped addresses.

Queues

Queues are primarily used for general incoming e-mails that are not related to a specific user. A common example is to use a queue to receive e-mails sent to your organization for queries related to general information, support, or customer support. In these cases, you could create queues with related e-mail addresses similar to info@yourdomain.com, support@yourdomain.com, and customerservice@yourdomain.com, for example.

To track the e-mails using these addresses, you must first create a queue by going to the Settings area, and then going to the Business Management option and selecting Queues.

Select New to create a new queue, and then set the e-mail options accordingly (see Figure 14.24).

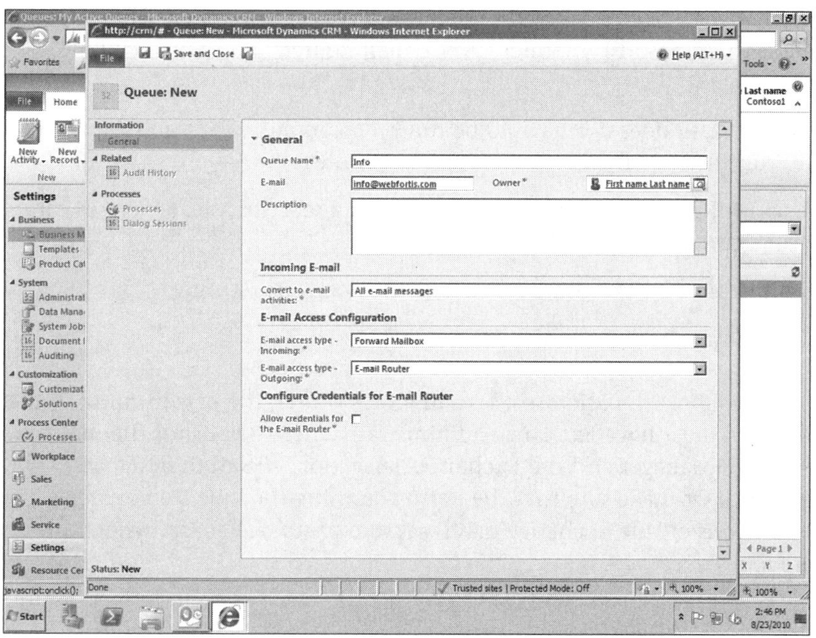

FIGURE 14.24 Creating a new queue for Info.

Rule Deployment Wizard

The Rule Deployment Wizard is used for the users or queues configured as forward mailboxes because they need server rules installed on Microsoft Exchange to forward e-mails to the Router mailbox. This rule sends a copy of each message received by a Microsoft Dynamics CRM user to the Microsoft Dynamics CRM system mailbox. From the Microsoft Dynamics CRM system mailbox, the E-mail Router retrieves the messages and creates an e-mail activity in Microsoft Dynamics CRM.

To deploy these Microsoft Dynamics CRM user inbox rules, you can use the Rule Deployment Wizard, which can be run at any time to add or change the inbox rules for your Microsoft Dynamics CRM users.

CAUTION

The Rule Deployment Wizard can only deploy rules to Exchange Server mailboxes. You cannot deploy rules by using the Rule Deployment Wizard with POP3 e-mail servers or Exchange Online. This also requires Owner access on the users' mailboxes.

If you selected to install this wizard as part of the E-mail Router installation, you can access this wizard by doing the following:

On the computer where you have installed the Rule Deployment Wizard, click Start, point to All Programs, point to Microsoft Dynamics CRM E-mail Router, and then click Rule Deployment Wizard.

The Rule Deployment Wizard does not have to be run on a computer with an instance of Exchange Server. To run the Rule Deployment Wizard, you must

- Be logged on as a Microsoft Dynamics CRM user with a security role. (The user can be in restricted access mode.)
- Be a local administrator on the computer where the wizard is running.
- Have Exchange administrative permissions.

To deploy rules to the mailbox of a Microsoft Dynamics CRM user, the person running the Rule Deployment Wizard must have Exchange administrative permissions for the mailbox. Use the Exchange System Manager and the Exchange delegation Wizard to designate Exchange Administrators. Or make sure that the person running the Rule Deployment Wizard has full permissions on the Exchange mailbox store or storage group, where the users' mailboxes are located.

Create the Rule Manually

For POP3 e-mail servers that support e-mail system rules where an e-mail message can be forwarded as an attachment, you can create the rule manually.

1. Open Outlook.
2. If you are working with Outlook 2007, on the Tools menu, click Rules and Alerts. When working with Outlook 2010, click Rules on the Ribbon.
3. On the E-mail Rules tab, click New Rule.
4. Select the Start from a Blank Rule option, make sure Check Messages When They Arrive is selected, and then click Next.
5. Select where my name is in the To or Cc box, and then click Next.

6. Select forward it to people or distribution list as an attachment, and then in the Step 2: Edit the rule description (click an underlined value) area, click people or distribution list.
7. Select the name of your E-mail Router forward mailbox, and then click OK.
8. Click Next two times.
9. Make sure that the Turn on This Rule option is selected, and then click Finish.
10. Make sure that the rule is at the top of the list, and then click Apply.

NOTE

For Exchange Online, you can create the rule manually (as described earlier) or by using Outlook Web Access.

Summary

This chapter described how Microsoft CRM processes incoming and outgoing e-mails and covered available options for sending and receiving e-mails that will be tracked as activities in Dynamics CRM. It also described the different system configuration options to track the incoming e-mails by reviewing the E-mail Router Service, Microsoft Outlook Client, and forward mailbox e-mail configuration and their deployment rules.

CHAPTER 15
Mobility

IN THIS CHAPTER

- Mobility Defined
- CWR Mobility
- Other Mobility Options

Mobility Defined

Mobility is becoming increasingly important for today's business users. Users expect to have access to their customer, sales, and marketing data anytime, anywhere. With the rise of smartphones and mobile devices such as the iPhone, BlackBerry, Android, Windows Phone, and also tablets such as the iPad that can access their banking information, home security network status, and even their favorite shows, Microsoft Dynamics CRM data is now available to users across these platforms.

NOTE

Although the full Microsoft Dynamics CRM is only available via the Outlook or Internet Client, a very rich and functional mobile client is available out-of-the-box (for both CRM Online and CRM On Premise) at no additional cost.

Mobile Express

CRM 2011 recognizes the need for mobile access across different devices by providing a mobile web client that runs on mobile browsers (as well as regular browsers) that support HTML 4, called Mobile Express for Dynamics CRM. Mobile Express is free and supported by Microsoft.

It is available by accessing your default instance of CRM, with a /m at the end of your URL.

For example, if you are using https://webfortis.crm.dynamics.com, simply enter the same URL, with /m at the end (https://webfortis.crm.dynamics.com/m) and you will see the mobile client, even on a regular web browser (see Figure 15.1). Figure 15.2 shows the same client rendered on an iPhone.

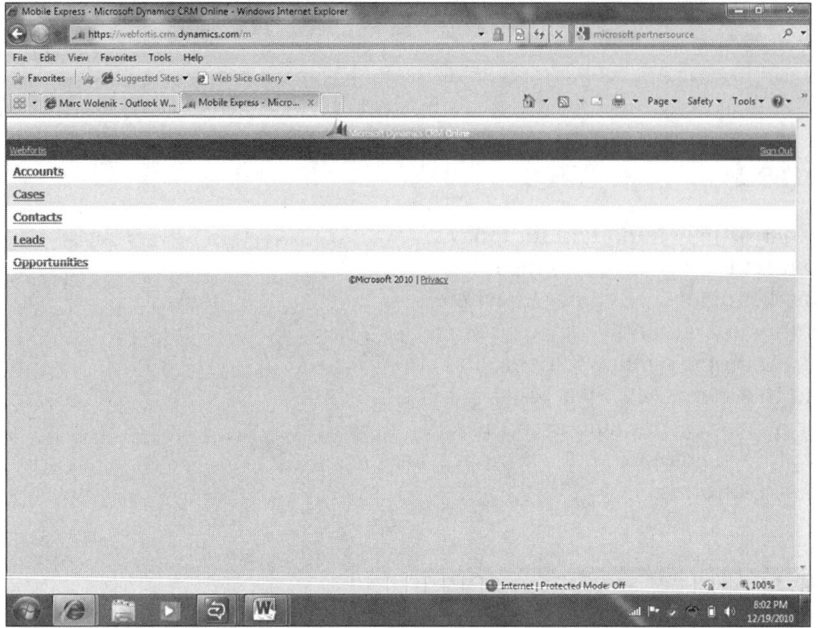

FIGURE 15.1 Screenshot of the mobility feature provided out of the box by Microsoft CRM Online on a regular web browser.

NOTE

A nice feature is that is also available is the redirection of the application to the mobile application when on an unsupported browser (that is, other than Internet Explorer).

Mobile Express is a web client, which means that you need to be online to use it, preferably using a fast Internet connection. So, generally, Mobile Express is sufficient when you want online-only, occasional access to your CRM data. The major upside to Mobile Express is its price—it is free.

Unlike in previous versions of Microsoft Dynamics CRM, almost every entity (including custom ones) have mobile forms available. Table 15.1 represents the available functionality of Mobile Express.

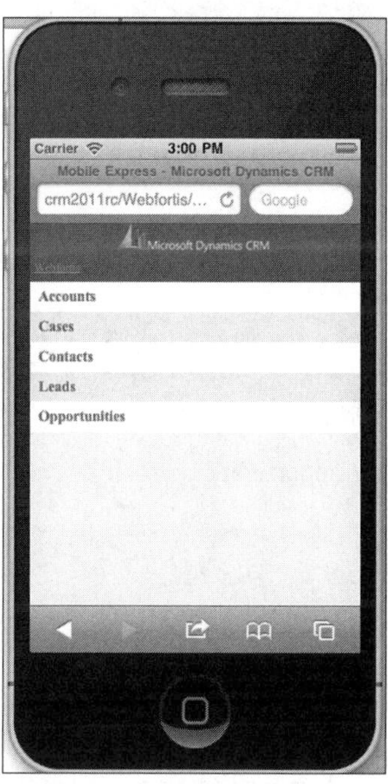

FIGURE 15.2 Screenshot of the mobility feature provided out of the box by Microsoft CRM Online on an iPhone.

TABLE 15.1 Mobile Express Functionality

Entity/Feature	Function
Accounts	Enter a new account or review an existing account, which contains information about companies that do business with your organization.
Addresses	Enter a new address or look up information for an existing account or contact.
Appointments	Review existing appointments. An appointment does not include service activities or check for conflicts, and you cannot search for available times.
Campaigns	Review existing campaigns.
Cases	Review existing cases.
Competitors	Review existing competitors.
Contacts	Enter a new contact or review an existing contact.
Contracts	Review existing contracts.
E-mail Messages	Review sent, received, and pending e-mail messages.
Faxes	Review faxes that have been entered into the system.

TABLE 15.1 Mobile Express Functionality

Entity/Feature	Function
Invoice Products	Review products associated with an invoice.
Invoices	Review existing invoices.
Leads	Enter a new lead or review existing leads.
Letters	Track when a letter has been sent or received.
Marketing Lists	Review existing marketing lists.
Notes	Add a new note to an activity or a record, or review an existing note.
Opportunities	Enter a new opportunity or review an existing opportunity.
Order Products	Review products associated with an order.
Orders	Review existing orders.
Phone Calls	Track when phone calls have been received or made. You cannot dial a phone number directly from this form.
Quote Products	Review products associated with a quote.
Quotes	Review existing quotes for opportunities, accounts, or contacts.
Service Activities	Review service activities.
Tasks	Create a new task or review an existing task.
Users	Review or search for people who have an active user account in Microsoft Dynamics CRM.
Local Data/Synchronization	Unavailable.
Internet Connection	Required.

Configuration of the client is very easy as well. To do so, follow these steps:

1. Navigate to Settings, Customizations, Customize the System.
2. Select the entity you want to work with and expand the view. Select Forms.

   You will see two forms here—notice the form type—one is for the Main application form, and the other is the Mobile form. Select the Mobile form to modify.
3. The attributes can be moved to a form by easily selecting them individually or all, as shown in Figure 15.4.

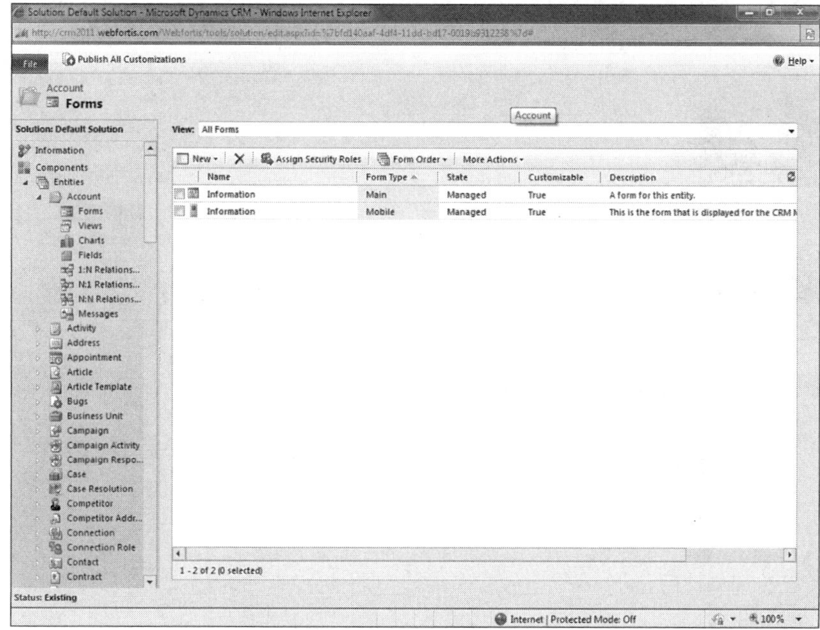

FIGURE 15.3 Mobile forms customization.

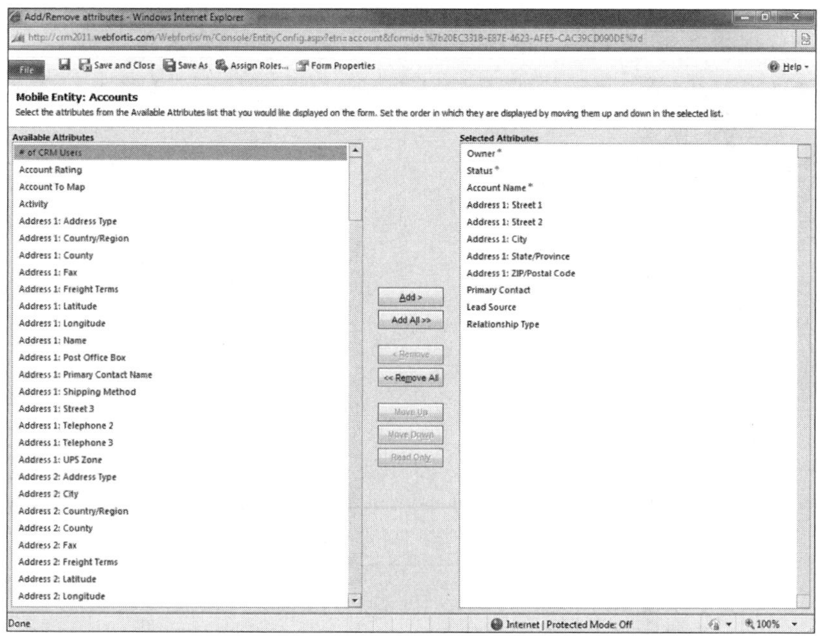

FIGURE 15.4 Mobile forms customization—adding attributes.

Figure 15.5 shows the mobile interface with a selected record, and Figure 15.6 shows the mobile interface in record edit mode.

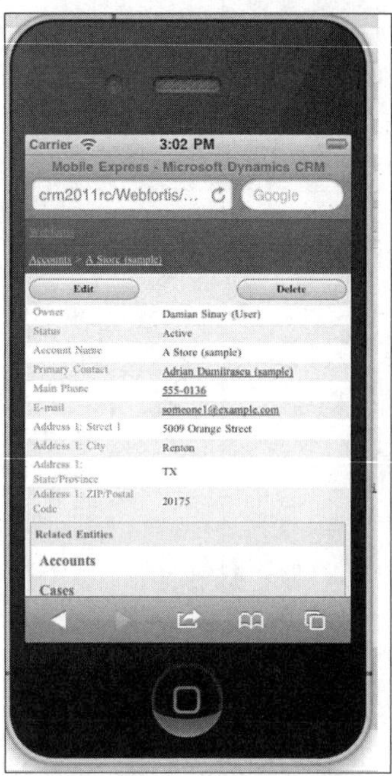

FIGURE 15.5 Mobile form record view.

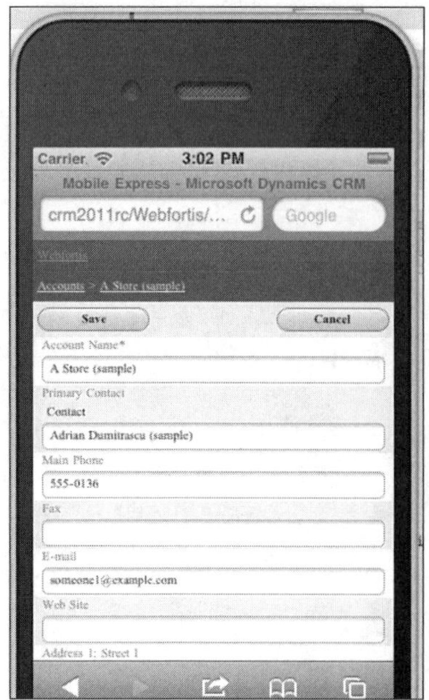

FIGURE 15.6 Mobile forms record edit view.

NOTE

Although initially planned for release, there is no out-of-the-box functionality for mobile form customization other than the attribute options shown previously.

However, despite its price, there are several scenarios where you need more than Mobile Express. An example might include when mobile access to CRM data is business-critical; you can't rely on an online-only web client. Users need to be able to access their data no matter whether or not there's network connectivity. In cases like this, an offline client is necessary and required.

CWR Mobility

Although Mobile Express is most suitable for the occasional user in an online environment that needs limited functionality, if you want to experience the full power of Dynamics CRM in the palm of your hand, your best option is an "occasionally connected" native rich client with comprehensive support of Dynamics CRM functionality.

CWR Mobility BV offers a mobile solution that addresses all the shortcomings of Mobile Express, and is available for virtually every mobile client on the market. CWR Mobility is a Microsoft Gold Certified Partner and winner of the 2011 Partner of the Year for Mobility Business-to-Business Application award and 2010 Partner of the Year for Mobility Solutions Business Application award.

CWR Mobility has a long history of working with Microsoft and with Dynamics CRM. CWR Mobile CRM launched in 2005 with version 1.0 for Dynamics CRM 3.0 on the Windows Mobile platform. It was followed by successive versions, including version 4.2 in January 2010, that added support for the Apple iPhone, RIM BlackBerry, and Microsoft Windows Mobile 6.5 device platforms, as well as an online-only web client that works on most mobile browsers, called CWR Mobile CRM Express. Following that, CWR Mobility released a client for the Apple iPad platform.

The most recent version CWR Mobile CRM 2011 was released in May, 2011. The CWR Mobile CRM 2011 architecture supports the new CRM 2011 features such as connections, custom activity types, and team ownership, among others. In addition, it provides new end user features such as dashboards, mapping, and navigation.

CWR Mobile CRM 2011 delivers extensive functionality leveraging all the power and flexibility of Microsoft Dynamics CRM 2011 and enabling that functionality across all mobile platforms.

Usage

The following represents how the CWR Mobility solution can be used:

- CWR Mobile Configurator is integrated into Dynamics CRM. No need for the CRM Admin to leave his familiar environment.
- All users of Dynamics CRM will immediately recognize their CRM on whichever device they have, and it will also mirror the experiences they are used to on their

mobile devices. So, iPad users will immediately recognize it as Dynamics CRM, but rendered within the native Apple iPad user interface. Similarly, users of Apple iPhone/iPad RIM BlackBerry or Windows Phone will also immediately recognize their CRM rendered within the native user interface of their mobile device.

- CWR Mobile CRM leverages the point-and-click customization model and tools for Dynamics CRM and extends them by seamlessly translating form and database changes on the server to the mobile clients. By leveraging a single development effort, customers can now mobilize their entire application.
- CWR Mobile WebServices intelligently optimizes communication to each specific mobile device.
- CWR Mobile CRM supports On-Premise, implementations as well as Cloud implementations (Partner Hosted, CRM Online). Beyond the existing CRM infrastructure, no additional servers are required.
- Mobile users are connected to their Dynamics CRM data, anytime, anywhere.

Components

CWR Mobile CRM is built using the Microsoft Dynamics CRM WebServices. It relies heavily on the CRM metadata and uses this metadata to configure the mobile application. There is no coding required to make changes to the mobile application, and everything is configurable from within Dynamics CRM. Making changes to the application is nothing more than changing a form or view and publishing the changes; the next time a user synchronizes, he will receive the updated application.

By taking advantage of the CRM metadata, CWR Mobile CRM can support practically all standard CRM entities, including custom attributes, custom relationships, and custom entities.

There are four major components to CWR Mobile CRM 2011:

- Mobile Configurator
- Mobile WebServices
- Smart clients
    - Native BlackBerry client
    - Native iPhone/iPad client
    - Native Windows Phone client
- Express clients

In addition, a separate product called CWR Exchange Connector is also available.

Figure 15.7 shows an overview of these components.

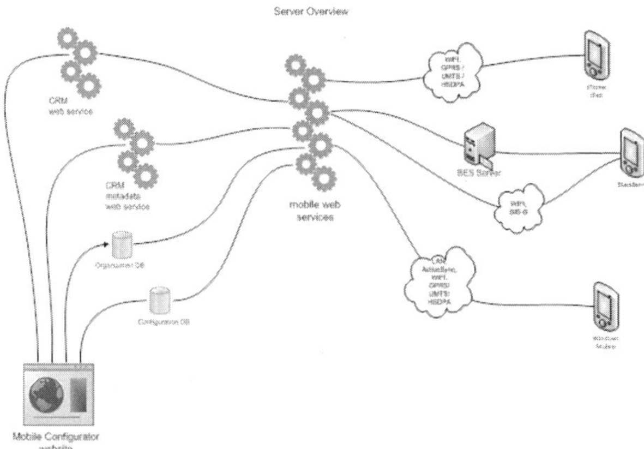

FIGURE 15.7 Components of CWR Mobile CRM 2011.

Mobile Configurator

The Mobile Configurator in CWR Mobile CRM enables you to configure the different aspects of the mobile application. It contains the following functions:

- **Manage Profiles**—For different user groups. Each profile can contain different configurations of forms, views, and filters.
- **Manage Views**—For navigating through the data on the device.
- **Manage Forms**—For displaying and editing data on the device.
- **Manage Synchronization Filters**—A synchronization filter defines what data is synchronized to the device.
- **Manage Users and Devices**—Each user can have multiple devices assigned to it. Users and devices can be activated, deactivated, wiped, resynchronized, and so forth.
- **Manage Client Sync Issues**—Sync issues that occur on the device can be handled by an administrator on the server.
- **Show Reports**—On synchronization statistics, error logging, and so on.

Figure 15.8 shows the CWR Mobile Configurator configured within Microsoft Dynamics CRM 2011.

Mobile Web Services

Mobile Web Services in CWR Mobile CRM is used for communication between the mobile devices and CRM. It acts as a gateway between the mobile device and CRM and performs functions such as executing the synchronization filters to retrieve the required data for each user, synchronizing metadata, and executing client requests (create, update, delete, and so on) on the CRM server.

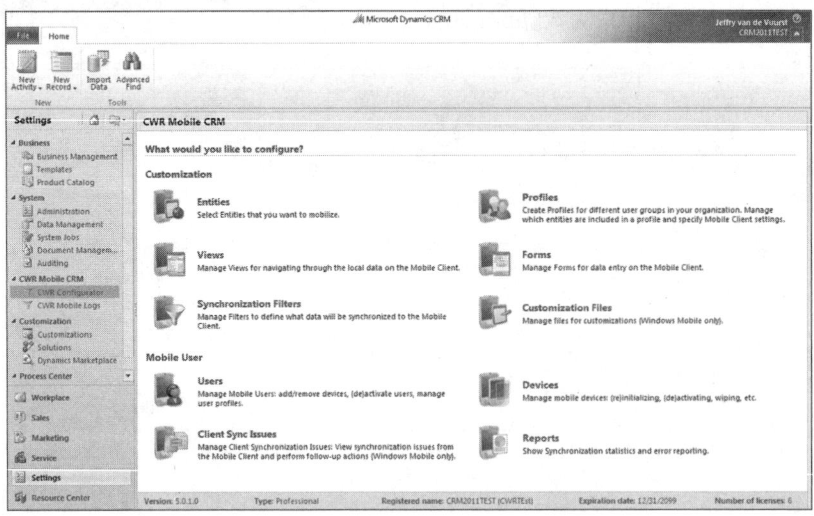

FIGURE 15.8 CWR Mobile Configurator integrated into Dynamics CRM.

The intelligent CWR Mobile Web Services optimizes the communication for each different mobile device. Data is compressed and sent in an optimized format per device type.

Smart Clients

CWR Mobile CRM native smart clients communicate with Mobile Web Services. Each mobile smart client retrieves the metadata and profile configuration and generates a user interface optimized for the specific mobile device.

The iPhone/iPad client is fully touch-optimized, whereas the BlackBerry client is optimized for easy navigation using the track ball. The Windows Phone client can be navigated using pen, keyboard, or touch.

Furthermore, the smart clients leverage the possibilities of each specific device. The BlackBerry and Windows Phone versions feature integration with the native e-mail and calendar clients. The iPhone/iPad version can integrate with the built-in Google Maps application.

The different clients are shown in the following sections.

BlackBerry

The BlackBerry smart client runs on BlackBerry devices with OS 5 and higher. Device specific features include integration with the native e-mail and calendar clients and phone call integration.

The client can be downloaded from a separate client installation website on the CWR server or from BlackBerry App World. The client in Blackberry App World has an option to run with sample data for demo purposes. Figure 15.9 shows the client within BlackBerry.

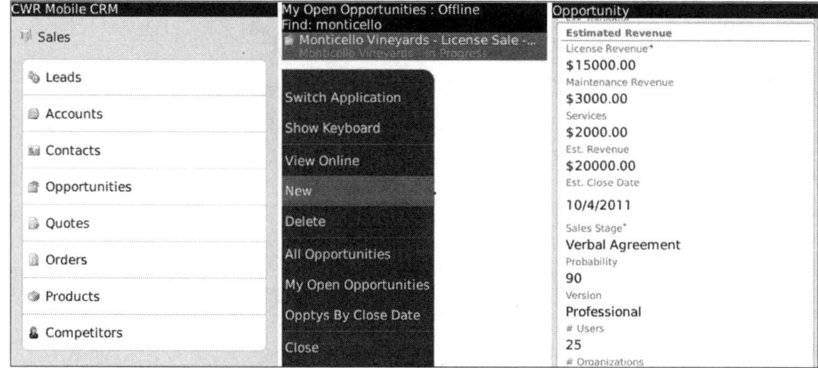

FIGURE 15.9 BlackBerry smart client.

iPhone/iPad Client

The iPhone/iPad client runs on iPhones and iPads with iOS 4 and higher. This client can be downloaded only from the Apple App Store and has an option to run with sample data. Figure 15.10 shows the client within the iPhone.

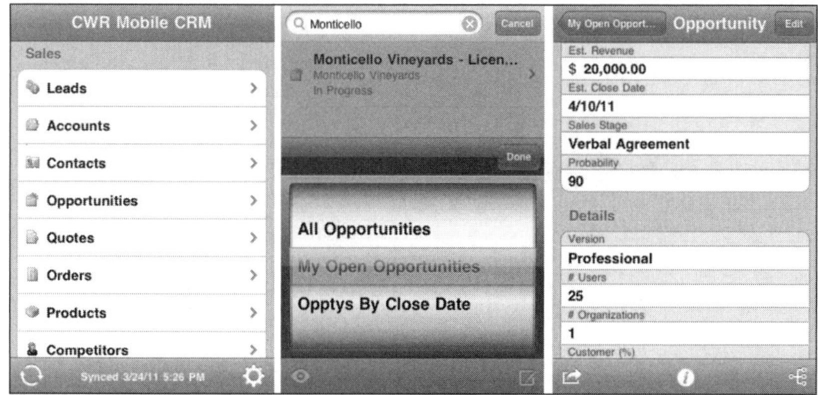

FIGURE 15.10 iPhone smart client.

iPad

Figure 15.11 shows the user interface that the iPhone/iPad smart client presents to users on the larger iPad device.

Windows Phone

The Windows Phone client is supported on Windows Phone 6.5. Just as with the BlackBerry, it integrates with the native e-mail and calendar client (Pocket Outlook) and phone call tracking. Integration with navigation software such as TomTom is also available. A Windows Phone 7 smart client is also in development. Figure 15.4 shows a prototype of the Windows Phone 7 smart client.

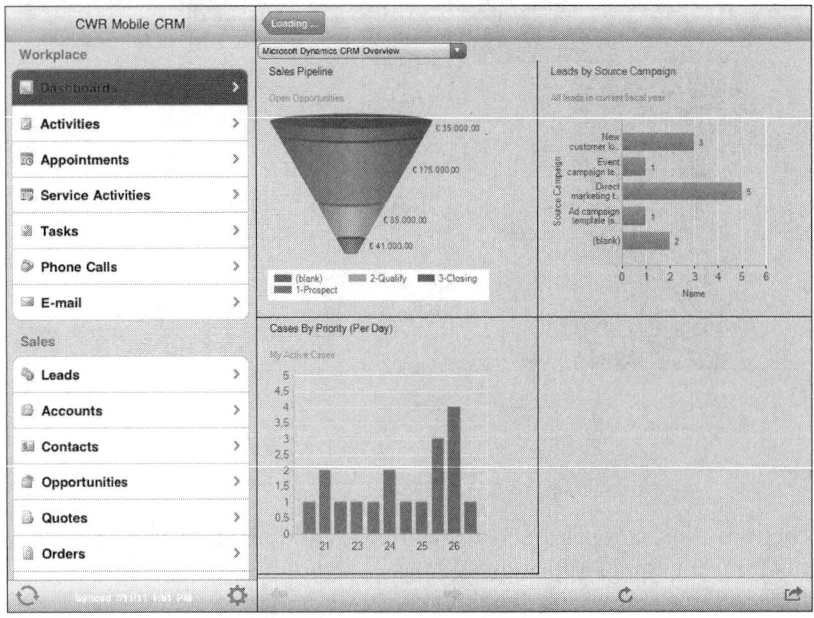

FIGURE 15.11 iPad smart client.

Figure 15.12 shows the client within the Windows interface.

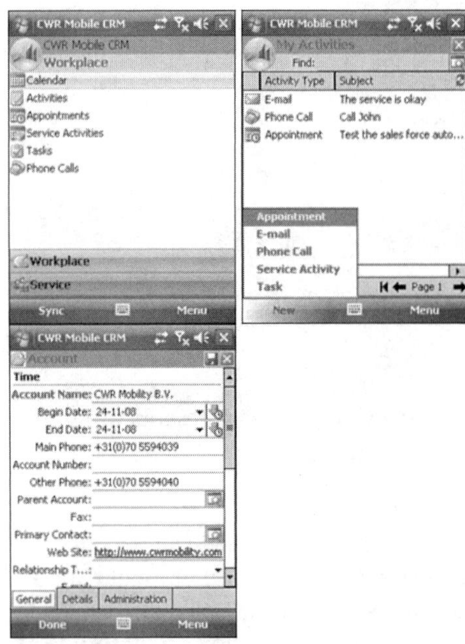

FIGURE 15.12 Windows Mobile client—touch screen.

CWR Mobile Express Client

The CWR Mobile Express client (not to be mistaken with the Microsoft Mobile Express client) is a feature-rich, online-only web client. Just as with the Microsoft version, it runs on mobile browsers that support HTML 4. However, instead of showing the same user interface on all browsers, it detects the browser and displays an optimized UI for each browser. For example, browsers that support the WebKit engine, such as iPhone Safari and the Android browser.

Furthermore, it doesn't have the same limitations as the Microsoft Mobile Express client, except of course that it's an online-only client. It is also fully configurable using the CWR Mobile Configurator.

Figures 15.13, 15.14, and 15.15 show the client for the CWR Mobile Express client.

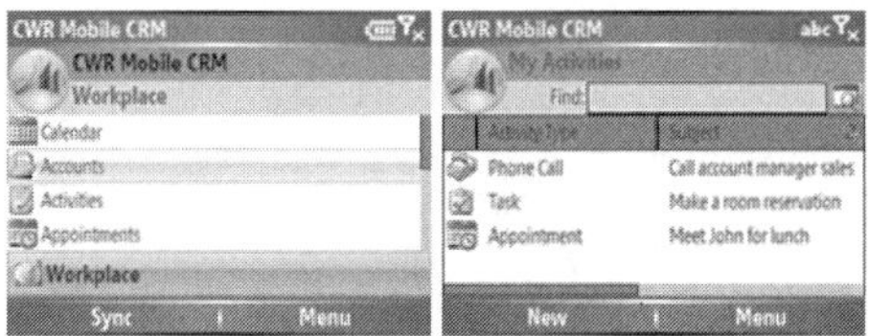

FIGURE 15.13 CWR Mobile Express client.

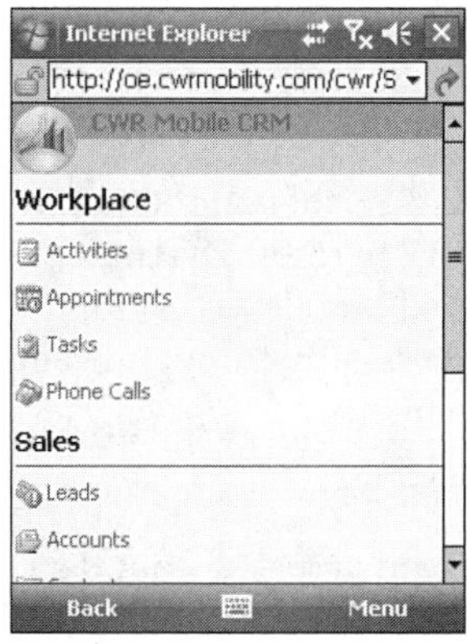

FIGURE 15.14 CWR Mobile Express on Windows Mobile browser.

CRM-Exchange Connector

This service synchronizes tasks and appointments between CRM and Exchange without the need for the CRM Outlook client. Using this, mobile users that want to see their tasks and appointments in their mobile calendar have the option to not use Outlook to synchronize these items to Exchange and from there to their mobile calendar.

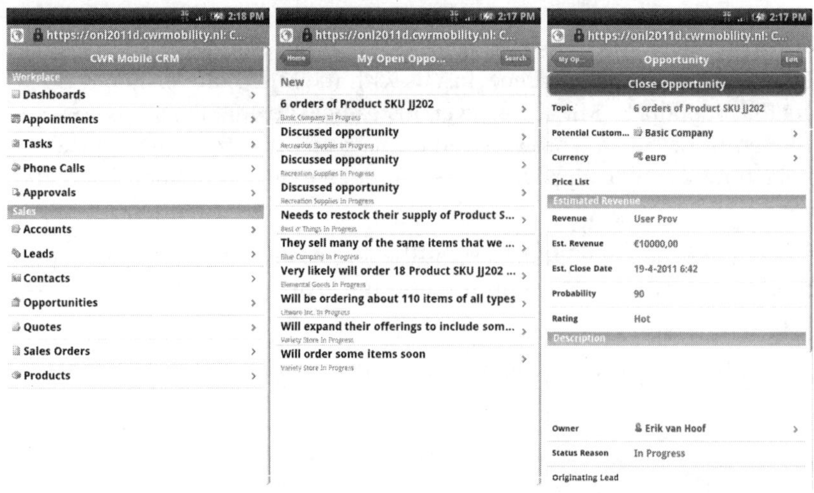

FIGURE 15.15 CWR Mobile Express on iPhone/WebKit browser.

Other Mobility Options

In addition to the options presented previously in this chapter, other companies have introduced products that provided limited mobility options.

TenDigits

Similarly to CWR Mobility, TenDigits, a Microsoft Gold Certified ISV Partner and Research In Motion (RIM) Preferred ISV Partner, provides a mobile version of Microsoft Dynamics CRM for both Windows Mobile and BlackBerry mobile devices called Mobile Access for Dynamics CRM. Mobile Access for Dynamics CRM delivers its functionality through Event Driven Push, which updates devices instantly without user involvement.

Additional features of the product include the following:

- **Always available wireless CRM**—Work anywhere with instant access to your data online and offline with full CRM functionality regardless of your location.
- **Multitasking graphical user interface**—Navigate instantly between various records, lists, tasks, and applications without losing track of anything.
- **Strong application integration**—Dial phone numbers, browse websites, and compose e-mails directly from fields. Log e-mails and phone calls from your BlackBerry to account and contact history in CRM. Gain access to internal applications such as AX, GP, and SAP to find timely information relevant to your CRM records.

- **Alert notifications**—Bring users' attention to important events with proactive alerts for action.
- **Copy/log to CRM**—Track handheld e-mails and phone calls using corresponding CRM activities with automatic, smart recipient linking.

▶ For more information about TenDigits, visit www.tendigits.com.

Summary

Mobility is a hot topic, and the day when full size computers are replaced by our handhelds is rapidly approaching. Microsoft Dynamics CRM 2011 and the products mentioned in this chapter enable users to step up and have the kind of functionality that is required to meet this challenge.

CHAPTER 16

Solution Concepts

IN THIS CHAPTER

- Solution Explained
- Best Practices When Working with Solutions
- Third-Party and Marketplace Solutions

Microsoft Dynamics CRM 2011 implements a new concept for extensibility called solutions that improves a mechanism for deployments of virtually any kind of system customization.

Solutions Explained

Previous versions of Microsoft Dynamics CRM allowed only for the customization of entities that you were able to export and import in one single XML file, but other customizations, such as reports, templates, and plug-ins had to be deployed separately. Microsoft realized that partners and clients were having a hard time trying to maintain CRM customizations because they usually involve modifying entities' views or forms or modifying and adding new attributes to the entities. Most of the solutions that currently exist on CRM and xRM environments involve other pieces of software such as plug-ins, reports, custom static and/or dynamic pages, images, scripts, Silverlight applications, flash animations, templates, and web services just to name a few.

A *solution* is a package that is a new and greatly welcome improvement that will help us in the deployment, support, upgrade, sale, and distribution of all the customizations we can think of. Each solution is compiled into one zip file containing the following components:

- Entities
- Option Sets
- Client Extensions

- Web Resources
- Processes
- Plug-in Assemblies
- Sdk Message Processing Steps
- Service Endpoints
- Dashboards
- Reports
- Connection Roles
- Article Templates
- Contract Templates
- E-mail Templates
- Mail Merge Templates
- Security Roles
- Field Security Profiles

By default each CRM organization has a hidden solution created with a friendly name of Default Solution. This is a system solution that cannot be deleted. To work with the default solution, go to Settings, Customizations, and then click on Customize the System as shown in Figure 16.1.

NOTE

Even though you can make any customization in the default solution, it is *strongly* recommended to create a custom solution and work with any customization from a new custom solution. The reason for this is that the custom solution can easily be rolled back, when imported as managed to another organization, reverting the application to its original state. Customizations in unmanaged solutions cannot be rolled back after the solution is removed.

To work with custom solutions, go to Settings, Solutions in the Customization group, as shown in Figure 16.2.

To create new solutions, complete the following steps:

1. Click on New; you will see a screen similar to Figure 16.3.
2. If this is the first time you will create a solution, you will also need to create a publisher for it. To do so, click on the lookup button, and then click on New (see Figure 16.4).
3. Enter a display name for the new publisher. When pressing the Tab key, the Name field will autopopulate with the same name in lowercase. You can also modify the prefix name, which is limited to eight characters. Click on Save and Close to close this dialog.

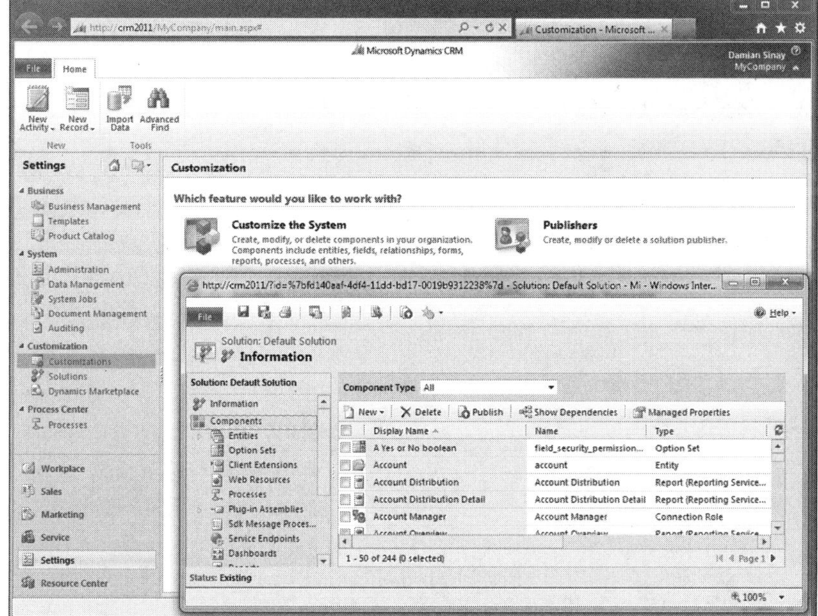

FIGURE 16.1 Default solution.

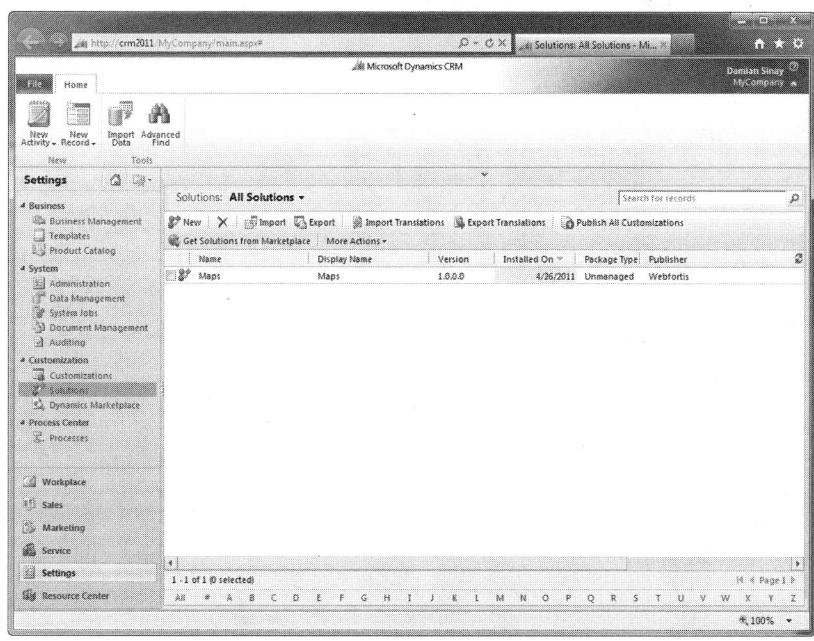

FIGURE 16.2 Solutions.

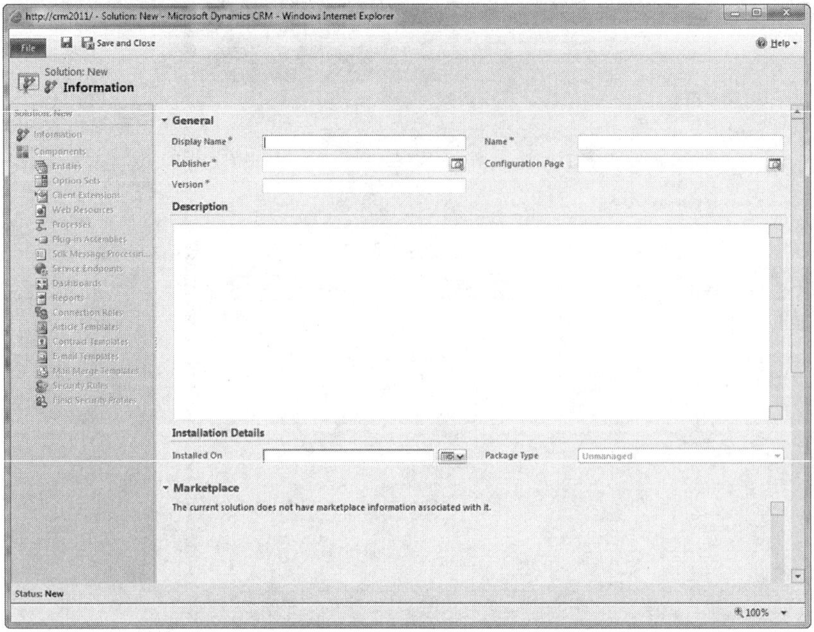

FIGURE 16.3 New solution.

FIGURE 16.4 New publisher.

NOTE

Even though the description is not required to create a publisher in CRM it will be required if you want to publish the solution to the Dynamics Marketplace as we will see later on this chapter, so it is recommended to enter a company description on this box as well as all fields that are inside the contact details tab like phone, e-mail, website, address, state, city and country.

TIP

To see the list of publishers, you can go to Settings, Customizations, and then click on Publishers.

4. Click OK on the Look up Record dialog as the new publisher we created in the previous step will be selected by default.
5. Enter a display name for your solution. Pressing the Tab key will autopopulate the Name field and also enter a version number (see Figure 16.5).

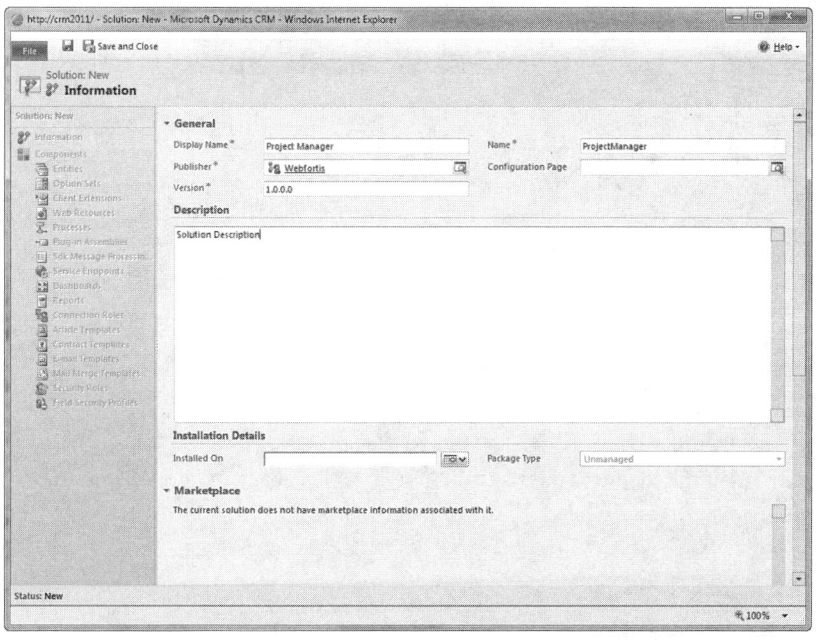

FIGURE 16.5 New solution.

6. Clicking on Save will enable all the items on the sidebar.

Each solution also has the ability to contain a *configuration page,* which is a web resource that can be used to provide general settings as well as license keys configuration for ISV providers. Those license keys can be managed and verified by custom plug-ins.

NOTE

Similar to the Publisher description, the Solution description is not required for creating a solution in CRM however it will be required if you want to publish the solution to the Dynamics Marketplace.

TIP

To create a configuration page, you can create an HTML file and add it as a web resource to the solution. To do this, click on Web Resources and then on New, enter a name and display name for the configuration page, select Web Page(HTML) in the type on the content area, and then select the language, and upload the HTML file you created (see Figure 16.6).

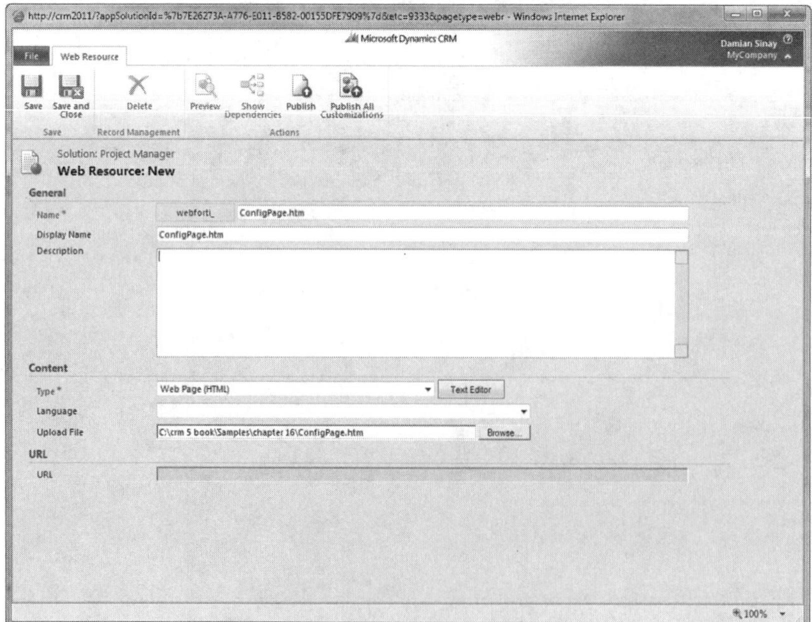

FIGURE 16.6 Creating a configuration page.

Click on Save and Close, and click on the Information link to assign the configuration page to your solution (see Figure 16.7).

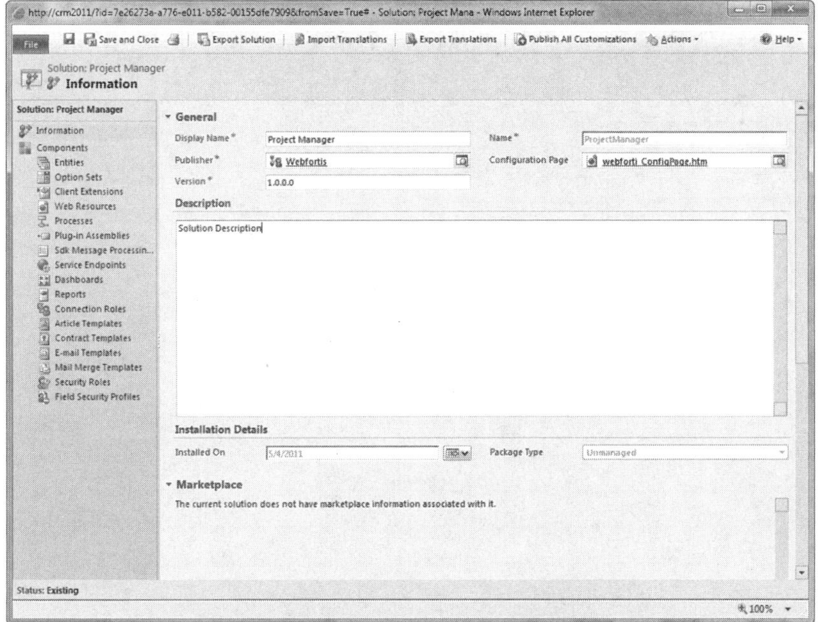

FIGURE 16.7 Adding a configuration page to the solution.

16

Click Save, and you will see the configuration page can now be accessed from a new link that appears in the Solution Form in the sidebar with the name of Configuration (see Figure 16.8).

Every solution component shares some functions, and some others depend on the component type. The functions shared by all components are the following.

Add Required Components

This function is available on all component types and requires you to select a component from the list before you can use it. It is useful, for example, when you create a Dashboard that contains a chart on the Account entity, or any other system or managed entity. Clicking this button will add the Account entity to the entity's components so that you can be sure it will be part of the solution (see Figure 16.9).

The same happens with reports and processes. If you have a workflow that needs to create a record of any of the system entities, this feature will add that entity to the entity's component.

NOTE

Note that this will not work for custom code, where you can add web resources with JavaScript or by calling the CRM Web Services from an event of a form or field.

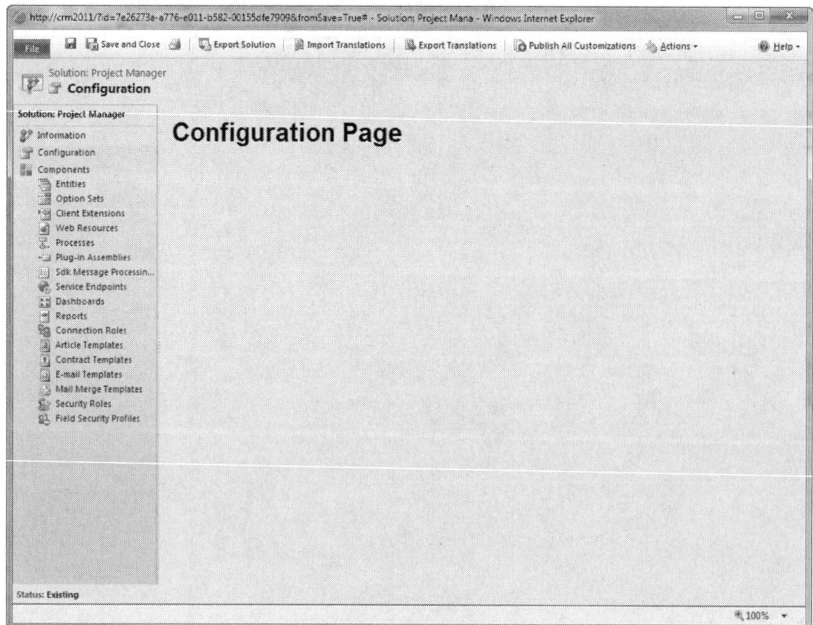

FIGURE 16.8 Solution configuration.

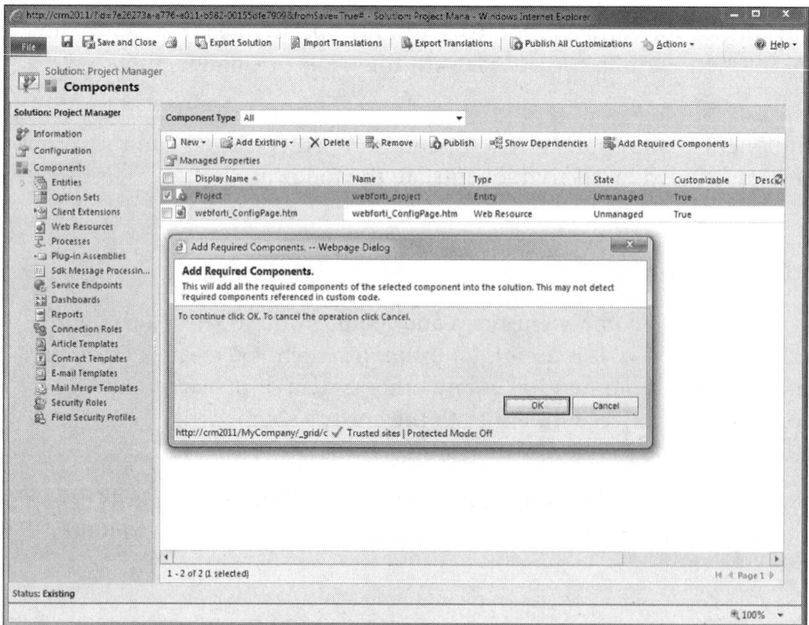

FIGURE 16.9 Add required components.

Managed Properties

There are two types of solutions; they are called managed and unmanaged. Unmanaged solutions are the ones that are used for development, whereas the managed solutions are the ones used for distribution.

Each component on an unmanaged solution has some properties called *managed properties* that depend on the component type selected. These properties enable you to specify the ability you want to give to the end users when the solution is exported as managed and then imported to another organization.

Figure 16.10 shows the solution properties you can set on a custom entity.

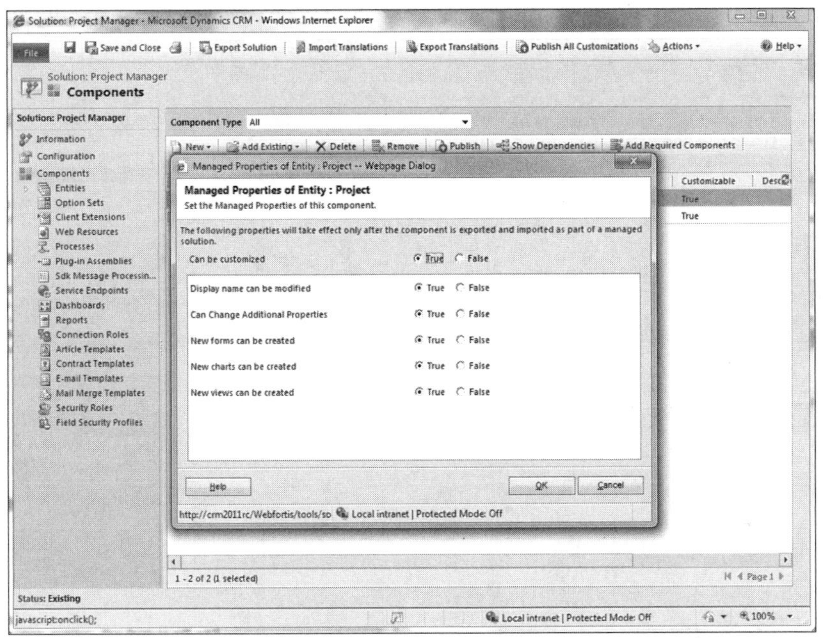

FIGURE 16.10 Solution properties.

If you set the first option, Can be Customized, to false, all the other options will be disabled. Notice that by default any customization you make will have this option set to true, allowing any person who implements your solution to make any customization, so it is good to change these values if you want to protect that.

For each solution component, you can perform some functions that depend on the component type. For example, you can create new entities from the solution form, new option sets, new security roles, new processes, new reports, new templates, new Dashboards, new web resources, new connection roles, and new field security profiles. But you cannot create new client extensions, plug-ins, SDK message processing steps, or service endpoints.

Plug-ins

If you want to include a plug-in on your solution, you must create the plug-in first in Visual Studio 2010 and then register the plugin with the Plug-in Registration Tool.

▶ Refer to Chapter 25, "Plug-Ins," for details on working with plug-ins.

After you successfully register the plug-in, you can go to the solution form, click on the plug-in Assemblies node, and click on the Add Existing button to include the plug-in on your solution (see Figure 16.11).

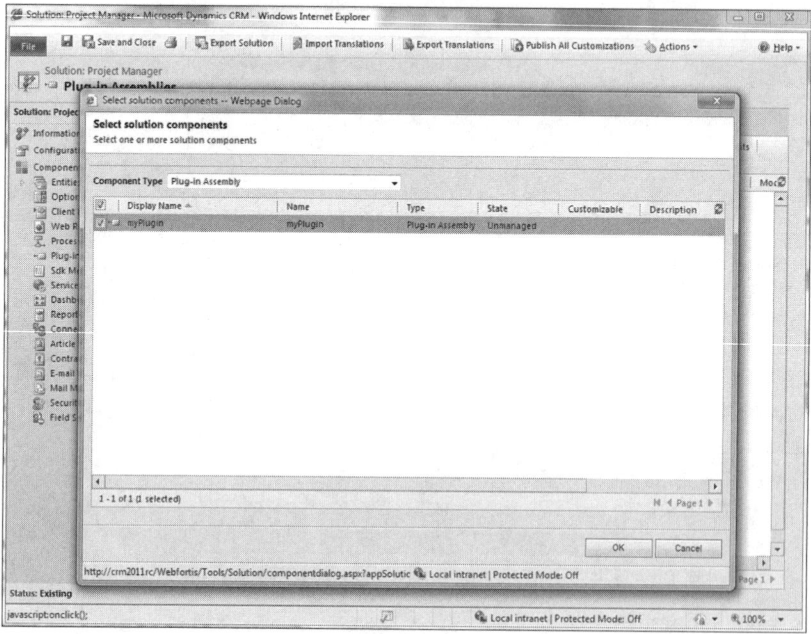

FIGURE 16.11 Adding plug-ins to your solution.

TIP

In the Plug-in Assemblies tab, you will see a button that says How to Register Assemblies. It will take you to the MSDN website with a detailed walkthrough about how to register plug-ins.

Keep in mind that plug-ins don't support managed properties, and the Add Required Components button won't work. If your plug-in refers to any entity missing on the solution, you will have to add it manually.

Adding a plug-in to the solution doesn't mean it adds all the steps you registered. If you only add the plug-in, export the solution, and implement your package on another CRM 2011 organization, the plug-in won't work as expected because there wasn't a step registered for the plug-in.

This means you will have to also include the steps you want to include on your solution right after adding the plug-in to the solution. To add the steps you need, go to the solution form, click on the Sdk Message Processing Steps node, and then click on the Add Exiting button. Find the steps you want to register, as shown in Figure 16.12.

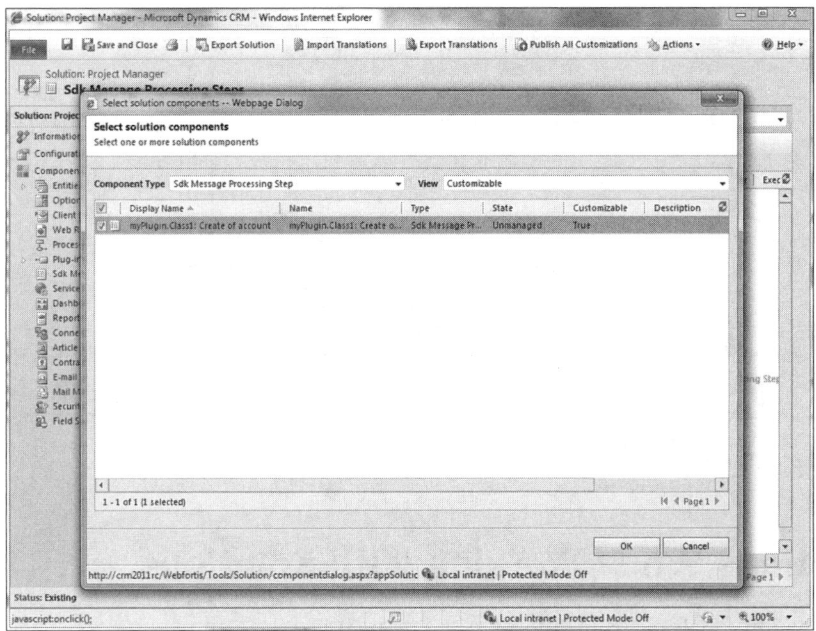

FIGURE 16.12 Adding SDK Message Processing Steps to your solution.

NOTE

In the SDK Message Processing Steps tab, you will see a button that says How to Register Steps. It will take you to the MSDN website with a detailed walkthrough about how to register plug-ins.

When adding the steps, you will be also asked to include the required components associated with the steps. For example, if you have a step created for the Create event of the

Account entity, you should include the Account entity within your solution (see Figure 16.13).

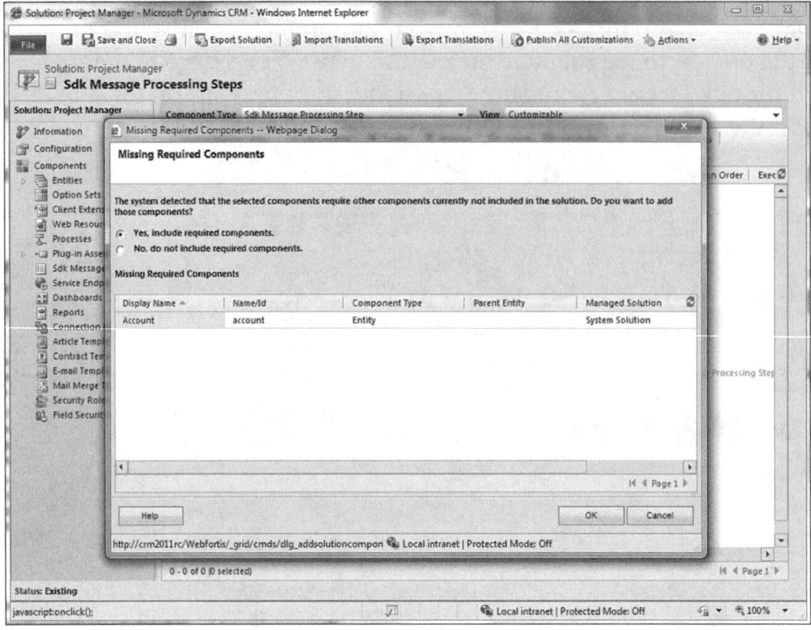

FIGURE 16.13 Missing required components.

Best Practices When Working with Solutions

Although every Dynamics CRM organization has a default solution from which you can start making customizations, we recommend making a backup of this solution by exporting it before you start making any customization on a fresh CRM deployment. Have in mind that any customization you make inside a custom solution will be also included on the default solution as well as any change you make on existing system entities. It is a good practice to start making any customization in a new custom solution, so they can be easily managed in the future. If you want to customize a system entity such as Account, you can do it by adding any existing entity to a custom solution.

To customize a system, complete the following steps:

1. Open your custom solution; be sure the Components node is selected on the sidebar.
2. Click on the Add Existing button and select Entity (see Figure 16.14).
3. Select the entity you want to add. In this case, we will select Account (see Figure 16.15).

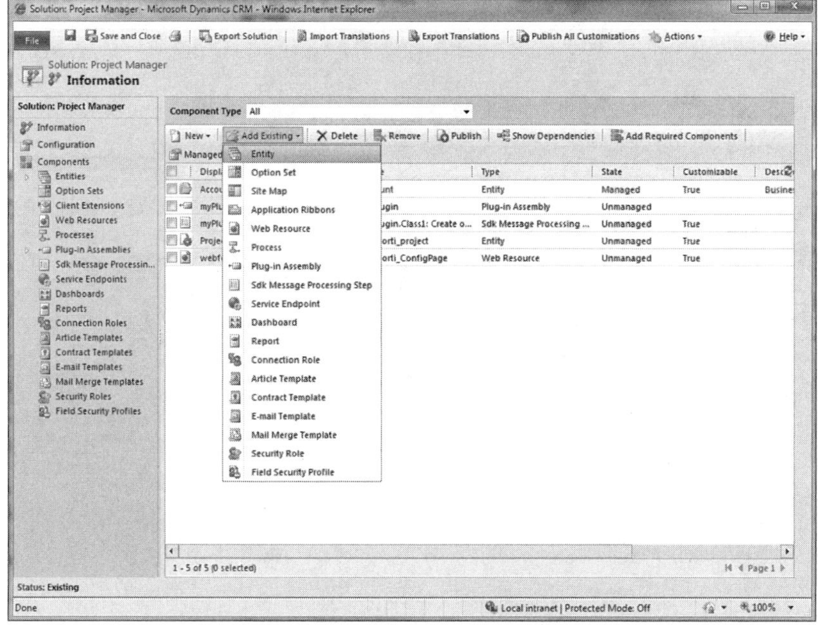

FIGURE 16.14 Add existing entity.

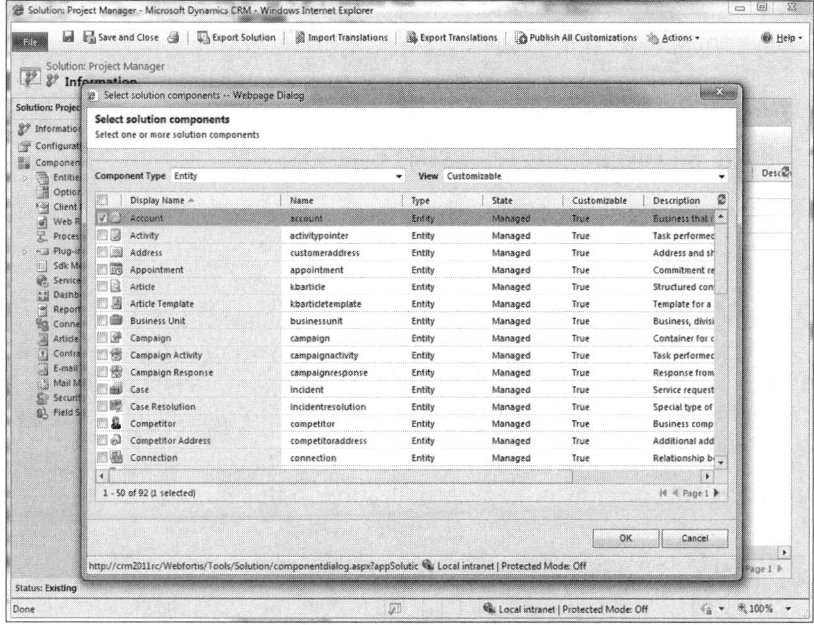

FIGURE 16.15 Select the existing Account entity.

4. Click OK to add the entity. You will see the entity added to the solution (see Figure 16.16).

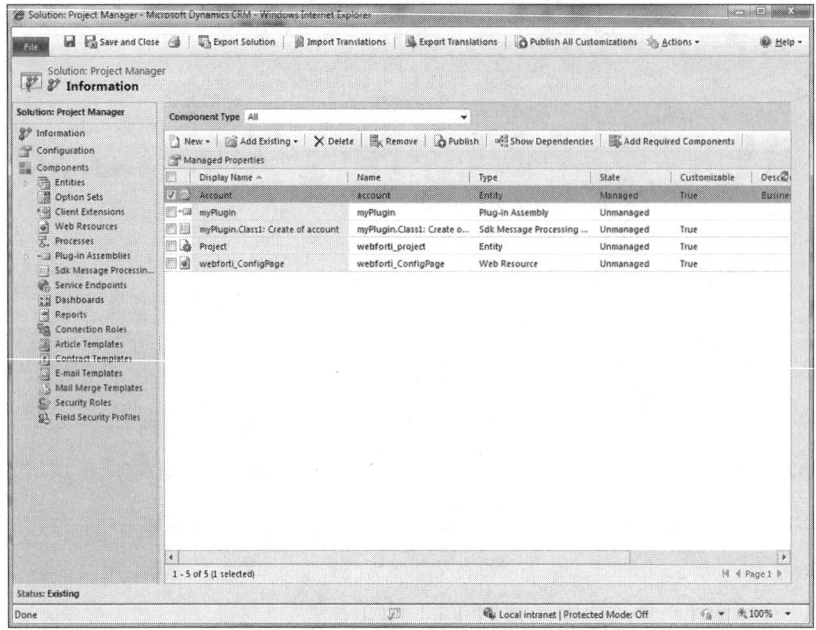

FIGURE 16.16 Existing entity added to the solution.

Exporting Solutions

Solutions can be exported in two different package types:

- Unmanaged
- Managed

Unmanaged is the option that enables developers to maintain backups of the customizations; they can be modified when applying them on any other environment. Note: when removing unmanaged solutions the custom entities are not removed; to remove the custom entities, you will need to remove them manually by going to the Default Solution.

If you want to be have other people deploy the solution, you will have to export the solution as managed so that people can't make any customization to the package.

CAUTION

Before exporting your solution, be sure you include the site map on the solution because it won't be added automatically by the entities you added or created. You can add the site map by going to the Client Extensions node and clicking on Add Existing, and then Site Map, as seen in Figure 16.17.

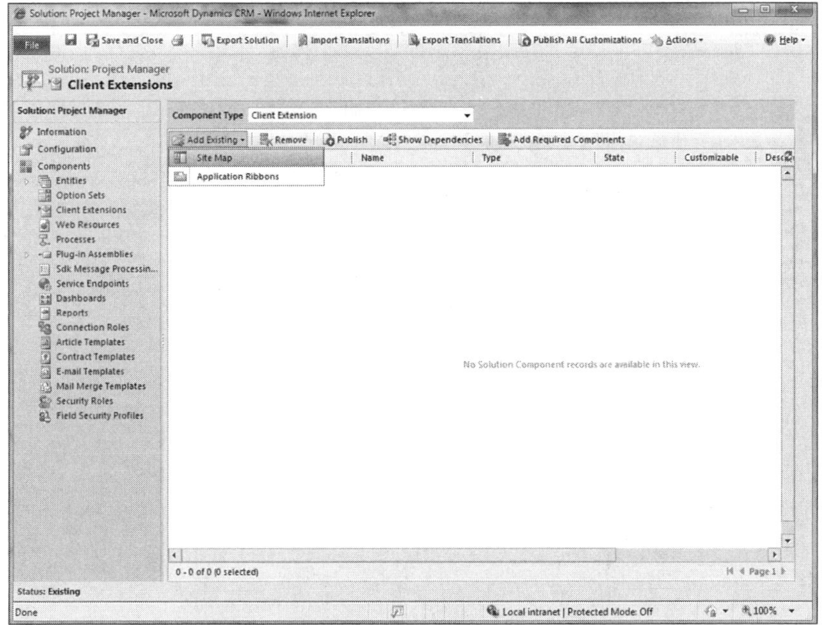

FIGURE 16.17 Adding a site map.

To export solutions, complete the following steps:

1. Open the solution you want to export, and click the Export button from the top toolbar (see Figure 16.18).
2. The Export Solution Wizard will open and will suggest to publish all customizations before continuing (see Figure 16.19).
3. Click the Publish All Customizations button, and then click on Next.
4. The next screen will enable you to select the settings you might want to export. The available settings are Auto-numbering, Calendar, Customization, E-mail tracking, General, Marketing, Outlook Synchronization, Relationship Roles, and ISV Config (see Figure 16.20).

CAUTION

Notice these settings won't be removed from the organization where you implemented this solution when you remove the solution even if you export the solution as managed.

5. Click Next to continue to the next step where you can set the package type to either unmanaged or managed (see Figure 16.21).

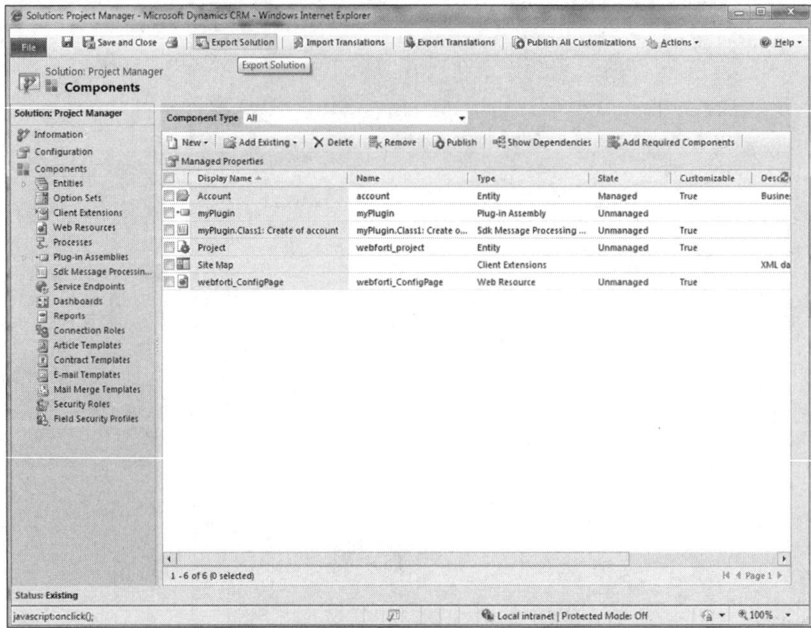

FIGURE 16.18 Export solution.

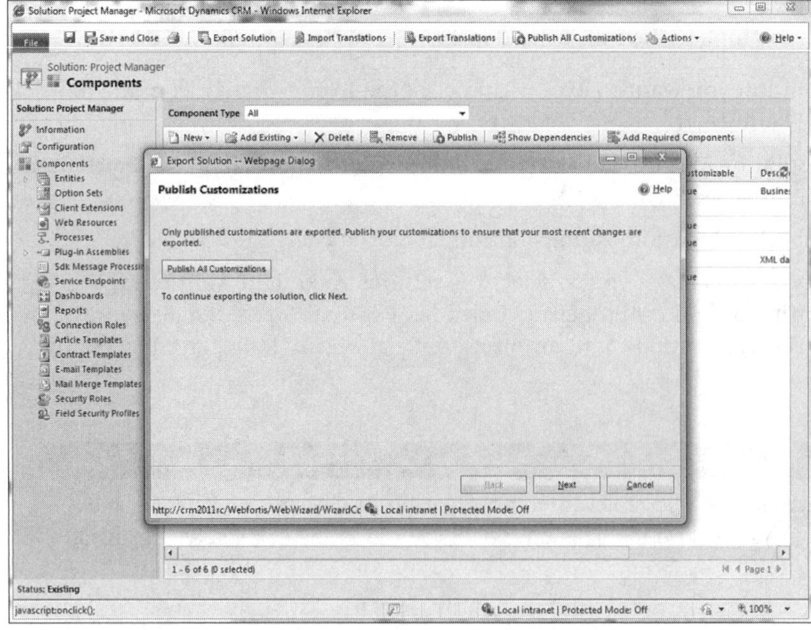

FIGURE 16.19 Export Solution Wizard.

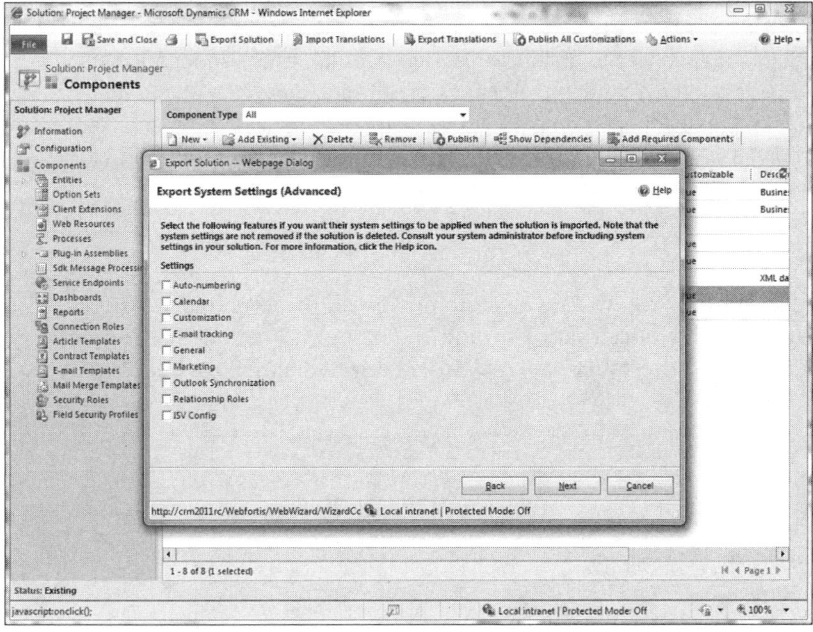

FIGURE 16.20 Export settings.

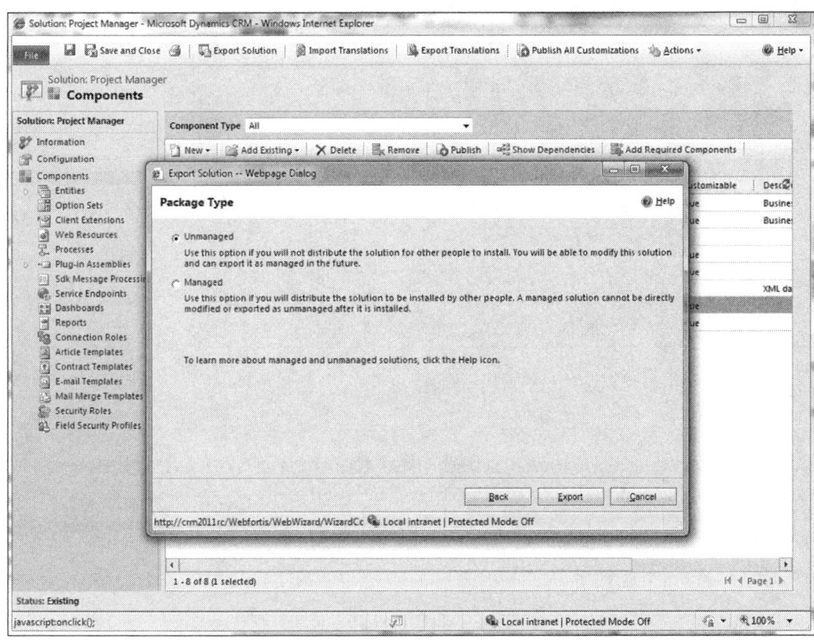

FIGURE 16.21 Package type.

NOTE

A managed solution is a good way to distribute packages for ISV and also for Microsoft partners to avoid the customers putting their hands on any customization whose functionality can be broken (as happened on previous versions of Dynamics CRM) and also to protect the copyright of the solution. For example, users won't be able to export or customize a managed solution they installed.

---

6. Click the Export button. You will be asked to download the exported solution as shown in Figure 16.22. Notice that by default the name will include the solution name, the version, and the suffix *managed*, if you selected a managed package type.

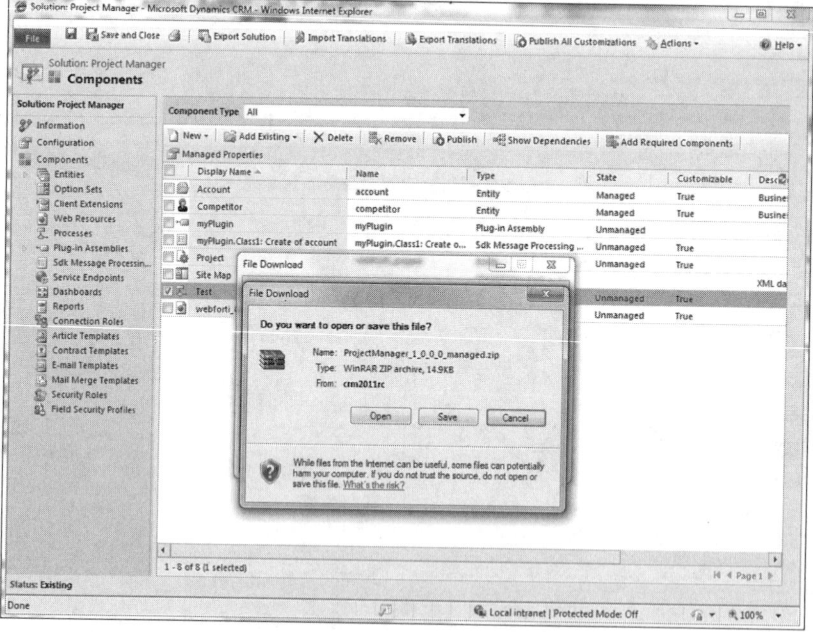

FIGURE 16.22 Export solution.

If you expand the compressed file you downloaded, after the import you will see it contains the following files and folders:

- WebResources
- Workflows
- Reports
- PluginAssemblies
- [Content_Types].xml

- Customizations.xml
- Solution.xml

The number of folders will depend on the type of components you added to the solution; if you added reports, you will see them inside the Reports folder, but if your solution doesn't include any reports, then this folder won't exist.

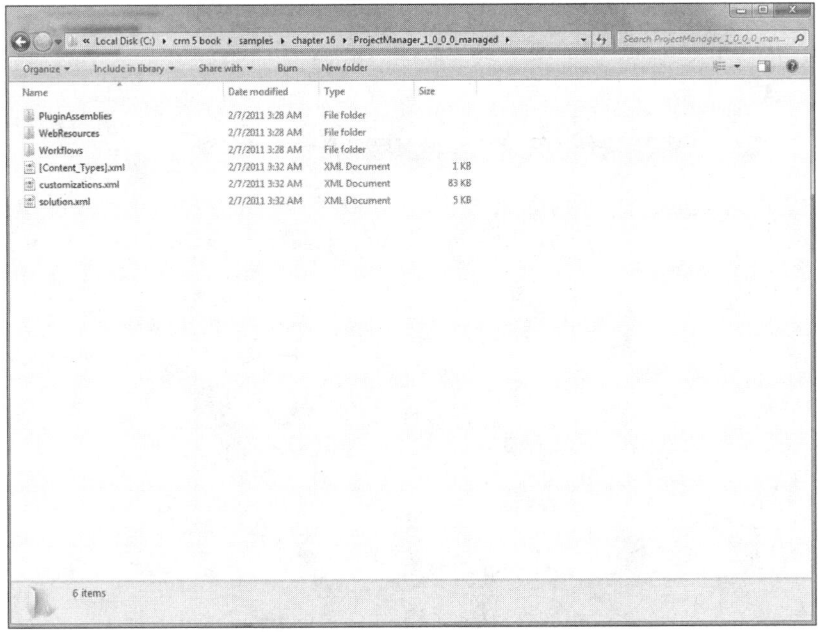

FIGURE 16.23 Expanded solution file.

It is important to maintain the solution version properly because this number is not automatically incremented every time you export your solution. You are responsible for incrementing this number on each export before publishing a new version to the public.

One consideration regarding versioning is that versions have four numbers separated by dots; for example, 1.2.3.4. Sequentially, each of these numbers is described as follows:

- Major version number
- Minor version number
- Build number
- Revision number

Use the first two numbers when you add new features to the solution and the last two numbers when you fix bugs or make improvements on existing features.

Importing Solutions

To import a solution on another organization, complete the following steps:

1. Go to Settings and then to Solutions in the Customization group, as shown in Figure 16.2.
2. Click on Import. You will see a dialog, as shown in Figure 16.24.

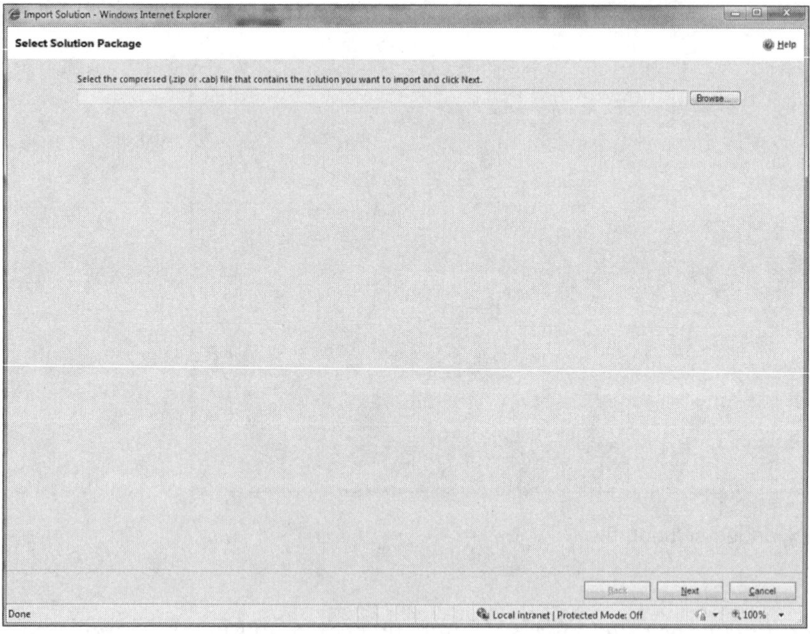

FIGURE 16.24 Import solution.

3. Click on Browse, locate the package zip file on your local hard drive, and click on Next (see Figure 16.25).
4. Optionally, you can check the solution package details by clicking on the View solution package details button. You will be able to see the detailed content of the package, as shown in Figure 16.26.
5. Click on Close to close the solution details dialog and click Next. You will see the Import Options from which you can activate the processes and plug-in SDK messages (see Figure 16.27).

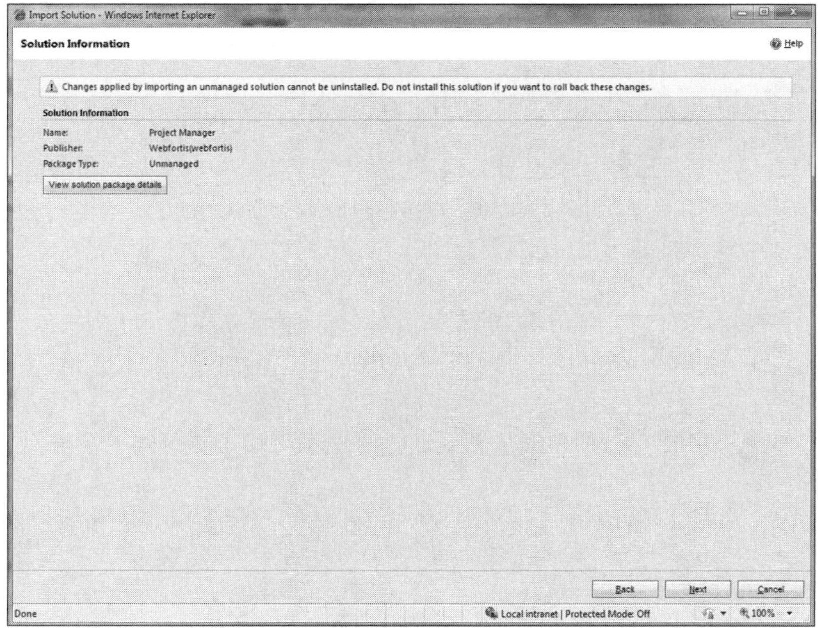

FIGURE 16.25 Solution information.

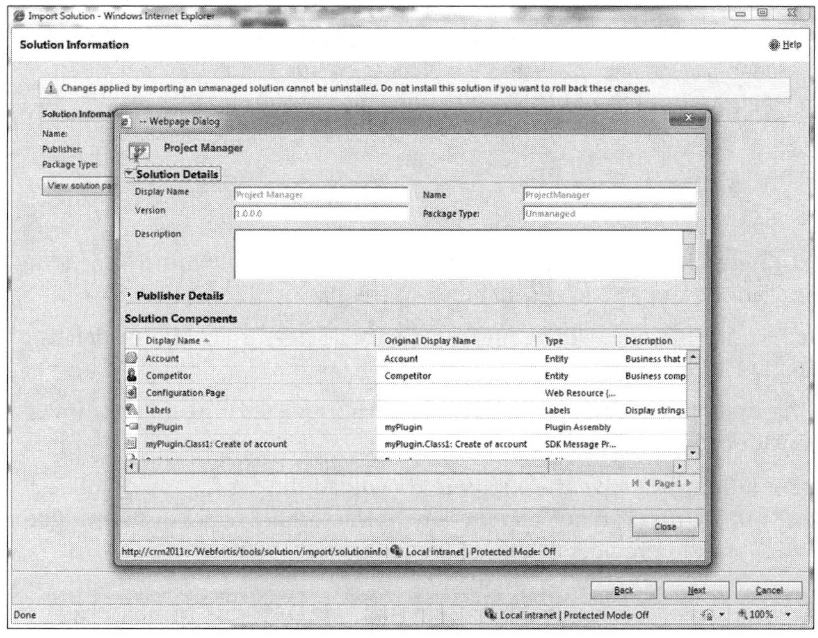

FIGURE 16.26 Solution package details.

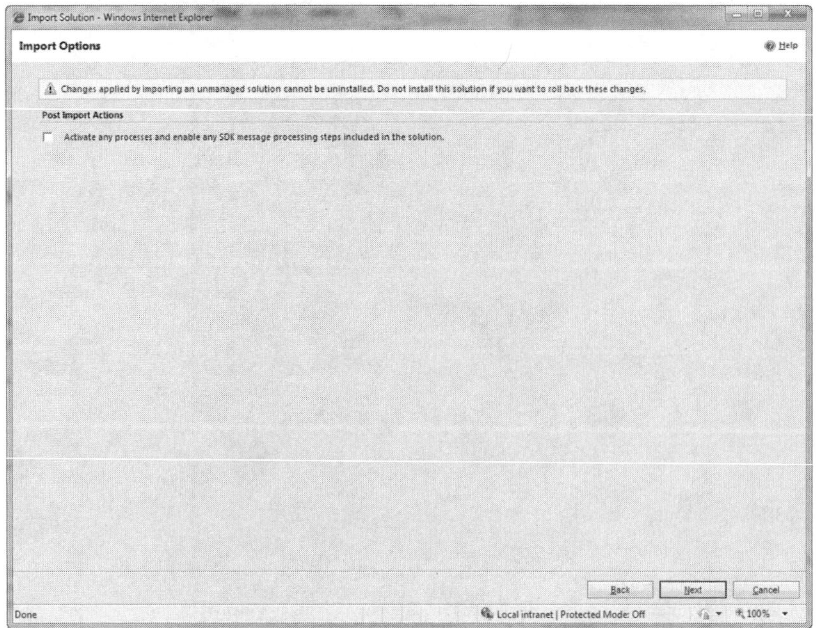

FIGURE 16.27 Import options.

TIP

If your solution includes plugins and SDK message processing steps, it is very important you select the Activate any processes check box and then enable any SDK message processing steps included in the solution, so the plugin steps will be registered successfully.

6. Click on Next to import the solution. This process might take some time, depending on the customizations and assemblies included in the package.
7. When the import finishes, you will be presented with a screen showing the details (see Figure 16.28).
8. After importing the solution, you will have to publish it by clicking on Publish All Customizations in order to start using it.

After importing the solution, you have the ability to download the log file (see Figure 16.29), which is an XML file that can be viewed easily in Microsoft Excel. This file will be helpful to send to the solution provider in case of any error.

CAUTION

If you don't have sufficient permissions and the solution you are importing contains plug-ins that are not configured with Sandbox isolation, you will get an error.

Import Solution - Windows Internet Explorer

Importing Solution Help

The import of solution: Project Manager completed with warning.

Date Time	Type	Display Name	Name	Status	Description	Detail
03:49:40.69	Process activation	Test	Test			None
03:49:40.61	SDK Message Pr...	myPlugin.Class1...	myPlugin.Class1...			None
03:49:39.61	Dependencies ...					None
03:49:36.53	Process	Test	Test			None
03:49:35.56	Process	Test	Test			The original proce
03:49:35.49	Client Extensions	Site Map			XML data used to control the application navigation p...	None
03:49:35.42	SDK Message Pr...	myPlugin.Class1...	myPlugin.Class1...			None
03:49:35.21	SDK Message Pr...	myPlugin.Class1...	myPlugin.Class1...			The original SDK r
03:49:35.13	Plugin Assembly	myPlugin	myPlugin			None
03:49:34.65	Chart		account		Entity that stores a chart attached with a view.	None
03:49:34.65	Chart		webforti_project		Entity that stores a chart attached with a view.	None
03:49:34.65	Chart		competitor		Entity that stores a chart attached with a view.	None
03:49:30.37	Relationship					None
03:49:27.26	Entity Ribbon	Project	webforti_project		XML data that represents the customized elements of t...	None
03:49:27.13	Entity Messages		webforti_project		Text that represents customized messages for an entity.	None
03:49:27.13	Form	Project	webforti_project		System-populated field for the XML representation of t...	None
03:49:26.90	System Views	Project	webforti_project		Query that is saved against the database.	None
03:49:26.68	Entity Ribbon	Competitor	competitor		XML data that represents the customized elements of t...	None
03:49:26.57	Form	Competitor	competitor		System-populated field for the XML representation of t...	None
03:49:26.57	Entity Messages		competitor		Text that represents customized messages for an entity.	None
03:49:26.35	Entity Ribbon	Account	account		XML data that represents the customized elements of t...	None
03:49:26.35	System Views		competitor		Query that is saved against the database.	None
03:49:26.14	Entity Messages		account		Text that represents customized messages for an entity.	None

Page 1

Download Log File | Publish All Customizations | Close

Local intranet | Protected Mode: Off 100%

FIGURE 16.28 Import solution details.

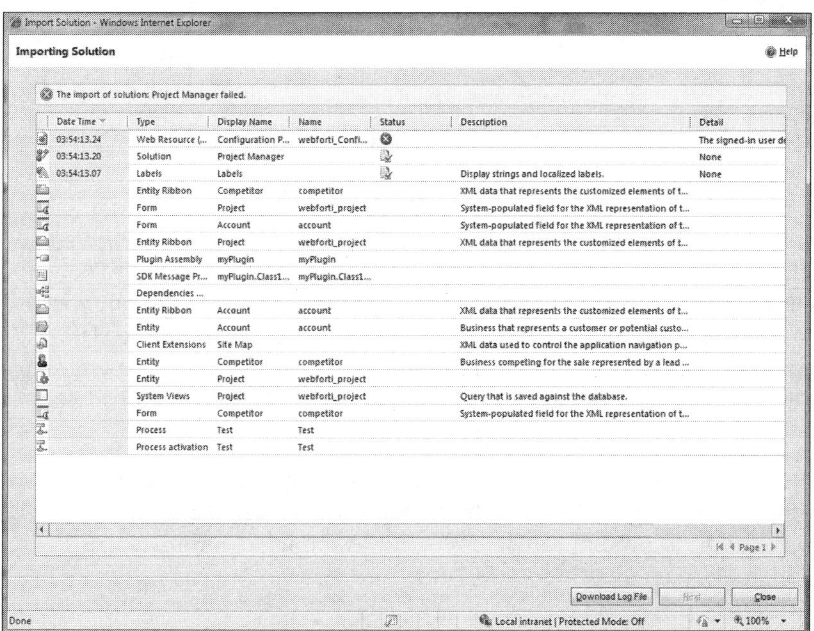

FIGURE 16.29 Import solution error.

To fix this error, you need to be added as deployment administrator in the CRM server with the Microsoft Dynamics CRM Deployment Manager (see Figure 16.30). If you are trying to use the solution on CRM Online, then the plugin will have to be deployed in a sandbox isolation mode.

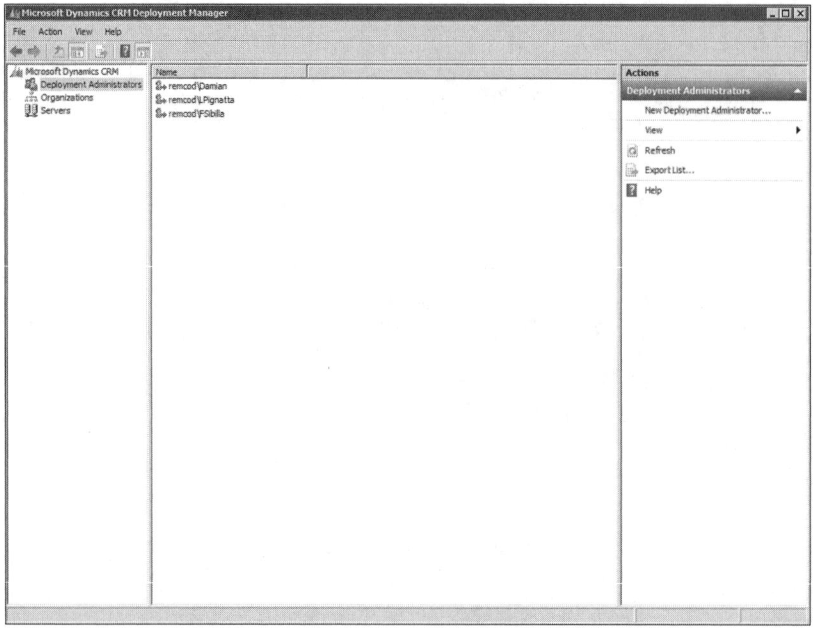

FIGURE 16.30 Microsoft Dynamics CRM Deployment Manager.

If you imported a solution that contains plug-ins and SDK message processing steps and you didn't check the check box that says Activate any processes and enable any SDK message processing steps included in the solution, you can activate them later but you will have to do that on the solution. When you open the solution and go to the SDK message processing steps node, you will have the ability to activate or deactivate any step you want to register on the plug-in assemblies installed by the managed solutions (see Figure 16.31).

All the functions that are on the solution's UI are also available on the API and the SDK, so you can automate the creation of solutions dynamically as well as manage the solutions from an external application that can be useful, for example, to automate the deployment of testing environments.

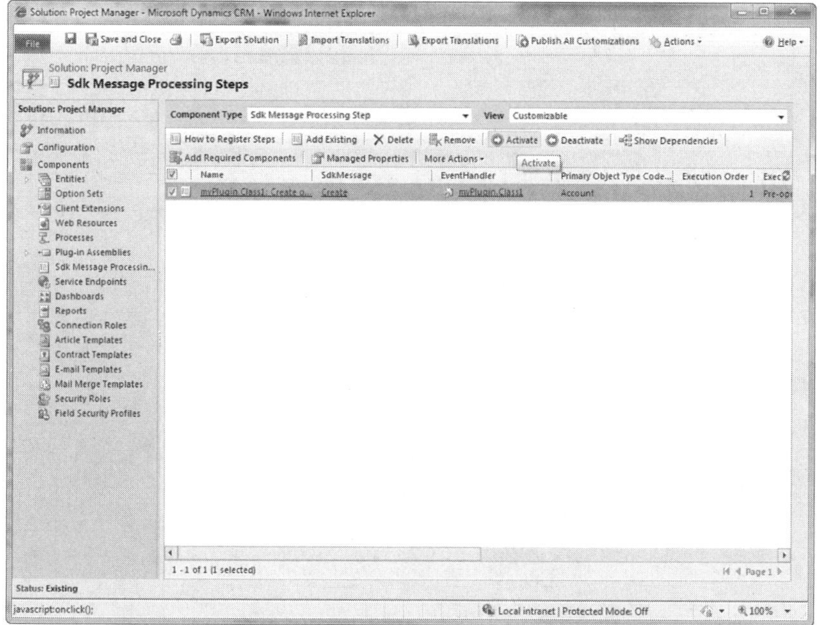

FIGURE 16.31 Activate or deactivate SDK message processing steps.

NOTE

Microsoft does not recommend using solutions such as ASP.NET, Silverlight, or Windows form application to package custom applications deployment that run outside of the CRM environment because they only consume the CRM resources through the Windows Communication Foundation (WCF) Web services. For those applications, it is recommended to use the old way for packaging by creating custom installers that can be generated by tools such as InstallShield.

A good practice is to add jQuery scripts as a web resource on your solution if you are going to use jQuery on your forms events. To add jQuery on your solution, download the most current version from http://docs.jquery.com/Downloading_jQuery, go to Web Resources, and click on New.

Enter the name and display name, select the type to script (JScript), and locate the jQuery file you downloaded (see Figure 16.32).

TIP

You can add the backslash character (/) on the Name field to simulate virtual directories. As you can see, in this example we used the script folder (see Figure 16.33).

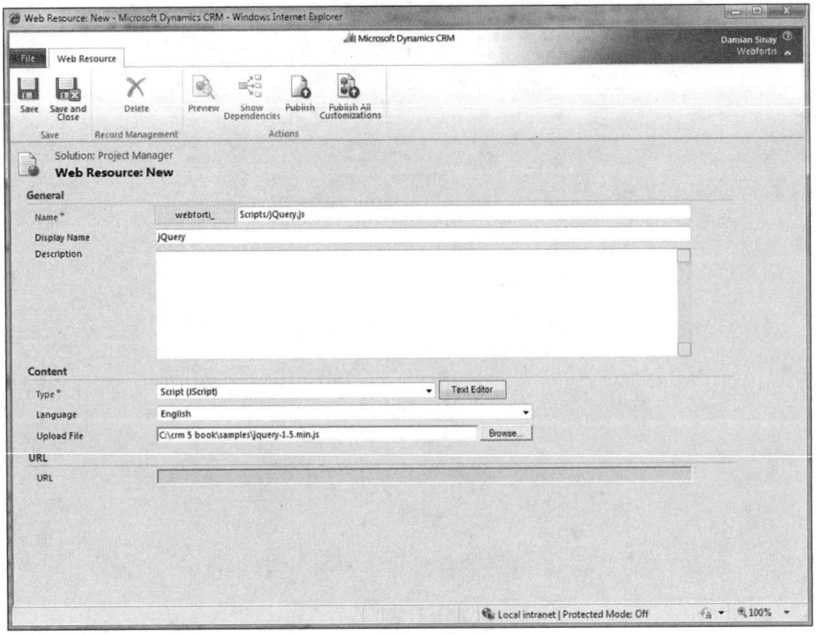

FIGURE 16.32 Creating a web resource for jQuery.

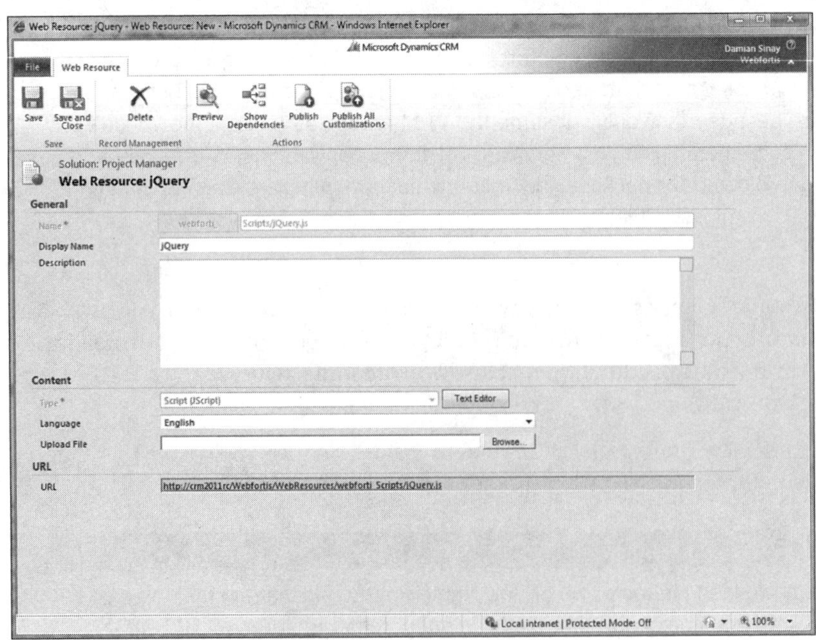

FIGURE 16.33 Adding jQuery with a custom virtual path.

Once you create this web resource, you can use jQuery on any form event.

▶ To see more details about web resources and forms customizations, refer to Chapter 23, "Customizing Entities."

CAUTION

You cannot import a managed solution on an organization that contains the same solution name in an unmanaged state. If you try to do that, you will see an error, similar to the one shown in Figure 16.34. If you want to test the managed package, you will need to import it on another organization.

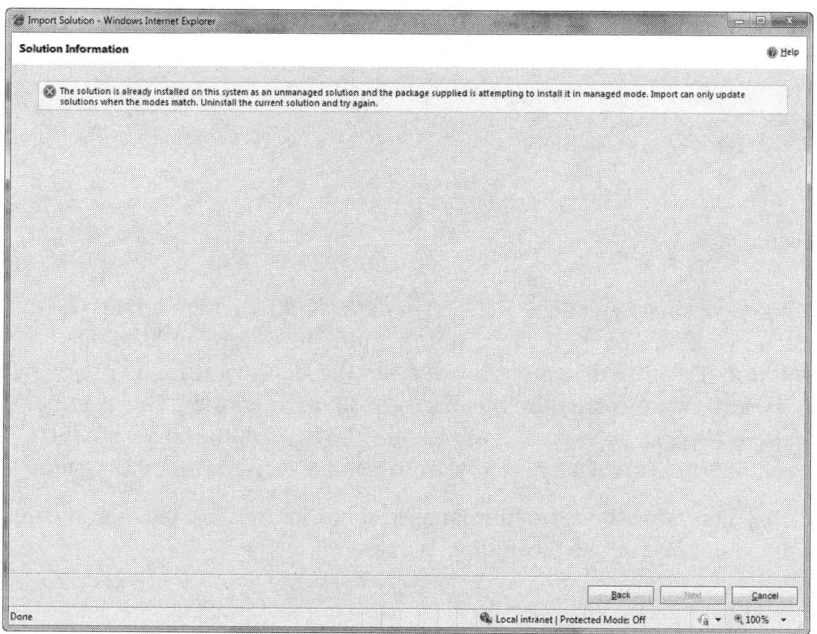

FIGURE 16.34 Import solution error.

Removing Solutions

After you import a custom managed solution to an organization that contains custom entities and you create records for those custom entities, CRM will delete all the records and SQL tables when you delete the managed solution. You will be alerted for confirmation before proceeding with the deletion operation, as shown in Figure 16.35.

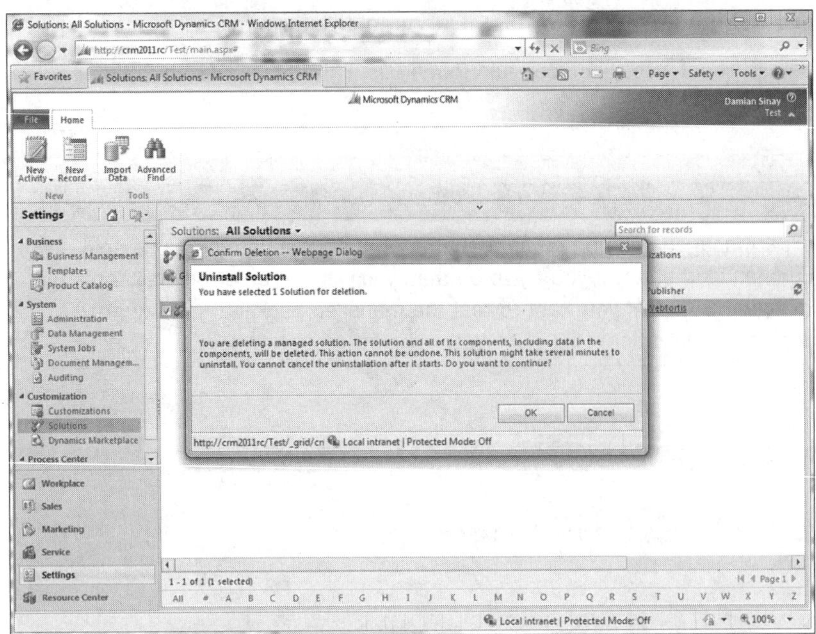

FIGURE 16.35 Confirm deletion.

It is recommended to make a backup of the SQL Server database (if you're working with an on premise version of CRM), or export the custom entities' records to an Excel file before deleting a solution. Deleting the solution will clean the CRM database by removing all the tables and views that were created by the managed solution entities. This is important to understand, especially if you are going to try a third-party solution on a production environment and after playing with it you want to remove it from the CRM system.

On the other hand, if you remove a custom unmanaged solution, the SQL tables and date of the custom entities won't be removed from the database.

To summarize what happens when removing solutions:

- **Managed solutions**—All customizations applied are removed, as well as all data.
- **Unmanaged solutions**—All customizations applied are removed. However, tables, views, and data remain in the Default Solution.

Working with Multiple Solutions

With this new concept of solutions, CRM implementations will probably contain more than one custom solution deployed. Not only might the CRM organizations used for solutions development contain more than one solution, but also the customer organizations that will finally use the solutions would probably be interested in deploying different solutions from different vendors.

When importing solutions, there are some considerations to take into account related to the predefined system entities. If we imported a solution that included a customized form of any system entity, for example, this could be by removing some fields and tabs on the Contact entity. These customizations will win on any other solution that included the same Contact entity without any customization. So, if we need to include the system Contact entity on our solution, we need to make at least one customization to the form so that we can be sure all the needed fields won't be overwritten by another solution.

TIP

As an Independent software vendor (ISV) developer who will work on a custom solution that will require a system entity, it would be good to consider adding new custom roles and creating new forms associated to this new security role. This will avoid other solutions overlapping with our solution customizations. So, users will have to use our custom roles to have a better experience with our solution.

Entity Forms Security

One important consideration when working with solutions that contain custom entities is the security configuration for the necessary roles. By default when you create a custom entity only the system Administrator and System Customizer are granted permission to use the custom entity. You are responsible to give the right permissions to any other role (such as the Customer Representative Role for example) so that users with that role can work with the custom entity you included on the solution.

To configure the security roles, open the solution and complete the following steps:

1. Navigate to the Components, Entities, your custom entity, and Forms (see Figure 16.36).
2. Click Assign Security Roles (see Figure 16.37).
3. Select the role you want to configure (in this example we will select the Customer Service Representative role) and click on the name to open the Security Role editor page.
4. Go to the Custom Entities Tab. You will see that all the solution custom entities are there with no permissions set, as shown in Figure 16.38.
5. Grant the permissions to the operations you want by clicking on the circles. Noticed if you click on the entity name, it will affect the entire row, meaning that it will configure all the operations at the same time (see Figure 16.39).

A new feature of CRM 2011 allows having different forms for each security role. So, you can create new forms with different fields and assign them to different roles. For example, you might have sensitive fields on an entity you would like to hide to a lower role such as a customer representative. You can now easily do that by creating a new form and designing it to show only the fields this user role should see.

Figure 16.40 shows an entity with more than one main form created to be used by different roles.

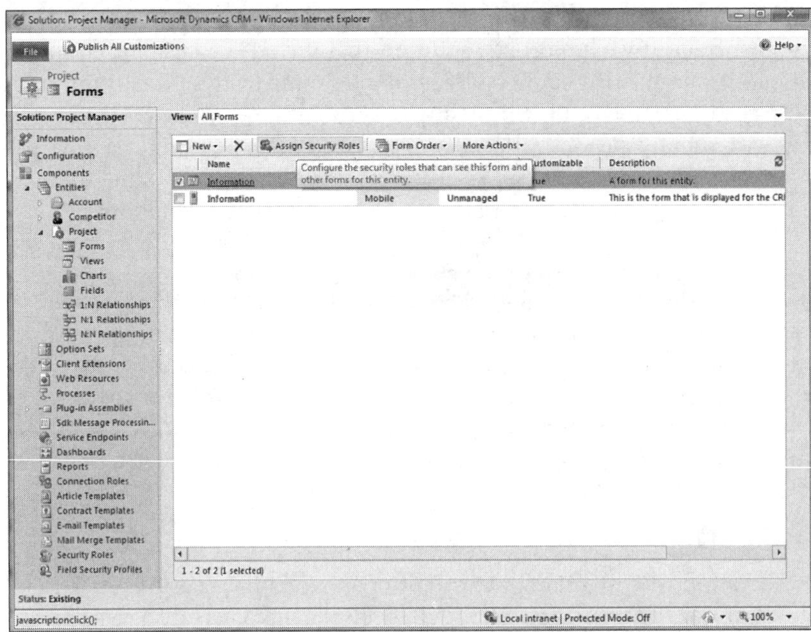

FIGURE 16.36 The Assign Security Roles button.

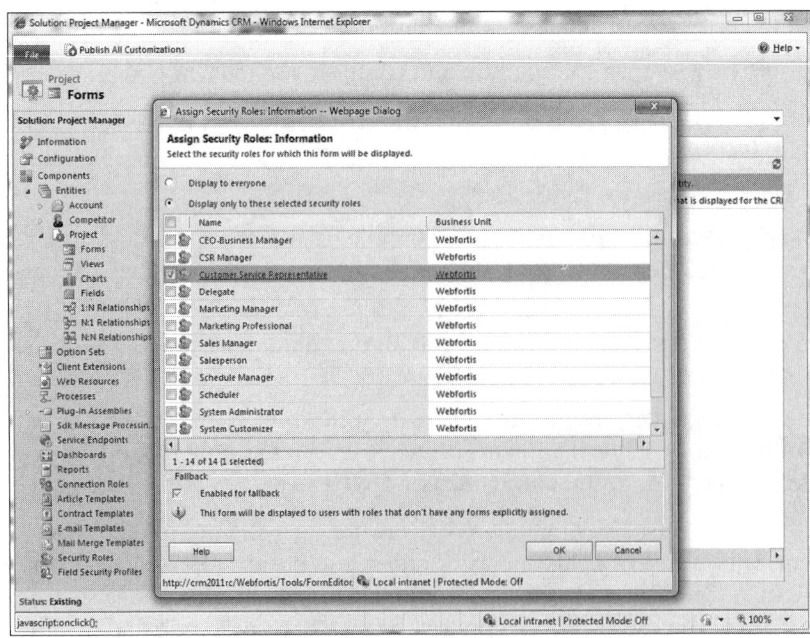

FIGURE 16.37 Assign Security Roles information.

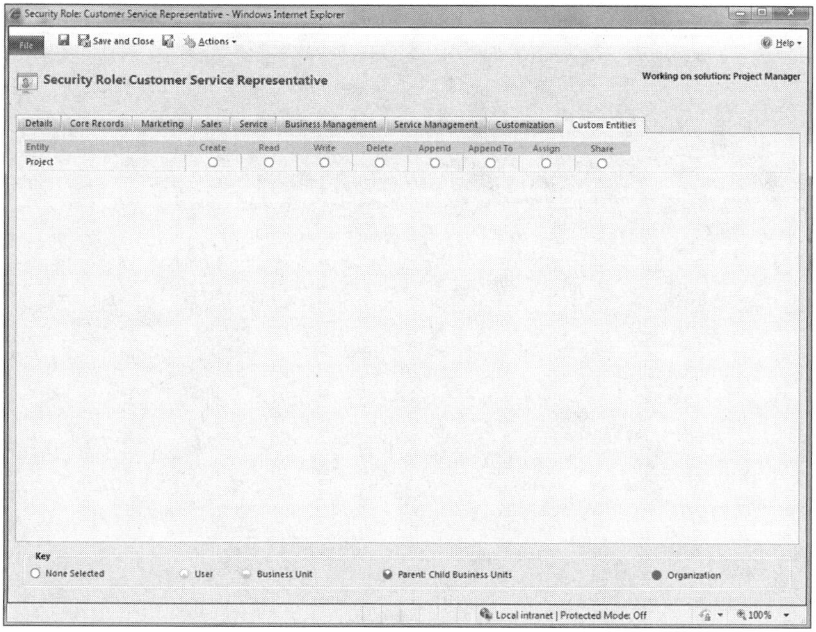

FIGURE 16.38 The Custom Entities tab.

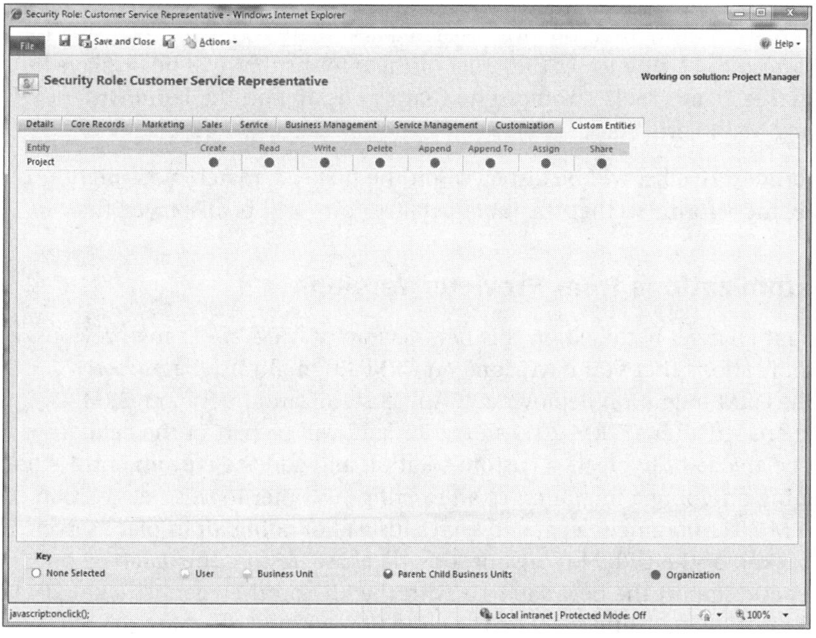

FIGURE 16.39 The Custom Entities tab with permissions set.

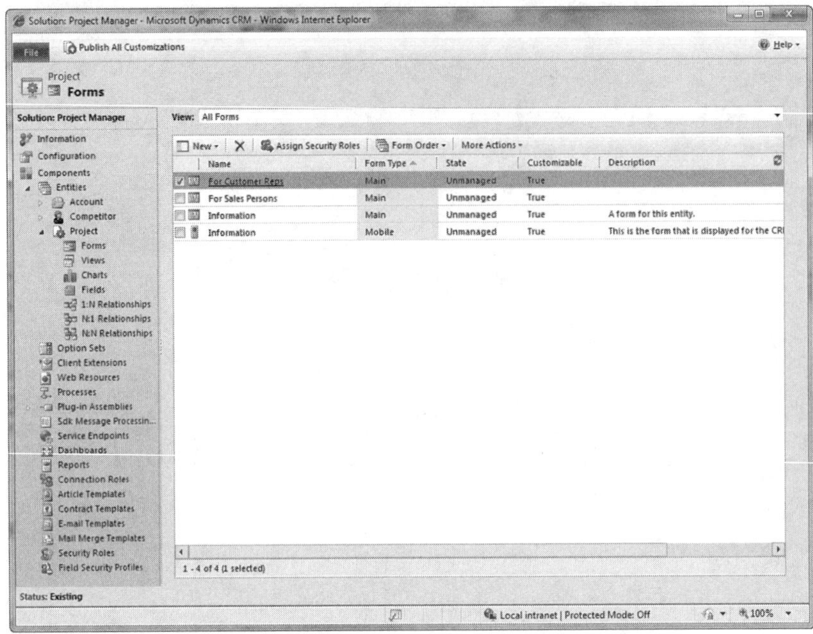

FIGURE 16.40 Entity with multiple main forms.

If you have a user that has more than one role assigned and there is one form created for each role, you will need to be sure to set the order of these forms that will be displayed first for those cases (see Figure 16.41). You can do that by clicking on the Form Order button and selecting Main Form Set.

Because the first form on this list will be displayed on the first role match, you might consider reordering these forms so that the more detailed form will be displayed first.

Migrating Customizations from Previous Versions

Due to the important changes included on this new version of CRM 2011, any previous CRM version customizations that you have done on CRM 4.0 might not be properly migrated during the CRM migration deployment. Any customization done on CRM 4.0 will remain as unmanaged after a CRM 2011 migration and will be part of the default solution, you will be able later to create a custom solution and add the custom entities on it. If you are planning on doing a migration of an existing customer to this new version, you can deploy CRM 2011 on a new separated server instead of doing an in place server upgrade, make a backup of the CRM 4.0 organization database, restore the database on another SQL Server and import the new database with the Microsoft Dynamics CRM 2011 Deployment manager to migrate and validate the migration without affecting the old CRM 4.0 deployment.

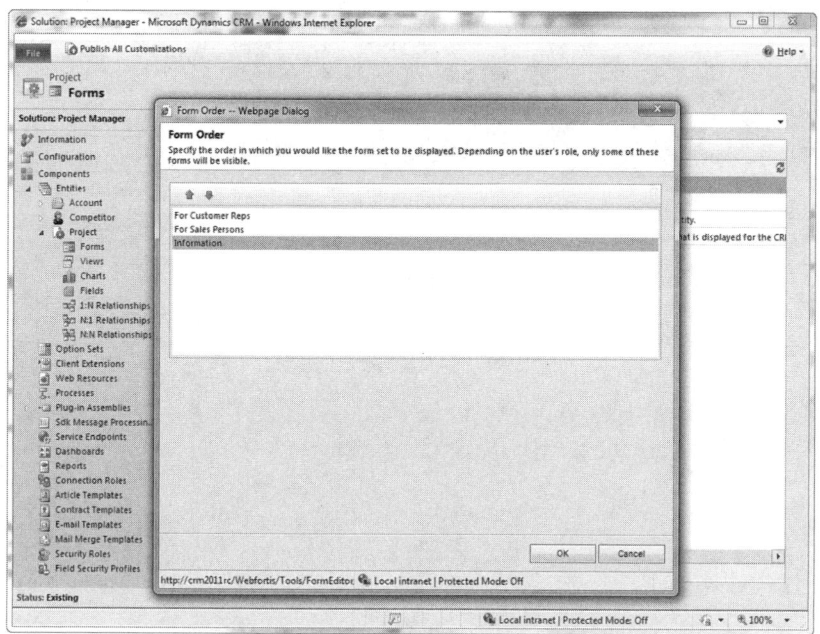

FIGURE 16.41 Form order.

For most cases, it would be a good idea to review all the new features implemented on CRM 2011 because they can be done more easily and with less code than any customization done for CRM 4.0. A good example would be a customization to make a field always visible on a form regardless of the tab the user has selected; on CRM 4.0, this required making a complex JavaScript code to move the fields outside the form tabs. This is something that now can be done with the new Header section of the CRM 2011 forms without involving any complex JavaScript code to do this customization. Other features, such as adding auditing, are now native to CRM 2011 and do not require any plug-in assembly to be loaded for this feature.

Third-Party and Marketplace Solutions

The Marketplace is a Microsoft website where Microsoft partners and ISV will be able to publish their solutions so that users of CRM 2011 and CRM 4.0 can easily find and install them on their environments.

For ISVs

In the Solutions area, you will see a button on the toolbar that says Get Solutions from Marketplace. Clicking this button takes you to the Microsoft Dynamics Marketplace website, as shown in Figure 16.42.

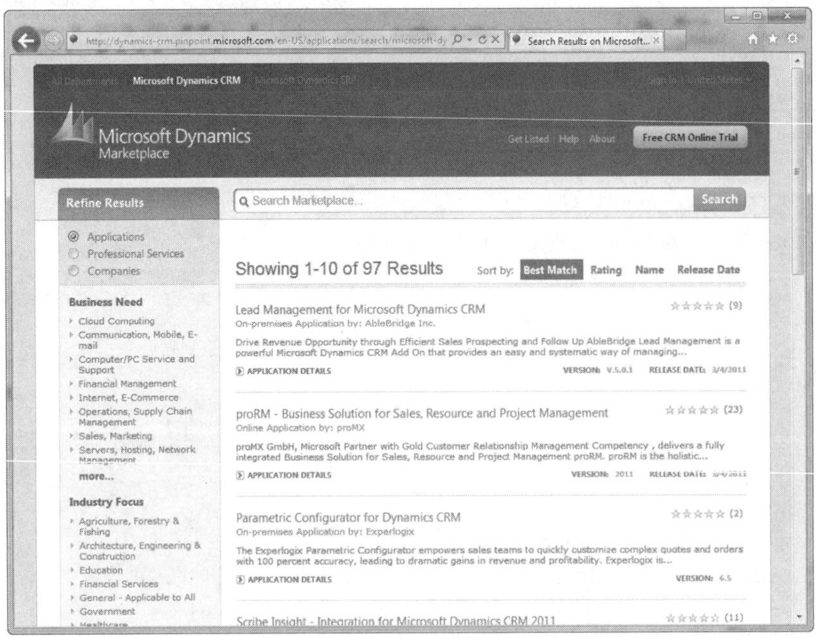

FIGURE 16.42 Microsoft Dynamics Marketplace.

▶ The direct URL for the Microsoft Dynamics Marketplace is http://dynamics-crm.pinpoint.microsoft.com/.

If you are an ISV and want to have your solution in this Marketplace, you will have to be listed first in Microsoft Pinpoint. To do that, your company needs to be first a Microsoft partner. Microsoft partners can list software solutions using the Solution Profiler tool and also be listed in the Microsoft Pinpoint website. There are two types of product registrations: For Microsoft CRM applications, go to the Microsoft Platform Ready website and test the application using free tools, and for Microsoft ERP applications, get the solution tested and certified with the CfMD (Certified for Microsoft Dynamics) certification.

▶ These tests and certifications are performed by the Lion Bridge company. More information is available at http://www.lionbridge.com/lionbridge/en-US/services/software-product-engineering/testing-veritest/product-certification-services/microsoft/certified-for-dynamics.htm.

The Microsoft Dynamics Marketplace will help you find the right customers by exposing your application to the worldwide Microsoft Dynamics users, who will be able to download your application from this site and also connect with your company.

ISVs have the ability to start working on new solution application since September 2010, when the first beta version of CRM 2011 was be available for the public. So, by the time CRM 2011 released, there would be lot of solutions added on the Marketplace.

For Customers

In the Settings area under the Customizations group is a link to the Dynamics Marketplace. From this link you will be able to see the most popular solutions ranked by customers as well as see the solution reviews to help you choose the best solution for your company (see Figure 16.43).

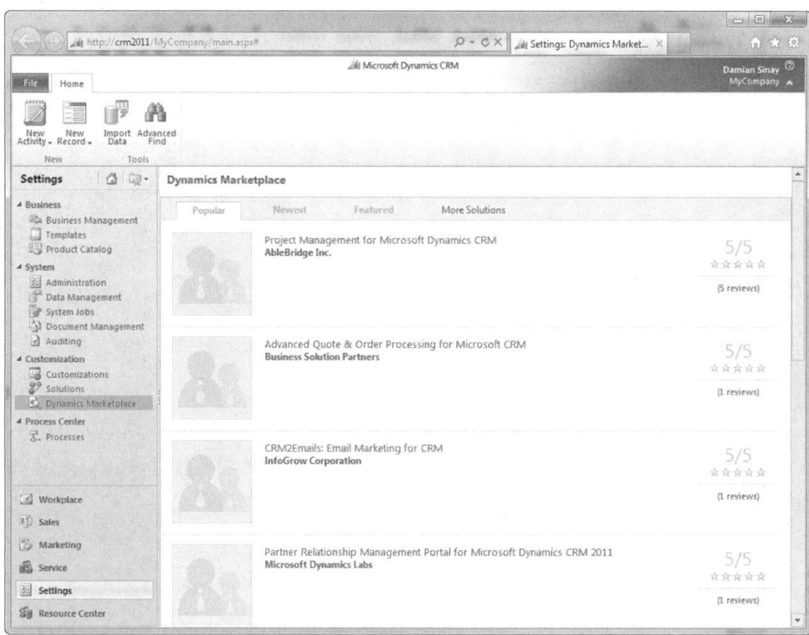

FIGURE 16.43 Microsoft Dynamics Marketplace for customers.

If you are a customer, the Marketplace will help you to discover and try custom solutions developed by third-party vendors that might be of interest and would be better to check before you start thinking about developing a new custom solution from scratch. Because the solutions that will be available in the Marketplace are verified and certified, you can feel confident installing them and not be worried about crashes on your system.

Microsoft will also maintain a blacklist for untrusted publishers to avoid any malicious code (that could be included on a plug-in assembly) being installed on your environment.

Summary

This chapter described the new way to customize Microsoft Dynamics CRM for deployment, support, and distribution by using solution packages. We reviewed the differences between managed and unmanaged solutions, as well as reviewed the Microsoft Dynamics Marketplace from which ISVs will be able to promote their solutions and customers will be able to find solutions easier.

CHAPTER 17

CRM 2011 SharePoint Integration

IN THIS CHAPTER

This chapter was researched and authored by Alex Aquila from Webfortis. Alex is an MCP and an accomplished developer in both Microsoft Dynamics CRM and SharePoint.

In this chapter, we cover the installation and configuration of CRM 2011 to SharePoint integration, focusing primarily on SharePoint 2010 integration components. Finally, we take a brief look at extending this integration by using C# and the SDK.

The "Basic Integration" section covers integrating SharePoint 2007 or SharePoint 2010 without the list components. The "Standard Integration" section explains how to install and configure the list components for CRM 2011 and SharePoint 2010.

TIP

With all levels of integration, if you are using Outlook, you must run in Online Mode to access SharePoint features.

What's New in Dynamics CRM 2011

Although SharePoint integration was an option with previous versions of Microsoft Dynamics CRM, it required configuration and even when deploying it based on best practices, there were still options that resulted in varied results (both in performance and implementation options). Microsoft Dynamics CRM 2011 now features native SharePoint integration options out-of-the-box. The document management integration is going to show up in two places. First, there is now a Documents view on every record in CRM, as shown in Figure 17.1.

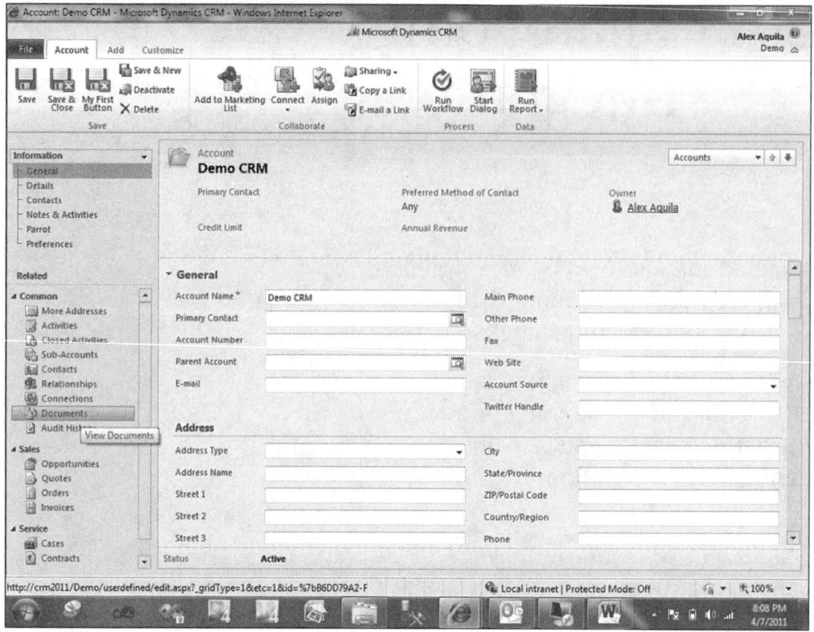

FIGURE 17.1 Documents available on entity in near navigation pane.

This integration option allows users to access SharePoint documents per entity across the application.

Secondly, there is now a Document Management section under System, located in CRM settings (see Figure 17.2).

This is where administrators set up and configure the SharePoint options that allow the SharePoint documents, as was shown in Figure 17.1, to be referenced and ultimately live.

The options in Document Management are

- **Document Management Settings**—This is where you specify which entities will use document management. You can also choose to apply auto-structuring around either the account or the contact.

- **Install List Component**—The entire purpose of this button is to download the latest version of the list components. As of the time of publication, this includes the crmlistcomponent.wsp and a PowerShell script to set up your SharePoint site. Although it is entirely possible to manage your CRM 2011 document structure and integration by hand, it does require that you first create the structure in SharePoint. Using the list component to automatically create document libraries is a much easier solution.

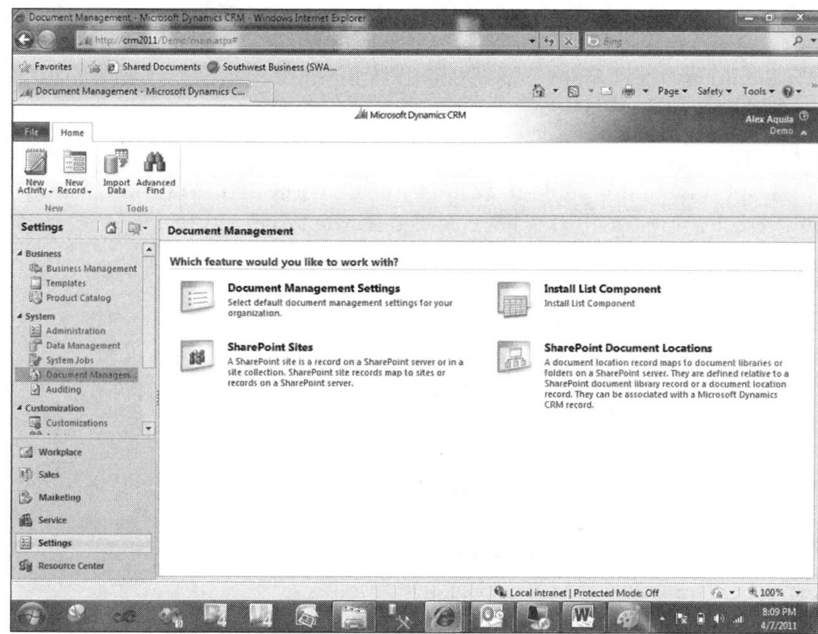

FIGURE 17.2 Document Management Console within CRM 2011.

The list components include the following features and benefits:

- Automatic Document Library Creation in SharePoint, applying a nested organizational structure specified in the Document Management Settings Wizard
- Automatic site object management in CRM
- A more secure and user friendly IFRAME view of SharePoint from within CRM
- **SharePoint sites**—When you run the Document Management Settings Wizard, a site is created here. You can also create sites by hand or modify sites created automatically.
- **SharePoint Document Locations**—This is where you view all the document locations that have been created, create new locations, and modify existing locations.

Even with these options, there are still several options when integrating with SharePoint.

Basic Integration

If you are using SharePoint 2007 (versus SharePoint 2010), you do not have the option to install the list components and are limited to basic integration. True integration requires the list components, and they are supported only in SharePoint 2010. If you have the capacity in your environment to implement them, doing so is highly recommended.

Your document locations will be saved and viewable in the Document Management section as records in CRM 2011. From inside CRM, navigate to Settings, Document Management, and you will see Document Management Options, which was shown in Figure 17.2.

Because you are using basic integration, the Install List Component and Document Management Settings options do not apply to you. If you are using SharePoint 2010 and you want to install the list component, this is explained in the next section.

Installing the List Component

To implement basic integration, follow these steps:

1. From inside Microsoft Dynamics CRM, open the record of your choice, and click Documents. You will receive the prompt shown in Figure 17.3.

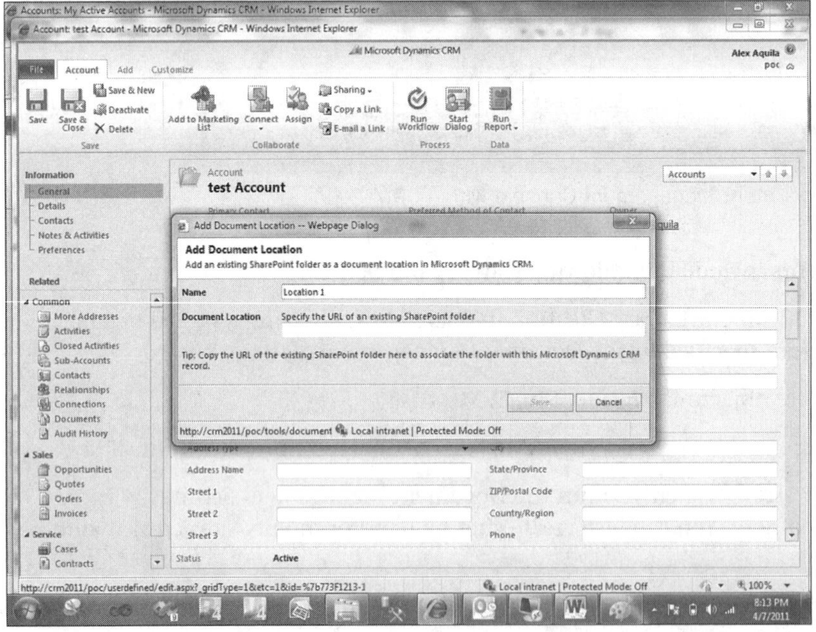

FIGURE 17.3 Prompt to link a CRM record to a SharePoint document location in basic integration.

2. Enter the name of the location and the URL to your SharePoint site where the documents will be stored, as shown in Figure 17.4.

TIP

Basic integration will not create the document library for you; it must already exist prior to attempting step 2.

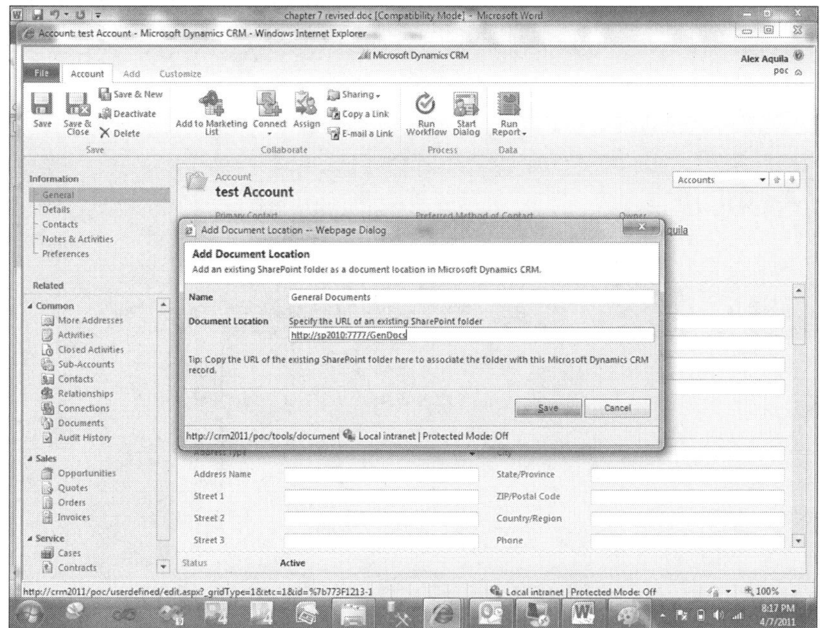

FIGURE 17.4 Type in the absolute URL used to access the pre-existing SharePoint document library.

When you click Save, you will now see an IFRAME that points to the SharePoint site and is open to the URL of the document library (see Figure 17.5).

You now can interact with the document library through this IFRAME and upload your documents. You can also add additional document locations using the drop-down at the top of the IFRAME and toggle among the different locations.

Open SharePoint Document Locations, and you will see the location we just made, the record it is regarding, and the URL (see Figure 17.6).

NOTE

The location is not paired with a SharePoint site record in CRM. You will learn how to do this manually in the "Integration Features" section later in this chapter.

This is the extent of basic SharePoint integration. If you are planning extensive document management integration solutions using Microsoft Dynamics CRM 2011, it is worth considering installing SharePoint 2010.

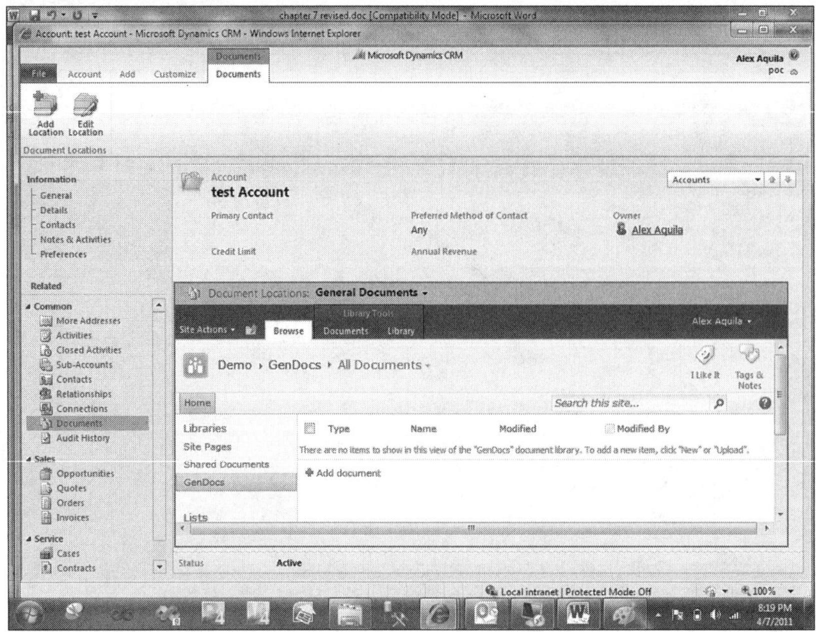

FIGURE 17.5 The record is now linked to the document library in SharePoint, and the IFRAME renders the page in SharePoint.

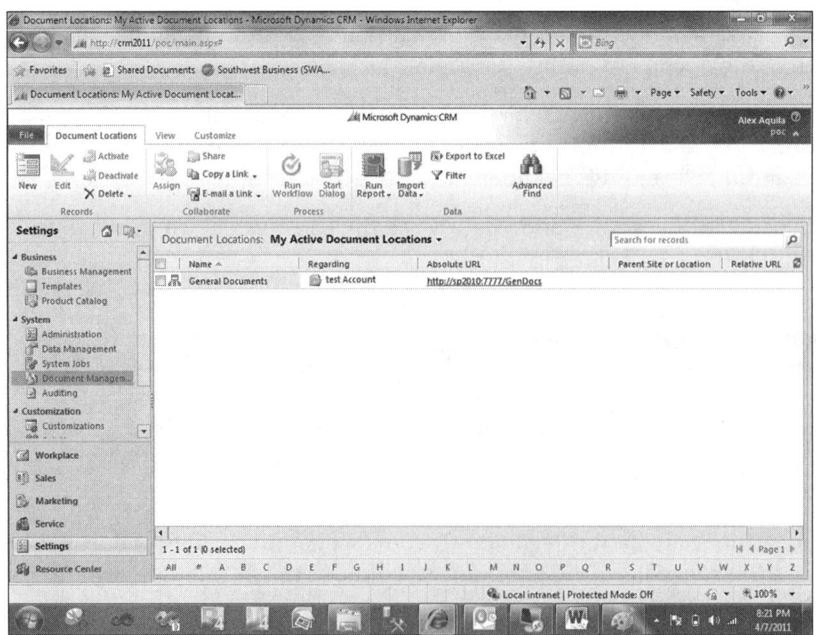

FIGURE 17.6 A document location record is created within CRM for you.

Standard Integration

Standard integration has numerous advantages over basic integration: The creation of document libraries is automated, the document library hierarchies in SharePoint are created automatically for you, and the document management interface on records in CRM 2011 is vastly improved.

We will now go through the process of integrating SharePoint 2010 and CRM 2011.

SharePoint Configuration

> **NOTE**
>
> You must be a SharePoint farm administrator to complete this installation.

Download the CRM 2011 list components by either getting the file from http://www.microsoft.com/downloads, or by clicking Install List Component in the Document Management section under Settings, System in Microsoft Dynamics CRM 2011, as shown in Figure 17.2.

Extract the AllowHtcExtn.ps1 file to a location on your SharePoint server. Open PowerShell as an administrator and navigate to the location of the script. Determine the URL of your SharePoint site, and enter the following command (see Figure 17.7):

```
.\AllowHtcExtn.ps1 http://<yoursite>
```

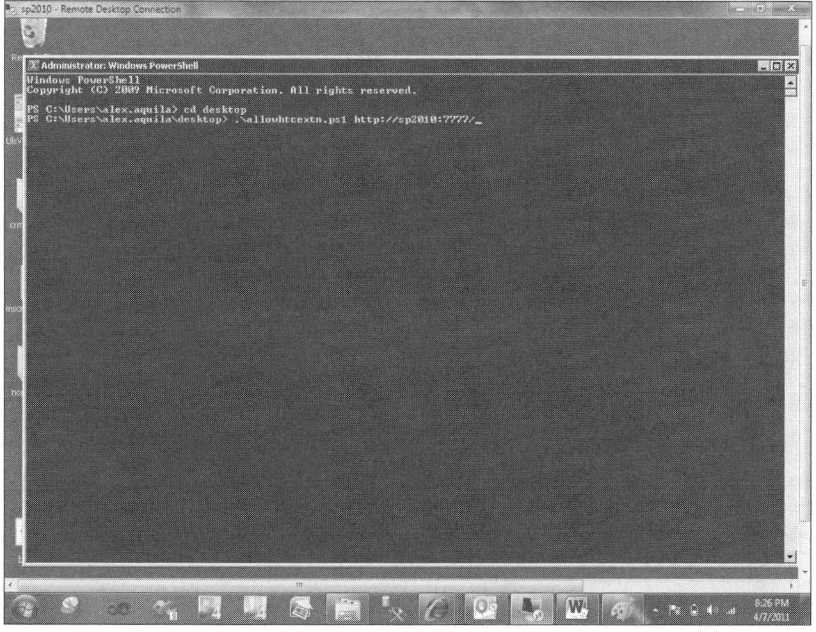

FIGURE 17.7 Execute the PS1 script provided in the installation package.

CAUTION

If you do not run this script, you will not be able to use the SharePoint buttons from inside Microsoft Dynamics CRM 2011. If this occurs, you must manually start the user code service and enable permissive browser file handling, which is explained later in this section.

Now, navigate to your SharePoint site. You will need to upload the crmlistcomponent.wsp to your solution library and complete the following steps to activate it.

1. Open your SharePoint site collection; that is, http://sp2010:7777/.

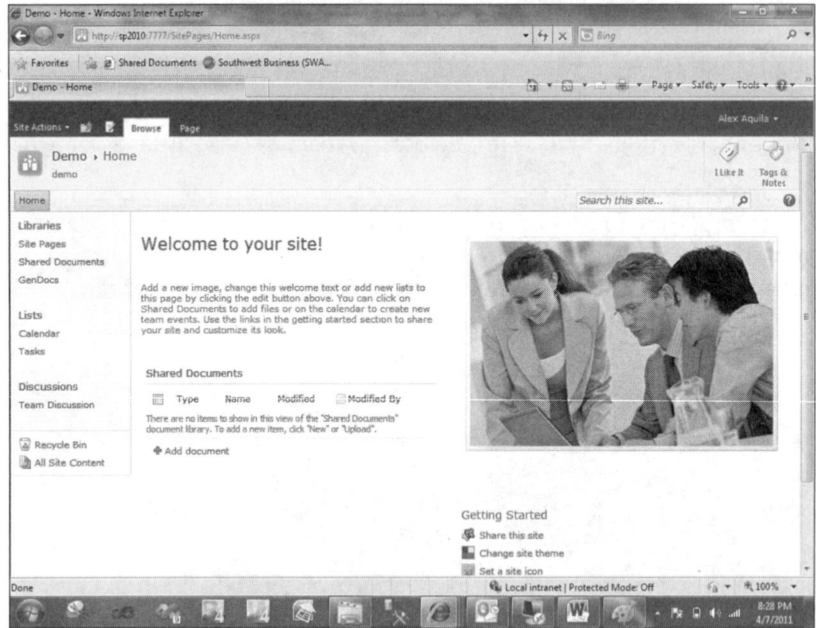

FIGURE 17.8 Open Internet Explorer and browse to your SharePoint site URL.

2. Click Select Site Actions, and then click Site Settings.
3. In the Galleries Section, click Solutions.
4. Click the Solutions tab on the Ribbon, and click the Upload Solution button.
5. Browse to the crmlistcomponent.wsp, select it, and click OK.
6. When the upload finishes, you will see the screen as shown in Figure 17.13.
7. Click Activate. This takes you back to the Solution Gallery, and you can see that the crmlistcomponent has a status of Activated.

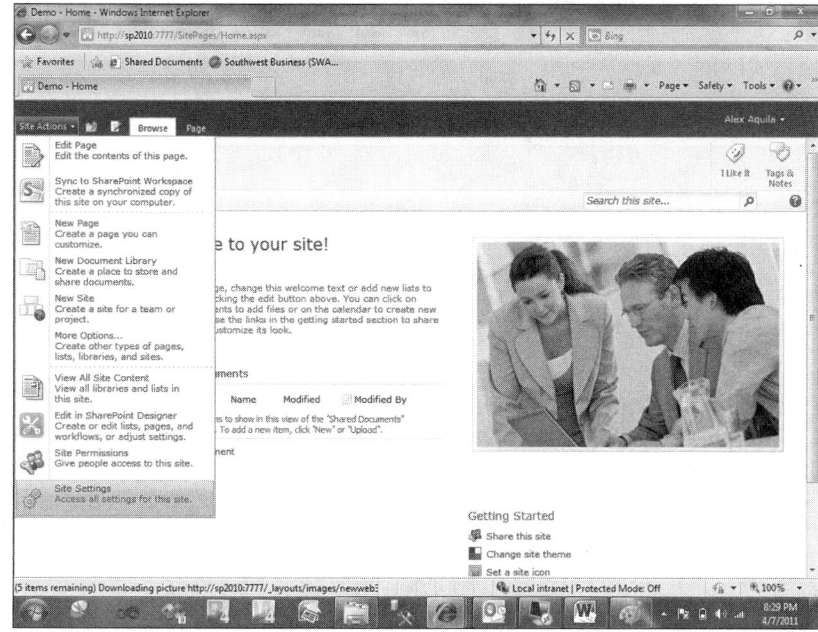

FIGURE 17.9 Open Site Settings, located under Site Actions.

Your SharePoint site is now properly configured. Note that deploying the crmlistcomponent.wsp file at a farm level is not supported by Microsoft.

If your SharePoint server is also a domain controller, you must run the following PowerShell Script provided by Microsoft:

```
$acl = Get-Acl HKLM:\System\CurrentControlSet\Control\ComputerName
$person = [System.Security.Principal.NTAccount]"Users"
$access = [System.Security.AccessControl.RegistryRights]::FullControl
$inheritance = [System.Security.AccessControl.InheritanceFlags/cr/lf
]"ContainerInherit, ObjectInherit"
$propagation = [System.Security.AccessControl.PropagationFlags]::None
$type = [System.Security.AccessControl.AccessControlType]::Allow
$rule = New-Object System.Security.AccessControl.RegistryAccessRule/cr/lf
($person, $access, $inheritance, $propagation, $type)
$acl.AddAccessRule($rule)
Set-Acl HKLM:\System\CurrentControlSet\Control\ComputerName $acl
echo "Finished."
```

You can also configure your SharePoint site manually, rather than executing the allowhtcextn.ps1 file.

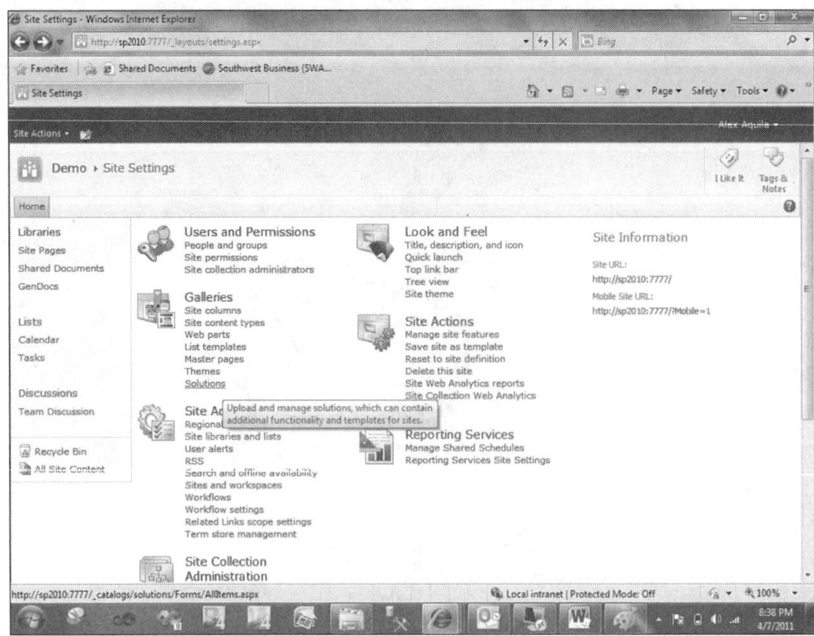

FIGURE 17.10 The SharePoint Solution Gallery Link is under Solutions.

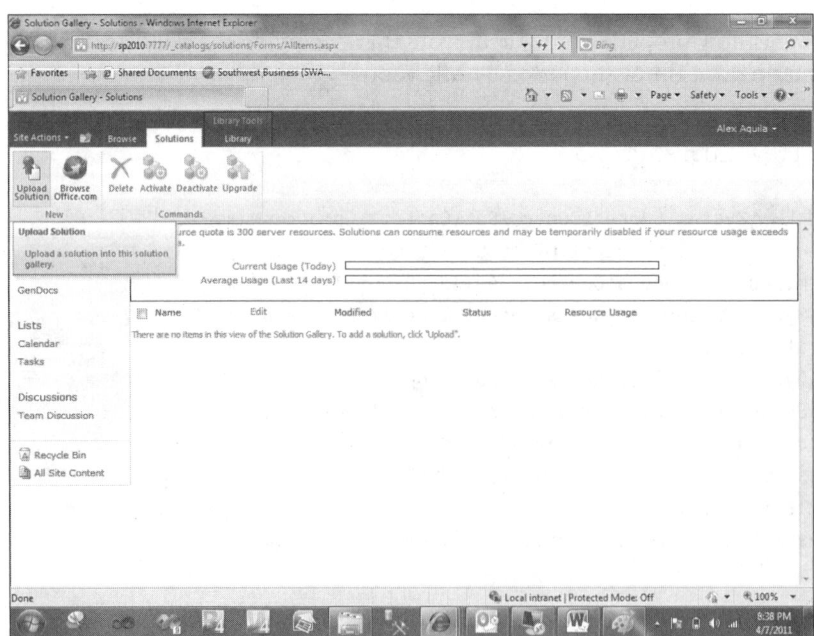

FIGURE 17.11 Click Upload Solution in the top left of the page.

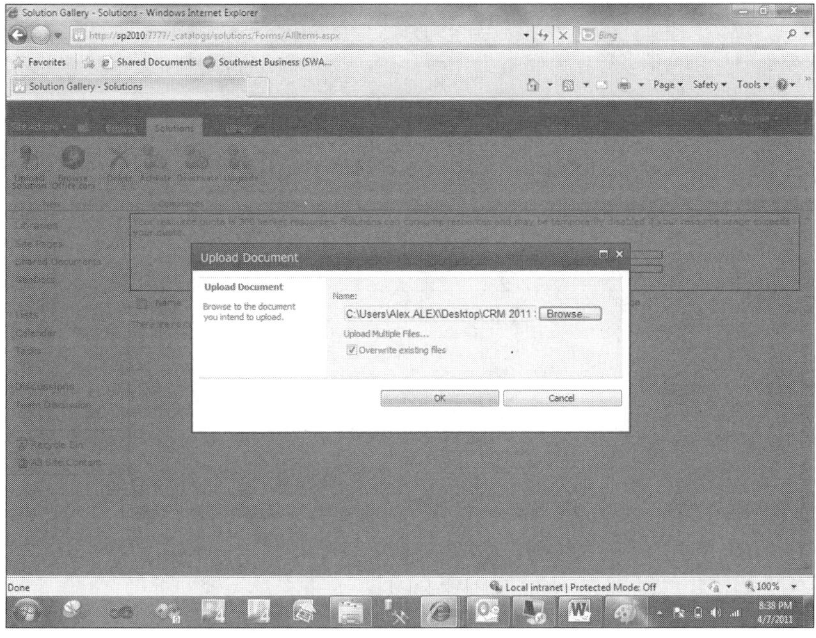

FIGURE 17.12 Load the crmlistcomponent.wsp file and click OK.

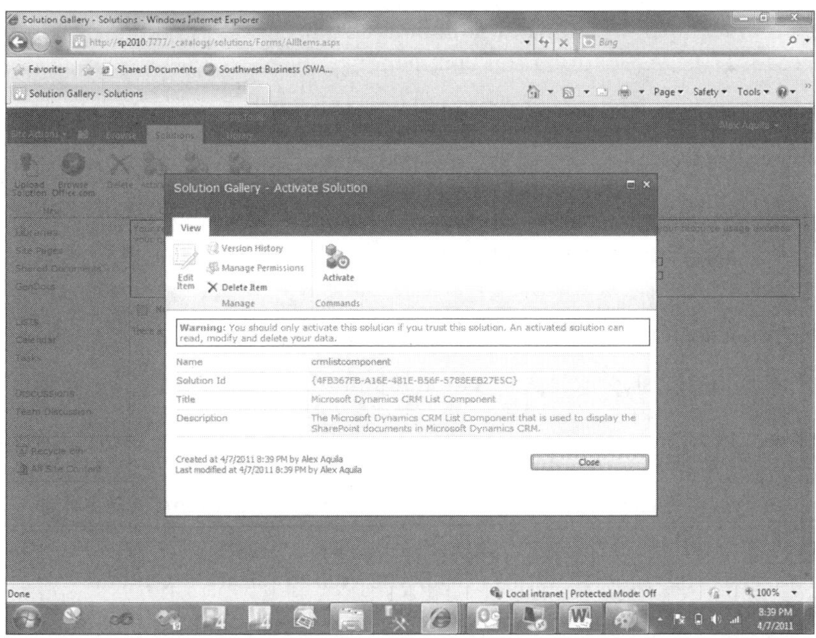

FIGURE 17.13 The solution has been uploaded, but it must be activated.

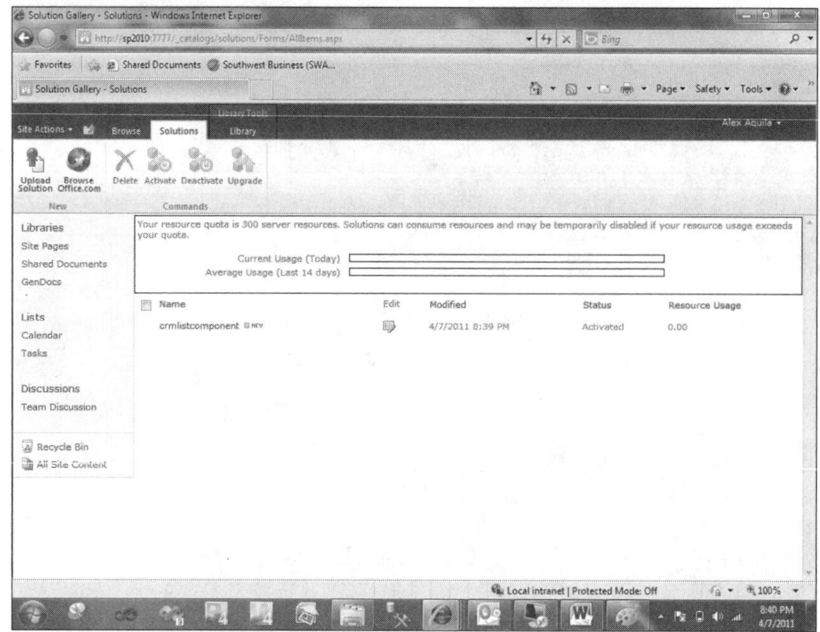

FIGURE 17.14 You can see the solution has been activated properly.

From the SharePoint server, open a command prompt as an administrator and navigate to the location of the STSADM.exe tool using this command:

CD C:\Program Files\Common Files\Microsoft Shared\Web Server Extensions\14\BIN

Next, run the following command:

```
stsadm -o provisionservice -action start -servicetype/cr/lf
Microsoft.SharePoint.Administration.SPUserCodeService/cr/lf
 -servicename SPUserCodeV4
```

Then enter iisreset /noforce and press Enter.

Finally, complete the following steps to open Central Administration and set Browser File Handling to Permissive:

1. Verify you are a SharePoint farm administrator.
2. Navigate to Manage Web Applications under Application Management. Select the web application you are using for this integration.
3. On the Ribbon, click the General Settings Gear. The Web Application General Settings will open. Scroll down to the Browser File Handling section, and set it to Permissive.

NOTE

These steps are required only if you were unsuccessful in executing the AllowHtcExtn.ps1 script.

Now that you have successfully configured SharePoint, you need to do some basic configuration in Microsoft Dynamics CRM 2011.

CRM 2011 Configuration

To configure Microsoft Dynamics CRM 2011, open CRM in your browser and navigate to the Settings, Document Management section, as shown previously in Figure 17.2.

1. Open Document Management Settings. This is where you will choose the entities that will have document management enabled. You can always come back to this screen and change these settings (see Figure 17.15).

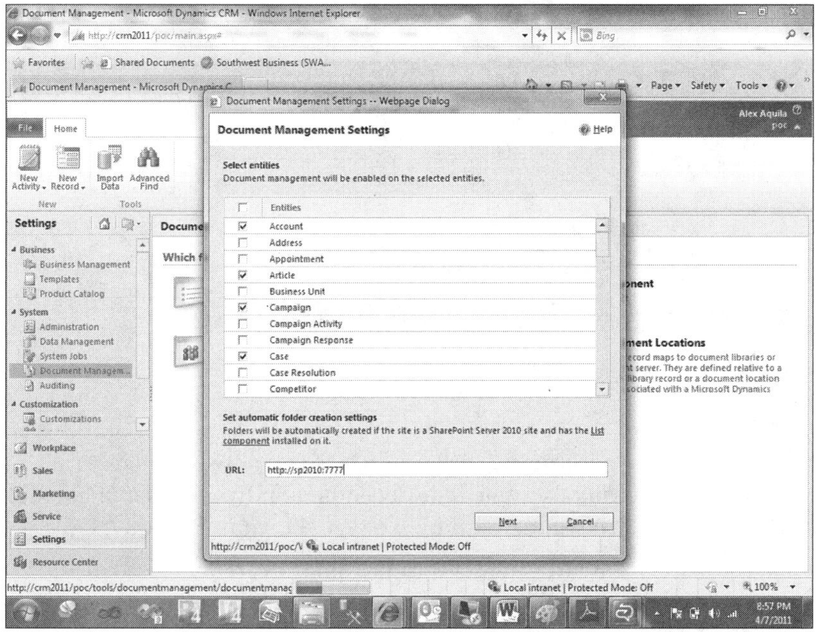

FIGURE 17.15 Choose which entities in CRM will have document management enabled.

2. In the URL field, type in the URL of your site collection that has the crmlistcomponent.wsp installed and activated. Click next. CRM will validate the URL, and you

can choose the base entity for a derived folder structure. Only Accounts and Contacts can be the base entity. So, for example, if you create an account (TestAccount) and an opportunity (TestOpp) as a child to TestAccount, documents for TestOpp will be stored in the: account\TestAccount\Opportunity\TestOpp library in SharePoint, but only if Account is set as your base entity type. If you do not want CRM to automatically apply a folder structure, leave the box unchecked (see Figure 17.16).

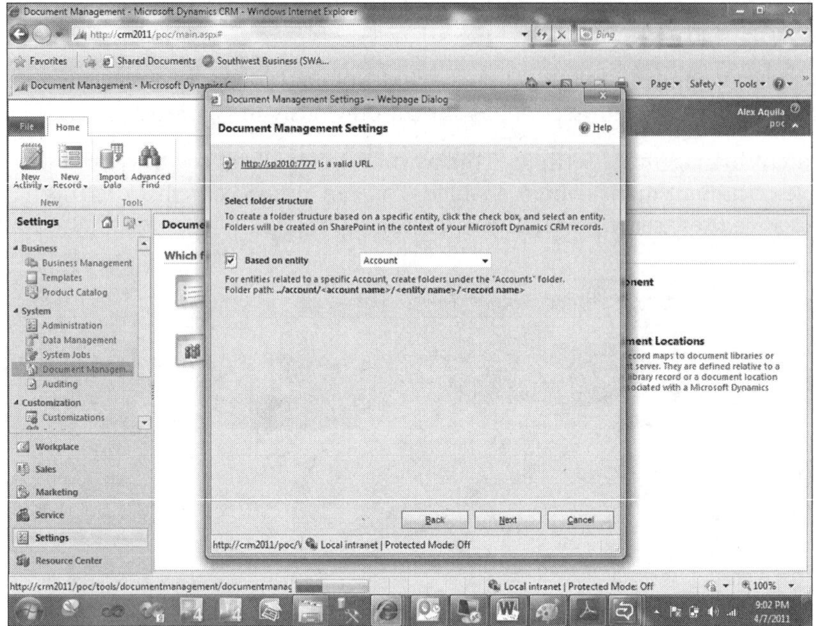

FIGURE 17.16 Select a base entity.

3. When you have decided on a base entity, click next. CRM will now try to create all the document libraries. This will take some time depending on the number of libraries that need creating, and you will see the warning message shown in Figure 17.17.

   You can also see the status, and error message, as the libraries are processed. Sometimes this process can time-out part way through the install; if it does, click back and rerun the wizard.

   When it is finished, close the wizard by clicking Finish.

4. Open SharePoint Sites. You will see that a site has been created and validated, as shown in Figure 17.18. It will have the name Default Site. You can rename this, and add a description if you choose.

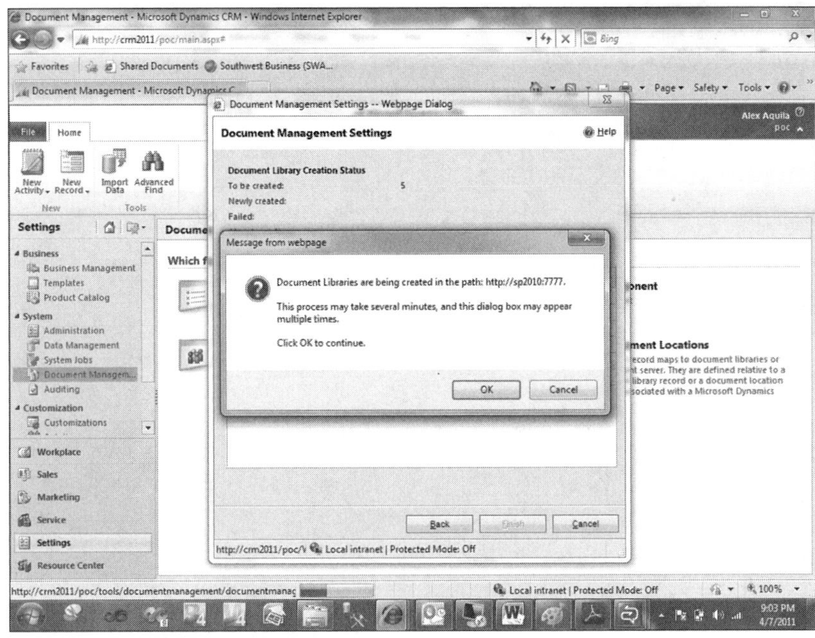

FIGURE 17.17 This box might reappear depending on the number of libraries you are creating.

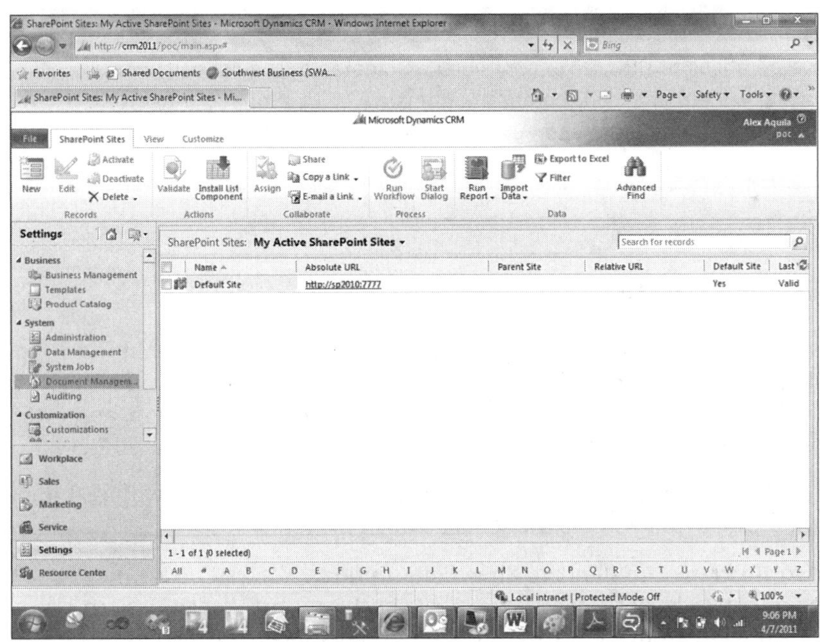

FIGURE 17.18 SharePoint site.

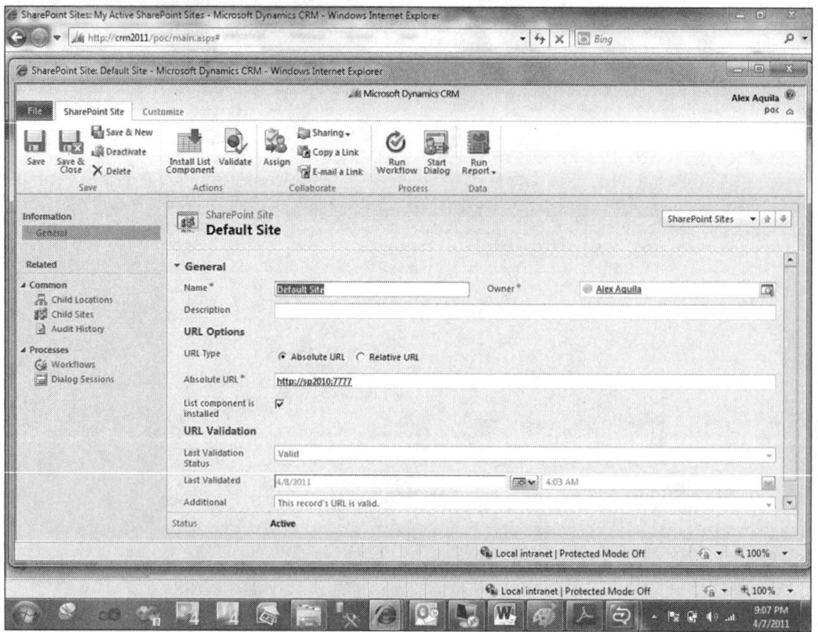

FIGURE 17.19 The information stored in the newly created site object.

NOTE

Your site will have an absolute URL. Document libraries created by the list component belonging to this site will automatically be assigned relative URLs. So, if your site URL changes, you only have to update the site object and not each individual document location object.

Integration Features

Now that you have installed the crmlistcomponent.wsp, creation of document libraries for records will be automated. Open a record of your base type, or of a type that you set to have integration features enabled in the wizard. Click on the Documents section, and CRM will detect that a document library for this record needs to be created (see Figure 17.20).

If you click OK, a folder will be created for you, and the document locations will load the library that was just created. You will see the screen shown in Figure 17.21.

The options listed in the frame are standard SharePoint options. You can create new folders, upload documents, edit documents, check in, check out, and so on. You can also open the documents directly from CRM without having to first open SharePoint. Any records created as child records to this account (after this step) will have their document libraries placed in the Test Account folder, provided Account was set as your base type.

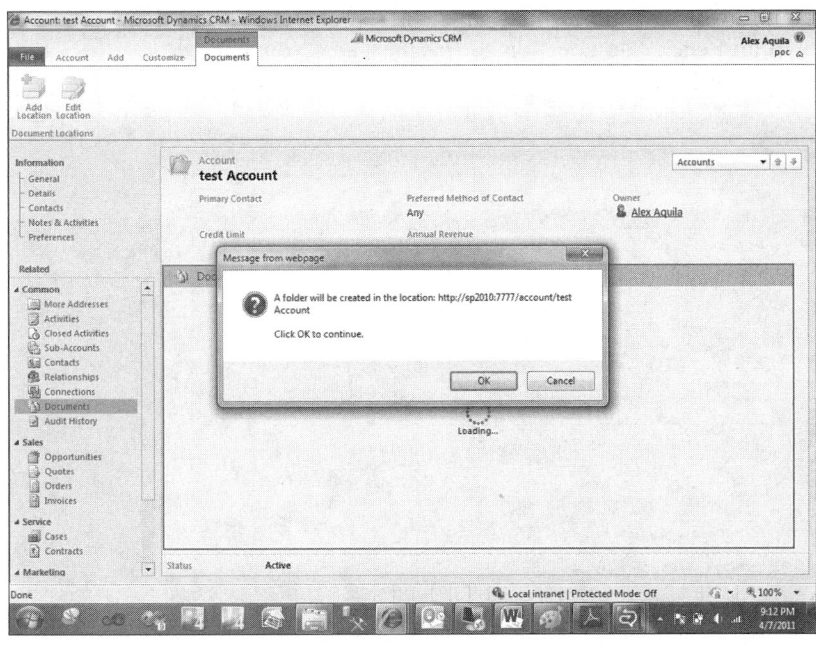

FIGURE 17.20 You will automatically be prompted to create a document library if none are paired with the current record.

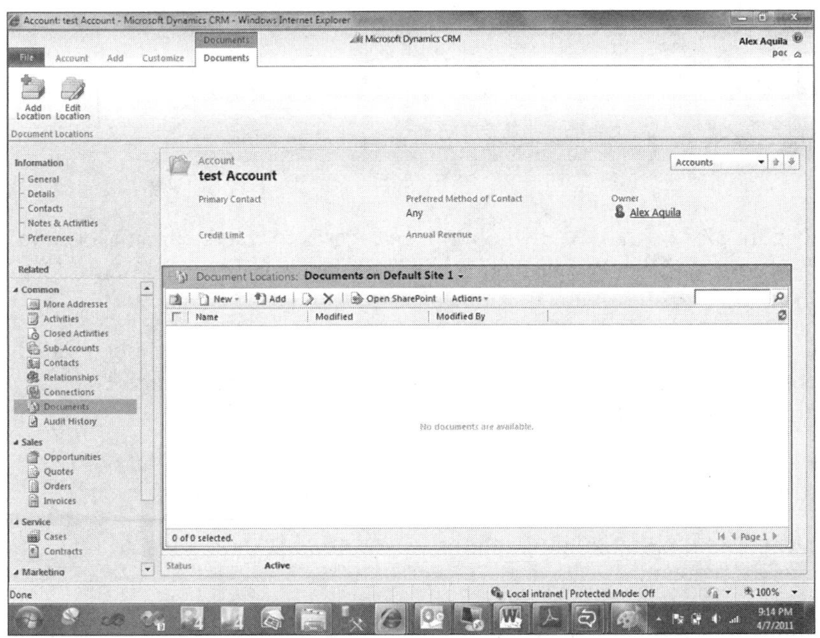

FIGURE 17.21 Your record now has its own document library that can be managed entirely from within CRM.

If you click Cancel, you will have no location created. You can open the Document Locations drop-down and click Add Location to specify where you want this document library to be, or link to another document library if it already exists (see Figure 17.22).

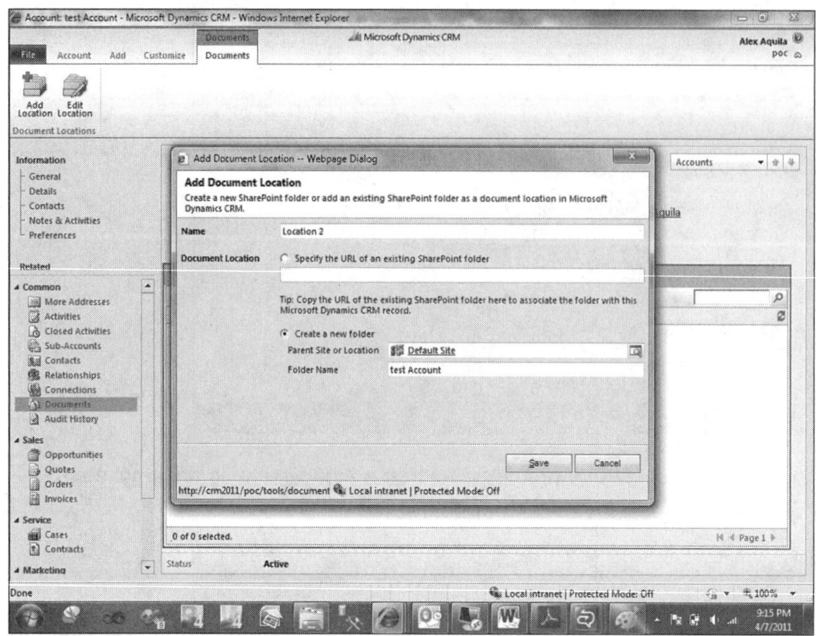

FIGURE 17.22 You can create a new library or link to a pre-existing library.

As you can see in Figure 17.22, you have two options in regards to the document location. You can specify a pre-existing SharePoint folder or you can have CRM create a new folder in a pre-existing location.

If you choose to create a new folder, you can specify its name and where it will be created. It can be at the root level or as a subfolder to any pre-existing document library. The parent or site location lookup can be either a site or a document location.

If we open the lookup and filter based on document location, you can see all of our current locations that will be available as a parent folder (see Figure 17.23).

When you are done, click save, and you can choose between the two locations in the Document Locations drop down.

You can view your document locations as they are created in Settings, Document Management, Document Locations in CRM (see Figure 17.24).

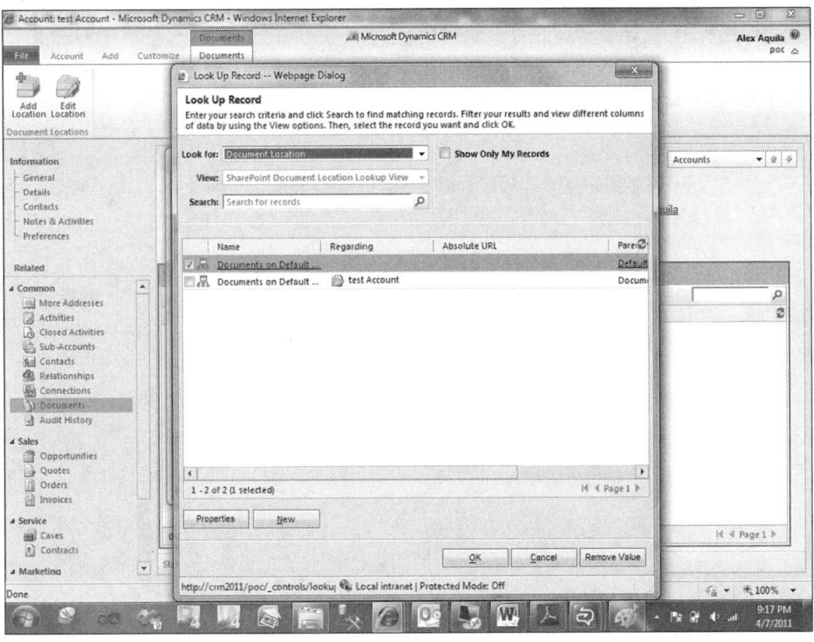

FIGURE 17.23 You can choose to create this under a site or a specific pre-existing document library.

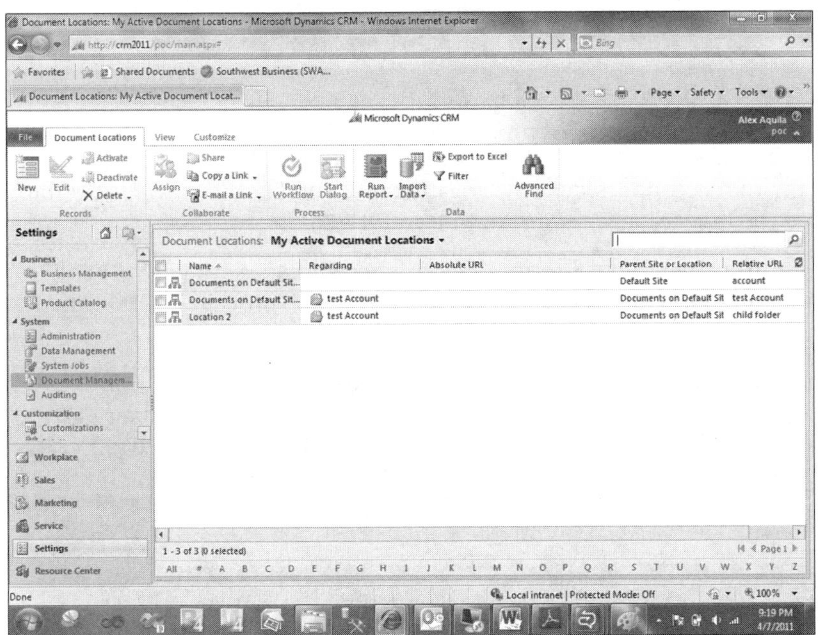

FIGURE 17.24 All the document locations we've created will be present in this section.

TIP

Notice that your document locations have automatically generated names. However, you can rename these here, as shown in Figure 17.25.

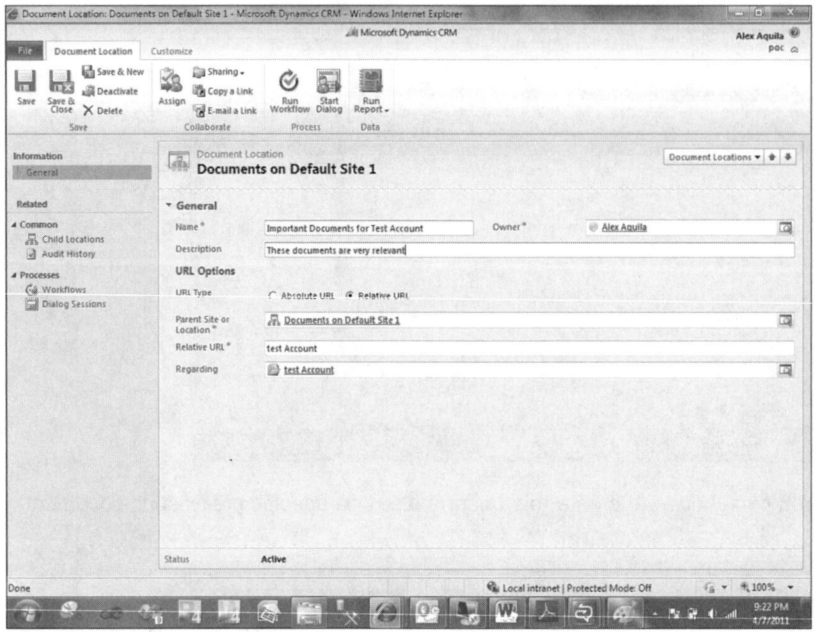

FIGURE 17.25 Renaming a document location.

Also note that you can view all of a document location's child locations. In Figure 17.25 we are looking at the root account folder, so navigating to Child Locations will show the folder we've created for Test Account, as shown in Figure 17.26.

You can manage the structure of your site and the document libraries entirely by hand through the Document Management section as well. Open SharePoint sites in Document Management, select your site, and click Edit (see Figure 17.27).

Open the child locations and click Add New Document Location. You will have to fill in the name and relative URL (see Figure 17.28). Relative URL is the document library URL, relative to the parent site or location. So, if my default site has URL http://Sp2010:7777/, and the document library has URL http://sp2010:7777/customLocation, customLocation is the relative URL.

CAUTION

Keep in mind that through this method, the folder must already exist in SharePoint. If it does not exist, you will be warned. If you create orphaned document locations, they will show up as failures when you validate your site.

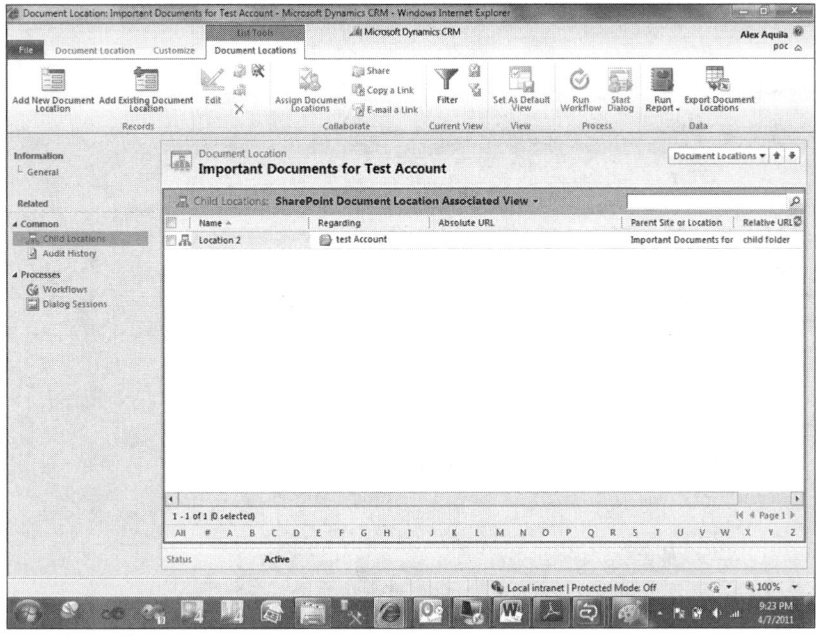

FIGURE 17.26 Child locations to this document location.

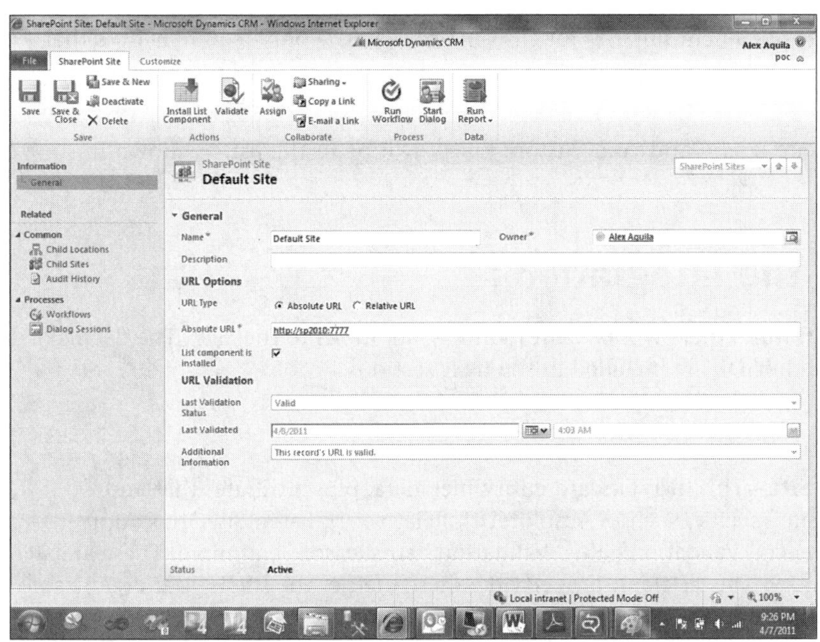

FIGURE 17.27 Edit site view.

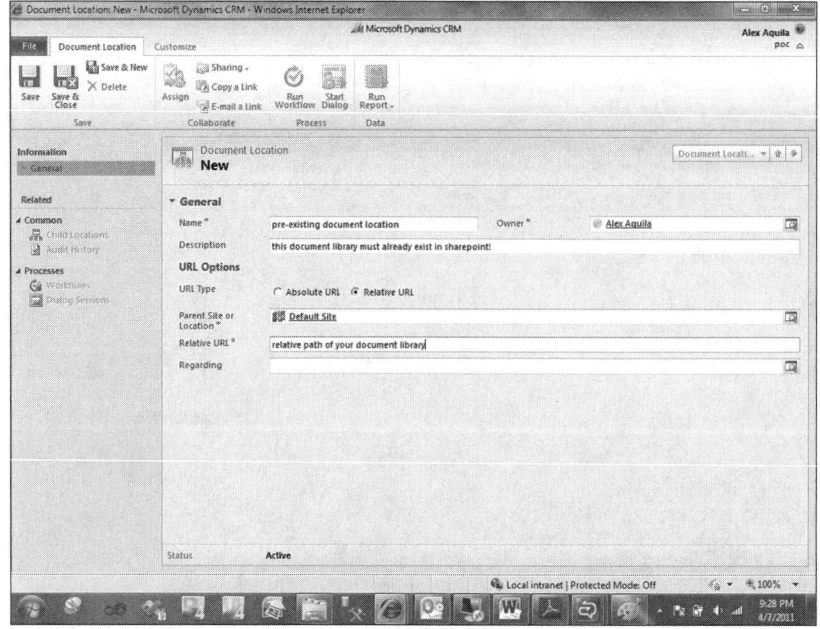

FIGURE 17.28 Creating a new document location in CRM, pointing to a document library that already exists.

You can also create document libraries for custom entities. The only requirement is that you enable Document Management in the Communication and Collaboration section (see Figure 17.29).

Next, run the wizard again, and your custom entity will be in the list, as shown in Figure 17.30.

Extending the Integration

As with any new feature, there will be corresponding additions to the SDK. The details of these additions to the SDK are included in the next sections.

New Entities

- **SharePointSite**—This has standard entity metadata, plus attributes that are SharePoint site specific, such as AbsoluteUrl, RelativeUrl, ParentSiteOrLocation (EntityReference), ValidationStatus, ValidationStatusReason, and more. These are all self-explanatory. The IsDefault property denotes whether the site is your organization's default location.
- **SharePointDocumentLocation**—This is basically the same as SharePointSite. The SharePointDocumentLocation entity makes use of the RegardingObjectId to associate a location with a specific record.

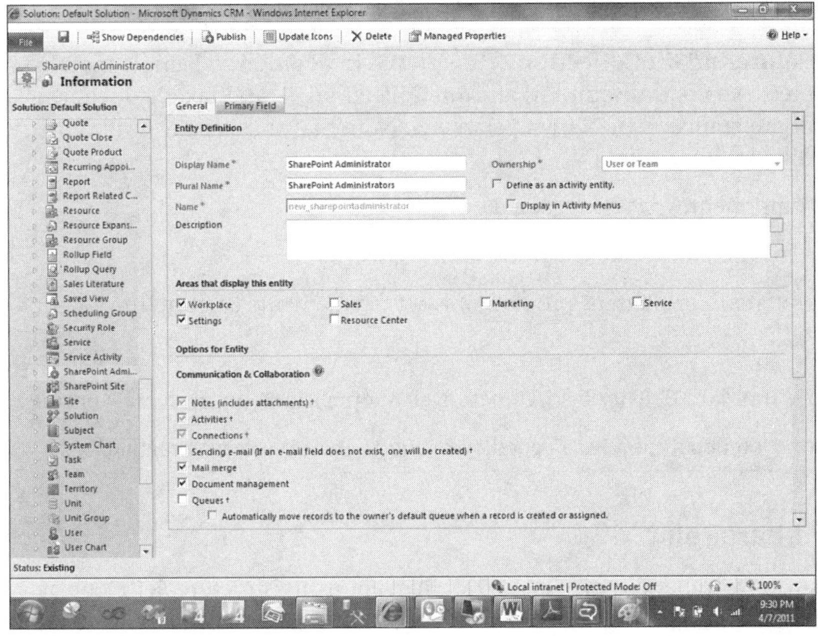

FIGURE 17.29 Check the Document Management check box on your entity to enable document management.

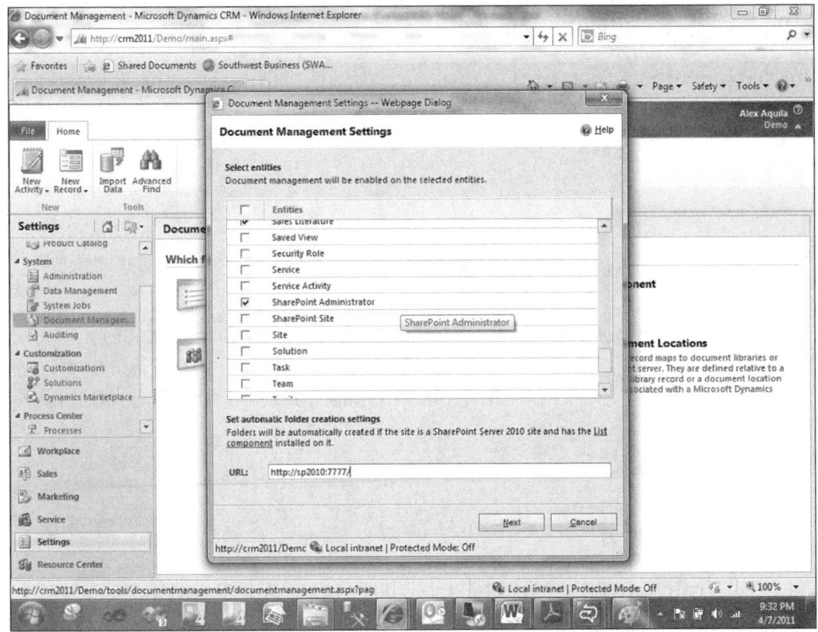

FIGURE 17.30 Now our entity shows up in the wizard.

New Message

- **RetrieveAbsoluteAndSiteCollectionUrlRequest**—In addition to being a mouthful, this will retrieve your AbsoluteUrl and SiteCollectionUrl, and takes a document location entity reference as the Target parameter. Note that this message will only work if the following are true:
- The crmlistcomponent.wsp was installed.
- The location for the parent site exists in CRM.
- The SharePointSite.IsGridPresent property was set to true while creating the parent location record.

You can perform all standard Create/Read/Update/Delete operations on these new entities.

► For more information about the CRUD operations, refer to the SDK documentation.

Operations in SharePoint

Now that you know how to handle the CRM 2011 SharePoint site structure, let's look at the corresponding operations in SharePoint 2010. SharePoint 2010 offers many services which allow you to interact with its contents. We will look briefly at the Lists Service and the Copy Service, as follows:

- **Lists Service**—Two useful functions are GetList and AddList. GetList will retrieve a list, and AddList will create a list. Here is a sample function that tries to retrieve a list, and if it does not exist, it will create the list:

```
public XmlNode processList(string listname, string listDescr, int libtype)
        {
            XmlNode result = null;

            try
            {
                result = listSvc.GetList(listname);
            }
            catch (System.Web.Services.Protocols.SoapException soExGET)
            {
                if (soExGET.Detail["errorcode"].InnerText == "0x82000006")
                {
                    try
                    {
                        result = listSvc.AddList(listname, listDescr, libtype);
                    }
                    catch (System.Web.Services.Protocols.SoapException soExADD)
                    {
                         ErrorLog.handle(soExGET.Detail.InnerText,/cr/lf
soExADD.Detail.InnerText);
```

```
                return null;
            }
        }
        else
        {
            ErrorLog.handle(soExGET.Detail.InnerText);
            return null;
        }
    }

    return result;
}
```

TIP

To create a Document Library, the libType should be set to 101.

- **Copy Service**—This service contains the CopyIntoItems function, which will upload content (as bytes) to a SharePoint library. Here is an example of this function in use:

```
public uint uploadFile(string fileName, string[] desinationUrl, byte[] stream)
{
    uint result = 0;
    bool Throw = false;
    CopyResult[] results = null;

    FieldInformation descInfo = new FieldInformation()
        { DisplayName = "Description", Type=FieldType.Text, Value=/cr/lf
"Automatic Upload from CRM"};
    FieldInformation[] inf = new FieldInformation[] { descInfo };
    try
    {
        result = copySvc.CopyIntoItems("http://crm2011",/cr/lf
 desinationUrl, inf, stream, out results);
        foreach (CopyResult cr in results)
        {
            if( cr.ErrorCode != CopyErrorCode.Success)
            {
                ErrorLog.handle("Error After File Upload Attempt: "/cr/lf
+ cr.ErrorMessage);
                Throw = true;
```

```
                }
            }
        }
        catch (System.Web.Services.Protocols.SoapException soExCopy)
        {
            ErrorLog.handle(soExCopy.Detail.InnerText, result.ToString());
            throw new Exception(soExCopy.Detail.InnerText);
        }
        if (Throw)
           throw new Exception("The upload file method has failed.");

        return result;
    }
```

So, for example, if you wanted a plug-in to retrieve an attachment as bytes and upload it to SharePoint, you're about 90% of the way there. If you were operating on an activitymimeattachment, you can use this line to retrieve the attachment as bytes:

```
byte[] filecontent = new UTF8Encoding(true).GetBytes(/cr/lf
(string)_this.Attributes["body"]);
```

As in CRM 4.0, the SDK is flexible, and you can write plug-ins that trigger on the Create, Update, and Delete of SharePointSite and SharePointDocumentLocation entities. Figure 17.31 provides an example.

So, now you should have enough tools to start exploring your own ways to extend this integration. Happy coding!

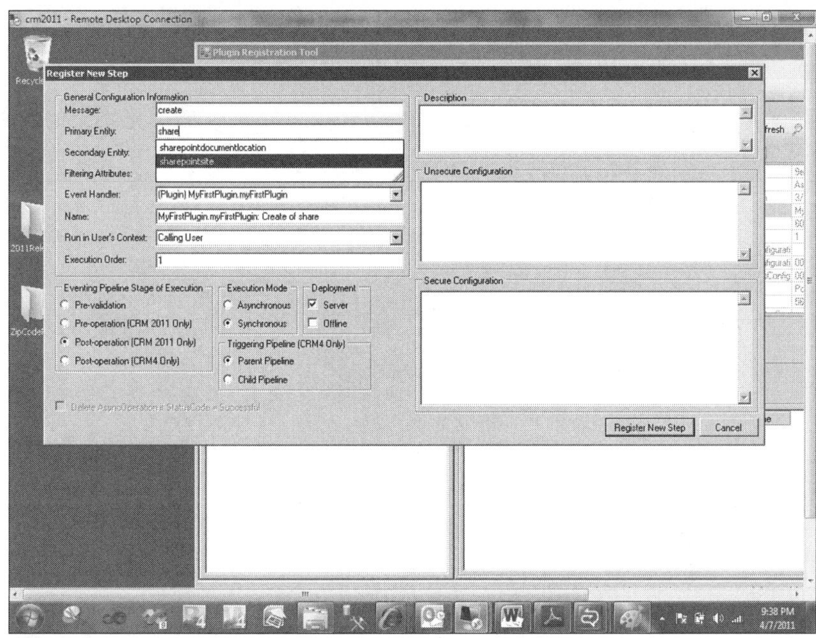

FIGURE 17.31 You have all the standard options in regard to extending the pipeline events corresponding to these new entities.

Summary

In this chapter, we explained how to integrate CRM 2011 with both SharePoint 2007 and SharePoint 2010, and how to manipulate these features to get the data structure you desire.

We took a brief look at the additions to the CRM SDK, and examined ways to connect to SharePoint and perform basic custom integrations.

CHAPTER 18
Azure Extensions

IN THIS CHAPTER

- ▶ Introduction to Azure
- ▶ Service Bus Configurations

This version of Microsoft Dynamics CRM features improved extensibility to cloud computing and Windows Azure.

Introduction to Azure

Azure is the Microsoft technology created to build and provide cloud-computing systems and applications. These applications will be hosted in the Microsoft datacenters and will give end users about 99.9% uptime, and the customer won't need to invest in any infrastructure or IT services for their environment.

The concept of cloud computing invites companies to alter their perspective with regard to procuring expensive on-premises equipment and hard-to-manage support and consider moving to a service-oriented service Software as a Service (SaaS) where they pay for the time and resources consumed (similar to what we currently do for electricity or phone calls services).

Azure is the set of tools and APIs that changes the way a system or application is designed to support the cloud-computing platform offered by Microsoft. This way customers can scale the system as needed by choosing the number of servers they want to have the same application running as soon as the usage demands it at a low cost per month.

Azure is divided in the following products that can be subscribed to separately:

- ▶ **Core**—This is the cheapest cost subscription that offers the platform without any database support.

With this version you can host a web application and a worker role and use the Azure storage to store the data in blobs, queues, or tables (without SQL support).

- **SQL Azure Core**—This includes only the database, and it might be useful for those customers that want to have only their data in the cloud but the application on another hosted or proprietary environment.

- **Extended**—This includes the Core and the SQL Azure database at a better price than getting either one of them separately.

NOTE

Windows Azure is not available worldwide yet. At the time this book was published, Azure was available in only 40 countries.

Service Bus Configurations

The service bus is the Azure component that can be used to integrate a CRM 2011 deployment to another legacy system. Because the CRM in these scenarios will usually be the online version and because we cannot call external web services from plug-ins deployed on the CRM 2011 Online sandbox, we will need to create a service bus application to communicate with our external application through the service bus.

TIP

The service bus subscription is not included in the windows Azure subscriptions just described; it uses a separate subscription and plan depending on the number of connections you need.

Currently there are packs of 5, 25, 100, and 500 connections. Each connection means an application that would be connected to the service bus to either receive or send messages. Microsoft doesn't charge for the number of messages sent to this service, but it charges for the number of simultaneous connections required by different applications. On any small implementation with CRM, you will need at least two connections: one for the Microsoft Dynamics CRM and another to your legacy application. However, to support redundancy and fault tolerance, you might need to think about more connections to the service bus in case your legacy application is configured for load balance.

This process of using the service bus to integrate a legacy system or application with Microsoft CRM 2011 involves the following:

- Creating a Windows Azure service bus account with a subscription
- Getting the CRM 2011 Online certificate
- Registering a service bus endpoint
- Creating a listener application

Creating a Windows Azure Service Bus Account with a Subscription

To create an app fabric service bus, follow these steps:

1. Go to https://windows.azure.com/ and log in with your passport. After you log in, you see the Windows Azure home page, as shown in Figure 18.1.

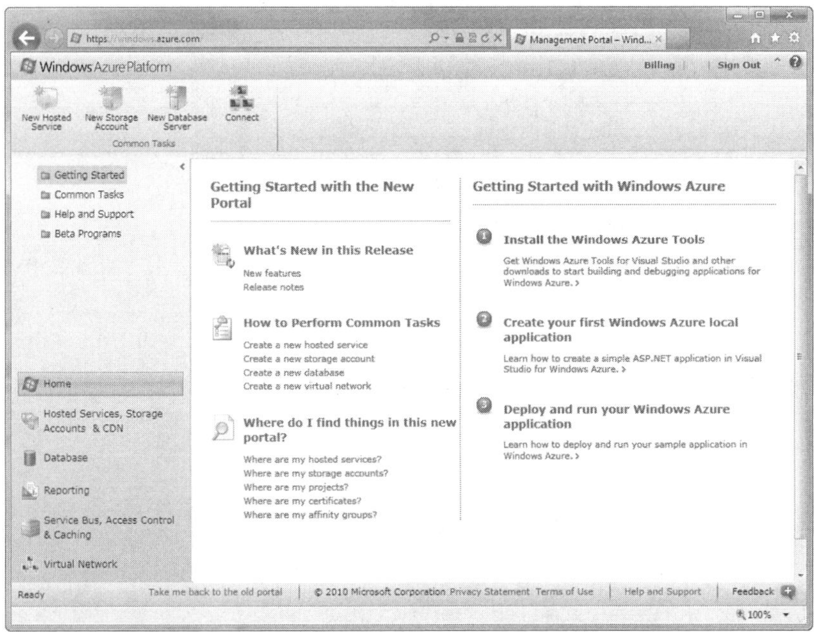

FIGURE 18.1 Windows Azure home page.

2. Click Service Bus, Access Control & Caching from the left menu options, as shown in Figure 18.2.

TIP

Be sure to use the new portal because the AppFabric configuration is no longer available on the old portal.

3. Click the Service Bus node that is listed in AppFabric tree view, as shown in Figure 18.3.
4. Click the New Namespace button link in the top Ribbon menu bar, as shown in Figure 18.4.
5. Enter a service namespace, the region, and the service bus connection packs, and click Create.

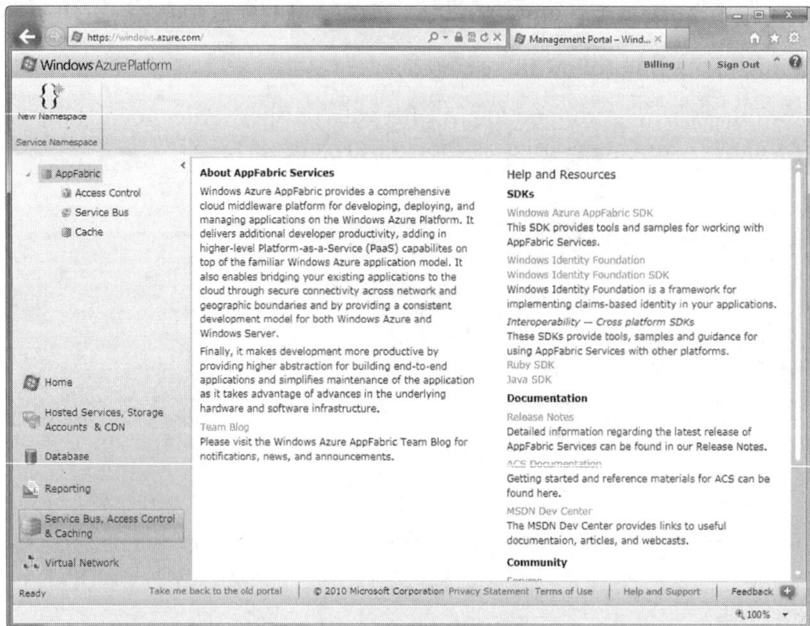

FIGURE 18.2 AppFabric home page.

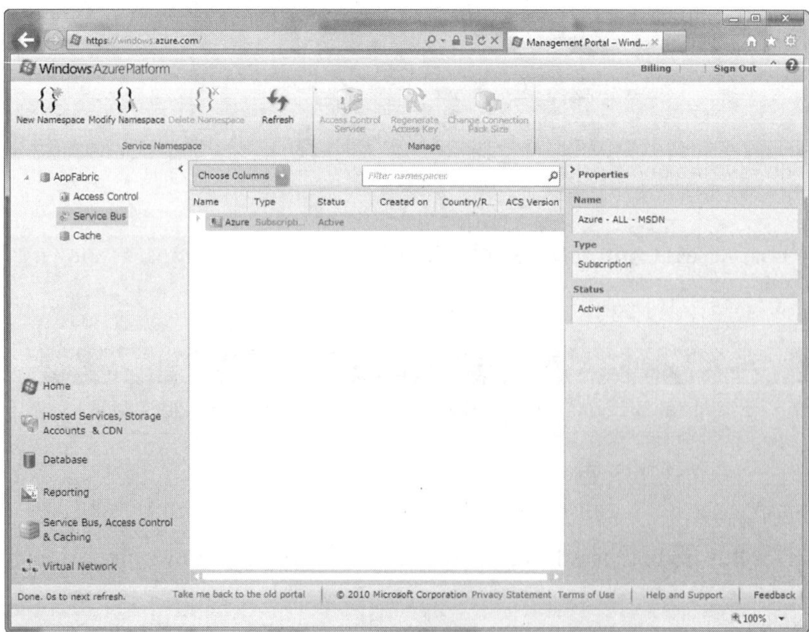

FIGURE 18.3 Service Bus project description.

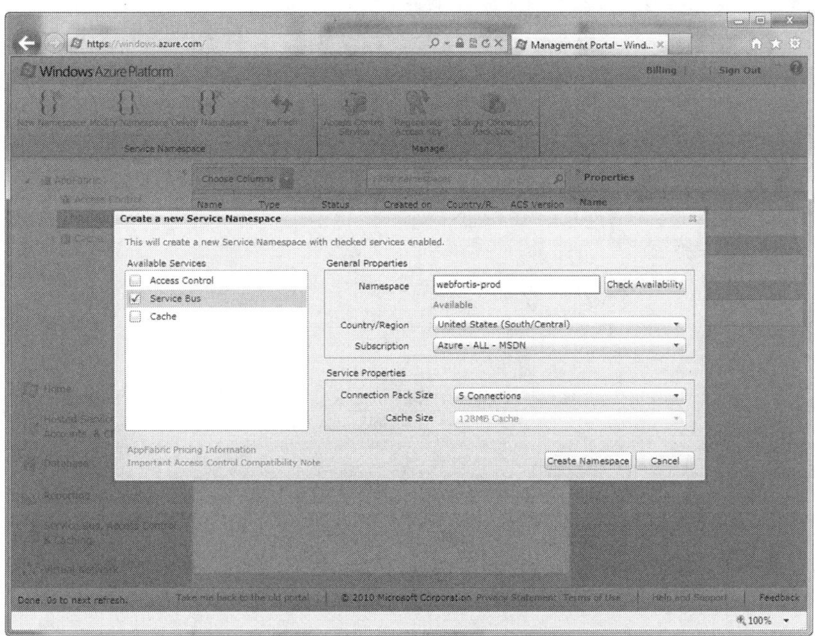

FIGURE 18.4 Create a new service bus namespace.

TIP

Remember to make a note of the service namespace you enter here because you will need it when registering the service bus plug-in.

6. After a few minutes the new service will be created, and its status will be active, as shown in Figure 18.5.

Getting the CRM 2011 Online Certificate

In this book, we explain how to connect an application with CRM Online, which would be the most suitable scenario. You can, however, connect with CRM on premises and in IFD environments, but to get a certificate you will need to follow other steps that are described in both the CRM 2011 SDK and in the CRM 2011 Developer Training Kit.

NOTE

The CRM 2011 SDK and the CRM 2011 Developer Training Kit can both be downloaded from http://download.microsoft.com.

1. Go to CRM Online and download the Windows Azure AppFabric Issuer Certificate by going to Settings, Customizations, and then Developer Resources (see Figure 18.6).

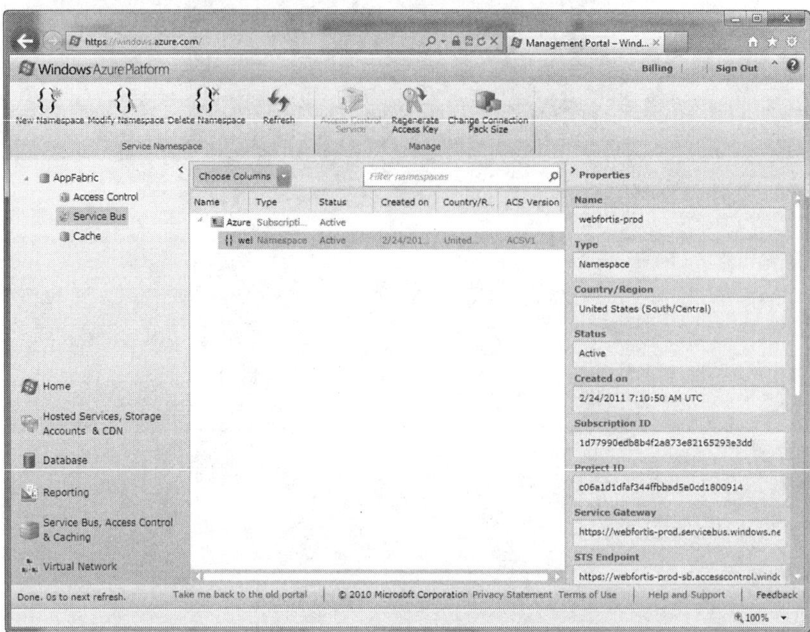

FIGURE 18.5 New service bus namespace created successfully.

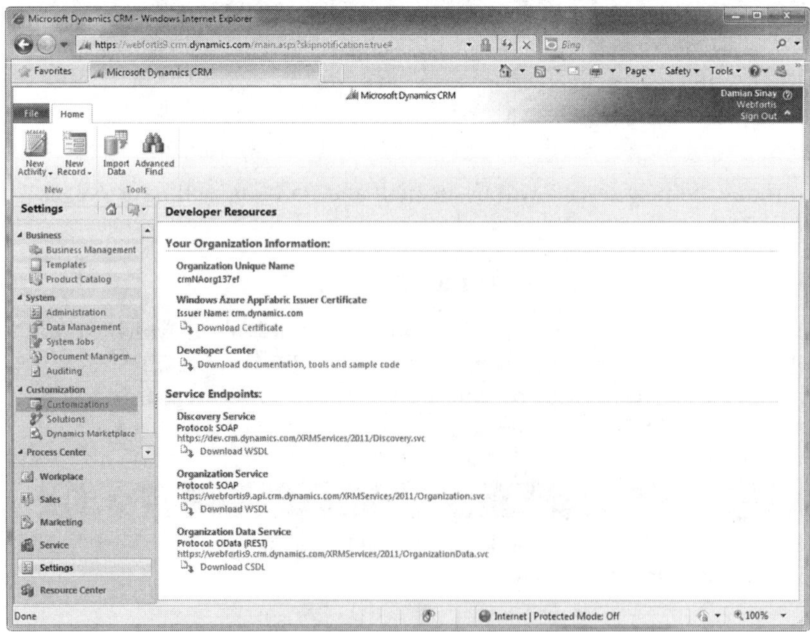

FIGURE 18.6 CRM 2011 Developer Resources.

2. Click Download Certificate under Windows Azure AppFabric Issuer Certificate, and store the certificate on your local hard disk.

Registering a Service Bus Endpoint

To register the service bus endpoint you will need to use the Plugin Registration Tool that is found in the CRM SDK under the sdk\tools\pluginregistration folder.

▶ To learn more about this application, which is the same one used to register any other CRM plug-in, refer to Chapter 25, "Plug-Ins."

You will need to use Visual Studio 2010 to open the pluginregistrationtool.sln solution file. After opening the solution in Visual Studio 2010, press F5 to run the project and follow these steps:

1. Enter the connection information, and click on Save (as shown in Figure 18.7).

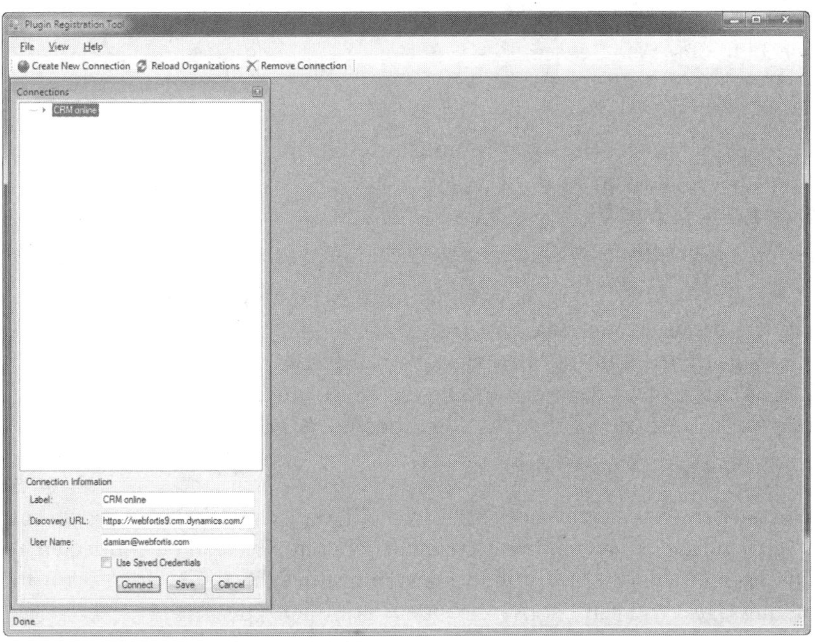

FIGURE 18.7 Plugin Registration Tool.

2. Click Connect, and enter your password (see Figure 18.8).

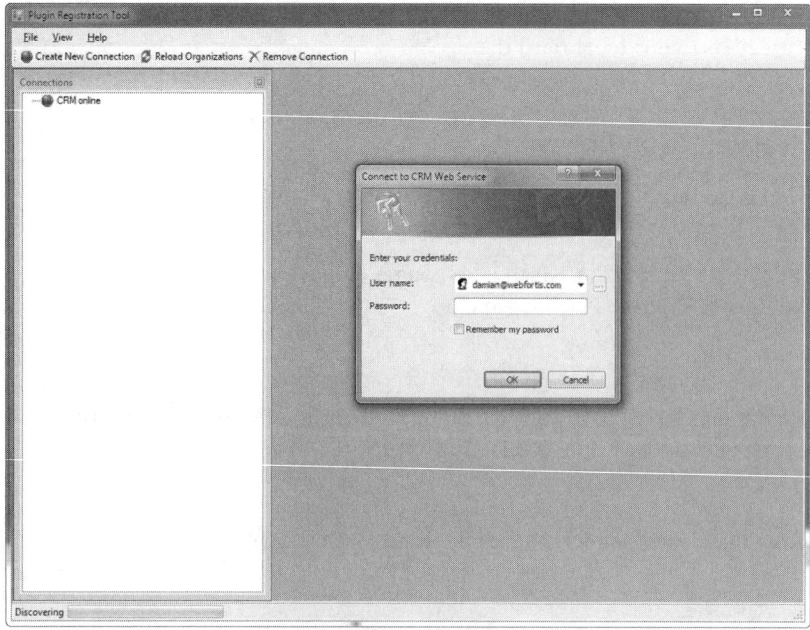

FIGURE 18.8 Connect to CRM Web Service.

3. When connected, you will see the organizations listed in the Connections list. Select the organization for which you want to register your service bus plug-in, and click Connect, as shown in Figure 18.9.
4. Click Register, and select Register New Service Endpoint, as shown in Figure 18.10.
5. The Service Endpoint Details will open (see Figure 18.11). Enter a name (this can be any name you want to use to reference your service), a description (optional), the solution namespace that is found in the windows.azure.com in the AppFabric/Service Bus section (refer back to Figure 18.5), and a path that can be any name that you want to be part of the URL used for the endpoint.

   The contract can be any of these types:

   - **One Way**—Used to send messages only from CRM 2011 to the service bus. For this type of contract, it is required that the listener application be connected at the time the message is sent or the message might be lost. If you don't want to lose the messages, you can choose the Queue contract type.
   - **Queue**—Where the messages will be queued; this will be useful for environments that are not fully connected at all times.
   - **Two Way**—Where the messages can be sent and received from CRM 2011.
   - **REST**—Creates a REST endpoint that works in a two-way fashion.

▶ To learn more about the REST protocol, refer to Chapter 26.

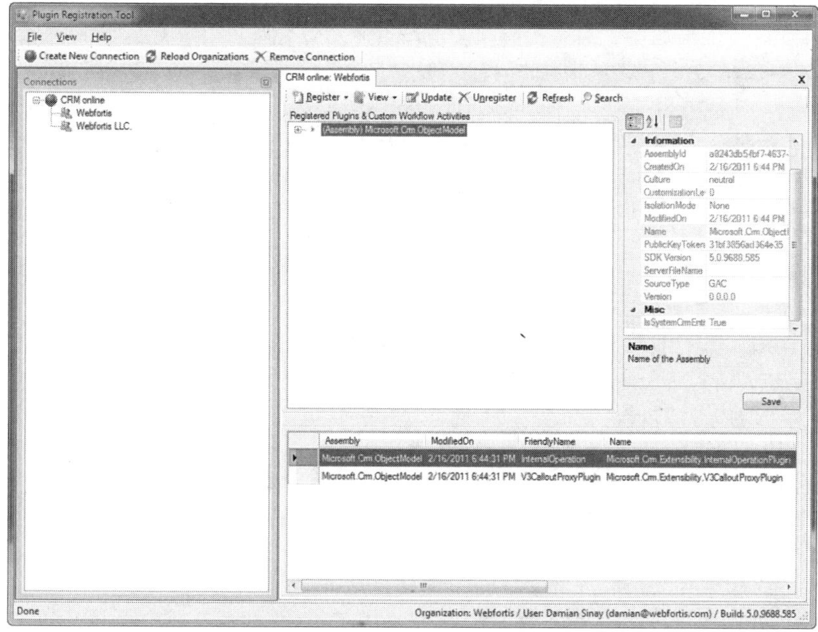

FIGURE 18.9 Connections.

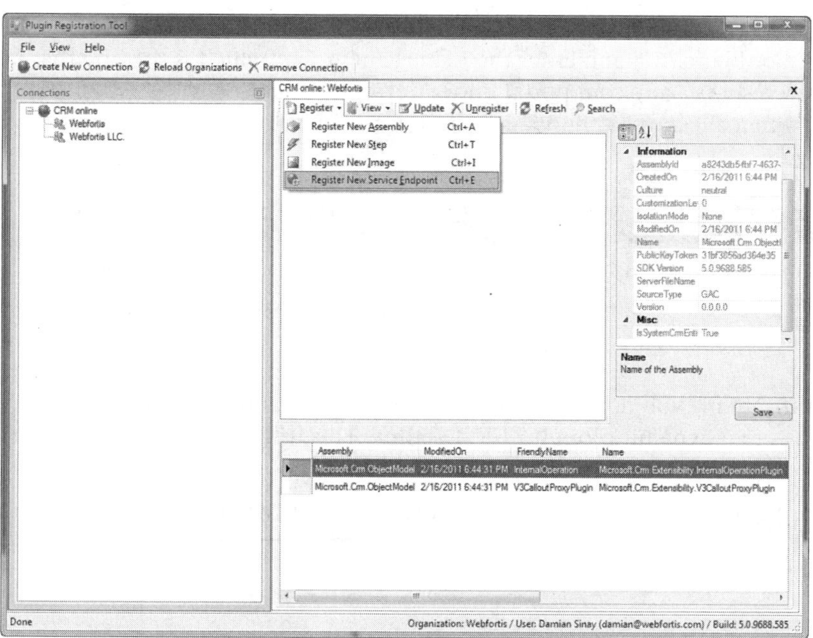

FIGURE 18.10 Register New Service Endpoint.

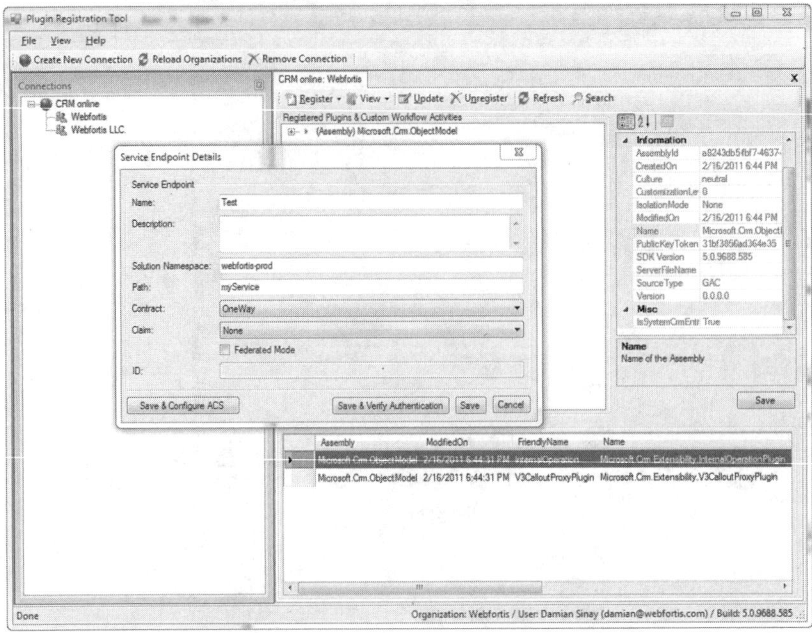

FIGURE 18.11 Service endpoint details.

6. Click Save & Configure ACS and enter the Management Key, which is the one that is found in the windows.azure.com portal under Current Management Key which can be displayed when clicking on the View button in the Management Keys property, as shown in Figure 18.12.

NOTE

The keys on Figure 18.12 and 18.14 are blurred on purpose as this key is private and cannot be shared.

7. Find the certificate file you downloaded from CRM Online, and enter the issuer name, which is crm.dynamics.com for CRM Online. This will be a different name for on-premises deployments (see Figure 18.13).
8. Click the Configure ACS button, and when a dialog appears warning that the action cannot be undone, click Yes.

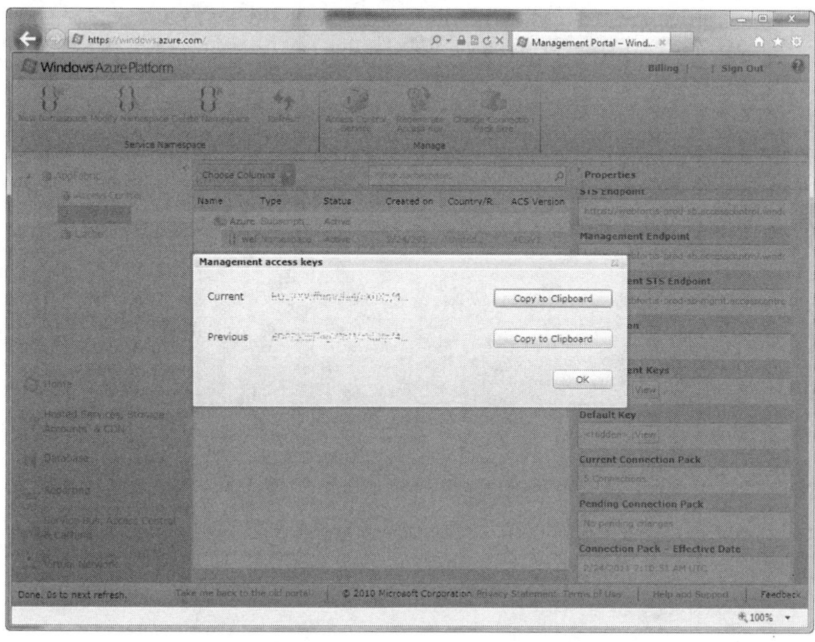

FIGURE 18.12 Current management key on Windows.Azure.com.

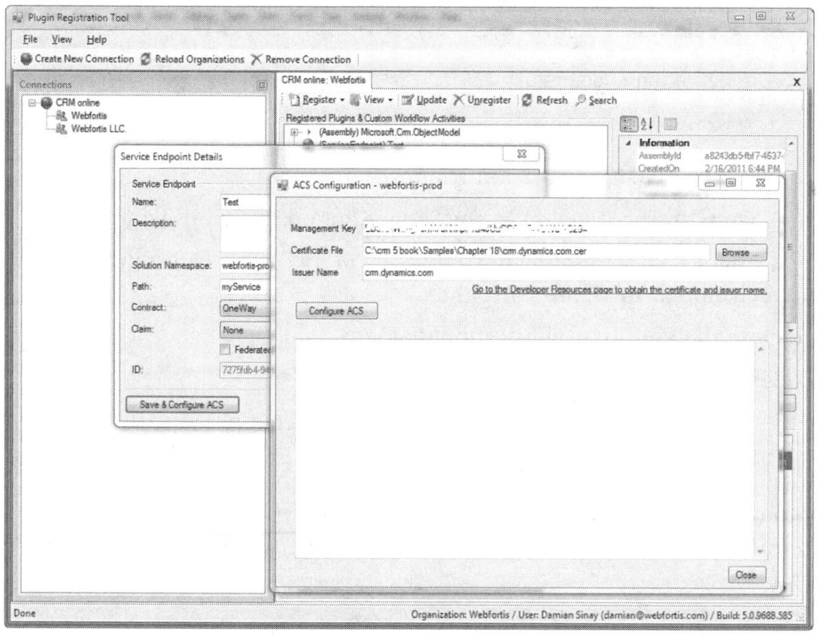

FIGURE 18.13 ACS configuration.

9. You see the detailed process messages with their statuses in the big text box. After successful configuration, you should see a screen similar to Figure 18.14.

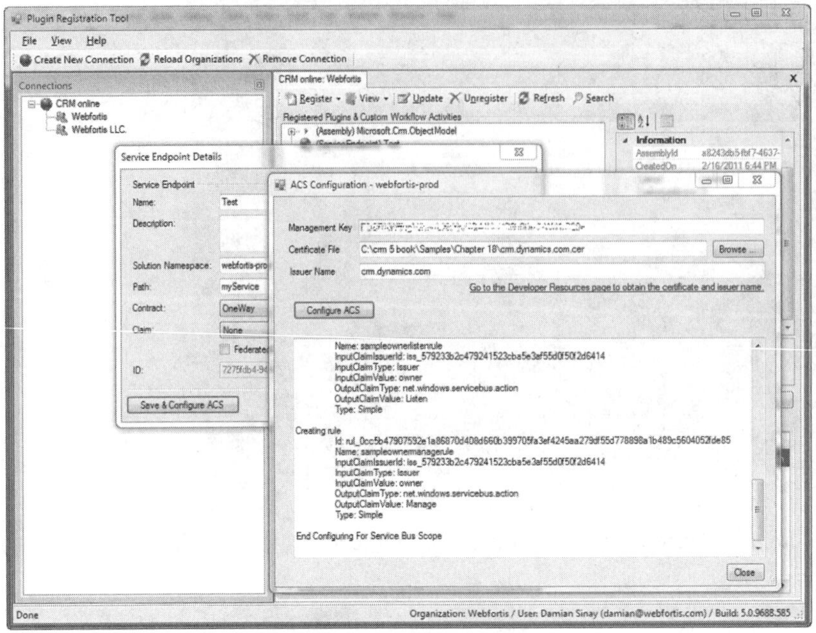

FIGURE 18.14 ACS Configuration successfully.

10. Click Close to close the ACS configuration window.
11. Click on Save & Verify Authentication in the Service Endpoint Details window.
12. The verification might take some time to complete. On successful verification, you should see a screen similar to Figure 18.15.
13. Click Close to close the Verify Authentication dialog.
14. Click Save to close the Service Endpoint Details dialog.
15. You now see the new service endpoint created in the registered plug-ins & custom activities list.

Now we are ready to configure the CRM events we want to listen to and have sent to the service bus. To do that, you need to create new steps for the service endpoint you created.

1. Select the service endpoint you created, click Register, and then select Register New Step, as shown in Figure 18.17.

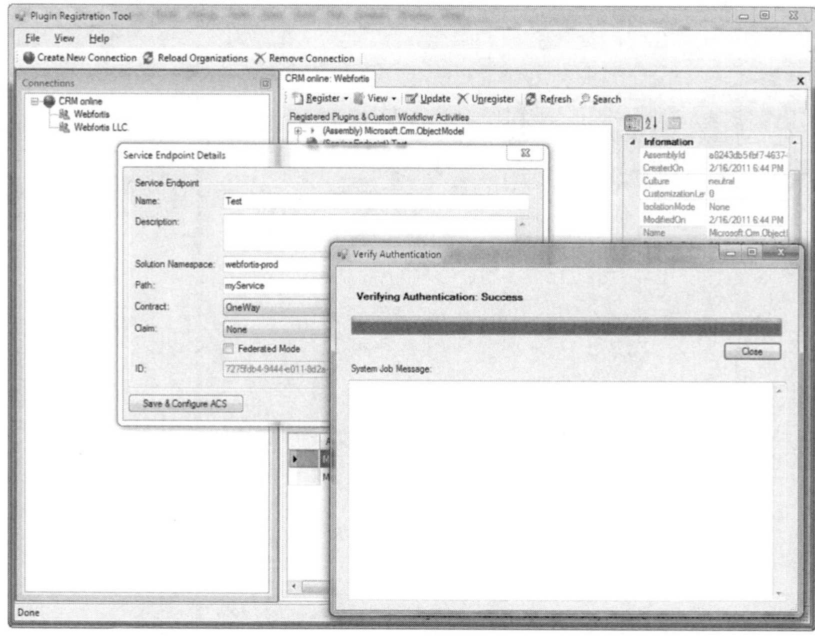

FIGURE 18.15 Verify authentication: success.

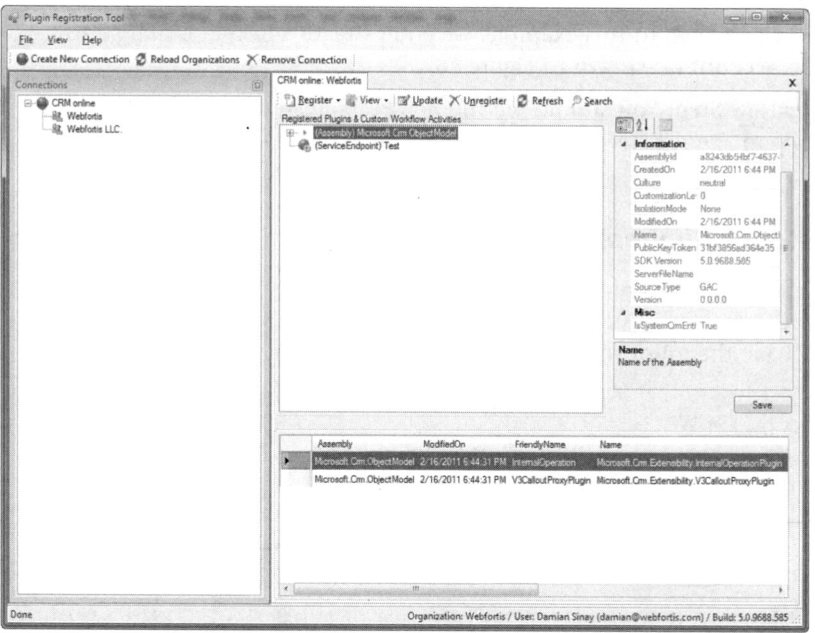

FIGURE 18.16 Service endpoint created.

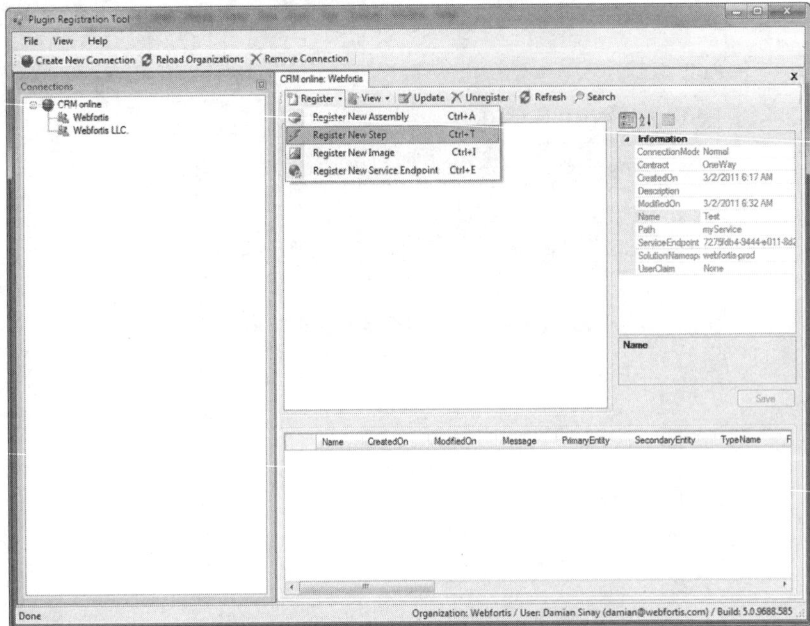

FIGURE 18.17 Register New Step.

2. Enter the message name. In this example, we enter Create and the primary entity, which will be Account (as shown in Figure 18.18).
3. Click Register New Step. You should see the new step created under the Service endpoint node in the registered plug-ins & custom activities list, as shown in Figure 18.19.

Creating a Listener Application

To start receiving the service bus messages, you need to create a listener application. To test the listener, you can create a simple console application with Microsoft Visual Studio 2010. You need to have the following SDKs downloaded and installed to follow this sample code:

- Windows Azure SDK
- Windows Azure AppFabric SDK
- Microsoft Dynamics CRM 2011 SDK

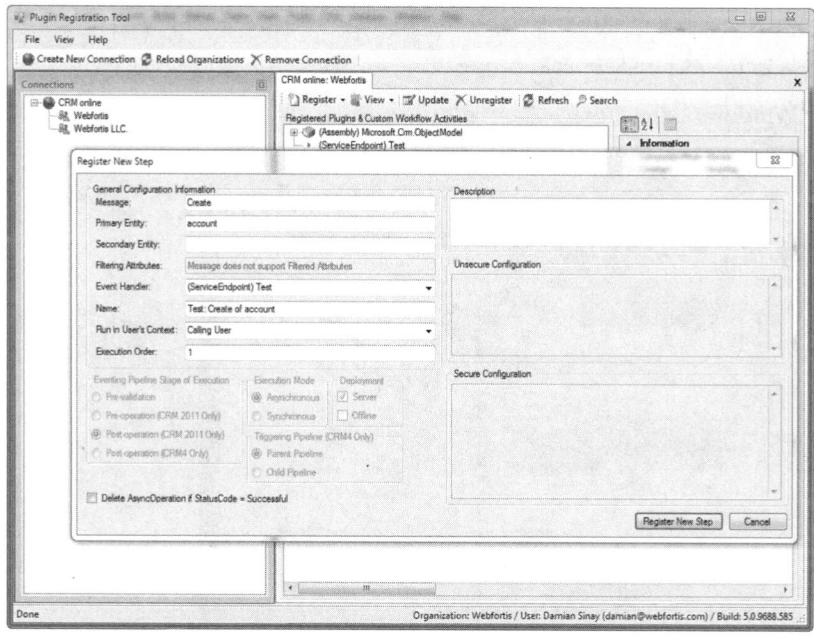

FIGURE 18.18 Create message for Account entity.

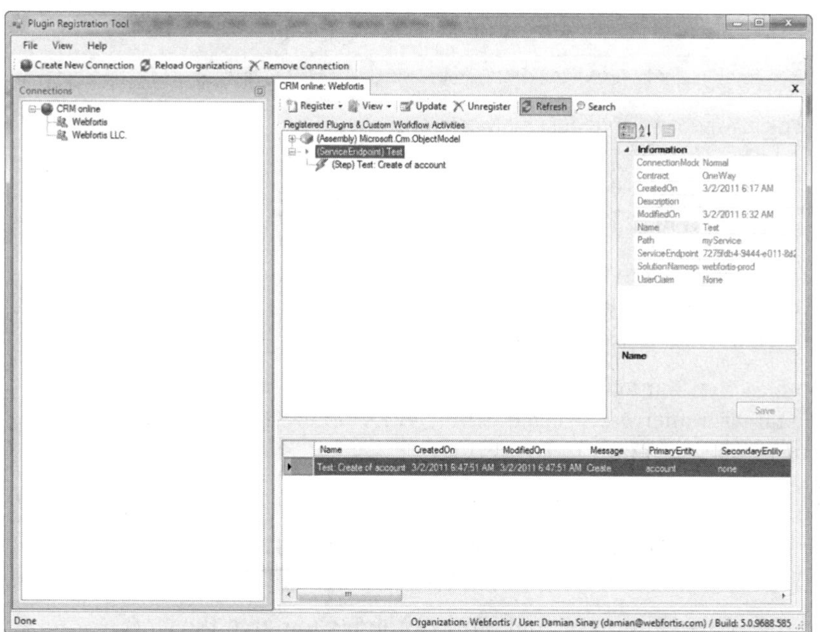

FIGURE 18.19 New step created successfully.

Add references to the following assemblies, as shown in Figure 18.20:

- Microsoft.WindowsAzure.ServiceRuntime.dll
- Microsoft.WindowsAzure.StorageClient.dll

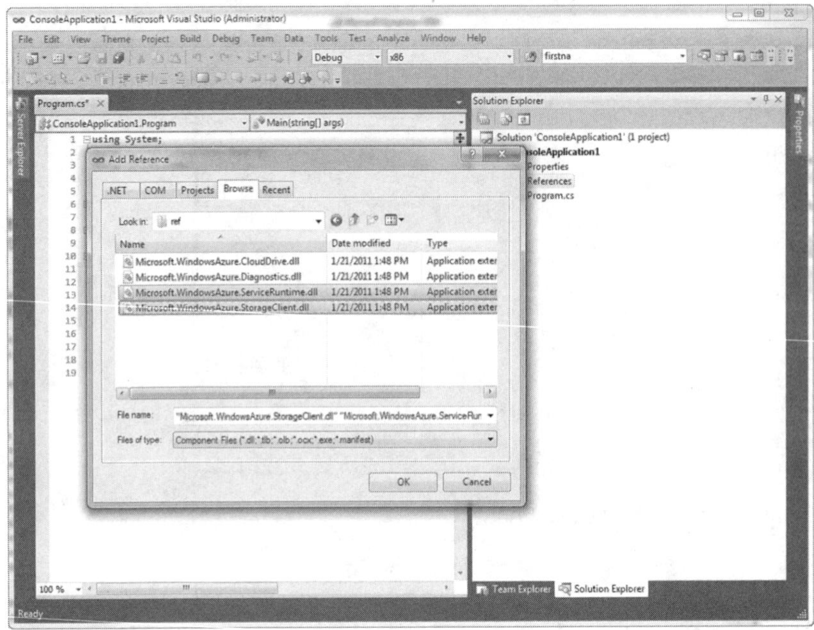

FIGURE 18.20 Adding Windows Azure assembly references.

These assemblies are found in the C:\Program Files\Windows Azure SDK\v1.3\ref\ folder that is created when you install the Windows Azure SDK.

You also need to add a reference to the Microsoft.ServiceBus.dll assembly located in the C:\Program Files\Windows Azure AppFabric SDK\V1.0\Assemblies\NET4.0\ folder that is created when you install the Windows Azure AppFabric SDK.

Go to the Solution Explorer, right-click on the project name, and select the Settings option. Be sure the target framework selected is the .NET Framework 4 and not the .NET Framework 4 Client profile, as shown in Figure 18.21.

Add a reference to the System.ServiceModel assembly found in the GAC (see Figure 18.22).

Add a reference to the microsoft.xrm.sdk.dll found in the CRM 2011 sdk\bin folder that is created when you installed the Microsoft Dynamics CRM 2011 SDK (see Figure 18.23).

Add a reference to the System.Runtime.Serialization assembly found in the GAC (see Figure 18.24).

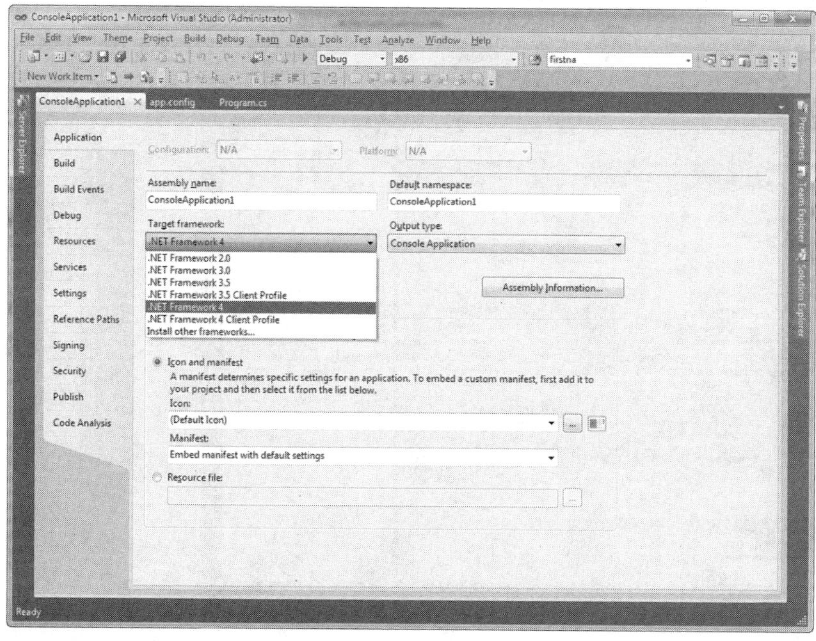

FIGURE 18.21 Target framework settings.

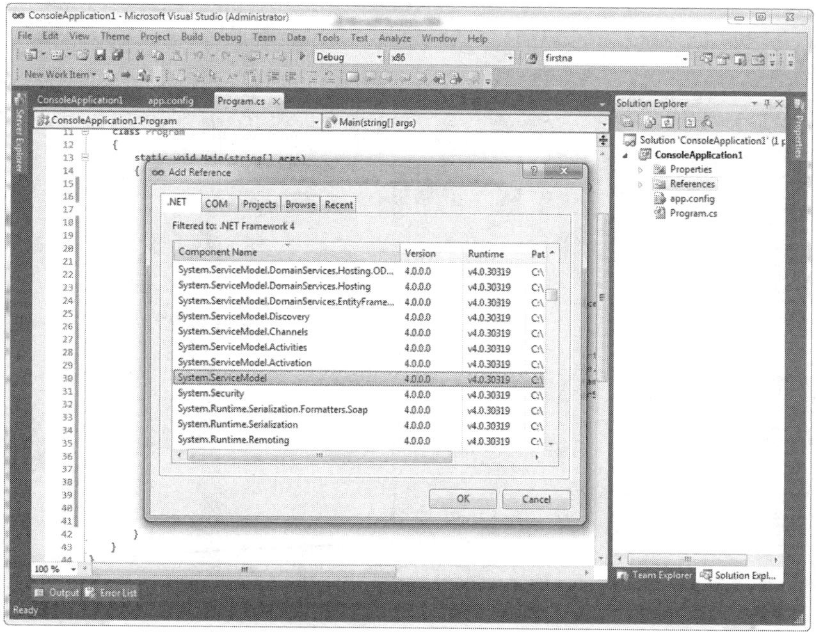

FIGURE 18.22 Adding reference to the System.ServiceModel assembly.

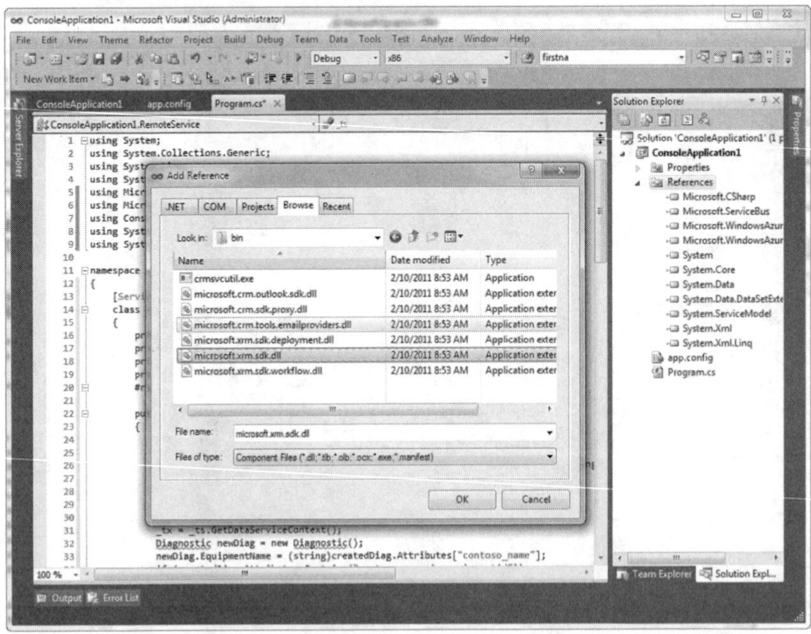

FIGURE 18.23 Adding reference to the microsoft.xrm.sdk assembly.

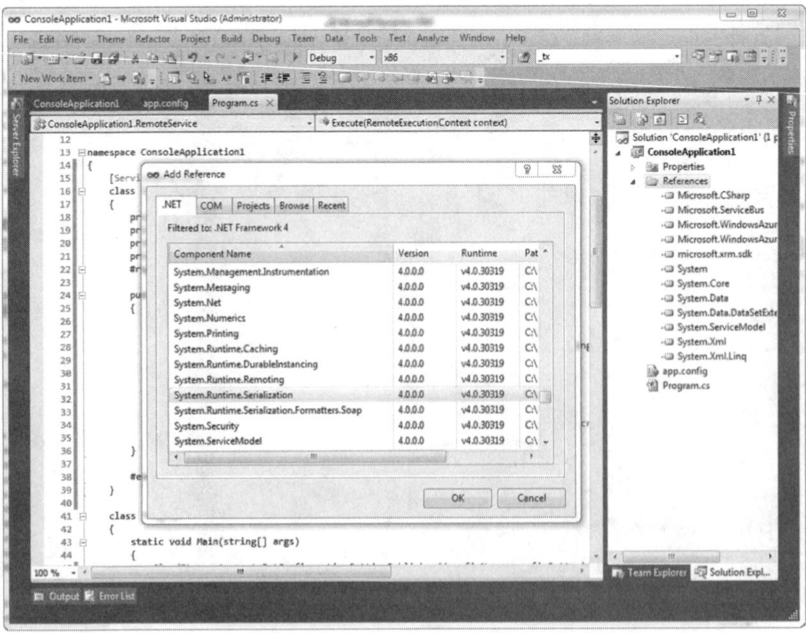

FIGURE 18.24 Adding reference to the System.ServiceModel assembly.

After we have added all the necessary references, we are now ready to insert the code. To do this, open the program.cs file and enter the following code:

```
using System;
using System.Collections.Generic;
using System.Linq;
using System.Text;
using Microsoft.ServiceBus;
using Microsoft.WindowsAzure;
using ConsoleApplication1.Properties;
using System.ServiceModel;
using System.ServiceModel.Description;
using Microsoft.Xrm.Sdk;
using Microsoft.WindowsAzure.StorageClient;

namespace ConsoleApplication1
{
    class Program
    {
        static void Main(string[] args)
        {
            ServiceBusEnvironment.SystemConnectivity.Mode =
            ConnectivityMode.Http;
            string serviceNamespace = "webfortis-prod";
            string issuerName = "owner";
            string issuerSecret = "321321";
            // Create the service URI based on the service namespace.
            Uri address = ServiceBusEnvironment.CreateServiceUri
              (Uri.UriSchemeHttps, serviceNamespace, "myService");
            Console.WriteLine("Service address: " + address);
            // Create the credentials object for the endpoint.
            TransportClientEndpointBehavior
               scb =
               new TransportClientEndpointBehavior();
              scb.CredentialType =
             TransportClientCredentialType.SharedSecret;
            scb.Credentials.SharedSecret.IssuerName = issuerName;
            scb.Credentials.SharedSecret.IssuerSecret = issuerSecret;
            // Create the binding object.
            WS2007HttpRelayBinding binding = new WS2007HttpRelayBinding();
            binding.Security.Mode = EndToEndSecurityMode.Transport;
            // Create the service host reading the configuration.
            ServiceHost host = new ServiceHost(typeof(RemoteServiceTest));
```

```
            host.AddServiceEndpoint(typeof(IServiceEndpointPlugin),
                  binding, address);
            // Create the ServiceRegistrySettings behavior for the endpoint.
            IEndpointBehavior serviceRegistrySettings =
            new ServiceRegistrySettings(DiscoveryType.Public);
            // Add the Service Bus credentials to
           // all endpoints specified in configuration.
            foreach (ServiceEndpoint endpoint in host.Description.Endpoints)
            {
                endpoint.Behaviors.Add(serviceRegistrySettings);
                endpoint.Behaviors.Add(scb);
            }
            try
            {
                // Open the service.
                host.Open();
            }
            catch (TimeoutException timeout)
            {
                Console.WriteLine(timeout.Message);
            }
            Console.ReadLine();
            // Close the service.
             host.Close();
        }
    }
    [ServiceBehavior]
    class RemoteServiceTest : IServiceEndpointPlugin
    {
        public void Execute(RemoteExecutionContext context)
        {
            Entity createdDiag = (Entity)context.InputParameters["Target"];
            Console.WriteLine("Account with name = " +
              createdDiag.Attributes["name"] + " was created");
        }
    }
}
```

Let's review and explain this code a little. For the service bus, we need to create a class that will implement the IServiceEndpointPlugin, which has a similar interface to the one we use for plug-ins (IPlugin).

▶ For more information about plug-ins, refer to Chapter 25.

This interface forces the implementation of the Execute method. This method will be called by the service bus and will send the context parameter. This parameter contains all the information we need for the entity we registered in the service endpoint. In our case, we registered the Create message for the Account entity, so we should expect to get the Account entity instance when a new account is created.

Updating Variables for the Main Method

There are three variables at the beginning of the Main method that you will need to update with your own service information: the serviceNamespace, issuerName, and the issuerSecret variables. You can find the values of these variables on the Windows Azure AppFabric portal, as shown in Figure 18.25.

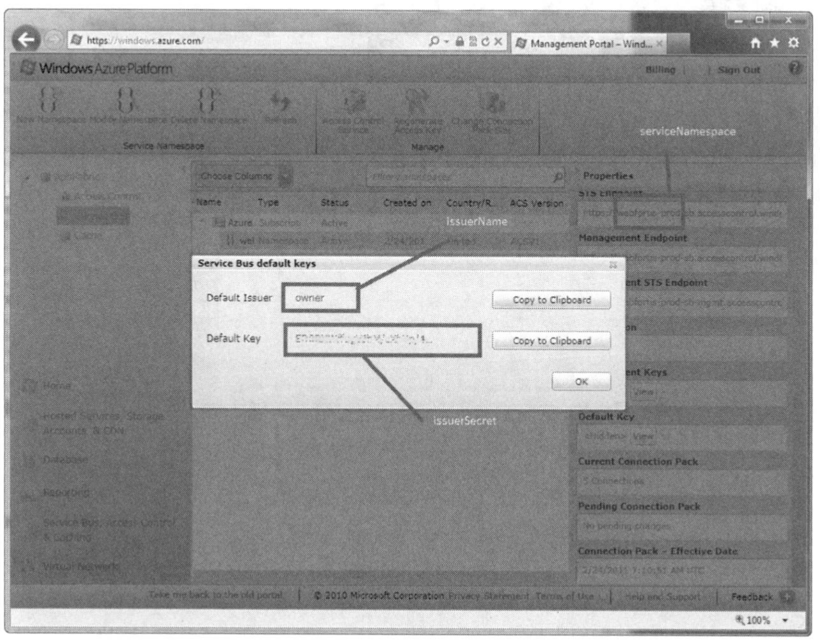

FIGURE 18.25 Windows Azure AppFabric portal.

The Main method starts with creating the service URI that will connect to your service; we used MyService here because that was the path we entered when we registered the service endpoint.

Then we create the credentials object that will need to be passed to the service endpoint. Notice the credentials are created using the issuer name and the issuer secret keys. We then create the binding object using the WS2007HttpRelayBinding class. Next, we instantiate the ServiceHost class, which is the object that will be connected to the AppFabric service bus. Here is where we specify the Service class that implements the IServiceEndpointPlugin interface. Finally we create and add the service bus credentials to all endpoints specified in the configuration and open the host service instance. Our sample application will run until a key is pressed, and it is important to close the service host when you are done.

To test the application, press F5 and you will see the console application running, as shown in Figure 18.26.

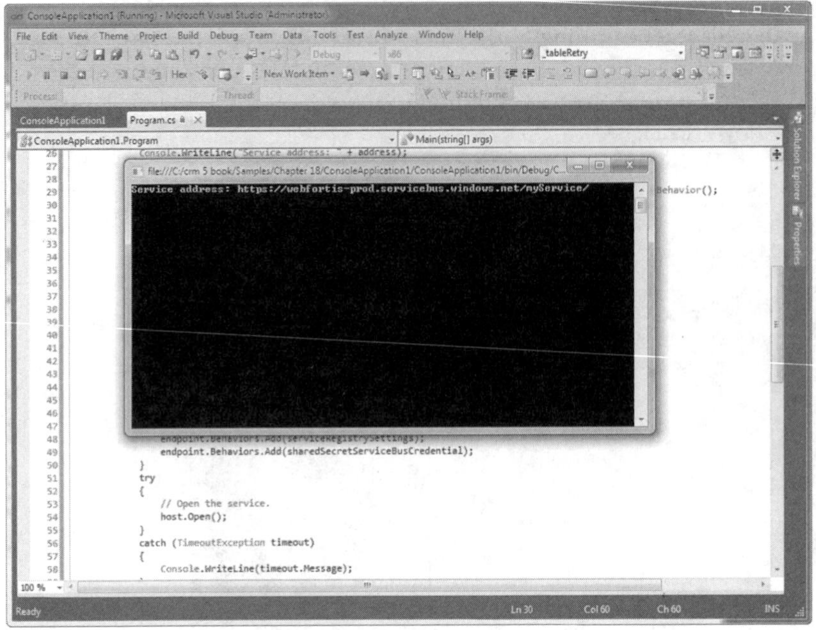

FIGURE 18.26 Testing service bus listener application.

Now go to CRM web UI, and go to Accounts, and then click New to create a new account, as shown in Figure 18.27.

After you click Save, you will see the message is sent to our custom console application and you will see the output, as shown in Figure 18.28.

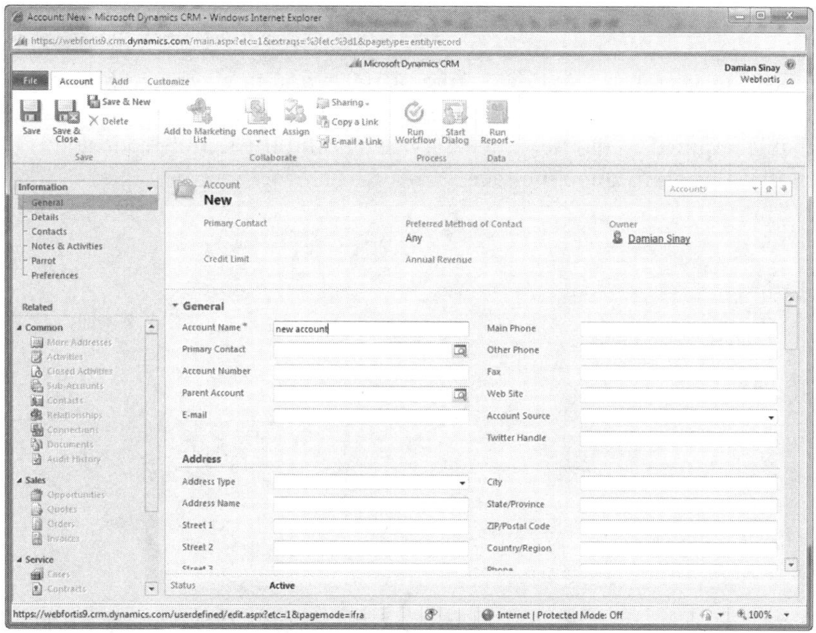

FIGURE 18.27 Creating a new account on CRM.

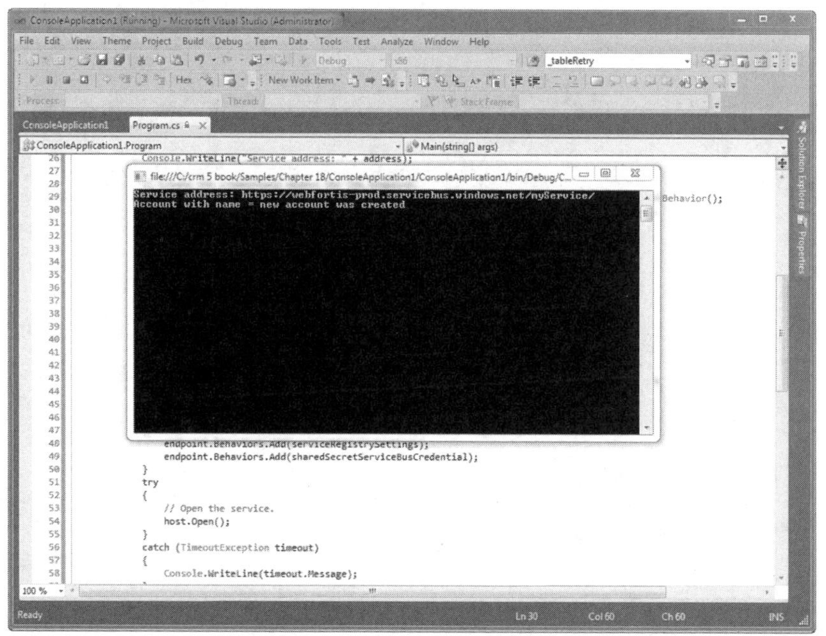

FIGURE 18.28 Account created event received on console application.

Summary

This chapter described the Microsoft Windows Azure platform and how we can interact with the Microsoft Dynamics CRM entity events through the AppFabric service bus. We've seen the process that is required to register a new service bus and the sample code and components necessary to listen to these messages.

CHAPTER 19

Advanced Views and Connections

IN THIS CHAPTER

- Views
- Connections

When working with Microsoft Dynamics CRM 2011, one of the most common questions is related to ease of use. This chapter explains the concepts of views and connections, which when properly used deliver an ease of use that can drive productivity.

Views

Views are how we interact with or view the data. When we look at the default configuration for Accounts, for example, we see the My Active Accounts view, as shown in Figure 19.1.

The views that are included by default in a vanilla implementation for Accounts are as follows:

- Accounts: Influenced Deals That We Won
- Accounts: No Campaign Activities in Last 3 Months
- Accounts: No Orders in Last 6 Months
- Active Accounts
- Inactive Accounts
- My Active Accounts
- My Connections

Additionally we have the option to create a personal view, which is demonstrated in the next section.

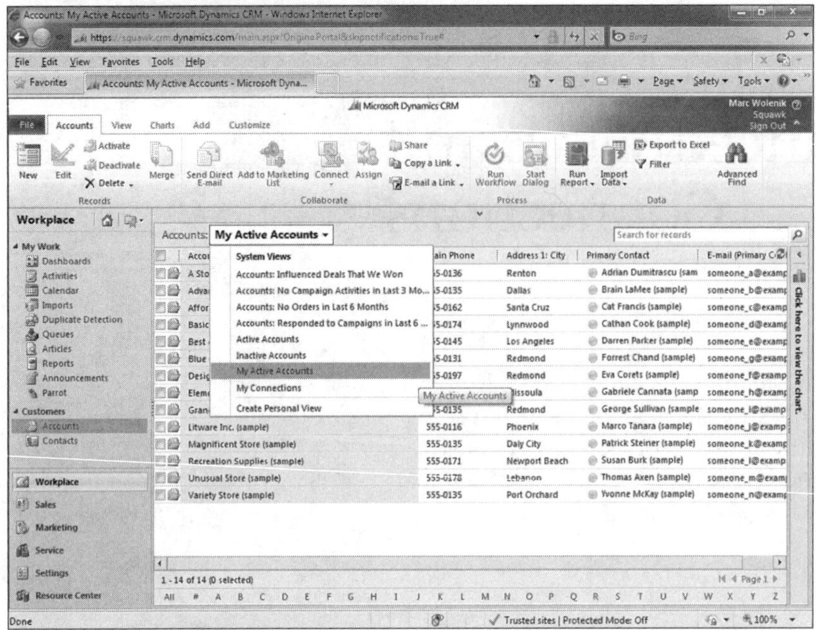

FIGURE 19.1 Standard Accounts view.

Create a Personal View

Creation of personal views are easy and provide a high level of usability to Microsoft Dynamics CRM 2011.

To create a personal view, follow the steps outlined:

1. To create a personal view, select Create Personal View from the drop-down shown in Figure 19.1. Alternatively, you can simply open the Advanced Find and select Accounts as the base entity, as shown in Figure 19.2.
2. The Advanced Find opens, and the base entity is Accounts, as shown in Figure 19.2.

NOTE

Advanced Find opens by default to the base entity from which it was launched. So, if you open the Advanced Find from Contacts, Contacts would be the Look For default value.

For our example, we are interested in seeing a view of all accounts that are in Redmond. Figure 19.2 has the logic added to the Advanced Find with that criteria. You could easily add additional logic that filters on orders placed, account status, or any other value.

3. Select Save As from the top of the Advanced Find.
4. Enter the friendly name of the view that you would like to refer to, as shown in Figure 19.3. (The default will be [new].) You can also add a description of the view.

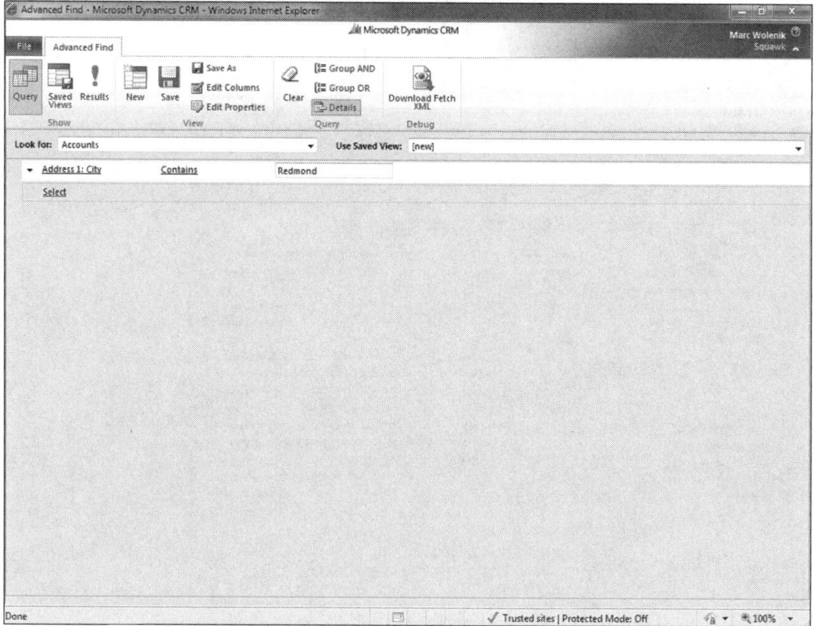

FIGURE 19.2 Advanced Find for Accounts.

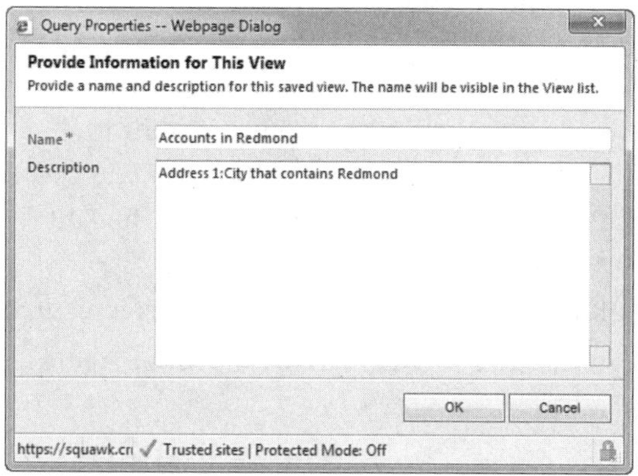

FIGURE 19.3 Set the query properties.

5. Select OK to save the Advanced Find.
6. Close the Advanced Find and navigate back to the Accounts page.
7. Select the views and notice the new view we created is displayed in the drop-down (see Figure 19.4) under My Views near the bottom.

FIGURE 19.4 New view displayed.

When the view is selected (see Figure 19.5), the columns selected are those that were chosen from the Advanced Find selection.

8. To modify the columns, select Advanced Find from the Ribbon menu, and then select the Saved Views from the Ribbon menu, and select the view you want to modify, as shown in Figure 19.6.

9. After you've selected a view, select Edit Columns from the Ribbon menu. The Edit Columns interface will open, as shown in Figure 19.7.

   Here we can see that we have the default columns that were displayed in Figure 19.5.

10. To delete a column, select the column so that it is highlighted (as shown in Figure 19.8), and then select Remove.

NOTE

This removes the column from the view only—it does not remove the attribute (or its related data) from the application.

11. To add a column, select Add Columns and select the desired column from the Add Columns view, as shown in Figure 19.9. In our example, we're going to add Account Number, Account Rating, and Account Source.

12. To add columns from the related records, select the record type from the drop-down, as shown in Figure 19.10.

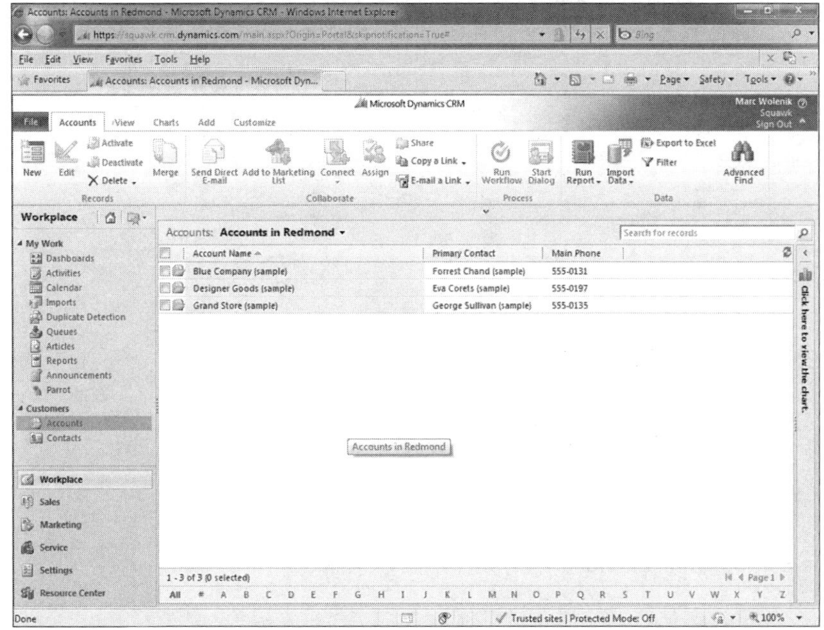

FIGURE 19.5 New view selected.

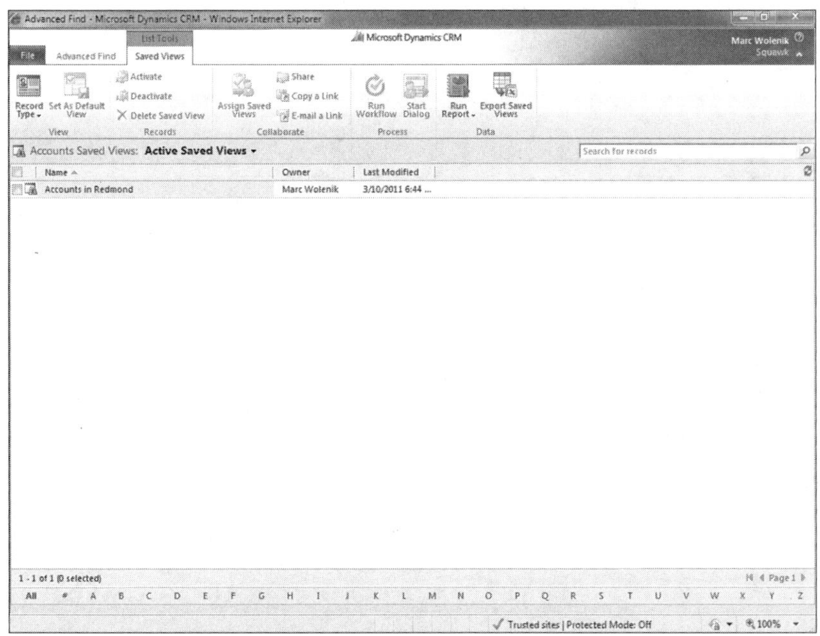

FIGURE 19.6 Select a saved view.

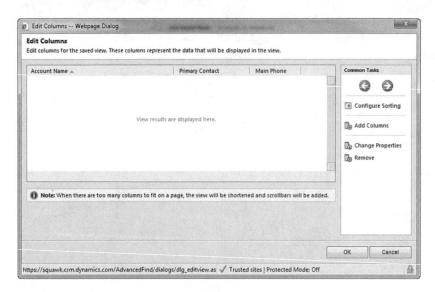

FIGURE 19.7 The Edit Columns interface.

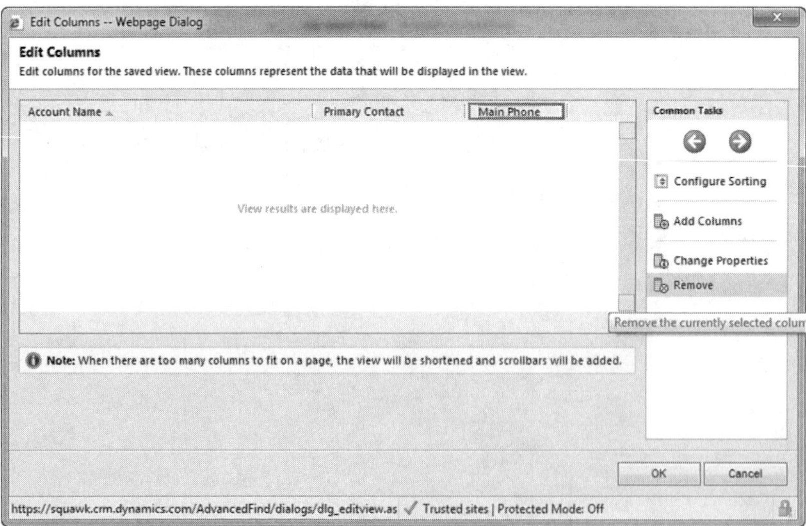

FIGURE 19.8 Removing a column from the Advanced Find.

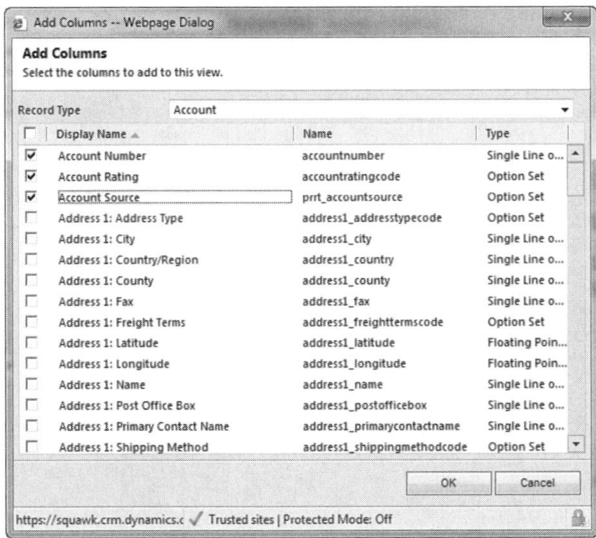

FIGURE 19.9 Adding columns from the Advanced Find.

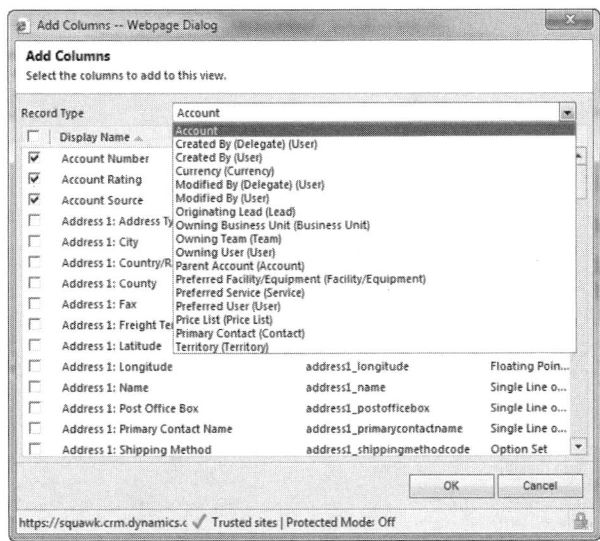

FIGURE 19.10 Adding related attributes from the Advanced Find.

In our example, we've selected the Created By (User) entity and the User Name (see Figure 19.11).

13. Selecting OK to save the query will show the Columns that will be displayed in the view (see Figure 19.12).

14. To move the columns, select the column so it is highlighted, and then navigate the columns by using the green left or right buttons.

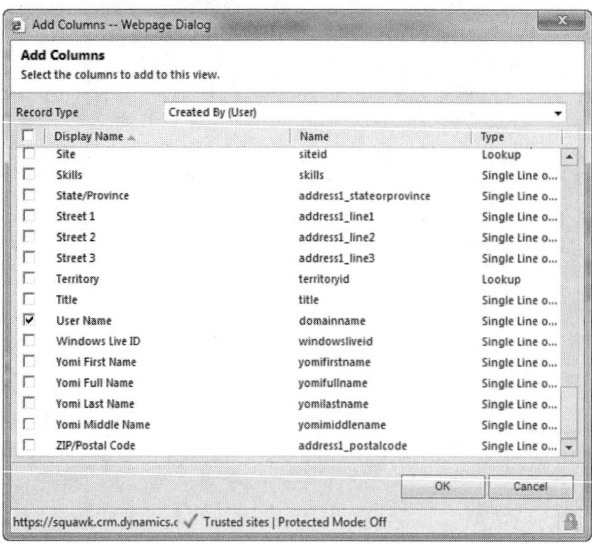

FIGURE 19.11 Adding related attributes from the user record to the Advanced Find.

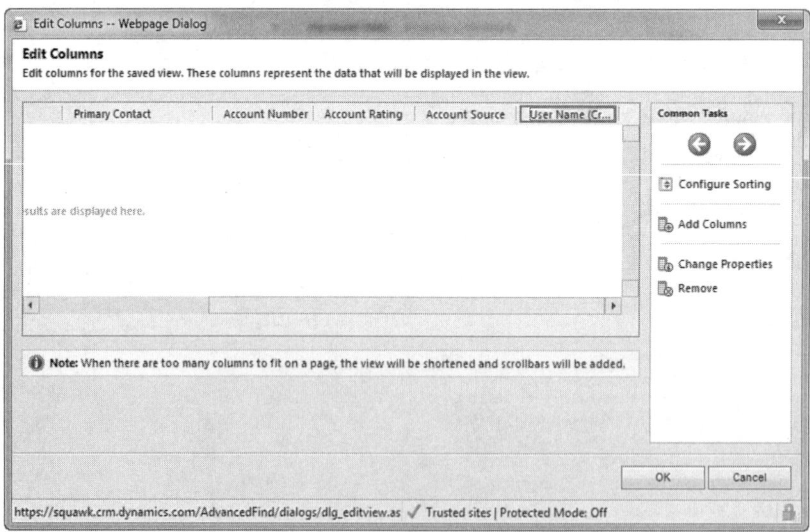

FIGURE 19.12 Selected columns shown on the Advanced Find.

15. Select OK to close the column editor, be sure to save the view by selecting Save (or Save As if you want to have a different version of the view), and then close the Advanced Find.

Selecting the view from the main Account page will show the columns we've selected now, as shown in Figure 19.13.

When working within Outlook, notice that the view we created is available near the bottom of the drop-down, as shown in Figure 19.14.

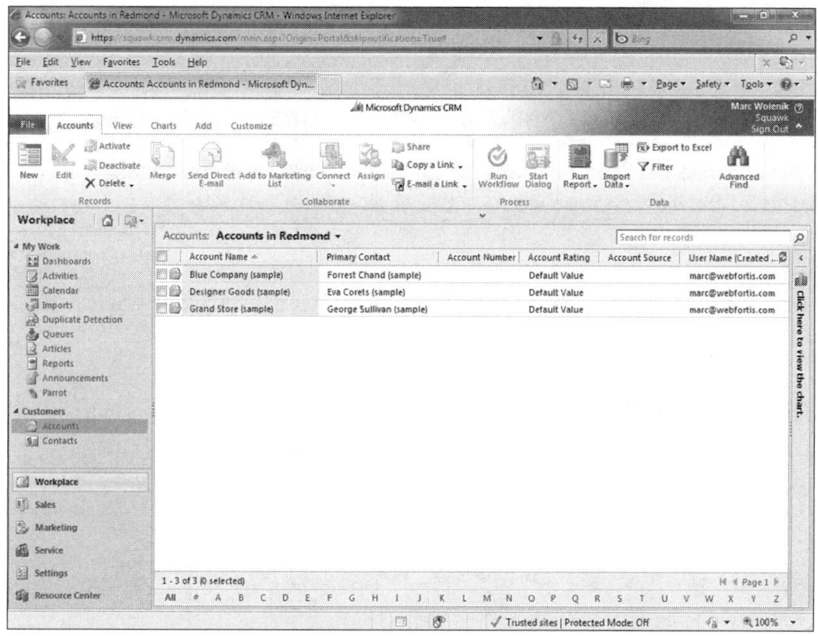

FIGURE 19.13 Modified view.

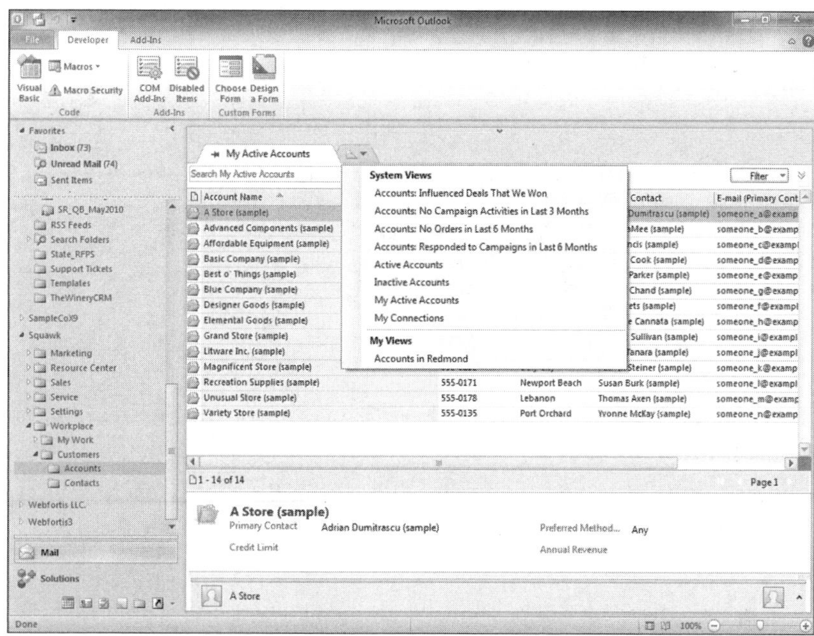

FIGURE 19.14 View in Outlook.

By default, views that are created are personal and not available to other users of the organization until they are shared or assigned.

NOTE

Assigning a view will change the owner of the view to the assignee, whereas sharing will retain ownership of the view and allow others to use it.

16. To share or assign the view, open Advanced Find, and select Saved Views. Select the view (or multiple views) by selecting it, as shown in Figure 19.15.

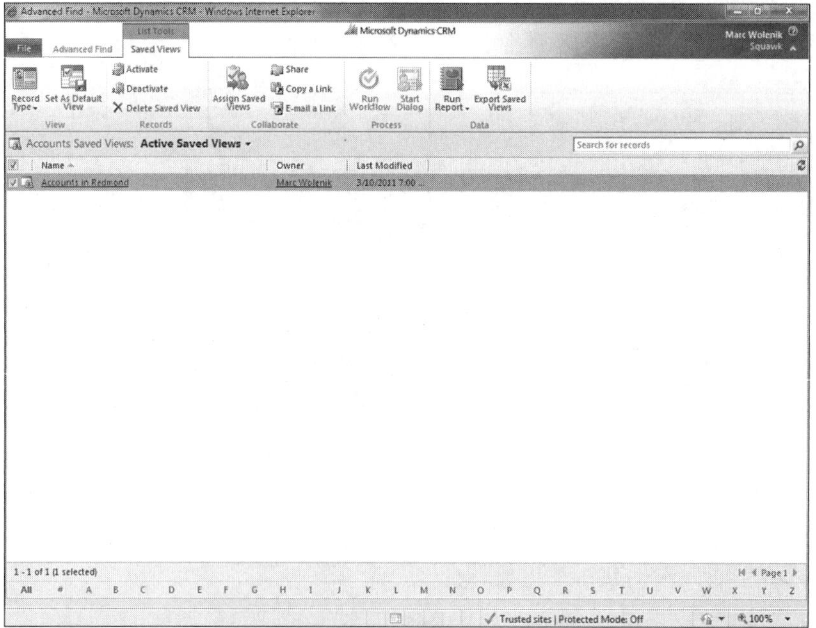

FIGURE 19.15 Selected view.

17. From the Ribbon menu, select Assign Saved Views (see Figure 19.16), and then select a user or team with which to share it.
18. To share a view, select the view, and then select Share from the Ribbon Menu. Select Add User/Team from the Common Tasks menu, and give the appropriate permissions for the view, as shown in Figure 19.17.

After it is shared or assigned, the view will be available immediately to the shared users.

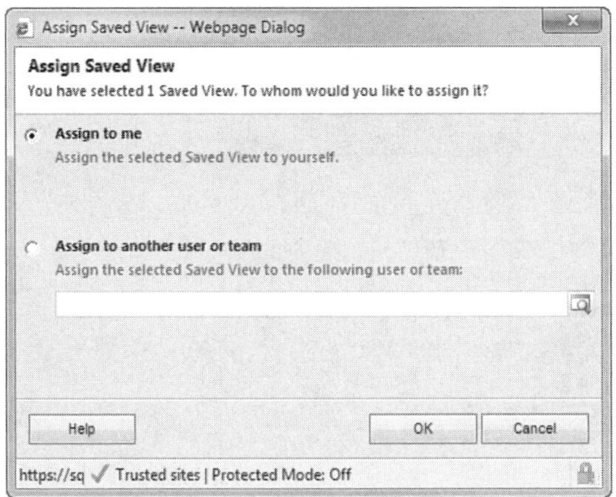

FIGURE 19.16 Assigning a view.

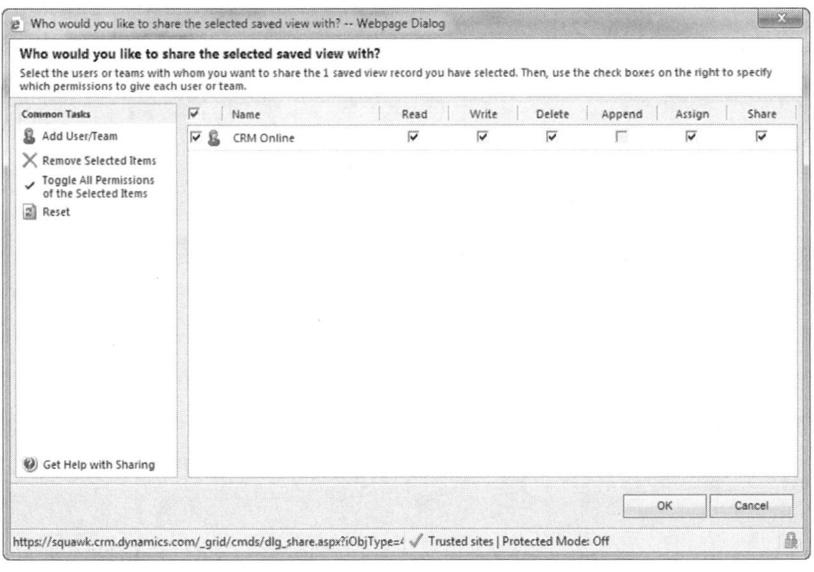

FIGURE 19.17 Sharing a view.

Modify the System Views

System Views are the same as custom/personal views. The important distinction is that they take precedence when selecting a view. Therefore, they are typically considered more important. Complete the following steps to create or modify the system views:

1. To begin, select Customize the System from Settings, Customizations, as shown in Figure 19.18.

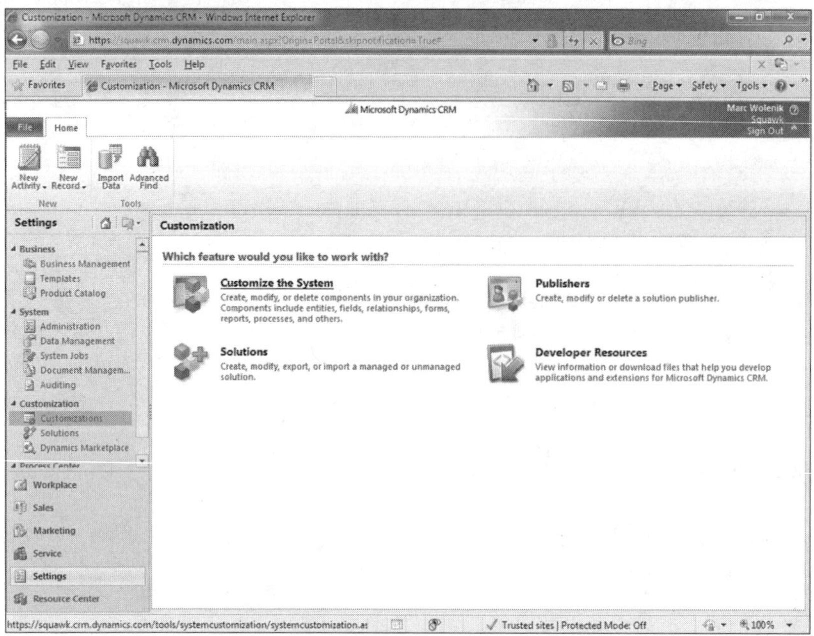

FIGURE 19.18 Customize the System.

NOTE

For best practices, consider making the modifications outlined in this section within a solution instead of customizing the base customizations.

▶ For more information about working with solutions, refer to Chapter 16, "Solution Concepts."

2. Navigate to the entity that has the view you want to modify. In our example, we're going to select Account and expand it (see Figure 19.19).
3. From here, views can be added by selecting New and following the same steps explained previously in this chapter on creating views.

TIP

To delete a view, select it and then click the Delete icon.

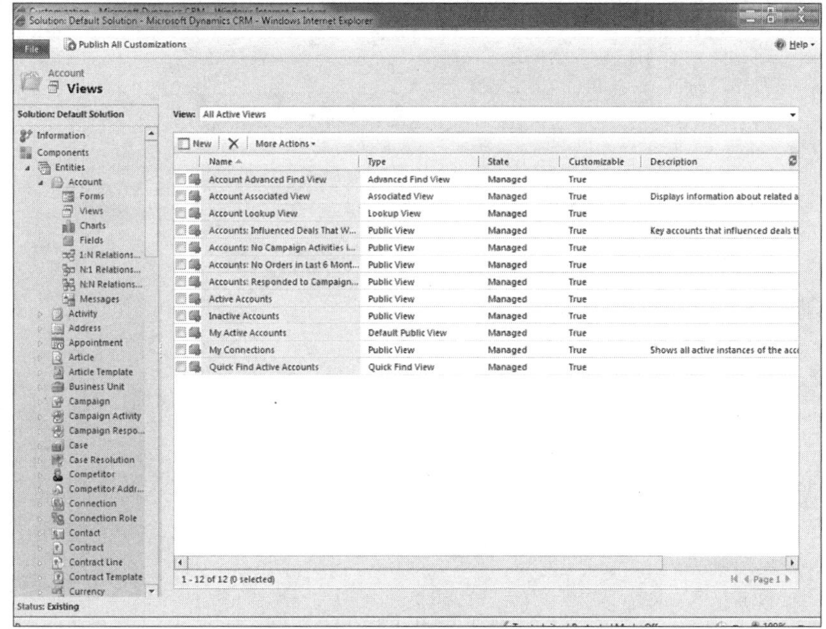

FIGURE 19.19 System views.

Additional commonly used options within the More Actions drop down enable you to set the default view (the view that opens by default when the entity is opened) as well as edit the system views.

Connections

Connections are new to this version of Microsoft Dynamics CRM, and although originally designed to replace Relationships, both are available as options in the system.

NOTE

Relationships were to have been deprecated in this version of Microsoft Dynamics CRM, and only available in upgraded scenarios. However, both are still available in the system. That being said, be sure to use Connections, and not relationships, going forward.

Connections (as the name implies) are the connections or relationships between one entity and another. Connections are established via connection roles. Connection roles are found in Settings, Business Management (see Figure 19.20).

Connection roles are very flexible and by no means limited to the roles that come out of the box.

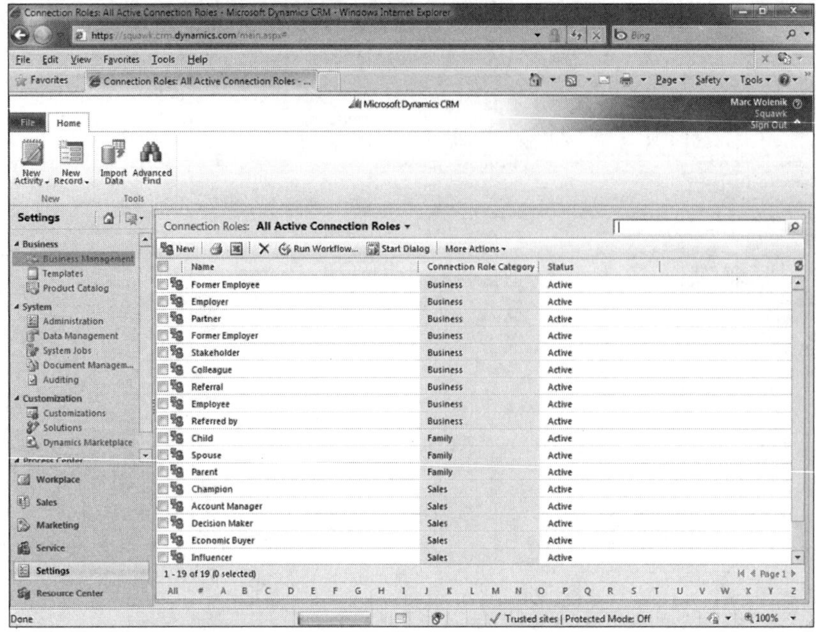

FIGURE 19.20 Connection roles.

Complete the following steps to make a new connection:

1. Select New, and follow the steps shown on the form, as shown in Figure 19.21.

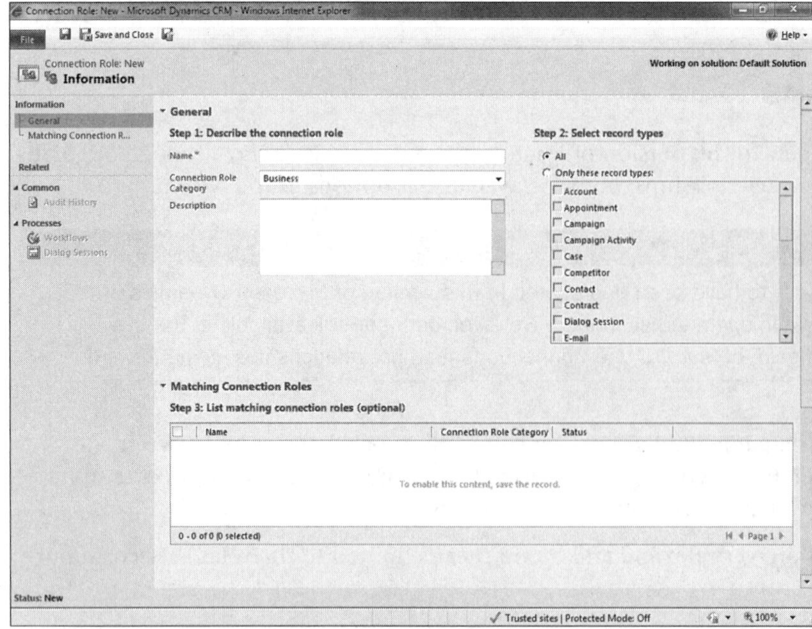

FIGURE 19.21 Create a new connection role.

2. Navigate to Customizations, and then select the Connection Role Category drop-down to configure the new connection.
3. Next, select the field Connection Role Category from the Connection Role entity to modify the options, as shown in Figure 19.22.

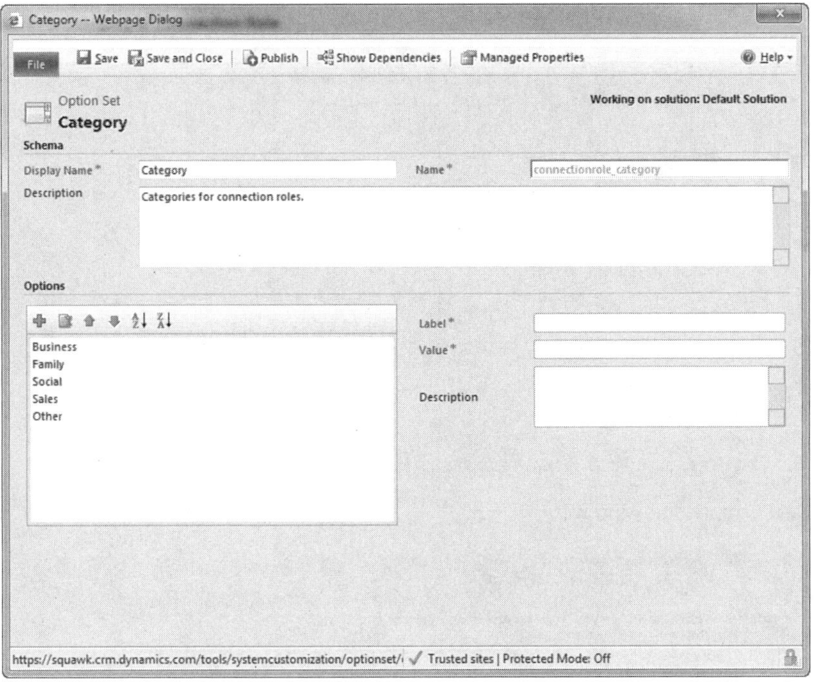

FIGURE 19.22 Modify the connection role categories.

4. To create a connection between one entity and another, navigate to the entity and either select Connections in the near navigation, or select Connect directly from the Ribbon menu.
5. When the Connection window opens, as shown in Figure 19.23, select the name of the connection. This is actually the entity to which the connection will relate.
6. From the options displayed, select the entity to which you want to make the relationship, as shown in Figure 19.24.
7. Next, select the connection roles. By default the view will be a custom view called Applicable Connection Roles (see Figure 19.25), which are the roles that are available to select between the two entities selected.

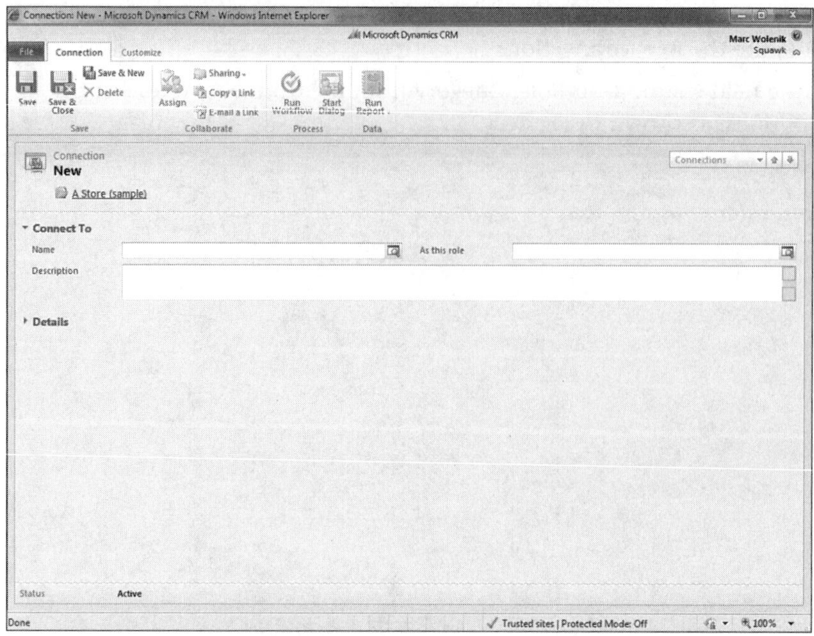

FIGURE 19.23 New Connection window.

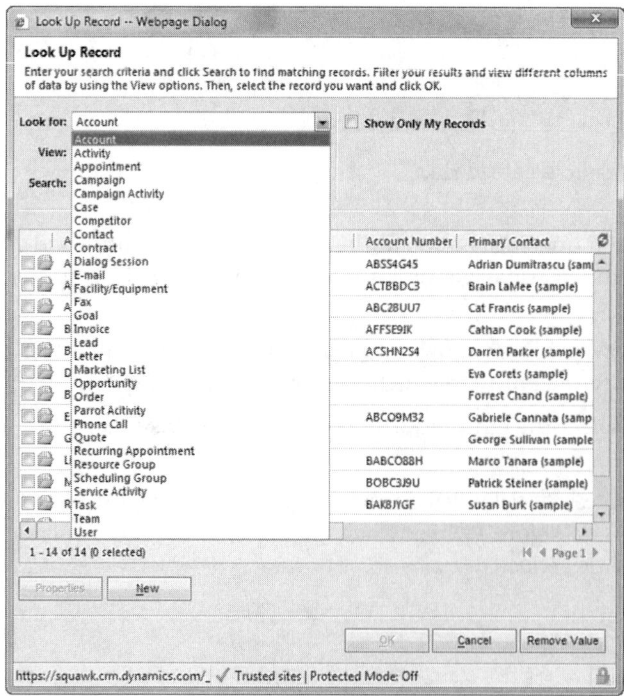

FIGURE 19.24 Connection options.

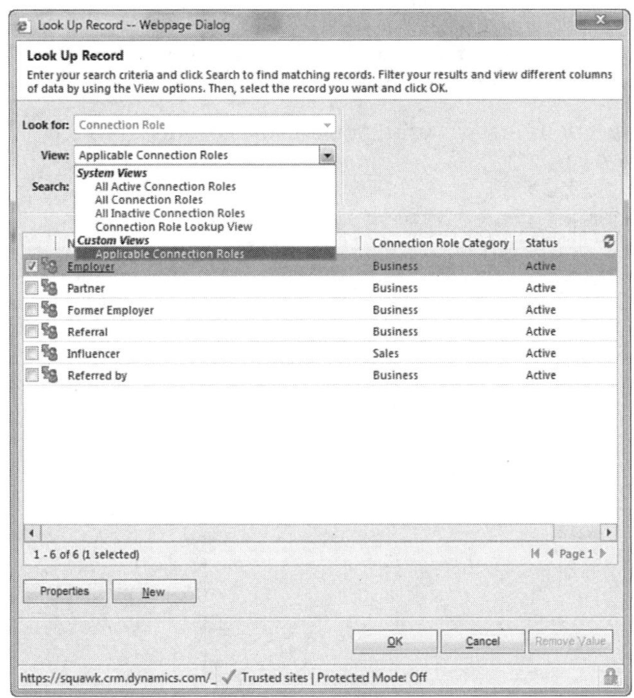

FIGURE 19.25 Connection role options.

CAUTION

If you try and create a connection between two entities that is not allowed, you will receive the error message shown in Figure 19.26.

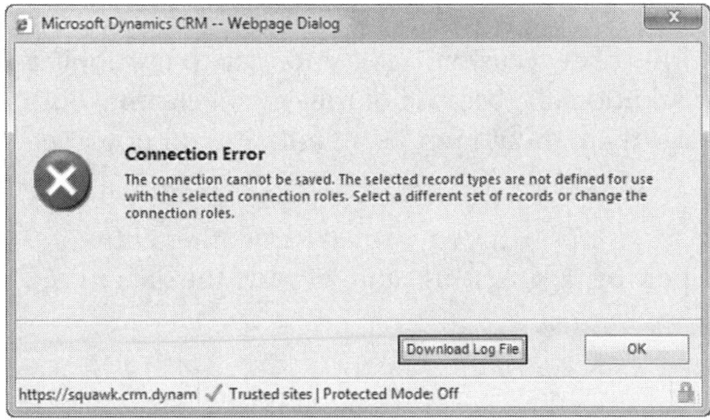

FIGURE 19.26 Connection error.

Figure 19.27 shows an Account with several connections. The flexibility is easy to see because we have added not just another company relationship but can set up the connection between former employees and add specific notes to the connection.

When you select the view My Connections for Accounts, you see all accounts to which you have a connection (refer to Figure 19.27).

FIGURE 19.27 Connections established on an Account level.

Summary

As we have shown, working with views will create a customizable and easy-to-use application by delivering specific data to users. Additionally, because of the ease in creating both custom views and modifying system views, there should not be a limitation on how the data is pushed to users.

Connections allow for users to create relationships between virtually any other entity in the system, allowing options for both reporting, aggregating, and viewing the data in a meaningful fashion.

CHAPTER 20

Filtered Lookups

IN THIS CHAPTER

- Availability of Filtered Lookups

Microsoft Dynamics CRM 2011 introduced the concept of lookups restricted to only what you need or filtered based on predefined criteria. In previous versions, when you had a lookup option, the only option you were presented with was every possible value for the lookup, restricted only to those records that your security settings prevented you from accessing. As such, if you needed to populate the parent account on the Account form, you would have to filter through every account record before finding the one you wanted.

Now we can define what records we want to choose from, making selection much easier.

Availability of Filtered Lookups

Filtered lookups are available on every entity where there is a lookup field. Figure 20.1 shows a new Account form. We're going to focus on the Primary Contact lookup, which is highlighted in Figure 20.1, as means of illustration for this chapter.

When you select the lookup icon, you are presented with the filtered view lookup, as shown in Figure 20.2.

To work with or modify a lookup, open the form in Design view. You can do this by either navigating to customization and selecting the entity and form, or by selecting Customize at the top of the form and then selecting Form.

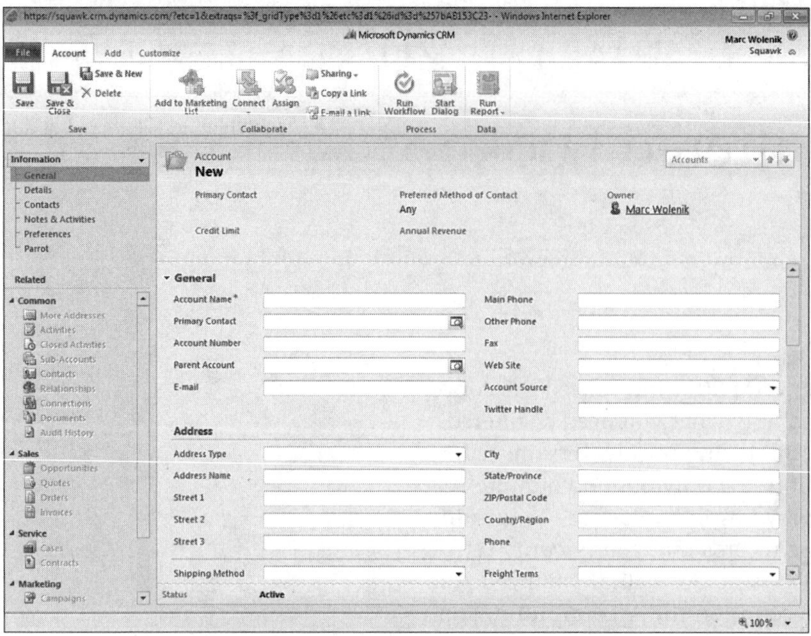

FIGURE 20.1 New Account.

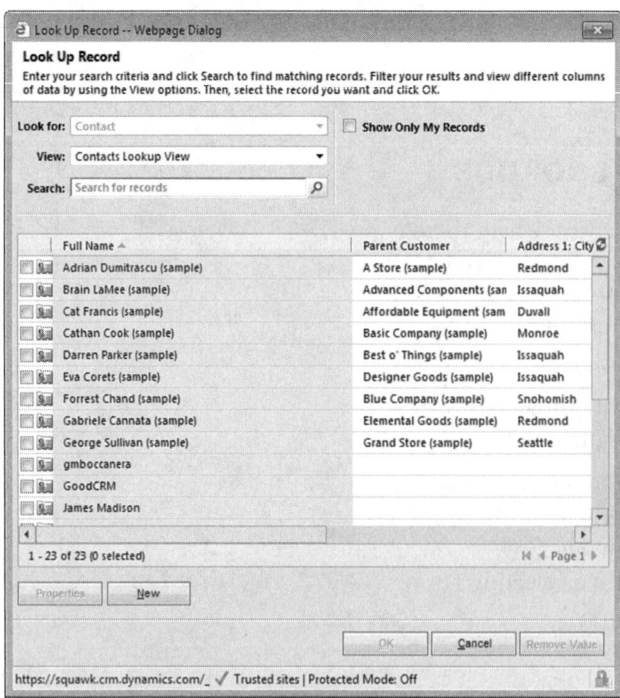

FIGURE 20.2 Filtered lookup for contacts.

When the form is opened in design mode, select Primary Contact from the form, as shown in Figure 20.3. Next, select Change Properties from the Ribbon menu.

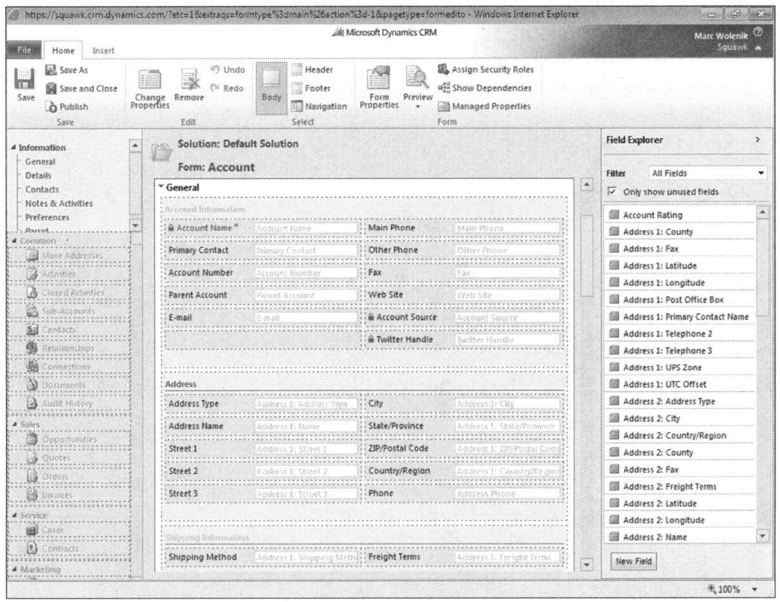

FIGURE 20.3 Account form in Design view.

When the Field Properties dialog is displayed as shown in Figure 20.4, scroll to the bottom of the Display tab. The filtering options are shown here.

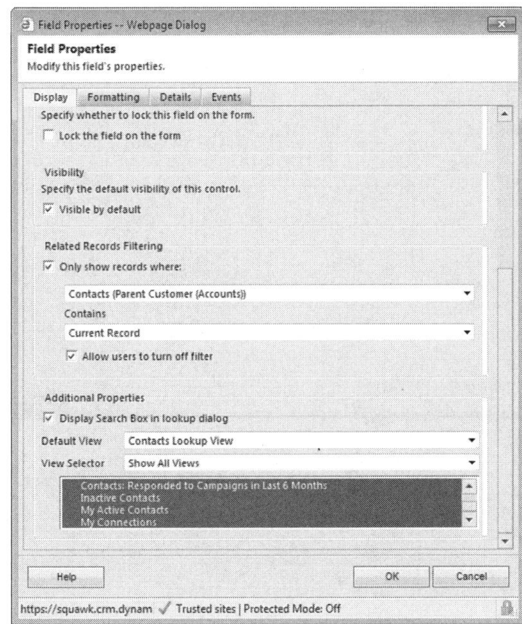

FIGURE 20.4 Field Properties dialog.

When the related records filtering Only Show Records Where is selected, you have the option to modify the lookup to show records specific to your filter requirements (see Figure 20.4). If this option is unselected, there is no filtering applied to the lookup field. (Search values are still limited to the relationship established.)

The first drop-down shows the options that can be selected for the lookup box (see Figure 20.5). When selected, the Contains drop-down is modified to show all relationships that connect to the first selection.

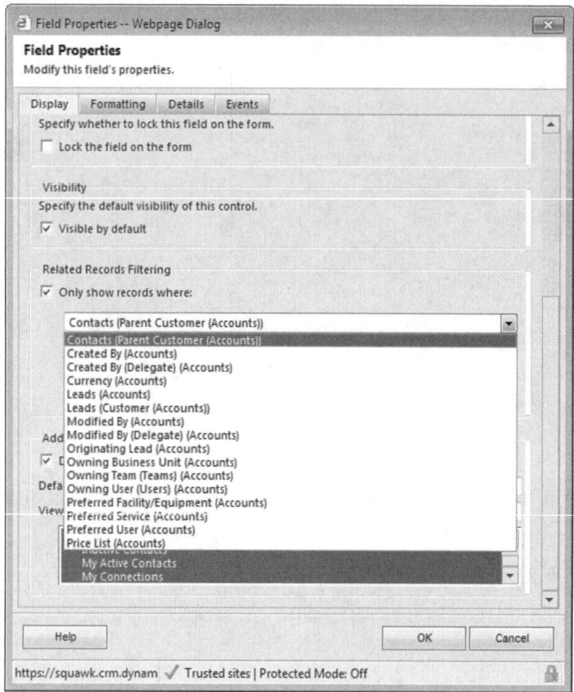

FIGURE 20.5 Filtered records selection.

When establishing the first drop-down, it is constrained to all potential relationship possibilities, as defined in Table 20.1.

TABLE 20.1 Possible Filtered Relationship Combinations

First Drop-Down	Second Drop-Down	Available
N:1	1:N	X
N:1	N:1	X
N:1	N:N	X
1:N	1:N	X
1:N	N:1	
1:N	N:N	
N:N	1:N	X
N:N	N:1	
N:N	N:N	

By selecting Allow Users to Turn Off Filter, users are given the option to search outside of the defined filters set.

Additional Properties enables you to select whether the search box is displayed in the lookup dialog (see Figure 20.6).

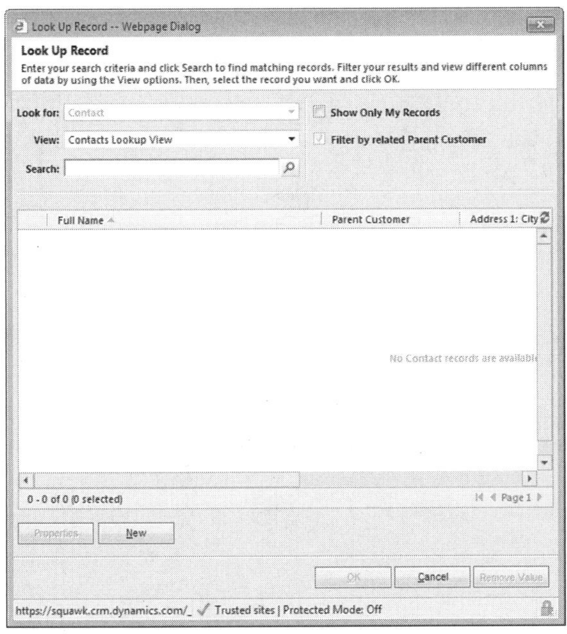

FIGURE 20.6 Filtered records selection.

The default view is the view returned by default for the lookup when selected, and you can show all, one, or some of the views by changing the View selector to Off, All or Some, and then defining (by selecting) views in the box below.

Be sure to publish all changes associated with changes made to have them pushed out to users.

CAUTION

It is possible in the way you define your filtered lookup that the results returned might be related in such a way as to return no results. This might or might not be the desired result (for example, forcing the user to create a new record), and careful testing and consideration should be given when setting up the filtered lookups.

Summary

With support for filtered lookups out of the box, Microsoft Dynamics CRM 2011 has increased the ease of use significantly by allowing administrators to push down to end users only data that they need.

An example where this type of behavior can be used with great benefit is not just when high security protocols are in place or necessary. Instead, views and related record contact can be defined and then the proposed underlying data can be presented, or proposed, to users to select without having to mine through numerous unrelated data.

CHAPTER 21

Reporting and Dashboards

IN THIS CHAPTER

Charts and Dashboards

CRM 2011 introduces a new way to represent data—native charts that can be also integrated into Dashboards, which provides a better representation of the data for some cases.

The first part of this chapter talks specifically about general charts, and then we'll discuss Dashboards, of which charts comprise a majority of how Dashboards work.

Charts

Charts are a new way to show data graphically in the following graphics types:

- Column
- Bar
- Line
- Pie
- Funnel

The core entities come with predefined charts that can be displayed by clicking on the entity from the sidebar list (for example, Accounts or Contacts) and then clicking the arrow on the right side of the grid, as shown on Figure 21.1.

The charts will be displayed in the right side of the Grid view. Figure 21.2 shows a bar chart of active accounts by industry.

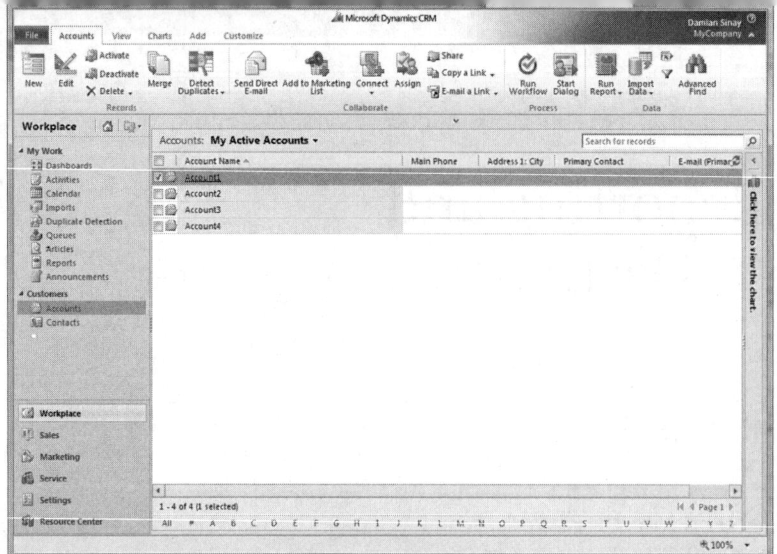

FIGURE 21.1 Showing charts in collapsed mode.

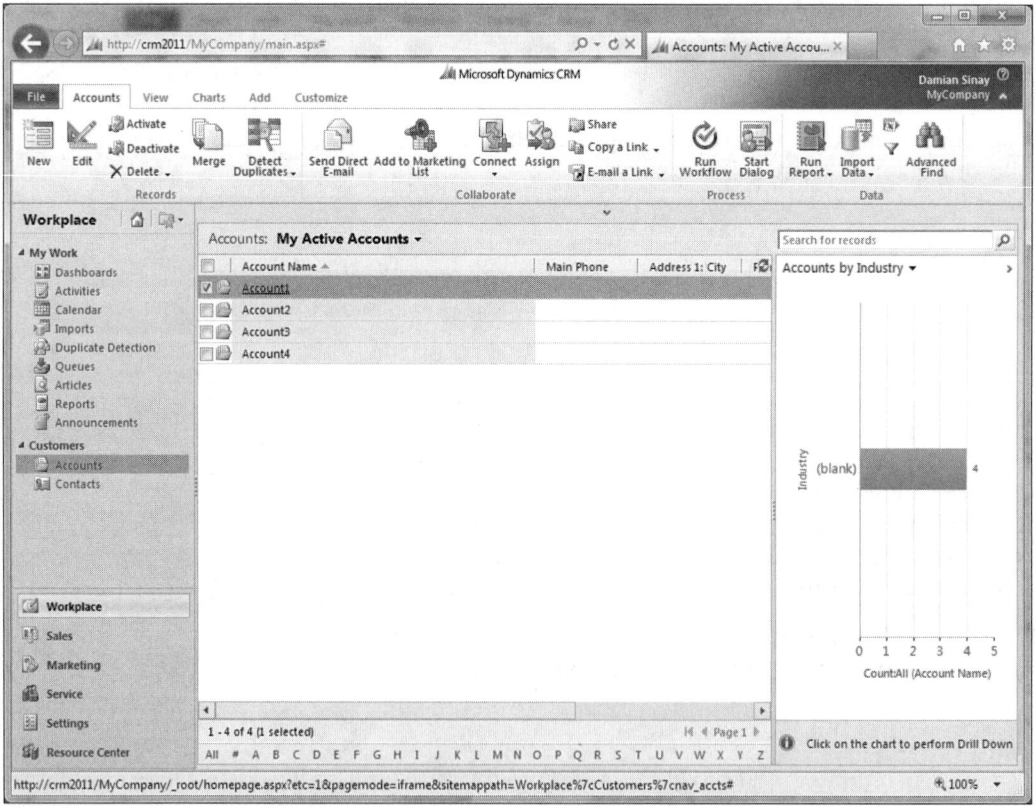

FIGURE 21.2 Accounts by industry chart.

Any system or custom view is also tied to charts and affect the results not only displayed on the grid but also on the chart. So, if you change the view to see the inactive accounts, this will also update the selected chart result. To change the view, you can click on the current view name and select a different view from the drop-down list. In this example we will select the Inactive Accounts view, as seen in Figure 21.3.

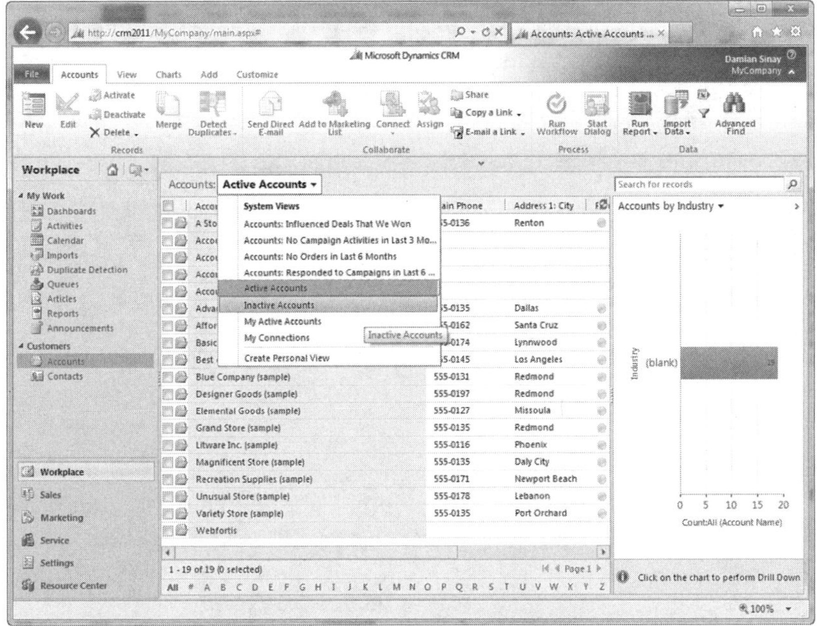

FIGURE 21.3 Changing views.

Also the chart bars can be drilled down and when clicked on any bar the underlying data of the grid will change to display the new data represented by the chart.

Because the chart results are tied to the results displayed on the grid, you can also use the new Filter feature to modify the chart results as well. This is a nice new feature that in some cases replaces the Advanced Find because it is easy to use with the predefined views. To use the Filter, go to the View tab on the Ribbon and click on Filter. Doing so adds filter controls to each of the column headers of the grid so that you can add specific or custom filters (see Figure 21.4).

After applying a filter, a button in the middle of the chart will appear asking you to refresh the chart (see Figure 21.5).

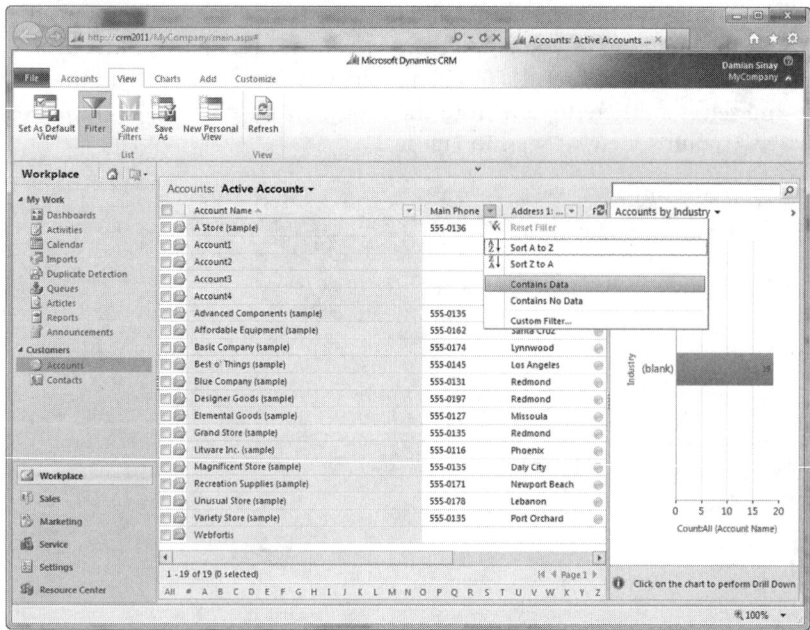

FIGURE 21.4 Working with the Filter.

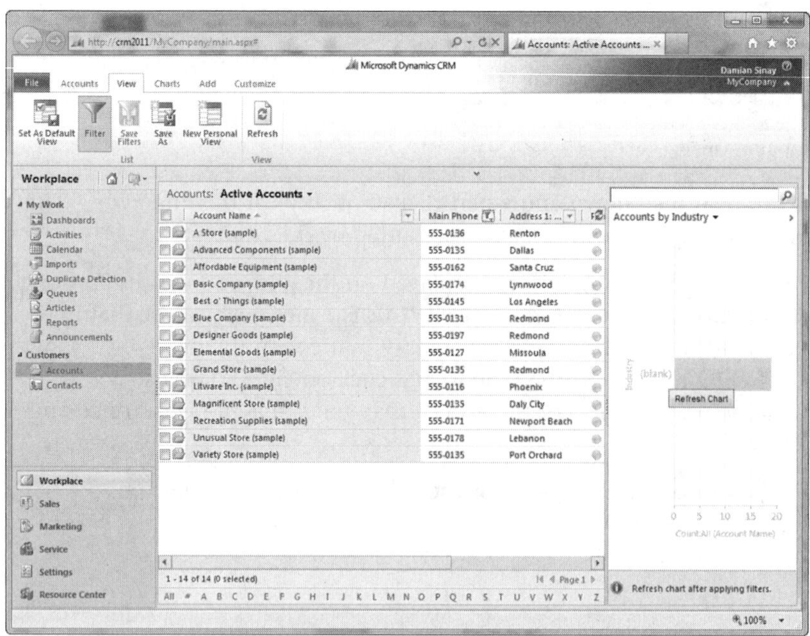

FIGURE 21.5 The Refresh Chart button.

There are two main types of charts: system charts and personal charts. System charts are ones that can be created with customizations and are available to all users. Personal charts are ones created by users (as explained in this chapter) and are visible only to the user who created them. 21

▶ To learn more about system charts, refer to Chapter 23, "Customizing Entities."

NOTE

Check the CRM 2011 SDK because there are other types of charts apart from the ones available to the user though the CRM 2011 web UI. You can also include Web Recourses as charts, as we explain later in this chapter; that is also documented on the CRM 2011 SDK.

Chart Tools

To create a new personal chart, click on the Charts tab of the Ribbon and then click on New Chart, as seen in Figure 21.6.

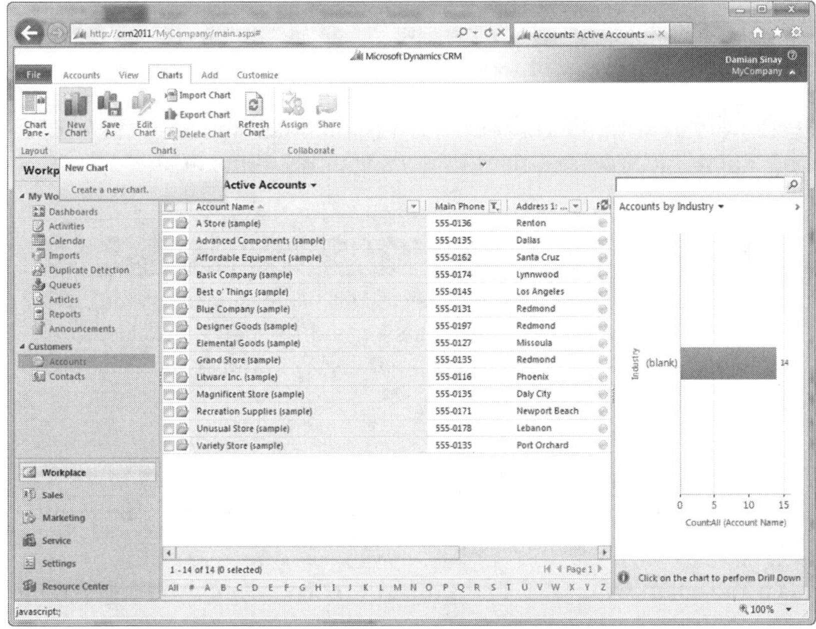

FIGURE 21.6 New chart.

The Chart Tools ribbon will be displayed as soon as you create or edit a personal chart (see Figure 21.7).

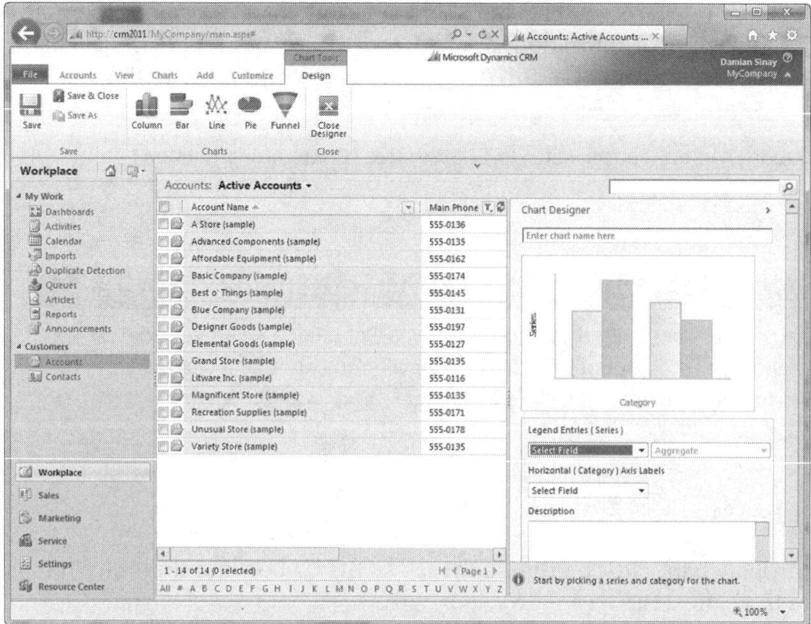

FIGURE 21.7 Chart tools.

When creating a new chart, you will need to specify a name for the chart, the Legend field, the aggregate function, and the Category field. Optionally you can add a description to the chart. If you are working with the core entities, it is important to review the current charts before creating a new one because a chart that fits your needs might already exist.

TIP

When creating a new chart, you can skip the Name field and it will be autocompleted with a name as Legend by Category when you select the Legend and Category fields. For example, if you select a Legend of Credit Limit and a Category of Owner, the Name will be autocompleted with Credit Limit by Owner.

The aggregate option changes depending on the type of the field you selected for the Legend. If the type of this field is numeric, you can use Sum, Average, Count: All, Count: Non-empty, Max, and Min for the aggregation type.

Figure 21.8 shows a custom chart we created that shows the Credit Limit by Owners of the Account entity.

Each chart also has some advanced options you can access by clicking the Show link, from which you can limit the X or Y items that will be displayed if the chart is hard to read because it contains a large amount of series (see Figure 21.9).

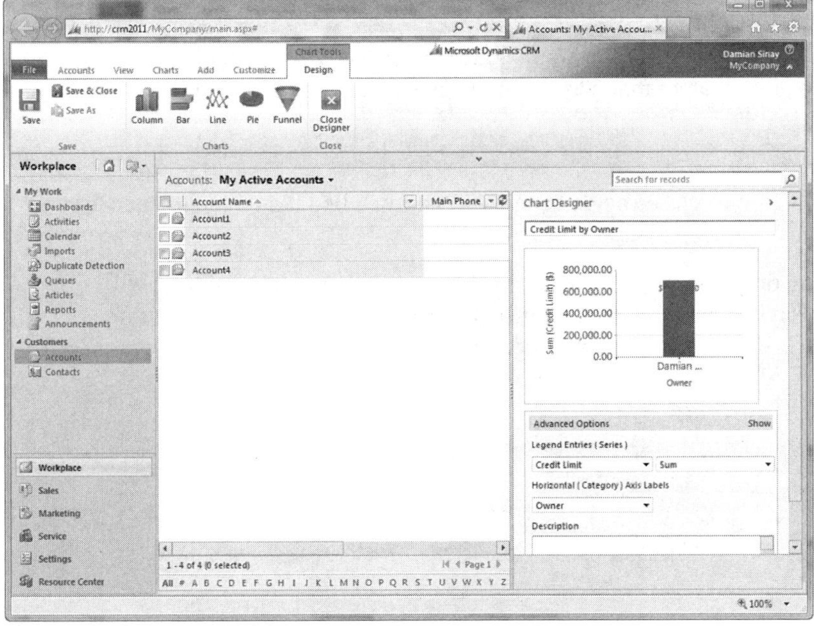

FIGURE 21.8 Custom personal chart.

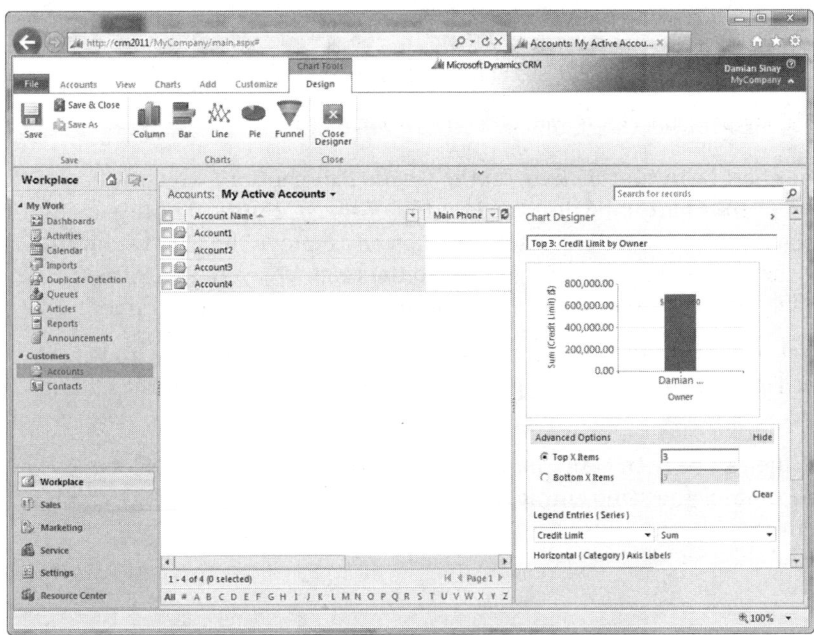

FIGURE 21.9 Advanced options.

NOTE

The advanced option allowing the top X and bottom Y options (as shown in Figure 21.9) is a great feature that allows the representation of data quickly and accurately.

Click on Save and Close to close the designer, and you will be taken back to the Charts tab on the Ribbon.

Personal charts, the ones the user creates from any entity view, can be shared with other users in different ways. If the user you want to share the chart belongs to the same organization you can click Share and select the users or teams you want to share the chart with (see Figure 21.10).

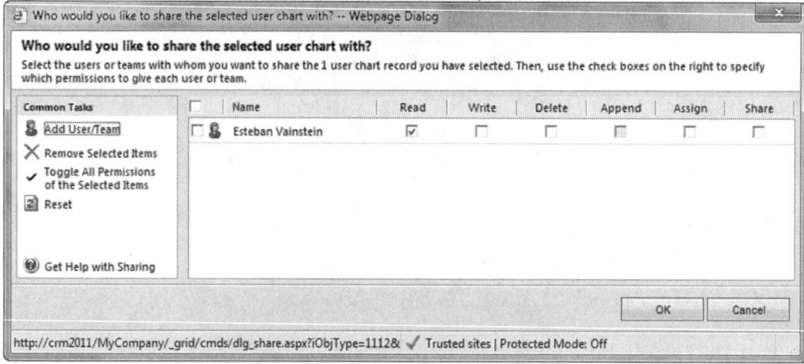

FIGURE 21.10 Sharing personal charts with other users or teams.

You can change the chart layout by clicking on the Charts Pane button, which will change the position of the chart to be displayed on top of the grid instead of displaying on the right (see Figure 21.11). Selecting Off will completely remove the Chart from the main view leaving the grid option only. To go back to the original layout, click the Chart tab of the Ribbon, click on the Chart Pane button again, and select the right option.

If the user you want to share with is in another organization, you can export the chart to an XML file (see Figure 21.12) by clicking on the Export Chart button in the Charts tab Ribbon.

The exported XML file can be then easily imported to another organization as long as the other organization contains the same entities and fields used by the originating organization where the chart was created.

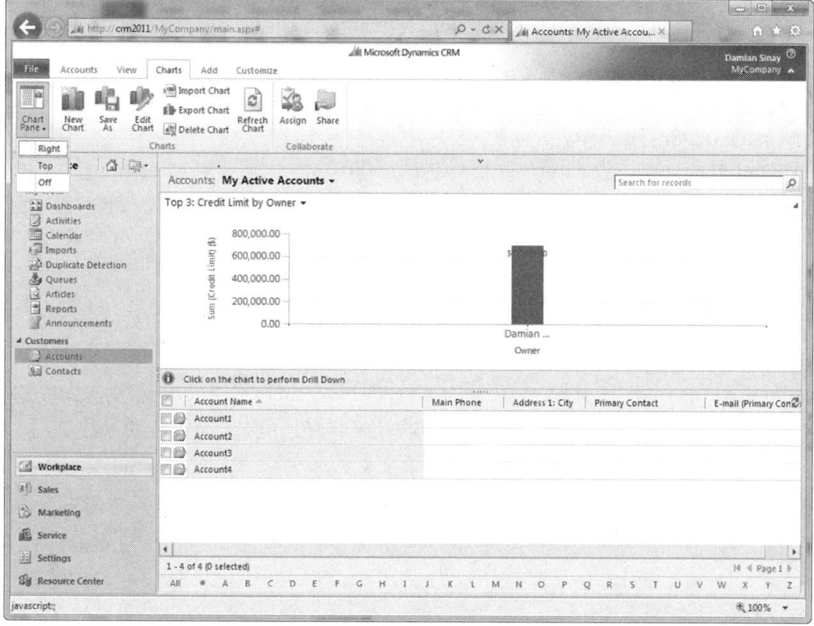

FIGURE 21.11 Change the chart layout.

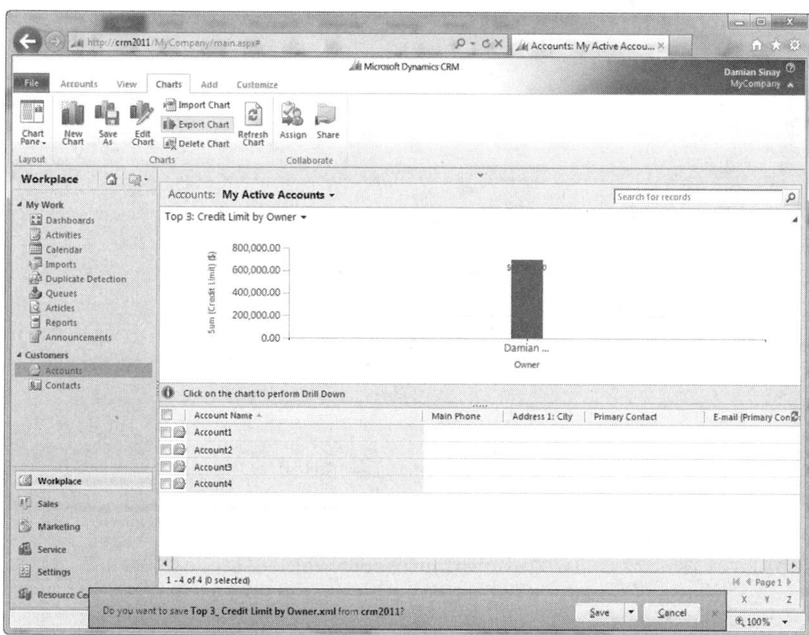

FIGURE 21.12 Exporting charts.

Here is an example of the XML generated for a chart:

```
<visualization>
  <visualizationid>{5D432D41-34C4-DF11-A19E-00155DFE7905}</visualizationid>
  <name>Credit Limit by Owner</name>
  <primaryentitytypecode>account</primaryentitytypecode>
  <datadescription>
    <datadefinition>
      <fetchcollection>
        <fetch mapping="logical" aggregate="true" count="3">
          <entity name="account">
            <order alias="aggregate_column" descending="true" />
            <attribute alias="aggregate_column" name="creditlimit" aggregate="sum" />
            <attribute groupby="true" alias="groupby_column" name="ownerid" />
          </entity>
        </fetch>
      </fetchcollection>
      <categorycollection>
        <category>
          <measurecollection>
            <measure alias="aggregate_column" />
          </measurecollection>
        </category>
      </categorycollection>
    </datadefinition>
  </datadescription>
  <presentationdescription>
    <Chart>
      <Series>
        <Series IsValueShownAsLabel="True" Color="55, 118, 193"
           BackGradientStyle="TopBottom"
           BackSecondaryColor="41, 88, 145" Font="{0}, 9.5px"
           LabelForeColor="59, 59, 59"
           CustomProperties="PointWidth=0.75,MaxPixelPointWidth=40">
        </Series>
      </Series>
      <ChartAreas>
        <ChartArea BorderColor="White" BorderDashStyle="Solid">
          <AxisY LabelAutoFitMinFontSize="8"
             TitleForeColor="59, 59, 59" TitleFont="{0}, 10.5px"
             LineColor="165, 172, 181" IntervalAutoMode="VariableCount">
            <MajorGrid LineColor="239, 242, 246" />
            <MajorTickMark LineColor="165, 172, 181" />
            <LabelStyle Font="{0}, 10.5px" ForeColor="59, 59, 59" />
          </AxisY>
          <AxisX TitleForeColor="59, 59, 59" TitleFont="{0}, 10.5px"
```

```
            LineColor="165, 172, 181" IntervalAutoMode="VariableCount">
          <MajorGrid LineColor="Transparent" />
          <LabelStyle Font="{0}, 10.5px" ForeColor="59, 59, 59" />
        </AxisX>
      </ChartArea>
    </ChartAreas>
    <Titles>
      <Title Alignment="TopLeft" DockingOffset="-3" Font="{0}, 13px"
             ForeColor="59, 59, 59"></Title>
    </Titles>
  </Chart>
</presentationdescription>
<isdefault>false</isdefault>
</visualization>
```

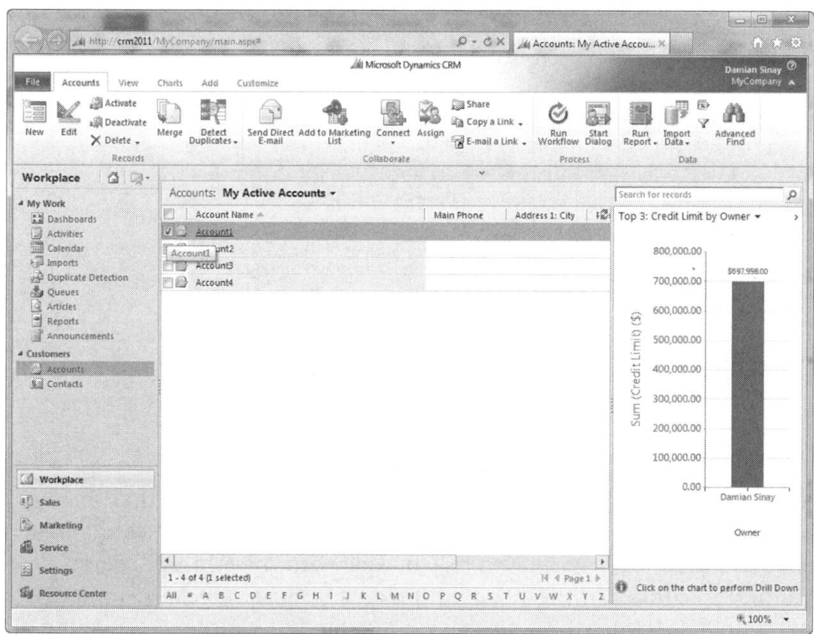

FIGURE 21.13 Chart with different title font.

For example, with little knowledge of XML, you could change the font type of the chart fonts and colors by changing the Font attribute of the AxisY node. The following line would make the text bigger and with red color (see Figure 21.13):

```
<AxisY LabelAutoFitMinFontSize="8"
                TitleForeColor="255, 0, 0" TitleFont="{0}, 15px"
                LineColor="255, 0, 0"
                IntervalAutoMode="VariableCount">
```

You can edit the XML file with any editor, such as Notepad, and then import the modified XML file to CRM. When importing the XML file, you will be asked whether you want to replace the existing chart or create a new copy (see Figure 21.14).

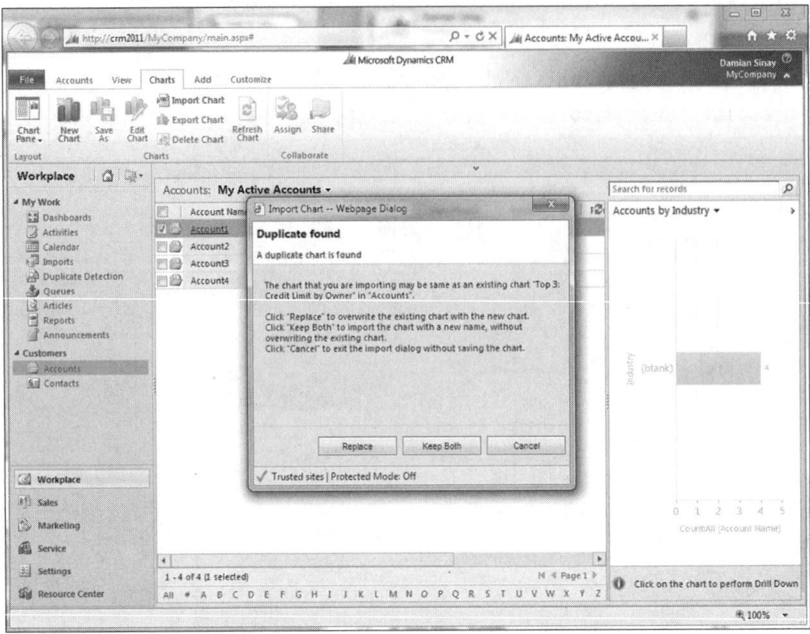

FIGURE 21.14 Importing a modified chart.

Visualizations

Charts are in the CRM SDK referred to as *visualizations*. The reason for this is that there is a tricky way to add other kind of charts by writing a little code. You can have charts that are actually web resources that will be displayed side-by-side with the grid. For example, you could show a Bing Map control in the visualization area instead of a chart. To do this, you need to create a simple XML file where you give it a name, a description, the name of the web resource you want to use, the primary entity where you want the visualization to be displayed, and whether it will be the default visualization for the entity. Here is an example of the XML file you would need to create for this:

```
<visualization>
  <name>BingMaps</name>
  <description>Bing Map</description>
  <webresourcename>webforti_map.htm</webresourcename>
  <primaryentitytypecode>account</primaryentitytypecode>
  <isdefault>true</isdefault>
</visualization>
```

Then you save this file with the .xml extension (for example, Customchart.xml) and you can import it just like any other chart as we explained earlier in this chapter. The result, however, will be what you have put on your web resource, which can be an image, an HTML file, and so forth. Figure 21.15 shows a visualization of a Bing Map that displays the pushpins of the account's cities on the map.

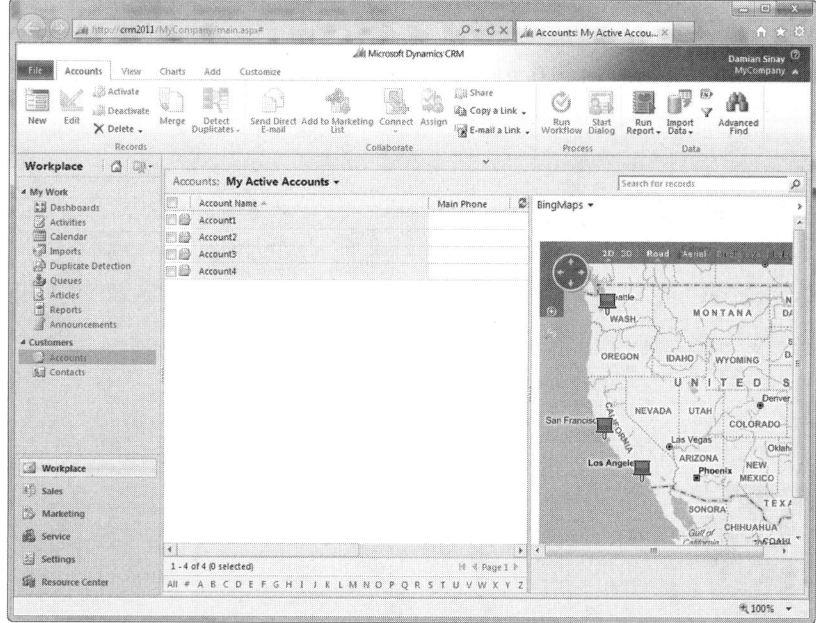

FIGURE 21.15 A visualization solution using a web resource.

Dashboards

Dashboards enable the user to see more than one chart from different entities on a one single page. Apart from adding charts that we've already discussed in this chapter, you can also add grids, IFRAMEs, and web resources to a Dashboard.

Grids are representation of underlying CRM data (for example, Activities that relate to an account or Leads that relate to a region), IFRAMEs are pass-through connections to other web pages (either externally or internally, or even self-referencing), and web resources are files that can be images, Silverlight applications, HTML pages, or script files.

The CRM system comes with seven predefined system Dashboards you can use as models.

- ▶ Customer Service Operations Dashboard
- ▶ Customer Service Performance Dashboard
- ▶ Customer Service Representative Dashboard
- ▶ Marketing Dashboard

- Microsoft Dynamics CRM Overview
- Sales Activity Dashboard
- Sales Performance Dashboard

In a similar way with the charts, there are two main types of Dashboards we can use: the system Dashboards that are available to all users in the organization and the personal Dashboards that a user can create.

Figure 21.16 shows a sample of how the Microsoft Dynamics CRM Overview Dashboard looks like.

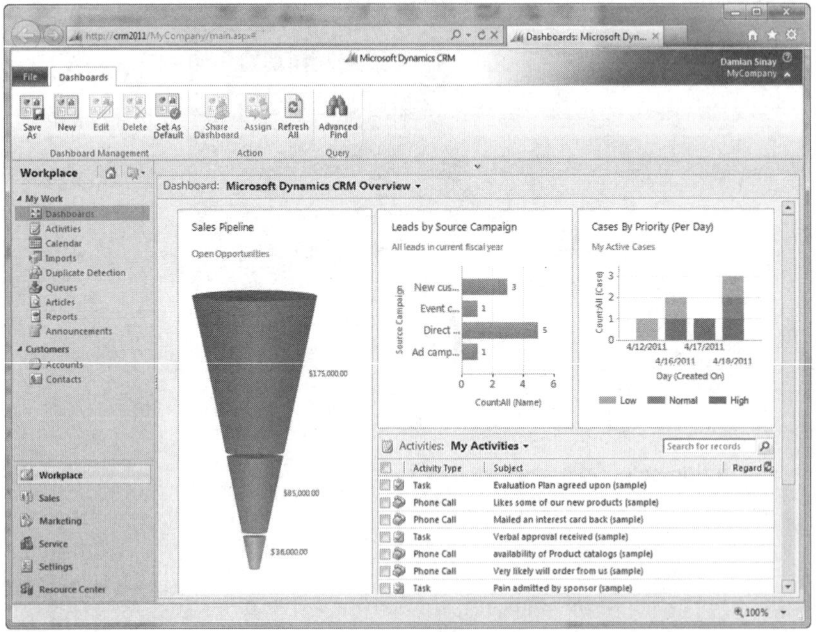

FIGURE 21.16 Microsoft Dynamics CRM Overview Dashboard.

Create a New Dashboard

To create a new Dashboard, follow these steps:

1. Go to the Dashboard area by going to the Workplace and then clicking Dashboards (as shown in Figure 21.16).
2. Click the New button located on the Dashboards tab on the Ribbon.
3. Select a layout from the predefined layouts on the left. You will see on the right how the layouts would look with sample charts.
4. Click the Create button. A new window will open with the Dashboard Editor.

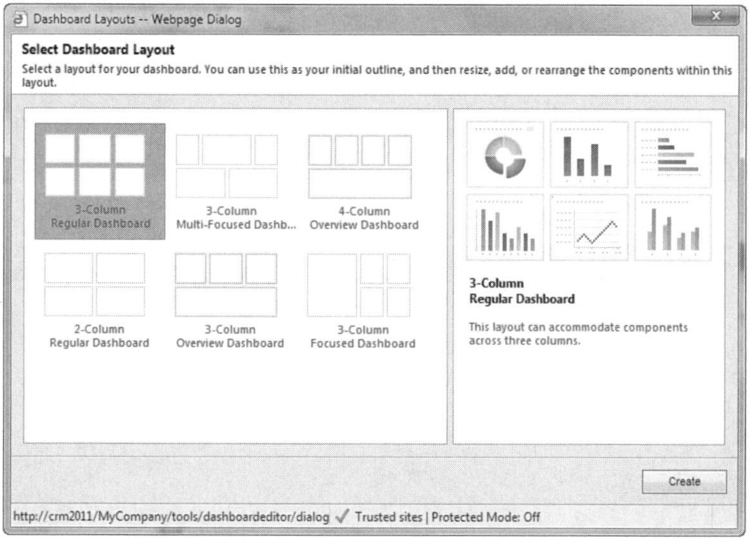

Dashboard Layouts -- Webpage Dialog

Select Dashboard Layout

Select a layout for your dashboard. You can use this as your initial outline, and then resize, add, or rearrange the components within this layout.

3-Column Regular Dashboard

3-Column Multi-Focused Dashb...

4-Column Overview Dashboard

2-Column Regular Dashboard

3-Column Overview Dashboard

3-Column Focused Dashboard

3-Column Regular Dashboard

This layout can accommodate components across three columns.

Create

http://crm2011/MyCompany/tools/dashboardeditor/dialog Trusted sites | Protected Mode: Off

FIGURE 21.17 Select Dashboard layout.

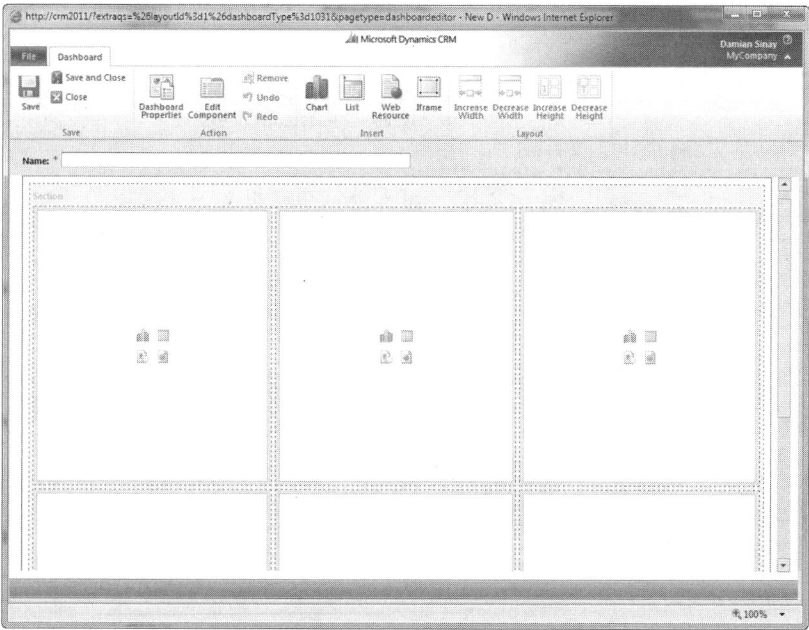

FIGURE 21.18 Dashboard Editor.

5. Click on the Chart icon that is inside of the first component to add a chart. Select the entity record type, the view, and the chart you want to display. In this example, we selected the Account entity to display the Accounts by Industry chart using the My Active Accounts view.

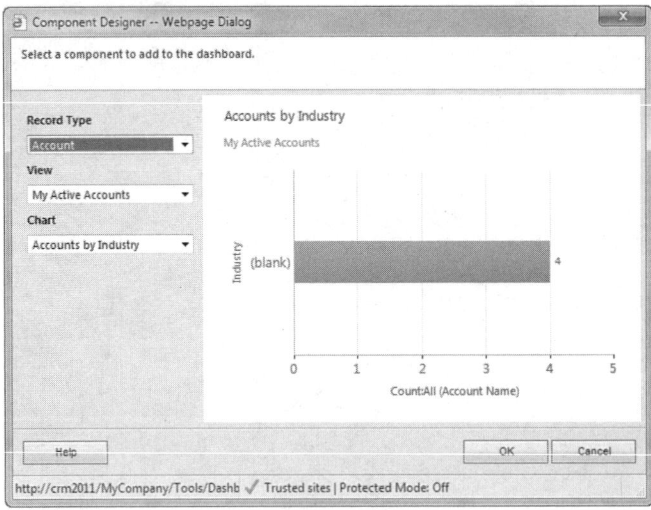

FIGURE 21.19 Adding charts to a component.

6. Click OK to add the chart. You will see the chart added to the Dashboard.

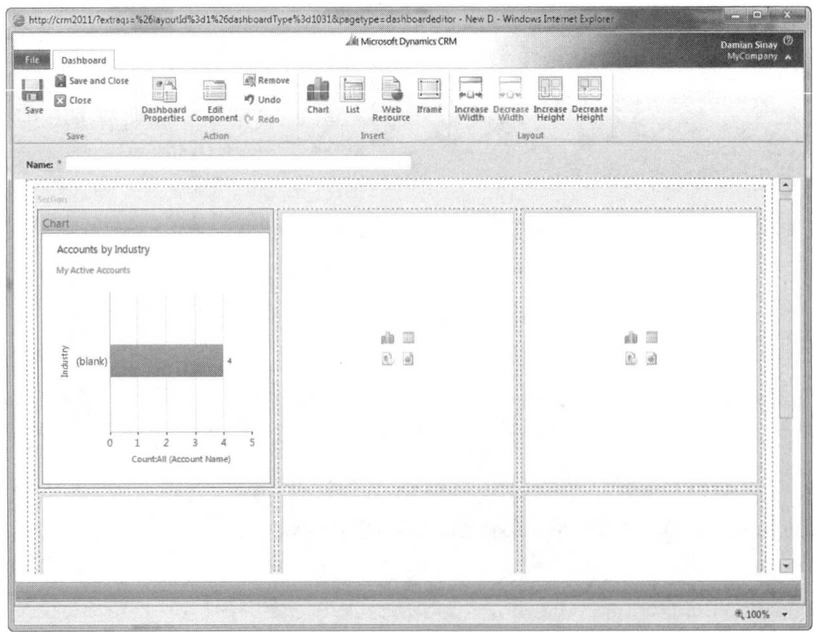

FIGURE 21.20 Chart added to a Dashboard.

7. Move to the next component and click the Grid icon. Select the entity and view you want to display.

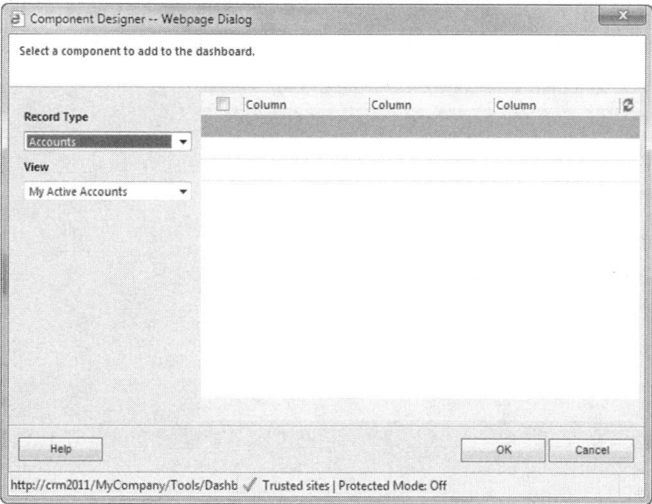

FIGURE 21.21 Adding a grid to a component.

8. Click OK to add the grid. You will see the grid added to the Dashboard.

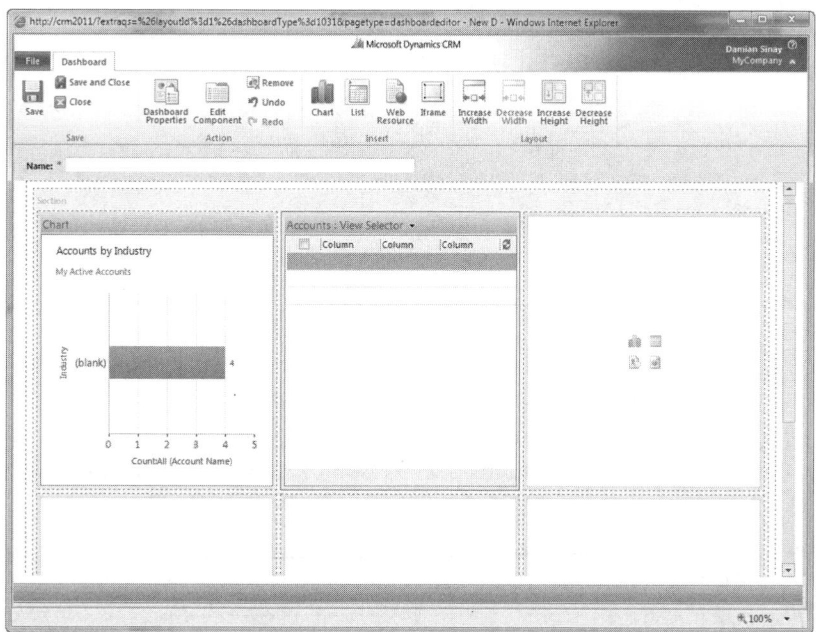

FIGURE 21.22 Grid added to a Dashboard.

9. Move to the next component and click on the IFRAME icon. Enter a name and the URL of the page you want to display. In our case, we don't want to pass parameters

to the URL, so we'll uncheck the check box that says Pass Record Object-Type and Unique Identifier as Parameters. This option can be useful if we enter an URL of a custom application we created that needs to know the record type and ID of who is calling it or similar information.

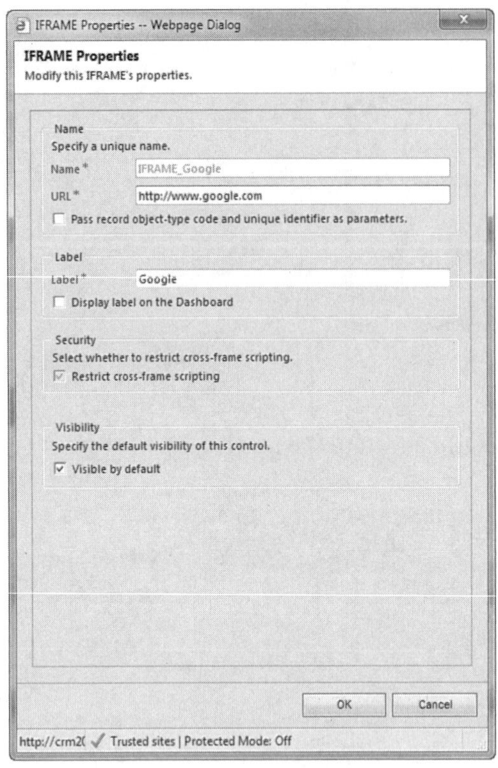

FIGURE 21.23 Adding an IFRAME to a component.

10. Click OK to add the IFRAME. You will see the IFRAME added to the Dashboard. Notice the URL will not be rendered in design mode (see Figure 21.24).
11. Move to the next component and click on the Web Resource icon. Select a web resource. For this example, we are selecting a web resource we created. Its type is a PNG image that will display our company logo (see Figure 21.25).
12. Click OK to add the web resource. You will see only the name of the web resource added to the Dashboard. Notice the image will not be rendered in design mode (see Figure 21.26).
13. To finish this sample, and because we are not going to add more components, we can select the other empty components and click the Remove button on the Ribbon to remove them. You will see the spot will remain empty (see Figure 21.27).
14. To clean the empty space, select the component where we added the image, and click the Increase Width button on the Ribbon twice.

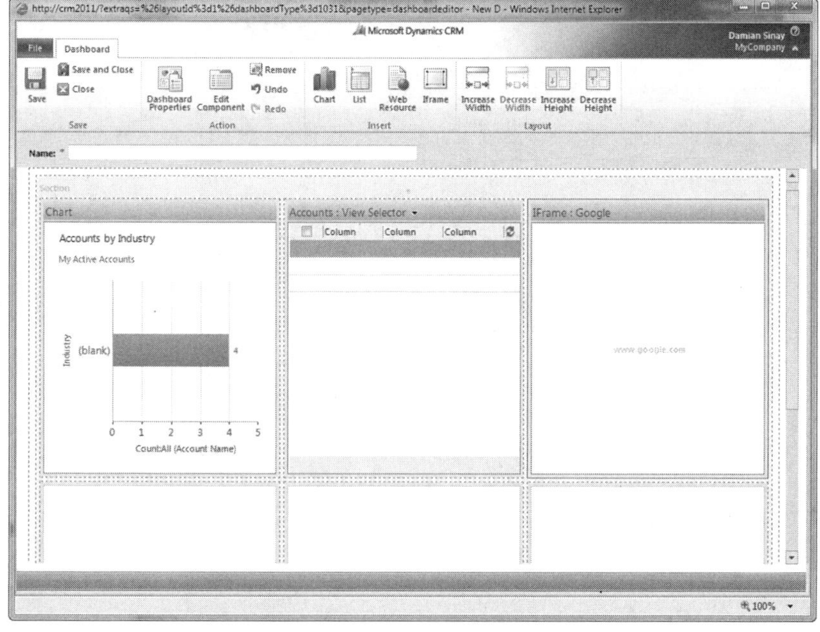

FIGURE 21.24 IFRAME added to a Dashboard.

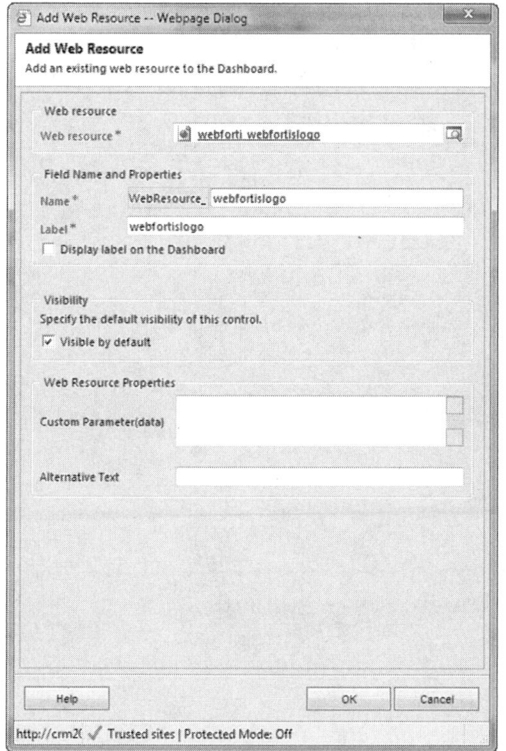

FIGURE 21.25 Adding a web resource to a component.

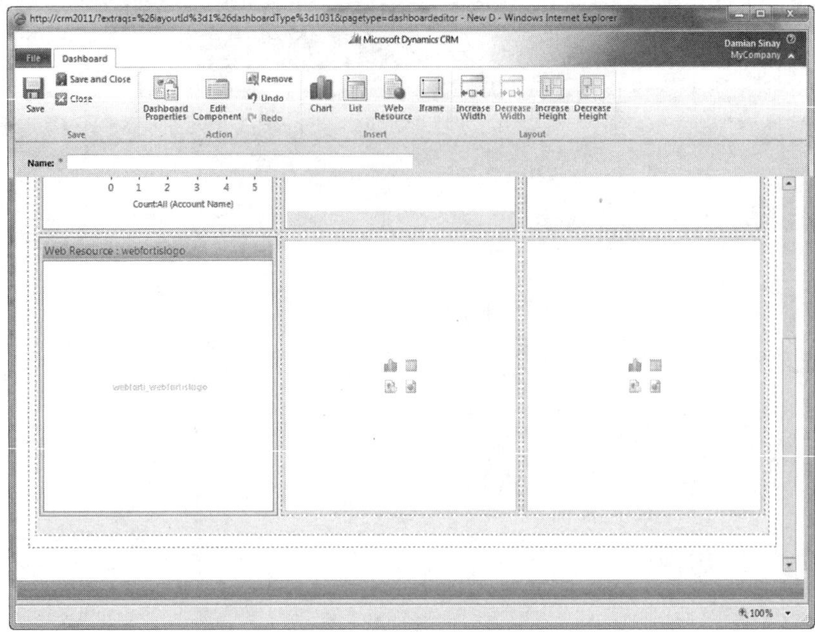

FIGURE 21.26 Web resource added to a Dashboard.

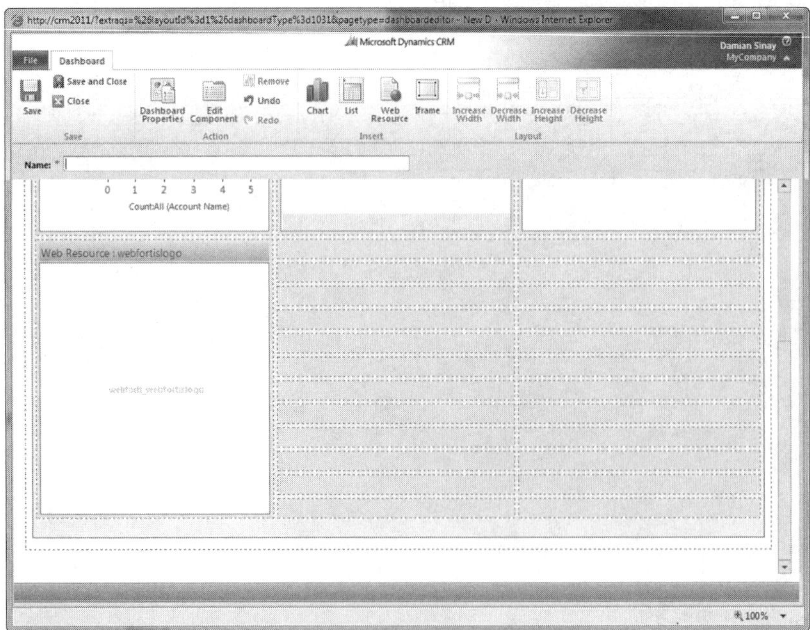

FIGURE 21.27 Removing empty components.

15. Click the textbox near the Name label to enter a name and click Save (see Figure 21.28).
16. Click on Save and Close to save the work, and the Dashboard will open in a new window showing the rendered content, as you can see on Figure 21.29.

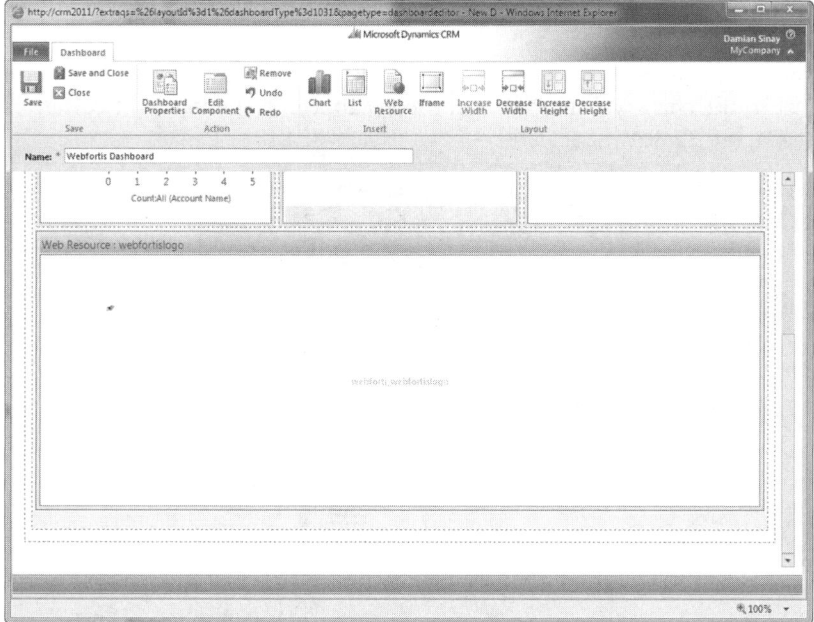

FIGURE 21.28 Adding a name to our Dashboard.

Dashboard Features

An interesting thing is that there is not an intuitive way to add new components to a Dashboard. If you start from one of the predefined templates, you can add from four to six components, depending on the layout you selected first. However, if you want to have a Dashboard with more components, you can do that, but you need to click on the section first and then clicking any of the Chart, List, IFRAME, or Web Resource buttons on the Ribbon. Clicking those buttons will add new components to a Dashboard, but if you have an empty component selected first (instead of the entire section) those buttons would replace the empty component space with the selected component.

TIP

You cannot change the component type once you select it; for example, you cannot change from Chart to IFRAME. You will need to remove the component and create a new one to change the type.

Dashboards can be shared with other users within the same organizations, but you also have the ability to assign them to other users. However, unlike charts, they cannot be easily exported or imported. If you want to export the Dashboard to be used in a different organization, you will have to create a solution and include the Dashboard inside that solution.

▶ To learn more about solutions, refer to Chapter 16, “Solution Concepts.”

When you add charts to a Dashboard, there are some cool features you can use. When you drag the mouse over to the chart, you will see three icons appear at the top-right corner of the component (see Figure 21.30).

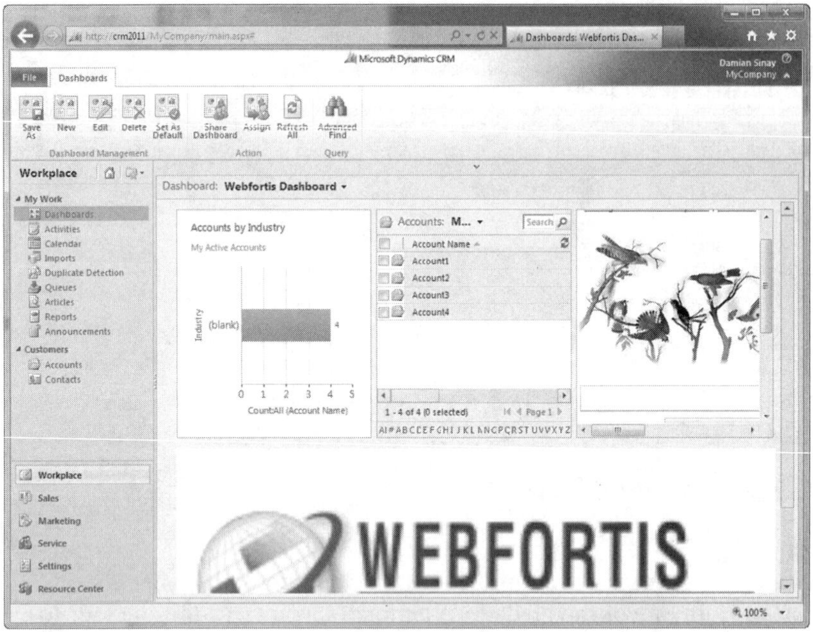

FIGURE 21.29 Rendered Dashboard.

The first icon refreshes the chart because the underlying data might have been changed, and you will have to manually click this icon to have an updated version of the chart. If you have more than one chart on the Dashboard, you can use the Refresh All button on the Ribbon to update all charts and components used in the Dashboard.

The second icon is a grid and enables you to see the list of records used by the chart. This enables you to see the details of the view used to generate the chart, as shown in Figure 21.31.

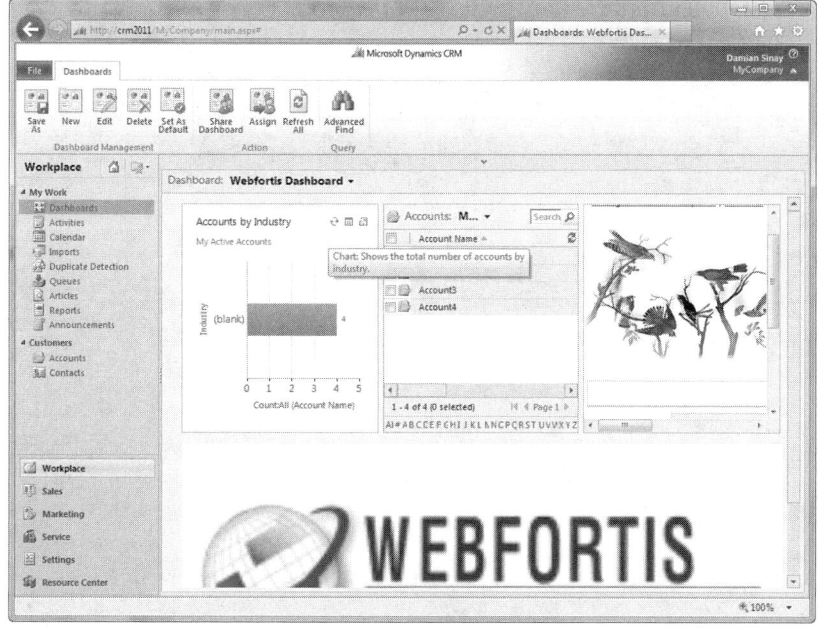

FIGURE 21.30 Chart tools on a Dashboard.

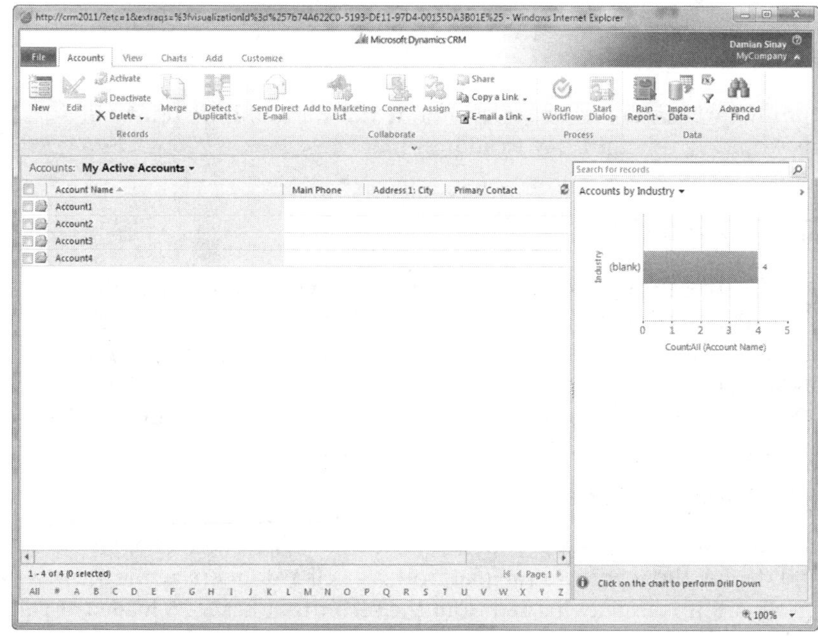

FIGURE 21.31 View details.

The last icon is an enlargement image that when clicked enlarges the chart to occupy the entire Dashboard, as shown in Figure 21.32.

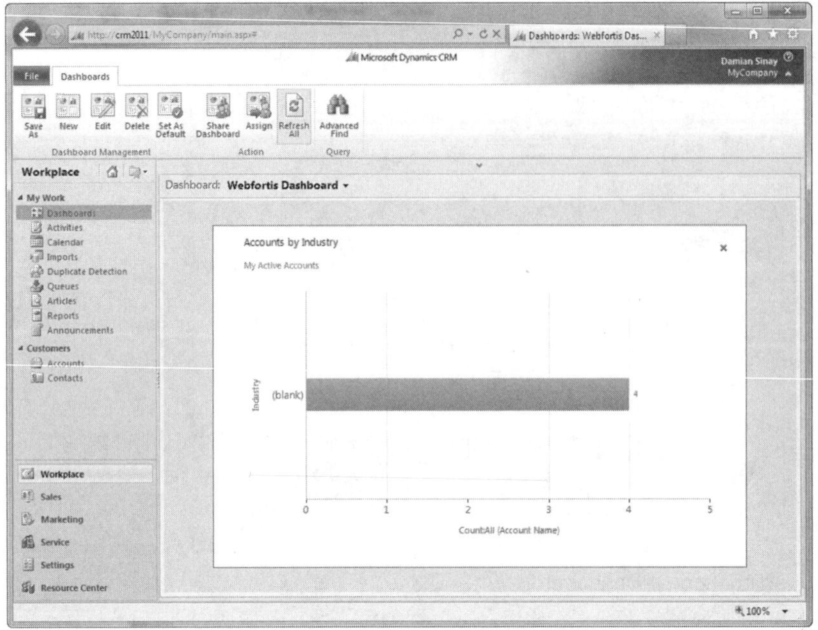

FIGURE 21.32 Chart enlarged.

Charts cannot be printed without taking a screenshot. If you want to have printable charts, SSRS reports would be the right way to address that.

Introduction to SSRS

SSRS, or Microsoft SQL Server Reporting Services, is a client/server reporting platform that is installed within Microsoft SQL Server. It is based on the Service Oriented Architecture (SOA), so it can be used as a service. SSRS was introduced within Microsoft Dynamics CRM 3.0 using Microsoft SQL Server 2000 (previously, CRM used Crystal Reporting). Microsoft Dynamics CRM 4.0 uses SQL Server 2005 or SQL Server 2008 and either version of SSRS. And CRM 2011 uses SQL Server 2008 and SQL Server 2008 R2.

SSRS consists of the following components:

- **Report Manager**—This is a web application that acts as a user interface application to manage and deploy the reports in the platform, as well as to manage the security access of each report. It is usually located from the server that has SSRS loaded at via http://localhost/reports.

- **Report Server**—This is a service that provides a common interface and entry point for all applications (including the Report Manager mentioned earlier, as well as Microsoft Dynamics CRM) to interact with the Report Server. It is usually located from the server that has SSRS loaded via http://localhost/reportsserver.
- **Report Database**—SSRS uses two databases stored in SQL Server as the repository of the deployed reports. They usually have the names of ReportServer and ReportServerTempDB.
- **SQL Server Reporting Services (using the Microsoft SQL Server instance name)**—This is a Windows service that is responsible for processing related functions, such as report scheduling.
- **Other components**—Configuration tools, Visual Studio 2008 projects templates for reports authoring, .NET controls to render and display the reports in Windows, and custom web applications and API documentation for extensibility and development.

Separate from these components, SSRS has the following features:

- Support for report snapshot creation.
- Support for scheduling of automated snapshot reports.
- Alerts so you can be notified via e-mail when a report is created.
- Capability for all reports to be exported in the following formats:
    - Microsoft Excel
    - Acrobat PDF
    - MSHTML (web archive)
    - TIFF images
    - Microsoft Word
    - XML file with report data
    - CSV (comma delimited)
- Capability to build reports with the open standard Report Definition Language (RDL), which is based on the XML standard. Reports then can be built not only with Visual Studio, but also with other third-party tools.
- Capability for each report to manage different data sources. This means that it is not necessarily tied to Microsoft SQL Server data. Reports can show data from any .NET-compatible data provider or from any OLEDB data provider.
- Capability to display data in either tabular, matrix, or graphical forms, as well as to use expressions to format the data properly.

Microsoft Dynamics CRM handles all the reports through this system and takes advantage of all its benefits.

CAUTION

SSRS controls are great to build reports with, but they do have some drawbacks. One of the most important is their inability to display HTML data properly. If you try to show data that was stored in HTML format, all formatting will be lost and the HTML will be displayed with HTML tags. The only way we've found to deal with this issue has been to create a function in SQL to clean the HTML tags so that the text can be easily read; however, all formatting is lost. This is an issue that Microsoft doesn't seem to have in its plans to fix with the next version of SQL.

NOTE

SSRS is a very complex platform, and the scope of detailing SSRS exceeds this publication. We recommend reviewing the Microsoft SQL Server books online, or similar topics by Sams Publishing for more detailed information about this product. To understand this chapter, you need only a basic understanding of SSRS and SQL.

Custom Reports

Custom reports are reports written with an external tool such as Visual Studio 2008. As explained in Chapter 11, "Reporting," you can easily build new basic custom reports with the Report Wizard in Microsoft Dynamics CRM; however, reports created are not so flexible. In some cases, you need to write more complex reports and have a more flexible page layout and design. With those cases, you need to use a tool such as Visual Studio to create and build your custom reports.

When Are Custom Reports Recommended?

Users can need custom reports for a variety of reasons. Some of these reasons are as follows:

- Special or custom designs such as those with complex layouts that can't be done with the Report Wizard.
- When you need to have a report with mixed data from data sources other than Microsoft CRM. For example, you might control the inventory counts of your products on a separated system that uses an Oracle database, and you want to have one report that shows the CRM orders with their product details from Oracle and their inventory counts.

You can build custom reports with SSRS or with any other report application, such as Crystal Reports, or even with a custom application built in ASP.NET. The range of applications that can be used to build custom reports exceeds the scope of this book.

Installing CRM 2011 BIDS Extensions

If you want to modify the reports generated by the Report Wizard or if you want to use Fetch queries on your report, you will need to install the CRM2011 BIDSExtensions (Business Intelligence Development Studio Extensions).

1. Download Microsoft Dynamics CRM 2011 Report Authoring Extension from the Microsoft website located at http://download.microsoft.com.
2. Run the file CRM2011-BIDSExtensions-ENU-i386.exe; the welcome wizard step will appear, as shown on Figure 21.33.

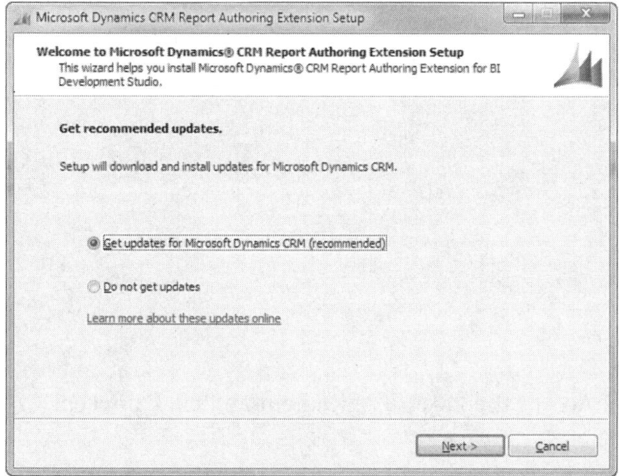

FIGURE 21.33 Welcome to Microsoft Dynamics CRM 2011 Report Authoring Extension Setup.

3. Click on Next so that the Setup Wizard can check for updates (see Figure 21.34).

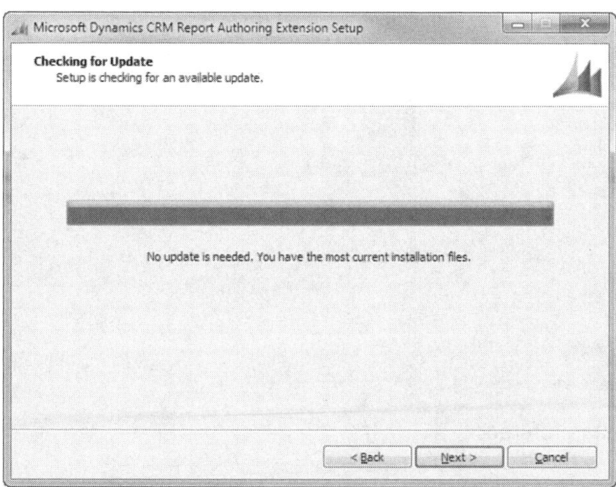

FIGURE 21.34 Checking for updates.

4. Click on Next to continue to the next step (see Figure 21.35).

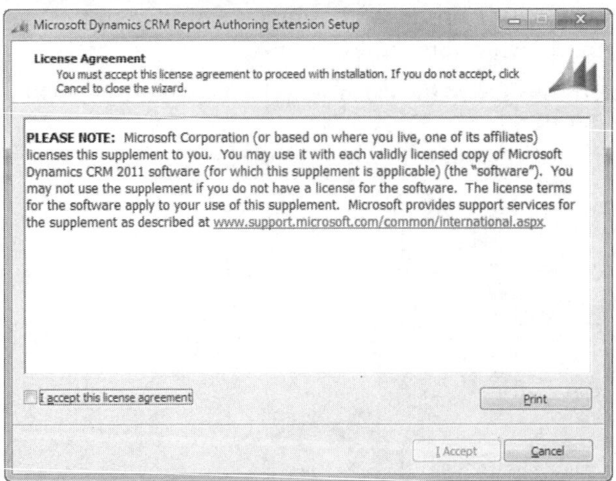

FIGURE 21.35 License agreement.

5. Check the check box that says I Accept the License Agreement and click I Accept (see Figure 21.36).

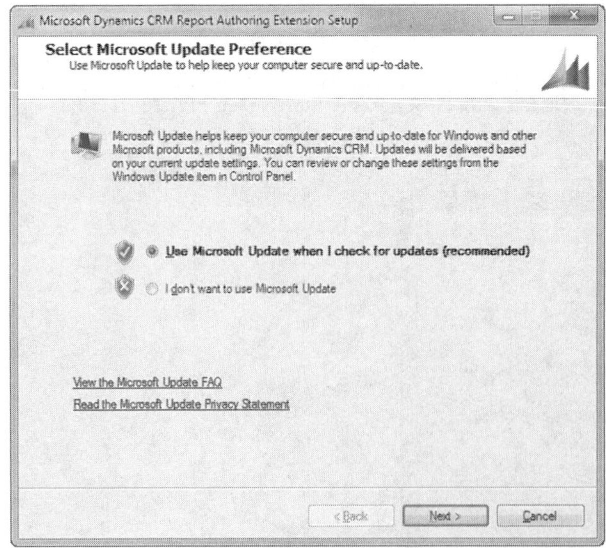

FIGURE 21.36 Select Microsoft Update preference.

6. Click on the Use Microsoft Update When I Check for Updates (Recommended) option and click on Next (see Figure 21.37).
7. Select the installation directory (or leave the one that is suggested) and click on Next. The setup will check the required software components necessary to run this

setup. If there are some missing components, you will be presented with a list as shown in Figure 21.38.

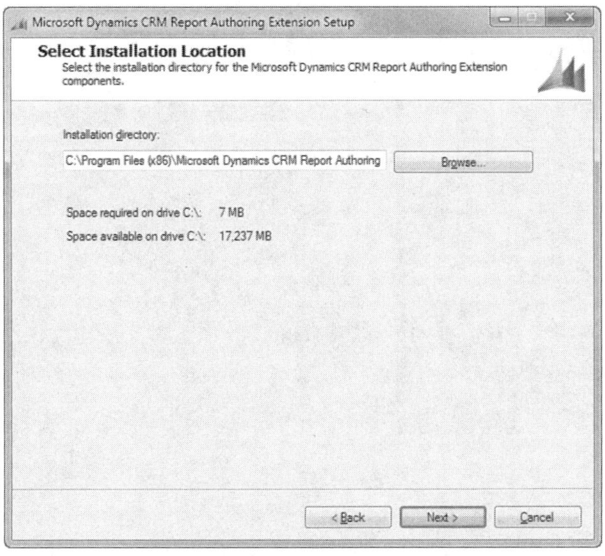

FIGURE 21.37 Select the installation location.

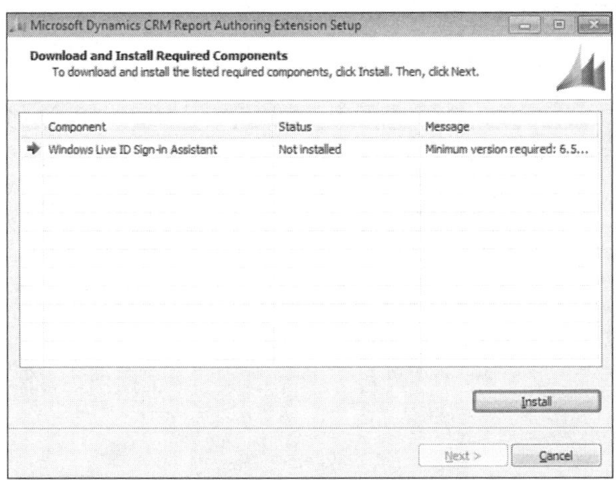

FIGURE 21.38 Download and install required components.

8. Click on Install when asked to download components. Then click on Yes (see Figure 21.39).

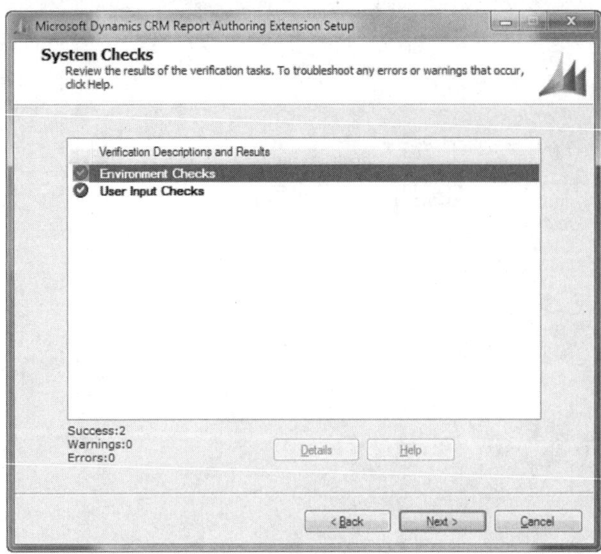

FIGURE 21.39 System checks.

9. Setup will check the required software components necessary to run this setup again. If everything is okay with your system, click Next (see Figure 21.40).

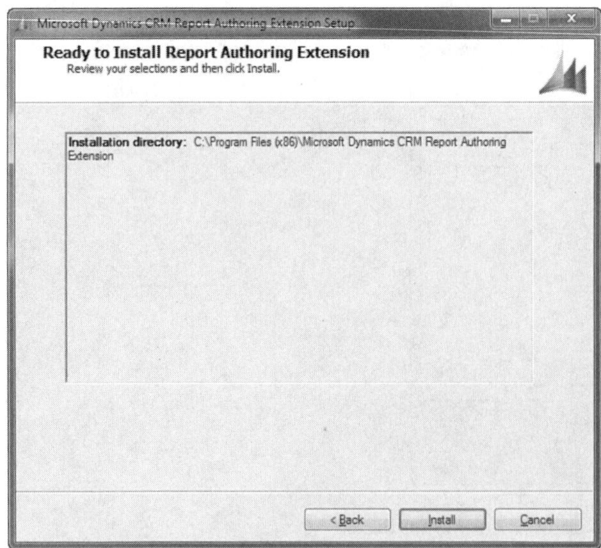

FIGURE 21.40 Review your selections.

10. If you are ready to install CRM Report Authoring Extension, click Install (see Figure 21.41).

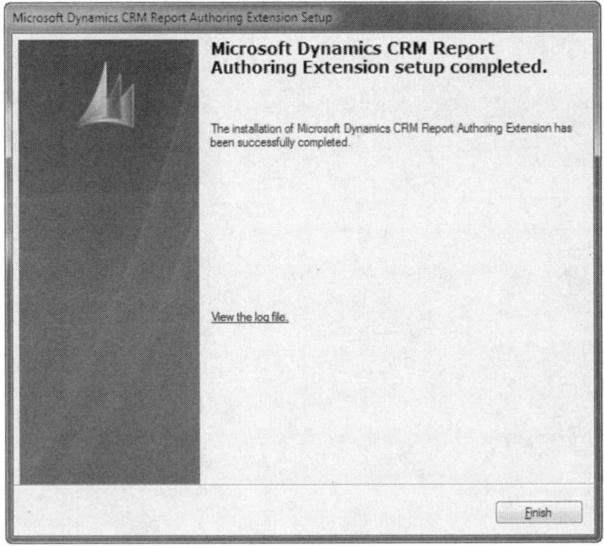

FIGURE 21.41 Setup Completed.

11. When Setup finishes, click Finish.

After the CRM 2011 Report Authoring Extension are installed, you can work with any report generated by the Report Wizard and open it with Visual Studio 2008. You will see the data source connection type is Microsoft Dynamics CRM Fetch and the connection string will point to the CRM 2011 organization URL.

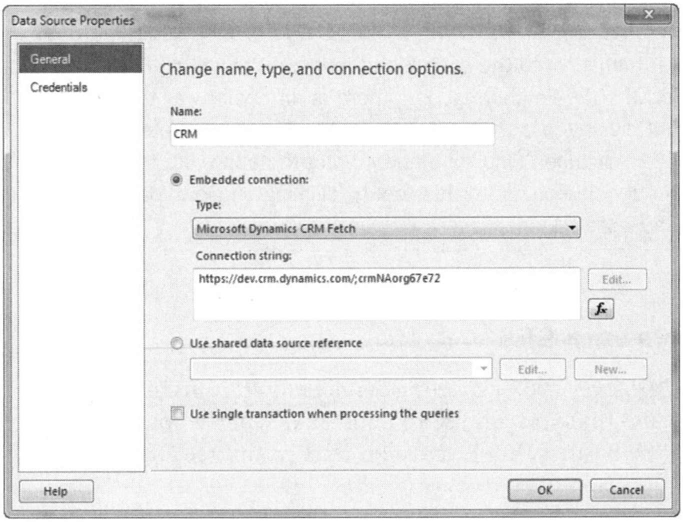

FIGURE 21.42 Microsoft Dynamics CRM Fetch data source type.

If you look at the data set properties, you will see the query is written in a Fetch mode.

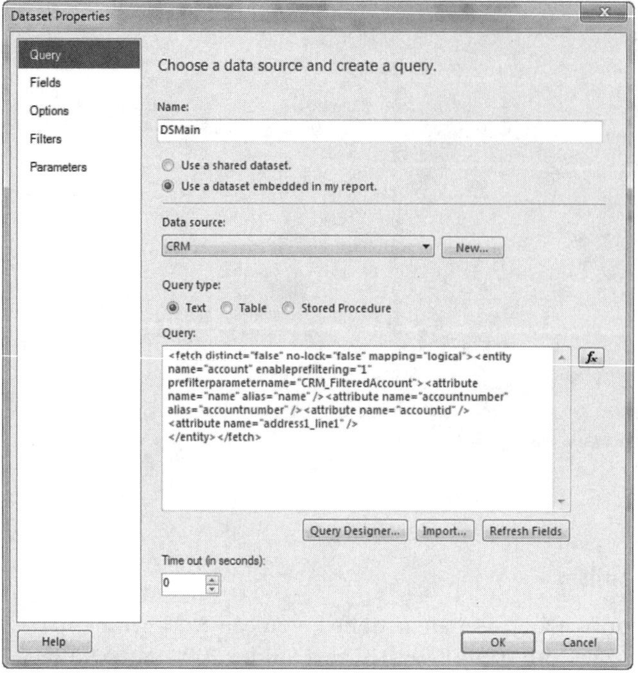

FIGURE 21.43 Fetch query.

NOTE

It might take some time to get familiar with the syntax and language of writing Fetch queries. For those not familiar with the Fetch language, there is an easier way to get the Fetch queries done without digging into the language details. You can create the queries by using the CRM 2011 Advanced Find tool, and if you are happy with the results you can get the Fetch query directly from this tool by clicking on Download Fetch XML button as shown in Figure 21.44.

Building Custom Reports with SRS

When you install Microsoft SQL Server 2008 Reporting Services tools, it installs Visual Studio 2008 and project templates that you can use to build SSRS reports. You can find these project templates under the Business Intelligence Projects group (see Figure 21.45).

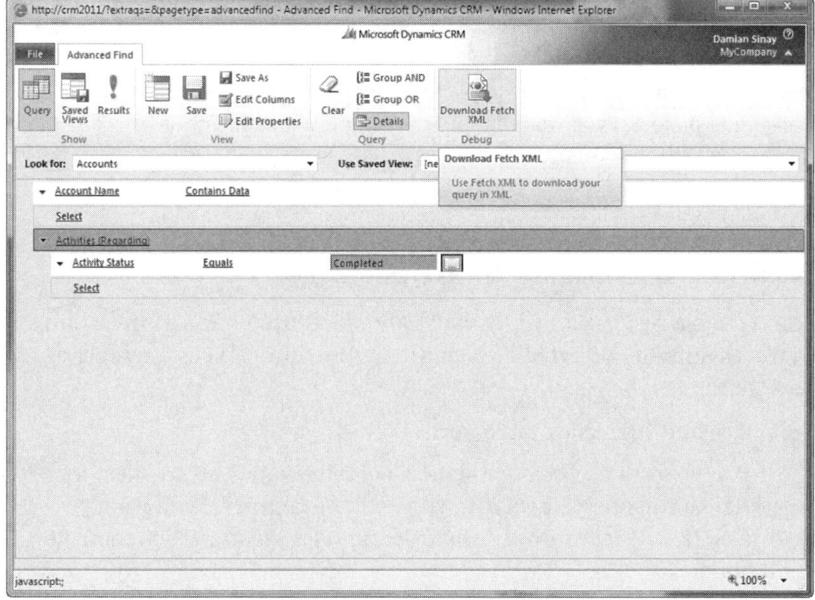

FIGURE 21.44 Download Fetch XML from the Advanced Find tool.

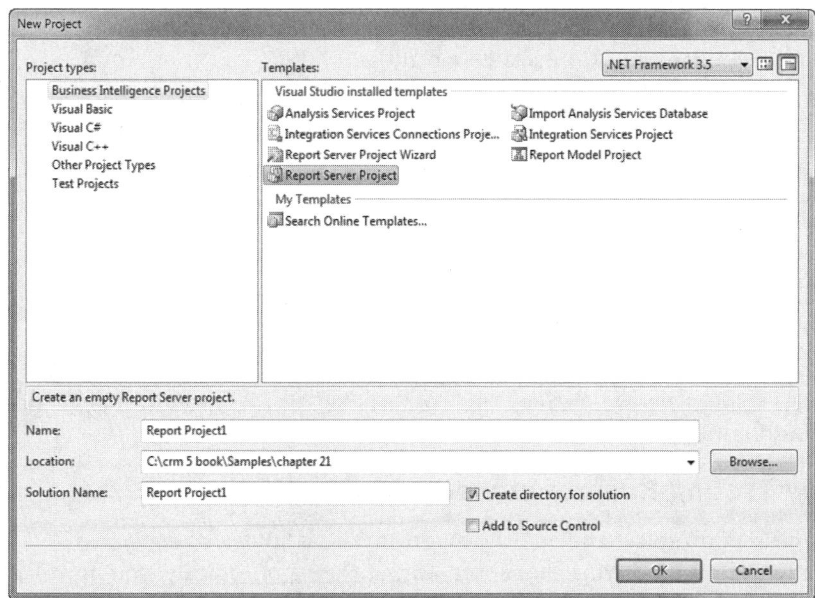

FIGURE 21.45 Business Intelligence Projects group in Visual Studio 2008.

NOTE

Notice that if you didn't have Visual Studio Installed, the SQL Server 2008 Setup would install a limited version of Visual Studio only applicable to building reports and using the Business Intelligence projects; you won't be able to create Windows Forms applications or custom websites with this version.

The Microsoft Dynamics CRM SDK comes with very detailed documentation about custom reports development (refer to the Reporting Writers Guide in the SDK).

Even though you can create a new report in Visual Studio 2008 from scratch, we recommend using one of the existing reports that are preinstalled within CRM as a template. To do that, follow these steps:

1. Go to the Workplace and then click on Reports.
2. Select the report you want to use as a template. Generally, you want to select a report that is similar to the one you want to create. For example, if you want to create a custom sales report, select one of the existing sales reports. Click the Edit button on the Ribbon.
3. Select the Actions menu from the top menu and select Download Report. For this example, use the Account Distribution report.
4. Save the report on your local machine.
5. Rename the file with the new name of the report you want to build. In this example, rename the report to Contacts Report.rdl.
6. Start Visual Studio 2008 from the Start Windows button, select All Programs, Microsoft Visual Studio 2008 program group, and Microsoft Visual Studio 2008 menu option.
7. Go to the File menu and select New, Project.
8. Click on Business Intelligence Projects in the project templates area, and select the Report Server Project template.
9. In the Solution Explorer, right-click on the Reports folder and click on Add, Existing Item.
10. Navigate to the folder where you stored the Contacts Report.rdl report in step 4, and click on the Add button.

Developing and Testing Reports in Visual Studio

After you create your report project and add the report in Visual Studio, as explained earlier, you are ready to start modifying the report. To test the report quickly, you must fix the dataset's connection strings to point to your CRM Server database. To do so, follow these steps:

1. Open the report you want to edit, go to the Report Data Explorer, and expand the Data Sources node. You will see there is a data source created with the name of CRM, as shown in Figure 21.46.

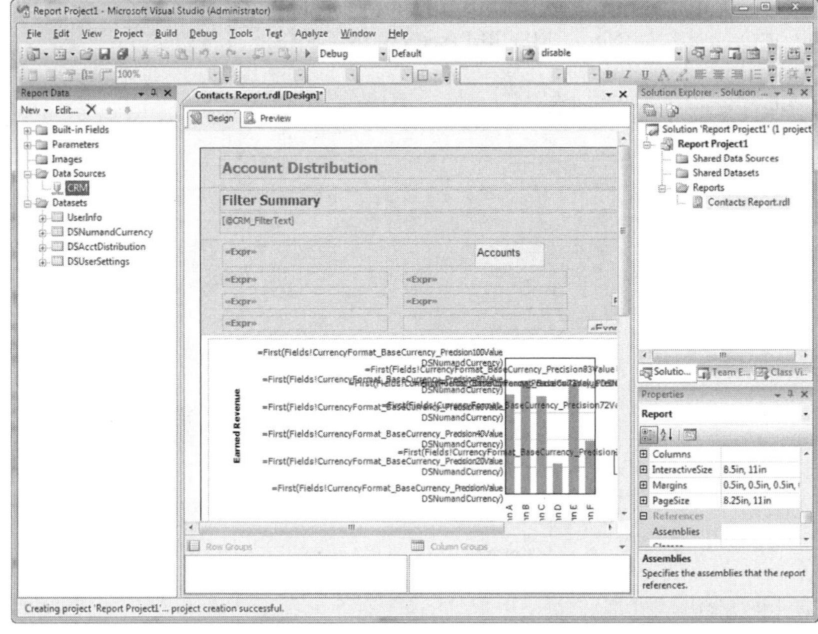

FIGURE 21.46 CRM shared data source.

2. Double-clicking the CRM data source will show the Data Source Properties dialog, as shown in Figure 21.47.

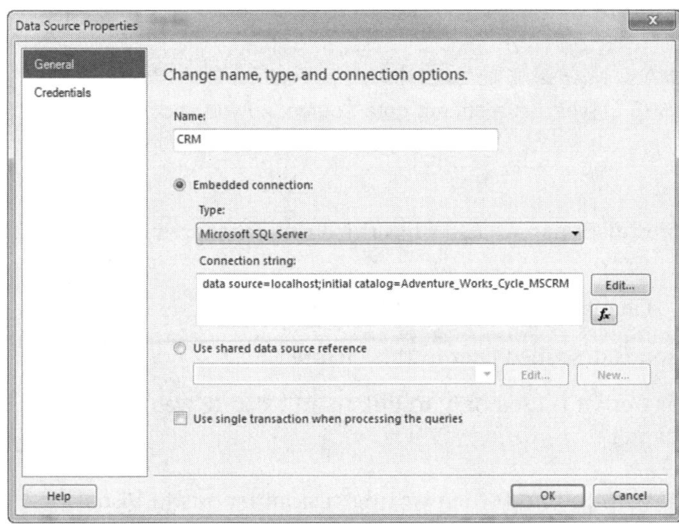

FIGURE 21.47 Data Source Properties.

3. Select your server name in the Server Name field and locate the CRM database that has the name of *OrganizationName*_MSCRM (see Figure 21.48).

FIGURE 21.48 Configuring the connection.

4. Click the Test Connection button to be sure it connects successfully.
5. Click OK three times to close the dialog.

CAUTION

The reports running on the SSRS server use a shared data source, so you should not deploy this data source.

As shown in Figure 21.49, Microsoft Dynamics CRM has three different types of custom reports.

- **Report Wizard Report**—Chapter 11 explained this option.
- **Existing File**—This option is described later in this chapter.
- **Link to Web Page**—This option is used only to link to an existing web page. It is explained later in this chapter.

Keep some important considerations in mind when writing custom reports in Visual Studio to take advantage of the benefits of the CRM prefiltering feature. These features are explained next.

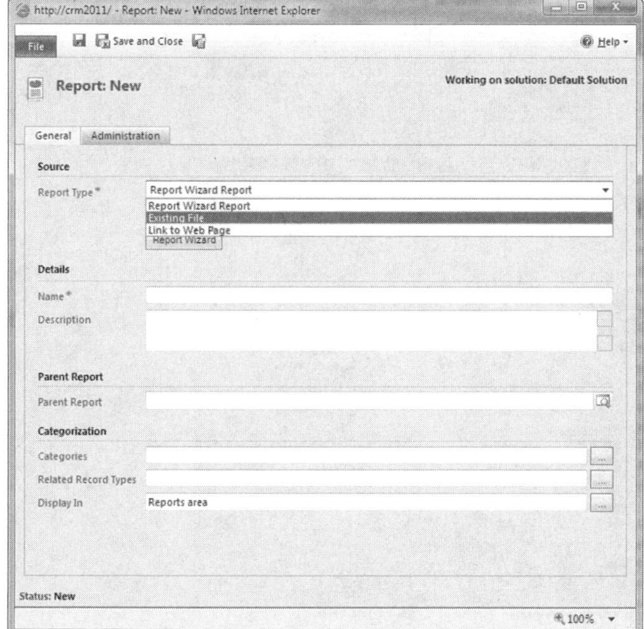

FIGURE 21.49 Custom report types.

Filtered Views

Although you can build your SQL queries by using the tables directly from the CRM SQL Server dataset, doing so is not recommended. The CRM SQL Server tables are shown in Figure 21.50, and you will notice that the Accounts entity has more than one table. The same is true for the other entities.

Instead of using these tables directly for SQL queries, predefined views make life a lot easier: You don't have to spend time trying to understand the complexity of the tables by studying an ERD. The views shown in Figure 21.51 will match the CRM entity diagram.

A lot of views have names similar to the CRM entity names. The views you should use with your reports are the ones with the Filtered prefix, as shown in Figure 21.52.

If you want to create a report that shows all the Contact names, your underlying query will look similar to this:

```
select fullname from FilteredContact
```

One of the advantages of using these views is that they are updated automatically every time you add a custom attribute to an entity from the CRM customizations interface. Additionally, when a custom entity is created in CRM, it automatically creates a filtered view for the new custom entity. In the preceding example, the database view name would be dbo.FilteredContact.

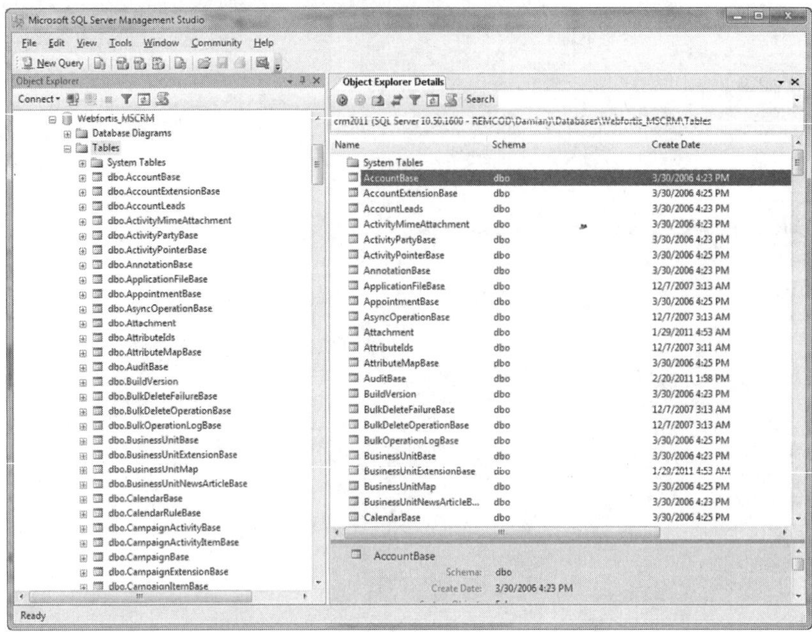

FIGURE 21.50 CRM SQL database tables.

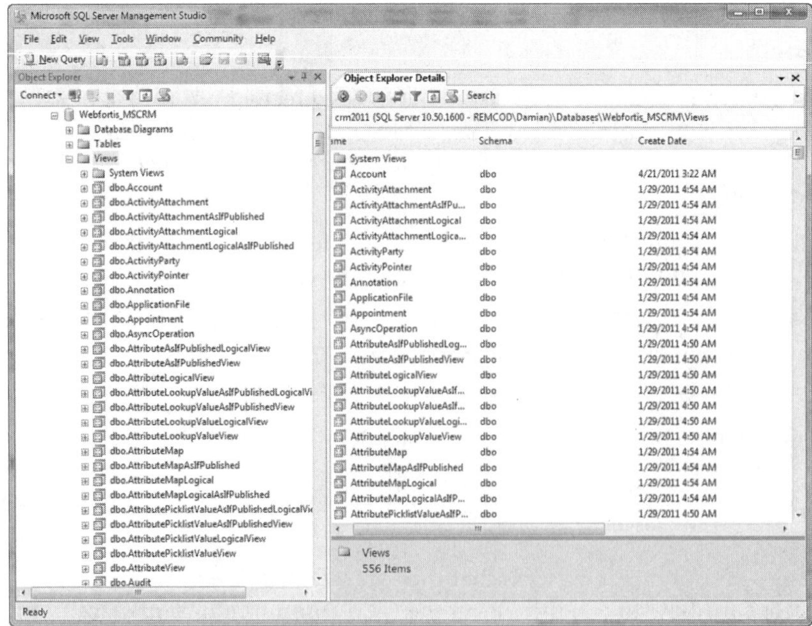

FIGURE 21.51 CRM SQL database views.

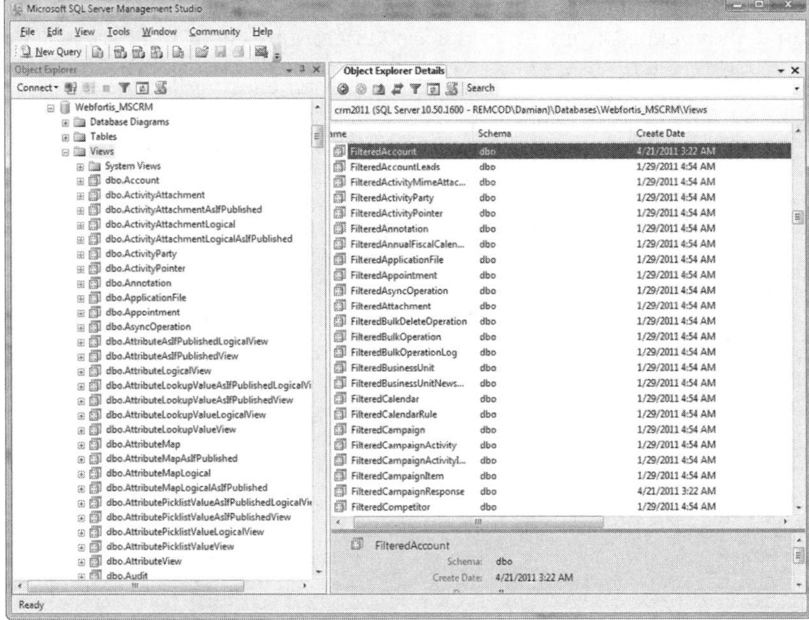

FIGURE 21.52 CRM SQL database filtered views.

Most important, filtered views provide security based on the user record permissions, so they show only the data that the user who is running the report has permissions to see as well as the fields the user has permissions to see as this new version of CRM 2011 also introduce field level security configurations.

NOTE

The custom properties and entities also have the prefix shown in the schema name. By default, this prefix is equal to New. However, you can change that in the Publisher setting of each solution. If you create a custom entity with the name of Event, the filtered view created will be dbo.FilteredNew_event by default.

▶ To learn more about customizing solution settings, refer to Chapter 16.

Deployment

To deploy a report in SSRS, you normally use the Report Manager web application. However, you should not use this option when working with custom CRM reports because you won't be able to see the report in CRM if you do.

To deploy a report for CRM, you must use the CRM client interface and follow these steps (notice that you can deploy reports from either the Web or Outlook client interfaces):

1. Go to the Reports area by going to the Workplace and then clicking Reports (as shown in Figure 21.53).

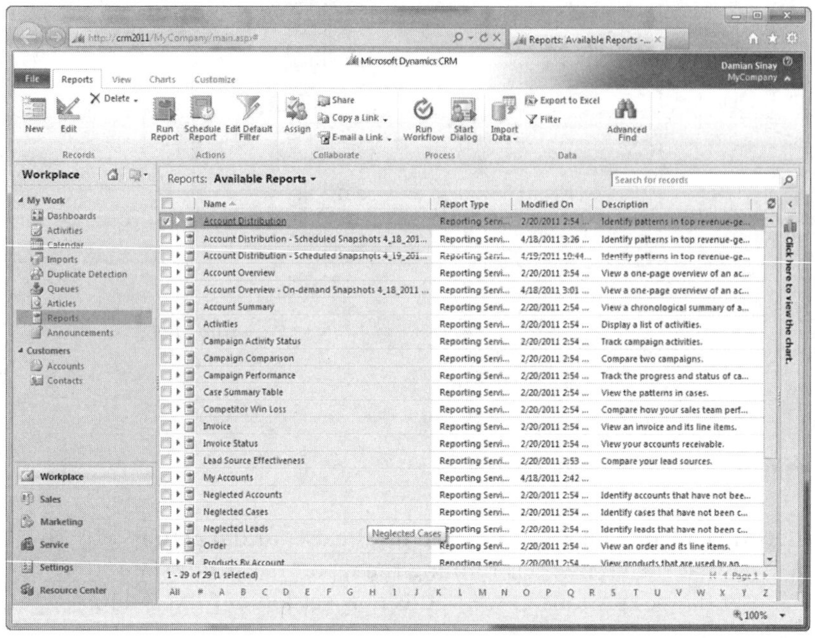

FIGURE 21.53 Reports area.

2. Click the New button located on the Ribbon.
3. Select Existing File in the Report Type property.
4. Under File Location, enter the full path of the report you built.
5. Optionally, change the name of the report; this will be autopopulated with the name of the report file, and the two don't need to be the same.
6. Optionally, you can select the categories, related record types, and display in the options.

▶ Refer to Chapter 11 for more information about customizing options in reports.

7. Click the Save and Close button on the top menu.

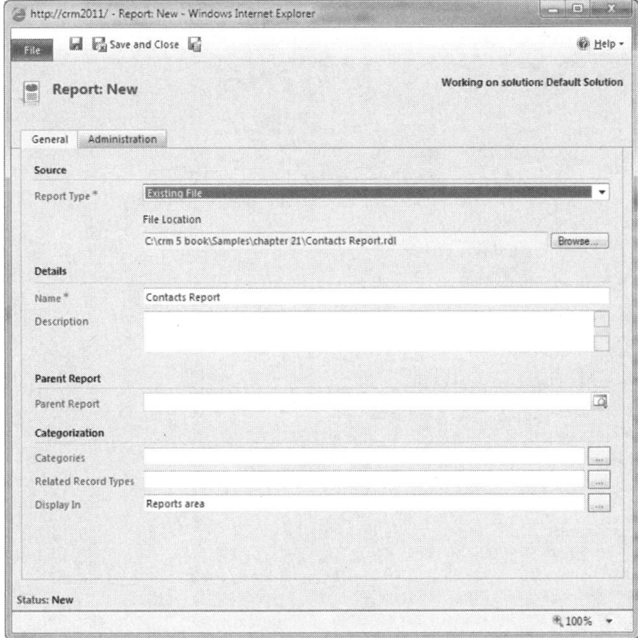

FIGURE 21.54 Deploying a new report.

Reports Parameters

To see the predefined report parameters from Visual Studio 2008, open the report you are authoring and expand the Parameters node on the Report Data window (see Figure 21.55).

The parameters include the following:

- **CRM_FilterText**—This parameter is used to display the Filter Summary text box (located in the report header), which display the prefilters selected by the User. Figure 21.56 shows this parameter value as Contacts: Parent Customer: Equals Webfortis.
- **CRM_URL**—This parameter provides drill-through capabilities on the CRM reports. This supplies quick links to edit the entities instances that you display on your report, for example. Figure 21.57 shows an example of a report that displays the Contacts; it has the Contact names as links so that the user can edit the Contact or see more details by easily clicking the links.
- **CRM_FilteredEntity**—This parameter is used to set up the default prefilters on your reports. You can add as many parameters as you like on the same report; you might have parameters such as CRM_FilteredContact and CRM_FilteredAccount, for example. When you deploy and run your report, you will see the prefilters, as shown in Figure 21.58.

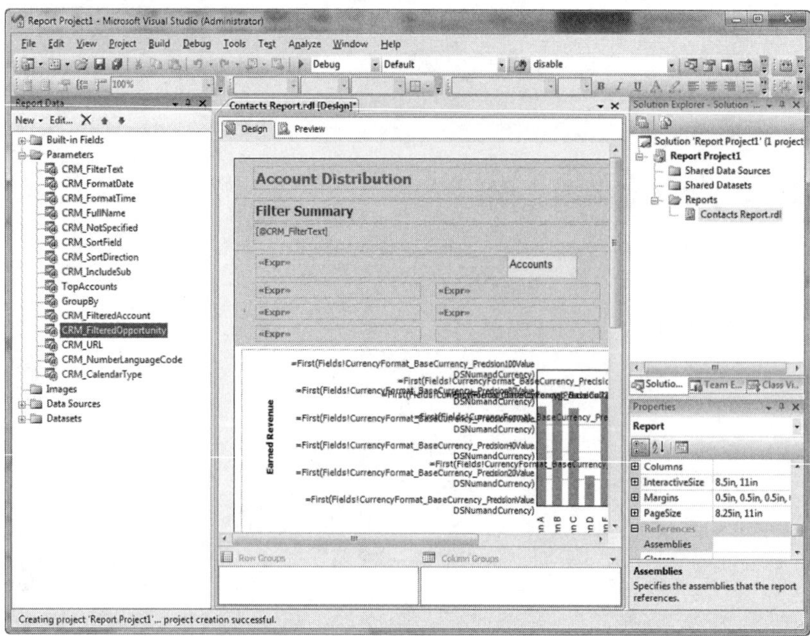

FIGURE 21.55 Report parameters.

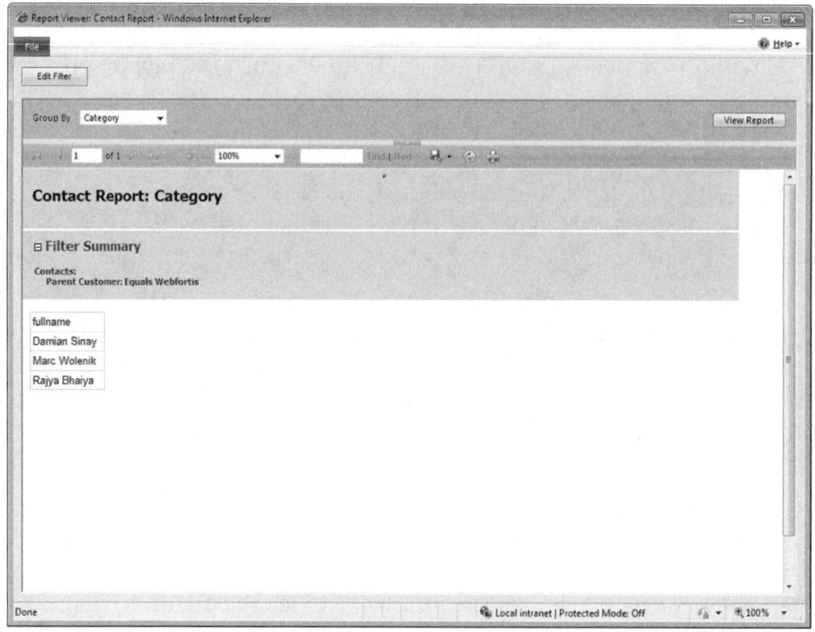

FIGURE 21.56 CRM_FilterText parameter.

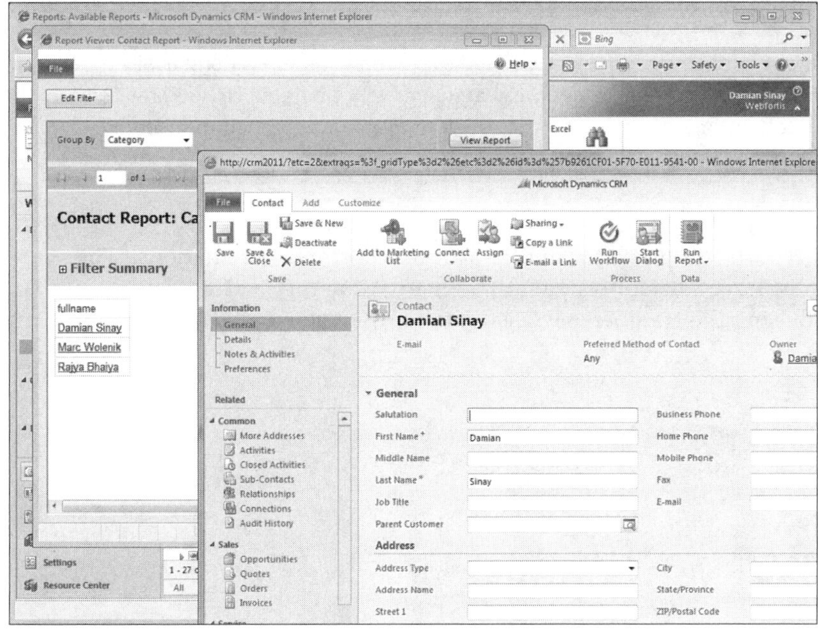

FIGURE 21.57 Drill-through with the CRM_URL parameter.

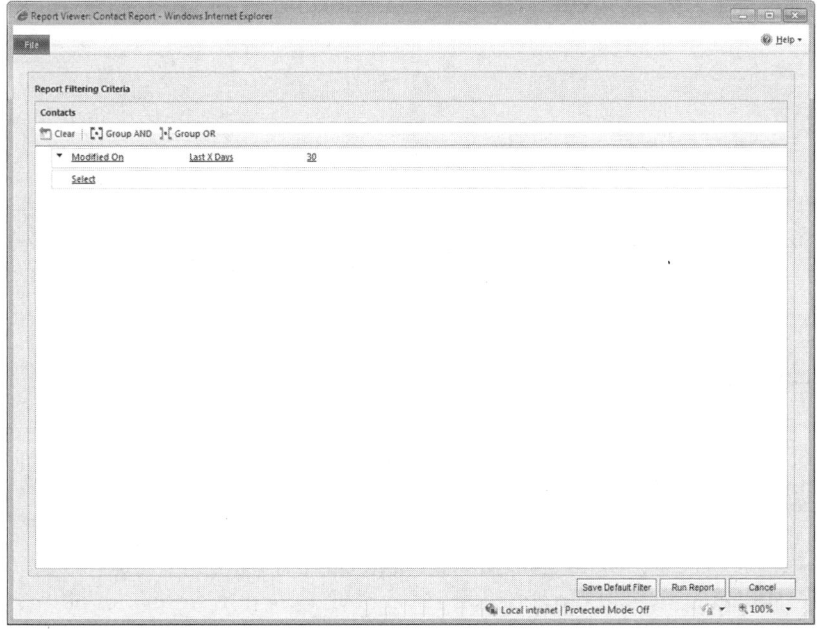

FIGURE 21.58 CRM_FilteredEntity parameters.

CAUTION

If you don't have any of these parameters defined, the report will run automatically without having the user select the prefilters. Also, users won't be able to add prefilters by modifying the default report filters from the CRM reports area through the Web or Outlook client interfaces.

- **CRM_NumberLanguageCode**—This parameter determines the language of the user running the report. It is useful for multilanguage report implementations. This parameter must have a default value from a query using the fn_GetFormatStrings() function and using the NumberLanguageCode for the Value field, as shown in Figure 21.59.

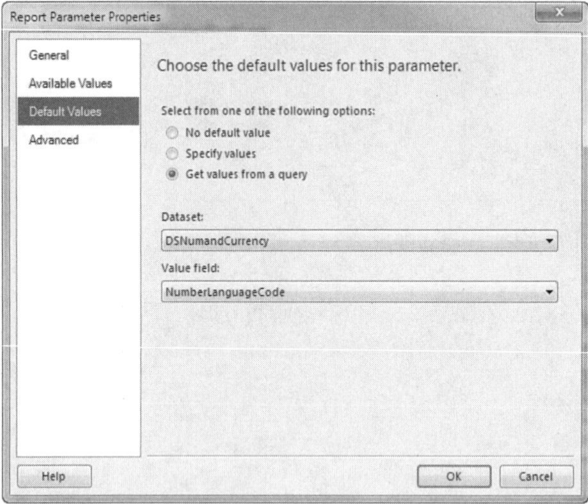

FIGURE 21.59 CRM_NumberLanguageCode parameter.

This function returns a value of en-US for English language in the United States.

Keep these important considerations in mind when using the `CRM_FilteredEntity` parameters:

- When adding these parameters, be sure to set them as internal and set a default value of distinct or null. This default value can be a nonqueried value or it might come from a query.
- Apart from adding the CRM_FilteredEntity parameters to the report, be sure to add the @CRMAF_FilteredEntity alias to the filtered views you use in your queries of the datasets. For example, if your query is as follows, the report will always show all the contacts, even though the user uses the prefilters:

```
select fullname from FilteredContact
```

To have the filters work properly, you must add the alias. Doing so affects our example as follows:

```
DECLARE @SQL nvarchar(Max)
SET @SQL = 'SELECT fullname FROM ('+@CRM_FilteredContact +') AS FC'
EXEC (@SQL)
```

After you add this query to the dataset, click the Refresh button so that you can start using the fields on your report, or you will get errors when you try to test and deploy it.

Another method in using the prefilters is to use the CRMAF_FilteredEntity alias to the filtered views. For example, you could build your query as follows:

```
select fullname from FilteredContact as CRMAF_FilteredContact
```

Using them this way, you don't have to add the CRM_FilteredEntity parameter.

Building Custom Reports with ASP.NET

Another way to create a custom report is to create an ASP.NET web application and then use the Link to Web Page option to deploy it, as explained earlier. Using this method doesn't allow you to use all the benefits inherent to SRS (including the capability to pass parameters to the reports and also use prefiltering), but enables you to extend a report with other features such as mapping or interactive reports not possible with SRS but easily to do with a custom ASP.NET application. If you need to create a report using this method, you must handle the filtering options in your application manually.

NOTE

It is *always* recommended to use the filtering views. With these types of reports, if you use Windows authentication in your application, the security will be in place.

This next example shows a custom report built in ASP.NET 4.0 that takes advantage of LINQ. You will need to have Visual Studio 2010 installed to follow this sample:

1. Open Visual Studio 2010 and create a new project by going to File, New, Web Site, as shown in Figure 21.60.

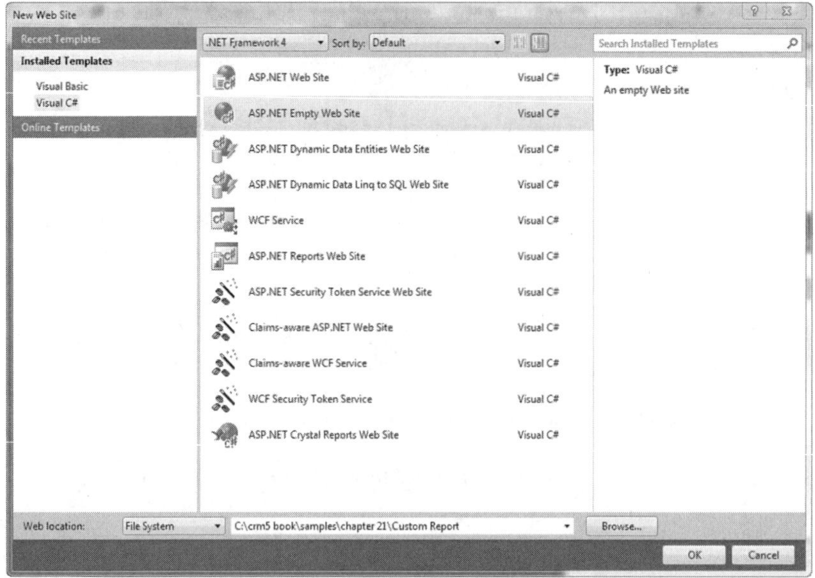

FIGURE 21.60 Creating a new website project.

2. Select ASP.NET Empty Web Site project and enter the location address where your website will be located. For the language in this sample, use C# and the 4 Framework.
3. Click OK to create the website.
4. Under the Solution Explorer, right-click your website URL and select Add New Item.
5. Select LINQ to SQL Classes, as shown in Figure 21.61.
6. Click the Add button.
7. Click the Server Explorer to see the data connections.
8. Click the Add Connection button to add a new connection, as shown in Figure 21.62.
9. Select your CRM database server and then your organization database name.
10. Click Test Connection to be sure you have access, and then click OK.
11. Expand the data connection you just created from the Server Explorer and expand the Views folder.
12. Locate the FilteredContact view, and drag and drop it into the Object Relational Designer, as shown in Figure 21.64.
13. Build your solution.
14. Go to the Solution Explorer, right-click your website URL and select Add New Item. Select Web Form and enter Default.aspx on the name, click on Add, and drag and drop a GridView control, as shown in Figure 21.65.
15. Under the GridView Tasks, choose a data source and select New Data Source.
16. Select LINQ and click OK, as shown in Figure 21.66.

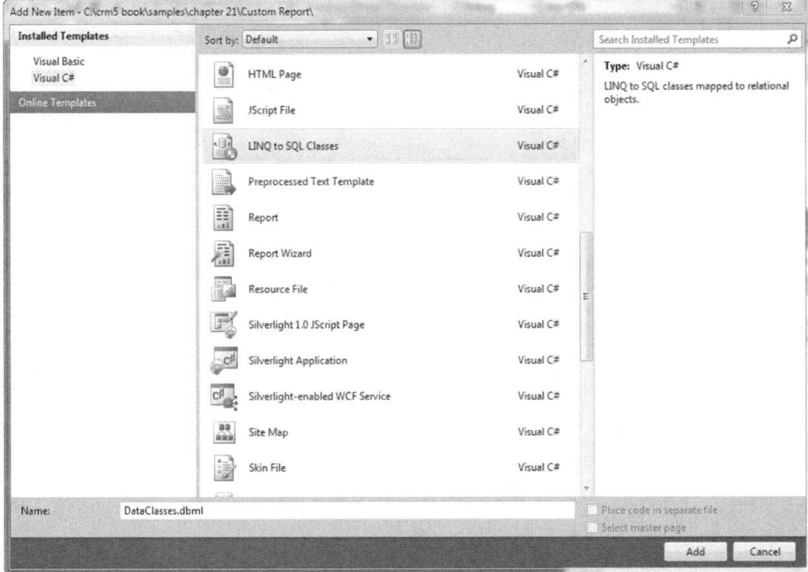

FIGURE 21.61 Adding LINQ to SQL classes.

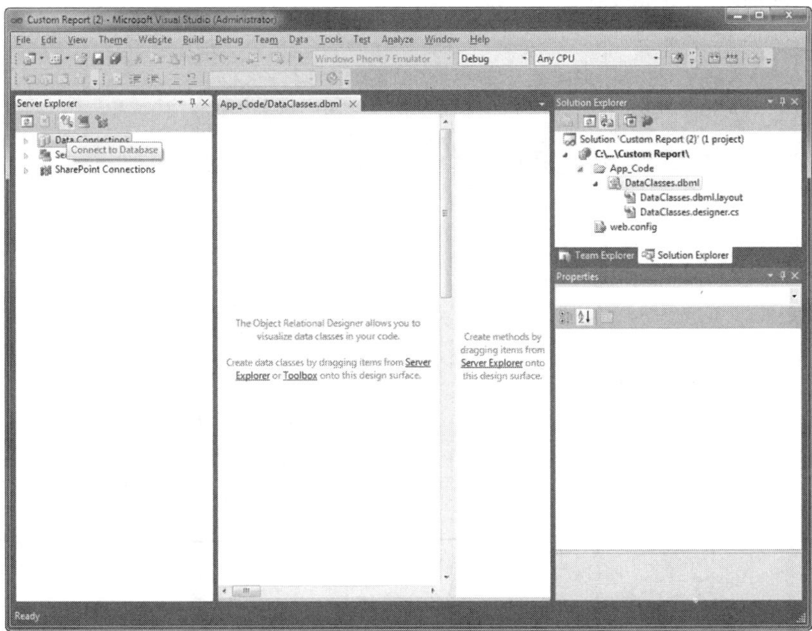

FIGURE 21.62 Adding the database connection.

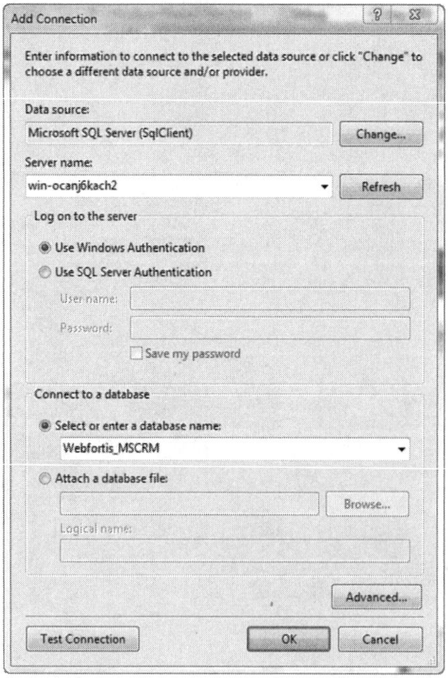

Add Connection

Enter information to connect to the selected data source or click "Change" to choose a different data source and/or provider.

Data source:
Microsoft SQL Server (SqlClient)
Change...
Server name:
win-ocanj6kach2
Refresh
Log on to the server
Use Windows Authentication
Use SQL Server Authentication
User name:
Password:
Save my password
Connect to a database
Select or enter a database name:
Webfortis_MSCRM
Attach a database file:
Browse...
Logical name:
Advanced...
Test Connection
OK
Cancel

FIGURE 21.63 Selecting the database.

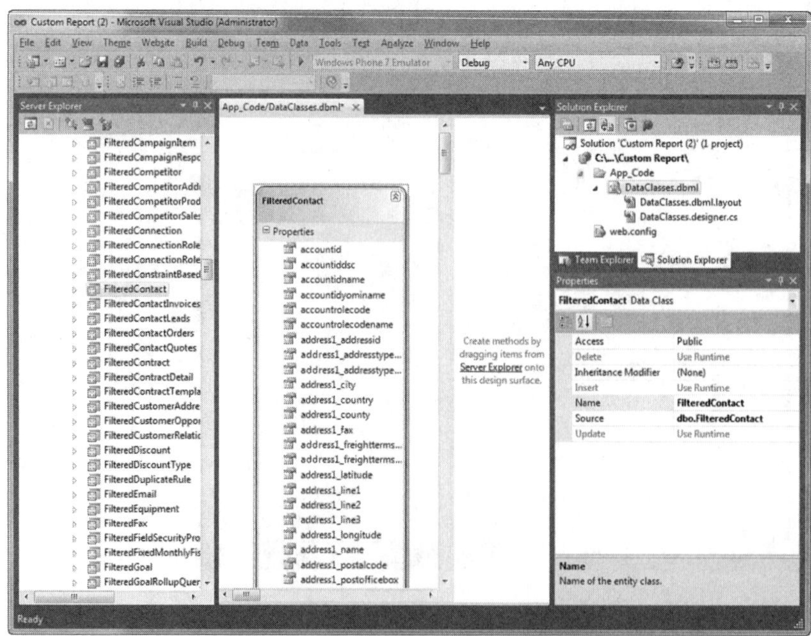

FIGURE 21.64 Adding FilteredContact to the Object Relational Designer.

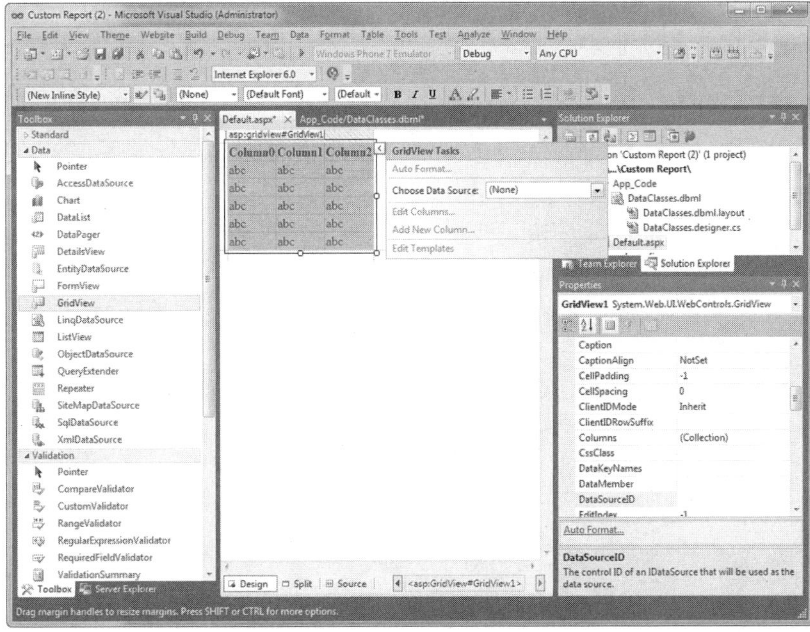

FIGURE 21.65 Adding a GridView control.

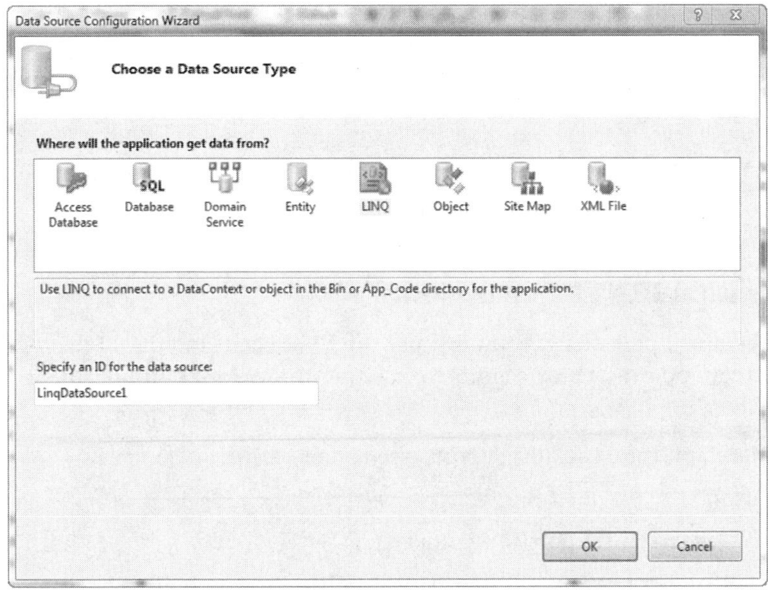

FIGURE 21.66 Adding a data source.

17. Leave the option that is displayed in the context object, as shown in Figure 21.67, and click Next.

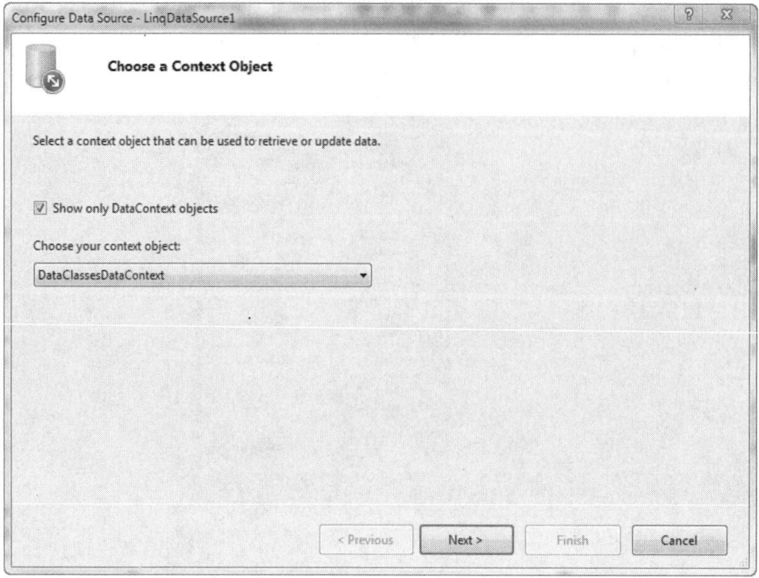

FIGURE 21.67 Choose a context object.

18. Select the fields you want to display in the GridView control. Here we select fullname and jobtitle, as shown in Figure 21.68.
19. Click the Finish button.

To test the application you created, press Ctrl+F5. You should get a page similar to the one displayed in Figure 21.69.

Custom Reports with ASP.NET Deployment

Similarly to what we explained previously, you must use the CRM client interface following these steps (notice that you can deploy reports from either the Web or Outlook client interfaces).

1. Go to the Workplace and then click on Reports (see Figure 21.70).
2. Click the New button.
3. Select Link to Web Page in the Report Type property.
4. Under Web Page URL, enter the URL of the custom application you built.
5. Enter a name for the report.

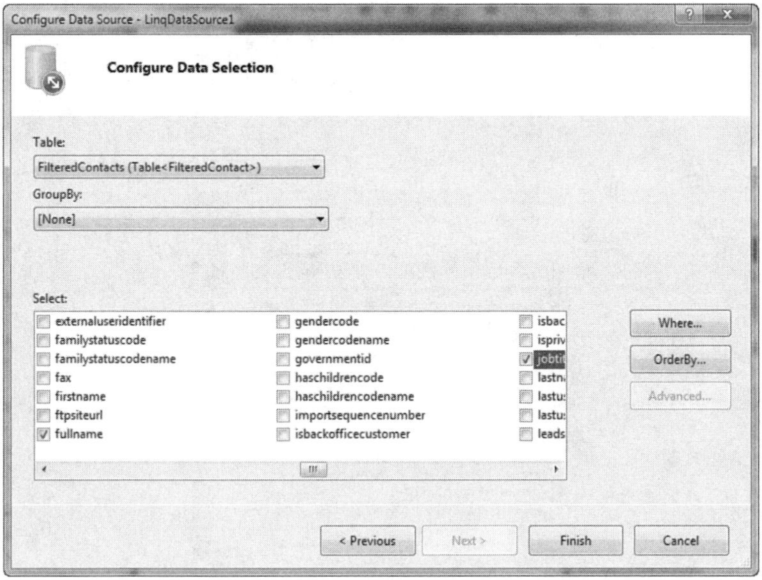

FIGURE 21.68 Configure data selection.

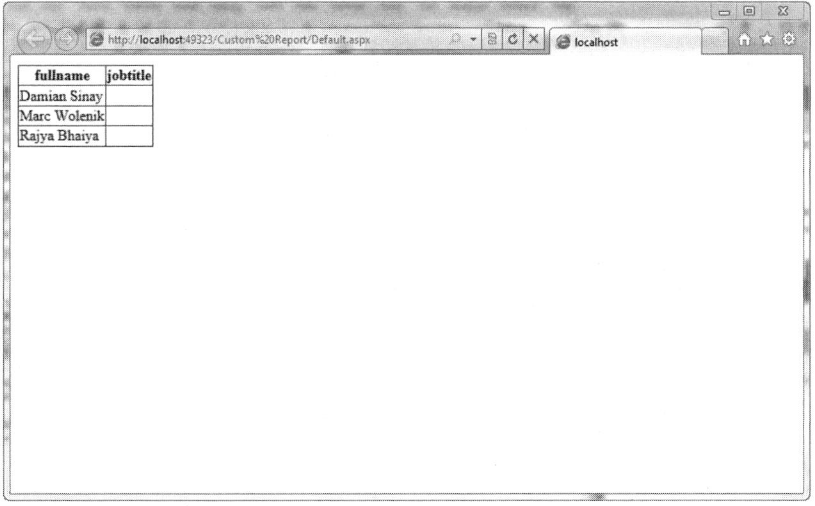

FIGURE 21.69 Testing the custom report.

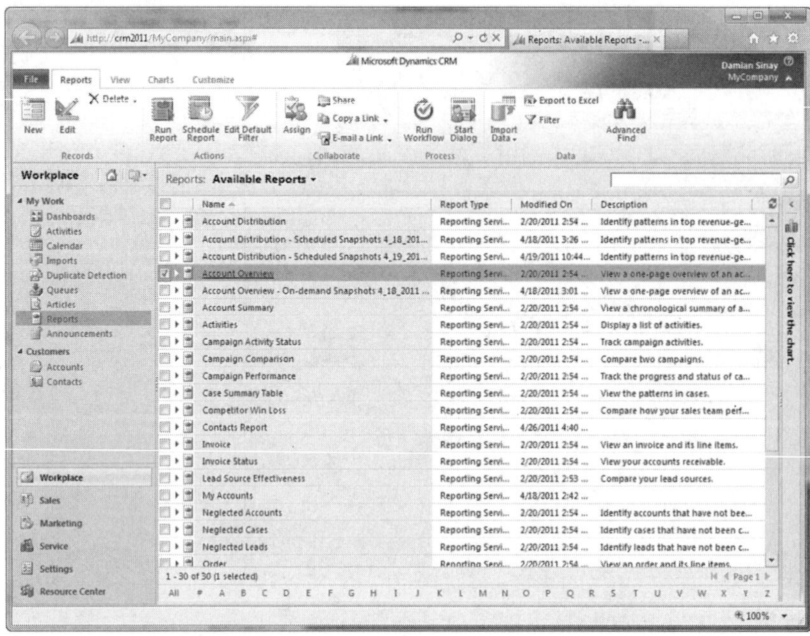

FIGURE 21.70 Reports area.

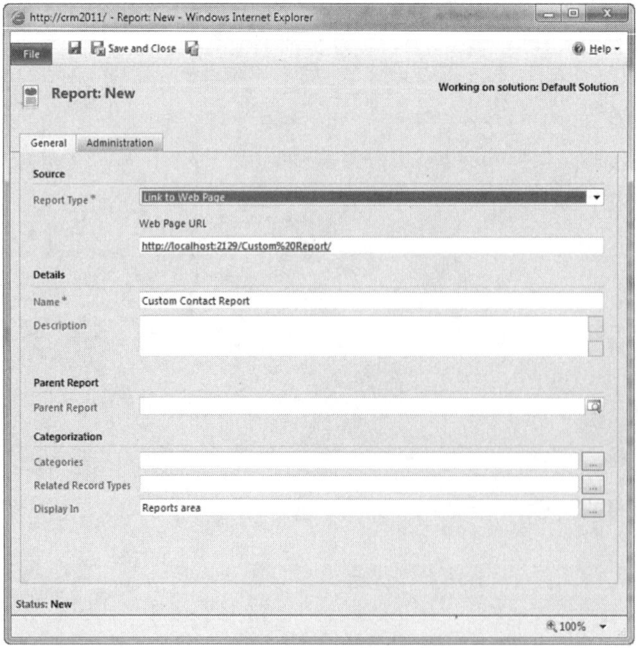

http://crm2011/ - Report: New - Windows Internet Explorer

File Save and Close Help

Report: New

Working on solution: Default Solution

General Administration

Source

Report Type * Link to Web Page

Web Page URL

http://localhost:2129/Custom%20Report/

Details

Name * Custom Contact Report

Description

Parent Report

Parent Report

Categorization

Categories

Related Record Types

Display In Reports area

Status: New

100%

FIGURE 21.71 Deploying a new report.

6. Optionally, you can select the Categories, Related Record Types, and Display In options.
7. Click the Save and Close button.

Now you will see the report added in the reports area and shown in the list. When you double-click the report, a new IE window opens with the custom application page, as shown in Figure 21.72.

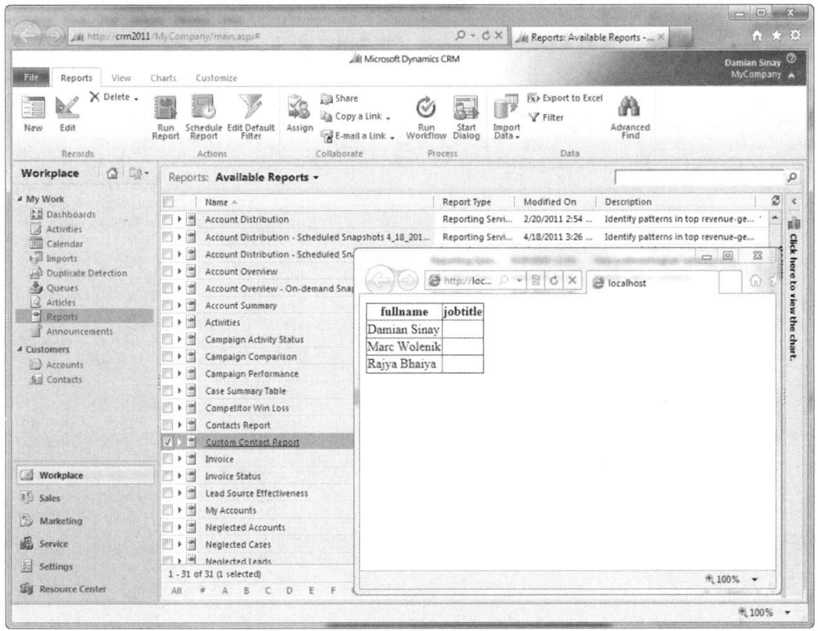

FIGURE 21.72 Testing the custom report in CRM.

Summary

This chapter covered charts, visualizations, Dashboard, and advanced SSRS functions, and described the components that are involved, such as the Report Manager and the Report Server. We discussed some of its features and benefits such as the snapshot creating and scheduling of automated reports. Finally we looked at different options to build custom reports with SSRS using Visual Studio and the Business Intelligence Projects or by a custom web application in ASP.NET 4.0 with Visual Studio 2010.

CHAPTER 22

Forms Authentication

IN THIS CHAPTER

- IFD Defined
- Claims Based Authentication
- Configuring IFD
- Working with IFD and Multiple Organizations

This chapter is specifically for on premise deployments of Microsoft Dynamics CRM 2011. This information can be used by those organizations that want to expose their CRM to Internet to provide public access to the CRM organization without having to use a Virtual Private Network (VPN) connectivity.

IFD Defined

Internet Facing Deployment (IFD) is a feature that enables users to log on to Microsoft Dynamics CRM with a type of authentication known in previous version as Forms Authentication that now is called Claims Based Authentication on this new version of CRM 2011. Claims Based Authentication is a method of authentication that prompts users with a web page interface instead of Integrated Windows Authentication. (The default installation for Microsoft Dynamics CRM is Integrated Windows Authentication.)

The advantage of Integrated Windows Authentication is that it is transparent for users who access the Microsoft Dynamics CRM server from computers that belong to the domain. These computers are not required to enter user information such as name and password because they are already authenticated by Active Directory when they initially log on. If you access the Microsoft Dynamics CRM server from a computer that doesn't belong to the domain, you get the Windows Authentication dialog (see Figure 22.1).

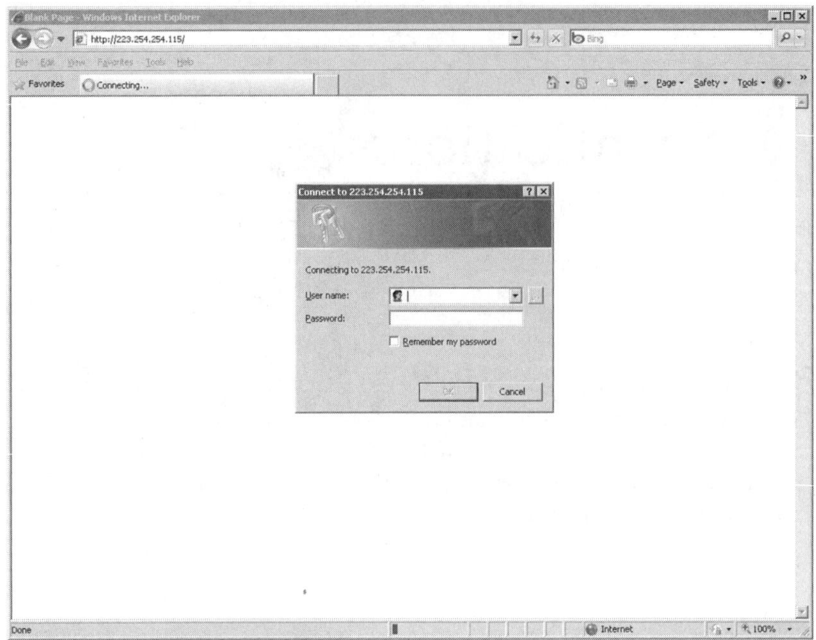

FIGURE 22.1 Windows Authentication dialog.

TIP

The automated login for users that belong to the same domain happens because a default setting in the Internet Explorer browser. If you want to use a different user, you should change this setting by going to the Tools menu of IE and then selecting Internet Options. Move to the Security tab and select the Local Intranet Icon, and then click on the Custom Level button. Move to the last option and select Prompt for user name and password. Click OK to close the dialogs.

If you want to access your CRM server from the Internet or from computers that are outside the network using Claims based Authentication, you must implement the IFD feature.

NOTE

If you don't desire Claims Based Authentication, you can leave the configuration set to its default configuration: Windows Authentication. Although IFD is intended to be used by Microsoft Dynamics CRM–hosted service providers to give their Users a customized login page. You can enable IFD for your own organization with an On-Premise installation, if you want. On the other hand CRM Online uses another type of authentication based on Passport authentication (see Figure 22.3).

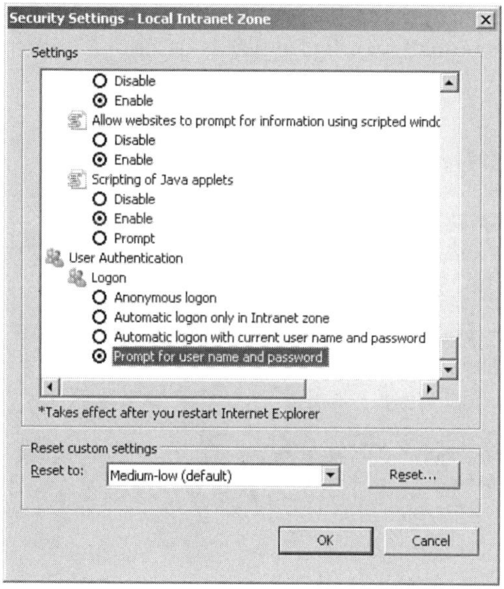

FIGURE 22.2 Changing automated Windows Authentication to prompt for the username and password.

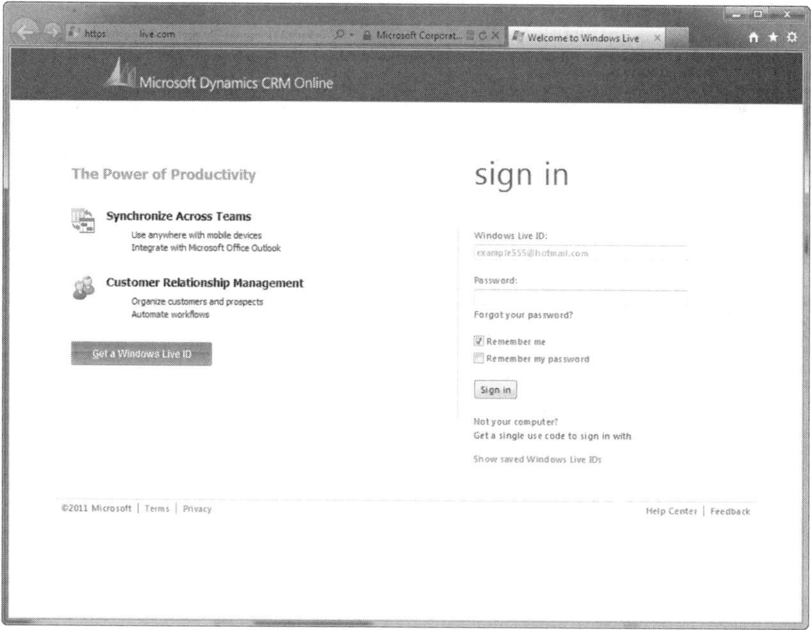

FIGURE 22.3 CRM Online with Passport authentication.

When Microsoft Dynamics CRM is installed using the Setup Wizard, you cannot enable IFD using the Setup Wizard. Instead, you must manually configure IFD as described in the next section.

Claims Based Authentication

IFD comes with another type of authentication, called IFD, that uses Claims Based Authentication With this method, the user may enters credentials (username and password) inside a form of a page instead of using the Windows Authentication dialog.

Figure 22.4 shows what happens when the user types the Microsoft Dynamics URL for an organization in the browser.

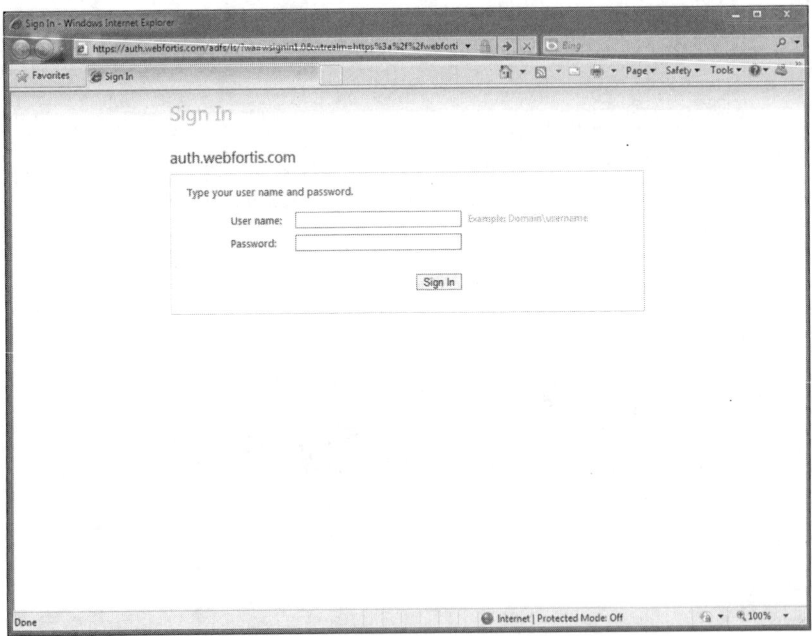

FIGURE 22.4 IFD with Forms Authentication.

Claims Based Authentication requires HTTPS for security reasons to protect the username and password to be transmitted over the network in clear text when making a POST method of HTTP, so you must use SSL (Secure Sockets Layer) to protect this sensitive data.

Configuring IFD

After installation, you have to open the Microsoft Dynamics CRM Deployment Manager application that is installed on the server to enable IFD. If you click in the root node, Microsoft Dynamics CRM, you will see a screen with the tasks containing the tools to configure IFD (see Figure 22.5).

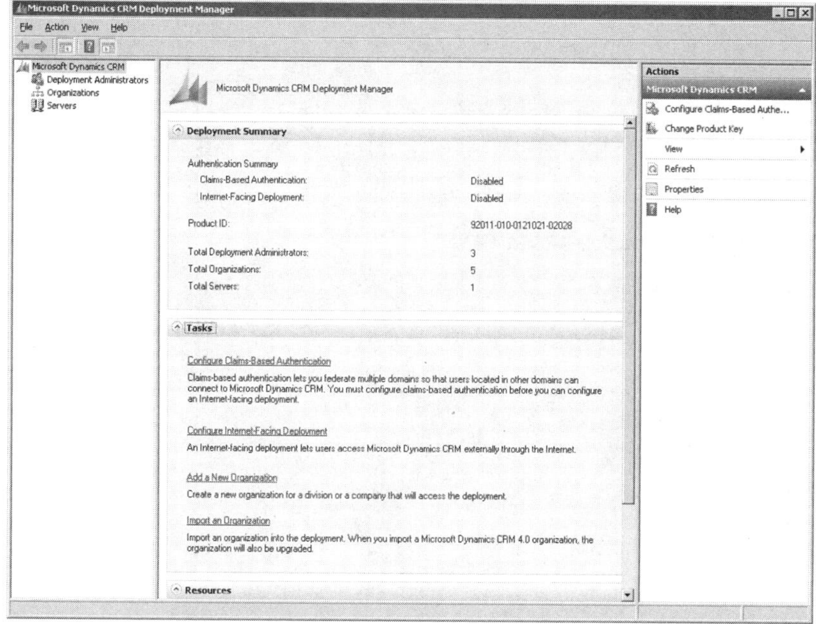

FIGURE 22.5 CRM Deployment Manager.

If you try to click the link that says Configure Internet-Facing Deployment under Tasks, you will get a warning dialog telling you that you must configure Claims-Based Authentication before you can configure IFD (see Figure 22.6).

So, you need to click OK to close this dialog and then click on the first task that says Configure the Claims-Based Authentication. However, clicking this link will show you another error (see Figure 22.7).

So, the first step you need to do is to go to the Properties link that is on the right of the Deployment Manager window, and then go to the Web Addresses tab and configure the HTTPS protocol as the binding type (see Figure 22.8).

The next sections explain these IFD components.

NOTE

For more details about configuring IFD you can download the Deployment and Operational Guidance for Hosting Microsoft Dynamics CRM 2011 from the Microsoft Download website http://www.microsoft.com/downloads/en/details.aspx?FamilyID=d609bb84-125e-4928-aa22-8f55c5a67a3f. There are also some cool videos published in YouTube if you search for IFD CRM 2011 with a step-by-step configuration.

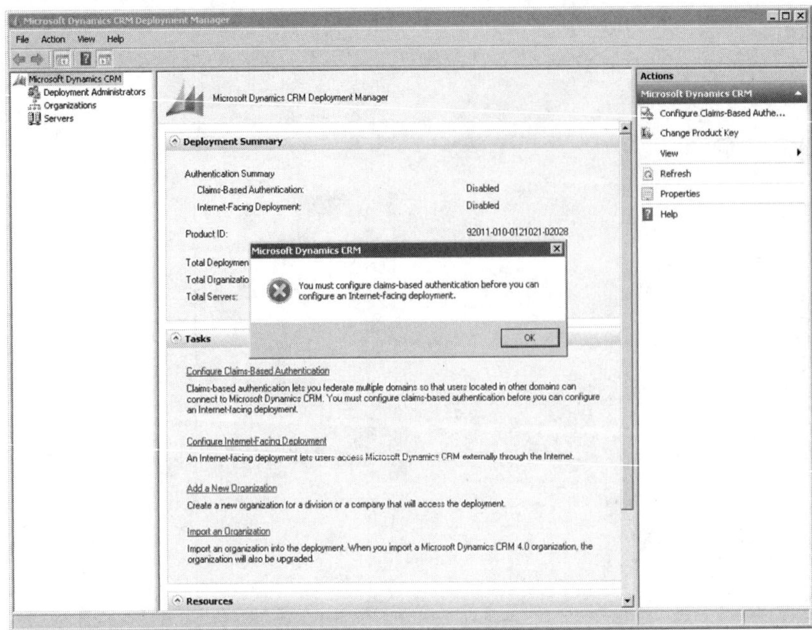

FIGURE 22.6 Configure IFD.

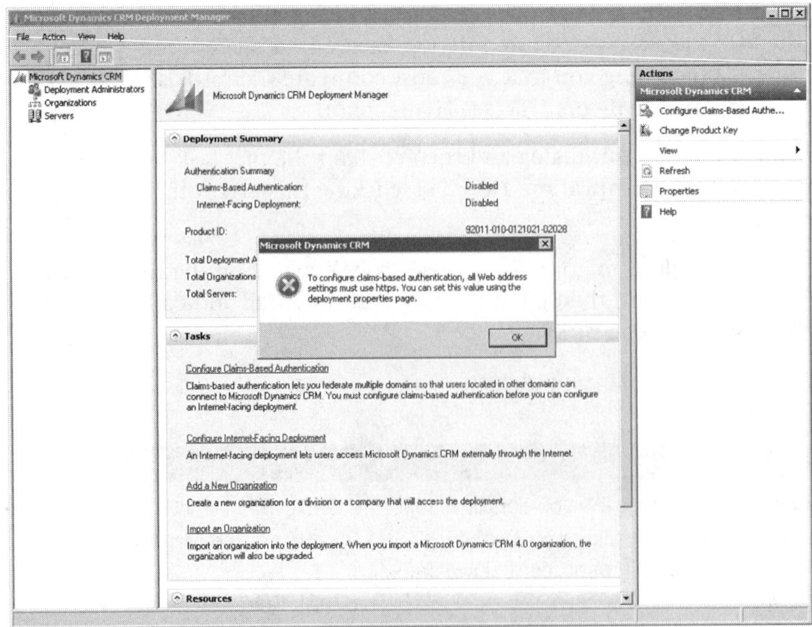

FIGURE 22.7 Configuring Claims-Based Authentication.

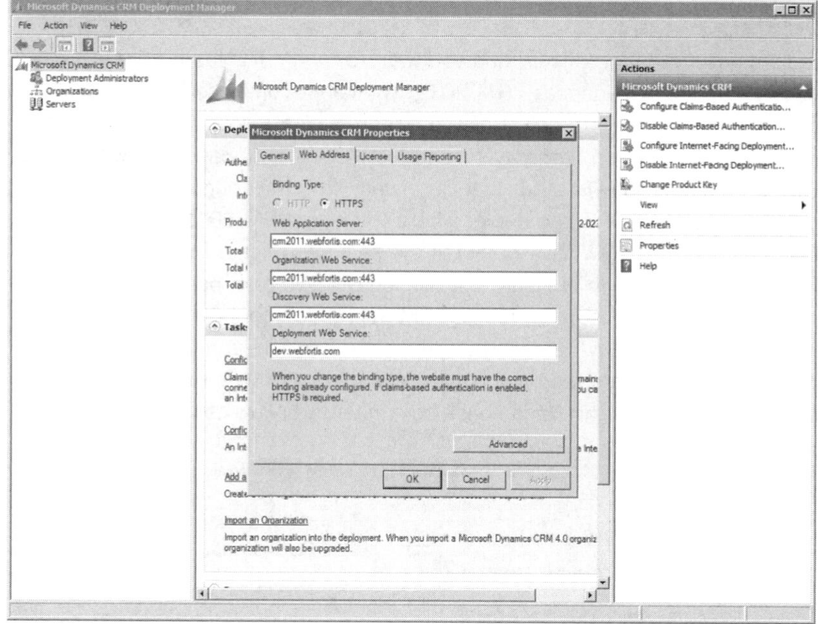

FIGURE 22.8 Configuring HTTPS.

SSL Certificate

Because IFD uses Claims Based Authentication as its authentication method, resulting in users' credentials being posted to the server, you must encrypt the credentials with a Secure Sockets Layer certificate. SSL encrypts information using 1024-bit or 2048-bit encryption and is the same level of protection used by major banking and financial institutions. A certificate of 2048 bits is recommended because it has the more secure level of protection. SSL uses port 443 by default but (you could use any other port), so this port must be set to allow traffic in your firewall—provided that you're using one.

You can obtain SSL certificates from a number of different certificate-issuing authorities, including www.verisign.com and www.thawte.com. Be sure to get a multiple-domain certificate or an unlimited subdomain (wildcard) certificate because you will need to use the certificate for at least two URL addresses, as explained in the DNS server configuration section.

NOTE

If you are not ready to get an SSL certificate and you want to try the IFD feature, as a difference on this new version of Dynamics CRM 2011, you cannot omit the SSL configurations and install the server with http only. However, you can create your own certificates using the Windows certification authority service (certsrv). In that case, you will have to import the certificate on the Trusted Root Certificate store for your local computer in the AD FS server as well as in the server where you have CRM 2011 installed, as shown in Figure 22.9. You will also have to install the same certificate in the Personal Certificates folder, as shown in Figure 22.10. You will give read permissions to the user that is running the Microsoft Dynamics CRM application pool (usually NETWORK SERVICE). This can be done by running the Certificates console in the CRM server, right clicking on the certificate, and selecting the Managing Private Keys option. Then add the user there and select the Read check box under the Allow column.

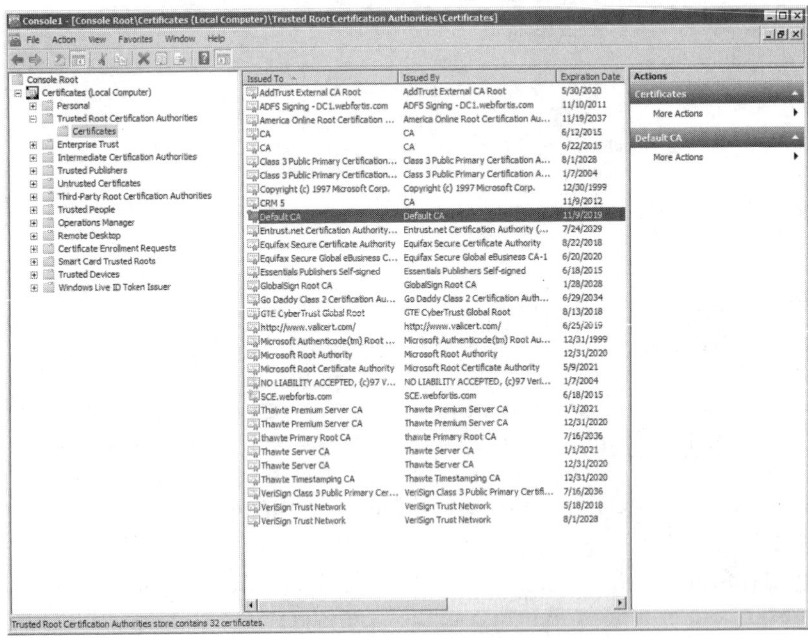

FIGURE 22.9 Trusted root certificate authorities.

TIP

We recommend you purchase the certificate from a trusted certificate authority so that you do not have to deal with the certificate stores.

Complete the following steps to request and install a new certificate through the Internet Information Services (IIS) Manager:

1. Open the Internet Information Services (IIS) Manager application by going to Start and then Administrative Tools.

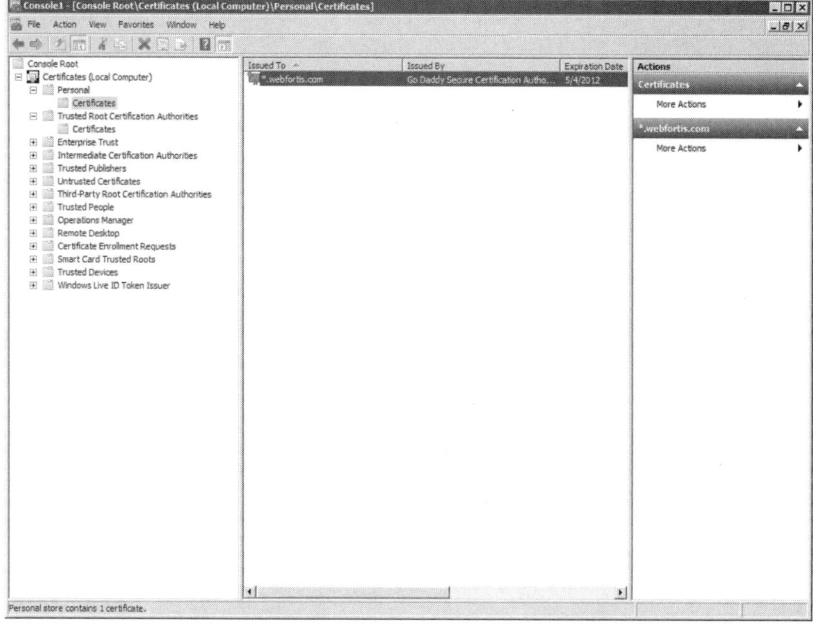

FIGURE 22.10 Personal Certificates folder.

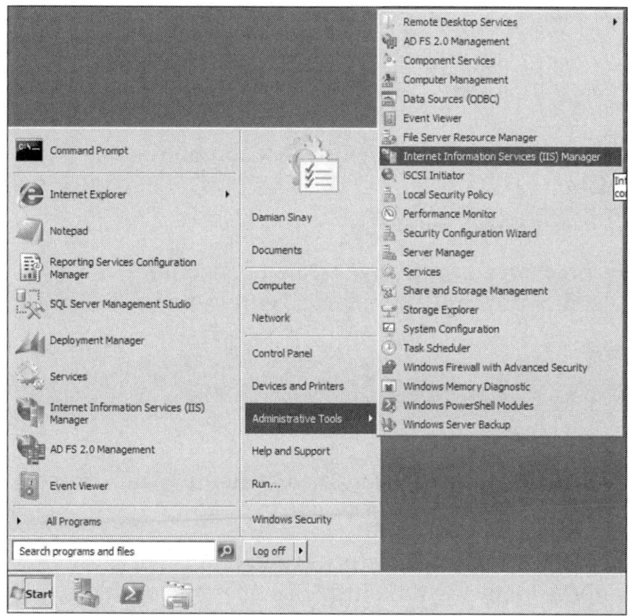

FIGURE 22.11 Locating the Internet Information Services (IIS) Manager.

2. Click the server name on the left, and then click the Server Certificates icon on the right.

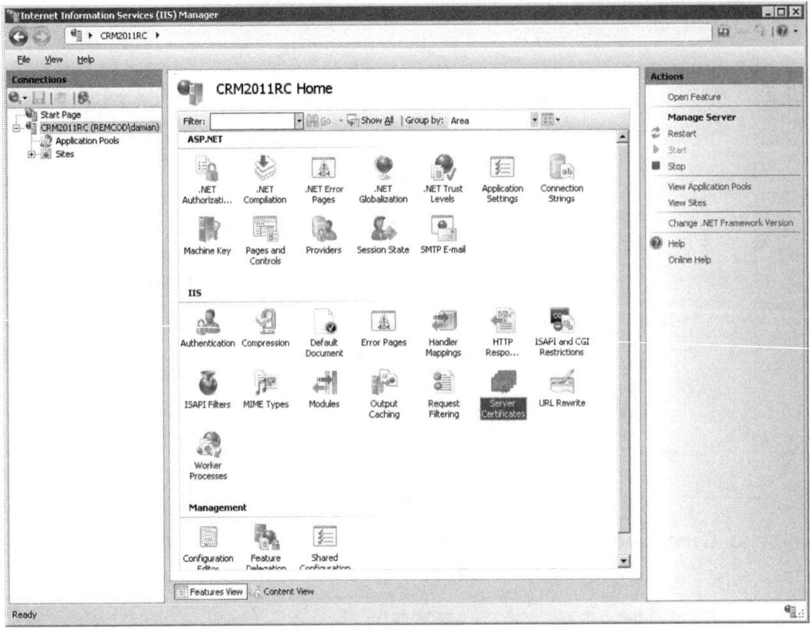

FIGURE 22.12 Internet Information Services (IIS) Manager.

3. Click the Create Domain Certificate link under the Actions section on the right, and enter your organization information.
4. Click Next and select an online certification authority.
5. Click Finish. When the process finishes, you will have created the certificate. Notice if you use a certificate from an online authority, it might take from hours to days to get the certificate created.

Installing AD FS 2.0

After this configuration is done, we are almost ready to start the Configure Claims-Based Authentication Wizard.

However, you must first install and configure Active Directory Federation Services 2.0 (AD FS 2.0). This can be downloaded from the following link: http://technet.microsoft.com/en-us/evalcenter/ee476597.aspx.

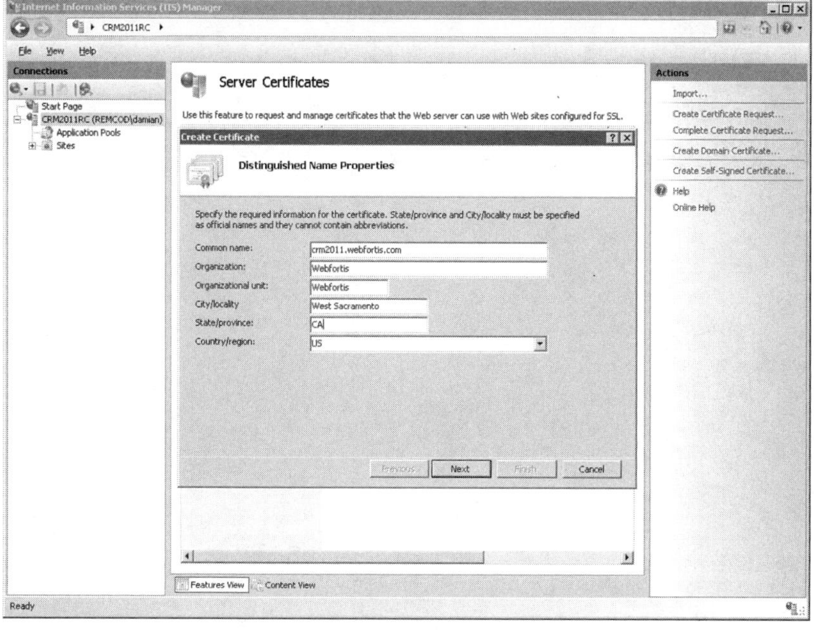

FIGURE 22.13 Create certificate.

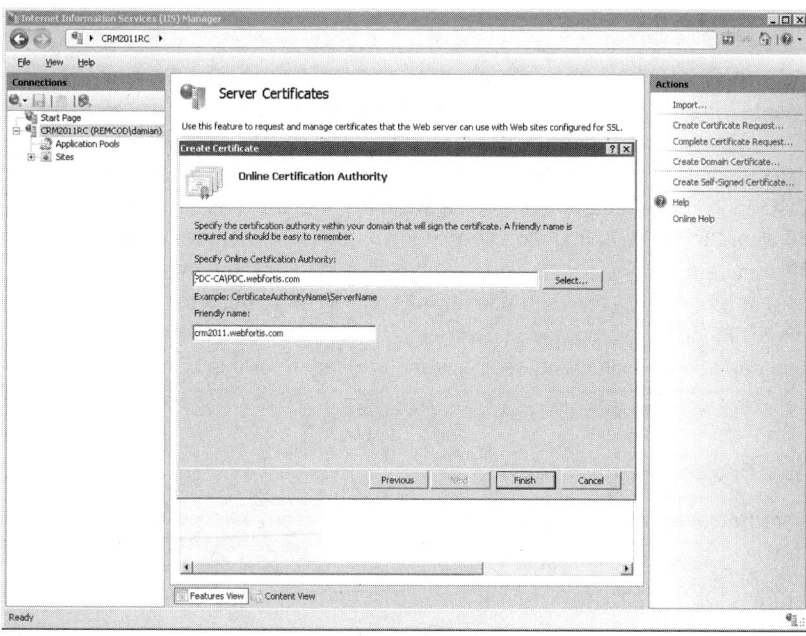

FIGURE 22.14 Online Certification Authority.

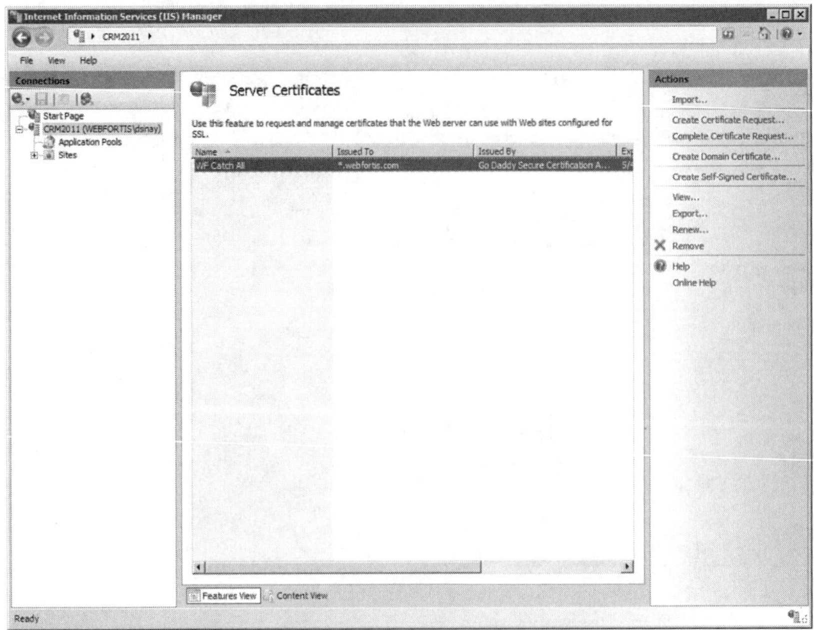

FIGURE 22.15 Server Certificate created.

NOTE

An important note is the server where you will install the AD FS 2.0 because it installs on the default website created on the IIS. If you try this on the same server where you installed the CRM, it won't run because the AD FS creates a virtual folder called adfs inside the default website, which needs the previous .NET Framework version 2.0. You can either install AD FS on a separate server with a clean IIS or create another default website on the IIS where the CRM is installed so that it won't overlap with the CRM server website. If you use the same server, you will have to either configure the new default website to use a port other than the default 443 for HTTPS or use host headers. Because deploying AD FS on the same server where the CRM lives requires the considerations mentioned earlier, we recommend using a separate server for this purpose.

To install the AD FS 2.0, complete the following steps:

1. Run the AdfsSetup.exe application that was downloaded from Microsoft. This opens the Setup Wizard.
2. Click Next and accept the terms in the license agreement.
3. Click Next and select the Federation server option.

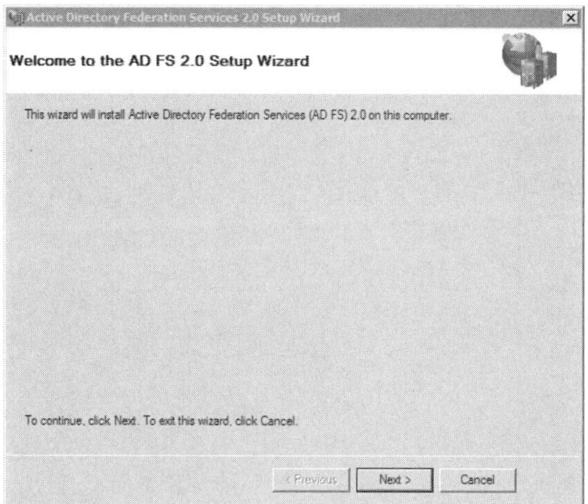

FIGURE 22.16 Welcome to the AD FS 2.0 Setup Wizard.

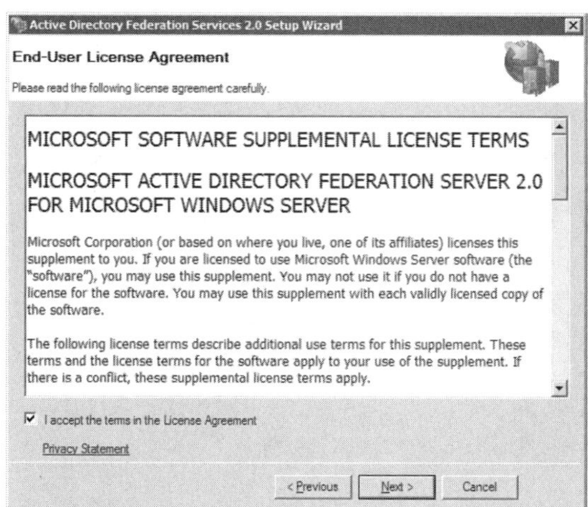

FIGURE 22.17 End-user license agreement.

4. Click Next. The next screen will show you the list of the prerequisite software that this component needs to be installed.
5. Click Next. The wizard will check the required software and install any that is missing. When it finishes, it will ask you to restart the server.

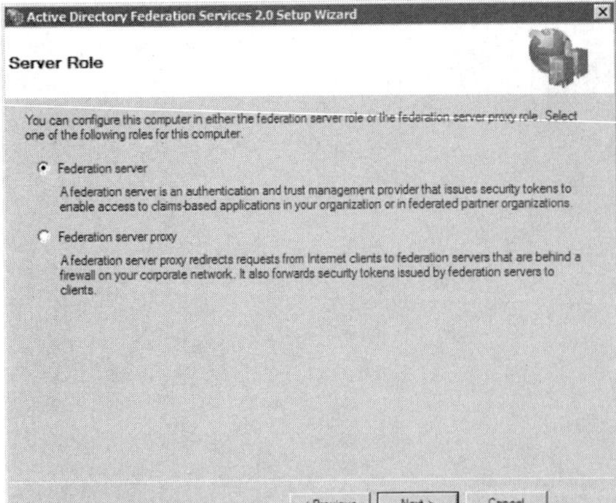

FIGURE 22.18 Server role.

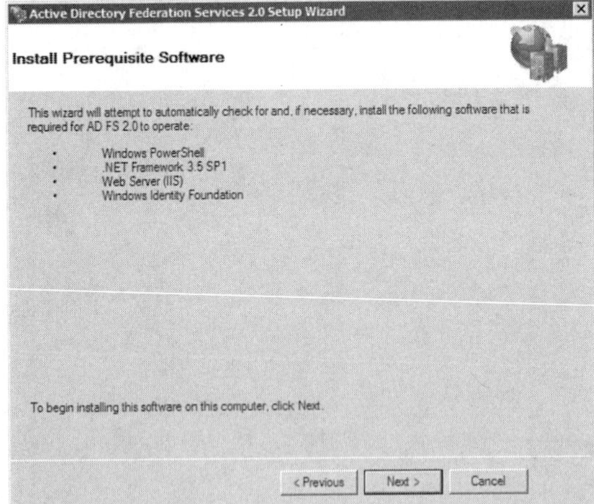

FIGURE 22.19 Install prerequisite software.

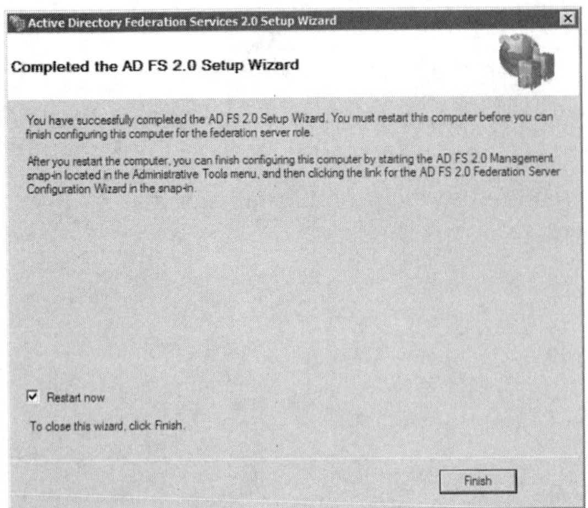

FIGURE 22.20 Completing the AD FS 2.0 Setup Wizard.

Configuring AD FS 2.0

After AD FS 2.0 is installed, you need to configure it. To do so, go to the Start menu and open the AD FS 2.0 Management application that is under the Administrative Tools group.

The AD FS 2.0 Management application will present a window, as shown in Figure 22.22.

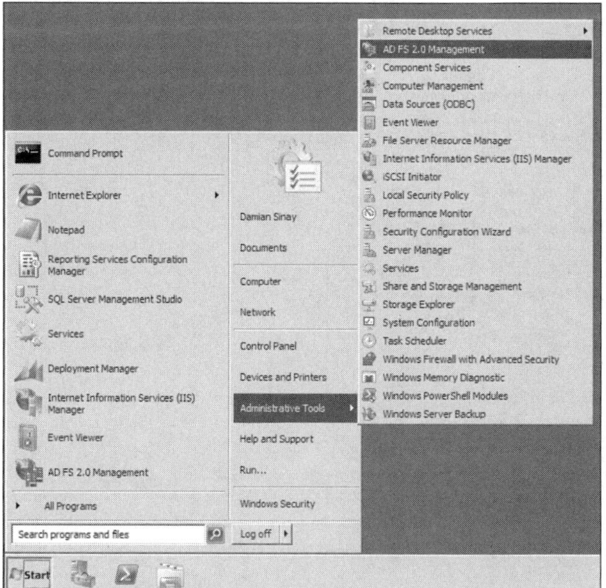

FIGURE 22.21 Locating AD FS 2.0 Management.

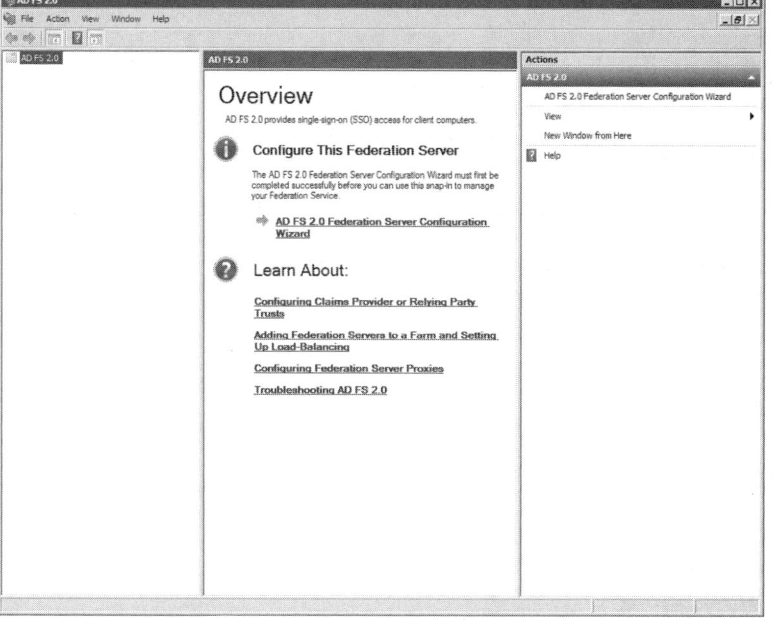

FIGURE 22.22 AD FS 2.0 Management.

To start the configuration, complete the following steps:

1. Click the AD FS 2.0 Federation Server Configuration Wizard link that is in the Configure This Federation Server section.
2. Select the option to create a new Federation Service and then click Next.

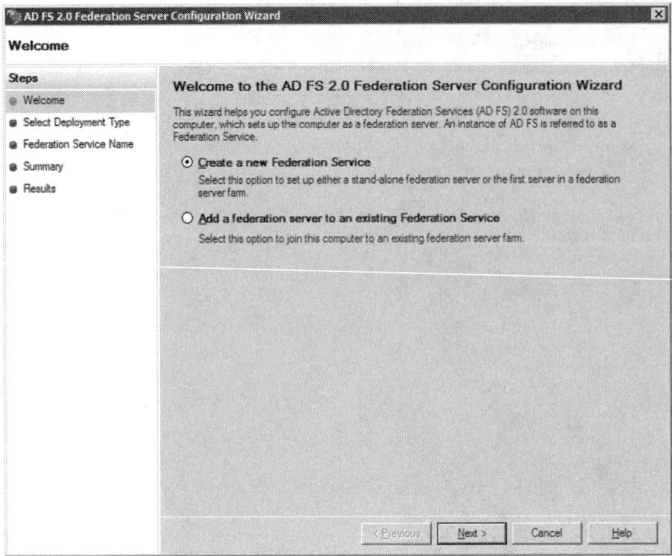

FIGURE 22.23 AD FS 2.0 Federation Configuration Wizard.

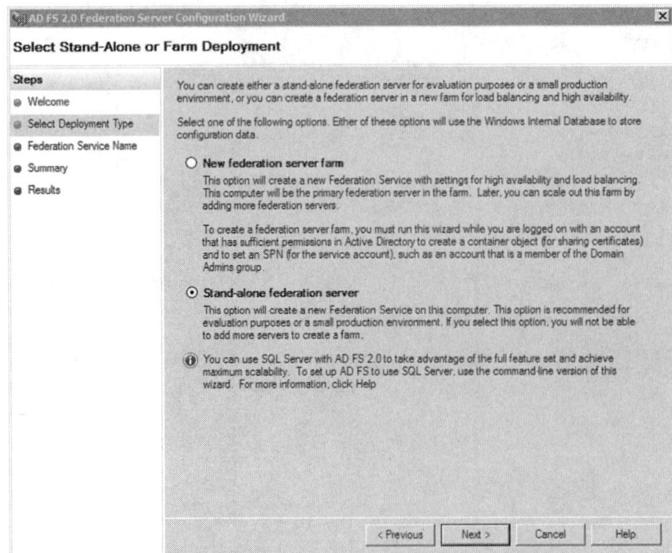

FIGURE 22.24 Select Stand-Alone or Farm Deployment.

3. For this sample we will create a stand-alone federation server that is the recommended setting for small implementations. For large organizations, you will need to create a server farm.
4. Click Next and select a certificate.
5. Review the settings that will be configure and click Next.
6. After the configurations are done, you will see the results of every task with the status in case of a failure.

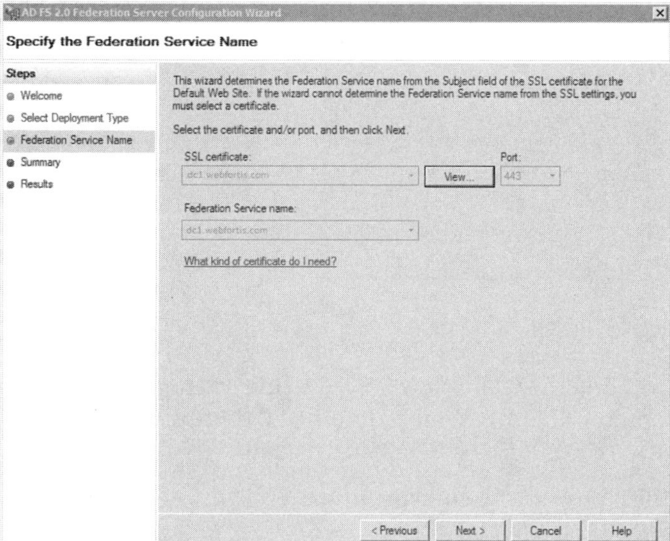

FIGURE 22.25 Specify the Federation Service Name.

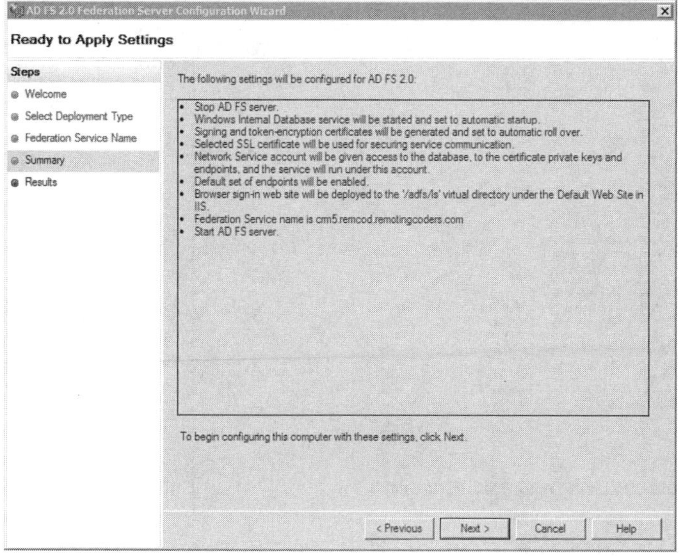

FIGURE 22.26 Ready to apply settings.

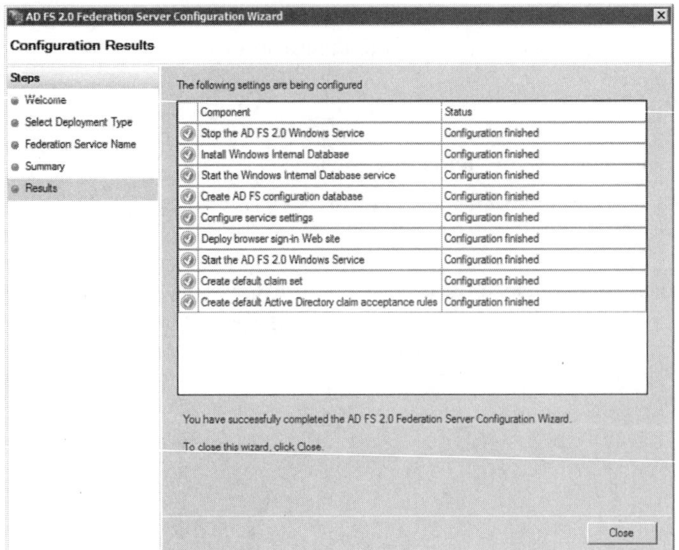

FIGURE 22.27 Configuration results.

7. Click on Close.

After the wizard finishes, you will find the URL you will need to use when configuring the Claims-Based Authentication on CRM. An example of this URL is https://crm2011.webfortis.com/FederationMetadata/2007-06/FederationMetadata.xml.

You can verify it has been installed properly by checking in the AD FS 2.0 Management application, as shown in Figure 22.28.

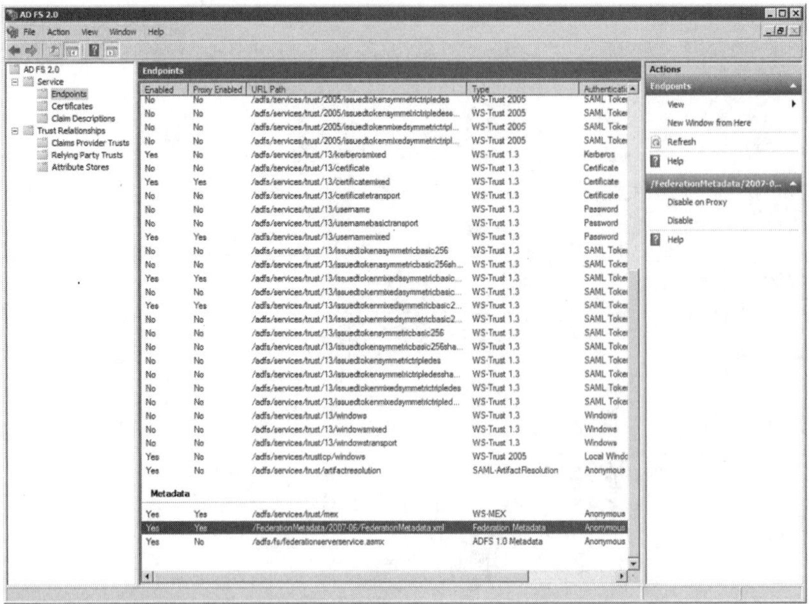

FIGURE 22.28 AD FS service endpoints.

Export the AD FS Token Certificate

Now we'll have to export the AD FS token certificate and import it to the trusted certificate authorities store on the CRM server. To do that, follow these steps:

1. From the AD FS 2.0 management application, go to the Server/Certificates folder, as shown in Figure 22.29.

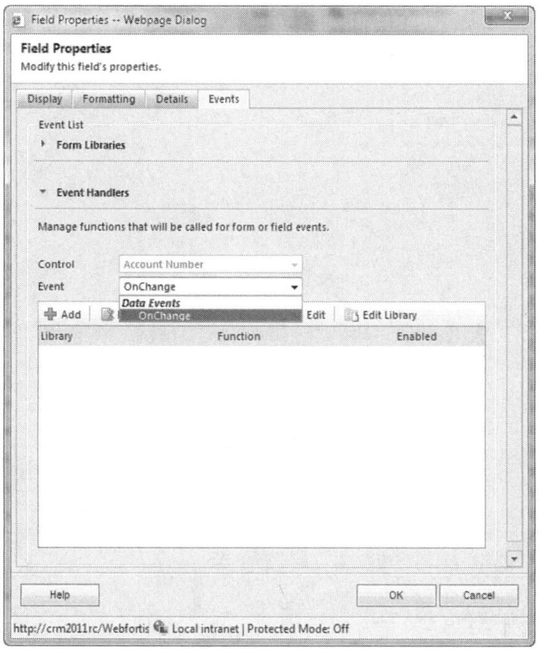

FIGURE 22.29 View the Token-Signing certificate

2. Select the Token-Signing certificate, and right-click and select View Certificate.
3. Go to the Details tab and click Copy to file.
4. When the certificate Export Wizard dialog opens, click Next (see Figure 22.30).
5. In the Export File Format step, select the default value of DER and click Next (see Figure 22.31).
6. Enter the filename with the full path where you want to store the certificate file, and then click Next (see Figure 22.32).
7. Complete the Certificate Export Wizard by clicking Finish (see Figure 22.33).
8. When the message box that says the export was successful appears, click OK.
9. Copy the file you exported to the Server where you have CRM2011 installed and open the Certificates Management snap-in and go to the trusted root certification authorities folder. Right-click the certificates folder inside and select All Tasks then Import (see Figure 22.34).
10. When the Certificate Import Wizard opens, click Next.

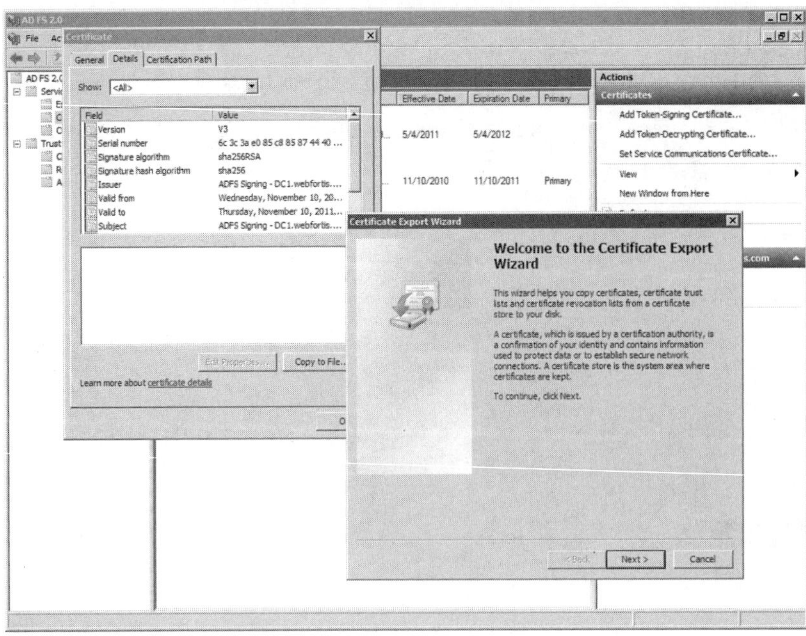

FIGURE 22.30 Certificate Export Wizard.

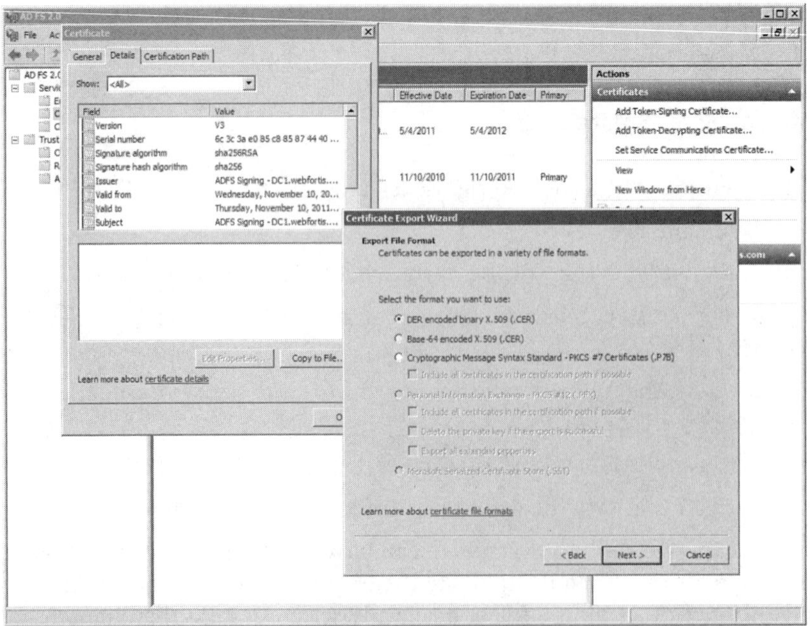

FIGURE 22.31 Export File Format.

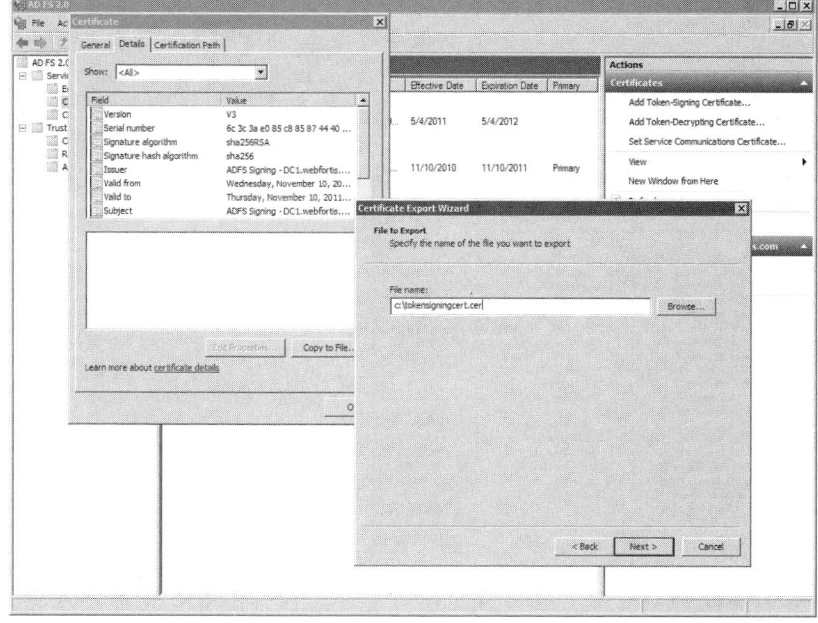

FIGURE 22.32 File to export.

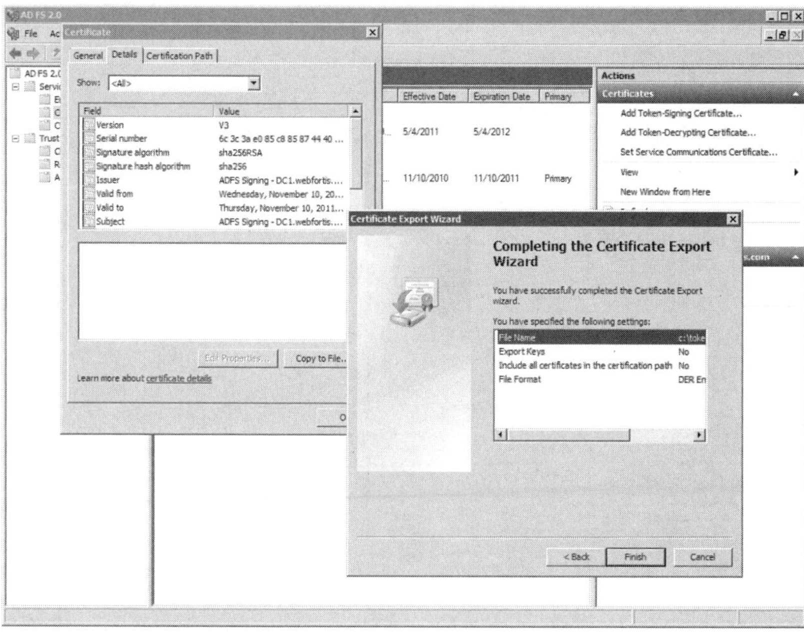

FIGURE 22.33 Completing the Certificate Export Wizard.

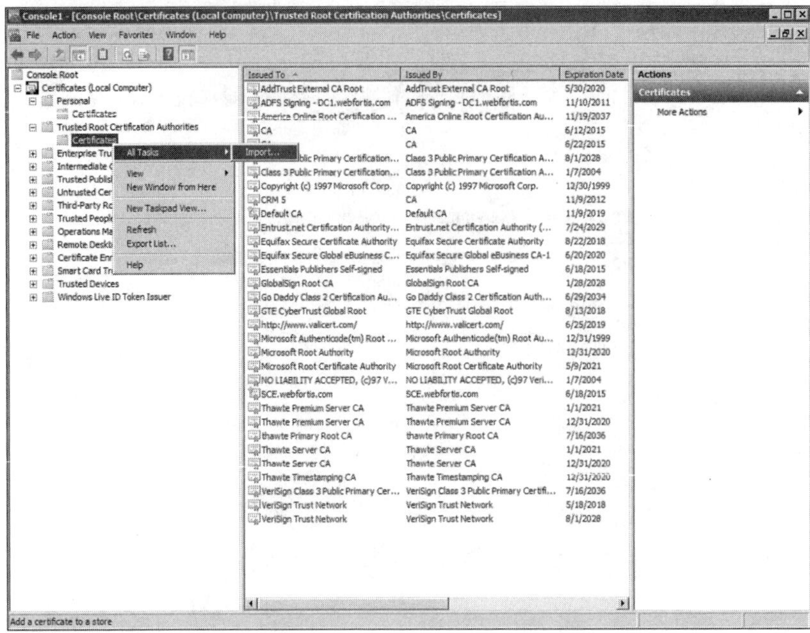

FIGURE 22.34 Importing the certificate.

11. Enter the file with the full path where you have the certificate file located and click Next (see Figure 22.35).

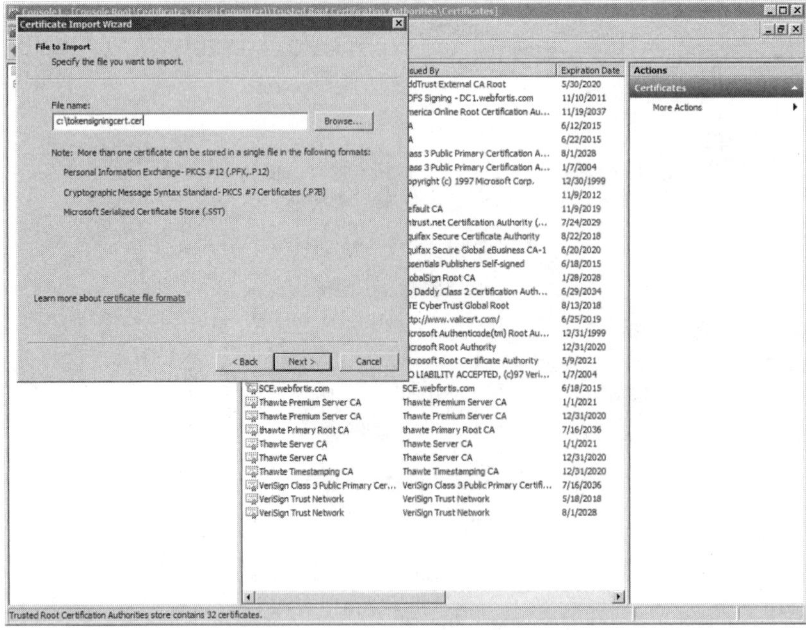

FIGURE 22.35 File to import.

12. Leave the default certificate store suggested, which is the Trusted Root Certification Authorities, and click Next (see Figure 22.36).
13. Click Finish (see Figure 22.37).
14. When the message box that says the import was successful appears, click OK.

Configuring Claims-Based Authentication on CRM

Complete the following steps to configure Claims-Based Authentication:

1. To open the wizard, click the Configure Claims-Based Authentication link that is in the Tasks pane (see Figure 22.38).
2. Click Next and enter the Federation URL you got when configuring the AD FS 2.0 (see Figure 22.39).
3. Click Next and select the SSL certificate (see Figure 22.40).
4. Click Next and select the SSL certificate (see Figure 22.41).
5. The wizard will validate the settings and system requirements and will show any error or warning to the user.
6. Click Next to review the configurations (see Figure 22.42).
7. Click Apply to apply the changes (see Figure 22.43).
8. Click Finish to close the dialog.

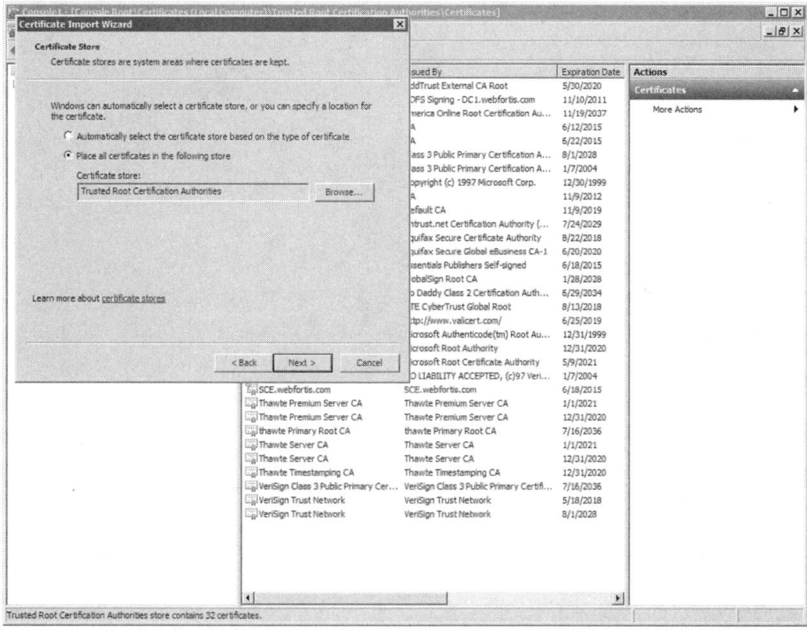

FIGURE 22.36 Certificate store.

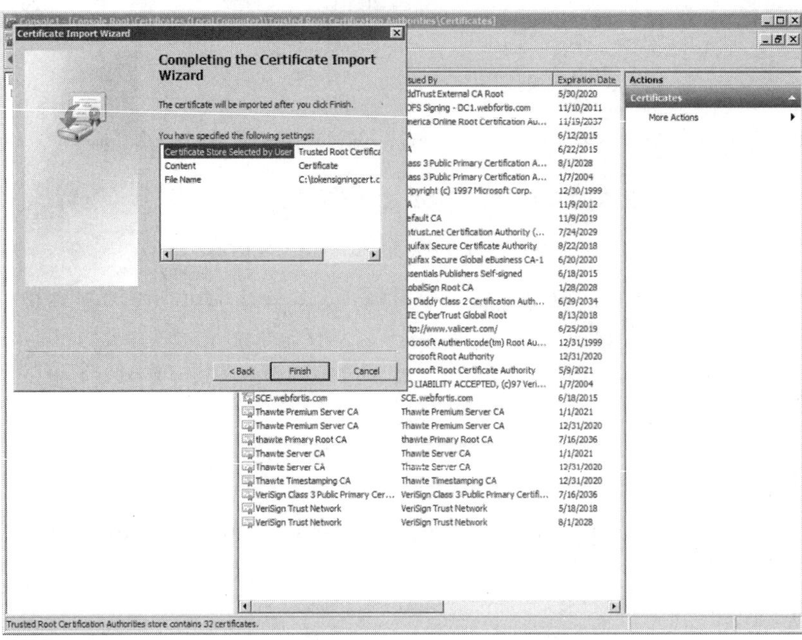

FIGURE 22.37 Completing the Certificate Import Wizard.

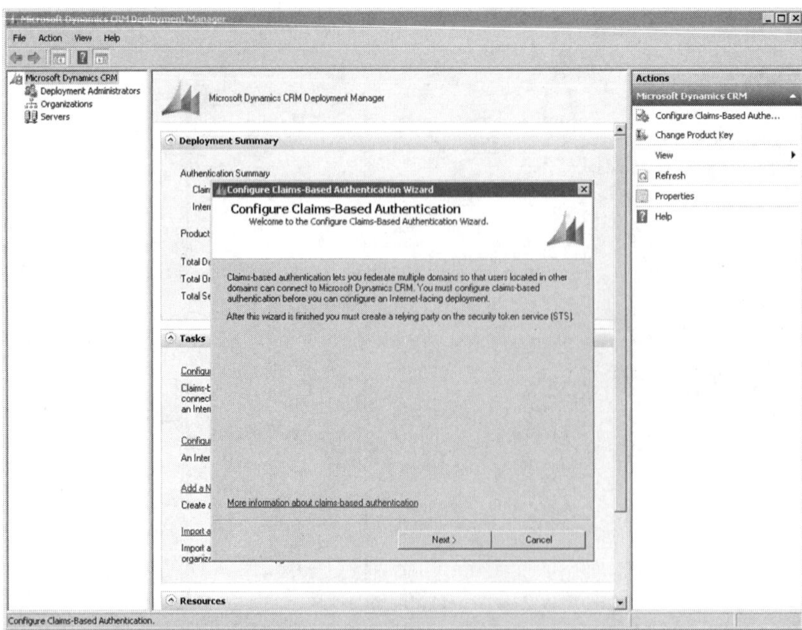

FIGURE 22.38 Configure Claims-Based Authentication Wizard.

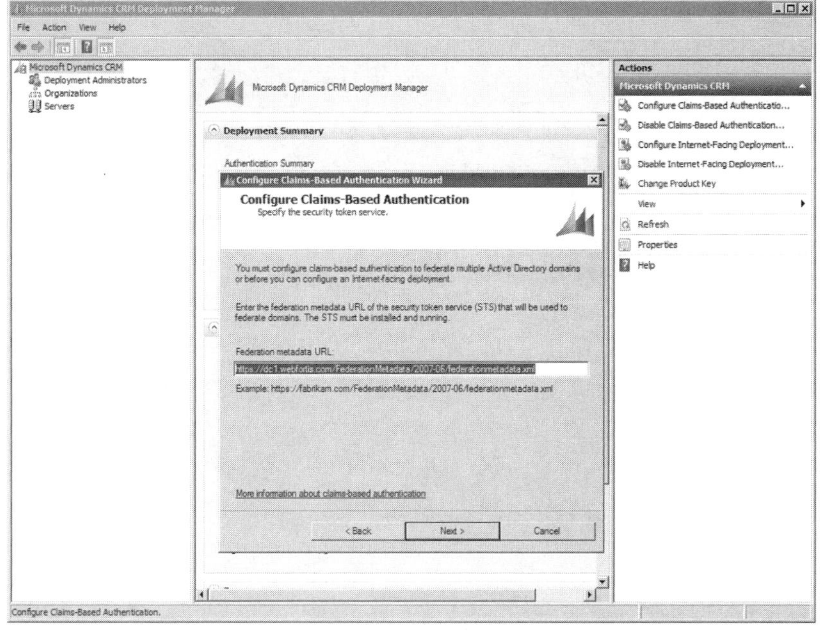

FIGURE 22.39 Configure federation metadata URL.

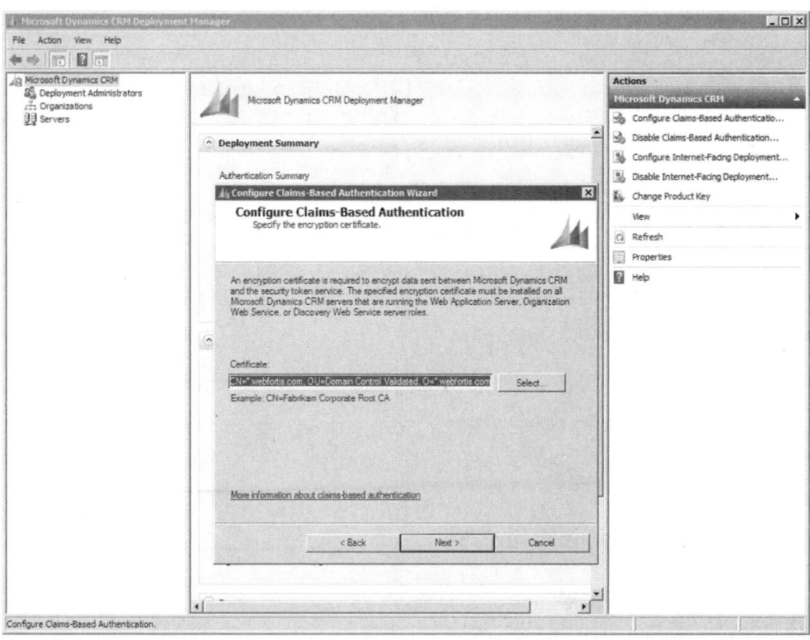

FIGURE 22.40 Configure certificate.

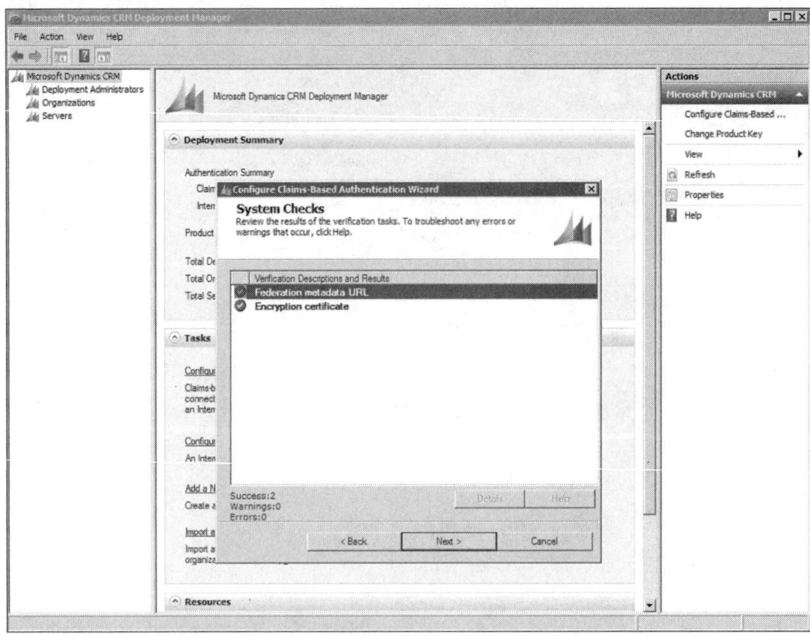

FIGURE 22.41 System requirements.

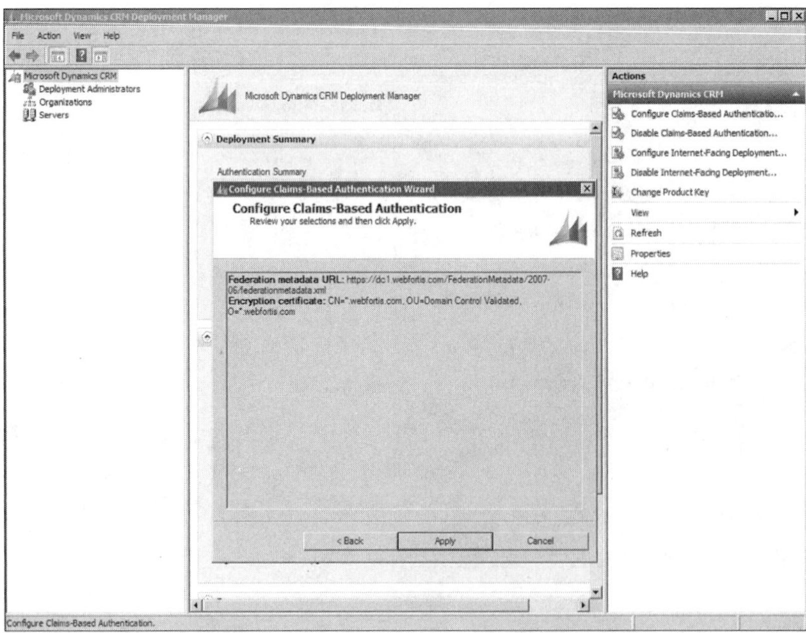

FIGURE 22.42 Review your selections.

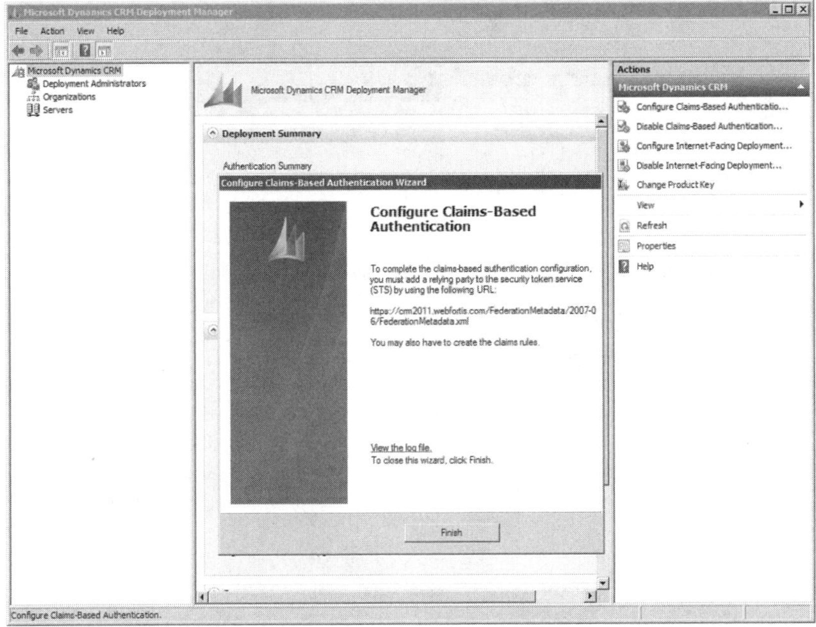

FIGURE 22.43 Wizard completed.

Add Relaying Party Trust on AD FS

After configuring Claims-Based Authentication on CRM, you will need to open the AD DFS application and add a relaying party trust. This is necessary for the AD FS to trust the CRM URLs uses by external users. Each organization has a unique URL that the AD FS needs to trust.

NOTE

If you have a multi-tenanted environment, every time you add a new organization you will need to manually update the relying part trust from the federation metadata if you want immediate access to your system via IFD, since ADFS only automatically updates this data every 24 hours. You can also do this programmatically or through PowerShell.

1. Open AD FS 2.0 by going to start administrative tools AD FS Management.

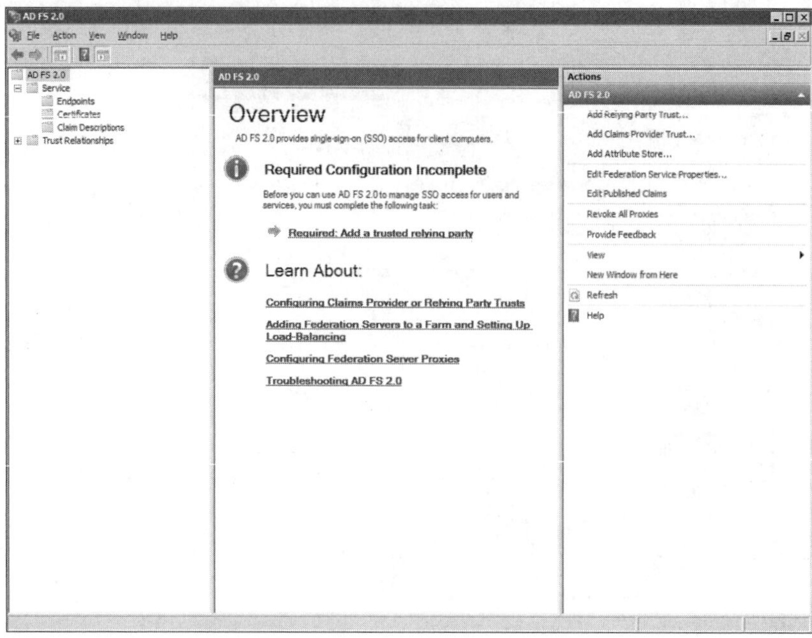

FIGURE 22.44 AD FS 2.0.

2. Click the Add Relaying Party Trust option that is on the Actions panel on the right. The Add Relaying Party Trust Wizard will open, as shown in Figure 22.45. You can also do this by expanding the Trust Relationships folder, right-clicking the Relaying Party Trust folder, and then selecting Add Relaying Party Trust from there.

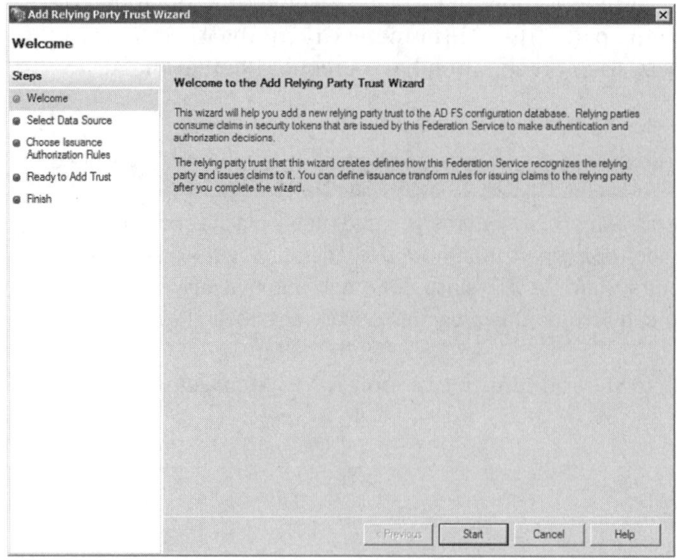

FIGURE 22.45 AD Relaying Party Trust Wizard.

3. Click on Start and in the select Data Source step; select Import data about the relaying party published online or on a local network, which would be similar to https://auth.webfortis.com/FederationMetadata/2007-06/FederationMetadata.xml.

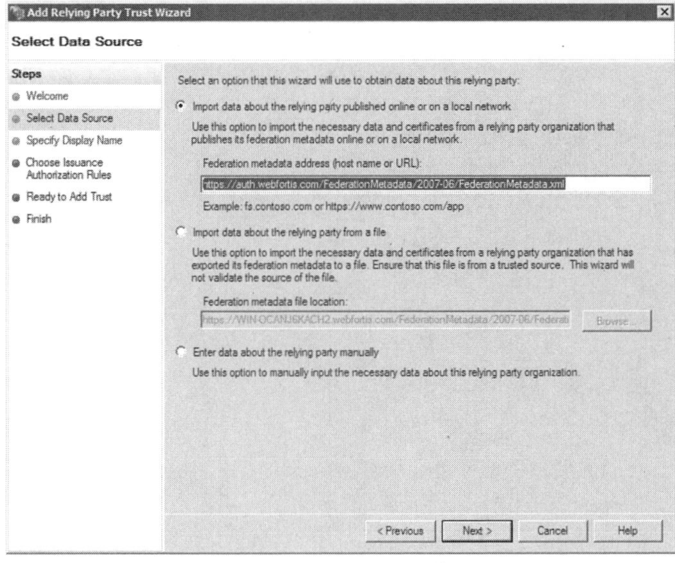

FIGURE 22.46 Select data source.

4. Click Next and enter a name for the display name.

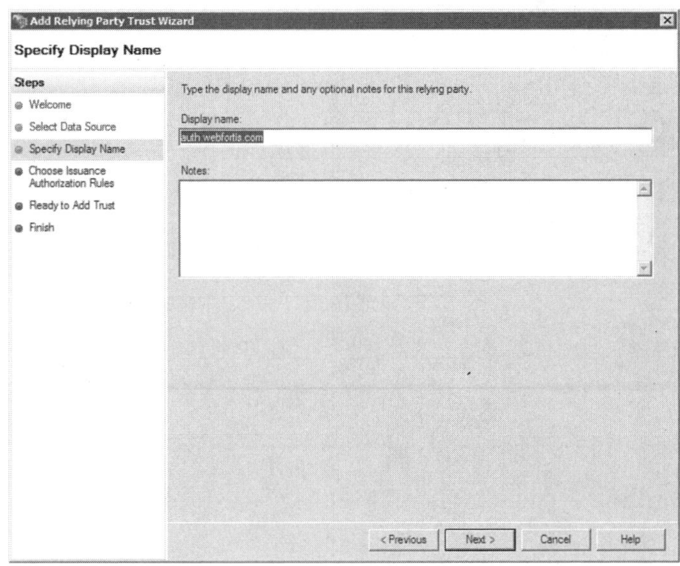

FIGURE 22.47 Specify a display name.

5. Click Next and select the first option that says Permit all users to access this relaying party.

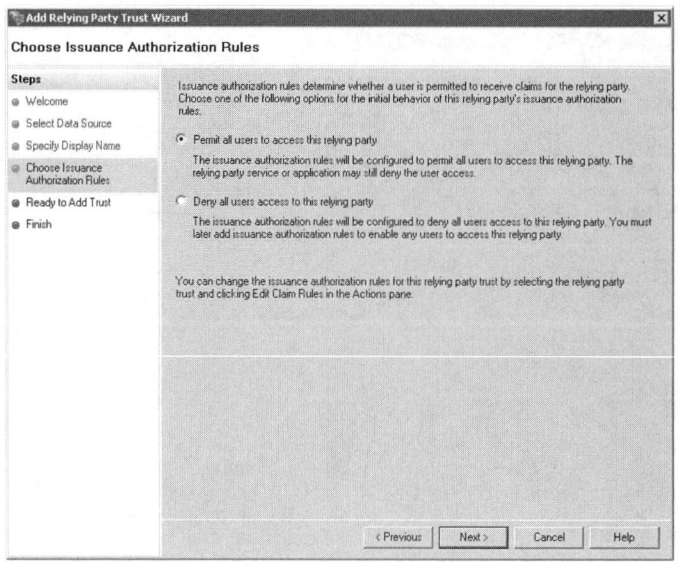

FIGURE 22.48 Choose issuance authorization rules.

6. Click Next to confirm the settings.

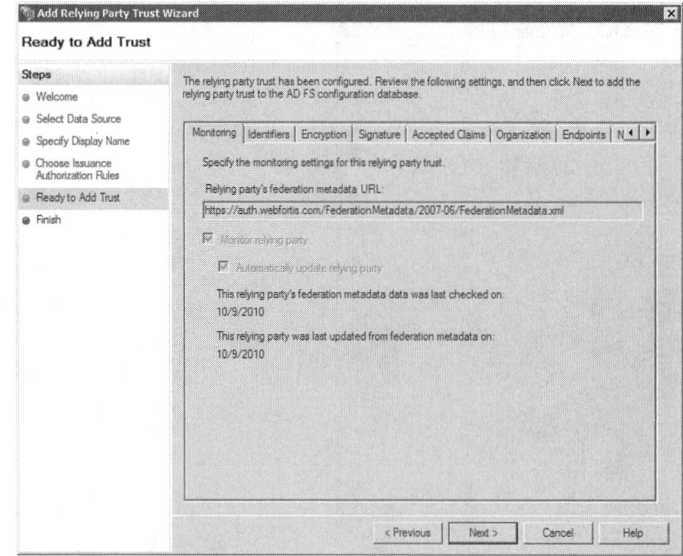

FIGURE 22.49 Ready to add trust.

7. Click Next to finish.

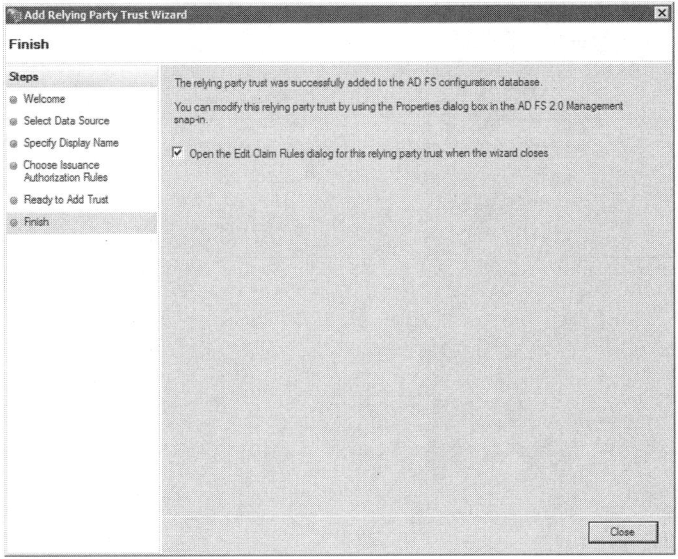

FIGURE 22.50 Finish.

8. Click Close.

When you click Close, the Edit Claim Rules dialog will open. Next, you need to complete the following steps to add a rule for this new relaying trusted party you created before (see Figure 22.51):

1. Click Add Rule (see Figure 22.52).
2. Select Pass Through or Filter an Incoming Claim and click Next (see Figure 22.53).
3. Enter a descriptive name for the claim rule and select UPN on incoming claim type.
4. Click Finish.
5. Create another rule for the primary SID, repeating the same steps as earlier but selecting the incoming type to Primary SID (see Figure 22.54).
6. Create another rule for the Windows account name, repeating the same steps as earlier but selecting the incoming type to Windows account name and using the Transaform an Incoming Claim rule template (see Figure 22.55).
7. At the end you should have three rules created, as shown in Figure 22.56.
8. Click OK to close the Edit Claim Rules dialog.
9. Now click the Claims Provider Trusts folder that is on the left, as shown in Figure 22.57.
10. Right-click the Active Directory item that is on the right and select Edit Claim Rules (see Figure 22.58).
11. When the Edit Claim Rules for Active Directory dialog appears, click the Add Rule button (see Figure 22.59).

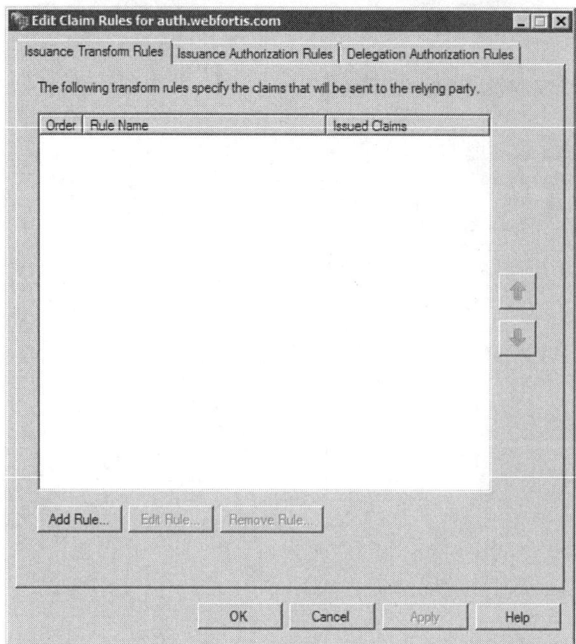

FIGURE 22.51 Edit Claim Rules for crm2011.webfortis.com dialog.

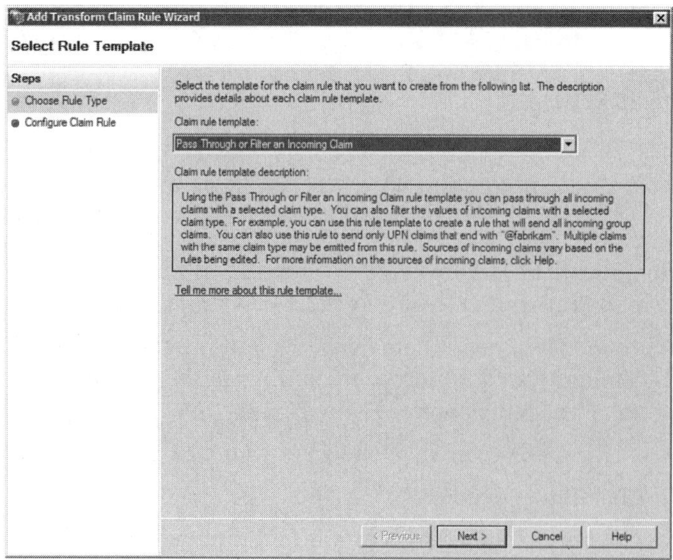

FIGURE 22.52 Select rule template.

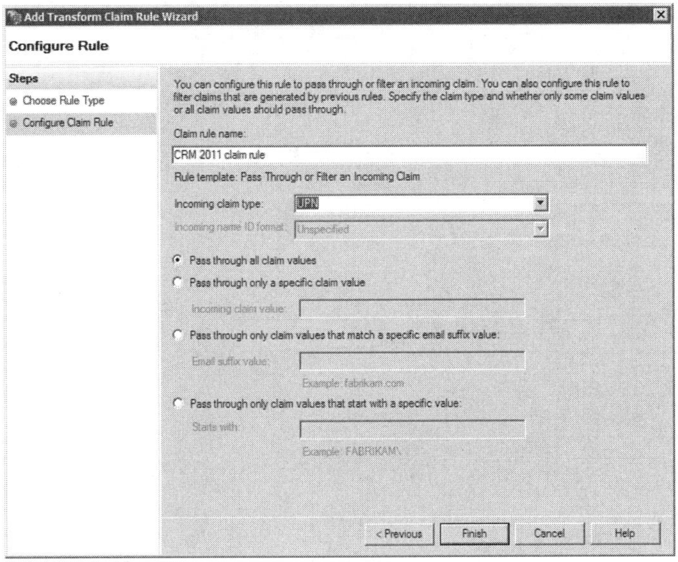

FIGURE 22.53 Configure rule for UPN.

12. In the Choose Rule Type step, leave the default option Send LDAP Attributes as Claims (see Figure 22.60).

13. Click Next and enter UPN in the claim rule name, select the attribute store to Active Directory, select the LDAP attribute to user-Principal-Name and the Outgoing Claim Type to UPN, as shown in Figure 22.61.

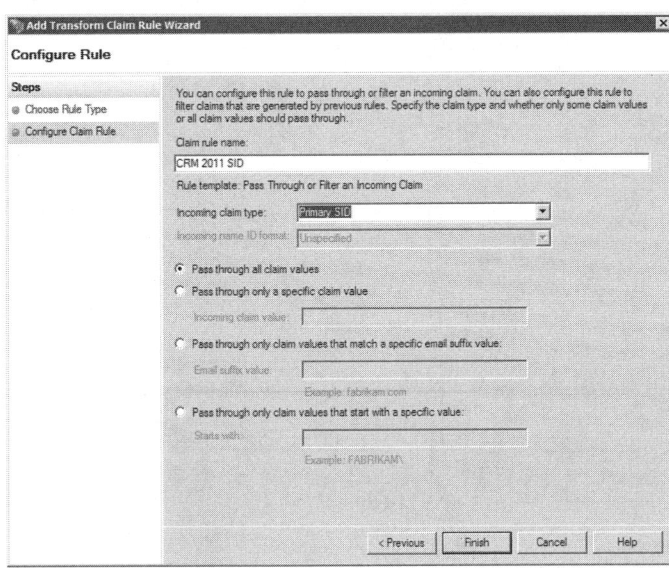

FIGURE 22.54 Configure rule for primary SID.

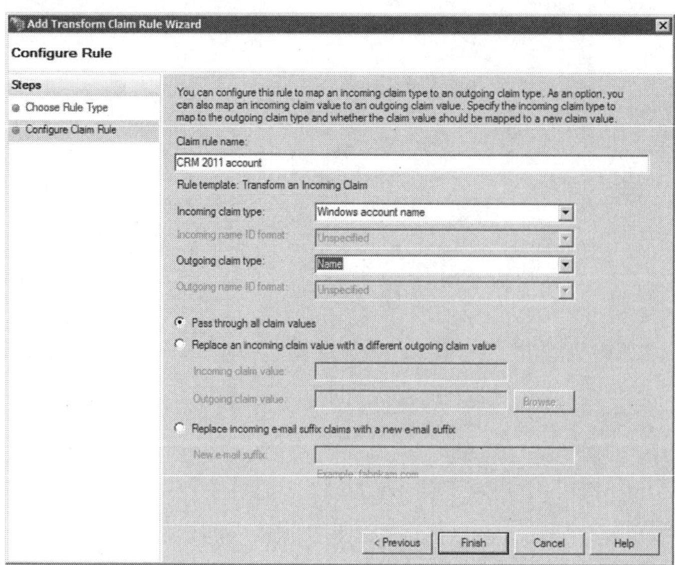

FIGURE 22.55 Configure Rule for Windows account name with Transform an Incoming Claim rule template.

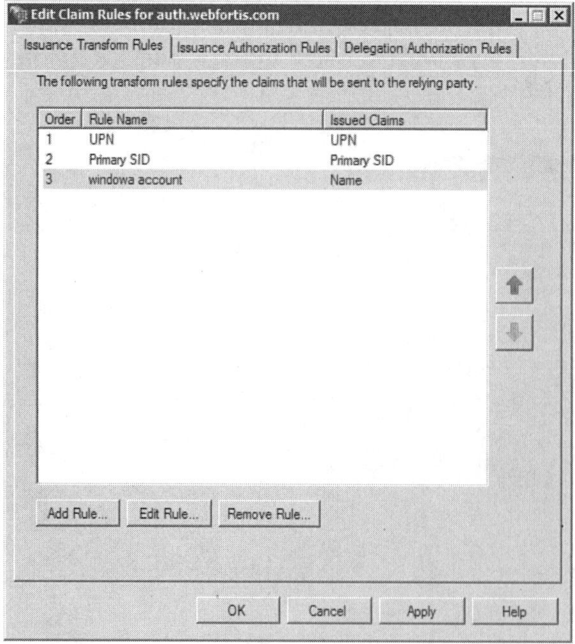

FIGURE 22.56 Three rules created.

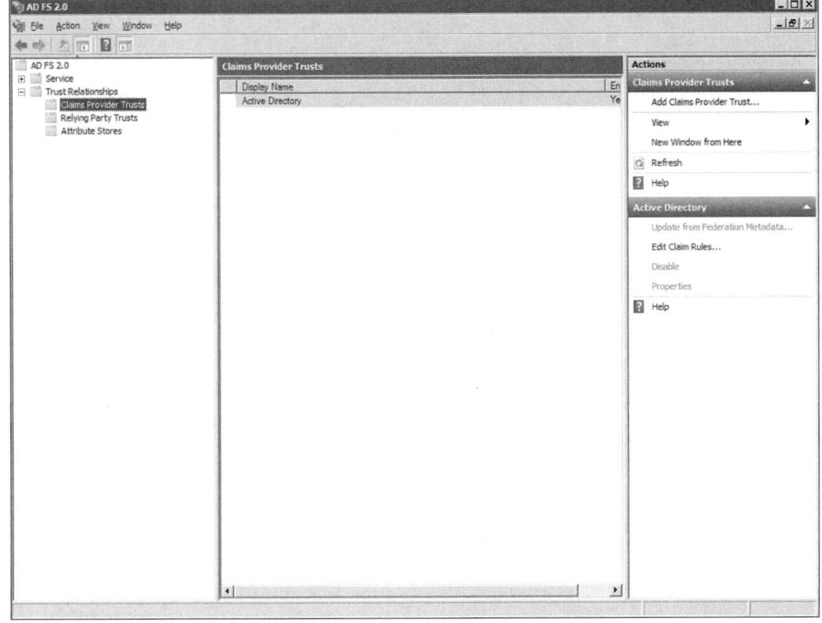

FIGURE 22.57 Claims Provider Trusts.

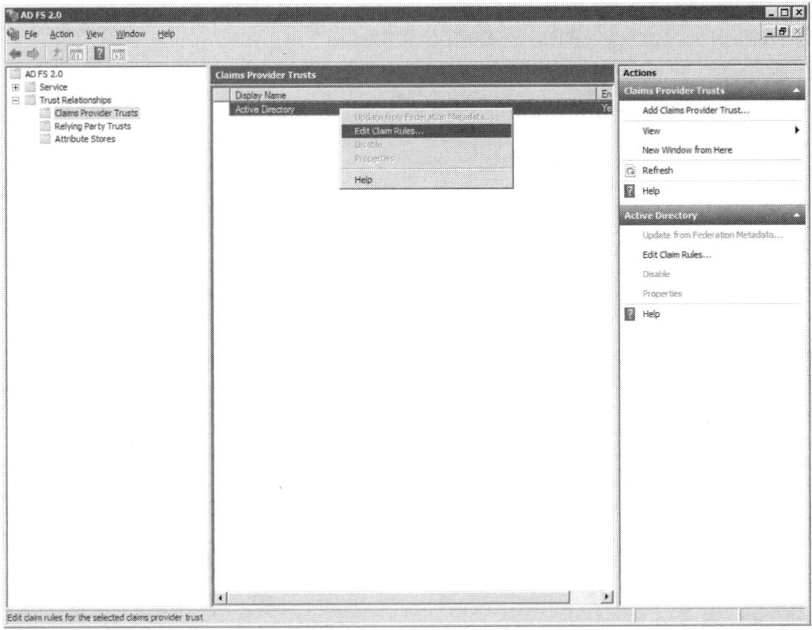

FIGURE 22.58 Edit Claim Rules.

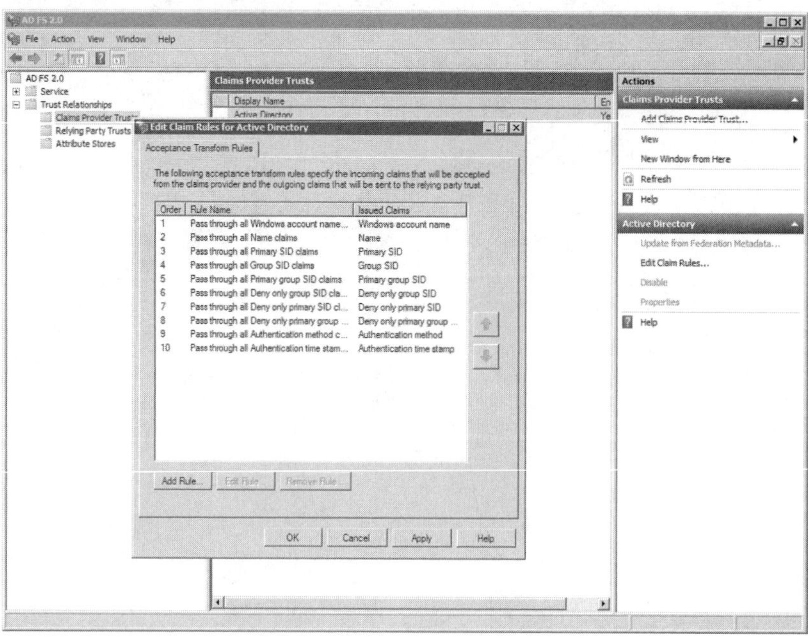

FIGURE 22.59 Adding new rule.

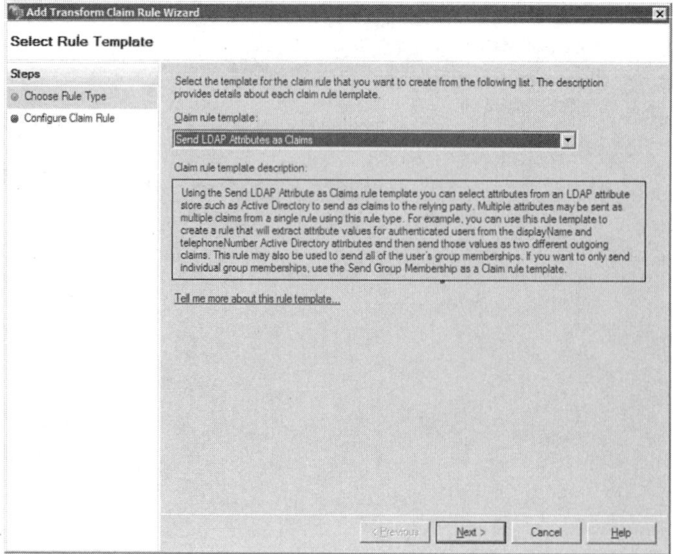

FIGURE 22.60 Adding new rule.

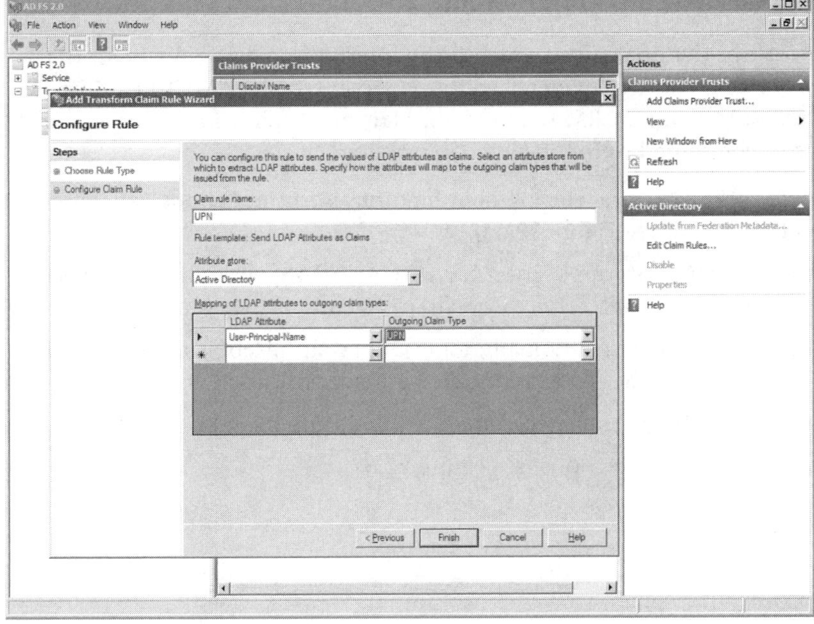

FIGURE 22.61 UPN Active Directory claim rule.

14. Click Finish to close this dialog. You should now have 11 rules for the Active Directory claims, as shown in Figure 22.62.

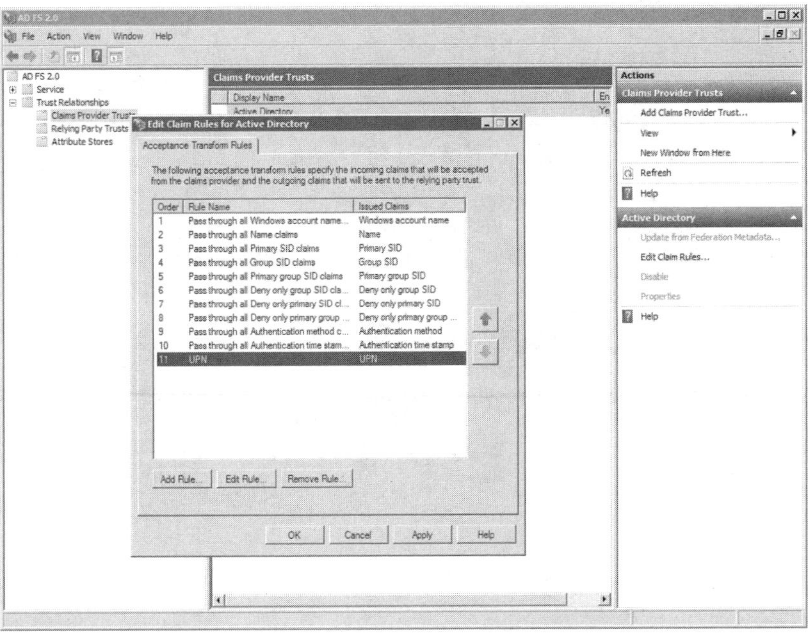

FIGURE 22.62 Eleven rules for Active Directory.

Configuring Internet-Facing Deployment

This section covers one of the final steps, which is the Internet-Facing Deployment (IFD) configuration. To configure this deployment, go to the server where CRM 2011 is installed and open the Microsoft Dynamics CRM Deployment Manager Application. Next, complete the following steps to configure Internet-facing deployment:

1. Click Configure Internet-Facing Deployment link that is in the Actions panel on the right to open the wizard (see Figure 22.63).
2. Click Next and enter the web application server domain, organization web service domain, and the discovery web service domain (see Figure 22.64).
3. Click Next and enter the external domain; for example, auth.webfortis.com. This is the domain address where the AD FS is installed for authentication (see Figure 22.65).
4. Click Next and verify the system checks are met (See Figure 22.66).
5. Click Next and review the selections (see Figure 22.67).

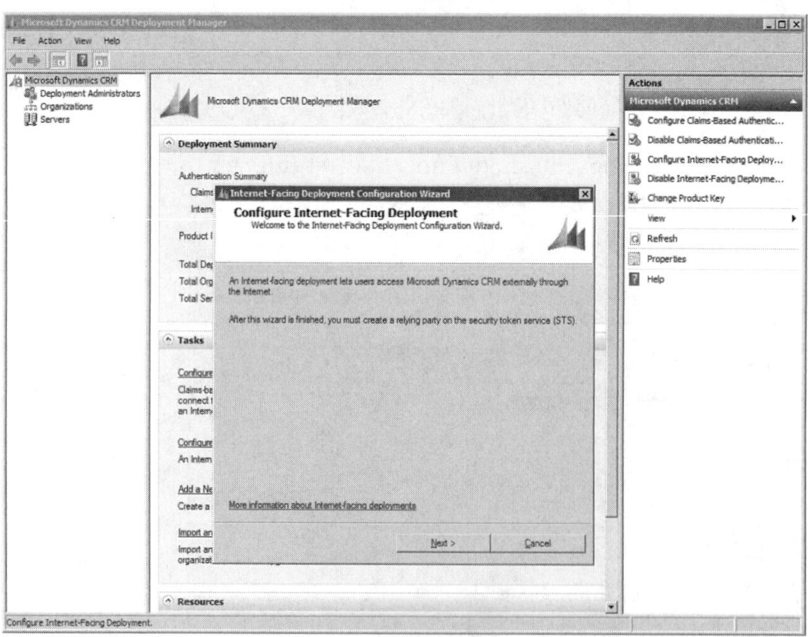

FIGURE 22.63 Configure Internet-Facing Deployment Wizard.

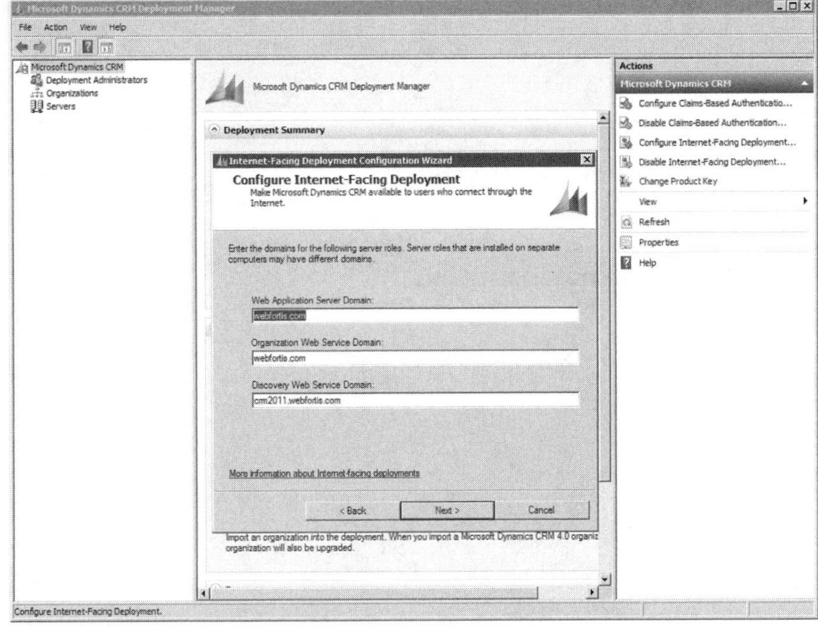

FIGURE 22.64 Configure server roles URL addresses.

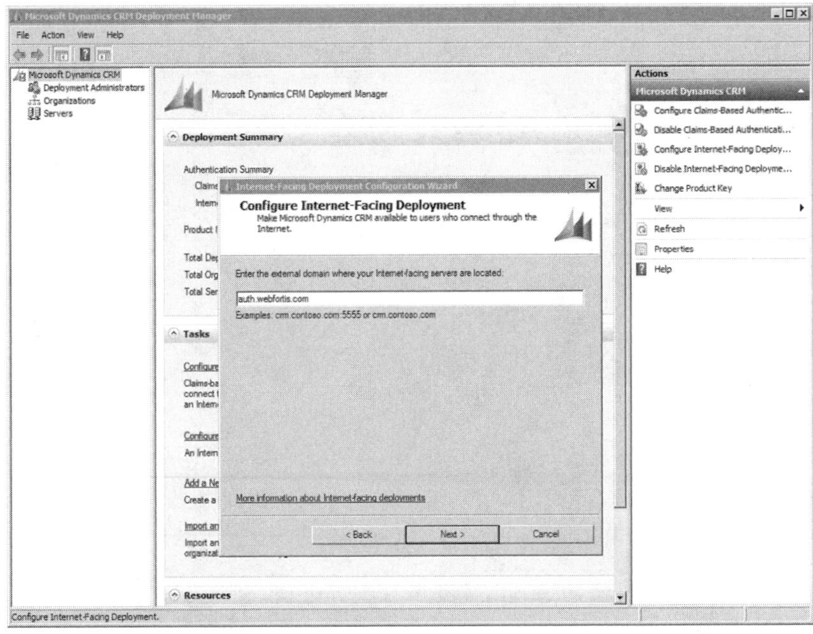

FIGURE 22.65 Configure external domain.

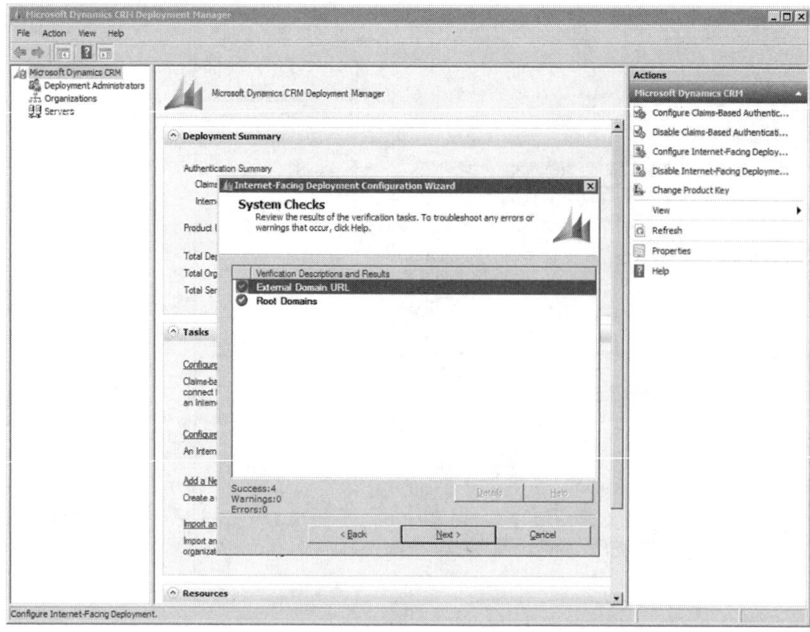

FIGURE 22.66 Verify system checks.

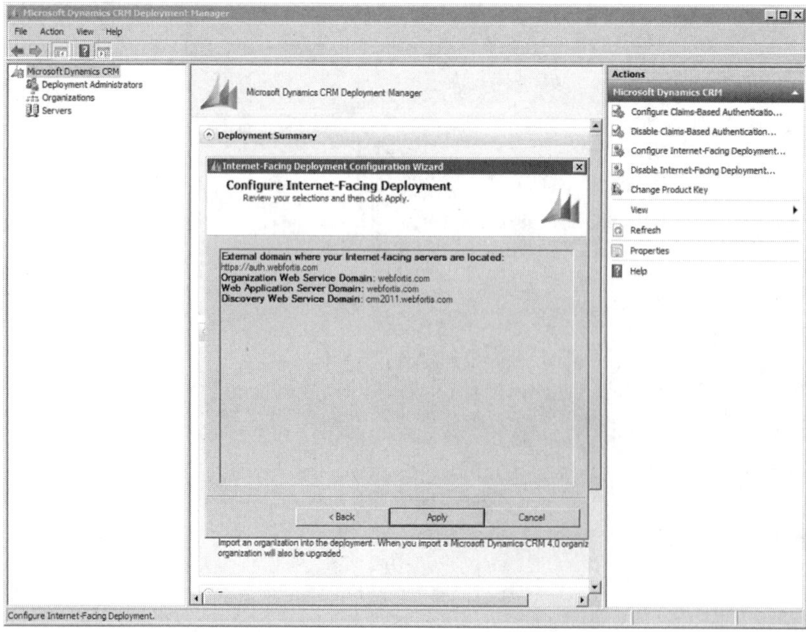

FIGURE 22.67 Review selections.

6. Clicking Apply will start the configurations. When they are done, you will see the results.

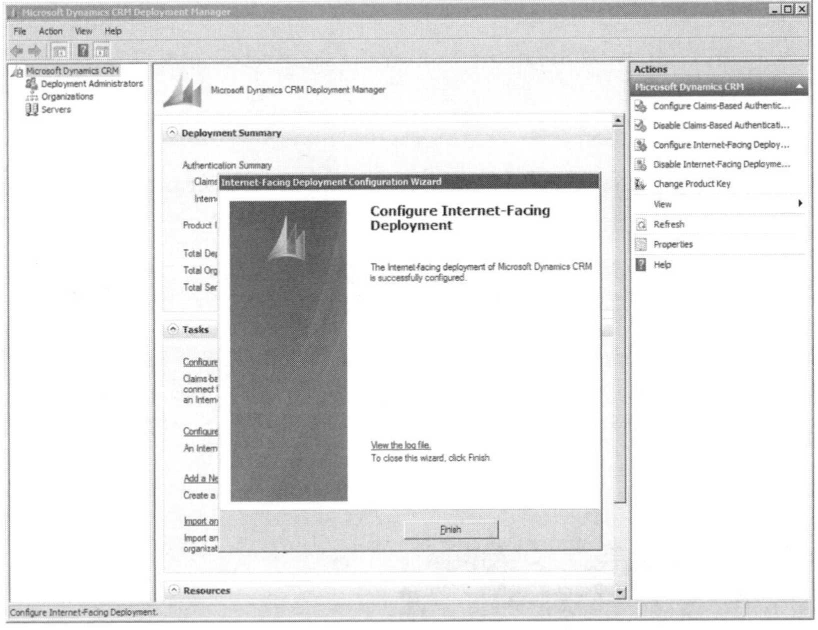

FIGURE 22.68 Wizard completed.

7. Click Finish to close the dialog.
8. Restart the IIS with the iisreset command prompt.

DNS Server Configurations

A very important consideration when implementing IFD is to configure the Domain Name Service (DNS) properly. Setup doesn't do this and the Forms Authentication page might not work without DNS properly configured. The DNS service is used to map a domain name to an IP address. Domains are mapped to IP addresses; for example, <www.domain name.com> equals 123.123.12.3. You can also add hosts below the domain as www, ftp, and so on, and map different IP addresses to them. An example of that might be <ftp.domain name.com> equals 123.123.12.4.

You must complete some necessary DNS configurations, and, depending on the DNS server you are using, the configurations could be different. You will see a sample in this section using the Windows DNS Server manager.

These configurations are required for every organization you will set up in Microsoft Dynamics CRM. If you are installing a version of Microsoft Dynamics CRM 2011, which supports multitenancy (in previous versions this was the Enterprise version), you must create a host entry in your DNS for each organization unless you use a wildcard host entry. This is because the IFD uses an URL in this format:

```
https://organizationName.CrmServerName.domainName.com.
```

If your domain name is webfortis.com, your server name is crm2011, and your organization name is Webfortis, this URL will be used:

https://webfortis.crm2011.webfortis.com.

If you have another organization with the name Test on the same server, it will be accessed using this URL

https://test.crm2011.webfortis.com.

You must configure your DNS so that crm2011.webfortis.com, webfortis.crm2011.webfortis.com, and test.crm2011.webfortis.com all point to the same IP address.

TIP

To verify the IP address resolved by DNS from a client computer, you can use the ping command from a command prompt window, as shown in Figure 22.69. Be sure to run this command internally on the network as most of the firewalls have this protocol blocked.

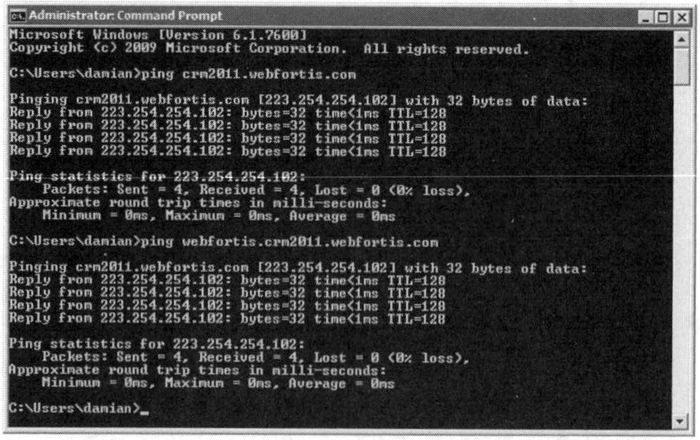

```
Administrator: Command Prompt
Microsoft Windows [Version 6.1.7600]
Copyright (c) 2009 Microsoft Corporation.  All rights reserved.

C:\Users\damian>ping crm2011.webfortis.com

Pinging crm2011.webfortis.com [223.254.254.102] with 32 bytes of data:
Reply from 223.254.254.102: bytes=32 time<1ms TTL=128
Reply from 223.254.254.102: bytes=32 time<1ms TTL=128
Reply from 223.254.254.102: bytes=32 time<1ms TTL=128
Reply from 223.254.254.102: bytes=32 time<1ms TTL=128

Ping statistics for 223.254.254.102:
    Packets: Sent = 4, Received = 4, Lost = 0 (0% loss),
Approximate round trip times in milli-seconds:
    Minimum = 0ms, Maximum = 0ms, Average = 0ms

C:\Users\damian>ping webfortis.crm2011.webfortis.com

Pinging crm2011.webfortis.com [223.254.254.102] with 32 bytes of data:
Reply from 223.254.254.102: bytes=32 time<1ms TTL=128
Reply from 223.254.254.102: bytes=32 time<1ms TTL=128
Reply from 223.254.254.102: bytes=32 time<1ms TTL=128
Reply from 223.254.254.102: bytes=32 time<1ms TTL=128

Ping statistics for 223.254.254.102:
    Packets: Sent = 4, Received = 4, Lost = 0 (0% loss),
Approximate round trip times in milli-seconds:
    Minimum = 0ms, Maximum = 0ms, Average = 0ms

C:\Users\damian>_
```

FIGURE 22.69 Verifying hosts with the ping command.

If you don't specify the organization name in the URL—for example, http://crm2011.webfortis.com—the Microsoft Dynamics CRM server redirects users to the default organization URL which on this version is the first organization that was created when deployment. In our example, this is https://webfortis.crm2011.webfortis.com/, assuming that Webfortis is configured as the default organization.

If you don't want to use a long URL, you can just avoid using the server name in the sdkrootdomain and webapplicationrootdomain parameters, and enter only the domain name there. For example, if you use webfortis.com, users would access the CRM by going to http://webfortis.webfortis.com and http://test.webfortis.com instead of http://webfortis.crmserver.webfortis.com and http://test.crmserver.webfortis.com. This is intended for use by domains with names such as crmhosted.com or mscrmsolutions.com, so the final URL for the organization will make more sense, as in http://webfortis.mscrmsolutions.com.

Disabling IFD

You can disable the IFD by going to the CRM Deployment Manager and selecting Disable Internet-Facing Deployment. You will be asked for a confirmation after clicking on this link. Click Yes to confirm, and then click disable Claims-Based Authentication. When you are asked for confirmation, click Yes again.

Working with IFD and Multiple Organizations

Only the Microsoft Dynamics CRM 2011 Server supports multitenancy or multiple organizations while the workgroup version does not.

For example, an organization with the name Brown would be able to access Microsoft Dynamics CRM at https://brown.crm2011.webfortis.com, and the organization Webfortis would be able to access https://webfortis.crm2011.webfortis.com from the same server.

The CRM web application is the same with or without IFD enabled. The only exception is that the user will see a Sign Out link below the organization name when IFD is enabled (see Figure 22.70).

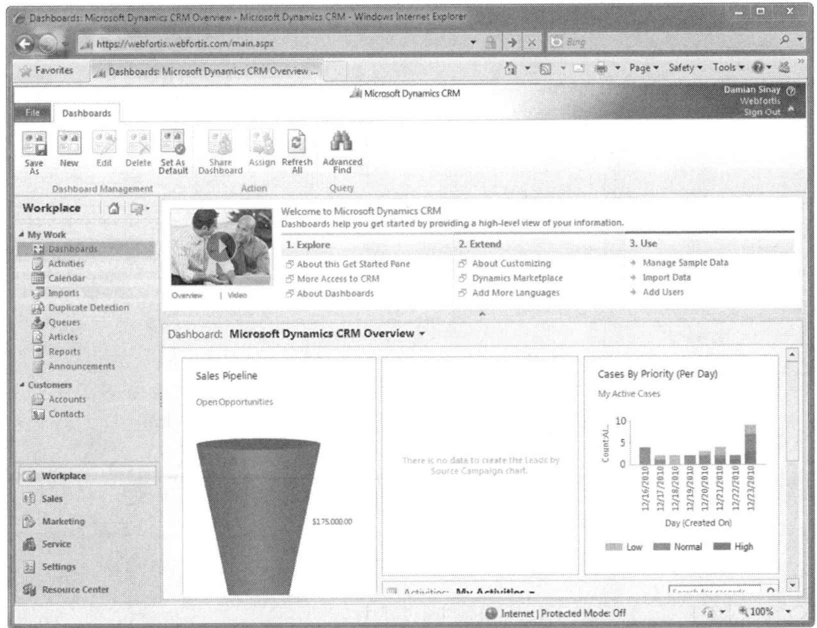

FIGURE 22.70 Sign Out link on IFD.

Summary

This chapter showed you how to expose a Dynamics CRM Server to the Internet by configuring the IFD feature so that users can authenticate via Claims Based Authentication over the Internet. We reviewed all the required components and configurations necessary to set up this feature, as well as how to enable and disabled the IFD on a Dynamics CRM 2011 installation.

CHAPTER 23

Customizing Entities

IN THIS CHAPTER

One of the most powerful features of Microsoft Dynamics CRM is that you can customize (or configure) all entities, such as Accounts, Contacts, and Opportunities.

Navigate to the main entities customization screen by going to Settings and Customizations, and you will see that you can customize entities in several ways (see Figure 23.1).

You can customize existing entities or create new entities. This version of CRM 2011 adds new ways to customize an entity without having to go this Setting area but going to any entity and either opening a Form of an entity and clicking on the customization tab on the ribbon will be enough to start making changes.

Customization Principles

The most basic principle is that Microsoft Dynamics CRM is built in an *n*-tier model with the user interface layers (web client and Outlook client) on the top, the application layer in the middle, and the database layer represented by the SQL Server on the bottom. Therefore, you should always make the customizations following the principles described in this chapter.

▶ Refer to Chapter 16, "Solution Concepts," to review some basic principles related to customizations.

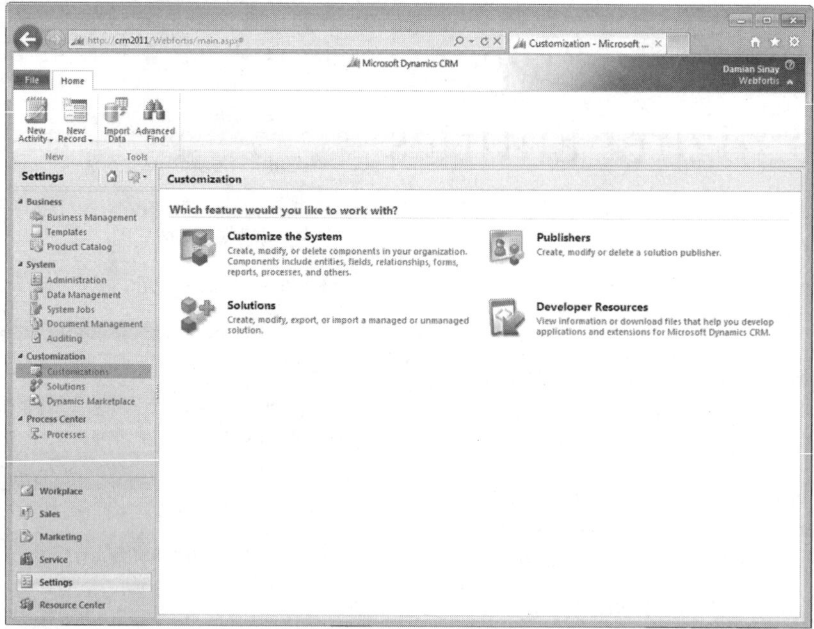

FIGURE 23.1 Customization interface.

CAUTION

If you are an expert SQL database administrator or developer, you might be tempted to create database triggers or stored procedures, or change the database schema. However, we *strongly* recommend that you *not* touch the database directly in any situation. Doing so is considered an unsupported customization and might cause the application to break or fail.

NOTE

Two kinds of customization characteristics exist when working with Microsoft Dynamics CRM: supported and unsupported. We outline only supported customizations that follow Microsoft best practices and will generally not fail when the product is upgraded. Unsupported customizations might perform any function, but they fall outside the range of Microsoft's testing when considering upgrades, database schema changes, and support rollups. Unsupported customizations can have the following results:

- Service packs might fail, break, or not install.
- Upgrades to the product might cause unexpected results or fail entirely.
- The application or database might become unstable and fail to work.

MS CRM Entity Model

Similar to an XML document, all objects in Microsoft Dynamics CRM are treated as an entity or an attribute. Account, Contacts, Activities, and so on are all entities in the CRM system, and every entity has attributes, related to the entity, which are now called *fields* on this new version of CRM. An example of this is Account and Account Name. Account is an entity and Account Name is a field (see Figure 23.2). This new version now enables us to create entities of type of activity, which was not allowed on previous versions.

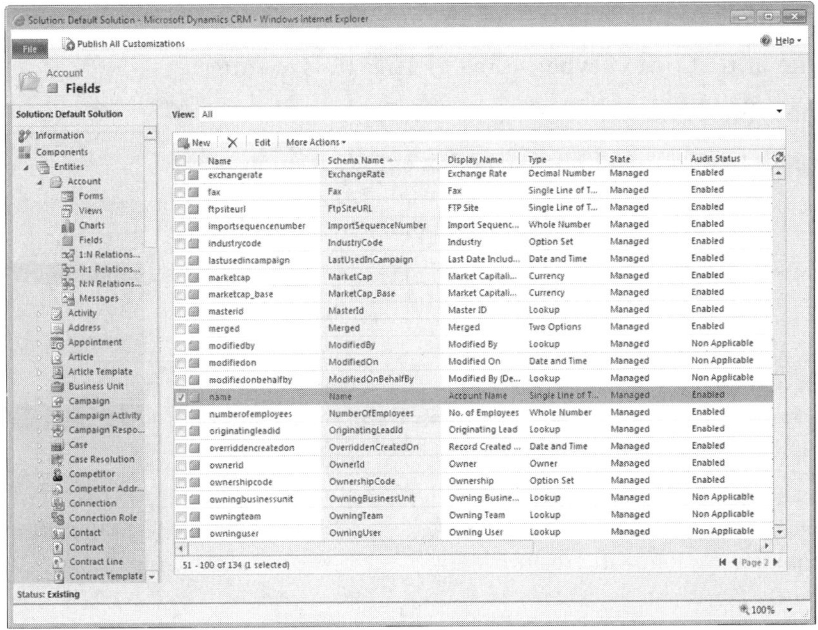

FIGURE 23.2 Fields of the Account entity

Fields

Fields can be of the following property types:

- **Single Line of text (nvarchar type)**—Used for small texts or strings.
- **Option Set (picklist type)**—Used for drop-downs or combo boxes, with a limited set of fixed options. This is what was called picklist on previous versions.

> **TIP**
>
> Because the picklist can display only simple, nondynamic options, you might want to use a new custom entity if you need something that is more dynamic or complex than the options provided.

Option sets on this new version of CRM are much more powerful and reusable than previous versions. You can reuse the same option set on more than one entity.

- **Two Options (bit type)**—Used for Boolean values such as yes or no
- **Whole Number (int type)**—Used for numbers
- **Floating Point Number (float type)**—Used for numbers with decimals with floating point
- **Decimal Number (decimal type)**—Used for numbers with decimals
- **Currency (money type)**—Used for amounts
- **Multiple Line of text (ntext type)**—Used for large texts or strings
- **Date and Time (datetime type)**—Used for dates and times
- **Lookup (lookup type)**—Used for lookup other entities relationships

Depending on which type you use, option sets have different properties.

Entities are associated with other entities via a customization referred to as a *relationship*.

Relationships

Not to be confused with relationships/connections as found on the interface level, relationships on the schema level are programmatic.

That being said, relationships are very user-friendly; you don't need to be a database system administrator expert to use and configure relationships between entities. Microsoft Dynamics CRM supports the following relationships:

- 1:*N* relationships (one to many)
- *N*:1 relationships (many to one)
- *N*:*N* relationships (many to many)

You can add as many relationships as you want and can also add more than one relationship to the same entity. For example, you can have a custom entity called Customer and add two fields called Primary Contact and Secondary Contact—both related to the entity Contacts.

Finally, another feature to relationships is the ability to relate an entity to itself, which is referred as *self-referential*. Using this type of relationship, you can use any type of relationship (1:N, N:1 or N:N) to relate an entity to itself.

1:*N* Relationships

Figure 23.3 displays the window where you can create a new 1:*N* relationship. With this type of relationship, the primary entity is the one you are customizing. For example, if you are working with the Account entity, you could use this type of relationship to specify the primary account for another entity, such as Contacts, for which the custom field defined by this relationship will contain only one account.

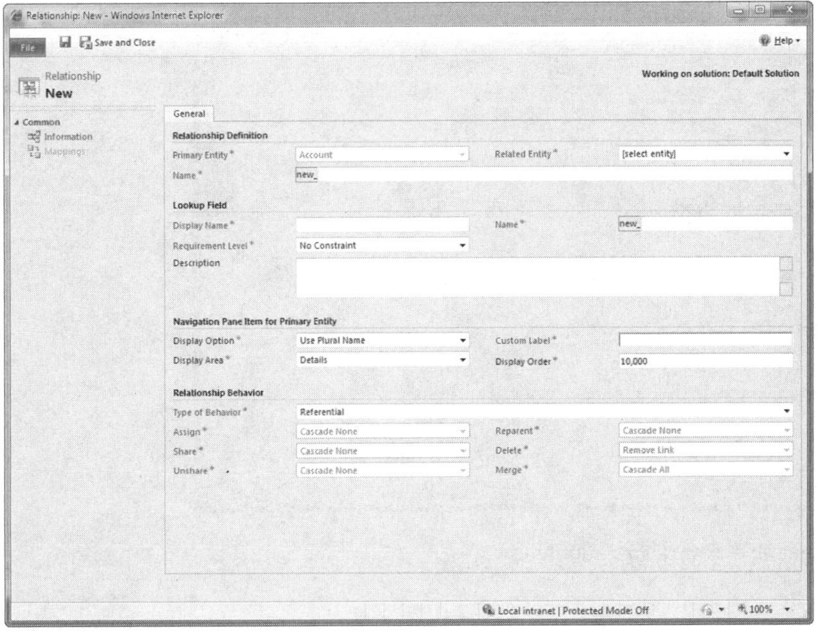

FIGURE 23.3 Creating a new 1: N relationship.

N:1 Relationships

With this type of relationship, the primary entity is the one you select. Therefore, the entity you are customizing is the related entity. For example, if you wanted a Contact to have multiple Accounts associated with it, you would apply this relationship to the Account entity.

N:*N* Relationships

With this type of relationship, there is not one primary entity and another secondary or related entity because they act as both types. For example, you might want to have one Contact related to many Accounts or one Contact related to many Contacts. In a real situation, you could have a Contact with a new person who works for two companies, and each company might have many Contacts apart from this one.

Relationship Behavior

For N:1 and 1:N relationships there are settings for the relationship behavior, also called *cascading rules*, which apply to the following operations:

- Assign
- Share

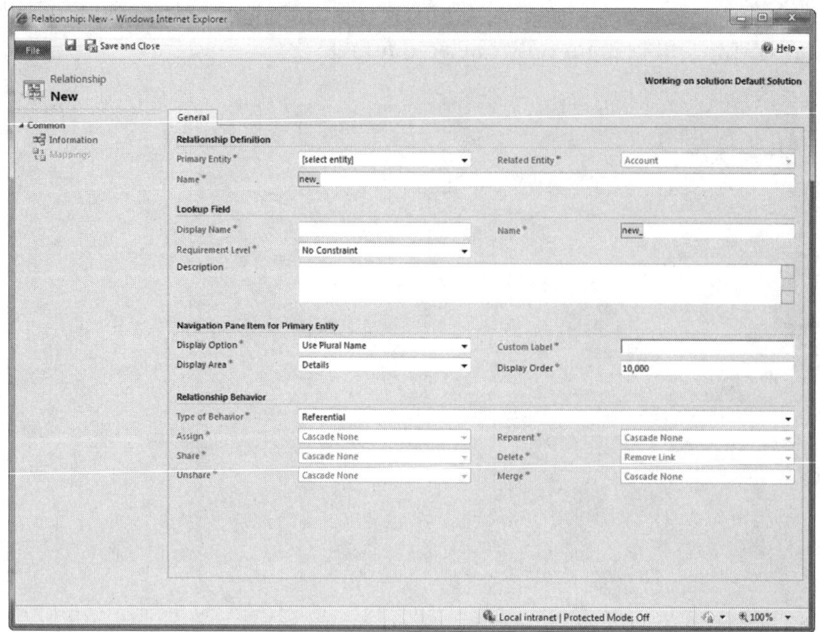

FIGURE 23.4 Creating a new N:1 relationship.

- Unshare
- Reparent
- Delete
- Merge

As shown in Figure 23.4, the Type of Behavior drop-down contains four options:

- Parental
- Referential
- Referential, Restrict Delete
- Configurable Cascading

The first three options are templates, and the last option Configurable Cascading allows you to configure the cascading manually for each operation.

The first four operations, Assign, Share, Unshare, and Reparent, shares these same cascading types:

- **Cascade All**—This option affects the current entity record and its related entity records. So, the operation is performed on both entities.

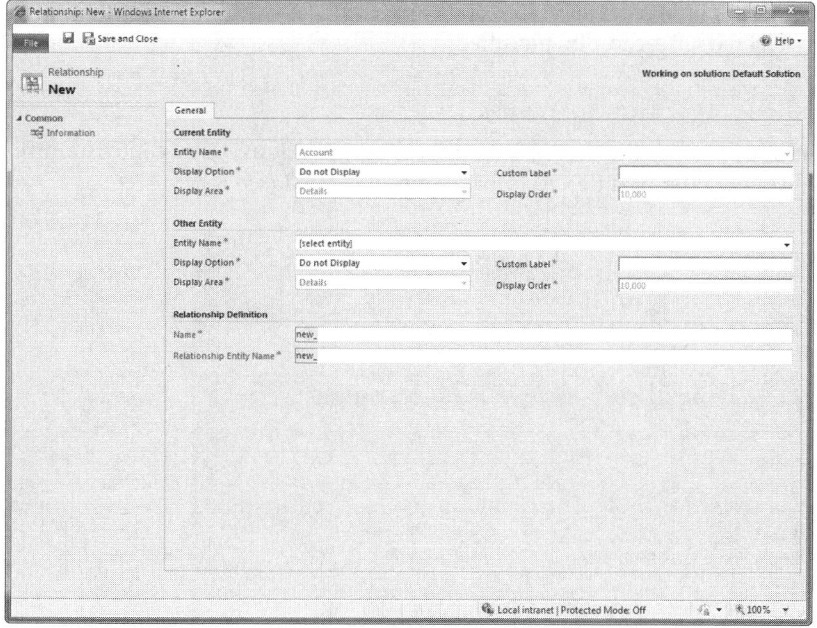

FIGURE 23.5 Creating a new N:N relationship.

- **Cascade Active**—This option affects the current entity record and its related entity records that have a status of Active.
- **Cascade User-Owned**—This option affects the current entity record and its related entity records that are owned by the user who is performing the operation only.
- **Cascade None**—This option affects only the current entity without affecting the related entity records.

The Delete operation has different cascading options as follows:

- **Cascade All**—This option is the same as explained for the other operations with the consideration that if you have a relationship 1:N between Account and Contact and you have one account record with 10 contacts related, when you delete the account, all 10 contacts will be also deleted.
- **Remove Link**—Using the preceding example, if you delete the account record, the contacts won't be deleted but the link between the contacts to the account will be removed.
- **Restrict**—Using the earlier example, you won't be able to delete the account until you delete all the related contacts manually first. Only when the account doesn't have any related records can it be deleted.

The Merge operation will change between Cascade None and Cascade All, depending on the primary entity selected, and can't be modified.

Messages

Messages display information to the user based on a variety of actions. Users can customize these messages to display richer or different information, if desired (see Figure 23.6).

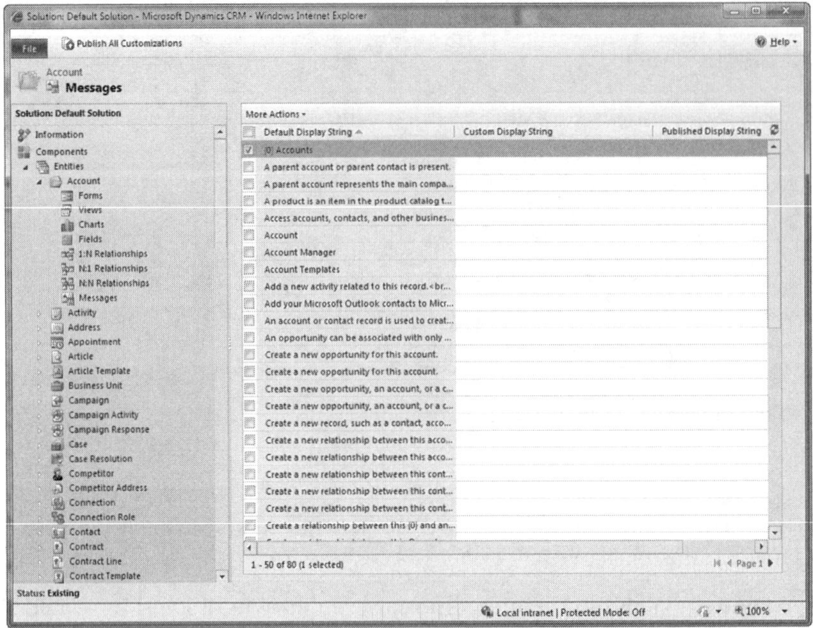

FIGURE 23.6 Message customizations.

Basic Customizations

Basic customizations are customizations to Microsoft Dynamics CRM that don't require any knowledge of programming or database design and configuration. Basic customizations include showing and hiding controls on a form, and hiding or showing columns in a view.

To make this type of customization, go to the entity you want to customize and go to the Forms or Views node in the left bar inside the Details section (see Figure 23.7).

Form Customizations

New and welcome features of CRM 2011 are that an entity now supports more than one form, and the default main and mobile forms can't be deleted. With this new version, you can create other forms with fewer or more fields displayed and assign them to specific CRM roles. This means that you can create another form if you want to show different fields for different users or roles.

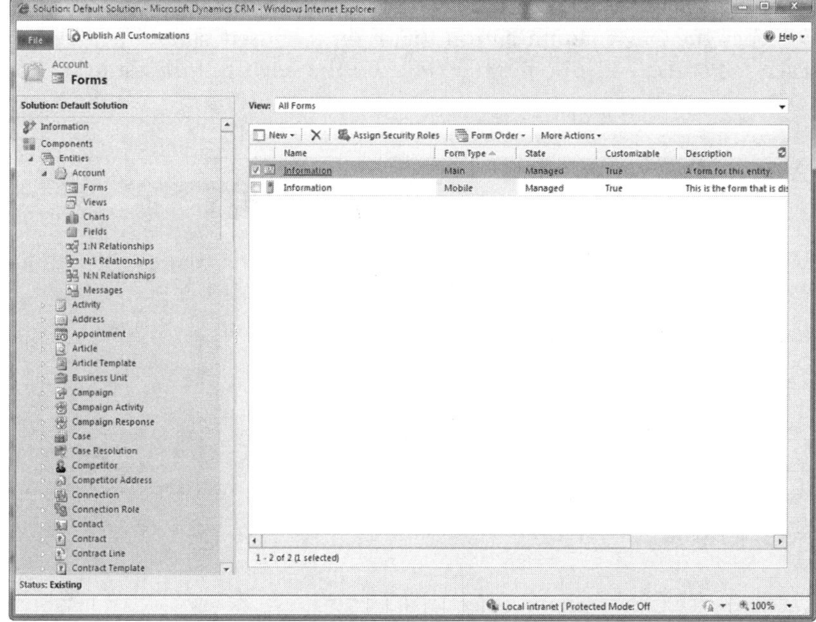

FIGURE 23.7 Forms and views customizations.

You can perform the following customizations to a form:

- Add, remove, or move tabs
- Add, remove, or move sections
- Add, remove, or move fields
- Add, remove, or move IFRAMEs
- Add, remove, or move notes
- Add, remove, or move spacer
- Add, remove, or move subgrids
- Add, remove, or move web resources (especially useful for images or custom pages)
- Edit the form navigation
- Change form properties

Add, Remove, or Move Tabs

The tabs in CRM 2011 behave different than the previous versions even though they are still called tabs, the tabs names are now displayed on the side navigation bar as links pointed to bookmarks in the form as all the tabs and fields controls are contained in the same form than can be also accessed using the scrollbar. This version enables you to add as many tabs as you want; there is no more limitation of a maximum of eight tabs as it used to have in CRM 4. Figure 23.8 shows a for with lot of new tabs with the label Tab, added to the form after you click the One Column button that is on the Insert tab of the Ribbon in the Tab group. Each tab is also added to the tree node on the sidebar of the form.

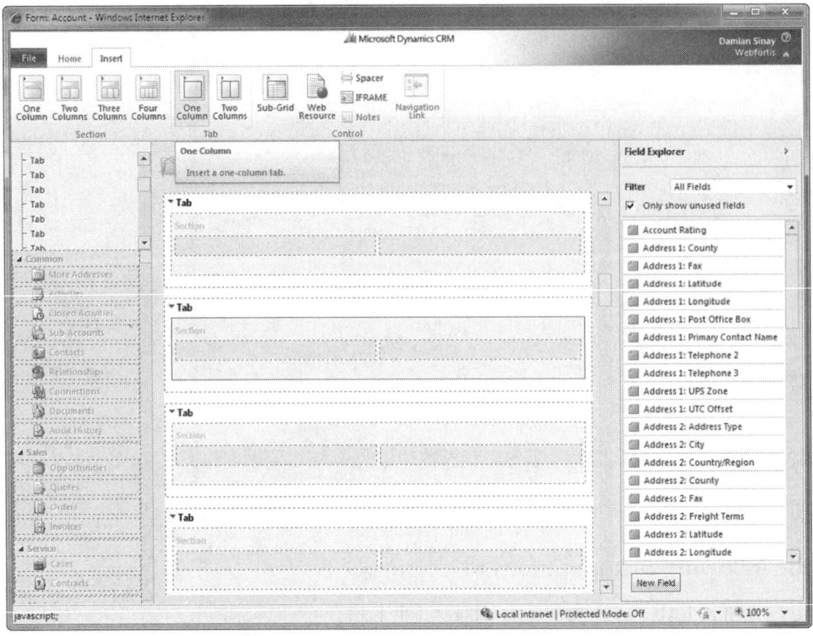

FIGURE 23.8 New custom tabs added called Tab.

As opposed to previous versions, now every time you add a new tab it will also add a new section inside the new tab.

Add, Remove, or Move Sections

Sections are used to group controls of related fields. The sections must be within a tab. To add a new section, click the buttons that are in the Insert tab under the Section group. When you double-click the new added section, you will be able to see the section properties (see Figure 23.9).

You can choose whether you want to have a label displaying the section name, and you can also specify the width of the field area, as shown in Figure 23.9.

You also have some limited layout options, as shown in Figure 23.10.

TIP

To move a section from one tab to another, just drag and drop the section.

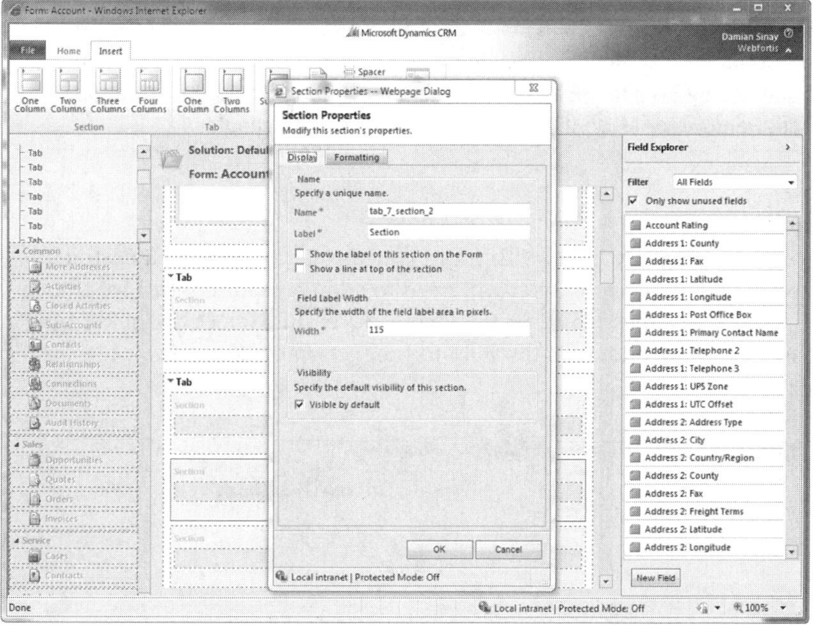

FIGURE 23.9 Adding a new section to the tab.

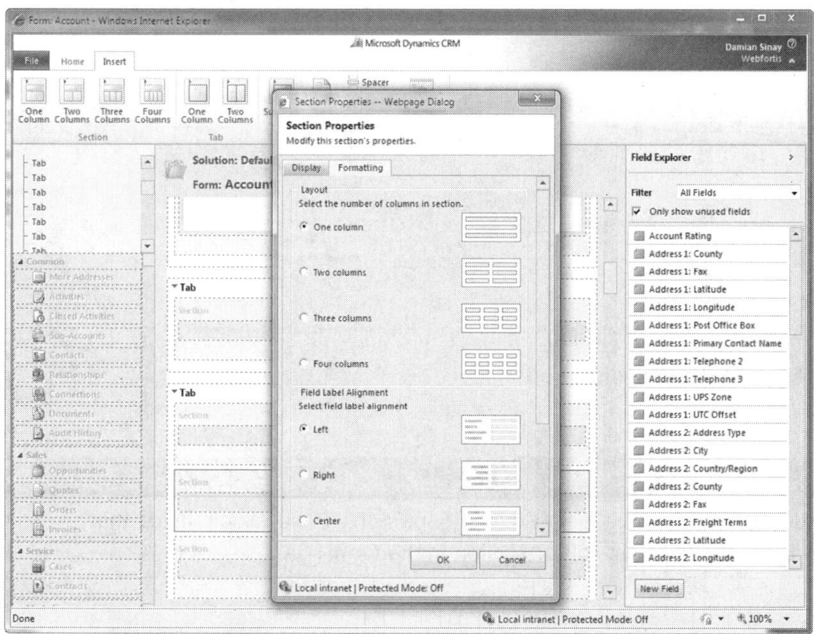

FIGURE 23.10 Selecting the layout.

NOTE

If the predefined layouts don't match your requirements, consider developing a custom page in ASP.NET and adding an IFRAME to display your custom page inside the form as detailed in the Add, Remove, or Move IFRAMEs section later in this chapter.

Add, Remove, or Move Fields

Fields are used to display the entity fields with input controls; if you created a custom field, as described earlier in this chapter, you will need to add an input control for that field to allow users enter the values. To add a field to the form, just select the field from the Field Explorer list, and drag and drop the field to the section or tab you want.

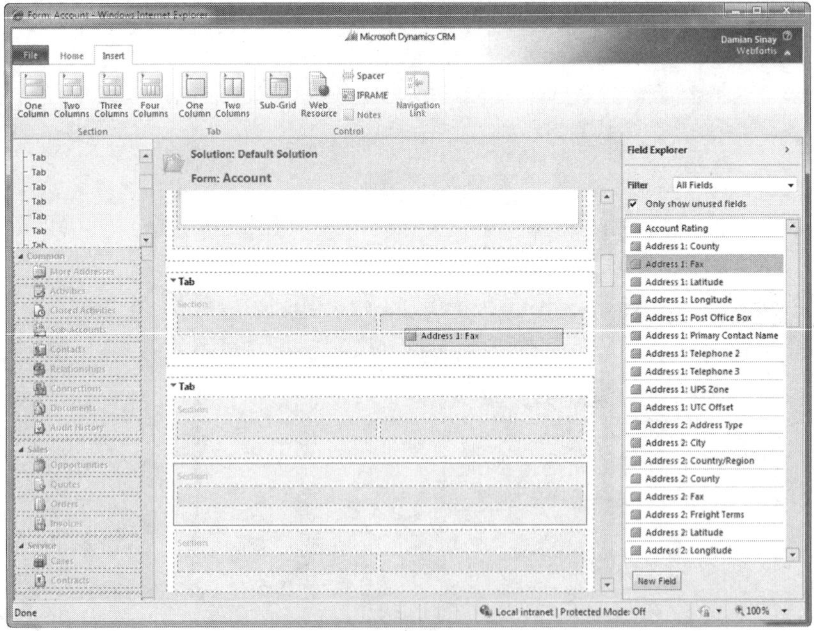

FIGURE 23.11 Adding fields to be displayed.

NOTE

To avoid adding duplicate fields, the Field Explorer shows only the available fields that have not already been added to any tab or section in the form.

You can also select the section where you want to place the field and go to the Field Explorer and double-click the field you want—it will be added to the selected section (see Figure 23.12).

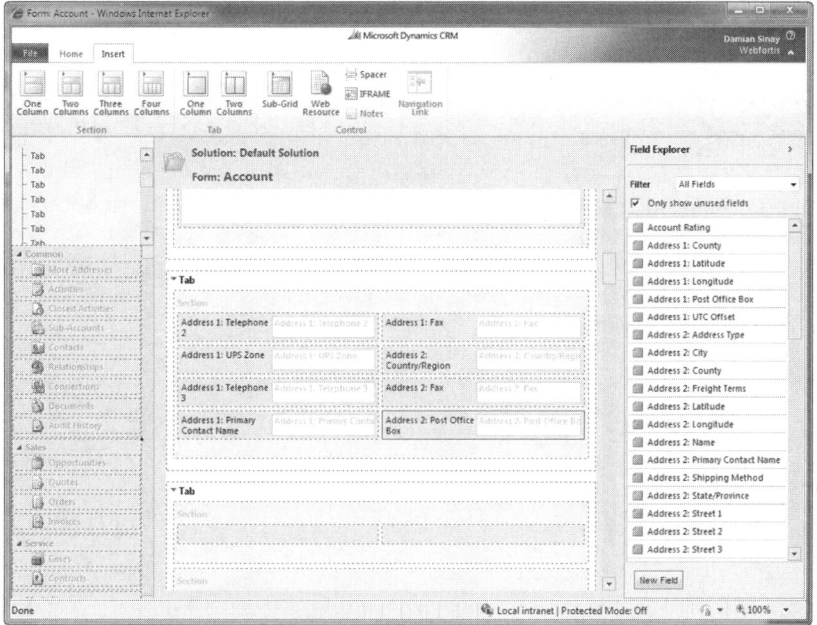

FIGURE 23.12 Fields added to the section.

TIP

You can drag and drop to move a field to any place inside the section. You can also add fields to the header or footer of a form, which will be always visible regardless of the tab the user has selected. This is a very nice feature available in the new version. Be sure you select the Header button that is on the Home tab on the Ribbon to be able to add fields on the header.

NOTE

This version also enables you to customize the navigation links when you click on the navigation button on the Ribbon. Change the navigation links and having fields displayed on a header/footer on previous versions required complex JavaScript added to the form load event—this is no longer needed. Be sure to take this into account when migrating customizations from old versions.

Add, Remove, or Move IFRAMEs

You can use IFRAMEs to display custom applications or pages inside the form. This is extremely helpful when you need to use advanced input/output controls that are not included in the CRM controls toolset. Examples include a complex grid, a picture control, or a movie control integrated with Flash or Silverlight. When you click the IFRAME button, you get the dialog in Figure 23.13, which requires the name for the IFRAME as well as the URL of your application.

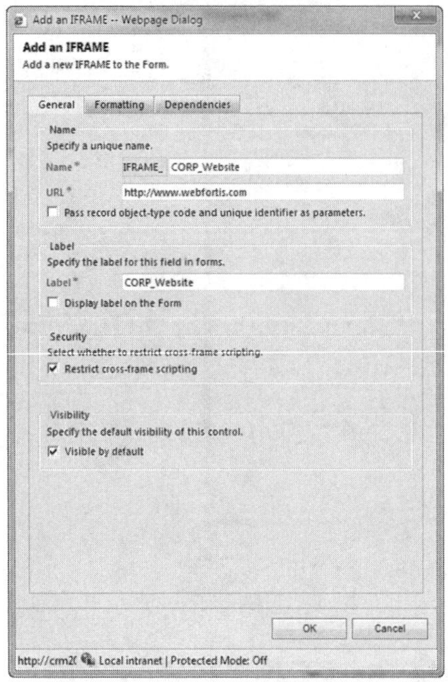

FIGURE 23.13 Adding an IFRAME.

For example, we are going to enter CORP_Website in the Name property and http://www.webfortis.com in the URL property. When adding the IFRAME with the default values, you will see the IFRAME inserted in the form, as shown in Figure 23.14.

Most of the times you want the IFRAME to expand vertically to fill the entire form. To do that, select the IFRAME and click on Change Properties, and then move to the Formatting tab. Under the Row Layout section of the dialog, check the Automatically expand to use the available space check box (see Figure 23.15).

In the Scrolling section, you can choose whether you want to have the IFRAME show the scrollbars (vertical and horizontal) as necessary (which is the default value), always, or never. Finally, you can specify whether you want to show a border around the IFRAME by clicking the Display Border property inside the Border section.

Click the OK button to accept this change. You will not see the IFRAME expand on the form in design mode, but it will be expanded when running the application.

To test the form with the IFRAME, click the Preview button on top of the window and select the Create Form menu option. If you use another URL, for example http://www.microsoft.com, which has both JavaScript and Silverlight controls in the page contents to be displayed in an IFRAME, we won't see the page render properly inside the IFRAME. Figure 23.16 shows the page with errors.

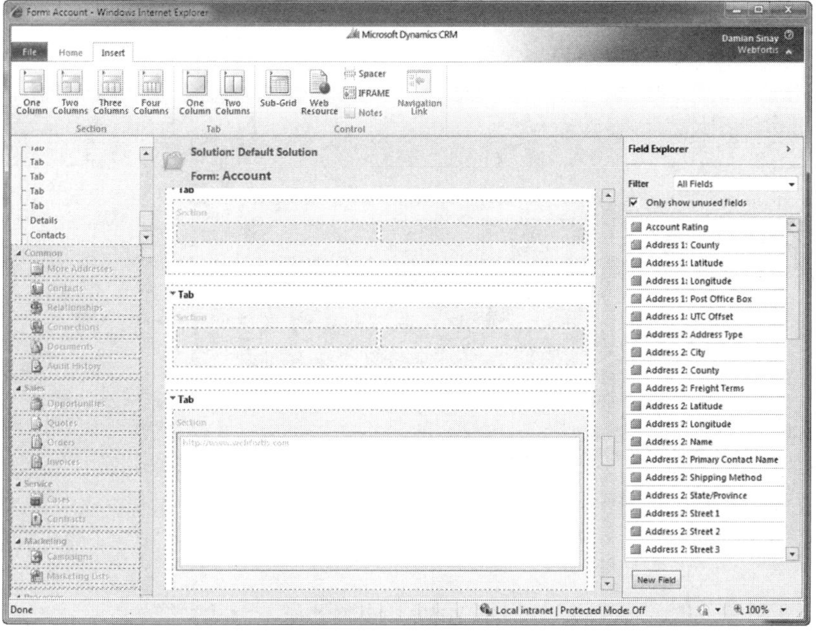

FIGURE 23.14 IFRAME added to the form.

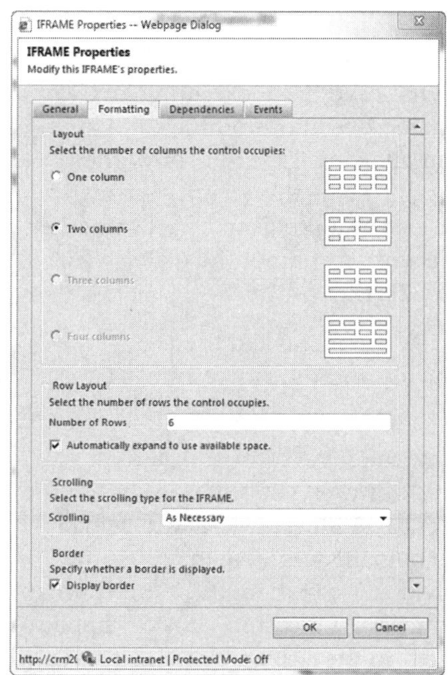

FIGURE 23.15 Making the IFRAME to expand to use the available space.

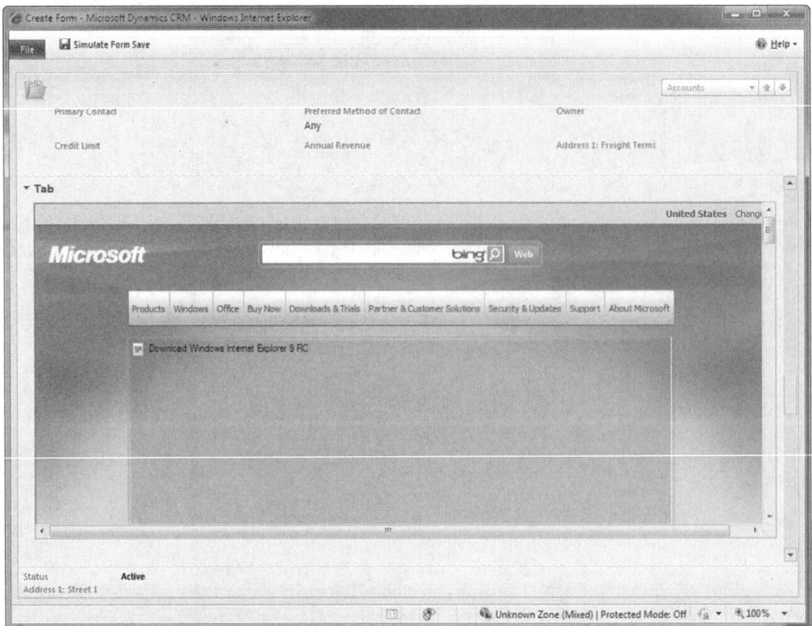

FIGURE 23.16 IFRAME test with errors.

Change Default IFRAME Properties

This behavior is normal. It is the default behavior because of the protection that is set by default on the IFRAME properties to prevent the external pages from executing JavaScript codes or ActiveX controls that might perform unintended operations on the CRM application, such as closing the form unexpectedly without allowing CRM to control the window and saving the data properly. However, you can change this security setting to have your page load correctly if you're sure there will not be a problem, by selecting the IFRAME and clicking Change Properties. Under the Security section of the dialog, clear the Restrict cross-frame scripting check box (see Figure 23.17).

Click OK to close the dialog and test it using the Preview top menu and then selecting Create Form. You will see the page loads properly without any warnings (see Figure 23.18).

For this sample, we used a web page URL that will show the same content regardless of when and where in CRM it is shown. Most of the time, however, you will want to use the IFRAME to show different content depending on the entity and record instance being displayed. For example, you might want to show the company web page in an IFRAME when working with Accounts, and then show an individual's picture in the IFRAME when working with Contacts. For those cases, you will need to create a custom ASP.NET application and read the GUID of the record that will be passed to the web application. This is accomplished by setting the check box that says Pass Record object-type Code and Unique Identifier as Parameters.

IFRAME Properties -- Webpage Dialog

IFRAME Properties

Modify this IFRAME's properties.

General | Formatting | Dependencies | Events

Name

Specify a unique name.

Name * IFRAME_CORP_Website

URL * http://www.microsoft.com

Pass record object-type code and unique identifier as parameters.

Label

Specify the label for this field in forms.

Label * CORP_Website

Display label on the Form

Security

Select whether to restrict cross-frame scripting.

Restrict cross-frame scripting

Visibility

Specify the default visibility of this control.

Visible by default

OK | Cancel

http://crm2(Local intranet | Protected Mode: Off

FIGURE 23.17 Removing the cross-frame scripting protection.

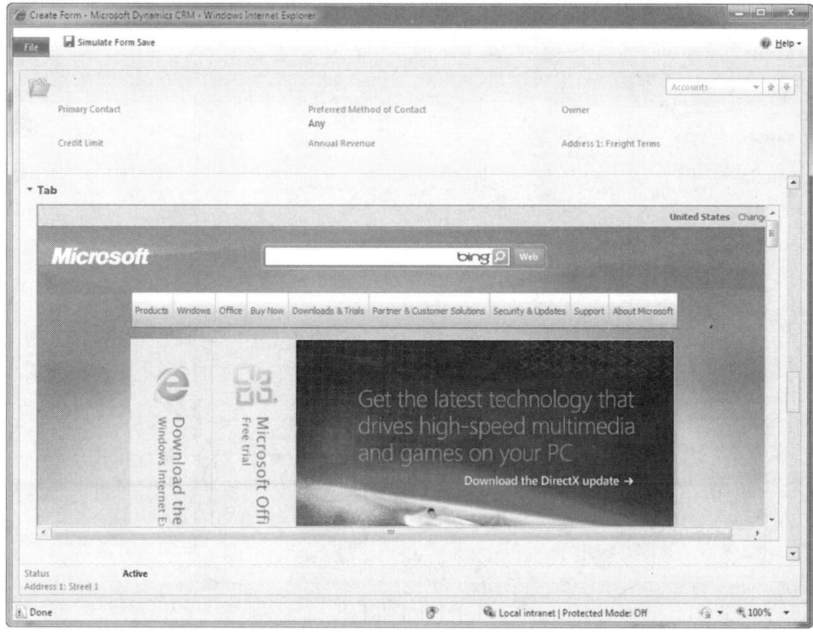

FIGURE 23.18 IFRAME test with active content displayed.

▶ For a complete sample of how this works, see Chapter 28, "Interacting with Custom Web Applications."

Change Properties of a Tab, Section, Field, or IFRAME

From this option, you can access the properties of the section you are positioning. For example, if you select a tab, you have access to the tab properties. If you select a field, the properties are related to the field selected.

Edit the Form Navigation

In this version, you can now easily modify the form navigation links without having to touch the site.map entity directly. By clicking the Navigation button, you can remove or add links to the form navigation bar.

Change Form Properties

From this option, you have access to the general form properties. These properties are not visible to the user; they include such events as the form assistance integration and the nonevent dependencies fields.

After you complete your customizations to the form, you can easily preview them by clicking the Preview button and choosing one of the form mode options, such as Create Form, Update Form, or Read-Only Form (see Figure 23.19). When you are done with the customizations, you can click Save and Close to save your work.

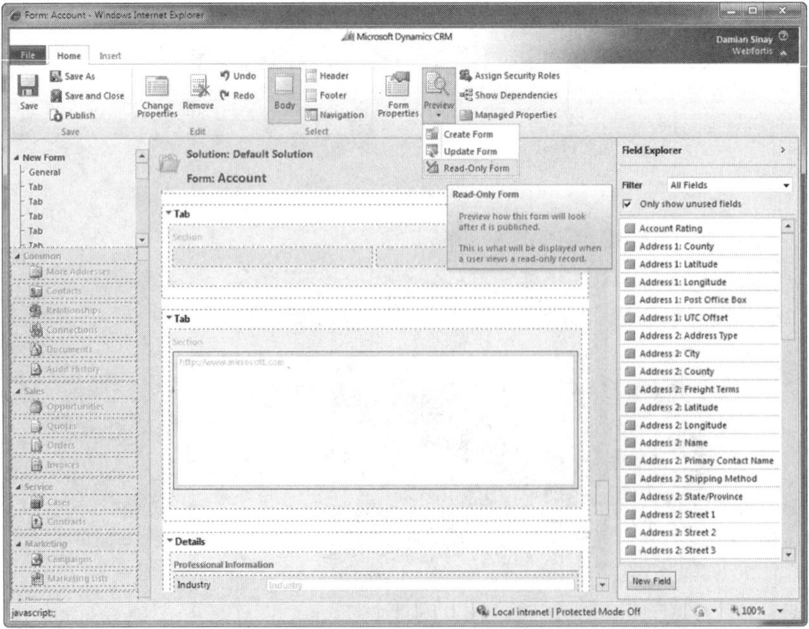

FIGURE 23.19 Preview Form menu items.

NOTE

For the customizations to be visible and usable by users, they must be published. See the "Publishing Customizations" section later in this chapter on how to do this.

View Customizations

A *view* is a read-only representation of the entity's records. It shows just a few of the entity's fields, and you can see them in the main screen of the entities in the Advanced Find results and in the Look Up Records results.

Several different types of views are created by default for each entity, and you can easily create new views. For each view, you can customize the fields to be displayed by adding, removing, or changing the display position of each column. You can also set the desired width in pixels for each column (see Figure 23.20). By default, the columns have a fixed width of 100 pixels.

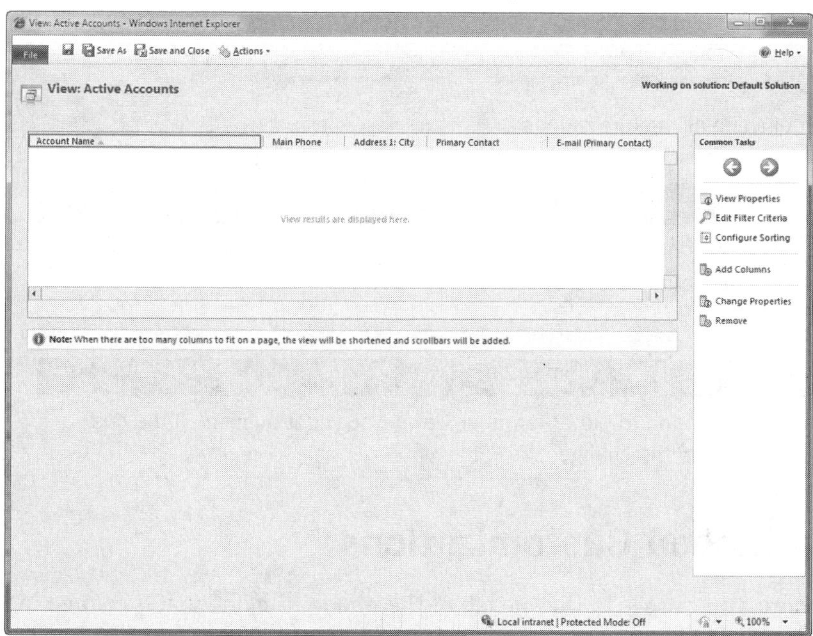

FIGURE 23.20 View customizations.

Publishing Customizations

When you have completed your desired changes to an entity, you must publish the customizations so that users can see and use the changes. To publish, select the entity you want to publish and click the Publish All Customizations button, as illustrated in Figure 23.21.

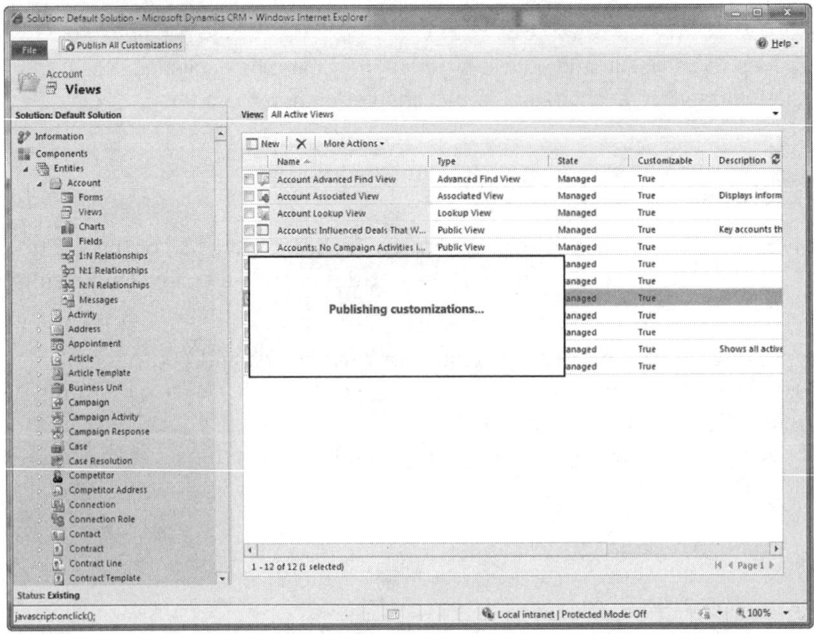

FIGURE 23.21 Publishing all customizations.

NOTE

If you delete an entity, you don't need to publish the customizations. It will be unavailable to users as soon as you delete it.

NOTE

After you make a customization to either forms or views, you must publish all the customizations for users to see the changes.

Menus and Ribbon Customizations

Menus are the options you can see in the File tab of the ribbon, the one that is colored in blue. From that tab you will have a menu, such as Save, New Activity, New Record, Tools, and Options. Notice that every entity has its own menu items as well when you go to create or update a record.

Ribbons are the buttons shown in the top bar below the menu. These buttons vary depending on the entity you are positioned on. Examples of these controls are New, Edit, and Export to Excel.

You can customize menus and controls in three ways:

- Site Map
- ISV.Config
- Ribbons

Each way requires a little knowledge of how to manage XML files because they are XML files. When working with XML files, remember the following rules:

- XML files are case-sensitive, so be sure to respect each node name case to avoid problems. This means that the node name <root> is not the same as <ROOT>.
- Each node needs to be closed. For example, if you open a node with <root>, you need to later close it with </root>. If the node doesn't contain children nodes, you can open and close it in the same line—for example, <root />.

23

▶ For more information about working with XML files and their specifications, visit http://www.w3.org.

TIP

Although XML files can be edited with any text editor, such as Notepad, we recommend using a richer text editor such as Visual Studio 2010. From there you cannot see not only the nodes colored, but you can also expand/collapse the nodes and also take benefits of the IntelliSense by assigning the schema files that are included in the CRM SDK under the sdk\schemas folder and using the customizationssolution.xsd file.

Site Map

The site map is the file that describes the items that will be shown on each area. For example, when you are in the workplace area, you can see on the left the site map options of Dashboard, Activities, Calendar, Imports, and so on. These options are quick links to the entities' administration that you can customize when you want to have another frequently used entity.

The site map is an XML file that needs to be exported first to be edited, and then it needs to be reimported to be updated. It is recommended to create a new custom solution with only the sitemap extension in order to update the site map quickly. Go to Settings, Solutions, New, and select the view Client Extensions, as shown in Figure 23.22.

▶ For more information exporting the site map, refer to the "Exporting and Importing Entity Customizations" section later in this chapter.

The following code illustrates the site map main nodes structure:

```
<SiteMap>
    <SiteMap>
      <Area>
         <Group>
           <SubArea>
```

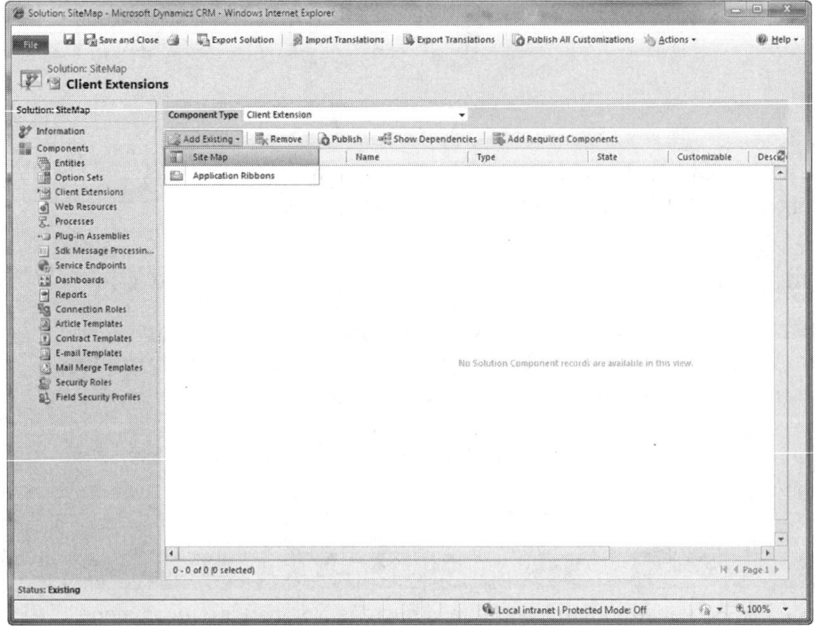

FIGURE 23.22 Locating the site map customization by using the Client Extensions view.

Site Map Node

This is the main and root entry-level node. Inside this node should be another node with the same name, SiteMap, which will contain all the Area nodes as children.

Area Node

Each area represents the main navigation buttons located on the near navigation that are displayed on the main interface. By default, the Site Map is configured with six main areas:

- Workplace
- Sales
- Marketing
- Service
- Settings
- Resource center

Figure 23.23 illustrates these navigation options or areas on the Web Application user interface.

The following code illustrates the area node with its default attributes for the Workplace area:

```
<Area Id="Workplace" ResourceId="Area_Workplace" ShowGroups="true"
Icon="/_imgs/workplace_24x24.gif" DescriptionResourceId="Workplace_Description">
```

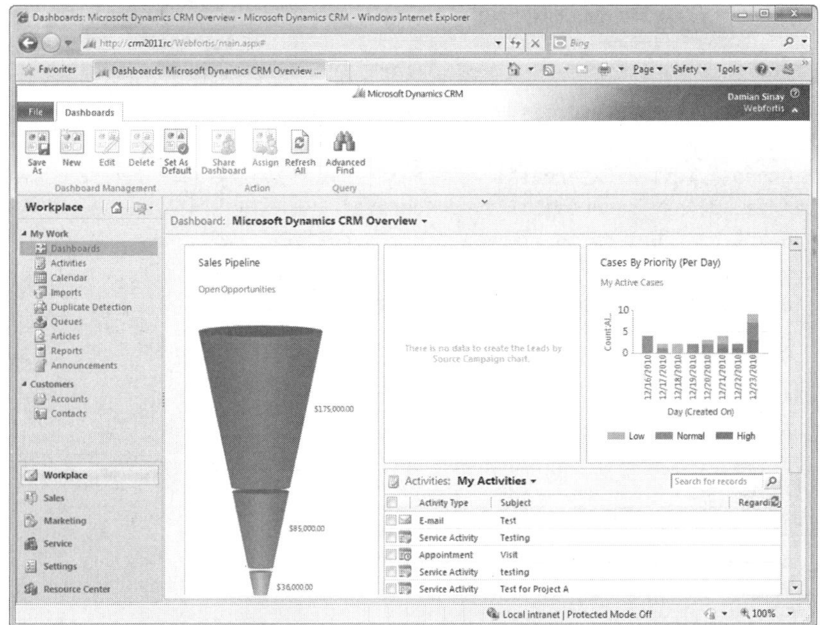

FIGURE 23.23 Areas displayed in the bottom-left corner of the screen.

These are the attributes of the Workplace area code:

- **Id**—The unique identifier name for each area.
- **ResourceId**—The ResourceId.
- **ShowGroups**—This attribute is necessary only if the area has more than one Group child node.
- **Icon**—The URL for the icon to be displayed near the Area title.
- **DescriptionResourceId** —This is for internal use only.

Group Node

This element is used to contain a group of subarea nodes. Each group will be displayed on the near navigation above the Area buttons with the ability to be collapsed or expanded. Samples of groups are My Work and Customers that are included by default in the Workplace area.

Subarea Node

These nodes are used to provide the links to the pages or websites (configured by its URL) inside the Group sections.

For example, suppose we want to add a new area to the sitemap called Webfortis to be used as a collection of links related to our organization and external application. We could add the following code into the Site Map file right after the last </Area> node and before the </SiteMap>.

```
<Area Id="WebfortisArea" Title="Webfortis" ShowGroups="true"
Icon="/_imgs/resourcecenter_24x24.gif" >
       <Group Id="Group1" Title="External"        >
              <SubArea Id="nav_subArea1" Title="Website"
Icon="/_imgs/ico_18_129.gif" Url="http://www.webfortis.com" />
              <SubArea Id="nav_subArea2"  Title="Microsoft"
Icon="/_imgs/ico_16_sales.gif" Url="http://www.microsoft.com"
AvailableOffline="false" />
       </Group>
       <Group Id="Group2" Title="Internal">
              <SubArea Id="nav_subArea11" Title="Intranet"
Icon="/_imgs/ico_18_129.gif" Url="http://www.webfortis.com/Internal"
AvailableOffline="false" />
              <SubArea Id="nav_subArea12" Title="Cost Control"
Icon="/_imgs/ico_16_sales.gif" Url="http://www.webfortis.com/CC"
AvailableOffline="false" />
       </Group>
</Area>
```

Save the changes and import the solution that contains the site map. To import the site map customizations, go to Settings, Solutions, Import, upload the XML file you edited and click the Import Selected Customizations button.

▶ For detailed instructions on how to import Site Map customizations, see the "Exporting and Importing Entity Customizations" section later this chapter.

After importing this customization you would see the result as shown in Figure 23.24.

NOTE

Important considerations when adding new areas, groups or subareas are to be sure to use unique names for the Id attributes, and not to use the ResourceId and DescriptionResourceID attributes in your custom elements because those are for internal use only. Instead use the Titles/Title elements to display the text for each different language.

ISV.Config

ISV.Config is an XML structure that is part of the customizations.xml file that is included on every solution. In earlier versions of Dynamics CRM, it was used to add custom menu items and controls to the toolbars. However, in this new version of Dynamics CRM 2011, that functionality has been moved to the Ribbon as we will see later in this chapter. The only functionality of the ISV.Config is to provide appearance and behavior of the Service Calendar.

FIGURE 23.24 Customized site map.

To be able to work with the ISV.Config XML, you need to explicitly specify it when importing the solution by selecting the ISV.Config option, as shown in Figure 23.25.

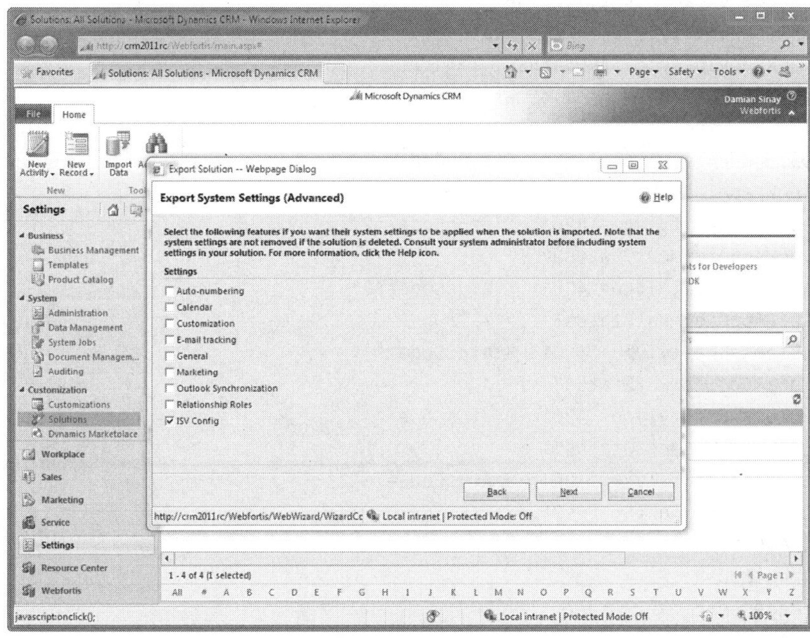

FIGURE 23.25 Custom menus and toolbars.

Noticed that because the ISV.Config is considered a system setting, any customization made here won't be removed when removing the solution.

The following code illustrates the ISV.Config main nodes structure:

```
<IsvConfig>
    <configuration version="3.0.0000.0">
      <Root />
      <ServiceManagement>
        <AppointmentBook>
          <SmoothScrollLimit>2000</SmoothScrollLimit>
          <TimeBlocks>
            <TimeBlock EntityType="4214" StatusCode="1"
CssClass="ganttBlockServiceActivityStatus1" />
            <TimeBlock EntityType="4214" StatusCode="2"
CssClass="ganttBlockServiceActivityStatus2" />
            <TimeBlock EntityType="4214" StatusCode="3"
CssClass="ganttBlockServiceActivityStatus3" />
            <TimeBlock EntityType="4214" StatusCode="4"
CssClass="ganttBlockServiceActivityStatus4" />
            <TimeBlock EntityType="4214" StatusCode="6"
CssClass="ganttBlockServiceActivityStatus6" />
            <TimeBlock EntityType="4214" StatusCode="7"
CssClass="ganttBlockServiceActivityStatus7" />
            <TimeBlock EntityType="4214" StatusCode="8"
CssClass="ganttBlockServiceActivityStatus8" />
            <TimeBlock EntityType="4214" StatusCode="9"
CssClass="ganttBlockServiceActivityStatus9" />
            <TimeBlock EntityType="4214" StatusCode="10"
CssClass="ganttBlockServiceActivityStatus10" />
            <TimeBlock EntityType="4201" StatusCode="1"
CssClass="ganttBlockAppointmentStatus1" />
            <TimeBlock EntityType="4201" StatusCode="2"
CssClass="ganttBlockAppointmentStatus2" />
            <TimeBlock EntityType="4201" StatusCode="3"
CssClass="ganttBlockAppointmentStatus3" />
            <TimeBlock EntityType="4201" StatusCode="4"
CssClass="ganttBlockAppointmentStatus4" />
            <TimeBlock EntityType="4201" StatusCode="5"
CssClass="ganttBlockAppointmentStatus5" />
            <TimeBlock EntityType="4201" StatusCode="6"
CssClass="ganttBlockAppointmentStatus6" />
          </TimeBlocks>
        </AppointmentBook>
      </ServiceManagement>
    </configuration>
  </IsvConfig>
```

ServiceManagement Node

This element customizes the Service Calendar. The ServiceManagement node contains only a child node with the name of AppointmentBook. The AppointmentBook node can have one of these nodes:

- **SmoothScrollLimit**—This option sets the maximum number of blocks to be displayed by a service activity before auto scrolling the appointment when it is selected or displayed.
- **ValidationChunkSize**—This option is used to configure the number of activities to be validated simultaneously by the server. The validation occurs in cases where more than one activity requires the same resource or materials.
- **TimeBlocks**

▶ Refer to Chapter 10, "Working with Service," for more information about the ServiceManagement node.

With each TimeBlock element, you can apply a different style to each status code of a service activity.

See this example:

```
<ServiceManagement>
   <AppointmentBook>
     <SmoothScrollLimit>2000</SmoothScrollLimit>
     <TimeBlocks>
       <!— All CSS Class mapping for Service activities —>
       <TimeBlock EntityType="4214" StatusCode="1"
[ccc]CssClass="ganttBlockServiceActivityStatus1" />
     </TimeBlocks>
   </AppointmentBook>
</ServiceManagement>
```

The EntityType attribute can be one of the following values:

4214—Service activity

4201—Appointment

Ribbons

Ribbons allow us to customize the Dynamics CRM Ribbon tabs to add custom buttons. Ribbons are more intelligent and smart that previous system menus. There are two main places where ribbons are located:

- HomepageGrid
- Form

Adding a simple button to the ribbon involves: touching the customization file to include nodes in the RibbonDiffXml node, adding web resources for the images to be displayed in the button, adding a web resource for the JavaScript method to be used when clicked the button.

HomepageGrid

The HomepageGrid is the place located in the home page of any entity where the main grid is located. Figure 23.26 shows the HomepageGrid for the Account entity.

Form

The Form is the place located in the entity record form of any entity where the Ribbon is located on top on the form. Figure 23.27 shows the Form location for the Account entity.

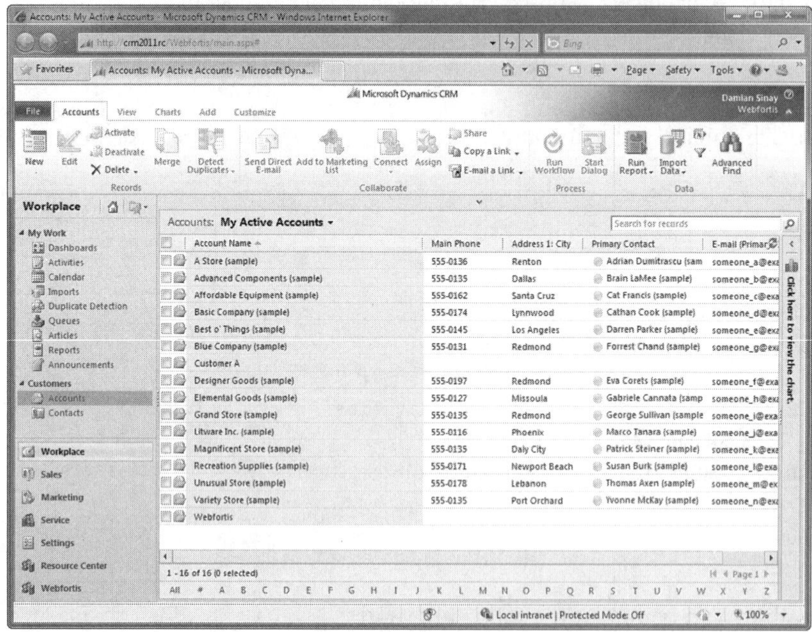

FIGURE 23.26 HomepageGrid for the Account entity.

There are three main controls for Ribbons:

- Tab
- Group
- Button

Every button must be contained on a group and every group must be contained on a Tab control.

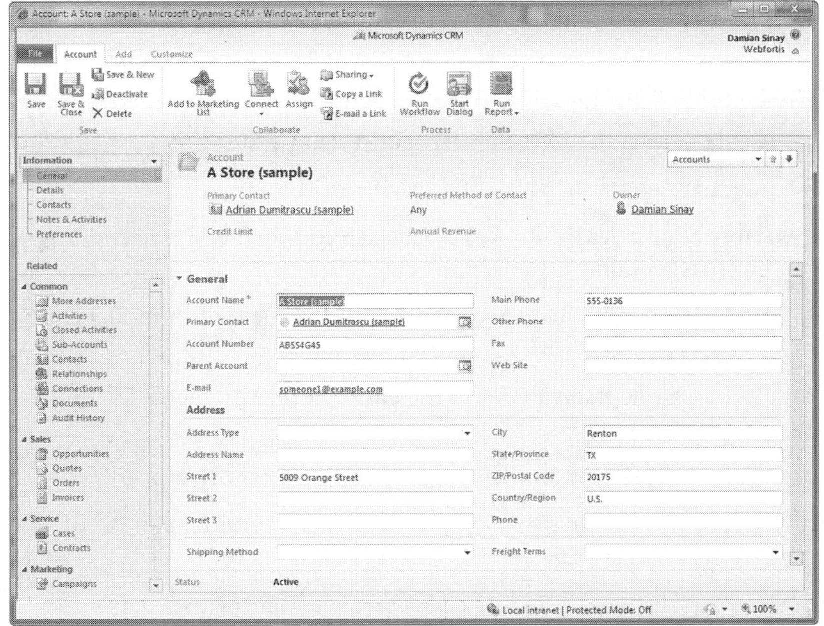

FIGURE 23.27 Form for the Account entity.

Because the Ribbon buttons are smart and can change while the user is using the application, there are some rules that will need to be configured for this case so that you can make the button visible or enabled depending on the following conditions:

- **Based on Form state**—Create, Existing, Read Only, Disabled, Bulk Edit
- **Configure Custom rules**—By JavaScript functions with parameters
- **CrmClientTypeRule**—Detects if running in outlook client or web client
- **CrmOfflineAccessStateRule**—Detects if outlook is running in offline or online mode
- **CrmOutlookClientTypeRule**—Types CrmForOutlook or CrmForOutlookOfflineAccess
- **OrRule**—A rule that contains a collection of rules so that this rule will evaluate as true if any of the rules in the collection evaluates as true
- **OutlookItemTrackingRule**—A rule that detects whether the item is enabled for items tracked in Microsoft Dynamics CRM in order to enable a Ribbon element
- **OutlookVersionRule**—A rule that detects the version of Microsoft Office Outlook client

- **PageRule**—A rule that evaluates the address of the current page
- **RecordPrivilegeRule**—A rule that detects a user's privileges for a specific record in order to enable a Ribbon element
- **SkuRule**—A rule that detects the Microsoft Dynamics CRM edition
- **ValueRule**—A rule that detects the value of a specific field
- **ReferencingAttributeRequiredRule**—A rule that detects whether the referencing attribute for an entity is required
- **RelationshipTypeRule**—A rule that detects whether a specific type of formal entity relationship exists between two entities
- **EntityPrivilegeRule**—A rule that can detect the current user's privileges for a specific entity
- **EntityPropertyRule**—A rule that can detect specific Boolean entity properties
- **FormEntityContextRule**—A rule that can detect whether a form Ribbon is displayed in the context of a specific entity
- **MiscellaneousPrivilegeRule**—A rule that can detect whether the user possesses a specific Microsoft Dynamics CRM privilege
- **OrganizationSettingRule**—A rule that can detect two specific organization settings within a DisplayRule; checks for IsSharepointEnabled or IsSOPIntegrationEnabled
- **OutlookRenderTypeRule**—A rule that can detect whether a form or list item is rendered as a web page or natively in Outlook in order to determine whether a Ribbon element should be displayed
- **SelectionCountRule**—A rule that detects how many items in a grid are selected

The SDK comes with samples that will help you easily add custom buttons to an existing group for all entities or add custom buttons to an existing group for specific entities. In addition you can add custom groups to an existing tab for specific entity, add custom tab to specific entity, add custom groups to the developer tab for all entities in a form, and hide Ribbon elements. These samples are located in the sdk\walkthroughs\ribbon folder.

NOTE

There is also a good source code sample in the SDK under the sdk\samplecode\cs\client\ribbon folder called exportribbonxml that will export all the entities' XML Ribbon data so that you can use it to easily locate each Ribbon tab, group, or button.

RibbonDiffXml

The RibbonDiffXml node defines the tabs, groups and buttons, and it contains the following child nodes:

```
<RibbonDiffXml>
        <CustomActions />
        <Templates>
          <RibbonTemplates Id="Mscrm.Templates"></RibbonTemplates>
        </Templates>
        <CommandDefinitions />
        <RuleDefinitions>
          <TabDisplayRules />
          <DisplayRules />
          <EnableRules />
        </RuleDefinitions>
        <LocLabels />
</RibbonDiffXml>
```


The CustomActions node defines the tabs, groups, and buttons and contains the following child Nodes:

```
<CustomActions>
  <CustomAction >
    <CommandUIDefinition>
      <Group >
        <Controls>
          <Button />
        </Controls>
      </Group>
    </CommandUIDefinition>
  </CustomAction>
</CustomActions>
```

The Button element node contains the following attributes:

- **Id**—the unique identifier for the button.
- **Command**—the Id of the command that will be defined in the CommandDefinitions node of the RibbonDiffXml root node. Each command definition is defined as follows:

```
        <CommandDefinitions>
          <CommandDefinition
    Id="Solution.all.HomepageGrid.MyGroup.Help.Command">
            <EnableRules />
            <DisplayRules />
```

```
          <Actions>
            <JavaScriptFunction FunctionName="ShowHelp"
Library="$webresource:webforti_Script.js" />
          </Actions>
        </CommandDefinition>
      </CommandDefinitions>
```

Inside the command deifintiions you can include the rules for enable or disable the buttons (inside the EnableRules node), show or hide the buttons (in the DisplayRules node) and the actions to be performed when the button is clicked.

- **Sequence**—The integer number of the sequence to define the position of the button related to the other buttons in the same group.
- **LabelText**—The Id of the localized label that is defined inside the LocLabels node for example:

```
<RibbonDiffXml>
    ...................
    <LocLabels>
      <LocLabel Id="Solution.all.HomepageGrid.MyGroup.Help.ToolTip">
        <Titles>
          <Title languagecode="1033" description="Help" />
        </Titles>
      </LocLabel>
   </LocLabels>
</RibbonDiffXml>
```

Inside the Title node you can enter as many Title node as languages you want. The languagecode used on this sample 1033 refers to the English language. For a complete list of codes refer to http://msdn.microsoft.com/en-us/library/0h88fahh.aspx

- **ToolTipTitle**—The Id of the localized label that is defined inside the LocLabels node, similar to the LabelText node
- **ToolTipDescription**—The Id of the localized label that is defined inside the LocLabels node, similar to the LabelText node
- **TemplateAlias**—The alias of the template to be used, this will affect the way the button will be displayed, o1 will display the button big, and o2 will display the button small.
- **Image16by16**—The id of the web resource used for the 16 by 16 pixels image, this is the image that is used for small buttons. If you use a web resource you need to enter a value as follows $webresource:<name of the web reosource>.png.
- **Image32by32**—The id of the web reource used for the 32 by 32 pixels image; this is the image that is used for big buttons. If you use a web resource you need to enter a value as follows: $webresource:<name of the web reosource>.png.

NOTE

You might wonder if you need to use either the Image16by16 or the Image32by32 attributes; however, it is recommended to set both as there are some templates that will use one of the other depending on the window's size.

JavaScript Events

JavaScript events are related to forms and the controls inside the forms only. Each form has OnLoad and OnSave events, which can accept JavaScript. Each field also has the OnChange event, which can also accept JavaScript. This new version of CRM 2011 also adds new events for the Tab control to track the tabStateChange event and to IFRAMEs to track the OnReadyStateComplete event (see Figure 23.28). This new version also introduces new javascript objects to easily access the from fields values and context information through the Xrm object. The previous version used to use the crmForm.all object collection, while this collection still exists in CRM 2011 for compatibility, the new Xrm.Page object collection is the recommended way for new CRM 2011 JavaScript customizations.

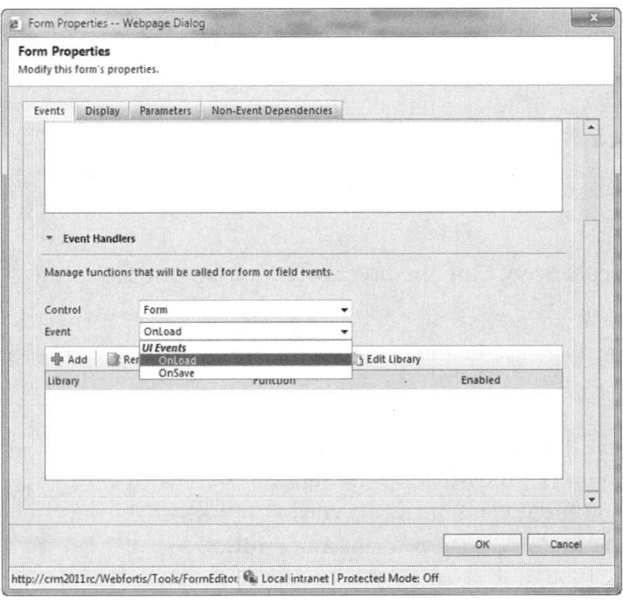

FIGURE 23.28 Form events that you can customize with JavaScript.

- **OnLoad event**—Occurs every time the window of an entity is open, either when you edit an existing record or when you create a new one

- **OnSave event**—Occurs every time the Save icon or the Save and Close button is pressed
- **OnChange event**—Is fired every time the value of the field is changed and after it loses the focus (see Figure 23.29)

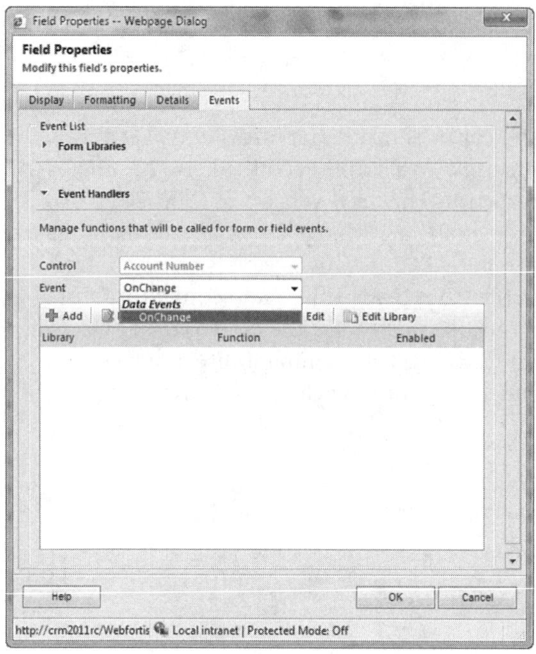

FIGURE 23.29 Form field events that you can customize with JavaScript.

- **TabStateChange Event**—Occurs every time the user switches from one tab to the other (see Figure 23.30)
- **OnReadyStateComplete event**—Is fired when the content of the IFRAME has been loaded (see Figure 23.31)

To start adding script to this event, you need to create a web resource of type JavaScript that you can use as a library where you can have a common repository for the event scripts you will handle. This is a good improvement in this version of CRM 2011 that allows as to reuse the JavaScript function on different forms and entities.

This new version has changed and added more powerful JavaScript objects that now can be accessible through the Xrm.Page.data.entity object; however, the old object model that uses the crmForm.all object still works for backward compatibility.

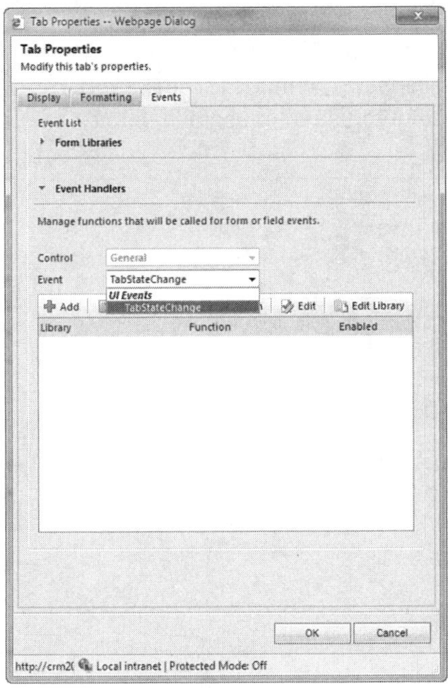

FIGURE 23.30 Form tab events that you can customize with JavaScript.

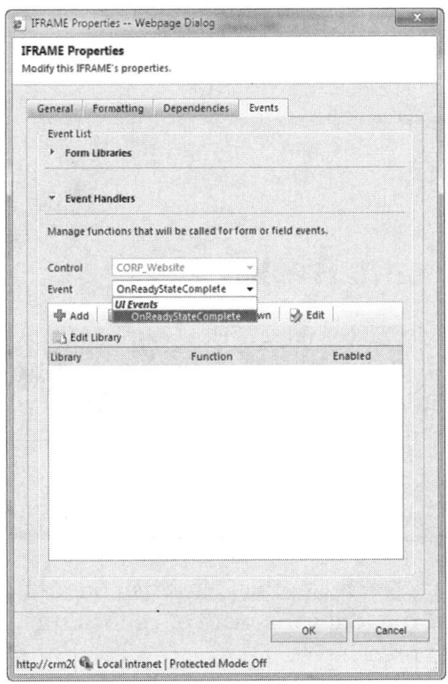

FIGURE 23.31 IFRAME events that you can customize with JavaScript.

▶ For people that need to migrate JavaScript code from CRM 4.0 to this new CRM 2011 version, there is a nice tool available at CodePlex called CRM 4 to CRM 2011 JavaScript Converter that you can download from this link:http://crm2011scriptconvert.codeplex.com/ (see Figure 23.32). This tool will be useful to use after upgrade, but it is not required.

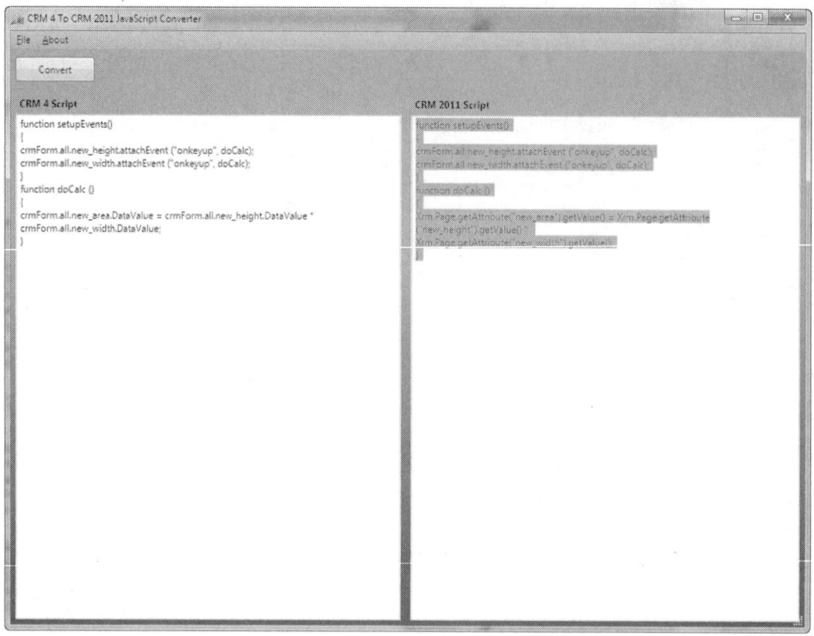

FIGURE 23.32 CRM 4 to CRM 2011 JavaScript Converter.

Advanced Event-Handling Tips and Tricks

If you are familiar with JavaScript and HTML, you might be thinking, "How can I add JavaScript code for all the other events that any regular HTML INPUT control has, such as the onkeypress, onkeyup, or onkeydown events?" Although you can have Microsoft Dynamics CRM perform these types of actions, it requires a little more effort. Let's look at an example of how to add the onkeyup event.

Suppose that you have a custom entity called House to which you have added the following custom fields: width, height, and area. You want to have the area automatically calculated from the width and height without forcing the user to move the focus from one control to the other to see the changes. You could add the following piece of code in the OnLoad event to attach a field control to the standard onkeyup event:

```
function setupEvents()
{
crmForm.all.webforti_height.attachEvent("onkeyup", doCalc);
crmForm.all.webforti_width.attachEvent("onkeyup", doCalc);
}
function doCalc()
{
crmForm.all.webforti_area.value = crmForm.all.webforti_height.value *
crmForm.all.webforti_width.value;
}
```


To see this sample working, follow these steps:

1. Go to Settings, Customizations, and then Solutions.
2. Create a new solution and go to Entities.
3. Click New to create a new entity.
4. Enter House in the Display Name field and Houses in the Plural Name field.

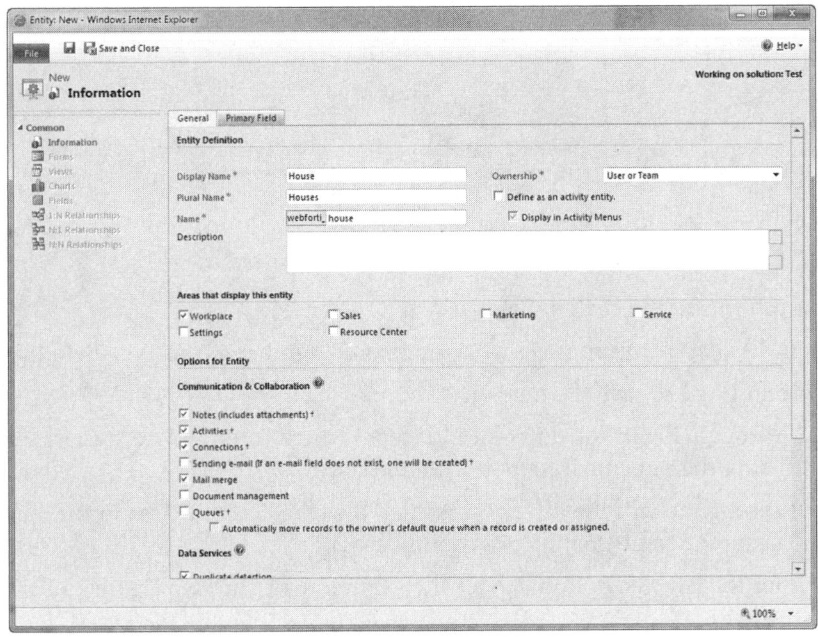

FIGURE 23.33 Creating the House custom entity.

5. Click the Save button, but do not close the window.

6. Click Fields from the left side options under the Common section, as shown in Figure 23.34.

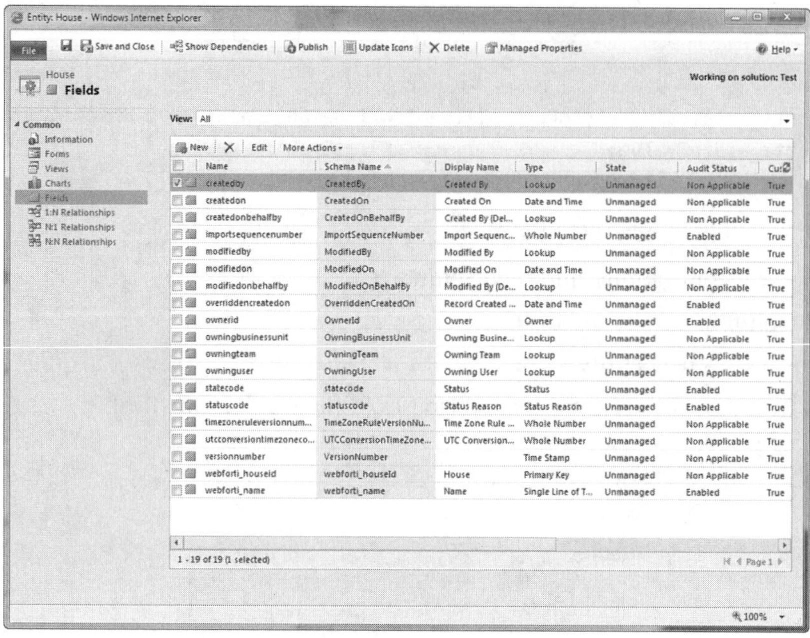

FIGURE 23.34 Attributes.

7. Click New button to add the custom field.
8. Enter Height in Display Name and select Floating Point Number in the Type field.
9. Click on Save and Close to save the field.
10. Repeat steps 7 through 9 with the difference in step 8 where entering Width in the Display Name using the same floating point number type.
11. Repeat steps 7 through 9 with the difference in step 8 where entering Area in the Display Name using the same floating point number type.
12. Click Forms from the left side options under the Common section (see Figure 23.36).
13. Select the Information Main type form record and double-click it to edit it.
14. Drag and drop the new attributes we created: Height, Width, and Area (see Figure 23.37).

TIP

Click the general section and double-click the fields to be added to the section easily.

FIGURE 23.35 Adding Height attribute.

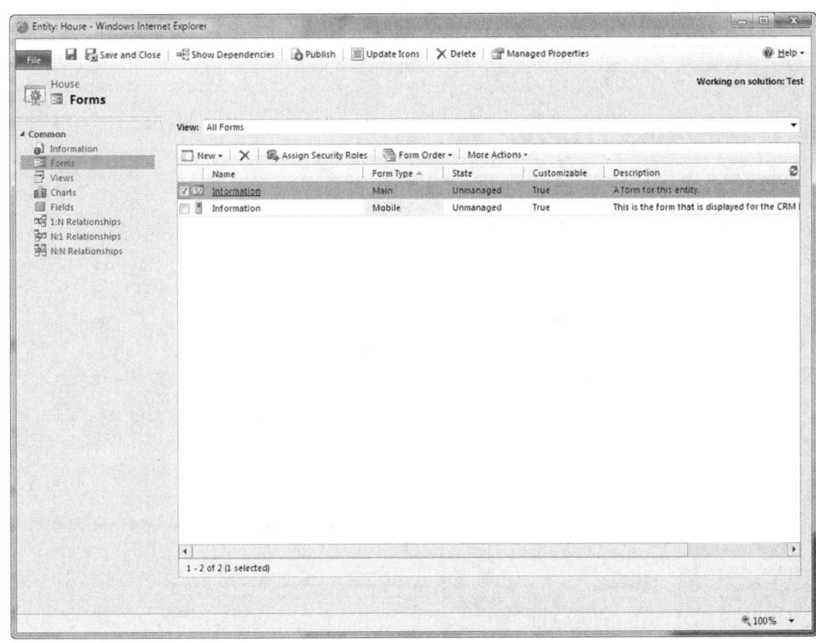

FIGURE 23.36 Forms.

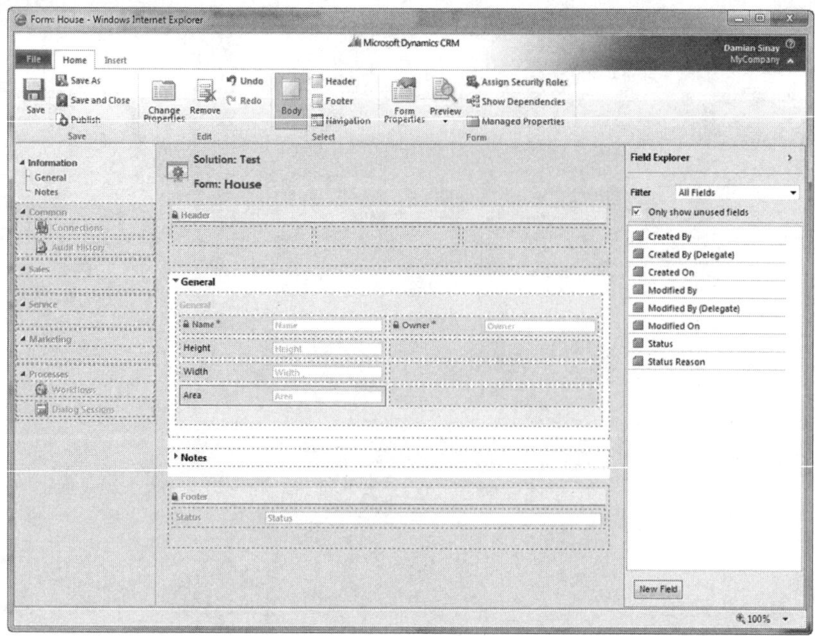

FIGURE 23.37 Adding the fields to the form.

15. Click on Form Properties on the Ribbon.

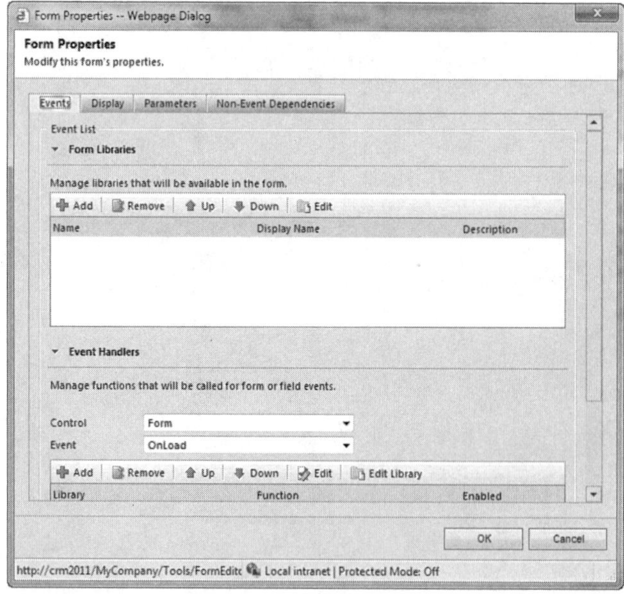

FIGURE 23.38 Form properties window.

16. Click Add under the Form Libraries section.

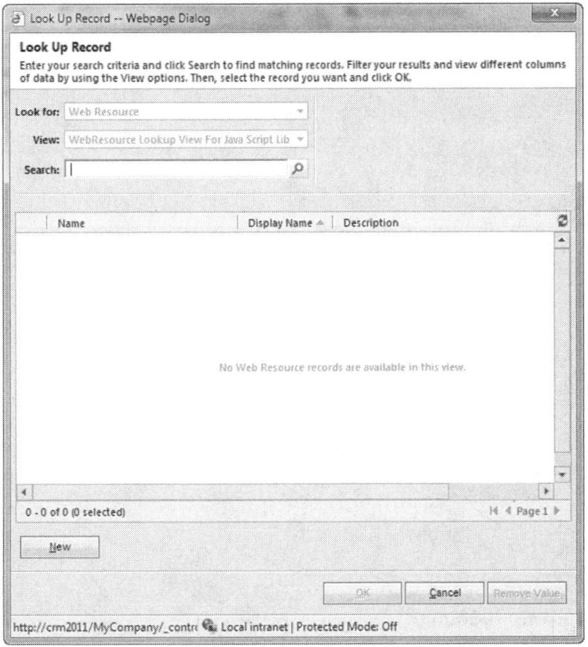

FIGURE 23.39 Web resources lookup.

17. Click New to create a new JavaScript file.
18. Enter mainlib.js on the Name and Display Name fields, and select the Script (Jscript) type, as shown in Figure 23.40.
19. Click Text Editor and enter the following code, as shown in Figure 23.41:

```
function setupEvents()
{
        crmForm.all.webforti_height.attachEvent ("onkeyup", doCalc);
        crmForm.all.webforti_width.attachEvent ("onkeyup", doCalc);
}
function doCalc()
{
crmForm.all.webforti_area.value = crmForm.all.webforti_height.value *
crmForm.all.webforti_width.value;
}
```

20. Click OK button to close the text editor.
21. Click Save, click Publish, then click Save and Close to close the Web Resource dialog.

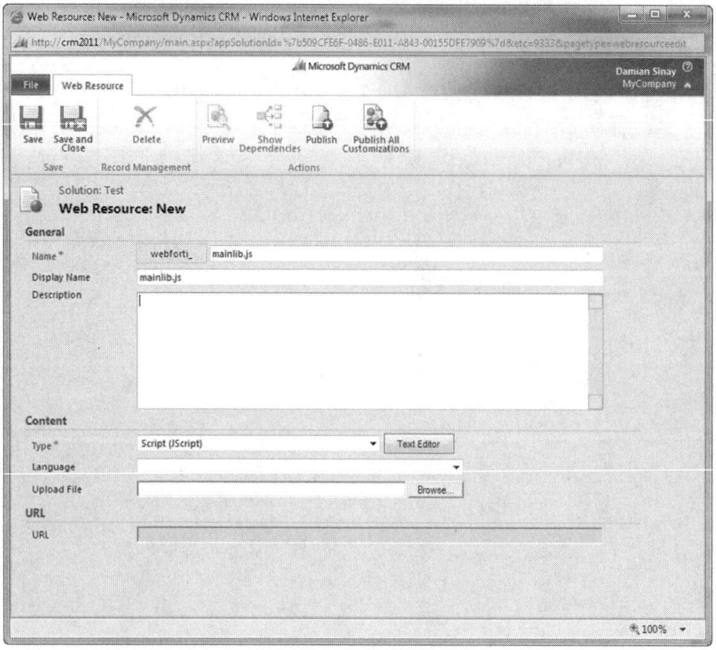

FIGURE 23.40 Creating a new JavaScript web resource.

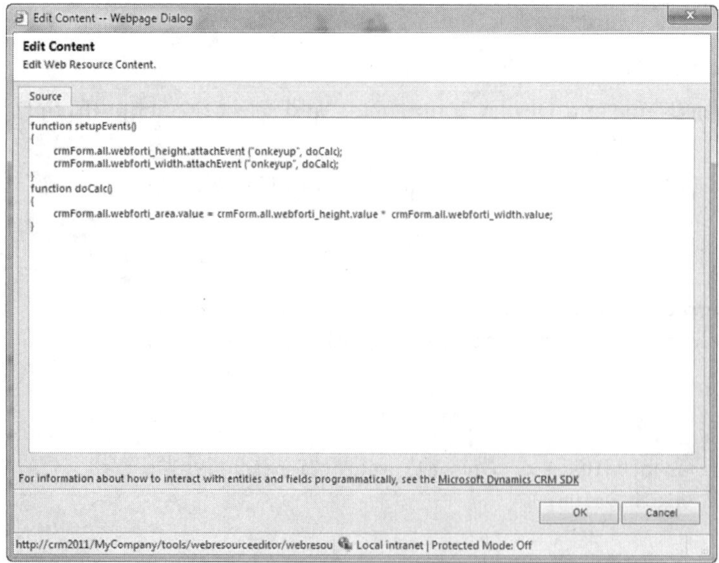

FIGURE 23.41 Adding code to the JavaScript web resource event.

22. Now press the Enter key on the search text box, select the new web resource we created, and click OK.
23. Because we added the form library we can now go to the event handlers and have Control selected to Form and Event to OnLoad. Click on Add.
24. Type setupEvents in the Function field.

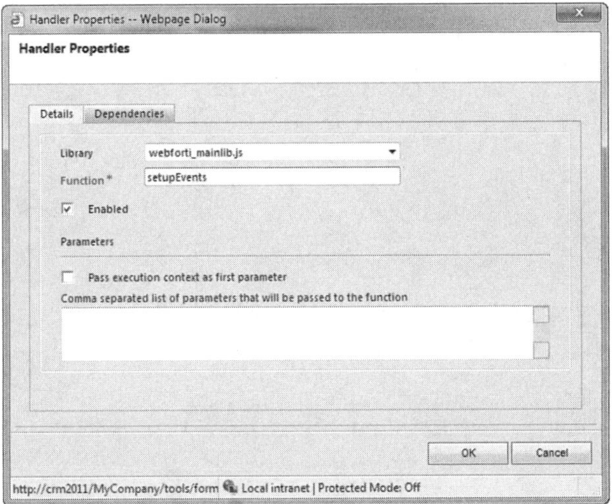

FIGURE 23.42 Handler properties.

25. Click the OK button to close the event handler properties dialog.
26. Click the OK button to close the Form Properties dialog.
27. Click the Preview menu button and then select Create Form to test the code, as shown in Figure 23.43.
28. Enter a value on the Height field (for example, 10) and enter a value to the Width field (for example, 10). You will see the Area field is set automatically with the calculated result, 100.

Notice the field names might vary depending on the solution prefix. We used webforti_ on this example, however you might use new_ or another different prefix.

When working with JavaScript code, it is important you publish the JavaScript web resource every time you make a change on it so that you can preview your changes. If you don't publish the web resource changes, you won't see the changes take effect on the preview window of the form.

▶ Check the MSDN library for full details of all the events supported in the HTML INPUT element (http://msdn.microsoft.com/en-us/library/ms533051(v=VS.85).aspx).

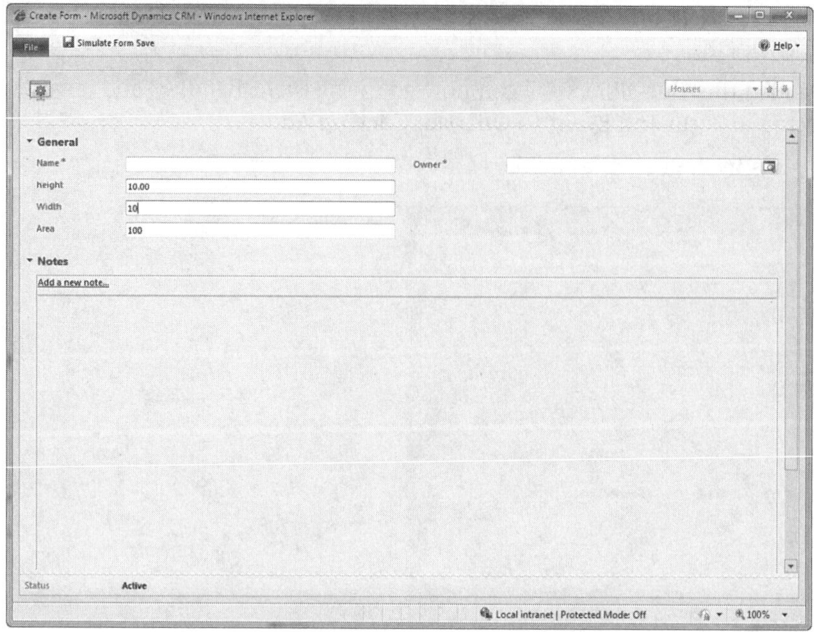

FIGURE 23.43 Testing the solution.

Tips and Tricks When Working with Events

When you work with JavaScript code, you encounter some disadvantages of using the regular web interface:

- The interface lacks IntelliSense.
- The JavaScript code is not colored for better understanding and manipulation.
- It is very tedious to debug and correct errors in some situations when you can't use the preview feature to simulate your changes because you need to touch the code, save the changes, publish the updates, and then see whether it works as expected.

To avoid all these disadvantages, you can use a richer JavaScript editor, such as Visual Studio. To be able to work with JavaScript within Visual Studio, having the script located in a separate web resources enables you to easily copy and paste the script from CRM to Visual Studio. That way you can get access to IntelliSense and colored code.

A good technique for debugging scripts is by enabling the Internet Explorer debugger. You can enable this by going to Tools, Internet Options, and then moving to the Advanced tab. Be sure you have unchecked the options that say Disable Script debugging (Internet Explorer) and Disable Script debugging (Other), as shown in Figure 23.44.

After you have script debugging enabled, you can put the sentence debugger on your code to start the debugger.

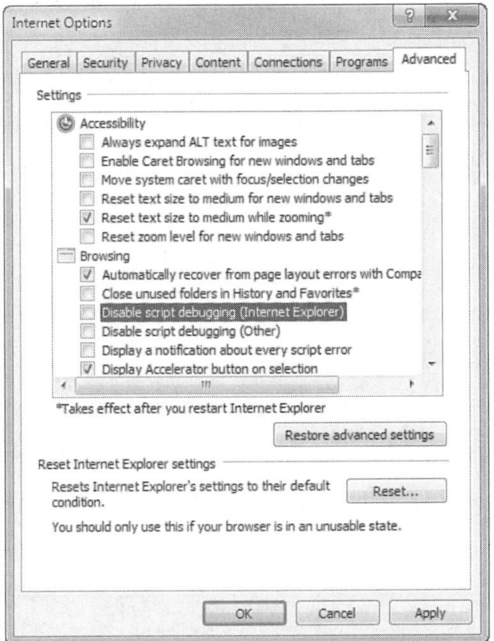

FIGURE 23.44 Disable script debugging.

For example:

```
function setupEvents()
{
        debugger;
        crmForm.all.webforti_height.attachEvent ("onkeyup", doCalc);
        crmForm.all.webforti_width.attachEvent ("onkeyup", doCalc);
}
```

When running this code on the onload event, you will see the dialog shown in Figure 23.45 open to enable you to select the debugger you want—this is in case you have Visual Studio installed on your machine.

This is a good technique to debug your JavaScript code because normal users will have the script debugger disabled by default and won't get these messages.

TIP

A good utility to work with JavaScript customizations is the Internet Explorer Developer Tools, which is available inside Internet Explorer, and you can use it by pressing the F12 key.

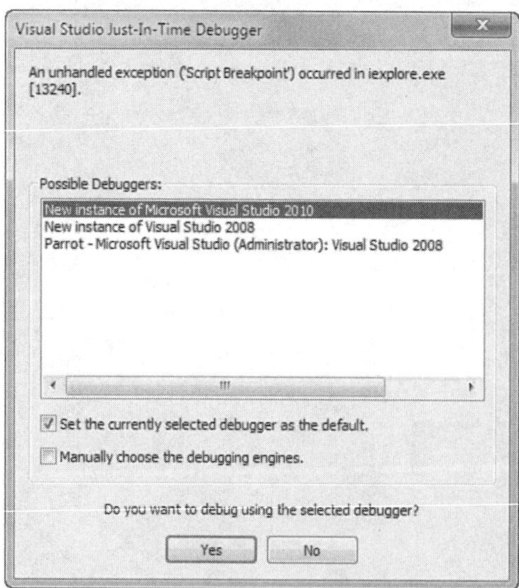

FIGURE 23.45 Launch debugger from JavaScript code.

Exporting and Importing Entity Customizations

You can export all customizations made on any entity out of the CRM system to be used on other CRM implementations or for backup purposes. This version changed the way the customizations are stored in CRM by using the Solutions concepts.

▶ Refer to Chapter 16, "Solution Concepts," for more details about how to work with solutions, as well how to export and import customizations as part of solutions.

NOTE

An important consideration about importing customizations is that they will only add or append new attributes to existent entities and won't delete any missing attribute or data. So, there is no risk of losing the data you or any other user added if you had previously added a new attribute and then you import an older version without that attribute. However, the new fields you might have added to the form or the views will be deleted in that case. Another difference happens when deleting solutions. If you delete a managed solution, then the new entities and data that belongs to that solution will be deleted; however, the data and entity is not deleted if you remove an unmanaged solution. To clean any custom entity you created with the data inside a custom solution you will need to also manually delete the entity in the Default Solution.

TIP

When importing customizations for the site map, you might accidentally delete the Settings area or import an error file that might break the web application to be accessed by the Import Customization interface to restore a backup and take the application to a good state. If that happens you can use the following link to access to this interface directly, as shown in Figure 23.46 (notice the direct URL):

```
http://<servername>:<port>/<organizationname>/tools/systemcustomization/system
customization.aspx
```

For example

```
http://crm2011/webfortis/tools/systemcustomization/systemcustomization.aspx
```

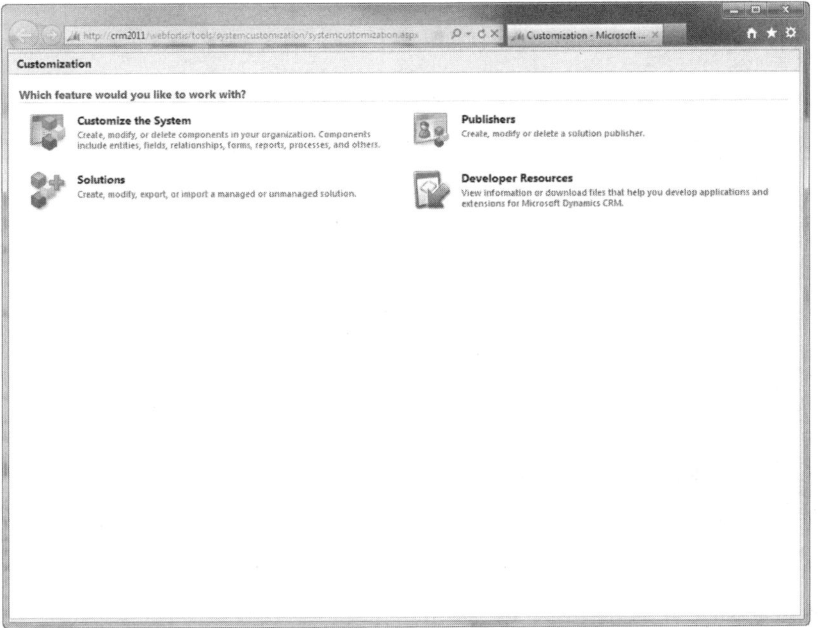

FIGURE 23.46 Customizations interface to recover a broken application.

Working with the SDK

The software development kit (SDK) is a compound of help files, documentation, binary tools, and code samples that gives developers the capability to extend and understand advanced Microsoft Dynamics CRM customizations. By "advanced customizations," we refer to all customizations that can't be done through the standard CRM user interfaces, such as the ones you saw earlier in this chapter. To develop these advanced customizations, you need a tool such as Visual Studio 2010, along with a solid knowledge and understanding of .NET development and programming in languages such as C# or VB .NET and JavaScript.

▶ The SDK does not usually come with the product media, so you must download it from Microsoft. It can be found by searching for "CRM 2011 SDK" at the following link: http://msdn.microsoft.com/en-US/.

Advanced customizations can include these:

- Server programming
  - Advanced workflow development

▶ For details about workflow development, see Chapter 24, "Processes Development."

  - Plug-ins development

▶ For details about plug-ins development, see Chapter 25, "Plug-Ins."

- Client programming
- Reports development
  - Advanced report development with SQL Server Reporting Services (SSRS).

NOTE

The main help file is the CrmSdk2011.chm file, which contains detailed documentation about all these topics.

Summary

This chapter looked at the CRM entity model, the attribute types we can use to add new fields to the entity forms, and the relationships between the entities that can be 1:N, N:1, or N:N. We made some basic customizations adding tabs, sections, and controls to the forms. We used and reviewed the IFRAME control and also added menus and controls to the toolbar using the site map, Ribbon, and the ISV.Config files, and explained how to use JavaScript events exposed by the Forms controls like the OnLoad and the OnSave events to extend the forms and the OnChange event for the fields. We discussed how to add other events manually such as onkeyup, and we explained how to easily debug scripts without having to publish the entity customizations. Finally we talked about how to import and export customizations, and reviewed the SDK and its uses.

CHAPTER 24

Processes Development

IN THIS CHAPTER

- Processes
- Dialogs
- Workflow basics
- Duplicate Detection Rules
- Creating Workflows in Windows Workflow Foundation with Visual Studio

Processes

Microsoft Dynamics CRM 2011 has changed and enhanced the concept of what used to be called workflows to what are now called processes. CRM 4.0 users will have to spend a little time trying to find the workflows locations the first time they use CRM 2011 because there is not a direct link on the Settings area for this as before. Instead they are now grouped inside the Processes node, which is in the Settings area under the Process Center group as shown in Figure 24.1.

Processes have been replaced to allow the addition of dialogs, which are also processes, but are different from workflows in that they are interactive and require user intervention in order to be completed and started. Table 24.1 shows the main differences between dialogs and workflows.

NOTE

Although dialogs can launch workflow, workflow cannot launch dialogs. In fact, unlike processes, which can be triggered automatically by an event, dialogs MUST be started manually. Additionally, dialogs run in synchronous state, whereas processes run asynchronously.

We are going to describe dialogs and workflows processes in the next sections of this chapter.

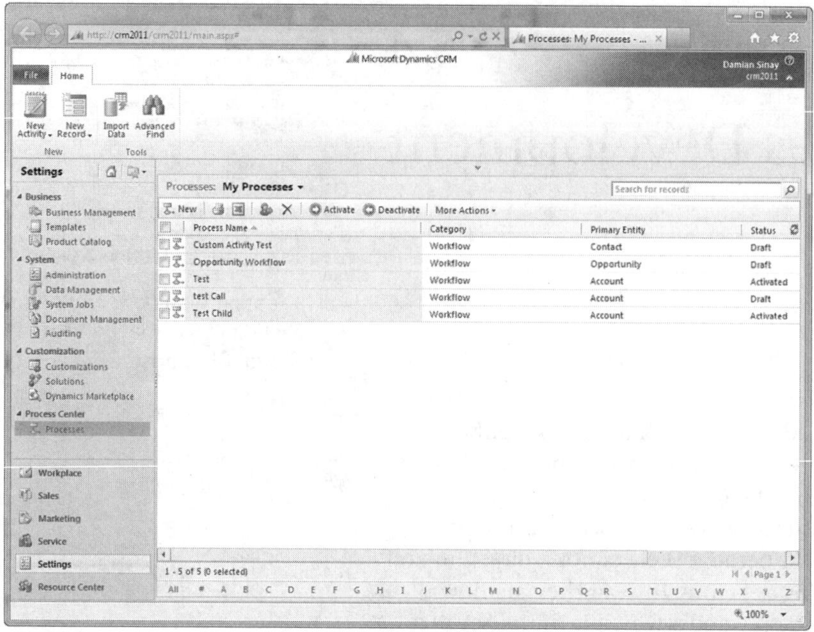

FIGURE 24.1 Processes.

TABLE 24.1 Differences Between Dialogs and Workflows

Dialogs	Workflows
Are synchronous	Are asynchronous
Interactive (require user interaction)	Unattended
Starts manually	Can start manually or triggered by an event like when a record is created, updated, deleted, and so on
Only supported on .NET Framework 4.0	Supported on Framework 4.0 and on Framework 3.5 for migration purposes

Dialogs

Dialogs are a good way to have users perform a business process in a way that we want and when a structured question flow is required. They are good for surveys where we want users to ask a customer to complete a customer satisfaction survey where the next question would depend on the current answer.

To create new dialogs, follow these steps:

1. From the main interface, navigate to Settings Processes, and then click on New.

2. Enter a name for the process; on our sample, we will enter Customer Satisfaction Survey. Select the entity—we will select Account—and select the category, which will be Dialog (see Figure 24.2).

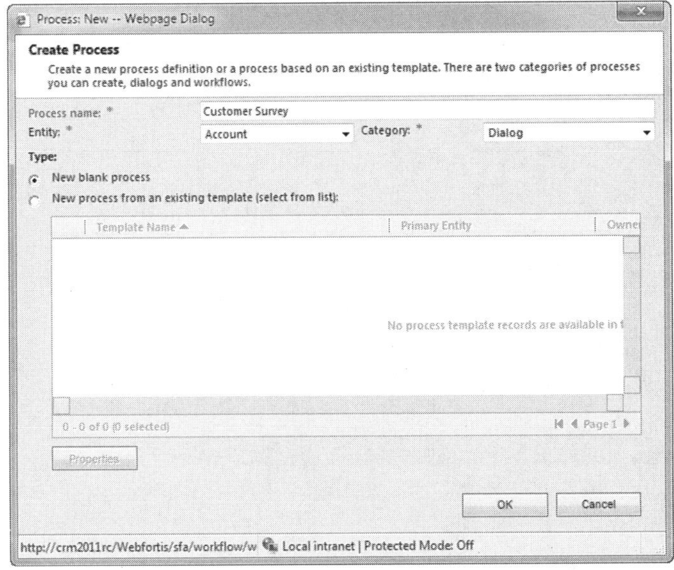

FIGURE 24.2 Create Process dialog.

This is the key step to creating dialogs: selecting the Category drop-down, as shown in Figure 24.2 as Dialog.

1. Click OK and you will see the Dialog Designer (see Figure 24.3).

We will stop the sample here to explain some basic things found on Figure 24.3.

Input Arguments

Input arguments are used for child dialogs to pass parameters from the parent dialog to the child. The input arguments can be a single line of text, a whole number, or floating point number types, as shown in Figure 24.4, and our sample in the Steps section in this chapter illustrates how to use this further.

When you try to add a new input argument, you will be alerted about the need to change the runtime to run as a child process if you didn't do it before.

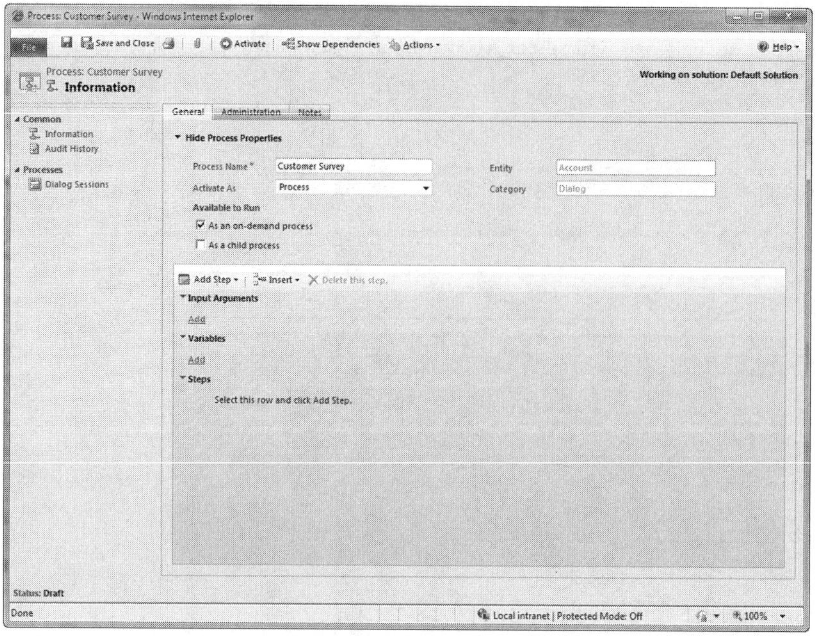

FIGURE 24.3 Dialog Designer.

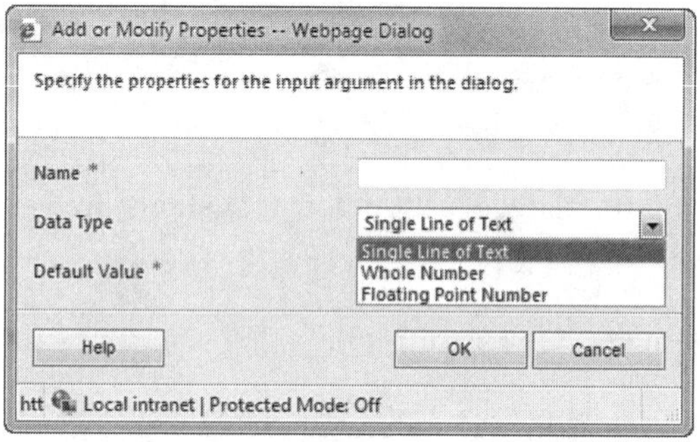

FIGURE 24.4 Input arguments.

Variables

Variables are used to store temporarily computed data or strings that would need to be concatenated on future pages of the dialog. Similar to input arguments, they can be a single line of text, a whole number, or floating point number types (see Figure 24.5).

Steps

Steps are similar to workflows with the exception of the main step, which gives you a Page option. Dialogs contain one or more pages that enable you to interact with the users by asking questions the user will need to answer. Based on the answer, you can change the flow of the entire process.

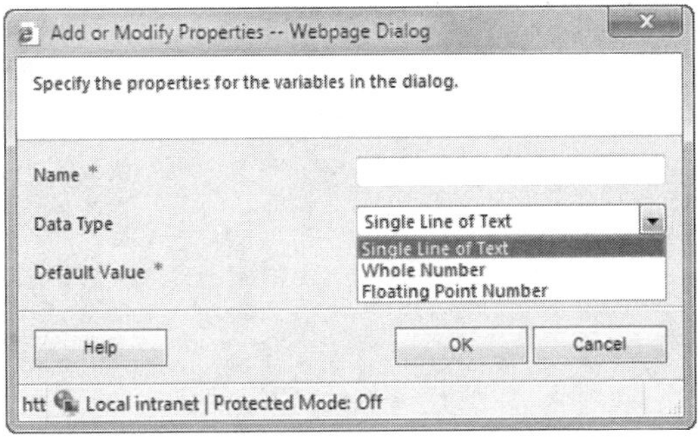

Add or Modify Properties -- Webpage Dialog
Specify the properties for the variables in the dialog.
Name *
Data Type
Single Line of Text
Single Line of Text
Whole Number
Floating Point Number
Default Value *
Help
OK
Cancel
htt Local intranet | Protected Mode: Off

FIGURE 24.5 Variables.

Think of pages as interfaces or pop-ups that are displayed to the user.

Now we are ready to continue with our sample, where we are going to create a welcome page. To do this, follow these steps:

1. Click Add Step and Select Page (see Figure 24.6).

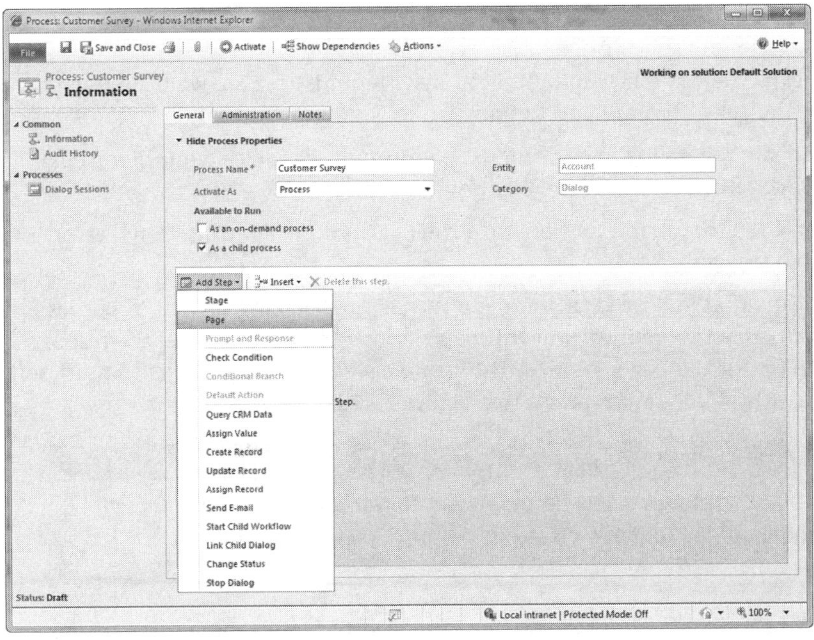

FIGURE 24.6 Adding page to steps.

2. After you add the page, you will see a red error icon (see Figure 24.7).

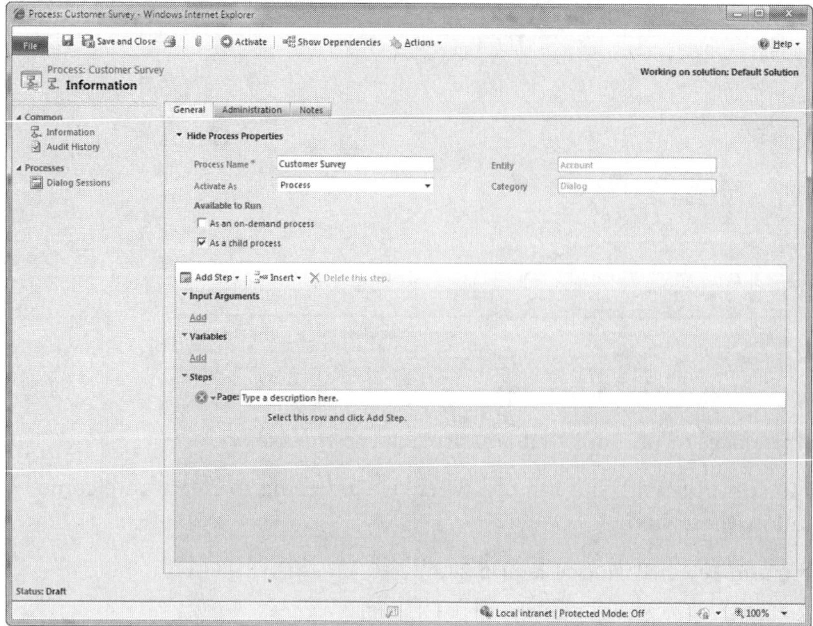

FIGURE 24.7 Page error.

3. This error means there is a Prompt and Response step missing. So, we need to click on Add Step and select Prompt and Response (see Figure 24.8).

Of course we can create the dialog in the order shown (input, variables, and then steps), but for the purposes of illustration, we are creating it backward.

4. After you add the Prompt and Response on the page, you will see also a red error icon, as shown in Figure 24.9.
5. This error means that you need to complete the step by clicking on Set Properties. After you click on Set Properties, you will be able to enter the question, the response type, and the tip for the page. We will first create a welcome page dialog that doesn't require the user to enter any response (see Figure 24.10).

NOTE

Notice in Figure 20.10 that the Response Type is set to None—hence all the related options at the bottom of the form are disabled.

6. Click Save and Close and add another page with another Prompt and Response step inside. On this page, we will select a response type of Option Set (radio buttons), as shown in Figure 24.11. So, we can ask whether the client is very satisfied, little satisfied, or not satisfied with our services.
7. Click Save and Close and add a Check Condition step (see Figure 24.12).

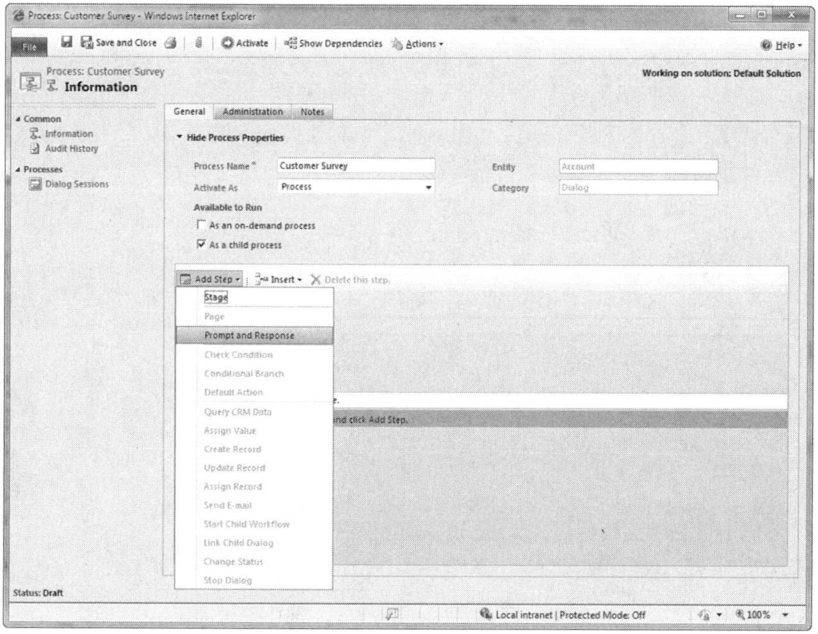

FIGURE 24.8 Adding Prompt and Response to page.

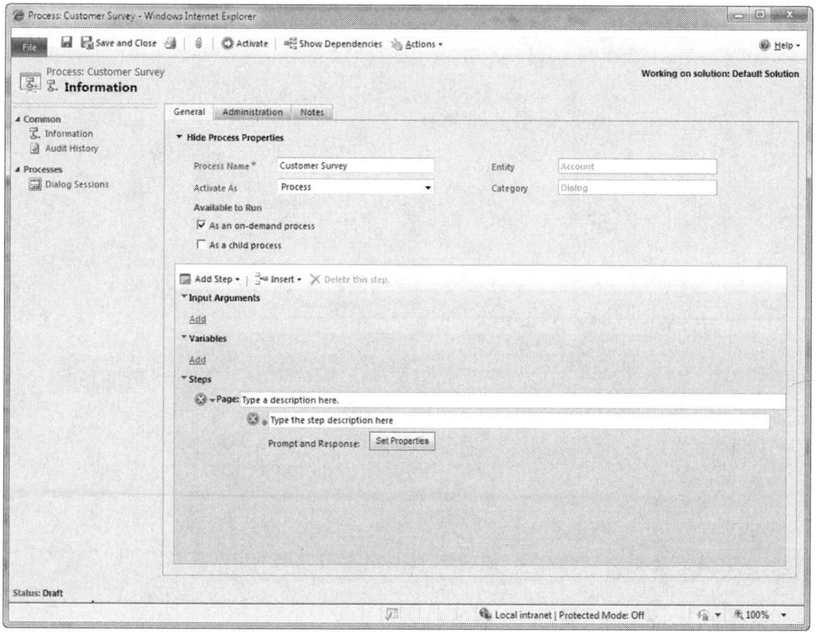

FIGURE 24.9 Prompt and Response error.

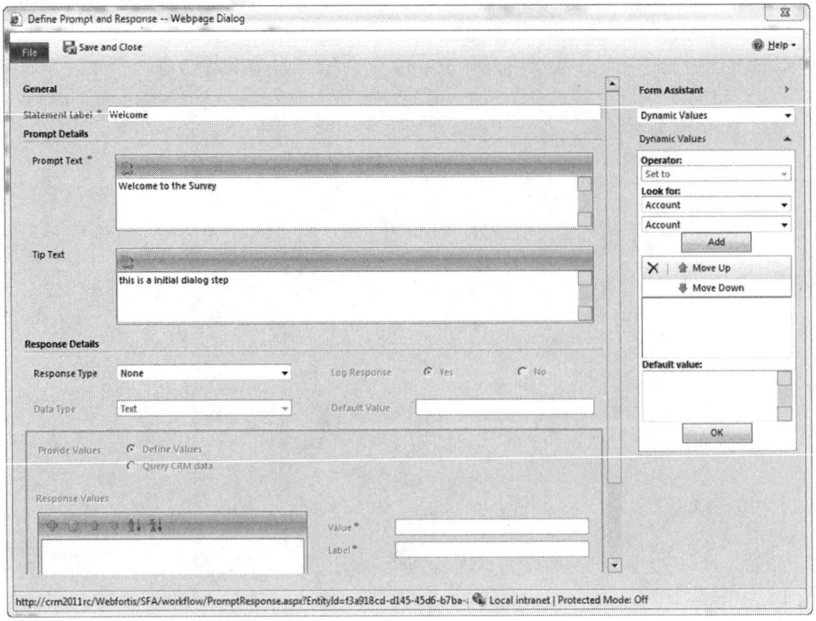

FIGURE 24.10 Welcome page.

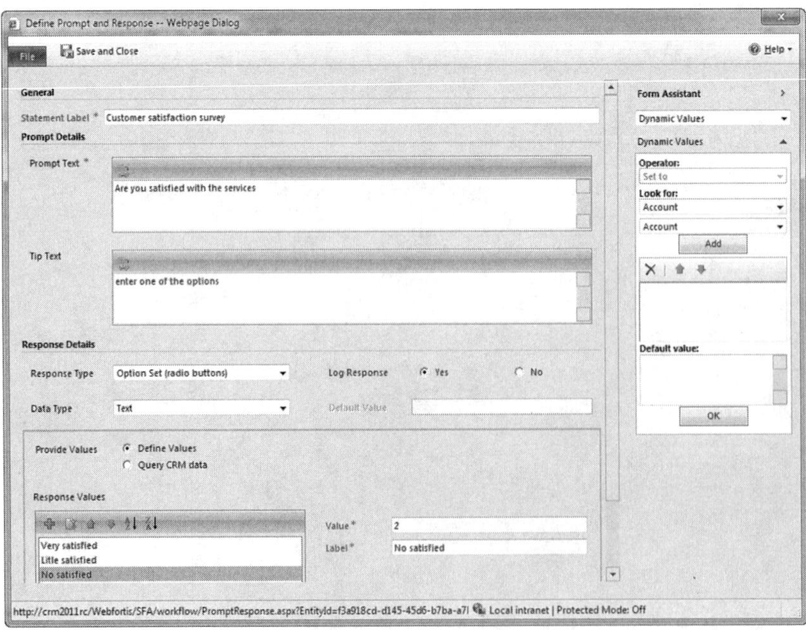

FIGURE 24.11 Option Set (radio buttons) response type.

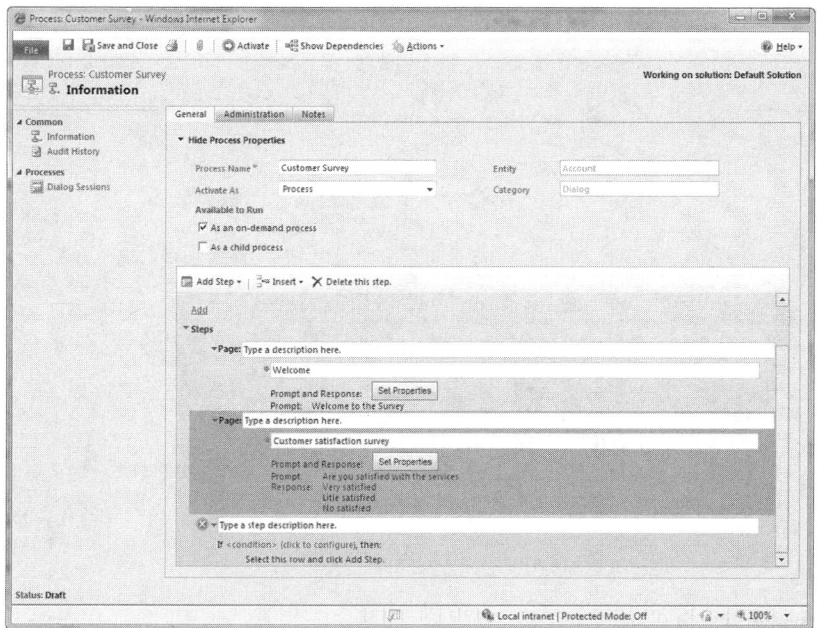

FIGURE 24.12 Adding check conditions.

8. We are going to ask a different question to those customers that are not satisfied. So, we click on the <condition> (click here to configure) to validate the previous page response. It is recommended to use the Response Value instead of the Response Label because it is likely we can change the labels but not the values of the options set.
9. Click Save and Close and add another page with another Prompt and Response step so that we can ask why the customer is not satisfied. For this question, we will allow the user to enter a free text description of the problem (see Figure 24.14). You could add more questions with fixed options on a real process.
10. It would be good to record the selections to a field on the entity, even though we can see the user response on the dialog sessions as we will see later on this chapter. But for the purpose of this sample we will record the text entered by the user on the Account Details field. To do this, select the entire last step, click on Add Step, and then Update Record.
11. Click on Set Properties, and in the Description field under the Details section we are going to set a dynamic value from the dissatisfaction response text.

We can update any field on the Account form with values from the dialog session.

This is an important piece to consider when using dialogs and processes—because we're updating the record, we can easily launch workflow on the field values set by the dialogs.

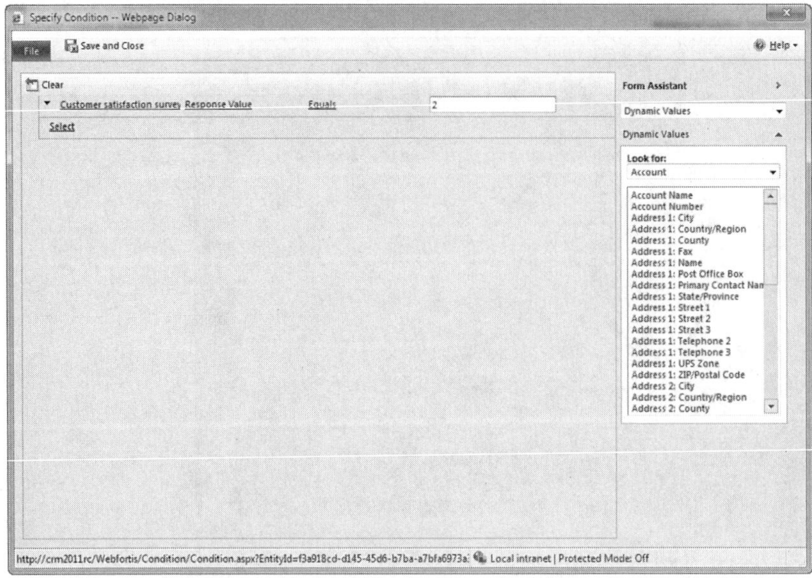

FIGURE 24.13 Validating response value.

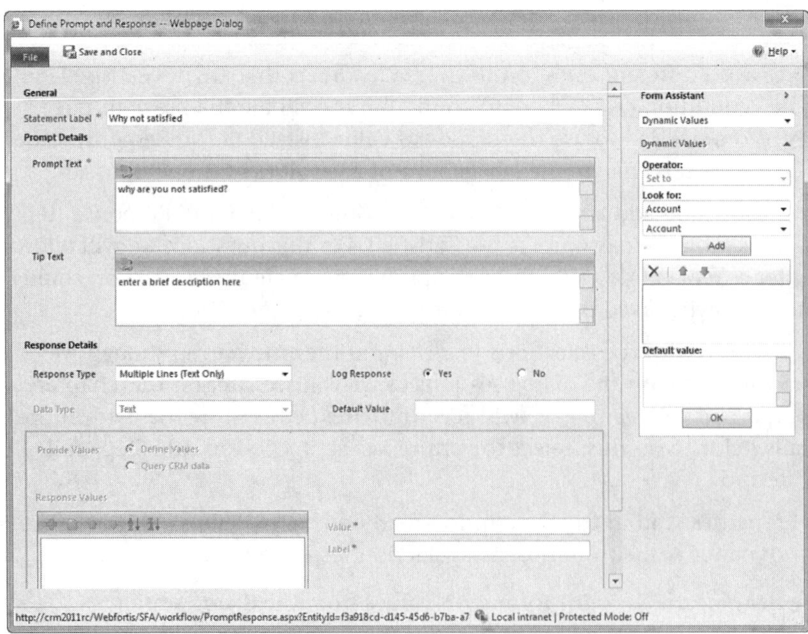

FIGURE 24.14 Multiple Lines of Text (ntext) response type.

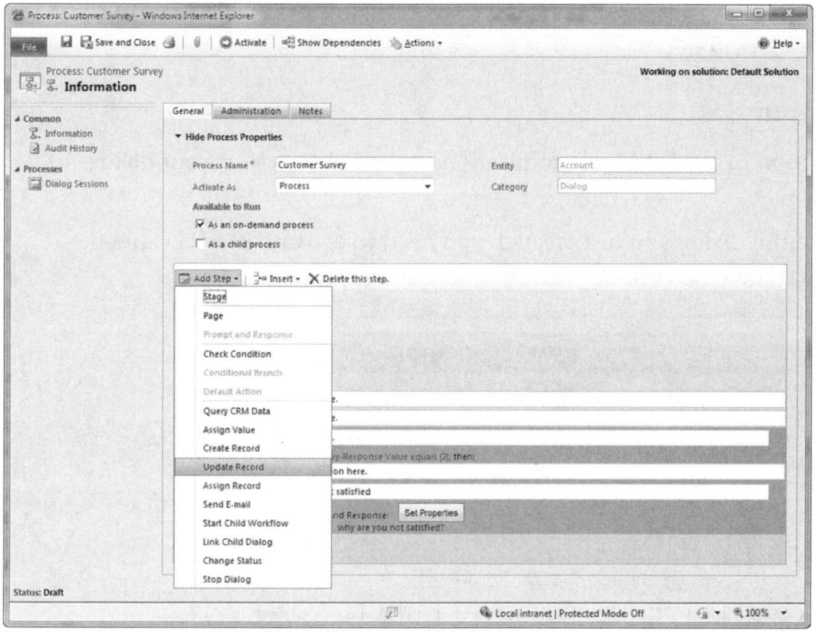

FIGURE 24.15 Adding update record step.

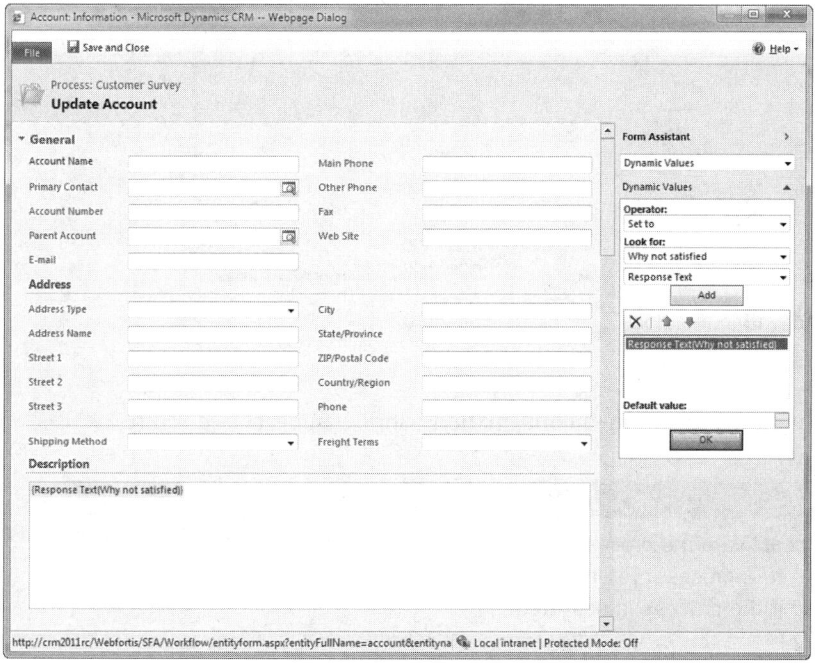

FIGURE 24.16 Updating the Description field based on the user response text.

12. Click Save and Close to close the update Account dialog and click Save and Close to close the Dialog editor.

Dialog Activation

Similarly to the action of publishing customizations, we need to activate our dialogs to make them available.

Before you can use the dialog you just created, you need to activate it by clicking the Activate button (see Figure 24.17).

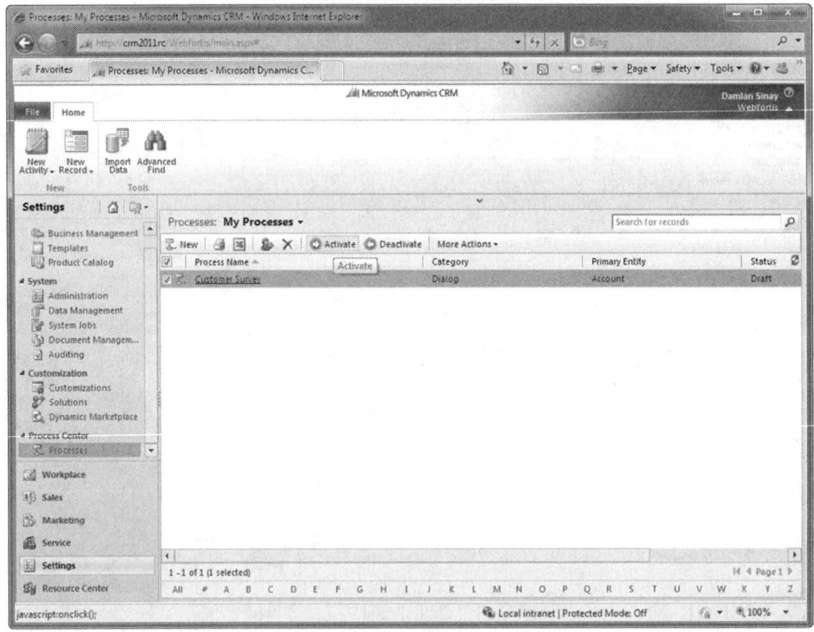

FIGURE 24.17 Activating a dialog.

When you click the Activate button, a confirmation window appears (see Figure 24.18).

TIP

You can always deactivate the process by clicking the Deactivate button. If you need to make any change to a process, you must deactivate it first because the capability to edit it is disabled if the process is activated.

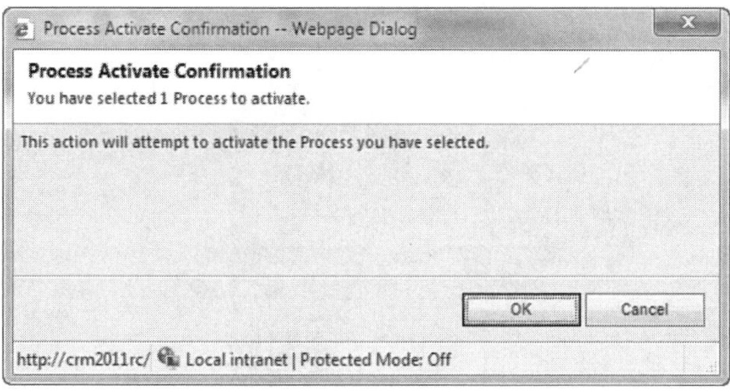

FIGURE 24.18 Process Activate Confirmation dialog.

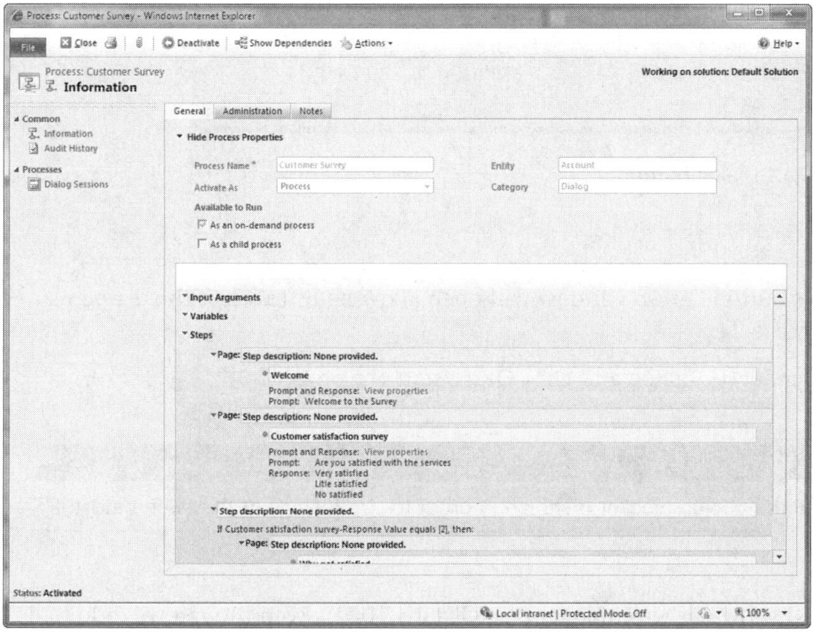

FIGURE 24.19 Viewing an activated dialog with the settings disabled.

Testing the Dialog

Dialogs must be started manually by the user because we want to test a dialog we made for Accounts, and then we need to go to the accounts, which are usually located in the workplace section. There we can select any account record and we will see a button on the ribbon that says Start Dialog (see Figure 24.20).

FIGURE 24.20 Start Dialog button.

When clicking this button, a new window will open allowing us to select the dialog we want to use (see Figure 24.21).

Select the Customer Survey dialog and click OK to start the process.

> **TIP**
>
> You need to have the pop-up blocker disabled in order to use dialogs or they won't start.

The first screen will show our welcome text (see Figure 24.22). Even though we didn't add any question on this page, the user will have the ability to enter a comment here. You will be able to see the comments and the dialog responses in the Dialog Sessions link that is related to the record we are running in the dialog.

Click Next to continue. You will be presented with the question we configured to allow the user to select one of the options (see Figure 24.23) because we added more logic for unsatisfied customers; select this option and click on Next.

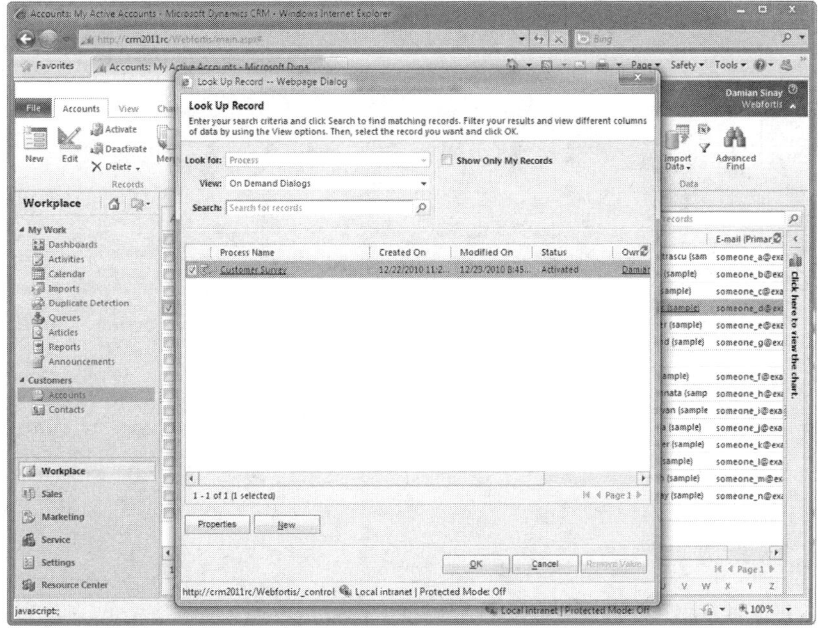

FIGURE 24.21 Select dialog.

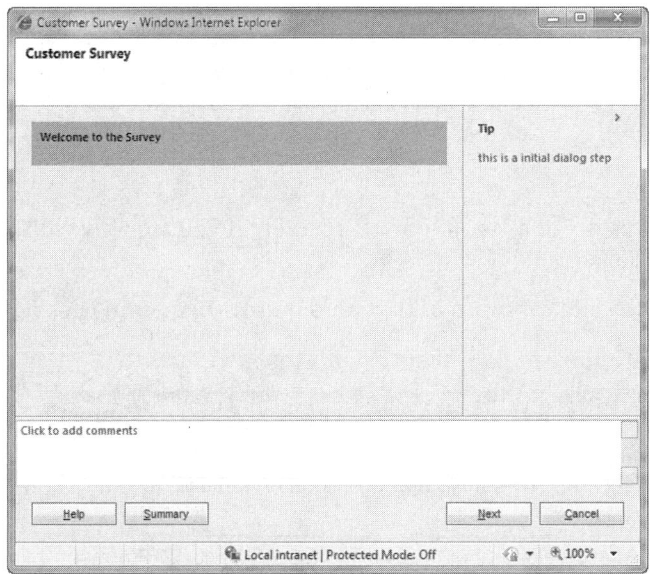

FIGURE 24.22 Welcome text.

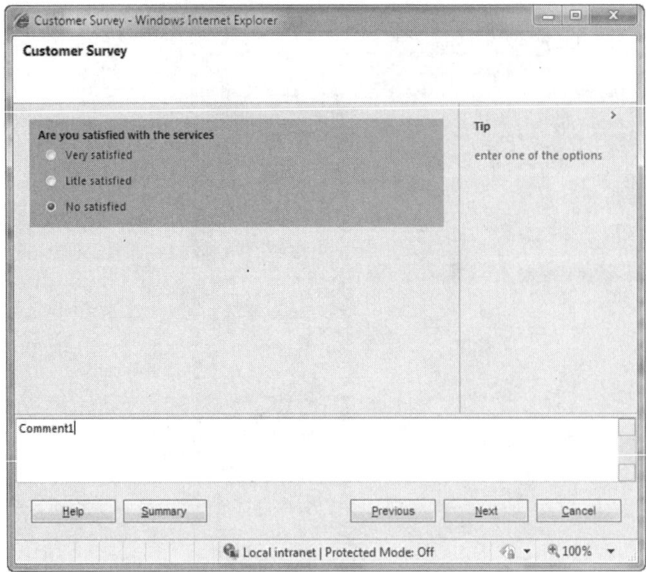

FIGURE 24.23 Option Set question page.

On the next page the user will be able to answer a question with a free text form explaining the reasons why he is dissatisfied on our example.

NOTE

Notice that this field is different from the comment text box that is on the bottom of the dialog because this is specifically related to this question, whereas comments are related to the entire dialog process.

Click Next to continue. The final page will ask you for confirmation. If you are okay with all the dialog responses, click on Finish.

During the dialog process, users can move forward or backward on the pages until clicking Finish on the last page.

NOTE

Dialogs can be also started by using a direct URL that will run the dialog (this is very helpful for programmatic access such as IVR software integrations or similar). You can access a dialog with an URL like this:

http://CRMServerName/OrgName/cs/dialog/rundialog.aspx?DialogId=DialogID&EntityName=EntityLogicalName&ObjectId=EntityObjectId where DialogID, EntityName, and ObjectID are the values found in the URL of the dialog. To grab this URL, you can launch the dialog and press Ctrl+N to get the dialog to open a new window where you can see the address bar.

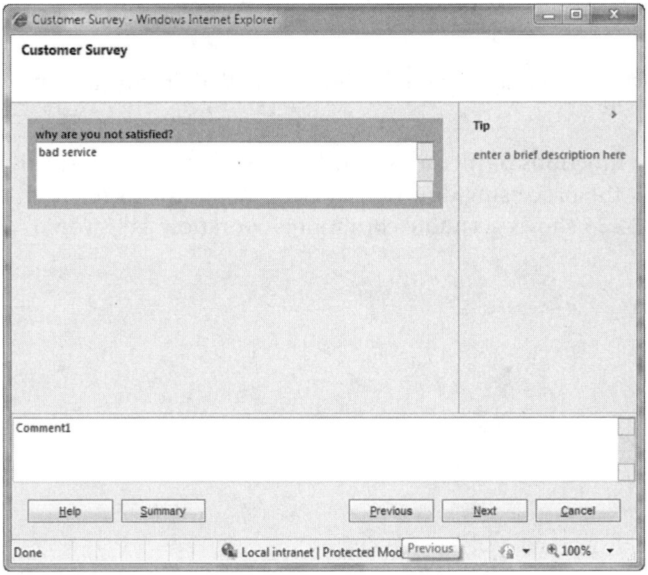

FIGURE 24.24 Free text answer page.

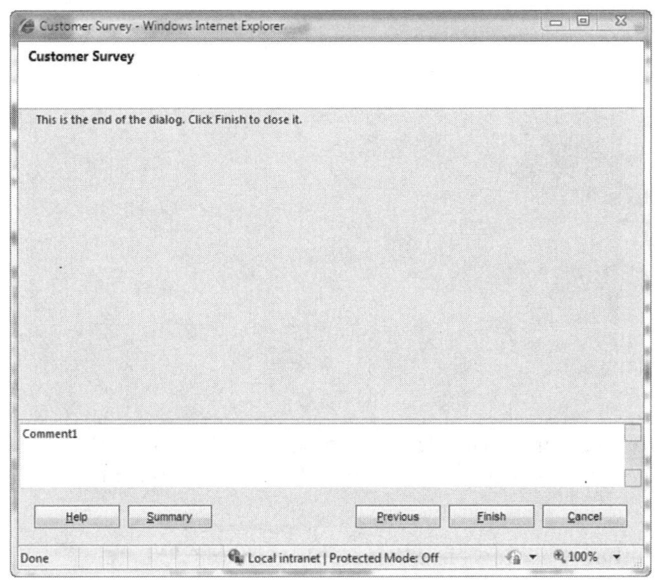

FIGURE 24.25 Final page.

Workflow Basics

Before digging into Workflow development, let's briefly review what Workflow means in IT terms.

A Workflow is basically a series of functions or methods called *steps*, which are performed sequentially. The flow can change the processing direction by using conditionals referred to as *conditional branches*. Figure 24.26 shows a sample conditional Workflow as it would appear on a flowchart.

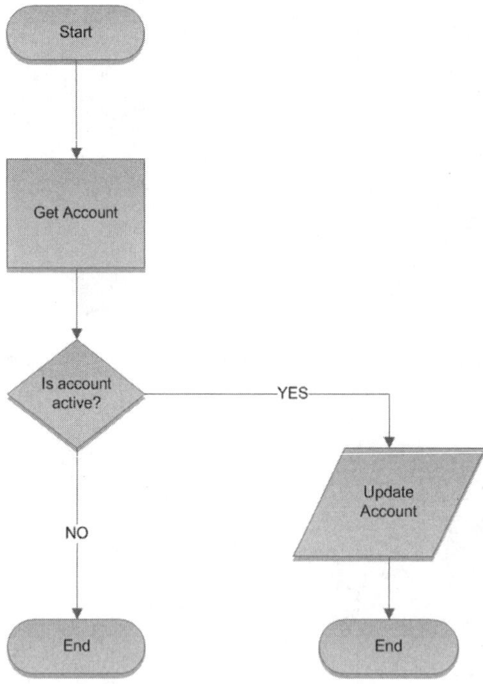

FIGURE 24.26 Workflow sample image.

A Workflow is an excellent tool for managing both data and processes. With Workflow rules, you can easily ensure that certain steps are followed and that required business processes are executed.

Two important considerations are that Workflows in Microsoft Dynamics CRM are executed asynchronous, and they use a Windows service to act as a host application for the Workflow engine to work. This Windows service has the name of Microsoft Dynamics CRM Asynchronous Processing Service and must be running on the server or the workflows won't be executed on time. Notice that if this service is not running, you won't see any of the workflows you are going to create through this chapter running properly on time, but they will run as soon as you start this service because the workflows are queued. So, it is a good idea to verify that this Windows service is running by going to Start,

Control Panel, Administrative tools, Services and start the Microsoft Dynamics CRM Asynchronous Processing Service if it is not running.

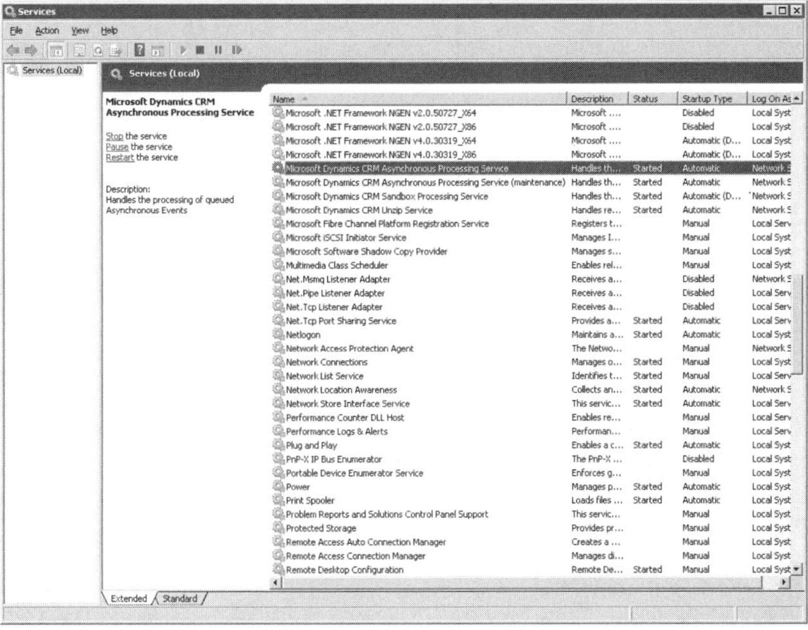

FIGURE 24.27 Checking that the Microsoft Dynamics CRM Asynchronous Processing Service is running.

Another consideration is that because Workflows are executed asynchronously, they might not run immediately and depending on the server overhead they might take some seconds or minutes to complete (or even start!). If you need a process to run immediately, it would be better for you to think about creating plug-ins, which can be set to be executed synchronously.

▶ Refer to Chapter 25, "Plug-Ins," for detailed instructions about how to use and create plug-ins.

Another feature related to workflows is that they are also treated as entities in CRM, so you can use the Advanced Find tool to lookup for workflows and you can also create reports based on them.

Creating Workflows with Microsoft Dynamics CRM

By default, any valid CRM user can create Processes; however, the permissions to create processes can be configured by roles to prevent users from creating new processes that might burden the system. Figure 24.28 shows where permissions are set in the Settings, Security Roles area for creating processes.

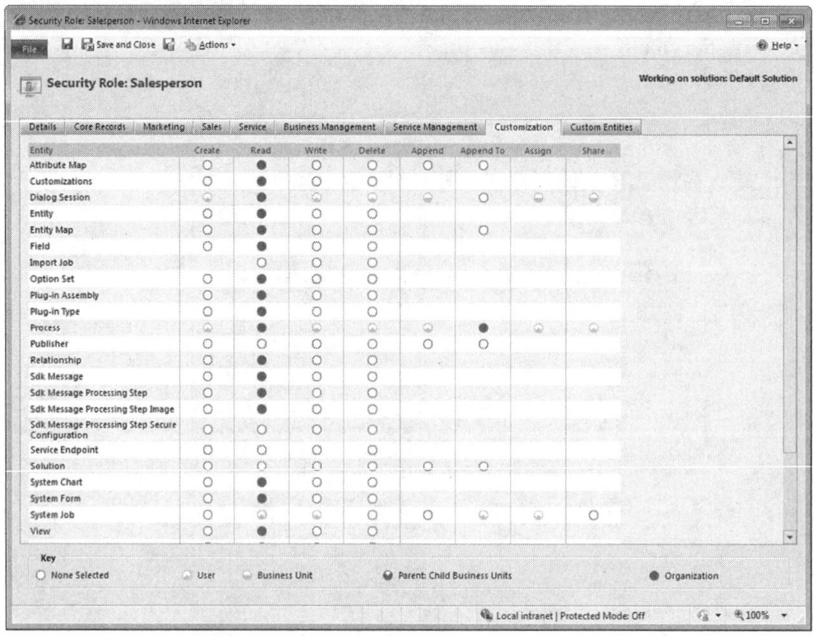

FIGURE 24.28 Process permissions configuration.

▶ Refer to Chapter 12, "Settings and Configuration," for more information about setting permission levels.

Workflows can be started by the following triggering events and run settings. These are the triggering events:

- Record is created
- Record status changes
- Record is assigned
- Record fields change
- Record is deleted

Notice that the "record fields change" event enables you to reference any field on the underlying entity. The details of each event are outlined later in this chapter. These are the run settings:

- As an on-demand process
- As a child process

As an On-Demand Process

If this option is specified, the process can be triggered manually by going to the associated entity and clicking the Run Workflow button that is in the Process section in the Ribbon.

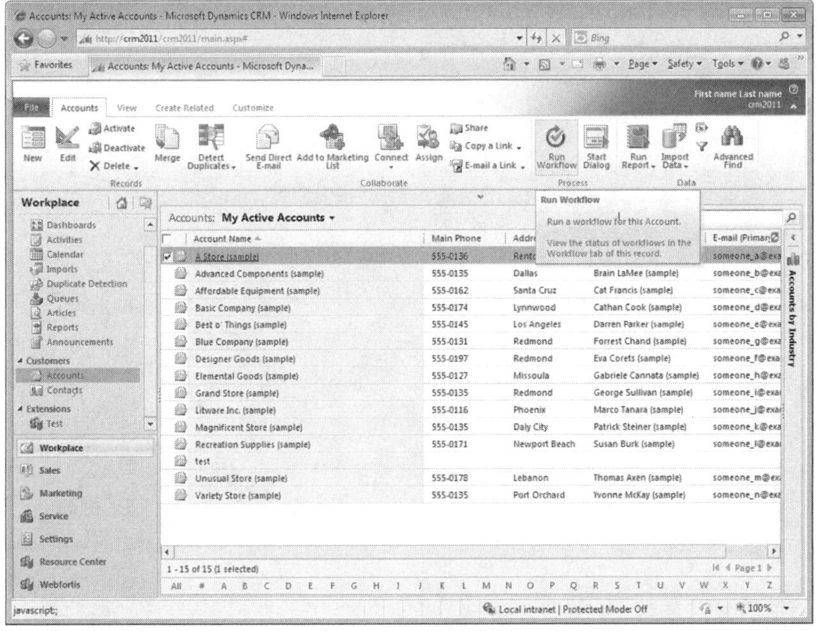

FIGURE 24.29 Running an on-demand workflow for the Account entity.

After clicking the Run Workflow button, the window shown on Figure 24.30 will appear, allowing the user to select which on-demand workflow to run.

As a Child Process

Child processes are not executed automatically when the associated events are triggered. Instead, they are executed only when they are called through the Start Child Workflow activity.

If you need to perform a series of steps that are common to other entities or to the organization, using a child workflow would make sense.

> **TIP**
>
> Only the related entities' workflows can be used to call a child workflow. For example, you can't call a child workflow associated with the Invoice entity from a workflow of the Account entity.

A good example of a child workflow is a child workflow created for the Contact entity that could be called from another workflow associated with the Account entity, which would be fired when an Account is created using the Primary Contact relationship. The same child workflow could also be fired from another workflow created for the Phone Call entity that would fire the related Regarding contact.

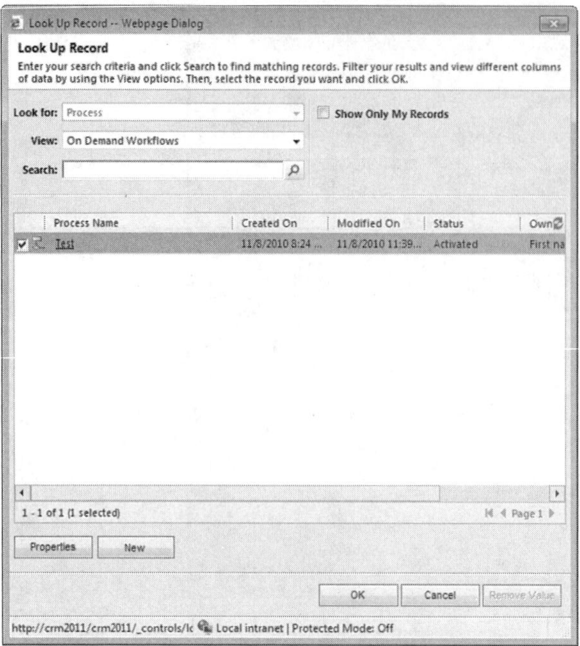

FIGURE 24.30 Running an on-demand workflow for the Account entity.

If neither As On-Demand nor As a Child process is selected, the workflow will run automatically when the triggering event is fired.

NOTE

If a workflow calls itself (on the same entity) more than 7 times in an hour, the 8th instance will fail. This failure was added to prevent a workflow from creating an infinite loop. For a birthday workflow sample (because the loop happens once a year), does not trigger any failure.

To access the Workflow Manager, follow these steps:

1. From the main interface, navigate to Settings Processes.
2. To create a new process of type workflow, click New, and the Create Process dialog window will appear (see Figure 24.32).

   There is also the option to create either a blank process or a new process from an existing template. For this example we're going to create a blank process; however, as explained further in this chapter, when working with the process, it can either be saved as a regular process or it can be saved as a process template. If saved as a process template, it can be referenced in this list for additional customization and/or other options.

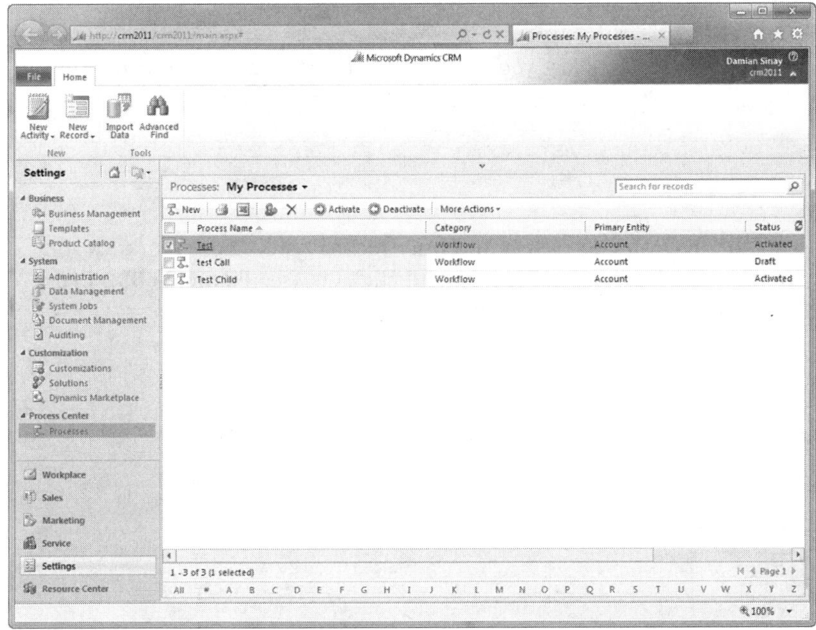

FIGURE 24.31 Settings, Processes screen.

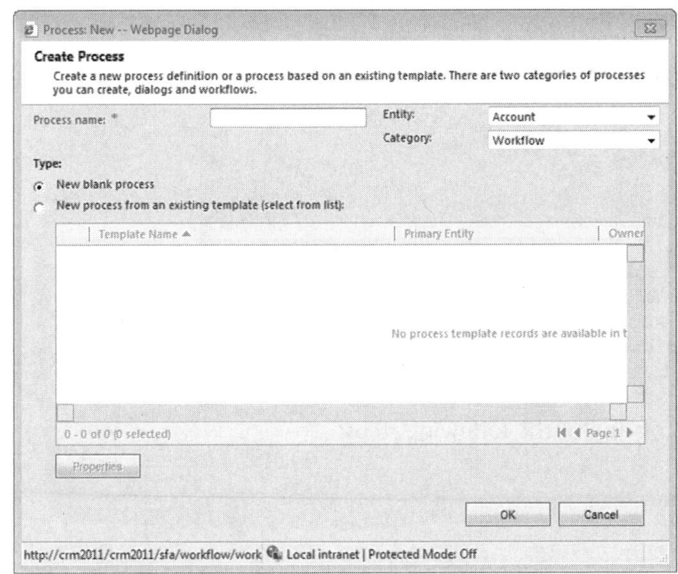

FIGURE 24.32 Create Process window.

TIP

Notice that when creating a new workflow, you must associate it to a base entity. The entity is a drop-down option that is found on Figure 24.32 and can be from any entity in the system.

3. Enter a name for the new process, select an entity record type, select Workflow on the Category field, select New Blank Process, and click OK (see Figure 24.33). Every workflow must be associated with an entity.

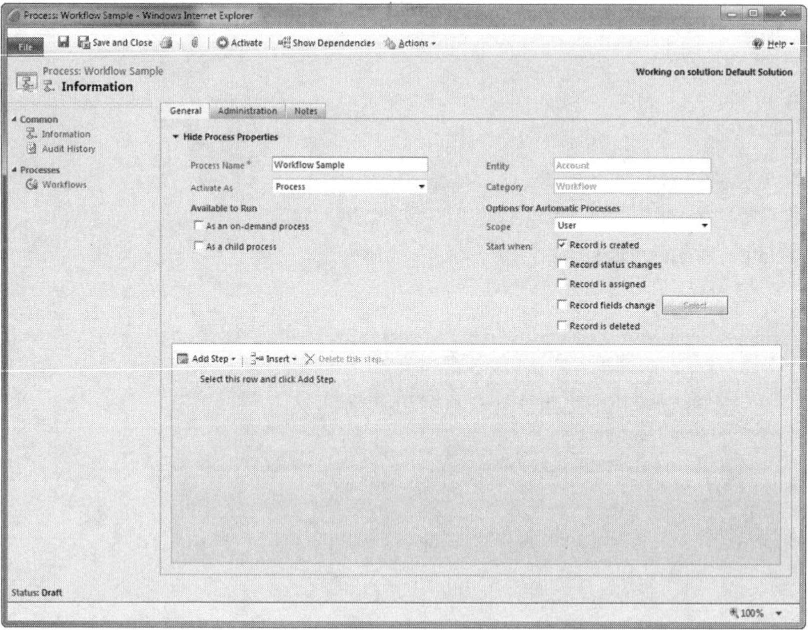

FIGURE 24.33 Workflow properties.

Now you are ready to start adding any of the following steps:

- Stage
- Check Condition
- Wait Condition
- Create Record
- Update Record
- Assign Record
- Send E-mail
- Start child Workflow
- Change Status
- Stop Workflow

Stage

Although stages are used for grouping purposes (see Figure 24.34), they are also stored in the database, enabling you to report on the different stages and various stage metrics, such as the number of records affected for each stage. If you have a complex workflow with several steps in it, grouping steps makes it easier to read and understand. You can collapse or expand the stages to fit the window screen (see Figure 24.34).

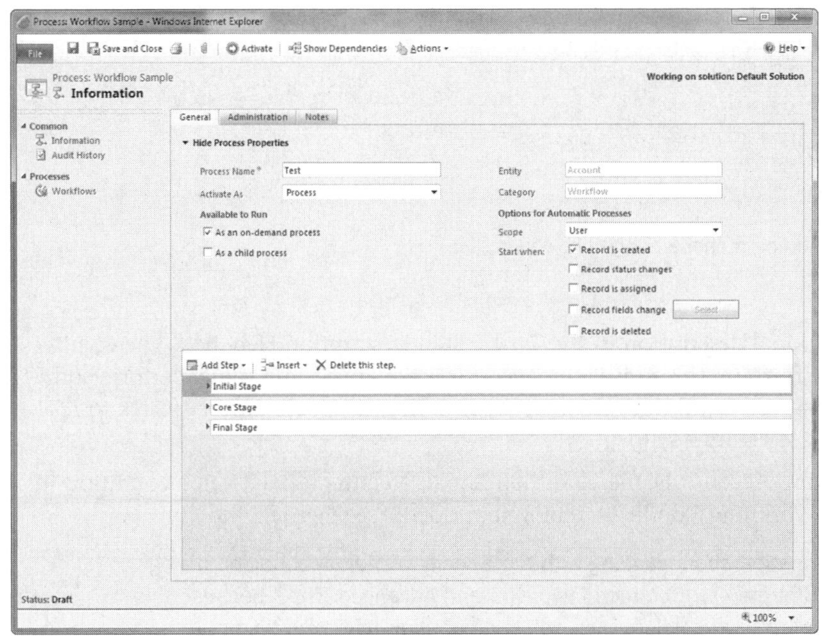

FIGURE 24.34 Workflow stages as shown on a three-stage workflow.

Check Condition

A check condition is a Boolean evaluation similar to the if/then conditional in programming. (For those unfamiliar with an if/then conditional, it is the way conditions are evaluated. For example if a=b, then c=d.). So, the condition to be evaluated can be either true or false.

To add a check condition, follow these steps:

1. Click Add step, and then select Check Condition (see Figure 24.35).

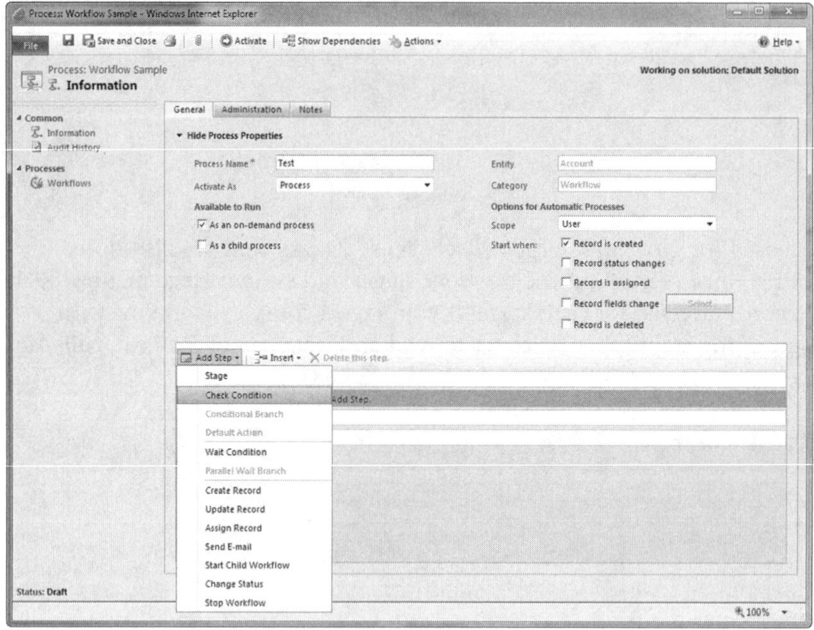

FIGURE 24.35 Adding a check condition.

2. Enter an optional description in the Type a Step Description Here box. The condition that we're going to add is if the Account is equal to some value, perform some action. To add this condition, click on the link that says <condition> (Click to Configure) (see Figure 24.36).
3. Select Account, Account Name, and then Equals to enter a fixed-value condition in the Specify Workflow Condition dialog that opens (see Figure 24.37).

▶ For more information about working with the Specify Workflow Condition dialog screen, refer to Chapter 7, "Common Functions and Advanced Find," because this chapter uses the same principles when selecting entities and conditions.

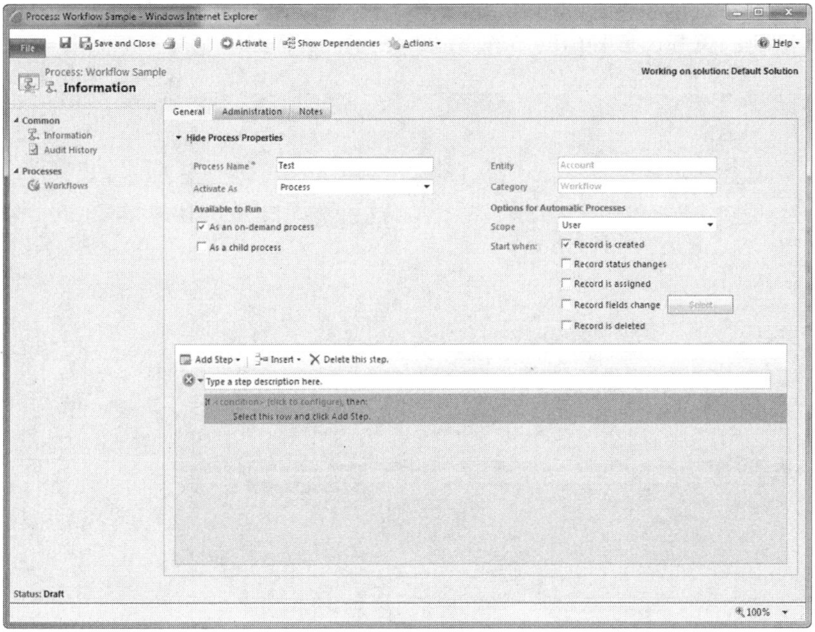

FIGURE 24.36 Using a check condition.

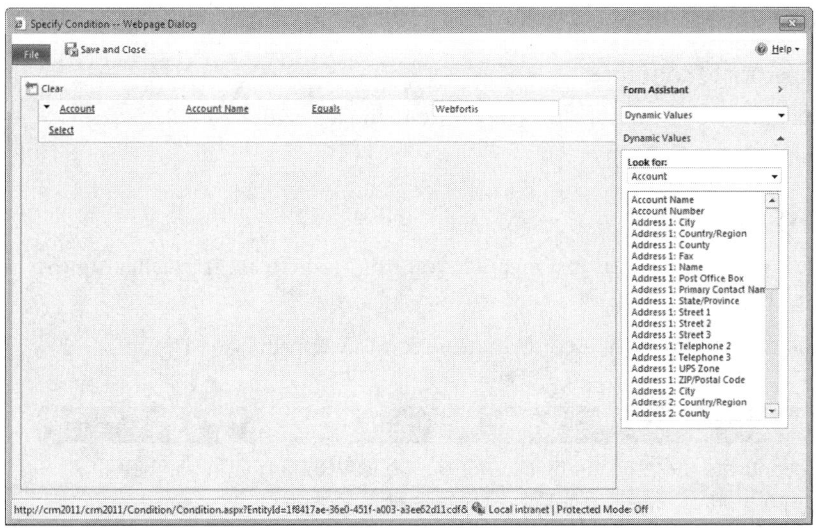

FIGURE 24.37 Configuring the evaluation expression based on a hard-coded value.

4. To set a dynamic value, select an entity from the drop-down, and then click on the desired field in the list box to set the condition (see Figure 24.38).

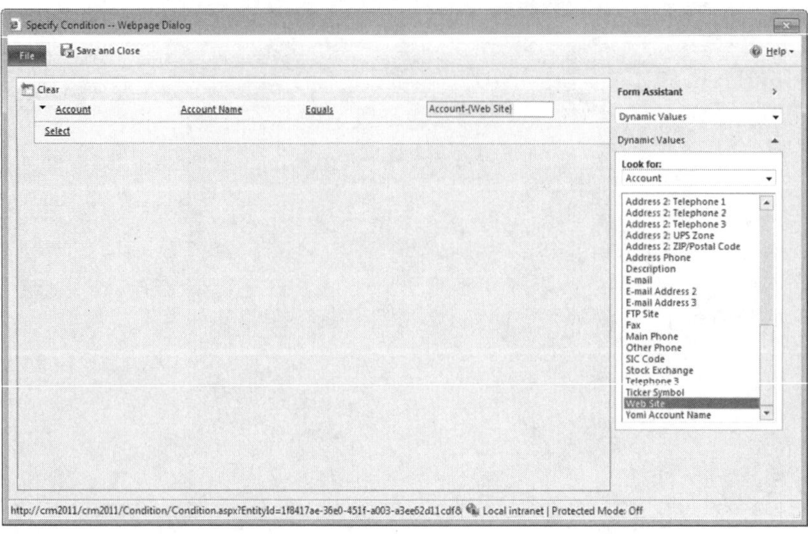

FIGURE 24.38 Configuring the evaluation expression based on an entity property.

5. Click Save and Close to continue.
6. Click Select This Row and then click Add Step. Then click Send E-mail (see Figure 24.39).
7. Click Set Properties to continue.
8. Enter a subject and body message for the new e-mail (see Figure 24.40).
9. Click Save and Close.

Workflow Activation

Before you can use the workflow you just created, you need to activate it by clicking the Activate button (see Figure 24.41).

When you click the Activate button, a confirmation window appears (see Figure 24.42).

TIP

You can always deactivate the process by clicking the Deactivate button. If you need to make any change to a process, you must deactivate it first because the capability to edit it is disabled if the process is activated.

Testing the Workflow

When a new Account is created using the same name as the website property, your process sample is fired. You can see the progress of a process by looking at the Status Reason. To do that from the CRM Web Interface menu, click on Settings and then System Jobs (see Figure 24.44).

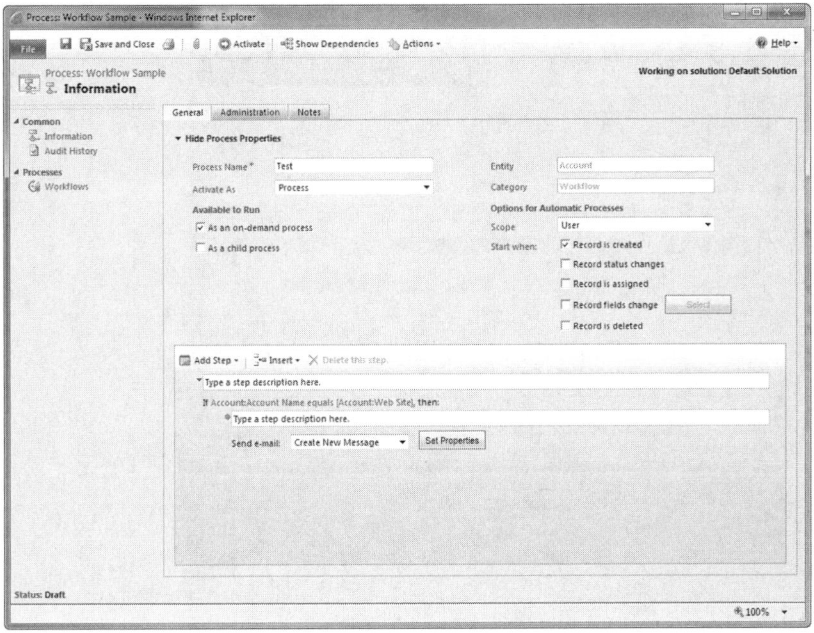

FIGURE 24.39 Creating an e-mail based on a conditional.

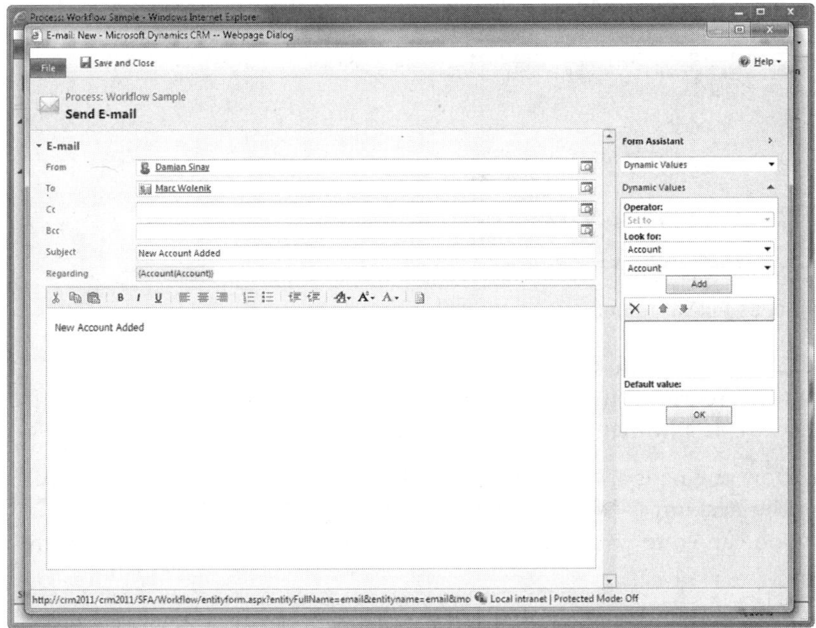

FIGURE 24.40 Configuring the e-mail properties

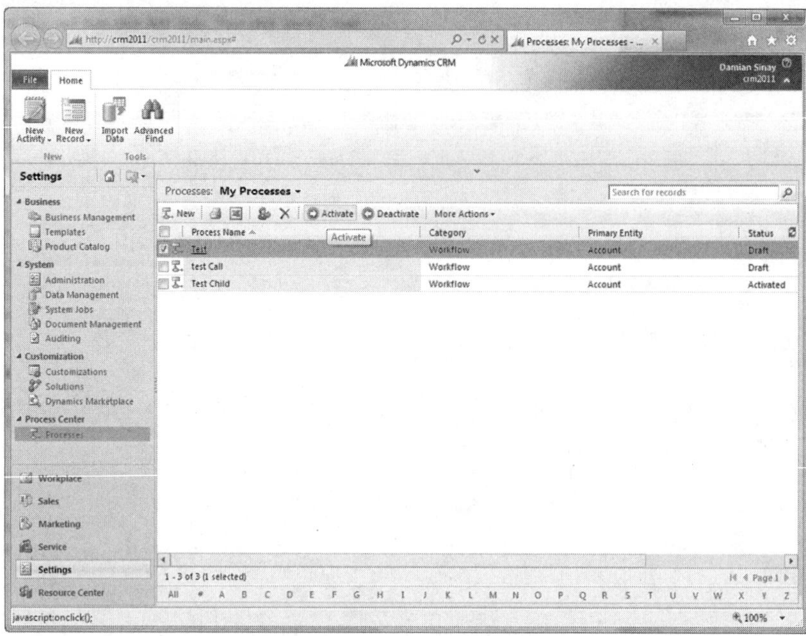

FIGURE 24.41 Activating a workflow.

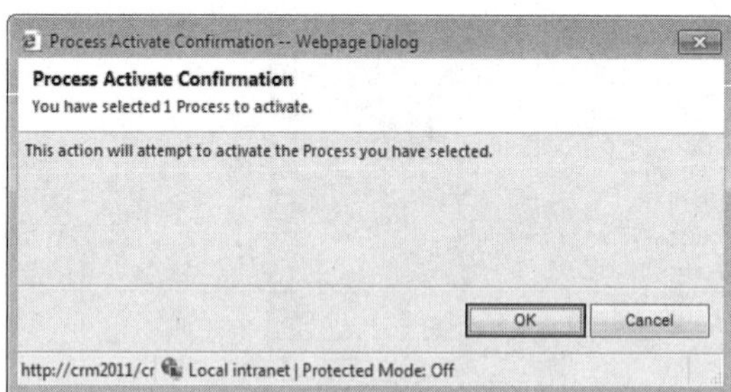

FIGURE 24.42 Process Activate Confirmation dialog.

When working with this screen, you have the option to select from the drop-downs at the top to filter the view. By default they are set to All System Jobs and All Entities.

Note that the workflow engine is asynchronous and the workflow might not be immediately trigged when the Account is created. When the process finishes, the new e-mail activity is created, you can go to your workplace and you will see the e-mail in the activities area.

Depending on your e-mail router configurations, the e-mail will be sent directly to the destination, or it will be queued as an activity (see Figure 24.45).

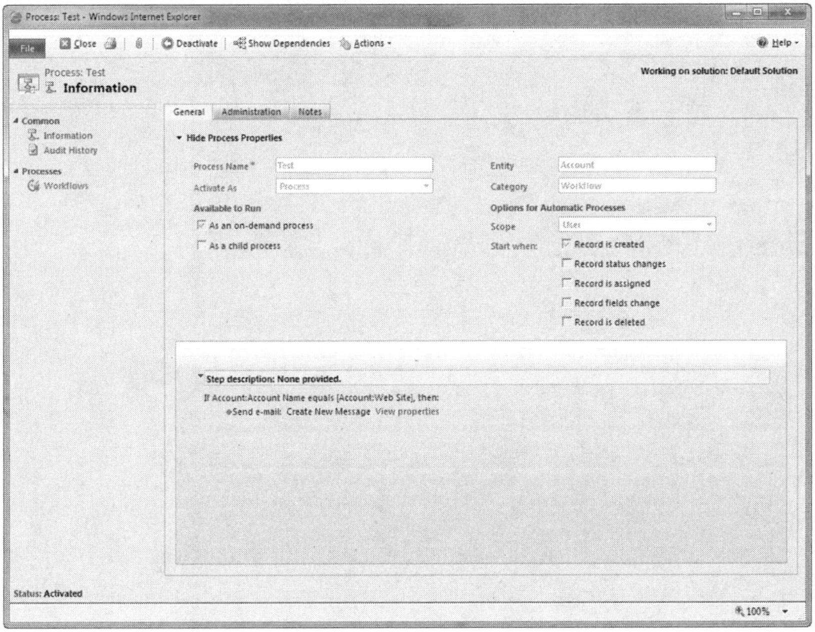

FIGURE 24.43 Viewing an activated process with the settings disabled.

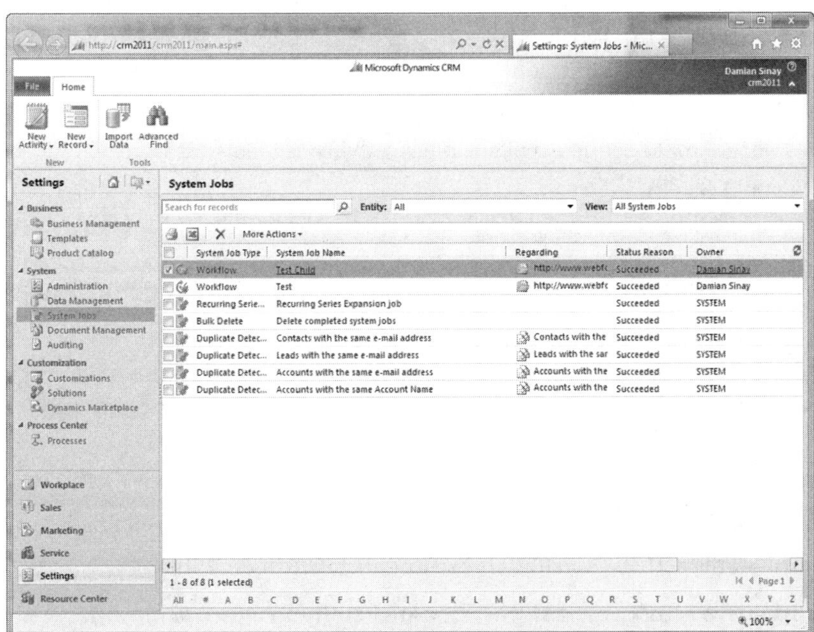

FIGURE 24.44 Monitoring process progress.

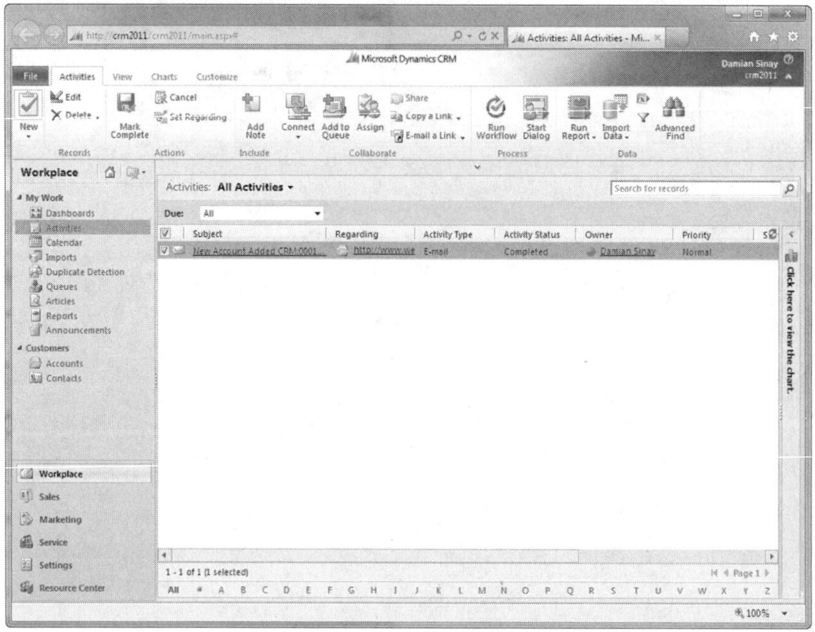

FIGURE 24.45 Workflow results with a new email activity created for the new account.

Notice you will have to change the Type drop down to E-mail to see the e-mail activities because they are not shown by default if your e-mail router is configured to send the e-mails automatically.

▶ For more details about how to set up e-mails and using the e-mail router, refer to Chapter 14, “E-Mail Configuration.”

The conditions described here are the conditions previously described earlier during workflow creation.

- **Wait Condition**—The wait condition can put the workflow to sleep until a condition changes, such as the property of the associated entity or after a period of time has elapsed.
- **Create Record**—Use this activity to create a new instance of any entity. The user can hardcode the properties or retrieve them from the associated entity.
- **Update Record**—This activity updates an existing instance of an entity.
- **Assign Record**—This activity assigns the associated entity to a user or a team.
- **Send E-mail**—This activity sends an e-mail by creating a new message or using a template. You can create a new e-mail message or use a predefined template as a recommended option.

▶ For additional information about how to create e-mail templates, refer to Chapter 12.

- **Start Child Workflow**—This activity calls a child workflow. As described earlier, a child workflow is one that needs to be created with the As a Child Workflow setting.
- **Change Status**—This step changes the associated entity status. The status type varies by entity. Table 24.2 lists the different entities and statuses affected by Change Status.
- **Stop Workflow**—This step stops the execution of the current workflow. You can change the result status of the workflow from Succeed to Canceled. Use this activity step inside a conditional to prevent the workflow from continuing if a property doesn't meet the criteria you expect.

TABLE 24.2 Entities Affected by Change Status

Entity	Status
Accounts	Active, Inactive
Appointments	Canceled, Completed, Open, Scheduled
Articles	Draft, Published, Unapproved
Article templates	Active, Inactive
Campaigns	Active, Inactive
Campaign activities	Canceled, Closed, Open
Campaign responses	Canceled, Closed, Open
Cases	Active, Canceled, Resolved
Connections	Active, Inactive
Connection Roles	Active, Inactive
Contacts	Active, Inactive
Contracts	Active, Canceled, Draft, Expired, Invoiced, On Hold
Contract lines	Canceled, Existing, Expired, Renewed
Currencies	Active, Inactive
Dialog Sessions	Complete, Incomplete
Discount lists	Active, Inactive
Document locations	Active, inactive
Goal Metrics	Active, inactive
Goals	Active, inactive
Imports	Active
Invoices	Active, Canceled, Closed (deprecated), Paid
Leads	Disqualified, Open, Qualified
Mail merge templates	Active, Inactive

TABLE 24.2 Entities Affected by Change Status

Entity	Status
Marketing lists	Active, Inactive
Opportunities	Lost, Open, Won
Orders	Active, Canceled, Fulfilled, Invoiced, Submitted
Orders	Active, Canceled, Fulfilled, Invoiced, Submitted
Price lists	Active, Inactive
Processes	Activated, Draft
Products	Active, Inactive
Queue Items	Active, Inactive
Queues	Active, Inactive
Quotes	Active, Closed, Draft, Won
Recurring Appointments	Canceled, Completed, Open, Scheduled
Rollup Queries	Active, Inactive
Sdk Message Processing Steps	Disabled, Enabled
Service activities	Canceled, Closed, Open, Scheduled
Services	Active, Inactive
SharePoint Sites	Active, Inactive
System jobs	Completed, Locked, Ready, Suspended
Unit Groups	Active, Inactive
Users	Disabled, Enabled
Views	Active, Inactive

Figure 24.46 shows the Change Status activity.

Workflow Events

Workflows can automatically start the execution when one or a combination of the events listed next is triggered.

▶ Refer to Figure 24.46 under Options for Automatic Processes.

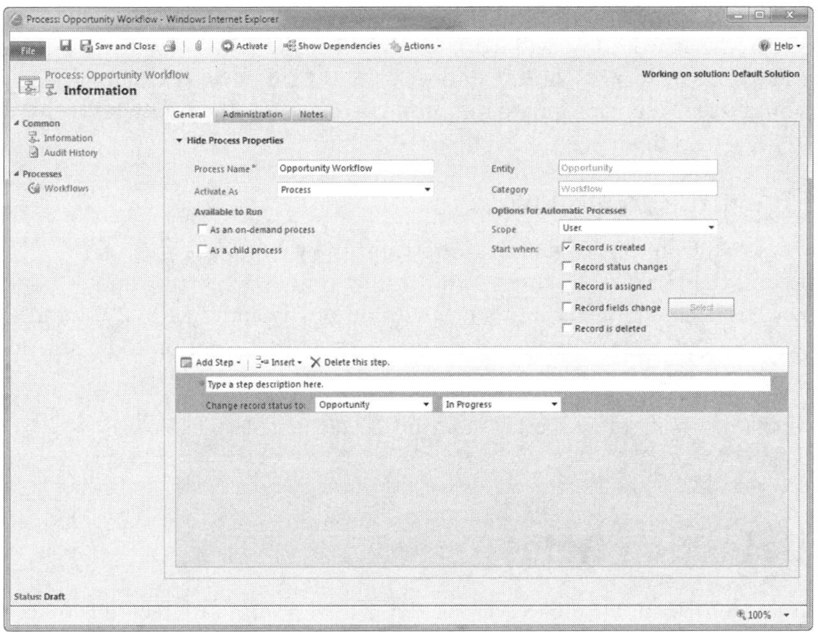

FIGURE 24.46 Change status step for an opportunity.

- **Record is created**—This event is triggered after a new record of the associated entity is created.
- **Record status changes**—This event is triggered when a record of the associated entity status changes, such as when a record of an Account is activated or deactivated, or when a record of an Opportunity entity status changes to Won. Refer to Table 24.2 for the various entity statuses.
- **Record is assigned**—This event triggers when an instance of the associated entity is assigned to a user.
- **Record fields changes**—This new event for Microsoft Dynamics CRM is very useful because you can trigger a workflow when any field of a record from the associated entity change.
- **Record is deleted**—This new event for Microsoft Dynamics CRM is triggered when a record of the associated entity is deleted.

Workflow Scope

Workflows created through this interface can be applied to the following areas:

- Users
- Business Units
- Parent: Child Business Units
- Organization

These items are the various scope options—what the workflow will apply to across the system. If you select User, this workflow will work for only the user who owns the workflow. If you want the workflow to work on the entire Business Unit or on the organizational level, you should select the appropriate option. Note that only the user who owns the workflow can see the tracking history.

Exporting and Importing Workflows

You can transfer workflows from one organization to another by exporting them as compressed zip files and then importing them into the new system. Exporting and importing workflows has been changed on this new version of Dynamics CRM 2011 and you will need to create a solution and include the workflows on that solution to be able to export them. Then you can import the solution to the destination organization.

▶ To learn more about how to create, export, and import solutions, refer back to Chapter 16, "Solution Concepts."

Duplicate Detection Rules

You can use the Duplicate Detection Rule to manage duplicates. A duplicate record can be defined in any manner applicable to your organization and is flexible. The following example illustrates Contacts that have the same e-mail address; however, if your business rules required unique addresses, we could easily add a Duplicate Detection Rule on Address.

To access the Duplicate Detection Rule interface, follow these steps:

1. Click Settings, Data Management, Duplicate Detection Rules (see Figure 24.47).
2. By default, four predefined rules exist:
    - Accounts with the same account name
    - Accounts with the same e-mail address
    - Contacts with the same e-mail address
    - Leads with the same e-mail address

These rules are published and running by default when Microsoft Dynamics CRM 2011 is loaded. If you don't want them, you should either unpublish them or delete them.

If you don't want to have duplicate Competitor names in the system, you can easily prevent that by creating a new rule by clicking on New and entering the required information in which the base record type and matching record type are both Competitors. If you wanted to ensure that no duplicate Competitor and Account names existed, you would change the base or matching record type appropriately (see Figure 24.48).

1. The new rule needs to be published to work. Clicking the Publish button publishes the rule.

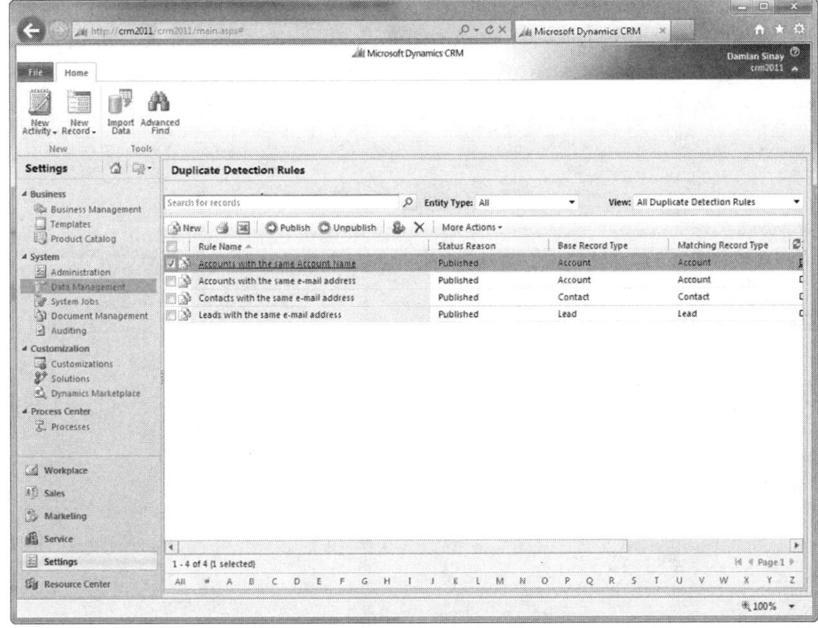

FIGURE 24.47 The Duplicate Detection Rules interface.

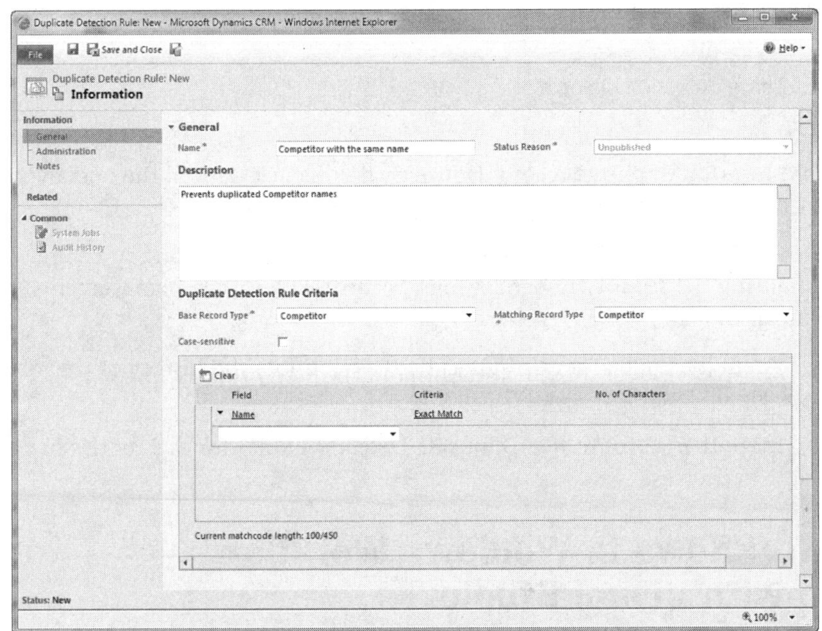

FIGURE 24.48 Creating a new rule to prevent duplicate account names.

After this rule is published, if a user tries to create a Competitor with a name that already exists in the system, a dialog alerting the user about the duplicate record appears after either Save or Save and Close is clicked on the Competitor record (see Figure 24.49).

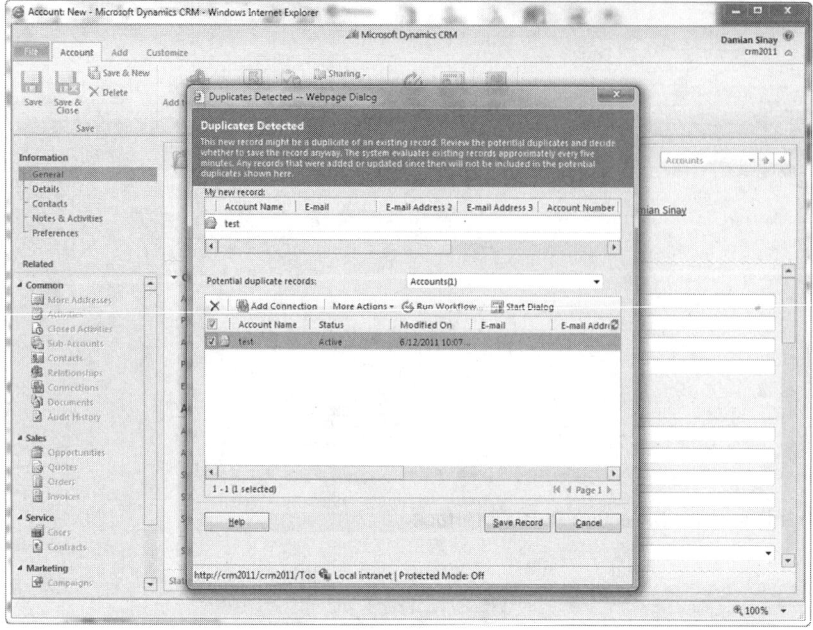

FIGURE 24.49 Duplicate detection dialog alert.

Clicking Save Record inserts a duplicate record. However, if you click Cancel, the operation ends and the Competitor is not created.

These rules apply to the Business Unit in the system by default. However, you can change this setting by configuring the security under Settings, Security Roles, Data management of each CRM role in the system.

When viewing the System Jobs node for any duplicate detection job, the history of the job will be displayed (see Figure 24.50).

You should have no more than three to five Duplicate Detection Rules for each entity or performance will start to decrease.

Creating Workflows in Windows Workflow Foundation with Visual Studio

You also can create processes by using Windows Workflow Foundation (WWF). WWF has been redesigned on.NET Framework 4.0, and you can create WWF projects using Visual Studio 2010. WWF project templates are included in the Visual Studio 2010 setup.

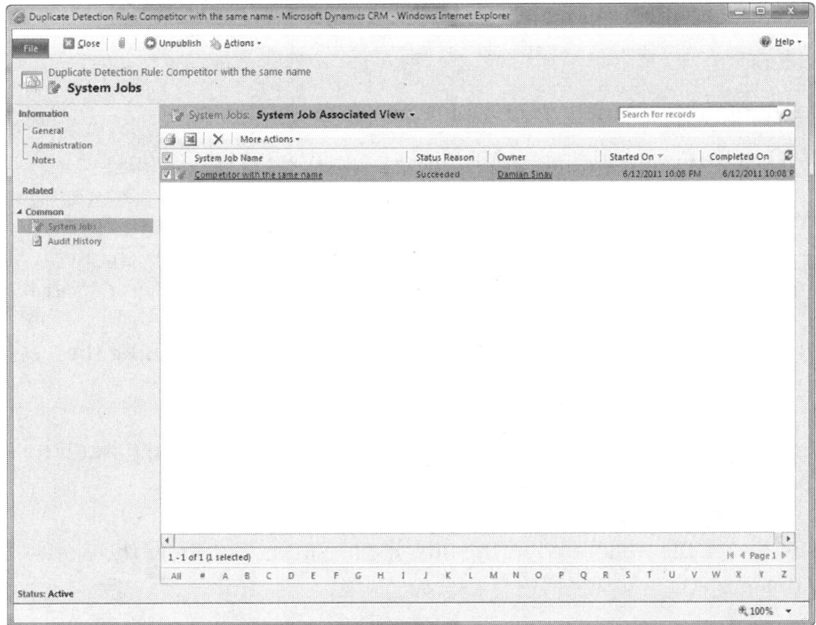

FIGURE 24.50 Duplicate Detection Rules jobs.

To start developing workflows with WWF, you must install the following components on the development machine:

- .NET Framework 4.0
- Visual Studio 2010
- Microsoft CRM 2011 SDK

▶ Although the scope of this book does not include all these components, users need to be aware that only Visual Studio 2010 Professional and above will work; the Express version is not supported. Chapter 23, "Customizing Entities," explains the Microsoft Dynamics CRM 2011 SDK in greater detail.

No-Code Workflow

The no-code workflows are XAML (Extensible Application Markup Language) files, they contain workflow markup in XML format.

The advantages of no-code workflows include the following:

- Can be deployed without compiling
- Easier to develop
- Can be deployed on live CRM servers or on-premise servers
- Can share WWF activities by adding parallel tasks or loop/while conditions

Before starting to be able to create a no-code workflow, we recommend you first create the workflow with the CRM workflow designer interface as explained early on this chapter and then create a new solution, include this workflow on the solution, and then export it.

1. Open the solution file with Visual Studio 2010 and create a new project using the Activity Library template.

2. Add the references to Microsoft.Xrm, Sdk.dll, and Microsoft.Xrm.Sdk.Workflow.dll to the project. These files are located in the SDK folder\bin folder.

3. Add the existing XAML file we located in the unzipped solution file under the workflow folder to this project.

4. Add the CRM workflow controls to the toolbox by adding the Microsoft.Xrm.Sdk.Workflow.dll file. Right-click on the General tab and click the Choose Items menu option. Then browse and add the Microsoft.Xrm.Sdk.Workflow.dll, which is located in the SDK\bin folder.

After you export the solution, you can unzip the solution file and locate the XAML file, which will be included inside the workflow folder.

When you add the controls to the toolbox, you will see a new group of activities specially designed to be used with CRM (see Figure 24.56).

The following example shows how to build a workflow that will create a Phone Call activity for every new contact added to CRM.

Development

To start development on the workflow, you first need a CRM Workflow activity (located in the General section on the toolbox), which is also included by default when you initially created an empty workflow. Add a CRM CreateEntity activity inside the first one. The workflow should look like the one shown in Figure 24.57.

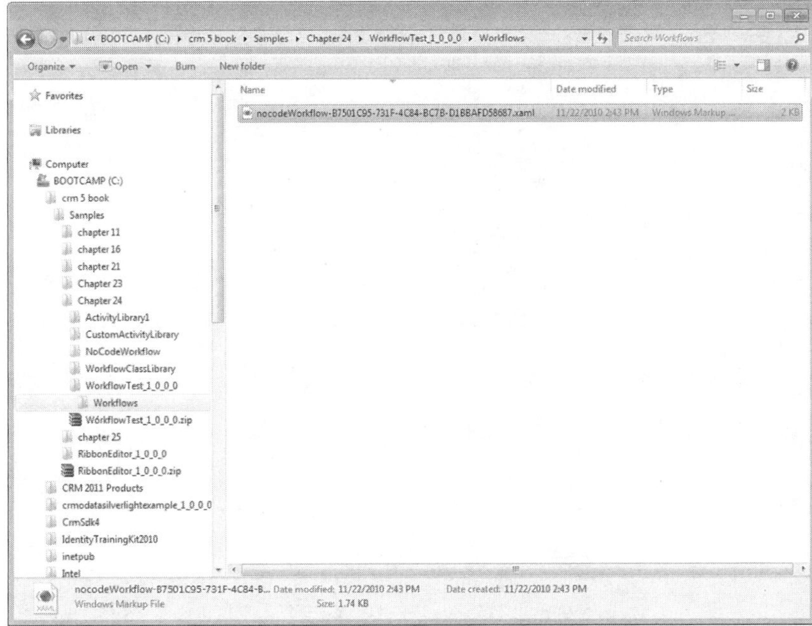

FIGURE 24.51 Locating the XAML file inside the workflow folder on the unzipped solution.

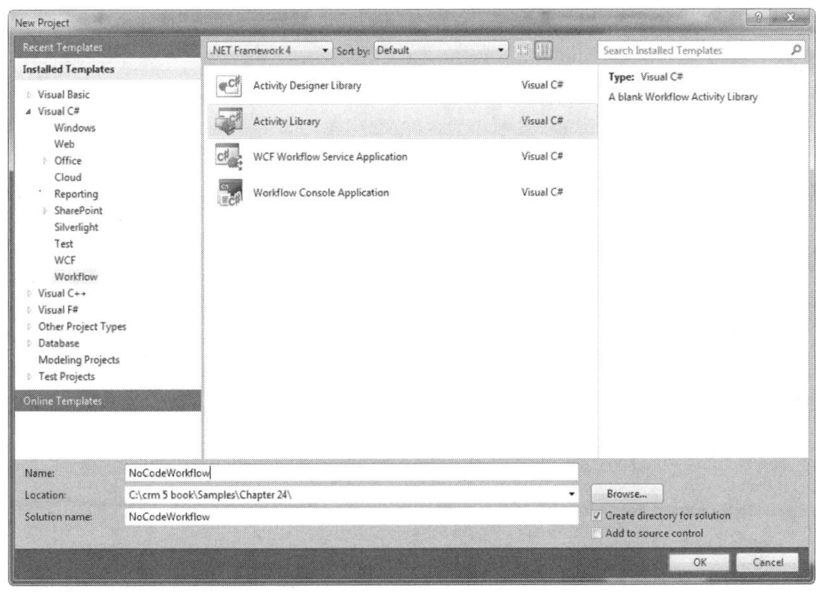

FIGURE 24.52 Activity Library project in Visual Studio 2010.

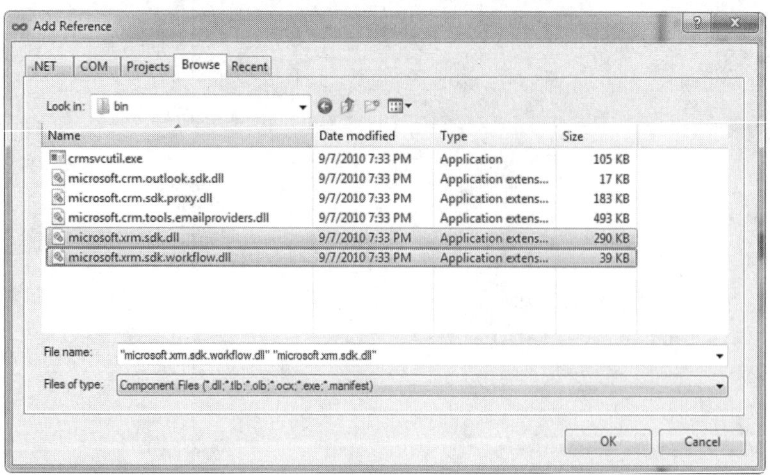

FIGURE 24.53 Adding CRM references.

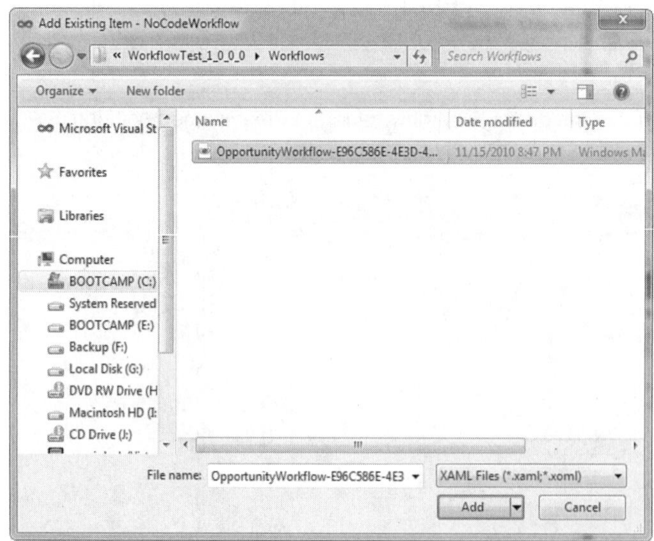

FIGURE 24.54 Adding existing XAML file to the project.

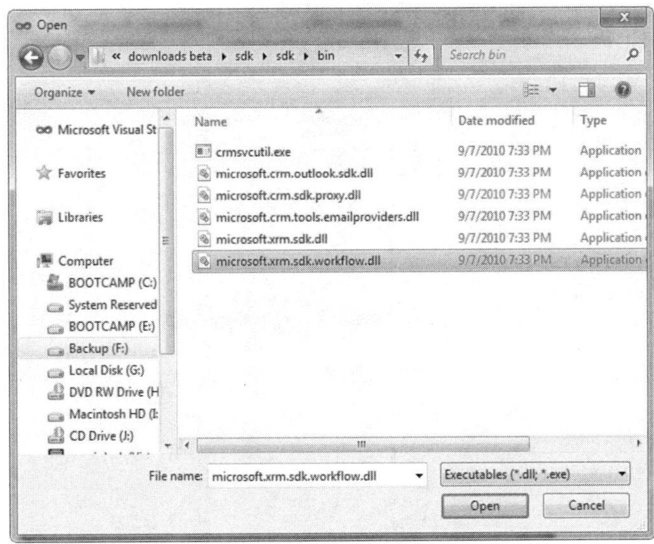

FIGURE 24.55 Adding CRM controls to the toolbox.

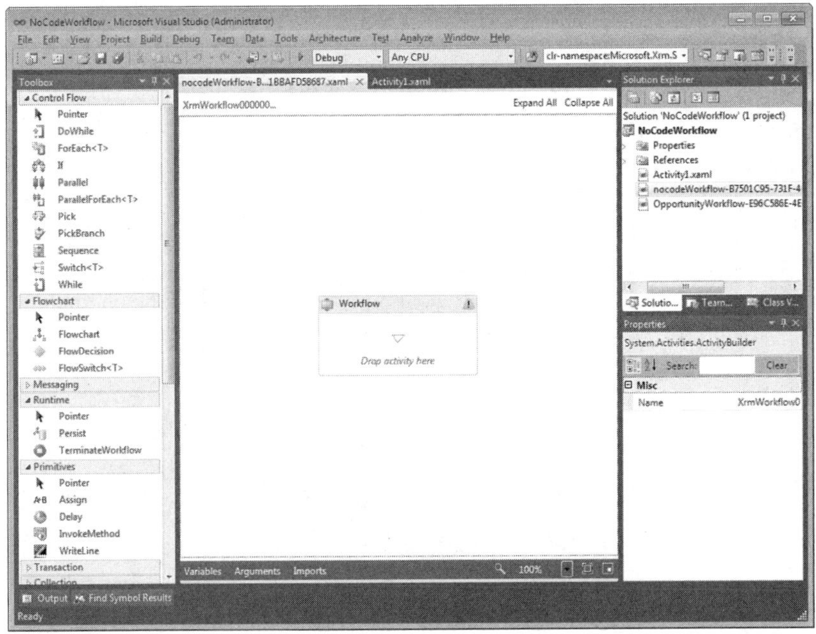

FIGURE 24.56 Workflow activities for CRM.

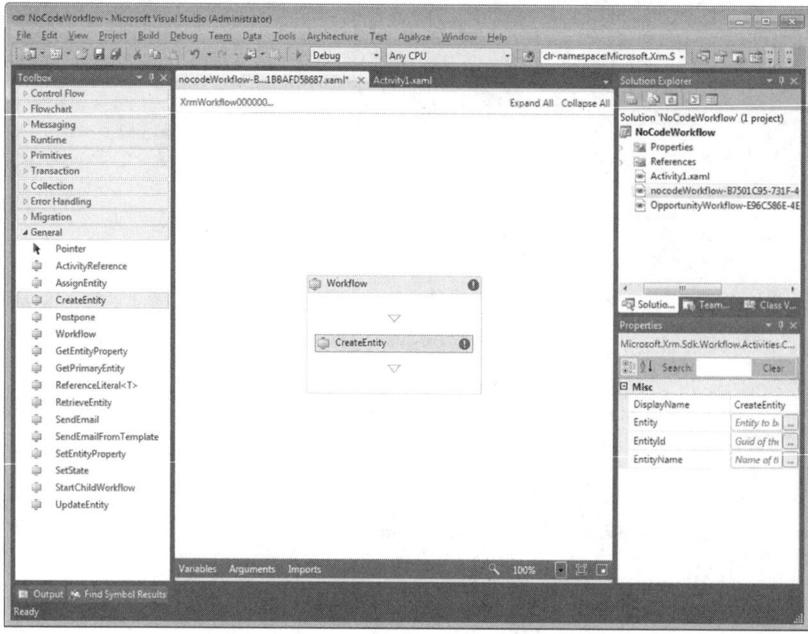

FIGURE 24.57 No-code workflow.

To continue with the workflow development, follow these steps:

1. Add an Assign activity, which is included in the Primitives group in the toolbox before the CreateEntity Activity (see Figure 24.58).

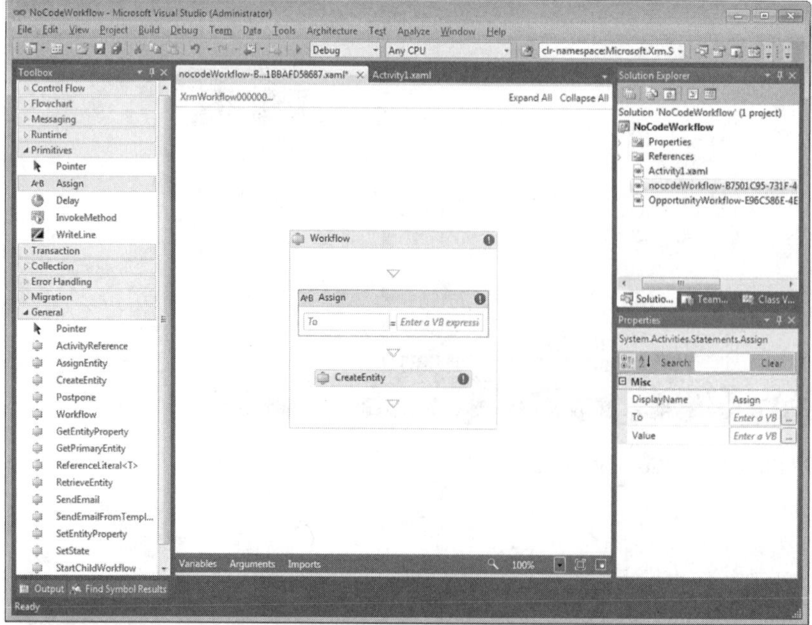

FIGURE 24.58 Adding Microsoft.Xrm.Sdk on Imports tab.

2. Click on the To property and enter CreatedEntities("localParameter") (see Figure 24.59).

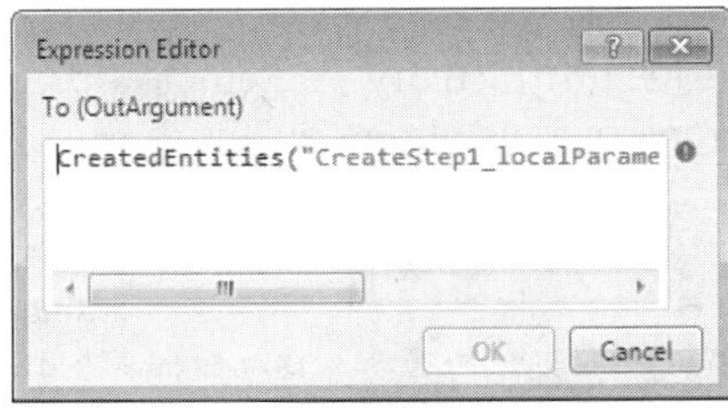

FIGURE 24.59 Assigning to variable.

3. Click on the Value property and enter New Entity("phonecall") (see Figure 24.60).

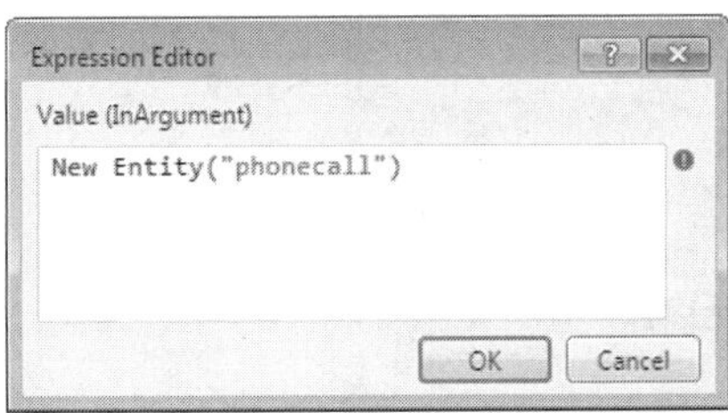

FIGURE 24.60 Assigning Value variable.

4. Add a SetEntityProperty activity after the Assign activity (see Figure 24.61).

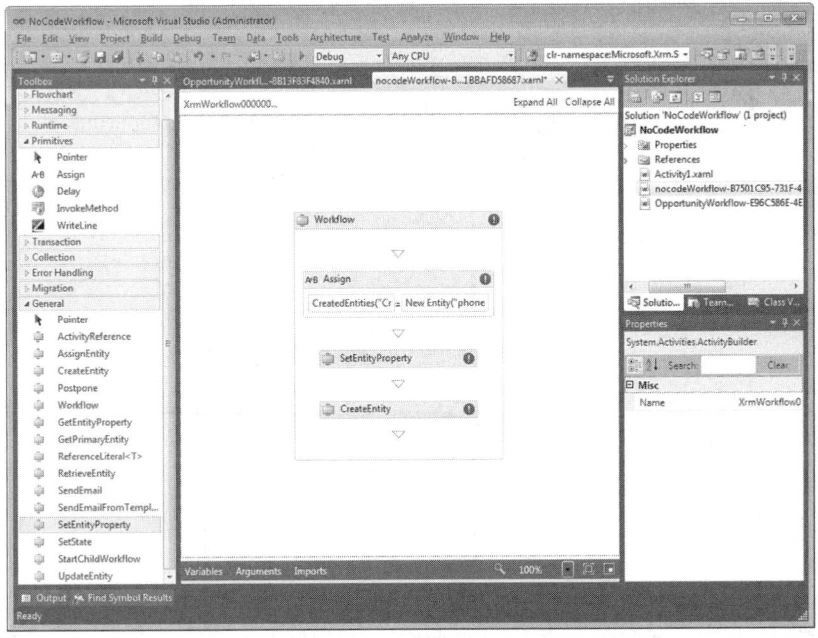

FIGURE 24.61 Adding SetEntityProperty.

5. Enter "subject" in the Attribute property, CreatedEntities ("localParameter") in the Entity property, "phonecall" in the EntityName property, and "Call this new Contact" on the Value property (see Figure 24.62).

6. Click on the last activity we added, that is the CreateEntity activity, and enter CreatedEntities("localParameter") in the Entity property and "phonecall" in the EntityName property.

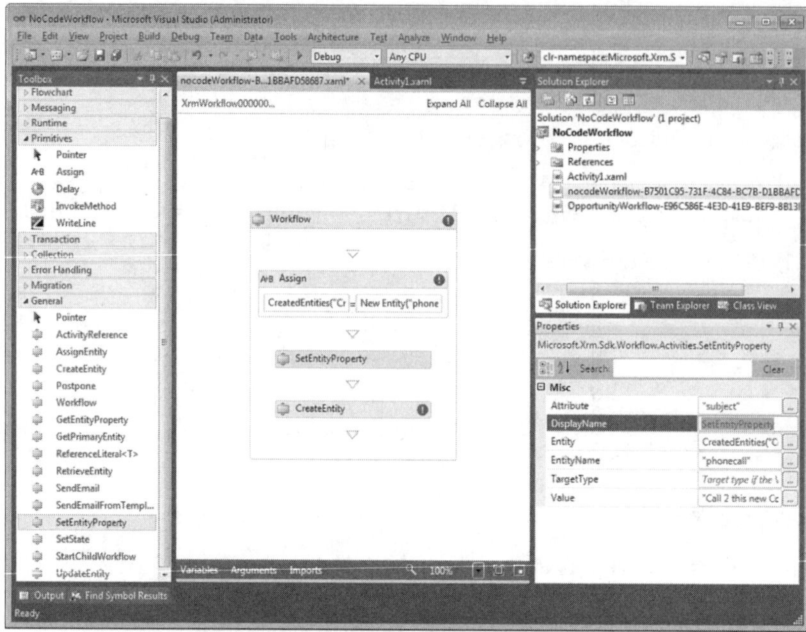

FIGURE 24.62 Setting properties to the SetEntityProperty activity.

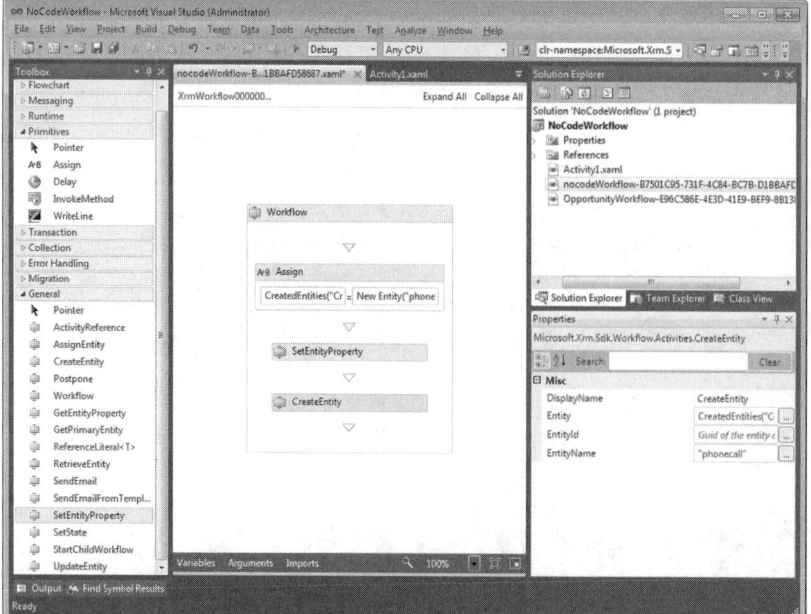

FIGURE 24.63 Setting properties of the CreateEntity activity.

7. Click Save.
8. Copy the XAML file to the one that was on the original solution you unzipped.
9. Compress the solution and import it back again to the CRM 2011 web interface.

TIP

To see the workflow that was just deployed, open Internet Explorer and go to the CRM web interface. Go to Settings and then to Processes (see Figure 24.64).

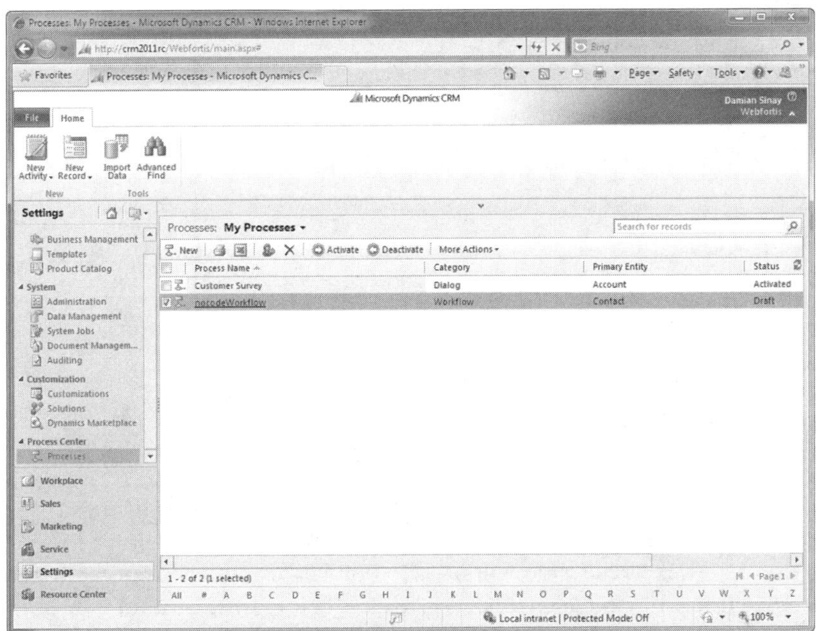

FIGURE 24.64 Reviewing no-code workflows.

From this interface, you can publish and unpublish the workflows in the same way as any regular workflow.

You can also see the deployed workflows and activate or deactivate them from the CRM 2011 web interface. Go to Settings, Solutions, select the solution you imported, and then select Processes (see Figure 24.65).

These kinds of workflows can be also created and deployed on CRM Online.

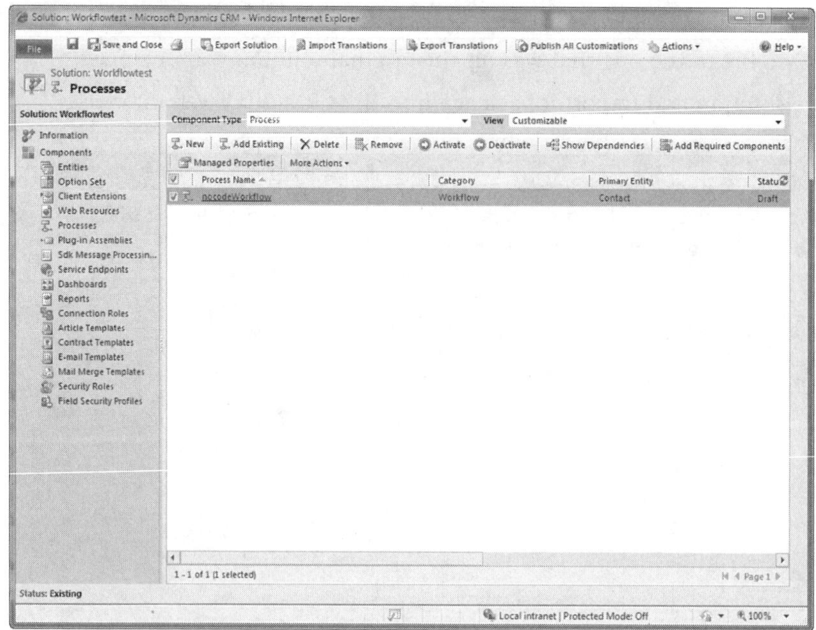

FIGURE 24.65 Reviewing no-code workflows with CRM 2011.

Custom Workflow Activities

Custom Workflow activities enable you to extend the steps available when you create a workflow. By default you can create steps for create, update, assign, send e-mail, and so on. For example, if you need to add a step that is not on this list, such as sending a SMS message or call an external web service, you will need to build a custom workflow activity to do so. As a difference from the no-code workflows we saw before this, Custom Workflow activities are compiled in dynamic link libraries (DLL) and you will be able to use them from the Workflow interface found in either the web or Outlook client applications as new steps. Custom Workflow Activities are not supported on CRM Online for security reasons. To create a custom workflow activity, you need to open Visual Studio 2010 and create a new project using the Activity Library template that is inside the Visual C#, Workflow project templates (See Figure 24.66).

After creating the project, you will have to add the references for Microsoft.Xrm.Sdk.dll and Microsoft.Xrm.Sdk.Workflow.dll. These files can be found in the CRM 2011 sdk\bin folder.

FIGURE 24.66 Creating a new workflow Activity Library project in Visual Studio 2010.

To use the CRM entities classes in the code, we will use what are called *early-binding entities*. We will need to generate the CRM classes using the crmsvcutil.exe tool that we can find in the sdk\bin folder. If we run this utility on the server with the minimum parameters as follows:

```
crmsvcutil.exe /url:http://localhost/Organization1/XRMServices/2011/
Organization.svc /out:GeneratedCode.cs
```

We will get an output file generated with all the classes needed on GeneratedCode.cs. We can include this file on our solution.

NOTE

The classes generated by the crmsvcutil.exe tool are .NET Language-Integrated Query (LINQ) supported.

We are going to see sample code using the same sample we used for the no-code workflow but this time using a custom activity. You will need to delete the Activity1.xaml file created by the Activity Library project template and create a new class file with the name you want. For our example, we will create a file with the name of CustomAcitivityLibrary.cs:

```
using System;
using System.Activities;
using Microsoft.Xrm.Sdk;
```

```
using Microsoft.Xrm.Sdk.Workflow;
namespace CustomActivityLibrary
{
    public class CustomAcitityLibrary : CodeActivity
    {
        [Input("My contact")]
        [ReferenceTarget("contact")]
        [Default("{575A8B41-F8D7-4DCE-B2EA-3FFDE936AB1B}", "contact")]
        public InArgument<EntityReference> inContact { get; set; }

        protected override void Execute(CodeActivityContext context)
        {
            // Get the tracing service
            ITracingService tracingService =
              context.GetExtension<ITracingService>();
            // Get the context service.
            IWorkflowContext mycontext =
               context.GetExtension<IWorkflowContext>();
            IOrganizationServiceFactory serviceFactory =
          context.GetExtension<IOrganizationServiceFactory>();
            // Use the context service to create an instance of CrmService.
            IOrganizationService crmService =
    serviceFactory.CreateOrganizationService(mycontext.UserId);
            //Get the Contact
            Contact myContact = new Contact();
            myContact.ContactId = inContact.Get(context).Id;
            // Creates the Phone Call activity for this conatct
            PhoneCall myPhoneCall =
                new PhoneCall();
            myPhoneCall.Subject = "Call this new contact";
            myPhoneCall.RegardingObjectId = new
                  EntityReference(Contact.EntityLogicalName,
                 (Guid) myContact.ContactId);
            crmService.Create(myPhoneCall);
            tracingService.Trace("PhoneCall created.");
        }
    }
}
```

Build the solution in debug mode to create the assembly.

To deploy the custom workflow activities, you need to register the compiled assembly as a plug-in using the same Plugin Registration tool we used in Chapter 25.

▶ If you have problems finding and building the Plugin Registration tool, refer to the "Plug-In Deployment" section in Chapter 25.

After deploying the custom workflow activity, you will be able to use it on any workflow. To do this, go to Settings, Processes and then click on New. Enter a name for the process; in the Entity, select Contact, and in the category, select Workflow. Click OK to move to the next step. Then click on Add Step and you will see the new group called Custom Activities Library with our custom activity inside (see Figure 24.67).

Add a step with the custom activity and click on the Set Properties button.

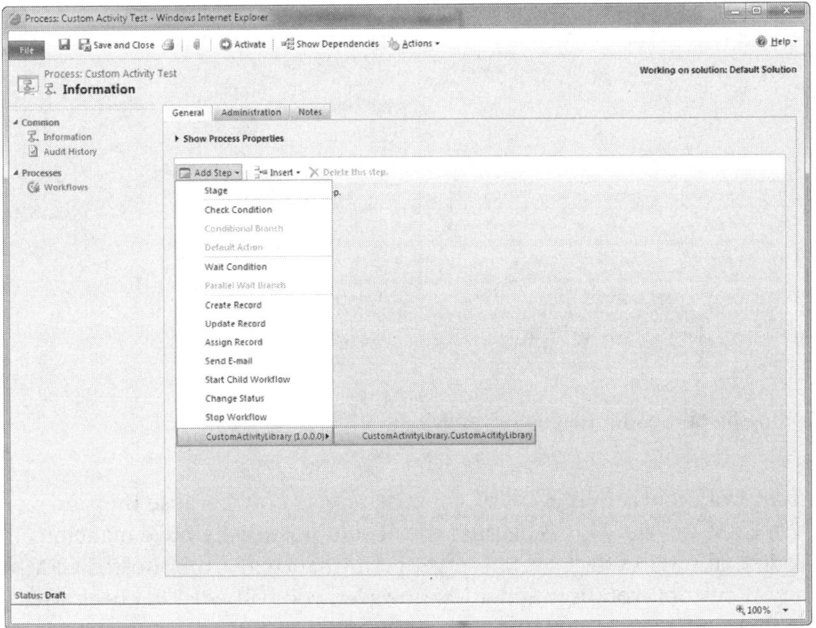

FIGURE 24.67 Using the custom activity on a workflow.

You will be able to set any custom property you added on the code—in our example, the My Contact property we used to send the current contact where the workflow will be running (see Figure 24.68).

Click Save and Close to close the Set Custom Step Input Properties and then click Save to save the workflow; click on Activate to test this solution.

NOTE

After you make any change on the codes and recompile the solution, you will have to restart the Microsoft CRM Asynchronous Processing Service. In some situations, you might also need to restart the IIS before redeploying the modified assembly.

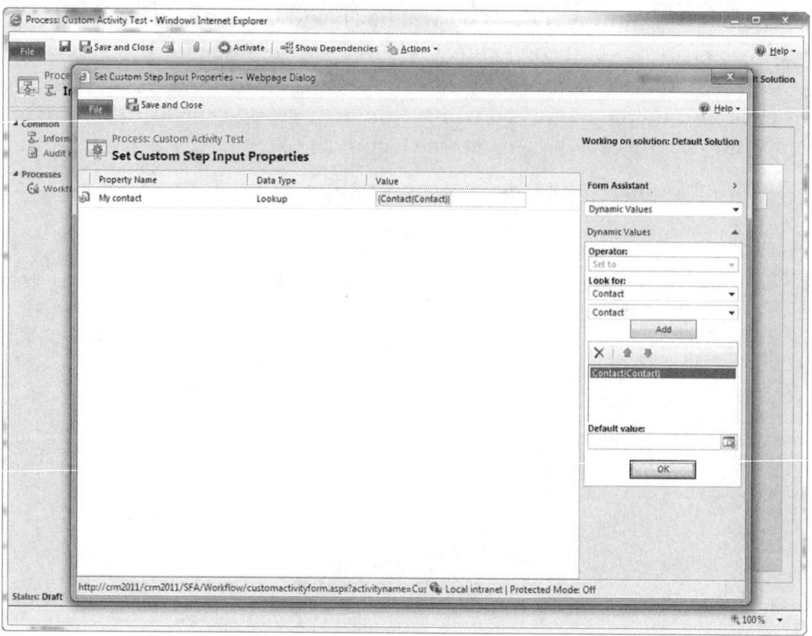

FIGURE 24.68 Setting properties to the custom activity.

You can install custom workflow activities on on-premise servers only because they are not supported by live CRM servers. This is because they could potentially have malicious or poorly written code that might affect overall server performance. (Partner-hosted CRM accounts might support custom workflow activities; however, you will need to check with you specific partner first.) to face this limitation on CRM online, Microsoft recommends the combination of workflows and custom plug-ins since now plug-ins can be deployed in Isolation mode.

- To learn more about .NET 4.0 and WWF development, check http://msdn.microsoft.com.

Summary

This chapter illustrated how to use and work with processes, which are now divided into dialogs and workflows in Microsoft Dynamics CRM 2011. We created dialogs and workflows with the CRM application interfaces as well as with Microsoft Visual Studio 2010. We learned that dialogs are synchronous and interactive processes, whereas workflows run asynchronously and they need a Windows service to run.

Process development is limitless—in fact, most organizations barely begin to take process development to the level that they could for not just sales force automation (SFA) tasks, but for alerting of almost anything.

CHAPTER 25

Plug-Ins

IN THIS CHAPTER

Overview of Plug-Ins

A *plug-in* is a .NET assembly that can be used to intercept events generated from the CRM system, to perform a variety of actions (previously referred to as *callouts* in earlier versions of CRM 3 and before). An example of event interception is an entity that will be created, updated, or deleted, and an action can be virtually anything. Some common plug-in uses might include

- Performing a complicated update routine on CRM entities and/or attributes when it might be impractical to use JavaScript
- Grabbing data from another system and updating CRM when an entity instance is being created or updated
- Updating another system programmatically from CRM (such as an accounting system)

Using plug-ins, you can fire a custom action or event on any entity, for example, on the account entity either before or after it has been created, updated or deleted. Additionally, other events can be handled from a plug-in, such as Assign, Merge, and Handle. Refer to the CRM SDK (Software Development Kit) for a complete list of events supported.

TIP

Not every event works in offline mode of the Microsoft CRM Outlook client. Although online mode supports all events, offline clients can manage only half of them. Refer to the CRM 2011 SDK for a complete list of events supported in offline mode, in the file called "message-entity support for plug-ins.xlsx" that is located in the sdk\tools folder.

Figure 25.1 shows the Event execution pipeline order in which the event and the plug-in calls are executed.

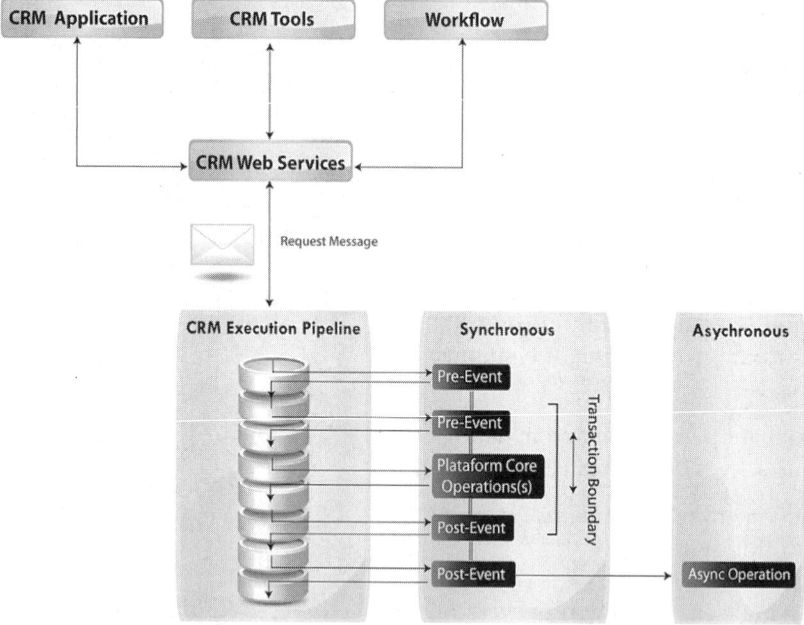

FIGURE 25.1 Event execution pipeline.

TIP

You don't need to restart the IIS or any other CRM Service when you register or unregister plug-ins.

Isolation

The concept of isolation is not new, however, it has not been available to Microsoft Dynamics CRM until now.

This new version adds the concept of isolation called the *sandbox*. Plug-ins can now be registered in normal mode, which means without having any kind of isolation. In other words, this mode will allow full trust on the code execution and full access to the server resources as the previous version of CRM 4.0 used to allow. If the plug-in is registered in the sandbox isolation mode, then it will run in partial trust and it won't be allowed to access to some resources on the server, such as files, registry, database, and so on. The level of isolation, however, allows the access to HTTP and HTTPS web resources for external web services communication.

The sandbox allows the plug-in to access the CRM services to create, update, or delete any entity on the system.

Developing plug-ins in sandbox mode is the recommended action, so they will be more secure and supported on all the CRM 2011 deployment types (Online and On premise). They are also monitored by the CRM system generated runtime statistics that can be queried using the PluginTypeStatistic entity records.

CAUTION

Thanks to a new sandbox isolation mode that allows partial trust with some limitations, CRM Online can now support plug-ins. CRM hosting providers might not support them for security reasons. Before you attempt to install it, check with your hosting provider if you want to use a plug-in.

Modes

You can set up plug-ins in synchronous or asynchronous mode.

Synchronous mode starts the execution of the plug-in when the event is fired and blocks the CRM application process until the executed method finishes. This option is not recommended if you are performing a process that might take a long time to execute. Regardless of the method used, synchronous or asynchronous, there is a timeout limit of 2 minutes for plugin executions. If your process needs more time, then you will have to consider using a workflow or another custom background process.

TIP

If you want to prevent a record from being created or updated, this should be the desired mode in conjunction with the Pre stage (see the next section for stages).

Asynchronous mode releases the application process, and the user can continue working while the code is executed.

Stages

Plug-ins can be set up in the Pre or Post stages:

The Pre stage sends control to the plug-in before the real event is executed in the core system. As an example, you might attach a plug-in to the Create event of the Account entity; your code would execute before the Account was actually created in the CRM system. With this method, you could prevent the Account or the entity record from being created.

The Post stage is executed after the real event has executed in the core system. So, following the example just described, your code would be executed only after the Account record is created.

This new version of Dynamics CRM 2011 allows these stages to participate on SQL transactions as well. So, you can use the Pre stage outside or inside a transaction as well as doing the same for the Post stage.

The concept of using transactions now allows the rollback of a plug-in operation. If you have two different plug-ins attached to the same message of an entity and the second plug-in fails, it can now roll back the successful operation performed by the first plug-in. This was not easily done with previous versions. You can check if the plug-in is running in a transaction by checking the IsInTransaction property of the IPluginExecutionContext. The stages 20 and 40 are the ones that guaranteed to be part of a transaction while the 10 and 50 might or not be part of it.

Deployment Types

There are three different ways to deploy a plug-in:

- Server
- Offline
- Both

Server means that the plug-in will execute on the server. Execution will occur when users use the web client or the Outlook Online client as well as when any workflow is executed.

Offline means the plug-in executes on the client's user machine where Outlook is running. This is especially useful when running in the Outlook client in offline mode.

The Both type executes the plug-in on the server and in the Outlook client in offline mode. Have in mind that the plug-in would be executed twice, once when Outlook is offline and again when it connects to the server.

The deployment type you select depends on what you want to do. If you need to grab data from an external system and need to have the user connected to the Internet or the network, you will want to have the plug-in run only on the server side and the Outlook client will not have network access in Offline mode.

When to Use a Plug-In

Use a plug-in when you need to integrate Microsoft Dynamics CRM with another legacy system or when you want to extend or customize the original functionality or behaviors of Microsoft Dynamics CRM.

Plug-ins are the best choice to enforce the business rules of your business. You could use JavaScript events to add validation on the rules you want to enforce; however those types of validations will work only when CRM is used through the native interfaces like web or outlook client. If we have in mind that there can be other applications interacting with the CRM system through the web services, service endpoints, and so on, the validations and rules enforcement will work always if we put them on plug-ins. Plug-ins runs on the server side, whereas JavaScript validations run on the client side. It is a good practice to put the validation logic in one place on the server side—that way we know the hardware and resources we can use. Clients will have a lot of different configurations of settings on their browser that might cause our validations to not work properly for some users.

TIP

Putting the business rules and validations on plug-ins doesn't mean you won't need to add validations with JavaScript events. In most cases, it would be good to have the validations in both places to avoid unnecessary server calls.

Plug-In Development

To develop a plug-in, you must download the Microsoft Dynamics CRM 2011 SDK from the Microsoft website. The SDK can be found by searching for "CRM 2011 SDK" from Microsoft.com.

Download the MicrosoftDynamicsCRM2011SDK.exe file, save it, and execute it (it is a Self-Extracting cabined file) by double-clicking on the file and entering the directory where you want to extract the files (see Figure 25.2).

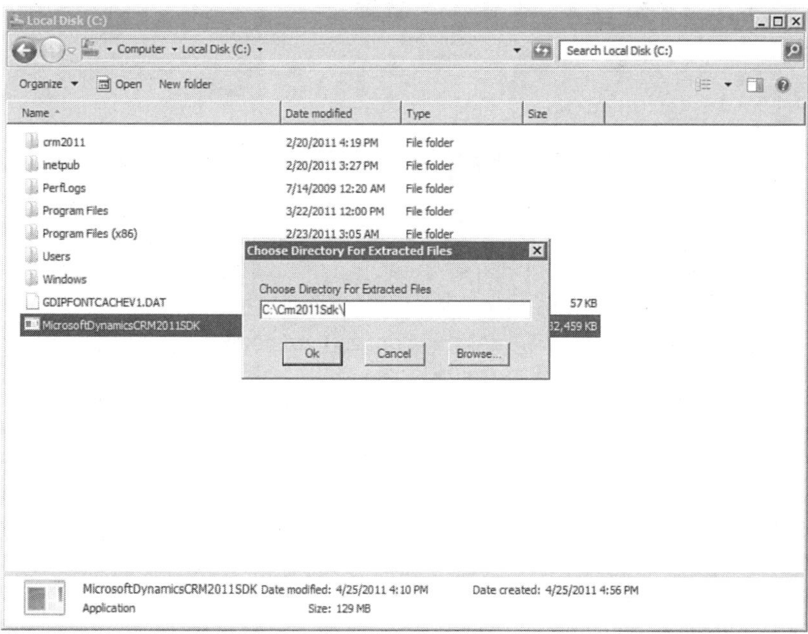

FIGURE 25.2 Extracting the SDK files.

To create a plug-in, you must create a new Class Library project in Visual Studio 2010 by going to the File menu, selecting New, and then choosing Project. Then select Visual C#/Windows in the project types on the left and select Class Library on the right. Enter a name for the project, and select the location and a solution name (see Figure 25.3).

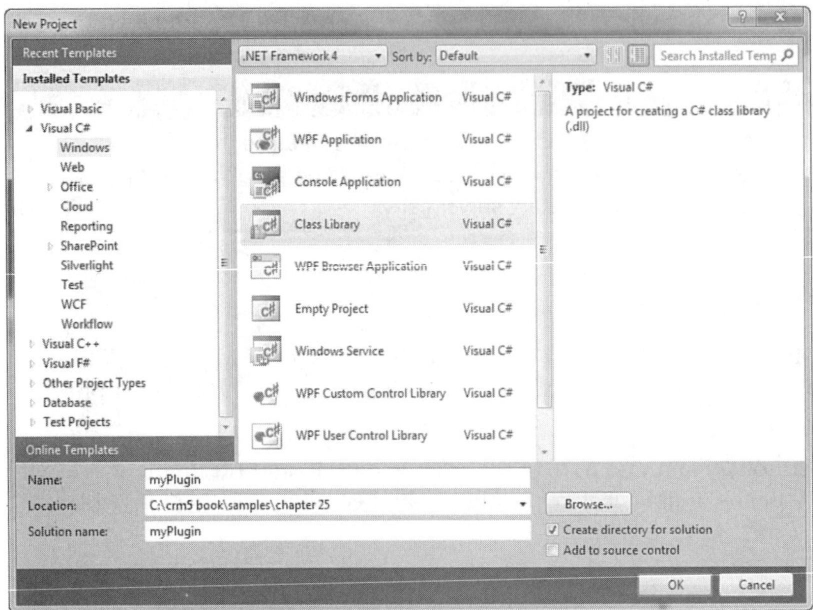

FIGURE 25.3 Creating a new Class Library project for a plug-in.

NOTE

This version of Microsoft Dynamics CRM 2011 is based on the .NET Framework 4.0, so we need to use Visual Studio 2010 to create class libraries. Although we can also create class library projects in a variety of languages, such as Visual Basic .NET or C#, for the examples in this book, we use C#.

The previous version of Dynamics CRM 4.0 was based on .NET Framework 2.0, and all plug-in assemblies had be to be created with Visual Studio 2005, Visual Studio 2008, or Visual Studio 2010. However, because CRM 2011 uses only Framework 4.0, all plug-ins must be created with Visual Studio 2010.

The project template creates a new public class by default. After you create the project, you must add a reference to the Microsoft.Xrm.Sdk.dll file to your project as well as a reference to Microsoft.Crm.Sdk.Proxy.dll. These DLL files are located inside the SDK\Bin\subfolder.

Adding References

To add these references, follow these steps:

1. Go to the Solution Explorer and select the project name (under the root node of the tree). Right-click and select the Add Reference menu option (see Figure 25.4).

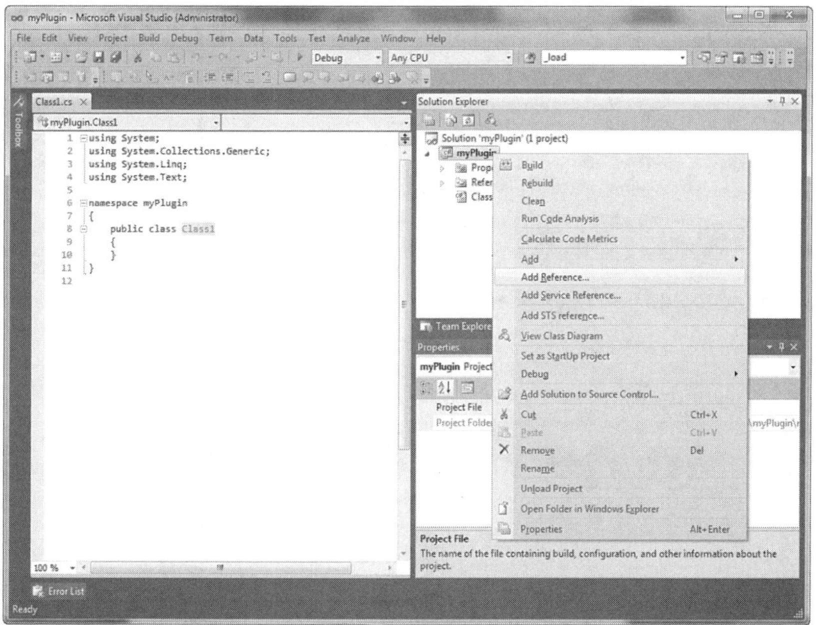

FIGURE 25.4 Adding references to the project.

2. Move to the Browse tab (see Figure 25.5).
3. Locate the SDK\Bin\ folder on your local drive and select both Microsoft.Xrm.Sdk.dll and Microsoft.Crm.Sdk.Proxy.dll files. (To select more than one file, hold the CTRL key.)
4. Click the OK button to add the references to your project. You will see these files inside the References folder of your project in the Solution Explorer (see Figure 25.6).

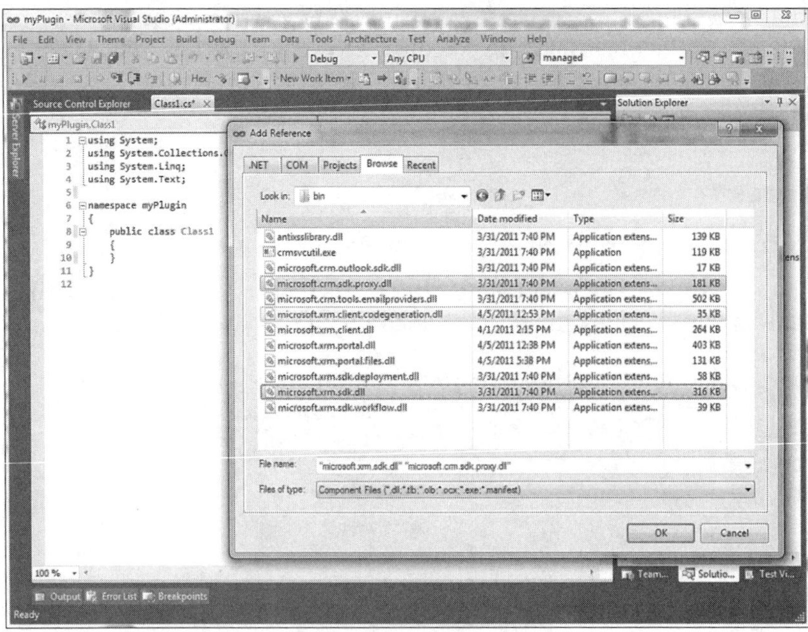

FIGURE 25.5 Browse tab to add new references.

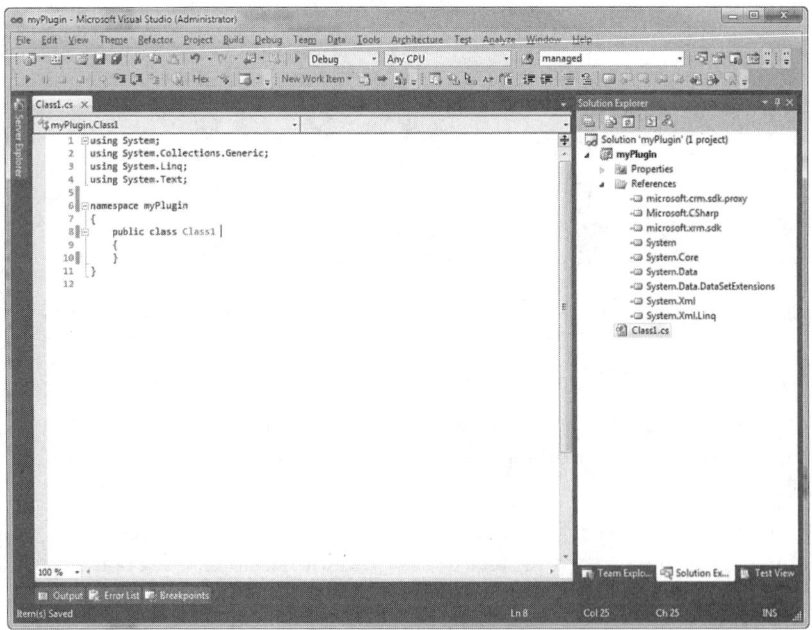

FIGURE 25.6 Checking that the new references were added.

5. Finally, add the using sentence to the Microsoft.Xrm.Sdk namespace, and implement the IPlugin interface, as shown in the following code (replacing myPlugIn with the name of your plug-in):

```
using System;
using System.Collections.Generic;
using System.Linq;
using System.Text;
using Microsoft.Xrm.Sdk;

namespace myPlugIn
{
    public class Class1 : IPlugin
    {

    }
}
```

TIP

You can implement more than one plug-in on the same assembly using different classes, if you want to.

As with any other interface, you must explicitly implement methods. In the case of the IPlugin interface, you must implement the Execute method, as shown in the following code:

```
namespace myPlugIn
{
    public class Class1 : IPlugin
    {
        #region IPlugin Members
        public void Execute(IServiceProvider serviceProvider)
        {
            throw new NotImplementedException();
        }
        #endregion
    }
}
```

Plug-In Deployment

Before explaining details about plug-in development, it is a good idea to review deployment options so that you can easily follow the sample code included with the development section of this chapter.

The first step in plug-in deployment involves registering your plug-in and signing the assembly with a strong name key file. A strong name key is necessary for security reasons so that the assembly can be trusted to execute external code, such as when invoking a web service. To sign your assemblies, follow these steps:

1. Go to Solution Explorer and select your project; right-click and select the Properties menu option (see Figure 25.7).

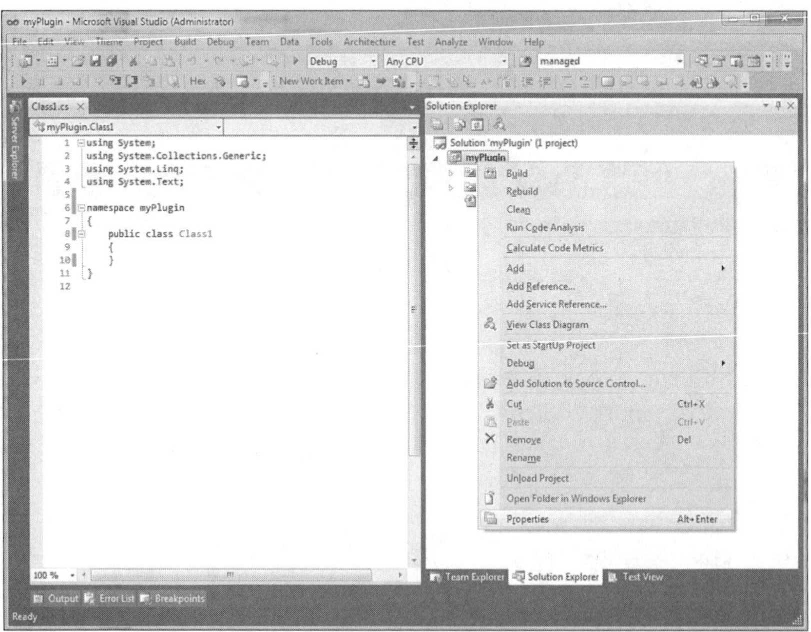

FIGURE 25.7 Properties menu item of the project.

2. Go to the Signing tab, and check the Sign the Assembly check box (see Figure 25.8).
3. Create a new string name key file by selecting New from the drop-down control (see Figure 25.9).
4. Enter a name for the key file, and optionally (but recommended) enter a password to protect the strong key (see Figure 25.10).

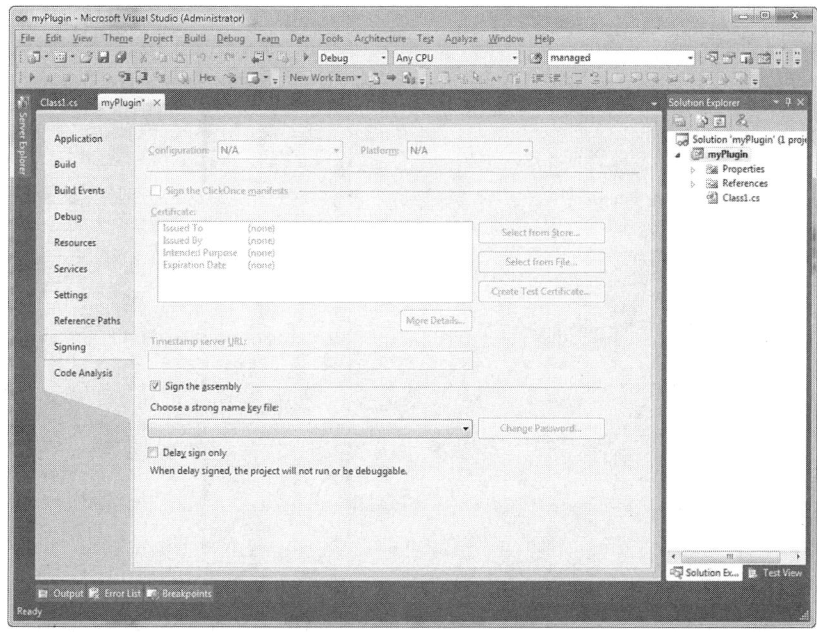

FIGURE 25.8 Signing tab.

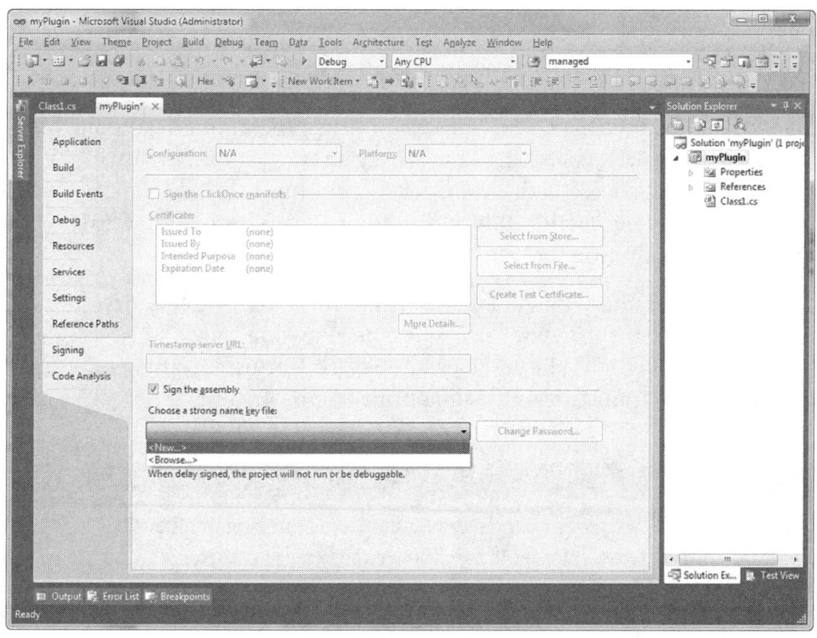

FIGURE 25.9 Selecting a new strong name key file.

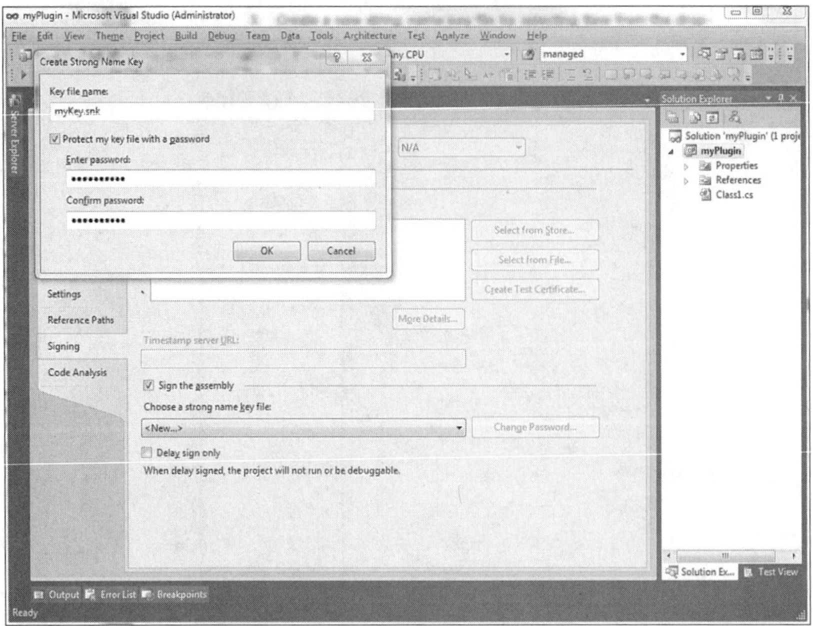

FIGURE 25.10 Creating a strong name key.

5. Click OK to close the dialog, and you will see the newly created strong name key will be added to your project in the Solution Explorer (see Figure 25.11).

To deploy your plug-in, you need to register it. You can do this programmatically or using a tool that comes with the CRM SDK called the Plug-in Registration Tool. Plug-in Registration Tool comes with the source code and is located in the Crm2011Sdk\SDK\Tools\PluginRegistration folder. You must have Visual Studio 2010 installed to open the PluginRegistrationTool.sln file located on that folder.

Before building the solution you must download and install the Windows Identity Foundation Runtime (WIF) from http://www.microsoft.com/downloads/details.aspx?familyid=EB9C345F-E830-40B8-A5FE-AE7A864C4D76&displaylang=en, or by searching for Windows Identity Foundation Runtime from Microsoft.com.

NOTE

For more information about WIF, we recommend downloading and installing the Identity Developer Training Kit from http://www.microsoft.com/downloads/details.aspx?displaylang=en&FamilyID=c3e315fa-94e2-4028-99cb-904369f177c0.

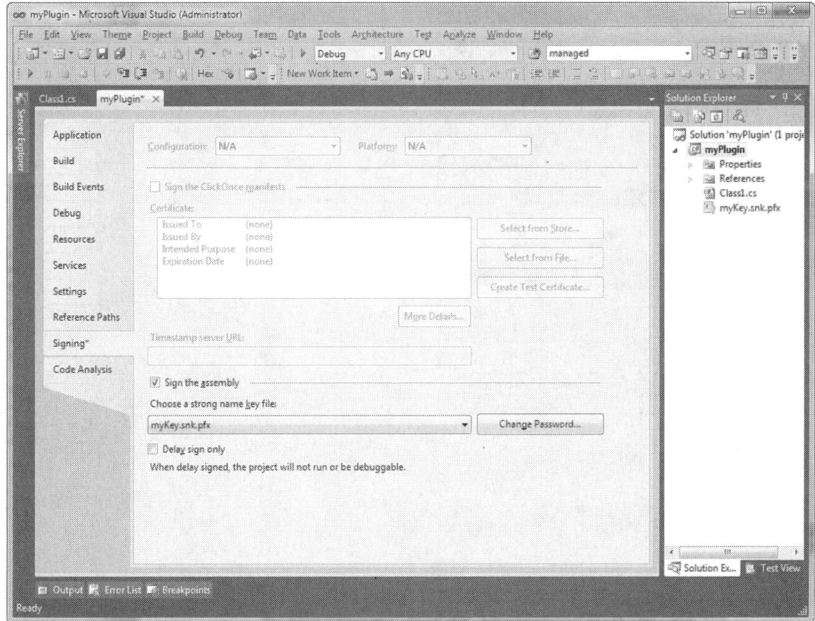

FIGURE 25.11 Signing the assembly.

Install WIF Runtime

To install WIF Runtime, follow these steps:

1. Execute the Windows6.1-KB974405-x64.msu file you downloaded. When the dialog in Figure 25.12 appears, click Yes.

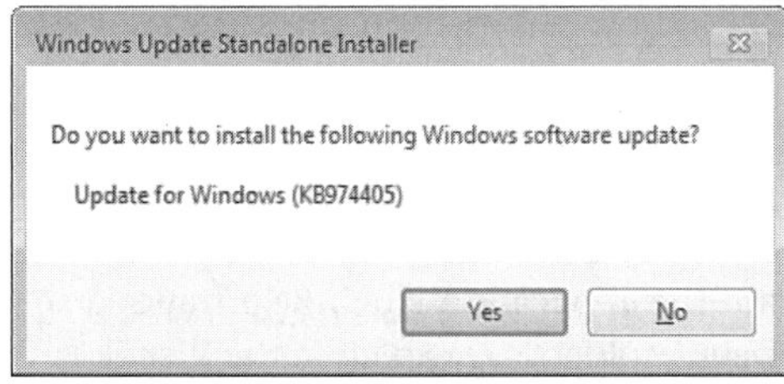

FIGURE 25.12 Windows Update standalone Installer.

2. Click I Accept to accept the terms in the license agreement (see Figure 25.13).
3. When the setup completes, the following screen will appear (see Figure 25.14).
4. Click Close.
5. Open the solution PluginRegistrationTool.sln file that is located in the CRM SDK under the SDK\Tools\PluginRegistration folder.

Download and Install Updates

Read these license terms (1 of 1)

You need to accept the license terms before installing updates.

Update for Windows (KB974405)

PLEASE NOTE: Microsoft Corporation (or based on where you live, one of its affiliates) licenses this supplement to you. You may use it with each validly licensed copy of Microsoft operating system products software (for which this supplement is applicable) (the "software"). You may not use the supplement if you do not have a license for the software. The license terms for the software apply to your use of this supplement.
Privacy statement: http://go.microsoft.com/fwlink/?LinkId=164072

Please note: As this software is distributed in Quebec, Canada, these license terms are provided below in French.
Remarque: Ce logiciel étant distribué au Québec, Canada, les termes de cette licence sont fournis ci-dessous en français.

REMARQUE : Microsoft Corporation (ou en fonction du lieu où vous vivez, l'un de ses affiliés)

Printable version | I Decline | I Accept | Cancel

FIGURE 25.13 Read the license terms.

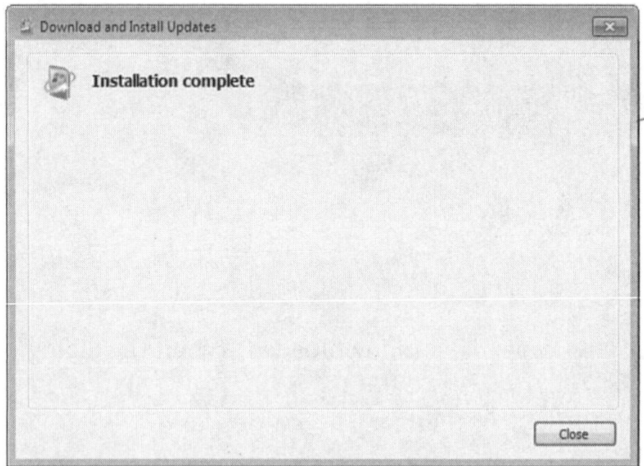

FIGURE 25.14 Installation complete.

6. Build the entire solution (see Figure 25.15).

After you successfully build the solution, you will find the application PluginRegistration.exe inside the SDK\Tools\PluginRegistrationTool\bin\Debug folder. You can close the Visual Studio application and run this tool directly from this folder, or you can follow these steps to integrate this tool into the Visual Studio 2010 application as a recommended option.

1. From Visual Studio 2010, go to the Tools menu, and click on External Tools (see Figure 25.16).
2. You will get the dialog shown in Figure 25.17.
3. Click the Add button, and change the title to CRM Plug-in Registration (see Figure 25.18).
4. Click the ellipsis (...) button near the Command field, and locate the PluginRegistration.exe application file that should be located in the SDK\Tools\PluginRegistrationTool\bin\Debug folder (see Figure 25.19).

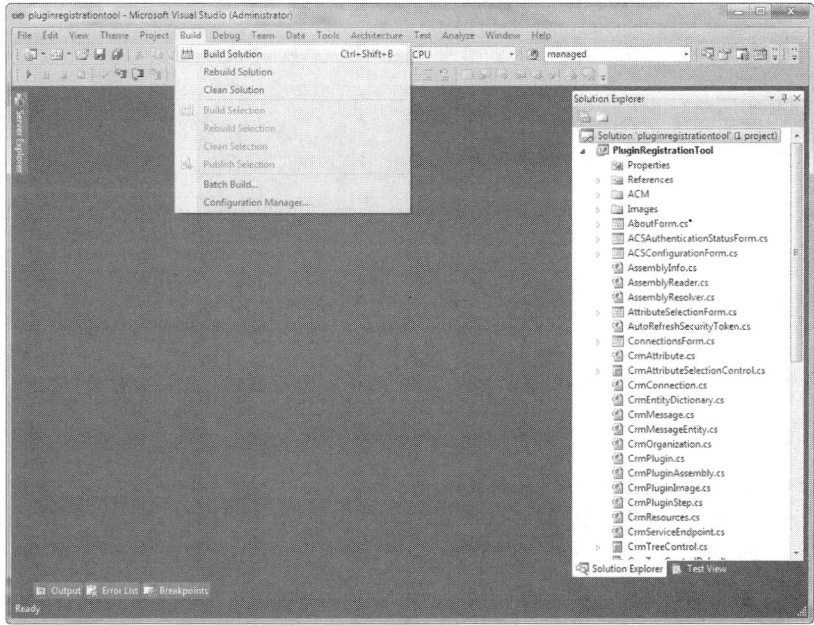

FIGURE 25.15 Building Plug-in Registration Tool.

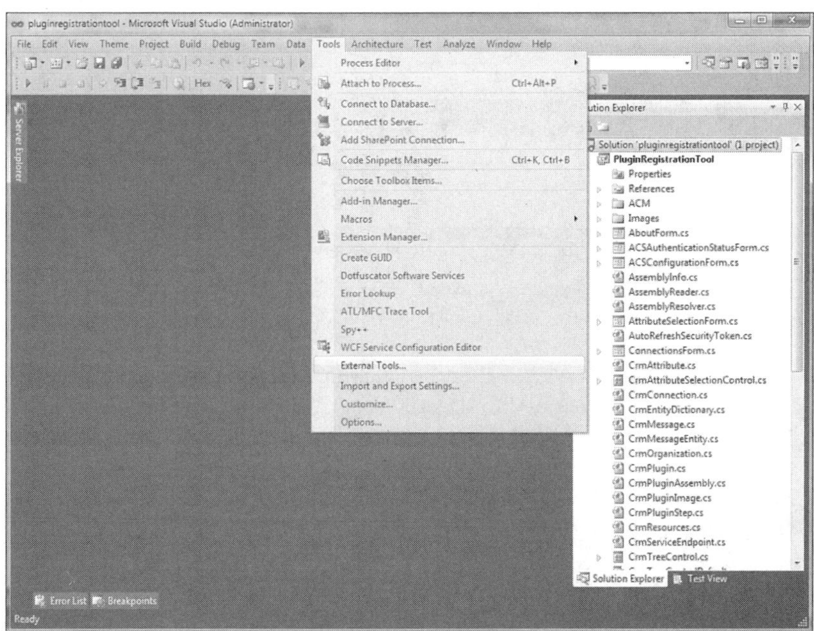

FIGURE 25.16 Visual Studio External Tools menu option.

5. Click on Open to close the dialog, and click on OK to close the close the External Tools dialog.

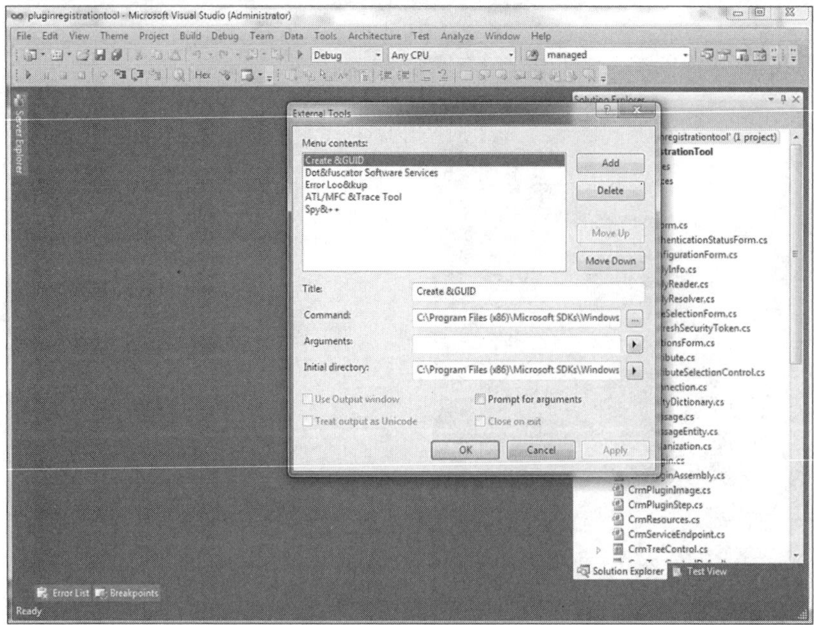

FIGURE 25.17 External Tools dialog.

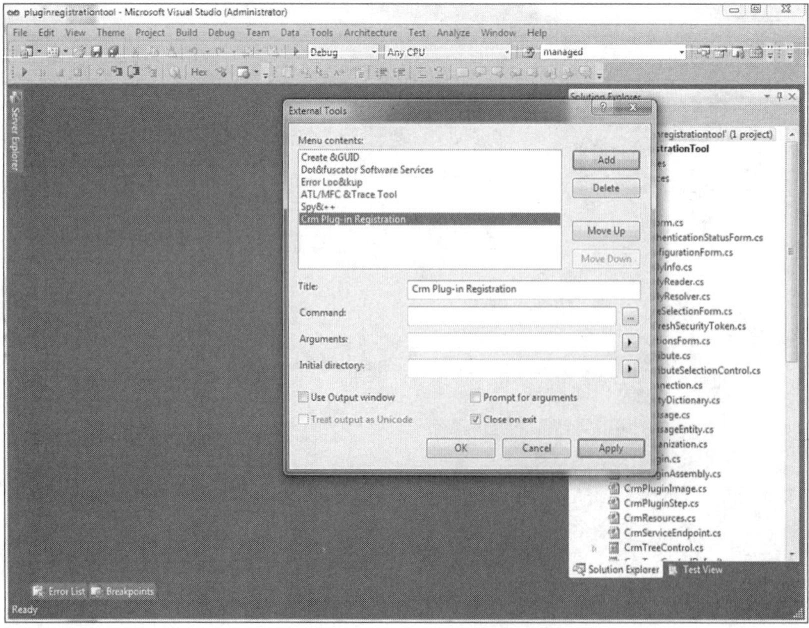

FIGURE 25.18 Adding CRM plug-in registration.

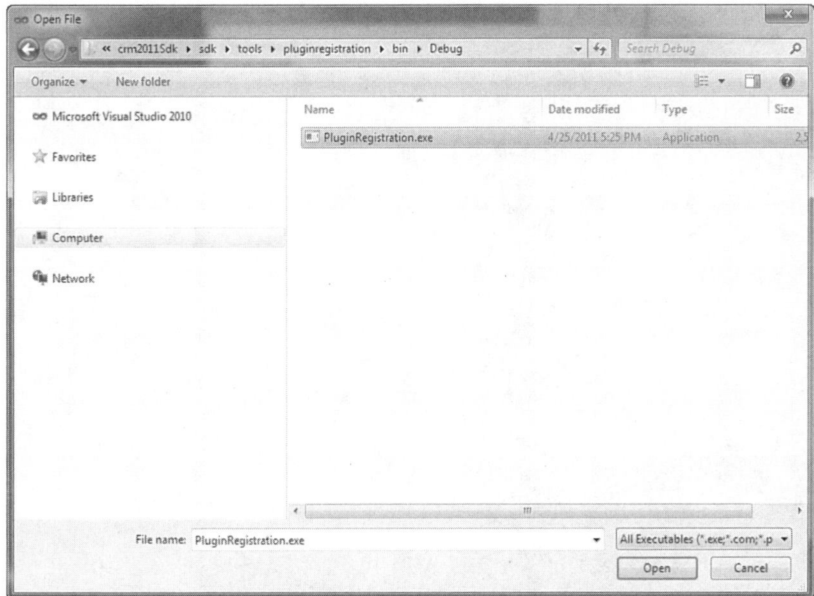

FIGURE 25.19 Locating the PluginRegistration.exe application.

This way you will be able to run the Plug-in Registration Tool from the Visual Studio 2010 application by going to the Tools menu and then CRM Plug-in Registration (see Figure 25.20).

Plug-In Registration

When you run this tool, you must click first on Create New Connection and enter information for the label and CRM Server discovery URL as shown in Figure 25.21.

TIP

Be sure to include the port number in the discovery URL if the port is different from the default port 80; for example, http://Server:5555.

This new version of the Plug-in Registration Tool has the option to use the credentials of the user you are already logged in as, so you don't have to enter the username and password every time you run this tool. If you want to use a different user credential, you can uncheck the check box that says Use Saved Credentials (as shown in Figure 25.21) and enter a valid username.

The username and password must be a valid Windows account and a valid Microsoft CRM user with Administrative roles assigned, as well as deployment administrator rights that can be added through the CRM deployment management application. If the plug-in is going to be registered with the isolation mode set to Sandbox, the user doesn't need to be a deployment administrator—the CRM System Administrator role will be enough.

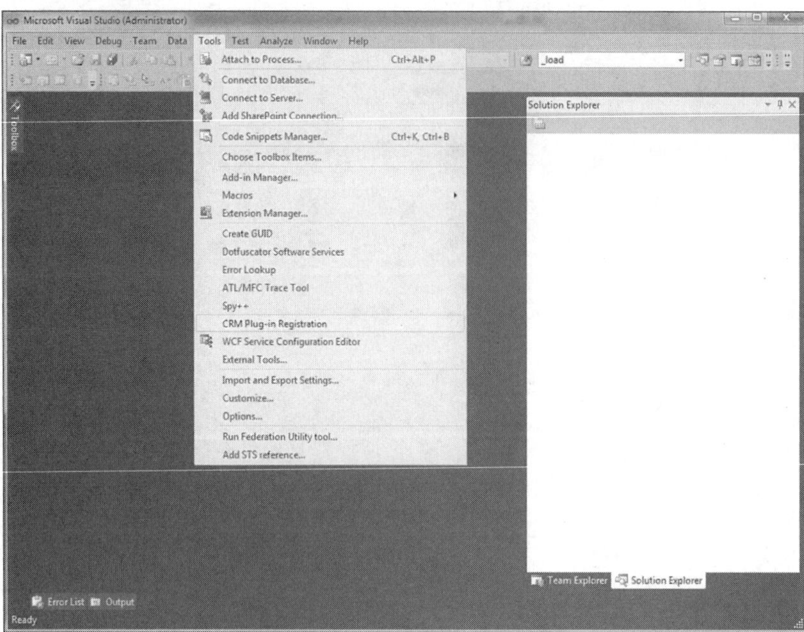

FIGURE 25.20 Accessing the Plug-in Registration Tool from Visual Studio.

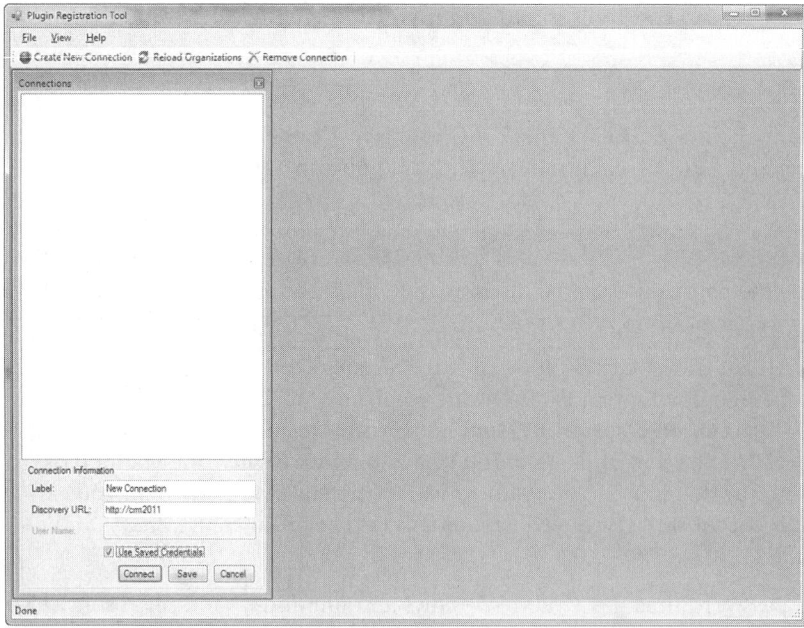

FIGURE 25.21 Registering the plug-in.

After you enter these values, you must click Connect. The organizations are listed as shown in Figure 25.22.

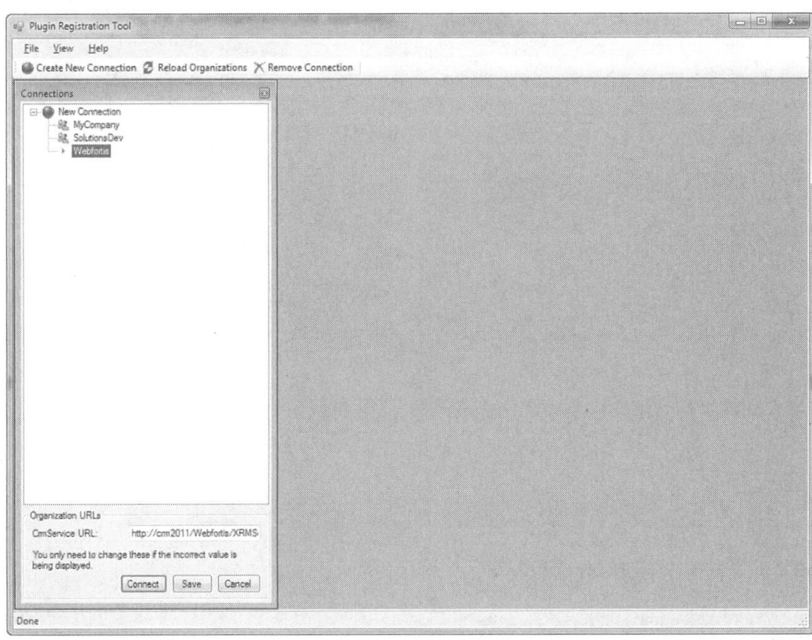

FIGURE 25.22 Selecting organizations to register a plug-in.

Select the organization where you want to deploy and register your plug-in, and click Connect. If you are connected successfully to the CRM organization, you will see the registered plug-ins and custom workflow activities, as shown in Figure 21.23.

To register your assembly, click the Register button, and then click Register New Assembly. The window in Figure 25.24 opens.

Locate your assembly by clicking the ellipsis (...) button near the Assembly location text box that is on Step #1. Set the isolation mode to None. (Remember the sandbox isolation mode is preferred when deploying to a CRM Online environment.) Select the Database option under Step #4 Specify the Assembly Location; be sure to select the class you want to register that appears on the list. Then click the Register button. When the assembly is registered, a confirmation window will appear, as shown in Figure 25.25.

Now expand the assembly you registered to see that your assembly was properly registered (see Figure 25.26).

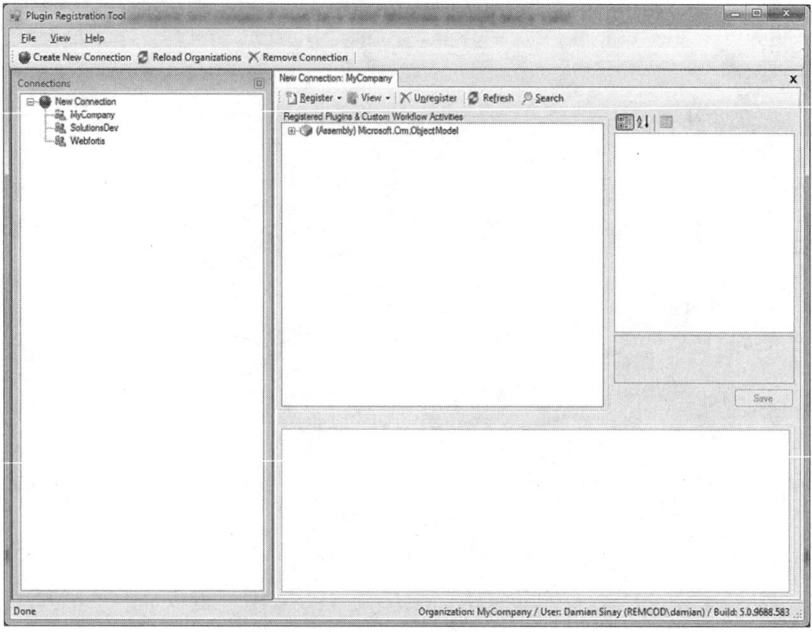

FIGURE 25.23 Successful organization connection.

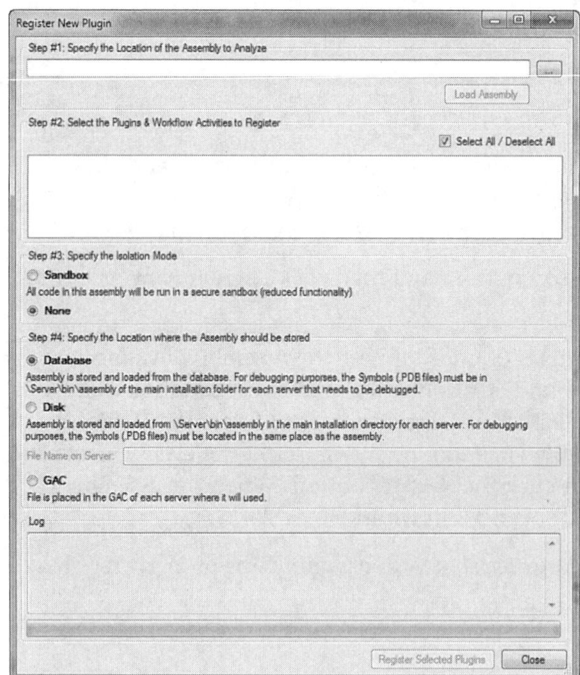

FIGURE 25.24 Assembly registration window.

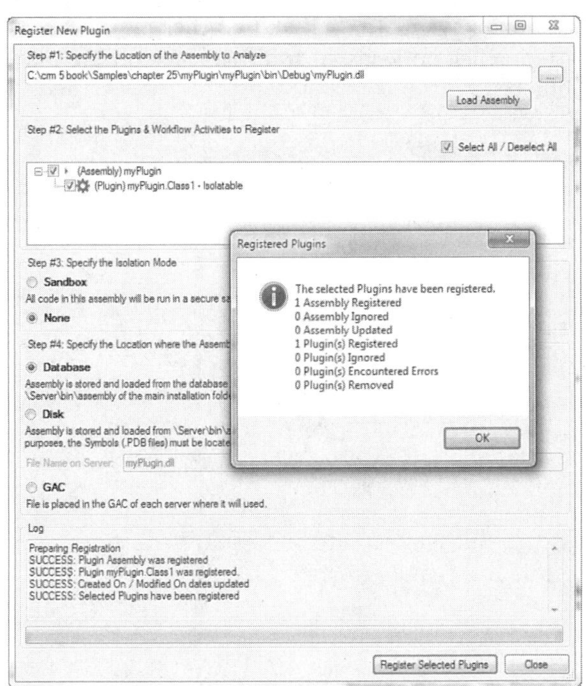

FIGURE 25.25 Registered assembly confirmation.

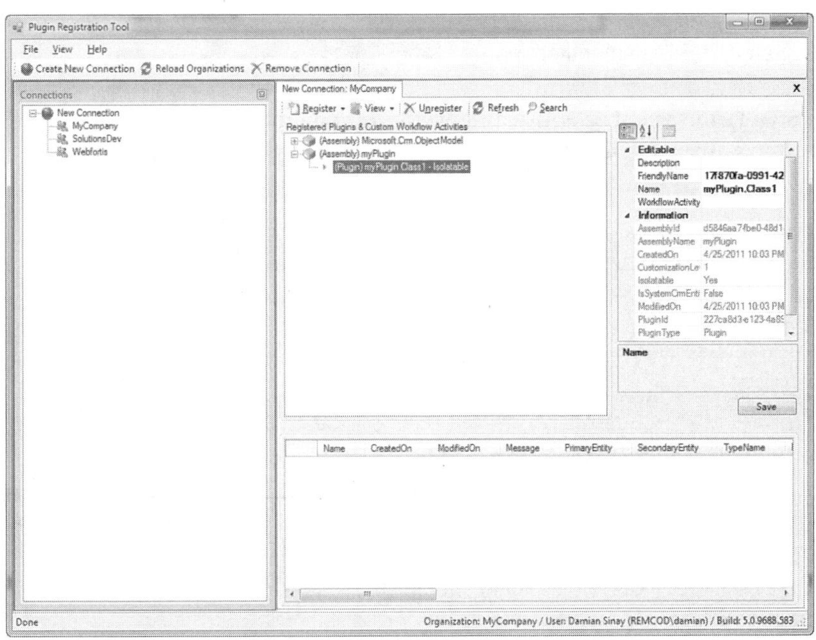

FIGURE 25.26 Reviewing assembly registration.

Now you must associate it with an entity and an event. To do that, first click on the assembly you registered in the previous steps, click on Register, and then click on the Register New Step menu option (see Figure 25.27).

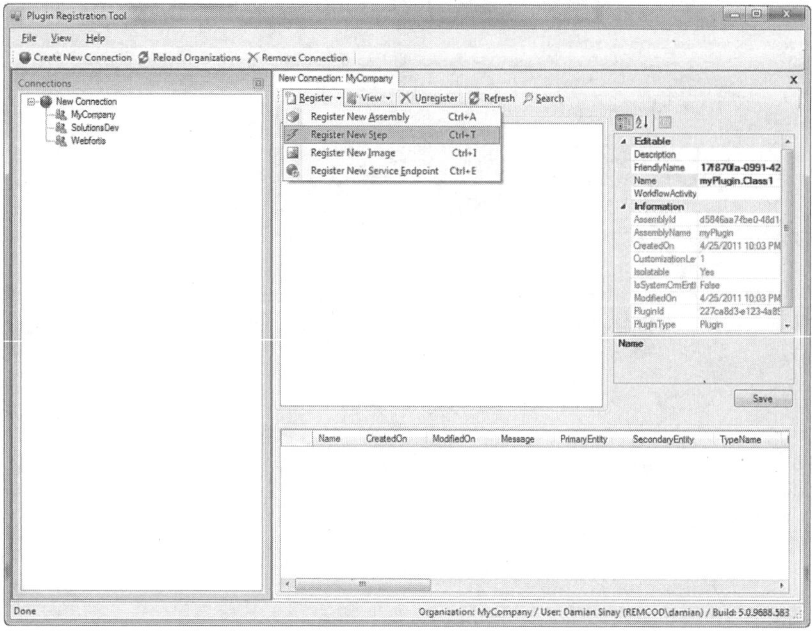

FIGURE 25.27 Register New Step menu option.

Then, to register a step (and select the entity and event), enter a message in the Message text box. In our example, we are going to enter Create for the message and Account for the primary entity by typing Account in the Primary Entity text box.

NOTE

The Message and Primary Entity text boxes have IntelliSense, so you will be presented with a list of values after entering the first characters.

TIP

If you don't enter a message name, the plug-in will be registered for all messages. You will be responsible to act for each message received by code. In the same way, if you leave the Primary Entity text box blank, the plug-in will be fired for any entity in the system.

Select Pre-operation(CRM 2011 Only) option from the Eventing Pipeline Stage of Execution radio button list and leave the other radio buttons on their default values, as shown in Figure 25.28

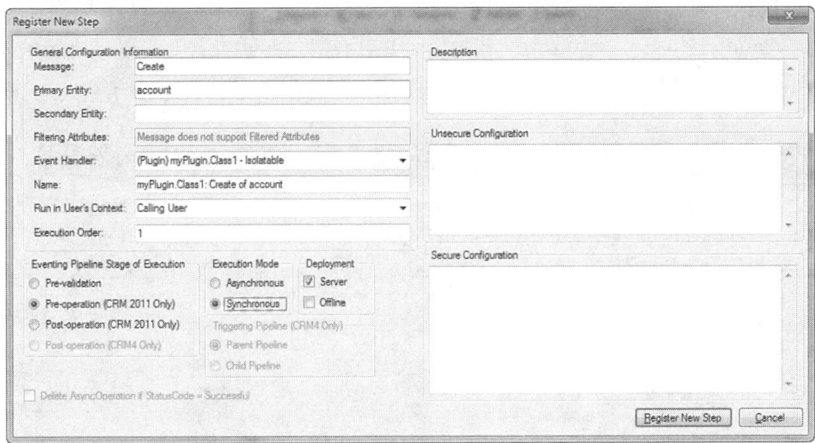

FIGURE 25.28 The Register New Step button.

Click Register New Step to close this dialog box. You will see the new step registered (see Figure 25.29).

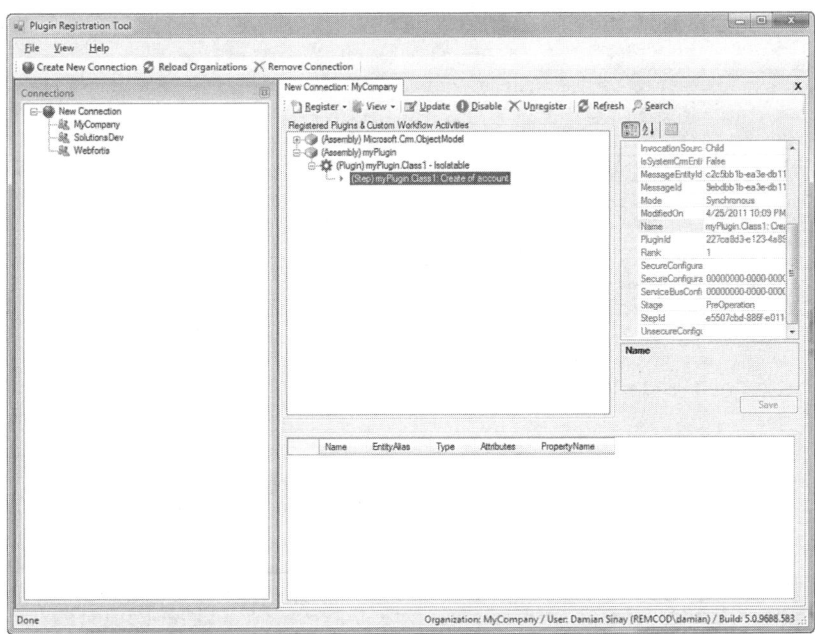

FIGURE 25.29 Step registrations review.

As you saw in Figure 25.29, you can deploy the assembly to either the local hard disk or the database server and to the GAC (Global Assembly Cache). Database is the recommended option for production environments that might be deployed on different servers like on a load balanced deployment.This way you don't need to deploy the assembly on every server. The local hard disk option is the recommended option for debugging purposes.

CAUTION

Be sure to properly debug and test your plug-in before implementing it to a production environment. If the plug-in has an error, users will not be able to create accounts if you attached the plug-in to the account Create event and the Pre stage (see Figure 25.30).

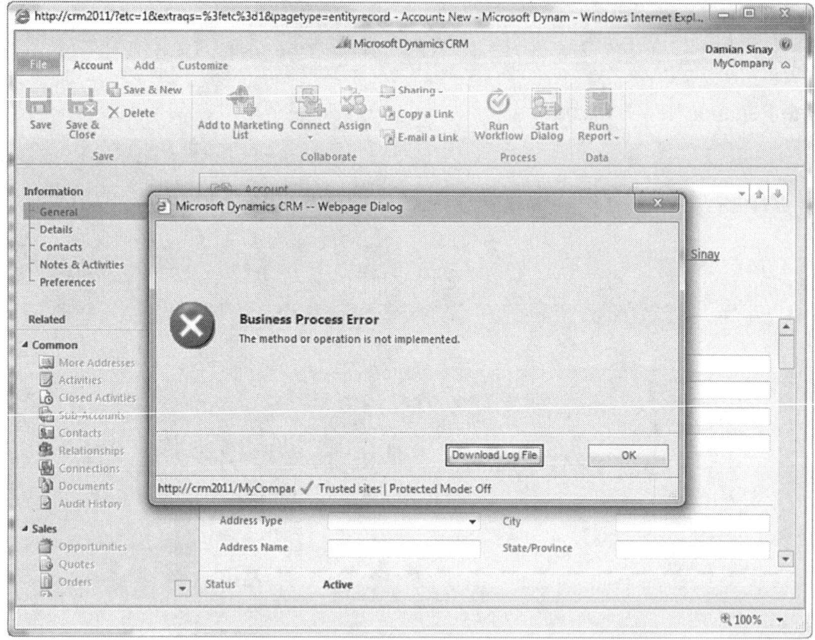

FIGURE 25.30 Plug-in errors and exceptions prevent users from creating records on Pre stage.

▶ See the "Plug-In Debugging" section later in this chapter for help on how to debug.

Plug-in Deregistration

To deregister your plug-in, select the plug-in you want to delete and click the Unregister button. Be sure to select the Assembly node as shown in Figure 25.31 before clicking the Unregister button.

Click Yes to confirm the operation, and a result dialog will be shown, as seen on Figure 25.32.

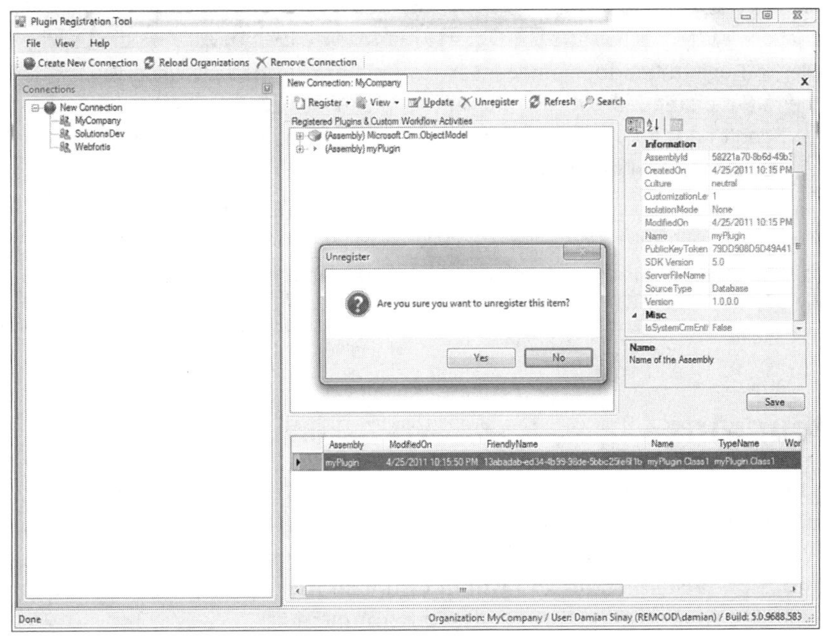

FIGURE 25.31 Successful plug-in deregistration.

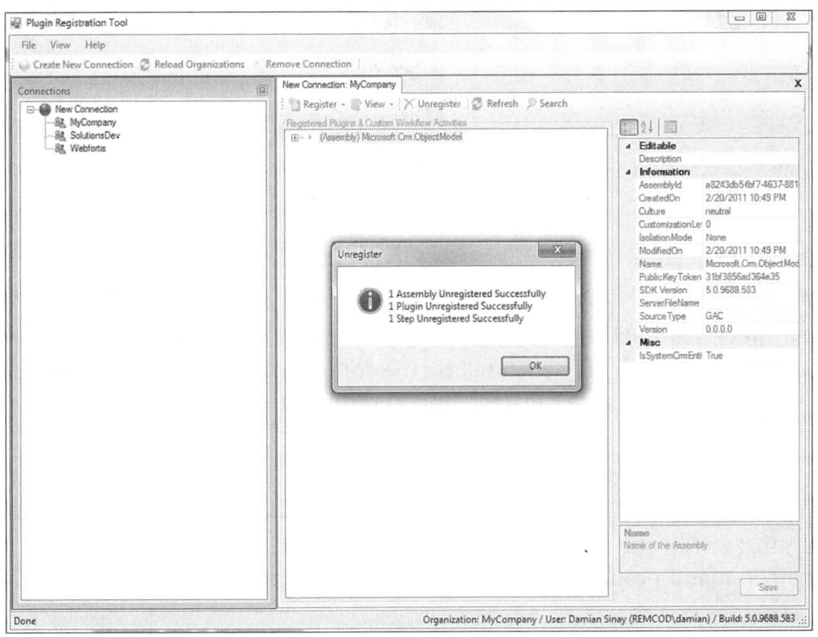

FIGURE 25.32 Successful plug-in deregistration.

NOTE

The use of the Plug-in Registration tool is necessary to register plug-ins only when you are developing them. For distribution of your plug-in to a production environment (or to another client), you don't need to use this tool because you can use solutions and deploy your plug-in for distribution that way.

▶ To read more about solutions and how to distribute your plug-ins, refer to Chapter 16, "Solution Concepts."

Plug-In Debugging

There are two ways to debug your plug-in. The first, as shown in Table 25.1, is attaching the debugger to the host process, and the other is forcing the plug-in to call the debugger. For either of these methods, it is recommended to try them in a testing environment because these methods use Visual Studio and will interrupt all user activity with the server if you attempt to enable debugging in a production environment.

TABLE 25.1 Attaching Debugger to Host Process

Plug-in Registration Configuration	Service Process
Online	w3wp.exe
Offline	Microsoft.Crm.Application.Hoster.exe
Asynchronous registered plug-ins (or custom workflow assemblies)	CrmAsyncService.exe
Sandbox (isolation mode)	Microsoft.Crm.Sandbox.WorkerProcess.exe

Before trying any of these methods, you need to build your plug-in with Debug mode and put the PDB (project database) file generated by the compiler in the following directory (assuming you have the CRM server installed on C:\Program Files\Microsoft Dynamics CRM.):

```
C:\Program Files\Microsoft Dynamics CRM\Server\bin\assembly
```

Unfortunately you must restart the IIS after copying the PDB file. This is something that can be done via the command prompt by running the following command:

```
Iisreset
```

You could also restart the IIS by using a PowerShell command:

```
Restart-Service W3SVC,WAS -force
```

TIP

You must copy the PDB file every time you rebuild the solution and restart the IIS.

CAUTION

You must have Visual Studio 2010 installed on the server where the CRM Server is installed, or you can only install the Visual Studio 2010 Remote Debugger on the server and debug from a development workstation. This sample assumes you have Visual Studio 2010 installed on the same server where the CRM Server is installed.

Attaching the Debugger to the host Process

With this mode you have to open your plug-in solution in Visual Studio 2010 first and put breakpoints where you want to stop and debug your code. To set a breakpoint, press F9 (see Figure 25.33).

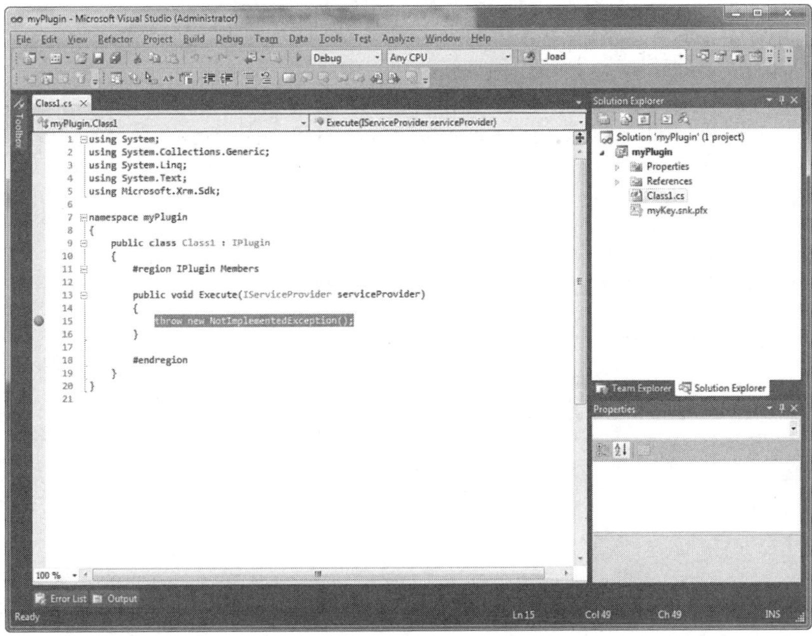

FIGURE 25.33 Setting breakpoints on your code.

You must start the debugger by attaching the Visual Studio debugger to the w3wp.exe process for example to debug an online plugin. To do that, go to the Debug menu, and select the Attach to Process option (see Figure 25.34).

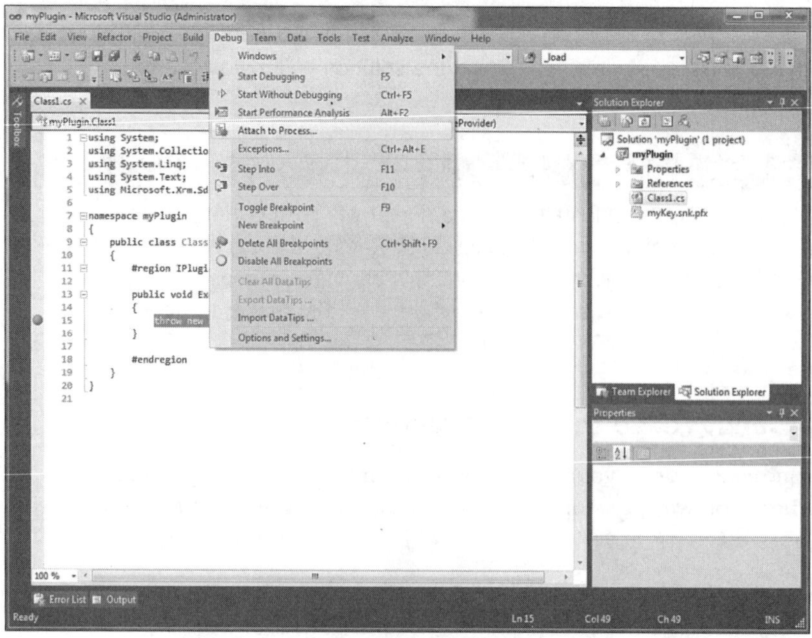

FIGURE 25.34 Attach to process menu option.

When the Attach to Process dialog appears, be sure to check the check boxes that say Show Processes from All Users and Show Processes in All Sessions. Locate the w3wp.exe process and select it (see Figure 25.35).

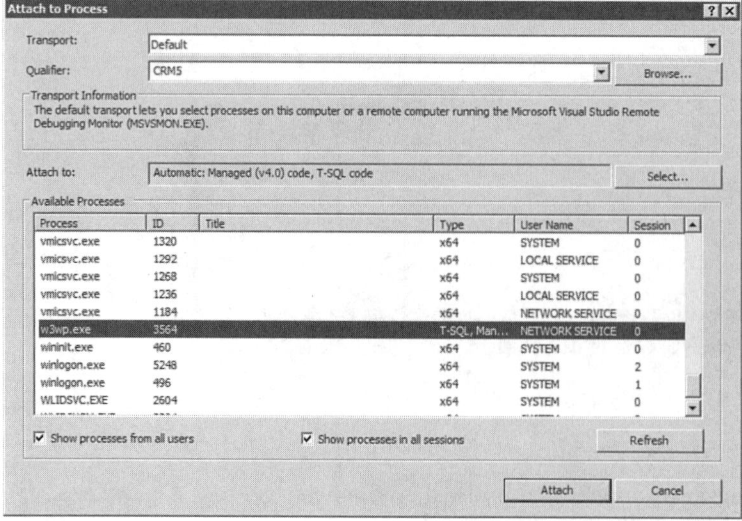

FIGURE 25.35 Attaching the debugger to the w3wp.exe process.

NOTE

If you don't find the w3wp.exe process, it is probably because you must first open an Internet Explorer window and browse to your CRM organization URL so that IIS will load the application pool represented by the w3wp.exe.

You might also find there is more than one instance of the w3wp.exe processes running; this might depend on the number of different websites and application pools running on the same IIS. Because it is hard to say on which one our application is running, we recommend attaching to all the w3wp.exe instances.

If you are using the Remote Debugger, you will need to change the qualifier name to the name of the computer where the CRM and the remote debugger are installed.

If the plug-in has been registered with sandbox isolation mode, you will need to attach to another process instead of the w3wp.exe process. The process that hosts the plug-ins on a sandbox is called Microsoft.Crm.Sandbox.HostService.exe.

Click the Attach button to start debugging the plug-in.

Assuming you registered a plug-in with a step associated to the Account entity on the Create event (as our example did), when you go to the CRM web application and try to create a new Account, you will be automatically switched to the Visual Studio 2010 application after you click the Save or Save and Close buttons on the Account form (see Figure 25.36).

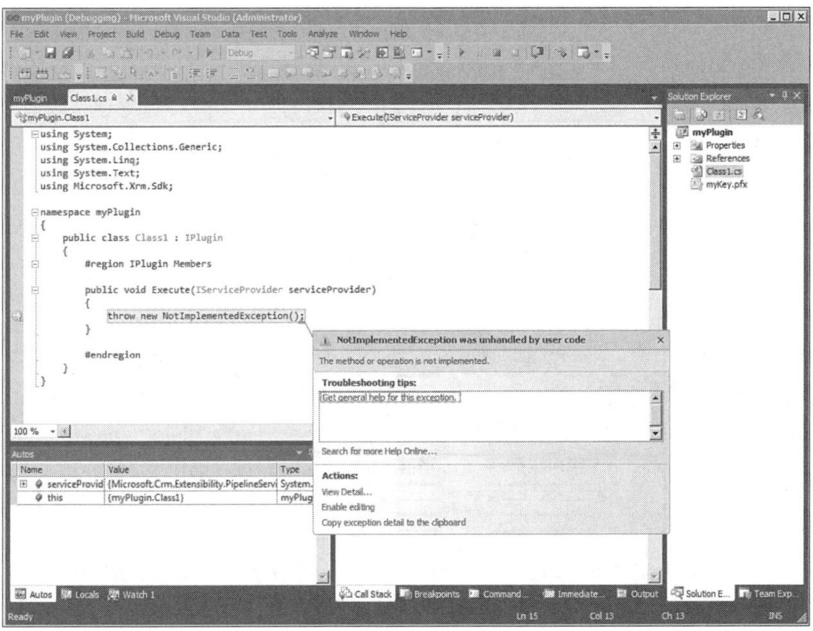

FIGURE 25.36 Debugging the plug-in.

Forcing the Add-In to Call the Debugger

To force CRM to call the debugger, you must add a line similar to the following in your add-in source code where you want to call the debugger:

```
System.Diagnostics.Debugger.Launch();
```

Assuming you registered a plug-in with a step associated to the Account entity on the Create event (as our example did), when you go the CRM web application and try to create a new Account, you will see the dialog shown on Figure 25.37 after you click the Save or Save and Close buttons on the Account form.

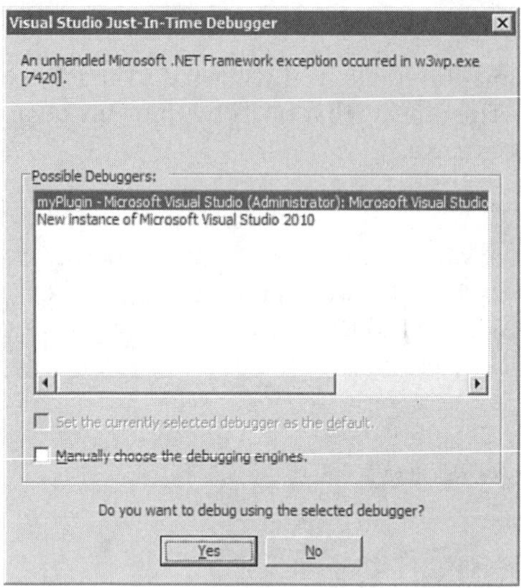

FIGURE 25.37 Visual Studio just-in-time debugger.

Click Yes to open a new instance of Microsoft Visual Studio 2010, and you will see the code of your plug-in stopped its execution right on the line of code we added to launch the debugger (see Figure 25.38).

NOTE

If you try saving the Account from a machine different than the server, the dialog shown on Figure 25.42 will be displayed on the server machine and not on the client machine.

Be sure to comment or remove all the lines where you put the Debugger.Launch() method after debugging and fixing your plug-in before deploying it to production.

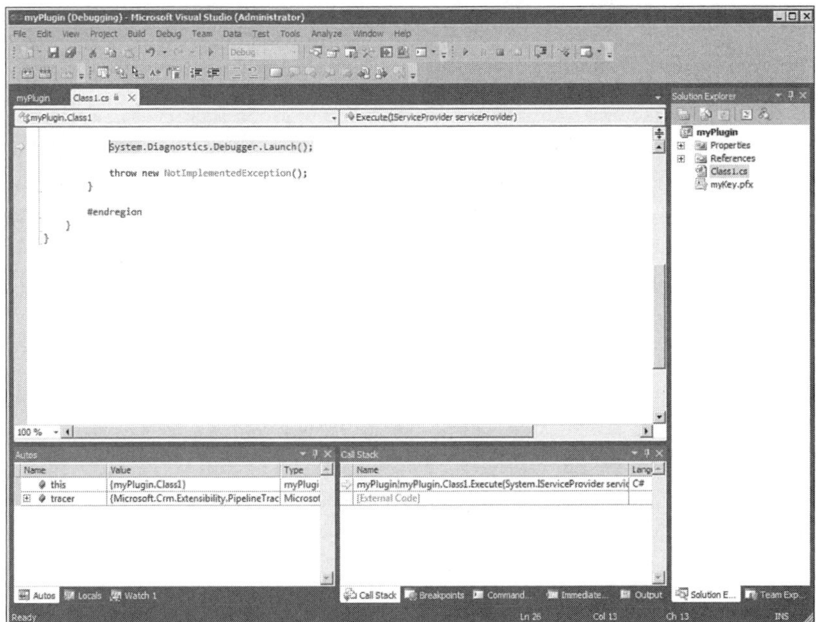

FIGURE 25.38 Plug-in debugging in Visual Studio.

IServiceProvider

The Execute method of the IPlugin interface has been updated and the only parameter received is the IServiceProvider, unlike the previous version where it was used the IPluginExecutionContext as parameter.

From this parameter, we can get the plugin execution context by typing this line of code:

```
IPluginExecutionContext context =
(IPluginExecutionContext)serviceProvider.GetService(typeof(IPluginExecutionContext));
```

This change of the main parameter has a method, GetService, that enables you to get other services from the service provider, such as the context of the organization and the context of the tracer service. This enables you to interact with the current CRM trace to add debugging information for the execution of your plug-in. For example, the following lines show the tracing.

The IPluginExecutionContext now inherits the IExecutionContext, which is a more generic interface that is also implemented by other classes like the RemoteExecutionContext class used for Windows Azure integrations.

IExecutionContext

From this object, you can query all the property values associated with the entity and event context where the method is being executed.

This class contains the following properties:

- BusinessUnitId
- CorrelationId
- Depth
- InitiatingUserId
- InputParameters
- IsExecutingOffline
- IsInTransaction
- IsOfflinePlayback
- IsolationMode
- MessageName
- Mode
- OperationCreatedOn
- OperationId
- OrganizationId
- OrganizationName
- OutputParameters
- OwningExtension
- PostEntityImages
- PreEntityImages
- PrimaryEntityId
- PrimaryEntityName
- RequestId
- SecondaryEntityName
- SharedVariables
- UserId

BusinessUnitId

This property returns the GUID (Global Unique Identifier) of the business unit of the entity. Notice that this is not the GUID of the entity's record. To return the GUID of the entity's record, there is a new property called PrimaryEntityId.

CorrelationId

This property returns the GUID of the plug-in event instance. Every time the event fires, it generates a new GUID that can be read from this property.

You can use this property for tracking and logging purposes, especially when you have more than one plug-in attached to the same event to see whether the codes execute for the same event pipeline.

Depth

This property returns the depth of the originated event. This property is of integer type and grows as the plug-in execution goes deeper. This can happen if your plug-in calls a web service to update another entity that also fires an event for another plug-in execution code.

InitiatingUserId

This property returns the GUID of the user who initially invoked the operation.

InputParameters

This property is a collection of the request parameters associated with the event. You can use this property to retrieve the entity of which the event is fired:

```
Entity entity = (Entity)context.InputParameters["Target"];
```

IsExecutingOffline

This property is used only for Outlook clients and returns whether the Outlook client is running in online or offline mode. This property is a Boolean type where true = offline mode.

IsInTransaction

This property is used to know whether the operation is participating on a SQL transaction. This property is a Boolean type where true = is in transaction.

IsOfflinePlayback

This property is used only for Outlook clients and returns whether the Outlook client is transitioning from offline to online mode. This property is a Boolean type where true = synchronizing with the server.

IsolationMode

This property returns the IsolationMode mode in which the plug-in is running. It can be none or sandbox. This parameter is an integer type where the following is true:

0 = None

2 = Sandbox

MessageName

This property returns the event's name that invoked the plug-in. It is a string—for example, Update, Create, Delete, and so on.

Mode

This property returns the mode in which the plug-in is running. It can be synchronous or asynchronous. This parameter is an integer type where the following is true:

0 = Synchronous

1 = Synchronous

OperationId

This property returns the operation GUID when the plug-in is running in asynchronous mode and will give you the ID of the current system job. In synchronous mode, this value will be always an empty GUID.

OrganizationId

This property returns the organization GUID where the plug-in is running.

Even though plug-ins are registered by organization ID, having this property helps if you have a generic plug-in developed that will be installed in different organizations and you need to perform different tasks depending on the organization the plug-in is running. This way, you can maintain only one Visual Studio solution and source codes.

OrganizationName

This property returns the name of the organization where the plug-in is running.

With this attribute you won't need to make an API call to get the organization name by given the Organization ID.

OutputParameters

This property is the collection of properties returned by the event. A common output parameter is the GUID returned when an entity is created. Be careful when adding parameters on Pre stages because they could be overwritten after the system processes the core event. As an example of this, imagine that you want to return the accountid property that is created when a plug-in is attached to the Create event of the Account entity in the Post stage:

```
Guid myAccountID = (Guid)context.OutputParameters["id"];
```

OwningExtension

This property returns the data associated with the step registration. This property type is an EntityReference class from which we can get, for example, the description of the step that is running where we registered the plug-in.

PostEntityImages

This property contains the collection of the images with the properties' names and values after the system executes the core operation.

> **NOTE**
>
> You need to specify the images and what properties you want to have on this collection when you register the plug-in.

PreEntityImages

This property contains the collection of the images with the properties and values before the system executes the core operation. This is very useful on Post stages to see what values the associated entity had before an update operation, for example.

> **NOTE**
>
> As with PostEntityImages, you also need to specify the images and what properties you want to have with this collection when you register the plug-in.

PrimaryEntityId

This property returns the GUID of the entity's record where the operation is performed. If you are working with Accounts, you should use the following code to get the entity record identifier:

```
Guid id = context.PrimaryEntityId;
```

PrimaryEntityName

This property gets the related primary entity name you specified when you registered the plug-in. This property is a type of string and returns the name of the associated entity—for example, account, contact, and so on.

RequestId

This property gets the id (GUID) of the asynchronous operation. It will return null for synchronous operations.

SecondaryEntityName

This property gets he related secondary entity name if you specified one when registering the plug-in. This entity is commonly used in the Parent Account or Contact of the

Account entity. This property is a type of string and returns the string none if no secondary entity name is specified.

SharedVariables

This property is used as a common repository to store properties that plug-ins will share. It is useful when you need to pass a parameter value from one plug-in to another that is being executed in the same event pipeline.

UserId

This property returns the GUID of the user who is invoking the operation.

IOrganizationService

Previously, the IPluginExecutionContext had methods to create the CRM and Metadata Services; now you will see these methods are gone. To use the CRM services you need to get an instance of the IOrganizationService as follows:

```
IOrganizationService service = factory.CreateOrganizationService(context.UserId)
```

The service instance returned by the IOrganizationService has the following methods:

- **Associate**—Used to create a link between records
- **Create**—Used to create records
- **Delete**—Used to delete records
- **Disassociate**—Used to remove a link between records
- **Excecute**—Used, for example, to execute Fetch queries
- **Retrieve**—Used to retrieve a record
- **RetrieveMultiple**—Used to retrieve more than one record
- **Update**—Used to update records

Plug-In Samples

The SDK comes with some plug-in samples: the AccountPluginSample, which creates a random account number when an account is created, the FollowupPlugin plug-in sample that creates a Task activity when an account is created, the PreEventPlugin that demonstrates the use of shared variables to send data through different plug-ins, and the WebClientPlugin that shows how to access a network resource in a sandoboxed plugin. You can find the code for these samples in C# within the SDK under the sdk\sample-code\cs\plug-ins folder.

The SDK can be downloaded from Microsoft by searching for CRM 2011 SDK at Microsoft.com.

TIP

The SDK is frequently updated by Microsoft, and we recommend checking the download site frequently for updated versions.

Summary

In this chapter, you learned about plug-ins, what they are, and when it is recommended to use them. You created a basic plug-in and reviewed all the development properties of the IServiceProvider, IExecutionContext, and the IPluginExecutionContext classes. You learned how to deploy and register the plug-ins using different tools such as the Plug-in Registration Tool with the UI. Finally, you learned how to test and debug your plug-in in different ways such as attaching the debugger to the w3wp.exe process or by forcing the add-in to launch a new debugger instance.

CHAPTER 26
Web Services

IN THIS CHAPTER

- Web Services Fundamentals
- Early Binding
- Samples of Web Services

Web Services Fundamentals

Microsoft Dynamics CRM 2011 uses the now common Service Oriented Architecture (SOA) concept for extensibility, which implements a series of Web Services to provide extensibility support. By using these web services, we can integrate other applications and systems with Microsoft CRM, as well as extend its capabilities.

Web services are based on Simple Object Access Protocol (SOAP) messages. This protocol uses Extended Markup Language (XML), which provides usability through Hypertext Transfer Protocol (HTTP) communication transports.

In simple terms, this gives applications and systems an easy way to communicate using standard protocols to interoperate and share functionalities.

Web services are language-and platform-independent, so they can be consumed by an application written in Java, Visual Basic, or C#. They also can be used on a Microsoft Windows–based OS, as well as UNIX and Macintosh platforms.

NOTE

The samples included in this chapter are written using C# with Visual Studio 2010. However, as shown with the Samples of Web Services section in this chapter, we could consume web services using JavaScript if desired.

CRM 2011 supports the same web service endpoints as the previous version of Microsoft Dynamics CRM (version 4.0) for backward compatibility; however, this new version implements some new communication frameworks that are important to understand.

The new components and standards available within Microsoft Dynamics CRM 2011 are as follows.

Windows Communication Foundation (WCF)

Windows Communication Foundation (WCF) is the next generation of web services that is independent of the protocol to be used, so it is not tied to the HTTP protocol as the old web services. WCF can be implemented and use other protocols such as TCP, HTTP, or peer-to-peer protocols that are configured on a configuration.

Representational State Transfer (REST)

Representational State Transfer (REST) is a modern and easy way to consume a web service without using the SOAP or WSDL protocols. By just using the query string for retrieve operations using the GET method of the HTTP protocol and the POST method for add, DELETE method for delete, and PUT method for update operations, you can quickly get the data you want in XML format without having to create any special proxy client as you would do it with SOAP.

JavaScript Object Notation (JSON)

JavaScript Object Notation (JSON) is a simplified way to send and receive messages that improves the amount of bytes being sent or received by a service comparing it with XML.

For example, an XML message like

```
<customers>
        <customer>Jhon</customer>
        <customer>Lucas</customer>
</customers>
```

would be formed like this in JSON:

```
"Customers" : { "customer" : "Jhon" , "Lucas" }
```

As you can see the JSON involves sending less numbers of characters than the corresponding XML message, and the result would be the same.

▶ For more information about JSON, visit http://www.json.org/.

Open Data Services (ODATA)

Open Data Services (ODATA) is a standard way of communication via the REST protocol that allows filtering, sorting, and choosing the columns returned and more.

The Microsoft CRM 2011 web services are divided and defined into three main groups:

- Discovery Service (SOAP protocol)
- Organization Service (SOAP protocol)
- Organization Data Service (ODATA protocol via REST)

To easily see these web services' definitions and get the URL addresses of the Web Services Description Language (WSDL) documents within Microsoft CRM 2011, follow these steps:

1. Go to Settings, Customizations (see Figure 26.1).

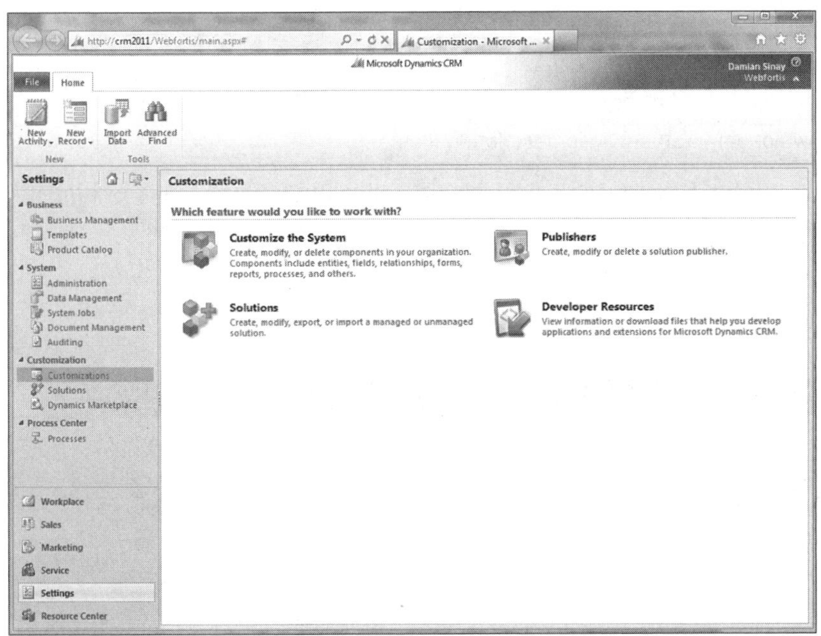

FIGURE 26.1 Navigating to Settings, Customization.

2. Select the option Developer Resources (see Figure 26.2).

As you can see in Figure 26.2, you can download the WSDL definitions for two web services: the Discovery and the Organization services. The Organization data service uses OData, so you can download the Conceptual schema definition language (CSDL) definition file for it.

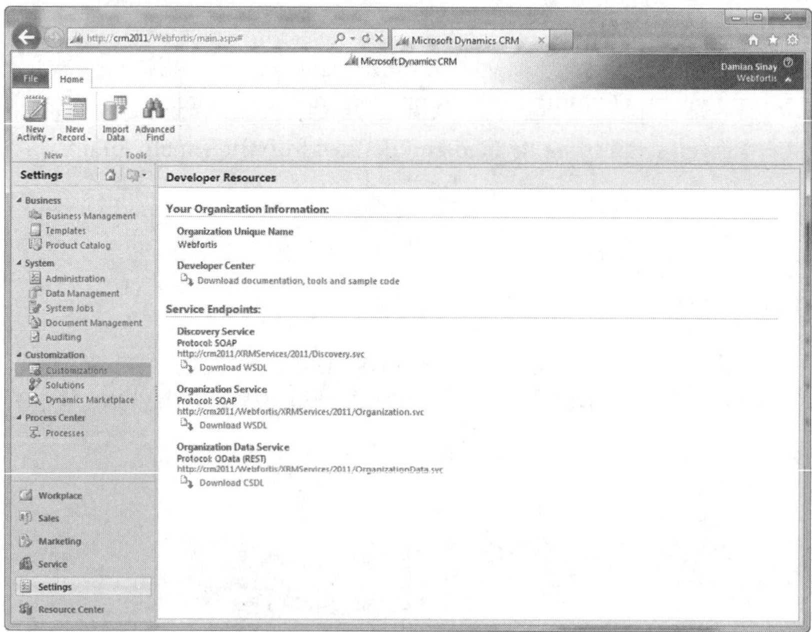

FIGURE 26.2 Downloading web services description files.

For backward compatibility there are still available the following services that are compatible with the previous version of CRM 4.0:

- Main Data web service
- Metadata web service

NOTE

To understand how to use these services, you will need to create a new console application in C# to follow the examples of this chapter. To do so, open Visual Studio 2010 and go to the File menu; select New and then Project. From the project templates, go to Visual C#/Windows, and select the Console Application in the right side where the templates are (see Figure 26.3).

The next section explains the web services definition files.

Discovery Web Service

As we explained previously, Microsoft CRM 2011 has multitenancy capability, which is support for more than one organization on the same server. Because of that, you need to query a general web service called CRMDiscoveryService that will give you the right web service for the organization you want to work with. You can find the query by navigating here:

```
http://<serername>:<portnumber>/XRMServices/2011/Discovery.svc?wsdl
```

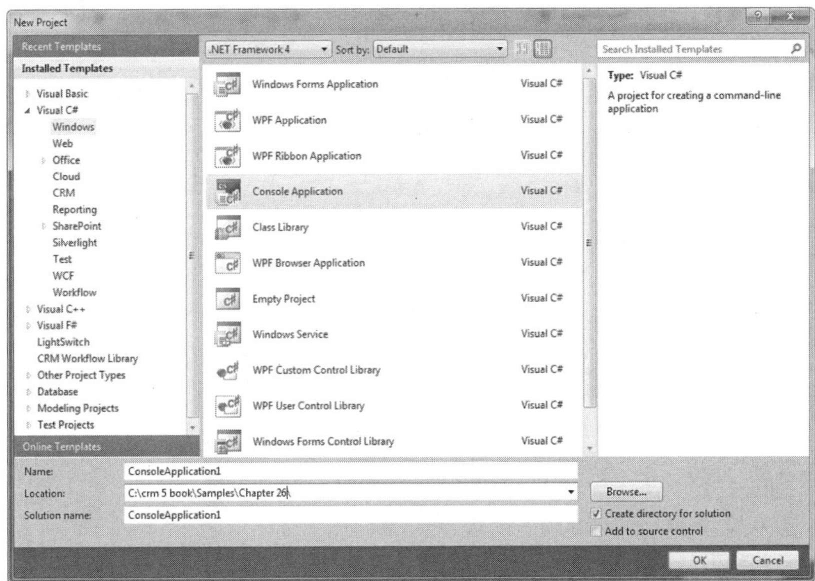

FIGURE 26.3 Creating a console application in Visual Studio 2010.

For example:

```
http://crm2011/XRMServices/2011/Discovery.svc?wsdl
```

TIP

The port number can be omitted for the default port 80 of the HTTP protocol on this sample.

To add a web reference for this service, go to Visual Studio 2010, and use the new console application project you created. Right-click the project name in the Solution Explorer, and choose Add Service Reference from the menu, enter the URL of the discovery service, click GO, and then enter CrmSdk.Discovery in the namespace text box (see Figure 26.4).

Click OK to finally add the WCF service reference to your project.

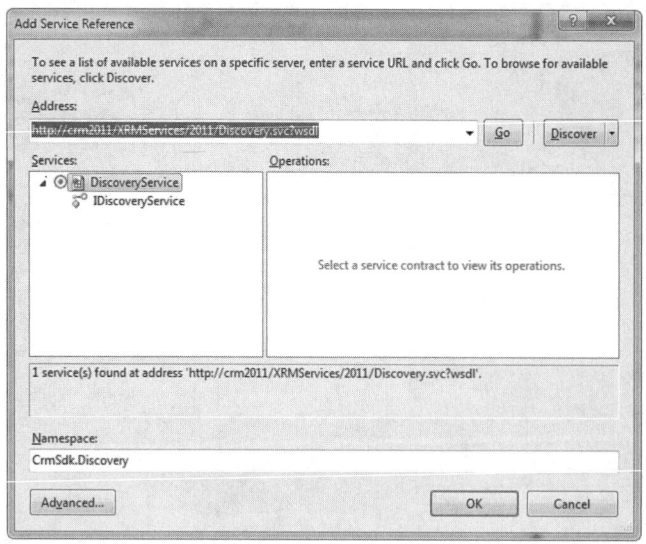

FIGURE 26.4 Adding a web reference to the Discovery WCF service.

By querying this service, you can retrieve all the organizations that a specific user belongs to and get the right services location. An example of this follows:

```
namespace ConsoleApplication1
{
    class Program
    {
        static void Main(string[] args)
        {
            Console.WriteLine(GetCrmServiceForOrganization("Webfortis"));
            Console.ReadKey();
        }
        private static string GetCrmServiceForOrganization
             (string organizationName)
        {
            using (CrmSdk.Discovery.DiscoveryServiceClient myCrm =
                new CrmSdk.Discovery.DiscoveryServiceClient())
            {
                myCrm.ClientCredentials.Windows.ClientCredential =
            System.Net.CredentialCache.DefaultNetworkCredentials;
                CrmSdk.Discovery.RetrieveOrganizationsRequest myRequest =
                    new CrmSdk.Discovery.RetrieveOrganizationsRequest();
                CrmSdk.Discovery.RetrieveOrganizationsResponse myResponse =
                    (CrmSdk.Discovery.RetrieveOrganizationsResponse)
                     myCrm.Execute(myRequest);
                foreach (CrmSdk.Discovery.OrganizationDetail
```

```
                 detail in myResponse.Details)
                {
                    Console.WriteLine("Organization = " + detail.UniqueName);
                    if (detail.UniqueName == organizationName)
                    {
                        return detail.Endpoints[1].Value;
                    }
                }
            }
            return "";
        }
    }
}
```

This function illustrates how to get the correct organization service endpoint address to use for the organization you want to work with.

Organization Service

The other service reference that is necessary for a custom application is the Organization service.

```
http://<servername>:<portnumber>/XRMServices/2011/Organization.svc?wsdl
```

For example:

```
http://crm2011/XRMServices/2011/Organization.svc?wsdl
```

Adding a Service Reference

To add a service reference for this service, go to Visual Studio 2010 and using the new console application project you created, right-click the project name in the Solution Explorer, and choose Add Service Reference from the menu. Enter the URL of the Organization service, click GO, and then enter CrmSdk in the namespace text box (see Figure 26.5).

Click OK to finally add the service reference to your project.

The Organization service has the following methods:

- Create
- Retrieve
- RetrieveMultiple
- Delete
- Associate
- Disassociate

- Execute
- Update

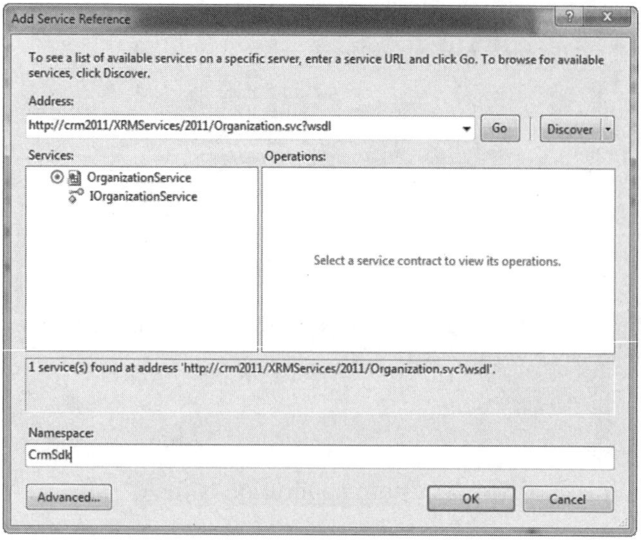

FIGURE 26.5 Adding a service reference for the Organization service.

Create Method

This method is used to create new instances of an existing entity, such as a new Account or Contact.

This method has only one implementation: It returns a Global Unique Identifier (GUID), which is the unique identifier of the new entity to be created; it accepts one parameter of type Entity, which is now replacing the old BusinessEntity used in CRM 4.0. Because all entities in CRM inherent from the BusinessEntity base class, you can pass any entity class to this input parameter.

This is an example of how to create a new account programmatically in Visual Studio 2010 with C#:

```
private static string CreateAccount(string organizationName,
          string accountName)
{
  using (CrmSdk.OrganizationServiceClient myCrm =
        new CrmSdk.OrganizationServiceClient())
  {
    try
    {
       myCrm.Endpoint.Address =
       new System.ServiceModel.EndpointAddress
```

```
        (GetCrmServiceForOrganization("Webfortis"));
         myCrm.ClientCredentials.Windows.ClientCredential =
         System.Net.CredentialCache.DefaultNetworkCredentials;
         CrmSdk.Entity newAccount = new CrmSdk.Entity();
         newAccount.LogicalName = "account";
         CrmSdk.AttributeCollection myAttributes =
          new CrmSdk.AttributeCollection();
         myAttributes.Add(new KeyValuePair<string, object>("name",
                        accountName));
         newAccount.Attributes = myAttributes;
         Guid newAccountId = myCrm.Create(newAccount);
         return newAccountId.ToString();
      }
      catch (Exception ex)
       {
          Console.WriteLine("General exception: " + ex.ToString());
          return "General exception: " + ex.ToString();
       }
    }
    return "";
}
```

To test this method, you need to pass the organization name and the name of the new Account you want to create to the method parameters as follows:

```
Console.WriteLine("New Account GUID = " + CreateAccount("Webfortis",
      "New Account"));
```

You can put the line above inside the Main function of your program to test it, so the Main function should look like this:

```
static void Main(string[] args)
{
    Console.WriteLine("New Account GUID = " + CreateAccount("Webfortis",
    "New Account"));
    Console.ReadKey(); //added for debugging purposes only
}
```

When running this code by either pressing F5 or by going to the Debug menu, and then Start Debugging menu option, you should see a similar output, as shown in Figure 26.6.

Now if you go to the CRM web client application, you will see the new Account (see Figure 26.7).

Be sure to assign *all* the Business Required fields for the entity you will create programmatically, to avoid exceptions.

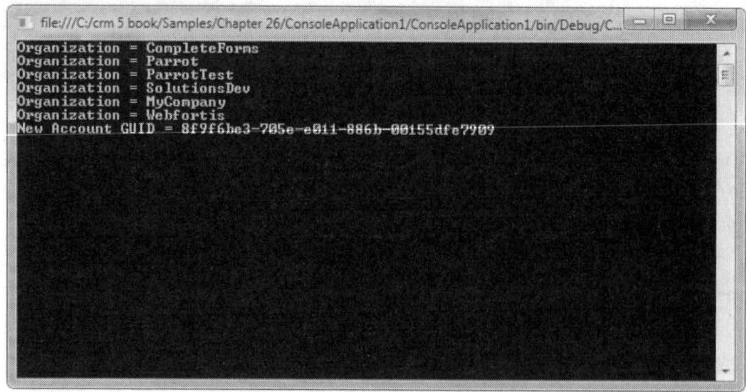

FIGURE 26.6 Creating an account through the Main Data web service.

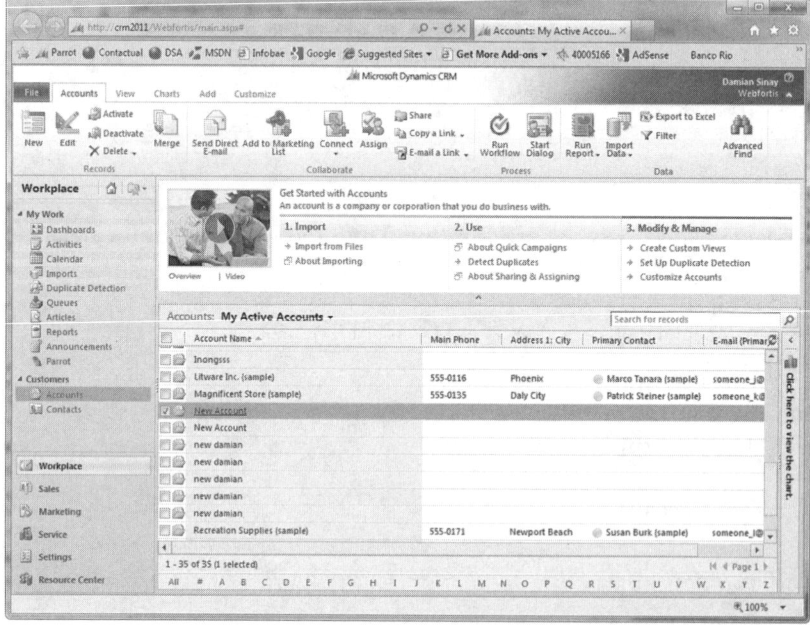

FIGURE 26.7 Reviewing the new account created through the Main Data web service.

Retrieve Method

This method gets an instance of an entity object. To get more than one instance of an entity, use the RetrieveMultiple method (explained in the next section).

This method returns a class type of Entity. The input parameters are the string of the entity name, the GUID of the instance of the entity, and a set of columns or fields you want to retrieve.

It is important to define the columns you want to retrieve in the last parameter, or you will get null values even though the instance in the CRM system has values.

This is an example of the Retrieve method:

```
private static CrmSdk.account RetrieveAccount(string organizationName,
             Guid accountId)
{
    using (CrmSdk.OrganizationServiceClient myCrm =
         new CrmSdk.OrganizationServiceClient())
    {
        try
        {
            myCrm.Endpoint.Address =
            new System.ServiceModel.EndpointAddress
           (GetCrmServiceForOrganization("Webfortis"));
            myCrm.ClientCredentials.Windows.ClientCredential =
            System.Net.CredentialCache.DefaultNetworkCredentials;
            CrmSdk.ColumnSet columns = new CrmSdk.ColumnSet();
            // add more attributes if you want separated by coma below
            columns.Columns = new string[] { "name", "accountid" };
            Guid myAccountId = accountId;
            CrmSdk.Entity myAccount =
            myCrm.Retrieve("account", myAccountId, columns);
            return myAccount;
        }
        catch (Exception ex)
        {
            Console.WriteLine("General exception: " + ex.ToString());
            return null;
        }
    }
    return null;
}
```


As you can see from this sample method, you need to know the GUID of the account record (or the entity we want to retrieve) in order to use this method. We can combine the CreateAccount method we created in the previous section to test this as follows: Remember to always replace Webfortis with your organization name.

```
static void Main(string[] args)
{
    string newAccountId = CreateAccount("Webfortis", "Test Account");
    Console.WriteLine("New Account GUID = " + newAccountId);
    Console.WriteLine("Checking new account created = " +
          RetrieveAccount("Webfortis", new Guid(newAccountId)
          ).Attributes[0].Value );
         Console.ReadKey(); //added for debugging purposes only
}
```

After running this test you will see the output, which should be similar to output shown in Figure 26.8.

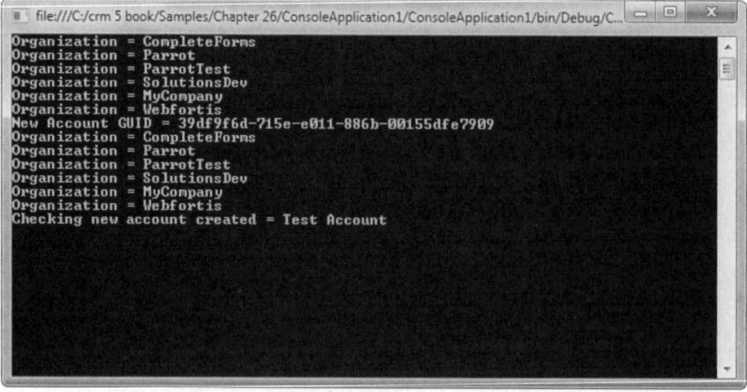

FIGURE 26.8 Testing the Retrieve method of the Main Data web service.

It is important to understand that you must know the GUID in order to use this code. This might not be practical when you only know the name and not the GUID. In these cases, you'll have to use the RetriveMultiple method as explained in the next section.

RetrieveMultiple Method

This method gets one or more than one instance of an entity.

For example, you can use this method to retrieve *all* the Accounts for an organization, as illustrated here:

```
private static void GetAllAccounts(string organizationName)
{
    using (CrmSdk.OrganizationServiceClient myCrm =
       new CrmSdk.OrganizationServiceClient())
    {
        try
        {
            myCrm.Endpoint.Address =
             new System.ServiceModel.EndpointAddress
             (GetCrmServiceForOrganization("Webfortis"));
            myCrm.ClientCredentials.Windows.ClientCredential =
            System.Net.CredentialCache.DefaultNetworkCredentials;
            // Creates a column set holding the names of the
            // columns to be retreived
            CrmSdk.ColumnSet colsPrincipal = new CrmSdk.ColumnSet();
            // Sets the Column Set's Properties
            colsPrincipal.Columns = new string[] { "accountid", "name" };
            // Create the Query Expression
```

```
            CrmSdk.QueryExpression queryPrincipal =
            new CrmSdk.QueryExpression();
            // Set the QueryExpression's Properties
            queryPrincipal.EntityName = "account";
            queryPrincipal.ColumnSet = colsPrincipal;
            /// Retrieve the accounts.
            CrmSdk.EntityCollection myAccounts =
            myCrm.RetrieveMultiple(queryPrincipal);
            Console.WriteLine("\nGetAllAccounts found {0} accounts\n",
                            myAccounts.Entities.Length);
            foreach (CrmSdk.Entity myEntity in myAccounts.Entities)
            {
                Console.WriteLine(myEntity.Attributes[1].Value);
            }
        }
        catch (Exception ex)
        {
            Console.WriteLine("General exception: " + ex.ToString());
        }
    }
}
```

To test this method, you need to pass the organization name to the method parameter. The Main function should be as follows:

```
static void Main(string[] args)
{
    GetAllAccounts("Webfortis");
    Console.ReadKey(); //added for debugging purposes only
}
```

TIP

Remember to always replace Webfortis with your organization name.

When running this code by either pressing F5 or by going to the Debug menu, and then the Start Debugging menu option, you should see a similar output, as shown on Figure 26.9.

You can apply filters on the data you want, as well as retrieve only the fields or properties you want to get.

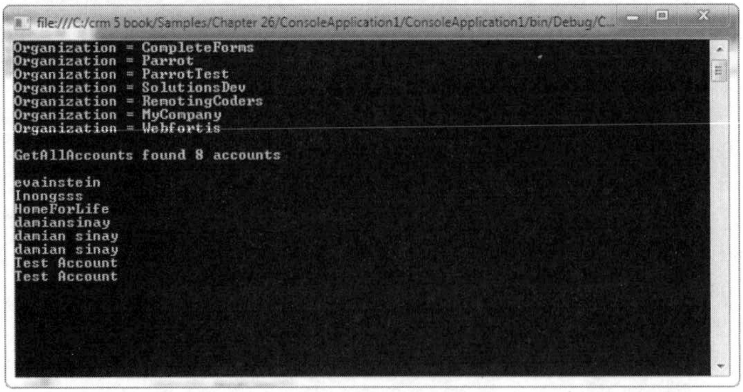

```
Organization = CompleteForms
Organization = Parrot
Organization = ParrotTest
Organization = SolutionsDev
Organization = RemotingCoders
Organization = MyCompany
Organization = Webfortis

GetAllAccounts found 8 accounts

evainstein
Inongsss
HomeForLife
damiansinay
damian sinay
damian sinay
Test Account
Test Account
```

FIGURE 26.9

For example, to retrieve all the Accounts whose name match or start with the first letters, use this code:

```
private static List<CrmSdk.account> GetAllAccountsByName(
       string organizationName, string accountName,
        CrmSdk.ConditionOperator conditionalOperator)
{
    List<CrmSdk.Entity> accounts = null;
    using (CrmSdk.OrganizationServiceClient myCrm =
      new CrmSdk.OrganizationServiceClient())
    {
        try
        {
            myCrm.Endpoint.Address =
           new System.ServiceModel.EndpointAddress
           (GetCrmServiceForOrganization("Webfortis"));
            myCrm.ClientCredentials.Windows.ClientCredential =
           System.Net.CredentialCache.DefaultNetworkCredentials;
            // Creates a column set holding the names of the
            // columns to be retreived
            CrmSdk.ColumnSet colsPrincipal = new CrmSdk.ColumnSet();
            // Sets the Column Set's Properties
            colsPrincipal.Columns = new string[] { "accountid", "name" };
            // Create a ConditionExpression
            CrmSdk.ConditionExpression conditionPrincipal =
            new CrmSdk.ConditionExpression();
            // Sets the ConditionExpressions Properties so that the condition
            // is true when the ownerid of the account Equals the principalId
            conditionPrincipal.AttributeName = "name";
            conditionPrincipal.Operator = conditionalOperator;
            conditionPrincipal.Values = new object[1];
```

```
            conditionPrincipal.Values[0] = accountName;
            // Create the FilterExpression
            CrmSdk.FilterExpression filterPrincipal =
            new CrmSdk.FilterExpression();
            // Set the FilterExpression's Properties
            filterPrincipal.FilterOperator = CrmSdk.LogicalOperator.And;
            filterPrincipal.Conditions =
            new CrmSdk.ConditionExpression[] { conditionPrincipal };
            // Create the Query Expression
            CrmSdk.QueryExpression queryPrincipal =
            new CrmSdk.QueryExpression();
            // Set the QueryExpression's Properties
            queryPrincipal.EntityName = "account";
            queryPrincipal.ColumnSet = colsPrincipal;
            queryPrincipal.Criteria = filterPrincipal;
            /// Retrieve the accounts.
            CrmSdk.EntityCollection myAccounts =
            myCrm.RetrieveMultiple(queryPrincipal);
            accounts = new List<ConsoleApplication1.CrmSdk.Entity>();
            foreach (CrmSdk.Entity myEntity in myAccounts.Entities)
            {
                accounts.Add(myEntity);
                Console.WriteLine(myEntity.Attributes[1].Value);
            }
            return accounts;
        }
        catch (Exception ex)
        {
            Console.WriteLine("General exception: " + ex.ToString());
            return null;
        }
    }
}
```

To test this method, you need to pass the organization name to the method parameter.

TIP

Remember to always replace Webfortis with your organization name.

The Main function should be as follows:

```
static void Main(string[] args)
{
    List<CrmSdk.Entity> accounts;
```

```
    Console.WriteLine("Accounts that starts with the letter A");
    accounts = GetAllAccountsByName("Webfortis", "A%",
        ConsoleApplication1.CrmSdk.ConditionOperator.Like);
    if (accounts == null)
    {
        Console.WriteLine("No accounts found");
    }

    Console.WriteLine("Accounts equal to 'Test Account'");
    accounts = GetAllAccountsByName("Webfortis", "Test Account",
    ConsoleApplication1.CrmSdk.ConditionOperator.Equal);
    if (accounts == null)
    {
        Console.WriteLine("No accounts found");
    }
    Console.ReadKey(); //added for debugging purposes only
}
```

When running this code by either pressing F5 or by going to the Debug menu, and then the Start Debugging menu option, you should see a similar output, as shown in Figure 26.10.

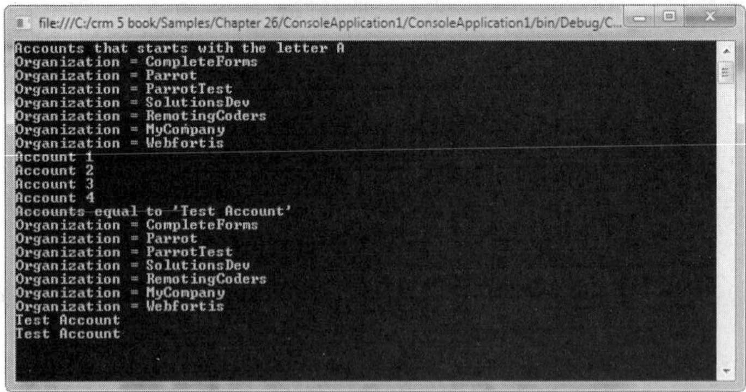

FIGURE 26.10 RetrieveMultiple method output.

Delete Method

This method deletes an existing instance of an entity. This method doesn't return any value and accepts two input parameters. The first parameter is a string containing the entity type, and the second parameter is the GUID of the instance of the entity you will delete.

This is an example of how to delete a new Account programmatically in Visual Studio 2010 with C#:

```
private static string DeleteAccount(string organizationName,
                Guid accountToDelete)
{
```

```
    using (CrmSdk.OrganizationServiceClient myCrm =
       new CrmSdk.OrganizationServiceClient())
    {
        try
        {
            myCrm.Endpoint.Address =
            new System.ServiceModel.EndpointAddress
            (GetCrmServiceForOrganization("Webfortis"));
            myCrm.ClientCredentials.Windows.ClientCredential =
            System.Net.CredentialCache.DefaultNetworkCredentials;
            myCrm.Delete("account", accountToDelete);
            return "Account successfully deleted";
        }
        catch (Exception ex)
        {
            Console.WriteLine("General exception: " + ex.ToString());
            return "General exception: " + ex.ToString();
        }
    }
}
```

To test this method, you need to pass the organization name to the method parameter as well as the GUID of the account to be deleted. Because you might not know the GUID of the account but you might know the account name, we will combine the GetAllAccountsByName method we created previously.

TIP

Remember to always replace Webfortis with your organization name.

The Main function to delete all the accounts that matches with the name Test Account should be as follows:

```
static void Main(string[] args)
{
    List<CrmSdk.Entity> accounts;
    Console.WriteLine("Accounts equal to 'Test Account'");
    accounts = GetAllAccountsByName("Webfortis", "Test Account",
    ConsoleApplication1.CrmSdk.ConditionOperator.Equal);
    if (accounts == null)
    {
        Console.WriteLine("No accounts found");
    }
    else
    {
```

```
        foreach (CrmSdk.Entity myAccount in accounts)
        {
            Console.WriteLine(
                DeleteAccount("Webfortis",
new Guid( myAccount.Attributes[0].Value.ToString())));
        }
    }
    Console.ReadKey(); //added for debugging purposes only
}
```

When running this code by either pressing F5 or by going to the Debug menu, and then the Start Debugging menu option, you should see a similar output, as shown in Figure 26.11.

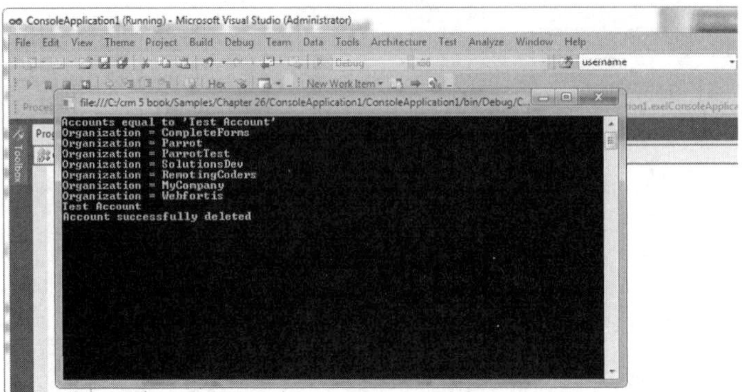

FIGURE 26.11 Account deleted example.

Execute Method

This method executes business logic.

It returns a Response object and accepts a parameter as the input of the Request type.

You can use this method as a wildcard for all the other methods. This means that you can create an Account by using this method because the class called CreateRequest derives from Request and can be used as the input parameter; you receive a CreateResponse as the result. The same happens for UpdateRequest, UpdateResponse, RetrieveRequest, and RetrieveResponse.

However, this method is usually used for things you can't do with the other methods. A good example is to close a CRM case. Although the case entity can be updated, you can't update the status by using the Update method. To close a case, you need to use this method.

▶ If you don not remember how to create a case, refer back to Chapter 10, "Working with Service."

```
private static bool CloseCase(string organizationName, Guid caseId)
{
    using (CrmSdk.OrganizationServiceClient myCrm =
      new CrmSdk.OrganizationServiceClient())
    {
        try
        {
            myCrm.Endpoint.Address =
            new System.ServiceModel.EndpointAddress
           (GetCrmServiceForOrganization("Webfortis"));
            myCrm.ClientCredentials.Windows.ClientCredential =
            System.Net.CredentialCache.DefaultNetworkCredentials;
            CrmSdk.Entity myIncidentResolution = new CrmSdk.Entity();
            myIncidentResolution.LogicalName = "incidentresolution";
            CrmSdk.EntityReference incidentId = new CrmSdk.EntityReference();
            incidentId.LogicalName = "incident";
            incidentId.Id = caseId;
            myIncidentResolution.Attributes = new CrmSdk.AttributeCollection();
            myIncidentResolution.Attributes.Add(
            new KeyValuePair<string, object>("incidentid",
            incidentId));
            CrmSdk.OrganizationRequest closeIncident =
            new CrmSdk.OrganizationRequest();
            closeIncident.RequestName = "CloseIncident";
            closeIncident.Parameters = new CrmSdk.ParameterCollection();

            CrmSdk.OptionSetValue statusValue =  new CrmSdk.OptionSetValue();
            statusValue.Value = -1;
            closeIncident.Parameters.Add(new KeyValuePair<string,
            object>("Status", statusValue));
            closeIncident.Parameters.Add(new KeyValuePair<string,
            object>("IncidentResolution", myIncidentResolution));
            myCrm.Execute(closeIncident);
            Console.WriteLine("Case successfully closed ");
            return true;
        }
        catch (Exception ex)
        {
            Console.WriteLine("General exception: " + ex.ToString());
            return false;
        }
    }
}
```

When you try to test this code, you will get a serialization error and the case won't be closed. To avoid any serialization error, you will need to update the reference.cs file associated with the CrmSdk service with the following directives on the OrganizationRequest method:

```
[System.Runtime.Serialization.KnownTypeAttribute(typeof(OptionSetValue))]
[System.Runtime.Serialization.KnownTypeAttribute(typeof(Entity))]
[System.Runtime.Serialization.KnownTypeAttribute(typeof(EntityReference))]
[System.Diagnostics.DebuggerStepThroughAttribute()]
[System.CodeDom.Compiler.GeneratedCodeAttribute(
 "System.Runtime.Serialization", "4.0.0.0")]
[System.Runtime.Serialization.DataContractAttribute(
Name="OrganizationRequest",
Namespace="http://schemas.microsoft.com/xrm/2011/Contracts")]
[System.SerializableAttribute()]
public partial class OrganizationRequest : object,
 System.Runtime.Serialization.IExtensibleDataObject,
 System.ComponentModel.INotifyPropertyChanged {
```

Fetch Method

This method executes a query defined by the FetchXML language. In this version, it used the RetrieveMultiple method, and the fetch XML is passed as a parameter using the FetchExpression class. In a difference from the previous version, instead of returning a string containing the XML representation of the entity's result set, it returns the entity collection, so you don't have to manage an XML result.

A few points to remember about the Fetch method:

- With Fetch you can get results in pages by limiting the number of records returned by page.
- With Fetch you can just query the record count or use any aggregation method such as Avg, Count, Max, Min, Sum.
- Fetch does not support a union join. To view all the tasks for an account by checking all the contacts of a contact, you need to perform separate Fetch methods—one on the contact tasks and the one on the account contacts—and then merge the results.
- The result set of records depends on the user privilege.

The following code example shows how to use this method to retrieve all contacts with all their properties:

```
private static void GetAllContacts(string organizationName)
{
    using (CrmSdk.OrganizationServiceClient myCrm =
        new CrmSdk.OrganizationServiceClient())
    {
        try
        {
            myCrm.Endpoint.Address =
            new System.ServiceModel.EndpointAddress(
            GetCrmServiceForOrganization("Webfortis"));
```

```
            myCrm.ClientCredentials.Windows.ClientCredential =
             System.Net.CredentialCache.DefaultNetworkCredentials;
            // Retrieve all Contacts.
            StringBuilder fetchStr = new StringBuilder();
            fetchStr.Append(@"<fetch mapping='logical'>");
            fetchStr.Append(
        @"<entity name='contact'> <attribute name='fullname'/>");
            fetchStr.Append(@"</entity></fetch>");
            CrmSdk.FetchExpression fetchexp = new CrmSdk.FetchExpression();
            fetchexp.Query = fetchStr.ToString();
            CrmSdk.QueryBase mq = new CrmSdk.QueryBase();

            // Fetch the results.
            CrmSdk.EntityCollection fetchResult =
            myCrm.RetrieveMultiple(fetchexp);
            Console.WriteLine("\nGetAllContacts found {0} contacts\n"
            , fetchResult.Entities.Count());
            foreach (CrmSdk.Entity entity in fetchResult.Entities)
            {
                Console.WriteLine("Contact fullname = {0}",
                entity.Attributes[0].Value);
            }
        }
        catch (Exception ex)
        {
            Console.WriteLine("General exception: " + ex.ToString());
        }
    }
}
```

26

TIP

If you are not familiar with the Fetch XML language, you can now create your query with the Advance Find window of the CRM Web UI and click a new button called Download Fetch XML to easily get the code you need for a programmatic call.

Update Method

This method updates data related to an instance of an entity.

This method has only one implementation and doesn't return a value. In the same way as the Create method, it accepts one parameter of type Entity. Because all the entities in CRM inherit from the Entity base class, you can pass any entity class to this input parameter. To use this method, you must set at least the ID property of the entity to be updated. For example, you would set the accountid property if you wanted to update an account.

This is an example of how to update an existing Account programmatically in Visual Studio 2010 with C#:

```
private static string UpdateAccountName(string organizationName,
              Guid accountId, string newName)
{
    using (CrmSdk.OrganizationServiceClient myCrm =
        new CrmSdk.OrganizationServiceClient())
    {
        try
        {
            myCrm.Endpoint.Address =
            new System.ServiceModel.EndpointAddress(
            GetCrmServiceForOrganization("Webfortis"));
            myCrm.ClientCredentials.Windows.ClientCredential =
            System.Net.CredentialCache.DefaultNetworkCredentials;
            CrmSdk.Entity myAcoount = new CrmSdk.Entity();
            myAcoount.LogicalName = "account";
            CrmSdk.AttributeCollection myAttributes =
            new CrmSdk.AttributeCollection();
            myAttributes.Add(new KeyValuePair<string, object>(
            "accountid", accountId));
            myAttributes.Add(new KeyValuePair<string, object>("name",
            newName));
            myAcoount.Attributes = myAttributes;
            myCrm.Update(myAcoount);
            return "Account successfully updated ";
        }
        catch (Exception ex)
        {
            Console.WriteLine("General exception: " + ex.ToString());
            return "General exception: " + ex.ToString();
        }
    }
}
```

CAUTION

Note that only the properties you set are updated. This means that, in the previous example, only the company name property will be changed and the other properties will keep their values. This happens even though they are not set and they have null values when sending them to the Update method.

Early Binding

As you can see, so far the method to use and access the Organization service is a little difficult, and also you need to type the entities' and attributes' names, making the code hard to write. Fortunately this version of CRM 2011 has a new way to use the services by using early binding that provides IntelliSense support and better use of the code and .NET technologies such as the .NET Framework language-integrated query (LinQ). To use early binding, you will need to generate the entity classes by using the code generation tool called CrmSvcUtil.exe, which is a console application found in the sdk\bin folder of the CRM 2011 SDK.

An example of calling this tool is as follows:

```
CrmSvcUtil.exe /url:http://crm2011/Webfortis/XRMServices/2011/Organization.svc
    /out:GeneratedCode.cs /username:damian /password:p@ssword!
```

TIP

This command will take some time to run as it generates code for everything you need to work with CRM 2011, so be patient.

26

If you get the GeneratedCode.cs file and include it on your solution, you can now work with the Organization service easily. You will also need to add references the following assemblies to your solution that are also found in the sdk\bin folder of the CRM 2011 SDK.

- microsoft.xrm.sdk.dll
- microsoft.crm.sdk.proxy.dll

The last assemblies you will need to reference are the System.Runtime.Serialization and System.ServiceModel that are found in the Global Assembly Cache (GAC).

Regular Operations for Early Binding

On this section we will look at the regular operations (create, retrieve, retrieve multiple, delete, and update) but by using the early access so that you can see the differences.

Create Method

To create any instance of an entity such as a new Account or Contact, instead of using the create method, you would do it this way:

```
using Microsoft.Xrm.Sdk.Client;
using System.ServiceModel.Description;
```

```
public static void CreateAccount(string organizationName, string accountName)
{
    ClientCredentials credentials = new ClientCredentials();
    credentials.Windows.ClientCredential =
     System.Net.CredentialCache.DefaultNetworkCredentials;
    OrganizationServiceProxy _serviceProxy =
        new OrganizationServiceProxy(new Uri("http://crm2011/" +
        organizationName + "/XRMServices/2011/Organization.svc"),
        null, credentials, null);
_serviceProxy.ServiceConfiguration.CurrentServiceEndpoint.Behaviors.Add(
new ProxyTypesBehavior());
    OrganizationServiceContext orgContext =
new OrganizationServiceContext(_serviceProxy);
    Account account = new Account()
        {
            Name = accountName
        };
    orgContext.AddObject(account);
    orgContext.SaveChanges();
    return account.AccountId.ToString();
}
```

Retrieve Method

To retrieve any record of an entity such as an Account or Contact, you could use LinQ. The code would look as follows:

```
private static Account RetrieveAccount(string organizationName, Guid accountId)
{
    ClientCredentials credentials = new ClientCredentials();
    credentials.Windows.ClientCredential =
    System.Net.CredentialCache.DefaultNetworkCredentials;
    OrganizationServiceProxy _serviceProxy =
     new OrganizationServiceProxy(new Uri("http://crm2011/" +
      organizationName + "/XRMServices/2011/Organization.svc"),
        null, credentials, null);

_serviceProxy.ServiceConfiguration.CurrentServiceEndpoint.Behaviors.Add(
new ProxyTypesBehavior());

    OrganizationServiceContext orgContext =
    new OrganizationServiceContext(_serviceProxy);
    Account account = (from a in orgContext.CreateQuery<Account>()
     where a.AccountId == accountId select a).Single();
    return account;
}
```

RetrieveMultiple Method

Retrieving multiple records can be also done with LinQ without the need to learn how to query and filter attributes in CRM 2011—the LinQ knowledge will be enough.

```
private static void GetAllAccounts(string organizationName)
{
    ClientCredentials credentials = new ClientCredentials();
    credentials.Windows.ClientCredential =
    System.Net.CredentialCache.DefaultNetworkCredentials;
    OrganizationServiceProxy _serviceProxy =
      new OrganizationServiceProxy(new Uri("http://crm2011/" +
      organizationName + "/XRMServices/2011/Organization.svc"),
        null, credentials, null);
_serviceProxy.ServiceConfiguration.CurrentServiceEndpoint.Behaviors.Add(
new ProxyTypesBehavior());
    OrganizationServiceContext orgContext =
     new OrganizationServiceContext(_serviceProxy);
    /// Retrieve the accounts.
    var accounts = from a in orgContext.CreateQuery<Account>() select a;
    foreach (Account myAccount in accounts)
    {
        Console.WriteLine(myAccount.Name);
    }
}
```

You can apply any filters you want as you would do it with any other LinQ filter.

Delete Method

To delete a record using the organization context, you would do it in the following way:

```
Account account = (from a in orgContext.CreateQuery<Account>()
where a.AccountId == accountToDelete select a).Single();
orgContext.DeleteObject(account);
orgContext.SaveChanges();
```

Without using the organization context:

```
Account account = (from a in orgContext.CreateQuery<Account>()
where a.AccountId == accountToDelete select a).Single();
_serviceProxy.Delete(Account.EntityLogicalName, accountToDelete);
```

Update Method

To update a record using the organization context:

```
Account account = (from a in orgContext.CreateQuery<Account>()
where a.AccountId == accountToUpdate select a).Single();
account.Name = "dddddddddddd";
```

```
orgContext.UpdateObject(account);
orgContext.SaveChanges();
```

Without using the organization context:

```
Account account = (from a in orgContext.CreateQuery<Account>()
where a.AccountId == accountToUpdate select a).Single();
account.Name = "dddddddddddd";
_serviceProxy.Update(account);
```

Metadata

Using the same Organization service described earlier, we can also access to the entire CRM metadata.

As opposed to its previous version where the metadata uses a different service, now the Organization service can be also used to create, update, or delete entities, as well as create or delete relationships within entities. You can also use it to add, delete, or modify attributes to an existing entity programmatically.

Using the metadata can be very useful for Independent Software Vendors (ISVs) to look up entities on a setup installer to see whether a solution was already installed or to check whether any conflict exists with the entities of the CRM system on which a customization would be deployed.

By using the Execute method, you can access to the sub methods necessary to interact with the metadata.

Execute Method

This method accepts the following submethods related to the metadata:

- CreateAttribute
- CreateEntity
- CreateManyToMany
- CreateOneToMany
- CreateOptionSet
- DeleteAttribute
- DeleteEntity
- DeleteOptionSet
- DeleteOptionValue
- DeleteRelationship
- InsertOptionValue
- InsertStatusValue

- OrderOption
- RetrieveAllEntities
- RetrieveAllManagedProperties
- RetrieveAllOptionSets
- RetrieveAttribute
- RetrieveEntity
- RetrieveOptionSet
- RetrieveRelationship
- RetrieveTimestamp
- UpdateAttribute
- UpdateEntity
- UpdateOptionSet
- UpdateOptionValue
- UpdateRelationship
- UpdateStateValue

Each of these submethods is called by using the OrganizationRequest and OrganizationResponse methods of the Organization service.

For example, you might use the following code to find out whether the custom entity new_MyNewCustomEntity already exists in a CRM implementation.

You can add the code for the sample where it has two parameters: the organization name and the entity name.

```
private static bool CheckEntity(string organizationName, string entityName)
{
    try
    {
        ClientCredentials credentials = new ClientCredentials();
        credentials.Windows.ClientCredential =
        System.Net.CredentialCache.DefaultNetworkCredentials;
        OrganizationServiceProxy _serviceProxy =
        new OrganizationServiceProxy(new Uri("http://crm2011/" +
        organizationName + "/XRMServices/2011/Organization.svc"),
            null, credentials, null);
_serviceProxy.ServiceConfiguration.CurrentServiceEndpoint.Behaviors.Add(
   new ProxyTypesBehavior());
        Microsoft.Xrm.Sdk.Messages.RetrieveEntityRequest myRequest =
```

```
        new Microsoft.Xrm.Sdk.Messages.RetrieveEntityRequest();
        myRequest.LogicalName = entityName.ToLower();
        Microsoft.Xrm.Sdk.Messages.RetrieveEntityResponse myResponse;
        myResponse =
(Microsoft.Xrm.Sdk.Messages.RetrieveEntityResponse)
       _serviceProxy.Execute(myRequest);
        return true;
    }
    catch (Exception ex)
    {
        Console.WriteLine("General exception: " + ex.ToString());
        return false;
    }
}
```

Now if you want to check whether the Account or new_MyNewCustomEntity entity exists on the organization with the name Webfortis, you could use the following code:

```
static void Main(string[] args)
{
        Console.WriteLine("Account entity exists = " +
        CheckEntity("Webfortis", "Account"));
        Console.WriteLine("new_ MyNewCustomEntity entity exists = "
         + CheckEntity("Webfortis", "new_ MyNewCustomEntity"));

        Console.ReadKey();
}
```

The preceding code should return true for the Account entity and false for the new_ MyNewCustomEntity entity (assuming you have not created any custom entity with the name of new_ MyNewCustomEntity on your CRM system).

The following code sample shows how to create a custom entity using this web service programmatically.

```
private static bool CreateCustomEntity(string organizationName,
        string entityName)
{
    try
    {
        ClientCredentials credentials = new ClientCredentials();
        credentials.Windows.ClientCredential =
        System.Net.CredentialCache.DefaultNetworkCredentials;
        OrganizationServiceProxy _serviceProxy =
        new OrganizationServiceProxy(new Uri("http://crm2011/" +
```

```
        organizationName + "/XRMServices/2011/Organization.svc"),
            null, credentials, null);
_serviceProxy.ServiceConfiguration.CurrentServiceEndpoint.Behaviors.Add(
      new ProxyTypesBehavior());
        // Creates new entity
        Microsoft.Xrm.Sdk.Metadata.EntityMetadata myNewEntity =
        new Microsoft.Xrm.Sdk.Metadata.EntityMetadata();
        myNewEntity.Description = CreateLabel(entityName);
        myNewEntity.DisplayCollectionName = CreateLabel(entityName);
        myNewEntity.DisplayName = CreateLabel(entityName);
        myNewEntity.IsAvailableOffline = true;
        myNewEntity.SchemaName = entityName;
        myNewEntity.LogicalName = entityName;
        myNewEntity.OwnershipType =
Microsoft.Xrm.Sdk.Metadata.OwnershipTypes.UserOwned;
        // creates primary attribute
        Microsoft.Xrm.Sdk.Metadata.StringAttributeMetadata
 myPrimaryAttr =
new Microsoft.Xrm.Sdk.Metadata.StringAttributeMetadata();
        myPrimaryAttr.DisplayName = CreateLabel("Name");
        myPrimaryAttr.Description = CreateLabel("this is the Name");
        myPrimaryAttr.MaxLength = 100;
        myPrimaryAttr.SchemaName = "new_Name";
        myPrimaryAttr.Format = Microsoft.Xrm.Sdk.Metadata.StringFormat.Text;
        myPrimaryAttr.RequiredLevel =
new Microsoft.Xrm.Sdk.Metadata.AttributeRequiredLevelManagedProperty(
Microsoft.Xrm.Sdk.Metadata.AttributeRequiredLevel.ApplicationRequired);
        myPrimaryAttr.LogicalName = "new_name";
        // prepare request
        Microsoft.Xrm.Sdk.Messages.CreateEntityRequest myRequest =
        new Microsoft.Xrm.Sdk.Messages.CreateEntityRequest();
        myRequest.Entity = myNewEntity;
        myRequest.HasActivities = true;
        myRequest.HasNotes = true;
        myRequest.PrimaryAttribute = myPrimaryAttr;
        Microsoft.Xrm.Sdk.Messages.CreateEntityResponse myResponse;
        myResponse = (Microsoft.Xrm.Sdk.Messages.CreateEntityResponse)
        _serviceProxy.Execute(myRequest);
        return true;
    }
    catch (Exception ex)
    {
        Console.WriteLine("General exception: " + ex.ToString());
        return false;
```

```
    }
}
```

The code uses a custom method called CreateLabel to simplify the code used to set up the labels. They must be managed in a collection because of the Multilanguage feature. This sample uses only the English language for the strings, but you can easily customize it to use other languages.

```
private static Microsoft.Xrm.Sdk.Label CreateLabel(string myString)
{
    Microsoft.Xrm.Sdk.Label myLabel = new Microsoft.Xrm.Sdk.Label();
    Microsoft.Xrm.Sdk.LocalizedLabel myLabels =
    new Microsoft.Xrm.Sdk.LocalizedLabel(myString,
    1033);// English code
    myLabel.LocalizedLabels.Add(myLabels);
    return myLabel;
}
```

Now if you want to create a new entity with the name of new_MyNewCustomEntity on the organization with the name Webfortis, you could use the following code:

```
static void Main(string[] args)
{
        CreateCustomEntity("Webfortis", "new_MyNewCustomEntity");
        Console.ReadKey();
}
```

TIP

Be sure the entity name does not already exist in the CRM system, or the Execute method will raise an exception. Alternatively, you can use the CheckEntity method you created before and use a code as follows:

```
static void Main(string[] args)
{
        if (!CheckEntity("Webfortis", "new_MyNewCustomEntity"))
        {
             CreateCustomEntity("Webfortis", "new_MyNewCustomEntity");
        }
        Console.ReadKey();
}
```

TIP

You must also set at least the primary attribute on the request, and this one must be required. In addition, you can use this web service if you wanted to show all the options from an Option Set attribute on another application.

As another example, imagine that you needed to retrieve all possible values for the Shipping Method property for Accounts. Because the shipping method is an Option Set, you would have to query the metabase to get the values. This method can be used as follows:

```
private static void GetShippingMethod(string organizationName)
{
    ClientCredentials credentials = new ClientCredentials();
    credentials.Windows.ClientCredential =
    System.Net.CredentialCache.DefaultNetworkCredentials;
    OrganizationServiceProxy _serviceProxy =
     new OrganizationServiceProxy(new Uri("http://crm2011/" +
     organizationName + "/XRMServices/2011/Organization.svc"),
     null, credentials, null);
_serviceProxy.ServiceConfiguration.CurrentServiceEndpoint.Behaviors.Add(
    new ProxyTypesBehavior());
    Microsoft.Xrm.Sdk.Messages.RetrieveAttributeRequest myRequest =
    new Microsoft.Xrm.Sdk.Messages.RetrieveAttributeRequest();
    myRequest.EntityLogicalName = Account.EntityLogicalName;
    myRequest.LogicalName = "address1_shippingmethodcode";
    Microsoft.Xrm.Sdk.Messages.RetrieveAttributeResponse myResponse;
    myResponse = (Microsoft.Xrm.Sdk.Messages.RetrieveAttributeResponse)
   _serviceProxy.Execute(myRequest);
    foreach (Microsoft.Xrm.Sdk.Metadata.OptionMetadata myOption in
((Microsoft.Xrm.Sdk.Metadata.PicklistAttributeMetadata)
   (myResponse.AttributeMetadata)).OptionSet.Options)
    {
        Console.WriteLine(myOption.Label.LocalizedLabels[0].Label);
    }
}
```

Now if you want to test this method on the organization with the name Webfortis, you could use the following code:

```
static void Main(string[] args)
{
        GetShippingMethod("Webfortis");
        Console.ReadKey();
}
```

Samples of Web Services

Because the WCF Web Services and REST are platform-independent, it is not strictly necessary to access the web services from a .NET assembly or a compiled application. You could access the web services using JavaScript, for example.

▶ Check the CRM 2011 SDK for more samples and also the Dynamics CRM 2011 Developer Training Kit.

JavaScript

This section provides an example of how to get and set the address from an account using JavaScript by querying the CRM ODATA (REST) Service. This sets the contact address when selecting an account as the parent customer field automatically (without requiring you to enter it again).

TIP

In order to have this sample working, you must select an account with the address fields populated with some data.

CAUTION

The following sample works only if you select a parent account for a contact and not a parent contact. However, after reviewing this sample, you can modify it to work with parent contacts if desired.

The purpose of this sample is to show how you can consume an OData (REST) service without having to build a .NET application or component to make some of your business customizations.

▶ For more details about working with JavaScript customizations, refer to Chapter 23, "Customizing Entities."

To create this sample, follow these steps:

1. Go to Settings, Customizations, Customize the System, and select the Contact entity in Microsoft CRM 2011.
2. Expand the Contact entity, and click on Forms on the left side of the window.
3. Double-click the Main Form type to open it.

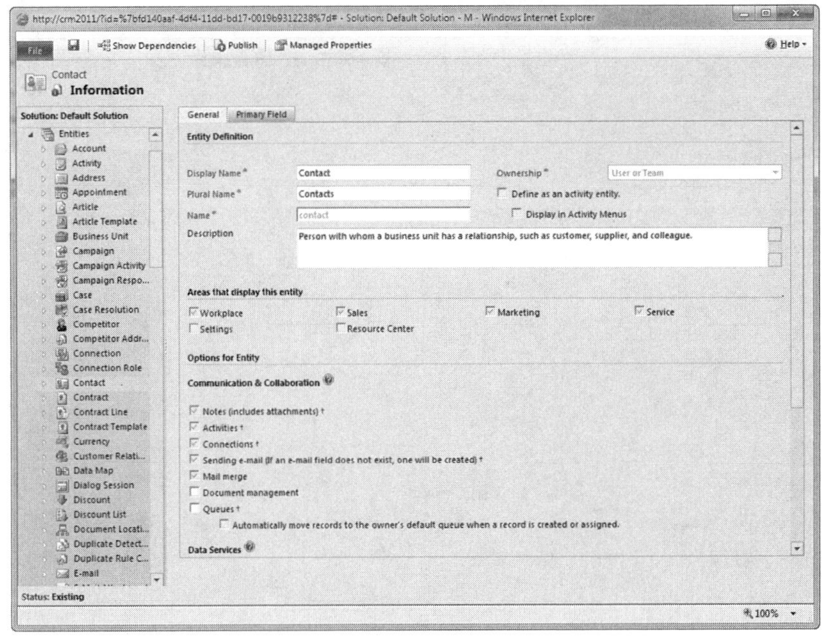

FIGURE 26.12 Contact customization.

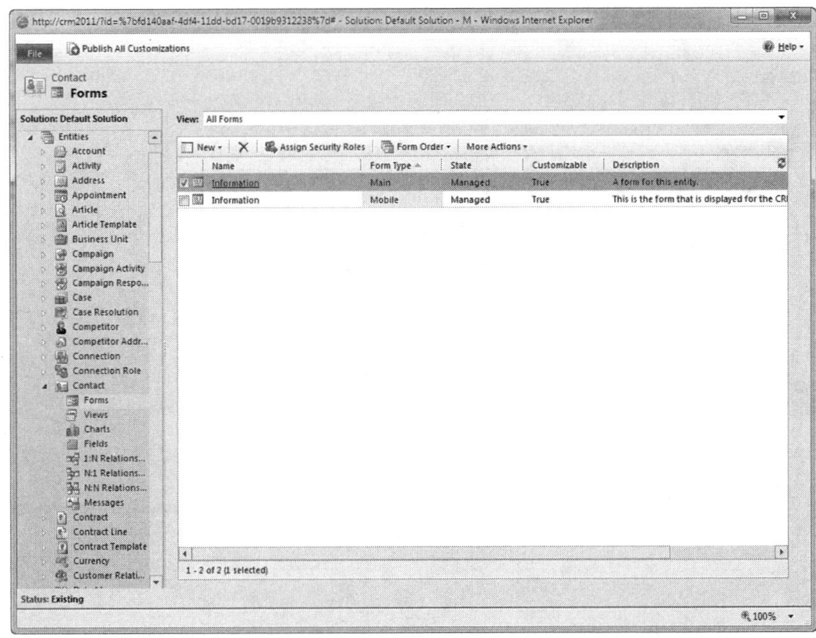

FIGURE 26.13 Forms customization.

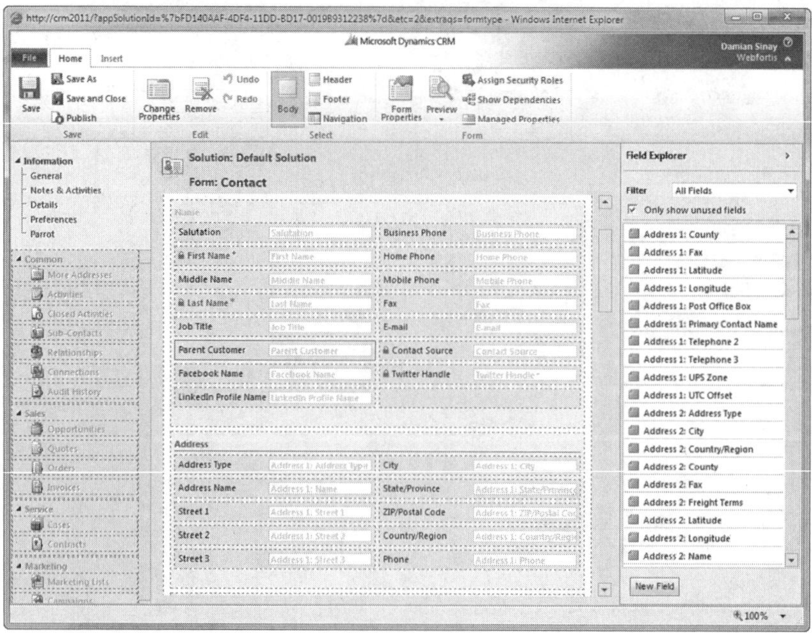

FIGURE 26.14 Main Form type customization.

4. Click the Parent Customer field and click Change Properties.

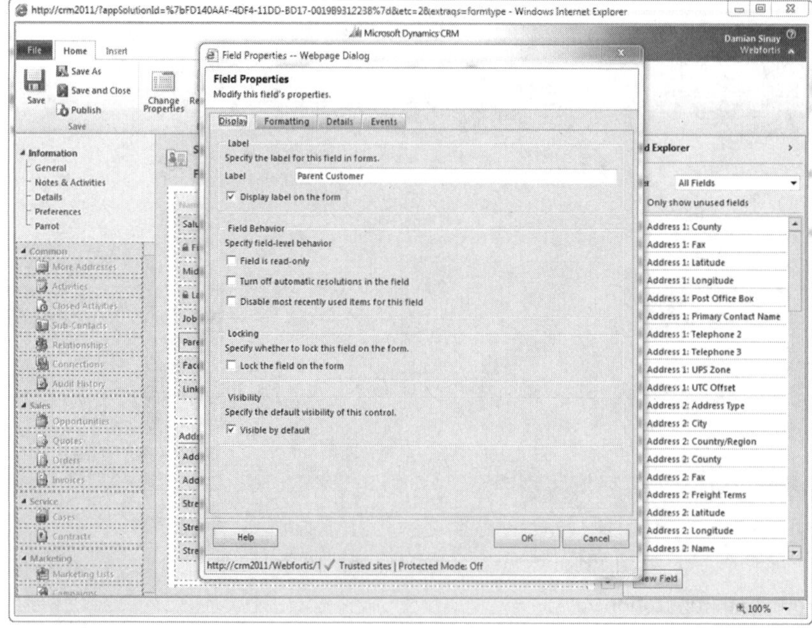

FIGURE 26.15 Parent Customer property page.

5. Select the Events tab.
6. Expand Form Libraries and click Add.

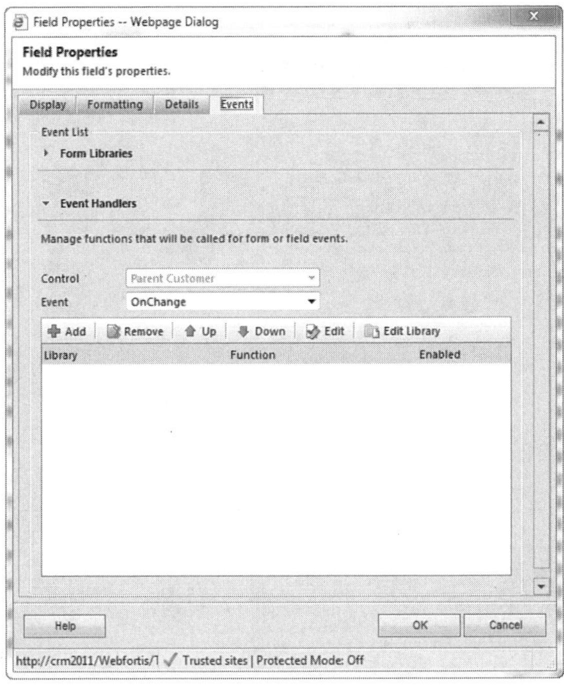

FIGURE 26.16 Events tab.

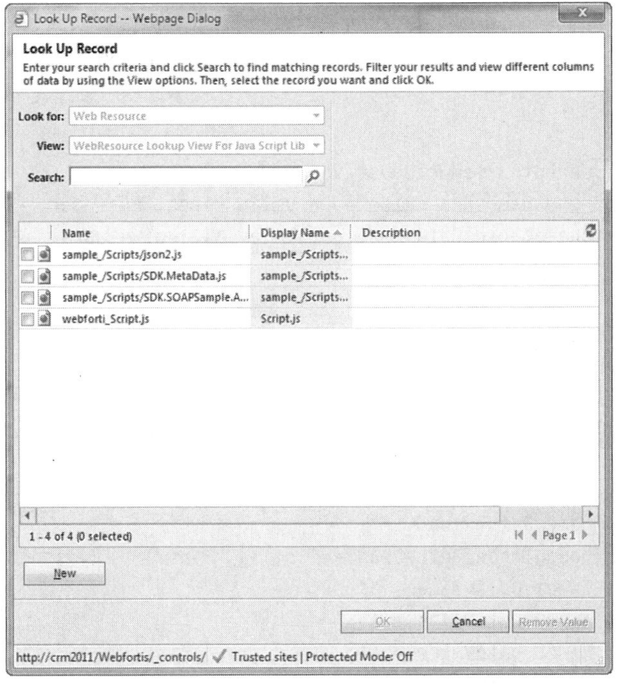

FIGURE 22.17 Adding Forms Libraries.

7. Click New and enter a name, usually with .js extension (for example sampleScript.js), enter a display name, and select Script (Jscript) on the Type.

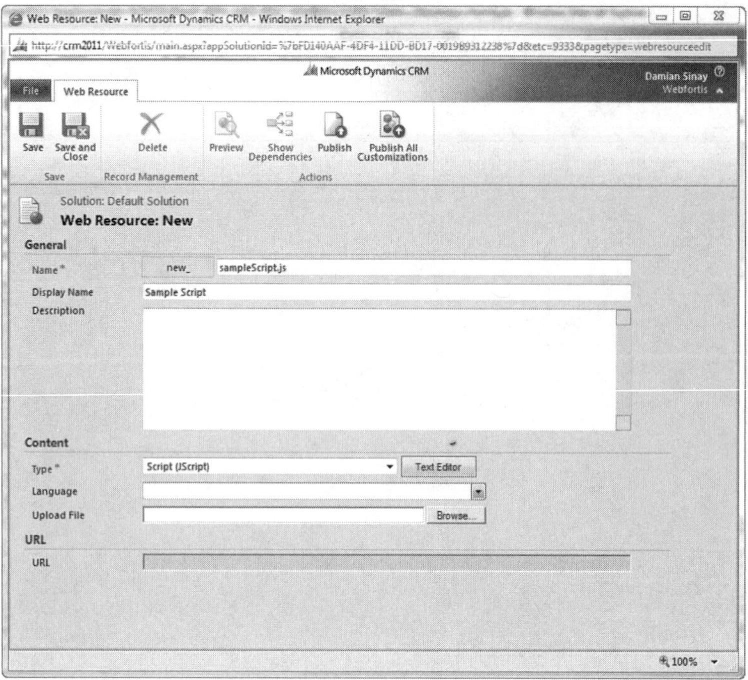

FIGURE 26.18 New Web Resource

8. Click the Text Editor button and insert the following code sample in the text box:

```
function GetAccountAddress() {
    var CustomerID;
    CustomerID = crmForm.all.parentcustomerid.DataValue;
    // first of all checks if the user has selected a valid parent customer
    // the crmForm.all.parentcustomerid.DataValue parameter will give us a
    // vector with
    // the GUID of the selected customer
    if (CustomerID != null) {
        var context = Xrm.Page.context;
        serverUrl = context.getServerUrl();
        ODataPath = serverUrl + "/XRMServices/2011/OrganizationData.svc";

        //Cleans the old address first
        crmForm.all.address1_name.DataValue = "";
        crmForm.all.address1_postalcode.DataValue = "";
        crmForm.all.address1_line1.DataValue = "";
        crmForm.all.address1_line2.DataValue = "";
        crmForm.all.address1_line3.DataValue = "";
```

```
        crmForm.all.address1_city.DataValue = "";
        crmForm.all.address1_stateorprovince.DataValue = "";
        crmForm.all.address1_addresstypecode.DataValue = "";
        crmForm.all.address1_country.DataValue = "";

        RetrieveAccountRecord(CustomerID[0].id);
    }
    else {
        alert("Select Parent Customer first!");
    }
}
function RetrieveAccountRecord(Id) {
    var retrieveAccountReq = new XMLHttpRequest();
    retrieveAccountReq.open("GET", ODataPath +
    "/AccountSet(guid'" + Id + "')", true);
    retrieveAccountReq.setRequestHeader("Accept", "application/json");
    retrieveAccountReq.setRequestHeader("Content-Type",
    "application/json; charset=utf-8");
    retrieveAccountReq.onreadystatechange = function () {
        RetrieveAccountReqCallBack(this);
    };
    retrieveAccountReq.send();
}

function RetrieveAccountReqCallBack(retrieveAccountReq) {
    if (retrieveAccountReq.readyState == 4 /* complete */) {
        if (retrieveAccountReq.status == 200) {
            //Success
var retrievedAccount = JSON.parse(retrieveAccountReq.responseText).d;
crmForm.all.address1_name.DataValue = retrievedAccount.Address1_Name;
crmForm.all.address1_postalcode.DataValue =
retrievedAccount.Address1_PostalCode;
crmForm.all.address1_line1.DataValue = retrievedAccount.Address1_Line1;
crmForm.all.address1_line2.DataValue = retrievedAccount.Address1_Line2;
crmForm.all.address1_line3.DataValue = retrievedAccount.Address1_Line3;
crmForm.all.address1_city.DataValue = retrievedAccount.Address1_City;
crmForm.all.address1_stateorprovince.DataValue =
retrievedAccount.Address1_StateOrProvince;
crmForm.all.address1_country.DataValue =
retrievedAccount.Address1_Country;
crmForm.all.address1_addresstypecode.DataValue =
retrievedAccount.Address1_AddressTypeCode.Value;
        }
    }
}
```

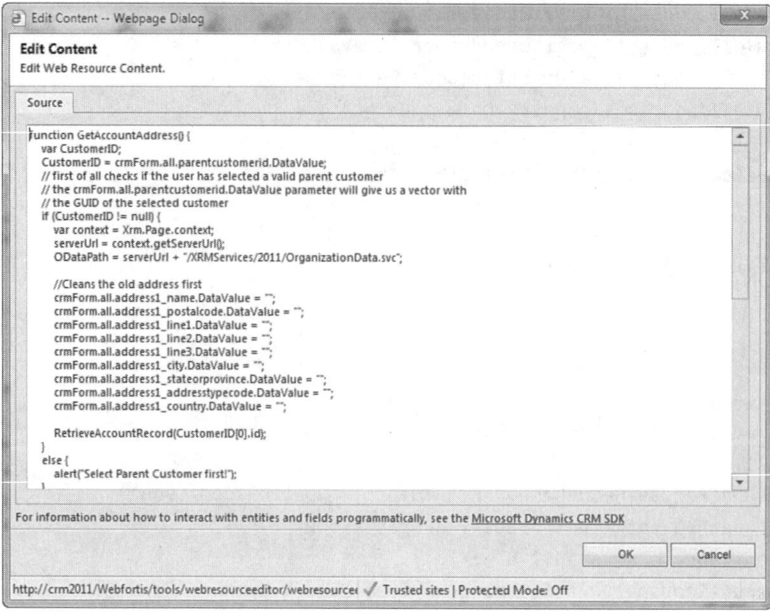

Edit Content -- Webpage Dialog
Edit Content
Edit Web Resource Content.
Source
function GetAccountAddress() {
var CustomerID;
CustomerID = crmForm.all.parentcustomerid.DataValue;
// first of all checks if the user has selected a valid parent customer
// the crmForm.all.parentcustomerid.DataValue parameter will give us a vector with
// the GUID of the selected customer
if (CustomerID != null) {
var context = Xrm.Page.context;
serverUrl = context.getServerUrl();
ODataPath = serverUrl + "/XRMServices/2011/OrganizationData.svc";
//Cleans the old address first
crmForm.all.address1_name.DataValue = "";
crmForm.all.address1_postalcode.DataValue = "";
crmForm.all.address1_line1.DataValue = "";
crmForm.all.address1_line2.DataValue = "";
crmForm.all.address1_line3.DataValue = "";
crmForm.all.address1_city.DataValue = "";
crmForm.all.address1_stateorprovince.DataValue = "";
crmForm.all.address1_addresstypecode.DataValue = "";
crmForm.all.address1_country.DataValue = "";
RetrieveAccountRecord(CustomerID[0].id);
}
else {
alert("Select Parent Customer first!");
For information about how to interact with entities and fields programmatically, see the Microsoft Dynamics CRM SDK
OK
Cancel
http://crm2011/Webfortis/tools/webresourceeditor/webresource Trusted sites | Protected Mode: Off

FIGURE 26.19 JavaScript code to call the CRM ODATA (REST) service.

9. Click OK to close the dialog.
10. Click Save and Close to close the Web Resource dialog.
11. Click OK to close the Look Up Web Resource dialog.
12. Under Event Handlers, click Add and enter GetAccountAddress in the Function text box.

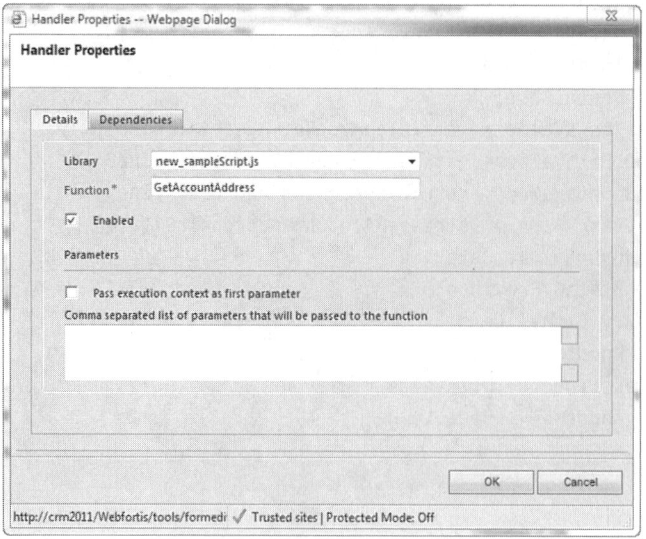

FIGURE 26.20 Handler properties.

13. Click OK to close the Handler Properties dialog.
14. Click OK to close the Field Properties dialog.
15. Click Save and Close to close the Entity Contact window.
16. Click the Publish All Customizations button to publish all the customization.

NOTE

In order to finish with this sample customization, you also need to create another web resource for the JSON JavaScript that can be downloaded from http://www.JSON.org/. Use the json2.js file and include this library on the Form Library as you did for the previous JavaScript code.

To test the solution, follow these steps:

1. Go to Workplace, Contacts.
2. Select a Contact and double-click it to open it, or click New to create a new Contact.
3. Click the icon button near Parent Customer to select an account.
4. Click OK to close the dialog. You will see the contact address automatically filled in with the selected account address.

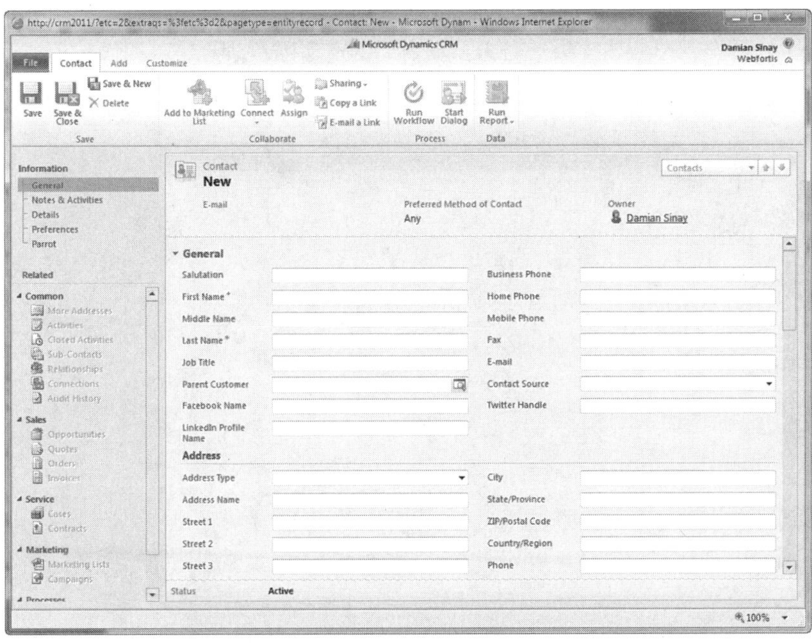

FIGURE 26.21 Creating a new Contact.

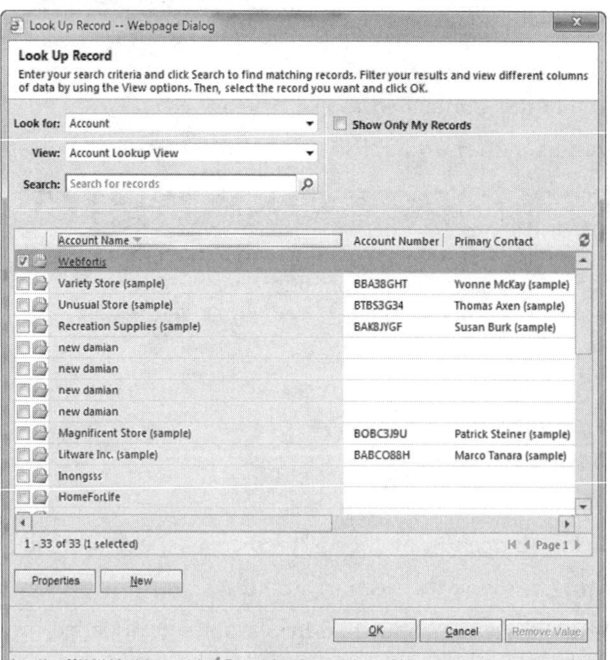

FIGURE 26.22 Select a parent account.

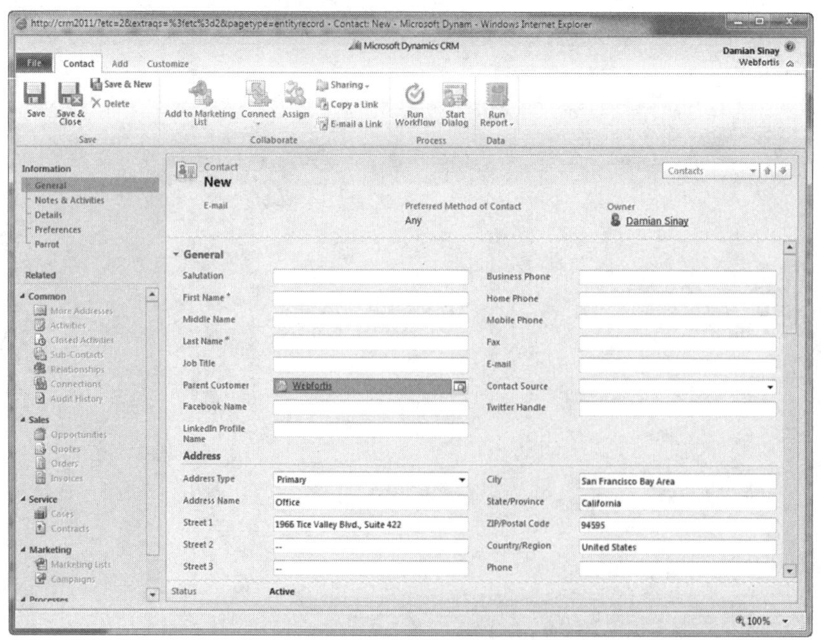

FIGURE 26.23 The new contact address filled automatically with the selected account address.

NOTE

If you are not familiar with ODATA protocol and queries and you want to implement similar customizations, you can use the Silverlight ODATA Explorer application that can be accessed via http://www.silverlight.net/content/samples/odataexplorer/. You can use this tool to build queries to filter data and select specific columns to be returned to improve the network traffic.

Summary

In this chapter, you learned about the web services that the Microsoft CRM 2011 system exposes and how to use them to extend the functionality and make customizations.

You explored the Discovery service that is used to find the right access endpoint of your organization especially useful for multitenancy environments, and you have seen how the Organization service manages the entity records with all the samples you will need to create new records for any entity, and update, delete, or retrieve existing records. You also looked at the metadata web service used to make customizations programmatically; for example, to create a new custom entity or attributes by calling this web service. We also viewed how to use the ODATA service by using REST on JavaScript code.

CHAPTER 27

Advanced Solution Management

IN THIS CHAPTER

- Solutions Explained
- Solution Layers

In Chapter 16, "Solution Concepts," we explored the fundamentals of solution development for Microsoft Dynamics CRM 2011. These concepts included the use of

- Customizations involving solutions
- Publishers
- Importing/exporting solutions

This chapter is dedicated to a deeper dive into solution management and best practices.

NOTE

The solution concepts explained in this chapter are a combination of recommendations from Microsoft and best practices derived by the authors. It should be noted that solutions and solutions management are evolving topics, and we expect changes to them (both small and significant) as they mature.

NOTE

Solutions cannot exceed 8MB in size; however, they can access external resources as necessary (web pages, web services, and so on).

Solutions Explained

Solutions represent the packages by which customizations are deployed in Microsoft Dynamics CRM 2011. The important take-away from that statement is that they are *packages*. They can hold a number of customizations that modify, customize, or extend Microsoft Dynamics CRM 2011.

Previous versions of Microsoft Dynamics CRM didn't allow for the logical grouping of customizations, and one customization was made on top of another with only the development prefix available to reconcile the modifications.

Solutions typically have one, many, or all of the following components as parts:

- Entity, attribute, or relationship modifications
- Modifications to the UI—form, site map, views, charts, and similar entities
- Developed code (processes, workflows, plug-ins, and so on)
- Templates
- Reports
- Roles
- System Settings

When working with solutions, they are available in two different formats: managed and unmanaged. Both have properties that affect the way they are loaded, merged with existing customizations, and depend on other system components.

Although the next section goes into the details of both formats, the highest-level explanation between the two is that managed solutions are locked down and can't be modified, whereas unmanaged solutions are available for editing.

Typically ISV or component developers will distribute their CRM customizations in managed solutions to protect the IP associated with their functionality.

TIP

It is easiest to think of a solution as the alternative to an installer program that developers typically create for distributing programs. Managed solutions are equivalent to programs that are compiled and whose code is unavailable (typically living within .DLL files), and unmanaged solutions are equivalent to open source programs (however unmanaged solutions could certainly contain compiled code).

In addition to availability of customizations, the solution formats interact in different ways with the underlying Microsoft Dynamics CRM system.

Managed

Managed solutions are available by exporting them from the base application in a managed state. They have the following properties associated with them:

- When installed, a managed solution cannot be exported. (But it can be deleted and re-installed if desired.)
- A managed solution cannot be directly modified.

> **NOTE**
>
> Managed solutions often introduce custom entities into an application. These custom entities will have their own tables, which are created to support them in the underlying database. When the solution is deleted, the tables are removed as well, which provides a higher level of security for managing and controlling IP.

To create a managed solution, follow these steps:

1. Navigate to Settings, Solutions, and select New, as shown in Figure 27.1.

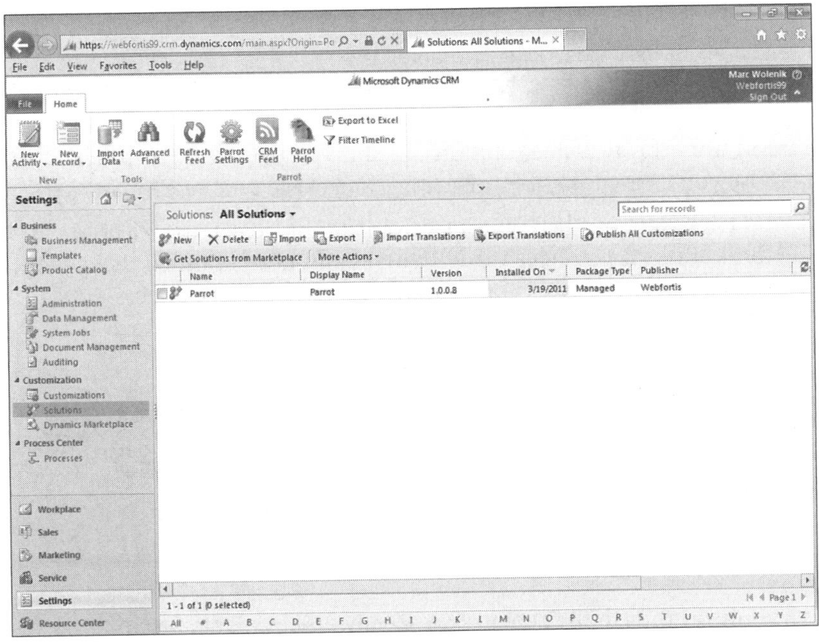

FIGURE 27.1 Solutions.

2. The new solution interface will open, as shown in Figure 27.2. Enter the required fields and select Save and Close.

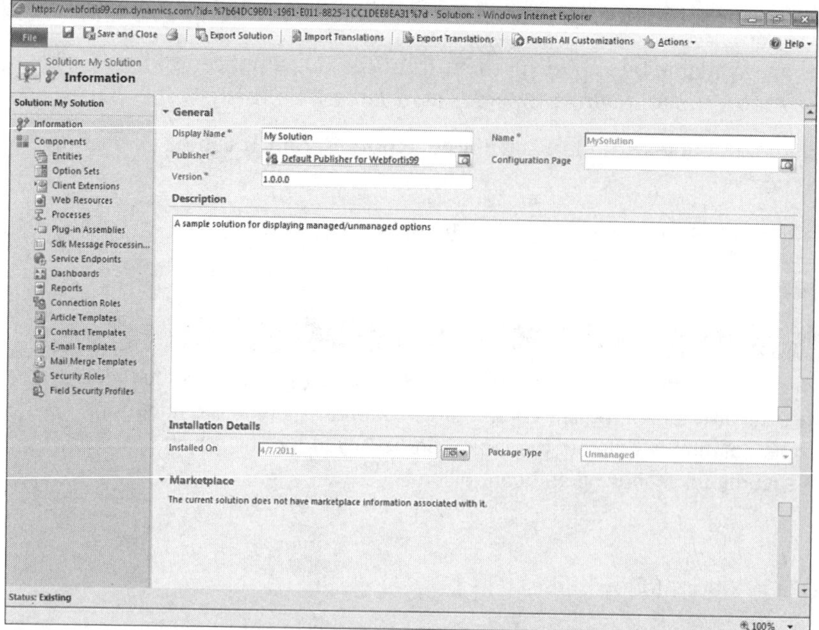

FIGURE 27.2 New solution.

▶ For more information about the fields, consult Chapter 16.

3. Select the solution from the available solutions, as shown in Figure 27.3. You'll notice that because you created the solution, it has a package type of Unmanaged.
4. Select Export, and click Next on the Publish Customizations screen (or select to Publish All Customizations if you have made changes and not published them—for our example we're not making any customizations, so this step is not necessary). Click Next on the Export System Settings, and you will arrive at the Package Type option, as shown in Figure 27.4.

TIP

In step 4, you need to select the solution type that is to be exported. Regardless of selection, the output will be a zip file that can be transported between applications for installation.

5. Selecting Next results in the zip file being saved locally and available for import.

CAUTION

Although the result of the export is a zip file that will be available for import into other systems, the zip files should not be modified.

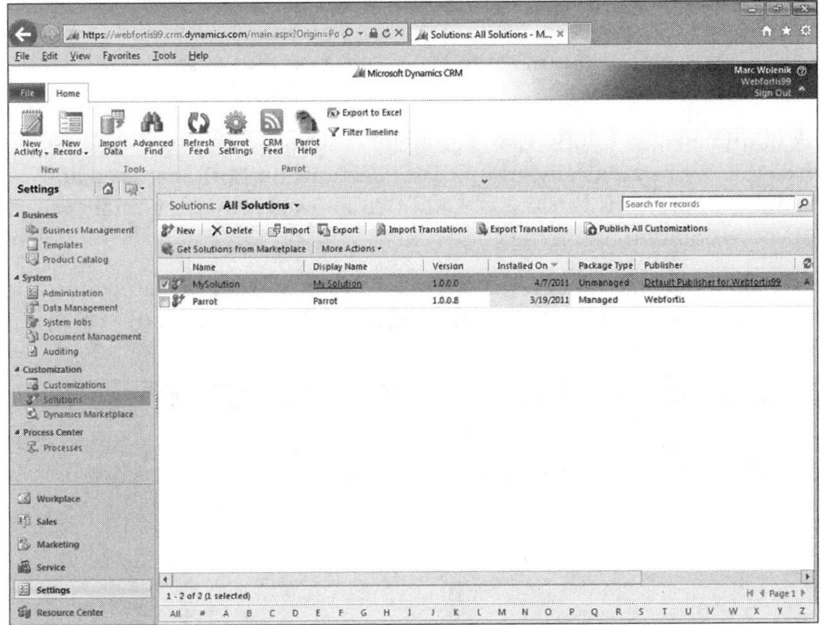

FIGURE 27.3 Existing solutions.

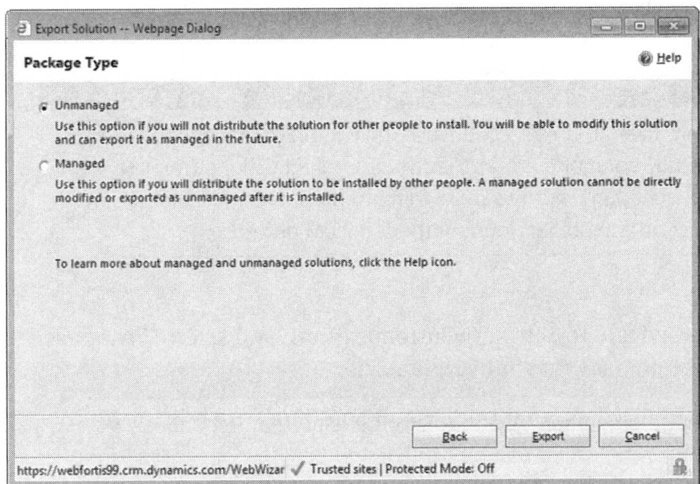

FIGURE 27.4 Solution package type.

CAUTION

The solution may export usernames, especially when workflows are part of the solution. Usernames may contain critical information such as domain information and should be thoroughly reviewed prior to distribution.

Unmanaged

Unmanaged solutions are customizations made to the application that allow for additional editing, viewing, or exporting.

It is easiest to think of unmanaged solutions as a group of customizations. And the best feature of solutions is that we can logically group customizations (in both managed and unmanaged state), unlike in previous versions of CRM that allowed only for unmanaged customizations with no visibility to grouping.

The steps for creating an unmanaged solution are the same as previously explained for managed solutions, except that the option for Unmanaged is selected instead of Managed.

NOTE

Unmanaged solution components that are already in use when applied will be overwritten by managed solutions and cannot be undone. For more information about this and the options related to it, refer to the section on layers later in this chapter.

System

The system solution, or *layer*, is the default or base solution that defines the default application behavior. It is the components from the system layer that are used within managed and unmanaged solutions, and it is possible to customize the system layer. Additionally, it is possible to export the system layer and import it into other organizations.

CAUTION

You *cannot* export the system layer in a managed type—only in an unmanaged type. This will have effects in the way solutions are applied to other applications (refer to the section on layers later in this chapter), but the main thing to be aware of is that it cannot be rolled back easily once it is installed into another application.

To export a system solution, navigate to Settings, Customizations, and select Customize the System (do *not* select Solutions), as shown in Figure 27.5.

Notice that the solution type is listed as Solution: Default Solution, which is shown in Figure 27.6 at the top left.

Export the solution by selecting Export Solution from the Ribbon menu and following the steps.

TIP

You will notice that there is no option for managed or unmanaged saving when navigating these options and the solution will be available in a zip file in an unmanaged state only.

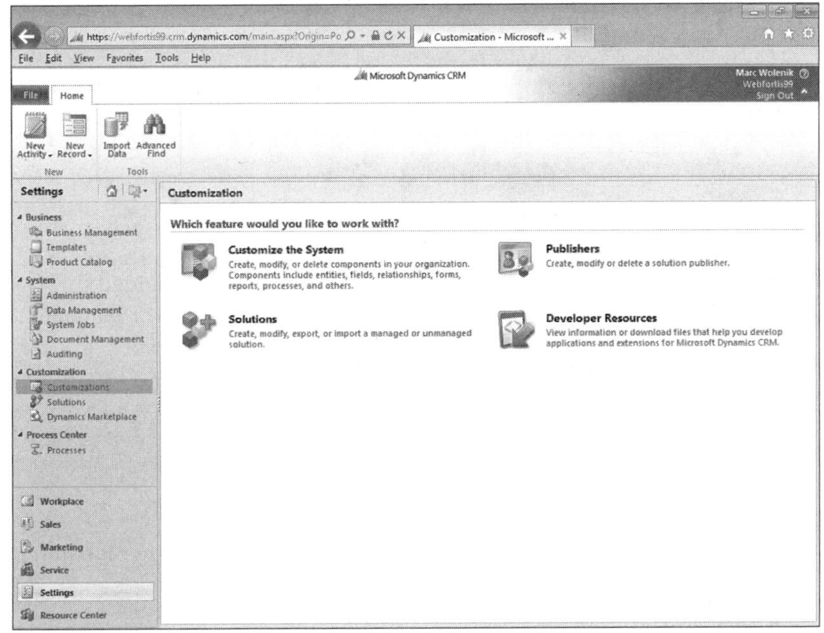

FIGURE 27.5 Customization.

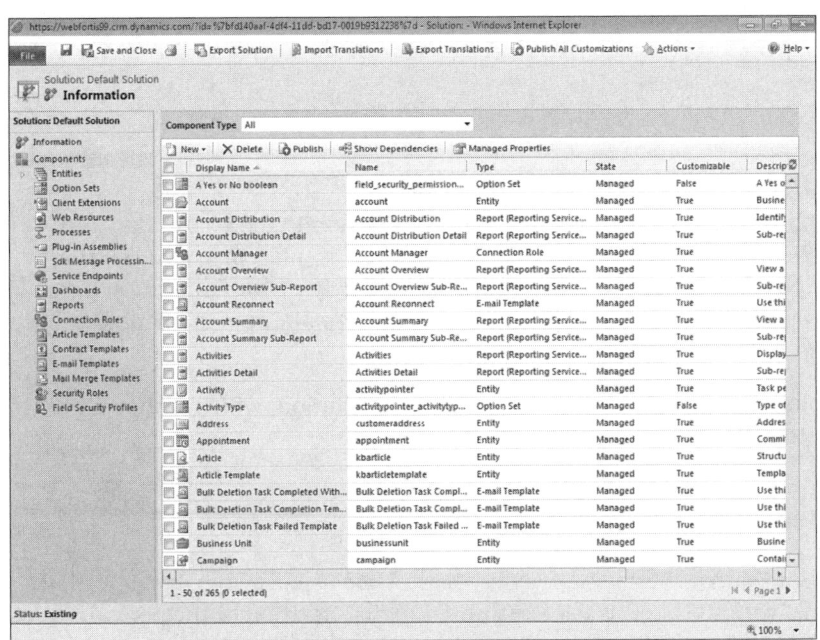

FIGURE 27.6 Solution: Default Solution.

Solution Layers

Solutions are *layered* in that solutions components operate in the context of previously installed solutions. Figure 27.7 shows how managed and unmanaged solutions work.

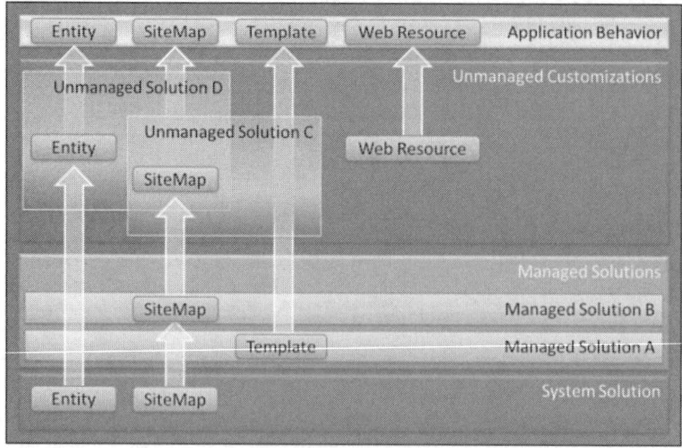

FIGURE 27.7 Solution interaction—available from http://i.msdn.microsoft.com/dynimg/IC443916.png

Four components make up the final application behavior (as shown in Figure 27.7):

- System (default) solution
- Managed solutions
- Unmanaged solutions
- Application behavior

The system solution is the base layer and can be heavily customized directly. Managed solutions are installed on top of the system solution, as well as other managed solutions. Unmanaged solutions are next in the layer, followed ultimately by the application behavior, which is the summarization of everything below it (that is, the system, managed, and unmanaged solutions).

Summary

Solutions provide the ability for custom functionality to be easily deployed, versioned, and managed.

It is important to realize that the solution concepts available in Microsoft Dynamics CRM will continue to evolve, and that this release is only the first iteration of the potential they offer.

For more/additional information, please consult the Microsoft MSDN website on Dynamics CRM 2011 Solutions, located at http://msdn.microsoft.com/en-us/library/gg334576.aspx.

CHAPTER 28

Interacting with Custom Web Applications

IN THIS CHAPTER

- Enhanced MS CRM Functionality with Custom ASP.NET Apps
- Sample IFRAME Customization

Enhanced MS CRM Functionality with Custom ASP.NET Apps

You can enhance Microsoft Dynamics CRM functionality by creating custom Active Server Pages .NET (ASP.NET) web applications to interact with Microsoft Dynamics CRM interfaces and data in different ways:

- Using the site map
- Using the Ribbon
- Using IFRAMEs
- Web Resources

Although Chapter 23, "Customizing Entities," thoroughly explained all four options, inline frames (IFRAMEs) are usually the easiest and best solution to embed in your custom web applications when you need to show or update data based on the entities' records.

You can create custom ASP.NET web applications using Visual Studio 2010. When you create a custom ASP.NET web application, you have some considerations to make.

You can host and deploy the custom ASP.NET web application on the following:

- Different server than the CRM web server
- In the cloud using Windows Azure
- Same web server where the CRM web server is installed, but on a different website
- Same CRM web server and website, but inside a new virtual folder

Depending on where you host your custom ASP.NET web application, there are some advantages and some disadvantages.

For the first two options, hosting the application on a different server than the CRM web server or in the cloud, the advantage is you don't need to be worried about the CRM website configurations. This is the best option when you're considering Microsoft Dynamics CRM Online implementations that don't allow you to host your applications on its servers.

The disadvantage is that you need another machine to host the custom application, and you are responsible for handling security properly.

If you host the custom ASP.NET web application on the same website as the CRM server, you must be aware of the following:

- Locate your application in a different folder than the CRM web folder. We do not recommend that you place your custom pages inside the CRM web folder list.
- Use a different application pool than the CRM web server, to provide isolation, as explained in the "ASP.NET Web Application Deployment" section later in this chapter. Isolation is important because if your custom code has a bug that can take the application offline, it will affect only your application, not the whole CRM website.

These configurations are explained further in the "ASP.NET Web Application Deployment" section later in this chapter.

Query String Parameters

Microsoft Dynamics CRM uses query string parameters to set values on pages. A *query string* is a set of variables and variable values appended to the URL. A sample URL follows:

```
http://crm2011/Webfortis/ContactPictures/Default.aspx?type=2&typename=contact&id
={3053F877-B9B4-DC11-9DC0-0003FF8924BE}&orgname=Webfortis&userlcid=1033&orglcid=
1033
```

Everything after the `.aspx?` is the query string.

These are the query string parameters:

- **`type`**—Parameter that passes the entity code identifier. It is an integer value where 2 equals the Contact entity. For all the out of the box entities type codes, see Table 28.1.

TABLE 28.1 Entities Type Code

Entity Name	Type Code
Account	1
Activity	4200
Address	1071
Appointment	4201
Business Unit	10
Campaign	4400
Campaign Activity	4402
Campaign Response	4401
Case	112
Case Resolution	4206
Competitor	123
Contact	2
Contract	1010
Contract Line	1011
Contract Template	2011
Currency	9105
Customer Relationship	4502
Discount	1013
E-mail	4202
E-mail Template	2010
Facility/Equipment	4000
Fax	4204
Invoice	1090
Invoice Product	1091
Lead	4
Letter	4207
Mail Merge Template	9106
Marketing List	4300
Opportunity	3

TABLE 28.1 Entities Type Code

Entity Name	Type Code
Opportunity Product	1083
Opportunity Relationship	4503
Order	1088
Order Product	1089
Phone Call	4210
Price List	1022
Price List Item	1026
Product	1024
Quick Campaign	4406
Quote	1084
Quote Product	1085
Report	9100
Report Related Category	9102
Resource Group	4007
Role	1036
Sales Literature	1038
Service Activity	4214
Subject	129
Task	4212
Team	9
Territory	2013
Unit	1055
Unit Group	1056
User	8

- **`typename`**—The schema name of the entity, such as `Contact`.
- **`id`**—The unique identifier of the record instance of the entity. This is also referred to as the global unique identifier (GUID). Note that this parameter is available only for existing records. If you are creating a new record, this parameter isn't available until you save the record.
- **`orgname`**—The name of the organization.
- **`userlcid`**—The language code identifier for the user who is running the application. For example, `1033` represents the English language.
- **`orglcid`**—The organization language code identifier. This is the default organization base language. For example, `1033` represents the English language.

TIP

The SDK comes with a solution named metadatabrowser that is found in the sdk\tools\metadatabrowser_1_0_0_1_managed.zip, which provides entity data as well as the object type codes for all entities including custom ones. This replaces the old sdk/list.aspx page used on previous version of CRM 4.0.

All customized entities type codes start from `10000`.

Sample IFRAME Customization

Chapter 23 illustrated a sample IFRAME customization using a URL that showed the same content for every record of the entity where we added the IFRAME. Most of the time you'll want to use the IFRAME to show different content, depending on the record instance of the form. For example, suppose you want to show a picture of your Contacts in the Contact form. This is a perfect scenario in which you would need to use an IFRAME in the Contact form because Microsoft Dynamics CRM has no built-in functionality to do this.

The example included in the next section illustrates how to perform a modification such as this one. You can modify or extend this example to work with other entities or application parameters.

Custom ASP.NET Web Application Development

To begin, you must build your custom ASP.NET application. To do so, follow these steps:

1. Open Visual Studio 2010
2. Go to New, Web Site.

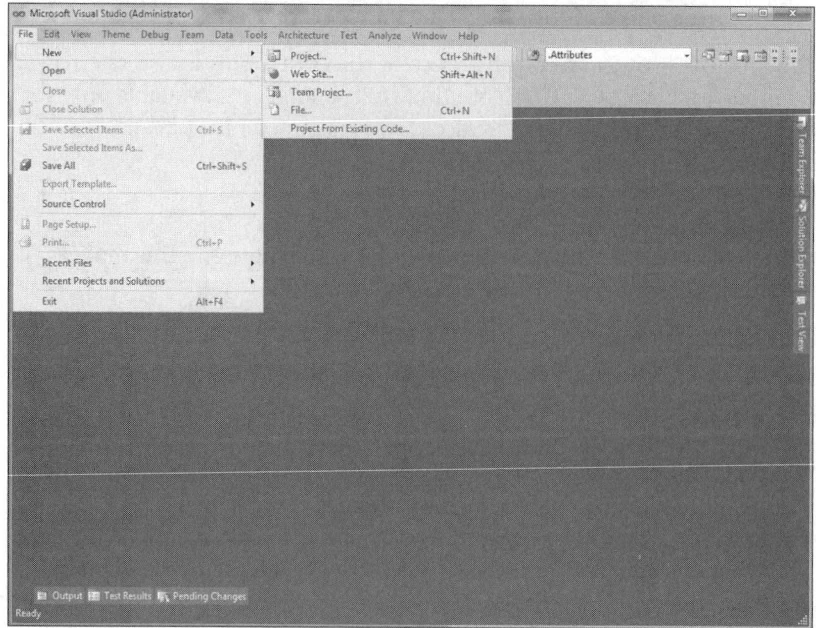

FIGURE 28.1 New Web Site menu.

3. Select File System for location and select Visual C# for language; then enter the path where you will place the application—for example, C:\Inetpub\ContactPictures and select the ASP.NET Empty Web Site project template.

NOTE

The path must be different from the path where the CRM website is installed.

4. Click OK.
5. Right-click the Solution Explorer, and select Add New Item menu option.
6. Select Web Form, and click Add.

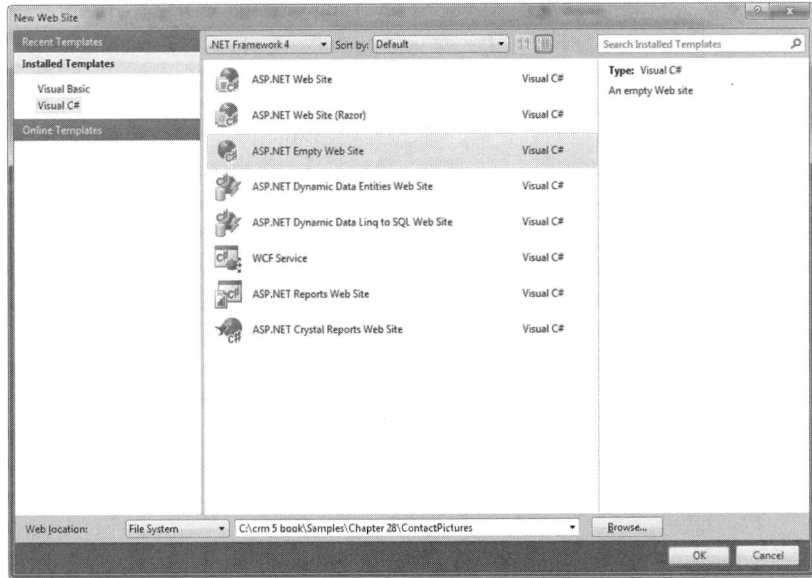

FIGURE 28.2 New Web Site properties.

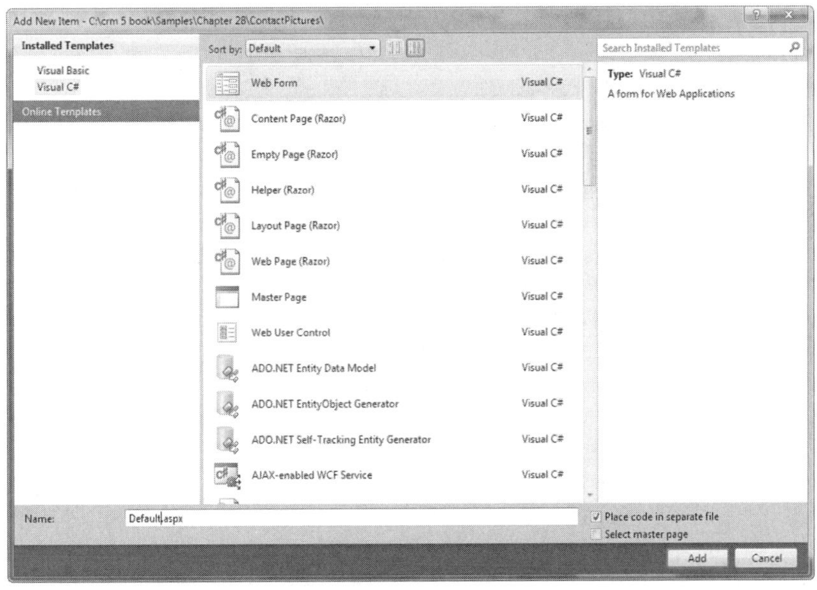

FIGURE 28.3 New Web Item Web Form.

7. In the `Default.aspx` page, replace the code with the following code. This adds an HTML table to the page, a picture control, a `FileUpload` control (so users can browse their local folders), and a `Button` control, so users can upload the selected image file:

```
<%@ Page Language="C#" AutoEventWireup="true"  CodeFile="Default.aspx.cs"
Inherits="_Default" %>
<!DOCTYPE html
PUBLIC "-//W3C//DTD XHTML 1.0 Transitional//EN"
"http://www.w3.org/TR/xhtml1/DTD/xhtml1-transitional.dtd">
<html xmlns="http://www.w3.org/1999/xhtml" >
<head runat="server">
    <title>Untitled Page</title>
</head>
<body>
    <form id="form1" runat="server">
    <div>
        <table>
            <tr>
                <td>
                    <asp:Image ID="Image1" runat="server"
                    Height="302px" Width="305px"
                    EnableViewState="False" /></td>
            </tr>
            <tr>
                <td>
                    <asp:FileUpload ID="FileUpload1"
                    runat="server"
                    Width="304px" /></td>
            </tr>
        </table>
        <asp:Button ID="Button1" runat="server"
            OnClick="Button1_Click"
            Text="Upload" />
    </div>
    </form>
</body>
</html>
```

8. Change to Design view. The page should look similar to Figure 28.4.

NOTE

Notice that the image control appears with a red X to indicate a broken link. This is normal behavior because no image has been uploaded yet.

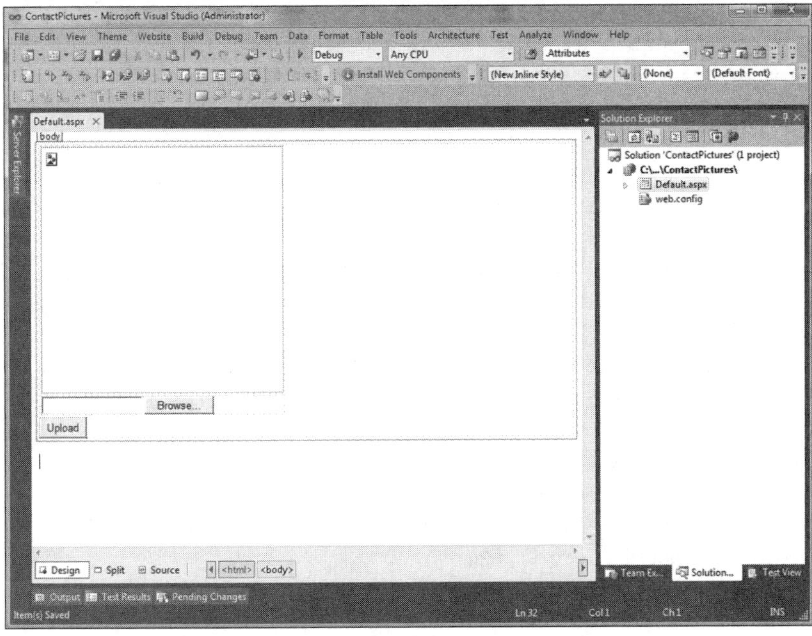

FIGURE 28.4 Default page in Design view.

9. Edit the code behind by right-clicking the page `Default.aspx` file from the Solution Explorer and selecting View Code, or by selecting Source from the bottom tabs.

10. Replace the code behind with the following code:

```
using System;
using System.Collections.Generic;
using System.Linq;
using System.Web;
using System.Web.UI;
using System.Web.UI.WebControls;
using System.IO;

public partial class _Default : System.Web.UI.Page
{
    protected void Page_Load(object sender, EventArgs e)
    {
      if (Request.QueryString["id"] != null)
      {
        string contactId = new Guid(Request.QueryString["id"]).ToString();
        string pictureFilename =
                Path.Combine(Server.MapPath("/ISV/contactPictures"),
                contactId + ".jpg");
        if (File.Exists(pictureFilename))
        {
```

```
            string pictureURL = "GetPic.aspx?id="
                + contactId + "&temp=" + Guid.NewGuid().ToString();
            Image1.ImageUrl = pictureURL;
        }
    }
}
protected void Button1_Click(object sender, EventArgs e)
{
    string contactId = new Guid(Request.QueryString["id"]).ToString();
    if (FileUpload1.HasFile)
    {
        string pictureFilename =
            Path.Combine(Server.MapPath("/ISV/contactPictures"),
            contactId + ".jpg");
        FileUpload1.SaveAs(pictureFilename);
        string pictureURL = "GetPic.aspx?id="
            + contactId + "&temp=" + Guid.NewGuid().ToString();
        Image1.ImageUrl = pictureURL;
    }
}
}
```

11. Create another page by right-clicking the project name in the Solution Explorer and selecting Add New Item.
12. Name the page `GetPic.aspx`, and click the Add button (see Figure 28.5).
13. Clear all the code on the page except for the first line. The code should have only this line:

```
<%@ Page Language="C#" AutoEventWireup="true"
CodeFile="GetPic.aspx.cs" Inherits="GetPic" %>
```

14. Edit the code behind by right-clicking the page `GetPic.aspx` file from the Solution Explorer and selecting View Code, or by selecting Source from the bottom tabs.
15. Replace the code behind with the following code:

```
using System;
using System.Collections.Generic;
using System.Linq;
using System.Web;
using System.Web.UI;
using System.Web.UI.WebControls;
using System.IO;

public partial class GetPic : System.Web.UI.Page
```

```
{
    protected void Page_Load(object sender, EventArgs e)
    {
        string picid = Request.QueryString["id"];
        string pictureFilename = Path.Combine(
              Server.MapPath("~/"), picid + ".jpg");
        Response.Clear();
        Response.ClearHeaders();
        Response.AppendHeader("content-type", "image/jpeg");
        Response.WriteFile(pictureFilename);
        Response.Flush();
        Response.End();
    }
}
```

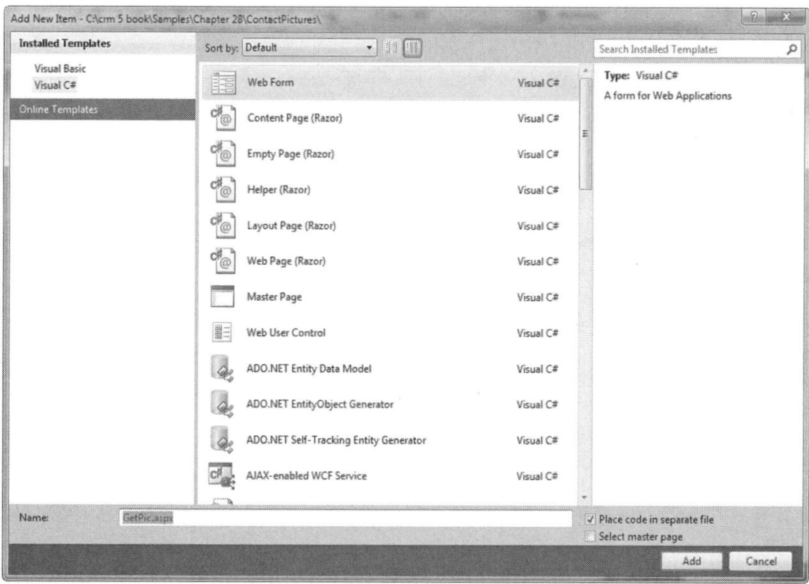

FIGURE 28.5 Adding a new page to the web project.

16. Build the solution by going to the Build menu and selecting Build Web Site.

In this application, we use a trick to display the picture by using a custom page called `GetPic.aspx` that is responsible for sending the image file to the `Image` control. This approach avoids having the picture cached on either the client browser or the web server; the users will see the image updated when a new image is uploaded. Alternatively, you can prevent this by altering the URL to use always a different query string. An example of this is to append a new GUID at the end of a `temp` parameter:

```
http://crm2011/Webfortis/contactPictures/GetPic.aspx?id=3053f877-b9b4-dc11-9dc0
0003ff8924be&temp=b4f18418-0d0d-401b-81c1-3196cf314a0d
```

28

ASP.NET Web Application Deployment

After you have built your custom web application and tested it, you are ready to deploy it. You must create the application virtual directory in Internet Information Services (IIS). Notice that, with this sample, you use the same web server as the CRM website. To deploy the web application, follow these steps:

1. Open the IIS Manager by going to Start, Control Panel, Administrative Tools, Internet Information Services (IIS) Manager.
2. Expand the server name (with this sample, it is CRM2011) and select the Application Pools folder. You will create a new application pool for the application to isolate it and not affect the CRM website application pool. Right-click the Application Pools folder and select Add Application Pool (see Figure 28.6).
3. Enter **`ContactPictures`** in the Application Pool ID text box, select .Net Framework v4.0.30319 in the .Net Framework version, select Classic in the Managed pipeline mode, and click OK (see Figure 28.7).

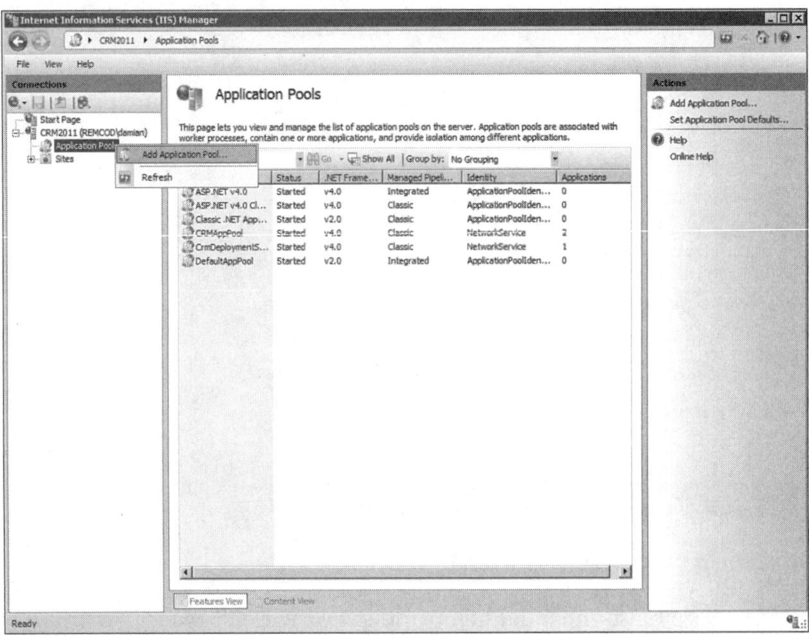

FIGURE 28.6 Creating a new application pool.

4. Expand the Web Sites folder.
5. Locate the website for your CRM system (see Figure 28.8).
6. Right-click the ISV folder and select Add Application (see Figure 28.9).

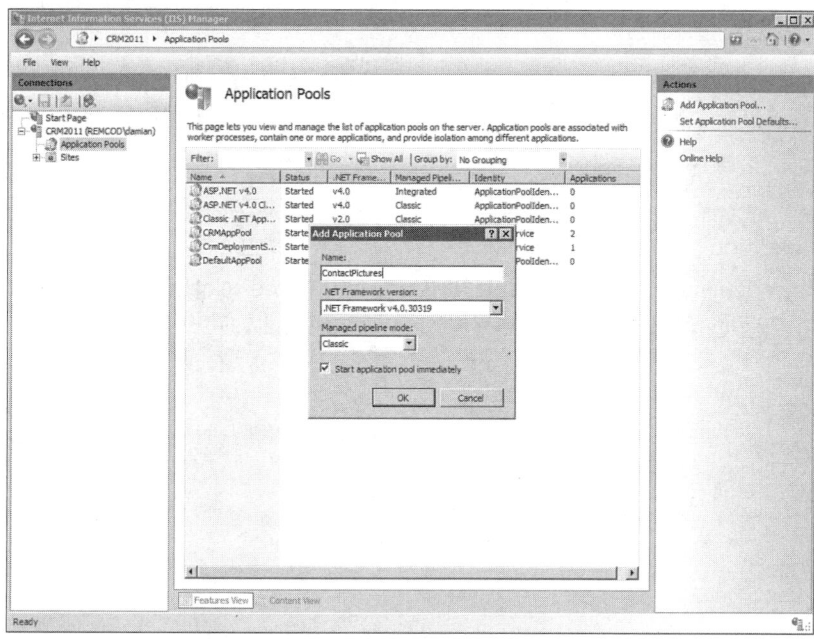

FIGURE 28.7 ContactPictures application pool.

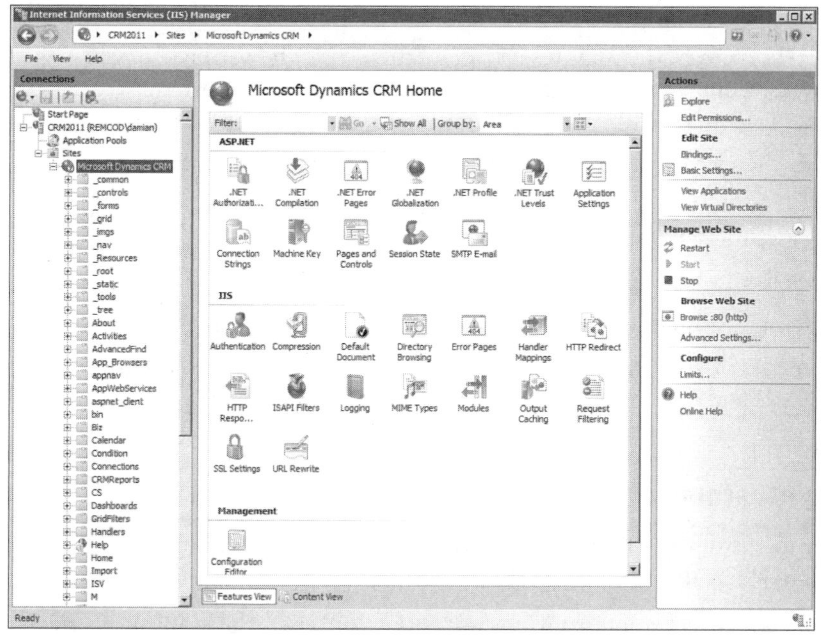

FIGURE 28.8 Microsoft Dynamics CRM website in IIS Manager.

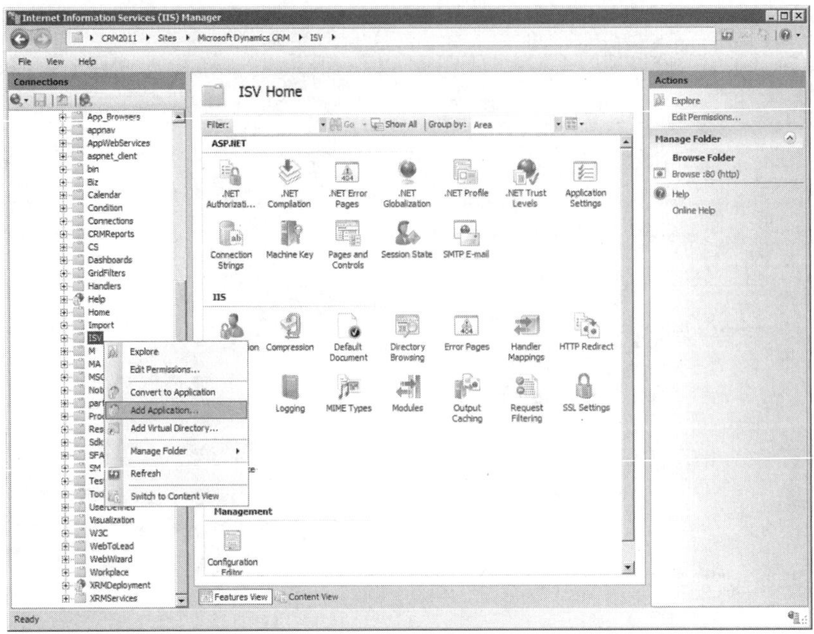

FIGURE 28.9 Add Application context menu.

7. Enter **ContactPictures** in the Alias text box, and then enter the path where you created the website application in Visual Studio—for example, C:\Program Files\Microsoft Dynamics CRM\CRMWeb\ISV\ContactPictures (see Figure 28.10).
8. Click Select to change the application pool and select **ContactPictures** (see Figure 28.11).
9. Click OK to close the select app pool dialog.
10. Click OK to close the Add Application pool dialog.
11. Close the Internet Information Services Manager.
12. Copy the contents of your published solution to the C:\Program Files\Microsoft Dynamics CRM\CRMWeb\ISV\ContactPictures on the CRM Server.

Contact Entity Customization

You are now ready to customize the Contact entity to show the application you've developed by creating a new tab and adding an IFRAME to it.

1. From the CRM web client application, go to Settings and then Customizations (see Figure 28.12).
2. Click Customize the System and locate the Contact entity (see Figure 28.13).
3. Click Forms, and then double-click the Main Form record.

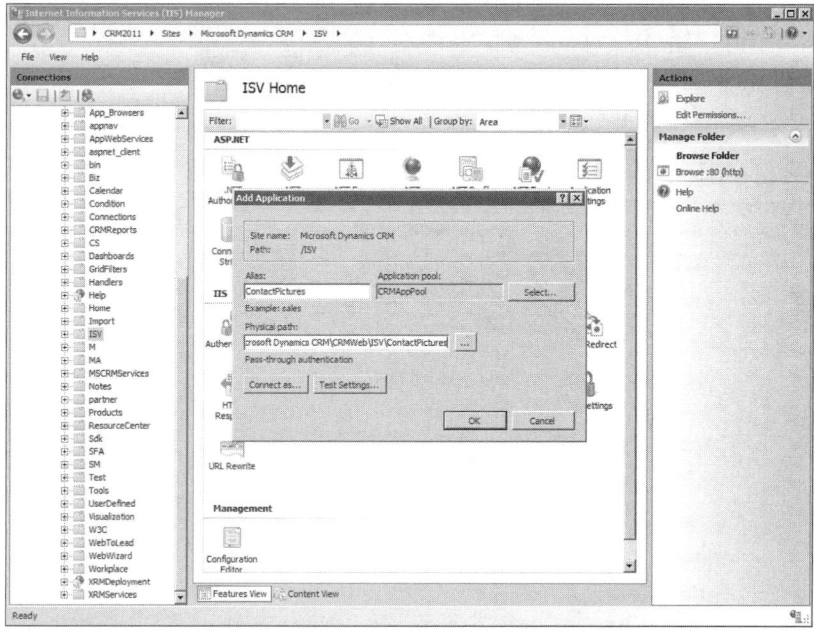

FIGURE 28.10 Virtual directory alias.

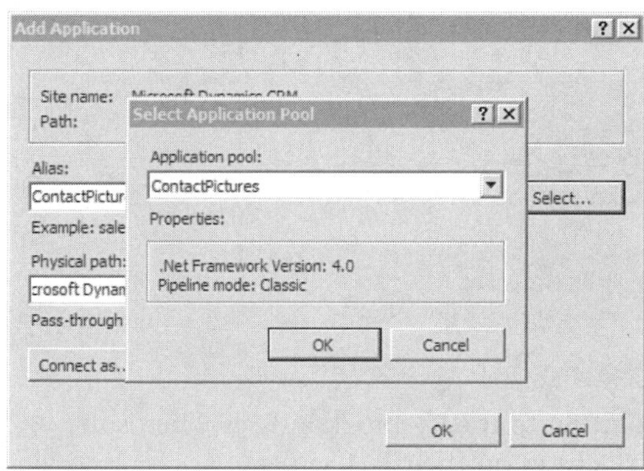

FIGURE 28.11 Application pool selection.

4. Click the Insert Tab on the Ribbon, and click One Column on the Tab group, double-click the new tab created, and enter **Picture** for the Name and Label; then click OK (see Figure 28.14).
5. Click the IFRAME button on the ribbon to insert an IFRAME inside the section of the tab.
6. In the Add an IFRAME properties, enter **Picture** for the name; in the URL, enter **/ISV/ContactPictures/Default.aspx**.

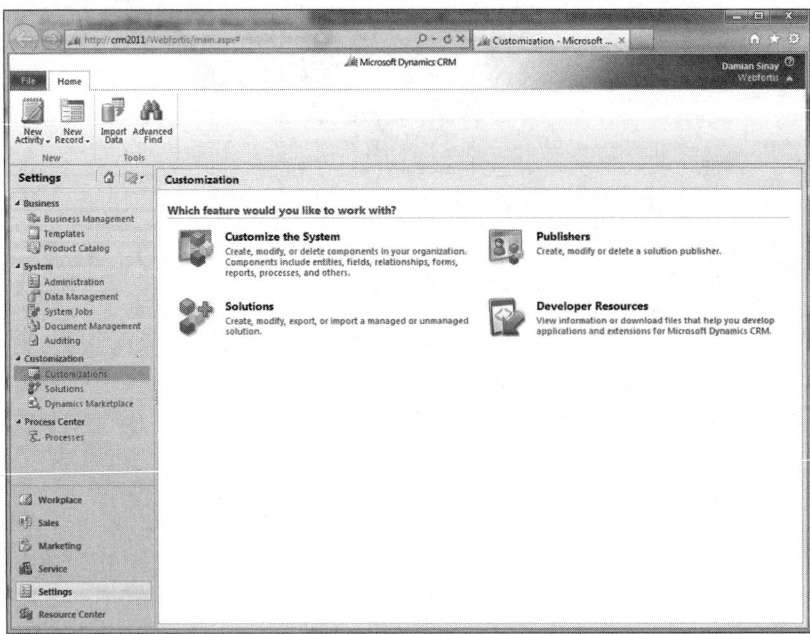

FIGURE 28.12 Customization interface.

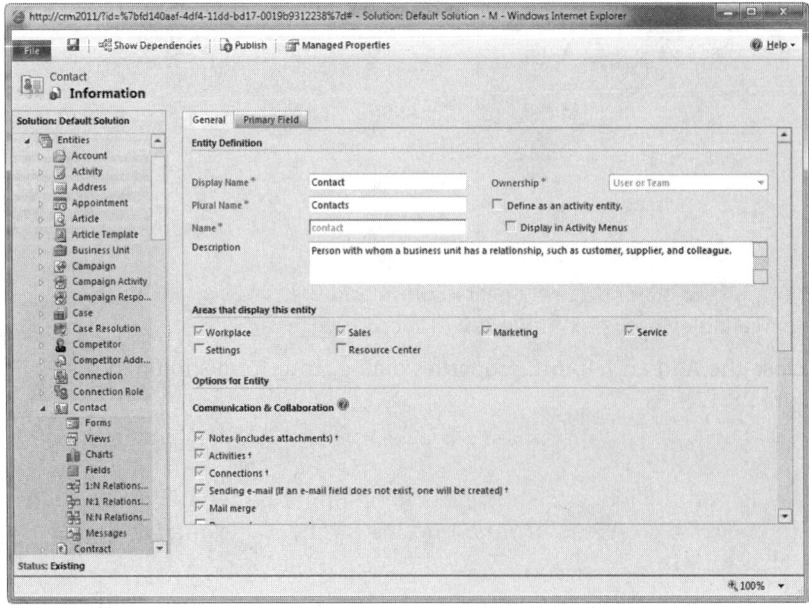

FIGURE 28.13 Contact entity.

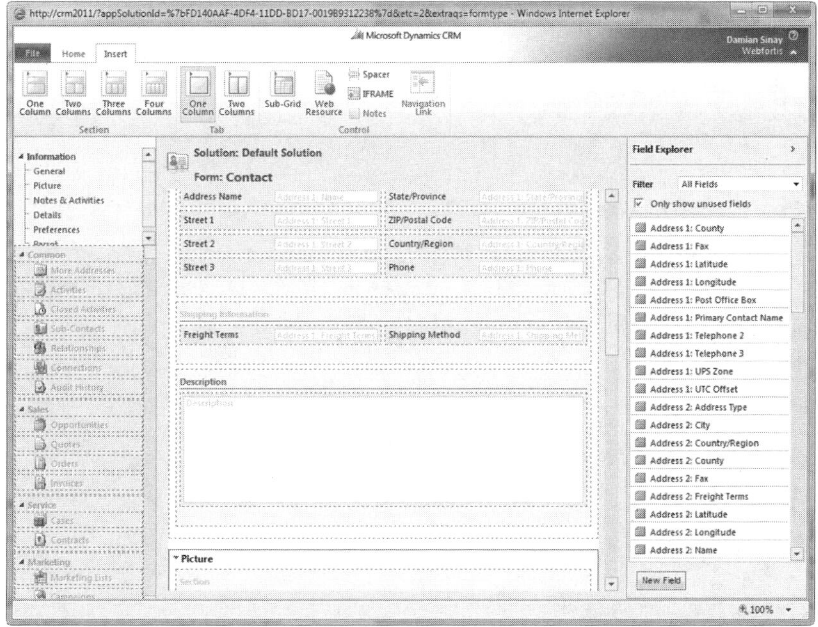

FIGURE 28.14 Adding a new tab for Picture.

7. Next, select the check box for Pass Record Object-Type Code and Unique Identifier as Parameters.

NOTE

This last property is the most important one for our purposes because it adds the GUID of the Contact in the query string for the Contact you are editing, enabling you to identify each Contact. Uncheck the box for Restrict Cross-Frame Scripting (see Figure 28.15).

8. Move to the Formatting tab and select One Column, and then check the Automatically Expand to Use Available Space box under Row Layout (see Figure 28.16).
9. Click OK to close the Add an IFRAME properties dialog. Your form should look similar to Figure 28.17.
10. Click on the Home tab on the ribbon and click Save and Close to save the form changes.
11. Click Publish All Customizations to publish your changes.

Testing

You are ready to test the customization.

1. From the CRM web client, go to the Workplace and then select Contacts.
2. Select a Contact and double-click to open it.

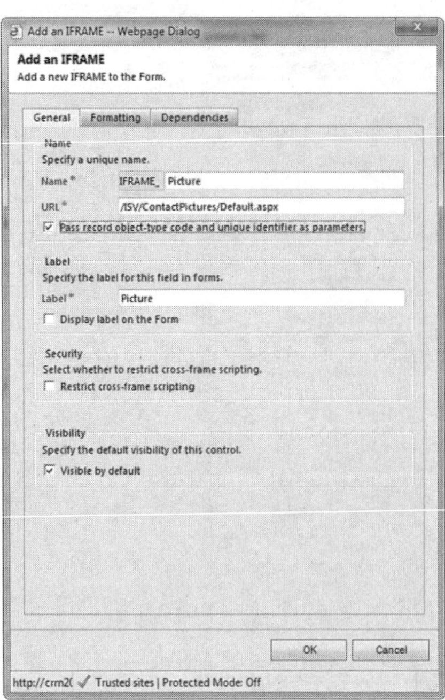

FIGURE 28.15 Adding a new IFRAME with the Pass Record Object-Type Code and Unique Identifier as Parameters option.

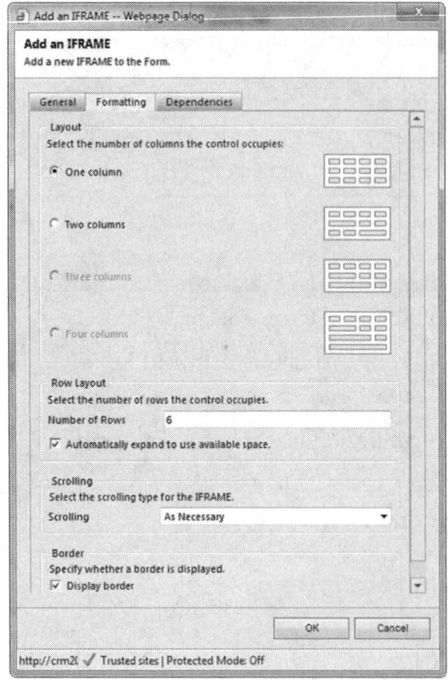

FIGURE 28.16 Automatically Expand to Use Available Space.

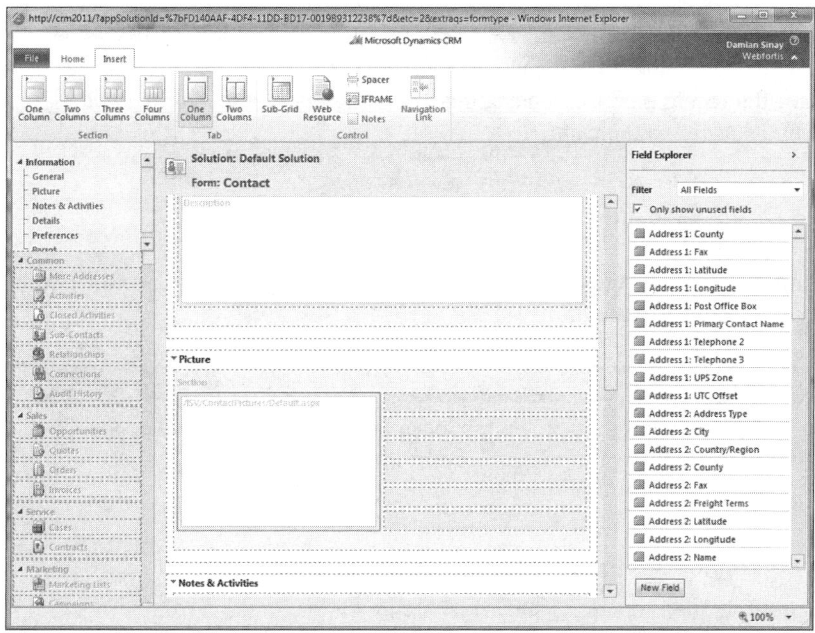

FIGURE 28.17 New IFRAME added to show the Contact picture.

FIGURE 28.18 Contacts list.

TIP

You must use an existing Contact to use this solution. If you are creating a new one, you must first save the record before uploading the picture so that the record will have a GUID that can be assigned to the picture.

3. Move to the Picture tab.
4. Enter the full path of the image file you want to upload, or click Browse to locate the file in your local disks (see Figure 28.19).

NOTE

At this point, the embedded application in the tab looks pretty rough. We address how to make it look more professional in the next section, "Improvements."

5. Click the Upload button.
6. You will see the uploaded image, as shown in Figure 28.20.

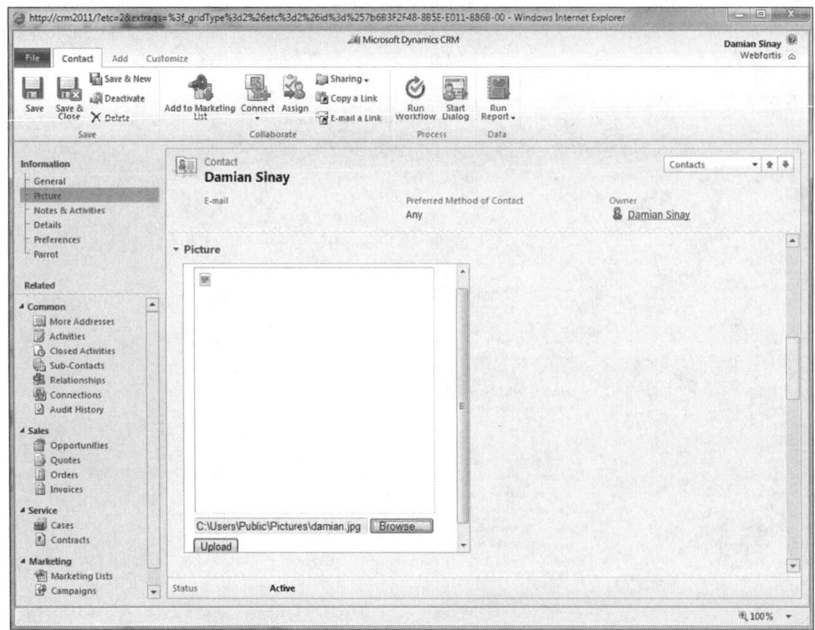

FIGURE 28.19 Uploading a picture to a Contact.

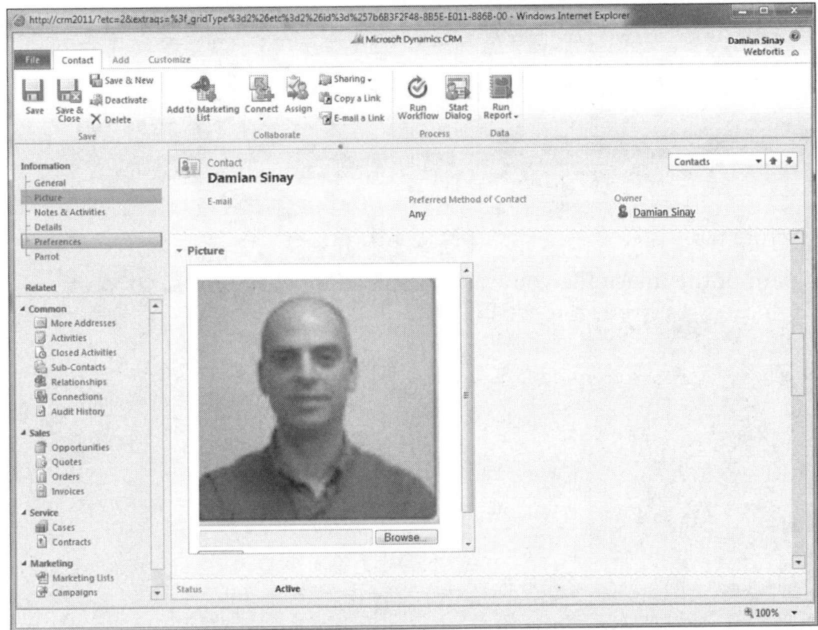

FIGURE 28.20 Contact with picture uploaded.

TIP

In this example, you don't need to save the record because the picture will be updated as soon it is uploaded.

Improvements

The sample we created may be basic, and you might want to add some improvements for this solution. For example, you would like to have the page looks more like any other CRM page by using the CRM styles to have similar fonts and colors as well as support for CRM offline.

Adding CRM Styles

The application looks strange and unprofessional inside the IFRAME. You will probably want to make the application look more like Microsoft Dynamics CRM. You can do that easily by applying the CRM cascading style sheet (CSS) to your application. To do this, add the following line inside the `<Head>` element in the `Default.aspx` page:

```
    <link rel="stylesheet" type="text/css"
href="../../_common/styles/theme.css.aspx?lcid=1033" />
    <link rel="stylesheet" type="text/css"
href="../../_common/styles/main.css.aspx?lcid=1033" />
```

After you apply the styles, your application will look as shown in Figure 28.21.

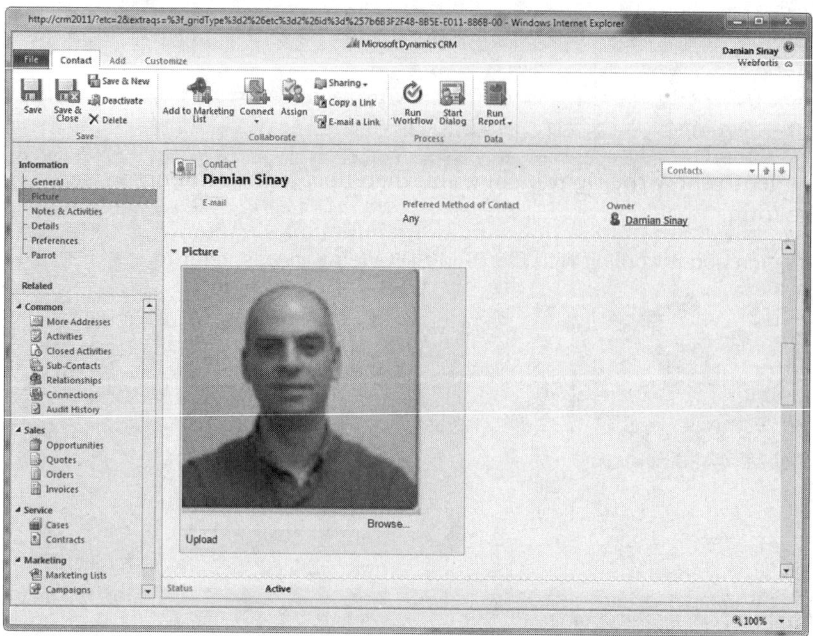

FIGURE 28.21 Contact with picture uploaded and Microsoft Dynamics CRM styles added.

Considerations for IFRAME in Offline Clients

When you implement IFRAMEs on the Microsoft Dynamics forms, they will not be accessible when the Outlook client is in offline mode. You can use the following code to detect whether the client is running in online or offline modes:

```
if ( Request.Url.ToString().StartsWith("http://localhost:2525") )
{
    // running in offline mode
}
else
{
    // running in online mode
}
```

Improving the Save Behavior

In the sample, the picture is updated automatically without the user having to save the record. We did that to simplify the code sample, but the user might expect to update the picture only when saving the record. To do that, you must create a new custom attribute for the Contact entity called `pictureid` (or similar), with a type of nvarchar and a length of 100, where you can store a unique identifier (for example a GUID) for the picture that is going to be uploaded. To do that, you use the CRM SDK Web Services to query the attribute value in order to show the right picture and then update the attribute in the `OnSave` event of the form.

▶ For more information about working with the CRM SDK Web Services, refer to Chapter 26, "Web Services."

TIP

You could use this same sample to show a company's logos and apply a similar customization to the Account entity.

CAUTION

This sample won't work on CRM Online because you don't have access to the file system; however, you could implement a similar feature by creating Web Resources programmatically via JavaScript and HTML code.

Summary

This chapter looked at how to integrate a custom ASP.NET web application with Microsoft Dynamics CRM using IFRAMEs. You learned how an entity form passes the parameters to an application so that you can determine which record, entity, and organization you are working on. Finally, you learned about some improvements, such as using cascading style sheets (CSS) files, to give your application the Microsoft Dynamics CRM look and feel.

CHAPTER 29

Data Management

IN THIS CHAPTER

- Import Templates
- Import Wizard
- Bulk Record Deletion
- Sample Data

As we explained in Chapter 7, "Working with the Workplace," the functionality to export data is persistent throughout the application. Similarly, so is the ability to import data in Microsoft Dynamics CRM 2011.

NOTE

Although a separate component for data migration (referred to as the *Data Migration Manager [DMM]*) existed in previous versions of CRM, there is no longer a separate component for data migration. Instead, the Import Wizard described in this chapter completely replaces the DMM.

Import Templates

Not found in Settings, Templates, but rather in Settings, Data Management, there exist data import templates, as shown in Figure 29.1.

When selected, users are presented with the option to download data templates for entities (including custom entities) by selecting the record type and clicking Download (see Figure 29.2).

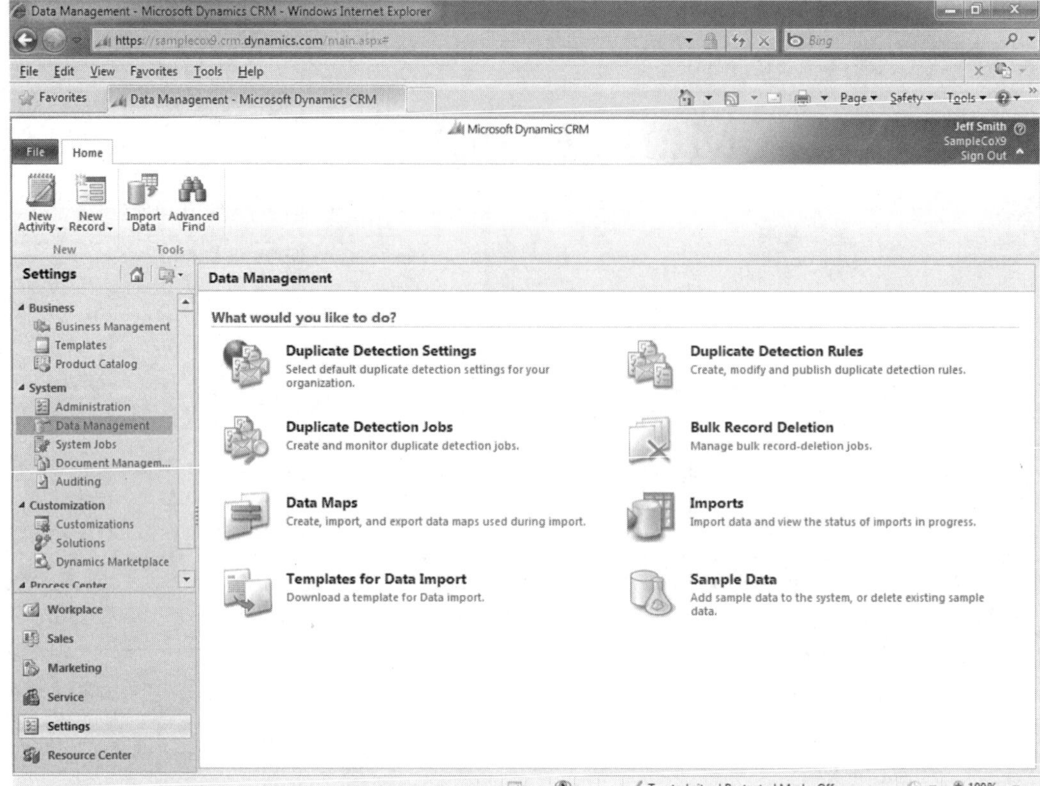

FIGURE 29.1 Data management interface.

TIP

You can also download the specific entity template from the entity directly by navigating to Import Data, and then choosing Download Template for Import from the Ribbon menu, as shown in Figure 29.3.

Save the export to your desktop and open in Excel. When you open the template in Excel, the attributes are available for population across the top of the spreadsheet (see Figure 29.4).

Where there are required attributes, such as Account Name, the column header is shown in bold. Additionally, there are tool tips on each of the columns that feature whether the field is required, and the character length and option sets are available in drop-down form.

Use the downloaded template to populate with data that can be easily migrated using the Import Wizard.

Templates for Data Import - Windows Internet Explorer

Templates for Data Import

Select the record type for which template is needed:

Account

Help

Download

Close

Trusted sites | Protected Mode: Off

100%

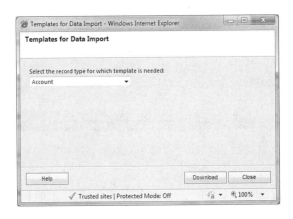

FIGURE 29.2 Templates for data import.

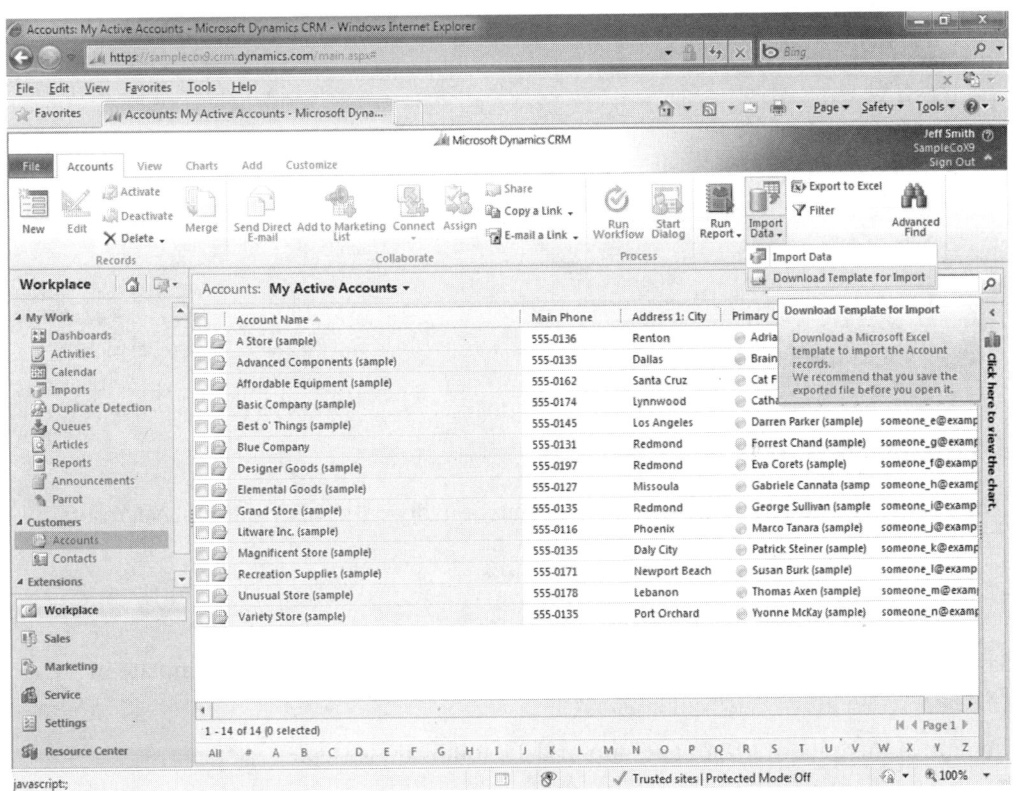

FIGURE 29.3 Templates for data import from the Account screen.

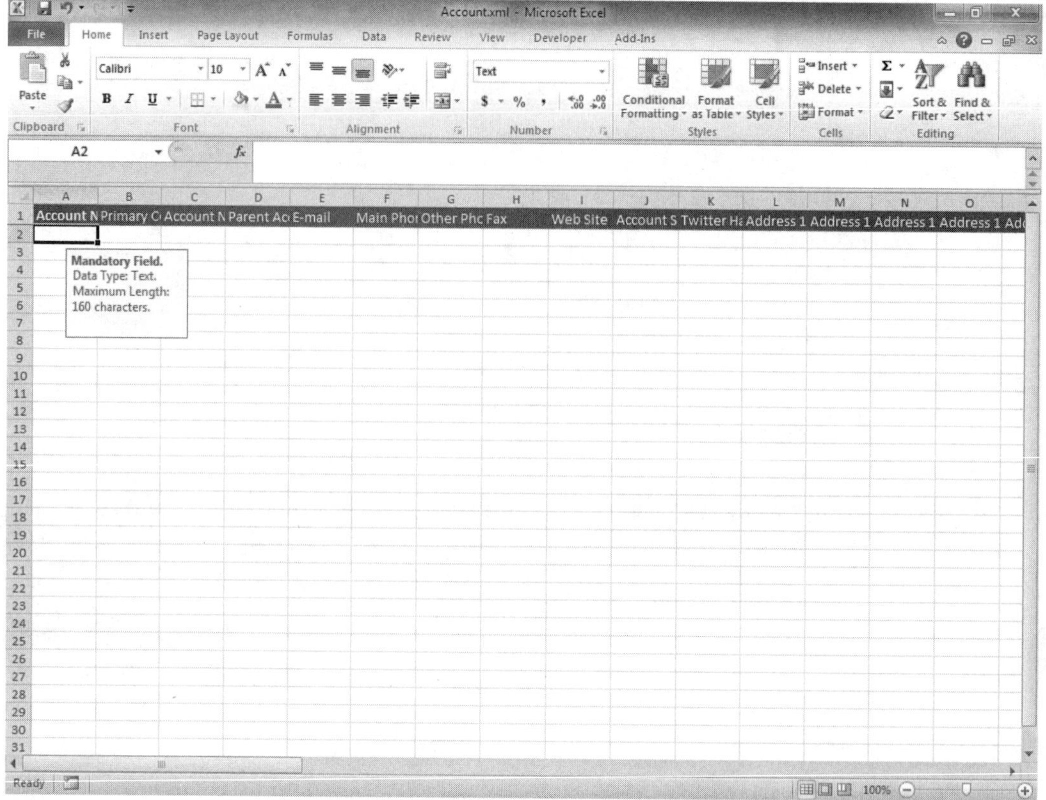

FIGURE 29.4 Data template for accounts.

Import Wizard

The Import Wizard has vastly increased in functionality with this version of Microsoft Dynamics CRM and now supports the following:

- ▶ Picklist and lookup mapping
- ▶ Multiple entity mapping from a single upload file
- ▶ Bulk update

To launch the Import Wizard and import data, follow these steps:

1. Either select Import Data from the Ribbon menu or select File, Tools, Import Data. The Data Import Wizard opens, as shown in Figure 29.5.

   The Import Wizard will take the following files:

   - ▶ CSV
   - ▶ TXT

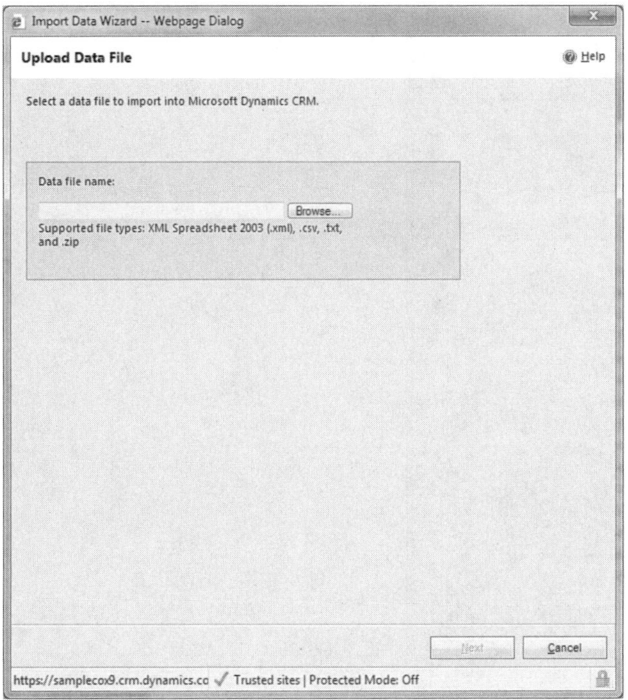

FIGURE 29.5 Data Import Wizard.

- XML
- ZIP

CAUTION

Although the upload size cannot exceed 8MB, you can have a zip file that contains multiple files. However, none of the included files can exceed 8MB and the entire zip file must not be greater than 32MB.

2. Select the file you want to upload—either a downloaded template or a custom import file—and select Next. If the system is able to recognize the data type, it will map to the target record automatically (see Figure 29.6).

TIP

If the system is not able to recognize the record type, you will receive an upload summary, as shown in Figure 29.7, which provides an option to set or change the delimiters.

3. Because the mapping is unknown in this case, unlike what we illustrated in step 2, we need to select the data map for the import.

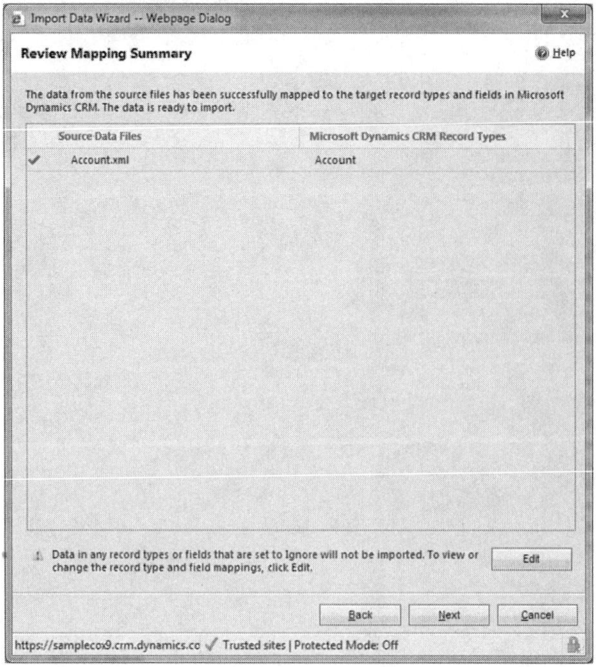

FIGURE 29.6 Data import mapping summary.

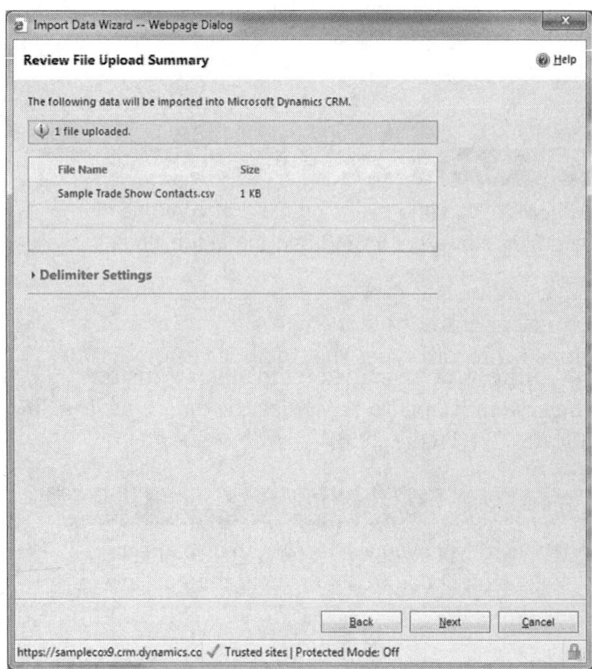

FIGURE 29.7 Data import upload summary.

NOTE

The data maps shown are those data maps that are available either out-of-the-box or maps that you created previously and activated, as shown in Figure 29.8.

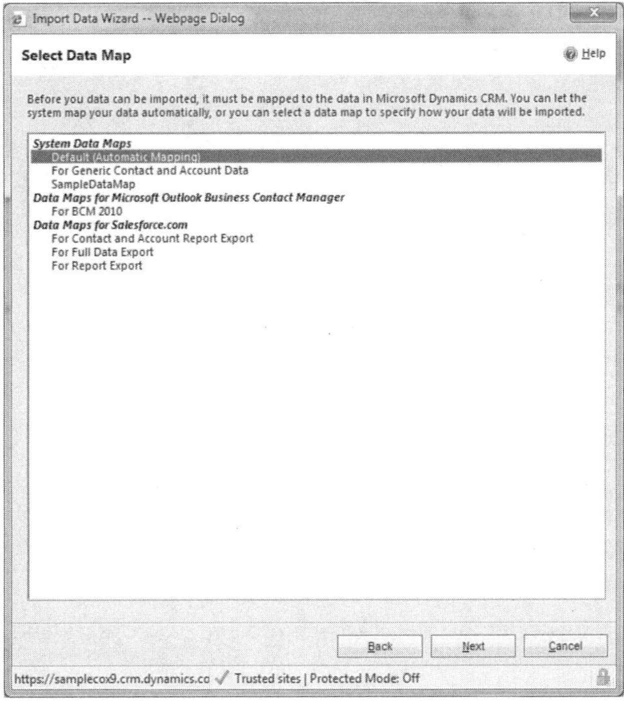

FIGURE 29.8 Data import data map selection.

4. Select the default data map for the import, and click Next to continue.

   Because we have only one source file uploaded, in step 5 we need to select the record type from the drop-down (or in the case of multiple file uploads, to not map the data). Figure 29.9 shows the options for record types that include custom entities.

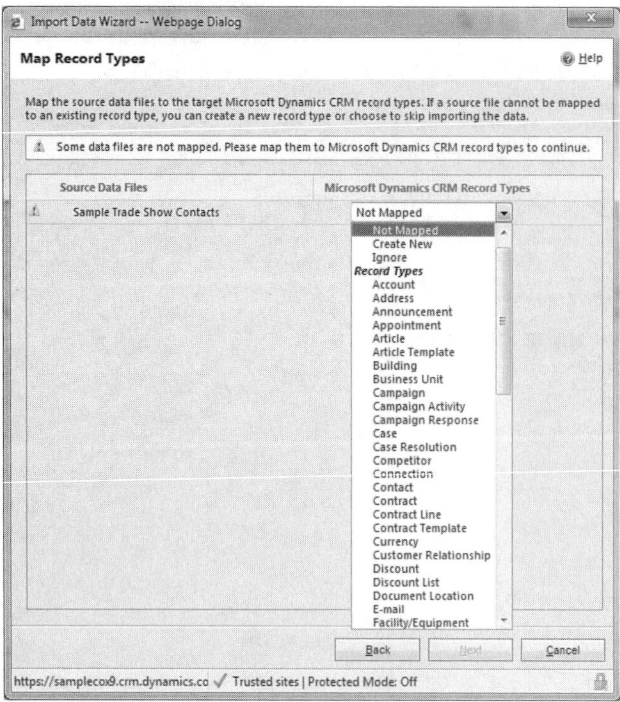

FIGURE 29.9 Data import map record types.

5. Because our records are Trade Show Contacts, select the Record Type as Contact, and then click Next to continue.

6. Because our source data is not able to map directly, we are prompted with mapping options as shown in Figure 29.10.

   Notice that the field mapping is broken down between required fields (the top part of the wizard) and optional fields (the bottom part of the mapping). Additionally, notice where mapping occurred—in our example, First Name was mapped automatically, but Email Address was not. Either fix or correct the mappings, and select Next to continue.

CAUTION

In this example, we have a field in our source data called Full Name. Notice that Full Name is an optional field from CRM. However, there is no way to import to this field because Full Name in CRM is an implied (that is, calculated) field, which means it cannot be imported.

We also have the option for mapping option sets directly in the interface.

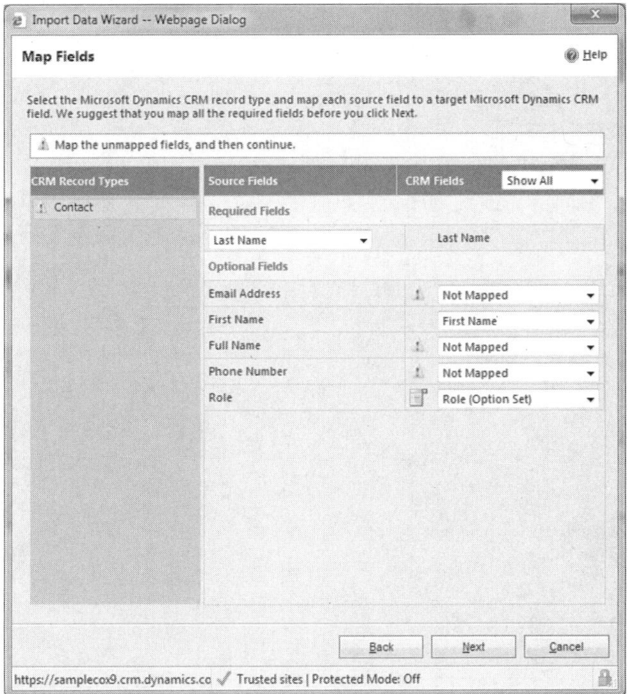

FIGURE 29.10 Data import map fields.

7. To map the option set, select the option drop-down icon next to the drop-down section. You will be prompted with the option set mapping for the field, as shown in Figure 29.11.

   You can select the mapping values based on what is on the underlying data source or map the underlying data to values that exist in the CRM system.

TIP

Option set imports will support a maximum of 400 options.

If we add Account to the data map, we have the option for a lookup reference, as shown in Figure 29.12.

You can select multiple reference fields for a lookup reference.

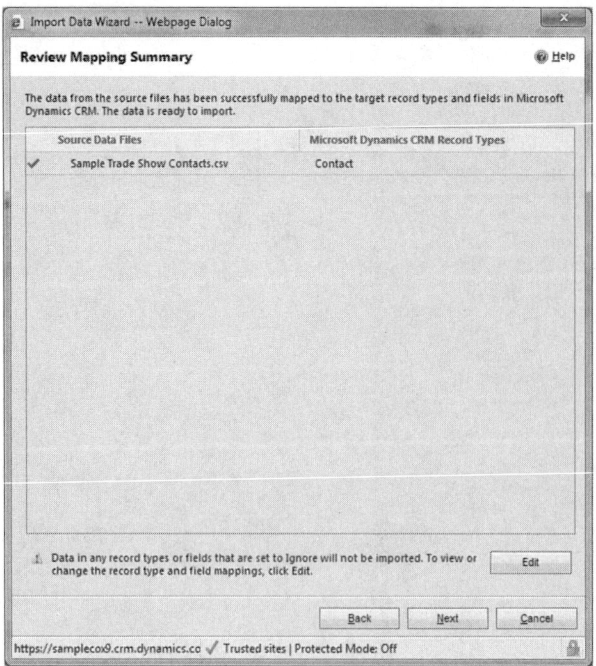

FIGURE 29.11 Data import map fields—option set options.

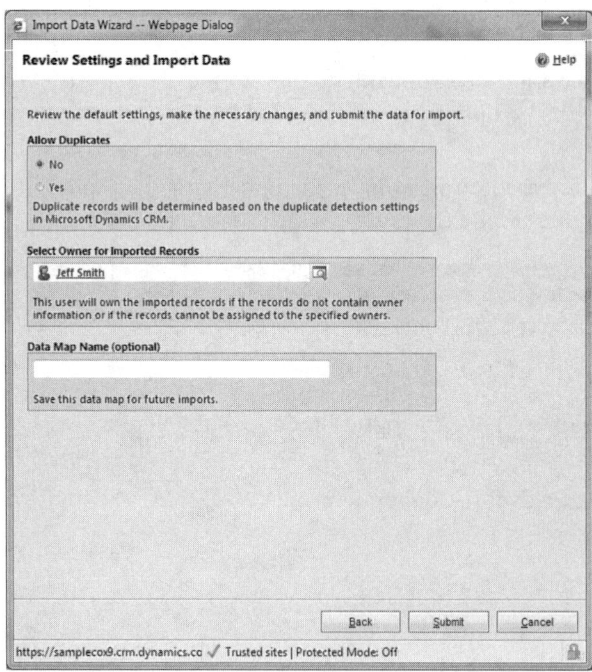

FIGURE 29.12 Data import map fields—lookup reference.

8. Next, review the mapping summary, as shown in Figure 29.13. You have the option to edit any field mappings by selecting Edit or canceling the import. Select Next to continue.

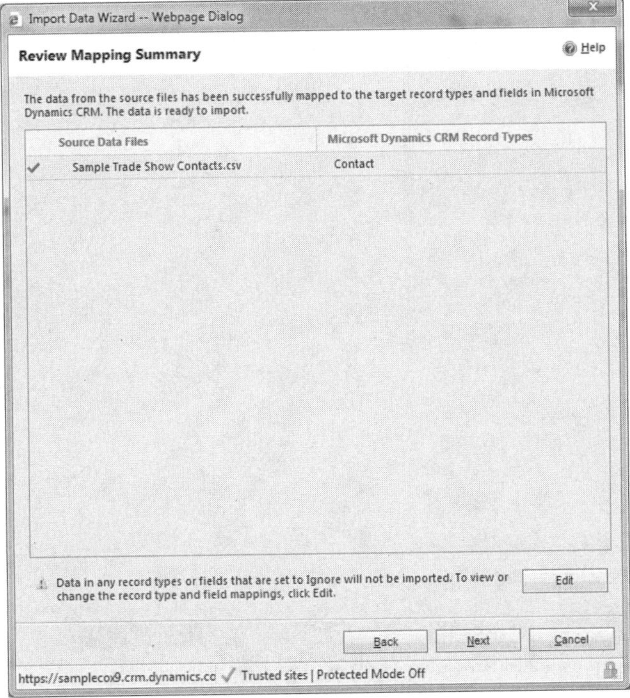

FIGURE 29.13 Data import mapping summary.

9. Finally, you have the option to allow duplicates to be created, assign the records to a different user, and save the data map for future imports, as shown in Figure 29.14.

10. Click Submit to submit the import. Now you can check the import by navigating to the workplace and selecting Imports, as shown in Figure 29.15.

View Import Status

Opening a record by selecting Imports shows the following status of the import:

- Name of the import
- Status of the import (success, failure, and so on)
- Who created it and when
- When the import finished
- What the source document was called and its size

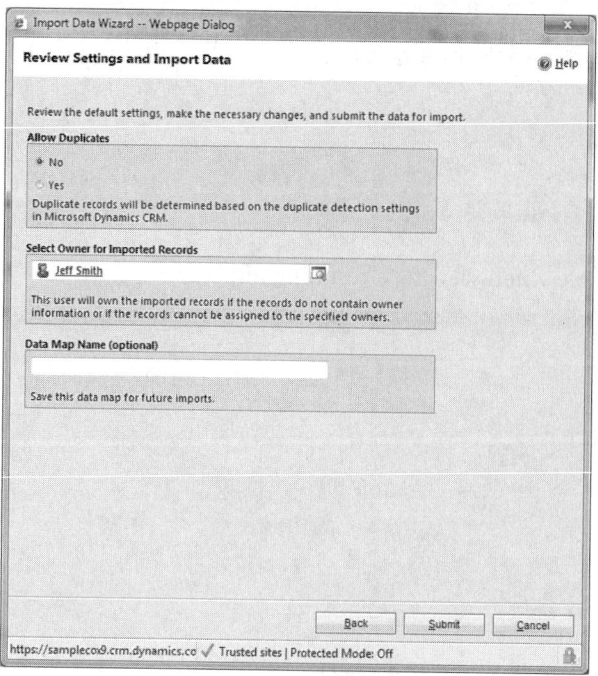

FIGURE 29.14 Data import review settings and import data.

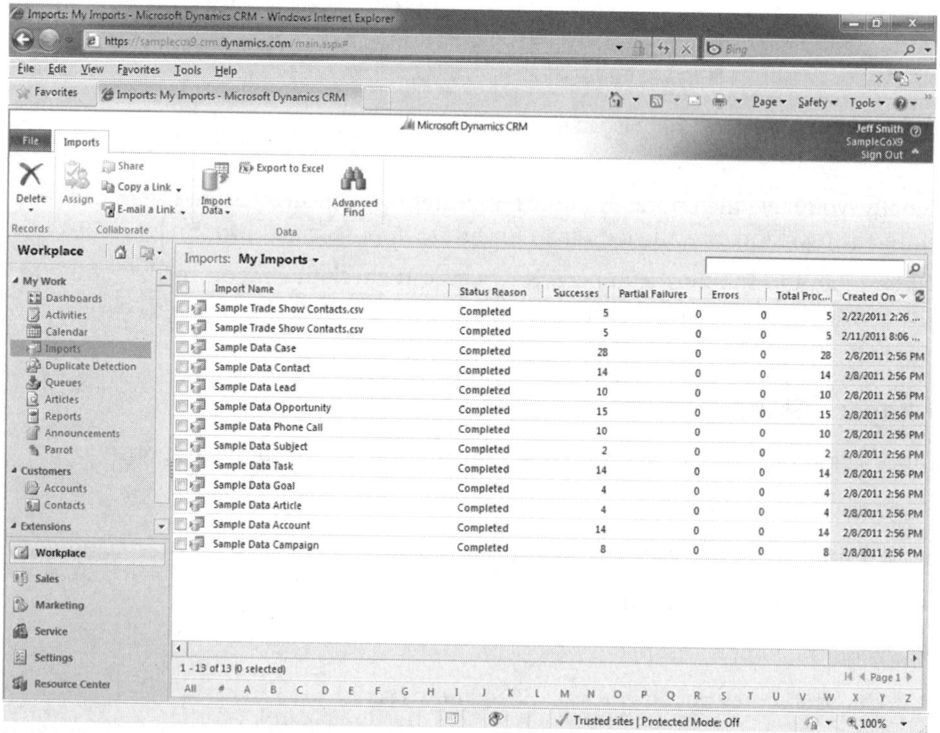

Imports: My Imports - Microsoft Dynamics CRM - Windows Internet Explorer

Imports: **My Imports**

Import Name	Status Reason	Successes	Partial Failures	Errors	Total Proc...	Created On
Sample Trade Show Contacts.csv	Completed	5	0	0	5	2/22/2011 2:26 ...
Sample Trade Show Contacts.csv	Completed	5	0	0	5	2/11/2011 8:06 ...
Sample Data Case	Completed	28	0	0	28	2/8/2011 2:56 PM
Sample Data Contact	Completed	14	0	0	14	2/8/2011 2:56 PM
Sample Data Lead	Completed	10	0	0	10	2/8/2011 2:56 PM
Sample Data Opportunity	Completed	15	0	0	15	2/8/2011 2:56 PM
Sample Data Phone Call	Completed	10	0	0	10	2/8/2011 2:56 PM
Sample Data Subject	Completed	2	0	0	2	2/8/2011 2:56 PM
Sample Data Task	Completed	14	0	0	14	2/8/2011 2:56 PM
Sample Data Goal	Completed	4	0	0	4	2/8/2011 2:56 PM
Sample Data Article	Completed	4	0	0	4	2/8/2011 2:56 PM
Sample Data Account	Completed	14	0	0	14	2/8/2011 2:56 PM
Sample Data Campaign	Completed	8	0	0	8	2/8/2011 2:56 PM

1 - 13 of 13 (0 selected)

FIGURE 29.15 Imports.

- What the mapping record type was
- Who owned the records after import
- The data map used
- Whether duplicate detection was enabled for the import
- Record results, consisting of failures, partials, and so forth

Figure 29.16 shows the options available when viewing a resulting import.

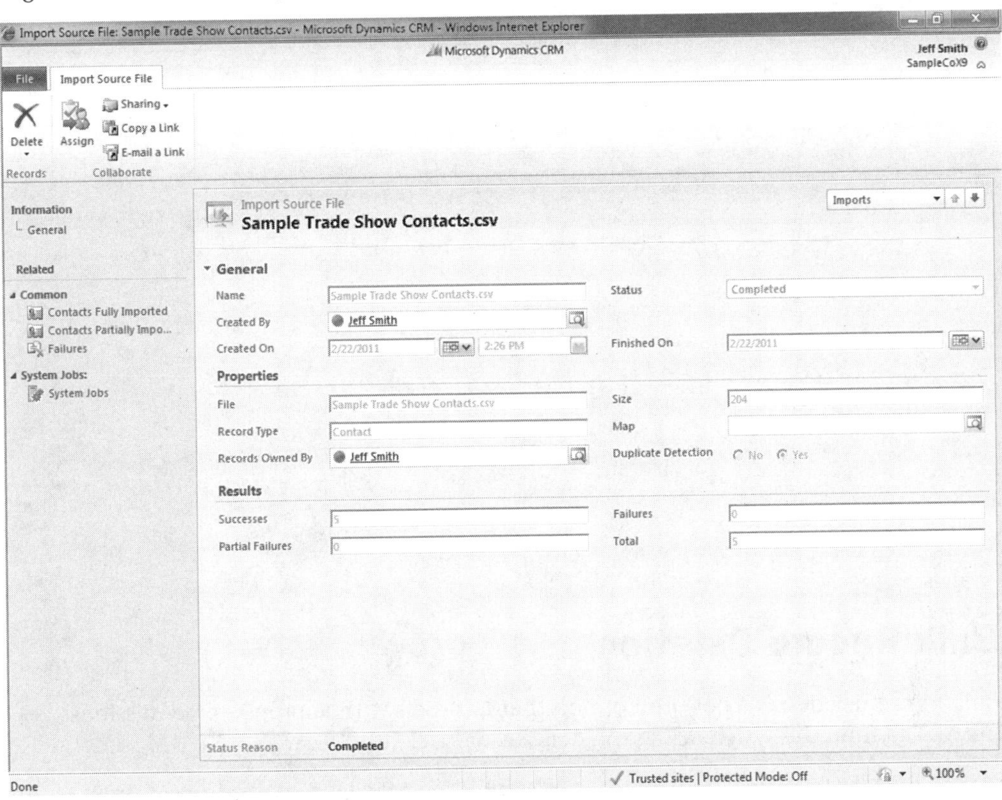

FIGURE 29.16 Data import details.

Additionally, a great feature to know about is the ability to roll back or delete the imported records. This is found by selecting Delete from the Ribbon menu, as shown in Figure 29.17, and selecting one of the options shown.

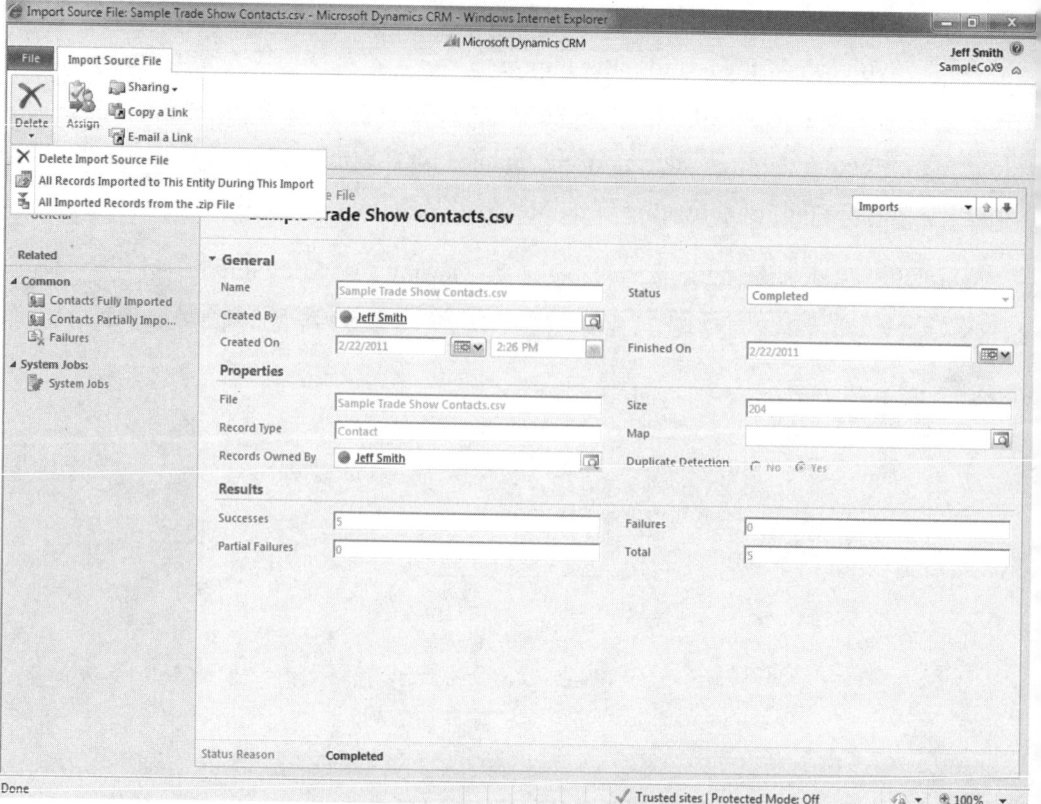

FIGURE 29.17 Data import delete options.

Bulk Record Deletion

Bulk record deletion is a powerful option that lets users with appropriate permissions purge data from the system using the Bulk Record Deletion Wizard.

To use the wizard, navigate to Settings, System, Data Management and select Bulk Record Deletion. There you will see any jobs that have run to clean or delete data (see Figure 29.18).

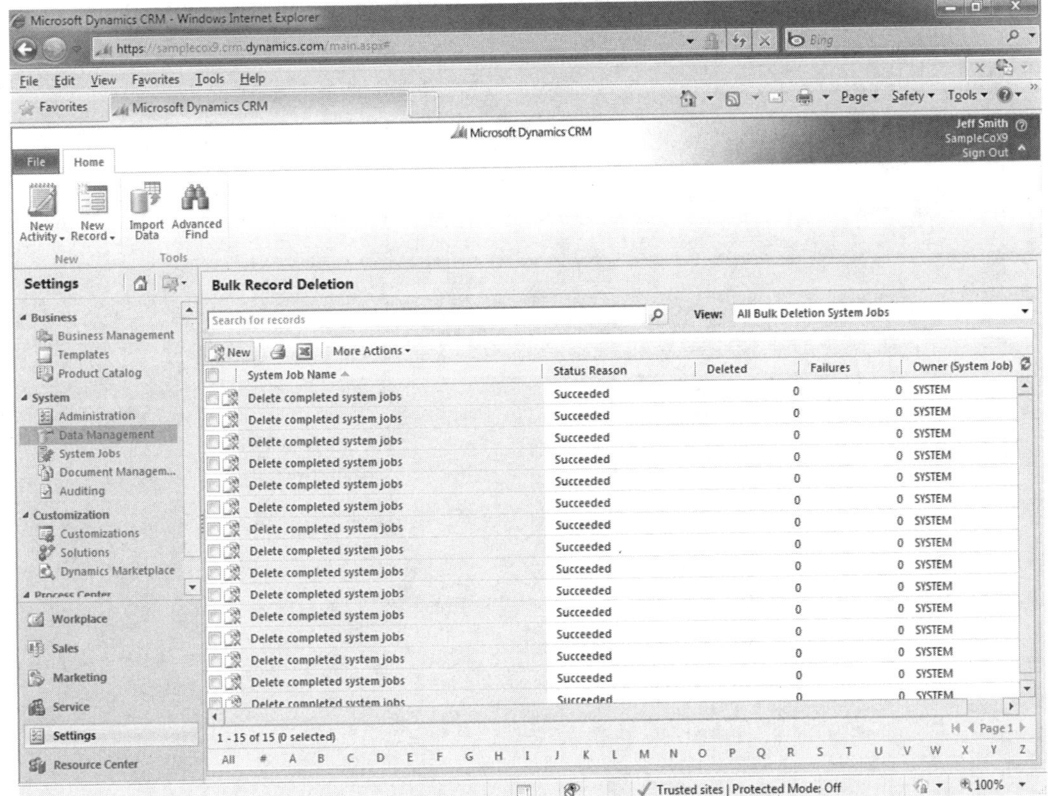

FIGURE 29.18 Bulk record deletion status.

Complete the following steps to use the Bulk Record Deletion Wizard:

1. To launch the wizard, select New from the menu bar on the middle of the screen (as shown in Figure 29.18).
2. When the wizard starts, as shown in Figure 29.19, click Next to continue.
3. Define the search criteria for the records you want to delete, as shown in Figure 29.20. You can select either existing Views from the Use Saved View option, or define criteria similar to how you define an advanced find.
4. In our example, we're going to delete the records we imported previously by selecting Contacts created in the last two hours. You can preview the records, which is always a good idea to confirm and validate that the records will be deleted as expected. Click Next to continue.

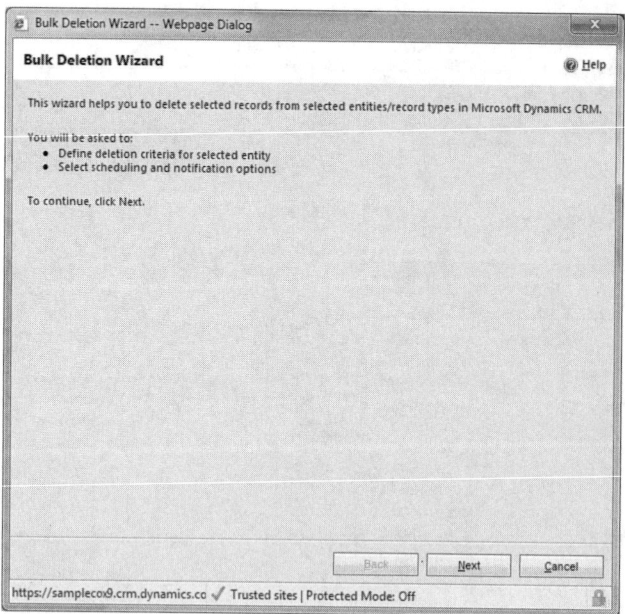

FIGURE 29.19 Bulk Record Deletion Wizard.

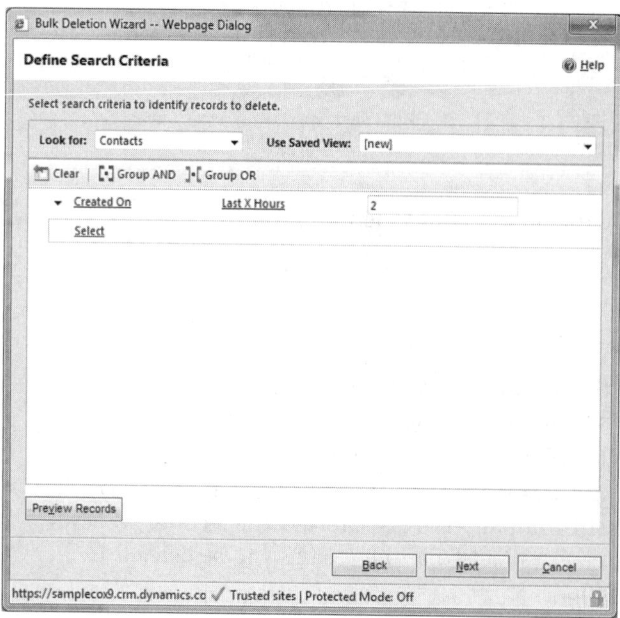

FIGURE 29.20 Bulk Record Deletion Wizard—define search criteria.

5. Select the name of the job, when you want the deletion to occur, how often it should run, and whether anybody should be notified when the job is complete (see Figure 29.21).
6. Select Next to continue, and then click Submit to fire the job.

The job will run in the background for all records that meet the criteria at the time, and if you elected, send you an email notifying you of the result.

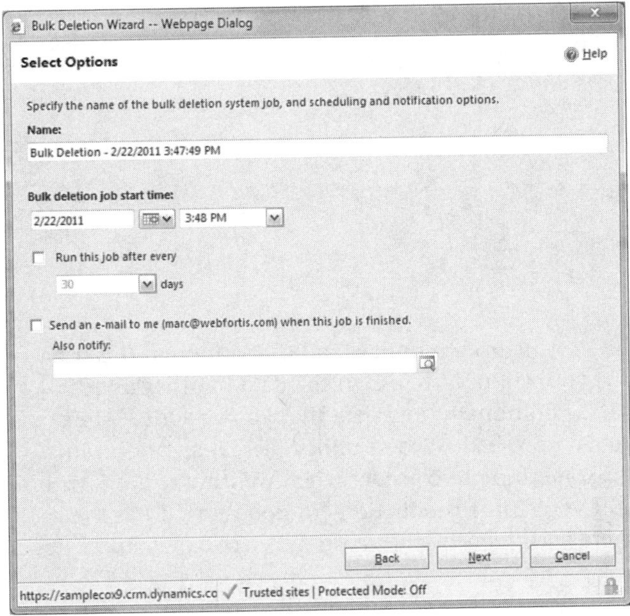

FIGURE 29.21 Bulk Record Deletion Wizard—select options.

Sample Data

Sample data can be loaded or removed from the Data Management page by selecting Sample Data. Figure 29.22 shows the option box when sample data is not loaded on the system and asks whether you'd like to have it installed.

Sample data loads data into the following entities:

- Account
- Contact
- Lead
- Opportunity
- Case
- Campaign

- Phone call
- Task

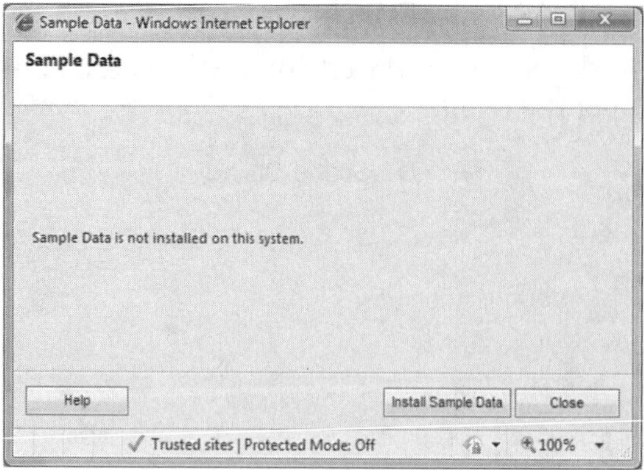

FIGURE 29.22 Load sample data.

When working with the sample data, it is helpful to understand that although it can be removed or added quickly and easily, you will need to assign the data to other users if they would like to work with the data. Additionally, any data that you've added while working with it will remain. Sample data can be loaded or uninstalled at any point in time, or as often as necessary. This is something to consider when wanting to work with a dummy dataset, but remember that if you're in a production environment, it has the potential to launch workflow, interfere with reports, and so on.

Summary

Data management has been vastly improved with the features included out of the box. The ability to quickly and easily import complex data has been streamlined and overall data management is less taxing.

CHAPTER 30

CRM 2011 and Scribe Online Services

IN THIS CHAPTER

This chapter is devoted to exploring the best-of-breed product used for integration—Scribe Software. Located at http://www.scribesoft.com, Scribe Software has long been the go-to company when performing integration development between both online and on premise systems.

Although much of the information in this chapter is around the product set delivered by Scribe, we have included some common usage scenarios.

▶ For an in-depth guide to working with Scribe and its related products, see our book *Microsoft Dynamics CRM 4.0 Integration Unleashed*, where we devote three chapters to working with Scribe.

Need for Integration

Companies that are most successful with their CRM deployments recognize the importance of integration. Integration enables your employees to be more effective and efficient at their jobs. Enabling companies to sell more and serve customers better is what CRM is all about, and that is what integration is all about.

So, how does integration do that? First, it enables your customer-facing employees to have more informed and meaningful interactions with customers. Having critical information at their fingertips gives them confidence to serve your customers efficiently and boosts your customer's image of your company with excellent service. Second, CRM systems are used by knowledge workers who spend much of their time interacting with customers. Nothing drives CRM adoption more than providing information to your employees that they care about and need to service their customers. Third, by integrating key information into your CRM system, you can use that information to drive better targeted marketing campaigns and programs to your customers. For example, if a company integrates information about what products their customers need, they can use that to drive up-sell campaigns targeted at customers of a particular product.

Integration should be one of the core value propositions of a CRM application and not a "nice to have" for your CRM implementation. You should plan for and build integration into all phases of your CRM application lifecycle.

Advent of Cloud Computing

The advent of cloud computing and the availability of cloud-based business applications such as CRM are dramatically changing the IT environment for companies of all sizes. The cloud offers simplification: simplification of the user experience and simplification for those responsible for managing the applications itself. The rapid adoption of the cloud, however, creates a perfect storm around data integration. On the one hand, the cloud has resulted in an explosion of data coming from employees, customers, partners, and influencers. Companies that can integrate, assimilate, and make sense of that information across the enterprise will be the winners. On the other hand, the creation of integration points is becoming more complicated by things such as limited bandwidth and limited access through the cloud application provider's APIs. Adding these issues to the already existing challenges around integration can be a daunting task.

Implementing an Integration Solution

So, how are companies going to make sense of it all? For some companies with highly sophisticated IT capabilities, they are tackling this challenge on their own. A large number of companies will be looking to outside partners, vendors, or consultants to help them through these challenges. When developing an integration plan around Dynamics CRM 2011, it is important to recognize the benefits of the relationship between the partner and customer as well as the changing roles between the two throughout the phases of a CRM deployment. Even if there isn't a partner involved, in many cases IT organizations act in a similar capacity as partner to the business to deliver a successful CRM project. A collaborative approach to integration between partner and customer best serves the integration needs of companies deploying Dynamics CRM 2011.

It is rare that one person has all the skills and knowledge necessary to fully implement an integration solution. To start, integration development requires a solid understanding of the design of the CRM system and the key customer processes that drive the integration need. It also requires detailed knowledge of the other applications, many of them complex back-office applications. The ability to allow multiple people to participate in the development and design of the integration solution in a coordinated manner is essential. Each of the parties should be able to design their discrete piece and simply fold it into the broader solution. The other members of the project team should be able to easily understand the work others have done and should be able add their input and comments. Team members that have moved on to other projects should be able to easily move back into an active role.

Essential Elements of Collaborative Approach

Beyond these team development capabilities, what does a collaborative approach to integration really mean? There are five essential elements: reusability, flexibility, transferability, supportability, and expandability.

Reusability

Partners invest heavily in developing the depth and expertise around the unique business requirements of their specific industry focus to provide solutions that deliver competitive advantage for their clients. A key question for any partner is how to take advantage of this industry knowledge and business process and distribute that quickly and easily to a broader set of clients without having to reinvent the wheel at every client site.

A packaged solution offered by a partner benefits the customer by offering a lower cost and lower risk integration option because they gain the benefit of the partner's expertise not only in the industry but also with the integration needs typical of customers in that industry. Customers may do an integration project once or not at all; the partner brings their experience and insight from many integration projects.

This sounds all well and good, but is not so easy to implement in practice. Invariably things get in the way. First, the project teams at partners are generally under a lot of pressure to complete their project and then move on to the next customer. They do not have the time to package the solution into something that can be reused. Even if they did have the time, not all the elements of a customer's specific solution are transferable to another customer.

A number of elements are very specific to the particular deployment. There might also be unique intellectual property within the solution that the partner wants to protect. The solution might also be implemented by an individual lacking the same depth of skills as the original designer of the solution, and so requires a more streamlined deployment experience. All these things stand in the way of achieving the great benefits of reusability.

A collaborative integration approach:

- Provides partners the ability to repackage an integration solution in a simple and easy manner. It should not add significant incremental effort to any project.
- Makes it easy to pick and choose the common elements of a solution implementation that can be packaged and reused.
- Protects the partner's intellectual property. A partner might invest significant effort to develop unique and innovative methods or approaches to solving particular industry or application integration challenges. Without some way to protect this intellectual property, partners may be reluctant to package the integration and spend the time re-implementing the integration at each client site, which increases cost and time for both the partner and customer.

- Allows customization, which might range from something as simple as a wizard-based UI where configuration choices are driven by metadata provided by the user to the use of a full suite of integration design tools depending on the complexity and uniqueness of the integration needed.

Flexibility

Integration requires a flexible approach. There are as many infinite varieties of integration needs as there are customers and business systems. Typical areas of variability include

- The data design of each business application involved and the transformations needed to resolve the design differences between those business applications
- The rules of data ownership: which system is the master of what data, which systems can insert or update certain records or fields, and so forth
- The actions that trigger integration events and the rules to process those integrations

Even if a customer can take advantage of a prepackaged integration solution, the solution will almost always require modification to address the customer's needs. These changes can range from minimal to extensive depending on how unique the business requirements are.

Custom code to achieve integration has a major advantage where it offers unlimited flexibility to meet a customer's needs. There is no limit to what can be accomplished provided that one has the resources with the skills and time necessary. The downside is cost in people, time, and money including the initial cost of the implementing the integration project and the ongoing costs of supporting and modifying the integration over time. The cost of custom code is always more expensive and can be out of reach for some customers.

For many customers, the right answer is a third-party integration tool that combines a graphical user interface with a significant depth of configuration capabilities. An integration tool gives customers to the ability get exactly what they need while significantly reducing (or in some cases, eliminating) the costs and complexity of a custom coded integration.

Transferability

In many cases, the people responsible for designing and implementing the integration processes are not the same people who will be administering them once they are put into production. Integration design and development is generally performed by business and/or data analysts who gather business requirements, create a design that meets those requirements, and develop the integration itself.

The design of the integration could include defining the events that initiate an integration process, capturing, filtering, and/or merging the relevant data affected by the events, mapping and transforming that data, establishing rules for data ownership, and designing error capture and remediation. The implementation itself involves completing the unit and system testing to ensure that the integration processes are ready for production. The final task of the integration developer is ensuring the integration is working in production and transitioning the ongoing ownership.

This handoff of the solution is very critical to the success of the integration project. How do you transfer ownership of the solution to someone that does not have intimate knowledge of the detailed design? Are there tools and dashboards that exist that can enable this person to know when things are working well and when they are not? Is there a straightforward mechanism in place for them to repair data issues? It is easy to identify which issues they can resolve or which issues they should contact the integration developer? If the original integration developer is no longer available, can someone else with integration design skills quickly understand the integration design and make modifications or enhancements to it?

This issue of transferability is also critical to the partner. It is very costly for a partner to pull their integration designers off other their other customer projects and have them fix an issue at an existing deployment. Depending on the issue, having to go back and fix or constantly maintain the integration can negatively affect the customer and partner relationship.

TIP

A good partner makes sure their customer understands the integration software and the design of their particular integrations, and that the customer can maintain it.

Supportability

Moving an integration process into production introduces the same set of challenges as moving any application or solution out of QA into production. Users always use application in ways that were not contemplated by the original integration design, resulting in unexpected errors and exceptions. Modifying the design of the endpoint applications after the integration is implemented may disrupt the integration processes. Changes to the overall IT environment might interrupt connections between the various applications.

In short, business happens and things stop working or do not work as intended. Your integration approach should include a robust set of error detection, diagnosis, and remediation tools.

Is there a way to proactively monitor the health of the integration and raise alerts when things are not functioning properly? Are there meaningful execution and error logs that enable someone to quickly identify the root cause of any issue? Does the integration process have built-in retry mechanisms that address any timing issues (for example, attempting to process an order transaction before the related customer record has been created in your target application)?

A major area to consider with any integration solution is the ability to handle gracefully upgrades to your business applications. For example, if a customer moves from Dynamics CRM 4.0 to Dynamics CRM 2011, what will the impact be on the integration? Is the upgrade simply a testing exercise where things for the large part continue to work, or does it require a rewrite of the integration?

The best integration solutions create an abstraction layer between the integration processes themselves and the API of the endpoint applications. The process sees only the abstracted interface and when the endpoint application is upgraded, it is simply a matter of modifying the interface between the API and the abstraction layer.

TIP

If you are looking at third-party adapter products, make sure you interrogate this question fully. You will be glad you did later.

At the risk of stating the obvious, the integration approach needs to be very reliable. In other words, "It just needs to work." The best integration is one that no one ever knows about or notices (of course, until it stops working and then it gets a lot of attention).

Integration solutions that are not rock solid are disruptive and costly to your business as well a significant drain on your resources. Users might not trust the data they are looking at and go to other methods that might be more time-consuming and costly to the business. They might stop using the CRM system all together and cobble their own system, which completely defeats the purpose of your CRM implementation and integration. Your resources that could be on other, more important projects are now working on fixing that integration—again.

Expandability

To coin the old adage, there is only one thing in business that is constant and that is change. What happens if you identify some other touch points that need to be integrated? What is the impact of adding a new business application that is integral to your business processes into the mix? What happens if you make significant changes to the way your people interact with customers? How do you deal with the replacement of one of the applications involved? What if you acquire another company with different business systems and processes? These things occur frequently and should account in your integration strategy.

CAUTION

A common mistake with data integration is trying to do too much the first time. Seeking to integrate any and all touch points that you can envision up front can weigh a project down and significantly increase risk.

A smart approach is to prioritize the different integration processes, particularly those things that will drive CRM user adoption in the initial phase, and then tackle a manageable number at the first phase. Additional integration processes can then be added over time.

This need for expandability requires that we think strategically and implement tactically when it comes to integration. It is important that the tools and approaches you utilize are nimble enough to meet your short-term needs without busting the budget while forming a strong foundation where future expansion can be easily accommodated.

Introduction to Scribe

The considerations when developing an integration strategy outlined previously are important regardless of the integration approach you choose; whether writing custom code or utilizing a third-party integration product. The remaining chapter will provide information on the most prevalent third-party integration product for customers of Dynamics CRM, Scribe Software. This will include a detailed discussion of Scribe's flagship integration product, Scribe Insight, along with a preview of the company's newest offering, Scribe Online.

Scribe Insight

With more than 5,000 Dynamics CRM customers, Scribe Insight is the proven software tool for data migration and integration needs. Scribe Insight enables companies to design any number of sophisticated integration processes within a graphical user interface, without having to write a line of code. There are more than 800 Dynamics CRM reseller partners worldwide that deliver integration solutions to customers using Scribe Insight. Scribe and many of its partners also offer pre-packaged templates for common integration scenarios that can be quickly modified to meet the needs of individual customers.

Figure 30.1 represents the topology of the components of Scribe Insight. The items labeled represent the five major Scribe Insight components: the Server, Workbench, Console, Adapters, and Templates.

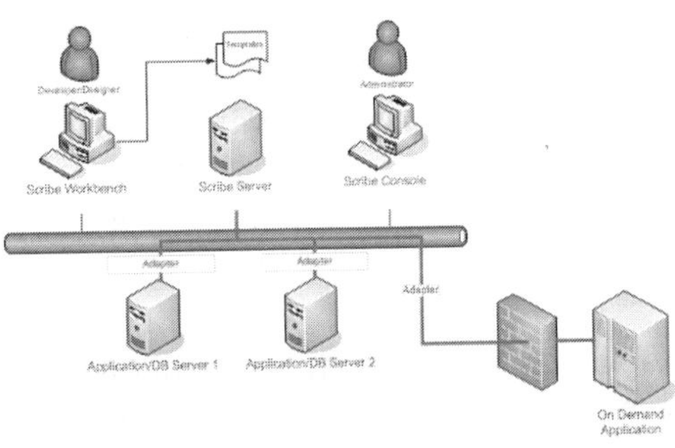

FIGURE 30.1 Integrated Scribe technology.

The core components of Scribe Insight are built using the Microsoft Visual Studio development platform for the Windows family of operating systems. The Scribe Server is the core engine that provides connectivity to the various applications, databases, and messaging systems within the integration environment (see Figure 30.1 for a graphic representation of the connectivity). Communications between the Scribe components and the applications being integrated is provided using the appropriate technology. For example, many of the Scribe Adapters for enterprise applications, such as Microsoft Dynamics CRM 2011 (online, hosted, or premised) utilize web services.

NOTE

Although Scribe Insight is an installed software product, it communicates simply and easily to cloud-based applications via a secure Internet connection to support the growing need for hybrid integration.

Scribe Insight is based on a loosely coupled, yet tightly integrated architecture that is highly adaptable to each customer's unique and constantly changing business environment. For example, each Adapter communicates to the Scribe Server in precisely the same way regardless of the application or database to which it is connecting.

This abstraction of the application or database details provides for a highly productive design environment—after users learn to use the Workbench, they can design integrations with a wide variety of applications and data stores. This abstraction also means that templates (representing specific integration processes between applications or databases) are insulated from most changes and updates to the application or database interface. For example, the same template that works with Dynamics CRM 4.0 will continue to work with Dynamics CRM 2011, requiring no reconfiguration except to accommodate substantive changes in the schema or functionality of that application.

The five other major Scribe components are explained in further detail in the following sections.

Scribe Server

The Scribe Server is the core of Scribe Insight–supported integration processes and facilitates the exchange of data between two or more applications or databases. Because Scribe Insight, in essence, brokers a conversation between these applications and databases, it can support a highly heterogeneous server environment of Windows, UNIX, Linux, on-demand applications, and so on. All that it requires is connection to these applications via a Windows client, a nonplatform-specific middleware protocol such as ODBC, via an MSMQ message queue, a public or private web service.

Underlying the Scribe Server are a number of Windows services designed to monitor and detect events, process messages, raise alerts, and provide an access point for the Scribe Console to the other services. The Scribe Server also includes its own internal database that stores all execution and error logging, persisted integration settings, cross-reference tables, and important integration statistics. The Scribe internal database can be configured to support the Microsoft SQL Express database (provided with Scribe Insight) or Microsoft SQL Server.

Scribe Workbench

The Scribe Workbench provides a rich graphical environment where users design and configure the data mappings and business rules that define the integration solution. All work completed in the Workbench is saved in a lightweight file that is referenced by the Scribe Server at runtime. This self-documenting, metadata-driven model allows for easy debugging during the deployment phase and rapid modification as the application environment or business needs change.

The workbench shown in Figure 30.2 enables you to connect to your applications, define a source result set, configure object-level target processing, and then simply point and click to modify or add data mappings.

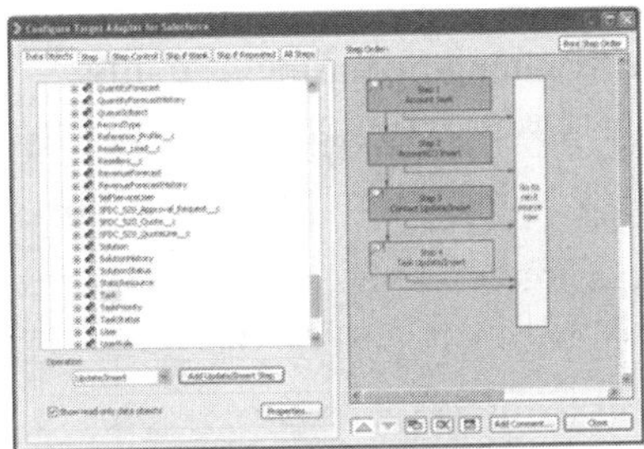

FIGURE 30.2 Scribe Workbench.

One of the key capabilities in the Workbench is the ability to normalize source data on the fly as it processed against the target application. In other words, single or multirow source data can have multiple operations executed per row on target data objects. These operations, referred to as *steps*, can be conditionally executed based on user-defined logic, allowing complex, transaction-enabled, multiobject operations.

With the Scribe Workbench, designing complex data transformations is a simple task. The Workbench provides more than 150 Excel-like functions (see Figure 30.3) for data translation, including

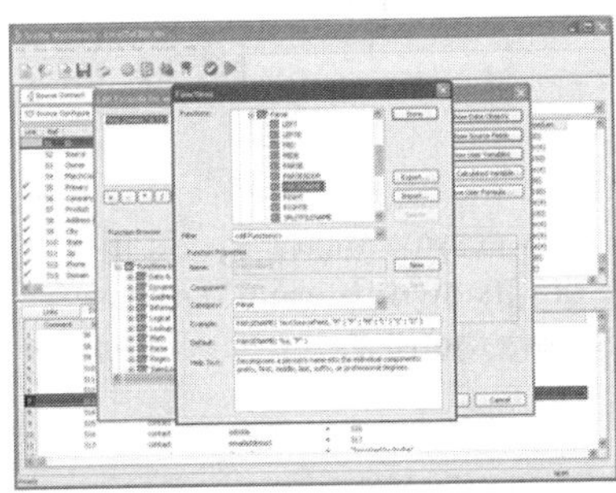

FIGURE 30.3 Scribe data transformations in action.

- Parsing functions for names and addresses
- Date and time conversions
- String manipulation

- Database and file look-ups for processing synonym values
- Logical if/then/else functions to support conditional processing

The Workbench was designed to support many advanced integration needs beyond data transformation and mapping and includes the following additional capabilities:

- A Test Window that displays the result of processing test data without committing the data to the target system. Users can view the results of data translations and object-level transaction processing for easy and efficient debugging of integration processes.
- Built-in system key cross-reference and management, designed to dynamically maintain data integrity between records across two or more loosely coupled applications.
- Built-in support for foreign key value reference management, designed to dynamically maintain data integrity between related records within an application.
- Net change tracking by updating or deleting successfully processed source records or by comparing a source-side update stamp against a variable last run date/time in the source query.
- Conflict detection and resolution to support bidirectional data synchronization.
- Formula-based lookups for fuzzy record matching logic .
- Value cross-reference and lookup support.
- Automatic data type mismatch resolution.
- Transactional support for Header-Detail type data sets.
- Configuration of target-side commit and rollback.
- Rich error handling and logical flow control, including support for user-defined errors.
- Rejected row logging to support automated repair and recovery processes.

Scribe Console

The Scribe Console provides the user interface to an array of powerful features used to set up, organize, and manage key aspects of any number of integration processes. The Scribe Console is the main user interface to the capabilities underlying the Scribe Server (see Figure 30.4).

The Console provides a single point of management for a company's various integration points, organizing them as discrete units of work or Collaborations. Each Collaboration is a series of related integration processes and instructions for how and when these processes should be automatically executed. Collaborations are organized in a graphical, user-defined tree and can be managed as independent objects with their own reporting, monitoring, and diagnostic functions. The Console also provides easy access and control of all integration processes running on the system through controls implemented at the Integration Server level.

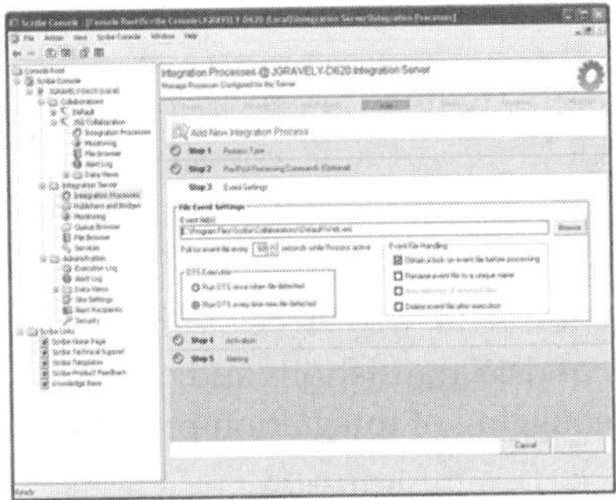

FIGURE 30.4 Scribe Console.

At the core of the Console are its sophisticated event management capabilities. The Console allows each company to precisely define the proper latency for each integration process from scheduling batch processes to run on a predefined time period, to establishing near real-time polling intervals based on a file drop in a directory or the results of a source-side query, to the real-time processing of messages arriving in an In Queue.

The Scribe Server is built with a modular, multithreaded architecture that allows for scaling of integration processes, based on the available CPU processing strength. It also features efficient connection sharing to maximize performance, where possible.

Additional capabilities of the Console include

- Access to the files on the Scribe Server that might need to be moved, copied, renamed, or deleted.
- Automated system monitoring of business level events or integration errors with configurable alerts via e-mail, page, and net send notification.
- For those data sources that do not have a built in net change mechanism (including event-based message publishing, time and date stamps for updates, or other forms of update stamps) the Console provides a Query Publisher that compares time-based snapshots of a source system and publishes the differences as an XML message.
- Settings to launch an executable file to run before or after an integration process. One example where this pre- or post-execution processing can be useful is the ability to move files into an archive directory after the process is executed.
- On-screen editable views of predefined queries that can be displayed in chart or list format.
- User interface for message viewing, moving, copying and deleting.
- Review execution history of what processes succeeded or failed, including detailed error reporting.

Scribe Adapters

Scribe Adapters enable Scribe Insight to communicate seamlessly to a variety of applications, databases, messages, and files. Scribe Adapters present rich levels of schema information, which is available through the available application interface (via a declare type function in an application API or in a WSDL in the case of web services interfaces) to the Scribe Server and Workbench.

This schema information includes object properties and interrelationships as well as detailed field attributes such as labels, data types, lengths, restrictions, and default/picklist values. Combined with the rich features in the Workbench, this information provides for unparalleled control over integration processes and eliminates the last mile coding required with other integration tools.

Figure 30.5 shows the Dynamics CRM schema as it is presented via its Adapter in the Scribe Workbench.

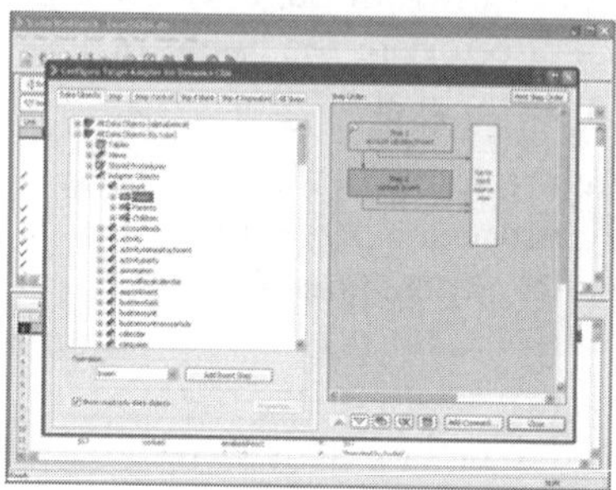

FIGURE 30.5 Dynamics CRM schema via the Scribe Workbench Adapter.

Enterprise Application Adapters are adapters that have been designed and developed to optimize Insight for use with Scribe targeted CRM and ERP applications including Microsoft Dynamics CRM 2011, Microsoft Dynamics GP, Microsoft Dynamics NAV, Microsoft Dynamics AX, Salesforce, and SalesLogix. Scribe's Enterprise Application Adapters are sold as add-ons to Scribe Insight.

Key features of these Application Adapters include

- The automation of common data loading tasks such as assigning primary ID values, setting default values, and validating input data, and setting object relationships all designed to eliminate runtime errors and provide for greater data integrity.
- Dynamic discovery that presents the unique configuration of each application or database instance to the Scribe Console and Workbench at runtime that adjusts to changes in the application or database schema without requiring recoding or recompiling.
- The seamless integration of application and database error messages to provide detailed exception reporting and handling from the Scribe Console's single point of management.

Connectivity Adapters are designed to complement the Enterprise Application Adapters by providing a wide variety of integration options to support connectivity to the varied applications and data stores within each company's computing environment.

Connectivity Adapters are used to support integration between the targeted applications served by Scribe's Application Adapters and a wide variety of other packaged enterprise applications and data sources including

- ERP and CRM systems from SAP, Siebel, Oracle (Oracle, Peoplesoft, JD Edwards,) Sage (MAS 90 / 200 / 500,) Epicor, and so on
- Packaged applications that serve a particular niche or vertical market
- Custom in-house developed systems

Scribe provides a number of approaches to integrating with these applications, depending on the business requirements and available technical resources including, but not limited to, the following:

- **Via Web Services**—By utilizing Scribe's Web Services Adapter, Scribe Insight enables a seamless integration between a variety of on premise and cloud based applications via a Web Service with a SOAP-compliant WSDL.

TIP

If available, this approach is preferred since it provides higher-level validation of business logic, ensuring a greater degree of data integrity.

- **Directly to the database**—This is a simple, straightforward approach if you are migrating from an application or your project is limited to a one-way feed of data from that application. Scribe Insight provides a number of methods to extract net change data from the application utilizing this approach.
- **Via interface tables**—Many applications support a set of interface or staging tables that provide for a safe way to integrate data into that application. After data is passed into the interface tables, an application process is initiated that validates the data and applies appropriate application rules. With Scribe Insight, you can write to these tables and initiate the application process automatically.
- **Via an XML/messaging interface**—Many enterprise applications provides an XML interface that is incorporated into the workflow engine within the application. Using this method, Scribe Insight can publish XML messages into a message queue for real-time integration with the other application. Scribe Insight can also receive XML transactions published by the application's workflow engine into a message queue in real-time.
- **Via the application's API**—Many applications expose a web services or COM-based API where transactions can be passed to the application. Data can also be queried via

this API. Out-of-the-box, Scribe Insight cannot natively integrate with this API; however, custom code can be written to convert these calls into an intermediate format. This intermediate format can be an XML message, a flat file, or a record in a database staging table.

Scribe Templates

Scribe Templates represent complete or partial data integration or migration processes that have been developed using Scribe Insight technology.

> Scribe provides a number of these Templates as free downloads from the Scribe Web Community to support the successful deployment of Scribe Insight, located at www.scribesoft.com/scribe-templates.asp.

Templates are comprised of the building blocks of a fully functional migration or integration solution as configured with Scribe Insight including

- Source-side net change processes and filtering
- Event and process automation
- Data mappings
- Record matching for updates and duplicate avoidance
- User/owner mappings
- Field ownership and update rules
- System key cross referencing and management
- Connection validation and security
- Data ownership and customizations
- Application customizations
- Transaction management
- Commit and rollback settings
- System monitors and alerts
- Business monitors and alerts

Certain templates offered by Scribe represent a complete, fully functional integration or migration solution between two applications. Scribe offers solution templates to integrate Dynamics CRM 2011 to three of the Microsoft ERP applications, Dynamics GP, Dynamics NAV, and Dynamics AX. Scribe also offers migration templates for customers moving from other CRM applications to Dynamics CRM 2011 including a template from Salesforce.

Scribe's unique template model provides out-of-the-box functionality for these integration scenarios, built over its industry-leading integration tool. Because most customers have business needs unique to them, these standard Templates can be quickly extended and customized utilizing the GUI-based mapping and development environment.

The component architecture of these solution templates also enables customers to implement Templates in phases or pick and choose the elements of the Templates that they require. In the front-to-back-office integration example, a customer might not want to implement order integration initially (or in some cases never), but can still synchronize customer activity (accounts, contacts, invoices) between the two systems. This modularity enables customers to implement an integration solution tailored to their exact needs.

Scribe in Action

Figure 30.6 1 provides just a few examples of customers that are using Scribe Insight to integrate Dynamics CRM with other applications in their enterprise.

Major Global Financial Services Provider	Major International Airline	Largest U.S. Steel Producer	Global Leader in Financial Protection	Major U.S. Government Agricultural Agency
7,000 seats initial 20,000 seats total	250+ seats	1,000 seats	750+seats	1,000 seats
Integrate three distinct CRM instances worldwide with legacy systems and data end points	Integration hub for Dynamics NAV, CRM, credit card processing, mileage points DB & online mileage redemption store	Roll up of 23+ divisions daily to corporate CRM system	Integration platform for all applications into Global Dynamics CRM	Integration hub for CRM and all legacy systems and data end points

FIGURE 30.6 Scribe Insight and Dynamics CRM Integration Usage

Although each of the customers listed here is a large, global enterprise, Scribe Insight is used by thousands of small and mid-sized companies as well. With Scribe Insight, the cost and complexity of integration is significantly reduced, enabling companies of all sizes to gain the strategic advantage that integration provides.

Scribe Online

The advent of cloud computing is enabling Scribe to take these collaborative design principals to the next level, with its new Scribe Online integration platform. Scribe Online takes advantage of the ease of use of web applications, the efficiency and scalability of a cloud computing architecture, and the rapidly evolving innovations in social media, crowdsourcing, push, and mobile to significantly lower the barrier to entry for data integration.

In addition to powerful data integration capabilities, Scribe Online will feature two major capabilities designed to significantly extend the openness and versatility of the integration platform.

- **Solution Builder**—This allows partners and customers to build and distribute repeatable solutions for a targeted industry, market, or client base. It will allow designers to easily and quickly wrapper any integration with configuration and installation wizards that are tailored to the needs of the target audience. And with the cloud deployment model, the ability to reach that target audience with a solution is unmatched.

  With Scribe Online, small and mid-sized businesses can enjoy the same level of integration of their much larger competitors. And because Scribe Online, running on Microsoft's Azure, is highly scalable and elastic, larger companies can take advantage of these new efficiencies as well. The Solution Builder will be available in early 2012.

- **Connector Development Kit (CDK)**—The CDK will allow developers to easily build and deploy connectors that enable any end point or data source to work with Scribe Online. The CDK can be used in conjunction with Solution Builder to create true integration solutions and packages for a targeted industry or market. The CDK will be available by the end of 2011.

- **Replication Services**—In the first quarter of 2011, Scribe introduced its inaugural service on Scribe Online called Replication Services, which enables customers to replicate the data from their Dynamics CRM Online 2011 instance to a local copy of SQL Server. Configuration of the solution is enabled through a simple wizard that can be set up in minutes. Creating a solution involves a few easy steps, such as providing log in credentials for Dynamics CRM 2011 and SQL Server and defining how often the replication process should run. In just a few short minutes of setup, the replication service will be creating a backup of your CRM Online data to a local SQL Server database. The service then maintains the currency of this back up data at the frequency that is defined (see Figure 30.7).

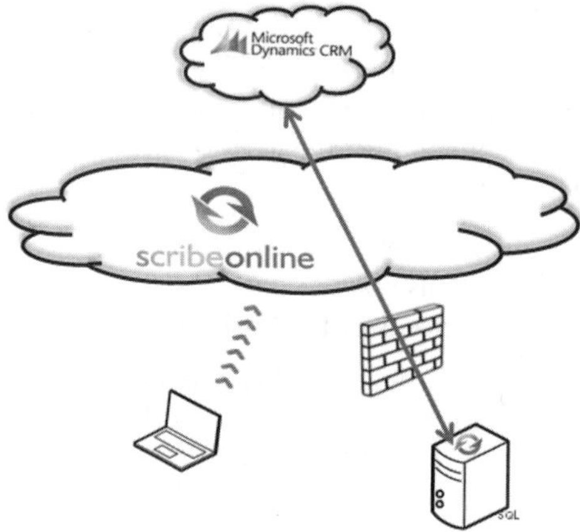

FIGURE 30.7 Replication Service.

All the user-facing elements of Scribe Online are served up in the cloud. The processing of data by the service, however, utilizes advanced agent technology. The agent approach recognizes that for this solution it is most efficient and secure for the processing to be done locally behind the customer's firewall. Installing a Scribe Online Agent locally ensures fast, secure data transfer without a heavy footprint and/or complex or difficult installation requirements.

Scribe Online Replication Services allow you to experience the benefits of the cloud CRM experience while maintaining complete control over your CRM data.

- Ensure Data Security and Compliance
    - Archive your customer data to meet compliance and governance.
    - Maintain your own backup for DR and business continuity.
- Meet Operational Reporting Needs
    - Use reporting tools including SQL Server Reporting Services (SSRS), Microsoft Excel, and Crystal Reports.
    - Provide optimized off-line access for Web sites, portals, and dashboards without impacting application users.
    - Merge your CRM data with other data sources.
- Deliver Advanced Business Intelligence / CRM Analytics
    - Quickly generate data cubes for use with BI platforms.

▶ The Scribe Online Replication Service is available in a "click, try, buy" experience and can be accessed at www.scribesoft.com/online.

Summary

Any customer looking to integrate Dynamics CRM 2011 with other business applications and data stores will benefit greatly from implementing a solution that meets the criteria for a collaborative integration approach. The benefits include faster and lower-cost deployments that deliver greater value to your business. They will also be less costly to support, more reliable, and can be adapted quickly to the changing needs of the business.

The collaborative integration capabilities outlined here are at the core of the design of Scribe's products.

▶ To learn more about Scribe and its collaborative integration products, go to www.scribesoft.com.

Index

Numerics

A

B

C

D

E

F

G

H-I

J

K-L

M

P

Q

R

S

T

U

V

W